# THE ROUTLEDGE HISTORY OF THE DEVIL IN THE WESTERN TRADITION

Covering a period of more than 2,000 years, this book offers an interdisciplinary exploration of the devil's role in the Western tradition and draws from history, religion, art, literature, media studies, and anthropology to provide a multifaceted view of the devil over time.

*The Routledge History of the Devil in the Western Tradition* examines topics such as the devil's scriptural origins, medieval development, and role in witch-hunting and possession cases, as well as the influence of the demonic on contemporary issues like terrorism, political polarisation, and digital culture. Collectively, this volume demonstrates that the demonological imagination has served as part of the glue holding Western societies together. While contexts, misfortunes, and anxieties have shifted according to time and place, many of the dynamics that underlie the devil's construction and detection have important continuities. This book, then, provides an innovative history of the anti-West—the West as seen through its anxieties, fears, and attempts to define and police itself and its boundaries.

With contributions from 28 leading scholars in the field, this volume is of interest to all students and scholars of the devil in the Western world.

**Richard Raiswell** is Professor of History at the University of Prince Edward Island, Canada. He has published works on demon possession, proof in witchcraft cases, rhetoric and demonism, and demonism and colonialism. His most recent book is *The Medieval Devil: A Reader* (trans. and ed. with David Winter, 2022).

**Michelle D. Brock** is Professor of History at Washington and Lee University, USA. She has published works on witchcraft and demonology, religious identity, and women and gender in early modern Scotland. Her most recent book is *Plagues of the Heart: Crisis and Covenanting in a Seventeenth-Century Scottish Town* (2024).

**David R. Winter** is Professor of History at Brandon University, Canada. His books include *The Llanthony Stories* (2021) and *The Medieval Devil: A Reader* (trans. and ed. with Richard Raiswell, 2022). He is currently working on a translation of 16th-century Icelandic bishop Oddur Einarsson's *Descriptio qualiscunque Islandiae*.

# THE ROUTLEDGE HISTORIES

*The Routledge Histories* is a series of landmark books surveying some of the most important topics and themes in history today. Edited and written by an international team of world-renowned experts, they are the works against which all future books on their subjects will be judged.

**The Routledge History of Antisemitism**
*Edited by Mark Weitzman, Robert J. Williams, and James Wald*

**The Routledge History of Happiness**
*Edited by Katie Barclay, Darrin M. McMahon, and Peter N. Stearns*

**The Routledge History of Irish America**
*Edited by Cian T. McMahon and Kathleen P. Costello-Sullivan*

**The Routledge History of the First World War**
*Edited by Paul R. Bartrop*

**The Routledge History of Religion and Politics in the United States Since 1775**
*Edited by Cara Lea Burnidge and Lauren Frances Turek*

**The Routledge History of Crime in America**
*Edited by James Campbell and Vivien Miller*

**The Routledge History of the Devil in the Western Tradition**
*Edited by Richard Raiswell, Michelle D. Brock, and David R. Winter*

For more information about this series, please visit: https://www.routledge.com/Routledge-Histories/book-series/RHISTS

# THE ROUTLEDGE HISTORY OF THE DEVIL IN THE WESTERN TRADITION

*Edited by Richard Raiswell, Michelle D. Brock,*
*and David R. Winter*

Routledge
Taylor & Francis Group

LONDON AND NEW YORK

Designed cover image: Le Songe de Tartini par Louis-Léopold Boilly,
1824 © Svintage Archive/Alamy Stock Photo

First published 2025
by Routledge
4 Park Square, Milton Park, Abingdon, Oxon OX14 4RN

and by Routledge
605 Third Avenue, New York, NY 10158

*Routledge is an imprint of the Taylor & Francis Group, an informa
business*

*British Library Cataloguing-in-Publication Data*
A catalogue record for this book is available from the British Library

*Library of Congress Cataloging-in-Publication Data*
Names: Raiswell, Richard, 1966- editor. | Brock, Michelle D., editor. |
Winter, David R., editor.
Title: The Routledge history of the Devil in the Western tradition / edited
by Richard Raiswell, Michelle Brock, and David Winter.
Description: Abingdon, Oxon ; New York, NY : Routledge, 2025. | Series:
History | Includes bibliographical references and index.
Identifiers: LCCN 2024058538 (print) | LCCN 2024058539 (ebook) | ISBN
9780367561420 (hbk) | ISBN 9780367561413 (pbk) | ISBN
9781003096603 (ebk)
Subjects: LCSH: Devil--History of doctrines. | Demonology--History. |
Civilization, Western--History.
Classification: LCC BT982 .R67 2025 (print) | LCC BT982 (ebook) | DDC
235/.47--dc23/eng/20250108
LC record available at https://lccn.loc.gov/2024058538
LC ebook record available at https://lccn.loc.gov/2024058539

ISBN: 978-0-367-56142-0 (hbk)
ISBN: 978-0-367-56141-3 (pbk)
ISBN: 978-1-003-09660-3 (ebk)

DOI: 10.4324/9781003096603

Typeset in Sabon
by KnowledgeWorks Global Ltd.

*In memory of Darwin, Gladys, Bridget, Isabel, Eleanor, Matilda, Octavia and Josie*

# CONTENTS

# Contents

# FIGURES

# ACKNOWLEDGEMENTS

We began work on this book in the summer of 2019. Through the autumn, we contacted authors, sent out contracts, and set deadlines aiming to have the book ready for publication at some point in 2022. Of course, the COVID-19 pandemic quickly put an end to that! Within a couple of months, libraries and archives across the world were closed, many not becoming fully accessible again for the best part of a couple of years. So we'd like to thank all of our contributors for bearing with us during these tumultuous times. It is a testament to their patience and commitment to this project that this book has finally come to fruition.

In a book as long and as far-reaching as this, our debts—as the devil said to Christ—are legion.

We are profoundly grateful to the Centre for Reformation and Renaissance Studies at Victoria University in the University of Toronto for the use of its fine collection of resources. At the University of Prince Edward Island, we would like to thank Christine MacLauchlan in Data and Research Services and Simon Lloyd, Archivist and Special Collections Librarian at the Robertson Library.

At Brandon University, we would like to acknowledge the administrative staff in the Dean of Arts' Office as well as the Arts Office. Over the course of the project, this has included Sally Mott, Shari Maguire, Hillary Campbell, and Laurence LeMoine.

At Washington and Lee University, we wish to acknowledge the work of the wonderful staff at Leyburn Library for quickly fulfilling our many interlibrary loan requests and the support of colleagues in the History Department and the Medieval and Renaissance Studies Program. We are also grateful to the Provost's Office for providing summer funding for this work.

Elsewhere, we would like to thank all the participants at the 2022 Scientiae Summer series, "Demonism and early Modern Knowledge-Making"—including Lu Ann Homza, Sari Katajala-Peltomaa, Jason Coy, Walter Stephens, Erika Gasser, Valerie Kivelson, and Gary Waite—and everyone who attended the "Devil 2024" conference. We have benefited enormously from many demon-inspired conversations over the last few years, and we owe particular debts of gratitude to, among many others, Stefano Gulizia, David Lawrence, Vera Kirk, Trinity Nylen, Jessica Old, Kay Edwards, Hans de Waardt, Sarah Hughes, Debbie Felton, Joseph Laycock, Peter Dendle, B. W. Bipps, Natasha Mikles, Kathryn Morris, Whitney Phillips, Mark Brockway, Brian Levack, and Michael Beverly.

We are grateful to the students in various devil-themed seminars and courses at UPEI, W&L, and Brandon who have helped us to calibrate the volume and position it, we hope, for maximum pedagogical effect. It is a pleasure to learn from those we teach.

We would also like to thank Laura Pilsworth at Routledge for her support and guidance.

Finally, we would like to thank our families—especially Jared Diener, Elizabeth Schoales, Allison and Xavier McCulloch—for their patience and support, and for enduring more conversations about the demonic than they signed up for.

Between us, there are too many dependent quadrupeds to acknowledge by name, but we appreciate all their suggestions, textual and otherwise.

In 1934, Dennis Wheatley felt it necessary to preface his classic occult thriller *The Devil Rides Out* with a note to reassure his readers: "I desire to state that I, personally, have never assisted at, or participated in, any ceremony connected with Magic—Black or White." We make much the same claim here about our involvement in demonism—but then, of course, we would say that.

RR, MB, DW
July 2024

# CONTRIBUTORS

**Michael D. Bailey** earned his PhD from Northwestern University and is now a professor of history at Iowa State University. His research focuses on magic, superstition, witchcraft and heresy in the later Middle Ages. Among his publications are *Battling Demons: Witchcraft, Heresy, and Reform in the Late Middle Ages* (2003), *Fearful Spirits, Reasoned Follies: The Boundaries of Superstition in Late Medieval Europe* (2013) and *Origins of the Witches' Sabbath* (2021). His research has been supported by fellowships from, among others, the DAAD, Humboldt Stiftung and the Mellon Foundation.

**Karl Bell** is an Associate Professor in Cultural and Social History at the University of Portsmouth in the United Kingdom. He is the author of *The Magical Imagination: Magic and Modernity in Urban England, 1780–1914* (CUP, 2012) and the award-winning *The Legend of Spring-heeled Jack: Victorian Urban Folklore and Popular Culture* (2012), and also the editor of *Supernatural Cities: Enchantment, Anxiety and Spectrality* (2019). His other publications have explored topics including Victorian ghosts, millenarianism, magical folklore, occult crime, Victorian proto-science fiction, and Surrealism. He was Director of the Supernatural Cities project between 2016 and 2022 and is now co-director of the University of Portsmouth's Centre for Port Cities and Maritime Cultures.

**Michelle D. Brock** is Professor of History at Washington and Lee University. A scholar of religion, gender and the supernatural in early modern Scotland, she is the author of *Satan and the Scots: The Devil in Post-Reformation Scotland* (2016) and *Plagues of the Heart: Crisis and Covenanting in a Seventeenth-Century Scottish Town* (2024). She is also the co-editor of *Knowing Demons, Knowing Spirits in the Early Modern Period* (2018). Currently, she is working on a new book about the sensational case of Margaret Dickson, an ordinary woman who survived hanging for infanticide in Edinburgh in 1724.

**Miranda Corcoran** is a lecturer in 21st-century literature at University College Cork, Ireland. Her research interests include genre fiction, popular fiction, comics/graphic novels, sci-fi, horror, the gothic, witchcraft and Satanism in pop culture. Her first monograph, *Witchcraft and Adolescence in American Popular Culture: Teen Witches*, was published in 2022 by the University of Wales Press. Her second (short) monograph, *The Craft*, was published in 2023 by Auteur/Liverpool University Press. She is currently editing a collection entitled *Satanism and Feminism in Popular Culture: Not Today Satan*.

**Peter J. Dendle** is a Professor of English at The Pennsylvania State University, Mont Alto. His research focuses on cultural expressions of the monstrous, including medieval demonology, zombies in film, and cryptozoology. His books include *Satan Unbound: The Devil in Old English Narrative Literature* (University of Toronto Press, 2001) and *Demon Possession in Anglo-Saxon England* (Medieval Institute Publications, 2014), and he is co-editor with Richard Raiswell of *The Devil in Society in Premodern Europe* (Centre for Reformation and Renaissance Studies, 2012).

**Bill Ellis** is Professor Emeritus of English and American Studies at The Pennsylvania State University. His publications include *Raising the Devil: Satanism, New Religions, and the Media* (Kentucky, 2000), *Aliens, Ghosts, and Cults: Legends We Live* (Mississippi, 2001), *Lucifer Ascending: The Occult in Folk and Popular Culture* (Kentucky, 2003), and (with Gary Alan Fine) *The Global Grapevine: Why Rumors and Legends about Immigrants, Terrorists, and Foreign Trade Matter* (Oxford, 2010). A Fellow of the American Folklore Society, he has served on that organisation's Executive Board. He holds a Lifetime Achievement Award from the International Society for Contemporary Legend Research.

**Per Faxneld** is Associate Professor in Study of Religions at Södertörn University. His research has focused on topics like Satanism, esotericism, secularity, and religious motifs in art, literature, and cinema. He is presently conducting a three-year project on spirituality among Swedish practitioners of Japanese martial arts, funded by the Swedish Research Council, while concurrently researching the Swedish spiritualist group Edelweissförbundet and the magical tradition of Scandinavian folk grimoires (ca. 1700–1900). Faxneld also writes fiction, and in 2020 published a collection of short stories that has been translated into several languages.

**Philip L. Frana** is Professor of Interdisciplinary Liberal Studies and Independent Scholars at James Madison University. He teaches subjects related to automation and society and has published numerous articles on the history of technology, science and medicine. He is the editor and contributor to the *Encyclopedia of Artificial Intelligence: The Past, Present, and Future of AI* published by ABC-CLIO in 2021. Dr. Frana received a doctorate in the History of Technology and Science from Iowa State University and completed post-doctoral training at the Charles Babbage Institute for Computing, Information & Culture at the University of Minnesota-Twin Cities.

**Eileen Gardiner** is an Honorary Research Fellow at the University of Bristol, Centre for Medieval Studies. She holds a PhD in Medieval Studies and English Literature. She is the author of *Visions of Heaven and Hell Before Dante; Medieval Visions of Heaven and Hell: A Sourcebook* and *The Pilgrim's Way to St. Patrick's Purgatory*. She is the curator of the website *Hell-on-Line* and editor of a series of books on the infernal otherworld in various religious traditions. She is also the former co-director of the Medieval Academy of America and the co-editor of its journal, *Speculum: A Journal of Medieval Studies*.

**Erika Gasser** is Director of Academic Programs at Historic Deerfield. She researches the history of gender in colonial New England, early modern England and the Anglo-Atlantic. She is the author of *Vexed with Devils: Manhood and Witchcraft in Old and New England* (2017) and "Possession and the Senses in Early Modern England" in *The Journal of the Canadian Historical Association/Revue de la Société historique du Canada* (2019).

**Marion Gibson** is Professor of Renaissance and Magical Literatures at the University of Exeter, UK, and author of nine books on witchcraft and magic. Her latest books are The Witches of St Osyth: Persecution, Betrayal and Murder in Elizabethan England (2022) and *Witchcraft: A History in 13 Trials* (2023).

**Sarah A. Hughes** is an independent scholar living near Philadelphia, Pennsylvania. She earned her PhD in American History from Temple University in 2015. Her publications include "American Monsters: Tabloid Media and the Satanic Panic, 1970-2000" in the *Journal of American Studies* (2017) and *Tabloid Media and the Satanic Panic, 1970-2000* (Palgrave MacMillan, 2021). She is currently working on her next book, *Nihilism & The New World Order: American Culture in the 1990s*. Her research interests include American conspiracy culture, commercial entertainment, suburbanisation, and corporate news media in the 1980s and 1990s.

**Linda C. Hults** studied art history and comparative religion at Indiana University, graduating in 1971, and received her PhD in Art History at the University of North Carolina in 1978. She taught at Northern Illinois University, the University of Tulsa, and finally at the College of Wooster in Ohio from 1987 to 2011. There, she contributed to both the gender studies and art history programmes. Now, she lives in Indianapolis with her husband. She has published numerous articles and two books on the history of prints and northern European witchcraft imagery.

**Robert L. Ivie** is Professor Emeritus in English and American Studies at Indiana University, Bloomington, Indiana, USA. He served as the founding editor of the journal *Communication and Critical/Cultural Studies* and earlier as the editor of the *Quarterly Journal of Speech* and the *Western Journal of Communication*. His research focuses on political rhetoric and war culture. His books include *Hunt the Devil: A Demonology of U.S. War Culture* (2015), with Oscar Giner. The working title of his current book project is *After Empire: Essays on a Path to Democracy*, with Oscar Giner.

**Johanneke Kroesbergen-Kamps** is a post-doctoral fellow at the University of Pretoria. Before that, she taught Religious Studies, Sociology and Research Methods at Justo Mwale University in Lusaka, Zambia, for six years. She has written extensively about narratives about Satanism in Zambia, exploring their persuasiveness and meaning in contemporary culture. Currently, her research is focused on the aesthetic formations of religious identity in pastors in the Reformed Church in Zambia, as well as their responses to the COVID-19 pandemic.

**David R. Lawrence** teaches in the History Department at Glendon College, York University and is a Senior Fellow at the Centre for Renaissance and Reformation Studies at the University of Toronto. He is the author of *The Complete Soldier: Military Books and Military Culture in Early Stuart England, 1603–1645* (2009) and a number of book chapters and articles on late 16th- and early 17th-century English martial culture.

**Jan Machielsen** is a historian working on early modern witches, demons and saints at Cardiff University. His publications include *The Science of Demons* (2020), *The War on Witchcraft* (2021) and *The Basque Witch-Hunt* (2024).

**Christopher S. Mackay** has been a Professor in the Department of History, Classics and Religion of the University of Alberta since 1996. He has written about ancient Roman history, medieval witchcraft, and the Anabaptist Kingdom of Münster of 1534/35, and has recently shifted his focus to Latin texts of the early modern period, especially ones pertaining to the history of Hungary.

**Charlotte-Rose Millar** is a Lecturer in History at the University of Melbourne. Her research focuses on supernatural beliefs and popular print in early modern England. She has previously held a research fellowship at the University of Queensland (2016–2020) and a visiting fellowship at the University of Cambridge (2018). She is the author of *Witchcraft, the Devil and Emotions in Early Modern England* (2017) and is currently working on a new, book-length project on ghosts in early modern England, as well as editing volume three of Bloomsbury's six-volume series *A Cultural History of Magic*.

**Ismael del Olmo** holds a doctorate in History and teaches early modern history at the University of Buenos Aires, the National University of General Sarmiento, and the National Pedagogical University, in Argentina. His research interests include the history of demonology, possession and exorcism from the late Middle Ages to the Enlightenment. He has published *Legio: Posesión Diabólica y Exorcismo en la Europa de los Siglos XVI y XVII* (2018).

**W. Scott Poole** has written books on the intersection of pop culture, politics, and all things spooky, including the 2009 *Satan in America: The Devil We Know*. He is best known for his book *Monsters in America* (2011, revised edition 2018) and *Wasteland* (2018). He has contributed to Salon, TodayOnline, *The Washington Post*, CNN and radio documentaries for the CBC. He lives in Charleston, South Carolina.

**Raiswell Richard** is Professor of History at the University of Prince Edward Island, Fellow at the Centre for Reformation and Renaissance Studies (Toronto), and a founding editor of the journal *Preternature* (Penn State). His research is concerned with questions about the construction and assimilation of knowledge in the late medieval and early modern periods, especially in relation to demonology. He has published works on demon possession, on proof in witchcraft cases, rhetoric and demonism, and on demonism and colonialism. He is co-translator (with David Winter) of a collection of primary sources on medieval demonology, as well as various articles and edited collections on aspects of premodern demonism.

**Justin Jeffcoat Schedtler** is Associate Professor of Religion at Wartburg College. His research concentrates on apocalyptic ideologies in early Jewish and Christian literature with an emphasis on the Book of Revelation. His most recent book, *Royal Ideologies in Revelation* (2023), explores royal motifs in the Apocalypse. With Kelly Murphy, he edited *Apocalypses in Context* (2016) which explores trajectories of apocalyptic motifs throughout history.

**Gary K. Waite**, Professor Emeritus, University of New Brunswick and a Fellow of the Royal Society of Canada, is a prolific, award-winning author/editor of ten books and dozens of scholarly articles and chapters. These have touched on the Protestant Reformation, Anabaptism, and spiritualism; the Dutch Chambers of Rhetoric and religion; demonology, magic, and witchcraft; and Christian European views of Jews and Muslims. His current research, "Amsterdamnified!", explores the contributions of religious dissenters to the rejection of the devil and the emergence of the early Enlightenment in England and the Low Countries (1540–1700). His latest book is *Anti-Anabaptist Polemics: Dutch Anabaptism and the Devil in England, 1531–1660* (2023).

**Arthur Williamson** did his PhD under the guidance of J. G. A. Pocock at Washington University in St. Louis. He has taught at the University of Chicago, New York University, and California State University, Sacramento. He served as the Assistant Dean at NYU's Graduate School of Arts and Science and as the Graduate Dean at CSUS. He has produced four books in addition to the two listed in the bibliography to his article. Currently, he is working on a large volume under the title, *Scotland and the Rise of Social Theory*, that examines the foundations of secular culture.

**Jutta Wimmler** is a historian and scholar of religion with a focus on Africa's impact on Europe from 1450 to 1900. She received her PhD from the University of Graz, Austria, in 2011 and currently heads the research group "The concept of slavery in African history" at the Bonn Center for Dependency and Slavery Studies in Germany. Her previous publications deal with early modern French, Central European and West African involvement with the early modern Atlantic economy. She has also investigated the movement of Christian religious concepts in that space and has taught several courses on the history of the devil.

**David R. Winter** is Professor of medieval and early modern European history at Brandon University in Manitoba, Canada. With an interest in popular religion and demonology, Winter has written and edited a number of works, including *The Llanthony Stories*, *The Medieval Devil: A Reader*, and *Knowing Demons, Knowing Spirits*. He is currently preparing a translation and study of Icelandic bishop, Oddur Einarsson's *Descriptio qualiscunque Islandiae*.

**Archie T. Wright** is the Executive Director of the Catholic Biblical Association of America. He is a Visiting Lecturer at Catholic University of America in Washington, DC. His doctorate is in the area of Second Temple Judaism and early Christianity. He earned his PhD at Durham University in England under the supervision of Professors Loren T. Stuckenbruck and C. T. Robert Hayward. Wright's research focuses on the relationship between 2nd Temple Period Jewish Literature and the New Testament, in particular the understanding of the New Testament in its 1st-century Jewish context. His publications include the *Origin of Evil Spirits, Satan and the Problem of Evil, Early Jewish Literature: An Anthology, An Introduction to Ancient Ethiopic Grammar,* and *The Spirit Says: Inspiration and Interpretation in Ancient Jewish and Early Christian Texts* along with other essays and journal articles. He is a member of the Editorial Board for the *Journal for the Study of the Pseudepigrapha* and serves as co-editor of Enoch Literature for the *Textual History of the Bible*, and as the General Editor for the forthcoming monograph series with Cascade Academic, *The NT in its Second Temple Jewish Context*. He also serves on the Board of Directors for the Enoch Seminar.

# INTRODUCTION

## Giving the Devil his Due

*Richard Raiswell, Michelle D. Brock,*
*and David R. Winter*

"Whatever the reality of evil is, it has a personal face."[1]
"Like Christianity depends on Satan. Without Satan, what the hell do you need Christianity for?"[2]

Around 1713, Giuseppe Tartini met the devil in a dream. Under the veil of sleep, the Italian composer offered up his soul in exchange for the fulfilment of his every mortal wish. Curious about the musical abilities of the evil one, he also proffered his violin, and soon the devil began to play. The music that flowed from Satan's talons was performed with such astonishing perfection that Tartini awoke from his dream with a start. He immediately wrote down all that he could remember from his diabolical encounter. These notes would form the basis for his most famous composition, the Violin Sonata in G minor, a technically challenging piece which became widely known as the "Devil's Trill Sonata."[3]

The general contours of Tartini's story were not new. The demonic pact has been imbedded in the Christian tradition since the earliest days of the faith, gradually growing in its folkloric and theological prominence through the medieval and early modern periods—an expression of anxiety about worldly ambition within the context of a morally constrained hierarchy. By the 18th century, deals with the devil had moved from the stuff of worldly popes, alchemists and witches to a mainstay of legends about artistic creation. Soon, the devil appeared at a crossroads in Mississippi to teach the blues before going down to Georgia to play the fiddle. The belief that the devil has preternatural knowledge and talent, musical or otherwise, is even older than the pact; indeed, construed as a fallen angel, Satan has been imbued from the beginning with abilities that exceed and beguile humans. Thus, when Tartini dreamed of the devil, he drew on a very long, dark and complicated history.

Louis-Léopold Boilly's 1824 lithograph of this encounter *Le Songe de Tartini*," depicted on the cover of the present volume, shows the devil perched at the foot of Tartini's bed. The fiend is depicted in all his gothic glory: batlike wings unfurled, horns sharp, his physique monstrous yet muscled like a grotesque David. For all its menace, though, the image is also humorous; the hint of a smile plays at the edges of Satan's mouth as Tartini

DOI: 10.4324/9781003096603-1

sleepily hums along. The viewer is not sure whether to laugh or recoil at the sight of this profoundly familiar figure.

It is a comfortable modern conceit that the Enlightenment signalled the end of any serious engagement with the idea that the devil as a force actively seeking to confound creation or to ensnare its human inhabitants. The likes of the Italian composer's nocturnal imaginings were increasingly consigned to the realm of anxious fantasy or anachronism. Indeed, Philip Almond has argued that by the middle of the 18th century, Satan had largely been relegated "to the distant corners of the educated European mind."[4] His wings ever-more clipped and his field of action progressively more circumscribed by the secularising forces of rationalism, the modern devil has been reduced to making cameo appearances in horror films, comic books and video games, or to selling vacuum cleaners and decadent desserts. Outside the demesne of a cadre of conservative Christians, he has even been deprived of whatever literal reality with which he had been invested in previous ages, diminished to the level of a symbol of evil or a metaphor for the weaknesses and failings of individuals.

Yet the devil has never really gone away. He remains lurking just below the surface of Western society, a force capable of breaking out of the shadows and the darkest reaches of the conscience to stoke fear and excite panic. Far from being eliminated by the Enlightenment, his very malleability as an explanatory resource means that he continues to be made and remade in response to circumstance. Whether that be with the Satanic panics of the 1980s and early 1990s, the growth of deliverance ministries and the revival of exorcism, or the apocalyptically framed war against "terror" and the West's demonically constructed opponents, the cultural niches he has always inhabited remain open to him. The devil matters still.

## The Devil's Role

For believers, the devil still matters because he solves some crucial problems at the heart of Christianity. In the first place, he gives meaning to sacred history. Had there not been a demonically inspired/possessed/allied snake—the way the relationship is construed varies—in the Garden of Eden, there would be no point in creation. Adam and Eve and their progeny would have remained in paradise, obeying God unquestioningly. There would be no original sin. Humanity would not need faith or a way to earn salvation, and so there would be no need of rewards and punishments. But with the arrival of the devil in some guise, the choices human beings make came to have consequences and became part of a grand, cosmological drama, with sacred history progressing towards some sort of inevitable showdown.

Second, with history construed as dynamic, the devil frees God from direct responsibility for evil. God may be the ultimate power in creation, but attributing the presence of evil to a distinct, malevolent principal maintains the pretence of his benevolence. From a human perspective, this framing is important, for it allows those suffering from affliction or misfortune to attribute their troubles to the machinations of Satan. To some, this recognition of the devil's presence in their lives serves as a starting point for uncomfortable introspection, an examination of both the individual's own sinfulness and the resilience of their spiritual armour in the face of demonic assault. To others, the effect is precisely the opposite, allowing them to contextualise their difficulties within a homogenising apocalyptic frame that frees them from seeking out human or naturalistic explanations for the circumstances in which they find themselves. For the latter type of self-identifying victim, the demonic functions as a complete and sufficient explanation for adversity—one which underscores for them their moral rectitude and, by extension, their confidence in their worldview. In this sense, then, the devil is both a necessary component of God's benevolence as construed within the frame of an uncompromising monotheism, and a means of explaining or projecting guilt for bad behaviour.

While the extent to which the devil is God's agent and so acting at the behest of the almighty has been debated over the centuries, in practical terms one important consequence of this separation of the divine from the infernal is to bridge the gulf between received revelation and people's lived experience. God may have created creation perfectly as implied by Genesis 1.31, but it is the presence of the devil that can explain much of the misfortune, pain, suffering and manifest injustice which afflicts humanity as it proceeds through time. To believers, the terminally ill infant, the shelling of a refugee camp, the capricious rule of a vengeful and sadistic dictator can all—under particular circumstances—be read as clear and unambiguous signs of the actions of the evil one. Indeed, that the number of apparent demonic assaults seems to be increasing over time merely underscores the idea that history progresses teleologically, and that the devil's rages become more extreme, more acute and more desperate as creation advances to its determined conclusion (2 Tm 3:1-13 and Lk 21:6-31). In this respect, the detection of the devil's presence within personal or worldly affairs is troublingly reassuring: it accounts for imperfection within what scripture proclaims to be perfect while confirming the inevitability of history's climax and resolution. Because the devil is bad, God can still be good—and his plan for creation proceeds apace.

But the devil is a problem solver for Christians in another important way, too. While it is difficult to offer rhetorically powerful, empirical examples that prove the existence of God without presupposing his existence as somehow axiomatic—that is, by having faith— apparent evidence of the devil's actions seems comparatively clear and ubiquitous. It is there in the individuals and communities pained, tormented or wiped out by a range of human and natural disasters. Yet while the obvious presence of evil in the world can be taken as vivid and moving evidence for the existence of a transcendent principal of evil, comparably convincing evidence for God is less forthcoming. Direct visions of the divine have historically proven both rare and limited, and exercises such as "counting one's blessings" can seem small when balanced against the manifest weight of the evidence of evil.

In certain contexts, this apparent evidence for the existence of the devil has also functioned as an impassioned defence of the reality of God. In one sense, at least, this dates to the New Testament: in the gospels, Christ repeatedly received people believed to be possessed by demons and demonstrated his divinity to those present by casting these spirits out. Indeed, this is also largely the case in subsequent possession narratives—both Catholic and protestant—into the Enlightenment. In these instances, the visually derived evidence of the presence of the devil precedes the divine, while its amelioration proves godly power. Walter Stephens has made a similar argument about the role of the devil in witchcraft theory as it coalesced from the second half of the 15th century. The testimony of confessed witches proved the possibility of the existence of a praeter- or supernatural realm of malevolent spirits. By extension, the effect of sacramental counter-magic on these spirits proved the reality of a transcendent antithetical power behind it.[5] Much the same style of argument underlies the American revivalist movements in the 18th and 19th centuries. As Scott Poole has argued, many of those who embraced this emerging form of evangelical Christianity came to their conversion experience by first understanding the extent to which their soul had been corrupted by Satan. Only the direct intervention of the Holy Spirit could free them.[6]

Thus, while the existence of God does not necessitate the existence of the devil, the abundant visible evidence of the reality of the devil can be argued to imply the existence of his moral opposite. In this sense, then, reasoning from effects, the devil and God become mutually authenticating and mutually contingent. As the Scottish king, James VI, argued at the end of the 16th century, "For since the Devill is the verie contrarie opposite to God, there can be no better way to know God, then by the contrarie."[7] To know the demonic is to know the divine.

## Demonologies and the Demonised

It has proven exceptionally difficult over the centuries to posit any coherent, philosophically robust definition of the devil and his powers. Insofar as they have been attempted, such definitions have tended merely to assert some version of his origin story—that is, that he was a being created at some biblically undefined point and that he turned evil through his own free will. This is the essence, for instance, of the definition of the devil posited by the Fourth Lateran Council in 1215. But this was not intended as a definition of the devil per se; rather, it was fashioned as a vigorous assertion of monotheism against the dualist Cathar heresy believed to pose an existential threat to the church at the time. Some 800 years later, Father Gabriele Amorth—the self-styled "chief exorcist of the Vatican"—was able to do little better.[8] Given that any meaningful definition of the devil has implications for the construction of divine power, omniscience and benevolence, those who have broached the topic philosophically have tended to do so primarily with a view to safeguarding the integrity of their conception of God. In the 5th century, for example, St. Augustine argued that the devil's ability to work apparent wonders was a function of his natural abilities as an angel, albeit a fallen one. For the saint, the devil's long experience of the natural world had given him the knowledge to exploit the properties of created things in novel ways to create effects that seemed miraculous to human beings.

Almost two centuries later, Pope Gregory the Great conceived of the devil as a mere tool of God, thus turning the devil's apparent evil into part of God's benevolent plan for creation—albeit in a fashion unfathomable to human beings mired within the confines of time. For his part, in the middle of the 13th century, Thomas Aquinas imagined a spiritual being with the ability to reify and condense air to the point where it can create human forms with the corporality necessary to copulate with people. In the middle of the 16th century, the physician Johann Weyer circumscribed the devil's abilities still further, arguing that the more fantastic-sounding claims of those who admitted commerce with demons were merely the product of demon-addled cognition. While these attempts to preserve almighty God's essential benevolence in the context of a devil whom—in the final analysis—he created and over whom he had power are all theoretically tidy, none is particularly satisfying in practice. [9] None provides much comfort or solace to those experiencing what they understood to be demonic trials or tribulations.

What this has meant is that the devil and his abilities are defined through the manifest empirical and experiential evidence of human suffering and injustice—and the fear and anxiety this understanding generates. As many of the chapters in this volume make clear, the bible has very little specific to say about the devil or Satan or Lucifer—and what it does say is often ambiguous and sometimes downright contradictory. Outside the few markers laid down by scripture—his absolute moral opposition to the good, his role as a tempter, deceiver and would-be subverter of the divine order—this imprecision implies that the devil lacks a stable identity. This has historically afforded those who believe in him a great deal of freedom. It allows that along with instances of human adversity, elements of folklore and patterns of traditional non-Christian belief systems can readily be assimilated into his nature as they were encountered as the faith spread. As Lyndal Roper has argued, this means that demonology "was to a large degree a science founded on the evidence of experience."[10] In effect, then, the devil is a composite being, a figure whose identity is a function of people's experience of adversity.

But if the devil is more a social construction than he is a figure whose identity is grounded in scripture, then diabology and demonology are borne of the process of the demonisation of experience rather from any theoretical premises. Indeed, this is implied in the gospel of Matthew which warns "every good tree bears good fruit, but a rotten tree produces bad fruit. A good tree cannot bear bad fruit, nor can a bad tree bear good fruit … Thus, by their fruits you will know them" (Mt 7:17-20). Thus, in discerning the presence of the devil, one should proceed from effects to causes—not the other way around. In practice, this has meant that the devil has been constructed and tokens of his presence expanded over the centuries according to shifting configurations of political, social and cultural power. Historically, at least, the Satan who reports to God, offering him advice in the Old Testament book of Job, does not look the same as the figure trapped in ice at the centre of the cosmos described by Dante in his *Inferno*. The devil with whom witches copulate at the sabbat described by the 17th-century Bordeaux judge Pierre de Lancre is not the same as that described in the second half of the 20th century by American evangelicals such as Hal Lindsay or Jack Chick. Yet in each case, his identity is an aggregate of each previous iteration. It might be argued that this merely implies that he adapts his schemes, tricks, ruses and stratagems to circumstances. But in practice, every reiteration of the devil serves to expand the devil's perceived field of operation.

But this experientially grounded construction of the devil has another consequence, for the devil is effectively the rubbish bin of the Western history. He is the embodiment of that which has been rejected by society, the foetid, corrupting stench from which people must be insulated and walled off. As St. Paul wrote to the Corinthians, "Can Christ ever be in accord with Beliar? What does a believer have in common with an unbeliever? Can there be an agreement between the temple of God and idols? … 'come out from their midst and separate yourselves from them,' says the Lord. 'Do not touch anything unclean, and I will welcome you'" (2 Cor 6:15-18; NCB). But like the refuse of any municipal dump, those things that have been discarded—those things that have been classed as "demonic" over the ages—have little in common with each other beyond the fact that they have been rejected. The polytheists of antiquity, Manichaean dualists, soothsayers, unruly women, Muslims, Scientologists, the Soviet Union, Freudians, the theory of evolution, "Dungeons and Dragons" players and the International Monetary Fund have all at various times been labelled as "demonic"; yet, it is hard to posit any essential connection between them beyond this arbitrary and historically particular classification. As a category, then, the demonic has become progressively more heterogenous over the centuries as every successive generation of believers has committed more of their fears and prejudices to the dump.

Using the demonic as a way of comprehending difference is a resilient strategy with a double origin: in the first commandment's emphatic condemnation of variant religious belief, and in early Christian attempts to distinguish their community from Judaism.[11]

It was employed to great effect in their dealings with rival wonder-working traditions (including competing groups within the Christian tradition), and with the traditional polytheistic practices of those whom they sought to convert as the faith moved more broadly across the Roman and then Northern European worlds.[12] It is not wholly surprising, then, that when Europeans took to the seas to find a maritime route to Asia, explorers, colonial propagandists and imperialists adopted precisely the same explanatory approach when trying to understand the foreign cultures they encountered, and then in the ways they tried to describe these peoples to those at back home. The Bolognese traveller, Ludovico di Varthema, who was in India in 1504 and 1505, for instance, described the religion of the king of Calicut as devil worship. The king, he continued, keeps an image of their God/devil in a chapel in his palace. This has four horns, hands like hooks and feet like those of a cockerel. All around the chapel are pictures of demons, and on each side there is an image of the devil seated on a chair in the midst of flames—he holds a soul in his right hand in his mouth, and with his left, he reaches to grab another.[13] A century later, in the "new" world, John Smith, one of the founders of the Jamestown settlement, was similarly emphatic about the religious practices of those he encountered: the indigenous people of Virginia, he asserted, worshipped the devil and adorned their temples with "his image evill favouredly carved, and then painted and adorned with chaines, copper, and beades, and covered with a skin, in such ma[n]ner as the deformity may well suit with such a God."[14]

Demonising the *other* in this way made difference readily comprehensible, for it placed it within a recognisable context, situating it within the economy of salvation. Far from facilitating any epistemological rupture or even engendering doubt, the encounters of these men with foreign cultures proved that the unfamiliar was, in fact, completely familiar. As Weyer argued, "the devil contrived that one in the same form of worship of him should be observed in the most widely separated parts of the whole world."[15] As was the case with early Christian encounters with *others*, there was no point in trying to understand the subtleties and nuances of the cultures with which these people came in contact. An extreme example is the early 17th-century English traveller Edward Terry. Commenting on the variety of religious practice he observed in India, he confidently proclaimed that there were 84 different sects of Hindus. This might fill one with wonder, he continued, if one fails to appreciate "that *Satan*, who is the author of division, is the seducer of them all."[16] For Terry and many of his contemporaries, ethnographic curiosity is, at best, a waste of time. At worst, it distracts, focusing people's attention on external appearance rather than the "real" transcendent significance of these people and their societies. Although lazily flattening difference into stultifying generalisations, demonising domesticates the strange, for it situates it within a familiar frame. To be sure, the discovery of the devil both within and without Europe was troubling, but it was not unexpected and was wholly comprehensible.

But the devil and the demonic play an important role within the community of the faithful, too, for they allow society to isolate and critically disengage from the repugnant or the deviant. Demonising the likes of Hitler or Stalin, or serial killers such as Fritz Haarmann, Richard Ramirez or Paul Bernardo reduces them effectively to stock characters in the pantheon of fallen angels as opposed to wholly human products of their societies. As figures believed somehow to be in league with the devil, their actions are literally *inhuman* or maybe even *anti-human*. They represent abhorrent yet precise, targeted intrusions of evil into the arc of sacred history. Accordingly, like cultural difference, the motivations of such people do not need to be probed or comprehended in any critical depth—and in by doing, demonisers can elide awkward questions about the human propensity for extreme violence. As David Frankfurter has put it, demonising these figures places them safely outside the realm of human identification and so "we no longer need to contemplate our own inclinations to such acts."[17]

While the demonisation of mass murderers preserves a particular conception of human goodness in this way, the process also functions as a means of comprehending social change, for threats to what is perceived to be the natural and proper order of society—the status quo—can readily be attributed to the master of disorder. Deviations from gender or sexual norms, or standards of behaviour deemed appropriate for particular individuals or cohorts—even unorthodox or foreign forms of political philosophy—could all readily be laid at the hooves of the devil. Even the seemingly unnaturally beautiful—Tartini's sonata, for example—could sometimes be attributed to the devil's machinations.[18] In this sense, whatever is perceived as different, new, socially or intellectually challenging, disruptive or which is perceived to threaten the received balance of power invites demonisation. Consequently, the self-identified "righteous" become acutely anxious about what they take to be the devil's social microaggressions, for through these he threatens to undermine society from within. The detection of the demonic, then, can be read as a sign of anxiety, a projection of people's fears about social integrity and a sign of a community's perception of its own moral health.

This view of the demonic as a marker of difference and disorder—or at least "new" order—has spurred some to embrace the devil publicly as an anti-reactionary, progressive force. It is the devil who is the lord of social development: it is he who embraces diversity, inclusivity of the marginalised, individuality, creativity and new ideas. As such, he represents a force capable of toppling traditional, conservative power structures, from oppressive morality and creatively stultifying monotony—he was, after all, the figure who first challenged arbitrary dictatorial power. While Anton LaVey argued that the devil could not be worshipped as a real entity, his Church of Satan, founded in 1966, adopted the prince of darkness as its symbol, contending that he better epitomised the real, carnal nature of humanity, its pride and quest for liberty and individualism.[19] Heavy metal musicians quickly found in the devil a transgressive symbol that framed the youthful rebellion of their audience in a way that assured them attention and notoriety. But for others, the decision to embrace Satan was more morally and personally empowering. For some of the young self-identifying Luciferians studied by Amy Slagle, the devil represents a "spiritual guide and ally." For the person Slagle identifies only as V, "[Lucifer's] like Lilith. He's very up in your face. He's very strong willed. And I feel like I look to those people because I want to be strong-willed … You have the feeling with them that they'll never disown you. There's no judgment. They're not just going to leave you … They force you to believe in yourself."[20] For V, Lucifer is not the epitome of evil; he is a powerful force, supporting her and forcing her to come out of herself. This embrace of the devil as a liberator has served, perhaps paradoxically, to reinforce the beliefs of traditionalists by reifying the threat of the demonic: Satanists are real and, thanks to the incorporation of the Church of Satan, the devil has not only minions, but an address: 6114 California St, San Francisco—or at least it was until the building was torn down in 2001.

But while this process of rejection-through-demonisation means that the contents of the category of the demonic are heterogeneous, the fact that they are all demonic means that they are ontological equivalent. In one sense, this means that classifying people, their values or their ideas as demonic serves not just as a description of them, but as a complete and omni-sufficient explanation of them. Yet the process of demonisation also creates new knowledge about the demonised through a process of dynamic nominalism. As groups operating at the behest of Satan in some way, knowledge about them is effectively inter-changeable. The tricks and schemes of the devil manifested in one cultural context can be uncritically reproduced as descriptive of other more recently demonised communities. A particular case in point is that of inversion and conspiracy. While it is hardly surprising to find that the demonised are regularly accused of various forms of transgressive and blas-phemous practice, including the desecration of Christian symbols, more sinister and more potent is the idea that they abuse and sacrifice children as part of their cultic practices. In many respects, it is hard to tell the difference between the accusations of ritual child murder levelled against medieval Jews, the confessions of infant cannibalism at the sabbat made by convicted witches in the early 17th century, and testimony of so-called "breeders" like Lauren Stratford in the late 1980s who claimed to have been forcibly impregnated by a sa-tanic cult so that its members could sacrifice their children. But the idea that the demonised engage in collective rituals at Satan's inspiration marks them out also as a self-aware, con-scious group—as a community or even a religion antithetical to the truth operating within the shadows of society. The ritual binds members of the group together through their col-lective participation in atrocities which are not just transgressive and socially abhorrent but illegal, too. Indeed, it is the secret, conspiratorial nature of these groups that allows them to operate undetected within the community of the "right minded." It purportedly allows them to hide their victims and their corpses; it allows them to infiltrate the highest orders of society, operating, for instance, a vast paedophilic conspiracy from the basement of a Washington, DC pizza restaurant. In the circular logic of the demonisers, that the demon-ised are subversive means that they are secret, and that they are secret means that they are necessarily subversive. In the end, this creates a sort of demonic Ouroboros, a starkly literal imagine of a snake eating its tail.

## Combatting Satan

While thinking with demons—to borrow Stuart Clark's phrase—can give meaning to mis-fortune in the here and now, it also endows wickedness and calamity with eschatological significance. St. Peter describes how the devil stalks humanity incessantly, prowling around, probing for weakened defences, looking to devour his prey (cf. 1 Pt 5:8-9). Thus, to the righteously minded, the tribulations inflicted upon them, the disordering forces they see gathering around them in their social spaces, all have apocalyptic meaning. In other words, such perceived assaults are demonic chevauchées—probing raids intended to wear down people's spiritual defences and to weaken their confidence in the efficacy of the forces of good. They are skirmishes in the great cosmic war that has been being fought between God and the forces of evil since the beginning of time and that will culminate in the ultimate tribulation—that described in the book of Revelations.

Amplified in this way, such torments cannot simply be tolerated. As St. Paul counselled the Ephesians, "Put on your armour of God so that you may be able to stand against the ambushes of the devil, for our struggle is not against flesh and blood, but against princes and powers, against the rulers of this world of darkness, against the spirits of wickedness in high places" (Eph 6:11-12). Thus, where the talons of the devil are discerned underly-ing human actions or failings, such activities must be actively resisted and overtly chal-lenged. Doing so is a moral imperative, for such apparent assaults are wily attempts by

Satan to subvert society, to replace hierarchy with pluralism, certainty with ambiguity, order with chaos.

This sense that Christian society is under siege dates from the earliest days of the new faith as it struggled to survive as an underground sect against the sporadic persecutions of Roman authorities. Despite the fact that Christianity became the official religion of the empire in the 4th century, the idea of the faith as embattled remained hardwired as Christians encountered and demonised new cultures and traditions as it spread across the tottering remains of the empire. The sense of being at siege with the devil is epitomised in the notion of monasticism, one of the central cultural and economic institutions of the Middle Ages into the 12th century. Indeed, the great Cistercian reformer Bernard of Clairvaux described the monastery as a fortress of the eternal king, a walled-off outpost in enemy territory defended by soldiers prepared to resist the assaults of the devil.[21] Spiritual combat continued to gird the thinking of Cold War fundamentalists like Billy Graham who tried to connect the external threat of communism with what he took to be the internal threats of Darwinism, feminism and sexual liberation. From this vantage, Graham crafted a heady narrative that presented America as hard-pressed by satanic forces internationally while simultaneously being subverted from within by the devil's morality-sapping agents.[22] For Ray Prichard, writing in the wake of the 9/11 attacks, Satan is the ultimate terrorist, waging incessant asymmetrical warfare against the faithful. In the battle between God and the devil, he continues, "we are all frontline soldiers"—and perhaps most worryingly, "no one gets a vacation[!]"[23]

In many ways, it is the apparent yet secret presence of the demonic within the community of the faithful that has proven most alarming. Jews, heretics and atheists, communists and terrorists, social reformers and LGBTQIA+ people all look like normal members of society, yet their presence represents an existential threat to rightly ordered society and the godly. One cannot discern a person's nature on the basis of mere appearances, St. Paul cautioned, for "even Satan masquerades as an angel of light" (2 Cor 11:13-15). Pritchard encapsulates the consequences of this mode thinking quite effectively: "don't negotiate with the devil. And don't talk it over with his representatives. Remember that his representative could be your best friend or a family member, a coworker, or someone else you know very well."[24] In that respect, it is the moral identity of individuals and groups that matter, and this can only be known by virtue of what these people are advocating and doing.

The effect is to galvanise the devil's opponents into a single front, united in thought and action, people whose antennae are precisely tuned to discern any perceived threat to the status quo. In this sense, the detection of the devil creates an army of variously credentialed experts—including saints, Christian clergy, inquisitors and witchfinders, exorcists or deliverance ministers, special investigators, social workers and child protection agents, and psychotherapists. Drawing on the testimony of what might be dubbed "expert" witnesses—Jewish magicians, confessed heretics and witches, the testimony of serial killers, former "breeders," "survivors" of "Satanic ritual abuse"—these crusaders find evidence of demonism all around them. Moreover, as the evidence they adduce confirms the presence of the demonic and the discovery of the demonic confirms the plausibility of their evidence, it becomes increasingly difficult to challenge. To question the authenticity of a witch's confession, for instance, is to challenge the legitimacy of the evidence-gathering practices of the legal system; challenging the testimony of the recovered memories of a Satanic ritual abuse (SRA) survivor is to retraumatise them—and to accept the word of the paedophiles they accused over that of their victims.[25]

As the evidence of demonism brought forward by these "experts" mounts and is determined to be essentially consistent with that from other places and times, it becomes self-authenticating. In certain times and under certain conditions, the result can be a moral panic—and the exposed activities of these secret sects become a problem not just for the moral crusaders but for society more generally. As the opening monologue to Geraldo Rivera's 1988 television special, "Devil Worship: Exposing Satan's Underground," proclaims, "It doesn't matter if you believe in Satan. It doesn't matter if you believe in demons. What's important to know is that there are people out there who do and they're willing to do anything to accomplish their goal."[26] Whether in the 12th century or the 21st, the consequences can be horrendous for the demonised. So construed, the devil has long been a very adaptable and dangerous fiction.

## A Satanic Renaissance?

Writing during the closing days of Vatican Council II in the mid-1960s, in his *Satanic Bible*, LaVey argued that humanity was entering what he called "a new Satanic age." His point was that the church's more liberal attitude towards some of the seven deadly sins signalled the beginning of the end of Christianity. For him, the church's move towards an accommodation of human weakness at the expense of its moral idealism represented a shift towards what he called "satanism"—an acknowledgement of humanity's need for physical, mental and emotional gratification.[27] At the same time, *Time* magazine asked the question "Is God Dead" on the cover of its 8 April 1966 edition. Obviously, LaVey's reading of religious politics has proven hopelessly wrong: organised religion has not perished; its adherents have not cast their "ecclesiastic vote" for a religion more consistent with their convictions. But in many respects we have entered a new Satanic age—or at least an age in which a renewed emphasis on demonism has seeped into mainstream public discourse. And this demonic resurgence is not merely about rhetoric; instead, it is a blueprint for active spiritual warfare, at times with deadly consequences.

Since his purported decline in the 18th century, the devil has lived on not only in popular belief and culture, but also in the revival movements of the fledgling United States with their emphasis on a staunch biblically adduced morality. He grew in importance to evangelical Christians as they took up Paul's advice to arm themselves against the snares and traps of the devil and came to construe creation as a battleground for a sempiternal struggle between the forces of darkness and those of light destined to last until the final days. The demonic gained ground in the conscience of many Americans with the perceived attacks on biblical literalism represented by the theory of evolution—and the subsequent attacks on morality posed by the banning of prayer and bible reading in public schools, and then the mandating of sex education. And it recast the geopolitical threat of communism in Manichean terms. As Billy Graham preached in Los Angeles in 1949, "Communism is not only an economic interpretation of life—Communism is a religion that is inspired, directed and motivated by the Devil himself who has declared war against Almighty God."[28]

The idea of a Satanic renaissance, then, is not necessarily about the devil's "rebirth," but rather about his resurfacing or reemergence into mainstream public discourse. In this way, the Satanic panic of the 1980s and 1990s—a cultural moment in which the devil was detected at the root of a series of abrupt social and political dislocations (many of them connected to or rooted in newly emerging gender patterns)—was in fact an epiphenomenon in a much larger process. Today, this resurfacing has been made manifest by two parallel yet seemingly contradictory phenomena. On the one hand, alongside the Church of Satan, the Temple of Set and, more recently, the Satanic Temple have carved an organised space for people to understand and even embrace the devil as a symbol of resistance or creative inspiration.[29] On the other, a far bigger embrace of the devil has emerged from the Christian right's backlash against cultural changes and shifting demographics—a trend that is most obvious in, but not limited to, the United States. Christian nationalism, once on the fringes of American political life, now has robust representation in the halls of Congress.[30] For its opponents, Satan looms large, with many espousing what Whitney Phillips and Mark Brockway have termed an "anti-liberal demonology."[31] New conspiratorial movements that replicate much of the demonic conspiracies of old have rapidly attracted followers as well as tacit nods from American leaders.[32] American Catholics too are increasingly invested in training exorcists and combating a purported rise in Satanism.[33] The devil, it seems, is being given his due.

Take, for example, a post that went viral on several social media sites in early 2024. "A televangelist from Arkansas claims Satan is engineering Taylor Swift's marriage to [American football quarterback], Travis Kelce," it reports, "so she can give birth to the antichrist and launch the apocalyptic thousand-year war against Christ." The post closes with two rhetorical questions related to Swift's popstar status: "Must she do everything? And during a world tour?"[34] The Arkansas preacher in question has not been identified, and no such Swift-Kelce offspring has been born; the whole thing is satire. But the crucial point about the televangelist's message is that it seems probable—it sounds like something someone might have said. And the truth is not far off. Swift has, in fact, been accused repeatedly of "doing satanic rituals during her shows," despite her open identification as a Christian. In April 2024, the spread of these claims prompted PolitiFact to publish a piece debunking them, which included an interview with Lucien Greaves, co-founder of The Satanic Temple, who dismissed such allegations as "incredibly asinine conspiracy theories."[35]

As we have seen, rumours of musicians being in league with the devil are nothing new. But to dismiss such allegations as the mere rantings of religious radicals on Facebook is to neglect just how influential the embattled worldview they reflect has become. For a significant subset of American Christians, spiritual warfare—the battle against ever-active demonic forces—is imperative, and the devil's minions countless. What might appear, at first glance, a primarily religious resurgence of demonic thinking is in fact intensely political; the central battleground for many of these believers is not the church, but Congress and the courts. Indeed, as S. Jonathon O'Donnell has pointed out, many who engage in spiritual warfare see "demons as central actors in world politics and everyday life."[36] As the Public Religion Research Institute survey reported in early 2024, some 25% of Americans agreed or mostly agreed with the statement, "The government, media, and financial worlds in the U.S. are controlled by a group of Satan-worshipping paedophiles who run a global child sex trafficking operation."[37] For many Americans, the devil is as active in the corridors of power as he is in the individual body and soul.

Nor has this Satanic resurfacing been confined to the United States. Throughout the Western world—as well as parts of the post-colonial global south that were Christianised—pastors, politicians and other public figures frequently and urgently claim to have detected the devil's operation in the activities of their political rivals and cultural opponents. For a period during the 2022 electoral rematch between the Brazilian presidential candidates Jair Bolsonaro and Luis Inacio Lula da Silva, for example, the devil "dominated traditional news outlets and blogs."[38] Lula supporters freely lobbed accusations at Bolsonaro, claiming that he mingled with Freemasons—the anti-Catholic fraternity claimed by its foes to have diabolical associations. A picture of Bolsonaro circulated online and in traditional media showing him below an image of Baphomet in a Masonic Temple. The image was clearly manipulated, but it served its discursive purpose: to show the former populist president as a figure of menace who had allied himself with occult forces. Meanwhile, Bolsonaro partisans claimed that Lula was consorting with evil spirits. Lula's election team was forced to issue a clarifying statement assuring Brazilians that their candidate was a Christian, and that "he does not have a pact nor did he ever talk with the Devil."[39] Both sides sought to contest the hustings "in heavenly places," however, and thus had to tread a very fine line, as their Catholic and Pentecostal constituencies were predisposed to interpret the old enemy's political interventions in very different ways.

Meanwhile, in sub-Saharan Africa, the devil has been repeatedly deployed in recent decades by those seeking to advance conservative cultural projects, particularly those that stigmatise sexual and gender minorities. Street-level deliverance ministries have played a major role in both shaping and responding to these anxieties. As scholar Naomi Richman warns, "Across West Africa, Pentecostal churches are becoming increasingly vocal in their warnings about the devil. Many share a growing concern that the existential threat he poses is becoming more widespread and more severe."[40] However, African political leaders are also paying attention. In a media interview in 2023, for example, the Catholic president of Burundi, Évariste Ndayishimiye, asserted that homosexuality was like "choosing between Satan and God."[41] Further north, in Uganda, a deeply entrenched moral panic surrounding queer identity led to the 2023 Anti-Homosexuality Act, in which those found guilty of "aggravated homosexuality" are liable to imprisonment or even the death penalty. Among Pentecostal and other groups seeking to position queerness within their understanding of the unfolding of providential history, gay and lesbian sexuality is unambiguously viewed as evidence of spirit possession and demonic activity. One queer man who fled Burundi for a United Nations refugee camp in Uganda noted ruefully, "LGBTQ refugees are living in constant fear of being attacked or even killed. Many people call us names; they mock us and say a demon and evil spirit of homosexuality possess us."[42] Here as elsewhere, the rising rhetoric of demonism matters; it consistently reflects and reinforces feelings of hate and an agenda of harm.

The response to the world-wide COVID-19 pandemic between 2021 and 2023 is the most recent, globalised example of the spread and influence of those who believe that "the devil has come down in great wrath." Throughout the global response to the public health crisis, populists and Christian-tinged conspiracy theorists frequently framed a general mistrust in government in the language of demonism. In Bolivia, vaccine misinformation was similarly derided by evangelical Christians in Satanic terms. In the United States, Naomi Wolf was suspended from the social media site, Twitter (now X), for alleging, among other things, that Chief Medical Advisor to the American President, Dr Anthony Fauci, was a Satanic actor. Other Americans claimed that the mRNA COVID-19 vaccine was the "mark of the beast," a pharmaceutical agent that, according to them, contains "a bioluminescent marker called LUCIFERASE so that you can be tracked"—its use portending the end time.[43] Further north, in the waning days of the pandemic, the anti-vaxx trucker convoy in Canada noisily adopted Satanic tropes to undergird its message of opposition to vaccination. Romana Didulo, a Q-Anon adjacent "sovereign citizen" and self-proclaimed "queen of Canada" repeatedly claimed that diabolical actors lead several Western governments in order to curtail citizens' rights.[44] Indeed, this Satanic resurfacing is what animates the whole of the Q-Anon conspiracy theory, which emerged during the first year of the Trump administration. Adherents believe, among other things, that "liberal elites"—from prominent Democrats to celebrities to progressive religious figures—are part of a Satanic cabal of cannibalistic paedophiles.[45] Unfortunately, such conspiratorial thinking—as powerful and dangerous as it is detached from reality—shows no signs of abating any time soon.

## Conclusion

The devil's relationship to humanity has long been complex: we fear and attempt to resist his earthly machinations, but we are also fascinated, entranced, seduced, repulsed and amused by him. This book is about why this is, how the devil became central to the Western imagination and why he remains there still. Its chapters span more than 2,000 years of history, a period in which the devil was made and remade alongside—and as an integral part of—the idea of "the west." This history is littered with dark chapters of political turmoil, war, natural disaster, persecution and more; throughout, the demonic has provided an explanatory frame through which to make sense of one's own experiences and identity, recasting instances of suffering and adversity into examples of his power in creation. The resultant discourses of public safety, purity and pollution against the demonised other, with its alien and sinister rites and rituals of inversion, often come to serve as justifications for horrendous atrocities.

Collectively, the chapters of this volume argue that the devil has been integral to the development of Western society and its sense of itself from the start of the first millennium. Indeed, the demonological imagination has served as part of the glue holding Western societies together, finding meaning in the world and spurring individuals and communities into specific behaviours—often with abhorrent consequences rationalised in terms of the loftiest moral rhetoric of the day. While contexts, misfortunes and anxieties shift according to the priorities of a period and the communities of practice in which he is made, many of the dynamics that underlie the devil's construction and detection and his use as a cultural resource have important continuities. This book, then, is a history of the anti-West—the West as seen through its anxieties, fears and attempts to define and police itself and its boundaries. It is the story of the devil we know, even if many of us no longer believe.

## Post-Scriptum

We wrote this piece just before the 2024 Republican Party national convention in Milwaukee, Wisconsin, where the devil has featured prominently as a foil for Christian nationalists. Only two days before its opening, former president and presidential candidate Donald Trump narrowly missed being assassinated at a rally in Butler, Pennsylvania. In his opening address to the convention, South Carolina senator Tim Scott declared that "our God still saves" and "still delivers" because that past Saturday, when "the devil came to Pennsylvania holding a rifle," Trump's life was spared.[46] Instead, a retired firefighter trying to protect his family was killed, and two others were seriously wounded. Later, Harmeet Dhillon, a Sikh and member of the Republican delegation for California, was asked to deliver a prayer to close the first night's proceedings. While the prayer had a universal message, she gave it in Punjabi, setting off a flurry social media commentary. Oklahoma state senator Dusty Deevers was apparently appalled, posting that, "Christians in the Republican party nodding silently along to a prayer to a demon god is shameful." Andrew Torba, CEO of the right-wing microblogging site *Gab*, declared that there can be "no tolerance for pagan false gods and the synagogue of Satan."[47] The next day, *ProPublica* reported on a closed-door speech given by vice-presidential nominee J. D. Vance to young conservatives in 2021 in which he proclaimed, "I believe the devil is real and that he works terrible things in our society. That's a crazy conspiracy theory to a lot of very well-educated people in this country right now."[48]

As Louisiana prepares to force every public-school classroom in the state to display the ten commandments with its proclamation of rigid monotheism and unambiguous prohibition against what it deems polytheism and "idolatry"—and with some other American states looking to follow suit—it seems the younger generation may be tempted to follow Edward Terry and his 16th-century brethren in seeing Satan lurking behind religious diversity. The devil of the past appears very present indeed.

## Notes

1 Peter Fink, S.J., Teacher of sacramental theology at the Weston School of Theology, as quoted in the *New York Times* 6 March 1990.
2 Varg Vikernes aka Count Grishnackh, founder of the Norwegian black metal band *Burzum* as quoted in Michael Moynihan and Didrik Søderlind in *Lords of Chaos* (Port Townsend, 2003), 126.
3 This story is recounted in many places, including Peter Egri, "Renaissance and Baroque Conceits: Literature, Painting and Music," *Hungarian Journal of English and American Studies (HJEAS)*, 3, no. 2 (1997): 89–105; 101; Carl Van Vechten, "On the Relative Difficulties of Depicting Heaven and Hell in Music," *The Musical Quarterly* 5, no. 4 (1919): 553–60.
4 Philip C. Almond, *The Devil: A Biography* (Ithaca, 2014), 196.
5 Walter Stephens, *Demon Lovers: Witchcraft, Sex, and the Crisis of Belief* (Chicago, 2002), 180–206.
6 Scott Poole, *Satan in America: The Devil We Know* (New York, 2009), 33–49
7 James VI, *Daemonologie* (Edinburgh, 1597), 55.
8 Gabriele Amorth, *An Exorcist Explains the Demonic: The Antics of Satan and his Army of Fallen Angels*, trans. Charlotte Fast (Manchester, 2016), 17–28.
9 See Chapters 3, 4, 5 and 11 in this volume. See also Richard Raiswell, "The Devil in Nature," ed. Katherine Edwards (Leiden, 2025), forthcoming.
10 Lyndal Roper, *Witch Craze: Terror and Fantasy in Baroque Germany* (New Haven, 2004), 52.
11 See Elaine Pagels, *The Origin of Satan: How Christians Demonized Jews, Pagans and Heretics* (New York, 1995), *passim*.
12 See Valerie Flint, *The Rise of Magic in Early Medieval Europe* (Princeton, NJ, 1991), *passim*.
13 Ludovico di Varthema, *Novum Itinerarium Aethiopiae, Aegipti, utriusque Arabiae, Persidis, Siriae, ac Indiae, intra et extra Gangem* (1511), fol xxvii$^v$–xxviii$^v$.
14 [John] Smith, *A Map of Virginia. With a Description of the Countrey, the Commodities, People, Government and Religion* (Oxford, 1612), 29.
15 Johan Weyer, *De praestigiis daemonum* (Basel, 1563), 46–8.
16 Edward Terry, *A Voyage to East-India* (London, 1655), 344–5.
17 David Frankfurter, *Evil Incarnate: Rumors of Demonic Conspiracy and Satanic Abuse in History* (Princeton, 2006), 11.

18 In attempting to create, imitating divine perfection by conjuring up images of unreal things intended to beguile those who viewed them, there was a Renaissance tradition that viewed the production of art as potentially suspicious. See, for instance, Michael Cole, "The Demonic Arts and the Origin of the Medium," *The Art Bulletin* 84, no. 4 (2002): 621–40, *passim*.

19 https://www.churchofsatan.com/

20 Amy Slagle, "The Many Devils of Luciferian 'Traditional Witchcraft'" (paper presented at "the Devil 2024" conference, Halifax, Nova Scotia, May 2024), 2.

21 Bernard of Clairvaux, *In dedicatione ecclesiae* (Migne, PL 183): 0523D–6B.

22 Sara Moslener, *Virgin Nation: Sexual Purity and American Adolescence* (New York, 2015), 48–76. See also Kristen Kobes du Mez, *Jesus and John Wayne: How White Evangelicals Corrupted a Faith and Fractured a Nation* (New York, 2020), 17–32.

23 Ray Prichard, *Stealth Attack: Protecting Yourself against Satan's Plan to Destroy Your Life* (Chicago, 2007), 15–29; quotation on 13.

24 Prichard, *Stealth Attack*, 35.

25 The examples are numerous. But see, for instance, Christian psychologist James G. Friesen, *The Truth about False Memory Syndrome* (Eugene, OR, 1996), 52–68.

26 https://www.youtube.com/watch?v=S_X-1age21E&t=12s

27 Anton LaVey, *The Satanic Bible* (New York, 1966), 46–54.

28 Billy Graham, "New Need Revival" in *Revival in Our Time: The Story of the Billy Graham Evangelistic Campaigns, Including Six of his Sermons* (Wheaton, IL, 1950), 69–80 on 73.

29 On the Satanic Temple, see Joseph Laycock, *Speak of the Devil: How The Satanic Temple is Changing the Way We Talk about Religion* (Oxford, 2020).

30 On the rise of Christian nationalism and its influence on politics, see, for example, Kristen Kobes du Mez, *Jesus and John Wayne: How White Evangelicals Corrupted a Faith and Fractured a Nation* (New York, 2020).

31 Mark Broadway and Whitney Phillips, *The Shadow Gospel: How Anti-Liberal Demonology Possessed US Religion, Media, and Politics* (Boston, 2025), forthcoming.

32 S. Jonathan O'Donnell, "Demons of the deep state: how evangelicals and conspiracy theories combine in Trump's America," *The Conversation*, 14 September 2020. https://theconversation.com/demons-of-the-deep-state-how-evangelicals-and-conspiracy-theories-combine-in-trumps-america-144898

33 See, for example, Solène Tadié, "Longtime Exorcist: Satanism Is Growing in Western Societies," *National Catholic Register*, 4 December 2020. https://www.ncregister.com/interview/longtime-exorcist-satanism-is-growing-in-western-societies and Jack Butler, "Demonic Possession Is Real and Exorcisms Can Work — And These Priests Do Them," *Los Angeles Times*, 7 May 2022. https://www.latimes.com/opinion/story/2022-05-07/demonic-possession-exorcism-the-exorcist-demons

34 Riley Utley, "There's A Wild Instagram Post Claiming Taylor Swift and Travis Kelce Are Engaged and Dad Ed Kelce Had a Funny Response," *CinemaBlend*, 26 April 2024. https://www.cinemablend.com/television/instagram-post-claiming-taylor-swift-travis-kelce-are-engaged-ed-kelce-response

35 Madison Czopek, "'Satanic Rituals' at Taylor Swift Shows? That's False. And Experts Say the Attack Isn't New," *PolitiFact*, 17 April 2024. https://www.politifact.com/factchecks/2024/apr/17/facebook-posts/satanic-rituals-at-taylor-swift-shows-thats-false/

36 O'Donnell, "Demons of the Deep State."

37 PRRI 2023 American Values Survey, question 41. https://www.prri.org/search-survey-questions/

38 Cede Silva, "Talk of Satan and Freemasons dominates social media in runoff campaign," *The Brazilian Report*, 5 October 2022 (updated 22 June 2023).

39 Silva, "Talk of Satan and Freemasons."

40 Naomi Richman, "Homosexuality, Created Bodies, and Queer Fantasies in a Nigerian Deliverance Church," *Journal of Religion in Africa*, 50, nos. 3–4 (2022): 249–77.

41 Samba Cyuzuzo, "Burundi's President Ndayishimiye hits out over gay rights and aid," British Broadcasting Corporation, 29 December 2023.

42 Doreen Ajiambo, "A life of 'constant fear': The plight of African LGBTQ refugees," *National Catholic Reporter*, 9 August 2023.

43 Matt Field, "What the hell? Newsmax correspondent thinks Satan is in COVID-19 vaccines," *Bulletin of the Atomic Scientists*, 3 November 2021. See also Julie Exline, Kathleen C. Pait, Joshua A. Wilt, and William A. Schutt. 2022. "Demonic and Divine Attributions around COVID-19 Vaccines: Links with Vaccine Attitudes and Behaviors, QAnon and Conspiracy Beliefs, Anger, Spiritual Struggles, Religious and Political Variables, and Supernatural and Apocalyptic Beliefs" *Religions* 13, no. 6 (2022): 519.

44 Mike Wendling, "A QAnon 'queen' and the Canada town that wants her gone," *British Broadcasting Company*, 27 September 2023.

45 For an excellent overview of QAnon and its growth, see https://www.theatlantic.com/magazine/archive/2020/06/qanon-nothing-can-stop-what-is-coming/610567/

46 Melissa Brown, BrieAnna J. Frank, Chris Ullery and Sudiksha Kochi, "'A Religious Rally': Trump's Republican Convention Fuses Faith and Politics," USA Today, 17 July 2024. https://www.usatoday.com/story/news/politics/2024/07/17/religion-at-2024-rnc/74408797007/

47 Kiera Butler, "RNC Delegates Sound Off on Whether America Should Be a Christian Nation," *Mother Jones* 17 July 2024. https://www.motherjones.com/politics/2024/07/rnc-delegates-sound-off-on-whether-america-should-be-a-christian-nation/

48 Andy Kroll and Nick Surgery, "In Private Speech, J.D. Vance Said the 'Devil is Real' and Praised Alex Jones as a Truth-Teller," *ProPublica: Investigative Journalism in the Public Interest*, 16 July 2024. https://www.propublica.org/article/jd-vance-alex-jones-leonard-leo-teneo-maddow-video

# 1

# SATAN IN BIBLICAL LITERATURE

*Justin P. Jeffcoat Schedtler*

The character of Satan as a divine adversary of God, who functions to instil and promote evil in the world—indeed as a figure who embodies evil itself—is no doubt grounded in biblical literature. The figure who rises from the depths of a hellish abyss in order to deceive and tempt the holy followers of God in Revelation 20, for example, is one of the more captivating images in all of biblical literature and one that has funded subsequent depictions of satanic figures throughout history.

However, the character of Satan is by no means consistent throughout biblical literature. Rather, the bible includes a number of figures who bear the name "Satan" but whose depictions, dispositions, and functions vary a great deal more than one might think. The image of Satan that appears in the Apocalypse, the one which has permeated the religious and popular consciousness for millennia, for example, looks very different from the "satans" who roam the pages of the Hebrew scriptures.

To put a fine point on it, the figure of Satan undergoes a radical transformation throughout the corpus of biblical literature, from the very first texts in the Hebrew scriptures to those of the New Testament. That much should not be terribly surprising, given the fact that these texts reflect worldviews of diverse groups of people spanning at least a millennium.

Thus, a review of Satan in biblical literature must traverse a variety of peoples, literatures, and ideologies. This survey will proceed chronologically, beginning with the earliest attestations of characters named "Satan" in the Hebrew bible and exploring their demeanour, function, and relationship with other characters in the text. This will provide a basis for analysing subsequent depictions of "Satan" figures in non-canonical Jewish literature, as well as the New Testament, paying attention both to common themes and to innovations across traditions.

## Satan in the Hebrew Bible

The word satan (Hebrew: śāṭān) appears several times in the Hebrew bible as a common noun to denote an adversarial figure. Most often, a "satan" appears to represent a human being, as in one of the earliest attestations of the term in 1 Sam 29.4, wherein David, who is

DOI: 10.4324/9781003096603-2

depicted as a temporary mercenary in the Philistine army, is identified as a potential threat because of his prior allegiances to King Saul and the Hebrews:

> But the Philistine commanders were angry with Achish and said, "Send the man [David] back, that he may return to the place you assigned him. He must not go with us into battle, or he will turn against us [lit. lest he become a satan] during the fighting. How better could he regain his master's [Saul's] favor than by taking the heads of our own men?"[1]

Though most English translations obscure the fact, David is characterised as a potential "satan" insofar as he is liable to "turn against" the Philistines.[2] This example presents a stark challenge to the notion of a satan as the unholy antithesis of God. Not only is this "satan" a human being, he is David, the one identified elsewhere as "... a man after [God's] own heart" (1 Sm 13.14)!

This episode provides the semblance of a functional definition of the term satan insofar as David is so identified by the fact that he is seen as a likely traitor to the Philistines. That is, the term seems to denote an antagonist, though the exact nature of the treachery is not elaborated. Subsequent uses of the term provide clarity. For example, after Absalom has failed in his bid to usurp his father David, Absalom's supporters are forced to own up to their treachery upon David's return to Jerusalem to retake the throne. One of these, Shimei, accosts David in an attempt to save his life. In response, one of David's subordinates, Abishai, proposes that Shimei be put to death for his treasonous participation in Absalom's rebellion. David responds to Abishai:

> What have I to do with you ... that you should today become an adversary (lit. a satan) to me? Shall anyone be put to death in Israel this day?
>
> *(2 Sm 19.22)*

Though again the English translation obscures the fact, David identifies Abishai as none other than a "satan" for his eager willingness to put Shimei to death. This episode corroborates the definition of satan as an antagonist, i.e., someone whose aims are at odds with the protagonist.[3] However, in this case, the precise nature of the antagonism is put into relief when David identifies Abishai as a satan because of Abishai's insistence on putting Shimei to death. In this way, the functional definition of a satan takes fuller form in this instance insofar as it denotes someone who would put another to death.[4] The definition of a satan as a person responsible for causing lethal harm to another is corroborated elsewhere in the Hebrew bible, as in 1 Kings 5.4, where King Solomon's reign is characterised as one in which there is neither "satan nor misfortune," as well as the Psalms, where the Hebrew verb *śṭn* characterises the actions of those who cause injury.[5]

Alongside depictions of human satans who function as earthly antagonists, satans who appear to be superhuman in form and function also appear in the Hebrew bible.

## Numbers 22.22-35

Likely, the earliest preserved example of a celestial satan in the Hebrew bible occurs in Numbers 22.22-35 as part of the story of Balaam and the ass.[6]

One morning, while the prophet Balaam is riding his donkey alongside the Moabite officials, God becomes angry with him and sends an angel of the lord to stand "in the road as his adversary" (Nm 22.22). Though Balaam does not see this heavenly figure, the donkey does and averts his path as a result. Angered, Balaam beats the donkey. Subsequently, the angel of the lord takes up another position further along the road, where Balaam's donkey is once again forced to take evasive action, thus injuring Balaam's foot. Angered, Balaam beats the donkey a second time. A final time, the angel of the lord blocks Balaam's path in such a way that the donkey is unable to evade him, with the result that the donkey simply falls to the ground. Angered, Balaam beats the donkey a third time. After the angel of the lord allows the donkey to ask Balaam about the beatings, the angel of the lord opens Balaam's eyes so that he is able to see the angel who is standing in front of him with his sword drawn. The angel of the lord says to Balaam:

> Why have you struck your donkey these three times? I have come out as an adversary (lit. "satan") because your way is perverse to me. The donkey saw me and turned away from me these three times. If it had not turned away from me, surely just now I would have killed you and let it live.

Though the English translation once again obscures the fact, this figure is identified as none other than a "satan" (Nm 22.22). Far from functioning as a hellish adversary to the God of Israel, this satan acts as an emissary of God and as such enacts God's own will in the encounter.[7] Indeed, it appears as if the angelic satan was sent by God in order to kill Balaam. This role makes some sense in light of the designation of this character as an "angel of the Lord" (Hebrew, mal'âk YHWH), a title that regularly denotes a figure (human or divine) sent by God in order to convey a message and/or to enact God's intentions—including lethal attacks—on earth.[8] However, the fact that this particular angel is designated a "satan" is a startling designation—at least from a contemporary perspective.[9]

## Zechariah 3.1-2

The fourth vision of the prophet Zechariah furnishes the next appearance of a celestial satan and provides an added dimension to this character. The vision consists of the high priest Joshua standing in heaven with "filthy clothes" before "the angel of the Lord" with "the Satan" standing "at his right hand to oppose him" (lit. "to satan him"). The lord says to the Satan, "The LORD rebuke you, Satan! The LORD who has chosen Jerusalem rebuke you! Is this not a brand plucked from the fire?" (Zec 3.1-2). The scene is most often understood to represent an investiture of the high priest Joshua, which functions as a cipher whereby Joshua represents the community of Judeans who have returned to Jerusalem after their 70-year exile in Babylon.[10]

Before turning to an interpretation of the role of the Satan in this episode, it is worth noting that this depiction of the Satan evinces several conspicuous differences with the narrative in Numbers 22. For one, in Zechariah's vision, the "angel of the Lord" and the Satan are not one and the same character. Rather, the Satan stands in clear opposition to the angel of the lord. Therein lies the second difference: here the character of the Satan appears to stand not only at odds with God's emissary but also with God as evidenced by the fact that God rebukes the Satan explicitly. Finally, this is the first time that a "satan" is identified as a titular character, i.e., "The Satan." Put another way, this is the first instance in which the definite article precedes the name (Hebrew, haśśāṭān). While previous instances of the term seemed to suggest a character (David, Abishai, or the angel of the lord) who happened to be playing the role of "a satan" in a particular instance, Zechariah 3 appears to introduce a character whose singular identity consists of being "The Satan."[11]

The position of the Satan in heaven alongside God and the angel of the lord suggests that this Satan occupies a position in the divine court of God.[12] The notion of a divine court is widespread in ancient Near Eastern literature and manifest in several texts of the Hebrew bible. Psalm 82, for example, depicts God presiding over a "great assembly" and rendering "judgment among the gods." Isaiah 6 presents God in a similar context surrounded by an angelic assembly:

> In the year that King Uzziah died, I saw the Lord, high and exalted, seated on a throne; and the train of his robe filled the temple. Above him were seraphim, each with six wings: With two wings they covered their faces, with two they covered their feet, and with two they were flying.
>
> *(Is 6.1-2)*

In 1 Kings 22.19-23, the prophet Micaiah has a vision of "the Lord sitting on his throne with all the multitudes of heaven standing around him on his right and on his left" (1 Kgs 22.19). A description of the multitude on either side of God itself appears to represent a divine heavenly council analogous with ancient Near Eastern counterparts, while the dialogue between members of the council describes one of its functions:

> And the LORD said, 'Who will entice Ahab into attacking Ramoth Gilead and going to his death there?' One suggested this, and another that. Finally, a spirit came forward, stood before the LORD and said, 'I will entice him.'
>
> *(1 Kgs 22.20-21)*

Here the function of the divine council mirrors that of a royal council insofar as it deliberates and advises God in order to manifest God's will in the world.

These examples provide a framework for considering the role of the Satan in Zechariah 3 as one who stands alongside God and an angelic host and whose role is primarily to advise God. Indeed, this scene has provoked widespread speculation that the Satan here functions as a kind of prosecutor in the divine court with God functioning as the judge.[13] Though in Zechariah 3 God ultimately sides with the angel of the lord and rebukes the Satan because of his position against Joshua, the Satan's own position is both legally defensible and reasonable. Joshua *was*, in fact, guilty before God as evidenced by his "guilt" and the "filthy garments" representative thereof (Zec 3.3-4).[14] Thus, the Satan certainly functions here as an adversarial figure, but only vis-à-vis the guilty high priest and his advocate, the angel of the lord, and *not* towards God. Put another way, the Satan is hardly out of place in this encounter; rather, the Satan appears to fulfil the role of a divine prosecutor who makes a (legally reasonable) case against the investiture of the high priest.

## 1 Chr 21.1

1 Chronicles 21 includes a scene in which "Satan" incites king David to take a census of the people, an action which angers God and results in God punishing David's people with pestilence.

The figure in 1 Chronicles 21 should certainly be understood within the trajectory of celestial satans elsewhere in the Hebrew bible. For example, Satan "stands against"

David in 1 Chronicles in a way that conjures the position of the Satan in Zechariah 3, who stands in an adversarial position "to the right" of Joshua. Likewise, the fact that Satan "incites" David in 1 Chronicles mirrors the language in Job 1-2 in which Satan "incites" God to test Job's faithfulness (see below).[15] Others, however, go further to suggest that this episode furnishes an example of a major development in the satan tradition, from one in which a number of figures could occupy the role of "satan" at any particular time into a singular celestial adversary, "Satan." This view rests in part on the premise that 1 Chronicles is the latest text chronologically within the Hebrew bible to mention a Satan-figure and in part on by the lack of a definite article and/or explicit identification as another individual or entity.[16]

Moreover, Satan's actions in 1 Chronicles 21 seem to suggest an adversarial character. While the reason for God's anger at David's census is not immediately clear,[17] Satan does appear to constitute a celestial adversary to David and to God insofar as Satan's actions compel David to act in such a way that would incite God's anger and punishment. However, a closer look reveals that Satan is acting in line with antecedent depictions in which he functions as an agent to bring about God's will on earth. This comes into view when 1 Chronicles 21 is viewed as a rewritten version of 2 Samuel 24:

| *2 Sm 24.1* | *1 Chr 21.1* |
|---|---|
| Again the anger of the lord was kindled against Israel, and he incited David against them, saying, "Go, count the people of Israel and Judah." | Satan stood up against Israel and incited David to count the people of Israel. |

That 1 Chronicles 21 is a rewritten version of 2 Samuel 24 is well accepted. Indeed, the introduction of Satan as the one who incites David and compels God's wrath is the most conspicuous modification of the Chronicler. Commentators have proposed a couple of explanations for this revision. Many conclude that the modification transfers the culpability for the violent actions taken against David and Israel from God onto Satan.[18] Others note that Satan here need not be understood as an adversary to God, but viewed rather as an intermediary acting on behalf of God.[19] At any rate, it appears that the Chronicler has transferred the agency responsible for inciting David from God to Satan in a way that suggests that Satan is functioning not so much as an adversary to God but as a representative thereof. In this way, Satan in 1 Chronicles 21 functions in a way that resembles antecedent satans who operate as agents of God who bring about God's will on the earth.

## The Book of Job

The final—and likely to be the latest chronologically—appearance of a celestial satan occurs in the book of Job, where the character resembles antecedent satans in a number of ways. For example, this satan presumably has a place in God's heavenly council:

One day the heavenly beings came to present themselves before the LORD, and the accuser (lit. "the satan") also came among them.

*(Jb 1.6; cf. 2.1)*

21

While some have suggested that the Satan is a trespasser in the scene, most commentators agree that he is included as one of the "heavenly beings" (lit. "sons of God") who present themselves before God. This would align most closely with antecedent depictions of satan in the Hebrew bible in which he appears as a functionary of God as part of God's own heavenly council.

It is in his capacity as a functionary of God that the Satan operates in the book of Job. After questioning the Satan as to his whereabouts (he had been "walking to and fro on the earth"), God asks the Satan whether he has "considered" Job, whom God describes as a "blameless and upright man who fears God and turns away from evil" (Jb 1.8). The Satan responds by questioning the integrity of Job's enduring faithfulness in light of the many blessings God has bestowed upon him (Jb 1.9-10), suggesting that Job might not be so faithful if some of these blessings were taken away. God then responds by saying that the Satan may do what he wants with Job's possessions as long as he doesn't touch Job himself (Jb 1.11-12). Much of the rest of the text details the ways in which the Satan does just this, and the extent to which Job and his friends try to make sense of why it is all happening.

The initial scene suggests that the Satan functions as an integral member of God's council who surveils the earth with an eye towards the moral dimensions (or lack thereof) of human beings.[20] In this way, Job's Satan recalls antecedent celestial satans who operate under God's authority to interact with humans, most often to antagonise and threaten humans on account of their behaviour. Job's Satan differs, however, both insofar as his primary function appears to be surveilling humankind and inasmuch as he antagonises a *righteous* man:

… you incited me [God] against him [Job] to destroy him for no reason.

*(Jb 2.3)*

In Job, then, we may be able to witness the inception of the notion that the Satan operates not as a means to satisfy God's will on earth but in opposition to it.

## God, Satan, and Evil

The preceding survey has not yielded a single portrait of the character of Satan in the Hebrew bible; rather, the literary record attests a degree of latitude with respect to characterisation. In some cases, Satan appears in human form, not as a character *per se* but as an epithet granted to a person—like King David or one of his subordinates—who happens to be performing the role of a "satan" in that particular moment. In these roles, characters dubbed "satan" take on adversarial roles but not in a cosmic sense; instead, a human "satan" seems to refer to an individual who, with a rather restricted scope, antagonises another. In certain instances, it appears the term functions as shorthand for an(y) antagonist. Regardless, human satans in the Hebrew bible functioned not as adversaries of God—their limited capacity would seem not to allow for the possibility of antagonising a deity—but instead as adversaries to humans within their sphere of influence, e.g., another solider or the king.

While a satan sometimes appears in human form, texts of the Hebrew bible also attest divine satans. However, the celestial satans of the Hebrew bible look little like those that have appeared throughout the subsequent historical record as the unholy antithesis of God who commands an army of demons and presides over souls who have been damned to the fiery pits of hell. On the contrary, the non-human satans of the Hebrew bible seem to function as agents *of* God, and often in ways that recall other celestial beings, e.g., spirits, and angels. Indeed, in perhaps the earliest attestation in the Hebrew bible, a celestial satan is identified *as* an "angel of the Lord" (Nm 22). Additionally, in some instances, a satan is manifest as a member of God's own divine council. In each of these ways, divine satans appear not as divine adversaries but as instruments through which the very will of God is enacted in heaven and earth. Far from occupying the realms of hell, the celestial satans in the Hebrew bible appear to occupy a privileged position among the angels and alongside God in heaven.

While the satans of the Hebrew bible do not align with stereotypical images of Satan-figures in subsequent Abrahamic traditions, neither do they comport with the characterisation of Satan-figures that appear in the earliest Christian texts, including especially those of the New Testament. In order to contextualise the satans who appear in the New Testament, it is necessary first to explore the texts composed in-between the time of the composition of the Hebrew bible and New Testament—the "intertestamental" period—including the so-called Pseudepigrapha, Apocrypha, the Dead Sea Scrolls, and so on. These texts, though not deemed canonical by (most) Jewish or Christian traditions, nevertheless provide a great deal of information about the ideologies of the people responsible for them in the period(s) intervening the composition of the Hebrew bible and New Testament. As such, in many important ways, these texts attest to developments in ideologies found in the Hebrew bible, and at the same time provide context for many of the ideational frameworks found in the New Testament. This can certainly be said of the satans who appear therein, as one can trace discernible lines from the heavenly satans aligned with God in the Hebrew bible to the hellish satans who antagonise God and God's people in the New Testament. This does not mean that the trajectories of this development are linear. Nevertheless, the ideologies of Satan-figures in the New Testament are not *sui generis,* and one can trace their roots which appear in antecedent Jewish literature.

It is profitable to consider this development through a lens focused on the relationship between God and evil. As we have noted, the celestial satans of the Hebrew bible did *not* embody evil, nor did satans—as in later traditions—promote evil for evil's sake. In fact, in several instances, it does not appear that the figure of satan does anything that could be considered *evil* in the first place. However, the figure does accomplish the will of God in ways that foreground his function as an adversarial figure—not to God but to other characters. In this way, satans function as a kind of medium between God and the world in such a way that preserves both God's ultimate control over the world and yet the transcendency of God vis-à-vis the world. Put another way, in this theological system, "evil" does not—indeed it cannot—exist outside of God's control of it.

For example, the "angel of the Lord," who as a "satan" functions as an adversary to Balaam in Numbers 22, manifests God's own anger at Balaam by standing in his path with a sword in hand ready to attack. Perhaps the clearest example of this occurs in the Chronicler's rewriting of 2 Samuel 24, whereby the "anger of the Lord" in 2 Samuel 24 becomes "satan" in 1 Chronicles 21. So, too, in the book of Job does a satan function to demonstrate this as he prods God to test righteous Job, resulting in God's decision to bring suffering upon Job and his family. In each of these examples, a satan functions as a kind of surrogate and/or instigator for the demonstration of God's power on the earth, all the while preserving the sovereignty and transcendence of God.

This also goes for "evil" and/or malevolent beings. Though there is no word for "demon" in the Hebrew bible, there are certainly spirits and angels—and even other, foreign deities—who are said to bring about calamities upon the world.[21] Deuteronomy 32 is often cited as a text that both acknowledges the powers of malevolent foreign deities and subsumes them under God's ultimate authority:

> Jeshurun grew fat and kicked; filled with food, they became heavy and sleek. They abandoned the God who made them and rejected the Rock their Savior. They made him jealous with their foreign gods and angered him with their detestable idols. They sacrificed to false gods, which are not God—gods they had not known, gods that recently appeared, gods your ancestors did not fear. You deserted the Rock, who fathered you; you forgot the God who gave you birth.
>
> *(Dt 32.15-18)*

Likewise, Psalm 82 speaks of God's superior place among the gods:

> God presides in the great assembly; he renders judgment among the "gods." How long will you defend the unjust and show partiality to the wicked? Defend the weak and the fatherless; uphold the cause of the poor and the oppressed. Rescue the weak and the needy; deliver them from the hand of the wicked. The "gods" know nothing, they understand nothing. They walk about in darkness; all the foundations of the earth are shaken.
>
> *(Ps 82.1-5)*

Just as malevolent deities fall under the auspices of God's ultimate control of the universe, so too do malevolent spirits roam the earth at God's command. 1 Samuel 16 narrates the story of an "evil spirit" (Hebrew, ru'aḥ ru'aḥ) sent from God in order to torment King Saul, the only relief from which comes in the form of David playing the lyre (1 Sm 16.14-23). Likewise, Judges 9 includes the story of God sending an "evil spirit" between King Abimelech and the sons of Shechem, which results in animosity and treachery between them (Jgs 9.23).[22] Thus, there is very little interest in what modern commentators would deem the "demonic" in the Hebrew bible; rather, *all* supra-human entities—whether they bring with them good or evil—operate under God's command.[23]

A major development in this theological system occurs, however, in the Book of Watchers, a text composed as early as the 3rd century BCE, which constitutes the first 36 chapters of the compilation of texts known as 1 Enoch. A significant portion of this text consists of a re-telling of the story told in Genesis 6.1-4:

> When human beings began to increase in number on the earth and daughters were born to them, the sons of God saw that the daughters of humans were beautiful, and they married any of them they chose.
>
> *(Gn 6.1-2)*

The Book of Watchers elaborates and modifies this story in significant ways. While the act of the sons of God marrying human women is not explicitly condemned in Genesis, the re-telling in the Book of Watchers leaves no doubt that it was considered an unholy act. The Book of Watchers characterises this as a "great sin" which results in all sorts of catastrophes for humans upon the earth. Not only do the angelic Watchers "defile" earthly women, they begin to teach them sorcery and other charms; moreover, they give birth to "giants" who consume all of the labours of humankind, eventually to the point where they begin devouring the humans themselves.

The more elaborate and prominent role given to the angels ("watchers") in the Book of Watchers reflects an increased interest in angels and demons more broadly in Jewish literature of this period. More angels are given specific names with specific functions, as in Tobit, a text roughly contemporaneous with the Book of Watchers, wherein seven angels are identified as especially close to God, while in Parables of Enoch and Jubilees heavenly angels are described in terms of their hierarchical organisation.

This is especially clear in Jewish texts that consist of rewritten texts of the Hebrew bible. To wit, the book of Jubilees—a work consisting primarily of modified stories from the book of Genesis—introduces angels into Genesis' story of creation as one of God's very first creations (Jub 2.2). Likewise, while in the book of Genesis it is God who makes a covenant with Abram on Mount Sinai (Gn 15.18), in the book of Jubilees it is an angel who makes this covenant (Jub 14.20). Moreover, while it is God who strikes the Israelites with pestilence in Numbers 14.22, the text of Pseudo-Phocylides attributes this attack to angels (Ps.-Phoc 15.5).[24] And so on.

Thus, the increased role of the angelic "watchers" in the Book of Watchers' re-telling of Genesis 6.1-4 fits within this broader trajectory. At the same time, this episode exhibits a couple of novel concepts. First, the Watchers themselves not only appear to function independent of God's will but at odds with it. Second, the hybrid offspring of the watchers, the giants, are said to have become "evil spirits" upon the earth:

> But now the giants who were begotten by the spirits and flesh
> They will call them evil spirits on the earth,
> For their dwelling will be on the earth ...
>
> The spirits of heaven, in heaven is their dwelling;
> But the spirits begotten on the earth, on the earth is their dwelling
> *(1 En. 15.8, 10).*

While the earthly element of the giants eventually passes away, their spiritual remnant remains and becomes "evil" to the extent that they:

> ... do violence, make desolate, and attack and wrestle and hurl upon the earth and make races ... These spirits rise up against the sons of men and against the women, for they have come forth from them ... Thus they will make desolate until the day of the consummation of the great judgments, when the great age will be consummated ....
> *(excerpt from 1 En. 15.11-16.1)*[25]

Critically, the giants operate clearly and totally independently from God's control. Thus, there appears for the first time a category of supra-human beings who may be characterised as "evil" insofar as they wreak havoc while doing so outside of the control of God.[26] Indeed, the giants (via the watchers) appear in the Book of Watchers in order to explain the origin and existence of evil in the world. For this reason, many have identified this as a watershed moment in Jewish demonology.[27]

The book of Jubilees also reflects continued innovation in terms of Jewish demonology. Jubilees attests to the increased attention given to supra-human beings in this period of Jewish literature, featuring a variety of such characters, including a number of "spirits" who function to vex humans as well as "demons" who are the object of illicit worship of foreign peoples.[28] Ryan Stokes has demonstrated how much more prominently these evil spirits and demons function within their narrative context than do their counterparts in antecedent

Jewish literature. Not only is the spirits' deceptive activity conspicuous but the extent of their ability to delude and mislead humans is expanded; indeed, Jubilees identifies the work of the spirits and demons as among the most potent threats to humankind.[29]

Corresponding with these innovations in Jewish demonology is a major development in Satan-characters. Jubilees employs the term "satan" as in 1 Kings 5.4 (see above), where it functions as a common noun to denote a(ny) human "attacker" or "adversary," as well as to denote supra-human entities who operate under God's control to carry out judgements and/or punishments as in Numbers 22, Zechariah 3, etc., most clearly insofar as Jubilees conflates the Satan with a character who at times appears to be the chief supra-human antagonist in the text, the Prince of Mastema (Jub 10.11).[30] The Prince of Mastema appears in Jubilees sometimes in ways that recall the supra-human satans in biblical tradition, i.e., as functionaries who act under the auspices of God's control in order to bring about God's intentions on the earth.[31] A clear example of this occurs in Jubilees' re-telling of the binding of Isaac from Genesis 22. While the biblical text confirms it was God who tested Abraham by commanding him to bind his son, Isaac, in Jubilees the Prince of Mastema compels God to test Abraham:

> Then Prince Mastema came and said before God, "Abraham does indeed love his son Isaac and finds him more pleasing than anyone else. Tell him to offer him as a sacrifice on an altar. Then you will see whether he performs this order and will know whether he is faithful in everything through which you test him."
>
> *(Jub. 15.17-18)*

This episode very clearly recalls the character of the Satan in the book of Job, who likewise makes the case to God to put a human being to the test.[32] And, as in the episode in Job, this character is depicted not as an adversary to God but as one who occupies a place in God's inner circle, the divine court, whereby he challenges God and thus carries out specific responsibilities within this court. Thus, a functional resemblance exists between Job's Satan and Jubilees' Mastema, a connection that is made explicit in *Jubilees* 10.11, where the Prince of Mastema is identified *as* Satan.

The major innovation occurs insofar as the Satan (Mastema) is identified as the supreme leader of the group of evil spirits identified elsewhere in Jubilees as deceivers of God's people.[33] Jubilees' re-telling of the flood narrative makes this connection explicit. In Jubilees 10.3-6, which takes up the narrative introduced in Genesis 6 and expanded in Book of the Watchers, Noah is speaking to God about the "wicked spirits" who have afflicted his people ever since they were born into the world by the "watchers." Noah asks God to bind the wicked spirits so they may cause no more harm. In response to Noah's plea, Mastema suggests instead that God bind only 90% of the spirits, leaving the rest under Mastema's control, so as to be able to "exercise the authority of [Mastema's] will," which includes "destroying and misleading" God's people on account of the peoples' "evil" (Jub 10.8).

Thus, at this point in the history of the Satan tradition, the Satan character is connected inextricably with a group of evil spirits. Nonetheless, however, in continuity with antecedent Satan traditions, Mastema and his evil spirits still appear to be enacting God's will on earth, punishing people for their sins. Though Mastema and his legion of spirits wreak havoc upon the earth, the figure does *not* yet represent the "diabolical enemy of God" familiar from later Satan traditions.[34] The relationship is not consistent; however, as even in other portions of Jubilees, this legion of evil spirits appears to act apart from, and in opposition to, God and God's people. This fact underscores an important conclusion about the character of Satan and demonology in early Judaism: it is neither uniform nor linear in its development.[35] At any rate, the system of demons and their satanic overlord manifest in Jubilees serves as a basis for subsequent commentators—Jewish and Christian—to imagine their own universe imbued with similar figures.[36]

Such texts speculate not only on the existence of such entities but on their relationship to evil in the world. While the Book of Watchers and Jubilees locate the origin of the world's problems in the diabolic activity of its own demons, subsequent authors expand the nature and scope of their activity. Moreover, the nature and function of Satan-figures continue to evolve. The Dead Sea Scrolls attest to robust speculation on the nature of demonic activity under the leadership of Satan-figures who go by many names.[37] Perhaps most importantly, there is a transformation of the character from one who operates under God's control to the figure recognisable from subsequent traditions—including those in the New Testament—who stands opposed to God as a cosmic adversary.

Among the most common names for Satan in the sectarian texts among the Dead Sea Scrolls is "Belial."[38] While this character resembles Satan-figures from antecedent Jewish literature in several respects, Belial is characterised in other ways that suggest an ideological shift in the way that Satan-figures are imagined to function vis-à-vis God and God's people. For example, while Jubilees characterises its Satan-figure as one who leads astray the peoples of foreign nations, Belial is characterised in the Damascus Document, a text which outlines many of the laws of the Dead Sea community, as one who has led astray away *even the people of Israel*.[39] This calamity is perhaps reflected in a similar text, the Community Rule—insofar as this period is labelled the "dominion of Belial" and the people under Belial's influence dubbed the "lot of Belial."[40]

Belial's role as a deceiver of God's righteous people is expanded in the War Rule. Consisting of a description of an eschatological war between the "sons of light" and the "sons of darkness," the War Rule identifies Belial as the leader of the sons of darkness insofar as he has led them to violate the covenant, putting Belial at odds with God's statutes and with those who follow them. More than this, however, Belial is portrayed in a way that identifies him as an enemy of God. In the description of the implements of war used by the sons of light, one of banners contains the words, "Wrath of God in outburst towards Belial and against all the men of his lot without any remnant" (1QM 4.1-2). Moreover, the description of the battle itself reports that "the great hand of God shall be lifted up against Belial and against all the forces of his dominion for an eternal slaughter" (1QM 18.1).[41]

The sectarian documents among the Dead Sea Scrolls manifest a shift in the way of thinking about Satan-figures from those who operate fully under God's authority to enact God's will upon the earth into an adversary of God and God's people. Moreover, Satan-figures—who go by many names—are imagined to rule over a "kingdom" of evil demons who are thought to wreak chaos and destruction upon the earth such that it requires militant resistance. This ideology provides a basis for the way that Satan and his legion of demons are imagined in the texts of the New Testament.

## Satan the Adversary and his Kingdom of Demons in the New Testament

Early Christian literature is replete with a dualistic theology that pits the evil forces of Satan against the benevolent forces of God. While Greek and Roman literatures—including Jewish traditions thereof—imagine a supernatural world imbued with spirits that oscillated regularly between benevolence and maleficence, early Christian texts nearly always reflect what David Frankfurter deems a "polarized ... supernatural cosmos."[42]

While earlier Jewish literature imagined celestial "satans" of many names—Belial, Mastema, etc.—the New Testament authors seem to have coalesced around two primary designations, (the) "Satan" and (the) "devil" (Greek, διάβολος), though other terms are occasionally used, including "the ruler," "the evil one," "Beelzebub," among others.[43] As in antecedent Jewish literature, the Greek designation for satan characters often includes the definite article (ὁ Σατανᾶς), which may signal reference to a title-holder, i.e., "the one holding the office of 'Satan'," rather than a proper name. With or without the definite article, it is difficult to determine whether a common or proper noun is indicated.[44]

The Greek term διάβολος ("devil") indicates an adversary who verbally or physically opposes another.[45] It is not surprising that the term was used to characterise Satan throughout the New Testament inasmuch as it was employed throughout the Septuagint (the Greek translation of the Hebrew scriptures) as a translation for the Hebrew śāṭān.

Thomas Farrar and others have argued that the terminological consistency of New Testament designations of Satan appears to be "paralleled by a conceptual consistency in functions and attributes assigned to the Satan."[46] This is not to say that there are no distinctions between individual New Testament texts, but that in general terms the figure of Satan had become more consistent in form and function when compared with antecedent depictions of (the) satans in Jewish literature. So, too, does the character figure more conspicuously and consistently throughout the New Testament, occurring 137 times in 19 different texts.[47]

Satan is imagined to preside over a "kingdom," which stands over and against the kingdom of God, and which is regularly identified as the world in which humans live.[48] For example, in promising Jesus "all the kingdoms of the world," Satan is depicted exercising power over them (Mt 4.8). Paul seems to conjure Satan when referring to the "god of this world" who blinds unbelievers from seeing the glory of Christ (2 Cor 4.4-5). Throughout, John's gospel identifies Satan as the "ruler (or prince) of this world," a claim that Jesus himself echoes (Jn 12.31; 14.30; 16.11), while 1 John states plainly:

The whole world lies under the power of the evil one.

*(1 Jn 5.19)*

While Satan's kingdom seems to have operated upon the earth, the figure was most often imagined to be supra-human in form and function.[49] The cosmic character of Satan in the New Testament is revealed in the scope and magnitude of his powers.[50]

The Synoptic Gospels and the book of Acts imagine that Satan regularly inflicted all sorts of illnesses upon people (e.g., Acts 10.38), which is explained in Luke's Gospel to be the result of having been "bound" by Satan (Lk 13.10-17). Paul understands his own sufferings, his "thorn" in the flesh, to be a result of (an angel of) Satan's work (2 Cor 12.7). In Revelation, Satan throws Christ-believers into prison (Rv 2.10), while John's Gospel characterises Satan as a "murderer" (Jn 8.44). In Hebrews, death itself is imagined to be under the control of Satan (Heb 2.14). This ideology makes some sense of the book of Hebrews' re-telling of the Passover scene from Exodus 12, in which Satan replaces God as the "destroyer of the firstborn" (Heb 11.28), as well as the notion that Satan was responsible for bringing about Jesus' own death (Lk 22.3; Jn 13.2, 27).

Satan regularly tempts individuals, e.g., Jesus to test God (Mt 4.1-11), Judas to betray Jesus (Lk 22.3; Jn 13.2), Peter to deny Jesus (Lk 22.31), husbands to cheat on their wives (1 Cor 7.5), etc.[51] Inasmuch as Satan is identified as a tempter who lures people into sin, it is not surprising that Satan is often in the New Testament associated with antagonists in the early Christian movement. For example, Paul's "false apostles" are identified as "ministers of Satan" (2 Cor 11.14-15), whereas Jesus identifies those who seek to kill him as offspring of the devil (Jn 8.44).[52]

In fewer instances, Satan is presented in less cosmic terms. In a pericope in John's gospel, Jesus identifies one of his twelve disciples as a "devil" insofar as he will soon betray Jesus (Jn 6.70). In response to Peter's rebuke of Jesus' declaration of his messiahship, Jesus famously commands Peter, "Get behind me, Satan!" (Mk 8.33). Each of these uses of the term conjures those texts of the Hebrew bible that characterise antagonistic humans as "satan(s)".[53]

In a very few instances, Satan appears as in the Hebrew bible and early Jewish literature as a functionary of God. For example, Paul's command to hand over to Satan the man who was sleeping with his father's wife in order that he might be "saved in the day of the Lord" (1 Cor 5.5) suggests the role of Satan as a functionary of God's good work. Likewise, 1 Timothy indicates that Paul handed over Hymenaeus and Alexander to Satan in order that they "be taught not to blaspheme" (1 Tm 1.20). Finally, Paul's own "thorn in the flesh," which is characterised as an "angel of Satan," appears to have been given to him by God in order to prevent Paul from becoming "too elated."[54]

More commonly, however, Satan is depicted in no uncertain terms as an antagonist to God and God's rule upon the earth. This dynamic is most conspicuous because Jesus was imagined to be Satan's dualistic counterpart. While early Jewish ideologies often presented angelic figures such as Michael as Satan's chief antagonist, early Jesus-followers identified Jesus as a cosmic counterpart in similar terms[55]:

> The one who sowed the good seed is the Son of Man. The field is the world, and the good seed stands for the people of the kingdom. The weeds are the people of the evil one, and the enemy who sows them is the devil. The harvest is the end of the age, and the harvesters are angels. As the weeds are pulled up and burned in the fire, so it will be at the end of the age. The Son of Man will send out his angels, and they will weed out of his kingdom everything that causes sin and all who do evil. They will throw them into the blazing furnace, where there will be weeping and gnashing of teeth.
>
> *(Mt 13.28-42)*

Satan's place as nothing less than the cosmic enemy of God and God's people is depicted in a myriad of other ways in early Christian literature where the lines between Satan's kingdom and God's kingdom are clearly drawn.[56] 1 John goes so far as to divide the entire world into two competing groups: the children of God and the children of the devil (1 Jn 3.10). In this ideological world, Jesus is often imagined as an antidote to Satan:

> The reason the Son of God appeared was to destroy the devil's work.
>
> *(1 Jn 3.8)*

Far removed is the notion evident in early Jewish scriptures of a Satan-figure who operated under God's own authority to bring about the will of God on earth; here, Satan is imagined as an antagonist to God.

The notion of Satan as a cosmic antagonist was reflected in dynamic ways. For example, the Synoptic Gospels imagine a world imbued with forces under the control of Satan. These forces go by many names, e.g., demons, unclean spirits. Sometimes, as in Matthew's gospel and in the book of Revelation, Satan is said to rule over "angels" (Mt 25.41; Rv 12.7-9).[57] While the designation of Satan's minions as "angels" may appear out of place in light of their nearly consistent designation as "demons" elsewhere, Paul's explanation may shed light:

> And no wonder, for Satan himself masquerades as an angel of light. It is not surprising, then, if his servants also masquerade as servants of righteousness.
>
> *(2 Cor 11.14-15)*

At any rate, these forces are often imagined to enter human bodies, manifesting physically in the host as skin sores, blindness, deafness, the inability to speak, seizures, etc. Often, demon-possessed hosts are imagined to be isolated, confused, or otherwise identified as abnormal in some way.[58] Some commentators have emphasised the degree to which demons made their hosts "unclean" and in need of ritual purification.[59]

In ways that can be compared with charismatic healers in antecedent and contemporaneous traditions, Jesus regularly casts out these demons from their human hosts.[60] Jesus' ability to interact with demons draws charges that he himself is in league with the master of demons, i.e., Satan.[61] Jesus' disciples are also imagined to be capable of defeating demons, as in Luke where the 72 who are sent ahead of Jesus proclaim:

> Lord, in your name even the demons submit to us!
>
> *(Lk 10.17)*[62]

Jesus' exorcisms were presented not only as instances of miraculous healing but as demonstrations of the dawning of the kingdom of God. The demon possession represented an attack of evil powers, while the exorcism demonstrated the power of God to attack Satan's dominion through Jesus' healing hands. For example,

> But if it is by the finger of God that I cast out the demons, then the kingdom of God has come upon you.
>
> *(Lk 11.20)*

Inasmuch as such interactions between Jesus and Satan's minions are imagined as worldly manifestations of a cosmic conflict, they demonstrate how Satan was viewed through an apocalyptic lens in which Satan represents the manifestation of ultimate evil at the end of the eschatological age. Put another way, Satan's worldly dominion had cosmic and universal dimensions. The notion that Jesus' resurrection constituted the defeat of Satan and with it the power of death itself is one manifestation of this belief:

> … by his death he might break the power of him who holds the power of death—that is, the devil.
>
> *(Heb 2.14)*[63]

Nowhere are the apocalyptic dimensions of Satan's rule clearer than in the book of Revelation. Drawing upon apocalyptic conventions for depicting cosmic warfare, the book of

Revelation identifies Satan as God's ultimate antagonist in a number of ways, e.g., as the "dragon" who gives power to the world's enemies of God (Rev 12-13), and as the adversary who leads legions of armies to fight God and God's people in the eschatological conflict (Rev 20). Christ's ultimate defeat of Satan means nothing less than the destruction of all worldly powers antithetical to God, including the power of death itself.

The preceding analysis demonstrates that the character of Satan in the early Christian imagination was certainly indebted to antecedent Jewish models. However, by the time of the composition of the New Testament, the character of Satan had developed considerably from its origins. For one, the variety of ways in which early Christian authors imagined Satan to function in the world, and the extent to which they depicted Christ's work as the antidote to Satan's destructive dominion, testify to the increased prominence Satan had attained by the 1st century CE.[64] Moreover, Satan's role as a functionary of God in antecedent Jewish literature had been almost wholly replaced with an ideology in which Satan functioned as the unholy antagonist of God, Christ, and Christ followers on earth. And yet, the character of Satan had not yet attained a fixed form. Rather, his character was adaptable to the theological and Christological concerns of individual authors, and one that was ripe for adaptation in subsequent Christian imagination.

## Notes

1 Parentheses added. All biblical translations are from the New International Version (NIV). unless otherwise noted.
2 Compare, for example, the more literal New King James translation: "… lest in the battle he become our adversary."
3 Peggy L. Day, "Abishai the śāṭān in 2 Sam 19.17–24," *Catholic Biblical Quarterly* 49.4 (1987): 543–7. This episode has funded the widely held definition of satan as an "accuser." However, as Stokes has successfully argued, Abishai is not branded a "satan" because he is "accusing" Shimei of anything; rather, Shimei himself had come to David admitting his part in Absalom's rebellion. "What is clearly in question here is not whether David will allow Abishai to serve as an accuser, but whether David will allow Abishai to put Shimei to death." Ryan E. Stokes, *The Satan: How God's Executioner Became the Enemy* (Grand Rapids, 2019), 9, n. 12.
4 Ryan E. Stokes, "Satan, YHWH's Executioner," *Journal of Biblical Literature* 133.2 (2014): 251–70.
5 Stokes, "Satan," 256–61; Stokes, *Satan*, 8–9.
6 Peggy L. Day, *An Adversary in Heaven: Śāṭān in the Hebrew Bible*, Harvard Semitic Monographs 64 (Atlanta, 1988), 45–56.
7 Others go further to associate this figure with God. See S.A. Meier, "Angel of Yahweh," *The Dictionary of Deities and Demons*, 53–9; Rivkah Schärf Kluger, *Satan in the Old Testament*, trans. Hildegard Nagel (Evanston, IL, 1967).
8 Karin Schöpflin, "YHWH's Agents of Doom: The Punishing Function of Angels in Post-Exilic Writings of the Old Testament," in *Angels: The Concept of Celestial Beings—Origins, Development, and Reception*, ed. Friedrich V. Reiterer, Tobias Nicklas, and Karin Schöpflin (Berlin, 2007), 125–37.
9 In fact, this is the only time in the Hebrew bible that an angel is identified as a "satan."
10 Day, *Adversary*, 118–26.
11 Stokes, *Satan*, 13.
12 M.S. Kee, "The Heavenly Council and its Type-scene," *Journal for the Study of the Old Testament* 31 (2007): 259–73; Antti Laato, "The Devil in the Old Testament," in *Evil and the Devil*, ed. Ida Fröhlich and Erkki Koskenniemi (London, 2013), 1–22, here 5–17.
13 See, e.g., Dominic Rudman, "Zechariah and the Satan Tradition in the Hebrew Bible," in *Tradition in Transition: Haggai and Zechariah 1-8 in the Trajectory of Hebrew Theology*, ed. Mark J. Boda and Michael H. Floyd (New York, 2008), 191–209. Day, *Adversary*, 25–43; Stokes, *Satan*, 7, n. 8.

14 Ryan E. Stokes, "Airing the High Priest's Dirty Laundry: Understanding the Imagery and Message of Zechariah 3:1–7," in *Sibyls, Scriptures, and Scrolls: John Collins at Seventy*, 2 vols., ed. Joel Baden, Hindy Najman, and Eibert Tigchelaar (Leiden, 2017), 2.1247–64.

15 See Psalm 109.6. Paul Evans, "Divine Intermediaries in 1 Chronicles 21," *Biblica* 85.4 (2004): 545–58. Stokes, *Satan*, 21–5. See also Ryan E. Stokes, "The Devil Made Me Do It … Or *Did* He? The Nature, Identity, and Literary Origins of the *Satan* in 1 Chronicles 21:1," *Journal of Biblical Literature* 128.1 (2009): 91–106.

16 Stefan Schreiber, "The Great Opponent: The Devil in Early Jewish and Formative Christian Literature," in Reiterer, Nicklas, and Schöpfin, *Angels*, 437–57; Kirsten Nielsen, *Satan: The Prodigal Son? A Family Problem in the Bible* (Sheffield, 1998), 100–5. Sydney H.T. Page, *Powers of Evil: A Biblical Study of Satan and Demons* (Grand Rapids, 1995), 33–7.

17 Some suggest that there was an Israelite taboo surrounding census-taking. Song-Mi Suzie Park, "Census and Censure: Sacred Threshing Floors and Counting Taboos in 2 Samuel 24," *Horizons in Biblical Theology* 35.1 (2013): 21–41.

18 See the summary in Day, *Adversary in Heaven*, 134–6.

19 Many note that the Chronicler inserts angels elsewhere into the narrative seemingly in order to depict a more transcendent deity. Day, *Adversary in Heaven*, 137–41.

20 Stokes, *Satan*, 41.

21 Anne Marie Kitz, "Demons in the Hebrew Bible and the Ancient Near East," *Journal of Biblical Literature* 135.3 (2016): 447–64.

22 Cf. other terms that are translated as "demon" or "evil spirit" by later Greek translators of the Hebrew text, e.g., Lev 17.2; 2 Chr 11.15; Isa 13.21; 34.14; Ps 106.27. Moreover, Azazel, Lilith, and Belial each function somewhat ambiguously in the Hebrew Bible but are viewed in later traditions as demonic forces who wreak havoc. See Ida Fröhlich, "Evil in Second Temple Texts," in *Evil and the Devil*, ed. Ida Fröhlich and Erkki Koskenniemi (London, 2013), 23–50, here 24–5. Karel van der Toorn, "The Theology of Demons in Mesopotamia and Israel: Popular Belief and Scholarly Speculation," in *Die Dämonen: Die Dämonologie der israelitisch-jüdischen und frühchristlichen Literatur im Kontext ihrer Umwelt*, ed. Armin Lange, Hermann Lichtenberger, and Dietmar Römheld (Tübingen, 2003), 61–83.

23 Annette Yoshiko Reed, *Demons, Angels, and Writing in Ancient Judaism* (Cambridge, 2020) 41–86; Anne Marie Kitz, "Demons in the Hebrew Bible and Ancient Near East," *Journal of Biblical Literature* 135 (2016): 447–64. Charles Stewart, *Demons and the Devil* (Princeton, 1991).

24 See the summary in Miguel De La Torre and Albert Hernandez, *The Quest for the Historical Satan* (Minneapolis, 2011), 58–61.

25 Stokes, *Satan*, 63–8;

26 Matthew Goff, "Enochic Literature and the Persistence of Evil: Giants and Demons, Satan and Azazel," in *Das Böse, der Teufel und Dämonen—Evil, the Devil, and Demons*, ed. Jan Dochhorn, Susanne Rudnig-Zelt, and Benjamin Wold (Tübingen, 2016), 43–57. Stokes, *Satan*, 61–74.

27 Kevin Sullivan, "The Watchers Traditions in *1 Enoch* 6-16: The Fall of the Angels and the Rise of Demons," in *The Watchers in Jewish and Christians Traditions*, ed. Angela Kim Harkins, Kelley Coblentz Bautch, and John C. Endres (Minneapolis, 2014), 91–104. Dale Martin, "When Did Angels Become Demons?," *Journal of Biblical Literature* 129 (2010): 657–77. Ryan Stokes, "What Is a Demon, What Is an Evil Spirit, and What Is a Satan?," in Dochhorn, Rudnig-Zelt and Wold, *Das Böse, der Teufel und Dämonen*, 259–72.

28 James VanderKam, "The Demons in the Book of *Jubilees*," in Lange, Lichtenberger, and Römheld, *Die Dämonen*, 339–64.

29 Stokes, *Satan*, 87–90.

30 See also *Jub.* 23.28–29; 50.5 for possible examples of a supra-human satan.

31 As with the noun "satan," the term "mastema" is found in the Hebrew bible where it is most often translated as "hostility." Devorah Dimant argued that this term perhaps referred to a category of angel, whereby it eventually morphed into a unique celestial character, as here in *Jubilees*. See Devorah Dimant, "Between Qumran Sectarian and Non-Sectarian Texts: The Case of Belial and Mastema," in *The Dead Sea scrolls and contemporary culture: proceedings of the international conference held at the Israel Museum, Jerusalem (July 6–8, 2008)* (Leiden, 2011), 235–56, here 247.

32 Reed Carlson, "Provocateurs, Examiners, and Fools: Divine Opponents to the Aqedah in Early Judaism," *Catholic Biblical Quarterly* 83.3 (2021): 373–89, here 377–81. Moshe Bernstein, "Angels at the Aqedah: A Study in the Development of a Midrashic Motif," *Dead Sea Discoveries* 7 (2000): 263–91, here 268.

33 Jan Willem van Henten, "Mastema," *Dictionary of Deities and Demons,* 553–4.

34 Todd Russell Hanneken, "Angels and Demons in the Book of Jubilees and Contemporary Apocalypses," *Henoch* 2 (2006): 11–25, here 21.

35 Annette Yoshiko Reed, "When did *Daimones* Become Demons? Revisiting Septuagintal Data for Ancient Jewish Demonology," *Harvard Theological Review* 116.3 (2023): 340–75.

36 Yoshiko Reed, *Demons, Angels, and Writing,* 87–101.

37 Loren T. Stuckenbruck, "The Demonic World of the Dead Sea Scrolls," in *Evil in Second Temple Judaism and Early Christianity*, ed. Chris Keith and Loren T. Stuckenbruck (Tübingen, 2016), 51–70; Cf. Bennie Reynolds III, "A Dwelling Place of Demons: Demonology and Apocalypticism in the Dead Sea Scrolls," in *Apocalyptic Thinking in Early Judaism: Engaging with John Collins' "The Apocalyptic Imagination,"* ed. Cecilia Wassen and Sidnie White Crawford (Leiden, 2018), 23–54; Douglas L. Penney and Michael O. Wise, "By the Power of Beelzebub: An Aramaic Incantation Formula from Qumran (4Q560)," *Journal of Biblical Literature* 113 (1994) 627–50; Bennie Reynolds III, "Understanding the Demonologies of the Dead Sea Scrolls: Accomplishments and Directions for the Future," *Religion Compass* 7 (2013) 103–14; Archie Wright, *The Origin of Evil Spirits: The Reception of Genesis 6:1–4 in Early Jewish Literature* (rev. ed., Minneapolis, 2015).

38 Corrado Martone, "Evil or Devil? Belial from the Bible to Qumran," *Henoch* 26.2 (2004): 115–27; Annette Steudel, "Der Teufel in den Texten aus Qumran," in *Apokalyptik und Qumran,* ed. Jörg Frey and Michael Becker (Paderborn, 2007), 191–200.

39 For example, CD 4.12–19. See Stokes, *Satan,* 156–60.

40 Stokes, *Satan,* 163–5. Cf. Miryam Brand, *Evil Within and Without: The Source of Sin and Its Nature as Portrayed in Second Temple Literature* (Göttingen, 2013), 243–8.

41 Stokes, *Satan,* 185–90. Stokes also draws a profitable comparison between the character of Belial in the War Rule and the "Angel of Darkness" in the Treatise on Two Spirits, which likewise posits a dichotomy between the righteous and the wicked and identifies the "angel of darkness" as the leader of the latter. See Stokes, *Satan,* 167–81.

42 David Frankfurter, "Master-Demons, Local Spirits, and Demonology in the Roman Mediterranean World," *Journal of Ancient Near Eastern Religions* 11 (2011): 126–31, here 127.

43 See Thomas J. Farrar and Guy J. Williams, "Diabolical Data: A Critical Inventory of New Testament Satanology," *Journal for the Study of the New Testament* 39.1 (2016): 40–71.

44 Douglas L. Penney, "Finding the Devil in the Details: Onomastic Exegesis and the Naming of Evil in the World of the New Testament," in *New Testament Greek and Exegesis: Essays in Honor of Gerald F. Hawthorne*, ed. Amy M. Donaldson and Timothy B. Sailors (Grand Rapids, 2003), 37–54.

45 Madeleine Wieger, "'Celui qu'on appelle διάβολος (Apocalypse 12.9): L'histoire du nom grec de l'Adversaire," in *L'adversaire de Dieu-Der Widersacher Gottes*, ed. Michael Tilly, Matthias Morgenstern, and Volker Henning (Tübingen, 2016), 201–18.

46 Thomas J. Farrar, "New Testament Satanology and Leading Suprahuman Opponents in Second Temple Jewish Literature: A Religio-Historical Analysis," *Journal of Theological Studies* 70.1 (2019): 21–68.

47 Thomas J. Farrar and Guy J. Williams, "Talk of the Devil: Unpacking the Language of New Testament Satanology," *Journal for the Study of the New Testament* 39.1 (2016): 72–96.

48 See Loren T. Stuckenbruck, "Satan and Demons," in *Jesus among Friends and Enemies: A Historical and Literary Introduction to Jesus in the Gospels*, ed. Chris Keith and Larry W. Hurtado (Grand Rapids, 2011), 173–97, here 181–2.

49 Thomas J. Farrar, "New Testament Satanology," 21–68.

50 For a summary argument for the supra-human dimensions of Satan in the New Testament, see Farrar, "New Testament Satanology," 21–68.

51 Cf. Mark 4.15; Acts 5.3; 2 Cor 4.4; 2 Tim 2.26; James 4.1–10; Rev 2.20; 12.9. Stokes, *Satan,* 204.

52 Stokes, *Satan,* 205.

53  See also 1 Timothy 3.11, in which women are characterised as "slanderers" (Gk. διαβόλους).
54  C David Abernathy, "Paul's Thorn in the Flesh: A Messenger of Satan?" *Neotestamentica*, 35.1–2 (2001): 69–79.
55  See Jude 9 and Revelation 12:7–10 for examples of ways in which early Christians promoted the ideology of archangel Michael as an antagonist of Satan.
56  Matt 13:38–39; Luke 11:18–21; Acts 26:18; 2 Cor. 6:14–15.
57  On the absence of exorcisms in John's Gospel, see Ronald A. Piper, 'Satan, Demons and the Absence of Exorcisms in the Fourth Gospel', in *Christology, Controversy and Community: New Testament Essays in Honour of David R. Catchpole*, ed. David G. Horrell and Christopher M. Tuckett (Leiden, 2000), 253–78; André Van Oudtshoorn, "Where Have All the Demons Gone? The Role and Place of the Devil in the Gospel of John," *Neotestamentica* 51.1 (2017): 65–82.
58  Lars Albinus, "The Greek δαίμων between Mythos and Logos," in Lange, Lichtenberger and Romheld, *Die Daimonen*, 425–46.
59  Stuckenbruck, "Satan and Demons," 185.
60  Amanda Witmer, *Jesus, The Galilean Exorcist: His Exorcisms in Social and Political Context* (London: Bloomsbury T&T Clark, 2012).
61  See Mark 3.22–27. Joel Marcus, "The Beelzebul Controversy and the Eschatologies of Jesus," in *Authenticating the Activities of Jesus*, ed. Bruce D. Chilton and Craig A. Evans (Leiden, 1999), 247–77.
62  Eric Eve, *The Healer from Nazareth: Jesus' Miracles in Historical Context* (London, 2009); Graham H. Twelftree, *In the Name of Jesus: Exorcism among Early Christians* (Grand Rapids, 2007).
63  Cf. Rev 1.18; cf. Rev 12.10–12. Klaus Wengst, "The Devil in the Revelation of St John," in *The Problem of Evil and its Symbols in Jewish and Christian Tradition*, ed. Henning Graf Reventlow and Yair Hoffmann (London, 2004), 68–74.
64  Gerd Theissen, "Monotheismus und Teufelsglaube: Entstehung und Psychologie des biblischen Satansmythos," in *Demons and the Devil in Ancient and Medieval Christianity*, ed. Nienke Vos and Willemien Otten (Leiden, 2011).

## Further Reading

Peggy L. Day, *An Adversary in Heaven: Śāṭān in the Hebrew Bible,* Harvard Semitic Monographs 64 (Atlanta: Scholars Press, 1988).
*Evil and the Devil* (ed. Ida Fröhlich and Erkki Koskenniemi; London: T&T Clark, 2013).
*Thomas J. Farrar*, "New Testament Satanology and Leading Suprahuman Opponents in Second Temple Jewish Literature: A Religio-Historical Analysis," *Journal of Theological Studies* 70.1 (2019): 21–68.
Annette Yoshiko Reed, *Demons, Angels, and Writing in Ancient Judaism* (Cambridge: Cambridge University Press, 2020).
Stefan Schreiber, "The Great Opponent: The Devil in Early Jewish and Formative Christian Literature," in *Angels: The Concept of Celestial Beings* (ed. Friedrich V. Reiterer, Tobias Nicklas, and Karin Schöpfin (Berlin: deGruyter, 2007), 437–57.
*Ryan E. Stokes*, *The Satan: How God's Executioner Became the Enemy* (Grand Rapids: Eerdmans, 2019).
Ryan E. Stokes, "What Is a Demon, What Is an Evil Spirit, and What Is a Satan?," in *Das Böse, der Teufel und Dämonen* (ed. Jan Dochhorn, Susanne Rudnig-Zelt, and Benjamin Wold; WUNT2 412; Tübingen: Mohr Siebeck, 2016), 259–72
Ryan E. Stokes, "Satan, YHWH's Executioner," *JBL* 133.2 (2014): 251–70.

# 2
# THE MYTH OF THE DEVIL IN THE EARLY CHURCH

*Archie T. Wright*

Christian literature in the mid- to late 2nd century reveals some noteworthy developments concerning the devil and other figures involved in the problem of evil. During the 1st century CE, Second Temple period terms such as Belial/Beliar, Mastema, or the "king of wickedness," amongst others, fell out of use. During the period of the early church, the theological views being considered concerning the origin of evil identified "the satan" or "the devil"[1] as the "leader" of the forces of evil. The question that is the centre of the debate amongst theologians and various Gnostic groups concerns the nature of this figure—good or evil—at his/its creation. The devil is identified with his own characteristics in the New Testament and other Jewish literature from the Second Temple period. One of the more common titles for the devil is "the ruler of this age."[2] It is unclear how he earned this title, but the idea of "this age" possibly reflects the phrase "dominion of Belial" found in various Dead Sea Scrolls in which Belial is at times referred to as the "prince," "chief," or "ruler," as in "the ruler of this age."[3] One of the more significant myths is that Satan is a fallen angel and the angels that fell with him are his demons.[4]

This view of the "fallen angel tradition" as the origin of demons of the world is the most substantial concept in the further development and understanding of the devil in the early church and ultimately in the modern church. However, prior to the late 1st and early 2nd centuries CE, the lack of language related to a supernatural demonology in the apostolic fathers led to an aetiology of evil and evil spirits that was not attributed to heavenly beings but derived from human activity.[5] The apostolic fathers do acknowledge the existence of a Satan/devil figure; however, close scrutiny of these early church theologians reveals that they did not have a consistent understanding of this figure. They generally acknowledged Satan during the numerous occasions when they were in dialogue with heretics and their teachings, which they ultimately blamed on Satan/the devil.[6]

One should also keep in mind the near disappearance of Satan from some Jewish apocalyptic texts at the end of the 1st century CE. The author of 2 Baruch 55.10-12, for instance, retells the story of the Garden of Eden without mentioning the devil. However, in the apocalyptic text of 2 Enoch 7, a figure identified as the "prince" of the fallen watchers from the watcher tradition in 1 Enoch is identified as "Satanail." This same figure is later identified in chapter 18 which, according to Andrei Orlov, "exhibits

DOI: 10.4324/9781003096603-3

familiarity with the Adamic mythology of evil by recalling some of features of the story of Satan's fall."[7] In addition, there is a lack of a distinct satanology in the New Testament; both issues are reflected in the lack of a singular satanology in the apostolic fathers (c. 50–150 CE) and the early church fathers (c. 150–450 CE).[8] It should be noted that these theologians of the early church serve as the modern church's interpretive lens to read or understand the Satan/devil found in the New Testament and the Old Testament. The apostolic fathers blamed much of the theology of the early heretical groups on the influence of a devil type figure, but as we will see, this figure is not necessarily to be identified as the modern church's "Satan" figure. We will next examine the prominent Gnostic groups from the early church period whose heresies these early theologians were attempting to refute.

## GNOSTIC GROUPS IN THE NEW TESTAMENT (TO C. 100 CE)

That heretical teachers and groups were a growing threat to early Christianity is apparent in various New Testament texts.[9] Minor distinctions in beliefs were becoming major differences. The author of 1 Timothy 6.20, for instance, warns the community to "Avoid the profane, foolish talk and the contradictions of the false knowledge." This is a clear warning against heretical teaching. In addition, the imperial authorities in Rome were beginning a programmatic denunciation of various forms of Christianity. This process appears to have forced the church towards some form of orthodox system of beliefs, but this would take considerable time with the wide range of theological communities that were emerging in the late 1st and early 2nd centuries CE. In the midst of this struggle for an orthodox identity against "heretical" groups, the devil or Satan figure became a central theological issue and weapon the church leadership used to battle the teachings of these heretics. The devil became identified as the "arch-heretic" due to the New Testament terminology associated with him such as the "ruler of this world" (Jn 16.11) or "father of lies" (Jn 8.44). It may be suggested that these various mythological monikers came about solely for the purpose of denouncing the Gnostics and other groups rather than being actual characteristics of the Satan figure. By applying these titles, those seeking an orthodoxy for the church were placing the heretical teachers in the camp of the devil that was opposed to God, at least in their eyes.

The early Christian leaders were doing all they could to defend "their" view of Christianity and the sovereignty and authority of God. Interestingly, there is not a single understanding of Satan amongst these heretics or the church leadership. The struggle with heresy in the early church appears to have been the driving force behind the emerging story of Satan's original apostasy and rebellion within the developing Christian mythos in the New Testament. The author of 2 Corinthians 4.4 calls him "the god[10] of this world who blinded the minds of the nonbelievers so that they will not see the light of the Gospel." In Ephesians 2.2, the author speaks of those who previously "followed the course of this world, following 'the prince of the power of the air',[11] the spirit now working in the children of unbelief." A form of ἄρχων (*archon*) is used in four other titles that the New Testament authors use allegedly to speak of the devil/Satan figures. These include the "*ruler* of this world" in John 16.11, 14.30 and 12.31; "*ruler* of the kingdom of the earth" in Revelation 1.5; and "*ruler* of the demons" in Luke 11.15, Mark 3.22, Matthew 12.24 and 9.34. Often the text of 1 Corinthians 2.6 and 8 has been used to identify the devil or Satan but it should be noted the Greek reads the plural *"rulers of this age"*[12] which is most likely referring to the human authorities rather than spiritual beings such as the devil. Except for the reference to 1 Corinthians, all these titles refer, in some way, to the origins story of the devil/Satan which was at the heart of the debate between the heretics and the church leadership.

There is clear evidence in the New Testament that heretical teachers were attempting to infiltrate the various Christian communities. 2 Thessalonians 2.7-12 speaks of "the mystery of lawlessness"[13] and "the lawless one"[14] who comes to deceive those who do not believe the truth. Verse 11 states that God has sent a "work of delusion"[15] to those who believe the lie. This "lawless one" is sent as part of "the working of the Satan."[16] This may suggest that the Satan is working on behalf of God, that is, that God has sent the "lawless one." 2 Peter 2.1 warns against the teachings of "false prophets" who are amongst the community who will secretly bring in "destructive heresies."[17] The author of 1 John 2.18-19 warns that the false teachers, although identified as "antichrists," are coming, ones who were previously believers in the community who now deny the truth of the Christ. In 1 John 3.8, we are told that these people were there to do the works of the devil to deceive the people. It appears that the "lawless one" may be the leader of these heretical teachers who are coming against the Gospel of Christ. There appears to be a growing interest or necessity amongst the New Testament authors to link the heresies of these teachers with the Satan figure, but exactly why is unclear.

## APOSTOLIC FATHERS (C. 50–150 CE)

Thomas J. Farrar has identified 160 "certain or probably references to Satan, under various designations" in the Apostolic Fathers and other Jewish Christian and gentile Christian literature dated c. 100–150 CE. These works include the *Ascension of Isaiah*, *Apocalypse of Peter*, *Odes of Solomon*, *Gospel of Truth*, Ptolemy's *Letter to Flora*, and the writings of Justin Martyr.[18] Farrar identifies numerous terms or phrases such as the familiar "the adversary,"[19] "the devil,"[20] "the Satan,"[21] and "the Ruler of this Age."[22] He identifies numerous others as either a certain or probable reference to the Satan figure. Farrar estimates there are over 300 references to the Satan figure, including those in the New Testament and "in extant Christian literature through the mid-2nd century CE."[23] In what follows, we will address the more prominent terms in the writings of the early church which are familiar to most readers.

### Clement of Rome

The earliest notable apostolic father to address the issue of a devil type figure is Clement of Rome who wrote his *Epistle of Clement* (*1 Clement*) to the Corinthians around 96 CE. He only makes one reference to such a figure in *1 Clement* 51.1 in which he speaks of seeking forgiveness of transgressions that were brought on by "suggestions of the adversary."[24] The term he uses, ἀντικειμένου (*antikeimenou*), is not the Greek term used in the New Testament term for the devil or the Satan, rather, a form of this term appears in the New Testament eight times and is used in the sense of a human adversary rather than a spiritual adversary (Lk 13.17 and 21.15, 1 Cor 16.9, Gal 5.17, Phil 1.28 and 2 Thes 2.4, "the "antichrist"[25]; 1 Tm 1.10; 5.14). It is similarly used in the Septuagint (that is, the Greek version of the Old Testament) to describe a human adversary twelve times[26]; it appears in the infinitive form, ἀντικεῖσθαι (*antikeisthai*), in the Septuagint version of Zechariah 3.1, translating the Hebrew לשטן (*lesatan*), "to be an adversary," the one who is opposing the appointment of Joshua as the High Priest. Interestingly, the Septuagint version of Zechariah 3.1 uses the term ὁ διάβολος (*ho diabolos*) to translate the Hebrew השטן (*hasatan*), "the adversary," rather than the term ἀντικειμένος (*antikeimenos*).

It appears from Clement's argument that there was a group within the Corinthian community causing disruption (acting as adversaries) amongst the church. Clement's Epistle to the Corinthians 51.1 suggests that some believers have fallen away and committed sins on account of the one who opposes the church. The "opposer" here is the ἀντικειμένου, the "adversary" who apparently is causing great jealousy amongst those in the community (see *1 Clem.* 3).[27] *1 Clement* 14.1 suggests this jealousy may be the result of the actions of a group who are sowing dissent amongst the community (see *1 Clem.* 15.5, 46.8-9 and 47.5-6); the "adversary" could be understood as the leader of this group rather than the supernatural "divine" adversary, the devil. Considering Clement's letter is 65 chapters long, it is surprising that he makes no clear reference to the work of Satan in a church with such dissent. In addition, the author attributes sin to the lusts of the "evil heart" rather than a supernatural being like the devil.[28]

### Ignatius of Antioch

The next figure we will examine is Ignatius of Antioch, c. 50–c. 117 CE, who served as the third bishop of Antioch following the apostle Peter and Evodius.[29] The seven epistles of Ignatius are thought to have been written between 110 and 117 CE.[30] Concerning the figure of the devil,[31] in Ignatius' *Epistle to the Ephesians* 10.3, he suggests that the devil has a role in the "purity"[32] or impurity of an individual and his or her "self-control."[33] Each person is to be an imitator of Christ (physically and spiritually[34]) "in order that no weed of the devil may be found in you."[35] The term "weed"[36] may be referring to the Parable of the Tares, although the Greek used in Matt 13.25-40 is ζιζάνια (*zizania*). A second use of the term "of the devil"[37] is found in his *Letter to the Trallians* 8.1 in which he warns the people that he "foresees the plots/traps of the devil"[38]; this may be an allusion to the "traps of Belial." The snares of the devil appear to be such things as "holding a grudge" or giving opportunity to the pagans through one's folly to blaspheme the lord. In *Trallians* 9, he goes on to identify the ways in which the pagans will blaspheme the lord. He emphasises the reality of Jesus' persecution under Pontius Pilate, "who really was crucified and died," "who really was raised from the dead"; all of these were ways in which the Docetist heretics were denying the humanity of Christ.

A third use of "of the devil" is found in the *Epistle to the Romans* 5.3 in a discussion of martyrdom in rather gruesome terms in which Ignatius attributes his torture to the "evil punishments of the devil."[39] This passage seems to attribute significant power to the devil, but what seems more likely in Ignatius' thinking is that the devil was at work behind the scenes rather than this being the devil's work. Ignatius is one of the earliest theologians to identify the Satan figure with the "ruler of this age." He writes in his *Letter to the Ephesians* 17, "Do not let yourself be anointed with the foul smell of the teaching 'of the ruler of this age'[40] lest he capture you and rob you of the life to come." In his *Epistle to the*

*Philadelphians* 6.1-2, he uses the phrase "ruler of this age" in what could be understood as an anti-Jewish polemic: he warns his readers not to listen to those who speak of Judaism without Christ for this is the deceit and plot of the "ruler of this age."

The writings of Ignatius suggest that the devil stands as a supernatural spiritual opponent to the believers in the late 1st to early 2nd centuries CE. The devil does not appear to be a personification of the internal human struggle with sin and temptation, but rather the devil is a major part of Ignatius' aetiology of sin and evil in his epistles to the various communities. However, one cannot rule out completely that the "ruler"[41] represents the human governments, pagan groups, or Jews who were opposed to Christianity. In addition, he sees the devil behind the teachings of the various heretical groups with which he is in debate.

## Polycarp of Smyrna

The third apostolic father of note is Polycarp of Smyrna, the disciple of John the Apostle and friend to Ignatius of Antioch. Like Ignatius, Polycarp was in an ongoing debate with the heretical Docetists. He was born in approximately 69 CE and died a martyr's death in 155 while residing in Smyrna as the city's bishop.[42] His martyrdom is the earliest recorded account of a martyr being burned alive, although it is alleged that because the flames would not harm him, he was stabbed to death. Only one of his writings survives, his *Epistle* to the church at Philippi, but we do have a letter written to him by Ignatius and the account of his martyrdom written by eyewitnesses.[43]

Polycarp's purpose in writing the *Letter to Philippi* was to address the improper behaviour of certain members of the church which he argues was a result of their wrong beliefs.[44] He uses the term "devils"[45] in his *Letter to Philippi* 5.2 in which his concern surrounds the office of deacon; however in this case, he appears to use the term to refer to human "adversaries" or possibly "slanderers." Polycarp, in all but one occasion, uses forms of the terms ὁ σατανᾶς and ὁ διαβόλος to refer to a heavenly adversary who meddles in the lives of the faithful ones.[46] The issues to which he connects these figures are related to heretical beliefs of Gnostic groups. On each occasion, the adversarial figure is attempting to cause disruption within one or more church. This raises an interesting point as to the "omnipresence" of the devil or the Satan figure in the early church. To this point in Jewish and Christian traditions, the figure has not had the ability to be in more than one place at a time. His role thus far is to test the faith of individuals on the earth and to incorporate a group of evil spirits (likely the spirits of the giants from the Enoch "watcher tradition") into his ongoing role upon the earth as the adversary to humanity. It appears that in the late 1st and early 2nd centuries CE, the figure could interfere with multiple churches and meddle in the lives of multiple individuals throughout the known world, but by using willing individuals (false teachers) or other evil spirits on his side. This may signal the beginning of the understanding of this figure as a semi-autonomous or even autonomous force of evil on the earth.

## *The Epistle of Barnabas*

The *Epistle of Barnabas* 2.1 offers the first allusion to the Satan figure (without naming it) in the author's claim that the people are in evil days and "the one who is at work has the power."[47] As a result, the people are told to be on guard and seek out the righteousness of the lord. His readers are warned in 2.10 to walk with care "so that the evil one does not work a creeping error in us."[48] This passage seems to suggest the Satan figure is tasked with testing individuals (or groups) with the temptation to sin, in this case to offer false oaths against one's neighbour (2.8).

*Epistle of Barnabas* 18.2 offers the clearest mention of a Satan figure within the author's discussion of the "Two Ways." He suggests there are two paths to follow, one of light guarded by "light-giving angels/messengers of God"[49] and one of darkness, watched over by "angels/messengers of the satan"[50]; again, both "angels" could be human messengers. Satan is identified in 18.2 as the one opposed to the lord and is "the ruler of the present time of lawlessness"[51]; this might refer to the period in which Belial/wickedness rules over Israel.

The next possible reference to the/a Satan figure is found in 19.11 in the context of a description of the "way of light" (19.1-12). Following a long list of "dos and don'ts" (more don'ts than dos) the reader is instructed that "to the end you shall hate *the evil one*."[52] In this context, it appears the role of this "evil one" is to try to cause the people to do the "don'ts" and thus turn away from "the way of light." In 20.1, the Satan figure is called "the black one." He is the one overseeing the "way of darkness" that is crooked and completely cursed and anyone who follows it will meet eternal death. The characteristics of people on this path are the opposite of those on the way of light. Those on the "way of darkness" commit idolatry, hypocrisy, adultery, murder, robbery; they are guilty of pride, sorcery, magic amongst many other sins culminating in a lack of fear of the lord (this list continues in 20.2 describing how these sinful actions manifest in actions towards others).

A reference to "the evil one," likely synonymous for the/a Satan figure (and the most common term used to describe him), is found in 21.3 which describes the end of days "in which everything will perish together with the evil one."[53] It appears that during this time the final judgement will take place and "the evil one" will meet the lord and God's recompense will be handed out to the righteous and the wicked. The author of the *Epistle of Barnabas* uses other appellations that seem to be identifying a supernatural evil being; however, if one considers the persecutions that were being carried out during the suggested time of the writing of the *Epistle of Barnabas*, the author may have been referring to the Roman Emperor or local government official.[54] It appears that the Satan figure is the key source for the author's aetiology of evil and sin and is part of the author's understanding and expectations during of the eschaton and the time of lawlessness.

## *The Shepherd of Hermas*

*The Shepherd of Hermas* offers a description of a series of visions given to the author that were mediated to him by an angelic figure identified as the shepherd, not unusual for the period in which the genre of apocalyptic flourished. The work is organised into a series of visions, mandates, and parables. The author presents various discussions concerning the issue of "repentance and forgiveness of postbaptismal sin" of a believer in light of God's justice and mercy.[55] In addition, the author contemplates the issue of social and economic justice or the lack thereof within his community. The *Shepherd of Hermas* was widely accepted as scripture by some prominent early church fathers, including Clement of Alexandria, Origen, and Tertullian. It was included in the canon of Didymus the Blind in the 4th century and, along with the *Epistle of Barnabas*, the *Shepherd of Hermas* is included in the Codex Sinaiticus following John's Apocalypse.[56]

The language of the author's diabology is scattered throughout the *Shepherd of Hermas*; it contains 24 instances of ὁ διάβολος or a form of it, but there is no reference to the term ὁ σατανᾶς in the 114 chapters. In addition, there is no mention of a devil figure or evil spirits in chapters 1–24 ("Visions"), the suggested earliest independent section of the book. Evil spirits are mentioned two times in chapter 33, three times in 34, once in 40, and once in 95. The term διάβολος, while significant in the "Visions" and the "Mandates," is found only once in the "Parables": 69.6.

The aetiology of evil in the world in the *Shepherd of Hermas* is anthropogenic in 6.2 in which the shepherd angel tells Hermas that all his children "have rejected God and blasphemed the Lord by their great evil." As a result, temptation and sin, normally attributed to the devil, is blamed on the "human passions" in 1.8; "evil desire" in 2.4; the "desire for riches" in 14.6, "licentious desires and evil deeds" in 15.2, and "weakness of the flesh" in 17.3.[57] However, the devil is still the one who comes "to test"(ἐκπειράζων—"the one testing") the servants of God (48.4), but according to 48.2 he cannot overcome the believer if he or she resists (cf. James 4.7) but, at the same time, if the person is "completely empty" then he will fear the devil and the devil will overcome him (48.7). In addition to a non-supernatural evil power, the way of salvation is not attributed to an eschatological supernatural being; rather it is accomplished through ethical instruction in 3.2, self-control in 6.1-2, repentance from double-mindedness in 6.4, walking in innocence and sincerity in 7.2 and 9.9, walking in righteousness in 9.6, and charity and almsgiving in 17.4-6.[58] Of course, all of these actions/characteristics are part of the teachings of Jesus in the Gospels.

The first reference to the devil is found in 31.4, in a discussion about forgiveness and repentance of sins in which he warns of "the cunning of the devil"[59] which can overcome the weakness of an individual. The shepherd tells Hermas that God knows the weakness of humans and that the devil behaves wickedly towards God's servants by doing some evil act to them, but that person can repent and be forgiven. There is no mention as to the authority of the devil to afflict these individuals although one might suggest that because the lord knows the weaknesses of individuals, he may want their faith tested in these areas and he permits the devil to test them. In 31.6, the author may be alluding to the idea that the lord has granted permission to the devil to test humanity (τις ἐκπειρασθεὶς); the shepherd states that should that person fail the test, he has one opportunity to repent of the sin. If a person repeatedly sins and repents it is of no use to him as he will attempt this with difficulty, perhaps suggesting he or she will live a hard life.

The second reference to the devil is found in 37.2 in the context of a discussion of keeping the lord's commandments. One's ability to resist the testing of the devil is accomplished by a healthy "fear of the Lord." If one has this fear, then he or she need not fear the devil but will be able to rule over the devil because the devil has no power/authority of his own. The shepherd says that if one rejects the devil then the devil has no power/authority over that individual (cf. the testing of Jesus in the wilderness—Mt 4 and Lk 4). In 37.3, the shepherd warns that a person should "fear the works of the devil, for they are evil." In contrast, when a person fears the lord, he or she will know to fear the works of the devil and avoid them.

The next reference to the devil is found in 39.11 in a discussion about being double-minded (διψυχίαν, "two souls"). The shepherd warns that "double-mindedness ... is evil and senseless" and has caused many to lose faith; it is "a daughter of the devil and does much evil to God's servants" (39.9). In 39.11, double-mindedness (doubt) is described as "an earthly spirit from the devil that has no power" in contrast to faith that is from the heavenly realm (39.12). This idea seems to suggest the influence of a spirit that is working alongside the devil to bring confusion to an individual. What is interesting is that here there is no mention of a spirit from the lord to counter this evil spirit until we get to chapter 43.

Chapter 43 presents a discussion on false prophets and the spirit from the devil and the divine spirit. In 43.3, the shepherd states that the false prophet is filled with emptiness, lacking the divine spirit, and gives empty answers to the double-minded who ask him to prophecy to them. Interestingly, the prophet does speak some true words, "for the devil fills him with his own spirit, to see if he will be able to breakdown any of the righteous." This perhaps alludes to the task of the devil, testing the faithful. Contrary to the actions of the false prophet, the true prophet operates "in the power of the divine spirit"[60] (43.5). He will never prophecy from a question of another person but will only speak when the Spirit wants him to speak (43.8). In 43.17, Hermas is warned to put his trust in the spirit from God and not on the earthly spirit that is from devil and lacks power. This idea may reflect the "lying spirit" concept (from the Ahab story) and add to the image of the devil being the father of lies.

In chapter 47, the shepherd returns to a discussion about keeping the commandments of the lord. In 47.5-7, he states that those who do not walk in the lord's commandments "walk in the devil's commandments"[61] (47.6), "which are difficult, bitter, wild and licentious," but there is no mention as to what these commandments are, but all those who walk in them are commanded to turn from them (repent—ἐπιστράφητε) and "be not afraid of him [the devil] and he will flee from you" (47.7). This language seems to reflect the idea, probably from the Qumran community (CD 16.4-5), that if one turns back to the Torah and follows God's commands, the adversary must flee, like the wilderness test of Jesus in the Gospels. Verses 48.1-2 seem to support this idea by suggesting that even attempts by those who desire to keep God's commandments are made difficult as "the devil is hard, and he oppresses them" presumably to test their faith. Verse 48.4 further supports the idea that the task of the devil is to test the servants of God ("the devil comes upon all the servants of God testing them").[62] He goes on to state that those full of faith resist him and he leaves and pursues those who are empty or partially empty, "he enters into them,"[63] which suggests "possession," but surely this cannot be speaking of the singular devil as he is only one spirit; rather the author must have in mind the evil spirits that are under the devil's authority. Is the author attributing, perhaps unknowingly, a sense of omnipresence to the devil figure? Can he "possess" more than one person at a time?

In 49.1, the author states that the "angel of repentance" was sent to strengthen the faithful and encourage them not to fear the devil. In chapter 63, the author introduces Hermas to the "angel of punishment"[64] as one of the angels of righteousness. Those who wander away from God are handed over to this angel to bring them back. One might ask if this is the angel that Paul speaks of when he hands individuals over to the devil to destroy the flesh and save the person's soul (e.g., 1 Cor 5 and 1 Tm 1.20).[65] This would support the idea that the devil is an angel of punishment who God uses to purify the wicked.

### The Fragments of Papias

The next writing of the apostolic fathers to discuss is the *Fragments of Papias*. Papias was the bishop of Hierapolis in Asia Minor and allegedly lived around the same time as Polycarp (c. 70–155 CE) and, according to Irenaeus in Frag. 14, Papias knew the apostle John. Since this is a collection of fragments, it is nearly impossible to date them as they come from not only Papias' writings but those of Irenaeus who allegedly cites him.[66] In the *Fragments of Papias*, the fall of the Satan figure is described as one that takes place prior to the creation of humanity as he states in verse 24.3, "He fell to earth, here to live; and when humanity came here, where he was, he did not permit them to live in natural passions; on the contrary, he led them astray into many evils."[67]

In verse 24.4, the reader is told that Michael and his legions of angels are also on the earth helping humanity, although this appears to be after the expulsion from the Garden during the period of the giving of the Torah and the days of the prophets (Dn 10, 12).[68] In verse 5, the author shares that there is now a war against the dragon in an effort to stop it from setting stumbling blocks for humanity. *The Fragments of Papias* 24.7 states, "Yet Christ came, and the Law, which was impossible for anyone else, he fulfilled in his body."[69] It appears from this reading that there is a battle occurring on the earth prior to Christ coming to the earth in bodily from. In verse 8, the author states that Christ "defeated sin and condemned Satan, and through his death he spread abroad his righteousness over all."[70] Then in verse 9 we have an allusion to the incident of Revelation 12 in which Michael defeats the dragon and he is cast down to earth defeated; this casting down, according to Papias in verse 24.10, is what we find in Luke 10 when Jesus said, "I saw Satan fallen from heaven like a lightning bolt."[71] If this is the case, then Papias may be suggesting that the dragon/Satan is battling Michael in the heavens (Rv 12), while Christ is on the earth in human form. But what then was the role of the dragon/Satan figure on earth prior to the battle breaking out between him and Michael? It seems from verse 24.5 that he was putting humanity through trials and perhaps got carried away with this authority which brought on the battle in verse 6 prior to Christ coming to the earth. In 24.11, Papias appears to identify two falls of the Satan figure; the first one is a spatial fall from heaven prior to the coming of Christ and the second fall is his judgement for perhaps exceeding his authority.

## Summary of the Apostolic Fathers

As we have seen in the writings of the apostolic fathers, these individuals should be understood as moralists who are attempting to instruct the early church as to the presence of a devil and evil spirits. They do not present a significant role of the devil in their theology, unlike the early church fathers and apologists. The apostolic fathers are concerned with the devil's role in the factionalism of the church, the heresies being spoken in the communities, and the right behaviour of the righteous. The apostolic fathers categorise the heretics such as Judaizers (see Ignatius, the *Martyrdom of Polycarp*, and *Epistle of Barnabas*), the Docetists (see Ignatius and the *Epistle of Polycarp*), and those refusing to obey the Bishop (Ignatius) as "tools of the devil."[72] We do see the devil and his minion of evil spirits apparently functioning as the tester of the righteous by attempting to lead believers into sin and manifesting vices, but these episodes are few in number. There is not a strong presence of a satanology in the apostolic fathers. Rather, they seem, with a few exceptions, more inclined to follow the Jewish "Two Ways" worldview in which humans have the responsibility to choose the right spirit to follow and allow that spirit to influence him or her.

## EARLY CHURCH FATHERS (C. 150–450 CE)

In the first or second decade of the 2nd century CE, apologists for the Christian faith began defending the doctrines of the early church due to a variety of opponents, the most prominent being the various heretical groups. The Gnostics and their unorthodox beliefs were a growing issue for the young church and many individuals entered the fray of defending the faith. One of the more prominent amongst this group was the apologist, Justin Martyr.

## Justin Martyr

Tradition tells us that Justin Martyr was born c. 114 CE in Samaria near modern-day Nablus. He was a follower of Socrates and Plato before converting to Christianity.[73] He was likely martyred in 165 CE during the rule of Marcus Aurelius. Although much of his writing has been lost, two very significant works survive, *First and Second Apologies* and his *Dialogue with Trypho*.[74]

Justin Martyr appears to be the first early church father to connect the devil/Satan with the myth of the serpent in the garden. In *1 Apology* 28.1 he notes, "Among us the chief [ruler] of the wicked demons[75] is called the serpent, and Satan, and devil, as you can learn from looking into our writings." This is the only mention of the Satan figure in Justin's *1 Apology* and *2 Apology*.

In *Dialogue with Trypho* 45, he again promotes the serpent myth of Satan: "the serpent that sinned from the beginning, and the angels like him, may be destroyed." Here, Martyr was likely alluding to the serpent in the garden (he identified the Satan as the serpent in *Dial. Try*. 45, 79, 100, 124). According to Jeffrey Burton Russell, Justin made the first major impact in discussing "the problem of evil in theological terms," in as much he saw that the church was in the midst of "a cosmic struggle" with the Satan and his followers.[76] In *2 Apology* it is clear he is very much aware of the fallen-watcher tradition of 1 Enoch, or at least a variation of it.[77] In *2 Apology* 5 he states that God appointed angels to watch over humanity, but the angels transgressed the laws of the cosmos and begat children with the daughters of humanity and produced offspring whom he calls demons (*2 Apol.* 5, cf., 1 En. 9.9; 19.1). These angels and the offspring are immediately called demons, subdue humanity and lead them into sin and idolatry and all wickedness. In addition, these demons have convinced humanity that they (the demons) are pagan gods (see *2 Apol.* 5).[78] He appears to suggest, however, that the fallen watchers are working alongside the demons to corrupt humankind, which, as we know, is not the case in the Book of Watchers; the watchers have been bound in the pit along with 90% of the evil spirits of the giants according to Jub. 10. He argues in *2 Apology* 7 and *Dialogue with Trypho* 140-41 that humans and angels are created with free will and can choose to follow God or reject him; interestingly, in *Dialogue with Trypho* 141, he seems to suggest that the angels who have sinned, along with the humans, can still repent and know God—and that would include the Satan figure.

In *1 Apology* 54, Justin contends that demons, the pagan gods,[79] are responsible for the Greek myths of Bacchus, Bellerophon and his horse Pegasus, Perseus, Heracles, and Aesculapius due to the prophecies foretold by the prophets of the coming Christ intending to show they (the prophecies) were "mere marvellous talks, like the things which were said by the poets." This idea that the pagan gods were demons was promoted by Justin and quickly adopted in the early church, to direct people to the true God of Israel. It may have been driven by Justin's early polemical interpretations of these texts in relation to the Jews and their rejection of Christ.[80] In addition to the Jewish question, Justin argues in *1 Apology* 56 that "the evil demons"[81] were attempting replace the Christ with other individuals such as Simon and Menander, who performed magic and claimed a divine status, and Marcion who denied God was the creator of all things and deceived many from following the Christ.

In the *Dialogue with Trypho* (160 CE), Justin offers a very different understanding of the origins of evil. Why are the two aetiologies in *2 Apology* and *Dialogue with Trypho* so different? Yoshiko Reed rightly suggests that *1* and *2 Apologies* and *Dialogue with Trypho* are directed towards two different non-Christian audiences—the *Apologies* are targeted at a pagan audience, probably Roman elite, in which he was "promoting Christianity as the true philosophy" while demonstrating similar Greco-Roman and Christian values.[82] The *Dialogue with Trypho* is directed towards the Jews and offers Justin's argument that the church is the true Israel and has since displaced the Jews from their legitimate heritage.

Throughout the *Dialogue with Trypho*, Justin offers his understanding of sin and the origins of evil by contrasting Christian piety and Jewish sinfulness.[83] With less emphasis on the fallen angel tradition to address sin (see *Dial.* 79),[84] he goes to the garden scene and the disobedience of Adam and Eve for his explanation. In *Dialogue with Trypho* 88.22-23, 10.36-43, and 125.21-29, Justin makes what is likely the earliest connection between Satan and the serpent in the garden, when he draws the parallel between the serpent and the Satan figure in 124.18 whom he identifies as one of the "Princes" (ἀρχόντων—this seems to imply a "heavenly being"). He argues the Satan figure was apostate from the will of God (125.26) and was "a sinner (as the serpent) from the beginning"[85] (*Dial. Try.* 45), a similar accusation he made concerning the fallen watchers in *2 Apology* (see also *Dial. Try.* 100 in which he groups the serpent, the angels, and men who are like Satan into a category of evil). As a result, Satan convinces Adam and Eve to turn away from God's will in the Garden that results in the eventual wickedness of humanity.[86] However, Justin does not give any reason as to how or why he makes this connection between the serpent and Satan in the midst of this polemic against the Jews (see esp. *Dial. Try.* 132-33). In the *Dialogue with Trypho*, he offers a story of Jewish history that reveals their ongoing disobedience and the punishment they faced from God.[87] Satan has deceived the Jews into thinking that they will be saved due to the fact they are the fleshly seed of Jacob (125.37), but this redemption is negated by their rejection of Jesus as the Messiah and their role in his death (*Dial. Try.* 16.4; 17.1; 32.3; 93.4; 103.2; 104.1; 133.6).[88] In *Dialogue with Trypho* 119, he accuses them of acting like the nations in Deuteronomy 32.17 in which "they sacrificed to demons which were not gods" (cf. Septuagint Ps 105.37 in *Dial. Try.* 19— "They sacrificed their sons and daughters to the demons"—τοῖς δαιμονίοις).

## Athenagoras

Athenagoras was an Athenian philosopher and apologist who wrote in the second half of the 2nd century. Only two of his writings survive, *Plea for the Christians* (176–177 CE) and *Treatise on the Resurrection* (176–180). The *Plea* was addressed to the Roman emperor Marcus Aurelius and his son Commodus and asked that justice be shown to Christians. *Resurrection* is possibly the first treatise on the Christian doctrine of the resurrection of the body.[89]

In our discussion in relation to the Satan figure, we begin with *Plea* 24 in which Athenagoras speaks of the belief in the divine amongst the poets and philosophers. For them, he argues, there were several gods, some were thought to be demons (δαιμόνων), others "matter" (ὕλης), while others believed these gods were once men (*Plea* 26). Amid this cosmology, Athenagoras contends that the heavenly angels were created by the *logos* and the so-called devil was one of these good-natured angels (*Plea* 24). Although Athenagoras does not use the term ὁ διάβολος or ὁ σατανᾶς, in *Plea* 25 he does speak of a being that could

45

align with the Satan figure. Much like the Gnostics),[90] he identifies this figure as the "ruler of matter" (τῆς ὕλης ἄρχων)[91] who is in control of the things that are outside of the "spirit" issues related to God. Interestingly, he operates in this arena with God's permission (*Plea* 25).[92] The original task of this "ruler," along with all other angels, was to exercise providence over creation and keep it and humanity in correct order for God; this sounds like the original task of the watcher angels in Jubilees. Athenagoras is also the first of the early church fathers to use the term ἀντίθεον, which is not something hostile to God, but rather the ruler of matter (otherwise, he would cease to exist—see *Plea* 24). The Satan controls the matter that is surrounded by the good that is God.[93] The adverse spirit (presumably the ruler of matter) attempts to move people and nations in various ways, some according to the things of matter and some according to the things divine. The character of each person and the direction he or she might take in life (good or evil) is affected by the attention given to him or her by the spirit and the demons who are pursuing that the person. Athenagoras may be one of the earliest theologians to identify Satan as one who tells many lies, but interestingly, he is not quoting Jesus from John 8.44; he quotes the words from Hesiod's Muses in *Theogony* 27.[94] This idea would of course make the connection to the pagan polytheism that had been associated with the demons in the 2nd century CE.[95]

In *Plea for the Christians*, Athenagoras contends that the fallen angels (the ruler of matter included) had the same freedom of choice over moral excellence and evil as do humans. Some of the angels, by their own accord, remained faithful in watching over what God made and ordained, while other angels corrupted the essence of their nature and the realm entrusted to them and followed their lust for the human women and created the giants of the watcher tradition. In *Plea* 25, Athenagoras discusses these two categories of spirits similar to those in the writings of Justin Martyr: the fallen angels and "the souls of the giants"[96] from the Enochic watcher tradition.

In *Plea* 25, Athenagoras contends the angels who fell from heaven still haunt the earth and the air and cannot rise again to the heavenly realm and the spirits of the giants are the demons (δαίμονες) that wander the earthly realm (see 1 Enoch 6-16). He does suggest that along with the spirits of the giants, the fallen angels haunt the air and the earthly realm, which would not align with the fate of the watcher angels in 1 Enoch who are bound up in the pit awaiting judgement. Athenagoras seems to be mixing the tradition of the watchers with that of the fall of the Satan figure in chapter 12 of John's Apocalypse in which we are told angels fall to earth with Satan.[97] In addition, Athenagoras alludes to the Ezekiel 28 "cherub" tradition by suggesting the fallen angel was dwelling in the "first firmament" of the earthly realm on the "holy mountain of God." Later church theologians interpret Ezekiel 28 and Isaiah 14 as the fall of the Satan figure due to his pride.[98]

## Irenaeus

Irenaeus was born around 140 CE in Asia Minor and died as a martyr in approximately 202.[99] His key writings focus on his conflict with the Valentinian Gnostics as recorded in the work entitled *Against Heresies* which he compiled around 180 CE. For Irenaeus, all heretics are part of the Satan's army that is in a war against Christ (*A.H.* 1.25.3). The Gnostic contention that the created world was a result of an evil creator, the demiurge (δεμιουργόν), was completely rejected by Irenaeus (*A.H.* 1.5) as neither the prophets nor the apostles identified another God involved in creation, only YHWH. The converse and far superior being, the true creator, was the *logos* (*A.H.* 1.5 and 4). In discussing the creation story,

Irenaeus, citing John 1.3, states that the heavenly beings (angels) were created good by God; since he considered Satan an angel, he too was created good (*A.H.* 3.8.3). The dualistic cosmology of the Gnostics is thus nullified in that Satan (the demiurge for the Gnostics) is inferior to God and Satan is not a God.[100]

Instead of raising the independence of Satan in the realm of sin, Irenaeus places the responsibility for sin on humanity.[101] This does not relieve the Satan figure of all responsibility in the process, in fact, he describes the task of Satan in similar terms as the figure in the Second Temple period Jewish texts and the New Testament. He is testing humans in an effort to persuade them to turn from God and stop following the Law, thus "emphasizing human responsibility for sin."[102] This does not, however, set up a cosmic dualism of the Satan as the enemy of God, but portrays him as the adversary of corrupt humanity (*A.H.*, 4.41.1-3 and 5.24.2), although even then his power over humanity is limited as he is only operating under the authority that is given by God (5.24.3). Following the storyline of Satan in the *Life of Adam and Eve*, the Satan figure is envious of humanity, Adam in particular, because God had put creation under Adam's authority. (*A.H.*, 3.23, 4.40, 5.21 and 5.24). Russell contends that due to this envy, the Satan figure fell from heaven following the creation of humans (*Apostolic Preaching* 17—the "rebel angel"—caused the sin in the Garden and caused Cain to slay Abel), but the apostate angels fell prior to the flood in the time of Enoch.[103]

In *A.H.* 3.23.3, Irenaeus, although in a convoluted way, contends that the devil either took on the form of a serpent or spoke through the serpent when Eve and Adam were tempted in the Garden. He quotes Jesus' words about the fire that is prepared for the devil and his angels, claiming that the devil is the one who beguiled Adam to sin. However, Irenaeus argues the devil did not compel the couple to sin—it was their own choice and weakness, which, strangely enough, Irenaeus attributes at least partially to God.[104] As a result of this human weakness, Satan empowers people to perform magic, create false doctrines, worship idols, and follow the stars; he does all this by one of the fallen watchers, Azazel from 1 Enoch (*A.H.* 1.15.6), once again maintaining the Enochic watcher tradition's role in the origins of evil in the latter part of the 2nd century CE.

For Irenaeus, the end of evil in the world will begin when the Antichrist appears and all who follow the devil will follow the Antichrist (see *A.H.* 5.25-30).[105] In the final battle the Antichrist will be defeated and Satan and his demons will be cast into the eternal fire.

## Tertullian

Tertullian was born around 155 CE in the city of Carthage into a wealthy family. No fewer than 31 works in Latin attributed to him survive dating from 196 to 212.[106] Even though he strongly rejected the Gnostic cosmological dualism of two gods involved in creation (God versus the Satan), he asserted a form of Jewish ethical dualism, which permeated his writings. As such, he stressed that an austere and regimented ethical lifestyle, avoiding all the wiles of the devil would be the only thing to assist one in resisting the devil (*De spectaculis* 1, 26).

Tertullian contends the physical world belongs to God, contrary to the Gnostics, while the sin in the world is a result of worldliness—that is, the love of the things of this world—and belongs to the devil (*De spec.* 15). He also understands that the devil is like the destroying angel of YHWH. In this role, he carries out the opposite of what God is doing in the world but with God's permission (*De anima* 57). He is not the ruler of the cosmos but has been given dominion over the earth or at least the part of it that he has corrupted (cf. Mt 13.18-30 and *De anima* 16 where he connects the weeds in the parable to the heresy of the Gnostics), but, according to Tertullian, the dominion of Satan over the earth was not enough. In *Adversus Marcionem* 5.17, speaking on the actions of the Satan, he draws on Isaiah 14.14, although not quoting the biblical text exactly (a mix of 14.13 and 14): "I will set my throne in the clouds, I will be like unto the Most High." Tertullian states that the devil has set himself up as a deity "this must be the devil … we shall recognize as the god of this world."[107] However, I see no overt identifying markers for the Satan figure in Isaiah 14 until we meet up with Tertullian and later early church fathers and their interpretations of this passage and Ezekiel 28, as discussed below.

Tertullian takes a very hard line on the devil whom he identifies as the primary cause of the fall in the garden. In *Adversus Marcionem* 2.5-10, we are told that Satan corrupted the image of God in Adam even though, according to Tertullian, they could have resisted by their own will, but they failed to stay on God's path and did not resist the temptation of the Satan. What is interesting in Tertullian's garden scene is there is no concept of Satan testing the faith of Adam and Eve, even though he does confess that he is given permission by God to do all that he does. Tertullian calls him a lying angel who corrupted humanity from the beginning (*De spec.* 2.12), but Satan does not stop with humans; he then turns to his fellow heavenly beings in an effort to turn them from God.

In *Adversus Marcionem* 2.9.3-4, Tertullian contends that the soul (נפש, ψυχή) is just a reflection of the "spirit," that is, the spirit that is from God. As such, humans are just a reflection of the image of God, for if they were the image of God then God would also be capable of corruption. He argues this makes humans of a lower quality than God, but at the same time, they can choose to do God's will. It is from here that he argues that angels are lower than humans because there is no mention that they too are created "in the image of God."

He begins in *Adversus Marcionem* 2.10 by stating that angels are inferior to humans as they are not created in God's image, unless of course one argues that God is speaking to the angels in Gen 1.26: "Let us make humanity in *our* image, according to *our* likeness." According to Jubilees 2.2, the spirits that serve before him (ἄγγελοι) were the only other beings in existence at the time. He goes on to say in 2.10 that God did not make the devil the devil, but rather that the adversary/accuser was made by himself, not created. That is, he became evil by self-transformation from good to evil due to his choices. This began with his accusation against God to Eve in the garden about forbidding them to eat from every tree in the garden (*Ad. Marc.* 2.10.2-3). This idea, of course, identifies the serpent as the devil. It is here that Tertullian turns to an allegorical interpretation of the Old Testament. Satan was originally a good angel full of wisdom who then, citing Ezekiel 28 and the story of the king of Tyre, chose to corrupt himself (2.10.2). Ernest Evans suggests in his translation that even though the devil, as an angel, was created in the "likeness" (assuming "of God"), he then annulled/unsealed the likeness.[108] Tertullian goes on to describe the devil as an archangel who was dwelling upon God's holy mountain, but sinned. He contends this is the description of the angel's transgression and not the king's, for no human was born in God's paradise, not even Adam, who Tertullian argues was "translated there" (2.10.3), which seems to contradict the biblical account of the creation of Adam in the garden. Nor was any human in the heights of heaven, (if one takes into consideration the "heavenly journeys" of Jewish apocalyptic texts, a person in the heights of heaven is a possibility), which he argues is where the Satan figure fell from and was cast down (2.10.3). Tertullian argues in 2.10.5

that God pre-condemned the Satan figure prior to the final judgement because he departed from his created nature of goodness due to his own free will.

In *Apology* 22, Tertullian describes the relationship between demons, the Satan figure, and humans.[109] He suggests that each human has a demon watching over him or her.[110] He contends that God allowed evil spirits to put humans to the test within the boundaries he had set for the evil spirits (*De fuga in persecutione* 1.1). However, at the onset of the passion of Christ, followers of Christ were granted authority over the evil spirits and given the ability to repel them during their continued testing and persecution until the final judgement (*Apol.* 27). In *Adversus Marcionem* 5.17, Tertullian turns Marcion's description of his God of this world towards that of the Satan figure whom Marcion thinks is "the creator" of creation, the demiurge. He describes Satan as the "god of this world," the "prince of the power of the air," and "a worker of disbelief." Here, Tertullian turns to the Isaiah 14.14 text to identify Satan as the prince of Tyre who has "filled the whole world with his lying pretence of deity."[111]

Amid Tertullian's diabology, people were invoking demons' names (idols or gods) when offering a curse and in doing so were invoking the name of the Satan, whom he identifies as the "ruler of evil spirits." Following the ideas of Justin Martyr, Tertullian links the demons to corrupt angels, who appear to be from the watcher tradition of 1 Enoch. He mistakenly argues these fallen angels are demons, led by their prince, and that their primary task is to bring about the ruin of humanity.[112] All of their actions are meant to lead people to idolatry and to turn them away from seeking the true God.[113]

## Clement of Alexandria

According to Epiphanius of Salamis in his *Against Heresies*, Clement of Alexandria's full name was Titus Flavius Clemens, and he was born c. 150 CE in Athens. He converted to Christianity at some point, but the date is not noted in any of his writings.[114] He died around 210 CE.[115]

Clement's explanation of the Satan figure starts with his view that evil was a contradiction to God's creation and offered an explanation of it "within a coherent philosophical system."[116] For Clement, Satan exists metaphorically and objectively, but perhaps more significantly, he sees him as the evil activity in the human soul. Satan is also active as an outside force or influence, perhaps a view influenced by the Jewish *yetser ra* in Second Temple period texts and early rabbinic thought. As a result, Clement stressed the non "being" presence of evil rather than the personified evil being—that is, the Satan figure. As with many other early Christian theologians, he suggested a view that could be categorised as a type of Gnostic dualism, in that Jesus came to disclose "the hidden deity to a select few and teach them saving knowledge."[117] However, his view of evil was in direct conflict with the Gnostic dualism of the time.

Clement argued in *Stromata* 5.14 that the devil was the first to choose by his own free will (he is also able to repent—*Strom.* 1.17) and he is the leader of demons (*Strom.* 5.14). He contends that the devil "generated evil nature"[118] and the angels and humanity followed him. The idea that the devil was able to "generate (give birth to) the evil nature" seems to suggest he was able, in some sense, to create, which does not fit into Clement's theology of the "principle being"; rather it would fit better in the Gnostic view of a second "evil" creator God. He argued that because of God's mercy there existed "salvation for all free and intelligent beings," along with the idea that free willed beings can opt for good at any time, as a result, Clement leaned towards a universal salvation that included the redemption of the Satan figure despite the idea that he sinned from the beginning. This idea of *apocatastasis* would be further developed by Origen in the early 3rd century CE (*Strom.* 1.17: "Now the devil being possessed of free-will, was able to repent and to steal").

## Origen of Alexandria

Origen was born approximately 185 CE in Alexandria to a wealthy family and as a result he was well educated.[119] In his 4th-century *Church History*, Eusebius of Caesarea records that he suffered torture under Emperor Decius in 251 and later died when Gallus was made ruler in 253 (*Church History* 6.39.5 and 7.1.1).

Origen discusses the fall of creation and the beings that occupy it considering what were once pure intellects who dwelled in the presence of God. However, these beings, through their free will, sought a greater measure of satisfaction (κόρος—*De principiis* 1.4.1) but because of original sin they fell to various levels of "being." The least fallen beings were angels, followed by humans, and the worst of all were demons.[120]

Origen's primary attack on the Gnostics is centred on his idea of an "ambitious angel," which he argues is already a prominent feature in the views of the church in the early 3rd century.[121] His purpose is to try to establish a consistent story of the origin of evil. In *De principiis* 6, he contends that the "most widespread opinion in the church, however, is that the devil was an angel and that once he became a rebel, he persuaded the greatest number of angels possible to revolt." It is here where we find the "replacement" for the fallen watcher myth. Despite carrying his own Gnostic ideas, his ongoing fight with pagans and Gnostics resulted in him establishing clear doctrines concerning the origins of evil to refute the Gnostic heresies of the demiurge. As a result of his teachings concerning universal redemption which implied that Satan could be redeemed,[122] Origen was later condemned for heresy.[123]

Many of Origen's ideas are found in his refutation of Celsus, a 2nd-century Greek philosopher who was a strong critic of early Christianity in his non-no longer extant *The True Word*. Celsus argued that Christianity perverted the words of the philosopher Plato, and the Jewish/Christian God was not all-knowing or all-powerful. He argued that the Satan figure was either a mortal fabrication thought up by Christians to scare others into believing their doctrines or if he did exist then God was not all-powerful, but a weak lesser God.[124] However, Origen contended that people like Celsus were under the influence of the devil and as a result they are unable to comprehend God or scripture. He argued that all knowledge of the devil needs to be collected from scripture and properly examined (*basanos*—"to test the validity of one's interpretation"). He claimed the heretics were examining scripture in a tortured fashioned—a secondary meaning for *basanos*. According to Neil Forsyth, Origen may have struggled with the idea that he had tortured the text "to extract the doctrine of Satan" from scripture.[125] In other words, he felt he did not hold the correct interpretive key to establishing a proper doctrine of the devil. The idea of the "correct interpretive key" sounds very Gnostic and may reveal Origen's Gnostic roots.

Origen's thoughts on the origins of evil evolved through three periods in his life. In the early stage his view seems to be influenced by the watcher tradition and such writers as Clement of Alexandria (*Strom.* 3.7; 5.1; 7.7) and Philo of Alexandria (*De gigantibus*). The middle stage of development is found in *De principiis* in which he presents a detailed discussion on the pre-cosmos fall of the Satan figure, which comes about in his refutation of the Gnostic view of the Satan; the final stage is presented in *Contra Celsum* a defence of the doctrine against the claim that Christianity was a primitive dualism which includes the fallen watchers. In 5.52, we are to understand that Celsus complained that Christians believed there were "many angelic visitations other than Christ's ... even sixty or seventy at a time, who were perverted and for punishment were chained under the earth." Origen refutes Celsus because he is misreading the book of Enoch or that it "is not generally held to be divine among the churches."[126]

Origen turns to the prophets Ezekiel and Isaiah to clarify the position of the devil in the hierarchy of rational (free will) creatures. He draws on Ezekiel 28 in support of his rebellion motif in relation to this evil power. He claims that the words of the prophet cannot be speaking of a man but rather a divine being who was cast from the heavens due to his change in nature not by his decision to change (*De prin.* 1.5.5; this appears to also be the cause of the watchers' fall). He uses the Isaiah 14 passage to argue against the Gnostic belief that the devil was evil at his creation—having once been light but was now a creature of darkness. He contends that Isaiah calls him the "prince of this world" and that he has power over all who follow his wickedness (1 Jn 5.19). Again, we see Origen using his understanding of the Satan figure as a rebellious being in order to refute the Gnostic view that he was created with an evil nature. Thus, he substitutes the lustful watcher motif with the rebellious motif of the Satan figure with the use of the Ezekiel 28 and Isaiah 14 passages. However, one should remember that the watcher motif was also one of rebellion involving a band of angels versus the single angel, the Satan.

In addition to the prophets, Origen draws on the words of Christ in his refutation of the Gnostics. He suggests that Luke 10.18 requires that Satan was once a creature of light who fell as lightning from heaven. He argues that the lord is stating that Satan once shared in the light as an angel. This passage of course can be argued as a prophetic vision given by Christ when he sees Satan falling from heaven in the future and not a previous event, but it does say that the Satan figure was created with a good nature and not an evil nature as the Gnostics argued.

Origen sums up his idea of the Satan figure and the origins of evil this way:

> Before the [Gnostic] aeons, all spirits were pure, demons, souls, and angels, serving God and fulfilling his commandments. The devil who is one of them, having free will, wanted to oppose God and God threw him out. All the other powers fell with him and the ones who had sinned a lot became demons, the others who had sinned less, angels, those who had sinned even less, archangels: thus, each received his lot according to his own sin. Only those souls [humans] were left who had not sinned enough to become demons, nor so lightly as to be angels. God therefore made the present world and bound the soul to the body in order to punish it.[127]

We see here a mix of a biblical "fall" myth and the Platonic view of the fall of the soul as espoused by philosophers such as Philo of Alexandria, all to counter the Gnostic narratives of the origins of evil.

## Augustine, Bishop of Hippo

Augustine, the Bishop of Hippo, was one of the most influential figures in the development of the Satan tradition in the early church fathers.[128] A number of Augustine's theological arguments were due to his confrontation with the teachings of Mani and his followers, a group of dualists called the Manicheans. The primary doctrine of Manichaeism was that of the divided cosmos: it focused on the struggle between a good spirit and an evil spirit.

Mani contended that in the beginning light and darkness, good and evil, and God and matter were separate. The darkness sought to fulfil hate and strife for itself, but at some point, the powers within darkness met light and through their envy for light went on the attack. Light was unable to repel the attack and God was "forced to create a new divine hypostasis more suitable for combat"—he called this figure "primal man." The knowledge of the primal man was part of the Gnostic secret knowledge.[129] The Manichaeans named this figure "Ormazd," similar to the God of light in the Persian Zoroastrianism, Ahura Mazda, who was opposed to Ahriman, the God of darkness. During the battle between light and darkness, the primal man was defeated by the Satan figure and light and darkness mixed, but the light had the adverse effect of making the darkness more evil. At the same time, the primal man of light was saved by the spirit of light—or, in the New Testament world, the event of the crucifixion.

The next phase of this Manichaean story describes how the so-called "prince of darkness" creates Adam and Eve (Gen 1.27) to imprison part of the divine light. As a result, humanity is now the major arena in which the forces of light and darkness battle, much like the situation in Zoroastrianism, the *Community Rule* texts of Qumran, and the possession stories in the New Testament. Interestingly, the procreation of humanity in Mani's theology resulted in a dissipation of the light in humanity. Adam must be warned and messengers are sent. One takes on the form of a serpent that Jesus speaks through to warn Adam and to convince him to eat from the tree of knowledge in order to begin his trek towards salvation through the revelation of many: Seth, Enoch, Noah, Buddha, Zarathustra, Jesus Christ, and finally Mani.[130] It is these teachings that Augustine attacked head on in his various works.

Augustine set the standard of orthodoxy for several major doctrinal issues, including "original sin," which involved the Satan figure.[131] In *City of God*, 11.13-15, he examines whether the Satan figure was evil from the beginning of his existence. He cites John 8.44 in establishing that the devil was a murder from the beginning of humanity in that he deceived Adam and caused his death and that from his creation he did not stand in the truth, nor was truth in him. The other angels were blessed because they submitted themselves to their creator.[132] The Manichaeans argued that the devil was created out of an evil nature, while Augustine insisted that he chose not to abide in the truth of his creator. He argues in stanza 14 that because he does not aide in the truth, there is no truth in him—not the other way around. The devil had the opportunity to abide in the truth, but his pride would not permit him.

In stanza 15, he rejects the Manichaean idea that 1 John 3.8, "the devil sinned from the beginning," means that "the devil was made with a sinful nature"; he maintains that if "sin is natural, then it is not sin." Augustine's early understanding of evil is seen through the nature of the devil's sin. In attacking Mani, Augustine argues that sin precedes evil and is the cause of evil; Mani, however, argued that evil is the cause of sin with each being an expression of the power of darkness. In addition, Augustine attacked the Manichaean and Gnostic idea that matter itself was evil by stating "that evil is corruption, not substance."[133] If matter were evil then it would have to be evil to everything and everyone; thus, fire, air, earth, and water would always be evil. It appears he made this argument to counter the Gnostic idea of the demiurge, which, as noted, was a divine being who is responsible for creating the material world. If this is the case, how then is the Satan figure able to enter the divine council in Job and have a conversation with God? If from the beginning he has rebelled, how is he able to remain in the role he has under God's authority?

Augustine asks how the Manichaeans could not recognise the nature of the devil in Isaiah 14 and Ezekiel 28 which, he asserts describe the fall of the Satan figure (*City of God* 11.15). He uses these prophetic texts to argue against those who believe the devil was created with a sinful nature (the Manichaeans). Thus, the devil was not created with a sin nature but according to Augustine he rebelled by his free will choice. Augustine is the first to identify Satan as "the fallen one, Lucifer, son of the morning" in Isaiah 14.12: "O how you fell from heaven, <u>shining one</u>,[134] son of the dawn."[135] Augustine combines this line with Ezekiel 28.13 in which he argues that Satan is the one who was in the Garden of God and every precious stone was his covering; he suggests that Ezekiel is saying that at some point in his existence the Satan figure was without sin—"You were perfect in your ways from the day you were created until iniquity was found in you" (Ez 28.15).

As for Adam and Eve, Augustine argues that the sin of pride, one of the vices of the devil (14.13), was the cause of the fall of Adam. The result of this pride was the soul being "enamoured of its own power" (including the fallen angels, 12.8; 11.33). This suggests that the fall of the Satan figure was the result of pride, but what was the origin of his pride? Was it due to his free will or was he created with pride? If it is through free will, this suggests the act of choosing to be prideful was the fall. Adam then becomes a victim of the Satan figure's pride and not his own will, as Augustine states in 13.14. Nevertheless, he suggests in 14.13 that Adam had already chosen "to live for himself" and thus, he was not actually deceived (14.11). Who is then at fault in this mythic event? The Satan figure or the first Adam? Or is it simply to be laid at the feet of "free will"?

The theological and philosophical views of Augustine appear to have been the primary source that finally established what would be the understanding of the Satan figure in the early church. With the conversion of the Roman Empire to Christianity and the end to the persecution by the Empire, Christians had to look elsewhere for an oppressor. Augustine turned to the spirit realm to set as doctrine a belief that early Christians had yet to solidify—where did the evil Satan figure come from? He claimed, in the *City of God*, that the devil was originally a sinner; that is, he refused to accept the righteousness of God. In *City of God* 11.13 he also contends Satan was originally good but that he, along with some other angels, fell away from the light of goodness. Augustine's apparent contradictions in matters concerning Christian doctrine leads to the question of how we can trust whether the things he considers as orthodox belief are actually true according to Scripture?

## Summary

The understanding of the function of the Satan figure in the apostolic fathers and early church fathers is based primarily on the understanding that God is not the cause of evil (countering Valentinian and Manichaean doctrines of the origins of evil), a doctrine established by Augustine. But scripture states otherwise in Amos 3.7, which suggests that if there is calamity in a city then it was certainly a result of the lord's doing. The Gnostic groups argued that another divine figure nearly equal in power to YHWH, the demiurge, was responsible for the evils in the world. The early church fathers and others were attempting to counter the Gnostic views by pressing the issue that the devil, created good, turned to evil through the sin of pride. As a result, the devil was trying to draw all humanity to himself and away from God. This autonomous or semi-autonomous evil figure is a significant shift away from the Satan figure that operated in the Hebrew bible, Second Temple period Judaism(s), and in the New Testament gospels.

## Notes

1 ὁ σατανᾶς (the satan) or ὁ διάβολος (the devil).
2 Gk., ὁ ἄρχων τοῦ αἰῶνος τούτου. Thomas J. Farrar suggests ἄρχων reflects the Hebrew term שׂר in Dn 10.13. See his "The Intimate and Ultimate Adversary: Satanology in Early Second-Century Christian Literature" *Journal of Early Christian Studies* 26, no. 4 (2018): 517–46.
3 Heb., שׂר.
4 See, for example, Tertullian's discussion concerning renouncing Satan prior to Christian baptism in *De Corona* 3.387: "When we are going to enter the water, but a short time before, in the presence of the congregation and under the hand of the authority, we solemnly profess that we reject the devil, and his pomp, and his angels." The Fourth Lateran Council in 1215 established the official church doctrine of the devil in canon 1: "The devil and the other demons were indeed created by God good by nature, but they became bad through themselves; [hu]man[ity], however, sinned at the suggestion of the devil." See Norman Tanner, *Decrees of the Ecumenical Councils*, vol. 1, Nicaea to Lateran V (London, 1990), 229.
5 See Jonathan Burke, "Satan and Demons in the Apostolic Fathers: A Minority Report" *Svensk Exegetisk Årsbok*, 81 (2016): 127–68.
6 See Ignatius of Antioch, *Epistle to the Ephesians* 17; cf. Ignatius, *Epistle to the Trallians* 10.
7 See Andrei A. Orlov, *Dark Mirrors: Azazel and Satanael in Early Jewish Demonology* (Albany, 2011), 90–1.
8 See Paolo Sacchi, *Jewish Apocalyptic and its History*, trans. William J. Short (Sheffield, 1990), 231; Sacchi notes the "various forms, from the tempter of Jesus to Peter's roaring lion, prowling around us (1 Pet. 5.8), and the first sinner of John (1 Jn 3.8), the cause of the terrifying cosmic drama...."
9 See Neil Forsyth, *The Old Enemy: Satan and the Combat Myth* (Princeton, 1987), 309–10.
10 Gk., ὁ θεὸς.
11 Gk., τὸν ἄρχοντα τῆς ἐξουσίας τοῦ ἀέρος.
12 Gk., τῶν ἀρχόντων τοῦ αἰῶνος τούτου.
13 Gk., τὸ μυστήριον ... ὁ ἄνομος.
14 Gk., ὁ ἄνομος.
15 Gk., ἐνέργειαν πλάνης. This term, ἐνέργειαν, is only used in relation to the work of a superhuman being, that is, God or the Satan figure.
16 Gk., ἐνέργειαν τοῦ σατανᾶ.
17 Gk. αἱρέσεις ἀπωλείας.
18 See Farrar, "Intimate and Ultimate Adversary."
19 Gk., ὁ ἀντικείμενος. See 1 Clem 51.1.
20 See 2 Clem 18.2; Ignatius, *Eph.* 10.3; *Trall.* 8.1; *Rom.* 5.3; *Smyrn.* 9.1; Polycarp, *Phil.* 7.1; *Martyr Polycarp* 2.4.
21 Gk., ὁ διάβολος, ὁ σατανᾶς. See Ignatius, *Eph.* 13.1; Polycarp, *Phil.* 7.1.
22 Gk., ὁ ἄρχων τοῦ αἰῶνος τούτου. See Ignatius, *Eph.* 17.1, 19.1; *Magn.* 1.2; *Trall.* 4.2; *Rom.* 7.1; *Philad.* 6.2.
23 See table 1 in Farrar, "Intimate and Ultimate Adversary," 522–33.
24 Gk., διά τινας τῶν τοῦ ἀντικειμένου. See Francis X. Gokey, *The Terminology for the Devil and Evil Spirits in the Apostolic Fathers* (PhD diss., Catholic University of America, 1961), 68.
25 See Burke, "Satan and Demons," 142.
26 See Ex 23.22, Heb, צרר; 2 Sm 8.10, לחם; Est 8.11; 9.2; 1 Mc 14.7; 2 Mc 10.26; 3 Mc 7.9; Jb 13.26, אִיב; Is 41.11, חרה; 45.16, צרר; 51.19, קרא; 66.6, אִיב.
27 Interestingly, the author of *1 Clem* in his rebuke of the Corinthians appears to cite a section of Wisdom 2.24, but omits the phrase φθόνῳ δὲ διαβόλου, "envy of the devil," and contends that their jealousy is due to "the lusts of their heart" which resulted in death entering the world.

28 Burke, "Satan and Demons," 142.

29 See Eusebius, *Church History* II.3.22.

30 Russell contends he was martyred in 107. See Jeffrey Burton Russell, *Satan: The Early Christian Tradition* (Ithaca, 1987), 34.

31 Ignatius uses other terminology that may make reference to a supernatural evil being or force. He uses "ruler of this age" in Eph 17.1, in reference to teaching (heretical); 19.1, birth of Christ; Magn 1, abuse by the "ruler"; Rom 7.1, being captive of the "ruler"; Phila 6.2, evil tricks and traps of the "ruler."

32 Gk., ἀγνεία.

33 Gk., σωφροσύνη.

34 Gk., σαρκικῶς καὶ πνευματικῶς.

35 Gk., ἵνα μὴ τοῦ διαβόλου βοτάνη τις εὑρεθῇ ἐν ὑμῖν.

36 Gk., βοτάνη.

37 Gk., τοῦ διαβόλου.

38 Gk., προορῶν τὰς ἐνέδραη τοῦ διαβόλου.

39 Gk., κακαὶ κολάσεις τοῦ διαβόλου.

40 Gk., τοῦ ἄρχοντος τοῦ αἰῶνος τούτου.

41 The title, "ruler" appears to be used for a leading evil figure: "ruler of demons" in Mt 12.24–29, Mk 3.22–27, and Lk 11.15–21; "ruler of this world" in Jn 12.31, 14.30, 16.11; "ruler of the authority of the air" in Eph 2.2; "evil ruler" in *Epistle of Barnabas*. 4.13, "ruler of the present time of lawlessness" in 18.2; and "unrighteous ruler" in *Martyrdom of Polycarp*. 19.2. But this could be referring to the local governor.

42 *The Apostolic Fathers: Greek Texts and English Translations*, trans. Michael W. Holmes, 3rd ed. (Grand Rapids, 2007), 298.

43 *Martyrdom of Polycarp*, in *The Ante-Nicene Fathers*, trans. and ed. Alexander Roberts and James Donaldson, vol. 1 (Grand Rapids, 1885), 15.1.

44 *The Apostolic Fathers*, 274. Here, Holmes argues that the letter was originally two letters written at different times: chapters 13 and 14 were written after Ignatius left Philippi, while chapters 1–12 were probably written around 135–137 CE due to its anti-Marcionite content. See P. N. Harrison, *Polycarp's Two Epistles to the Philippians* (Cambridge, 1936). This idea is still debated. See *The Apostolic Fathers*, 275–6.

45 Gk., διάβολοι.

46 The use of the term "teaching" could suggest that he is warning against the teaching of the Gnostics, for the epistle is warning against being corrupted by evil teaching that corrupts one's faith in God. If this is the case, then Polycarp and other apostolic fathers appear to see the Satan figure behind the teachings of the various Gnostic groups.

47 Gk., καὶ αὐτοῦ τοῦ ἐνεργοῦντος ἔχοντος τὴν ἐξουσιαν. The *Epistle of Barnabas* is dated sometime between 70 and 135 CE and, according to Michael Holmes, it is difficult to be more precise. See *The Apostolic Fathers*, 373. See also the discussion in James N. Rhodes, *The Epistle of Barnabas and the Deuteronomic Tradition* (Tübingen, 2004), 75–87.

48 Gk., ἵνα μὴ ὁ πονηρος παρείσδυσιν πλάνης ποιήσας ἐν ἡμῖν.

49 Gk., φωταγωγοὶ ἄγγελοι τοῦ θεοῦ.

50 Gk., ἄγγελοι τοῦ σατανᾶ.

51 Gk., ὁ δὲ ἄρχων καιροῦ τοῦ νῦν τῆς ἀνομίας.

52 Gk., εἰς τέλος μισήσεις τὸν πονηρόν.

53 Gk., ἐν ᾗ συναπολεῖται πάντα τῷ πονηρῷ.

54 In *Epistle* 2.1, he is "the ruler who is at work in the age of evil"; he is the "evil one" in 2.10, 19.11, and 21.3; the "evil ruler" in 4.13; the "lawless one" in 15.5; and the somewhat enigmatically "the black one" in 4.9 and 20.1.

55 *The Apostolic Fathers*, 443.

56 *The Apostolic Fathers*, 444–5.

57 Burke, "Satan and Demons," 145. This is a similar line of argument for many Alexandrian theologians, including Philo of Alexandria, a Jewish exegete. *The Shepherd* suggests that the "vices" are demons, or better yet δαιμόνια; for example, "slander" and "vain confidence" are identified as *daimonian*. In 27.3, the author speaks of "slander" as a "restless demon" (ἀκατάστατον δαιμόνιόν) and in 99.3, "vain confidence" and "self-will" are identified as great demons (μέγα . . . δαιμόνιόν). This personification of vices as demons in *The Shepherd* is not seen in other

apostolic fathers, but the author is often inconsistent in his dialogue about evil spirits. This may be an idea that could be part of Philo's or an Alexandrian demonology, although Philo does not make this connection. See Gokey, *Terminology of the Devil*, 127.

58 It appears that the author of *The Shepherd* may have been influenced by the letter of James and the idea that faith without works is not much good and that failure to follow the acts of righteousness allows an open door for trial by the adversary, the Satan. See Oscar J. F. Seitz, "The Relationship of the Shepherd of Hermas to the Epistle of James," *Journal of Biblical Literature* 63.2 (1944): 131–40; Patrick J. Hartin, *James* (Collegeville, 2003).

59 Gk., τὴν πολυπλοκίαυ τοῦ διαβολοῦ.

60 Gk., τῆς δυνάμεος τοῦ θείου πνεύματος.

61 Gk., οἱ ταῖς ἐντολαῖς πορευόμενοι τοῦ διαβόλου.

62 Gk., ὁ διάβολος ἔρχεται ἐπι πάντας τοὺς δούλους τοῦ θεοῦ ἐκπειράζων αὐτούς.

63 Gk., εἰσπορεύεται εἰς αὐτούς.

64 Gk., ὁ ἄγγελος τῆς τιμωρίας.

65 See the discussion of Satan as "the attacker" in Ryan E. Stokes, *The Satan: How God's Executioner Became the Enemy* (Grand Rapids, 2019), 205–7.

66 Holmes suggests that Papias' major work *Expositions of the Sayings of the Lord* (see frag. 3.1) was written around 130 CE. See *The Apostolic Fathers*, 722.

67 *The Apostolic Fathers*, 763.

68 This could be an allusion to the original tasks of the watcher angels in Jubilees prior to the fall of the group from the Enochic tradition.

69 *The Apostolic Fathers*, 763.

70 *The Apostolic Fathers*, 763.

71 *The Apostolic Fathers*, 763.

72 See Gokey, *Terminology of the Devil*, 175.

73 Russell, *Satan*, 63.

74 *St. Justin Martyr: The First and Second Apologies*, trans. Leslie William Barnard (Leuven, 1997), 3–5.

75 Gk., ὁ ἀρχηγέτης τῶν κακῶν δαιμόνων.

76 Russell, *Satan*, 63–4.

77 See Annette Yoshiko Reed, "The Trickery of the Fallen Angels and the Demonic Mimesis of the Divine: Aetiology, Demonology, and Polemics in the Writings of Justin Martyr" *Journal of Early Christian Studies* 12, no. 2 (2004): 141–71 on 141 to 153; also, Forsyth, *Old Enemy*, 351. This connection is also addressed by Athenagoras (c. 133–190). See his *An Embassy for the Christians*, trans. by J. H. Crehan (Westminster, 1956), section 25. In this, he contends that the fallen angels had intercourse with the virgins and begot the "so called giants." However, Athenagoras veers from the watcher tradition to suggest that the fallen angels haunt the air and the earth and "they are the demons which wander about the world" and are servants of the prince of matter—that is, of the Satan.

78 He blames the same demons for the death of Socrates who attempted to tell people that they were demons and not gods.

79 The idea that δαιμόνια are pagan gods is found in biblical texts such as Ps 96.5, which reads "for all the gods of the nations are idols" (אלילים, Heb. "idols"; Septuagint 95.5, δαιμόνια, Gk. "demons") and Dt 32.17, "They sacrificed to demons (לשדים, Heb. 'demons'; Septuagint, δαιμονίοις, 'demons'), not God, to deities (אלהים, θεοῖς) they did not know."

80 Forsyth, *Old Enemy*, 352.

81 Gk., οἱ φαῦλοι δαίμονες.

82 See Yoshiko Reed, "Trickery of the Fallen Angels," 154. Reed also suggests that perhaps the two approaches to the origins of sin were already circulating in the likes of Jubilees and 3 Baruch, 159.

83 See discussion in Judith Lieu, *Image and Reality: The Jews in the World of Christians in the Second Century* (Edinburgh, 1999), 177–82.

84 In *Dialogue 79*, Tyrpho responds to Justin by calling his idea that the angels sinned against God as blasphemy. Justin replies that evil angels dwell in Tanis Egypt. The princes of Tanis are evil angels, but it is unclear what the position or role of the princes hold in Tanis; however, Justin clearly sees them as demonic: "The gods of the nations are demons." Justin cites Is 30.1–5 in stating that the evil angels are in Tanis. Here, the Masoretic text reads: "For his [Pharaoh's] Princes [likely political leaders] and his messengers [מלאכיו] were in Tsoan." This connection between the princes and the evil angels appears again in 124.18, here ἀρχόντων.

85  Gk., ὁ πονηρευσάμενος τὴν ἀρχὴν ὄφις.

86  See Reed, "Trickery of the Fallen Angels,"155.

87  See Justin's condemnations of Israel in *Dialogue* 19, of circumcision in 92, and dietary laws in 20. Reed, "The Trickery of the Fallen Angels," 156.

88  See Reed, "The Trickery of the Fallen Angels," 156.

89  Leslie Barnard, "Notes on Athenagoras." *Latomus*, 31, no. 2 (1972): 413–32.

90  See Forsyth, *The Old Enemy*, 353.

91  Athenagoras uses the term ἄρχων in reference to the devil four times in his *Legatio pro Christianis*, ed. Miroslav Marcovich (Berlin, 1990): 24.24, 14. 27, 25.4 and 25.

92  Athenagoras acknowledges the existence of other powers (δυνάμεις) that exercise dominion over matter, but there is one that is opposed to God (although nothing is really opposed to God because it would cease to exist). This is an interesting term in this context. Besides hostile or opposed to God, it can also mean equal to the gods or godlike. This could suggest the divine nature of the Satan figure. Athenagoras is clear that God created this "spirit that is over matter" along with all the other angels some of which rebelled against their nature. See Athenagoras, *A Plea for the Christians*, trans. by J. H. Crehan (Westminster, 1956), 24.

93  See Gerhard Ruhbach, "Zum Begriff 'Katholisch' in der Alten Kirche" in *Handbuch der Dogmengeschichte*, vol. 1, ed. Michael Schmaus, Alois Grillmeier, and Leo Scheffczyk (Freiburg, 1975): 1–45. Ruhbach contends the epithet was later applied to the devil.

94  Cf. Homer, *Odyssey* 19.203.·

95  See Forsyth, *The Old Enemy*, 354.

96  Gk., αἱ τῶν γιγάντων ψυχαί.

97  Cf. the Latin version of the anonymous *Life of Adam and Eve* which is also known as the *Apocalypse of Moses*.

98  Forsyth, *The Old Enemy*, 353–5. Athenagoras connects the fallen watchers and the evil spirits of 1 Enoch as servants of the Satan due to the idea that negligence and forgetfulness were the causes of the fall of the Satan, which Forsyth argues were factors in later interpretations of the Ezekiel 28 and Isaiah 14 stories of the "fall of the Satan." See Origen, *De principiis* 2.8.3 and 2.9.2.

99  Russell, *Satan*, 80.

100  In his *Adversus Haereses*, Irenaeus does identify the Satan as a liar (5.22–4), the adversary (3.18.7 and 5.22.1), a serpent (4.40.3), murderer (3.8, 3.18 and 5.22), an apostate (3.23.3, 4.40.1 and 5.25), and the devil (3.8.2 and 4.40.1).

101  Also, Theophilus, bishop of Antioch (c. 169), emphasised human responsibility over demonic influence in his *Discourse to Autolycus*. In that work, he notes that the devil was at first an angel who envied humanity. However, he also alludes to a work he wrote about the devil that is now lost. See Russell, *Satan*, 78–9.

102  Russell, *Satan*, 81.

103  Irenaeus argues in *Adversus Haereses*, 4.16.2 (also *Apostolic Preaching* 18) that the story of the fall of the watcher angels in 1 Enoch, along with their teachings that corrupted humanity, are events we learn from scripture, perhaps alluding to the acceptance of 1 Enoch in the early church. See St. Irenaeus: *Proof of the Apostolic Preaching*, trans. Joseph P. Smith (London, 1952), 58, 155–6, n. 100. Also, Russell, *Satan*, 81–2. In *Adversus Haereses*, 3.23.3, Irenaeus suggests that the devil and the angels fell at the garden episode, but while the eternal fire had been prepared for the devil and the apostate angels, it was not for humanity. But in this text, there does not appear to be a connection to the Enochic watcher story.

104  See Russell, *Satan*, 82, n. 10.

105  Russell, *Satan*, 88.

106  Russell, *Satan*, 88–89. See especially n. 24.

107  *Tertullian: Adversus Marcionem*, trans. and ed. Ernest Evans (Oxford, 1972), 617.

108  *Adversus Marcionem*, 116–7. See particularly n.1 in which Tertullian contends that the angels were created at the same time as the animals in Gen 2.18–20.

109  *The Apology of Tertullian*, trans. William Reeve (London, 1709). Interestingly, here, in *Apology*, 22 Tertullian appears to refer to the Enochic watcher story as "sacred literature" perhaps hinting at his view of its place in the church.

110  Tertullian, *De anima* 57. Russell, *Satan*, 97.

111  *Adversus Marcionem*, 617.
112  Tertullian offers an analogy between a pandemic that infects the air and scatters its deadly potion throughout the world as a "contagion that walks in the darkness" and the way that demons and evil angels "blast the minds of men." *Apology of Tertullian*, 71.
113  See *Apology of Tertullian*, 72. He contends that "every spirit, angel, and demon . . . may be said to be winged for they can be here and there and everywhere in a moment" giving the illusion that they are omnipresent.
114  John Ferguson, *Clement of Alexandria* (New York, 1974), 13.
115  Russell, *Satan*, 107.
116  See W. E. G. Floyd, *Clement of Alexandria's Treatment of the Problem of Evil* (London, 1971).
117  Salvatore R. C. Lilla, *Clement of Alexandria: A Study in Christian Platonism and Gnosticism* (Eugene, 2005).
118  Gk., τῶν κακῶν φύσιν γεννήσας.
119  See Eusebius, *Church History* 6.3.1 and 6.7–8.1. Mark Edwards, "Origen of Alexandria" in *The Wiley Blackwell Companion to Patristics*, ed., Ken Perry (Oxford, 2015), 98–110.
120  In *First Principles* 3.5.6 in which he discusses Eph 1.4, Origen alludes to the soul's descent from God's hand, although not in the sense of a fall due to sin. This idea of the descent of the soul follows a similar track to Philo of Alexandria and the separation of souls from the divine, see his *Who is the Heir of Divine Things* in *The Works of Philo*, trans. C. D. Yonge, new edition (Peabody, 193), section 240.
121  Forsyth, *The Old Enemy*, 358.
122  See Mark J. Edwards, "The Fate of the Devil in Origen," *Ephemerides theologicae Lovanienses* 86, no. 1 (2010): 163–70.
123  This was condemned by Justinian in 543 and at the second council of Constantinople in 553. See Forsyth, *The Old Enemy*, 359.
124  See Celsus, *On the True Doctrine: A Discourse Against the Christians*, trans. Joseph Hoffman (Oxford, 1987). One might ask how much truth lies behind this suggestion by Celsus; should we accept Origen's criticism of Celsus or give it careful consideration?
125  Forsyth, *The Old Enemy*, 361.
126  Forsyth, *The Old Enemy*, 368.
127  Origen, *De principiis* 1.8.1–4 and 1.6.1–3.
128  Christian Tornau, "Saint Augustine," *Stanford Encyclopedia of Philosophy*, ed. Edward N. Zalta (Stanford, 2018): 424–7.
129  Forsyth, *Old Enemy*, 391–2.
130  Forsyth, *Old Enemy*, 393.
131  See Augustine, *Confessions*, II.4.9. Augustine still needed to offer reasons for sin and suffering amongst humanity. In so doing, he challenged the Manichaean idea that evil dwelt in humanity by insisting that humanity was responsible for sin through the exercise of free will and not by a cosmic power (of darkness). See his *De duabus animabus*, 10.14. However, in the following years, he realised that free will was not the sole cause of sin in humanity. This change in thinking was brought about by reading Romans 5.12: "Death came into the world through one man and death through sin." Augustine continually mistranslated the last part of the verse that reads, "In that all men sinned" (ἐφ᾽ ᾧ πάντες ἥμαρτον). He translated it as, "In whom [Adam] all men sinned. See his *Contra Julianum* 1.3.10 and 1.4.11. Thus, Augustine argued that original sin is transmitted through sexual intercourse and as a result a person is damned from birth. See Kenneth Wilson, *Augustine's Conversion from Traditional Free Choice to "Non-free Free Will": A Comprehensive Methodology* (Tübingen, 2018), 93, 127, 140, 146, 231–3 and 279–80. This seems contrary to God's command to go forth and populate the world, and would seem to suggest that God wanted to intentionally spread sin and death. According to Augustine, self-gratification causes one to turn away from God which causes guilt which causes sin. Because the devil is the cause of this sin, then the entire human race was in servitude to the devil.
132  See the Latin *Life of Adam and Eve*.
133  Forsyth, *Old Enemy*, 399.
134  ὁ ἑωσφόρος, "Morning Star," likely signifies the planet Jupiter. A form of this word (φωσφόρος) is used in 2 Pet 1.19 to refer to Jesus as the morning star that rises in one's heart, which leaves the question if this can be referring to the Satan figure in Isaiah 14.12.
135  Heb. (שחר בן הילל משמים נפלת איך and Gk: ὡς ἐξέπεσεν ἐκ τοῦ οὐρανοῦ ὁ ἑωσφόρος ὁ πρωὶ ἀνατέελλων.

## Further Reading

Jonathan Burke, "Satan and Demons in the Apostolic Fathers: A Minority Report" *Svensk Exegetisk Årsbok* 81 (2016): 127–68.

Thomas Farrar, "The Intimate and Ultimate Adversary: Satanology in Early Second-Century Christian Literature" *Journal of Early Christian Literature* 26, no. 4 (2018): 517–46.

Neil Forsyth, *The Old Enemy: Satan and the Combat Myth* (Princeton, NJ: Princeton University Press, 1987).

*Der Kölner Mani-Kodex, Über das Werden seines Leibes. Kritische Edition* eds. L. Koenen and C. Römer (Opladen, Germany: Westdeutscher Verlag, 1988).

Birger A. Pearson, Early Christianity and Gnosticism in the History of Religions" *Studia Theologica* 55 (2001): 81–106.

Andrei A. Orlov, *Dark Mirrors: Azazel and Satanael in Early Jewish Demonology* (Albany, NY: State University of New York Press, 2011).

Annette Yoshiko Reed, "The Trickery of the Fallen Angels and the Demonic Mimesis of the Divine: Aetiology, Demonology, and Polemics in the Writings of Justin Martyr" *Journal of Early Christian Literature* 12, no. 2 (2004): 141–71.

Jeffery Burton Russell, *Satan the Early Christian Tradition* (Ithaca, NY: Cornell University Press, 1981).

Hector M. Scerri, "Augustine the Manichaean and the Problem of Evil" *Augustinian Panorama* 5–7 (1988–1990): 76–86.

# 3

# EXPERIENCES OF EVIL

## The Devil in the Early Middle Ages

*Peter Dendle*

The devil of the early Middle Ages was an organic, fluid entity. If he is the author of strife, it is perhaps fitting that his various roles were in perpetual conflict with each other. Rather than reducing its utility, such internal tension gave the protean figure adaptive power and resilience. This can be seen in the different ways the devil is formulated in competing spheres of discourse, spheres only imperfectly captured with the modern concept of "genre." The devil of the charms and medical literature is primal and visceral: it is worms, seizures, ravings, and elf-shot. The devil of literature is a stylised figure in highly conventionalised genealogies of mannered tropes. The devil of the liturgy betokens a flattened procedural element of sacramental praxis, codified over centuries of traditions marbled with diverse regional practices. The devil of theology and commentary literature reflects the attempt to understand scripture through the application of reason, hinting also at ongoing rhetorical disputations and power struggles. The devil of sermons and exempla is educed to encourage basic morality and adherence to church values, reflecting various levels of sophistication or orthodoxy on the part of the author. Generic context largely determines the devil's manner and characterisation. This diversity of functions ensured that the old enemy was an ever-changing entity, adapting to different times and places.

What would the experience of the demonic be like for a person chosen at random from the fields, villages, and towns of the early Middle Ages, someone far from the centres of literacy and learning? We cannot know, although we can perhaps catch refracted glimpses in the charms, sermons, saints' lives, material arts, and residual folk traditions. The popular devil of later medieval stonework and stage bristles with electricity. The devil has always found a comfortable home in curses, idioms, ditties, and jokes—the vast majority of which would never be recorded in writing. Folk traditions thrived independently of the theological commentary literature or doctrinal treatises. The former reflects the varied social and emotional needs of a diverse populace, while the latter reflects, among other things, a desire to define and maintain orthodoxy in Christian belief and practice. The result was always a patchwork compromise, lending creative power to medieval demonology: "Where the scholastics would have formulated learned arguments about the demonic, the average Christian was free to construct more wide-ranging demonologies."[1] The demonic occupies a space elusive to strict definition, categorisation, or control by

DOI: 10.4324/9781003096603-4

those seeking to contain it, a space in which it can express the darker and more painful sides of the human condition authentically.

## Physical Forms of the Devil

Some who believe in the devil conceive of him as an intangible force, while others believe him to be capable of real, localised manifestation. We can glimpse how people in the early Middle Ages might have visualised the old enemy through a variety of artistic portrayals and narrative descriptions. Through the medieval period, the devil was represented with a wide range of attributes and behaviours, only a few of which would crystallise into the forms more familiar today. Jeffrey Burton Russell suggests that there are no visual depictions of the devil prior to the 6th century in Western art, and Louis Jordan and Luther Link argue that demons are not portrayed prior to the 9th century.[2] Sophie Lunn-Rockliffe nuances these claims further, observing that the devil is implicit in early portrayals of type scenes such as exorcism, and in animals understood to have demonic resonance.[3] The 9th-century Utrecht Psalter depicts the demons as tormenting souls in hell. The *Leofric Missal* (Bodley 579, fol. 50r), compiled in the 10th and 11th centuries, depicts the devil with horns, but with feathered angel wings rather than the more common bat wings. Goats' horns and hooves—whose origins lay in their association with demonised pagan gods such as the Greco-Roman Pan and the Celtic Cernunnos—become more common after the 9th century. Early medieval representations of the devil drew from myriad colours, traits, animal forms, many of which will seem quite strange to today's readers.[4] As well as a lion, wolf, serpent, and whale, the devil could also appear as a bee, deer, boar, goose, sheep, or mouse. In early paintings and sculptures, he is most often seen as black in hue and commonly appears naked or in a loin cloth. The early medieval devil was as likely to have talons as hoofs, and by the 10th century, claws, animal hair, and a tail are common.[5] Demons carry agricultural instruments of torture such as tridents and pitchforks. They feature physiological distortions and sport wings growing out from the "wrong places" (such as wrists, ankles, and backside): "the most striking and consistent feature of demons in medieval art is their combination of animal and human physical forms to create a bestial perversion of God's image."[6] In the Middle Ages, "representations of Satan and his minions took on a new physicality, a new tangibility, a new immediacy."[7] Link writes of a Romanesque capital at St. Benoît-sur-Loire, France, in which the devil is struggling with an angel over a soul in between them. He relates that he waited for many hours to be able to observe the figure in full sunlight, but that it never came: it was designed such that the devil's face always remains in shadow.[8] The 6th-century Pope Gregory the Great offers a description of what he claims is the devil in his own true form, without any pretence:

> This time he did not appear to the saint in a dream or under a disguise, but met him face to face ... According to the saint's own description, the Devil had an appearance utterly revolting to human eyes. He was enveloped in fire and, when he raged against the man of God, flames darted from his eyes and mouth.[9]

The demonic also appeared as a gigantic animal mouth—most resembling a lion—beginning around the end of the 10th century in manuscripts and even earlier in ivory.[10] The hellmouth in the Junius manuscript is a notable example, with the gaping maw of zoomorphised hell calmly sucking in the rebellious angels of heaven as a bound Satan watches helplessly from his shackles. The hellmouth remained a prominent and quite terrifying icon of Christian visual art for the remainder of the Middle Ages. Satan could also appear as a serpent in reference to the Garden of Eden, or a dragon in reference to Revelation. Grotesque figures in sculpture adorning churches and cathedrals would render the demonic grotesque, at once terrifying and laughable.[11] This multiplicity of forms sometimes reflected underlying tensions in theological discussions of the devil's power, presence, and significance.

## Demonologies of the Early Middle Ages

There was little attempt in the early Middle Ages to construct anything resembling a unified demonology.[12] Of course, there are some early medieval texts that do wind up serving as precursors to systematic demonology. By the time of Augustine—a key transition figure from Late Antiquity to the Middle Ages—the broad strokes of the devil as a central character in Christian "salvation history" were largely in place. A parascriptural narrative gradually evolved in which the archangel Lucifer, either prideful of God's supremacy or jealous of Adam as God's most recent creation, turned against God along with a host of other apostate angels and were exiled from heaven. Now reframed as the devil and his demons, these wicked spirits seek only to spite their Creator's will by turning as many humans away from him as possible, and by creating a hostile environment on earth in which prayer, meditation, and attention to God are frustrated at every step. Writers such as Irenaeus of Lyon, Tertullian of Carthage, and Origen of Alexandria were integral in crafting this demonology, which developed not in a vacuum of abstract thought but in theological dialogics that also reflected secular conflicts of authority and diverse local beliefs.[13] "Irenaeus' definition," as Russell pointedly observes, "is a pragmatic one: a heretic is one who is designated by a bishop as a heretic."[14] Figures such as Ambrose, Jerome, John Cassian, and Augustine helped translate the Greek contours of early Christian thought for the Latin West. Gregory the Great's more parochial exegesis and homiletics served as a practical pattern for over 200 years, in which priests and missionaries with little access to libraries had to contend with the challenges of daily preaching in remote locations across Europe.

Early medieval writings are often creative patchworks that reflect whatever material is available at hand. Visions of the other world such as *The Vision of Paul* (*Visio Pauli*) draw from traditions of noncanonical apocalyptic literature. Miscellanies such as the *Solomon and Saturn* dialogues, rich in demonological imagery, often preserve tropes from Enochian literature and other works portraying Solomon as a great keeper of esoteric magic and knowledge.[15] In the 10th-century Old English prose *Solomon and Saturn* dialogue, the devil appears in fifteen forms, each matched against a unique form of the Pater Noster as the two are locked in combat. In the first instance, the devil appears as a child, while the Pater Noster appears as the Holy Spirit. Their transformations are as imagistic as they are diverse. Some forms the devil assumes include darkness, a nightmare, an evil woman, bramble, murder, strife, an evil thought, and death.[16] The apocryphal *Descent into Hell* (*Descensus ad inferos*) tradition firmly establishes the "I will not serve" (*non serviam*) trope in literary and popular milieus, and fixes Satan as a character in Hell—where Dante Pilgrim will later find him. The *non serviam* devil asserts defiance against God with rhetorical power and even dignity: "I will no longer be his servant." Thus, the devil of the Old English poem *Genesis*

B—though of course perverse in nature—is a compelling rhetor and a worthy dialogical opponent of God.[17] His resilience and vitality have long invited comparisons with Milton's Satan in *Paradise Lost*.

Diana Walzel observes that early medieval demons "did have an important place in the thoughts of the people. [Yet] there really were no great debates, doctrinal splits, or even Church councils devoted to the subject."[18] This is not because writers shared a common understanding of the figure, but because the concept was versatile in its artistic and literary forms. The devil is bound in hell, and yet he roams the earth, "like a roaring lion" (1 Peter 5.8). He is at once a singular entity, the fount of all evil, and yet he is interchangeable with his armies of demons: "My name is legion, for we are many" (Mark 5.9; for more on the Gerasene Demoniac, see David R. Winter, Chapter 7). St. Hilarion casts out a crowd of demons from a wealthy man named Orion, asserting to God, "It is yours to conquer many just as to conquer one."[19] The devil is a created being with a clearly articulated narrative in salvation history, and yet an expansive and nebulous metaphor for all sin. He is the Principle of Evil itself and yet a physical gremlin taking gratuitous swipes at people who are simply in the wrong place at the wrong time. He can even represent natural evils such as storms and drought. The needs of a specific generic, narrative, or rhetorical situation will dictate how the devil is characterised at any given crux, and this multifaceted utility has outweighed the need for a specific theological delineation of what the devil is, and is not, even to this day.

## The *Life of Anthony* and the Desert Saints: Narrative as Theology

In the late 3rd century, an Egyptian monk named Anthony gave up his worldly possessions and family attachments to retreat to the wilderness in pursuit of the holy life. His continued search for solitude and ascetic living drew the attention of other spiritual seekers, who eventually grew around him in communities. He is thus a key figure of both the eremitic and communal monastic lives in their nascent stages, and his powerful biography by Bishop Athanasius of Alexandria became a template for both saints' lives and for excerpted spiritual tropes through the Middle Ages. The devil explodes onto the scene with full force and vigour in the *Life of Anthony*: he embodies at the very outset a variety of functions and portrayals, and also exhibits the contradictions that would give these disparate functions such ongoing vitality. Athanasius was influential at the Council of Nicaea and is known for theological treatises in addition to his *Life of Anthony*. His treatment of the devil would set the tone for the next 1,000 years of Christianity, while revealing already some of the contradictions and conceptual fissures. Athanasius worked in both expository and narrative modes, thus embodying the interplay between generic modalities that would characterise much of medieval religious thought, and the inability of any one literary form to contain the devil.

Roughly, a third of the *Life of Anthony* consists of a first-person discourse the saint delivers to the monks gathered around his dwelling. He relates his experiences regarding temptation and the many forms of approach the devil can take, but more than this, he also offers an expository model for the operation of demons. In the *Life of Anthony*, the devil is ever-present as the saint's nemesis and as the catalyst for Anthony's spiritual growth. The early ascetics leaving behind friends and family for a life of solitude in the desert saw themselves not as fleeing from temptation, but as braving the front lines of spiritual warfare. The devil's first mode of attack is to plant seeds of doubt: he "raised the greatest of doubtful thoughts" in Anthony's mind.[20] Throughout the monastic traditions of the Middle Ages, the devil would come to represent everything a spiritual aspirant might encounter: drowsiness, wandering thoughts, boredom, or doubt. The "noonday demon" of Psalm 91.6 would become associated with *acedia*, or "spiritual sloth"—finding oneself distracted from the persistent urgency of prayer and supplication. The devil appears to Anthony at night "transformed into the shape of a beautiful woman, omitting no signs of lewdness" to lure him astray.[21] Lust is among the most common demonic temptations that afflict the desert monks in the early centuries. Anthony overcomes the threat by turning his thoughts to "the flames of Gehenna and the ravaging worm."[22]

The devil also tempts Anthony with greed. He invokes the phantasm of a silver dish along Anthony's path. The saint resists this by reasoning how improbable it is in the first place: "How is there a dish here in the desert? ... This artifice, devil, is yours."[23] Next, Anthony encounters real treasure along his path: "a huge pile of gold lying in his path—not phantasmal as before."[24] Here even Athanasius comments that he does not know if it was the devil who left it. The juxtaposition of phantasmal and real treasure presages a key facet of early medieval demonology. For Augustine and for many theologians of the early Middle Ages, Satan and his demons are not capable of interfering substantially with the physical workings of God's created world: they are principally effective by causing phantasms and illusions in people's perceptions. This limits demonic power, and helps minimise any sense that God has created for humans an impossible trap. The threat is ostensibly over the convictions of one's faith, not the endurance of one's body. The crux of Anthony's lengthy sermon is that the demons "are weak and can only threaten, not do anything."[25] In practice, however, the two are hopelessly intertwined from the very outset: demons tempt and demons hurt alike.

The ability to discern good spirits (or impulses) from bad ones becomes a preeminent virtue in the early desert saints. The 4th- to 5th-century monastic pioneer John Cassian, notably, devotes significant attention to "discernment" in Book 2 of the *Conferences*: "discretion is in some way the source and root of all the virtues ... how it can be known whether it is true and from God or false and diabolical."[26] Gregory the Great, an influential exegete in his own right, explains, "The saints can distinguish true revelations from the voices and images of illusions through an inner sensitivity."[27] Athanasius is committed to the materialism of most early church figures. That is, the demons are physical substances of a sort, and they operate in the physical world. To this, he adds a psychological overlay: "Such as they found us and our state of mind, that's how they were inclined to present themselves to us."[28] Desert spirituality borders on the metaphorical, with demons representing the temptations of the human heart.

Occasionally, there are implications in early Christianity that the demons are the impulses towards sin and perhaps no more than the impulses towards sin: that they are "thought hypostasized."[29] The 4th-century monk Evagrius of Ponticus arranged his *Antirrheticus* according to the eight deadly sins commonly listed in Late Antiquity, detailing the demonic presences and influences associated with those. His succinct and captivating *Praktikos* similarly breaks down the machinations of demons and their distinctive provinces. The spiritual warrior is to remain vigilant against the demons of *acedia* and sadness, of pride and vainglory, and their compatriots. Above all, however, the demons of impurity and blasphemy are "the two swiftest demons—they are nearly more swift than the speed of thought."[30] Cassian was instrumental in translating the eastern Mediterranean tradition of the desert monks to western Christianity, and he too signals that "particular spirits brood over particular vices."[31] Later writers such as the 10th-century homilist Ælfric of Eynsham will flirt with the idea as well: "however many sins a person obeys, that many devils are the person's masters."[32]

However much Anthony insists that demons "can only threaten, not do anything," demons in early medieval hagiography are clearly capable of physical assaults that have real effects and that can leave lasting damage. They raise storms at sea in Constantius of Lyon's 5th-century *Life of Germanus of Auxerre*: "The ocean was assaulted by the violence of demons, haters of religion, who were livid with malice at the sight of such great men."[33] The demons confess this themselves: "As they were being cast out of the bodies of the possessed ... they acknowledged that they had contrived the storm and its dangers."[34] The 8th-century polymath Alcuin of York's *Life of Willibrord* (c. 796) speaks of a wicked spirit infesting a house: "it would suddenly seize food and clothing and other household goods and throw them into the fire."[35] It also throws a little boy into the fire, though the vigilant parents are able to retrieve him. The devil beats holes in the walls and roof of a monastery with stones in the 6th-century *Life of Romanus*.[36] The demons, then, do not merely tempt: they claw, they strike, and they kill. They leave marks. When the devil causes St. Germanus to fall and break his leg in Bede's *Ecclesiastical History*, the leg remains broken.[37] Moreover, it is a two-way fight: Dunstan grabs the devil by the nose with red-hot tongs, and Saint Benedict simply slaps the devil out of a fellow monk.[38] Despite psychological and metaphorical interpretations, the demonic always reasserts itself periodically as obdurately visceral, biological, and violent. It is not a metaphor or a shorthand for something else: the demonic is an irreducible monad of early medieval thought.

It would not be until the 13th century that angels and demons were systematically conceived as purely immaterial rather than physical beings. For the first thousand years of Christianity, spirits were understood as corporeal beings, although comprising a much more rarefied substance. They were creatures of the lower air, seemingly capable of supernatural feats because they were composed of a sort of attenuated vapour.[39] The devil appears to Anthony on one occasion in one of his most common forms in early medieval iconography, a boy of dark hue (ch. 6). Shortly afterwards, Anthony is assaulted by the demons who shake the walls of his cell and make tremendous noise in the form of beasts and snakes: "All of a sudden the place was filled with phantasms of lions, bulls, wolves, asps, snakes, scorpions and leopards and bears."[40] The "temptation of Anthony" would become a common type scene for representing a saint's internal spiritual struggles. Gregory the Great recreates the scene in his account of Bishop Datius of Milan: while sleeping in a house that had been given up to the devil by locals, the bishop is assaulted by "the roaring of lions, the bleating of sheep, and the screaming of mules, as well as the hissing of serpents and the squealing of pigs and mice."[41]

These dramatic scenes exhibit one of the primary developments of the New Testament in formative Christianity: the zoomorphic multiplicity of ancient Near Eastern demons have become united into a single kingdom of evil, unified under the great apostate Satan.[42] After the New Testament, the devil and his demons are one. No longer do they reflect the chaotic forces of an elementally hostile world, as in the stark incantations of the Sumerian "forerunners to Udug-Hul" collection: they have intelligence and purpose.[43] Indeed, Gregory the Great describes a remarkable council of demons witnessed by a traveller along the Appian Way. Stopping at a temple of Apollo, the man sees the devil sitting in the middle of the temple, surrounded by a parade of demons. The demons approach the old enemy one by one, each accounting for what wickedness it has done and what souls it has ruined. The devil revels in these accounts, offering prizes for those demons sufficiently accomplished in wickedness.[44] Such anecdotes can sometimes draw as much from the writer's imagination as from source material, but it is from such threads that the tapestry of medieval demonology was woven over time.

## Possession, Exorcism, and Baptism

The demons in Gregory the Great or Gregory of Tours' miracle stories still pulse with the spirits of the classical world, such as spirits of rivers, wells, groves, stones, and crossroads. During the period of conversion in any given region across Central, Western, and Northern Europe, the indigenous cultures' pre-Christian gods and spirits were systematically recast by missionaries as demonic. Local rites were reframed to the populace as idol worship: demons, it was explained, have been posing as gods and accepting the sacrifices in an effort to pervert human souls. In a letter of 738/9 to the Saxons, Pope Gregory III urges the local populace to give up their adherence to their traditional gods and spirits, which the expanding church characterised as demon worship: "These lying deities, called gods by the heathen of old, are well known to be the dwelling place of demons. For all the gods of the Gentiles are demons, saith the Scripture."[45] A synod of 742 specifies some of the pagan practices to be prohibited. They include: "sacrifices to the dead, casting of lots, divinations, amulets and auguries, incantations, or offerings of animals."[46] Missionaries encounter local populations making sacrifices to trees and springs.[47] The hagiographic literature valorises the saints who cut down these sacred trees and groves, erecting Christian churches in their places.[48] Aldebert of Soissons, a preacher whose visibility and public confidence perhaps outpace his orthodox credentials, attempts to clear his name before church officials by proclaiming that the lord God is the one and almighty father with an attestation before eight angels of God: Uriel, Raguel, Tubuel, Michael, Adinus, Tubuas, Sabaoc, and Simiel. The synod notes that the errant preacher has only gotten one out of the eight right: "The eight names of angels which Aldebert calls upon in his prayer are not names of angels, except Michael, but rather of demons whom he has summoned to his aid."[49] Exorcism served as a tangible, dramatic proof of Christianity's authority to newly converted peoples. As Christianity spread it brought the exorcism paradigm to cultures that either had no inherent possession tradition or that had possession traditions very different from those of Hellenistic Palestine and the ancient Near East. The possession and exorcism dyad travelled to converted regions as a single package.[50]

Recent ethnographic work by Éva Pócs can serve as an instructive reminder of how diverse folk beliefs largely disconnected from official theologies can thrive in thoroughly Christianised areas for centuries. Her research focuses on forms of spirit possession in Central and Southeastern Europe, with special attention to Hungarian villages in Transylvania. She reports: "The outcome was rather surprising: in the Roman Catholic villages under study we found a variety of quite lively notions relating to possession, as well as a living practice of purificatory rites with the exorcism ceremonies of Romanian priests and monks, and narratives about people who had been possessed … What was even more surprising was that in addition to possession by the devil, possession by the dead also played a fundamental role."[51] Historically, there is little sanction for possession by ancestors in Christian theology, though it is well attested in many non-Christian traditions worldwide. Here it survives under the radar, as it were: "possession by the dead—closely related to notions of the body and soul described here—was the archaic deep structure of all other systems."[52] As Nancy Caciola makes clear, possession by the deceased is widely documented in classical antiquity, and then only appears piece-meal in later medieval accounts. She cites instances from specific regions of Italy and Portugal.[53] During the first half of the Middle Ages, it is unlikely the phenomenon disappeared entirely. More likely, it was ignored, minimised, or rebranded by more orthodox-minded writers.[54] Furthermore, Pócs documents local practices in the 20th century that bear more than a passing resemblance to the elf-shot of early medieval English charms or to fairy possession of Celtic lore, though separated from those cultures by a thousand miles and a thousand years. Rites of exorcism and prophylaxis that in the western Church are largely restricted to consecrated priests, monks, or saints are far more broadly shared among the local populace. In Western Europe, a church initially hesitant to entertain too many tales of ghosts gave way after the development of the liturgy of the dead: "Thus in the 9th century the entire apparatus—institutional, liturgical, narrative—was in place ... It was henceforth admitted that the dead could indeed appear to the living, much to the benefit of both groups."[55]

In the early 8th-century *Life of Gregory the Great* by an anonymous monk of Whitby, even a horse can be demon possessed. A disgruntled man excommunicated by the pope hires two sorcerers who then conjure some demons (*"arte sua demonia excitantes"*) to possess Gregory's horse: "at once the fearsome enemies entered the horse he was riding and made it go instantly mad."[56] The demonic assumes the form of hostile birds in the 6th-century *Life of Caesarius of Arles*, written by Caesarius' disciples. A woman cannot leave her house without being ferociously attacked by crows: they tear at her face, neck, and any exposed parts. The authors marvel that she has discovered "a new kind of demon."[57] Jerome's *Life of Hilarion* relates that possessed animals as well as humans were brought to the saint for healing.[58] It takes 30 people to hold down a certain camel brought to him enraged, but Hilarion calmly addresses it: "You do not scare me, devil ...."[59] Jerome explains that the devil "burns with such hatred for people that he desired to destroy not just them but whatever belongs to them."[60] In other cases, the devil does not seem especially inclined to wish ill on anyone. The devil minding his own business on a lettuce in Gregory's *Dialogues* presents something of a moral enigma: "What did I do? I was sitting on this lettuce, when she came along and bit me."[61] In the 7th-century *Life of Aldegund*, the devil begrudgingly offers that he does not want to make the saint suffer, but is forced to: "I have been compelled by angelic threats and that is why I dare once more to make you suffer."[62] Demons are simply fulfilling their assigned roles in the unfolding of the cosmos, in which human souls are to be judged amidst the swirling vicissitudes of the moral and natural world.

One of the principal means by which the demonic was manifest in the daily lives of medieval Christians was through baptism. Baptism was the definitive sacrament for the formation of Christian identity. In his *De ecclesiasticis officiis* (598–615 CE), Isidore of Seville explains: "Exorcism is a stated rebuke against the unclean spirit of the possessed or the catechumen, through which the most wicked power of the devil—his never-ending malice and violent assaults—is expelled from them."[63] During the early periods of conversion, this would mean adult baptism, but gradually the exorcisms would mostly be performed over the infants within Christian communities. In a typical ceremony, there would be an exorcism and then blessing of the salt, the water, the oil, the ashes, the host, and other materials. The items are *adjured* (the core meaning of "exorcise" is to implore or entreat) to be free of evil spirits and thus to be consecrated. A parent or godparent would be on hand to answer the scrutinies on behalf of the child:

Do you renounce Satan?
I renounce.
And all his works?
I renounce.
And all his pomps?
I renounce.
*Abrenuntias Satanae?*
*Abrenuntio.*
*Omnibus operibus eius?*
*Abrenuntio.*
*Omnibus pompis eius?*
*Abrenuntio.*[64]

The exorcistic prayers themselves vary in length and content, and there is substantial overlap in exorcisms used in baptisms and those recited over the possessed. A number of the prayers address the devil directly, rather than the baptismal candidate or God: "Hear, accursed Satan, adjured by the name of eternal God and of our savior the son of God; depart along with your envy, trembling and groaning, conquered."[65] Henry A. Kelly has traced the evolution of the extent to which medieval theologians viewed the devil as literally inhering in the infant, or to what extent the rhetoric signalled more metaphoric conceptualisation.[66] In either case, the rhetoric must have struck the participants as direct and powerful: "these references [to the devil] do bring home to the congregation the 'real presence' of Satan in their lives."[67]

Aside from procedural baptisms, many early medieval communities encountered the devil in daily life through possession and exorcism. Exorcism was among Jesus' most common healing miracles, and he indicated that his followers will also show themselves by casting out demons.[68] In alignment with the New Testament and of ancient Near Eastern understandings of illness, many cases of "demon possession" in the early Middle Ages refer to muscle disorders, convulsions, seizures, blindness, paralysis, and a range of what would now be considered physiological conditions. This continued through the Middle Ages as well. In addition, psychiatric disturbances and chronic behaviour disorders could be interpreted as invasive demons. Violent outbursts, uncharacteristic behaviour shifts, or ongoing symptoms of psychosis could be attributed to an indwelling demon that has supplanted the individual's personality. Mediterranean cultures in the 1st century had a rich tradition of exorcism as cultural expression—what may be called functional possession. This includes a highly choreographed ritual of explosive emotional outburst on the part of the possessed, countered by ordered, authoritative response on the part of the priest or saint. The dramatic exorcism paradigm at once allowed a systematised means for addressing conflict publicly, while simultaneously reinforcing the central role of the Church and its ministers in the cosmic fight against evil. Exorcisms may at first seem confrontational and chaotic, but in fact the possession-exorcism dyad is a performative rite in which all participants—energumen, exorcist, and audience—must understand their roles and be versed in background narrative. In functional exorcism (which the modern Catholic Church refers to as "major exorcism"), the sufferer and the exorcist alike draw from a common repository of tropes to enact and reinforce the manifest authority of God, and of the Church, on earth. Such possession rituals are well documented globally in a wide variety of societies, but in Christianity possession is regarded as an exclusively negative phenomenon.[69] The demon is never to be cajoled or supplicated as in many other traditions, only cast out. In this context, the possessed appear in miracle narratives alongside the blind, the lame, and others suffering from natural ailments. The behaviours of the energumen waiting to be healed are not generally regarded as the individual's fault, because another agency has supplanted their own.[70]

It is important to note, however, that for all of these conditions, the demon possession paradigm was never the only one available. The early Middle Ages inherited a vocabulary for mental and behavioural impairment referring exclusively to natural processes, without necessary recourse to the demonic. Hippocratic and Galenic models continued to inform regimens of diet, bleeding, and other therapeutics well into the early modern period. Thus, the decision to label a seizure, an outburst of violence, or an unpopular political view as demonic was always made by individuals, in the context of a particular time and place. This could sometimes be seen as absolving the person of fault: as Anthony tells his acolytes, "this rage comes from the possessor, not the possessed."[71] In other cases, demon possession can imply guilt: St. Rusticula draws confessions from a group of demoniacs, asking each one, in turn, to name his sin.[72] In later centuries, the Catholic Church would try to codify specific features of demonic instigation or possession to distinguish them from natural illness, psychological motivations, or other causal mechanisms, but in the early Middle Ages the demonic remained a system of interrelated metaphors kinetic and fertile even in its inconsistencies.

In Late Antiquity, *exorcista* appeared as one of the minor orders of the evolving church hierarchy: doorkeeper, reader, exorcist, and acolyte.[73] The duties originally associated with this procedural office are poorly understood, although we know they were to commit exorcisms to memory.[74] The exorcism of water, oil, salt, and other materials for baptism and other rites are documented earlier and more extensively than adjurations to be spoken over a possessed person, so it is likely those were under the *exorcista's* province to some extent. In narrative sources such as saints' lives, however, it is not these lower functionaries who are shown driving demons out of raging energumens: there, of course, it is the missionary or saint whose inherent gift is highlighted. In hagiography, exorcisms of possessed people are not portrayed as lengthy rites with various stages of prayers, fasting, and *materia liturgica* as detailed in liturgical books, but as immediate expressions of the saint's holy charisma. Allowances must be made for the genre: the point of a saint's life is to show how a given representative of the faith is more exceptional than local healers or than less gifted clerics in the region (for instance, other priests who have tried and failed to exorcise the demon). Over time, contact relics associated with the holy person—or the burial location itself—could serve just as well for the expulsion of demons, as well as the healing of wounds and illnesses. Throughout the Middle Ages, the Church continually reshaped its own internal structures against a perceived backdrop of combatting demonic assaults. The nebulous form and presence of the devil's representations allowed for dynamic interplay between ecclesiastical institutionalism and popular religious expression.

## Conclusion

The rhetoric of the demonic pervaded many aspects of early medieval experience of pain, illness, natural evil, misfortune, and moral sin. None of these facets of quotidian life were reductively equated to the demonic, nor was the devil implicated in each and every instance of these. The use of medicinal herbs was ubiquitous in the early European landscape, for instance, but would only be termed "demonic" in as much as the expanding Church felt the need to assert authority over the rhetoric employed by local healers. The teachings of an author or bishop would be deemed as diabolically instigated only when they conflicted with a given author's needs and purposes. The early medieval liturgy includes prayers and exorcisms for a wide variety of misfortunes that are entirely divorced from human intentionality or sin: storms, draughts, blights. The devil simultaneously retains a dual role in Christianity as primordial evil demiurge, and the seemingly incongruent role of petty threat whom the devout can send packing with a prayer or the sign of the cross. He is a powerful entity to be feared, dyed into the very ontological fibre of experience, and yet one that even the humblest Christian can easily defeat day to day. Throughout the Middle Ages the devil retained force and vitality drawn in part from studied literary and theological templates, but just as much from the people themselves, who wove their hopes, fears, and uncertainties into those forms of cultural expression meaningful to them and available to them.

## Notes

1  Ed Simon, *Pandemonium: A Visual History of Demonology* (New York, 2021): 74. He adds, "The result was a rich and complex visual language of the wicked, which still provides the base for the demonological imagination," 102. Simon refers to "demonic poetics," through which "medieval literature and thought embraced complex world-building in its demonology," 78.

2  Jeffrey Burton Russell, *Lucifer: The Devil in the Middle Ages* (Ithaca, 1984), 129; Louis Jordan, "Demonic Elements in Anglo-Saxon Iconography," in *Sources of Anglo-Saxon Culture*, ed. Paul Szarmach (Kalamazoo, 1986), 283–317, 284 and Luther Link, *The Devil: The Archfiend in Art from the Sixth to the Sixteenth Century* (New York City, 1995), 38 and 72.

3  Sophie Lunn-Rockliffe, "Visualizing the Demonic: The Gadarene Exorcism in Early Christian Literature," in *The Devil in Society in Premodern Europe*, eds. Richard Raiswell and Peter Dendle (Toronto, 2012), 439–57.

4  See also Russell, *Lucifer*, 61–77.

5  Link, *The Devil*, 68–70.

6  Debra Higgs Strickland, *Saracens, Demons, and Jews: Making Monsters in Medieval Art* (Princeton, 2003), 63 and 64.

7  Simon, *Pandemonium*, 77.

8  Link, *The Devil*, 47–8.

9  *Dialogues* 2.8. Odo John Zimmerman, trans. *Saint Gregory the Great: Dialogues* (New York, 1959), 74–5. See *Grégoire le Grand: Dialogues*, vol. 3, ed. Adalbert de Vogüé and Paul Antin (Paris, 1980), "*Non occulte uel per somnium, sed aperta uisione eiusdem patris se oculis ingerebat... corporalibus eius oculis isdem antiquus hostis teterrimus et succensus apparebat, qui in eum ore oculisque flammantibus saeuire uidebatur,*" 168–70.

10  Joyce Ruth Galpern, *The Shape of Hell in Anglo-Saxon England* (PhD dissertation, University of California at Berkeley, 1977), 119.

11  By the later Middle Ages, visual representations of the devil were likely drawing from costumes in mystery plays and liturgical drama (Link, *The Devil*, 60–1, 69–70). John D. Cox reminds us that most dramatic portrayals of the devil in the cycle plays are serious rather than comedic, although it is the comedic roles that draw the most critical attention because they stick more in the imagination and they fulfil a preconceived narrative about the alleged secularisation of the devil. Cox, *The Devil and the Sacred in English Drama, 1350-1642* (Cambridge, 2000), 24. In fact, Cox reminds

us that demons are not especially prevalent in the cycle plays as a whole. See 23–4. Demons would prance about the stage in exaggerated costumes, performing pixie-like antics. In the early 15th-century *Castle of Perseverance*, Belial appears on stage with pipes of burning gunpowder in his hands, ears, and posterior: "And he that schal pley Belyal loke that he have gunnepowdyr brennynge in pypys in hys handys and in hys erys and in hys ars whanne he gothe to batayl." See *The Castle of Perseverance*, ed. David N. Klausner (Kalamazoo, 2010), 9. On the devil on the later medieval stage, see M. D. Anderson, *Drama and Imagery in English Medieval Churches* (Cambridge, 1963), 171–7. C. S. Lewis' concern that it is hard for the general populace to take Satan seriously when they imagine him in red tights refers more to 19th-century costuming. See C.S. Lewis, *The Screwtape Letters* (New York, 1952), 40.

12 Alain Boureau notes, "Until the end of the thirteenth century, theology had shown little interest in demons … the situation seems to have changed rather abruptly beginning in the 1270s." See Alain Boureau, *Satan the Heretic: The Birth of Demonology in the Medieval West*, trans. Teresa Lavender Fagan (Chicago, 2006), 94–5.

13 Some concise overviews of the formative history of the devil include Philip C. Almond, *The Devil: A New Biography* (Ithaca, 2014); Everett Ferguson, *Demonology of the Early Christian World* (Lewiston, 1984); Henry Ansgar Kelly, *The Devil, Demonology and Witchcraft* (Garden City, 1968); Jeffrey Burton Russell, *Satan: The Early Christian Tradition* (Ithaca, 1981); and Archie T. Wright, *Satan and the Problem of Evil* (Minneapolis, 2022). Many of primary documents now appear in *The Medieval Devil: A Reader*, eds. Richard Raiswell and David R. Winter (Toronto, 2022).

14 Russell, *Satan*, 87.

15 Daniel Anlezark, "The Fall of the Angels in *Solomon and Saturn II*," in *Apocryphal Texts and Traditions in Anglo-Saxon England*, eds. Kathryn Powell and Donald Scragg (Cambridge, 2003): 121–33.

16 *The Old English Dialogues of Solomon and Saturn*, ed. and trans. Daniel Anlezark (Cambridge, 2009), 72, "ðystres, atoles swefnes, yfles wifes, bremles, sleges, wrohte, yfeles geðohtes, deaðes … onlicnisse."

17 According to Colleen Donnelly, *Genesis B* provides the first instance of the *non serviam*. "Ne wille ic leng his geongra wurþan," line 291; "Apocryphal Literature, the Characterization of Satan, and the *Descensus ad Inferos* Tradition in England in the Middle Ages," *Religion & Theology* 24 (2017): 321–49, 333. See the visions translated and catalogued in Eileen Gardiner, *Visions of Heaven and Hell before Dante* (New York, 1989) for the relative absence of the old enemy as a central figure in hell in the early Middle Ages. Hell is rather a place to which the devil is sent back over and over again, rather than a place he spends any time.

18 Diana Lynn Walzel, "Sources of Early Medieval Demonology," *Rice University Studies* 60 (1974): 83–99 on 97.

19 *Vita Hilarionis*, ch. 10. *Jérôme: Trois vies de moines*, eds. Edgardo M. Morales and Pierre Leclerc (Paris, 2007), 240, "Ut unum, ita et plures uincere tuum est."

20 Athanasius of Alexandria, *Vitae Antonii versiones Latinae*, ed. P.H.E. Bertrand (Turnhout, 2018), 9 (ch. 5), "prorsus maximam ei cogitationum caliginem suscitabat." The *Life of Anthony* was first translated into Latin around 357, perhaps by the monk Ammonius, but is best known to Western Europe in the Middle Ages through Evagrius of Ponticus' Latin translation of 373.

21 Athanasius, *Vitae Antonii*, 9 (ch. 5), "in pulchrae mulieris vertebatur ornatum nulla omittens figmenta lasciviae)."

22 Athanasius, *Vitae Antonii*, 9 (ch. 5), "gehennae flammas et dolorem vermis."

23 Athanasius, *Vitae Antonii*, 18 (ch. 11), "Vnde hic in deserto discus? … Hoc artificium, diabole, tuum est."

24 Athanasius, *Vitae Antonii*, 18 (ch. 12), "non ut ante phantasiam, sed ingentem massam auri iacentem in itinere."

25 Athanasius, *Vitae Antonii*, 34 (ch. 27), "sint debiles, minantur cuncta, nec faciunt."

26 John Cassian, *Conferences* 2.9. See *John Cassian: The Conferences*, trans. Boniface Ramsey, (New York, 1997), 90; *Iohannes Cassiani opera*, part 2, ed. Michael Petschenig (Vienna, 1886), 47, "discretionem fontem quodammodo radicemque cunctarum esse uirtutum … utrum uera et ex deo, an falsa et diabolica sit possit agnosci."

27 Gregory, *Dialogues* 4.50. See Zimmerman, 262; cf. de Vogüé and Antin, *Dialogues*, 174–6, "sancti autem uiri inter inlusiones atque reuelationes ipsas uisionum uoces aut imagines quodam intimo sapore discernunt."

28 Athanasius, *Vitae Antonii*, 48 (ch. 42), "*quales nos et nostras repererint cogitationes, tales se nobis praestare consueuerunt.*"

29 Evagrius Ponticus, *The Praktikos and Chapters on Prayer*, trans. John Eudes Bamberger (Kalamazoo, 1981), 8.

30 Evagrius, *The Praktikos and Chapters on Prayer*, 30.

31 John Cassian, *Conferences*, 7.17: "Not every demon imprints every passion in human beings ... particular spirits brood over particular vices" (Ramsey, 258–9); cf. Petschenig, "*non omnes daemones uniuersas hominibus inurere passiones, sed unicuique uitio certos spiritus incubare*, Petschenig," 195.

32 "*Dominica V in Quadragesime*," in *Ælfric's Catholic Homilies: The Second Series Text*, ed. Malcolm Godden (Oxford, 1979), 129, "*swa manegum leahtrum swa he gehyrsumað, swa manega deofla him beoð to hlafordum gesette.*" Godden has not identified a source for this passage. See Godden, *Ælfric's Catholic Homilies: Introduction, Commentary, and Glossary* (Oxford, 2000), 469. In a vision of hell related in St. Boniface's letters, a monk of Wenlock describes demons coming up to him one by one, each one identifying itself as a sin. See *Die Briefe des Heiligen Bonifatus und Lullus*, MGH, *Epistolae Selectae* 1, ed. Michael Tangl (Berlin, 1955), 9.

33 *Soldiers of Christ: Saints and Saints' Lives from Late Antiquity and the Early Middle Ages*, eds. Thomas F. X. Noble and Thomas Head (University Park, 1995), 86; *Vie de Saint Germain d'Auxerre*, ed. René Borius (Paris, 1965), 146 (ch. 13), "*occurrit in pelago religioni inimica uis daemonum, qui tantos ac tales uiros ... liuidis iniquitatibus inuiderent.*"

34 *Soldiers of Christ*, 87; *Vie de Saint Germain d'Auxerre*, 148 (ch. 13), "*dum ab obsessis corporibus detruduntur, et tempestatis ordinem et pericula quae intulerant fatebantur.*"

35 *Soldiers of Christ*, 206; *Passiones vitaeque sanctorum aevi Merovingici*, ed. B. Krusch and W. Levison, (Hanover and Leipzig, 1920), 133 (ch. 22), "*nam subito cibos vel vestimenta vel alia domui necessaria rapere solebat et in ignem mittere.*"

36 *Vita S. Romani*, ch. 53; *Vie des Pères du Jura*, ed. François Martine (Paris, 1968): 296 8.

37 Bede, *Ecclesiastical History of the English People*, ed., trans., Bertram Colgrave and R.A.B. Mynors (Oxford, 1969), 60 (ch. 1.19).

38 Osbern of Canterbury, *Vita Dunstani*, ch. 13, in *Memorials of Saint Dunstan, Archbishop of Canterbury*, Rolls Series 63, ed. William Stubbs (London, 1874), 84–85; Gregory the Great, *Dialogues* 2.30 (de Vogüé and Antin, *Dialogues* 2, 220).

39 Augustine of Hippo, *De divinatione daemonum*, in *Fathers of the Church* 27, ed. Roy Deferrari, trans. Ruth Wentworth Brown (New York, 1955), 417–40.

40 Athanasius, *Vitae Antonii*, 15 (ch. 9), "*omnem protinus locum repluere phantasiis leonum, taurorum, luporum, aspidum, serpentium, scorpionum, necnon et pardorum atque ursorum.*"

41 *Dialogues* 3.4. See Zimmerman, *Dialogues*, 117; de Vogüé and Antin, *Dialogues*, 270, "*rugitus leonum, balatus pecorum, ruditus asinorum, sibilos serpentium, porcorum stridores et soricum.*"

42 Everett Ferguson, *Demonology of the Early Christian West* (Lewiston, New York, 1984), 20.

43 Markham J. Geller, *Forerunners to Udug-Hul* (Stuttgart, 1985).

44 *Dialogues* 3.7; de Vogüé and Antin, *Dialogues*, 2. 278–82. Cf. Chapter 7 of the current volume.

45 *The Letters of Saint Boniface*, trans. Ephraim Emerton (New York, 2000), 24. See *Die Briefen des Bonifatius und Lullus* 1, 35: "*Qui falsidica numina a paganis antiquitus quasi dii vocati sunt, in quibus demones habitare noscuntur; quoniam omnes dii gentium, ut ait scriptura, demonia sunt.*" Cf. 1 Corinthians 10.20.

46 *Letters of Boniface*, 70, "*sacrificia mortuorum sive sortilegos vel divinos sive filacteria et auguria sive incantationes sive hostias immolaticias.*" Cf. Tangl, *Die Briefe des Heiligen Bonifatus und Lullus*, 100.

47 Willibald, *Vitae sancti Bonifatii*, ed. Wilhelm Levison (Hanover and Leipzig, 1905), 30–1 (ch. 6).

48 Willibald, *Vita Bonifatii*, ch. 6; see also Eigil, *Vita Sturmi*, MGH *Scriptorum*, vol. 2.22, ed. George H. Pertz (Hanover, 1829), 376.

49 *Letters of Boniface*, 83. Cf. *Die Briefen des Bonifatius und Lullus* 1, 117, "*Quia octo nomina angelorum, quae in sua oratione Aldebertus invocavit, non angelorum praeterquam Michaelis, sed magis demones in sua oratione sibi ad prestandum auxilium invocavit.*" For Aldebert and the origins of his off-brand angel names, see Jeffrey Burton Russell, "Saint Boniface and the Eccentrics," *Church History* 33 (1964): 235–47.

50 Eric Sorensen, *Possession and Exorcism in the New Testament and Early Christianity* (Tübingen, 2002), 94–5. Wesley D. Smith, "So-Called Possession in Pre-Christian Greece," *Transactions and Proceedings of the American Philological Association* 96 (1965): 403–26 on 415.

51 Éva Pócs, "Possession Phenomena, Possession-Systems: Some East-Central European Examples," in *Communicating with the Spirits*, eds. Gábor Klaniczay and Éva Pócs (Budapest, 2005): 84–151 on 89.

52 Pócs, "Possession Phenomena, Possession-Systems," 93.

53 Nancy Mandeville Caciola, *Afterlives: The Return of the Dead in the Middle Ages* (Ithaca, 2016), 302–45. See also Sari Katajala-Peltomaa, *Demonic Possession and Lived Religion in Later Medieval Europe* (Oxford, 2020), 111–3.

54 As Caciola notes, Tertullian insists that the demons are simply pretending to be the deceased: "This imposture of the evil spirit lying concealed in the persons of the dead ... when in cases of exorcism (the evil spirit) affirms himself sometimes to be one of the relatives of the person possessed by him." Caciola, *Afterlives*, 306. See Tertullian, *De anima*, ch. 57, trans. Peter Holmes, in *Ante-Nicene Fathers*, vol. 3, eds. Alexander Roberts, James Donaldson, and A. Cleveland Coxe (Buffalo, 1885), 233. Cf. Tertullian, *De anima* (PL 2.748A-B), "*Hanc quoque fallaciam spiritus nequam sub personis defunctorum delitescentis ... cum in exorcismis interdum aliquem se ex parentibus hominem suis affirmat.*"

55 Jean-Claude Schmitt, *Ghosts in the Middle Ages: The Living and the Dead in Medieval Society*, trans. Teresa Lavender Fagan (Chicago, 1998), 34.

56 Anon., *The Earliest Life of Gregory the Great*, trans. Bertram Colgrave (Lawrence, 1968), 112 (ch. 22), "*statimque hostes magni equum eius intrantes quem sedebat, cito insanire fecerunt.*" The monk draws this story from an interpolated version of a life of Gregory by Paul the Deacon. See Paul the Deacon, *Sancti Gregorii magni vita*, ch. 25 (PL 75.56A).

57 *Vita S. Caesarii*, 2.21 in *Sancti Caesarii Arelatensis opera varia*, ed. Germain Morin (Bruges, 1942), 333, "*novi generis daemonium.*" The unknown author continues: "I have never read, nor seen, nor heard of this kind of demon ambushing someone" ("*Numquam isto genere diabolum insidiatum alicui vel legi vel vidi, vel audivi*").

58 *Vita Hilarionis* (ch. 14), 252, "*bruta quoque animalia quotidie ad eum furentia pertrahebantur.*"

59 *Vita Hilarionis* (ch. 14), 252, "*non me terres, diabole.*"

60 *Vita Hilarionis* (ch. 14), 254, "*tanto eorum ardere odio, ut non solum ipsos, sed et ea quoque, quae ipsorum essent, cuperet interire.*"

61 *Dialogues* 1.4. De Vogüé and Antin, *Dialogues*, 44, "*Ego quid feci? Sedebam mihi super lactucam. Venit illa et momordit me.*"

62 *Sainted Women of the Dark Ages*, trans and ed. Jo Ann McNamara, John E. Halborg, and E. Gordon Whatley (Durham, 1992), 248. For the *diabolica bonitas* trope, see Valerie Edden, "Devils, Sermon Stories, and the Problem of Popular Beliefs in the Middle Ages," *Yearbook of English Studies* 22 (1992): 213–5.

63 Isidore of Seville, *De ecclesiasticis officiis* 2.21. *Sancti Isidori Episcopi Hispalensis: De ecclesiasticis officiis*, ed. Christopher M. Lawson (Turnhout, 1989), 96, "*Exorcismus autem sermo increpationis est contra inmundum spiritum inerguminis siue caticuminis factus, per quod ab illis diabuli nequissima uirtus et inueterata malitia uel uiolenta incursio expulsa fugetur.*"

64 *The Gelasian Sacramentary: Liber Sacramentorum Romanae Ecclesiae*, ed. Henry A. Wilson (Oxford, 1894), 79.

65 *Gelasian Sacramentary*, 48, "*Audi maledicte Satanas adiuratus per nomen aeterni Dei et Salvatoris nostri Filii Dei; cum tua victus invidia tremens gemensque discede.*"

66 Henry Ansgar Kelly, *The Devil at Baptism: Ritual, Theology, and Drama* (Ithaca, 1985). See also Peter Cramer, *Baptism and Change in the Early Middle Ages, c.200-c.1150* (Cambridge, 1993) and J.D.C. Fisher, *Christian Initiation: Baptism in the Medieval West* (London, 1965).

67 Kelly, *Devil at Baptism*, 210.

68 Mark 16.17. See also Roy Yates, "Jesus and the Demonic in the Synoptic Gospels," *Irish Theological Quarterly* 44 (1977): 39–57 on 45.

69 Sorensen, *Possession and Exorcism*, 169.

70 Peter Brown argues that exorcism supplanted sorcery as the predominate paradigm in Late Antiquity, shifting blame from the human to a suprahuman agent: "if there is misfortune, it is divorced from a human reference and the blame is pinned firmly on the 'spiritual powers of evil'." See Peter Brown, "Sorcery, Demons, and the Rise of Christianity from Late Antiquity into the Middle Ages," in *Witchcraft, Confessions & Accusations*, ed. Mary Douglas (London, 1970), 17–45 on 33.

71 Athanasius, *Vitae Antonii*, 70, "*furor iste obsidentis est, non obsessi.*"
72 *Life of Rusticula*, ch. 13, in *Sainted Women*, 129.
73 Louis Duchesne, *Christian Worship: Its Origin and Evolution*, trans. M.L. McClure (New York, 1949), 345–50. In the 9th century, Hrabanus Maurus lists these in *De clericorum institutione*, ch. 4, for instance. See *PL* 107.299B.
74 *Gelasian Sacramentary*, 145.

## Further Reading

Boureau, Alain. *Satan the Heretic: The Birth of Demonology in the Medieval West*, trans. Teresa Lavender Fagan (Chicago: University of Chicago Press, 2006).

Caciola, Nancy Mandeville. *Afterlives: The Return of the Dead in the Middle Ages* (Ithaca: Cornell University Press, 2016).

Ferguson, Everett. *Demonology of the Early Christian World* (Lewiston, 1984).

Katajala-Peltomaa, Sari. *Demonic Possession and Lived Religion in Later Medieval Europe* (Oxford: Oxford University Press, 2020), 111–3.

Kelly, Henry Ansgar. *The Devil at Baptism: Ritual, Theology, and Drama* (Ithaca: Cornell University Press, 1985).

Schmitt, Jean-Claude. *Ghosts in the Middle Ages: The Living and the Dead in Medieval Society*, trans. Teresa Lavender Fagan (Chicago: University of Chicago Press, 1998).

Strickland, Debra Higgs. *Saracens, Demons, and Jews: Making Monsters in Medieval Art* (Princeton: Princeton University Press, 2003).

Wright, Archie T. *Satan and the Problem of Evil* (Minneapolis: Fortress Press, 2022).

# 4

# THE DEVIL THEORISED AND RATIONALISED

## Christopher S. Mackay

Scholasticism refers to the method of academic teaching, reasoning and discourse that held sway in the universities of medieval Europe, particularly between c. 1100 and 1450. This was a heavily regimented and formalised way of thinking, and while the devil may have been a vivid character in popular culture, he is a much more abstract figure in scholasticism. In order to understand how the devil is presented in scholastic thought, we have to consider the origin and development of the medieval university, and the intellectual discourse that characterised medieval universities.

The institution of the medieval university is the ancestor of modern universities and can be defined as a permanent establishment for the training of students that hired its own in-structors and awarded to those who completed a prescribed course of studies degrees that certified their competence as instructors and were generally recognised at other universities. The new institution soon replaced the monastery as the main centre of intellectual life. Universities began to be established at the end of the 12th century, and in the succeed-ing century universities were founded across Western Europe (first in Italy, France and England, later in Germany).[1]

The main disciplines of the medieval university were the older literary programme known as the liberal arts, and the three technical fields of law, medicine and theology. Like their modern equivalents, medieval scholars were jealous of their privileges, and there was much dispute about the hierarchical ranking of these disciplines. Not surprisingly (given the importance of religion in the medieval mind), theology claimed precedence as the "queen of sciences" (*regina scientiarum*).

"Scholasticism" is a somewhat vague term used to characterise the intellectual atmos-phere that dominated the universities of the later Middle Ages. It refers not to a particular doctrine but to the methodology that characterised the pedagogy and argumentation used in the universities. Prior to the 12th century, the thought of Augustine provided the basic framework for Christian philosophical analysis in Western Europe. However, early scho-lastics such as Peter Abelard adopted an active interest in the use of logic as an analytical tool and they relied on a few works from Late Antiquity for their knowledge of Greek philosophy. This knowledge depended upon the 6th-century author Boethius, who trans-lated into Latin two of Aristotle's works on logic—the *Categories* (*Praedicamenta*) and

DOI: 10.4324/9781003096603-5

*On Interpretation* (*Peri hermeneisas*)—and Porphyry's *Isagoge*, which was a commentary on the *Categories*. This interest in logic blossomed into a virtual mania after a large number of Aristotle's works as well as Arabic commentaries on them were translated into (often rather dubious) Latin in the period from the later 12th to the early 13th centuries. The abstract application of the fixed principles of logic became the obligatory method of interpretation and analysis in the late medieval universities. This methodology involved the precise use of terminology to define the issue at hand and then the (theoretically) rigorous resolution of the issue through logical analysis.

One of the fundamental principles of scholasticism that not infrequently makes its logical reasoning seems strange to the modern mind is the use of deduction. In deduction, logic is used to derive new conclusions on the basis of accepted premises, and since scholasticism recognised a rather disparate group of authoritative texts (e.g., the works of Aristotle, the bible and the writings of previous figures in the church, especially the "Church Fathers" from antiquity), totally separate texts with no relationship to each other could be combined to reach conclusions that had little to do with the original thought of the works being quoted. Furthermore, if it was a question about the natural world, conclusions could be reached without any reference to observable reality (e.g., statements about the physical nature of angels and demons, who by definition did not even exist in the real world). This sort of a priori reasoning is opposed to the basic methodology of modern scientific thought, which involves inductive reasoning. Inductive reasoning is the derivation of general rules or principles on the basis of observed instances of practice or behaviour (i.e., data). Thus, while deduction attempts to explain phenomena in terms of accepted doctrine, induction formulates general principles as a result of observing and analysing the phenomena independently in their own right. The reason why certain texts came to be held as authoritative and pretty much unquestioned in scholastic thinking (such as Ptolemy's understanding of the cosmos or Galen's of the human body and medical practice) can be seen in this deductive method of reasoning. The scholastics' aim was to apply abstract reasoning to a body of accepted facts. Thus, they not only had no interest in questioning traditional beliefs but were constitutionally opposed to doing so. The facts of the faith and the world as laid out in the excerpted statements of traditional authorities were taken for granted and used as the basis for Aristotelian battles of wit.

The use of (derivative) Aristotelian logic is the main feature of scholasticism, and with surprising swiftness the logical principles acquired from the newly translated works of Aristotle were incorporated into a new Christian understanding of the world. The first work in this adaptation of the ancient pagan philosopher was undertaken by men like Alexander of Hales (c. 1185–1245), Albertus Magnus (c.1200–1285), Bonaventure (1217–1274) and Duns Scotus (c. 1266–1308), but undoubtedly the most prominent figure of this movement was Thomas Aquinas (c. 1225–1274). The attempt to use the tool of pagan philosophy for the interpretation of Christian doctrine met with opposition (mainly from those who objected to this deviation from traditional Augustinian forms of interpretation), but certain attempts in the later 13th century to prohibit the use of Aristotelian logic in the universities were fleeting and ineffectual. Before long, this logical mode of thought was taken for granted as the natural vehicle for intellectual discourse. Thus, in the 14th and 15th centuries, the main issue of debate was not whether to use logic in answering questions but by which principles this new logic was to be applied.

In modern studies, one often sees the works of Aquinas described as dealing with philosophy, but (to borrow a conceit of scholasticism) this depends upon what one means by "philosophy." If philosophy is conceived of as the use of logical argument to determine the origin and nature of physical reality and of human morality, then in the abstract Aquinas was a philosopher in the modern sense. Such study was, however, firmly grounded in the absolute conviction of the accuracy of the doctrines of the Christian Church, and in fact the impulse for the use of logic among the scholastics was to expedite biblical exegesis. At the same time, since scholastic theology strove to understand and explain God's creation in light of the Church's teachings, it entered into areas of discussion that ranged far beyond what a narrow conception of theology would encompass. Thus, while in the modern period the natural sciences became separate and independent fields of study, medieval theology dealt with a total interpretation of the universe as understood at the time, including both natural and moral philosophies. Aquinas's views about the natural world were no doubt based upon the soundest theories of his time, but the often elaborate conclusions that he derived from scientific ideas that have since been completely disproved are frequently vitiated.

Although scholastic methodology permeated all aspects of the medieval university, in no discipline was this truer than theology. The early opponents of the adoption of Aristotelian logic in theological discussion were worried that this would lead to unorthodox conclusions. To some extent such concerns were not without foundation, but it soon transpired that the logic did not serve so much to come up with novel interpretations of the Christian religion as to provide (often specious) rationales to buttress pre-existing dogma. Since Aristotelian logic was thought to be capable of determining the answer to any valid question, then it followed that every conceivable theological question not only was susceptible of solution but in fact demanded an answer. It was this sort of irrepressible urge to ask and answer the most esoteric questions that led to the fabrication of the mock scholastic issue of how many angels could dance on the head of the pin.

A standard practice of scholastic writing is to present arguments in the form of a "disputed question" (*quaestio disputata*). The issue at hand is often presented in the form of a reply to a theoretical question: "If it is asked why ..., then it should be said/responded that ...." Such phraseology does not imply that anyone had actually raised the stated question. Rather, it was a natural procedure for someone trained in the scholastic tradition to present his argument as the response to a putative debating opponent. The disputed question was a standard mode of discourse in the scholastic tradition and had its origins in actual debates that took place under the presidency of a senior scholar. After an oral debate on a specific topic (hence the phrase "disputed question"), the presiding scholar would formally summarise the debate. This mode was a very convenient way to lay out an issue, and hence could be used as a formal way to present an issue without reference to an actual debate.

As part of scholastic argumentation, the disputed question takes on a formal scheme. It normally begins with an indirect question, which describes the issue at hand (this is called the *titulus* or "title" of the question). This title gives the correct answer to the question, which begins by giving the incorrect negative answer that author will eventually refute and then presenting one after the other various arguments in favour of this false initial answer. Each argument is at most a few sentences long and is generally based on or corroborated with a quotation from some authority, though sometimes it appeals to some principle of reason or observation of the natural world. After the arguments in favour of the false answer comes contradictory evidence in the form of one or more quotations from relevant authorities who indicate that the initial answer to the question was not correct. After the various arguments pro and con have been set out in this way, the presiding scholar (or author) gives his "determination" of the issue. Here he gives a discussion of some length explaining his reasoning in rejecting the false answer to the question and then answering the question affirmatively. After this, the question is concluded with a direct refutation of the individual arguments made in favour of the false conclusion at the beginning of the question.

The early scholastics made use of earlier *florilegia*, that is, collections of short quotations from accepted authors (mainly the major Patristic writers of Late Antiquity) that were drawn up during the Carolingian period. In short, the Carolingian monks made collections of pithy excerpts from a given author and the quotations thus culled were then selected and arranged in other collections in which the items were listed under various topics. In this way, the early scholastics were able to find relevant quotations for their arguments on a given topic (say, the nature of grace or original sin).[2]

Two problems arose from this procedure. First, the quotations themselves were sometimes adapted or otherwise modified in the process of excerpting and transmission, and at times quotations were falsely ascribed to authors who never said any such thing (sometimes the correct origin of these falsely attributed quotes can be determined but sometimes they are of indeterminate origin). Second, even if the quotation in question actually is recorded accurately in terms of the directly cited words, these words have been literally taken out of context and thus often mean something rather different if read in their original setting. The scholastics for the most part had never read the original context of the words at all, and in the case of the later scholastics simply reused the short quotations provided for them in previous scholastic discourse.

Now that we have considered the broader context of scholastic discourse, we will look carefully at a few representative authors to get sense of the general picture of the devil that appears in scholasticism. The first writer we will look at is a sort of transitional figure. Anselm of Aosta (1033/4–1109) was an Italian Benedictine, who became abbot of the monastery of Bec in France and eventually archbishop of Canterbury in Norman England.[3] He was actively involved in church affairs and also was a remarkable intellectual who engaged in much philosophical and theological reflection. He lived at the very beginning of the spread of scholastic thought and is considered a founding figure of scholasticism. Among a large number of works on theological topics, he composed several dialogues. The dialogue format that was prevalent in the Middle Ages took the form of an interaction between a teacher and a student. In this case, the teacher is clearly Anselm himself. The student is not a real interlocutor, but rather a literary device, never seriously challenging the teacher. Rather, he poses questions and raises objections, which allows the teacher to hold forth on the matter at hand. This mode of presentation is different from the "disputed question" that characterises the more developed period of scholasticism.

Anselm wrote a series of three interrelated dialogues, one of which is directly related to the notion of the devil: *On Truth* (*De veritate*), *On Free Will* (*De libertate arbitrii*) and *On the Fall of the Devil* (*De casu diaboli*).[4] The last work is much longer than the other two, but surprisingly enough, gives pretty much no information about the devil at all. It is rather an extended discussion of the question of whether God is responsible for the devil's evil. In effect, the malevolent activities of the devil are entirely taken for granted and left unexamined. The issue is the theoretical one of how the devil can be held responsible for his own misfortunes in the context of God's omnipotence. As is typical of scholastic thought, the matter is treated in a manner that revolves around the clarification of terminology and the logical working through of the issue at hand on the basis of these definitions.

The devil originally had, like the other angels, the proper attitude of love towards God, but at some point, turned against God. The question therefore is, why did he not "persevere" in that correct attitude? With no introduction, the dialogue begins with the student citing 1 Corinthians 4:7 ("What do you have that you didn't receive?"), which could be taken as meaning that whatever the devil "had" he got from God, who is therefore responsible for his actions. The long discussion that follows is basically intended to show that God is not in fact responsible for the devil's fall from grace. Part of this has to do with the issue of the status of "nothing." Is there actually such a thing in a "substantive" sense? No, not really. "Nothing" is actually the absence of something positive, and does not in and of itself signify anything. This ultimately is relevant because it turns out that evil is not in fact a meaningful concept, but simply the absence of good. And this, in turn, has to do with the nullity of evil as such, which means that it is simply an absence of good. And the good is what comes from God. So why did the devil not receive good from God? The answer is not that God withheld it, but that the devil declined to accept it. Thus, it is his own fault that he does not receive God's goodness, not God's fault for not offering it.

The entire discussion is very arcane, theoretical and convoluted, and ultimately unsatisfying in showing how God is not responsible for what the devil does since whatever abilities he may or may not (in this instance his ability to "accept" God's grace) were created by God. It resembles later scholastic treatment in being focused on the abstract issue of the devil's relationship to creation and having no particular interest in the actual interaction of the devil with humans.

The next author we will examine is Peter Lombard (ca. 1100–1160).[5] He was born in northern Italy and after beginning higher studies there moved to France, where he became an educator, eventually settling in Paris, where he taught at the school associated with the cathedral of Notre Dame. He held various ecclesiastic positions and was appointed bishop of Paris just before his death. Lombard had a huge, one might say fundamental, influence on the development of scholastic theology with his *Four Books of Sentences* (*Libri quattuor sententiarum*). There were of course huge amounts of theological discussion in the previous centuries of the Christian tradition, but this was generally of an ad hoc nature.[6] In his *Books of Sentences*, Lombard endeavoured to produce a broad handbook on Christian theology. He did so on the basis of the individual "sentences" on individual topics provided by the *florilegia* discussed above. Lombard expounded on specific topics, discussing opposing views and generally coming to a conclusion about the correct view (though sometimes he is uncertain about how to resolve contradictions).[7] In the subsequent centuries of scholasticism, academic theologians would frequently write commentaries on Lombard's *Sentences* (as the work is known in short). The individual books of the work were divided by Lombard himself into sentences. These are arranged in groups, unmarked by Lombard, and in the start of the 13th century, Alexander of Hales divided the books according to these sense groups, which he called "distinctions."

Book Two of the *Sentences* treats the "creation."[8] This is meant in two senses. First, it deals with the current nature of the "created" world that humans occupy, and, second, the way in which this world was brought into existence ("created") by God in the beginning. The whole discussion is basically anthropocentric. The entire world exists for the benefit of people, and the purpose of the account is to explain how the world serves as the stage on which is played the drama in which humans lead either a good and pious life for the glory of God or a wicked and impious one in defiance of God. The devil and his subordinate squad of demons play a role in the failure of humans to live up to the role God intended for them.

The discussion of the devil and demons thus has a very specific and narrow purpose in terms of explaining how they fit in with the struggle over the human soul, and there is no particular interest in the devil as such. The discussion is very colourless and abstract, mostly treating the role that the demons play in corrupting human souls. A major aspect of this is how the demons came into existence in the first place, and how, paradoxically, they acquired from the omnipotent creator of the world the ability to act contrary to his will. The colourful and exciting stories, attested elsewhere in the medieval world, about how demons interact with humans are not relevant to this intellectual discussion of the way the world is put together and how it functions.

Let us now consider what we learn about the demons from Lombard's treatment (the parenthetical numbers refer to distinctions, questions and subsections). Demons began their existence as angels, literally supernatural beings created by God at the start of the world (2.1.4; 2.3), whose substance is different from that of the living creatures of the world inhabited by humans, so that their powers are vastly superior to those of humans (3.1, 2, 5). That is, they were good like all the angels (3.4), but came to "fall" (literally and metaphorically) from their position as favoured creatures through a rebellion against God. A vexing issue was how creations—whether human or supernatural—could come to act in disregard of the wishes of their all-powerful, all-knowing, entirely good creator. The answer is that they had the "free will" to make their own decisions, and chose to exercise this in an evil way (5.1, 2). The mechanics of this free will was an issue that the scholastics spent a lot of energy on. The issue was of fundamental importance to them, as the fall of the rebellious angels was basically the same as the question of how mankind fell from grace through the sin of Adam and Eve. Lombard spends a lot of time on the mechanics of how the "confirmation" of the good angels (5.3, 4) and the "turning away" (*aversio*) of the bad ones happened, what the role of God in this was, and how it was the fallen angels' fault (5.5). What they actually did in the world was of no particular interest from an intellectual point of view. The question was not "what?" but "why?" With their rebellion, the demons were cast down from their previous position in the "empyrean" heaven, which is a fiery realm in the heavens above the "firmament," where the stars are located. In the fullness of time (that is, in the eschatological drama of the end days laid out in the Book of Revelation), they would be cast down into hell (6.2, 3), but until then, their residence was not in hell or on earth, which they would otherwise make uninhabitable for humans), but in the "foggy" air above the earth.

The leader of the fallen angels is the devil himself, known as Satan or Lucifer (6.1). He led the rebellion as a result of his pride (his resentment of God's supremacy and the desire to become his equal: 2.6). Their fall had two consequences in terms of their being. First, it appears that they became weakened in their powers (8.1, an uncertain position). While still superior to humans (7.5), they were now inferior in power to the angels who had remained loyal to God (and whose powers were enhanced as a result of their confirmation). Second, they became obdurate in their wickedness and malice (7.1, 2). They were now the implacable enemies of God and his creation.

Just as there would be an "anti-Christ" in the end times who was a sort of "reverse" of the real one, the devils act in ways that reflect the activities and traits of the angels, but in a malicious direction. Like the angels, the demons have a leader (the devil in place of the archangel Gabriel), and a hierarchy among themselves, so that there are various demons deputed to preside over various sinful practices (6.4; 10.2.1). In particular, the demons are behind the apparent operation of magical arts (7.6). They can only do so with God's permission (7.7), and "create" nothing by their own powers. Indeed, their own powers, even if somewhat reduced as a result of the fall, are so great that they would wreak havoc on earth if they were not prevented from doing so by God's withholding of his permission (7.10).

Why, then, does God give his permission at all? There are three reasons (7.6). The magical practices of demons deceive the unjust, serve as a warning to the faithful, and allow a venue for the righteous to show their virtue by resisting the demons' trickery. In effect, the purpose of God's allowing these apparently evil things to happen is to reinforce the divine order of the world by thwarting evil humans in their mistaken faith in God's opponents and by demonstrating the superiority of those who retain their faith in God. For this reason, there is no particular interest in the demons and the procedures as such. They are simply a vehicle by which humans are tempted to rebel against God, either succumbing or prevailing. The major interest of book two is on the nature of human propensity towards evil and the ways in which they either resist or yield to temptation. Half of the 44 distinctions into which the book is divided are devoted to examining temptation from a human perspective. Distinctions 22–33 treat the nature of the original sin of Adam and Eve, which is viewed almost entirely from their perspective, and the way that this is passed on to future generations via sexual intercourse. Distinctions 34–44 then deal in depth with the nature of sin and vice. The role of demons in this discussion is ignored.

Yet, there is a role for the demons to play in this human drama. Temptation takes two forms. There is inner temptation, which operates via people's sensual appetites (22.6). In effect, this is a natural weakness in human character. Then there is external temptation. This may take the form of a demon assigned to each human. Just as there is a guardian angel assigned to look after a person, there is a demon whose job is to encourage that person to act evilly (11.1). There is no real explanation of how exactly this demon operates, nor is it clear how these relate to the demons who preside over the various sins. Clearly, there is much greater focus on the human side of the process of temptation rather than the ways in which demons attempt to subvert them. It is argued at some length that demons do not physically occupy human bodies, despite a fair amount of description in texts on the matter that they do in fact have a presence with a person possessed by them (8.4). Perhaps a reason for this somewhat unexpected conclusion is to undercut any sense that the demon is actually responsible for the person's misdeeds through taking "possession" of them (literally). In effect, while Lombard cannot deny the role of demons in urging people to wickedness because there was so much textual attestation of that, he nonetheless wished to emphasis humans' own responsibility for their actions.

There is a fair amount of interest in the devil's role in subverting Adam and Eve in the paradigmatic failure of humans to adhere to God's ordinances, which, in turn, is the ultimate cause of human wickedness in later generations. To some extent, this event is a stand-in for the ways in which later demons would attempt to tempt Adam and Eve's posterity. The devil envies Adam and Eve because of their close approximation to God, something he had lost through his fall from grace (21.1.1). He chose to undermine the couple by working his wiles on Eve, because as a female she has less reason and is therefore less able to resist his suggestions (21.1.2). He decided to approach in the form of the serpent because he needed to be deceptive rather than violent (21.2). His method of subversion operates by presenting his evil advice as something seemingly good (22.5.5). As already noted, temptation takes two forms, and one might think that the devil's bad advice to Eve would be characterised as an external suggestion rather than an internal one. Yet, Lombard takes the position that for all humans, the serpent's deceit represents an inner temptation (24.7). This paradoxical interpretation reflects the general tenor of the discussion as concentrating far more on the interaction of humans and demons as reflecting the moral failing of the humans. In effect, while there was no doubting the existence of demons, who are attested clearly and repeatedly in both testaments of the bible[9] and in the traditions about Christian saints, their role in human depravity is definitely played down, with the result that the paradigmatic example of the devil's malicious effect on humans is conceived of as an instance of human failing as a result of moral weakness as a result of human nature. The devil and his minions do have a role to play in human corruption, but this is entirely subordinate to the human side of the equation. Ultimately, humans are still redeemable via the salvific power of Jesus's sacrifice on the cross, whereas the greater nature of the demons' sins is such that there is no hope for them (22.7). The book ends by noting that humans' ability to sin is ultimately granted through the power of omnipotent God, and the devil is incapable of doing anything without God's consent (44.1.3). This then leads to the final, somewhat quirky issue of whether it is wrong to resist the power of evil if the devil (and evil men) get their power from God (44.2). The answer is that evil is to be resisted when it goes against God's ordinance, regardless of the source of the power wielded by the evildoer. The main issue of human behaviour in the face of the evil in the world is how humans do or do not choose to reject evil and stay loyal to God's ordinance, and the nature of the forces of evil is only of subordinate interest.

One of the towering figures of scholasticism is Albert the Great (Albertus Magnus).[10] Born in Germany around 1193, he became a Dominican friar and received an education in theology in Italy and at the prestigious University of Paris, becoming one of the major academics to incorporate the logical procedures from the newly translated works of Aristotle into the western theology. He was an important leader within the Dominican Order, and made a significant contribution to establishing scholastic institutions of education within the Dominican Order. Albert's interests extended far beyond the narrow confines of theology. A very prolific writer, he composed works on disparate topics like astronomy and the nature of matter. He died after a very successful career in 1280.

Albert wrote a commentary on Lombard's *Sentences*.[11] This was a common practice among scholastic theologians. The purpose of the exercise was not to challenge the views of the authoritative work (it was, after all, the accepted handbook on the matters it treats), but to shed new light on the text. In particular, in Albert there are now references to a broader range of authorities going beyond those cited by Lombard. Aristotle puts in a number of appearances, but so do other scholastics as well as the official commentary ("gloss") on the text of the bible. Not surprisingly, Anselm's previous discussion is cited a number of times by Albert in connection with the question of the fall of the demons. As a random example of Albert's mode of discussion, in connection with the issue of what the fault was because of which grace was not given to the angels that fell (2.5.F), one question is whether the evil angels always sin, and whether their every act is evil. The format of the "disputed question" is now used. The incorrect answer is backed up with six separate one-line quotations and a syllogism (a form of reasoning to scholastic thought was very prone). A syllogism is a logical proposition consisting of two premises, an initial "major" one, which gives the general framework, and a second, "minor" one, which specifies the major premise, the combination of the two premises then leading to a conclusion.[12] In this case, Albert asserts that the confirmation of the good and the obstinacy of the wicked are opposing concepts, so evil creatures cannot be the origin of a good act; they must always be bad. Somewhat paradoxically, the correct answer is no, they are not always wicked, which is backed up with one quotation, six logical arguments and one interpretation of a quotation. Not surprisingly, none of this leads to any clearer idea of the demons, just quibbling about the details.

Albert also turned his hand to the kind of work known as a *summa* ("summary"), a synthesising treatment that dealt systematically with all the various aspects of a topic. One such work was his *Summa de creaturis*, dealing with the creations of God.[13] Tractate (i.e., major subdivision) 4 of the work deals at length with the angels. The tractate contains 50 separate questions, most dealing with the angels as a whole, with questions 62–69 devoted specifically to the devil and demons. Of these eight questions, seven are devoted to the mechanics of the actual fall (62–68). Only one question (69) pertains to the devil's actual functions in terms of humans. It contains four articles (subordinate issues): what is temptation? who is the tempter? in what part of the soul or body is a person tempted? and what are the methods of temptation and how many of them are there? The first is a pedantic discussion of the various meanings of the word "temptation" (in Latin, the word can also mean "attempt"). The incorrect answer to the second article (the identity of the tempter) is the devil. The correct answer is God (everything is dependent on his omnipotence, so the devil does not really do anything). The third article is divided into two subdivisions (particles). The first is subdivided into two subordinate questions. First, does the devil enter a person's heart? As one would expect from Lombard's treatment of the same question, the answer is no. The second subordinate question of the particle is what functions of the human mind the devil exercises his temptation on. The false answer is that he cannot do so at all, but the correct answer is that while angels operate on the intellect but not the will of a person, the devil can only work on the physical senses and the power of fantasy (a function of the mind in scholastic understanding of the operation of the human mind). That is, angels work on the "higher" functions of the mind, but the devil works on the baser bodily functions. The second particle of the third article contains three subordinate questions. The first is a discussion of a quotation from Augustine in which he distinguished "steps" (*gradus*) in the original sin of Adam and Eve (the serpent/devil, the woman, and the man). This question shows how the scholastic format of the "disputed question" is artificial in that sometimes it is used for discussion of an idea without any actual question. In any event, this pseudo-question involves various discussions (some quite extensive) of aspects of the original sin, such as a treatment of aspects of the human psyche, like sensuality and appetite, and the ways in which Adam and Eve separately sinned. The second subordinate question is a treatment of "morose delectation." This is term for mental concentration on wicked thoughts (more or less "dirty thoughts" in modern parlance), and again contains elaborate subsidiary discussions of topics like what was going on in Eve's mind at the time of the temptation by the serpent, and how such thoughts take place in the medieval understanding of the mind. The third question of the second particle of the third article is the amount of sin in each of the three steps posited by Augustine (that is, the serpent, the female/Eve, and the male/Adam). Finally, the fourth article concerns the various methods of temptation and their number. If one were expecting to finally get some concrete examples of the devil's practices, one would be disappointed. Again, this is basically an elaborate piling up of various ways in which misbehaviour can be characterised as "temptation." Basically, it is another discussion of terminology and no real treatment of concrete functioning of the devil. In sum, one can see how the inherent tendency of scholastic thought to concentrate on matters of definition and strictly logical analysis results in a very abstract and theoretical treatment that leaves the devil a colourless, vague entity. The scholastic is more interested in applying his Aristotelian logic to come up with a tidy explanation for why the world is set up as it is rather than any discussion of the actual world itself.

Thomas Aquinas (1225–1274) was Albert's student (and fellow Dominican), and in some ways he comes to be the final synthesiser of scholastic thought.[14] He is a much clearer and more orderly thinker than Albert, laying out his discussion in a tidier and more concise manner. Like Albert, he was an extensive writer, and his monumental *Summa theologica* was a summation of scholastic thought that eventually came to be a replacement for Lombard's *Sentences*. The devil gets mentioned in many passages in Aquinas's extensive corpus of work, but we will examine the *Summa theologica* to get a sense of how his treatment compares to the tradition we have examined so far.

Book one of the *Summa theologica* is basically about the nature of the world. The first 49 questions mostly concern the nature of God, where the extensive treatment of angels begins (questions 50–64). Of the fifteen chapters devoted to angels, only the final two are devoted to the bad angels specifically (though some of the previous questions touch on them as well). The first question (63) concerns the issue of how some of the angels fell and consists of nine articles. Let us look at first article (whether the evil of sin [*malum culpae*] can exist in angels). There are four points raised in favour of the (false) idea that it cannot. These do not consist of any cited text. Instead, they are all matters of abstract reasoning. For instance, the second one takes the form of a syllogism: the wicked angels are more worthy (*digniores*) than the heavenly objects, but according to the philosophers, there cannot be anything evil among heavenly objects. Therefore, there cannot be any such thing among the angels either. This is a silly argument, and all of them give the impression of being unconvincing arguments crafted by Aquinas himself to give a supposed opposition to the right answer, since scholastic method demands such a presentation. The whole lame edifice is then rebutted with a single quotation, from Job 4:18: "in his angels he found depravity" (*in angelis suis reperit pravitatem*). Aquinas then gives his reasoning in a long paragraph beginning with the idea that any rational creature, including angels, by nature can sin, and the ability not to sin comes only from the gift of God. In effect, this is the only substantive part of the argument, and the rest is just show. In the rebuttals of the individual points, it is explained that the heavenly bodies operate by invariable natural operations, but the free will operating in the angels' works by a different principle. The whole issue of the question comes from the unnatural attempt to fit the drama of Christianity into the abstract mechanism of the cosmos derived from ancient astronomy.

To get a general sense of Aquinas's preoccupations and concerns, the devil's only sins are pride and envy (2); the devil sinned by wanting to be "like" God, but there are various ways this can be understood (3); as rational beings, angels (including the evil ones) cannot have a natural inclination towards evil (4); the demons were not evil from the beginning, because they were in existence at the time when God said that everything in his creation was good in Genesis 1:31 (5); it is hesitantly argued that the rebellion of the bad angels took place immediately after creation (6); uncertainty about the question of whether the higher angels sinned more than the lower ones (7); a discussion of the causality by which the sin of the "first angel" led to the sinning of the lesser ones (8); and the fact that the angels who remained loyal to God outnumbered those who rebelled (9). As so often in scholastic thought, one can see here the great emphasis on definition and classification. Interest is not focused on how the devil and his minions operate among humans in the present age, but on using abstract reasoning to explain how such a situation, which is taken for granted, came into being in the distant past. Question 64 then examines the way in which the fallen angels were harmed (the "punishment" they received) compared to those who remained loyal. The answers are similarly abstract.

Questions 103–119, which form the end of book one of the *Summa theologica*, lay out the "government" by which God rules his creation. There are a number of questions pertaining to how angels interact with people (like 107 on how they talk), and these also pertain to the fallen angels. Only one pertains directly to the operations ("assaults") of demons on humans (114). This question consists of five articles, which show that (1) demons do in fact assail humans; (2) the devil is able to "tempt" humans, the phrase meaning to "put to the test," and the "temptations of the flesh" are simply the vehicle by which the devil tempts; (3) the devil is not the cause of all temptation, some of it being "internally" generated by people themselves; (4) the devil can lead people astray via seemingly "miraculous" feats, though in reality these are just "supernatural" acts that the supernatural demons can perform, rather than "real" miracles; and (5) the idea that a demon can no longer tempt people once he is overcome by a human is rejected, and the narrower conception that he can no longer tempt his vanquisher is guardedly accepted. Once again, the treatment is very abstract, pertaining to theoretical considerations of demonic power rather than any clear analysis of how it relates to actual events in the current world.

Aquinas is thus the culmination of the traits of the scholastic understanding of the devil and his minions. Their operation in the human world is taken for granted, as this is amply attested in the New and Old Testaments and in the stories of the saints. It was, moreover, a general feature of popular belief. But the scholastics were entirely focused on using Aristotelian logic to explain the presence of such evil in the creation of an omnipotent good God and had no interest in considering the practical issues about how the devil exercised the power he acquired through his fall. In Goethe's tragedy *Faust (Part One)*, the title character, a medieval academic who comes to be involved with the devil, is dissatisfied with his understanding of the world, saying the following:

> There I am, a bloody fool,
> I am no wiser than before,
> My title's "master," or even "doctor,"
> And for ten years now,
> It's back and forth, and up and down,
> By the nose, I drag my students round ...
> And I see we can't know anything!
> That would burn me to the core.[15]

Perhaps he would have been less dissatisfied with his knowledge of the devil if he were not so immersed in the dreary issues of scholasticism. But this "bloodless" interpretation of the devil and his works, so unfulfilling to Faust's curiosity about the world, would give an intellectual justification to the horrifying witch hunts that would sweep across Western Europe in the 16th and 17th centuries.

*Malleus Maleficarum* is the best known work on witchcraft from the period of witch hunting.[16] Written in 1486 by the Dominican inquisitor Heinricus Institoris, it was the first printed book to disseminate in a systematic way the novel idea that witchcraft was part of a world-wide effort by the devil to subvert God's creation through undermining the fidelity of Christendom to its creator and master, God Almighty.[17] The devil knew that the world would come to an end (and he would be cast into the pits of hell) once the number of the elect (that is, souls admitted to heaven) equalled that of the fallen angels. Therefore, he had to do everything he could to lessen the number of saved souls. An easy way to do this was to convince humans (especially more easily manipulated and less rational women, who thereby play the role of latter-day Eves) of the reality of witchcraft and persuade them to commit it. In using witchcraft, the devil has two goals. First, in the immediate sense, those engaged in witchcraft will be condemned to eternal damnation and thereby lower the number of the elect. But at the same time, any failure on the part of the secular authorities to thwart the witches angers God, which, in turn, encourages him to give the devil further permission to carry out acts of apparent witchcraft (which only work through his intervention, which, in turn, is dependent on God's permission), these subsequent acts of witchcraft being a punishment for the authorities' failure to stamp out the earlier acts of witchcraft. The work is meant specifically to encourage the secular authorities to do their duty and execute convicted witches. The work has three basic sources. One is a procedural manual for inquisitors (Nicholas Eymeric's *Directorium inquisitorum*) and is meant to give a legal framework for secular judges (this is the third division of the work). A second is the scholastic understanding of the world, which is basically derived from Thomas Aquinas.[18] This forms the basis of the first part of the work, which is meant to demonstrate the reality of witchcraft. This part of the work provides its intellectual heft. A lot of the theoretical discussion of the powers of the devil and demons is probably mind-numbingly boring to modern readers. But for contemporary readers, whose higher education generally took the form of the scholastic learning that had dominated European universities for centuries, the logical arguments laid out according to (and frequently in imitation of) the firm regimentation of Aquinas's formulations would have proved at the very least worthy of consideration if not absolutely convincing. But to the dry logic of Aquinas is added a much more colourful layer of contemporary reality. Some of this comes from the *Formicarius* ("Anthill") of the Dominican Johannes Nider. That work was a denunciation of heretical practice in general, and book five discusses instances of witchcraft known personally to Nider.[19] This is combined with personal stories from Institoris's own activities as an inquisitor in Ravensburg in 1484 and Innsbruck in 1485, as well as anecdotal material of unknown derivation. This material provides the substance to Part Two of the *Malleus*, which covers the deeds of witches and the methods of remedying them. In effect, the dry intellectual constructs of scholasticism are given the vividness and immediacy that is so lacking in the abstract discussions of authors like Anselm and Aquinas. Part of the impact of the work derives from its presenting its case in a way that answers both intellectual and emotional needs at once. From a modern perspective, the intellectual arguments seem to be wrong-headed and based on false premises, while the vivid anecdotes seem unreal. But we are not the audience for whom the work is intended. In effect, the *Malleus* served three functions is setting the stage for subsequent witch hunts. First, the scholastic argumentation of the work (so tiresome to modern sensibilities) gives intellectual respectability to the pressing need to suppress witchcraft.

Second, the anecdotal material "fleshes" out the abstract, colourless understanding of demons in scholasticism. In effect, the eschatological aspects of the scholastic view of the devil are given a vividness by interpreting the anecdotes about witchcraft from regular life in the framework of the scholastic view of the devil. Finally, the combination of the theoretical and the anecdotal managed to convert the pretty much universal belief in some sort of folk magic into an existential threat to the Christian order and necessitated the most drastic actions to thwart the attempt by the devil and his minions (both demons and witches) to subvert Christendom.

The *Malleus* itself was a sort of bridging vehicle, transmitting and modifying the scholastic tradition. The book was soon replaced by later handbooks on witchcraft, like Jean Bodin's *De la démonomanie des sorciers* (1580) or Martin Del Rio's *Disquisitiones Magicae* (1599–1600).[20] In effect, the *Malleus* gave intellectual legitimacy to viewing common witchcraft as an existential threat to civilisation. Yet, it is easy to make too much of it. While it would undoubtedly be horrible to be caught up in an instance of witch hunting, it was a limited phenomenon, and most people in Western Europe lived their entire lives without encountering it. And it was also limited in scope temporally. There was an upsurge in witch hunting from the late 15th century until around 1520, when the religious disorders accompanying the Reformation occupied people's attention. Witch hunting then resumed on a large scale in the last quarter of the 16th century and the sort of heyday of the attack on witches took place in the first third of the 17th on the continent (England, with its distinctive tradition about witchcraft, and Massachusetts lagged behind events on the continent). By that point, the scholastic world of Thomas Aquinas was giving way to a much different conception of the world and of the place held in it by the devil.[21]

During the period of the witch hunts, it was up to local individuals (whether governmental or judicial figures or preachers or commoners) to come up with their own conception of witchcraft on the basis of their readings and absorption of cultural understandings. The *Malleus* played a major role in complicated and prolonged process of converting the abstractions of scholastic understanding of the devil into a lethal mixture of eschatology, folk beliefs and state power.

## Notes

1 A convenient general introduction to the origins, development and structure of the medieval university is provided in *A History of the University in Europe: Volume 1, Universities in the Middle Ages*, ed. Hilda de Ridder-Symoens (Cambridge, 1992). Though dated, Hastings Rashdall's work, *The Universities of Europe in the Middle Ages* (Oxford, 1936), is still useful for its greater detail. Anders Piltz gives an excellent presentation of the medieval learning as it was conceived of at the time in *The World of Medieval Learning* (Oxford, 1981).

2 In connection with the Carolingian *florilegia*, Clifford Lawrence makes the amusing observation that "It was unoriginal work, but in the end it served a wider purpose than its authors could have foreseen: the patristic anthologies of the 9th century provided a compost in which the Schoolmen [an old-fashioned term for scholastics] of a later age were able to grow strange plants as yet undreamed of." See Clifford H. Lawrence, *Medieval Monasticism: Forms of Religious Life in Western Europe in the Middle Ages* (London, 1984), 73.

3 For a general introduction to St. Anselm, see R. W. Southern, *Saint Anselm: A Portrait in a Landscape* (Cambridge, 1990).

4 For a translation, see Jasper Hopkins and Herbert Richardson, *Truth, Freedom and Evil: Three Philosophical Dialogues by Anselm of Canterbury* (New York, 1967).

5 For a general introduction to Lombard, see Philipp W. Rosemann, *Peter Lombard* (New York, 2004).

6 Of course, some works like Augustine's *City of God* did treat the broadest questions of the nature of the Christian cosmos, but these were not meant as comprehensive treatments of all aspects of theology. Later medieval discussions tended to take the form of commentaries ("glosses") on individual passages.

7  In this context, the Latin world *sententia* does not signify a grammatical "sentence" but an authoritative "pronouncement" (a sense reflected in the English use of "sentence" to signify the decision made by a judge in a criminal case about the punishment of the accused once he is convicted).

8  For a translation of book two plus an introduction, see *Peter Lombard: The* Sentences, *Book 2: On Creation*, trans. Giulio Silano (Toronto, 2008).

9  From a Jewish point of view, the statement about the Old Testament could be disputed, but the apocryphal Book of Tobit was accepted in the Catholic tradition and it does involve an encounter with the demon Asmodeus. In addition, various stories in the Old Testament were interpreted in the Catholic tradition as involving demons (e.g., Moses's competition with pharaoh's magicians in Exodus 7–8 and the evil spirit afflicting King Saul in 1 Samuel 16:23.

10  For general introductions to Albert, see Irven M. Resnick, *A Companion to Albert the Great* (Leiden, 2013). See also Kevin Vost, *St. Albert the Great: Champion of Faith and Reason* (Charlotte, NC, 2011).

11  There is no English translation of the work. For the Latin text, see *B. Alberti Magni, Ratisbonensis Episcopi, Ordinis Praedicatorum Opera Omnia*, vol. 27, *Commentarii in II Sententiarum*, ed. S. Bourget (Paris, 1894).

12  For instance, humans are mortal (major premise), and Socrates is human (minor premise). Therefore, Socrates is mortal.

13  There is no English translation of this work either. For the Latin text, see *B. Alberti Magni, Ratisbonensis Episcopi, Ordinis Praedicatorum Opera Omnia*, vol. 34, *Summa de Creaturis*, ed. S. Bourget (Paris, 1895).

14  The scholarship on Aquinas is massive. For a recent general treatment, see *The Oxford Handbook of Aquinas*, eds. Brian Davies and Eleonore Stump (Oxford and New York, 2012).

15  Da steh ich nun, ich armer Tor!
Und bin so klug als wie zuvor;
Heiße Magister, heiße Doktor gar
Und ziehe schon an die zehen Jahr
Herauf, herab und quer und krumm
Meine Schüler an der Nase herum—
Und sehe, daß wir nichts wissen können!
Das will mir schier das Herz verbrennen.

16  Of course, the *Malleus* gave intellectual respectability to notions of a diabolic aspect to witchcraft and played a major role in disseminating the ideas that gave rise to the major witch hunts of the 16th and 17th centuries, but these ideas predated the *Malleus*. For the Latin text, English translation plus extensive introduction, see *Malleus Maleficarum*, 2 vols, trans. and ed. Christopher S. Mackay (Cambridge, 2011).

17  The eschatological interpretation of witchcraft is first attestable around 1400. In 1484, Institoris asked Pope Innocent for a ruling about an administrative/judicial matter, and this resulted in the papal bull *summis desiderantes*. This document was based on Institoris's own petition, including the introductory material, whose inclusion in the document was taken by Institoris as proof that the pope approved of Institoris's views about the Satanic nature of witchcraft. While the pope (like pretty much everybody at the time) would have accepted the reality of witchcraft in general, he would no doubt have been surprised to see Institoris's assumption that this document had any significance beyond the immediate context. For the novel theory, see Mackay, *Malleus*, 1.46–62, and for the bull, see 1.121–126.

18  See Charles Edward Hopkin, *The Share of Thomas Aquinas in the Growth of the Witchcraft Delusion* (Philadelphia, 1940) for an old-fashioned attempt to blame Aquinas for the work; it is nevertheless a convenient collection of passages in Aquinas that are used by Institoris.

19  For a treatment of Nider's role in the development of conceptions of witchcraft, see Michael D. Bailey, *Battling Demons: Witchcraft, Heresy, and Reform in the Late Middle Ages* (Philadelphia, 2002).

20  For Bodin, see Jean Bodin, *On the Demon-Mania of Witches*, trans. Randy A. Scott (Toronto, 1995). For Del Rio's text, see Martin Del Rio, *Investigations into Magic*, trans. P. G. Maxwell-Stuart & J. M. García Valverde (Leiden, 2022–3). For a general discussion of the man and his work, see Jan Machielsen, *Martin Delrio: Demonology and Scholarship in the Counter-Reformation* (Oxford, 2015).

21 The classic treatment of the decline of the belief in witchcraft is Keith Thomas, *Religion and the Decline of Magic: Studies in Popular Beliefs in Sixteenth- and Seventeenth-Century England* (London, 1971).

## Further Reading

Bailey, Michael D., *Battling Demons: Witchcraft, Heresy, and Reform in the Late Middle Ages* (Philadelphia: Penn State University Press, 2002).

Del Rio, Martín, *Investigations into Magic*, trans. P.G. Maxwell-Stuart & J.M. García Valverde (Brill: Leiden, 2022–23).

Hopkin, Charles Edward, *The Share of Thomas Aquinas in the Growth of the Witchcraft Delusion* (Philadelphia: University of Pennsylvania, 1940).

Hopkins, Jasper and Herbert Richardson, *Truth, Freedom and Evil: Three Philosophical Dialogues by Anselm of Canterbury* (New York: Harper & Row, Publishers, 1967).

Machielsen, Jan, *Martin Delrio: Demonology and Scholarship in the Counter-Reformation*. (Oxford: Oxford University Press, 2015).

Mackay, Christopher S., *Malleus Maleficarum*, 2 vols. (Cambridge: Cambridge University Press, 2011).

Silano, Giulio, *Peter Lombard: The* Sentences, *Book 2: On Creation* (Toronto: Pontifical Institute of Mediaeval Studies, 2008).

# 5

# DEVILS, COMMUNITY, AND ITS BOUNDARIES

*Michael D. Bailey*

Association with the demonic has served as a mechanism for exclusion from Christian society throughout history. The devil is, of course, Christianity's great oppositional force. For as much as he sometimes acts as God's agent, most famously in scripture against the long-suffering Job, he is also an implacable opponent of proper behaviour and approved morality.[1] Ever since the apostle Paul warned that all pagan deities were actually demons and expressed his fervent hope that Christians would have no "fellowship" with them, Christian authorities have demonised perceived enemies of the faith.[2] This is nowhere more apparent than in Augustine of Hippo's endlessly influential division of the *City of God* from the earthly city held in the devil's thrall. The several chapters he spent describing how that city was saturated with demonic malevolence forms the most important expression of early Christian demonology in the Latin West.[3]

The devil and his minions continued to serve as fierce antagonists for pious monks struggling to perfect their devotion into the early Middle Ages, and Christian writers long associated first real pagans and then the perceived remnants of pagan practices enduring within Christianised lands with the demonic.[4] Yet the threat that the devil was imagined to represent was not unchanging over time. Many scholars have identified a sharp increase in concern over the demonic emerging in the late medieval period (generally, the 14th and 15th centuries) and enduring into the early modern era.[5] Fear of demonic possession grew tremendously in the late medieval centuries, with the early modern period constituting a "golden age" for possession.[6] The experiences of mystics, particularly women mystics, were increasingly regarded with suspicion, and for the most anxious authorities, almost any kind of intense female spirituality came to represent a potential gateway to hell.[7] Perhaps the greatest indicator of this growing concern was the emerging stereotype of diabolical witchcraft and rising numbers of witch trials across much of Western Europe. Notions of moral and social inversion proved central to conceptions of witchcraft, and the imagined demonic society of witches served in countless ways as a loathsome antithesis of and useful foil for properly ordered Christian communities.[8]

Here I want to explore association with demons and diabolism as a mechanism for exclusion from Christian society from a slightly different angle. The medieval historian R. I. Moore's analysis of the development of a "persecuting society" during the central Middle

DOI: 10.4324/9781003096603-6

Ages has proven to be enormously influential in a number of fields.[9] Moore began with a well-known fact in the study of medieval heresy: while early Christian authorities had identified and condemned various heresies, for several centuries after the patristic period, there was a long lull in the identification or persecution of perceived heretics, until shortly after the year 1000 when accusations and official acts of repression begin to appear again in historical records.[10] Over the next few centuries, large-scale heretical groups were imagined to exist and increasingly centralised mechanisms for the investigation and control of heresy, in the form of inquisitorial tribunals, were created.[11]

Other groups faced increasing repression in the same period, Moore argued. Jews had always stood somewhat apart from their Christian neighbours, but in the course of the 11th, 12th, and 13th centuries, they were subject to more focused ostracisation: required to wear certain identifying badges, to live clustered together, and ultimately expelled from many realms. Likewise, lepers, a designation that in these centuries could encompass a variety of diseases or conditions, and that also implied moral as well as physical degeneration, were segregated into special hospitals and communities. Male homosexuals and female prostitutes also faced more pronounced condemnation for what were regarded as their sexual transgressions.

Moore's most important insight was not just that different groups perceived as diverging from various Christian norms were subject to similar systems of repression at roughly the same time, however. He also discerned a more fundamental conceptual coherence. All these groups were described by the authorities who sought to punish them through similar metaphors of contagion and corruption. They were not just bent on living their lives in ways Christian authorities (whether within the church or operating through secular systems of power) disapproved of, but rather they aimed (so those authorities claimed with increasing ferocity) to subvert the very order of Christian society. The thought then naturally extended itself that they did so because they were all agents of the ancient enemy, servants of the devil.[12]

Likewise, European society did not begin to repress all these groups at roughly the same time through some dark serendipity or because mechanisms of persecution developed against one group gradually engulfed others. Instead Moore saw these developments as part of a single, coherent response to tremendous, indeed revolutionary, social changes underway in medieval Europe.[13] The most important perpetrators of persecution were a newly powerful group, the *litterati*—Latin-literate clerical officials operating within increasingly bureaucratic political and ecclesiastical regimes. These men developed modes of persecution, segregation, and exclusion in order to expand the control of the regimes they represented over society as a whole. This made Europe, in Moore's estimation, not just a society that was subject to periodic instances of persecution, but one in which certain "mentalities" and "mechanisms" of persecution became absolutely fundamental, and among these was a necessary "demonisation of the accused."[14]

These dynamics would continue into later periods, and Moore himself repeatedly cited late medieval and early modern witchcraft as the most obvious subsequent manifestation of the persecutorial trends he identified in the high medieval period prior to about 1250.[15] Surprisingly, however, his framework has generated relatively little direct engagement among scholars of magic and demonology. Perhaps the seeming obviousness of the connection was itself to blame. Insofar as the persecution of witches stemmed in many ways directly from the persecution of heretics, particularly in the late medieval period when many witch trials were conducted by ecclesiastical inquisitions, little more attention seemed necessary.[16]

This chapter, however, looks beyond structural connections between heresy trials and witch trials and seeks to test Moore's insights as they pertain to the growing persecution of putatively demonic magic more broadly in the 14th and 15th centuries, immediately subsequent to the period of his main focus. It will present key steps in the demonisation and hereticisation of magic across these centuries, from papal actions against relatively highly placed ritual magicians to the emerging stereotype of diabolical witchcraft. For each episode, it will highlight how the supposedly demonic nature of magical practices was deployed to exclude its practitioners from decent, tolerable Christian society. Finally, in the conclusion, it will explore the extent to which the authorities who developed these dynamics did so in order to expand the reach of whatever power structure they represented. In this way, it will test not just the general contours but also some more specific components of Moore's "persecuting society" as it relates to the devil, demonisation, and community.

### Dilemmas of Necromancy

Ironically, given that our story focuses on exclusion from Christian society based on association with demons and the diabolical, the first important shift driving this development occurred among the clergy and within privileged institutions at the heart of western Christendom. What Richard Kieckhefer has described as a "clerical underworld" of demonic ritual magic, commonly termed necromancy, began to develop at emergent schools and universities in medieval Europe in the 11th and 12th centuries.[17] Christian authorities had, of course, always maintained that most if not all magical practices involved demons in some way. Yet for centuries they had dismissed many magical rites, especially those used by ordinary Christians, as empty superstition rather than any kind of real demonic threat. When educated clergymen began to claim that they invoked demons through more complex forms of ritual magic, however, authorities could hardly remain dismissive; especially not when knowledge of such magic derived from cutting-edge scholastic learning grounded in ancient texts or newly imported Arabic ones.[18]

One early example of this development comes from the Italian scholar Anselm of Besate. In a work on rhetoric composed in the mid-11th century, he accused his own cousin Rotiland of practising such magic. Rotiland had supposedly performed an elaborate invocation which involved taking a young boy to a field outside a certain city and burying him up to his waist. He then lit fires around the boy, filling the air with smoke, and performed an elaborate conjuration to summon a demon. He knew of this rite from a book of magic that he possessed, and he was also in contact with a "Saracen physician" from whom he learned other diabolical practices as well.[19]

Knowledge of this art soon spread from schools to courts. In the 12th century, for example, the English clergyman John of Salisbury offered what became a relatively famous account of how he had been conscripted into a demonic rite in his *Policraticus*, a handbook for princes and courtiers. As a young boy, John related, the priest from whom he learned Latin took him and another pupil aside. Anointing their fingernails with oil, the older man then spoke a conjuration involving various unknown names which, because of the revulsion they inspired in him, John was sure designated demons. In the end, the conjuration fizzled. John saw nothing, and the other boy saw only "cloudy figures."[20] John's larger point, however, was that such demonic rites were rampant at many courts, and wise rulers should either disregard or more aggressively censure those who practiced them.

Conjurers such as these rarely occupied the highest echelons of either academic or political power. Instead they tended to be found among more middling ranks of the educated clergy who staffed both ecclesiastical and secular institutions.[21] They were, however, hardly at the fringes of Christian society. Indeed, they were far closer to its heart. Conceptually as well, these people need not have thought of themselves as operating outside the bounds of intellectual or spiritual norms.[22] Critics like Anselm and John presented them as dangerously outré, and no doubt some of them saw their own flirtations with the diabolical as alluringly illicit. Yet when pressed, they could offer a startlingly orthodox defence. When they summoned and sought to command demons, they were only deploying the power of exorcism, which Christ himself has conferred upon all the faithful.[23]

No less an authority than the great 13th-century scholastic theologian Thomas Aquinas addressed this problem head-on. His point was a simple one, but it had to be made. As Christ's own actions in scripture demonstrated, the only proper form of exorcism available to a Christian involved commanding a demon *to go away*. Seeking to attract a demon or compel it into any kind of service, as magical rites obviously did, meant stepping outside the bounds of proper Christianity and entering into fellowship, *societas*, with demons instead.[24] Aquinas's reasoning became a mainstay of all subsequent ecclesiastical arguments against any but the most limited form of engagement with demons.[25]

The accusations levelled by both ecclesiastical and secular authorities against supposed "invokers of demons" provide much of our information about them, inevitably in a confrontational and condemnatory way. But we are fortunate not to be limited entirely to such sources. Scholars of medieval magic have uncovered a number of remarkable texts written by clerical magicians themselves.[26] Some of these are relatively straightforward and unphilosophical in their presentation of demonic conjurations, dwelling not at all on the nature of the interaction or the moral quality of the act itself.[27] Others, however, offer considerable insight into the real difficulties some pious Christians faced when trying to demarcate the tenuous boundary between appropriate spirituality and diabolical sorcery.

Perhaps no one left so detailed a record of his struggles along these lines as the Benedictine monk John of Morigny, whose grand magical and mystical treatise *Liber florum celestis doctrine* (Flowers of Heavenly Teaching) survives in multiple forms.[28] Shortly after entering the monastery of Morigny in the mid-1290s, John went to study canon law at Orléans. While there, he obtained "a certain book from a certain cleric containing many nefarious things of necromantic art."[29] He moved even deeper in the "clerical underworld" associated with the schools when he learned of another famous magical text, the *Ars notoria* (Notory Art, so-called for its inclusion of various figures or signs, *notae*, in its rites), from a Lombard physician. This work was not explicitly demonic; indeed, it presented itself as a ritual system for invoking angelic spirits in order to obtain knowledge.[30] "Through it, omnipotent God promises and imparts to operators attainment, in a brief time, of all knowledge of scriptures and arts."[31] What more could any budding scholar want?

Enraptured by this new learning, John instructed his friend and fellow monk John of Fontainejean and even his own younger sister Bridget in the *Ars notoria*. Yet throughout the time he worked with this text, he was beset by visions of demons, as were his friend and sister. Only gradually did he come to suspect that there "might be something evil" in its rites, but eventually he renounced it completely.[32] Remarkably, he continued to practice more explicitly demonic necromancy for some time after this, but eventually he turned his back on that practice too.[33] All along, he had been cultivating a devotion to the Virgin Mary, and he attributed his eventual salvation to her, at one point explicitly comparing himself to

Theophilus, the legendary early Christian clergyman who contracted with the devil but was saved through the Virgin's intercession.[34]

John's devotion to Mary, which both preceded his dabbling in the demonic and eventually saved him from it, was intensely visionary in nature. Nor was it an entirely passive form of mysticism. Sometimes the Virgin would appear to John unbidden, but he also set about devising a series of rites to call her to him. He called these rites "prayers," but they involved elaborate figures not unlike the *notae* that gave the *Ars notoria* its name. One rite in his *Liber florum* even entailed crafting a ring that many might see as a magical token.[35]

John was no fool. Having returned from Orléans to Morigny, apparently with necromantic texts still in his possession, he worried that his fellow monks might suspect that his Marian visions were actually demonic conjurations.[36] Yet he went ahead and circulated an early version of his *Liber florum*, wanting to share what he considered to be a good and pious practice. In 1315, his work was condemned by a group of clerics, unknown except for John's own description of them but seemingly from outside the monastery of Morigny. Unsurprisingly, they asserted that his images "had been composed in the manner of necromantic figures."[37] Perhaps more remarkably, John acknowledged that they had a point. Although his figures had been revealed to him by the Virgin herself, he admitted that they did resemble those in the *Ars notoria*.[38] He therefore scrapped the first version of his work and set about composing anew.

Through John we can see just how uncertain and permeable were the boundaries that separated the realm of Christian piety from the diabolical. What is clear, though, is that John always considered himself a pious Christian, albeit one who briefly strayed into error. He worried that his immediate community at Morigny would reject him if they learned of his involvement with necromancy, but he also wanted to share his visionary experiences and ritual methods. Rebuked by some authorities in 1315, he complained loudly that his work was misunderstood, but he revised. He wanted there to be no danger of misunderstanding. Unfortunately for him, his writings were condemned again and burned in Paris in 1323, having been declared to be "false and evil, and against Christian faith."[39]

### Excommunicating Demonic Magicians

All things considered, John could hardly have picked a worse time to try to spread his particular devotional message, for powerful institutions within western Christendom were mobilising in the early 14th century to impose clearer boundaries on exactly the sort of nebulous practices in which he at least at times explicitly engaged. Near at hand to John (Morigny is 30 miles from Paris), the French royal court underwent a spasm of concern about demonic sorcery in the early 14th century. When Queen Joan died in 1305, at just 32, charges of poisoning and harmful sorcery were eventually brought against a bishop, Guichard of Troyes.[40] When King Philip IV died in 1314, suspicions again swirled of a plot against the royal family involving sorcery, and charges were brought against such high-ranking individuals as the royal chamberlain Enguerrand of Marigny and the bishop of Châlons.[41] Various diabolically tinged magical intrigues continued to erupt until, in 1331, King Philip VI complained to Pope John XXII about sorcerers plotting against him at his court, and the pope ordered the bishop of Paris to investigate.[42]

Pope John was himself deeply concerned about diabolical sorcery at his own court. In 1317, almost immediately after he had assumed the papal throne, his agents accused Bishop Hugues Géraud of trying to assassinate the pope through magical rites involving wax images. Then in 1318 John appointed a commission to investigate a number of clergy in Avignon, where the papal court then resided, for practising "necromancy, geomancy, and other magical arts."[43] In 1320, a plot was uncovered in which the Visconti rulers of Milan supposedly had hired magicians to kill the pontiff.[44] What matters for our story, however, is not these individual cases but rather actions taken in response by Pope John that ultimately positioned anyone who performed demonic magic, regardless of intent, as an enemy of Christendom and set them outside of the bounds of the Christian community.

In 1320, the same year as the supposed Visconti plot against him, John XXII ordered inquisitors in nearby Carcassonne and Toulouse to begin investigating all cases of demonic magic within their territories.[45] Such cases were only tenuously under the jurisdiction of papal inquisitors up to this point. More than 60 years earlier, in 1258, Pope Alexander IV had ordered inquisitors to avoid cases of "divination and sorcery" unless they "clearly savoured of manifest heresy."[46] Due to some of the complexities sketched above, the question of whether invoking demons in magical rites was "manifestly" heretical remained open, but John XXII aimed to draw clear boundaries if he could.

Also in 1320, the pope convened a special committee of ten theologians and canon lawyers at the papal court in Avignon. They were to determine whether demonic magic, particularly the elaborate ritual magic thought to be employed by clerical necromancers, automatically entailed heresy.[47] The issues were complex and the opinions presented varied. Even if a magician should offer a consecrated eucharist to a demon, one committee member argued, this need not be heretical. Since it stood to reason that a demon would want to see a host desecrated, the creature might very well be willing to perform some service in exchange for such an act. Thus the summoning magician would have committed a clear sacrilege but not one involving any incorrect belief (since the position that demons were evil and eager to defile holy items was clearly in accord with Christian doctrine).[48] Another expert even imagined a situation in which a magician might use a eucharist wafer to entice a demon into some service that would not actually defile the host in any way, in which case the person would not even have committed sacrilege, let alone heresy.[49]

At the crux of the matter, ultimately, lay the nature of the magician's interaction with the demon, akin to what has been sketched out above regarding exorcism. That is, if a human could either compel a demon into service or obtain its cooperation by offering it something in exchange, the behaviour might be loathsome and sinful, but it need not be heretical, and in that sense not inherently unchristian. Interaction with demons became heretical only if one displayed any reverence or worship to the creature. Even here there was a rub, for again it was possible at least theoretically to imagine a scenario in which a magician performed some rite that appeared to offer reverence to a demon, for example baptising an image in its honour, but still did not wilfully *intend* to offer reverence.[50]

This objection, at least, could be, and was, brushed aside. Only God could know all the mysteries of the human heart. The church in this world had to judge by external signs, and the signs that magicians gave to demons in the course of their ritual conjurations—the mysterious images and figures they employed, the objects they consecrated through baptism or other means, as well as the explicit offerings they sometimes made—were deemed to signify reverence, worship, and a necessarily heretical attachment.[51] This was the judgement on which John XXII would seize when he ordered the inquisitors of Carcassonne and Toulouse into action later that year, and again in 1326 when he composed the proclamation *Super illius specula* (Upon His Watchtower). Here he lamented that many people were "Christian in name only" because they "offer sacrifices to demons, worship them, [and] make or cause to be made images, a ring, a mirror, a phial, or some other thing to bind demons by magic." Against such people, he issued an automatic sentence of excommunication.[52]

## Demonic Magic and Inquisition

With John's ruling, a line had been drawn and a seemingly firm boundary erected between the community of faithful Christians and those who entangled themselves with demons, at least through elaborate magical rites. *Super illius specula*, however, was not immediately influential. It was not entered into official canon law, and it remained curiously uncirculated. There are some who suggest John never even authored the document, and that it was only later attributed to him.[53] Certainly neither John nor any pontiff immediately subsequent to him fully unleashed papal inquisitors against the perceived threat of demonic magic.[54] Only decades later did the inquisitor Nicolau Eymeric integrate within an effective legal framework the position that almost any kind of engagement with demons in magical rites made one a heretic and set one unquestionable outside the Christian community. He did so in the course of arguing that magicians who invoked demons fell firmly within the jurisdiction of church inquisitors.[55] Eymeric based his position explicitly on *Super illius specula*, quoting the earlier papal decree in full in his enormously influential inquisitor's manual *Directorium inquisitorum* (Directory of Inquisitors) in 1376.[56]

Nicolau Eymeric would be important enough in our story if all he did was serve as the means by which John XXII's decree against demonic magicians was promulgated and began to influence inquisitorial practice. Beyond this, however, he also marks another significant expansion in the underlying notion that involvement with demons inevitably set one outside the bounds of one's religious community, or, to see the process more actively, that religious authorities could deploy accusations of demonic entanglements to draw boundaries around communities and set certain people outside them. Remarkably for a Christian inquisitor, he argued that this process should by no means be restricted to the Christian community alone.

A native Catalan, Eymeric served for most of his career as an inquisitor in the crown of Aragon.[57] As such, he was particularly well-placed to address the issue of Christian authority over non-Christian peoples, for Aragon and other late medieval Iberian kingdoms had substantial Jewish and Muslim populations. In secular matters, these communities were under royal jurisdiction, being considered the special property of the crown, or "royal treasure."[58] Regarding spiritual matters, however, the question of jurisdiction was more complicated. A fairly straightforward argument existed that individuals could not be subject to the authority of the Christian church if they were not, in fact, members of that community. Specifically regarding the jurisdiction of inquisitors, one standard position was that no one could be a heretic who had not been baptised into the Christian faith.[59] Such a fundamental limitation did not satisfy Eymeric, who looked to expand the jurisdiction of papal inquisitors in every way possible, arguing that they should be empowered to respond to almost any perceived threats to Christian society.[60]

Various mechanisms existed by the late 14th century whereby an inquisitor could act against a non-Christian. In the main, these applied to Jews and Muslims who had converted to Christianity and then were suspected of reverting to the practices of their former faith.[61] Inquisitors could also act against Jews or Muslims who sought to win converts from Christianity, or if they degraded or disparaged Christian teachings in any public way.[62] Eymeric championed a broader principle, as well. He argued that if non-Christians violated any basic tenet of their own faith while living under overarching Christian control, Christian inquisitors could and should step in to discipline them.

This position was not entirely unknown in inquisitorial thinking, but Eymeric focused on his favoured issue of demonic invocation. Since honouring or worshiping demons in any way clearly violated a tenet common to all three Abrahamic monotheisms, the Catalan inquisitor found it an ideal test-case to work with, and he continued to refine his arguments in this area for much of his career. Having written first about demonic invocation among Christians in a treatise *Contra christianos demones invocantes* (Against Christians Invoking Demons) in 1359, he then extended his arguments against non-Christians (mainly Jews) in *Contra infideles demones invocantes* (Against Infidels Invoking Demons), written probably around 1370.[63] He returned to the issue again in *Tractatus brevis super iurisdictione inquisitorum contra infideles fidem catholicam agitantes* (Short Treatise About the Jurisdiction of Inquisitors Against Infidels Troubling the Catholic Faith), written in the 1380s.[64] As with Christian demonic invocation, however, his most influential statements on this subject came when he summarised these more focused treatises in certain sections of his *Directorium inquisitorum*.[65] Here was a Christian authority arguing that involvement with demons was inevitably so pernicious that it served to set any person—Christian, Jew, or Muslim—outside of any religious community. And again, more practically, this line of argument meant that authorities could use allegations of demonic entanglements to cast people out of those communities as well.

Most importantly of all, perhaps, Eymeric fully articulated a theory whereby any act of magic that authorities could conceive as entailing some kind of interaction with demons could and indeed must then be deemed heretical. The nature of the heresy was not the interaction with demons per se, but rather, as John's commission had previously determined, the suspicion that some demonstration of adoration or reverence adhered to that interaction. As he so often did in his manual for inquisitors, Eymeric simplified a complex point. Merely "to invoke is considered an act of adoration," he wrote, and "therefore, if a demon is invoked by a Christian...such people must be considered heretics."[66] He gave many examples of overt worship and sacrifice that he thought magicians offered to demons: "by genuflecting, by prostrating themselves, by observing chastity out of reverence for the demon...by lighting candles, by burning incense or spices or other aromatics, by sacrificing birds or other animals."[67] Such demonstrative rituals were not necessary, however, and "from this it is clear that to invoke and consult demons, even without sacrifice, is apostasy from the faith, and as a consequence, heresy."[68]

In support of this idea, Eymeric could draw on a tradition extending back to Christian thinkers such as Thomas Aquinas, and ultimately to Augustine, that one could enter into a pact with demons tacitly as well as expressly.[69] This meant in practice that authorities did not need to limit their suspicions of demonic entanglements to instances of complex ritual magic, such as John XXII had feared at his court. Even the simplest magical acts performed by ordinary Christians might be thought to mask full-blown diabolism. This development would find its grim conclusion in an intensely demonised notion of witchcraft that coalesced in the 15th century.

## Diabolical Witchcraft

The emergence of what has often been called diabolical or conspiratorial witchcraft in the early 15th century is well-studied.[70] Within just a few years, numerous authorities developed the notion that witches were not individual malefactors working discrete harm by magical means (*maleficium*) but rather members of large, overtly heretical sects meeting at secret conventicles to worship demons or the devil himself. What became the most pervasive stereotype, ultimately spreading across much of Europe, was first articulated in a tightly clustered group of sources all describing sects of witches operating in regions around the western Alps.[71] The number of alleged witches can be startling. One magistrate conducting witch trials around Briançon, in the French region of Dauphiné, claimed to have identified and convicted more than 100 in just a few years.[72] Another author, writing about trials in the nearby region of Valais, asserted more than 100 executions in just over a single year, and stated that convicted witches testified to there being more than 700 members of their sect in this region overall.[73]

At their imagined diabolical conventicles, eventually referred to as sabbaths but more typically labelled synagogues in the earliest sources, witches performed any number of horrific acts. They engaged in depraved sexual orgies with each other and attendant demons, "join[ing] together carnally, man with woman, or man with man, and sometimes father with daughter, son with mother, brother with sister, and with the proper order of nature scarcely being observed," as one text described it.[74] They also murdered children, spirited the corpses away to their gatherings, and cooked and devoured them. As one particularly gruesome passage would have it, they "boil them [children] in a cauldron until, with the bones removed, nearly all the flesh is rendered such that it can be slurped up or drunk."[75] Not least, they submitted themselves to the devil, body and soul, renouncing their Christian faith and often trampling on or otherwise desecrating the cross or eucharist to demonstrate their apostasy.

The point of these horror stories was to make ostensibly manifest how associating oneself with the devil led to all other perversions and represented the complete inversion of what a good Christian should be.[76] The components of the stereotype came from folklore (particularly in terms of night-time journeys and interaction with spirits of various kinds), but also, as Moore observed, from allegations long deployed in the persecution of heretics and Jews.

There is one notable difference, however, between diabolical witches and those previously persecuted groups. Leaving imagined associations with the devil aside, Jews were nevertheless obviously not Christians. That did not, of course, necessitate their increasingly harsh separation from the Christian communities that surrounded them, but a basic and real boundary did stand between them and their neighbours. When authorities invented diabolical connections, they enhanced a separation that already existed. With heretics, scholarly arguments rage about whether or not the essential features of many heresies were just as completely imagined by authorities as were sects of diabolical witches.[77] Yet at least within the minds of those authorities, there was some fundamental error of belief, aside from attendant allegations of diabolism, that separated heretics from the larger community of the Christian faithful.

With charges of diabolism directed against magicians, we see something different. Learned magicians—whether they actually engaged in ritual magic or were merely accused of such crimes—were almost always clerics, for in the Middle Ages generally only clergy had the requisite Latin literacy and ritual training to perform such magic. In the absence of any allegations of demonic entanglements, they were very much members of their respective communities, ensconced within ecclesiastical institutions and often in the ambit of courtly centres of power. Admittedly, they often existed at the margins of these communities, but it was only the charge of diabolism that set them fully outside.[78]

What of witches? Here too I would suggest that it was the charge of diabolism that fundamentally created a boundary that otherwise would not have existed or even been imagined to exist. Minus entanglement with demons, a person simply was not a witch (in terms of the stereotype of diabolical witchcraft examined here). Indeed, during the height of the early modern witch trials in many jurisdictions it was possible for a person to be identified as a witch—that is, as a member of a diabolical sect—without any allegation of witchcraft in the sense of some discrete act of harmful magic or *maleficium* having been brought. The dark brilliance of this system, as a mechanism for exclusion and persecution, was precisely the fact that anyone could theoretically fall victim.

In practice, of course, most accused witches shared certain demographic and social characteristics: old more often than young, poor more often than rich, women more often than men, and generally already in some way marginalised or disreputable within their communities. In some cases it may have been an association with magical practices that made them so. One of our earliest sources for diabolical witchcraft describes what many experts would accept as exemplifying later patterns as well. Beyond the horrors that they supposedly committed at their sabbaths, accused witches also "relieve many troubled people from [some] kind of malady, on account of which relief they say that previously, before such an investigation as this, people called upon them as soothsayers and they received responses from the dead."[79] That is, they were healers and diviners offering their communities what were originally regarded as mostly positive, beneficial magical services, until "such an investigation as this," conducted by authorities who strove to associate them powerfully with the devil.

Like learned magicians described above, such cunning-folk, as they are often called in English, might not have been the most respected members of their communities.[80] While they offered useful services, they claimed to wield uncanny power that could make their neighbours more than a little nervous. They did still operate within those communities, however, and the purpose of wild charges of diabolism that could be brought against them in the course of witch trials was precisely to create a fundamental boundary between them and their neighbours where none had previously existed.

## Agents of Persecution

Why was this terrible mechanism of exclusion developed and deployed? The reasons are manifold.[81] To keep the issue contained, let me return to Moore and hew closely to one of his explanations for the development of a "persecuting society" in Europe overall. While some classic sociological models argue that the impetus to persecute and exclude certain groups can arise more or less organically from a community as a whole, Moore rejects this. He sees the process as more top-down, driven by powerful institutions seeking to restrict to themselves the right to employ violence and coercion. One consequence is that authorities often reframe individual infractions against specific victims as more abstract offences against the entire social order.[82] We certainly see this in the diabolisation of witchcraft, with the figure of the witch elevated from someone who supposedly performed discrete acts of *maleficium* that harmed individuals to an agent of cosmic evil. We have also seen that, while individual practitioners of magic might have been viewed with some trepidation by their communities, it took powerful agencies to impose the idea that they were heretical servants of the devil.

Moore then went further, arguing that it was not powerful institutions per se that drove persecution, but rather a particular set of agents within them: the newly ascendant literate clerks of the 11th, 12th, and 13th centuries.[83] These men staffed the increasingly bureaucratic courts of this period. They developed the new methods of coercion and exclusion that characterised the "persecuting society" precisely because they, as a class, were new to power, compared to their masters, the traditional secular aristocracy and princes of the church. As newcomers, they were uncertain about the extent of their power and their place.

Since originally articulating his theory, Moore himself has questioned and reconfigured certain aspects of it.[84] To what extent, though, do his ideas apply to growing concern over demonic magic in the 14th and 15th centuries? We might observe an immediate contradiction, as the first sections of this chapter outline concerns about demonic magic at the very upper end of certain echelons of power: kings and princes, intellectual and theological elites, and ultimately the papal court under John XXII. We should note, however, that while such elites provided a basis for later action, they were rarely the immediate agents of much effective persecution. Even the fulminations of John XXII lay idle for half a century before they were revived by Nicolau Eymeric.

With Eymeric we have a figure who fits Moore's pattern more closely. Not that he was a bureaucrat trying to carve out a place for himself within a courtly power structure. As an inquisitor, however, he frequently clashed with the crown of Aragon over the scope of his authority. He repeatedly found himself removed from and then reinstated to office, and he also endured several periods of exile from Aragon.[85] His efforts to extend inquisitorial jurisdiction over groups he presented as engaging with demons emerged from this fraught context. Half a century later, some of our earliest sources articulating the idea of diabolical witchcraft were also associated with inquisitors attempting to establish the scope of their jurisdiction, specifically new inquisitorial tribunals in Lausanne and Lyon. While inquisitors in Lausanne seem to have succeeded rather spectacularly, the attempt in Lyon appears to have failed, as traditional elites, including the bishop and secular city officials, rejected this fabulous new stereotype and the claim to power that it represented.[86]

Secular officials who deployed the idea of diabolical witchcraft fall into a similar pattern. A cluster of trials was reported in the Simme Valley, which lay in the mountains south of the city of Bern, in the early 15th century. Civic magistrates were, in fact, just beginning to extend their authority into the city's Alpine hinterland at this time.[87] At roughly the same time in the Alpine regions of French Dauphiné, a royal magistrate was using witch trials to extend his jurisdiction there, arguing that witches' supposed affiliation with the devil represented not just heresy against the church but also a form of treason against the crown.[88] Towards the end of the 15th century, and returning to the inquisitorial side of things, the infamous Heinrich Kramer had just been stymied in his attempt to conduct a witch hunt around Innsbruck by the local bishop when he retreated to Cologne to pen his diabolical masterpiece, *Malleus maleficarum* (Hammer of Witches).[89]

Charges of demonic magic and diabolical witchcraft were far from the only ways that fear of the devil manifested in late medieval and subsequently in early modern Europe. Nor were magicians and witches the only people to find themselves cut out of their community by allegations of some supposed association with the devil. Yet magicians and witches may represent this process in its purest form, for without the implication of diabolism that persecuting elites laid on them, there was almost nothing to set these people apart from their neighbours. John of Morigny thought he had safely rejected all illicit magic and practiced only appropriate Christian devotion until other groups forcefully condemned his writings. Likewise, at least some accused witches were probably people who claimed particular expertise in common magical practices that their neighbours might also have employed to some degree themselves.

The persecuting society that Moore saw developing in the 11th, 12th, and 13th centuries was founded on the demonisation of what were already perceived, in one way or another, as outsider groups. The late medieval period saw this process of demonisation expand into a primary criterion that created new groups open to persecution and exclusion. Throughout the early modern period, at least until the intellectual shifts wrought by the Enlightenment, this particular imagining of the devil stood at the boundaries of many Christian communities and marked those within from those without.

## Notes

1  Richard Raiswell and Peter Dendle place the devil in various "cultural contexts" based on his relative "potency" and "malevolence" in "Epilogue: Inscribing the Devil in Cultural Contexts," in *The Devil in Society in Premodern Europe*, ed. Raiswell and Dendle (Toronto, 2012), 537–51.
2  1 Corinthians 10.20.
3  Mainly in book 8 of *City of God*; Augustine also addressed demonic power in *De divinatione daemonum*.
4  See e.g. David Brakke, *Demons and the Making of the Monk: Spiritual Combat in Early Christianity* (Cambridge, MA, 2006). For a brief sketch of paganism in this period, see Ian N. Wood, "Pagan Religions and Superstitions East of the Rhine from the Fifth to the Ninth Century," in *After Empire: Towards an Ethnology of Europe's Barbarians*, ed. Giorgio Ausenda (Woodbridge, 1995), 253–68. On pagan survivals within Christian society, see Yitzhak Hen, *Culture and Religion in Merovingian Gaul A.D. 481–751* (Leiden, 1995), chap. 6; Bernadette Filotas, *Pagan Survivals, Superstitions and Popular Cultures in Early Medieval Pastoral Literature* (Toronto, 2005).
5  Jeffrey Burton Russell, *Lucifer: The Devil in the Middle Ages* (Ithaca, 1984), esp. chap. 10; Philip Almond, *The Devil: A New Biography* (Ithaca, 2014), chap. 4. Robert Muchembled, *A History of the Devil: From the Middle Ages to the Present*, trans. Jean Birrell (Cambridge, 2003), essentially begins in the late medieval period.
6  See the foreword to *Dämonische Besessenheit: Zur Interpretation eines kulturhistorischen Phänomens*, eds. Hans de Waardt et al. (Bielefeld, 2005), 7. On late medieval developments, see Nancy Caciola, *Discerning Spirits: Divine and Demonic Possession in the Middle Ages* (Ithaca, 2003), 312–3; Dyan Elliott, *Proving Woman: Female Spirituality and Inquisitional Culture in the Later Middle Ages* (Princeton, 2004).
7  Caciola, *Discerning Spirits* and Elliott, *Proving Woman*, both have much to say about women mystics. Barbara Newman, "Possessed by the Spirit: Devout Women, Demoniacs, and the Apostolic Life in the Thirteenth Century," *Speculum* 73 (1998): 733–70, identified a key shift as early as the 13th century. See also Dyan Elliott, *The Bride of Christ Goes to Hell: Metaphor and Embodiment in the Lives of Pious Women, 200–1500* (Philadelphia, 2012), esp. chap. 7.
8  Stuart Clark, "Inversion, Misrule, and the Meaning of Witchcraft," *Past and Present* 87 (1980): 98–127; Clark, *Thinking with Demons: The Idea of Witchcraft in Early Modern Europe* (Oxford, 1997), esp. chaps. 2–6.
9  R. I. Moore, *The Formation of a Persecuting Society: Authority and Deviance in Western Europe, 950–1250*, 2nd ed. (Oxford, 2007), addresses its own influence in a new chap. 5 (pp. 144–71) and its concluding "Bibliographical Excursus" (pp. 172–96). Further on its reception, see *Beyond the Persecuting Society: Religious Toleration Before the Enlightenment*, eds. John Christian Laursen and Cary J. Nederman (Philadelphia, 1998); and *Heresy and the Persecuting Society in the Middle Ages: Essays on the Work of R. I. Moore*, ed. Michael Frassetto (Leiden, 2006), although the latter focuses mainly on Moore's earlier work on medieval heresy.
10  Charges of heresy never completely disappeared. For an informative case study, see Matthew Gillis, *Heresy and Dissent in the Carolingian Empire: The Case of Gottschalk of Orbais* (Oxford, 2017), reference to Moore at 6–7.

11 Aside from Moore's own summary, see standard surveys such as Malcolm Lambert, *Medieval Heresy: Popular Movements from the Gregorian Reform to the Reformation*, 3rd ed. (Oxford, 2002); Christine Caldwell Ames, *Medieval Heresies: Christianity, Judaism, and Islam* (Cambridge, 2015).

12 Moore, *Formation*, 61.

13 Addressed more broadly by Moore himself in *The First European Revolution, c. 970–1215* (Oxford, 2000).

14 Moore, *Formation*, 154.

15 Moore, *Formation*, 4–5, 85 and 137. For some further connections, see Raisa Maria Toivo, "The Witch Craze as Holocaust: The Rise of Persecuting Societies," in *Witchcraft Historiography*, ed. Jonathan Barry and Owen Davies (Basingstoke, 2007), 90–107.

16 On connections between heresy and witchcraft in the 14th and 15th centuries, see Kathrin Utz Tremp, *Von der Häresie zur Hexerei: "Wirkliche" und imaginäre Sekten im Spätmittelalter* (Hannover, 2008).

17 Richard Kieckhefer, *Magic in the Middle Ages*, 3rd ed. (Cambridge, 2022), 208–12. The term most commonly employed in medieval texts is *nigromantia*, which might also be translated as "black magic," but it seems clear that *nigro-* was a garbling of the Greek *necro-*, technically referring to divination via spirits of the dead. See also Frank Klaassen, "Necromancy," in *The Routledge History of Medieval Magic*, ed. Sophie Page and Catherine Rider (London, 2019), 201–11.

18 For an overview of this process, see Michael D. Bailey, "Diabolic Magic," in *The Cambridge History of Magic and Witchcraft in the West: From Antiquity to the Present*, ed. David J. Collins (Cambridge, 2015), 361–92; on earlier conflation of this kind of magic with superstition, see Michael D. Bailey, *Fearful Spirits, Reasoned Follies: The Boundaries of Superstition in Late Medieval Europe* (Ithaca, 2013), 35–70. As an example of one influential Arabic magical text translated into Latin, see *Picatrix: A Medieval Treatise on Astral Magic*, ed. and trans. Dan Attrell and David Porreca (University Park, 2019).

19 Karl Manitius, "Magie und Rhetorik bei Anselm von Besate," *Deutsches Archiv für Erforschung des Mittelalters* 12 (1956): 52–72; Edward Peters, *The Magician, the Witch, and the Law* (Philadelphia, 1978), 21–8.

20 John of Salisbury, *Policraticus* 2.28, in *Corpus Christianorum Continuatio Mediaevalis* 118, ed. K. S. B. Keats-Rohan (Turnhout, 1993), 167–8.

21 In addition to Kieckhefer on the "clerical underworld," see Peters, *Magician*, 112–25, on the magical "demimonde" at many courts.

22 For a broader argument about how magic, even demonic magic, might be situated as a part of Christian spiritualty rather than opposed to it, see Michael D. Bailey, "Was Magic a Religious Movement?" in *The Sacred and the Sinister: Studies in Medieval Religion and Magic*, ed. David J. Collins (University Park, 2019), 143–62.

23 Mark 3.15, Luke 9.1.

24 Aquinas, *Summa theologiae* 2.2.90.2, 2.2.92.2. The terminology of *societas* with demons goes back at least to Augustine, *De doctrina Christiana* 2.23(36), *Corpus Christianorum Series Latina* 32, ed. Joseph Martin (Turnhout: Brepols, 1962); and more basically to Paul's injunction (see note 2) that Christians not make themselves "fellows" of demons (*socios* in the medieval Vulgate).

25 In the 14th century, the inquisitor Nicolau Eymeric referenced it in his *Contra demonum invocatores*, MS Paris, Bibliothèque nationale de France, Lat. 1464, fols. 100r-161r, at 156r-159v. In the 15th century, it was picked up by many others, including the chancellor of the University of Paris, Jean Gerson, *De erroribus circa artem magicam*, in Gerson, *Oeuvres complètes*, ed. P. Glorieux, 10 vols. (Paris, 1960–73), 10:84–5; the Dominican theologian Johannes Nider, *Preceptorium divine legis* 1.11.29 (Milan, 1489); and the Carthusian Jakob of Paradise, *De potestate demonum*, MS Munich, Bayerische Staatsbibliothek, Clm 18378, fols. 245r-272r, at fols. 259v-260r. See Bailey, *Fearful Spirits*, 167.

26 See Nicolas Weill-Parot, "Cecco d'Ascoli and Antonio da Montolmo: The Building of a 'Nigromantical' Cosmology and the Birth of the Author-Magician," *The Routledge History of Medieval Magic*, ed. Sophie Page and Catherine Rider (London, 2019), 225–36.

27 For example, the so-called Munich Handbook, examined in Richard Kieckhefer, *Forbidden Rites: A Necromancer's Manual of the Fifteenth Century* (University Park, 1998).

28 For the text and extensive introductions, see John of Morigny, *Liber florum celestis doctrine: The Flowers of Heavenly Teaching*, ed. Claire Fanger and Nicholas Watson (Toronto, 2015). On the

reconstruction of textual variants, see Claire Fanger, *Rewriting Magic: An Exegesis of the Visionary Autobiography of a Fourteenth-Century French Monk* (University Park, 2015).

29  John of Morigny, *Liber florum*, 158.

30  Julien Véronèse, *L'Ars notoria au Moyen Âge: Introduction et édition critique* (Florence, 2007).

31  John of Morigny, *Liber florum*, 158–9.

32  John of Morigny, *Liber florum*, 161.

33  On John's complicated view of necromancy, see Fanger, *Rewriting Magic*, esp. chap. 5; also Claire Fanger, "*Libri Nigromantici*: The Good, the Bad, and the Ambiguous in John of Morigny's *Flowers of Heavenly Teaching*," *Magic, Ritual, and Witchcraft* 7 (2012): 164–89.

34  John of Morigny, *Liber florum*, 154.

35  John of Morigny, *Liber florum*, 336.

36  John of Morigny, *Liber florum*, 168.

37  John of Morigny, *Liber florum*, 298.

38  John of Morigny, *Liber florum*, 320.

39  Nicholas Watson, "John the Monk's *Book of Visions of the Blessed and Undefiled Virgin Mary, Mother of God*: Two Versions of a Newly Discovered Ritual Magic Text," in *Conjuring Spirits: Texts and Traditions of Medieval Ritual Magic*, ed. Claire Fanger (University Park, 1998), 163–215 at 164.

40  Alain Provost, "On the Margins of the Templars' Trial: The Case of Bishop Guichard of Troyes," in *The Debate on the Trial of the Templars (1307–1314)*, ed. Jochen Burgtorf, Paul F. Crawford, and Helen J. Nicholson (Farnham, 2010), 117–27.

41  William R. Jones, "Political Uses of Sorcery in Medieval Europe," *The Historian* 34 (1972): 670–87, esp. 676–81; Peters, *Magician*, 120–2.

42  Documents in *Quellen und Untersuchungen zur Geschichte des Hexenwahns und der Hexenverfolgung im Mittelalter*, ed. Joseph Hansen (1901; reprint Hildesheim, 1963), 7–8.

43  Hansen, *Quellen*, 2–4.

44  For various perspectives, see Anneliese Maier, "Eine Verfügung Johannes XXII. über die Zuständigkeit der Inquisition für Zaubereiprozesse," *Archivum Fratrum Praedicatorum* 22 (1952): 226–46; Frans van Liere, "Witchcraft as Political Tool? John XXII, Hugues Géraud, and Matteo Visconti," *Medieval Perspectives* 16 (2001): 165–73; Alain Boureau, *Satan the Heretic: The Birth of Demonology in the Medieval West*, trans. Teresa Lavender Fagan (Chicago, 2006), 8–42; Rainer Decker, *Witchcraft and the Papacy: An Account Drawing from the Formerly Secret Records of the Roman Inquisition*, trans. H. C. Erik Midelfort (Charlottesville, 2008), 23–31.

45  Hansen, *Quellen*, 4–5.

46  Hansen, *Quellen*, 1.

47  The fullest studies are Boureau, *Satan the Heretic*, 43–67; and Isabel Iribarren, "From Black Magic to Heresy: A Doctrinal Leap in the Pontificate of John XXII," *Church History* 76 (2007): 32–60. Documents have been edited in *Le pape et les sorciers: Une consultation de Jean XXII sur la magie en 1320 (Manuscrit B.A.V. Borghese 348)*, ed. Alain Boureau (Rome, 2004).

48  Boureau, *Pape et les sorciers*, 6–7. It should be noted that this argument rests on a highly intellectualised understanding of heresy. In other situations, church authorities often branded people as heretics for what might be called "bad behaviour." See Richard Kieckhefer, "Witchcraft, Necromancy, and Sorcery as Heresy," in *Chasses aux sorcières et démonologie: Entre discours et pratiques (XIVe-XVIIe siècles)*, ed. Martine Ostorero, Georg Modestin, and Kathrin Utz Tremp (Florence, 2010), 133–53.

49  Boureau, *Pape et les sorciers*, 32–3.

50  Boureau, *Pape et les sorciers*, 39.

51  Boureau, *Pape et les sorciers*, 34–5, 64–5, 132–3.

52  Hansen, *Quellen*, 5.

53  Patrick Nold, "Thomas Braunceston O.M./O.P.," in *Kirchenbild und Spiritualität: Dominikanische Beiträge zur Ekklesiologie und zum kirchlichen Leben in Mittelalter*, ed. Thomas Prügl and Marianne Schlosser (Paderborn: Schöningh, 2007), 179–95. Against this, see Boureau, *Satan the Heretic*, 12–4; Bailey, *Fearful Spirits*, 79–80. The best analysis is now Derek Hill, *Inquisition in the Fourteenth Century: The Manuals of Bernard Gui and Nicholas Eymerich* (York, 2019), 182–6.

54  Hill, *Inquisition in the Fourteenth Century*, 187.

55 His fullest consideration of the issue is in *Contra demonum invocatores* (see note 25) written in 1359, on which see Julien Véronèse, "Nigromance et hérésie: Le *De jurisdictione inquisitorum in et contra christianos demones invocantes (1359)* de Nicolas Eymerich (O.P.)," in *Penser avec les démons: Démonologues et démonologies (XIIIe-XVIIe siècles)*, ed. Martine Ostorero and Julien Véronèse (Florence, 2015), 5–56. His most influential statement came in *Directorium inquisitorum* 2.42–43, ed. F. Peña (Rome, 1587), 335–48, written in 1376. For recent analysis, see Hill, *Inquisition in the Fourteenth Century*, esp. 180–205; Pau Castell Grenados, "The Inquisitor's Demons: Nicolau Eymeric's *Directorium inquisitorum*," in *The Science of Demons: Early Modern Authors Facing Witchcraft and the Devil*, ed. Jan Machielsen (London, 2020), 19–34.

56 Eymeric, *Directorium inquisitorum* 2.43.9, pp. 341–2.

57 Regarding the scope of his authority, see Claudia Heimann, *Nicolaus Eymerich (vor 1320–1399), praedicator veridicus, inquisitor intrepidus, doctor egregius: Leben und Werk eines Inquisitors* (Münster, 2001), 18–9.

58 A classic study is John Boswell, *The Royal Treasure: Muslim Communities Under the Crown of Aragon in the Fourteenth Century* (New Haven, 1977).

59 Michael D. Bailey, "Muslims in Medieval Inquisitorial Thought: Nicolau Eymeric and His Contexts," *Church History* 90 (2021): 1–20 at 2.

60 Hill, *Inquisition in the Fourteenth Century*, 172–3.

61 Eymeric summarised these in *Directorium inquisitorum* 2.44–5, pp. 348–52.

62 The central papal pronouncement here, addressing Jews, was *Turbato corde*, issued in 1267. See Jeremy Cohen, *The Friars and the Jews: The Evolution of Medieval Anti-Judaism* (Ithaca, 1982), 48–9.

63 First identified in Josep Perarnau, "Tres nous tractats de Nicolau Eimeric en un volum de les seves 'Opera omnia' manuscrites procedent de Sant Domènec de Girona," *Revista Catalana de Teologia* 4 (1979): 79–100; now partially edited in Katelyn Mesler, "The Jurisdiction of Medieval Inquisitors over Jews and Muslims: Nicholas Eymeric's *Contra infideles demones invocantes*," in *The Sacred and the Sinister: Studies in Medieval Religion and Magic*, ed. David J. Collins (University Park, 2019), 163–99.

64 Josep Perarnau i Espelt, "El *Tractatus brevis super iurisdictione inquisitorum contra infideles fidem catholicam agitantes* de Nicolau Eimeric," *Arxiu de Textos Catalans Antics* 1 (1982): 79–126.

65 Eymeric, *Directorium inquisitorum* 2.46, pp. 352–58.

66 Eymeric, *Directorium inquisitorum* 2.43.14, p. 343.

67 Eymeric, *Directorium inquisitorum* 2.43.2, p. 338.

68 Eymeric, *Directorium inquisitorum* 2.43.7, p. 339.

69 Aquinas, *Summa theologiae* 2.2.90.2, 2.2.92.2.

70 Recent overviews include Hans Peter Broedel, "Fifteenth-Century Witch Beliefs," and Richard Kieckhefer, "The First Wave of Trials for Diabolical Witchcraft," both in *The Oxford Handbook of Witchcraft in Early Modern Europe and Colonial America*, ed. Brian P. Levack (Oxford, 2013), 32–49 and 159–78; Martine Ostorero, "Witchcraft," in *The Routledge History of Medieval Magic*, ed. Sophie Page and Catherine Rider (London, 2019), 502–22; Martine Ostorero, "The Rise of Witchcraft Doctrine," in *The Routledge History of Witchcraft*, ed. Johannes Dillinger (London, 2020), 61–78.

71 These sources are translated and analysed in Michael D. Bailey, *Origins of the Witches' Sabbath* (University Park, 2021). On the spread of the stereotype, see Martine Ostorero, *Le diable au sabbat: Littérature démonologique et sorcellerie (1440–1460)* (Florence, 2011). Another stereotype developed in northern Italy and proved influential in Mediterranean lands; see Richard Kieckhefer, "Mythologies of Witchcraft in the Fifteenth Century," *Magic, Ritual, and Witchcraft* 1 (2006): 79–108.

72 Bailey, *Origins of the Witches' Sabbath*, 42.

73 Bailey, *Origins of the Witches' Sabbath*, 32.

74 Bailey, *Origins of the Witches' Sabbath*, 46.

75 Bailey, *Origins of the Witches' Sabbath*, 64.

76 See note 8.

77 I refer mainly to debates about 12th- and 13th-century Catharism. For Moore's position, see his *The War on Heresy* (Cambridge, 2012). For an overview, see Antonio Sennis, ed., *Cathars in Question* (York, 2016).

78 See Kieckhefer, *Magic in the Middle Ages*, 208–12; or Peters, *Magician*, 112–25.

79 Bailey, *Origins of the Witches' Sabbath*, 38. Unfortunately, the text, as least as it survives, offers no clue as to what malady is meant.

80 An early and still essential study is Keith Thomas, *Religion and the Decline of Magic* (New York, 1971). Into the modern period, see Owen Davies, *Cunning-Folk: Popular Magic in English History* (London, 2003). Most recently on the subset of "service magicians," see Tabitha Stanmore, *Love Spells and Lost Treasure: Service Magic in England from the Later Middle Ages to the Early Modern Era* (Cambridge, 2023).

81 See Robin Briggs, "'Many Reasons Why': Witchcraft and the Problem of Multiple Explanation," in *Witchcraft in Early Modern Europe: Studies in Culture and Belief,* ed. Jonathan Barry, Marianne Hester, and Gareth Roberts (Cambridge, 1996), 49–63.

82 Moore, *Formation*, 100–6.

83 Moore, *Formation*, 127–32

84 See esp. the final chapter and "excursus" on "Debating the Persecuting Society" he added to the second edition; Moore, *Formation*, 144–96.

85 The fullest account of his life and career is Heimann, *Nicolaus Eymerich*. On his political difficulties, see also Michael A. Ryan, *A Kingdom of Stargazers: Astrology and Authority in the Late Medieval Crown of Aragon* (Ithaca, 2011), esp. chap. 5.

86 Franck Mercier and Martine Ostorero, *L'énigme de la Vauderie de Lyon: Enquête sur l'essor de la chasse aux sorcières entre France et Empire (1430–1480)* (Florence, 2015), 260–70.

87 Arno Borst, "The Origins of the Witch-craze in the Alps," in Borst, *Medieval Worlds: Barbarians, Heretics, and Artists in the Middle Ages,* trans. Eric Hansen (Chicago, 1992), 101–22.

88 Pierrette Paravy, *De la chrétienté romaine a la Réforme en Dauphiné: Évêques, fidèles et déviants (vers 1340-vers 1530)*, 2 vols. (Rome, 1993), 2:795–97.

89 Richard Kieckhefer, "Magic at Innsbruck: The Case of 1485 Reexamined," in *Religion und Magie in Ostmitteleuropa: Spielräume theologischer Normierungsprozesse in Spätmittelalter und Früher Neuzeit*, ed. Thomas Wünsch (Münster, 2006), 11–29; Christopher S. Mackay, *"An Unusual Inquisition": Translated Documents from Heinricus Institoris's Witch Hunts in Ravensburg and Innsbruck* (Leiden, 2020).

## Recommended Readings

Bailey, Michael D., "Diabolic Magic," in *The Cambridge History of Magic and Witchcraft in the West: From Antiquity to the Present*, ed. David J. Collins (Cambridge: Cambridge University Press, 2015), 361–92.

Boureau, Alain, *Satan the Heretic: The Birth of Demonology in the Medieval West*, trans. Teresa Lavender Fagan (Chicago: University of Chicago Press, 2006).

Fanger, Claire, *Rewriting Magic: An Exegesis of the Visionary Autobiography of a Fourteenth-Century French Monk* (University Park: Pennsylvania State University Press, 2015).

Kieckhefer, Richard, *Magic in the Middle Ages*, 3rd ed. (Cambridge: Cambridge University Press, 2022).

Moore, R. I., *The Formation of a Persecuting Society: Authority and Deviance in Western Europe, 950-1250*, 2nd ed. (Oxford: Blackwell, 2007).

Utz Tremp, Kathrin, *Von der Häresie zur Hexerei: "Wirkliche" und imaginäre Sekten im Spätmittelalter* (Hannover: Hahnsche Buchhandlung, 2008).

# 6

# PLACING SATAN

*Eileen Gardiner*

This chapter will seek to define the physical place that, in the Western imagination, Satan is thought to inhabit. It will first reflect on gods and spirits from other traditions who function in similar capacities and may have influenced our notion of Satan or share an archetypal essence with him. It will then examine Satan's emergence from Western sources. Biblical texts, both canonical and non-canonical, present a complex narrative that reveals Satan as a contradictory character. Certain episodes show him wandering the earth either testing humanity in the service of God or tempting humankind as a free agent of evil. Others, including the fall of Satan, the harrowing of hell, and the Last Judgement, place and restrain the devil in hell, where he is locked as a prisoner without hope of freedom or change. This chapter will examine those texts and their relationship to the literature and graphic arts that interpret those texts during the medieval period. It will consider the nature and purpose of the underworld to which Satan, as the embodiment of evil, is ultimately consigned as well as the role that he plays therein. This underworld evolved from the land of the dead into a vast and complex terrain of pain and punishment. To understand this transformation, we will also consider the literature and imaginative geography of otherworld visions, which flourished from the 6th century to their culmination in Dante's *Divine Comedy*.

## Underworld Gods before Satan

In whatever way we choose to parse the origins of Satan in the West, we will discover that this multifaceted devil emerges from a long and ancient complex of analogous traditions. He is related to the Greek god Hades, the Roman Orcus, and the Scandinavian Hel, all gods of their eponymous underworld. These gods rule over that world, which is the ultimate destination of the dead. It is not so much a place of pain and punishment as a place of want and lack, a grey region encircled by rivers, where the shades or souls of the dead wander without hope. These ancient Western gods dwell in their palaces in the underworld, but their roles are otherwise vague. They do not seem to be prisoners of their realms. They oversee neither judgement nor punishment. For punishment, it is necessary to go even deeper, into the Greek Tartarus, a section of the ancient underworld separated from the neutral dwelling place of the dead. Although initially it was the place for the punishment of the rebellious

DOI: 10.4324/9781003096603-7

Titans, by the time of Plato's *Republic* (c. 375 BCE), it would already begin to emerge as a place for the punishment of wicked mortals.[1]

The ancient Near Eastern chthonic gods and goddesses, with names like Death or Irkalla, also ruled over a dark underworld: Kur, a joyless place where there was only dust to eat and drink. Like Hades' bride Persephone, Inanna and Ishtar, goddesses of the ancient Near East, and Baal, a god of the Canaanites, were principally associated with fertility cycles in the plant kingdom. Legends told how these goddesses and gods descended into the netherworld where they were captured and imprisoned. Their subsequent rescue and resurrection would restore fruitfulness to life on earth. Kur may also have served as a great warehouse for dead mortals. This ancient Near Eastern underworld was not conspicuously a place of punishment, although hints of judgement and punishment are evident.[2] Underworld punishment is more obvious in Hinduism, Buddhism, and Taoism, where Yama, the God of death and justice, rules. It is a place where severe torments are inflicted on spirits guilty of crimes, sins, and even trivial misdemeanours as they await the rebirth and reincarnation that are fundamental tenets of these religions of cyclical rather than linear time. This cyclicality means that sometimes, although not always, Yama is also associated with fertility.[3]

The West forges together aspects of these various ancient and often foreign underworld rulers and mixes in its own traditions. Such a fabric of various threads contributed to the contradiction and confusion implicit in the figure of Satan who rules over the world of the dead. Like some, he punishes the dead; unlike others, he is neither a god nor the first human to have died. He is neither a judge of the dead nor a fertility god. This devil is instead an eternal being, once benevolent, who has also served as tester and tempter but is now deprived of power over his own destiny despite his ability to entangle the fate of others to the point of damnation.

## The Biblical Origins of Satan

Satan's long history in the West is an "extraordinary mixture of confusion,"[4] an amalgam of various ideas that might prevail individually at any moment or might even all coincide simultaneously. This complexity is the result of the devil's dual history in the Western tradition. On the one hand is the established textual tradition of the bible. At its broadest, this tradition extends from the Hebrew and Greek Testaments and the Latin Vulgate to all their associated translations and commentaries as well as to the considerable body of non-canonical or semi-canonical texts, apocalyptic and otherwise.[5] On the other hand is the amorphous tradition of poetry, plays, novels, songs, film, paintings, manuscript illuminations, prints, and sculpture. The interplay of these two traditions results in both a tangled history and a multifarious figure variously known as the devil, Satan, Lucifer, Mephistopheles, Belial, and Beelzebub. Except for the fact that he appears to be undeniably male, he is not restricted to any one form and manifests himself as he chooses: from a handsome youth or a beguiling dog to a snake, a worm, or a dragon.

Within the corpus of literary, artistic, and theological works, we also find that Satan is not only associated with hell. Indeed, he is not restricted to any one location. He occupies ever-changing locations as a function of his ever-changing nature. He could be a ruler of the underworld or its most preeminent prisoner. But he could also be in constant motion, wandering in the dark and foggy air. He could be in the forest, within us, or within our enemies. According to the Western perception of his ever-changing location, he appears to be free. Unhindered he may travel through the space of air and earth. At one time, he may have found a place in heaven. But not satisfied with his role there, he risked all and lost, showing himself prone to the very human sins of pride, envy, greed, and arrogance. In the discourse that now surrounds him—one that developed in the West from the Axial Age into Late Modernity—the devil eventually acquired an essential, rather than an ever-changing, nature and became the personification of evil. According to this essential nature, hell has become his place, and there he is bound.[6] In terms of human geography, hell is the space that Satan can be said to inhabit as a *place*.

If we consider the bible, one source for uncertainty about the devil's location becomes clear. It provides few references to the devil that are consistent enough to determine a straightforward narrative. In the Hebrew scriptures, the name *satan*, like the Greek *diabolos*, indicates an individual's role as adversary rather than an individual's name, and the name has been applied to any number of beings, often angels, who block or obstruct individuals.[7] So this Hebrew *Satan* does not correspond to the individual personality of later writings.

While three biblical episodes—the fall of Satan, the harrowing of hell, and the Last Judgement—can be construed to place the individual referred to as Satan in the underworld, other episodes in the bible are less secure in this proposition. For instance, the bible also presents Satan as an active agent on earth. In Job (1:6–7; KJV),[8] the "sons of God" present themselves before God on an appointed day, and *Satan*, so named, is among them. It is unlikely that he is burdened with the reputation of Lucifer, who has presumably already been expelled from heaven, or with the reputation of the serpent, who has certainly already been expelled from paradise. God asks him: "From whence comest thou?" and he responds: "From going to and fro on the earth, and from walking up and down upon it." Although the text indicates that Satan the tester, son of God, will continue walking up and down on the earth, he does not appear again under any of his names in the Hebrew bible. When he emerges in the New Testament, he again walks the earth in the role of tempter. His temptation of Jesus is mentioned briefly in Mark (1:13) and more fully described in both Matthew (4:1–11) and Luke (4:1–13). While the temptations of Job and Jesus present Satan as an adversary and a tester on earth, Matthew (25:41) prepares the way for Satan in hell, mentioning the "everlasting fire, prepared for the devil and his angels."

The apocryphal tradition occasionally hints at a devil in hell. The Coptic *Apocalypse of Zephaniah*[9] (100 BCE–c. 70 CE), a Judeo-Christian text, mentions an accusing angel located in Hades. Although he has been identified as Satan, the identification is not firm.[10] The Judeo-Islamic *Greatness of Moses*[11] (*Gudulat Moshe*, as early as the 1st century CE) describes an angel, the chief of hell, although his name is Nasargiel. Both the *Apocalypse of Peter*[12] (Greek/Ethiopic, mid-2nd century) and *Apocalypse of Paul*[13] (Greek, early 3rd century) mention an angel of torment, who may be Satan. He is named Tartaruchus or Tatîrokos (Greek, Temeluchus), and he is set over hell's torments.

Early Christian texts from the desert fathers often include scenes of Satanic temptation on earth, but evidence of Satan's place in hell emerges as well. In his *Discourses*, Shenoute the Great of Egypt (c. 347–1 July 465) specifically mentions Satan in hell: "What affliction will the sinner not find in hell if he dies in his sins? He is with Satan and his angels in the fiery furnace, which is filled with frost and nakedness, groaning and grief, contempt and condemnation and shame."[14] Shenoute may have believed that this scenario would not occur until the future, after the Last Judgement. Without the concept of the "particular judgement" at death, there would be no need, until the end of time, to place Satan in hell overseeing punishment. However, the idea of the particular judgement is already evident in the New Testament parable of Dives and Lazarus (Lk 16:19–31) and in Jesus' promise to the Good Thief (Lk 23:43): "Verily I say unto thee, today shalt thou be with me in paradise." While the notion of a particular judgement had its roots in Egyptian monastic literature and many Church Fathers, including Tertullian (c. 200) and Augustine (d. 430), held to this view, the particular judgement, which would necessitate Satan's residence in hell before the last days, was slow to develop into dogma.[15]

## The Fall of Satan

The bible refers, or seems to refer, twice to Satan's fall from heaven with his angels. Taken literally, Isaiah 14:4–17 describes the fall of the king of Babylon. However, this has often, although not always, been interpreted as a figurative description of the fall of Lucifer. The Latin text even refers to this king as *Lucifer*, the Morning Star: "How art thou fallen from heaven, O Lucifer, son of the morning? How art thou cut down to the ground." Revelation (12:7–10) mentions the devil's fall, but to earth, not to hell: "And the great dragon was cast out—that serpent of old called the Devil and Satan, which deceiveth the whole world. He was cast out onto the earth, and his angels were cast out with him."

Medieval texts and images embellish this slim history of the devil's fall as found in the bible. Genesis, which describes the serpent tempting Adam and Eve in paradise before their fall, does not equate the serpent with Satan, nor does it mention the fall of Satan, either before or after creation. In the medieval period, however, Satan and his fall were often tied to the creation story. Medieval illuminations of Satan's fall would be included within an assemblage of images depicting the seven days of creation.[16] They show a sky above full of bright, heavenly creatures, including God and the archangel Michael, and black creatures plunging headfirst into a lower world, often depicted as a pit or lake, sometimes with flames, but always full of darkness, a place where Lucifer may already be restrained in chains or even in a cage.[17]

The Old English verse retelling of Genesis provides clear evidence of Satan in an infernal abode. The poem comprises two parts, *Genesis A* and *Genesis B*.[18] Unlike its biblical prototype, *Genesis B*, dating from c. 880 or afterwards, describes Lucifer and his followers cast from heaven into hell before the temptation of Adam and Eve in the Garden of Eden:

> He exiled him then from his favour and cast him into hell,
> into the deep chasm where he changed into a devil,
> the enemy with all his allies. They fell from heaven
> a very long time: three nights and days,
> those angels from heaven into hell—the Lord debased them all into demons.
>
> *(304–9a)*

Once "dearest to his Master," he is now called Satan and is tormented in a dark, narrow place, referred to as "a corpse bed," clearly the abode of the dead. While he is said to rule "over that black abyss of hell," he complains:

> … iron bonds lie about me; I swing in looped chains.
> I am without power—
> These harsh fetters of hell have been clapped fast about me.
> Here is a great fire from above and below.

I have never seen a more loathsome region;
the flame does not blow past. It is hot throughout hell.
A tormenting chain of rings has prevented me from moving,
depriving me of my power to fare forth—my feet are fettered,
my hands are bound. The ways to these hell-doors are barred,
so, I cannot escape at all from these limb-chains.
Huge bolts lie about me, heated and hammered of harsh iron
and with them God has chained me by the neck ....

*(371–85)*

In the Old English poem, *Christ and Satan*,[19] possibly from the late 8th to early 9th century, along with other events involving these two adversaries, the devil is cast from heaven into hell immediately after the story of creation.

English mystery-play cycles of the later Middle Ages put Satan on stage to reenact his fall.[20] These plays again connect the Fall of Satan with the creation myth. The Satan plays always occupy the first place in the lists of plays. The York cycle includes Lucifer's fall as a play of its own presented by the barkers or tanners, *The Fall of the Angels*, where Satan falls into a hell that "... shall never lack darkness."[21] In York's *The Fall*, unlike in Genesis, a devil *(diabolus)* explains how he will assume the form of "a worme" and is thereafter referred to as *Satanas*. He may represent Satan, but this could simply be a reference to the role of a devil as a tempter.[22]

The N-Town and Chester plays combine the fall of Lucifer with the creation play. In the former, God proclaims Lucifer's fate:

Thou, Lucifer, for thy great pride
I bid thee fall from heaven to hell
And all those that chose your side
In my bliss never more to dwell.
At my commandment, now down you slide
With mirth and joy never more to mell.
In mischief and menace ever shall you abide
In bitter burning and fire so fell.
In pain that ever shall bite![23]

Both these plays treat the Fall of Adam and Eve, and each includes a serpent, who, however, is distinct from the demon or devil, who also plays a role.

Although it never mentions "hell," the first play of the Towneley cycle, "The Creation," includes Lucifer's fall along with the creation of the heavens and earth in one long play. Within the play, Adam and Eve are warned about the tree of life, but their fall is not recounted, providing no role there for either devil or serpent.[24]

## The Harrowing of Hell

In addition to Satan's fall, the Western tradition provides another episode placing Satan definitively in hell: the harrowing of hell. Here Jesus, immediately after his death, descends into Hades, the world of the dead, to release the worthy pagans from imprisonment. Several New Testament texts are alleged to refer to the fact that the righteous fathers would be delivered from Hades, and by the 2nd century, the notion was quite widespread. The story might derive from or be related to a group of generic underworld myths like the Sumarian descent of Ishtar, who threatens to break down the doors of Kur to conquer the realm of her sister Ereshkigal.[25]

A full narrative of the Christian harrowing is found in a document attached as an appendix to the 4th-century apocryphal Gospel of Nicodemus (sometimes called the Acts of Pilate).[26] The appendix describes Satan as "the prince of death" and also as the prince of Tartarus and holder of the keys of hell. The scene opens as Satan warns the princes of hell of Christ's imminent arrival. Satan's first impulse is to order his ministers to shut the gates and bar them closed. But he also advises Hell, now personified: "Make thyself ready to receive Jesus." Satan fully expects Jesus to enter the realm of the dead and be subject to both Hell and Satan. Hell is unconvinced and fearful of the man whom he recognises as the one who released Lazarus from his control. Hell tells Satan that this Jesus "is a God strong in command and mighty in manhood, and that he is the savior of mankind. And if thou bring him unto me, he will set free all that are here shut up in the hard prison."[27] He warns Satan that if Jesus enters hell: "Lo, thy destruction draweth near, and I shall at last be cast down and remain without honor; but thou wilt be tormented under my dominion."[28] Satan next announces that the gates of hell should be thrown open, but Hell resists: "Depart from me and go out of mine abode: if thou be a mighty man of war, fight thou against the King of glory."[29] Hell casts Satan out of hell and commands that the gates again be shut and locked. But Jesus bursts open the doors. First, He released the righteous men and women of the past, figures such as Abraham, David, Methuselah, Solomon, the Queen of Sheba, and even Adam and Eve. He left behind the wicked, notably Cain and Judas, in a place of punishment. When he "laid hold of Satan the prince and delivered him unto the power of Hell," Jesus tells Hell: "Satan the prince shall be in thy power unto all ages."[30]

The juxtaposition of Satan and Hell in this narrative separates Satan from his predecessors like Hades and Hel. Here Satan is not identical to the realm that he rules. Instead, he becomes its prisoner, and Hell becomes personified as distinct from Satan. This personification is rare in the Western tradition, but hints of it might be found in the hellmouth motif, a notable motif in the West.[31]

Medieval images of the harrowing of hell use several details mentioned in the Gospel of Nicodemus. A triumphant Christ, who resembles the resurrected Christ bearing a standard topped by a cross and decorated with a flowing banner, bursts the locks on the gates or door of hell as depicted in Fra Angelico's fresco at the Convent of San Marco in Florence. The gates swing into a space occupied by a hellmouth or they are broken apart and cast to the side. Satan may be found either inside the gate, trapped under the feet of the liberated souls, or pinned beneath the fallen hell gates. He might also be pictured outside the gate trampled under Christ's feet. Satan is in chains; these are reminiscent of the ones that restrain Cerberus, the hound of hell, who guards the gates so the dead do not escape. The archangel Michael is sometimes included in the scene. He may be depicted standing by Christ's side and attacking the devil with a spear, reminiscent of his role in the fall of Lucifer, or even with a key opening the hell gate. The Winchester Psalter depicts Michael in both roles.[32]

The hellmouth image, mentioned above, appears in depictions of the harrowing of hell, but also within other scenarios as well, such as the Last Judgement. This mouth seems perennially stretched wide open to receive the damned, fostering the illusion that the damned are swallowed and eaten by this beast. The mouth is large enough to encompass hoards of the dead. The open mouth reveals teeth or fangs, and flames often flash out. Within the mouth, a cauldron set above a fire might contain sinners. And although it is referred to as a hellmouth, it is often more than that: an entire head with staring, wide-open eyes. The mouth is often shaped like a round-hulled boat at the bottom edge of the image so that what lies below the mouth is invisible. Sometimes, it is opened towards the viewer and what is behind the mouth is shrouded in darkness or flames. This animal-like head with whiskers and ears can resemble a dog or perhaps a crocodile with a long pointy snout or even a great fish, somewhat like the leviathan in the story of Jonah. These images can be found in books of hours[33] or in Last Judgement sculptures.[34]

The harrowing of hell story was popular in medieval Europe. In England, the *Gospel of Nicodemus*, mentioned above, was translated into both Old and Middle English. Several Middle English harrowing of hell poems survive.[35] In *Christ and Satan*, Satan is specifically consigned to a place in hell after the harrowing: "at the very bottom/[h]e looked about without hope across that hateful hole …."[36] Among the English mystery plays, Satan appears in the York *Harrowing of Hell*. The stage set would probably have included a hellmouth with Jesus appearing before doors that will fall so he can rescue the righteous. Rather than being in dialogue with the personification of Hell at the approach of Jesus, Satan's interlocuters include Belial, Beelzebub, and two devils. Satan's fate is sealed when Jesus tells him:

> No, fiend, you shall be tied,
> So not far shall you go ….
> Michael, my angel, make him bound.
> Tie down that fiend. He shall not flit.
> And, Devil, I command you go down
> Into your cell where you shall sit.
> Satan is left to acknowledge his fate:
> Alas, for dole and care!
> I sink into Hell's pit![37]

The Towneley cycle's *Harrowing of Hell* tells a similar story, without, however, including Michael.[38] The Chester and N-Town cycles also include a harrowing of hell play. The latter is extremely brief, only 48 lines,[39] while the former is longer, over 300 lines, and includes Satan in conversation with two demons about securing hell against Christ.[40]

Since the creation of hell was not included in the Genesis account of the seven days of creation, when the fall of Satan is told in the context of the creation story, the archfiend is cast out of heaven into the world below. Hell is not always specified as his destination. The harrowing of hell, however, is a clear *terminus ante quem* for finding Satan in hell. With Christ's victory over death, Satan is bound in hell, subject to hell, and yet also its ruler.

## Satan at the Last Judgement

As previously mentioned, Revelation alludes to Satan's fall (12:7–10), but it is less clear about his role in the Last Judgement. He seems to dissolve—if he is there at all. He may be represented by any one or a combination of all of the following: the angel of the church of Ephesus (Rv 2:1–6), a fallen tester; the angel of the church of Smyrna (Rv 2:8–10), a punisher and rehabilitator; the angel of the church of Pergamum (Rv 2:13–14), an angelic ruler of the Roman Empire; the angel of the church of Thyatira (Rv 2:18–23), associated with the "depths of Satan"; or the angel of the church of Sardis (Rv 3:1–5), Philadelphia (Rv 3:7–12), or Laodicea (Rv 3:14–21). He might also be found among the four horsemen in the figures of Death and Hades: "And I looked, and behold a pale horse: and his name that sat on him was Death, and Hell followed with him" (Rv 6:8). He may be the beast from the bottomless abyss or the great dragon. At the end of time, this Satan of the book of Revelation functions as an accuser working with the forces of heaven. He has fallen but is not bound in hell. He has been working on earth, he will be imprisoned in the abyss for a millennium and will return to earth again (Rv 20:1–8); he will be punished eternally in the lake of fire (Rev 20:9–10). The book of Revelation switches tenses, and the gap between what has happened already and what is still to come is fathomless.[41]

Other Apocalypse texts are tied to the names of Zephaniah (100 BCE–c. 70 CE), Peter (mid-2nd century), Ezra (150–850 CE), Paul (3rd century), Baruch (after 550), and Mary (9th century). Though they too fail to delegate a role to Satan at the end time, they are important for the development of ideas about hell. They provided descriptions of gruesome torments that were transferred from a hell at the end of time onto visions of a contemporaneous hell.[42] Fire is the basic element of the end-time punishment, but punishment-by-hanging augments it. Apocalyptic works also informed the landscape of the netherworld—previously described simply as a pit—with rivers, abysses, valleys, and gorges. To simple fire, they added brimstone, pitch, and smoke as well as fiery devices in the hands of demons.[43]

A 4th-century Latin apocalypse called the *Vision of St. Paul* was strongly influenced by Greek ideas of the afterlife found in the earlier *Apocalypse of Paul*. The legend enjoyed widespread dissemination with earlier versions in Syriac, Coptic, and Ethiopic and later versions in almost every European language, including Italian, German, Provençal, Old French and Anglo–Norman, Danish, and Old and Middle English. It had a great influence on later visions and is often referred to within other apocalyptic and otherworld texts.[44] The legend is based on the raptus of Paul (2 Cor 12:1–5) and begins with the discovery of a sealed lead box under Paul's house in Tarsus in 388 CE. The box contains Paul's story of being taken bodily into the otherworld. In hell, he sees a range of sinners: unworthy priests, bishops, deacons, and lectors. Punishments include immersion in a river of fire up to various parts of the body, but there are also worms and dragons that devour sinners and vile pits into which sinners are cast. Paul's vision presents a very early instance of the judgement of individual souls at death.

When the Last Judgement was treated as the final play in the mystery cycles, Satan was notably absent. The Chester and Towneley Last Judgement plays include two demons; the York and N-Town plays bring three devils on stage. But none of these demons takes on the role of the archfiend. In the medieval visual arts, Last Judgement scenes provide more evidence of the devil in the underworld. On the remarkable Romanesque Last Judgement tympanum at the church of Sainte Foy, Conques (after 1120), in addition to a hellmouth, the arch-demon appears raised above those around him, sitting as if enthroned and even crowned with a circle of flames. He appears to be bound by snakes entwined around his legs. Another remarkable medieval image of Satan in a Last Judgement scene is the mosaic ceiling in the Florentine baptistery of San Giovanni (1271–c.1330). To the left of an enthroned Christ, the figure is seated, perhaps even enthroned, on two serpents devouring condemned souls. This group is ensconced in a valley of flames with mountains rising on either side. In other depictions, Satan often appears full-frontal as the central figure in hell. Occasionally a hellmouth is used to represent Satan as the arch-demon, and then it is almost always viewed from the side, with the mouth in the lower right.

## Satan and Hell in the Medieval Imagination

Aside from works based on biblical texts, the Middle Ages also produced works that vastly extended the descriptions of the devil and his place. Early Christian apocalypses fed the imagination of those eager to depict or describe the otherworld fate of sinners. At first, the development of both hellish punishments and landscapes took precedence over the devil himself. These subjects were tempting challenges to writers and artists, each one building upon existing notions and embellishing them, seeking new ways to make netherworld locations and tortures more graphic. As writers described their perceptions of the underworld in works such as the *Vision of Ezra*,[45] artists depicted them on the pages of illuminated manuscripts and on the walls of churches in frescoes and mosaics.[46] These verbal and visual descriptions conjured up a place below, a deep, dark place either at the centre of the earth or at the bottom of the universe. Behind a hellmouth entrance, dungeons, caves, rocky mountains, and gorges with rivers and lakes formed hell's natural environment. Furnaces, ovens, grills, cauldrons, and mills provided constructed places of torture. In this realm inhabited by demons and devils, ice was added to fire as a means of torment.

Measure-for-measure punishment became applied to each sin or crime. Individual parts of the anatomy complicit in these acts became the points for specific retaliation, such as suspension points for hanging. With ropes or chains, souls were suspended over fire by their tongues for sins of the mouth: slander, lying, and blasphemy; by their hair, breasts, or genitals for sexual sins: immodesty, fornication, and adultery; by their ears for eaves-dropping and gossip; by their hands for stealing; and by their eyelids for incest.[47] Hanging could be replaced or supplemented by immersion up to the sinful body part in boiling caul-drons or flaming rivers. Textual banners or captions within images often identify sinners by their sins, while some identified those in hell as Jews, Tartars, and pagans. Sometimes the poses of naked sinners or something they carried served to identify them: naked men and women chained face to face were fornicators; naked men with sacks over their shoulders were thieves; unbalanced scales indicated a dishonest tradesperson. Head coverings could identify the sinner or his or her role in society: crowns for kings and queens, escoffions and chaperons, wimples and helmets, bishops' mitres, cardinals' hats and papal tiaras, hoods and turbans.[48]

The medieval genre of otherworld visions reveals much about the ideas of hell that circulated in Europe from the 6th to the 13th century, providing a vivid roadmap to the development of the netherworld. At least 40 of these visions survive, recording the out-of-body or near-death experiences of religious and lay people who witnessed the rewards and punishments of the afterlife.[49]

From the time of Gregory the Great (c. 540–12 March 604), Christian visions of hell included bridges that spanned the depths. This motif might derive from, but is certainly related to, the Zoroastrian Chinvat Bridge, the place where the soul is judged after death. The bridge stretches from an earthly mountain to heaven above a river. The bridge mani-fests itself as a wide walkway for the good, allowing them to ascend easily, or a sharp and narrow razor-edge for the wicked, who fall into hell. Gregory's vision of the soldier in *Dialogues* 4.37 tells of a bridge over a dark river that emitted a stinking vapour. The wicked, in attempting to cross it, fall into the river, with evil spirits pulling them down by their legs and binding them with weights of iron.

Gregory of Tours' *Vision of Sunniulf,* which dates from 563, describes how the abbot of Randau saw:

> a flaming river, in which from one part of the bank people were streaming ... and there were others up to their waists and still others up to their armpits, and some even up to their chins, crying out with weeping that they were fiercely burned.[50]

The text does not explicitly state how the depth of submersion was tied to individual sins, but such distinctions generally indicated differences of either type or gravity.

Only a fragment survives of the brief late 8th–early 9th-century Old Irish *Vision of Lais-rén*, probably seen by the abbot (d. 638) of the monastery of Leighlin in Carlow. A guardian angel explains to the abbot the differences in the punishments that they see in hell, as:

> the man's soul went into hell itself, even a sea of fire with an unspeakable storm and unspeakable waves upon it. And he saw the souls aflame in that sea, and their heads all above it; and they were wailing and lamenting, crying woe without ceasing throughout the ages. Some of the souls had fiery nails through their tongues, which were sticking out of their heads; others through their ears, others through their eyes.

> Again, he saw others with their mouths gaping, and the demons compelling them with fiery forks .... The man desired to know the difference of the torments. The angel answered at once: "The folk whom thou seest with the fiery nails through their tongues, those are they who have not been praising God or blessing and worshipping Him, and [...] and perjuring themselves and blaspheming and talking vaingloriously and ...."[51]

The text breaks off just as we are about to discover what sins are associated with nails sticking into heads, ears, and eyes.

In time, this single-location underworld of otherworld vision literature expanded with related sinners congregated together and separated from others: *segmented* is the term used by art historians to describe these hells. The texts clearly identified the sinners—calling out murderers, thieves, traitors, and adulterers—or indicated the sins themselves: pride, gluttony, avarice, lust, sloth, wrath, and envy. Eventually each class of sinner had its own location, and these locations became even more specifically defined. By the 12th century, hell had transformed into multi-layered landscapes, each layer addressing a different type of sin. Hell was a long way from being a place of lethargic souls pining away in darkness. It was now inhabited by vicious creatures, as small as insects or as large as giants, who were equipped with every imaginable means of inflicting unending torture, anything from their own sharp teeth and claws to knives, awls, axes, spears and saws, ropes and chains. Although devils and demons abound in these narratives, few, except for several works originating in Ireland, mention Satan or Lucifer specifically, so that much of the development of hell proceeded without any direct allusion to them. The *Fis Adamnán* (Irish, early 10th century) describes a landscape of mountains, caverns, and thorny brakes; plains, bare, and parched, with stagnant, serpent-haunted lakes. The soil is rough and sandy, very rugged, ice-bound. Broad fiery flagstones bestrew the plain. Great seas are there, with horrible abysses.

This vision identifies this as "the devil's constant habitation and abiding-place."[52] According to the *Vision of Merlino,* an undated Irish work, hell has two kings, Lucifer and Beelzebub. Without specifying who rules over which, each rules over five of the ten kingdoms of hell: the lake of death, the land of darkness, lowest hell, the marsh of fire, the land of horror, the unfilled lake, the land of affliction, the dwelling of pains, the fire of poison, and the land of oblivion.

The presence of two devils recurs from time to time within various texts. Sometimes they provided foils for each other, their dialogues helping to elucidate the workings of the underworld. Evidence for this type of dramatic embellishment can be traced to the *Gospel of Nicodemus* where we find the devil in dialog with Hell itself. A second figure also expands the master devil's capabilities and locations, broadening his role in the underworld. This second figure, in addition to either Satan or Lucifer, is sometimes called Beelzebub or Belial. In a handful of works, as we will see later, another beast altogether mirrors the role of the devil.

A Spanish vision from the late 7th century, *The Vision of Bonellus,* includes another rare mention of the devil. The monk Bonellus has told Valerius of Bierzo, who records his vision, how an angel brought him up to heaven where he is promised a place after he dies. Before he returns to this life, however, devils conduct him on a tour of hell where they lead him from precipice to precipice until he is finally shown an imprisoned devil:

> I had come into the depths of hell. And so, they led me before the face of the most impious devil. He was moreover terrible and fearsome, secured by the strongest chains. On his head sat a bird of iron in the likeness of a raven, from the top of which hung his chains.[53]

Another otherworld vision, the *Vision of Tundale,* was an Irish monk's record of the vision of a knight from Cashel in Tipperary. It includes the most thorough description of the devil in this literature before Lucifer in Dante's *Divine Comedy. Tundale* is a lengthy otherworld vision (over 10,000 words). It was emblematic and enormously popular, translated into at least thirteen languages. Copies survive in hundreds of manuscripts.[54] It includes many features found in similar works but here fashioned with greater skill and vividness. Its structuring of hell is particularly remarkable: a highly delineated, multi-layered, segmented place where sinners are punished gruesomely in ways that particularly fit their sins. And while some visions give the sense of passing through a landscape of punishment, this one provides a dynamic sense of descent deeper and deeper into the pit of hell.

Before Tundale finally encounters Lucifer, he meets an auxiliary devil named Acheron, traditionally the name of Hades' river of woe. His most remarkable feature is his mouth, which is just like a hellmouth. He is not, however, at the entrance to hell, but in the fourth level, where he is occupied specifically in tormenting the greedy with his wide-open mouth ingesting as many as nine thousand souls at a time:

> Inextinguishable flames ... belched forth from his mouth, which was divided into three parts by the three gates, and into this flame the condemned souls were compelled to enter. An incomparable stink also came from his mouth. It was no wonder that both the crying and the howling of the multitude in his stomach were heard through his mouth since there were many thousands of men and women atoning in dire torment inside.[55]

While Tundale is witnessing eight different types of torment, he thinks he is in hell, but just before descending further into the depths, his angel guide reveals: "All you saw above still wait for the judgement of God, but those who are below in the depths are already judged."[56] If God has not made these preliminary judgements, who has? In many of these visions, this after-death judgement before the Last Judgement is left to wrangling angels and devils to sort out on a case-by-case basis. When Tundale first entered the otherworld, he was repeatedly encircled by devils trying to drag him down to hell. His guardian angel appeared just in time to rescue him and arrange his reprieve. Descending from the depths of hell to the deepest depth, Tundale is again encircled by devils. Like a swarm of inflamed bees, they taunt and threaten him, promising that he will burn forever in hell.

These taunting devils finally say, "Let's take him to Lucifer for devouring." Passing into the depths of hell, Tundale sees the Prince of Shadows, a black beast, like a raven, but shaped like a human, except that he has a thousand hands, each a thousand cubits long and ten cubits wide, with twenty enormous fingers that ended in long iron claws with a thousand points. His feet have just as many claws. He also has a great long beak and a long and sharp tail.

> This horrible stooping spectacle was seated on a forged iron wicker-work placed over coals inflamed by the inflated bellows of an innumerable number of demons … this enemy of humanity was attached through each member and at their joints with very large and flaming iron bonds.[57]

The angel tells Tundale that here he sees "Lucifer, and he is the prince of the creatures of God." The text refers to him alternately as "Lucifer" and "Satan." This beast turns from side to side in his wrath, clutching and crushing the souls of the damned. With his breathing he sucks souls into his mouth, and he devours them with smoke and sulphur. Tundale asks "why this monster is called the Prince of Shadows when he can defend no one, and he is not able to free himself."[58] The angel explains that this Prince of Shadows is called *prince* not because of his power but because of his primacy in the shadows. This is an early example of the devil not only in hell, but as a bound prisoner torturing sinners in the deepest depths of hell.

In depicting otherworld visions, medieval artists often devoted great attention to specific textual details. An excellent example is provided by the deluxe illuminated manuscript of *The Visions of Tondal* (Getty Museum Ms 30) created for Margaret of York (1446–1503), duchess of Burgundy (1468–77), and illuminated by Simon Marmion (1425–89).[59] It includes twenty miniatures, each one devoted to an episode of the narrative. This artist explored his subject to great effect, especially in his depiction of Lucifer (fol. 30v). In the depths of hell, a naked Tundale, on the left, stands behind a golden-haired angel in a blue garment with blue wings. Darkness surrounds them and before them massive, bronze-like doors are thrown open. In front of the open doors are demons peering into a chamber with a red-hot floor. In the near distance on the floor is a grill or a bed of nails and on top of that is a black Satan. His form is humanoid, but he is much more beast-like. He has a distinct red mouth. He is depicted to convey the multi-handed, multi-fingered monster of the text. Those hands reach up to grasp the souls of the dead while behind them lurk more demons.

Only one illustrated manuscript of the *Vision of Tundale* survives, but an early printed edition of the text from c. 1483 illustrates this scene differently. Although the text is quite clear about the physical nature of the devil, here we find instead a hellmouth representing Lucifer, his huge mouth is crammed with souls. And, like the text, his arms have multiple hands, which are multi-fingered. He is atop a gridiron above a bed of coals. This would lead one to suspect that there may have been some confusion or conflation between the devil and the hellmouth in medieval depictions. Perhaps the hellmouth served as a metonym for Satan, a way of representing him in space as well as a synecdoche for both the realm and its ruler.

Compared to these *Tundale* illustrations, the almost contemporary *Hortus delicarum* (1180) by Herrad of Landsberg, shows four levels with several different punishments on each, some of them with captions identifying the sinners. In the bottom row, at the right, is a cave, above which is the inscription "Lucifer or Satan." We find him sitting above a fire with a chain about his neck. In addition to the head on his shoulders, he has an extra one on each hip swallowing souls. An early 13th-century Oxford psalter[60] depicts hell's separate places for punishment with twelve scenes in four rows of three. These scenes include three hellmouths, the largest occupying the panel at the bottom right.

Finally, a rare, frescoed representation of a medieval otherworld text survives in the Convent of San Francesco in Todi. It is a rather damaged depiction of the "Purgatory of Saint Patrick" (1179), another Irish otherworld text. A knight named Owein visits a cave that serves as a portal to the otherworld. There he encounters a series of locations, apparently on a single plain, where souls are tortured with quite specific tortures, although the text does not identify the sins and crimes. An otherwise unknown pilgrim, Louis of Auxerre of France, visited this cave in 1358. Although the Todi fresco by Jacopo di Mino del Pellicciaio has been dated to 1346, and predates the Louis of Auxerre text, some version of it is the likely basis for this painting, since, unlike the Owein version, this details the sins for which the sinners are punished:

> The first group of individuals … for murder and usury …. The second group … that sort of person who is a false witness, cruel, and blasphemous of God and the saints …. The third group … adulterers and fornicators …. The fourth … heretics, pagans, and the perversely unfaithful …. The fifth … tyrants and other lords who ruled … as well as judges and lawyers of any type who judged and advocated unjustly, and even clerics exercising the perquisite of passing unjust ecclesiastical laws … to be prepared afterwards as edibles for the insatiable and malignant Lucifer. The sixth group … the envious and the slanderers. The seventh punishment is for those … who were bereft of the divine mercy.[61]

The Todi painting features seven caves—one of them damaged beyond reading—and each cave is marked with a caption: *avaricia* (greed), *lusuria* (lust), *superbia* (pride), *invidia* (envy), *ira* (wrath), *accidia* (sloth), and the mostly obscured *gula* (gluttony). Although the scenes include demons, a bridge, and cauldrons, there is no evidence of the devil or a hellmouth.

Although the devil is absent from the Todi fresco, most visual artists of the Middle Ages took advantage of the challenge of depicting Satan. He often appears in a central position, chained and bound on a throne or a grill. He reaches out to capture souls and either crush them in his claws or stuff them into one of his mouths, because, like Cerberus, he is often depicted with three heads, each with a mouth that devours sinners. In addition, no matter how many heads he has, he is sometimes depicted with an extra face on his belly where his mouth regurgitates regenerated sinners. They fall, as if they were emerging from his entrails, ready to be tormented anew.[62]

In conclusion, we turn to Dante's *Divine Comedy*. This early 14th-century work (c. 1308–20) marks the end of the medieval tradition of otherworld vision literature. None of the other surviving examples approached its level of literary sophistication. Dante perfects the vision of evil in his *Inferno*, where Lucifer sits devouring souls. Like its predecessor, the *Vision of Tundale*, the *Inferno* refers to the devil by two names: here Beelzebub and Lucifer. He is also described as enthroned and bound in the pit of hell. Rather than layers, Dante employs circles, and his hell has nine. The first is Limbo, the place of the unbaptised, while the next seven are designated the locations for the punishment of some version of the seven deadly sins: lust, gluttony, greed, wrath, heresy, violence, fraud, and treachery. Canto 34, the final canto of the *Inferno*, describes the pilgrim's encounter with the devil: "The emperor of the woeful realm stood forth from mid-breast out of the ice; and I in size compare better with a giant than giants with his arms."[63] He is a huge, winged giant. Dante describes how:

I saw three faces on his head: one in front and it was red, and the other two joined to this just over the middle of each shoulder, and all three were joined at the crown. The right one seemed between white and yellow, and the left one was such in appearance as are those who come from whence the Nile descends. From under each one came forth two mighty wings, of size befitting such a bird—sails at sea I never saw so broad. They had no feathers, but were like a bat's. And he was flapping them, so that three winds went forth from him.[64]

This three-headed monster is again reminiscent of the three-headed dog Cerberus, who guarded the entrance to the Greek underworld to prevent the dead from leaving.

Virgil and Dante climb down the beast's shaggy, frozen, matted flanks to where "the thigh turns just on the thick of the haunch."[65] At that point, they turn around. Dante expects to be now climbing back up to hell and expects to see Lucifer's head again but finds himself looking instead at Lucifer's feet extended into the air. Virgil explains to a perplexed Dante that "the evil worm that pierces the world" marks the axis of the earth. They have passed the centre point of gravity and now are on the other side. He explains how Lucifer:

… fell down from heaven; and the earth, which before stood out here, for fear of him made a veil of the sea and came to our hemisphere; and perhaps in order to escape from him that which appears on this side left here the empty space and rushed upwards.[66]

Before Lucifer fell, dry land was opposite Jerusalem, but it escaped from the devil by rushing to the other hemisphere. This beast is wedged into the centre of the earth. As in the *Vision of Tundale*, he is a prisoner of the deepest depths of hell. Above him are hell's upper regions as well as the habitable earth, while below him is a hemisphere of water where the only land is the mountain of purgatory.

In contrast to the *Vision of Tundale*, there are uncountable illustrated versions of the *Divine Comedy* in both manuscript and print. Dante and Virgil generally appear as onlookers at the side of each scene, both fully clothed, Dante in blue and Virgil in red. When they encounter Beelzebub, he is, according to the text's description, fully erect, a hairy monster with wings but just one pair of hands. The mouths in his three heads are engorging Cassius, Judas, and Brutus. This same image is repeated, again and again, with fascinating variations, in almost all illustrations for Canto 34 of the *Inferno*: from medieval manuscripts[67] to Gustave Doré's Romantic mid-19th-century engravings[68] and Rachel Owen's radical 21st-century collage/prints,[69] we find Satan in the place where we expect to find him, in the deepest pit of hell.

Texts and images reveal Satan in heaven, Satan falling, and Satan flying through the air. He is found wandering the earth in numerous temptation stories from Job to Jesus and from the Desert Fathers to the early saints. However, hell is the place where we truly find the devil, the place most vividly described and depicted: Satan in his designated space, his destined abode, the place where he is bound to his fiery throne. For the most part, the development of hell raced ahead without taking full account of Satan, but once the segmented, multi-level structure of hell reached its ultimate expression, then Satan had his natural, designated spot as the denizen of the very bottom of the pit, enthroned and enchained.

# Notes

1 John Casey, *After Lives: A Guide to Heaven, Hell and Purgatory* (Oxford, 2009), 65–102; *Greek and Roman Hell: Visions Tours and Descriptions of the Infernal Otherworld*, ed. Eileen Gardiner (New York, 2019), xv, xvii–xix.

2 For an introduction and collection of relevant texts, see *Ancient Near Eastern Hell: Visions, Tours and Descriptions of the Infernal Otherworld*, ed. Eileen Gardiner (New York, 2013), ix–xiv; for an analysis, see Alan E. Bernstein, *The Formation of Hell: Death and Retribution in the Ancient and Early Christian Worlds* (Ithaca, NY, 1993), 4–11.

3 For an introduction to these traditions and a selection of relevant texts, see *Buddhist Hell: Visions, Tours and Descriptions of the Infernal Otherworld*, ed. Eileen Gardiner (New York, 2012), xii–xv; and *Hindu Hell: Visions, Tours and Descriptions of the Infernal Otherworld*, ed. Eileen Gardiner (New York, 2013), viii–xi.

4 Representations of the devil are thoroughly examined in Luther Link, *The Devil: The Archfiend in Art, from the Sixth to the Sixteenth Century* (New York, 1995), 183.

5 For the overall background on the development of Satan, see Neil Forsyth, *The Old Enemy: Satan and the Combat Myth* (Princeton, NJ, 1987); Elaine Pagels, *The Origin of Satan* (New York, 1996); and Henry Ansgar Kelly, *Satan: A Biography* (Cambridge, 2006).

6 Jeffrey Burton Russell, *The Devil: Perceptions of Evil from Antiquity to Primitive Christianity* (Ithaca, NY, 1977), 254; Link, *The Devil*, 126.

7 Pagels, *Origin*, 39.

8 Biblical references are to 21st-century King James Bible (KJ21).

9 Martha Himmelfarb, *Tours of Hell: An Apocalyptic Form in Jewish and Christian Literature* (Philadelphia, 1985), 176–7 and *passim*.

10 Richard Bauckham, *The Fate of the Dead: Studies on the Jewish and Christian Apocalypses* (Leiden, 1998), 37, 91.

11 Himmelfarb, *Tours of Hell*, 182 and *passim*.

12 Himmelfarb, *Tours of Hell*, 175–6 and *passim*.

13 Himmelfarb, *Tours of Hell*, 177 and *passim*.

14 *Selected Discourses of Shenoute the Great: Community, Theology, and Social Conflict in Late Antique Egypt*, eds. David Brakke and Andrew Crislip (Cambridge, 2015), 259.

15 See "Jugement" in the *Dictionnaire de théologie catholique*, eds. A Vacant, E. Mangenot, É. Amann, et al., 18 vols (Paris, 1889–1950), 8:1742–812.

16 Examples can be found in the Crusader Bible of 1240 (Morgan MS 638, fol. 1), the French *Bibles Moralisées* of 1402–04 (BNF Fr 166, fol. 1r) and of 1455–60 (BNF FR 897, fol. 1r) and the historiated bible of Guiard des Moulins of 1410 (Royal Library of Belgium MS 9024).

17 For example, the *Silos Apocalypse* (1091–1109), London, BM Add MS 11695, fol. 148r; the *Huelgas Apocalypse* (1202), New York, Morgan MS M.429, fol. 102r; or the *Apocalypse of Saint-Sever* (1028 and 1072), Paris, BN MS lat. 8878, fol. 159r.

18 Aaron K. Hostetter, *Genesis A and B*, "The Old English Poetry Project." https://oldenglishpoetry.camden.rutgers.edu/genesis-ab/

19 Hostetter, "Old English Poetry Project." https://oldenglishpoetry.camden.rutgers.edu/christ-and-satan/

20 John D. Cox, "The Devil and the Sacred in the English Mystery Plays," in *The Devil and the Sacred in English Drama, 1350–1642* (Cambridge, 2000), 19–38.

21 "The Creation of the Angels and the Fall of Lucifer," in "The York Corpus Christi Plays," ed. Clifford Davidson (Kalamazoo, MI, 2011). https://d.lib.rochester.edu/teams/text/davidson-play-1-the-creation-of-the-angels-and-the-fall-of-lucifer at line 149.

22 "York Corpus Christi," *The Fall,* at https://d.lib.rochester.edu/teams/text/davidson-play-5-the-fall

23 Modernised from "The N-Town Plays," ed. Douglas Sugano (Kalamazoo, MI, 2007), ll. 66–74, at https://d.lib.rochester.edu/teams/text/sugano-n-town-plays-play-1-creation-of-heaven-fall-of-lucifer

24 "The Creation," in *The Towneley Plays*, ed. Garrett J. P. Epp (Kalamazoo, MI, 2017) at https://d.lib.rochester.edu/teams/text/epp-the-creation

25 Gardiner, *Ancient Near Eastern*, 29–35.

26 This appendix is no earlier than the 5th century. M. R. James, *The Apocryphal New Testament* (Oxford, 1924), 94–6, 117–44.

27 James, *Apocryphal*, 132.

28 James, *Apocryphal*, 126.

29 James, *Apocryphal*, 132.

30 James, *Apocryphal*, 136–7.

31 For the identification of the hellmouth as Satan or as hell, compare Gary D. Schmidt, *The Iconography of the Mouth of Hell: Eighth-Century Britain to the Fifteenth Century* (Selinsgrove, PA, 1995), 88–9; and Petra Hoffman, "Infernal Imagery in Anglo-Saxon Charters" (PhD diss, University of St Andrews, 2008), 82–6.

32 London, British Library, Cotton MS Nero C IV, fols. 24r, 39r.

33 For instance, *The Book of Hours of Catherine of Cleves*, Morgan Library and Museum, New York, MS M.945, fol. 168v.

34 For example, the tympanum of the Church of St Foy at Conques.

35 See Karl Tamburr, *The Harrowing of Hell in Medieval England* (Cambridge, 2007), ch. 3, 4.

36 Aaron K. Hostetter, "Old English Poetry Project." https://oldenglishpoetry.camden.rutgers.edu/christ-and-satan

37 Chester N. Scoville and Kimberley M. Yates, "The York Plays: A Modernization," 2003. https://users.pfw.edu/flemingd/yorkplays/york.html#pag, ll. 335–48.

38 Epp, "Towneley Plays," ll. 363–70 at https://d.lib.rochester.edu/teams/text/epp-the-harrowing-of-hell

39 Sugano, "N-Town," at https://d.lib.rochester.edu/teams/text/sugano-n-town-plays-play-33-harrowing-of-hell

40 "The Chester Plays," ed. A.F. Johnston (2010) at https://pls.artsci.utoronto.ca/wp-content/uploads/2015/09/chester16.pdf

41 See Kelly, *Satan*, 141–59, for an analysis of Satan in Revelation.

42 For a thorough examination of hell in apocalyptic texts, see Himmelfarb, *Tours of Hell*.

43 Himmelfarb, *Tours of Hell*, 114.

44 Bernstein, *Formation*, 292–3; Theodore Silverstein, *Visio Sancti Pauli: The History of the Apocalypse in Latin together with Nine Texts* (London, 1935), 23, 91; Hell-on-Line, ed. Eileen Gardiner, http://www.hell-on-line.org/TextsJC.html#Paul

45 Richard. Bauckham, "Hell in the Latin *Vision of Ezra*," in *Otherworlds and Their Relationship to This World: Early Jewish and Ancient Christian Traditions*, ed. Tobias Nicklas, Joseph Verheyden, et al. (Leiden, 2010), 323–42.

46 For manuscripts, notably the illuminated manuscripts of the *Commentary on the Apocalypse* by 8th-century monk Beatus of Liébana, see John Williams, *The Illustrated Beatus* (London, 1994); for frescos, notably, Pietro Cavallini's "Last Judgment" in Sta Cecilia, Rome, see Alessandro Tomei, *Pietro Cavallini* (Milan, 2000), ch. 3; and for mosaics, notably S. Maria Assunta, Torcello (Venice), see Liz James, *Mosaics in the Medieval World: From Late Antiquity to the Fifteenth Century* (Cambridge, 2017), 344–9.

47 Himmelfarb, *Tours of Hell*, 87.

48 Almost any painting of the Last Judgement will display many of these elements, but a particularly fine example for the use of head coverings for both the damned and the saved dates from 1480 and is in the German National Museum at Nuremberg: https://objektkatalog.gnm.de/wisski/navigate/8792/view

49 For a listing of these otherworld visions, see *Medieval Visions of Heaven and Hell: A Sourcebook*, ed. Eileen Gardiner (New York, 1993), and http://www.hell-on-line.org/TextsJC.html

50 *History of the Franks,* book 4, ch. 33, English translation mine.

51 "The Vision of Laisrén," ed. and trans. Kuno Meyer, *Otia Merseiana* 1 (1899): 113–9. https://celt.ucc.ie//published/T207003/index.html

52 From C. S. Boswell, *An Irish Precursor of Dante: A Study of the Vision of Heaven and Hell Ascribed to the Eighth-Century Irish Saint Adamnán* (London, 1908; rpt. New York, 1972), 43.

53 *Visioni dell'Aldilà in Occidente*, ed. Maria Pia Ciccarese (Florence, 1987), 290–1, English translation mine.

54 Gardiner, *Medieval Visions,* 210–1.

55 Gardiner, *Visions,* 159.

56 Gardiner, *Visions,* 174.

57 Gardiner, *Visions,* 177–8.

58 Gardiner, *Visions,* 180.

59 Thomas Kren and Roger S. Wieck, *The Visions of Tondal from the Library of Margaret of* York (Malibu, 1990); Thomas Kren, *Margaret of York, Simon Marmion, and the* Visions of Tondal (Malibu, CA, 1992).

60 Munich, Bayerische Staatsbibliothek, Clm 835, fol. 30v.

61 Max Voigt, *Beiträge zur geschichte der visionenliteratur im mittelalter I-II* (Leipzig, 1924; rpt. New York: Johnson Reprint, 1967), 226–45; translation by Darius Matthias Klein, http://christianlatin.blogspot.com/2009/01/vision-of-louis-of-france.html

62 For instance, see "Hell" from the Paul, John, and Herman Limbourg, *Les Très Riches Heures du Duc de Berri,* (1415), Chantilly, Musée Condé Ms 65/1284, fol. 108r, or the fresco in the Florence Baptistry; for a discussion of depictions of the devil, see Link, *The Devil,* ch. 3.

63 Dante Aligheri, *The Divine Comedy,* vol. 1, *The Inferno*: Text and vol. 2, *The Inferno: Commentary,* ed. Charles Singleton (Princeton, NJ, 1970), 1:363.

64 Dante, *Inferno,* 1:363.

65 Dante, *Inferno,* 1:365.

66 Dante, *Inferno,* 1:369.

67 For example, the Chantilly *Inferno* of 1345 (Chantilly, Musée Condé Ms 597/1424) and the British Library Yates-Thompson 36 of 1444-c. 1450.

68 Dante Aligheri, Gustav Doré, and Lawrence Grant White, *The Divine Comedy: The Inferno, Purgatorio, and Paradiso* (New York, 1963).

69 Rachel Owen, *Illustrations for Dante's Inferno* (Oxford, 2021).

## Further Reading

*Ancient Near Eastern Hell: Visions, Tours and Descriptions of the Infernal Otherworld*, ed. Eileen Gardiner (New York, NY: Italica Press, 2013).

Bernstein, Alan E. *The Formation of Hell: Death and Retribution in the Ancient and Early Christian Worlds* (Ithaca, NY: Cornell University Press, 1993).

Casey, John. *After Lives: A Guide to Heaven, Hell and Purgatory* (Oxford: Oxford University Press, 2009).

*Greek and Roman Hell: Visions Tours and Descriptions of the Infernal Otherworld*, ed. Eileen Gardiner (New York, NY: Italica Press, 2019).

Hell-on-Line, ed. Eileen Gardiner, http://www.hell-on-line.org

Himmelfarb, Martha. *Tours of Hell: An Apocalyptic Form in Jewish and Christian Literature* (Philadelphia, PA: Fortress Press, 1985).

*Medieval Visions of Heaven and Hell: A Sourcebook*, ed. Eileen Gardiner (New York, NY: Garland Publishing, 1993).

# 7

# THE DEVIL'S MINIONS

*David R. Winter*

"The Evil One is seldom alone, muttered the boy ...."[1]

When the Romantic poet and artist William Blake observed that John Milton was "of the devil's party" for his sometimes astonishingly sympathetic portrayal of Satan in his 1667 *Paradise Lost*, he articulated an assumption that was, by that time, deeply rooted in the Western psyche.[2] It was not simply that created beings, through their thoughts and actions, tended to align themselves with a particular cosmic fate, but rather that, in uniting himself with Satan's cause, Milton had in fact joined *a society*. While often imagined as fundamentally antisocial or the consummate loner, from very early in his story, the devil has stood at the head of a vast company of evil actors.[3]

Though subordinate and subject to him (i.e., there are no wicked spirits outside his dominion), the devil's demonic followers were, in a sense, his moral (and ontological) equals.[4] Indeed, at the instant of his defiance, God's formerly most glittering cherub swapped service for lordship and assumed command over a mighty and terrifying host. As Milton's Lucifer put it, it was "better to reign in Hell, than serve in Heaven" (1.261-3). Although the precise sequence and timeline of Satan's fall remain open to diverse readings, various authorities—both scriptural and extrabiblical—agreed that when Satan was thrown from heaven, he took a multitude of refractory beings with him.[5] Shaped originally by their creator to offer adoration and worship, this faction of angelic beings wilfully rejected its original purpose and joined itself to mutiny and rancour.

For the earliest Christians, these rebel angels quickly assumed new identities as Satan's factotums and deputies: they became the infernal cohort of demons, imps, and fiends.[6] Though normally invisible to mortal humans, they infested all parts of the sublunary cosmos: the earth, the air, and the subterranean world all teemed with demonic activity. Their fate was to toil unceasingly in a variety of capacities on their master's behalf. Whatever their assigned task or station, however, it was incumbent on each infernal subordinate—from the greatest named archfiend to the most debased and minor imp or bogey—to labour without respite, to promote the destruction of humanity, to stimulate everywhere misery and discord and, ultimately, to speed the final confrontation between the forces of cosmic good and evil.

DOI: 10.4324/9781003096603-8

This chapter focuses not on Satan himself, but rather on his subordinates, deputies, and followers. It canvasses the scope and extent of the devil's legions as Christianity's cultural and institutional weight increased through the medieval and early modern eras. It discusses (1) the general nature of demons according to dominant premodern readings of them; (2) the shape of the devil's government; (3) the ranks and offices purported to be under Satan's command; and, importantly, (4) how these offices were reimagined and extrapolated as Christianity solidified its claims over the emerging idea of Europe. In other words, it deals with the demonisation of indigenous/local deities and spirits as Christian evangelists sought to bring rival systems within the scope of their understanding and control.[7] These issues are fundamental to a basic appreciation of how premodern people conceptualised their place in creation; together, they offer a sense of how Christians imagined the scale of the threat that was arrayed against them. A single enemy can be exceptionally formidable, but one who has access to near inexhaustible reserves of support (as Christians supposed the devil had) is more alarming by several orders of magnitude. Indeed, the early "atomisation" of cosmic evil had implications for everything from how the medieval political order was imagined, to social relations among individuals and communities, to the premodern view of the natural world. Even if Satan himself were preoccupied with grand attempts to frustrate the divine plan, the existence of an army of demonic helpers portended a threat that was much closer to home. It transformed the mundane world of Europeans' daily lives into an eschatological terrain. The borders of the rural village became a haunted topography—one that was firmly situated within the ambit of sacred history. So, while the lord of this world, Satan, might connive with his lieutenants to bring down popes and princes, his minor vassals lurked in the forests beyond the meadow, by the manorial forge, in the rafters of the tithe barn, and even between the sheets of the marital bed.[8] It was a dangerous and thoroughly demon-thronged world, one that had to be traversed carefully, with discernment and care. The landscape that medieval Christians erected for themselves demanded a meticulous knowledge of the habits of devils: a sense of where they might linger, how they might seek advantage, and the surest means of turning back their enticements and advances.[9]

Before considering these matters, however, some caveats are necessary. For modern readers, the term "devil's minion" can be so broadly construed as to mean virtually any entity that exists in the service of Satan. Conceivably, this could include any beings—including humans—who do not exist in a state of grace with God.[10] Thus, it could incorporate all sinners, heretics, witches, necromancers, worshippers of foreign gods, and other mortal beings whom Christians believed dedicated themselves to evil ends. Indeed, in Blake's estimation, John Milton was a particularly conspicuous member of the devil's *human* entourage. So conceived, the term "devil's minion" could also incorporate monsters, prodigies, spectral creatures and revenants. The conceptual distance between the monstrous and the demonic is certainly not great and, from earliest times, it has been repeatedly bridged by those seeking to account for the actions of creatures that appear to slip between categories of being. While there are no doubt arguments for the inclusion of all such creatures under the rubric of demonic "minion," this chapter, out of necessity, does not extend to a discussion of human agents of the devil. Nor does it treat the monstrous or the prodigious—at least not monsters *qua* monsters. Instead, it will concentrate on entities explicitly identified by Christians as fallen angels or spirit-servants of Satan.

## The General Nature of Demons

Though Christian understandings of the nature and operation of demonic forces are unique, with their own cultural and theological tensions, they also exist within a much broader historical context. Belief in minor spirits was attested almost universally in premodern societies. In virtually every culture worldwide, it existed prior to the establishment of formal or organised religion.[11] Spirits appear in animistic, pantheistic, dualist, monotheistic, and other cosmologies. Most early societies detected—and sought to understand, describe, and even control—the operation of these unseen forces that appeared to exist just at (or beyond) the limits of normal human perception. In most systems, interaction between the visible and spirit worlds was deemed possible. Spirit beings sometimes entered the human realm voluntarily, while in other cases, they had to be coaxed or compelled into this world by human specialists in spectral or occult knowledge. These same experts were also deployed to exorcise or adjure spirits who had overstayed their welcome. In pan- and polytheistic systems, minor spirits were often viewed as morally ambiguous. While they sometimes required appeasement or reverence to maintain the peace, they were seldom wholly good or evil. Though they often appeared in human or animal form, the physical and intellectual capabilities and powers of these entities varied considerably. Some spirit creatures were godlike in their ability to manipulate the forces of the cosmos while others possessed only a modest ability to affect the natural world. Some spirits acted in the service of supernatural beings greater than themselves while others were independent actors seeking their own ends. In many instances, they were unformed or inchoate presences, appearing abstractly as signifiers of cosmic imbalances, of divine wrath or favour, or as some other disturbance of nature.[12]

Christian belief in evil spirits (and reliance on them as causal and explanatory agents) ultimately originates in a worldview grounded fundamentally in magic and enchantment. Premodern people believed that self-aware beings of greater-than-human ability operated normally in the universe, and Christians, in many respects, simply took prior belief and shaped it to their theological needs.[13] They appropriated and redefined spirit beings, endowing them with motives, powers and abilities that aligned with the Christian theodicy. As they did so, scholars erected a view of creation that had a far more stripped-down order of being than that of the classical world. They divided all animate creatures into a small number of existential categories. They were either God, angels, humans, animals, demons, or the devil. Each category had intrinsic properties particular to its station. Ideas, beings, and situations that appeared to contradict the emerging system of categorisation or which fit uncomfortably within its dimensions had to be nudged into coherence. This frequently meant the demonisation of whole classes of beings, particularly those that inhabited rival systems. But it was a complex and protracted process, one that extended into the Middle Ages and beyond. It was also a process that met with sustained resistance from many quarters, both within and outside the established church.

The word commonly used in modern English to denote Satan's deputies and subordinates, that is, "demon," derives via medieval Latin, *demon*, from the Greek, δαίμων (*daimon*). In the Greco-Roman "pagan" view, the term connoted a wide range of good, evil, and morally ambiguous spirits and supernatural entities.[14] Sometimes, the word *demon* was also used to denote intellectual abstractions or concepts; for example, ideas such as "goodness," "abundance," "vengeance," or "strife" could take demonic form.[15] While there was some disagreement within Greco-Roman philosophical and religious traditions with respect to the function and nature of demons, by the classical era, they appear in most instances to have occupied an intermediate space between the mundane and the divine, serving as messengers and intermediaries of the gods.[16]

The use of *daimon* and its cognates to specify the unclean spirits of the Judeo-Christian tradition can probably be traced to Hellenistic Egypt. There, between c. 250 and 132 BCE, Hebrew scholars prepared a *koine* Greek translation of the Tanakh.[17] There is some debate as to whether this was done to serve the community of Jewish exiles whose facility in Hebrew had begun to decline or so that other philosophical and faith traditions could have access to Jewish sacred texts. Regardless, the version that resulted is the *Septuagint*: the book of the 72 scribes and translators (conventionally abbreviated as "LXX").[18] While, on the one hand, translators were careful to retain the richness and variety of Hebrew spirit lore, on the other, in an attempt render Semitic "categories of being" intelligible to a broader audience, they were sometimes forced to erode or collapse linguistic subtleties.[19] For example, the translators of the *Septuagint* used *daimonia* in the well-known passage from Deuteronomy 32.17 to indicate alien gods: "They sacrificed to demons which were no gods, to gods they had never known, to new gods that had come in of late, whom your fathers had never dreaded."[20] Because of their status in Greco-Roman traditional religion as intermediaries between the visible and invisible worlds, the term "demon" increasingly became a convenient lexical repository for any spirit who was alienated from Yahweh.[21] Pagans could fulminate against this view and claim that it fundamentally (and perhaps maliciously) misconstrued the nature of the spirit world, but to Jews and early Christians, it made sense.[22]

Thus, the semantic legacy of the *Septuagint* was passed more or less intact to the first Christians, including the apostle Paul and the gospel authors, who deployed a constellation of related terms to denote minor spirits in the service of Satan. Three terms in particular became the primary signifiers of wicked spirits in the New Testament and the earliest auxiliary texts of the church. The foremost was *daimonion* or *daimon* (demon), which occurs at least 60 times in the New Testament, mostly in the Synoptic gospels. The other terms used most frequently included *pneuma ponera* (evil spirit), and *pneuma akatharta* (unclean spirit). Thus, for example, in the famous story of the Gerasene demoniac, the authors of Matthew and Luke employed *daimon* to denote the evil entity(-ies) identified in the text as Legion, while Mark used *pneuma akatharta* to refer to the same spirit(-s).[23] *Daimon* was a direct borrowing from earlier usage; the gospel writers made recourse to the term because rabbis immersed in the Hellenistic milieu had done so before them. The other terms, however, *pneuma ponera* and *pneuma akatharta*, were almost completely unknown to Levantine monotheism.[24]

The emerging demonological lexicon of the New Testament reflected an urgency among its writers about the shape and scope of demonic activity in their world. While demon-like actors had appeared with regularity throughout the Tanakh and in early Hebrew lore, their intrusions into human affairs achieved a prominence—and even coherence—in the gospels almost completely unseen in mainstream Judaism of the Hellenistic period.[25] Christ's earthly mission against Satan and his followers, and his absolute dominance over all supernatural agents of darkness (and their human allies), became one of the overriding motifs of those who first wrote about the reform-minded rabbi and thaumaturge. Jesus' ability to discern the presence of unclean spirits, to resist their temptations, and to cast them out of his fellow human beings became a hallmark of his ministry.[26] So, from a very early moment in the Christian story, there was an intrinsic focus on themes of opposition, betrayal, and the pressing need to identify the enemies of God, both natural and supernatural. Notions of demonic obstruction and contrariety bind and charge the gospel narrative. The cosmic struggle against elemental evil began to organise the Christian worldview at a fundamental level.[27] In this context, it should also be noted that most early followers of Jesus unreservedly believed that the pagan gods and the creatures who attended them were deceptive spirits in the service of Satan.[28] Thus, Christians deemed the use of the Greek lexicon of minor spirits as singularly appropriate to their circumstances.

As they sought to articulate the view that the story of Jesus represented the fulfilment of Old Testament prophesy regarding the long-promised messiah, and as they asserted the premise that the hand of God operated with purpose through time, Christian apologists and theologians began to impose a new, largely *ex post facto*, reading on the demonology of the Tanakh. Foremost among their tools for this project was a hermeneutics (i.e., system of literary exposition and analysis) developed largely by Jewish scholars of Alexandria. There, authors such as Aristobulus of Alexandria (d. 125 BCE) and Philo Judaeus (d. c. 47 CE) sought to reconcile Hebrew theological ideas with prevailing trends in Greek thought and to cloak their beliefs in a veneer of intellectual rigour and respectability. Using traditional exegetical principles of *Midrash* and *Aggadah* together with ideas derived from Stoicism, Philo imposed a typological or allegorical reading on scripture.[29] He asserted, for example, that Mosaic and Platonic accounts of the generation of the world could be harmonised.[30] Early Christians, in turn, developed Philo's ideas further, asserting the "fourfold sense" of scripture, an interpretive model that prioritises the allegorical reading of sacred texts. Its widespread application to biblical texts has enabled Christians to adduce patterns and continuities between the Old and New Testaments. It was subsequently transmitted to Origen, Augustine, and the other Christian doctors of the Patristic era, who, in turn, passed it to the Middle Ages. According to the "fourfold sense," each verse of scripture can be read on four different, but complimentary, levels: the literal, the typological, the moral (or tropological), and the anagogical.[31] By reading scripture on these levels and making very careful textual comparisons, events, figures, images and ideas could symbolically "stand in" and represent other things. This is an extraordinarily powerful systems-building tool for theologians, and it permitted early Christians to erect a compelling discursive framework around the body of historically and thematically disparate texts they deemed sacred. Indeed, by juxtaposing Old and New Testament verses on virtually any topic, an essayist or commentator could draw a line back into the past and extend it into the future, making credible claims of continuity between traditions.

Importantly, this hermeneutical tool also enabled early Christians to construct a far more systematic and stable demonology from the sometimes inconsistent (or even discordant) literary materials of their world. While the writers of the New Testament had clearly presupposed a degree of correspondence between the activities of the unclean spirits in their own era and the imps and fiends of the Tanakh, the fourfold exegetical model facilitated the ability of the earliest theologians to draw precise parallels and to detect continuities in the actions and intentions of demonic actors old and new. In this way, individual episodes of "demonic" activity in the Old Testament became epiphenomena of a much larger, more ordered worldview: one in which the heretofore standalone fiends and spirits of Genesis, Ezekiel and Isaiah were endowed with origins, objectives, and a consummation. So, for example, it was famously the 2nd-century Christian apologist, Justin Martyr (d. c. 165), who first applied a typological reading to the serpent in the Garden of Eden story (Genesis 3) and equated the talking reptile with the devil. In his *Dialogue with Trypho*, Justin discussed the relationship between various scriptural villains, including lions, the serpent, the devil, and Satan, and he drew them all, perhaps for first time, into a tidy affinity. In his extended rumination on the meaning of Christ's sacrifice, Justin wrote:

> Or He (i.e., God) meant the devil by the lion roaring against Him: whom Moses calls the serpent, but in Job and Zechariah he is called the devil, and by Jesus is addressed as Satan, showing that a compounded name was acquired by him from the deeds which he performed. For 'Sata' in the Jewish and Syrian tongue means apostate; and 'Nas' is the word from which he is called by interpretation the serpent, i.e., according to the interpretation of the Hebrew term, from both of which there arises the single word *Satanas* … For as he [Satan] had deceived Adam, so he hoped that he might also contrive some mischief against Christ.[32]

Allegorical readings have become such an intrinsic feature of demonological exegesis (and even casual understandings of how biblical demons "work") that it is sometimes difficult to appreciate the extent to which some ancient authors deliberately reshaped or rendered the scriptural material they were deploying into meaningful discursive structures. In the process, they were sometimes forced to ignore or distort the historical or literary circumstances of a given text's original production in order to create a functional and internally consistent metaphysics. In the passage above, Justin conflated distinct images and figures of evil to align with his understanding of how providential history was *supposed* to unfold. Yet, the *nāḥās* (serpent) of Genesis was produced in vastly different historical, cultural, and linguistic circumstances from the *satanas* of Job, which, in turn, was created in a very different context from the *diabolos* of the Septuagint or the prowling *aryeh* (lions) of Daniel. Still, Justin's understanding of the salvific trajectory of history compelled him to discern patterns of malice and to interweave them into a dense, multitextured fabric. In the evocative phrase of Tudor lexicographer Richard Mulcaster, the attempt to forge an enduring coherence in allegory rests on establishing "the likeness of unlike things."[33]

Because of this robust hermeneutical frame, by the early Middle Ages there existed among Christians a clear sense of what cosmic evil looked like—and minor spirits figured prominently in this view. There could be disagreements about the precise shape and scope of demonic interference in the lives of Christians, and sometimes learned views clashed with popular understandings of demonic activity, but there was a broad consensus about basic issues such as: what demons were, where they came from, what constituted their essential natures, and what their ultimate trajectory was within the Christian eschatological scheme.

Most premodern Christians started from the premise that scripture contained authentic revelations about the nature, activities, and motives of evil spirits. Moreover, they believed that it provided an internally consistent record of the history and destiny of fiends and that it could help the faithful recognise wicked spirits when they encountered them. For Christians, the bible was the first and best "field guide" for those seeking to identify Satan's minions and to keep them at bay. Indeed, the dominant demonological discourses that emerged in medieval and early modern Europe—at least among learned Christians—were ultimately grounded in scripture and the hermeneutical reading of sacred texts described above. Before the era of the Reformation, this view was supplemented by the notion that the Church was God's instrument for salvation in the world and that, on this account, it was the repository of all authority in matters of interpretation and exegesis.

This meant that, for Christians living before the modern age, demons were believed to be an ontologically distinct class of self-aware being, subordinate to the devil and serving him in a variety of capacities. Like other animate creatures (including angels, humans, and animals), demons were individual entities, possessing their own faculties of apprehension, intelligence, and will, as well as a capacity for movement and change. They had bodies of aerial or spiritual substance. This endowed them with abilities that sometimes appeared to humans as super- or preternatural. They were able to travel at speed, course through the air, change and reconstitute their appearance. They could enter spaces inaccessible to other types of created beings. They could move through solid obstacles and enter the bodies of humans and animals. They were able to interact with or manipulate the natural world in a variety of ways: they could move the air, churn oceans, enflame conflagrations, or move objects. Accordingly, through the subtle composition of their own airy bodies, they could affect the humours of human and animal bodies, promoting illness and instilling thoughts and emotions of every type. They could distort memories, produce hallucinations, and cause humans to experience delusions.

Demons were once angelic beings, but through an act of rebellion against the creator, they fell from heaven and therefore inhabit the cosmos below the heavenly sphere: that is, they dwell in the lower air, upon the ground, in water, and in darkness below the surface of the earth.[34] While they retain certain aspects of their former angelic natures, in their fallen state, they labour to frustrate God's plan for humanity, and do so under the direction of their chief, Satan. They use their abilities and powers to tempt, taunt, thwart, and otherwise defeat human attempts to live a godly life. However, they work entirely under God's permission and authority. They can be repelled and ejected in God's name. Demons will be defeated by God at the end of time and thrown, together with the devil, into the lake of fire. They are, in the orthodox understanding of things, entirely bereft of hope for redemption.[35]

According to most accounts, the size of the Satanic cohort is vast. Using Revelation 12 and other texts, early exegetes asserted that fully a third of the heavenly host joined in the angelic rebellion.[36] They would remain in the devil's ranks until the final consummation. No doubt most Christians living before the modern age agreed with the Cistercian abbot, Richalmus of Schöntal, who asserted that demons were like "specks in the sunlight such is the multitude of them that surround every man—perhaps even more."[37] While many thought that the number of demons was fixed or constant, some Christians averred that the cohort was supplemented through the coupling of fallen angels with human women. They cite the story of the Nephilim in Genesis 6 as the evidentiary basis for these claims.[38]

## The Form and Composition of the Devil's Government

Historically, among Christians, there has been broad agreement that, after their rebellion, the fallen angels arranged themselves (in a surprisingly compliant manner for such mutinous beings!) under Satan's government.[39] Moreover, it has been widely accepted that the devil established some kind of settled polity over his charges. While the nature and complexity of this arrangement have been conceptualised in various ways, the devil's portion has typically emulated the forms of hierarchical government that dominated the late ancient and medieval worlds. It also very quickly came to mirror—albeit darkly—the heavenly court of Yahweh. Indeed, before the modern period, Satan's realm was imagined primarily as a kind of despotic or monarchical regime. That is, the devil acted, in most understandings of his operation, as the unquestioned lord over his demons, who were believed to do his bidding, typically without hesitation or demur. While he was capable of breathtaking cruelty towards those who served him, he presided over a regime that was remarkable for its efficiency, discipline, and dedication to its objectives. In short, the devil never faced the sort of insurrection that Yahweh did.

The monarchical "principle" appeared early. Its source can probably be traced to biblical passages such as Isaiah 14, a prophecy concerning an unnamed king of Babylon. There, the prophet scorned the monarch, calling him "the son of morning," or "Lucifer," in Latin.[40] The author of Isaiah proclaimed that, despite the Babylonian king's intention of setting his throne above the stars of heaven's vault, this Lucifer had been brought down into the depths of Sheol, the Hebrew abode of the dead. While the passage is unambiguously about the mundane fortunes of the Israelites and their relationship with political rivals on the eve of the Babylonian captivity (597 to 538 BCE), perhaps unsurprisingly the author placed these events in a cosmic register. By the early Christian period, exegetes and theologians elided the Isaiah passage with Luke 10.18, in which Christ asserted "I saw Satan fall like lightning from heaven." In this way, despite its single occurrence in the canon of scripture, the name "Lucifer" established itself as one of the primary signifiers for the devil (or less commonly, for one of his leading henchmen). In turn, this helped to entrench in Christian cosmology the notion that there existed a diabolical "throne" to rival God's, and this became a starting point for an idea that was elaborated throughout the premodern age.

Though New Testament authors did not address the matter directly, they nevertheless seem to have made several assumptions about how the devil wielded government. In his letter to the Ephesians, for example, Paul asserted that Satan presided over a regime whose structure corresponded substantially to common understandings of how coercive powers were distributed among human governments:

> For we are not contending against flesh and blood, but against the principalities, against the powers, against the world rulers of this present darkness, against the spiritual hosts of wickedness in the heavenly places.
>
> *(6.12)*[41]

This is a view of diabolical power that extends outwards from Satan in ranks, offices, or graded tiers. In Romans, Paul went so far as to imply that there existed a kind of structural continuity between the government of the infernal and the celestial spheres: "Do you not know that if you present yourselves to anyone as obedient slaves ($\delta o \tilde{v} \lambda o i$), you are slaves of the one whom you obey, either of sin, which leads to death, or of obedience, which leads to righteousness?" (Rom 6.16). The gospel writers appear to have largely agreed with this view, accepting the idea that demons are ordered according to their particular level of menace:

> When the unclean spirit has gone out of a man, he passes through waterless places seeking rest, but he finds none. Then he says, "I will return to my house from which I came." And when he comes he finds it empty, swept, and put in order. Then he goes and brings with him seven other spirits more evil than himself, and they enter and dwell there; and the last state of that man becomes worse than the first. So shall it be also with this evil generation.
>
> *(Matt 12.43-45)*

This strongly intimates an ordered hierarchy of demonic rank and service.

Further, the Satan of the New Testament was styled as the "lord (*archon*) of this world," that is, as a prince who possessed an identifiable imperium and demesne—one that had physical and temporal dimensions.[42] The devil's God-given dominion extended throughout the created order in its fallen state and embraced the visible and invisible worlds below the celestial realm.[43] It was given to Satan until Christ reclaimed his patrimony upon his return in glory. While in Satan's possession, however, creation was a divisible kingdom: Satan could administer it as he saw fit. In Matthew and Luke's versions of Christ's temptation, for example, Satan offered Jesus "all the kingdoms of the world and the glory of them" in exchange for his submission (Matt 4.9). He did this on the premise that, in the world's fallen condition, such endowments were his to dispense. Indeed, this episode firmly established the principle that the devil could distribute gifts, boons and commissions to whomsoever he pleased in return for loyalty and service.[44]

The idea that the devil presided as lord over a structured and densely populated regime allowed Christians to render the demonological side of their cosmology with a complexity and nuance that otherwise would have been difficult. It created conceptual space for elements of the biblical narrative (as well as for cultural materials from other sources) to be interwoven relatively effortlessly through the fibres of monotheism. So, while the vast majority of the devil's legions toiled anonymously as perdition's drudges, and while these minions would multiply in the approaching apocalyptic battle between good and evil, by the early medieval period, the devil's court became a place to accommodate alien gods as well as biblical figures of special malevolence.[45] Indeed, through their prominence or persistence in the Hebrew canon, many of the numinous figures of the Tanakh were recast by Christians as the patrician class of Satan's blasted company.[46] Fiends such as Belial, Lilith, Asmodeus, Leviathan, Beelzebul, and others became governors and princes under the devil's rule. Indeed, demonic entities with Canaanite, Philistine, Babylonian, Assyrian, or Greco-Roman pedigrees came to be identified as seraphim or cherubim—or other angelic beings—who had become partisans against God in the heavenly civil war. This was a process that began in the intertestamental period with the development of new ideas about angels and demons in *Jubilees* and the *First Book of Enoch*; however, it was helped along by the rapid development of a distinctive Christian angelology under the 6th-century Neoplatonist, Pseudo-Dionysus, and others in the early medieval period. It might even be said that the principle of diabolical contrariety—the notion that Satan's realm should substantially reflect God's—increasingly demanded it.

By the early medieval period, scholars, preachers, and theologians had begun to speculate about the structure and design of the diabolical kingdom as well as about the sort of powers and duties disbursed to Satan's powerful lieutenants. In *The Dialogues*, for example, Pope Gregory I (d. 604) related a tale that was retold repeatedly throughout the Middle Ages concerning a pious bishop of Fondi in Lazio named Andrew. Gregory told how Bishop Andrew had been tempted by the presence of a particular holy woman in his household. This, according to Gregory, provided the "ancient enemy" with an opportunity to lure the bishop into sinful thoughts. A traveller, who was on his way from Campania to Rome, became caught up in the situation. Unable to find lodging for the night, the traveller took refuge not far from the bishop's palace in an abandoned temple of Apollo by the wayside. Uneasy about his decision to remain in this pagan space, the traveller, who was Jewish, rather unaccountably signed himself with the cross. Suddenly, around midnight, however

> there appeared before his eyes a crowd of evil spirits parading along like a guard of honor before some potentate. The master spirit himself sat down in the middle of the temple and began a formal investigation of each of his followers in order to find out how much wickedness each had done. As the spirits came up one by one to be tried, they reported what harm they had done to virtuous souls. One of them jumping up before the assembled crowd proclaimed how he had stirred up in the heart of Bishop Andrew a temptation of the flesh … The master spirit listened with avid ears … His attitude encouraged the spirit on trial to add a further detail, by relating how on the previous evening he had induced the holy man to give the woman a caressing pat on the back. Then the [master] spirit … encouraged his minion to complete what he had begun and win for himself an outstanding prize in ruining this great man.[47]

In this telling, the traveller reported the occurrence directly to Bishop Andrew, who tearfully admitted his lustful feelings and dismissed the nun—and all other women—from his service.

The traveller had clearly stumbled upon the council of a very great demon and his retainers. Readers of Gregory's era would no doubt have interpreted the encounter as an appearance of Lucifer or Abaddon, who frequently embodied himself as the Olympian god, Apollo—hence the setting. The conclave appeared to be a formal meeting, one that was rich in symbolism and demonstrations of dominance and authority. The "master spirit" demanded that his subordinates render accounts and justify themselves and their actions, presumably since their last meeting. There were opportunities to claim preferment and gifts, a ritual display of power, and evidence of dutiful service on the part of the master spirit's underlings (as well as, presumably, the master spirit's own hope for recognition from *his* superior). In short, the scene evoked the sort of political pomp that would have been immediately recognisable to post-Roman readers, as well as to subsequent audiences immersed in the symbolic vocabulary of feudal obligation and display. Doubtless, this is why the story was told in dozens of versions throughout the medieval era.[48] To update the tale and render it more familiar to readers of their own times, many authors added narrative elements. In the early 14th-century moral compendium *Handlyng Synne*, for example, Robert Manning of Brunne elaborated on the master spirit's interrogation of his inferiors. For their failure to live up to the expectations of their superior, they were subjected to a kind of rough feudal justice: one demon was beaten, while another was sent to trial.

The locus classicus for the monarchical view of the devil in the medieval period is perhaps *Genesis B* in the Junius Manuscript. This is an Old English reworking of the creation story from 10th-century England. The unknown author clearly understood Satan as a pretender, a usurper, and the lord of a rival kingdom to Yahweh:

> 'Why am I to toil?' said he. 'I have no need of a master; I can work as many wonders with my hands [as God]. I have great power to prepare a better throne, higher in heaven (cf. Isaiah 14). Why am I to wait upon his favor, bow before him with such homage? I can be a God like him. Strong comrades, bold-hearted heroes who will not fail me in the fight, stand by me. They, brave men, have chosen me for their master. With such comrades, a man can lay a plan, carry it out with such companions in war.

They are keen in their friendship to me, loyal in their hearts; I can be their leader, rule in this kingdom.[49]

There is very little doubt about the sort of regime the author of this text imagined for Satan and his angels. This is personal government bound by perverse notions of fealty and promises of service.

The trappings of diabolical monarchy proliferated throughout the medieval period and, in the process, authors increasingly made recourse to the vocabulary and symbols of the emerging feudal regime. Human degradation, particularly in relation to interactions with Satan, was frequently expressed through the idea of the sinister pact. While oaths and pacts were typically the devil's instruments of *human* control, verbal and written promises were often strictly enforced by his demons, who recognised the solemnity and legal weight of such promises. In James of Voragine's extremely popular 13th-century version of the deeds of St. Basil, for example, a slave turned to a sorcerer to help him win the love of a noble lady. The magician crafted a letter in which the man agreed, in return for the woman's affection, to renounce his Christian faith and to serve the evil one:

When [the sorcerer] gave the letter to the slave, he said: "Go and stand on the tomb of a heathen at midnight and cry out to the demons. Hold this letter up in the air, and they will come right away!" So the youth went and summoned the demons, throwing the letter into the air. In an instant the prince of darkness, surrounded by a swarm of demons, was at hand; and when he had read the letter, he asked: "Do you believe in me, that I can bring about what you want?" "I believe, my lord!" he answered. The devil: "And do you renounce your Christ?" The slave: "I renounce him!" [The devil then said] "If you want me to fulfil your desire, write me a script in your own hand, in which you profess to renounce Christ, your baptism, and the Christian faith; to be my servant; and to be condemned with me at the Last Judgment."[50]

The man repudiated Christ and indentured himself "to the service of the devil," at which point, Satan dispatched "spirits of fornication" to enflame the young woman with love for the slave. The two people subsequently married (against the wishes of the young woman's father); however, in the course of events, the bride also discovered her husband's deception. After he repented, the couple sought St. Basil's assistance to put things right. The saint signed the man with the cross and sealed him in a cell for three days and nights. Throughout his time enclosed, the man was tormented by the demons who had borne witness to his oath. They held the script before his eyes—proof of his committal to Satan's service. The matter culminated in a quasi-judicial confrontation between Basil and the devil, both with their entourages in tow. Upon securing the man's release from Satan's clutches, the magician's parchment descended from the lower air into Basil's outstretched hands. The saint destroyed the script and restored the man to his wife.

The entire affair was saturated with the symbols and assumptions of feudal obligation. Satan's demons offered their lord counsel and service throughout—from the moment the man sought the devil's aid upon a heap of heathen bones (in implicit mockery of the use of holy relics in commendation rites), to his public recognition of Satan's lordship before a court of demonic attendants, to the inviolable nature of the sworn contract. Throughout it all, Satan's minions supported their liege by attending him, bearing witness to the slave's infeudation, acting as his agents and proxies and intervening in support of their master's legal claims.

The resemblance of Satan's regime to a royal court was especially conspicuous in the literature of medieval preaching and folklore. Exemplary tales of the 13th to 15th centuries provide numerous allusions to demonic tournaments and processions, the chase (particularly in folkloric accounts of the Wild Hunt), not to mention the defence of hell's battlements by an army of hellish fiends. Satan is often greeted by human and demonic subordinates with a mocking kiss of peace, and, of course, the language of contracts and legal rights is deployed repeatedly. Satan has great lords and foot soldiers, counsellors and juridical officers. One particularly notable embellishment is the gradual emergence—at least in the folk traditions of medieval Europe—of a kind of infernal "royal family." Thus, the Satan of medieval preachers is often given a mother or grandmother—one whom he typically fears or loathes. He is also given daughters, usually seven or nine—often they preside over the cardinal vices. In some tales, Antichrist serves as the devil's "dauphin." While he has no hope of inheriting his sire's throne, he nevertheless fulfils the role of apparent heir. This is a kingdom that stood in opposition to God's heavenly court, preparing itself for the final confrontation between the elect and the damned.

## Offices and Ranks

The idea that the devil presided as a kind of monarch, together with the notion that he distributed powers unevenly among his retinue, prompted medieval Christians to imagine a diabolical host that was extremely stratified in its roles and offices. Accordingly, the demonic entities under Satan's command ranged in the Christian imagination from powerful princely devils who presided over whole realms of wickedness, to trifling bogies who seemed barely evil. While some demons might be given jurisdiction over entire kingdoms or nations, orders of society, or classes of sin, others could be tasked with far more modest assignments: instigating a conflict between neighbours, raising a windstorm, or even wracking some poor soul with a toothache. Some fiends appear to have acted as infernal handymen, pitching in wherever their malicious talents were needed—but having no fixed responsibility of their own. There were imps who appeared spatially bound, haunting particular locations or regions. There were devils who promoted specific illnesses or afflictions. There were demons who lingered for decades in the shadow a single individual, and others who manifested themselves only fleetingly to tempt a person to commit a particular sin.

Because they could take so many forms and assert their malevolence in such a variety of ways, the urge to identify wicked spirits and their objectives appeared early in the history of the church. The author of I John, for example, advised the faithful to "believe not every spirit, but to test the spirits to see whether they are of God" (I John 4.1), while the apostle Paul declared that, because Satan sometimes disguised himself as an "angel of light," it was not strange that his minions might also disguise themselves as "servants of righteousness" (2 Cor 11.14-15). In this way, the desire to disentangle the attributes and motives of spirits—that is, the desire to *discern* them—represents the beginning of Christian demonology, the science of knowing demons.[51] And because their cunning and persistence were so great, the need to know them fully and precisely was acute. It was inextricably tied to the matter of how souls are saved from eternal torment.

While New Testament authors appear to have developed primitive typologies of demons, proposing, for example, the existence of fiends which presided over "specialisations" such as divination (Acts 16.16), jealousy (James 3. 13-16), and possession of human beings (Matt 12), the first Christian attempts to devise systematic demonological schemes occurred in the works of Patristic-era monastic writers such as Athanasius of Alexandria and Evagrius Pontus.[52] While Athanasius' *Life of Antony* was probably the earliest text to dwell on the great variety, order, and seeming ontological instability of demonic spirits, it was the Anatolian solitary (and later, heretic) Evagrius of Pontus (d. c. 400) who, in *The Monk* (*Praktikos*), proposed one of the earliest formal typologies.[53] Here, he listed eight vices, calling them variously "demons" and "tempting thoughts." He warned that these spirits waged unrelenting combat against hermits, that there were no humans who equalled them in their bitterness, and that, to confuse and exhaust the monks, they undertook all their stratagems at once. Evagrius' list included the demons of gluttony, sexual immorality, love of money, sadness, anger, acedia (a kind of slothfulness particular to monks), vainglory, and pride.[54] He described each of them in detail, particularly how they worked on the human soul to produce evil. Evagrius' characterisations show a sometimes surprising level of sophistication and psychological insight.

It became common by the medieval period for Christians to link spheres of sin (or other dominions) to specific named demons—typically, princely fiends. The impulse to do so was no doubt initially connected with the desire to gain dominance or mastery over them, in the hope of ultimately defeating them. In the Christian view, the authority to give things names was inherently powerful: it was a responsibility given to Adam by Yahweh before the fall. Indeed, it was so potent that, when rites of exorcism began to emerge, many of them adjured demons to reveal their identity—just as Christ had commanded in the case of the Gerasene demoniac. Knowing precisely which fiend one was confronting helped the faithful to diagnose and treat demonic vexation. Indeed, through a protracted process of trial and error, medieval exorcists devised regimes of treatment and cures that pertained to specific demons. In a sense, then, by aligning vices with specific demonic "sponsors," Christians attempted to ascertain and describe predictable forms of deliverance, forms which efficiently and reliably adduced the workings of grace. The 15th-century Lollard text, the *Lanterne of Light*, offers insight into the classificatory priorities of Christian demonology during the late medieval age. Echoes of Evagrius' moral concerns are still detectable throughout, though the author has also implied connections with sacramental offices:

These seven sacraments: baptism, confirming and penance, orders, Christ's body, matrimony and the last anointing. These help us in this fighting church against seven deadly sins that are seven cruel devils. The first is Lucifer that rules in his malice over the children of pride. The second is called Beelzebub that lords over envy. The third devil is Satan and wrath is his lordship. The fourth is called Abaddon. The slothful are his retinue. The fifth devil is Mammon and (he) has with him the avaricious and also one that is his fear, a foul sin, covetousness. The sixth is called Belphegor. That is the god of gluttons. The seventh devil is Asmodeus, who leads the lecherous. But the seven sacraments cast out these devils from the servants of God that rescue effectively and establish in them seven gifts that are called those of the Holy Ghost.[55]

In some instances, scripture offered the key to a demon's presumed identity: the spirit Mammon was originally connected with love of money in the gospel of Matthew (6.24).[56]

In the deuterocanonical book of Tobit, the fiend Asmodeus prevented Sarah from consummating her marriage (and thus was presumed to have responsibilities over carnal matters). In other instances, demonic connections with spheres of influence were traditional or speculative and varied somewhat in surviving taxonomies.

The tendency to align particular demons with jurisdictions and offices reached its fullest expression between the 15th and 17th centuries, largely in the context of debates over witchcraft and learned magic, particularly the necromantic tradition.[57] Throughout the period, theologians, exorcists, inquisitors and natural philosophers fashioned increasingly complex demonological taxonomies, which were devised largely via idiosyncratic readings of scripture, hermetic and Neoplatonic literature, and, to a lesser extent, the book of nature. Many existed in dialogue with the angelological traditions of pseudo-Dionysius. The anonymous *Lesser Key of Solomon* (sometimes called the *Lemegeton*), a grimoire written in the middle of the 17th century, for instance, offers a sense of the encyclopaedic aspirations of late medieval and Renaissance demonologists. Here, the author proposed the existence of 72 named demonic "nobles," each of which was opposed by a corresponding angel from the Christian Kabbalah. Each demon was identified by name, rank, their appearance, function(s), and the number of legions they had at their command. The author also included sigils or staves to identify the spirits and to assist those consulting the book to summon or repel the fiends (using arcane rituals and forms of binding). A partial list offers a sense of the scale and range of demonic personalities and their priorities:

| Name | Rank | Appearance | Function | Number of legions |
|---|---|---|---|---|
| 44. Shax | marquis | stock dove, with a hoarse and subtle voice | takes away sight and hearing; steals from kings | 30 |
| 45. Vine | king and earl | lion, riding a black horse with a viper in his hand | finds hidden things; reveals the past and future; throws down walls; makes seas rough | 35 |
| 46. Bifrons | earl | monster, then a man | teaches trivium and quadrivium; teaches herbs and stones; switches bodies in their graves | 6 |
| 47. Vual | duke | dromedary, then an Egyptian-speaking man | Procures the love of women; tells of things past, present, and future; procures friendships | 37 |

These sorts of plans survive in various forms in dozens of different grimoires and demonological manuals from the period.[58] However, the ideas and worldview that underpin them can also be seen—often implicitly—in the works of those charged with identifying and prosecuting those who were believed to consort with demons. Thus, the demonologies of witch-finders, inquisitors, and exorcists, while they often do not list Satan's minions in such precise or fulsome detail, nevertheless start from the proposition that vast, complex networks of demons were labouring in different capacities to frustrate the salvation of Christians. In condemning their recourse to demons, for example, the Catalan

Dominican inquisitor Nicholas Eymeric (d. 1399) stated in his *Against those Who Invoke Demons* (*Contra demonum inuocatores*) that necromantic practitioners praised "superior demons," and that others, slightly less culpably, unwittingly mixed the names of demons with the names of the saints in lesser forms of magic.[59] In the well-known *The Hammer of Witches*, Heinrich Kramer (d. c. 1506) and Jacob Sprenger (d. 1495) distinguished the habits of lower demons from those of higher ones. They stated that only lower demons could bring themselves to have sexual relations with humans because, for more exalted demons, "the nobility of their nature caused [them] to balk at committing certain actions and filthy deeds."[60]

While most premodern Christians were not especially engaged in cataloguing the names and habits of demons, the idea that demons manifested themselves in diverse forms and could specialise in specific types of mischief was widespread. Two common "species" of medieval demons, drawing on far older ideas, were thought to vex the faithful: seducing demons and personal fiends. Christians described the activities of the *succubus* (a night demon that seduced men) and the *incubus* (a fiend that preyed on women). While there could be great regional and chronological variation with respect to what kind of threat they represented, there appears to have been some agreement regarding their habits and presentation: *succubi* and *incubi* were unwanted nocturnal spirits who presented themselves to humans for the express purpose of engaging in sexual relations with them. Though they were sometimes thought to appear in dreams or visions, in many instances, they were believed to take corporeal form, rousing their intended target in order to assault them physically. They often proffered themselves in alluring guises, though they could revert to other forms (such as hags or gremlins) at will. Their intention was to corrupt and befoul the souls of Christians and to incite them to more conscious and deliberate perversions, as well as to habituate their victims to sexual excess and impropriety. The figure of the nocturnal demon was probably used to explain a number of concerns, including sleep paralysis, erotic dreams, and nocturnal emissions.[61] They could also be deployed to account for more tragic circumstances, including unwanted pregnancies, birth defects, or developmental delays in newborns. Accusations of demonic coupling were also regularly advanced to impugn the reputations of people considered disreputable. Although theologians such as Thomas Aquinas denied that demons could in themselves have any procreative power, stories abounded about folkloric and historical figures presumed to be "cambions," or *cambiti*, the hybrid offspring of demonic coupling. Robert the Devil, Sir Gowther, and Merlin were among the literary and folkloric figures tainted by the accusation. Historical figures included Eustace the Monk and Eleanor of Aquitaine. Eleanor was a particular target of polemicists and the prurient. Matthew of Paris suspected that she was something akin to the water-spirit, Melusine, while the great Cistercian raconteur, Caesarius of Heisterbach, claimed that she was descended from a "phantom mother."[62]

One of the critical issues, however, for those who promoted the idea that demons could seduce humans was the matter of demonic "biology." The mechanics of such liaisons were not entirely clear. Because demons were widely held to have aerial bodies, questions lingered over their sexual compatibility with humans, particularly in matters pertaining to fertility. Several authors, including William of Auvergne, Thomas Aquinas, and Heinrich Kramer, appear to have argued that, on balance, the possibility of demonic sex was real. Some cited as proof the story of angelic-human unions in Genesis 6. The prodigious offspring known as the Nephilim established a clear basis for belief in the sexual compatibility of humans and spirits.[63] Others had difficulty imagining that such couplings were in any way possible, asserting that those who claimed intimacy with demons were simply deluded. For those who believed that demon sex could be "productive," various circumlocutions were proposed for successful conceptions. The 15th-century Castilian scholar, Alfonso Tostado, for example, claimed:

> Once in a while procreation can happen … through the agency of incubus and succubus demons … For in the form of a succubus the demon can gather the semen thus emitted; thence, having turned himself into an incubus, he can deposit it in the vessel of a woman, and the woman will conceive.[64]

Some Christians appear to have believed that, during the sexual act, demons could interfere with the human seed to assist in the creation of monstrous offspring. Others argued that they simply procured semen from hellacious human figures in a kind of abominable "husbandry" programme.[65]

Regardless of how it might have worked, the fear of demonic sex with humans—generative or otherwise—was, of course, pernicious. Moral panics surrounding the notion that women had carnal relations with demonic spirits (or Satan himself), and that they received sexual pleasure from the activity, in no small way contributed to the fevered climate of the witch prosecutions after c. 1540.

The notion that spirits can attend or serve specific humans is also very old. It has several antecedents, including the household gods of Rome such as the *lares* and *penates*, as well as the fetches, *fylgjur* and other "following" spirits of Celtic and Germanic heathenism.[66] Thus, while in medieval folkways, spirit beings sometimes attached themselves to persons to protect or serve them, in the strictly orthodox understanding of their activities, they did so invariably as demonic presences. While personal demons could manifest themselves in a variety of ways, they are perhaps best known—particularly in premodern Britain—for their supposed offices to sorcerers and those practising *maleficium* (i.e., witchcraft). In this instance, they are often called familiars or familiar spirits, and their service was provided according to the terms of a formal or implicit pact. According to late medieval understandings of their operation, they could take a great variety of forms (and could change their shape at will). In most accounts, they appeared as animals. Typically, they manifested themselves for their master in the constant shape of a cat, raven, dog, hare, hedgehog or some other small mammal. Sometimes they took the form of more frightful animals such as lizards, horseflies, frogs, or toads. There are also instances of familiar spirits appearing as larger animals: wolves, horses, bears, etc., or even as human companions. In the case of the latter, they would generally take the form of slightly "exotic" human figures such as Moors, Spaniards, woodsmen, or Sami shamans.[67] To underscore the regular service provided by the familiar—as well as the complicity of those employing such fiends—early modern accounts sometimes emphasise a familiar's homely or unassuming pet name: Bomelius, Vinegar Tom, Krütli, Federwisch, to name a few.[68] In 1582, an accused Essex witch, "Mother Bennet," confessed to having two familiars, a black dog named Suckin, and a creature called Lierd, who was "red like a lion."[69] In witchcraft accusations, familiars tended to exist in a symbiotic relationship with the witch. The demons provided care and service, and, in return, the witch nourished them, often through a superfluous nipple or teat that could be located on any part of the witch's body. Witchcraft investigations frequently included invasive searches for these teats.

## Reimagining Demons

While attempts to establish demonic typologies were clearly an element of the Christian desire to understand and explain the order of the cosmos, and while they stemmed, in large measure, from the impulse to contain wicked spirits in order to effect salvation, classification was also a necessary outgrowth of the collision between Christian ontology and the persistent beliefs of former times. Indeed, creatures such as *succubi* and *incubi* or familiar spirits already brush against the attempts of learned Christians in the Middle Ages to understand and assimilate beings from rival cosmologies within their ways of knowing. Many theologians understood seducing demons to be identical to creatures that originated outside the framework of Christian categories of being, creatures that many Europeans still knew as the fae, fairies, *dusii*, hidden people, the good ladies, and so on. Moreover, as noted above, "familiar spirits" almost certainly had their origins, at least in part, in *lares* and *penates*, *fylgjur*, Doppelgangers and the like.

Like many of those who gathered and catalogued popular stories for preaching, Caesarius of Heisterbach confronted this issue in his 1223 work *The Dialogue on Miracles* (*Dialogus miraculorum*). There, he recorded a number of exemplary tales about demons who seem somehow less than demonic—at least in the conventional understanding of how wicked spirits are supposed to operate. In one *exemplum* designed to show the fundamental deviousness of Satan's followers, for example, Caesarius told of a diabolical minion who bound himself in service to a Christian knight.[70] The knight did not know the demon's identity and "found his new servant to be extremely helpful, respectful, and faithful."[71] The servant was of course able to offer aid that was beyond the capabilities of a human retainer, so, in the course of the story, Caesarius had his knight interrogate the underling about his true nature. When the imp told him "I am a demon, one of those who fell with Lucifer," the knight enquired: "If you are by nature a demon, why is it that you serve a man so faithfully?" The demon answered, mournfully, that it was his greatest consolation to serve the sons of men. He went on to assure the knight that he would never harm him. As a good Christian, however, the knight had no recourse but to dismiss the imp from his service with full pay. The demon returned the coins proffered, however, and asked the knight to use the money to purchase bells for a nearby church to call the faithful to prayer. With this tale, Caesarius appears to have stumbled upon the European fairy tradition.

In trying to make sense of the creature's behaviour, Caesarius stated that the demon was not an *active rebel* against God but had merely "consented to join the proud ones" who had risen up against him during the war in heaven. He went on to state that there are angels who fell with the rest of the demons, but "they are less evil, and can do less harm to men."[72] While the idea that demons could pose a greater or lesser threat was consistent with the teachings of the Church, the notion that they could be good and faithful servants was troubling to many Christians. And the view that some spirits remained neutral in the angelic rebellion crossed the line into heterodoxy. Indeed, in the moral universe of orthodox belief, there was very little room for non-partisans, conscientious objectors, or those who simply got caught up in the heavenly revolt. From the Patristic period forward, theologians stressed the binary choice available to both humans and angelic beings: goodness or evil. Christ had said that those who were not against him were with him, but he never made provisions for a middle ground.[73]

With *daimones*, *lares*, and other Mediterranean spirits folded into the Christian understanding of the demonic during the classical period, it is not surprising then that, when

Christian theologians encountered other cultures, they assimilated the spirit beings of these cosmologies within the scope of their understanding. Indeed, when Christians encountered the fauns, goblins, elves, gnomes, trolls, huldufolk, and other spirits of the Celtic and Germanic traditions, they launched a similarly vigorous campaign of demonisation against the godlings of heathenism. There was no question of denying the reality of these tenacious small gods of earlier times; it was instead a matter of how to construe the evidence. As Francis Young puts it, it was not so much an issue of "diametrically opposed" cosmologies as it was a case of different interpretations of the same set of beings.[74] And these godlings remained an important presence for many Europeans both within and outside the Christian tradition, particularly in contexts that appeared cosmologically ambiguous or morally ambivalent. Their existence could account for small hardships, minor boons, unexpected windfalls, and the daily accidents of an uncertain world. These uneasy creatures of the gloaming created spaces for negotiation with the spirit world, spaces that many medieval Christians appear to have longed for. Indeed, as with Caesarius, the appeal of ambiguous spirits permeated medieval society at a number of levels—and even extended to places that should have proscribed them.

The need to reconcile "the heathen numinous" within the framework of orthodox Christian cosmology resulted in many creative attempts at accommodation. However, as Richard Firth Green has shown in *Elf Queens and Holy Friars*, virtually all attempts at accommodation that were *not* forms of demonisation were met with contempt and resistance by the theological elite. Indeed, the official church issued repeated condemnations of fairy belief and sought to re-channel errant believers towards orthodoxy. In Burchard of Worms' 11th-century penitential work, *The Corrector*, for example, pastors attempted to police belief (and thereby demonise ambiguous spirits) by asking penitents, "Have you believed what some are accustomed to believe that there are rural women whom they call sylvans?"[75] For such ideas, he prescribed a penitential fast of ten days on bread and water.[76] Later, in the anonymous 14th-century Franciscan preaching text the *Fasciculus Morum*, under the rubric "People who go against the faith," the author inveighed against evil spirits who were said to appear, variously, as elves or by night as "beautiful queens and dancing girls."[77] From the perspective of medieval clerics, the ability of demons to cloak themselves in the guise of such ambiguous or even pleasing forms was disconcerting, but it was also readily overcome through the application of the correct forms of religion. Firth Green relates a story from Thomas of Cantimpré's moral tome, *Bonum universale de apibus* (*On the Good Society of Bees*, c. 1260), that outlines how Christians ought to construe and rebuff fairy belief. The tale concerns a heretic who claimed that he had visited Christ and his mother in a palace deep inside a mountain, one that, despite its subterranean seclusion, "shone with a wonderful brightness." The heretic asked a Dominican friar to join him in his adoration of the Virgin Mary inside the mountain. The canny friar, however, suspected a demonic illusion, so only agreed to visit the site after secreting a consecrated host in the folds of his habit. When they arrived at what was apparently Mary's glittering throne, they were met by an impressive host of patriarchs and angels. Falling down in reverence, the heretic beseeched the friar to do likewise. Instead, the Dominican held up the host and the illusion vanished. The heretic repented of his error.

These sorts of stories must have been written as much for preachers and confessors as for their presumed lay audiences. Indeed, the widespread acceptance of the existence of such beings was remarkably enduring, both in the folkways of premodern Europe and in the literary canon. Thus, if anything, ecclesiastical admonitions against fairy belief and the demonisation of numinous beings gathered momentum as the medieval period proceeded. One of the critical moments in the largely unsuccessful endeavour to stamp out the intrusion of heathen godlings into orthodox belief came in 1398, when the theological faculty of the University of Paris issued a charter listing 28 errors. Most of the articles concerned *maleficium*, the summoning of spirits for necromantic purposes, the use of images and so on. Many scholars have viewed the document as one of the ideological or theoretical frames around which the European obsession with *maleficium* began to intensify in early modernity—an obsession which would ultimately culminate in the gruesome spectacle of the witch hunts more than a century later. But article 23 stated explicitly, "It is an error [to believe] that some demons are good, some are friendly, some are all-knowing, and that others are neither saved nor damned."[78]

The clarity of the message and the urgency of its delivery accelerated towards the end of the Middle Ages. Thus, these sorts of opinions were carried by scholars and prelates to the Councils of Constance (1414–18) and Basel (1431–42), and thence, to the universities, cathedral schools, and monasteries of Europe through the 15th and early 16th centuries. They informed discussions concerning the sorts of spirits that the 14th-century Swedish saint, Birgitta of Sweden, had encountered (and whether her cult should be recognised); they appeared in the theological discourses of those seeking to stamp out the proposed reforms of the 15th-century Bohemian reformers, the Hussites; they were no doubt mixed among the sheaves of learned opinions carried by Joan of Arc's interrogators when they questioned her about the fairy tree at Domrémy-la-Pucelle. Ultimately, they were situated in tomes like Johannes Nider's *Formicarius* and Kramer and Sprenger's *Hammer of Witches* (*Malleus maleficarum*)—works that would have an increasingly decisive and material impact on the affairs of the 16th and 17th centuries.

## Conclusion

Despite his malevolence, brutishness and lack of fidelity, in virtually every version and rendering that has survived, the devil of the Middle Ages and early modernity commanded a steadfast host of wicked vassals. To be sure, his status as a governor of preternatural beings was a core facet of his identity. And he was a lord who brooked no opposition from his subordinates. His minions could range from fiends of unparalleled viciousness to imps of passing menace. Satan's ability to govern this motley swarm with such pomp and authority was necessary, though, for it inversely mirrored the lord's greatness and it magnified Christ's victory on the cross. Indeed, God gave succour to his Church against not only the assaults of his aggrieved former archangel, but also against the incessant barrage of Satan's near inexhaustible reserve of fallen angels. These foul creatures relentlessly besieged the faithful and occupied virtually every corner of the world in its fallen state. God's ability to hold them at bay and repel them, even as this boundless cohort stood in readiness to test every corner of the sublunary cosmos, spoke to the creator's unparalleled power, his ubiquity, and his care for his creation. Thus, Satan's minions fulfilled the roles allotted them, and they did so as much to amplify God's glory as to stand in defiance against the divine plan for humanity's salvation. After all, as St Paul observed, where sin abounded, grace did much more abound (Rm 5.20-1).

It was largely for this reason that the fiends of the Middle Ages were such fungible, pliable creatures, standing where they were needed and taking whatever shape was required of them. Indeed, in many respects, the less precisely the category "demon" was defined, the more useful it was as an explanatory tool. It filled gaps, smoothed over flaws, and reconciled inconsistencies in the narrative of sacred history with exceptional utility and ease. This is also the reason that one of the central projects of medieval Christendom was to refine, extend, and continuously reinvent the scope of the church's demonological claims. Theologians of the period systematised and rationalised the dimensions of Satan's kingdom to meet the exigencies of shifting political, cultural and cosmological terrain—but also so that it might be brought into alignment with Christendom's increasingly hegemonic claims.[79] Thus, as Christians encountered rival and competing religious systems, the numinous beings of their opponents' imaginations were subsumed within the vocabulary and categories of being of the church. It was an inflationary process, however: the more that Christians watched for and detected signifiers of the demonic, the more demons they were able to detect. As Christians increased their ability and willingness to patrol the limits of ecclesiastical discipline and to impose their claims upon the daily lives of the Europeans towards the end of the medieval period, they endowed the devil's realm with a far greater sense of menace and immediacy.

## Notes

1 Jón Kalman Stefánsson, *Heaven and Hell* (London, 2011), 16.

2 William Blake, *The Marriage of Heaven and Hell* (Boston, 1906), 10.

3 See Fabian Campagne, "Demonology at a Crossroads: The Visions of Ermine de Reims and the Image of the Devil on the Eve of the European Witch-Hunt," *Church History* 80, no. 3 (2011): 467–97.

4 See Justin P. Jeffcoat Schedtler, "Satan in Biblical Literature," in this volume.

5 For the scriptural basis of these ideas, see, for example, Isaiah 14 and Ezekiel 28 (fall of the king of Tyre); in the New Testament, see Matthew 25, 1 Corinthians 6, and 2 Peter 2. Cf. Revelation 12 as well as the extrabiblical books of Enoch and Jubilees. All biblical references in this chapter are based on the Revised Standard Version, Catholic edition (RSVCE).

6 See, for example, John of Damascus, *Exposition of the Orthodox Faith*, trans. E.W. Watson and L. Pullan, 2.4 "Concerning the devil and demons."

7 On demons and the assimilation of difference, see Euan Cameron, *Enchanted Europe: Superstition, Reason, and Religion, 1250–1750* (Oxford, 2010), ch. 5; Michael Bailey, *Fearful Spirits, Reasoned Follies: The Boundaries of Superstition in Late Medieval Europe* (Ithaca, 2013), ch. 1, "The Weight of Tradition"; Francis Young, *Twilight of the Godlings: The Shadowy Beginnings of Britain's Supernatural Beings* (Cambridge, 2023), esp. chs. 3 and 4.

8 It also escalated the stakes: because he had so many agents at his disposal, if one managed to arouse the focus of Satan himself, then that person must be an exceptionally great sinner!

9 See Nancy Caciola, *Discerning Spirits: Divine and Demonic Possession in the Middle Ages* (Ithaca, 2003) and Moshe Sluhovsky, *Believe Not Every Spirit: Possession, Mysticism, and Discernment in Early Modern Catholicism* (Chicago, 2007).

10 See, for example, 2 Cor. 6.15: "What accord has Christ with Belial? Or what has a believer in common with an unbeliever?"

11 See Rudolf Otto's understanding of the numinous in *The Idea of the Holy: An Inquiry into the Non-Rational Factors in the Idea of the Divine and its Relation to the Rational*, trans. John W. Harvey (Oxford, 1923).

12 For example, evil spirits that bring sickness. Or the satyrs (*se'irim*) who dance and gambol in the wastes of the Negev in Isaiah 14 and 34. See Schedtler, "Satan in Biblical Literature." See also John H. Walton and J. Harvey Walton, *Demons and Spirits in Biblical Theology: Reading the Biblical Text in its Cultural and Literary Context*, (Eugene, Oregon, 2019), 55–85.

13 As Valerie Flint notes, demons "were one of the features of the old pre-Christian magical world most enthusiastically transferred." See Valerie Flint, *The Rise of Magic in Early Medieval Europe* (Princeton, 1993), 157. Cf. Martha Rampton, *Trafficking with Demons: Magic, Ritual, and Gender from Late Antiquity to 1000* (Ithaca, 2022).

14 See Homer, *The Iliad*, trans. A.T. Murray, 3.420, 8.66, 11.792, 17.98; cf. Hesiod, *Works and Days*, trans. Hugh G. Evelyn-White, 121–6; 252–5 and *Theogony*, trans. Hugh G. Evelyn-White, 991.

15 In its Greek and Latin forms, the term δαίμων/demon could often be used interchangeably with θεός or deus, -a. So, for example, in his *Apology of Socrates*, Plato famously referred to the unseen entity that guided his master as a θεοῦ σημεῖον (godlike sign) or δαιμονίου σημεῖον (demonic sign).

16 See, for example, Hesiod *Works and Days*, 122–6.

17 Tanakh is an acronym or portmanteau for Torah, Nevi'im, and Ketuvim (i.e., the Law, Prophets, and Writings). It is the word used by Jews for the Hebrew canon of scripture, roughly, what Christians refer to as the Old Testament.

18 Anna Angelini, "Δαίμονες and Demons in Hellenistic Judaism: Continuities and Transformations," in *Demons in Early Judaism and Christianity* (Leiden, 2022), 54–73.

19 See James E. Hogg, "'Belial' in the Old Testament," *The American Journal of Semitic Languages and Literatures* 44, no. 1 (October 1927): 56–8. It is an exceptionally complex matter. See, for example, Annette Yoshiko Reed, "When did *Daimones* become Demons? Revisiting Septuagintal Data for Ancient Jewish Demonology," *Harvard Theological Review* 16, no. 3 (July 2023): 340–75.

20 Angelini, "Δαίμονες and Demons in Hellenistic Judaism," 57.

21 See, Ryan E. Stokes, *Satan: How God's Executioner Became the Enemy* (Grand Rapids, 2019). See also Robin Lane Fox, *Pagans and Christians* (London, 1986), 117, 130, 297; John H. Walton and J. Harvey Walton, *Demons and Spirits in Biblical Theology* (Eugene, 2019); Anna Angelini, "Naming the Gods of Others in the *Septuagint*: Lexical Analysis and Historical-Religious Implications," *Kernos: Revue internationale et pluridisciplinaire de religion grecque antique* 32 (2019). https://journals.openedition.org/kernos/3150

22 As best as we can reconstruct from Origen of Alexandria's *Contra Celsum*, for example, in the now lost *Logos Alethes*, Celsus the Philosopher accused Origen and other Christians of fundamentally misconstruing the nature of *daimones* and the gods of Greece in their writings. See esp. Origen, *Contra Celsum*, trans. Frederick Crombie, 7:68–8:63. Cf. Bernhard Pick, "The Attack of Celsus on Christianity," *The Monist* 21, no. 2 (1911): 223–66. This view can also be discerned in Justin Martyr's *Apology*, trans. Marcus Dods and George Reith, 1.5–6, in which the author rebuts pagan objections to Christians' characterisations of demons as evil actors. He even seems to suggest that Socrates' belief in the goodness of demons made him vulnerable to their attacks and eventually led to his death. See also Elaine Pagels, *The Origin of Satan* (New York, 1996), 143–5.

23 See Matthew 8.28–34; Mark 5.1–20; Luke 8.26–39. The story does not appear in John.

24 *Pneuma ponera* does not occur in LXX. The only occurrence of *pneuma akatharta* in the Greek Old Testament appears in the minor prophet, Zechariah 13.2.

25 See Schedtler, "Satan in Biblical Literature."

26 See Reed, "When did *Daimones* become Demons?"

27 Pagels, *Origin of Satan*, chs. 3 and 4.

28 See Book of Wisdom, chs. 13–15. Cf. Pagels, *Origin of Satan*, ch. 5; see also Ramsay MacMullen, *Christianizing the Roman Empire (AD 100–400)* (New Haven, 1984), 17–8.

29 See Naomi G. Cohen, "Philo and Midrash," *Judaism* 44, no. 2 (1995): 196–207. Cf. Edmund Stein, *Philo und der Midrasch. Philos Schilderung der Gestalten des Pentateuch verglichen mit der des Midrasch* (Gießen, 1931).

30 Philo, *On the Creation: Allegorical Interpretations of Genesis 2 and 3*, trans. F. H. Colson, G. H. Whitaker (Cambridge, 1929).

31 On the fourfold sense of Scripture, see Henri de Lubac, *Medieval Exegesis: The Four Senses of Scripture*, trans. Mark Sebanc and E. M. Macierowski, 2 vols. (Grand Rapids, 1998–2000).

32 Justin Martyr, *Dialogue with Trypho*, trans. Marcus Dods and George Reith, 103.

33 Quoted in C. S. Lewis, *The Discarded Image* (Cambridge, 1964), 1.

34 See Thibault Maus de Rolley, "Putting the Devil on the Map: Demonology and Cosmography in the Renaissance," in *Boundaries, Extents and Circulations: Space and Spatiality in Early Modern Natural Philosophy*, eds. K. Vermeir and J. Regier (Cham, 2016), 179–207.

35 Augustine of Hippo provided a comprehensive description of demonic attributes in *De divinatione daemonum* (*On the Divination of Demons*, trans. Charles T. Wilcox and others). See also Joseph Lycha, ed., *Corpus scriptorium ecclesiasticorum Latinorum* 41 (Prague, 1900), 599–618. See also *Dictionnaire de spiritualite*, s.v., "Demon."

36 According to John, the dragon's tail "swept down a third of the stars of heaven, and cast them to the earth." Read in conjunction with texts such as Daniel 7, Christian scholars interpreted the passage as an indication of the scale of the heavenly rebellion.

37 Richalmus of Schöntal, *Liber Revelationum*, quoted in *The Medieval Devil: A Reader*, eds. Richard Raiswell and David R. Winter (Toronto, 2022), 129. During the early modern era, some scholars attempted to scientifically calculate the precise number of demons at Satan's command. Johannes Weyer asserted that Satan commanded 1,111 legions of 6,666 demons each. This produced a total number of 7,405,926 diabolical auxiliaries. A Swiss theologian named Martin Barrhaus disagreed, putting the number at 2,665,866,746,664. See Maximilian Rudwin, "The Number of Devils" in *The Devil in Legend and Literature* (La Salle, 1931), 290–1.

38 See Genesis 6.1–4 and Numbers 13.32–3. Their role was greatly elaborated in the pseudepigraphic Book of Enoch and other intertestamental writings. On the tradition of the watcher angels coupling with human women, see Schedtler, "Satan in Biblical Literature," and Wright, "The Myth of the Devil in the Early Church," in this volume.

39 According to the 17th-century scholar, Thomas Browne, the "empire of truth" is so large that "it hath place within the walls of Hell, and the Devils themselves are daily forced to practise it." In other words, the lord of misrule ruled by order. See Browne, *Pseudodoxia Epidemica* (London, 1646; 6th ed. 1672) 1.11 on 45–6.

40 In the Septuagint, *Eosphoros*, "the dawn bringer," from the Hebrew, *helel*.

41 Cf. Ephesians 1.21 in which Paul lists the orders of angels.

42 See John 12.31; cf. 1 John 5.19, 2 Corinthians 4.4.

43 In Ephesians 2.2, Satan the prince of the power of the air.

44 Cf. Luke 4.6, "… for it has been delivered to me, and I give it to whom I will."

45 See Esther Hamari, *God's Monsters* (Minneapolis, 2023), esp. "Part 1: God's Entourage."

46 Satan's "great commands" often retained elements of their biblical name: thus, the Hebrew *B'liya'al* became Belial; the Canaanite *Ba'al z'vuv* became Beelzebub; the Avestan *Aesma-daeva* became Asmodeus; *Livyatan* became Leviathan.

47 Gregory the Great, *Dialogues*, trans. Odo John Zimmerman, 3.7.

48 The tale appears in Caesarius of Heisterbach, *Libri octo miraculorum*, 2.56, Jacques de Vitry (Crane, no. 131), and Odo of Ceriton, *Parabolae*, no. 32. Versions of it also appeared in the *Speculum Laicorum*, no. 188, the Seelentrost, 150.17, the *Liber exemplorum ad usum predicantium*, no 26, and at least a dozen anonymous collections of preaching tales from the 13th to 15th centuries contained in the British Library. On these, see Tubach, *Index Exemplorum* (Helsinki, 1969), no. 1663, 136, and Herbert, *Catalogue of Romances*, vol 2, *passim*.

49 R. K. Gordon, *Genesis B* from *Anglo-Saxon Poetry* (London, 1922), 100–4.

50 James of Voragine, *The Golden Legend: Readings on the Saints*, vol. 1, trans. William Granger Ryan (Princeton, 1993), 109–2.

51 See Caciola, *Discerning Spirits*, introduction; see also Brian Levack, *The Devil Within: Possession and Exorcism in the Christian West* (New Haven, 2013), chs. 1 and 2.

52 See, for example, Juanita Feros Ruys, *Demons in the Middle Ages*, 14–7, 20–2.

53 Athanasius described Antony's encounters with demonic spirits in graphic and striking terms. See Athanasius of Alexandria, *Life of Antony*, trans. H. Ellershaw, chs. 22–3, 88. Cf. *The Medieval Devil: A Reader*, 106–10.

54 See Evagrius, *Praktikos* chs. 6–14. Evagrius elaborates on each of these demons in the *Antirrhetikos* (*The Counter-Arguments*), *passim*. Another early demonological text is the anonymous and pseudepigraphical Testament of Solomon; however, its place in the development of demonological typologies is uncertain, and the text's date of composition is disputed. Some claim that the text is Patristic era, while others assert that it did not achieve its final form till the 12th or 13th century. For a translation of the relevant sections, see *Medieval Devil: A Reader*, 62–6.

55 *The lanterne of lizt*, Ed. from *MS Harl. 2324*, ed. Lilian M. Swinburn (London, 1917), 59–60 (modernised).

56 Cf. Luke 16.11.

57 Necromancy is a category of magical practice that sought to communicate with (and control) the spirits of dead humans and preternatural beings, including angels and demons. See Frank Klaassen and Sharon Hubbs Wright, *The Magic of Rogues: Necromancers in Early Tudor England* (University Park, 2021), introduction.

58 See, for example, Richard Kieckhefer, *Forbidden Rites: A Necromancer's Manual of the Fifteenth Century* (University Park, 1997). I have used Kieckhefer's list of demonic princes as a template for the one I offer here.

59 Michael Bailey, "From Sorcery to Witchcraft: Clerical Conceptions of Magic in the Later Middle Ages," *Speculum* 76, no. 4 (2001): 972–3.

60 See Heinrich Kramer and Jacob Sprenger, *The Hammer of Witches: A Complete Translation of the Malleus maleficarum*, trans. Christopher Mackay (Cambridge UK, 2006), 25B.

61 See Nadine Metzger, "Incubus as an Illness: Taming the Demonic by Medical Means in Late Antiquity and Beyond," in *The Devil in Society in Premodern Europe*, eds. Richard Raiswell and Peter Dendle (Toronto, 2012), 483–510.

62 See Richard Firth Green, *Elf Queens and Holy Friars* (Philadelphia, 2016), esp. ch. 4 "Christ the Changeling," 110–46.

63 Cf. Justin P. Jeffcoat Schedtler, "Satan in Biblical Literature," and Archie T. Wright, "The Myth of the Devil in the Early Church," in this volume.

64 Quoted in Walter Stephens, *Demon Lovers: Witchcraft, Sex, and the Crisis of Belief* (Chicago, 2003), 69–70.

65 See, for example, Thomas Aquinas, *Commentary on* The Sentences *of Peter Lombard*, Book 2, Distinction 8.

66 According to Jeffrey Burton Russell, "the small demons that became the witches' familiars of the later Middle Ages were originally dwarves, trolls, fairies, kobolds, or the fertility spirits called Green men, any of whom could be either frightening or funny." Russell, *Witchcraft in the Middle Ages*, (Ithaca, repr. 1984), 52. See also Thomas B. De Mayo, *The Demonology of William of Auvergne: By Fire and Sword* (Lewiston, 2007), 84–5.

67 In Iceland, the familiar spirit elides with a strange creation known as the *tilberi* or *snakkur*; these were "enlivened" contrivances made by winding sheep's wool around the rib bone of a recently dead farmer, then suckled on a cunning-woman's thigh. They were sent out to steal milk from neighbouring farms.

68 Russell, *Witchcraft in the Middle Ages*, 255–7.

69 Emma Wilby, "The Witch's Familiar and the Fairy in Early Modern England and Scotland," *Folklore* 111, no. 2 (2000): 296–7.

70 Caesarius of Heisterbach, *Dialogue on Miracles*, trans. Ronald E. Pepin (Collegeville, 2023), 5.36.

71 Coree Newman, "The Good, the Bad, and the Unholy: Ambivalent Angles in the Middle Ages," in, *Fairies, Demons, and Nature Spirits: 'Small Gods' at the Margins of Christendom*, ed. Michael Ostling (London, 2018), 103–4.

72 Caesarius, *Dialogue*, 5.36.

73 Mark 9.40.

74 Francis Young, *Twilight of the Godlings: The Shadowy Beginnings of Britain's Supernatural Beings* (Cambridge, 2023), 148.

75 Burchard of Worms, *Die Bussordnungen der abendländischen Kirche*, ed. F. W. H. Wasserschleben (Halle, 1851) 658, quoted in Firth Green, *Elf Queens and Holy Friars*, ch. 1.

76 As Frith Green notes, later versions of the *Corrector* became more explicit about the presumed identity of such creatures. In one 13th-century adaptation, they are "*diaboli ... quos faunos vocant* (devils ... which are called fauns)." See Firth Green, *Elf Queens and Holy Friars*, ch. 1.

77 *Fasciculus Morum: A Fourteenth-Century Preacher's Handbook*, trans. and ed. Sigfried Wenzel (University Park, 1989), 579. See A. G. Little, *Studies in English Franciscan History* (Manchester, 1917), 228–31. See also Keith Thomas, *Religion and the Decline of Magic* (New York, 1971), 728.

78 See *Chartularium universitatis Parisiensis*, ed. H. Denifle (Paris, 1889), 35.

79 See David Frankfurter, *Evil Incarnate: Rumors of Demonic Conspiracy and Satanic Abuse in History* (Princeton, 2006), 25–6. See also Rampton, *Trafficking in Demons*.

## Recommended Readings

Bailey, Michael D. *Fearful Spirits Reasoned Follies: The Boundaries of Superstition in Late Medieval Europe* (Ithaca and London: Cornell University Press, 2017).

Caciola, Nancy. *Discerning Spirits: Divine and Demonic Possession in the Middle Ages* (Ithaca and London: Cornell University Press, 2003).

Cameron, Euan. *Enchanted Europe: Superstition, Reason, and Religion 1250-1750* (Oxford: Oxford University Press, 2010).

Green, Richard Firth. *Elf Queens and Holy Friars: Fairy Beliefs and the Medieval Church* (Philadelphia: University of Pennsylvania Press, 2016).

Hamori, Esther. *God's Monsters: Vengeful Spirits, Deadly Angels, Hybrid Creatures, and Divine Hitmen of the Bible* (Minneapolis: Broadleaf Books, 2023).

Rampton, Martha. *Trafficking with Demons: Magic, Ritual, and Gender from Late Antiquity to 1000* (Ithaca and London: Cornell University Press, 2022).

Ruys, Juanita Feros. *Demons in the Middle Ages* (Kalamazoo and Bradford: Arc Humanities Press, 2017).

Walton, John H and J. Harvey Walton. *Demons and Spirits in Biblical Theology: Reading the Biblical Text in Its Cultural and Literary Context* (Eugene: Cascade Books, 2019).

Wilson, Stephen. *The Magical Universe: Everyday Ritual and Magic in Pre-Modern Europe* (Hambledon and London: Continuum International Publishing, 2000).

Young, Francis. *Twilight of the Godlings: The Shadowy Beginnings of Britain's Supernatural Beings* (Cambridge: Cambridge University Press, 2023).

# 8

# SATAN AND THE DIVINE PLAN

## Politics, the Devil and the End of Days[1]

*Arthur H. Williamson*

"I can't believe that there is still such great perversity in human nature that a majority does not want to see all these principles adopted at once, or that, if some are reluctant, they cannot be taught ... or ... persuaded."

*David Hume of Godscroft, 1605*[2]

"Yet again, a messianic movement provided a bridge to a secularist ideology."

*Karen Armstrong, 2000*[3]

In his light-hearted film *The Fearless Vampire Killers* (1967), Roman Polanski injects at one point the story of a 19th-century Polish Jew who gets bitten by a vampire and thereby becomes one himself. When the vampire hunters subsequently encounter him and try to frighten him away, they adopt cinema's time-honoured ploy in such situations: they hold up a cross. The vampire, unfazed, replies in a suitably east European accent, "You got da vrong vempire." Similarly, believers in the past and perhaps even today will assure you that Satan can adopt disparate forms and multiple guises. Yet two stand out in the Western tradition, becoming highly articulated in the early modern period (1500–1800). Both these manifestations of the satanic participated prominently in the culmination of history and fulfilment of human destiny at the last judgement—both guises meeting their prophesied end in the lake of fire and brimstone. Nevertheless, their political, social and cultural implications differed dramatically, enjoining different strategies of confrontation.

The first, imagined as the New Testament's prophesied Antichrist—often described as Satan's "lieutenant" (occasionally, by Protestants, as his "vicar" or "legate")—loomed in the great confessional conflicts of the 16th century. Identified by Protestants as the papacy, Antichrist proved "secularising" in the sense that he participated immanently and continually within the *saeculum*, offering intelligibility and meaning to the Reformation's hard-fought, often convulsive struggles. At the same time, Antichrist framed for Protestants the rise and development of the false Christianity that they thought had emerged as the medieval Roman church. In this way, the devil became an institutionalised agency of evil with a history whose course might be studied and revealed, indeed one lying at the very core of the European (and hence human) experience. The rise of Antichrist and thereby the rise of

DOI: 10.4324/9781003096603-9

medieval Christendom formed a linear, non-recurring narrative, one serving as the spine for what became the Protestant understanding of the Reformation.

The second envisioned the devil as the universal tempter, the serpent ever lurking in the garden, a much less time-bound, much less political figure. Although the Satan of this manifestation would also experience the nasty end scripture had foretold and would become prominent at the end of days, this latter devil could surface without any special reference to the divine plan, indeed he functioned altogether independently of it. He was always there, and, crucially, always the same. Even though these two demonic forms were inherently joined in the sacred drama, they actually pulled in different—and ultimately conflicting—directions. The first, Antichrist, drove an activist world and might eventually come to encourage civic identities. The latter, a personal and even intimate devil, stoked a much more conservative and authoritarian world. Both shapes of the satanic organised experience and gave it intelligibility, yet they focused differing sorts of activity, prioritised different kinds of event and spoke to different needs. The choice of devil carried wide-reaching implications, opening contrasting vistas and obligations, alternate prospects and procedures. The wrong "vempire" could prove devastating.

## The Divine Plan: From Prophecy to Eschatology

The ancient New East was a region awash with prophecy and perhaps no faith arising there embraced divine prophecy more centrally than did early Judaism. Prophecy, often understood as a promise, emerged as its core doctrine—arguably more central than even monotheism. By accepting the lord God and then by following his instructions, good things would happen (and bad ones would be avoided). One's seed would be multiplied and the success of the individual was bound up inextricably with the peoplehood that was Israel. The lord God meant the promise of success in battle, liberation in moments of defeat and, in time, literally a promised land. Only later still did ethical notions become integrated into the prophetic.

By the middle prophets, beginning in the 8th century BCE, the faith had acquired a good deal more complexity. The lord God of Israel had now grown to be the God of the nations as well, a universal deity. Moreover, God's revealed will manifested itself through an underlying programme, as part of a narrative framework—an apocalypse. The Jewish apocalypse comprised a great sacred drama, possessing a beginning, a middle and an end. That culmination, the eschaton—eschatology is the study of final things—would mean the realisation of Israel's destiny and, increasingly, that of humankind as well. History thereby provided the story of redemption, the trials and triumph of righteousness and, fundamentally, the framework of meaning.

Three features stand out. Both prophecy and eschatology validated this life, not the next. As the Psalmist declares, "The dead do not praise the Lord,/nor do any that go down into silence" (Ps. 115:17; ESV). No temporary veil of tears, we encountered God here, not in anything that might follow. Even, eventually, the promise of another life took shape as resurrection within this world. With only limited exceptions, the prophetic has continued to focus on the *saeculum* rather than away from it.[4]

Second, the apocalypse and attendant eschatological projects arose as a courtly development and spoke to royal contexts. Jonathan Z. Smith has persuasively argued that it was "a learned rather than a popular religious phenomenon" that did not derive from deprivation or "reflect lower class interests."[5] As Bernard McGinn and others have shown, the apocalypse rarely fired social revolution during the Middle Ages, though it neverthe-less rested uncomfortably with mainstream medieval civilisation.[6] Only in the later 15th century did eschatological expectations emerge dramatically within Catholicism, Judaism, Orthodoxy, both Sunni and Shia Islam, and later, most enduringly, in Protestantism.

Finally, the entire increasingly complex range of Old Testament prophecy and escha-tology fails to portray the devil as the Christian era imagined it, or as we would visualise that figure today. The book of Daniel (c. 150 BCE) projected a series of evil empires that blocked out world chronology. It also spoke about the dream of the powerful Babylonian king Nebuchadnezzar (605–562 BCE) in which a gigantic statue of a human figure, layered in various metals and materials, is struck and destroyed by a little stone. Here too would be found the periodisation of Jewish experience and human history. Daniel never portrays the empires, however grotesque, as embodying some larger principle or force of evil. His culmination, the coming of "the Son of Man" at the end of days, includes no final retribu-tion. The apocalypse without the devil turned out to be eminently possible.

That would change profoundly during the Intertestamental period (c. 150 BCE–200 CE), immediately following Daniel. Then inter-Jewish conflict fractured Judaism into a range of competing sectarian movements, including the Jesus movement and, eventually, Christianity, as well as rabbinic Judaism. This led to highly developed images of Satan, Antichrist and demonic spirits. Moreover, their history, deeds and fate became articulated in rich, symbolic detail. Building on Daniel, John of Patmos' Revelation (c. 95 CE), espe-cially, depicted the devil's career through multiple dramatic symbols and, in one of the New Testament's more fraught lines, spoke of this figure being bound for a thousand years, prior to the last judgement and the final resolution of time (Rv. 20.1-10). The text projected or seemed to project a grand era of triumph, righteousness and justice on earth, before a de-monic breakout and final conflict would conclude the realm of nature altogether.

These lines of apocalyptic thought became increasingly attenuated in later antiquity, especially in the West where church fathers like St. Augustine tamed John's heated im-aginings. Yes, there would be a final wrap-up and a great conflict wherein the devil, Antichrist and their demonic associates would meet their prophesied fiery fate. To deny these events altogether comprised atheism or total heresy. But they lay far off in the indeterminate future and did concern the present world. Moreover, the projected age of righteousness was not a future era, but the current Christian age. Nevertheless, if the apocalypse retreated to the margins, taking Antichrist with it, the personalised devil, of course, remained altogether vibrant, omnipresent and actively suffused throughout Christian civilisation. Moreover, scholasticism's naturalising of theology through Aris-totelian categories in the 13th century endowed the devil (and much else) with a pro-found physically he had not previously enjoyed. Thus, Thomas Aquinas' (1225–1274) arguments about the real presence of Christ in the eucharist provided the devil with a real presence as well—or, rather, gave the figure an intellectual foundation, at once new, powerful, and "natural."

To be sure, the medieval world did produce one major apocalyptic thinker in the ab-bot Joachim of Fiore (c. 1135–1202). However, his arresting, highly pictorial vision of the apocalypse as an organic process had only limited impact. Although he was an elite figure, advising popes and consulted by kings, the intellectual mainstream came together in the following century with projects like Henry de Bracton's (c. 1210–c. 1268) consolidation of legal tradition and Aquinas' timeless, universal categories of naturalised theology. Joachite thought moved to the margins, as had the apocalypse itself. From time to time major figures such as the Emperor Frederick II (r. 1220–1250) or a range of medieval popes, or even Islam and Muhammad might be deemed for a while to be the prophesied Antichrist, and radical Franciscans might even embrace Joachim. Yet these lines of thought never shaped core assumptions or informed the medieval spirit.

## Politics in the Age of Antichrist

After about 1450, the Iberian kingdoms of Portugal and Spain began a seaborne expansion that would subsequently be joined by all the great Western powers, only culminating in the early 20th century. Underwriting these extraordinary activities were apocalyptic expectations that now acquired an unprecedented prominence. The peoples of Spain and more generally Iberia had received the "grace of election" that rendered them latter-day Israelites. Their ruling dynasties became endowed with messianic mission. Moreover, their triumphs in Asia and the New World did indeed create the first genuinely global empires. For many, this led to the conviction—from scripture as well as traditional sources—that there would emerge a Last World Empire, Daniel's fifth monarchy, a universal order that would presage the end of days and the return of the Nazarene.

The extraordinary successes of the Habsburg dynasty gave these claims increasing plausibility. By the 1530s, this rapidly expanding superstate, now headed by Charles V (r. 1519–1556), appeared to promise the prophesied universal monarchy of one faith, one head. Its iconography declared *plus ultra* (yet further) and portrayed it as breaking through the boundaries of the antique Roman Empire to realise an altogether new, sacred order. Iconography later in the century would declare that Charles' son, Philip II (r. 1556–1598), brought light to the world (*iam illustrabit omnia*), and that the world itself was not enough (*non sufficit orbis*).[7]

But if the apocalypse powered mission, expansion and exhilaration, no less did it frame and articulate dread and terror. In 1453, the Ottoman Turks conquered Constantinople, one of Christendom's greatest citadels, along with much of the Middle East, and were now charging into Europe. Their target was nothing less than the Habsburg capital, Vienna, and their religious expectations were no less messianic. As Cornell Fleischer and his students have shown, Sultans Mehmed II (r. 1444–1446 and 1451–1481) and Süleyman (r. 1520–1566) also saw themselves as building the prophesied Last World Empire at the end of days.[8] Charles and Süleyman confronted one another in the 1530s with remarkably similar apocalyptic expectations constructed from largely overlapping materials. Viewed from Vienna, Christ encountered Antichrist as a total inversion. The devil who rode out of the east looked oddly like the people on the battlements who witnessed his approach.

Apocalyptic expectation reached across the globe in a great arc, running from Portugal to India, and from Sweden to Yemen. It spoke to all the children of Abraham. Yet nowhere did it reach more deeply, nor to more telling effect than it did with the Protestant Reformation. Protestant reformers faced a formidable challenge, at once epistemological and historical, that reached far more deeply into the textures of European culture than did the claims for dynastic mission, or any threatening individual figure who might be deemed the prophesied Antichrist. For the reformers needed to explain the existence of an *institution*, the medieval church. How in the world did Christianity go so wrong and lead to this massive, powerful structure that falsified Christianity, that indeed was anti-Christianity and satanic? Further, why was the present generation charged with the responsibility of setting things right—and that somehow saw more clearly than any previous generation ever had. Reform mandated a vocabulary that could envision qualitative change—how today might be one way, but tomorrow would be radically different. The only vocabulary available for that purpose in the 16th century was prophecy, eschatology, the apocalypse. The story of the Roman church then emerged as the working out of both Old and New Testament prophecy, a linear non-recurring process now reaching its climactic moments in the "latter days." A great "master narrative" developed that told the story of the rise of Antichrist, effectively a critical account of the Middle Ages and medieval civilisation. Here lay the meaning of the 1,000-year binding and loosing of Satan: the rise of the anti-Christian church recounted nothing less than Satan's reemergence from the bottomless pit. Nor would the apocalypse simply be available as a strategic tool in the confessional struggle, but instead proved integral to the meaning of Protestantism itself. Just as Protestantism did not replicate Christ's sacrifice in the sacraments, but collectively recalled its efficacy in the past, so time became the frame for truth in the master narrative. And there the issue would be joined: prophecy confronting miracles, history challenging the sacrament, time battling the *nunc stans*, the eternal now.[9] This intellectual moment is altogether unprecedented and would prove the hinge to modernity and secular culture. Europe had invented its first historicism. Such thinking breaks with the medieval world, even at its most radical. Reformers might occasionally reference Joachim, but they had come to inhabit an altogether different intellectual frame. Institutions supplanting visual images, documents marginalising numerical parallelism became the guiding principles.

This monumental face-off between Reform and Counter-Reform shattered and then foreclosed what had been a widely shared eschatological mindset at the end of the 15th century. Even so, the apocalypse had never played well at the Vatican. As early as 1513, well before the Reformation, the Fifth Lateran Council decried popular preaching about Antichrist. The Council of Trent (1545–1563) declared decisively against the new eschatology, while Robert Bellarmine, (1542–1621), Francisco Ribeira (1537–1591) and other Jesuits turned out massive works that tore into the Protestant master narrative and worked to revive the medieval understanding of the issue. Bernard McGinn has shown how apocalyptic spirituality ceased to inform Catholic religious thought after 1600.[10] Embattled outliers such as Tomasso Campanella (1568–1639) and Antonio Viera (1608–1697) would crop up on occasion, but the Protestant-Catholic confrontation had become highly articulated and defining, indeed fully confessionalised. The issue of the apocalypse ran unbridgeably deep.

### Demonology and the Assault on Prophecy

Historians have generally agreed that the European fascination with witchcraft largely flourished during the two centuries between 1480 and 1680. This is also a period of the most serious apocalyptic speculation. A number of scholars have consequently come to believe, *post hoc, propter hoc*, that apocalyptic expectations led to witch-hunts. They do not. Just the reverse: witch-hunts lead away from apocalyptic concerns. Instead, the phenomenon needs to be seen as a reaction against the prophetic, rather than a manifestation of it. Some of the greatest witch panics occurred in regions where Counter-Reform had triumphed—one thinks of Lorraine, the Spanish Netherlands, Bamberg and more generally the lands along the "Spanish Road."[11] In the Protestant world, the situation was more ambivalent. It is certainly true that the John of Patmos had alerted his readers to the intensified activity of the devil when he realised his time was short in the "latter days" (Rv. 12.12). For the late 16th century, such activism included, centrally, the enlisting of followers, witches notable among them. Surely, action needed to be taken in response.

But did it? That activist devil was not the figure Protestants had identified in their master narrative, not the institutionalised agency of evil that was the Catholic Church, nor the political order against which Protestantism struggled on the broad stage of confessional confrontation. No pope ever slipped into little old ladies' bedrooms at night to spirit them away to kinky parties in the neighbouring woods (possibly to their disappointment). No Jesuit ever wasted his time with impoverished nobodies. To pursue witches was to realign priorities and meet with a different devil.

At the same time, Revelation alerted its (Protestant) readers to the existence of a large number of "necromantic" popes, popes who nefariously worked with black magic to forward the Vatican's agenda. Yet wicked popes from past centuries were woven into historical analysis and grand narratives rather than providing present prescriptions. Such figures documented the loosing of Satan, the developmental narrative, not the dangers from problematic neighbours. To focus on putative witches and, still more, on demonic exorcism, reframed the discussion ultimately away from prophecy. It was to play a Catholic game.

We can see this clearly with French demonology in the late 16th and early 17th centuries. The Wars of Religion produced only one Protestant demonologist, Lambert Daneau (d. 1590), and his approach to the subject was scriptural rather than scholastic. Indeed, Daneau became much exercised to distinguish his *De veneficis ... Dialogus* (1574), founded on the word of God, and not on "these vayne babbling proofes and curious disputations" arising from vanity rather than spirituality. He had no patience for "curious quiddities" and the "many other such trifling matters," nor the endless disputes of "the schoolmen and Doctors, and others," who "would reach aboue the heavens, and search all things that are beneath the bottome of hell." It would not do to "runne and wander freely without [beyond] the true boundes of the faith."[12]

Daneau's *Dialogus* is part of a response to Counter-Reformation demonology, and specifically the work of the Spanish Jesuit, Juan Maldonat (1533–1583), who began lecturing at the new Collège de Clermont at Paris in 1564. Maldonat rapidly emerged a major figure in French Counter-Reform, whose lectures by the 1570s linked witchcraft with the Protestant heresy and proved enormously effective. We need to see the *Dialogus*, in part, as an effort to contain the Jesuit onslaught, validating witchcraft and Protestant opposition to it, while framing it within the "precinct" of reformed religion. The matter became still more urgent because Maldonat was apparently promising to publish a book on the subject.[13] The *Dialogus* appeared in anticipation to this work, seeking to blunt its effect. It will not surprise us that the tract saw print when, in the years following the St. Bartholomew catastrophe of 1572, Maldonat toured the Poitou region, reconverting significant numbers, especially from the elites. The *Dialogus* emerges, then, as a fundamentally defensive work, a response to a deepening crisis.

To be sure, like all French demonologists, Daneau was also much exercised by the frequent acquittal of witchcraft cases appealed to the Parlement de Paris. The minister conceded that, "For all that are accompted commonly witches and sorcerers are not so in deede, and many there are that haue been suspected thereof undeservedly." Yet that did not deter him from seeking prompt sentencing and execution of those convicted at the local level. The great magistrates of the court did not doubt the reality of witches, but they unflinchingly insisted on the dignity of the *noblesse de robe* and the authority of the parlement.[14] The preoccupation with status rather than enlightened principles foreclosed the rush to judgement.

No less arresting, the *Dialogus* contains not a trace of apocalyptic thinking, even where we might expect it. Daneau repeatedly notes that there are today more witches than in the past, an observation that cries out for the commonplace explanation from Revelation 12.12: we live in the latter days of the world, and the devil is redoubling his efforts, realising that time is running out. Instead, Daneau simply comments, "Truly this is the terrible judgement of God agaynst us, the cause whereof is unknown unto us." God's decrees are inherently righteous and just, but, in a deeply Calvinist spirit, beyond us.[15] Daneau took a great interest in the Protestant master narrative, writing at length about Antichrist. But as the *Dialogus* visibly indicates, it simply did not inform his understanding of witchcraft.[16]

The Wars of Religion also produced one demonologist with a faith all his own, Jean Bodin (c. 1530–1596), but he was no less troubled by appeals to the Parlement de Paris. All the rest, significant in number and influence, were militant Counter-Reformers. Outstanding among them were Maldonat and his students, the most prominent of whom were Louis Richeome, Pierre de Lancre and Martin Del Rio. Del Rio (1551–1608) became the most influential demonologist of the 17th century and his writing, among much else, informed Philip II's 1592 order on witchcraft. Far from a dispassionate theological study, the entire burden of the new demonology, the Huguenots soon learned, served to attack Protestantism. As Jonathan Pearl has shown, validation of such witchcraft beliefs as the transportation of witches to sabbaths, the use of ointments created from murdered infants, the ability of witches to make themselves invisible with the help of the devil, also validated the mysteries of the church. Seeing was not believing, for the senses could be deceived. After all, transubstantiation remained true despite appearances. For Maldonat, Protestantism with its time-based, historical spirituality seemed to undermine the immortality of the soul.[17] And in a way the Jesuit had a point. The Reformed emphasis on prophecy and thereby the *saeculum* might easily appear to devalue the life to come.

Of course, the devil and his demons worked through natural means to alter the appearance of things. Only God could actually suspend the laws of nature. But that in no way impugned the reality of demonic "false miracles," as Maldonat called them. Such naturalism was important, for the witch phenomenon became amenable thereby to scholastic reasoning. Hierarchy could be shown to be a common principle, suffused through the universe, obtaining in all planes of being—extending even to that of the damned. One could learn the structure of things from God's "opposite."

Moreover, even if Catholic demonology carried heavy spiritual and political implications, its effects were nevertheless severely depoliticising. By stressing authority, stability, tradition, even accepting folklore, against those who would overturn them all, demonology reinforced a consolidating monarchy. Hierarchy and headship emerged as natural and inevitable, curbing notions of civic action and local autonomy. Although the demonologists were consistently militant *Ligueurs* (even Bodin enlisted in the *Ligue*), nearly all their writings nevertheless saw print during the years of Henri IV's (r. 1589–1610) rule. Perhaps no surprise, for despite his earlier Protestantism, Henri found he needed to have recourse to the royal touch: the coronation-derived power that late medieval French and English kings claimed for curing scrofula and related illnesses by laying hands on the afflicted. Possessing this wondrous healing capability served to validate Henri as the legitimate king.[18] Thaumaturgic kingship joined with a sacerdotal clergy to promote a world of wonder—and witchcraft.

Only exorcism, that most dramatic and successful form of ultramontane rite-theatre, faded with the *Ligue*. With demonic possession, as with all matters demonic, what we see and what we have were two different things. Always uneasy about possession, miracle-bereft Protestantism could only offer prayer and fasting as a solution. Catholicism claimed something far more powerful and that power depended on the reality of demons. If demons disappeared, so too, it seemed, might Catholicism. The stakes could hardly be higher: at issue was the *verba operanda* confronting the bare historical word in context. Protestants constantly denounced the "conjuring mass" as anti-Christian and even devil-inspired, but to them the rite itself remained inert and fraudulent. Demonic possession by contrast reached out to other worlds. The thunderously successful 1566 exorcism of Beelzebub from a young woman at Laon was a major Catholic triumph that confounded Protestant scoffers. The "miracle of Laon" made demonology a major weapon in the Catholic arsenal and thereafter an exclusively Catholic property. But possession was potentially explosive: could we always count on Beelzebub to be there, saying the right things about "my Huguenots" (whom the great demon regarded as more damaging to Christ "than the Jews")? Del Rio and others worked to promote and at the same time contain the phenomenon within naturalistic terms that the clergy might control. But, in the end, this form of demonology unlike the others largely fell before its inherent dangers.[19]

Two decades later, a team of Jesuits performed an exorcism at Denham and Hackney in England, and its purpose, to expel "the unclean spirit of the Calvinist heresy," directly served the Counter-Reformed struggle much as it did in France.[20] Yet the spectacle proved significantly lower key, producing nothing of the convulsive drama in much more prophecy-suffused England. Some 15 years later, the Protestant minister John Darrell (1562–after 1602) undertook a series of exorcisms that also led to witchcraft prosecutions. In part, Darrell sought to validate prayer and fasting as effective exorcism methods in the face of Catholic procedures and their apparent success. Darrell's activities, however, brought down the wrath of England's clerical establishment, notably the Archbishop John Whitgift (d. 1604), in concert with Richard Bancroft (d. 1610) and Samuel Harsnett (d. 1631). A protracted struggle and pamphlet war ensued, one that ultimately marginalised both exorcism and Darrell.

Although discomfort with exorcism might be found with almost any government, this apparent confrontation between a "puritan" minister, ostensibly a reformer, and a reactionary hierarchy is unusual. With remarkable consistency, witch beliefs and witch-hunting attracted religious and political conservatives. Far more representative was the deeply conservative Elizabethan judge, Lord Chief Justice Sir Edmund Anderson (1530–1605), who declared, "The land is full of witches, they abound in all places, I have hanged five or six and twenty of them." Yet, significantly, Anderson too would reject the exorcism discoveries of Darrell's demoniacs.[21] The clash between Darrell and the authorities—Harsnett served as their lead person—formed part of an ongoing struggle from the late 1580s about church government and the intellectual values associated with it. It had devolved into a species of *kultur-kampf* in which ecclesiology became interwoven into debate about scholastic learning and traditional modes of cognition.[22] Yes, exorcism was a Catholic phenomenon, predicated on a world of miracles that had altogether ceased with Christ. But Darrell had provided an opening for conservatives to attack critics of church hierarchy, individuals who promoted "their Presbyteriall conceits." Such people needed "to thinke more reverently of those that be in authoritie."[23] In fact, the entire episode, like so much demonology on the continent, turned on political issues. We encounter no dispute about Calvinist theology.

Harsnett proved at least as "puritanical" Darrell. Significant reformist ministers such as John Deacon and John Walker dissented from Darrell's activities.[24] Crucially, the apocalypse and the prophetic narrative were not in play.

We will better understand the Darrell phenomenon by considering his contemporary, the puritan minister and witchcraft commentator, William Perkins (1558–1602). As Patrick Collinson pointed out long ago, figures like Perkins wrote at a time when the English puritan movement had experienced defeat and found itself largely "diverted" from institutional reform and the larger apocalyptic project of the master narrative.[25] Instead, the reformers turned inwards, focusing on personal piety and individual salvation, in large part as articulated through Perkins' enormously popular federal theology. And there was nothing in the least apocalyptic about federal theology. This realigned spirituality brought with it a realignment of the devil, both now inhabiting a world upfront and intimate. It is in this context that we need to understand Darrell.[26] A charismatic preacher who appeared to discount the gravitas of hierarchy would naturally outrage figures as authoritarian as Whitgift, Bancroft and Harsnett. That formed the crux of the issue, rather more than a principled rejection of witch beliefs that might anticipate the Enlightenment.[27]

A similar pattern occurred on the continent where the struggle against the prophetic and reform devolved into witch-hunting. The infamous witch-hunter Friedrich Föner (1568–1630) helped lead a successful struggle against Protestantism in Bamberg, and much of his attack focused on the prophecies—or "divinations" as Föner called them— of the reformers. Against Protestant apocalyptic, Föner offered miracles: the former were the work of false prophets, the latter the visible hand of God. The attack on the prophetic was integrally linked to the (by then) very familiar charge: where was your church before Luther? To discredit prophecy was to discredit a crucial element in the Protestant vision. Following the destruction of Bamberg Protestantism, Föner became obsessed with large-scale witch-hunting, for heresy and witchcraft formed parts of a common package, both being assaults from the devil on the true faith. William Bradford Smith has observed that the most intense moments during the witch-hunt coincided with dramatic moments of Catholic activism: the Catholic victory at White Mountain at the outset of the Thirty Years War and later the imperial edict restoring the secularised church lands.[28]

The pattern remains broadly comparable in Lutheran Sweden. Apocalyptic excitement never reached more deeply into the cultural tissues of Swedish society than during the reign of Gustavus Adolphus (r. 1611–1632). Yet this period, "so choked with eschatological expectation," saw little witch activity. Gustavus' theoretician for Sweden's emerging *dominium maris Baltici* and the Vasa dynasty, Johannes Bureus (1568–1652), had a different agenda, and the great Swedish hunts lay over the horizon.[29]

Yet perhaps no country at this juncture better illustrates the politics of the witch-hunt, and still more the ways witch panics lead away from eschatology—the transition from one manifestation of Satan to another—than does the experience of Europe's only Calvinist kingdom: the Kingdom of the Scots.

### Scotland: From Melvillian Moment to Royal Witch-Hunt

Scotland's largest witch-hunt, by far, occurred in that moment of intense political, spiritual and cultural reaction that accompanied the Restoration of the monarchy in 1660. At that juncture, miracles acquired an altogether new cogency in the context of an increasingly catholicised spirituality, while institutions became sacralised. The royal touch would be performed more frequently during the reign of the restored Charles II than at any time in British history, before or since. Concurrently, eschatology, the master narrative, and Calvinism became increasingly qualified, marginalised, if not discounted altogether, while in the same process secularising attitudes experienced "slippage."[30]

It was a decisive moment whose effects in surprising ways are still with us, yet the pattern for the great Restoration witch-hunt took shape almost exactly a century earlier. From the later 16th century onwards—effectively from the outset of the Reformation in Scotland—the witch phenomenon attracted religious and political conservatives with remarkable consistency. Key figures in the witch-hunts during the 1590s came from elite members of the Catholic peerage: William Douglas, 9th earl of Angus (1533–1591), George Gordon, 6th earl of Huntly (1562–1636) and Francis Hay, the 9th earl of Errol (1564–1631). The last two played a commanding role in the great hunt of 1597.[31] Crucially, witch panic and witch-hunting at once tracked and propelled the growing conservatism of King James VI (r. 1567–1625) through the course of the decade.

Even so, the pattern of witchcraft and conservatism surfaced earlier still with the contrasting fathers of the Scottish Reformation: John Knox (d. 1572) and John Erskine of Dun (d. 1590). Although both were determined Protestants, their spirituality differed in ways subtle yet significant. Knox was fully immersed in Protestant apocalyptic: his earliest and best remembered sermons introduced the Protestant narrative to Scotland; he never lost sight of the end of days. He certainly accepted the reality of witchcraft and prosecuted the occasional witch as part of the programme to create a "disciplined" Christian society. Yet he never spoke much about it and at one point simply declined to elaborate on "why mannes nature is affrayed for spirites, and so vehementlie abhorreth their presence and company." His latest and most authoritative biography at no point mentions witchcraft.[32] Antichrist remained the focus, and his last great (abortive) project had him join his friend Christopher Goodman in an evangelising mission to Ireland.

Erskine cut a quite different figure. He surely accepted the Protestant narrative but has not left any comment on it. His preoccupation was clerical authority and his role as Superintendent of Angus and Mearns, which he saw as fundamentally episcopal. He had no sympathy for the Presbyterian discipline that became embraced by many reformers in the 1570s, and he was regarded by them as a "pest" during the great struggle for reform in 1584. His administrative responsibilities caused him to focus on "marks" by which one could identify a true believer, rather than the larger apocalyptic struggle for the "invisible" church.[33] This sharply focused concern brought out the priorities separating them, when in 1568 Erskine presided over the first major witch-hunt in the British Isles: one that involved some 40 individuals "and all utheris ... delatit or suspecit of certain abhominable crymes of sorcerye and wychecraf."[34] Erskine's conservatism contrasted with Knox's radicalism in still other ways apparent throughout their careers. While Knox participated in political revolution at St. Andrews, looking to English aid and promoting a British vision, Erskine fortified Montrose against possible English invasion. In the 1559–60 revolution, Erskine continued negotiating with the French regent until last possible moment. Knox's last major project was the Irish mission; Erskine's last major project, also abortive, was an appointment in 1587 to lead yet another great witch-hunt, directed against "the greit wichcrafte necro[mancie] and sorcery daylie comittit within oure burgh of montrose and boundis adicent."[35] Knox's career finds itself bookended by apocalyptic revolution, Erskine's by witch-hunts. In the end, Knox emerges a better

Calvinist. Although Knox and Erskine were lifelong friends, they often did not combat a common enemy or encounter the same devil.

The 1568 witch-hunt appears not have left any visible mark on Scottish public consciousness. Still, the experience at Angus and Mearns and the contrast between Knox and Erskine offers insight into the highly visible events of the 1590s.

The years immediately before the 1588 Spanish Armada and for more than a decade thereafter witnessed an ever-growing body of literature about the apocalypse, literature that projected an increasingly articulated prophetic future. King James' line by line paraphrase of Revelation, followed up by two apocalyptic "meditations," the first in the year of the Armada crisis, the second celebratory immediately after. These are well known. Less noticed is that they form elements within this broad tissue of writings that included in Scotland John Napier of Merchiston, Robert Pont and James Maxwell, and in England most notably Andrew Willet, Hugh Broughton and Thomas Brightman. This would prove the high point of the king's immersion in apocalyptic thought, the moment at which he celebrated the Scottish church before the General Assembly (and lamented the one south of the Border), the moment at which he asked the professor, preacher and poet Andrew Melville (1545–1622) to prepare poetry for the coronation of his new bride Anna of Denmark.[36] All of them variously looked to the creation of a British state that in alliance with Henri IV would lead the "free" (i.e., Protestant) world against the Habsburg universal monarchy and its papal sponsor. As the Huguenot poet, Guillaume de Sauluste du Bartas, a friend of both James and Melville, put it in a 1588 letter home to Henri and others, "it seems to me that I see the walls of Rome tremble and the entire papacy twist in fear, hearing of the alliance of two such brave princes."[37]

The key figures were Melville and the Edinburgh minister Robert Bruce (1554–1631). Contemporaries saw the struggle against Antichrist as much more than the working out of prophecy diplomatically and on the battlefield, but also as a cultural flowering involving "learned poets" (*poetae docti*), who made the moment articulate and compelling: among them Melville, David Hume of Godscroft (1558–1629), Robert Pont (1524–1606), and, signally, Edmund Spenser (1552/53–1599).[38] Still more, the coming age entailed new, faster teaching methods such as Ramism, and, most important, the powerful truths derived from mathematics particularly the outstanding works associated with Napier and the Englishman Thomas Digges (1546–1595). No neutral undertaking, mathematics in this period normally elided into such magical traditions as astrology, alchemy, Jewish mysticism and carried prophetic and eschatological implications.[39]

There existed, then, an extraordinary intellectual range and great promise to what we might call the Melvillian Moment. Like Knox, Melville took witchcraft seriously, and, again like him, Melville was prepared to enquire into cases of putative witches.[40] Yet he said nothing at all about witchcraft in the surviving record, while his apocalyptic expectations were far more highly articulated than Knox's. Melville's devil manifestly lay elsewhere. We can see this clearly in his poem celebrating the birth of James' son Henry in 1594, even though prospects had turned much darker than they had been four years earlier. Prince Henry with his "Scoto-Britannic champions" from the emergent British state would lead the Protestant world against Spain's universal empire and the "Roman Cerberus." "This farthest land in the world [Scotland]" would make known what could be achieved against "Iberian pride" and "the legions of Antichrist." Melville looked to the time when Henry "dear to heaven and dear to his fellow citizens" would "rejoice to have buried the insolent spirit of empire in its tomb." Not a prophetic Last World Empire, but the end of empire altogether; not preoccupation with "Europe's inner demons," but in some sense liberation. Or, as Melville's younger associate, David Hume, later put it with reference to the British union, it was "heavenly and lasting accomplishments ... this is how we should wish to see ourselves."[41] Neither reprobation and depravity nor the dangers of witchcraft seemed to limit the power of apocalyptic prospects.

The Melvillian Moment began to unravel with the witch crisis in 1591 that became huge with the threat to the king and his subsequent involvement in it. The abrupt transition appears clearly with Bruce. Close to James and playing a prominent role in government, Bruce had shortly before given a prominent series of sermons that sought to reconfigure social connection: just as we did not connect with Christ through the papist "grosse and carnal conjunction" of the mass, so we did not join with one another through "a carnall band of blood and allya [alliance]." Instead, Scottish people linked with one another through "ane spiritual band." Christ's blood relations did not form his community, but those joined to him through the spirit. In much the same way, Scots were joined through a "celestial glue" and the law, rather than through kin-ties and traditional blood obligations.[42] From this, the minister set about exhorting a reform programme for the nation.

Bruce sought to break up Scottish tribalism for a law-based civic society. His focus away from "blood" fit well the Calvinist preoccupation with motives rather than good works and the "carnal." Accordingly, the devil normally appeared as seducing through the "affections" and working through people's minds. But in 1591 something had clearly changed, pointing in new and unexpected directions and causing Bruce to reverse course. He now spoke with palpable shock as he set about explaining to his listeners that the devil actually operated in two ways. He could work "covertly" as "he insinuates himself into our affections by reason of the corruption that is in us." Or, Bruce explained, "he oppones himself openly that by thy outward sense thou may take him up." With clear alarm, Bruce held forth against "gross devilry" and the newly emergent corporeal devil. "Gross devilry" raised still further issues. For there then arose the danger of a rush to judgement. Bruce, a lawyer as well as a minister, insisted that "iniquity being discovered, it may be punished without respect to persons," yet "the innocence of others being discovered, they may be justified ... For I am not of mind that the innocent should be punished, but only the guilty." The minister went on to promote his social programme, urging the elites "to have feeling for and be touched by the oppression of their subjects," but the intellectual alignment had visibly shifted. [43]

The witch-hunt of 1591 loomed as that of 1568 did not in part because it happened in and about Edinburgh, but mainly because of the heavy involvement of the king. James' extended terror-fascination with witch-hunting in 1591 and again in 1597 made the pursuit of witches a national affair and gave it a public visibility and importance that it otherwise would not have had. More than that, his ongoing preoccupation with witches enabled his transition away from the apocalypse to more traditional formulations of kingship. James faced or felt he faced a problem of legitimacy, for Scotland had experienced two successful revolutions, the first overthrowing his grandmother, the second his mother—who was ultimately be tried and executed in England for treason. The latter threatened to attaint his blood, potentially jeopardising his succession to the English crown. In the face of all this as well as the chronic instability that had characterised his reign, James became increasingly exercised to establish that his authority was derived from blood, right and due descent, rather than from revolution and civic action, something Melville's poem for Anna's 1590 coronation had left distressingly open. Had apocalyptic direct action set him on the throne?

Surely not. As he declared at the trial of the accused witch Barbara Napier, his authority arose "not because I am James Stuard and can raise so many thousandes of men, but because God hath made me a king and judge to judge righteous judgement."[44]

Scots law did not accept the testimony of "infamous persons," and that would clearly extend to witches. But if witchcraft became viewed as *lèse majesté*, a form of treason, then their testimony became admissible. Thereby conviction became vastly easier.[45] It led to the 1597 debacle whereby witches were carted from town to town to identify further witches—a process denounced by the St. Andrews Presbytery as a "horable abuse." But far more than that, it made the crusade against witchcraft a struggle for the crown, its legitimacy, its safety and its status. Witches became integral to the validation of expansive regal authority. Only in this context can we understand the king's extraordinary and otherwise inexplicable personal involvement in witch-hunting. Accordingly, in 1597 James turned up in St. Andrews to purge the university's Presbyterians and to hunt witches.[46] Both proved integral to the consolidation of authoritarian monarchy.

In his apocalyptic writings, James spoke of the *patrie* and referenced King David, but at no point did he ever put himself forward as yet another prospective Last World Emperor. Instead, he now looked to something far more traditional: an underlying natural order that withstood all the flux of time and contingency, one that maintained hierarchy and authority against all claims for parity, whether civil or clerical, and against all claims of custom and privilege, however "ancient." To this end, he produced the series of works for which he is known today: the *Daemonologie* (1597), the *True Lawe of Free Monarchy* (1598) and the *Basilikon Doron* (1599). All three works are atemporal, seeking to found authority beyond the reach of time. All three proclaim hierarchy. All three are also deeply hostile to prophecy.

The *Daemonologie* is key because it delineates the transition from the earlier 1590s to the resolutely un-apocalyptic other two writings and the outlook they embody. On the margins we encounter traces of historical development and reference to the apocalypse as it works to quite different purposes. In the time of "blinde Papistrie," the devil accosted people through ghosts and spirits, while today with sincere religion people understand the truth and seek out the devil knowing full well the implications of their actions. Further, this wilful seeking out of the devil through witchcraft and magic has intensified because the devil is aware that time is running out and has redoubled his efforts (Rv. 12.12).[47] Yet the entire thrust of the *Daemonologie* is to foreclose the prophetic future that his countrymen (and their English allies) were projecting in ever more articulated form. Again and again, James emphasises, all prophecies, oracles and visions have ended. Those who pretend otherwise are "euill." Scholars who seek "to creepe to credite with princes by fore-telling them manie greate thinges" are agents of the devil. Astrology, necromancy and implicitly all of the occult traditions that seek to predict the future are demonic. Their practitioners should meet the same fate as the humble practitioners of witchcraft. Their so-called wisdom was learned in "the deuils schole," their techniques "the deuilles rudiments."[48] James concedes, almost certainly thinking of the eminent astrologer and chronologist Robert Pont, that "yet manie of the learned are of the contrarie opinion." Then he scurried off without a rebuttal—space did not permit further examination of the issue—departing simply with a citation from Jeremiah.[49]

James recognised that the central issue was mathematics, which, though no mathematician, he sought to detach from the occult, along with its reformist and apocalyptic implications. James' attack on the occult led not to proto-Enlightenment rationalism, but promoted a bloodthirsty, scholastic crusade against the devil, witchcraft and the full range of attendant belief.[50] No less central to the king's purpose, his focus on witches foreclosed prophecy and led away from the apocalypse. He thereby challenged Scotland's intellectual elite and some of the brightest minds in the realm.[51] In the process, he went in a direction altogether contrary to his earlier writing and sought to overthrow the cultural foundations of the Melvillian Moment. Unsurprisingly, the *Daemonologie* at no point mentions Antichrist.

To be sure, James did not jettison the apocalypse, but it became much more marginalised than it had been a decade earlier, an attenuating process that would continue throughout his life. The witch-hunting pattern, initially surfacing in 1568, then resurfacing in 1591 and 1597, would prove the Scottish pattern into the late 17th century. Witch panics occurred during moments of conservatism and reaction, moments that enjoined a personalised devil, and led away from his institutionalised manifestation as Antichrist and the apocalyptic master narrative—notably in 1629–1631 and 1660–1662.

A striking counter-instance seems to have occurred during the 17th-century Scottish Revolution (1638–1651). A revolt against London-based religious and political authoritarianism, the revolution founded itself on an apocalyptically charged National Covenant driven by a vision of human redemption. The ensuing upheaval in the British isles would become part of the European revolutionary tradition. The more radical revolutionaries briefly held power in 1649–1650, a juncture that witnessed a surge in witch prosecutions (if hardly on the scale of the Restoration). Yet the moment appears anomalous: 1629 and 1660 experienced powerful and effective assertions of royal authority (the first launching the prerogative rule of the "11 Year Tyranny"; the second launching the most determined establishment of hierarchy and monarchical rule that century). The revolutionary government existed in a context of decentralised rule, with large swathes of the country effectively beyond its control.[52] The outbreak, current research suggests, assumed shape as a series of localised outbreaks quite unlike 1629 or 1660, and still more in contrast with the great royal hunts of the 1590s. Central authorities apparently approached such matters with caution.[53] At the same time, the one place the government could control utterly was the revolutionary capital Edinburgh, and in the capital it is striking just how few witchcraft cases actually arose. That seems the case generally in Edinburgh, with the most evident contrast occurring with conservative Aberdeen.[54] Moreover, if we look at the revolutionary government, the Committee of Estates that ruled between sessions of Parliament, we find two members with genuinely millenarian commitments to be John Hope of Craighall and his younger brother James Hope of Hopetoun. John subsequently served on the Cromwellian replacement for the Court of Session Scotland's Supreme Court. Witchcraft prosecutions were consistently rejected at the new court, and today this is often attributed to its "English judges."[55] Yet not all the judges were English, and those Scots who agreed to serve were not such as could be steamrolled by English *force majeure*.[56] In the end, the (temporary) defeat of Scottish witchcraft rather than its promotion may owe much to Scottish apocalyptic radicalism.

## A Final Judgement

The apocalypse and witchcraft are founded on two quite contrasting conceptions and images of the satanic. Although both manifestations of evil inevitably meet together a common fate in the concluding acts of the sacred drama, they operated differently within the *saeculum* and ultimately worked to different ends. Historians might do well to ensure they have the right vampire.

## Notes

1 My thanks to William Burns, Malcolm Smuts and Nina Straus for their comments and insight.
2 "Nec certe tanta adhuc hominum perversitas, ut non haec omnia simul iuncta plures velint: aut siqui nolint errore aliquot, et possint ... doceri; et ... persuaderi," David Hume of Godscroft in *The British Union: A Critical Edition and Translation of Godscroft's "De unione insulae Britannicae,"* eds. P. J. McGinnis and A. H. Williamson (London: Ashgate, 2002), 313.
3 Karen Armstrong, *The Battle for God* (New York, 2000), 132.
4 See A. H. Williamson, *Apocalypse Then: Prophecy and the Making of the Modern World* (Westport, 2008), 1–35.
5 Jonathan Z. Smith, "Wisdom and Apocalyptic," in Jonathan Z. Smith, *Map Is Not Territory: Studies in the History of Religion* (Chicago: University of Chicago Press, 1993, originally 1975), 74, 81 and 86.
6 B. McGinn, "Early Apocalypticism," in *The Apocalypse in English Renaissance Thought and Literature,* eds. C.A. Patrides et al. (Ithaca; Cornell University Press, 1984), 2–39, at 5 and 14–6.
7 Within a vast literature, see especially Marie Tanner, *The Last Descendent of Aeneas: The Hapsburgs and the Mythic Image of the Emperor* (New Haven:Yales University Press, 1993), 119–30, 154–61 and 223–309.
8 C. H. Fleischer, "Seer to the Sultan: Haydar-I Remmal and Sultan Süleyman," in *Cultural Horizons: A Festschrift in Honor of Talat S. Halman,* ed. J. L. Warner (Syracuse, 2001), 290–9; Fleischer, "The Lawgiver as Messiah: The Making of the Imperial Image in the Reign of Süleyman," in Giles Veinstein (ed.), *Süleyman the Magnificent and his Time* (Paris, 1992), 159–77; Fleischer, "Shadows of Shadows: Prophecy and Politics in 1530s Istanbul," *International Journal of Turkish Studies* 13 (2007), 51–62; Tijana Krstić, *Contested Conversions to Islam: Narratives of Religious Change in the Early Modern Ottoman Empire* (Stanford, 2011), 7–8, 11–3, 75–97; Krstić, "Reimagining Religious Identity: Dutch and English Pamphlets, 1550–1620," *Renaissance Quarterly* 64 (2013), 1250–95 at 1278–81; Krstić, "Illuminated by the Light of Islam and the Glory of the Ottoman Sultanate: Self-Narratives of Conversion to Islam in the Age of Confessionalization," *Comparative Studies in Society and History* 51 (2009), 35–63; Mercedes Garcia-Arenal, *Messianism and Puritanical Reform: Madhis of the Muslim West,* trans. M. Beagles (Leiden, 2006), 269–313. Space does not allow notice of Shia eschatology of the Safavids that challenged the Ottomans at the other end of their empire. Nor will it be possible to discuss the Jewish apocalypses, the emergence of Moscow as the third (and final) Rome or the efflorescence of popular prophecy that occurred especially in Italy.
9 See R. J. W. Evans, *The Making of the Hapsburg Monarchy, 1550–1700* (Oxford, 1979), 394.
10 B. McGinn, "Wrestling with the Millennium: Early Modern Catholic Exegesis of Apocalypse 20," in *Imagining the End: Visions of the Apocalypse, from the Ancient Middle East to Modern America,* eds. A. Amarat et al. (London, 2002), 148–67, at 158, 161, 162 and 166.
11 B. P. Levack, *Witch-Hunting in Scotland: Law, Politics, and Religion* (New York, 2008), 2; Jonathan L. Pearl, *The Crime of Crimes: Demonology and Politics in France, 1560–1620* (Waterloo, 1999).
12 Lambert Daneau, *De veneficiis quos olim sortilegos, nunc autem vulgò Sortiarios vocant, Dialogus* (1574), trans. by Thomas Twyne as *A Dialogue of Witches* (1575), sigs. B5v, B6r, B7r. As Daneau phrased it, "... we may only haue understanding therof by the most holy word of God," sig. B6r. Reference is occasionally made to a 1564 edition, but this appears to be a ghost, possibly the result of a typo. See L. J. Watson, "The Influence of the Reformation and Counter Reformation upon the Key Texts in the Literature of Witchcraft" (PhD diss., University of Newcastle Upon Tyne, 1997). 14–5.
13 *A Dialogue of Witches,* sig. B4r-v.
14 *A Dialogue of Witches,* sigs. K8v-L1r and L5r-v. Alfred Soman, "The Parlement of Paris and the Great Witch Hunt (1560–1640)," *Sixteenth Century Journal* 9 (1978), 30–44, esp. 39. The *noblesse de robe* preoccupation with status especially in regard to the higher ranked military aristocracy, the *noblesse d'epée,* emerges in a range of literature at this juncture, including Charles Loyseau, *Traité des orders et simples dignitez* (1610).
15 *Dialogus,* sigs. D5v, D7r. For Daneau's Calvinist orthodoxy, see Olivier Fatio, "Lambert Daneau (1530–1595)," in *Shapers of Religious Traditions in Germany, Switzerland, and Poland, 1560–1600,* ed. J. Raitt (New Haven, 1981), 105–19.
16 See Daneau, *Tractatus de Antichristo* (Geneva, 1576), translated as *A Treatise Touching Antichrist* (London, 1589). In Chapter 22, Daneau discusses the "deuilishe and deceiptful" (*satanicum & fraudulentum*) practices used to set up Antichrist's kingdom. He discusses the importation of pagan rites, but at no point mentions sorcery or witchcraft. See *A Treatise,* 90–2; cf. *Antichristo,* 109–11.

17 Pearl, *Crime of Crimes*, 62–3, 67, 73, and *passim*.
18 Marc Bloch, *The Royal Touch: Monarchy and Miracles in France and England* (New York, 1961, originally in French as *Les Rois Thaumaturges* [Paris, 1923]), 193.
19 Pearl, *The Crime of Crimes*, 43–6.
20 Described by Alexandra Walsham, "Miracles in Post-Reformation England," *Studies in Church History* 41 (2005), 273–306 at 281.
21 William E. Burns, "Anderson, Sir Edmund (1530–1605)," in William F. Burns, *Witch Hunts in Europe and America: An Encyclopedia* (Westport, 2003), 6–7; David Ibbetson, "Anderson, Sir Edmund (1530?–1605)," *Oxford Dictionary of National Biography* (Oxford, 2004); Allen Boyer, *Sir Edward Coke and the Elizabeth Age* (Stanford, 2003), 63; Keith Thomas, *Religion and the Decline of Magic* (London, 1973), 541–2.
22 A. H. Williamson, "Roman Past, Jewish Future: Prophecy, Poetry, and the End of Empire," *Huntington Library Quarterly* 30, no. 2 (2020), 567–89, at 583–89; Glynn Parry, "The Academic, the University and Cultural Warfare: The Case of Thomas Digges (1546–1595)," in *Early Modern Universities: Networks of Higher Learning: Scientific and Learned Cultures and Their Institutions*, eds. A-S. Goeing and M. Feingold, (Leiden, 2021), 99–121. Reactionaries such as the Scot George Mackenzie (d. 1691) and the Englishman Robert Filmer (d. 1653) fully discounted witchcraft, but their politics and outlook were unusual.
23 Samuel Harsnett, *A discovery of the fraudulent practices of John Darrell* (London, 1599), 15.
24 Harsnett wanted women to be veiled in church, going well beyond any normal "puritan" repression. Nicholas W. S. Cranfield, "Harsnett, Samuel," *Oxford Dictionary of National Biography*; Brendan C. Walsh, *The English Exorcist John Darrell and the Shaping of Early Modern Protestant Demonology* (New York, 2020), 8, 11, 17, 21, and passim.
25 Patrick Collinson, *The Elizabethan Puritan Movement* (London, 1967), 432–47, notably 434–5.
26 Collinson, *Elizabethan Puritan Movement*, 437–8. See A. H. Williamson, *Scottish National Consciousness in the Age of James VI* (Edinburgh, 1979), 75–9.
27 Exorcism would only resurface significantly in New England and Scotland within the transformed environment at the very end of the 17th century.
28 William Bradford Smith, "Friedrich Föner, the Catholic Reformation, and Witch-Hunting in Bamberg," *Sixteenth Century Journal* 36 (2005), 115–28.
29 M. Roberts, *Gustavus Adolphus: A History of Sweden, 1611–1632*, vol. 1 (London, 1953), 379; cf. Göran Malmstedt, *Premodern Beliefs and Witch Trials in a Swedish Province, 1669–1672* (London, 2021); Robert Muchembled, "Satan ou les Hommes? La chasse aux sorcières et ses causes," in *Prophètes et Sorciers dans les Pays-Bas, XVIe-XVIIIe siècle*, eds. Marie-Sylvie Dupont-Bouchet, Willem Frijhoff and Robert Muchembled (Paris, 1978), 17; W. Monter, "Witch Trials in Continental Europe, 1560–1660," in *Witchcraft and Magic in Europe*, vol. 4, *The Period of the Witch Trials* eds. B. Ankarloo and S. Clark (London, 2002), 26.
30 A. Walsham, "Skeletons in the Cupboard: Relics after the English Reformation," *Past & Present* supplement 5, 206 (2010), 123–43, at 136–7; Christopher Highley, "Charles II and the Meaning of Exile," *Stuart Succession Literature: Moments and Transformations* eds. Paulina Kewes and Andrew McRae (Oxford, 2019), 75–94 esp. 91–2. Historians who believe witch-hunting originates with eschatology have found this hunt, Scotland's greatest, to be "somewhat surprising." B. P. Levack, *Witch-Hunting in Scotland*, 80.
31 Julian Goodare, "The Aberdeenshire Witchcraft Panic of 1597," *Northern Scotland* 21 (2001), 7–37 at 22, 29–30. Goodare notes, importantly, that both at both Aberdeen and St. Andrews "there is no actual evidence that the … trials were initiated by the church," 31. Huntly, Errol and the king were decisive. In 1591, the Catholic 9th earl of Angus featured prominently. Goodare, "Introduction," and V. Carr, "The Countess of Angus's Escape from the North Berwick Witch-Hunt," in *Scottish Witches and Witch-Hunters*, ed. J. Goodare (Houndmills, 2013), 3, 40–6; B. Levack, *Witch-Hunting in Scotland*, 37.
32 John Knox, "An Admonition to the Professors of God's Truth in England," in *The Works of John Knox*, vol. 3, ed. D. Laing (Edinburgh, 1846–52), 279; J. Dawson, *John Knox* (New Haven, 2015).
33 G. Donaldson, *The Scottish Reformation* (London, 1960), 127, 161–2, 214 and n. 1; F. Bardgett, "John Erskine of Dun: A Theological Reassessment," in *Scottish Journal of Theology* 43 (1990), 59–87 at 81 and n. 86.

34 SRO: GD 16/25/4, discussed in Williamson, *Scottish National Consciousness*, 56.

35 Angus Archives: M/18/33/12. For a further discussion of the contrast between Knox and Erskine, see Williamson, *Apocalypse Then*, 129–30.

36 Andrew Melville, Στεθανεςκιου (Edinburgh, 1590), discussed below. See D. Calderwood, *The History of the Kirk of Scotland*, vol. 5, ed. T. Thomson (Edinburgh, 1842–49), 106.

37 "Il me semble que je voy trembler les murs de Rome et que toute la papauté tressle de peur oyant parler de l'alliance de deux princes si braves." Du Bartas to J. Segur, 14 February 1587/8, in *The Warrender Papers*, vol. 2, ed. A.I. Cameron (Edinburgh, 1931), 69–70. I am grateful to Malcolm Smuts for this reference.

38 For many Philipp Melanchthon provided the model. See M. P. Fleischer, "Melanchthon as Praeceptor of Late Humanist Poetry," *Sixteenth Century Journal* 20 (1989), 559–80.

39 A. H. Williamson, "Number and National Consciousness: the Edinburgh Mathematicians and Scottish Political Thought and the Union of Crowns," in *Scots and Britons: Scottish Political Thought and the Union of 1603* ed. R. Mason (Cambridge, 1994), 187–212; Parry, "The Academic, the University and Cultural Warfare."

40 M. C. Smith, *The Presbytery of St Andrews, 1586–1605: A Study and Annotated Edition of the Register of the Minutes of the Presbytery of St. Andrews*, vol. 1 (Ph.D. thesis, University of St. Andrews, 1985), 41.

41 Andrew Melville, "*Principis Scoti-Britanorum natalia* ('On the Birth of the Scoto-Britannic Prince')," in *George Buchanan: The Political Poetry*, eds. P. J. McGinnis and A. H. Williamson (Edinburgh, 2000), 276–81; Hume, *De unione insulae Britannicae*, 262 and 263.

42 *Sermons by the Reverend Robert Bruce*, ed. W. Cunningham (Edinburgh, 1843), 56, 59, 66, 154, 355 and passim.

43 *Sermons*, 389, 394, 396 and 397. Long ago Christina Larner recognised the stark transition at this juncture. See Christina Larner, *Witchcraft and Religion: The Politics of Popular Belief* (New York, 1984), 7–9. Also see Williamson, *Scottish National Consciousness*, 59–60.

44 *Calendar of State Papers Relating to Scotland*, vol. 10, ed. by J. Bain et al. (Edinburgh, 1898–1952), 129–30.

45 James Balfour, *The Practicks of Sir James Balfour of Pittendreich*, vol. 2, ed. P. G. B. McNeill (Edinburgh, 1962, 1963), 503; Thomas Hope, *Hope's Major Practicks*, vol. 2, ed. J.A. Clyde (Edinburgh, 1938), 268 and 304; Williamson, *Scottish National Consciousness*, pp. 60–1.

46 Goodare, "Aberdeenshire Witchcraft Panic," 57 and 59.

47 James VI, *Daemonologie* (Edinburgh, 1597), 53–4, 81. The contrast with Daneau is striking.

48 James, *Daemonologie*, 14, 15, 16, 20, 22, 53, 62, 65, 75 and passim.

49 James, *Daemonologie*, 14. See A. Williamson, "Robert Pont," in *Astrology through History: Interpreting the Stars from Ancient Mesopotamia to the Present*, ed. W. E. Burns (Santa Barbara, 2018), 73–6.

50 James describes his work as speaking "scholasticklie" and "in the logick schools." See *Daemonologie*, xii and 2. He imagined the devil as "God's ape," an inverted parody of the sacred from which one could learn about it. The king's Calvinism was sufficiently robust as prevent him from positing an inverse hierarchy. See *Daemonologie*, 21 and 35.

51 Williamson, "Number and National Consciousness," 210–2.

52 A. I. Macinnes, "The Scottish Constitution, 1638–51: The Rise and Fall of Oligarchic Centralism," in *The Scottish National Covenant in its British Context*, ed. John Morrill (Edinburgh, 1990), 106–33, at 127; Levack, *Witch-hunting in Scotland*, 59.

53 Paula Hughes, "Witch-Hunting in Scotland, 1649–1650," in *Scottish Witches and Witch-Hunters*, 85–102, at 90, 93 and 98.

54 Alistair Henderson, "The Urban Geography of Witch-hunting in Scotland," in *Scottish Witches and Witch-Hunters*, pp. 177–95 at 181 and 188–90.

55 B. P. Levack, "Witchcraft and the Law in Early Modern Scotland," in *Witch-Hunting in Scotland*, 15–33 at 21. A preliminary perusal the Committee minutes suggests that they were not present at meetings when commissions for witch trials were issued.

56 A. H. Williamson, "Union with England Traditional, Union with England Radical: Sir James Hope and the Mid-Seventeenth-Century British State," *English Historical Review* CX (1995), 303–22; A. H. Williamson, "Hope, Sir James of Hopetoun (1614–1661)," in *Oxford Dictionary of National Biography*.

## Further Reading

Cornell H. Fleischer, "Shadows of Shadows: Prophecy and Politics in 1530s Istanbul," *International Journal of Turkish Studies* 13 (2007): 51–62.

Bernard McGinn, "Wrestling with the Millennium: Early Modern Catholic Exegesis of Apocalypse 20," in A. Amarat et al. (eds.), *Imagining the End: Visions of the Apocalypse, from the Ancient Middle East to Modern America* (London, 2002): 148–67.

Elaine Pagels, *The Origin of Satan* (New York, 1995).

Jonathan L. Pearl, *The Crime of Crimes: Demonology and Politics in France, 1560-1620* (Waterloo, Canada, 1999).

Jonathan Z. Smith, *Map Is Not Territory: Studies in the History of Religions* (Chicago, 1975, repr. 1993).

A.H. Williamson, *Scottish National Consciousness in the Age of James VI* (Edinburgh, 1979, repr. 2003).

A.H. Williamson, *Apocalypse Then: Prophecy and the Making of the Modern World* (Westport, CT, and London, 2008).

# 9

# PRODUCING DEVIL KNOWLEDGE

## Experience, Theory and Evidence

### *Richard Raiswell*

*Qui credit cito levis corde est, et minorabitur.*[1]

By 21 October 1477, Antonia, the wife of Jean Rose of Villars Chabod, a small community towards the western banks of Lake Annecy, was ready to confess. She had been in jail for at least six weeks by this point and had been questioned repeatedly—about her orthodoxy, her acquaintances and whether or not she had ever attended what her interrogators termed "the synagogue of heretics."[2] Though she had repeatedly pleaded her innocence over the weeks following her arrest, now, before the Vice-Inquisitor General, she was willing to admit the truth and confess to being a willing participant in the criminal heresy of which she stood accused.

Calling upon the grace of God and the church's mercy, she admitted that some eleven years earlier she had been approached by a certain Masset Garini after a portion of her land had been seized in payment of a debt. Garini—who was later drowned as a heretic himself—comforted the distraught Antonia, promising to help her redeem her property if she did as he ordered. Antonia agreed, and so that evening Garini came to the woman's house and took her to a place called "laz Perroy" where a band of heretics had gathered. There, she reported, she saw a great number of men and women shrieking and dancing backwards in a circle—their backs towards each other. Although she claimed to have been afraid, Garini explained that were she to do everything he told her, she would gain whatever she wished. And at that, Garini pointed to a demon in the form of a black man who, he said, was named Robinet, explaining that for her wishes to be realised she must first deny the creator, her Catholic faith, "that red-headed woman called the Virgin Mary," and do homage to the demon, accepting him as her lord and master. This she did, kissing the demon on his foot, pledging to pay him one vienne every year at the synagogue as tribute. With this, Robinet placed a mark on the little finger of her left hand, and she—at his "unnatural insistence" (*importunam instantiam*)—gave him her soul.[3] The demon then invested her with a small bag of gold and silver—although, she lamented, when she got home later that night, she found it empty. He also gave her a staff about a foot and a half long and a small box full of ointments. Any time she wanted to go to the synagogue, the demon continued, she was to anoint the staff with the ointment, straddle it between her thighs, and repeat the

DOI: 10.4324/9781003096603-10

phrase "Go, on behalf of the devil. Go!" ("Vade ex parte diaboli, vade!"). And at that, the demon claimed, she would be transported through the air at great speed to her destination.

Her initiation complete, she joined with the other heretics, eating, drinking and dancing with them. After a time, Robinet transformed himself again, this time into the guise of a black dog, and everyone did homage and reverence to the animal, kissing it on the anus. Then the fire that had been illuminating the synagogue was extinguished, and the demon commanded "Meclet! Meclet!"[4] At this, the men joined with the women in the manner of beasts. She herself admitted to having sex with Garini.

Over the next few days, Antonia elaborated on the details of her confession. She claimed that after her initiation, she attended synagogues across the region regularly, committing all manner of atrocities, blasphemies and crimes. And, in the process, she implicated many of her acquaintances, claiming to have seen them at these gatherings. Several times, she said, she saw pieces of human flesh—even the flesh of infants—eagerly eaten by attendees. On another occasion, her demon master gave her an ointment which she later applied to the hand of a four-year-old child, causing him to languish and die. Others at the synagogue, she said, ground the bones of exhumed corpses into powders which they used to work malevolent magic, harming both people and animals. Finally, she confessed, when the body of Christ (referring here to the consecrated eucharist) was smuggled into the synagogue, the heretics abused and debased it, dragging it along the ground and stamping on it with their feet. Significantly, though, she admitted that when they tried to grind it into dust, it vanished from their sight in a great flash of light.[5]

The outrages and sacrileges to which Antonia confessed never happened. Her confession was the result of a deadly combination of leading questions posed under juridical torture. Indeed, the records indicate that Antonia had been subjected to the strappado twice over her the term of her imprisonment: each time, her hands had been tied behind her back before she was hoisted up by a rope attached to her wrists. On the first occasion, she was left to hang suspended above the ground for half an hour. The second time, her tormentors attached weights to her feet to compound the intensity of her suffering. It was this second session that finally induced her to confess and to tell the inquisitors what they wanted to hear.

But much of what Antonia admitted were relatively new additions to the litany of atrocities associated with the devil. The witches of the high Middle Ages were women of a very different kind. The sorceresses described by the 12th-century Benedictine chronicler William of Malmesbury, for instance, used various unspecified demonic arts, but they did so in order to ameliorate their wretched status—not to scandalise or destabilise the faith. The so-called witch of Berkeley he describes was a solitary recluse who turned to sorcery and auguries to stave off destitution.[6] Similarly, the two unnamed women of Rome who were apparently able to turn unsuspecting travellers into animals did so in order to have the beasts perform public tricks, allowing the women to sell them on to wealthy townsfolk as amusing novelties.[7] In both cases, though, these women are not a mortal threat to anyone but themselves. To be sure, the Berkeley sorceress was dragged off by demons at the end of the tale, but she is not described as having harmed anyone or anything. And—significantly— these stories are presented not so much as literal truths but rather as entertaining and morally illuminating anecdotes.

From the beginning of the 15th century, though, there is increasing evidence for a series of disparate beliefs progressively coalescing into what scholars have dubbed "the cumulative" or "elaborated" theory of witchcraft. Noticeable in a series of writings from the 1430s that purport to describe the activities of witches in the regions around the western

Alps, these texts describe a devil who is a much more immediate and fundamental threat to the whole of Christian society than the figure who promised poor women relief from their poverty, who skulked in the shadows of medieval monasteries, who seduced would-be magicians by pandering to their greed or baser instincts, or whose efforts to frustrate the saints were thwarted by divine power.[8] Central to this new, reworked conception of witchcraft is the idea that a witch was a willing partner of the devil, part of a secret sect of women and men who had renounced their homage to God, taking the devil as their lord instead. At certain times of the year, these witches would travel through the air, as Antonia described, to the synagogue—increasingly coming to be known as the *sabbat*—a large assembly of witches presided over by demons, and sometimes even by Satan himself. There they would provide reports to their demonic lords about their recent nefarious dealings, make new ointments and powders to wicked ends, and practice maleficent magic. The climax of the sabbat would come with a great, atrocious feast, featuring as one of its most eagerly anticipated dishes, the flesh of infants.[9]

But by the time Antonia confessed to having made her pact with Robinet, the cumulative conception of witchcraft was beginning to spread from its Alpine base. Just seven years after her trial, the Dominican inquisitor Henricus Institoris sought to find evidence for it in the southern German city of Ravensburg and then the next year in Innsbruck. His experiences in these jurisdictions profoundly coloured his thinking about witchcraft and its prosecution, and is reflected in the first great witch-hunting manual of the age of print, the 1486/7 *Hammer of Witches* (*Malleus maleficarum*) which he described in the work's foreword as co-authored with the Kölner theologian Jacobus Sprenger.[10] It is this notion of witchcraft that fomented anxiety amongst zealous inquisitors and magistrates across Europe between roughly 1430 and 1650 and which stoked the periodic, localised bouts of intense prosecution—the so-called witch "panics" or "manias"—that justified circumventing aspects of standard legal procedure intended to protect an accused to ensure his (and increasingly her) conviction. It is this notion of witchcraft that underlies the European witch hunts.

In this sense, then, thinking about the devil as it developed in the second half of the 15th century was inextricably woven into witchcraft discourse. Indeed, as the cumulative notion of witchcraft developed and spread, and more witches were discovered and confessed to ever-more outrageous outrages, crimes and blasphemies, so too did the body of evidence attesting to the devil's powers and his perceived field of operation.

## Devil Information

In his seminal 1997 study of early modern demonism and its relationship to witchcraft, *Thinking with Demons*, Stuart Clark argued that demonology was never a closed system of dogmatic and uncritical assertions.[11] It was always a product of debate and negotiation. More recently, Gerhild Scholz Williams has argued that demonologies comprise a distinct literary genre which draws on material from history, theology, law and medicine to define and describe the relationship between the devil, demons and people.[12] While there is certainly an unbroken tradition of texts that purport to assess the power and wiles of the devil that can be catalogued from the early Christian period up to the present day and can be grouped together based on their common subject matter, this gives an artificial sense of the homogeneity of the field.

As much recent work in the history of science has stressed, though, the construction of knowledge is a socially embedded process. Here, it is useful to distinguish between *data* and *knowledge.* Following Ann Blair, I treat *datum/a* as raw information. That is, data is a set of unprocessed facts, information that has not been assimilated into any explanatory scheme and so has no meaning beyond its value as a particular truth claim. By contrast, *knowledge* is data processed towards a specific end. In short, *data* is knowing that X happened; *knowledge* is knowing how X happened.[13]

This distinction has a number of important consequences. First of all, it implies that *knowledge* is owned—it is a function of the epistemic practices of a particular set of like-minded people striving in a methodologically similar fashion towards much the same goals. Put differently, *knowledge* is not universal in the sense a group of knowers might claim; rather, it is a product of their concerns and needs—the questions for which they seek to find answers. It also implies that the significance of *data* is far from unambiguous. *Data* only get their meaning by virtue of the arguments they are appropriated to make or the epistemic claims they are intended to bolster. But the corollary matters here, too, for where certain points of information cannot readily be assimilated into a particular community's knowledge—where on a superficial basis at least *data* seem to contradict the axioms and precepts it accepts—the community either has to face the prospect of a fundamental paradigm shift or, as is more likely, argue that the processes by which the data were adduced were somehow flawed, or that the data actually points to some deeper, non-literal meaning.

Tied to this is the space in which knowledge is generated and where it is consumed. On one level, what we might—at the risk of anachronism—call "the research environment" helps shape what sort of data are sought, the standards which inform how it is collected, and the interpretative frame into which it is assimilated. But for the subsequent knowledge generated to have any resonance, it also needs to conform to epistemic practices and natural (and supernatural) assumptions of the people who encounter it. If it does not, it will either be ignored or challenged. In this sense, then, the social construction of credibility tends to mirror that of the knowledge producers.[14]

This matters for devil knowledge, for despite the fact that, as numerous modern scholars have noted, there was a broad consensus about the nature of the devil and demons amongst late medieval theologians, this claim is too tightly focused.[15] From its earliest period, devil knowledge had never been confined to theologians. It had always had an important experiential dimension to it which was not always easy to reconcile with the theoretically tidy devil deduced by the university masters from biblical exegesis and premises lifted from Aristotelian natural philosophy. It was at odds in many ways with the devil of early saints' lives, or that of the monasteries. But by Antonia's period, new sites of devil data were coming becoming important, too. Chief amongst these were courtroom and the deck of the carrack.

And with the coming of printing, this data—sometimes reconstructed as knowledge—was being widely reproduced, creating new communities of practice, mediating people's anxieties and experiences of misfortune in new ways to new ends. These communities were less concerned than the university masters with reconciling their data with the more subtle elements of scholastic demonology. Operating in a different intellectual environment and to different ends, they treated their data literally—that is, as facts. But as Frances Dolan has argued, the effect of such relations is to serve as a substitute on the reader's part for reality. That is to say, they allow the reader to experience empathetically much of the information conveyed—sometimes as it has been rearranged into narrative—vicariously.[16]

In this sense, then, the enormous influx of new evidence about the devil amassed in the courtroom, garnered from his confessed human confederates and spread from the 1450s through the new technology of printing, raised difficult questions about the nature of evidence: its production, meaning and significance and, by extension, its relationship to received natural philosophical theory. It created a new devil—one at odds with the comparatively tame beast constructed by the university masters of the 12th and 13th centuries. But it also created one who, through print, came to assume a larger, more immediate presence in the minds of a widening circle of people encountering accounts of his machinations.

But the weight of this new evidence pushed both the devil of the masters and the devil of the courtroom to absurdity. To accommodate this new data, the masters had to ascribe an ever-widening ability to the devil to confound the senses to the point at which certain knowledge was no longer theoretically possible. To the lawyers, the devil's power seemed so great that God must either be impotent or a sadist. Either way, the devil was tied up intimately to the debates over knowledge production and authentication that characterise the early modern period—what Susan Schreiner has called the 16th-century's "clanging, clashing certitudes," the methodological and epistemological reconfiguration that earlier generations of historians dubbed "the scientific revolution."[17]

## Producing Devil Knowledge in the Middle Ages

As earlier chapters have shown, the patristic and early medieval devil was known from something of a hodgepodge of disparate sources. Some of this data was sensory, taken from the testimony of those who claimed to have had encounters with demons. As vividly recounted by Athanasius, bishop of Alexandria in the middle of the 4th century, for instance, Saint Anthony spent much of his time while a hermit engaged in an intense, personal struggle with the devil. But the information adduced from this account pointed to a devil who seemed paradoxically to have the characteristics and abilities of both a physical and spiritual creature. On the one hand, he and his minions were able to assault the future saint—on one occasion beating him all over and leaving him in such pain that he could neither move nor speak. But on the other, this apparently corporeal devil was also able to change forms, and to create apparitions and illusions. Despite this apparent and fundamental contradiction as to their nature, Athanasius made little attempt to explain how demons could have the properties of both spiritual and physical creatures. That that was the case was a function of his data. He had witnessed some of what he related first hand or had heard it from the saint himself; other data he had garnered from the testimony of learned people who had spent a great deal of time with him.[18] In other words, for him, what he related was data acquired from good, reliable sources. The result was an aethereal devil capable of transforming himself into a woman, a black boy, a monk, various beasts and even fire, but sufficiently physical as to be able to smash down the door of the saint's cell and beat him senseless. Athanasius' devil, though, was produced by and for monks. It was intended to memorialise the deeds of a great man and to serve as an exemplar for those who strived to follow in his footsteps. But in the process, he made known a devil who defied some of the principles of natural philosophy and whose apparent power raised awkward questions about divine omnipotence and benevolence.

In this sense, the devil of the early medieval centuries was primarily a monastic construction. Indeed, Pope Gregory I, a former monk himself, warned monks always to expect new battles with the ancient enemy, noting that such confrontations represented an occasion for God's servants to earn a victory.[19] Accordingly, monks regularly detected his presence in the temptations they faced in their daily life and in the great and petty tribulations within and without their community's walls. Theirs was an antagonistic devil who, finding their sanctity and that of the cloistered space of the monastery especially odious, assailed them night and day in a myriad of different ways. Demonic conflict was central to the construction of monastic identity, part of what Sari Katajala-Peltomaa calls their "lived religion"—an integral element that conditioned how monks experienced their vocation and participated in their community.[20]

But this devil had little theoretical grounding. He was a creature known through experience and the testimony of trustworthy authorities. The great 12th-century monastic reformer, Bernard of Clairvaux, for instance, described the monastery as a fortress under constant sieged from demonic enemies.[21] Some 70 years later or so, Richalm, the abbot of the Cistercian abbey of Schöntal, saw enormous numbers of demons roaming his house—"like specks in the sunlight such is the multitude of them that surround every man"—accompanying the monks everywhere they went, disturbing their sleep, causing them to seem to stutter during the sacred reading, emitting foul odours, tempting them with lust-inducing forms, and speaking through thunder.[22] Neither of these monks was particularly interested in how the devil did these things. All they had was data about his actions lifted from their own lived experience as monks, and what they set down in manuscript about his doings was intended to be consumed by like-minded readers.

However, this experiential devil came increasingly to be challenged from the 11th century by the schools and then from the early 13th century by the universities. In this very different intellectual environment, the schoolmen were more interested in explaining the devil's power than in compiling a compendium of instances of his action. They sought to rationalise the devil in order to produce *devil knowledge*, refracting received data about him through the lens of Christian Aristotelianism, reconciling this with truths derived from particular interpretations of scripture. The result was a theologically neater devil, one whose abilities were deduced from contemporary understandings of nature and which more comfortably squared with contemporary thinking about the divine omnipotence and benevolence.

To Thomas Aquinas writing in the middle of the 13th century, for instance, creation was a form of communication, a statement by the creator to humanity about his omnipotence. However, as an infinite being, it was not possible for God to express his limitless goodness fully through the medium of any single, finite created form. Thus, he created a hierarchy of progressively more perfect things, reaching from the base elements—earth, air, fire and water—through stones, plants, animals and people, up to the heavenly bodies.[23] At the top of this hierarchy, juxtaposed against the material but inanimate forms at its base, it was necessary, he argued, that there be some order of immaterial but animate beings. This order was that of angels.[24]

In this view, every order of created thing had its own particular God-given nature that defined its place, position and potency within the cosmos.[25] The universe that results from this reading, then, is necessarily ordered and regular, with every order of being behaving according to its nature. Indeed, it cannot do otherwise, for nothing can operate in a fashion contrary to the way it was made. Thus, while scripture has nothing explicit to say about the creation of angels, it was clear to Aquinas that they were part of nature: they occupied a place at the top of the created order, endowed with their own distinct nature. While their fall from heaven had isolated the devil and his confederates from grace, it had not changed their angelic nature; in formal terms, at least, they maintained their position on the ladder of creation. This meant that as naturally (if not morally) superior beings, their abilities were considerable, far surpassing those of animals, birds and people—characteristics they exploited to beguile and confound the gullible and unwary.

To St. Augustine in his early 5th century *On the divination of demons* (*De divinatione daemonum*), it was clear that unencumbered by the weight of a physical body, demons could naturally move at exceptional speeds. They also largely maintained their angelic intellective powers after the fall and so their natural perception was far sharper and keener than that of other creatures. This, combined with the fact that they were sempiternal and so had long experience of the world, meant that they were well familiar with nature and its operation and had a far more complete understanding of the natural properties of things. By virtue of this occult knowledge, demons were able to perform all manner of strange and curious feats. While such effects might seem amazing from the perspective of human beings with their more limited perception and acuity, as Augustine stressed, they were wholly natural, simply a consequence of the nature of demons and their long experience observing the regular course of the world.[26]

A case in point is the apparent ability of demons to make predictions about the future. Appearances to the contrary, such prognostications cannot rise to the level of prophecy, Augustine asserted, for demons no longer have access to immutable divine knowledge. Thus, at best, anything that a demon might claim to know about the future can only ever be contingent. That said, their nature does allow them to offer well-informed guesses about the course of future events. They can do this, the saint argued, in a number of different ways. The fact that they can flit almost instantaneously from one region to another allows them to see things occurring in one place that might later have consequences elsewhere. Seeing an enemy mustering his army, for instance, might allow a demon to predict an invasion to the people of a neighbouring region. But demons can also use their long experience reading and interpreting signs in nature to make reasonable inferences about the future. Here again, though, what they say is necessarily contingent, differing only in sophistication from the well-seasoned sailor's ability to predict the next day's weather on the basis of natural signs, or the experienced physician's ability to predict the course of an illness from a patient's symptoms. Demons may like to feign supernatural power to win or astound human followers, but as Augustine stressed, there is nothing *super*natural about them; the devil cannot go beyond his nature.[27]

Still, Job shows that the devil has the power to manipulate the elements to cause real harm in the world, sending down fire from on high, raising terrible storms, even inflicting horrible, disfiguring sores on people. But as Job 2.6 makes clear, while it is within the devil's nature to be able to create appalling torments for people, he can only do so insofar as he is permitted by God. Thus, it is quite possible that there are things that demons are naturally capable of doing which they cannot do because they do not have divine permission. For Augustine as later for Peter Lombard in the 12th century and Aquinas in the 13th, this was what happened in the course of the wonder-working contest between Pharaoh's magicians and Aaron described in Exodus 7.10-8.19. At the start of the contest, both sides were able to turn their staffs into serpents. But while Aaron was later able to turn dust into lice, when Pharaoh's magicians tried to do the same thing, their conjuration failed, causing them to remark that they had been thwarted by "the finger of God." To Augustine, in producing serpents—and later frogs—the demons who worked the magicians' wonders had not actually created anything. They had merely used their speed and agility to gather up the seeds of those creatures left on the land or in water, and then used their knowledge of nature to cause them to germinate almost instantaneously. Magical though the process may have seemed from Pharaoh's perspective, unbeknownst to him, there was nothing unnatural about it.[28] From this, it is clear that the power of the devil is limited by his nature and by the will of God. While as Aquinas argued, the power and operation of any thing is always contingent upon its nature, potentiality does not translate into actuality without the permission of God.[29]

With some qualification as to details, most learned theologians into the 17th century—Catholic and Protestant—accepted the broad outline of the position laid out by the schoolmen. Most would be familiar with it from the works of Augustine, Lombard's hugely influential *Four Books of Sentences* (*Libri Quattuor Sententiarum*), effectively the standard textbook for divinity in the medieval university, and Aquinas' voluminous writings—either directly or through the critiques of his critics.[30] This, then, was the devil created by the schoolmen. To them, part of the great strength of this devil lay in the fact that he maintained the integrity of nature and, by extension, eliminated any possibility of dualism. The devil may be able to manufacture all manner of apparent wonders intended to seduce would-be followers and beguile his disciples, but ultimately, as a natural being anything he was able to do he did within the realm of nature. Such effects, then, could never be real miracles, for the devil did not have the ability to breach nature in the way that God did when, for instance, he made the sun stop moving as recounted in Joshua 10.12-15 or when he made a donkey speak, as related in Numbers 22.28-30. Following the language of 2 Thessalonians 2.9, they were "lying wonders" (*prodigiis mendacibus*)—tricks wrought by the devil by virtue of his natural capacity as a fallen angel or by virtue of his knowledge of nature amassed over the centuries since his creation. These tricks may be impressive even stupefying to human beings confined within the bounds of the capacities of their physical bodies, but they were never miraculous.

In terms of the construction of devil knowledge, then, this meant that any information about the devil had to be naturalised in some way in order to be made consistent with the implications of this position. From this perspective, it was difficult to accommodate new powers within demonic discourse, for ultimately anything asserted of the devil needed to be—in the final analysis—wholly natural. Yet this was never always an easy position to maintain. In particular and for different reasons the issues of transmutation and transvection posed particular challenges. In both cases, the way the schoolmen sought to naturalise these notions, known from the encounter with traditional religion, popular belief and saints' lives—and increasingly from the 15th century the legally adduced confessions from the devil's co-conspirators—opened the door to what would become a fundamental epistemological crisis.

## Transmutations

As scripture makes clear, all creative power is restricted to God.[31] By extension, this means that the devil must have no ability to create. Certainly, the devil can use his knowledge of nature to cause natural things to come forth in an untimely manner, as the demons serving Pharaoh's magicians had done. But the question as to whether demons could transform people into animals was more complicated, for there were plenty of examples where this seemed to have happened. In scripture, there was the story of Nebuchadnezzar who was apparently changed into a wild beast.[32] Turning his attention to the subject, Augustine pointed to the story of Circe, the witch who transmuted Ulysses' companions as an example. Indeed, the saint claimed to have some direct knowledge of the issue, for when he was in Italy, he heard of women who, working through the power of demons, gave drugs to passing travellers hidden in chunks of cheese that turned them into pack animals.[33]

To the schoolmen, such transformations were naturally impossible for demons. They were not just beyond their capacity, as Aquinas argued in *On Evil* (*De malo*), they were contrary to the general order of nature.[34] Accordingly, he attributed apparent information about demon-wrought transformations to some form of deception—more lying wonders. For Aquinas, this was how demons were apparently able to raise the dead. It was, of course, impossible for demons to bring the dead back to life. But it was clear from scripture that despite being insubstantial, both angels and demons could take on bodies from time to time in order to appear visible. Demons did this, Aquinas argued drawing analogies to the formation of steam and clouds, by condensing or otherwise compounding air to make it solid in such a way that it was able to refract light and so take on colours. The resultant mass was then manipulated into the shape of a deceased person.[35]

In an assumed body, a demon could mimic many of its faculties, appearing, for instance, both to eat and to speak. However, as Aquinas argued, given that angels neither need to feed nor talk, such actions when they are enacted in a body would be imitations of real processes, a point he supported with reference to Tobias where an angel admits to feigning eating with the eponymous patriarch, using some invisible means to consume food and drink.[36] In much the same way, Aquinas allowed that it was quite possible for demons in assumed bodies to have intercourse. While he did not doubt that it was impossible for demons to procreate with human women, he thought that it was not unreasonable to hold that demons might impregnate them. They might do this, he suggested, by having intercourse with a human male in the form of a succubus—a female demon—capturing the discharged semen and then, upon assuming the guise of an incubus—a male demon—inseminating it into a woman. While any child born from such a union would necessarily be human, the demon might capitalise on his knowledge of the occult properties of the stars to impregnate his victim at an especially advantageous time in order to ensure the child was born with a particular complexion.[37]

In making these arguments, though, Aquinas granted broad explanatory powers to illusion. Indeed, it seems that any data about demonic powers that appeared to challenge accepted ideas about nature and its operation was not to be read literally. Rather, to maintain the integrity of nature as it was understood, and the exclusive omnipotence of God, it needed to be read simply as an example of the power of demonic illusion.

### Transvection

Perhaps more problematic, though, was the issue of transvection, for scripture contains a number of references to spirits transporting people. Daniel, for instance, describes how a good angel transported Habakkuk from Judea to Chaldea.[38] In the New Testament, the apostle Philip is described at one point as having been transported to Azotus.[39] More crucially, the gospel of Matthew has Christ carried by the devil first to the top of the temple in Jerusalem and then on to an exceedingly high mountain.[40] But the idea that demons could physically transport people was challenged by the canon *Episcopi*. Believed to be early 4th century, the canon was first attested in the early 10th century by Regino of Prüm, Abbot of Trier. Incorporated into the law collections of Burchard of Worms and Ivo of Chartres in the 11th century, it came to be included in Gratian's great compendium of ecclesiastical law, the *Decretum*, in the middle of the 12th, and so became part of the *Body of Canon Law* (*Corpus iuris canonici*). The canon took issue with the idea that on certain nights, groups of wicked women believed themselves to ride out on beasts, traversing enormous distances with the goddess Diana in response to her summons, condemning this belief as pagan error. The women who thought themselves transported, it declared, were actually dupes of the devil, seduced by illusions and phantasms impressed upon their minds by demons. Significantly, it also condemned those who accepted such accounts as literal truth, asking "who is so stupid and foolish as to think that all these things which happen in the spirit happen in the body," and concluding that whoever believes such things is "beyond doubt an infidel" (*proculdubio infidelis est*).[41]

To those keen to maintain the integrity of nature against the devil, *Episcopi* offered a way to address the direct testimony of those who claimed to have had experiences with the devil that did not conform to the tenets of natural philosophy. Rather than reworking conceptions of nature to accommodate the devil, the data garnered from such people could readily and comfortably be assimilated within the ambit of illusion. Indeed, as the canon counselled, it was accepting such counsel that was problematic. But as ever-more apparently reliable data about the power of the devil accrued in the early modern period, it was increasingly clear that the devil's ability to occlude the senses and to manipulate the cognitive faculties of people to cause them to see and experience unreal things was seemingly without limit.

## Producing Demon Knowledge in the Age of the Witch Hunts

The historiography of early modern demonology has tended to focus disproportionately on the devil of the theorists—that is, the naturalised devil as he was deduced by the schoolmen. Indeed, Clark goes so far as to assert that "in Renaissance Europe, it was virtually the unanimous opinion of the educated that devils, and, *a fortiori*, witches, not merely existed in nature but acted according to its laws."[42] As noted above, the strength of this position was that it preserved the realm of the miraculous for God and made the idea of some form of modified dualism untenable. But the second half of the 15th century saw the increasing importance of new centres for the generation and assimilation of devil knowledge. Outside the rarefied space of the university lecture halls, new devil knowledge was being uncovered by magistrates and inquisitors in the courtrooms, by physicians and cunning folk at the bedsides of apparent demoniacs, and by merchants and mariners plying the seas. Unlike the theoreticians, the primary concern of these men was not theoretical tidiness or to keep the devil bound up in natural philosophical knots. Rather, these men were informed principally by what they heard and what they saw. They saw in the lands of the east and the west myriad signs of the devil's handiwork: hideous idols being worshipped as gods, inverted ceremonies clearly mocking Christianity, and ritualised cannibalism. In Europe, as Chapters 5 and 12 show, the torments of those diagnosed as possessed seemed to foreshadow the final struggle between God and the devil enacted in microcosm. And in courtrooms across the continent, men heard the confessions of people who, like Antonia, (seemingly) freely and openly admitted to serving as the devil's accomplices, who had drawn on his power to work *maleficium*, who had rendered people and animals impotent, and who had even copulated with the ancient enemy. While the theorists took the accounts these witnesses supplied as merely more evidence of the apparently unlimited scope of demonic illusion, the approach of these new men was analogous to that of the monks of earlier centuries. That is, they believed that they had an increasingly large volume of high quality, sensory data attesting to a host of hitherto uncontemplated demonic powers adduced from reliable sources. They were realists.

In his *Enchanted Europe*, Euan Cameron asserts that what distinguishes the authors who worked with such data from the theorists is that they tended not to apply a rigid scepticism to the phenomena they recounted, taking such data literally, rarely challenging their veracity.[43] But to some extent, this is to critique the approach of men of the 16th and 17th centuries according to the methodological practices and concerns of the 13th and 14th. As Richard Serjeantson has stressed, different standards of proof were expected of different disciplines, and so what counted as evidence was wholly dependent upon the discipline in which it was expected to function, and the ends to which it was put.[44] This matters because while the works they produced were often in dialogue with those of the theoreticians—and vice versa—these men came to their knowledge of the devil and his powers through the courtroom, and the procedures and practices that had developed over the preceding centuries to winnow and weigh respective accounts in order to reconstruct events of the past.

In this respect, in the context of the law—either canon or secular—what mattered was methodological rigour. Through the early Middle Ages, triers of fact could resort to the juridical ordeal in order to determine whether an accused was guilty of an alleged offence. While ordeals were never common and tended only to be used when other evidence was unclear, ambiguous or contradictory, the strength of these rituals was that they called upon God to subvert the ordinary course of nature to indicate if an accused party was innocent. In that sense, ordeals provided secure, incontestable proof: if God caused blessed water to reject a person submerged in it or did not intervene to heal the burns of someone who had carried a red-hot piece of iron three paces, it was clear that he was not prepared to prevent the accused from being punished. The result of an ordeal, then, was a sign of God's judgement.[45] That was the theory, at least.

But in 1215 the Fourth Lateran Council formally prohibited clergy from participating in ordeals.[46] Without the blessing of the elements of the ordeal—the water, the iron—as a prerequisite to the ritual, the process could no longer be deemed reliable, and so had to be abandoned. The result was a revolution in legal procedure that saw it increasingly left up to fallible, human judges to determine what constituted evidence and the weight it should be accorded in reconstructing events.[47] In England, the prohibition spurred the development of the jury trial.[48] On the continent, though, it hastened the adoption of inquisitorial procedure.[49] Adapted from Roman and canon law, this was a process by which magistrates sought to obtain proof of an offence according to the standard laid down in the 6th-century *Body of Civil Law* (*Corpus iuris civilis*): proof clearer than daylight.[50]

Once an individual was denounced, inquisitorial proceedings comprised two parts. The first, known as the *general inquiry* (*inquisitio generalis*), saw a judge determine if a crime alleged by a complainant had actually occurred and, if it had, whether the offence was punishable at law. Unlike the situation under English common law, the *general inquiry* saw the judge take an active role in proceedings, calling witnesses and taking testimony to help him identify a possible suspect. The second phase—the *special* or *particular inquiry* (*inquisitio specialis*)—saw the accused brought to court, and charges formally levelled against him or her.

While strong suspicion was enough to cause a suspect to be arrested, the law required full proof to convict. This was formally defined as the testimony of two disinterested eye-witnesses or a confession. In the case of secret crimes—such as heresy or witchcraft—eyewitnesses were exceptionally difficult to acquire. Moreover, when eyewitnesses were available, it was not always clear what they were meant to have witnessed: the *concocting* of a presumably maleficent powder or its *effects*—effects which may only become evident at a later time some distance away? Similarly, what did two eyewitnesses have to have seen for their testimony to be deemed consistent? Did they both have to see the same necro-mantic conjuration performed, for instance, or did separate instances of some demonically sacrilegious outrage constitute consistency? There was also the related question of witness reliability, for it was highly likely that were a witness to admit to having seen the accused do homage to the devil, she was also a participant at the sabbat. If she was a co-conspirator with the accused and, by extension, a vassal of the devil—the father of lies—could she in any sense be judged a reliable and disinterested witness?

Given these difficulties, in practice, a confession was deemed the more desirable mode of proof. Contemporaries dubbed them "the queen of proofs" (*regina probationum*), for unlike other forms of evidence, the epistemic value of a confession was unambiguous.[51] But for obvious reasons, few people accused of witchcraft or related crimes were willing to ad-mit to what was alleged against them. Yet by the time an accused was hauled up into court, the judge had already determined through the *general inquiry* that there was some evidence against her. In such cases, where there were sufficient partial proofs—the testimony of a sin-gle witness, or sufficient *indicia* (indications, or what we would generally class as "circum-stantial evidence")—torture was licit. As Edward Peters has stressed, though, torture was not intended as a method of proof in itself; rather, it was a way of obtaining a confession which was the method of proof.[52] Indeed, torture was intended as a method of last resort, to be employed only after all other methods had failed. And even then, any confession made under such duress had to be repeated freely in open court.[53]

To be sure, as Lyndal Roper and many others have shown so effectively, the dynamic in the torture chamber between suspect and inquisitor saw the latter reshape the testimony of the former through leading questions based upon what he thought he knew about witches and demons.[54] And here, the circulation of inquisitors' manuals such as that of Bernard Gui from the 1320s and Nicholas Eymeric from the 1370s which included formulae for inter-rogating those suspected of commerce with demons, were crucial in colouring testimony and go a long way to explaining why much of the information elicited from witches seems broadly consistent. But this is an *effect* of the process, something that was not immediately apparent to most of those eliciting testimony at the time.

This is certainly not to excuse the process—obviously, the character of the judge and the accused's position within the social geography of her community were all important in fac-tors in shaping how a trial proceeded and whether it led to a conviction. And I would not go as far as Henry Angsar Kelly who described inquisition as "a brilliant and much-needed innovation in trial procedure," going on to declare that the "abusive practices that came to prevail in the special heresy tribunals do not merit the name of inquisition, but rather should be identified as a perversion of the inquisitorial process caused by overzealous and underscrupulous judges."[55] But I would argue that what developed over the centuries after the suppression of ordeals was a system of rationalised inquiry premised upon evidence which was (in theory at least) assessed, evaluated, and weighed according to the shifting epistemological standards of the day.[56] The veracity of the evidence that emerged was a function of the legal process through which it was adduced. And in the growing volume of witch confessions that developed from the middle decades of the 15th century, what the experiential demonologists thought they had was a body of evidence extracted from people who were, in Stephens' terminology, *expert witnesses* (*testes expertae*) to the power of the devil. Indeed, their testimony was all the more valuable—all the more credible—by virtue of the fact that it was elicited from people *not* trained in theology, not tainted by the naturalising concerns of university theoreticians.[57]

Ultimately, what these experiential demonologists of the 15th and 16th centuries thought they traded in were *facts*. Although the term "fact" came to be appropriated by the natural philosophers of the 17th century, it came into early modern discourse from law where it was used to distinguish questions about what actually happened (*de facto*) from matters of law (*de iure*). That is to say, *fact* was used to denote an action or an event in which an individual participated, related in bald terms, unencumbered by any theoretical baggage that might situate it within some broader discursive frame.[58] It was a point of data from which—if combined with other, similarly constructed *facts*—general inferences might be made. These juridically adduced facts were in sharp contrast to how the deductive demonologists treated accounts of experience: they treated such material merely as illustrative of particular, accepted knowledge claims.[59]

Certainly, there was a problem epistemologically with singular experiences. As Peter Dear has argued, when Aristotle talked about *experience* as a source of knowledge about the natural world, he considered the idea only in the context of commonly accepted, regular experiences: *the sun rises in the east* was an unproblematic observation, for it was something upon which there was universal agreement. Because they were common, such experiences were sufficiently secure to serve as premises from which other truths might logically be deduced—and so could function as the basis for whole branches of knowledge.[60] Singular experiences, though, particularly those known only through historical report, were more problematic, for they were an inadequate base from which to draw more general inferences. But as a number of 16th-century scholars and their followers were beginning to assert, facts were useful in that they provided operational knowledge about how things actually behaved.[61] Certainly, this was how experiential demonologists treated the facts they unearthed. What they discovered were real examples of the devil's power, independent of rationalising constraints.

But it is also important to note that to their minds, the men who related these facts were certainly *not* dealing with singular experiences in the Aristotelian sense, for what they uncovered about the extent of the devil's powers and his field of operation was confirmed by multiple sources. Moreover, it was broadly consistent with facts garnered from other jurisdictions and regions—and sometimes from other periods of time.[62] In witch confessions, then, experiential demonologists had material which, under some circumstances, could be profitably mined for facts about the devil and his minions. They were given by people who had participated in the events that were being described under circumstances that did not permit collusion.

All of these factors made the data gleaned from such accounts of high evidentiary value. As the Toulouse lawyer Pierre Le Loyer explained in his 1605 *Treatise on Spirits* (*Discours des spectres*), witch confessions were highly unlikely to come from a demon-addled brain: witches were interrogated separately and in private, he noted—yet they all confessed to the same thing, agreeing in the circumstances, time and manner of events without variation.[63] In his 1613, *The Inconsistency of Evil Angels and Demons (Tableau De L'Inconstance des Mauvais Anges et Demons)*, the Bordeaux judge Pierre de Lancre made a similar point. The work was a detailed treatise that discussed the manifold depravities, abominations and sacrileges to which witches had confessed in engaging at the sabbat during the course of his investigation in the French part of the Basque country several years earlier. While he noted that much of what his witches confessed was corroborated by external physical evidence—when witches confessed to infanticide, parents found children suffocated; when they confessed to cursing people, their reputed victims were often found ailing—for him, the fact that the confessions he extracted were in agreement not just with those offered by other Basque witches, but across the world, proved that what was admitted had actually happened, and was not a delusion.[64]

Indeed, the facts these experiential demonologists amassed through legal process came close to meeting the maxims identified by Steven Shapin for the evaluation of testimony he found in his survey of 17th-century literature: they were plausible in that they were consistent with what other judges had found; they were multiple, for many witches confessed to much the same sort of thing; they were immediate in that they came directly from the people involved in the events described; they were given in a manner that inspired confidence, for they were freely admitted under oath; and they were presented by learned men of integrity—men whose position afforded them social capital.[65] In that sense, Roper is unquestionably right in arguing that early modern demonology "was to a large degree a science founded on the evidence of experience."[66]

The shift towards a more unmediated, experientially grounded form of devil knowledge is clear from at least the second third of the 15th century through a series of tracts from figures associated with the early sessions of the Council of Basel (1431–1449). While the council was called ostensibly to deal with questions about authority within the church, as Michael Bailey and Edward Peters have argued, it also seems to have served incidentally as an informal meeting place for clerics interested in what they took to be the emergence of diabolical heresy. In that capacity, it is significant that many of the early tracts describing the central elements of what would coalesce into the full-fledged elaborated concept of witchcraft over the subsequent decades were written by men who had attended the council.[67]

One of the earliest of these is the *Errors of the Gazarii (Errores gazariorum)*. Although the work is anonymous, Martine Ostorero has argued that it was likely written by the Franciscan Ponce Feugeyron, an inquisitor who had attended the council intermittently between 1433 and 1437.[68] In lurid detail, the text describes the initiation ceremony for novices into the devil's sect, and includes most of what would become the diagnostic features of demonic witchcraft: demonic homage and fealty; transvection; the cannibalism of infants; orgies involving incestuous or homosexual couplings; ritualised sacrilege; and the making of various necromantic potions and powders. Significantly, though, the author made no attempt to analyse or explain what he related—nor did he try to fit the information he related into any received theoretical frame. He seems to have been wholly untroubled by the fact that the devil's devotees are described as having to fly to the sabbat whenever summoned despite the fact that this assertion was at odds with *Episcopi*. Instead, as Ostorero points out, the text reads as if it was based upon a series of answers to questions reworked into the form of a narrative. If so, she suggests, the text is most likely based on the confessions of Jeanne Vacanda and Jean d'Etroubles, both of whom are specifically mentioned in the tract.[69]

In this sense, the *Errores* stands as a collection of facts about the devil's dealings garnered from his co-conspirators, and so of high evidentiary value.

Some 30 years later, Arras in northern France saw the trial and execution of a number of apparent devil-worshipping heretics which spurred the composition of a number of new, experientially grounded devil tracts.[70] One of the more interesting of these is the *History of the Case, State and Condition of the Waldensian Idolaters* (*Recollectio casus, status et conditionis Valdensium ydolatarum*) likely written in the summer of 1460 shortly after the first accused had been executed. As with the *Errores*, this text is anonymous, but Ostorero has argued convincingly that it was likely authored by one of the judges at the trial, Jacques Du Bois.[71] While this cannot be proven definitively, the *Recollectio* was clearly written by someone close to proceedings, for the author makes clear that his account is based upon the notes compiled by inquisitors and other experts, and that he relied, too, on the confessions of the accused and other trial records. In other words, the tract is grounded on information gleaned from experience which, he stated, had been faithfully reported.[72]

Amongst the various atrocities and outrages described, the author seems to have been particularly concerned with the issue of transvection. The truth and reality of the fact that people are consciously transported—mind and body—to the sabbat, he declared, cannot be denied given the confessions of witches and the proceedings conducted against them.[73] These confessions ought to be treated as certain evidence (*indicium certum*), enough not just to persuade but to prove that witches can be transported in body and soul from one place to another by a demon—and, in a nod to the standard of proof laid down in the *Corpus iuris civilis*, the evidence is clearer than daylight.[74] His argument was obviously a swipe at *Episcopi* which he casually dismissed, stating merely that it pertained to a completely different set of circumstances, and not to demonic witchcraft. That said, the author did turn at several points to discuss some of the arguments of the theologians, but he treated their deduced devil knowledge not as providing a frame into which to assimilate his evidence; rather, he used their arguments to support the reality of what his evidence described, thereby safeguarding it from dispute.[75] For the author of the text, as Ostorero indicates, inquisitorial procedure in itself is enough to uncover the reality of transvection—and where the evidence adduced through that process contradicts the conclusions of the theoreticians, it is their arguments that must be explained away, not the evidence.

This emerging tension in the construction of devil knowledge comes perhaps most sharply into relief in the *Malleus maleficarum*.[76] While much of the material upon which Institoris and Sprenger grounded their arguments was lifted from earlier sources, what was important about the text was the way it was structured, for the authors went to some lengths to try to strike a balance between truths deduced from authorities and those admitted by the devil's co-conspirators.[77] But in their ham-handed attempts to reconcile these two types of truth, they unwittingly created a far more powerful devil—one who tends to be defined according to his moral character, rather than in terms of his capacity as a created being.

The *Malleus* is divided into three parts distinguished by virtue of subject matter and modes of argumentation and proof.[78] Section one comprises a series of abstract, theological arguments made in the classic scholastic fashion. Here, the authors mustered an eclectic variety of authorities for and against stated propositions in order to deduce the veracity of various assertions about witchcraft and the relationship of witches to demons. While poorly and inconsistently argued, it is fairly conventional in its approach, borrowing heavily from scripture, canon law and the writings of fellow Dominicans such as Aquinas, Eymeric and Johannes Nider. The second part, though, shifts to investigate how witches are able to work their malice. As the subject matter is moral and not strictly theological, the authors explicitly eschewed a scholastic approach, beseeching their readers, in the section's preface, "not to ask for an explanation for all matters, when suitable likelihood is sufficient if facts are generally agreed to be true either on the basis of one's experience from seeing or hearing or on the basis of the accounts given by trustworthy witnesses are adduced."[79] A scholastic proof is not necessary, they asserted, because the section is based upon *common experience* and evidence garnered from reliable witnesses—after all, they assert, experience is "the teacher of reality."[80] The implication is clear: while certain facts gathered from witness testimony may seem to confound the arguments of theoreticians, they should be accepted at face value. It is up to others to explain how such things might be possible. Because they placed such a premium upon such direct evidence, the third section of the work is given over entirely to questions concerning how evidence should be elicited, from whom and under what circumstances.

Institoris and Sprenger never doubted the reality of demon sex. However, it seems to have been clear to them in comparing the evidence supplied by modern witches to that provided by historical ones, that the notion that women wilfully copulated with incubi demons was a relatively new development—something not known before 1400.[81] "It is not so much our pronouncement that advocates this," they asserted, "as the testimony of experience given by the sorceresses themselves, who have rendered all these things believable."[82] To support this, they provided the example of a woman from Ravensburg, identifiable as Agnes the bath keeper (*balneatrix*). On her way to meet her boyfriend for sex, the woman admitted at her trial that she came upon a demon in human form who promised to serve her every desire. And so, for the next 18 years, until her arrest, prosecution and execution, she dedicated herself to lechery with the devil.[83] Of this, they asserted, "all the inhabitants of the city can bear witness"—and so, along a series of other prosecutions across the diocese, belief in the reality of demon sex "is based upon either our own experience or the reports of trustworthy witnesses."[84]

As experience tends to trump authority for Institoris and Sprenger, *Episcopi* emerges as a possible stumbling block. As it was for the author of the *Recollectio*, taking the canon at face value would mean discounting the testimony of those who confessed to having been carried by demons to the sabbat as illusory. But rather than interpret the meaning of their evidence, they reinterpreted the canon, arguing that it should be construed in a very narrow sense. Their argument hinged upon the authority of Isidore of Seville who distinguished 14 different types of superstition in his early 7th-century *Etymologiae*. Amongst these various groups, Isidore identified one he called "pythons" (*Pythones*), an allusion to the woman who called up the spirit of the prophet Samuel for Saul.[85] These are people through whom demons speak or through whom demons perform wondrous works. They are quite different from the sorcerers (*malefici*) who are defined according to their ability to work malicious magic by means of spells.[86] While Institoris and Sprenger did not bother to probe this distinction too deeply, it was enough for them to assert that in its condemnation of the followers of Diana, the canon was actually intended to apply to pythons, for as idolaters they were demonstrating their lack of faith in such an overt form that they had left their minds open to demonic manipulation. Thus, the canon clearly did not apply to sorcerers.[87]

The authors returned to the issue of transvection later in the text. That people can be transported by demons through the air is not only well attested in the writings of other trustworthy authors, but, they assert, "one of us has very often seen and discovered such people."[88] As with the author of the *Recollectio*, Institoris and Sprenger seem to have felt obliged at this point to insulate their evidence from criticism by providing a theoretical justification for what they claimed to have seen. But their argument is curious, turning the devil of the theoreticians on its head. If witches are unable to be transported by the devil, they contended, this would either be because God had not given him his permission, or because the devil was limited in his abilities by virtue of his nature. To the first point, they argued that it was clear from observation that God sometimes gives the devil permission to perpetrate all sorts of atrocities some of which are morally more offensive than simply moving a witch from one place to another. For instance, he occasionally allows demons to torment righteous children and adults who are in a state of grace. Accordingly, they reasoned, if God allows these "greater" acts to occur, how could he not permit demons to perform the far lesser act of changing the location of one who has dedicated himself to the devil?[89]

Their argument here rests on upon the word "greater." While the theoreticians had construed the devil in terms of his position on the ladder of creation, arguing that by virtue of his nature he was greater than that of human beings, Institoris and Sprenger construed the term purely in a moral sense. Indeed, boiled down, their point was merely that because God allows demons to do morally more repugnant things, he can also permit them to do things that are less nasty. The devil's nature does not enter into it. Indeed, when they turned to discuss whether his abilities as a creature limit his capacity, the authors fell back on Job 41.24, "there is no power on earth that can be compared with him." While medieval commentators had tended to read the passage as a statement about the devil's natural power over earthly things and his knowledge of its occult properties, Institoris and Sprenger took it to mean that Lucifer's natural powers surpass those of every other created thing—even, they say, those of good angels. The fall from heaven had cut the devil off from grace to be sure, but his awesome power as chief of the angels remained intact.[90]

But this devil defined exclusively according to his moral character rather than his created capacity means that the testimony of confessed witches can be taken literally. Certainly, demonic illusion was always a possibility—not all confessions necessarily reflect reality. But where confessions and eye-witness testimony were properly adduced according to the method they laid out in the *Malleus'* final section and where it was consistent with that garnered from other jurisdictions, it was clear that—with God permitting—the devil's field of action in the natural world was effectively unlimited.

While Institoris and Sprenger stood at the cusp of this new, experiential devil and struggled to balance two quite different types of source material, during the most virulent phase of the witch hunts, the French jurist, natural philosopher and historiographer Jean Bodin was struck by what he saw as the apparently common experience of demonic witchcraft through history. Although he never presided over any witch trials, he was moved to write his 1580 *On the Demon-mania of Witches (De la démonomanie des sorciers)* after serving as a consultant at the trial of Jeanne Harvillier two years earlier.[91] According to Bodin, Jeanne freely confessed that at age 12 she had been given by her mother to the devil. From then, until her arrest some 40 years later, she claimed to have served her new master faithfully, having intercourse with him regularly, and being transported by him to the sabbat, where he gave her all manner of ointments and noxious powders to work her *maleficia*. Certainly, the details Jeanne confessed were strange and seemingly contrary to nature and canon law, but, Bodin pointed out, they were consistent with what was known about witches and their relationship to the devil from other documented accounts.

In making this claim, Bodin drew upon an eclectic array of sources which he read with a demonising eye. Certainly, he referred to the seminal patristic, medieval and early modern accounts of the devil. But he also found the devil behind incidents and anecdotes described in much pre-Christian material. He wrote that one finds described in Orpheus and in Homer—men who lived almost 3000 years ago—the kind of demonic sorcery that is consistent with the evidence garnered from confessed witches in the present day.[92] In effect, Bodin demonised the material he lifted from the likes of Herodotus, Livy and Pliny the Elder, transforming it into information about the operation of the devil's power in earlier periods. The result, of course, is a mutually authenticating circle: what modern witches confess about their relationship with the devil confirms the demonism underlying classical accounts, while the apparent demons of classical accounts confirm the reality of modern witchcraft. But the process allowed him to conclude that—whether reading Greek or Latin histories, ancient or modern works—every country, every people has had reports about the kind of things witches do—including being transported in soul and body to the sabbat by evil spirits almost instantaneously.[93] In effect, by reading his pre-Christian authorities through the lens of demonism, Bodin levelled his source material, making it all evidence fit to be assimilated into his burgeoning discourse of the demonic. The effect of this process is important. In the first place, he turned demonic witchcraft into a trans-historical, world-historical problem. But he also—and surprisingly—turned the devil into a stable entity, one who—like God—reveals himself through his actions.

Here, Bodin seems to be adapting the historical method he developed in his 1566 *Method for the Easy Understanding of History* (*Methodus ad facilem historiarum cognitionem*). In this work, he argued that the way to ascertain the plausibility of any particular historical data was to compare it against generally accepted truths known from other sources. Here Bodin was principally concerned with understanding nations and their relationship to universal history. In order to determine the accuracy of information reported in a specific source about the actions of a particular people at a particular point in time, he argued that it should be compared with general knowledge about the people's nature as deduced from the principles of geography and cosmography. His assumption was that nature acts in a heterogeneous but regular fashion across space and time, fixing the complexion and character of peoples. Therefore, if information about a people is inconsistent with what is known about their nature, then it should be rejected as implausible.[94]

His point in the *Démonomanie* was that the devil functions in a fashion analogous to nature in the *Methodus*. That is to say, the devil acts constantly if differently on people and the world through time; therefore, what is known about his actions in one place or time implies the likelihood that any later account of his actions alleging the same or analogous actions should be construed at least as plausible. As Bodin wrote in the *Démonomanie*, for some 3,000 years, witches have reported their actions—their sacrifices, dances, night flight, murders, charms and sorceries. In this, all who had recently been burned in Italy, Germany and France agreed, point by point. Thus, he continued, "if the common agreement of the law of God and the human laws of all peoples, of judgements, convictions, confessions, re-examinations, collations, executions—if the common agreement of the wise is not adequate, what greater proof ought one demand?"[95] In other words, what modern witches confessed was wholly consistent with what was documented about the devil from a litany of sources reaching back into the mists of antiquity. The evidence of the past authenticated that of the present.

While precedent may serve as a guide for discerning the devil's power, in a swipe against the theologians Bodin stated explicitly that what is alleged about the devil should not be assessed against the axioms of natural philosophy. "It is also quite ridiculous to gauge natural things against supernatural things," he asserted, "and the actions of animals against the actions of spirits and demons."[96] Again, here he drew upon the process he laid down for the production of historical knowledge in the *Methodus*. In this earlier work, he distinguished three different types of history, each defined according to their object of study: human, natural and divine.[97] But just as their subject matter varies, so too does the sense of causation proper to each branch of inquiry. Human history chronicles the acts of people in society, its causes a function of the vacillations of the human mind. Natural history, by contrast, depicts the actions of nature through time, a process determined by natural albeit sometimes secret causes. Divine history is the most noble form of history, for it records the strength and power of the almighty, its cause always the operation of providence.[98] Trawling through the records of the past, Bodin continued, the diligent historian must extract information about similar sorts of events, grouping them together according to the appropriate mode of historical analysis, as if in a commonplace book.[99] With information stripped from its narrative context and arranged with other facts about similar but chronologically or temporally distinct occurrences, it ought to be possible to make inferences about specific causation. When it came to the devil and his actions, though, Bodin was clear that they ought not to be treated as part of natural history, for the devil is not part of nature. Indeed, he wrote in the *Démonomanie*, those who have tried to argue in physical terms about supernatural or metaphysical matters have committed the greatest of all errors and fallen in absurdity, "for each science has its own principles and foundations which are different from one another."[100] The devil's actions, then, are part of divine history, and so should be assessed according to supernatural causation.

Consequently, Bodin had little problem attributing to the devil a host of new powers. Chief amongst these was lycanthropy. While the idea of demons turning men into beasts may have been difficult to believe, it was well attested in modern witch confessions and in historical descriptions from the likes of Homer, Herodotus, Pomponius Mela, Strabo, Virgil, Ovid and others.[101] Indeed, he asserted, not only was there no evidence to suggest that such accounts were the product of demonic deception, there was no evidence that God did *not* give such a power to Satan, for the counsel of God and the power he gave to the devil is unknown to human beings. All we know about the limits of the devil's power comes from Job 41.24, and—as it had been for the *Malleus* authors—that makes clear that he is peerless in his abilities in the created world.[102] Witch confessions assessed against what is known of the devil's actions from divine and human histories are "undeniable proof" (*preuue trescertaine*) that Satan can change people into beasts.[103] The problem with those who discount lycanthropy, according to Bodin, was that they treat the devil as part of nature—and, as he said, that is ridiculous.

Bodin's sense of history and method of historical analysis, then, resituate witch confessions as a species of divine history, a demesne historians should try to understand only through the lens of extra-natural causation. But of course, if the standard against which witch confessions are ultimately to be evaluated is the power of God, then, quite literally, anything is possible, and for Bodin, this was precisely the point.[104]

## Epistemological Difficulties

This tension as to how the devil should be known—deduced through theory or experienced directly or vicariously through the senses—was part of the broader debate through the 16th and early 17th centuries about the gathering and assessment of data and the construction of knowledge on the one hand, and the role of knowledge-making spaces and interpretative communities on the other—debates, ultimately about how truths should be discovered and confirmed. But unlike the debate over geo- or heliocentrism, for instance, the debate over devil knowledge was urgent and had immediate implications: if the data amassed by the realists reflected reality, then all of Christian society had been infiltrated and subverted by the devil. The end times must surely be at hand.

This pressing debate engaged ever-more people, for the period of the witch hunts coincided with Europe's first information revolution. As a result, texts grounded in the confessions of witches were a favourite offering of Europe's printing presses. While some of these were intended as serious, sober works, a good many were clearly intended to cater to the baser, more scandalous tastes of the popular market. But as Dolan has expertly shown, even the latter were frequently coded as what she terms "true relations," shoring up the truth claims of their narrative with references to official documents and other details such as the names of witnesses.[105] In either case, though, what this meant was that the evidence adduced and then set forth by the realist demonologists had a wide circulation. Moreover, the apparent consistency of this material was striking—and as so many of them pointed out, Aristotle, in his *Nicomachean Ethics*, argued that what seems true to most people cannot be altogether false.[106]

But the construction of this new, more immediate devil—a figure who seemed no longer constrained by either nature or his nature—was not without its critics. Chief amongst these was the Low Countries physician, Johann Weyer in his *On the Tricks of Demons* (*De praestigiis daemonum*) first published in 1563. Drawing heavily on the writings of Augustine and many other church fathers, Weyer accepted that the devil was a fine, subtle spirit, endowed by virtue of his nature with incredible speed and keenness of perception. However, for him, the devil's power was constrained by both his nature and divine permission. He accepted that by virtue of his longevity the devil had an extraordinary knowledge of nature and used this to perform wondrous and fearsome feats—to make prodigies appear in the sky; to generate the sound and sight of clashing armies; to inflict horrible afflictions.[107] But he stressed that the devil's actions—even at the most trivial level—were always contingent upon God's assent. Drawing upon the story of the Garasene demoniacs described by Matthew, he noted that the demons possessing the girls had to appeal directly to Christ to be allowed to enter even into a herd of swine.[108]

For Weyer, this meant that the devil was wholly a creature of nature: he operated within its realm and was limited by the capacities bestowed upon him as a created spirit. Indeed, he went so far as to argue that even were God to grant him explicit permission to work something beyond his nature, he could not do so because nothing can ever exceed how it is made. As Weyer wrote of himself:

> if I were permitted by divine majesty to fly through the air with birds, or crawl through the bowels of the earth with worms, or live in the waters with fish, I would certainly be unable to do so, for that would contravene the order of God established from the beginning, and the natural power given to me by God who created me a man from the mud of the earth, and out of bones, nerves, ligaments, flesh, veins, arteries, blood and spirit all joined together.[109]

Like a cat permitted to do algebra, the devil simply lacks the ability to do things he was not created to be able to do.[110]

However, Weyer admitted that as God's ape, the devil was keen to imitate many of the creator's wonders, and exploit what capacity he had as a spirit to confound the unwary. He could use his speed and agility, for instance, to put things like cloth, iron nails, brass clasps, needles, pins, thread, even bits of bone secretly into the back of the throats of those believed to be possessed, so that they might appear to void them spontaneously to the great wonderment of those present. But for Weyer, the devil's power to beguile went far beyond this sort of petty sleight of talon, for he had the natural power to confound human senses.[111] He could distort the imagination, for instance, that faculty of the soul that fashions likenesses of external things for the mind from impressions left on it by the senses. This he could do either by implanting his own images there, or by causing the imagination to retrieve older images it has stored, making them seem immediate.[112] Alternately, he could manipulate his victim's optic or aural nerves, causing her to perceive things that were not there.[113] With their senses or cognitive faculties compromised in one of these ways, what this means is that the devil's victims were actually experiencing what he had made them perceive. In a witch's mind, she really was an ass shut up in a bag, an eagle in flight—or being carried to the sabbat by Diana in the company of many other silly women.[114] In admitting such things, the confessions of such women may have been genuine, but what they confessed to were things that never happened—and that never could have happened.

For Weyer, this was as far as the devil could go. As a spirit, he had powers far beyond those of human beings, but they were limited by his own nature and by God. Indeed, in Weyer's mind, God did not permit everything Satan wishes, or of which he is capable by virtue of the subtlety of his nature. Because God was good and just, he allowed only those things which he himself decreed. God did not collude with demons.[115]

While Weyer squared the pentagram, as it were, maintaining the integrity of witch confessions while denying their value as descriptions of reality, he did so at great epistemic cost, for he granted the devil seemingly unlimited powers to create illusions. It was not just that demons could manipulate the air into seemingly familiar forms, but he allowed them to manipulate the process of cognition at its most fundamental level. As a result, accused witches did not know and had no way of knowing that what their senses perceived and what they consequently experienced—albeit virtually—was not real. But his argument's implications were more profound than even this. How could witnesses be certain that what they claimed to have observed actually was what had happened—and taking another step back, how could those weighing witness testimony be sure that the testimony they thought they heard was what was attested? Indeed, taken to extremes, Weyer's argument was utterly devastating, for if the devil has the kind of powers Weyer ascribed to him, if he could so confound the cognitive faculties that illusion is perceived as reality, could any human being ever be certain of anything? In his 1676 *Doctrine of Devils*, the English physician Thomas Ady characterised this position as "a senseless Doctrine," for it would mean that "We have eyes and see not, ears but cannot hear or know we do so—Seeing, hearing tasting, smelling, feeling, may all deceive us according to this doctrine of Devils."[116] Weyer's argument and that of the theoreticians who followed him implied that no form of cognition or discernment could ever be deemed secure.

The epistemological crisis implied by the scope afforded to illusion was the starting point for René Descartes' 1641 *Meditations on First Philosophy* (*Meditationes de prima philosophia*).[117] In this text, the philosopher set out to find a certain, unshakeable foundation for human knowledge—one that could not be subject to demonic subversion. To do this, he subjected every source of information humans gather through their senses—along with the cognitive faculties used to assess it—to a radical scepticism, deliberately finding reason to challenge their reliability. In the work's most striking section, Descartes turned to the problem of the devil.[118] Here, he took Weyer's position to its logical extreme. What if, he asked rhetorically, reality was governed by an omnipotent but malevolent spirit who deceives him in everything he sees, thinks and thinks he does? Were this the case, could he be certain of anything, for all perception, all experience, all thought would be of something other than it actually is? But were the devil to have such power, deceiving and deluding him in every thought and with every sensation, he would not be able to deceive him into thinking that he did not exist. That is to say, even under this most epistemologically dire scenario, Descartes concluded that he knew for certain that he was a thing that could think. About this, he could never be deceived, for deception is contingent upon existence.

One certain, unfalsifiable truth does not constitute a system of knowledge about reality, but for Descartes, it served as a premise from which other truths might be deduced. Moreover, knowing how he knew this nugget of certainty—this first principle of philosophy—allowed him to recognise other truths when he encountered them.[119] The devil might still be the master of illusion, but for Descartes, at least, it was still possible to construct a system of knowledge that was certain. In that sense, at least, the devil's delusory powers must be finite.

For their part, the realists needed to maintain the integrity of witch confessions in order to justify the extraordinary measures taken to root out the existential threat they alleged was posed by demonic witchcraft. Yet, in so doing, their privileging of the epistemological value of first-hand testimony undermined the role of nature in creation and effectively opened the door to a form of Manichaeism that granted the devil all but immediate, direct creative power. Ady argued that those who gave heed to such doctrines made demons "as honourable as Christ himself, equalizing them and him, if not preferring them before him, for power and mightiness of operations."[120] By extension, the benevolent God of the gospels was aloof, callous and uncaring, leaving individual souls to fend for themselves against demonic adversaries with supernatural powers.[121]

While the likes of Institoris and Sprenger, Bodin and Pierre de Lancre were at pains to argue that the method by which they adduced their evidence was rigorous and could produce facts that accurately described reality, without any sense of the nature of that reality, and with their data not ordered towards any final cause, what resulted was epistemological chaos. This point was appreciated in the field of medicine where, for instance, the physician John Cotta took aim at those who relied exclusively on empiricism in his 1612 *Short Discoverie*. Such empirics, he asserted—those who endeavour to heal without reference to theory and accept only that which they discern as evidence—are reasonless. While the evidence of experience is certainly important, it needs to be tempered by understanding and right reason to translate it into certain knowledge about the affliction to which the patient has succumbed. It is this that turns symptoms into evidence of a particular disease, and which—by extension—implies a course of treatment.[122]

Cotta was also concerned with the problem of witchcraft and demonically induced illnesses in this work. He did not deny the reality of witchcraft and the ability of demons to cause disease, but, he argued, to find witches and devils lurking everywhere is a "base proclivitie and unlearned lightnesse."[123] Again, as in the context of medicine, the key, he asserted, is that the apparent evidence of demonic action needs to be filtered through rational premises. Where adduced evidence apparently defies what is rationally possible, it is the significance and value of the evidence that should be reconstrued. For Cotta, then, it was theory that ordered the data of experience, translating it into facts that describe reality—it is a theory that made evidence *evidence of something.*

In his 1620 *Great Instauration (Magna instauratio),* Francis Bacon called for a general reformation of knowledge in order to set natural history on more epistemological footings. Here, he was particularly concerned about the relationship between empirical evidence, reason and certain knowledge. For him, up to his day, those who had endeavoured to investigate nature had proceeded either as empirics or dogmatists. The empirics, he argued, were like ants, mindlessly heaping up data to no particular end. By contrast, the dogmatists were like spiders, spinning ever more elaborate theoretical webs from inside themselves. The better, but hitherto untried way of proceeding, was that of the bee, a mean between the two extremes. Bees extract matter from the flowers of the field, but then fashion it by means of their own efforts. This is the way to more certain knowledge, Bacon argued, for it draws on both the evidence of experience and the rationalising powers of the mind. It is a method that constructs axioms from sense particulars, only ascending gradually to offer general propositions.[124]

## Conclusion

The debate over the way of constructing demon knowledge that took place through the later Middle Ages and early modern period constituted an important early chapter in the scientific revolution. To those concerned primarily with safeguarding the integrity of nature in their reasoning, the devil that resulted was one powerful enough to subvert human cognition completely, making certain knowledge impossible. But to those concerned with determining the devil's power based upon the growing volume of evidence as to their operation in the world, demons become deities. Taken together, the manifest absurdities of the positions of the demonologists—both the senseless and the reasonless—opened the door to the more rigorous assessment of the relationship between observation, experience and reason that emerged in the second half of the 17th century.

## Notes

1 "He who believes quickly is light of heart and will not be taken seriously." Ecclus. 19.4.
2 The term "synagogue" is an allusion to the phrase "synagogue of Satan" used by John of Patmos in Revelations to condemn his opponents. See Revs 2.9 and 3.9. As David Frankfurter has argued, John used the term not intended to refer to Jews *per se* but rather to those Jews who had yet to accept the brand of Jesus-Judaism to which he subscribed. David Frankfurter, "Jews or Not? Reconstructing the 'Other' in Rev 2.9 and 3.9," *Harvard Theological Review* 94.4 (Oct. 2001), 403–25 on 403 and 409.
3 A coin from the Archbishopric of Vienne.
4 Likely from the French *mêlez* meaning "mingle." Here, though, the sense is clearly a command for the participants to have sex.
5 Joseph Hansen, *Quellen und Untersuchungen zur Geschichte des Hexenwahns und der Hexenverfolgung im Mittelalter* (Bonn, 1901), 487–99. Henry C. Lea provides a précis of this case in his *Materials Toward a History of Witchcraft,* Part 1 (Philadelphia, 1939), 238–40.
6 Though William's chronicle is mid-12th century, he places the story after an account the miraculous burial of Pope Gregory VI in 1048, suggesting that he thought the story of the sorceress was roughly contemporary to that. William of Malmesbury, *Gesta Regum Anglorum atque historia novella* (London, 1840): I. 351–4.

7 This story is described as taking place around the reign of (anti) pope John XVI. This places it around the turn of the first millennium. William of Malmesbury, *Gesta Regum Anglorum*, I: 282–3.

8 For a useful introduction to the development of the elaborated concept of witchcraft and its early dissemination, see Richard Kieckhefer, "The First Wave of Trials for Diabolical Witchcraft," in *The Oxford Handbook of Witchcraft in Early Modern Europe and Colonial America*, ed. Brian Levack (Oxford, 2013), 159–78.

9 Brian Levack, *The Witch-Hunt in Early Modern Europe*, 3rd edition (Harlow, 2006), 32–51.

10 Both of these sets of proceedings are recounted together with the most important extant primary material in Christopher S. Mackay, *"An Unusual Inquisition": Translated Documents from Heinricus Institoris's Witch Hunts of Ravensburg and Innsbruck* (Leiden, 2020).

11 Stuart Clark, *Thinking with Demons: The Idea of Witchcraft in Early Modern Europe* (Oxford, 1997), 184.

12 Gerhild Scholz Williams, "Demonologies," in *Oxford Handbook of Witchcraft in Early Modern Europe and Colonial America*, ed. Brian Levack (Oxford, 2013): 69–83 on 69.

13 Ann Blair, *Too Much to Know* (New Haven, 2010), 2. Cf. Peter Burke, *Social History of Knowledge: From Gutenberg to Diderot* (Cambridge, 2000), 13. I follow Blair in treating *information* as a convenient, unspecific term.

14 See Livingstone, *Putting Science in Its Place: Geographies of Scientific Knowledge* (Chicago, 2003), 1–16. See also James Lancaster and Richard Raiswell, "Evidence before Science," in *Evidence in the Ages of the New Sciences* eds. James Lancaster and Richard Raiswell (Cham, 2018): 1–29 on 3.

15 For instance, Euan Cameron, *Enchanted Europe: Superstition, Reason, and Religion, 1250–1750* (Oxford, 2010), 270.

16 Frances Dolan, *True Relations: Reading, Literature and Evidence in Seventeenth-Century England* (Philadelphia, 2013), 12–18.

17 Susan Schreiner, *Are You Alone Wise? The Search for Certainty in the Early Modern Era* (Oxford, 2011), ix.

18 Athanasius, *Vita Beati Antonii Abbatis* (Migne, *PL* 73: 0125-0128).

19 Gregory the Great, *Dialogi* in *Opera Omnia* vol. 6 (Venice, 1769): II.viii.

20 Sari Katajala-Peltomaa, *Demon Possession and Lived Religion* (Oxford, 2020), 2.

21 Bernard of Clairvaux, *In dedicatione ecclesiae* (Migne, *PL* 183: 0523D–526B).

22 Richalm von Schöntal, *Liber revelationum* (Hannover, Hahnsche Buchhandlung, 2009), *passim*. Quotation from "Besieged by Demons," in *The Medieval Devil: A Reader*, trans. R. Raiswell and D. R. Winter (Toronto, 2022): 127–31 on 129.

23 In his *De veritate Catholicae contra Gentiles*, III. 97, Aquinas draws an analogy to language: when someone develops a concept in the mind which cannot be adequately communicated in a single word, the speaker uses multiple words in an attempt to make the idea more fully comprehensible.

24 Aquinas, *Summa Theologicae* 1ᵃ q. 47 a.1–2 and 1ᵃ q. 50 a.1–2.

25 Aquinas, *De malo* q. 16 a. 1.

26 Augustine, *De divinatione daemonum* (Migne *PL* 40.0584–0587).

27 Augustine, *De divinatione daemonum* (Migne *PL* 40.0584–0588); cf. his *De Genesi ad litteram* (Migne *PL* 34.0278–0279) and *De Trinitate libri quindecim* (Migne *PL* 42.0878).

28 The underlying assumption here is that imperfect creatures such as frogs, lice and serpents scattered their seed in the elements. Augustine, *De trinitate* (Migne *PL* 42.0878–0879). See also Peter Lombard, *Sententiarum Libri Quattuor*, 2.7.10.1–2 and Aquinas, *De malo*, 16.9.

29 Aquinas, *De malo*, 16.1.

30 For a fuller treatment than is necessary here, see Jeffrey Burton Russell, *Lucifer: The Devil in the Middle Ages* (Ithaca, 1984), 159–207 and Henry Ansgar Kelly, *Satan: A Biography* (Cambridge, 2006), 237–9 and 242–8. Clark, *Thinking With Demons*, 160–72 provides an extensive summary of the position of early modern theologians who accepted the broad strokes of the medieval scholastic tradition.

31 See Col 1.16: "For in him [i.e. God] were all things created in heaven and on earth, visible and invisible, whether thrones, or dominations, or principalities, or powers: all things were created by him and in him."

32 Dn 4.23-33.

33 Augustine, *De civitate dei*, 18.17–18.

34 Aquinas, *De malo*, 16.9.

35 Aquinas, *Questiones disputatae de potentia dei*, 6.7.

36 Tob. 12.19 and Aquinas, *Questiones disputatae*, 6.8.

37 Aquinas, *Questiones disputatae*, 6.8.

38 Dn. 14.35.

39 Acts 4.39–40.

40 Mt 4.5–8.

41 The women are described as "daemonum illusionibus et fantasmatibus seductae." Gratian, *Decretum* (Graz, 1959), II. c. 26, q. 5, cap. 12 (p. 1030). For a full translation, see "The Possibility of Night Flight" in *The Medieval Devil: A Reader* eds. Richard Raiswell and David Winter (Toronto, 2022): 99–100. For the history of the canon, see Cameron, *Enchanted Europe*, 133.

42 Stuart Clark, "The Rational Witchfinder: Conscience, Demonological Naturalism and Popular Superstitions," *Science, Culture and Popular Belief in Renaissance Europe* (Manchester, 1991): 222–48 on 223.

43 Cameron, *Enchanted Europe*, 106 and 271. Virginia Krause, *Witchcraft, Demonology and Confession in Early Modern France* (Cambridge, 2015), 127.

44 Richard W. Serjeantson, "Proof and Persuasion," in *The Cambridge History of Science, Volume 3: Early Modern Science*, ed. Katherine Park and Lorraine Daston (Cambridge, 2006): 132–75 on 136, 138, 150–4.

45 Robert Bartlett, *Trial by Fire and Water* (Brattleboro, 1986; 2014), 26–33. As Bartlett points out, the determination of whether a person was received by the water or whether a burn showed signs of healing tended to be left to the community and so rather than reflect the judgement of God, the verdict reflected the accused's position within the social geography of the community judging him.

46 See "Fourth Lateran Council," in *Decrees of the Ecumenical Councils*, vol. 1: *Nicaea I to Lateran V* ed. Norman Tanner (London, 1990), canon 18 (p. 244). One of the main arguments against the ordeal was that it placed necessity in God. That is, it forced God to cause a miracle to avoid an injustice. Bartlett, *Trial by Fire and Water*, 86–8.

47 Edward Peters, *Inquisition* (Berkeley, 1989), 52.

48 Medieval juries in England were self-informing. That is, they comprised men who were expected to know the details of a case before coming to trial. Richard Groot, "Early Thirteenth-Century Criminal Jury," in *Twelve Good Men and True*, ed., J. S. Cockburn and Thomas Green (Princeton, 1988), 3.

49 As Kelly has stressed, it is important to distinguish between *inquisition* as a legal procedure and *The Inquisition*—a tribunal for investigating particular crimes, particularly heresy and later witchcraft. He also points out that *The Inquisition* was not a permanently constituted tribunal before the 16th century. Medieval inquisitors were appointed on an *ad hoc* basis. See Henry Ansgar Kelly, "Inquisition and the Prosecution of Heresy: Misconceptions and Abuses," *Church History* 58, no. 4 (1989): 439–51 on 439–41.

50 "Clearer than daylight" is an allusion to 4.19.25 of Justinian's *Corpus iuris ciuilis*, ed. A. Kriegel and E. Osenbrüggen (Leipzig, 1848), 236.

51 Edward Peters, *Torture: Expanded Edition* (Philadelphia, 1996), 44.

52 Peters, *Torture*, 55.

53 The above description relies on Peters, *Inquisition*, 64–7. Walter Stephens points out that in the Catholic context at least, confessions at law were also considered sacramental, meaning that inquisitors knew that for witches what was at stake was not just their place in this life, but in the next one as well. Stephens, *Demon Lovers: Witchcraft, Sex and the Crisis of Belief* (Chicago, 2002), 104.

54 Lyndal Roper, *Witch Craze: Terror and Fantasy in Baroque Germany* (New Haven, 2004): 44–66.

55 Kelly, "Inquisition and the Prosecution of Heresy," 450.

56 See also Lancaster and Raiswell, "Evidence before Science," 12–3.

57 Stephens, *Demon Lovers*, 96.

58 Serjeantson, "Proof and Persuasion," 158–9. Barbara J. Shapiro has also dealt with the issue of the construction of certainty in witchcraft cases in her *Probability and Certainty in Seventeenth-Century England: A Study of the Relationship between Natural Science, Religion, History, Law and Literature* (New Jersey, 1983). However, as her title suggests, her examination is limited to England.

59 Barbara Shapiro, "The Concept 'Fact': Legal Origins and Cultural Diffusion," *Albion* 26, no. 2 (1994): 227–52 on 228. See also Peter Dear, "Miracles, Experiments, and the Ordinary Course of Nature," *Isis* 81, no. 4 (1990): 663–83 on 663.

60 Peter Dear, "The Meanings of Experience," *The Cambridge History of Science, Volume 3: Early Modern Science*, ed. Katherine Park and Lorraine Daston (Cambridge, 2006), 108–9. Steven Shapin, *The Scientific Revolution* (Chicago, 1998), 80–5.

61 Dear, "The Meanings of Experience," 110–1.

62 Virginia Krause, *Witchcraft, Demonology and Confession in Early Modern France* (Cambridge, 2015), 37.

63 Pierre Le Loyer, *Discours, et Histoires des Spectres, Visions et Apparitions des Esprits, Anges, Demons, et Ames* (Paris, 1605), 136. Krause, *Witchcraft, Demonology and Confession*, 37.

64 Pierre De Lancre, *Tableau De L'Inconstance des Mauvais Anges et Demons* (Paris, 1613), 534–5.

65 Steven Shapin, *A Social History of Truth: Civility and Science in Seventeenth-Century England* (Chicago, 1994), 212–42.

66 Roper, *Witch Craze*, 52.

67 Michael D. Bailey and Edward Peters, "A Sabbat of Demonologists: Basel: 1431–1440," *The Historian* 65, no. 6 (2003): 1375–95 on 1377–81.

68 Martine Ostorero, *Le diable au sabbat: Littérature démonologique et sorcellerie (1440–1460)* (Firenze, 2011), 33–9.

69 Vacanda was burned for witchcraft on 11 August 1428. Ostorero, *Le diable au sabbat*, 34–5. The full text is available in [Anon], *Errores Gazariorum, seu illorum qui scopam vel baculum equitare probantur* from *L'imaginaire du sabbat: Edition critique des textes les plus anciens (1430 c.–1440 c.)*, (Lausanne, 1999), 277–99, and translated by Raiswell and Winter as "The Synagogue of Satan" in *The Medieval Devil*, 369–73.

70 The defendants are described as being involved in *vauderie*—a heresy that bears all the hallmarks of diabolical witchcraft. See *The Arras Witch Treatises*, trans. and ed. Andrew Gow, Robert Desjardins and François Pageau (University Park, 2016), 1–2.

71 Ostorero, *Le diable au sabbat*, 666.

72 The *Recollectio* can be found in Hansen, *Quellen*, 149–83. The reference here is to 149. The text is available in translation as "A History of the Case, State, and Condition of the Waldensian Heretics (Witches)" in *Arras Witch Treatises*, 18–79.

73 Hansen, *Quellen*, 151.

74 Hansen, *Quellen*, 153.

75 Ostorero, *Le diable au sabbat*, 669.

76 *The Hammer of Witches: A Complete Translation of the* Malleus Maleficarum, trans. Christopher S. Mackay. (Cambridge, 2009), 34–7.

77 I am certainly aware of the arguments that attribute the *Malleus* almost exclusively to Institoris. See, for instance, Albrecht Classen's review of *The Medieval Devil: A Reader* in *Sehepunke* 23, no. 10 (2023). However, I accept Mackay's view who states in his introduction "only an imbecile would have fabricated a claim to joint authorship in a sworn document [the Approbation of the work by the theology faculty at Cologne of which Sprenger was a member and which names both Institoris and Sprenger as authors] that would be included with the forgery and which it would be impossible to keep from coming to the notice of the man who was being falsely associated with the work," *The Hammer of Witches*, 5.

78 Hans Peter Broedel, *The* Malleus Maleficarum *and the Construction of Witchcraft: Theology and Popular Belief* (Manchester, 2003), 20–1.

79 *The Hammer of Witches*, 86A. See also Broedel, *The* Malleus Maleficarum, 20–1.

80 *The Hammer of Witches*, 20D. Hans Peter Broedel has argued that the authors shift evidentiary registers because the point of the *Malleus* was to assimilate popular witch lore into an extended discourse of maleficent witchcraft. This seems likely, for what is adduced through the trial process as evidence is frequently popular, unnaturalised demon knowledge. Broedel, *The* Malleus Maleficarum, 21.

81 *The Hammer of Witches*, 108A–B.

82 *The Hammer of Witches*, 108B.

83 *The Hammer of Witches*, 94B–C.

84 *The Hammer of Witches*, 108D.

85 I Kgs [AV 1 Sm] 28.7–19. See Isidore, *Etymologiarum libri XX*, 8.9.21. (*PL* 82.0313A).

86 Isidore, *Etymologiae*, 8.9.9. (*PL* 82.0312A).

87 *The Hammer of Witches*, 10C–11B.

88 *The Hammer of Witches*, 101C–103A. The author who had apparently seen the man who claimed to have flown was likely Institoris. He was the active inquisitor.

89 *The Hammer of Witches*, 101C–103A.

90 The section concludes by quoting the gloss to the section from Job, which asserts that although Satan is superior to all things, he is still subordinate in terms of merits to the saints. This does not mediate the argument of Institoris and Sprenger, for they are discussing power and capacity, not grace. *The Hammer of Witches*, 103A–B.

91 Jean Bodin, *De la démonomanie des sorciers* (Antwerp, 1593), 3–5. Virginia Krause notes that there were 13 French editions of this work published before 1616, along with translations into Italian, German and Latin. Krause, *Witchcraft, Demonology and Confession*, 1–3 and 7.

92 Bodin, *De la démonomanie*, 13.

93 Bodin, *De la démonomanie*, 13–14.

94 Jean Bodin, *Methodus ad facilem historiarum cognitionem* (Geneva, 1590), 79–80.

95 "si le co[m]mun consenteme[n]t de la loy de Dieu, des loix humaines de tous les peuples, des iugemens, conuictions, co[n]fessions, recolemens, confrontations, executions: si le commun consentement des Sages ne suffit, quelle preuue demanderoit on plus grande?" Bodin, *De la démonomanie*, 20.

96 "Aussi est ce chose bien fort ridicule de mesurer les choses naturelles aux choses supernaturelles, & les actions des animaux, aux actions des espirts & Daemons," Bodin, *De la démonomanie*, 202

97 Bodin, *Methodus*, 22. As Donald R. Kelley has pointed, the basic categories of history were identical to those of the law. See "Theory of History," in *Cambridge History of Renaissance Philosophy*, ed. Quentin Skinner and Eckhard Kessler (Cambridge, 1988), 746–61 on 757.

98 Bodin, *Methodus*, 22–5.

99 Commonplacing was a technique of arranging information garnered from any reading and observation according to content. See Ann Blair, "Humanist Methods in Natural Philosophy: the Commonplace Book," *Journal of the History of Ideas* 53, no. 4 (1992): 541–51.

100 "Car chacune science a ses principes & fondeme[n]s, qui sont diuers les vns des autrès," Bodin, *De la démonomanie*, 20.

101 Bodin, *De la démonomanie*, 197.

102 Bodin, *De la démonomanie*, 204

103 Bodin, *De la démonomanie*, 192.

104 Weyer, *De praestigiis daemonum*, 128.

105 Dolan, *True Relations*, 10–2. For a case study, see my "Writing Demon Possession: The Case of the *Witches of Warboys*," *Preternature* 10, no. 2 (2021): 163–94.

106 Stephens, *Demon Lovers*, 71, 83 and 173.

107 Johann Weyer, *De praestigiis daemonum, & incantationibus ac veneficiis libri sex* (Basel, 1583), 47–54.

108 This is an allusion to Mt 8.28–32 which describes how the demons possessing several girls besought Christ to be expelled into a herd of swine. Weyer, *De praestigiis daemonum*, 124.

109 Weyer, *De praestigiis daemonum*, 128.

110 Weyer, *De praestigiis daemonum*, 128–34.

111 Weyer, *De praestigiis daemonum*, 393–9.

112 Weyer, *De praestigiis daemonum*, 260–5.

113 Weyer, *De praestigiis daemonum*, 241–2.

114 Weyer, *De praestigiis daemonum*, 264.

115 Weyer, *De praestigiis daemonum*, 279.

116 Thomas Ady, *Doctrine of Devils, Proved to be the grand Apostacy of these later Times* (London, 1676), 91.

117 Richard H. Popkin has suggested that Descartes was moved to tackle the issue in the wake of the case of Urbain Grandier, a priest who was convicted and burned in 1634 for causing the possession of a number of nuns in an Ursuline convent in Loudon. See his *History of Scepticism: From Savonarola to Bayle* (Oxford, 2003), 149–50.

118 Clark notes that both Pascal and David Hume found Descartes' argument rooted in contemporary demonology that seemed to allow the possibility of total deception. Clark, *Thinking with Demons*, 175.

119 Popkin, *History of Scepticism*, 150–7.
120 Ady, *Doctrine of Devils*, 9.
121 Cameron, *Enchanted Europe*, 126–30.
122 John Cotta, *A Short Discoverie of the Unobserved Dangers of seuerall sorts of ignorant and unconsiderate Practisers of Physicke in England* (London, 1612), 10–7.
123 Cotta, *Short Discoverie*, 55–6.
124 Francis Bacon, *Novum Organum* (London, 1620), 51–2 and 115.

## Further Reading

Cameron, Euan. *Enchanted Europe: Superstition, Reason, and Religion, 1250-1750*. Oxford: Univ. Press, 2010.

Dear, Peter. "Miracles, Experiments, and the Ordinary Course of Nature," *Isis* 81.4 (1990): 663–83.

Krause, Virginia. *Witchcraft, Demonology and Confession in Early Modern France*. Cambridge: Univ. Press, 2015.

Peters, Edward. *Inquisition*. Berkeley: Univ. of California Press, 1989.

Popkin, Richard H. *History of Scepticism: From Savonarola to Bayle*. Oxford: Univ. Press, 2003.

Schreiner, Susan. *Are You Alone Wise? The Search for Certainty in the Early Modern Era*. Oxford: Univ. Press, 2011.

Stephens, Walter. *Demon Lovers: Witchcraft, Sex and the Crisis of Belief*. Chicago: Univ. Press, 2002.

# 10

# COMMUNICATING THE DEVIL

*Marion Gibson*

Ideas about the devil were spread through a multitude of media in the late medieval and early modern era. These implanted and strengthened the notion of the devil's power over human life. In this chapter, our focus will be on the impact of this notion on the imaginative world of Christian Europeans. With them, demonic media appearances reached across the social and cultural spectrum and influenced thinking over a large part of the Christianised globe. The centrality of the devil in oratory, print culture and theatre ensured that an understanding of Satan's significance and methods extended well beyond powerful elites, blending with historic popular conceptions of supernatural phenomena and drawing in imagery from subjected peoples. It is not too strong a claim to say that the devil haunted the thoughts and dreams of all medieval and early modern people who encountered him. That was his function in culture: it was what he was made to do. And a very large proportion of people living during those periods of history did encounter him. Children and adults, men and women, urban and rural people, people from different religious and racial groups, enslaved and free people, colonised and colonisers, clergy and laypeople, irregular and regular churchgoers all heard about the devil in various educational settings.

The devil was communicated widely, then, and with an intent that those who heard about him should act upon the messages. This was especially true of the pious: clergy and other Christians who attended extra preaching, festivals and fasts. The more pious people were, the more exposure they had to devil stories. Laypeople could enhance their demonic knowledge by bible readings, conversations with ministers and in prayer groups. But even the impious could not escape hearing or reading about the devil. Ministers of all sects, particularly fundamentalist ones, discussed him frequently in sermons, conduct literature and verbal advice, so he was often imagined as vividly present. Stories of his power were also read privately or narrated publicly from printed news pamphlets: true crime accounts of murderers, witches and traitors supposedly inspired by him.[1] The devil appeared in ballads, treatises, folk customs, jokes.[2] Named demonic characters and troupes of lesser devils also danced before playhouse audiences, indeed anywhere theatre was produced from the Cornish *plen an gwari*—an open air, circular "playing place"— to inn yards and country houses.[3] Medieval plays featured devils such as Belzebub and

DOI: 10.4324/9781003096603-11

Lucyfer, actors emerging from smoky onstage Hells smothered in black paint.[4] In the late 16th-century, stagings of Christopher Marlowe's play *Doctor Faustus* also included these traditional devils with "vile long nails," "horns," fireworks, a dragon and a hell.[5] Medieval representations of the devil continued after the Reformation and even increased in significance: Matthew J. Smith has argued that in *Faustus* devils not only gambolled among the audience but *are* the audience, near-constantly onstage, watching their human prey.[6] Outside the theatre too, there was no escape from the devil's omnipresence. He was, literally, everywhere.

In this context, this chapter surveys the dynamic ways that educated Europeans communicated ideas about the devil to an array of readerships and audiences through the written and spoken word. For its examples it draws on British sources from around 1500 to around 1700—these are especially important because Britain was a major cultural producer of fictions and expository writing about the devil during this time, some of which has been influential globally. Although the chapter does not imply that knowledge about the devil was communicated exclusively top-down, it does examine how text and performance produced by educated people was intended to shape belief and behaviours. But it also looks at more ambivalent examples of communication and at accounts of the devil that challenged the elite world because they came from beyond it.

As this volume explores, communicating the devil is a tricky business. Although demonic agency was an adaptable explanation for misfortune in the medieval and early modern world, its very slipperiness was a problem. Both what were regarded as truths and what were regarded as myths of demonic attack spread widely and fast. Officially sanctioned stories were not being broadcast by elites to an unreceptive public—instead, they were consumed, reworked, changed and acted upon, with new elements added. These elements could spawn or shape events that were difficult to control: witch trials, claims of demonic possession, moral crusades. A shared resolve to combat demonic agency was a centripetal force that held together medieval and early modern societies and allowed some Europeans to unite against a common enemy. But it could also blow societies apart.

It was appropriate that communication about the devil was unpredictable—and therefore dangerous—because that echoed the character ascribed to him. The devil was imagined as a trickster and liar. He specialised in luring sinners with false promises and remained ill-defined by evading close scrutiny. So communication about him was often contradictory: the communicators had different impressions of him and argued about his nature and being. Their communicative efforts were also multiform and multivocal, with great internal variety of images, narratives and doctrines. While some texts were forthright in depicting the devil—for example, as a named individual imagined to be present in a directly threatening manner—others were remarkably opaque. This ambiguity echoed the devil's shadowy and protean nature. Was he singular or multiple? What were his key attributes, adjectives, verbs? Which biblical verses best described him? How might his body, if he had one, best be represented in a poem, tract or play and what kinds of auditory, aerial and visual effects might be needed? Which of his many names might best fit? Might there be dangerous sectarian implications in interpreting him, anything that would get the writer or speaker into trouble? How could his vast complexity be communicated helpfully in a pamphlet, treatise or sermon to relatively uneducated audiences? (and so on). No wonder medieval and early modern texts feature a wide variety of depictions of the devil, a sample of which are surveyed here.

## Sermons: Warnings and Instructions

At their simplest, representations consisted of warnings and instructions. A favourite biblical extract providing clear mental images of resistance and self-defence against the devil was Ephesians 6.11-17, believed to be the Apostle Paul's letter to the people of Ephesus. One section was among the most oft-quoted texts about the devil in medieval and early modern times, chosen as a theme for sermons and tracts by ministers and demonologists. This is the version from the "King James" bible of 1611:

Put on the whole armour of God, that ye may be able to stand against the wiles of the devil.
For we wrestle not against flesh and blood, but against principalities, against powers, against the rulers of the darkness of this world, against spiritual wickedness in high places.
Wherefore take unto you the whole armour of God, that ye may be able to withstand in the evil day, and having done all, to stand.
Stand therefore, having your loins girt about with truth, and having on the breastplate of righteousness;
And your feet shod with the preparation of the gospel of peace;
Above all, taking the shield of faith, wherewith ye shall be able to quench all the fiery darts of the wicked.
And take the helmet of salvation, and the sword of the Spirit, which is the word of God.

Preaching in 1536 to the English court, the reformist Bishop of Worcester Hugh Latimer expanded on the text, urging his congregation:

Be ye therefore armed at all points with the armour of God, that ye may stand strongly against the assaults of the devil. "That ye may stand," saith he [Paul]. Ye must stand in this battle, and not sit, nor lie along; for he that lieth is trodden under foot of his enemy. We may not sit, that is, not rest in sin, or lie along in sluggishness of sin; but continually fight against our enemy, and under our great Captain and Sovereign Lord Jesus Christ, and in his quarrel, armed with the armour of God, that we may be strong. We cannot be strong unless we be armed of God. We have no power of ourselves to stand against the assaults of the devil. There St Paul teacheth what our battle is, and wherefore we must be thus armed.

Like a fitness instructor, Latimer encouraged his listeners to feel the assaults of the devil as real bodily experiences, prompting them to easily understood movements. He broke down the images of armour into body parts: the loins must be defended by guarding against sexual temptation, the body held upright in a mailshirt of justice, faith grasped firmly as a shield in the hand, God's word ready to be wielded as a sword, and so forth. This fully visualised antagonist devil—a heavily armoured, attacking soldier—must be resisted physically and in this sermon Latimer applied his text particularly to those he saw as pro-papal enemies of the reformist Anglican church and its king, Henry VIII. If necessary, he explained, Christians could combat the devil by raising an army against these militant papists. Many Protestants regarded the Pope as demonic, an Antichrist who had corrupted the Christian church from within, betraying it to the devil. In 1536, Latimer saw this anti-Christian threat embodied in activists opposing the closure and sacking of monasteries in northern England, a rebel group known to history as the Pilgrimage of Grace.

Latimer's sermon offers a simple, visual, visceral picture of the devil communicated with the straightforward kinetic appeal of a video game and directed against individuals: here, participants in the Pilgrimage. It exemplifies both the devil's power to unify (here, reformist proto-Protestants against Catholic conservatives) and to divide (one Christian against another, with the result being mutual murder). It's an image of the devil designed to make people do things, taking violent action, including actions explicitly forbidden by the Ten Commandments. Here is the devil as a cartoon villain, an obviously evil presence against whom it is the duty of all good Christians to fight. Appropriately, Latimer's sermon therefore concludes with a call to arms:

> Let us fight manfully, and not cease; for no man is crowned or rewarded but in the end. We must therefore fight continually, and with this sword; and thus armed, and we shall receive the reward of victory.[7]

All very clear, then. The Pilgrimage of Grace was routed in battle and at the negotiating table, its leaders captured and executed along with around two hundred of their followers. In the terms of the sermon, all were depicted as demonic enemies of good religion and therefore to be straightforwardly defeated.

But even the zealous simplifier Latimer—one of the reformation's great communicators of complex ideas in accessible terms—admitted here and in other sermons that the devil was "a crafty warrior," not as transparently readable as he appeared. The word "crafty" was a favourite descriptor of demonic strategy. All was well if good Christians could identify their enemy easily, as Latimer intended them to do in 1536. But what if the devil confused them with his craftiness and they could not tell who was their enemy and who was their friend? Sermons like Latimer's were aimed at delivering a punchy message to listeners with varied levels of engagement and so tended to communicate the simpler elements of resistance. Other preachers attempted to address Satanic deceit more fully. How should Christians respond if instead of all-out attack Satan tried persuasion? In the 1580s the vicar of St Giles Cripplegate in London, Lancelot Andrewes, dramatised a verbal joust between Christ and the devil in seven sermons on temptation. He noted how, in response to Satan's demands and promises, Christ turns his back and "gives him hard words … words of bitter reprehension." Ordinary politeness and deference was to be cast aside, Andrewes showed his listeners, in favour of resolute rejection. "There is a time when we are to keep the devil before us, and have our eye still upon him," but there is also "a place, a time, and a sin, that we are to turn our backs on, and not once look at his temptation." Telling Satan to "avaunt," he counselled, would rout him since "we stand not at the devil's courtesy … God hath the devil on a chain, and will not suffer him to tempt us above our strength." This, he told his congregation in dismissing them at the end of his seventh sermon, should be "a comfort to us."[8] While acknowledging demonic craftiness, Andrewes attempted to keep his message simple: resisting Satan would deliver results.

## Poetry: Seduction and Anxiety

Writers in other genres, particularly those intended for private reflection by highly educated minds, had the luxury of further anxious elaboration. As the reformation dragged on, it claimed victims on both Protestant and Catholic sides and split those sides into factions.

Surveying this devastation, thoughtful writers wrestled with how to communicate the seductive, confusing nature of evil more persuasively to sophisticated readers. For example, poems like Edmund Spenser's *The Faerie Queene* (first three books, London 1590) presented themselves as militantly Protestant, implying they offered a simple, functional depiction of the devil rather like Latimer's. But in fact, Spenser dwelt obsessively on mistake and false appearance. His version of the devil was anything but simple and he admitted himself that many readers would be displeased with how his religious message was "clowdily enwrapped" in allegory. Book One of *The Faerie Queene* begins with an easily legible image: a Protestant knight, Redcrosse, riding out to combat Antichrist/demonic evil. It was imagery Latimer would have recognised: the metal-clad Redcrosse is literally wearing God's armour, carrying the shield of faith, etc. But instead of a simple boss battle with Satan, the knight encounters a series of deceptive, hard-to-read characters named Errour (Error), Duessa (Doubleness) and Archimago (Arch-magician, a manipulator of images). They represent demonic forces but are elusive and often have to be defeated by prudent restraint, wit or careful scrutiny rather than in battle. These characters lurk in dark forests or hide beneath beautiful disguises. Their devilishness is communicated only in flashes of alarming imagery, perplexing both Redcrosse and the poem's readers.

For example, the character of Duessa or Doubleness—deceit, untrustworthiness—is introduced as:

A goodly Lady clad in scarlot red,
Purfled with gold and pearle of rich assay,
And like a Persian mitre on her hed
She wore, with crowns and owches garnished,
The which her lavish lovers to her gave;
Her wanton palfrey all was overspred
With tinsell trappings, woven like a wave,
Whose bridle rung with golden bels and bosses brave.[9]

She is "goodly" (pleasing to look at), a "lady" of high birth and beautifully dressed, but words such as "scarlot," (scarlet) "Persian mitre," "lavish lovers" and "wanton" flag to the reader something is amiss. "Lovers" and "wanton" suggest immorality. Persia was associated with demonic magic in the early modern mind because of a misunderstanding of "pagan" Islam and Zoroastrianism. The pope wears a "mitre," so Duessa is also linked to Catholicism. And although she introduces herself to Redcrosse as "Fidessa" (faithfulness), the headnote to this section of the poem has already informed the reader that Redcrosse will encounter "faire Falshood" soon. This is she. Later in the poem, we learn Duessa's true name and that she is a witch, so her identity is made clearer.[10] But Spenser's more attentive readers seem to be expected to unmask her at the first encounter. Likely they are meant to feel clever for becoming suspicious, but also to experience a frisson of fear: suppose they had missed the signs of Satan's presence?[11] This is a good illustration of the anxiety that communicating the devil created in early modern minds, complicating depictions of evil. In *the Faerie Queene* Spenser communicates that anxiety by mimicking it, putting the reader through a test. If they recognise Duessa's devilishness, they have passed. If they are deceived by her beauty, wealth and her false name then they have fallen into the devil's trap and that should indeed make them anxious. Later, John Milton would use the same literary trick in his poem *Paradise Lost* (1667, second version 1674).[12]

Spenser's worries about the devil, and his desire to communicate these to readers, were drawn from biblical extracts that were more complicated than Ephesians 6 but were also favourite quotations deployed in early modern religious education. In 2 Corinthians 11.13-15, also notionally written by the Apostle Paul, a particularly troubling passage remarks that:

> ... such are false apostles, deceitful workers, transforming themselves into the apostles of Christ.

> And no marvel; for Satan himself is transformed into an angel of light.

> Therefore it is no great thing if his ministers also be transformed as the ministers of righteousness; whose end shall be according to their works.

Not only ordinary churchgoers but ministers struggled to understand and interpret this cryptic warning. If the devil could appear to be an angel, then how were they to perceive his evil and resist him? If he did not come to them as a hostile thug but as an apparent friend, offering help or dropping thoughts into their minds, what should they do?[13] Characters like Spenser's seductive Duessa embodied early modern people's growing sense that things could not be as simple as polemics like Latimer's sermon insisted. By the 1580s, when Spenser wrote his poem, it was common knowledge that Latimer had been executed as a heretic. He had used demonic imagery to whip up hatred of Catholics and had fallen victim to that demonisation coming back in reverse against Protestants. So was Latimer not also a suspect "angel of light," at least to some readers? Early modern British culture was increasingly haunted by such fears of misidentification and poets and dramatists responded. Such writers communicated the devil most straightforwardly when they imagined him as an easily recognisable antagonist—a dragon or a hideous giant, and Spenser does both later in his poem—but their poems reflected their awareness that identifying evil was not so simple in real life.

## Drama: Complexity and Multivocality

William Shakespeare's plays are among the most complex—you might say uncommunicative—texts about the tricksy devil of his time. While they give us some of the most evocative and shocking early modern depictions of devilish figures and their evil activities, they also withhold clarity and specificity in a way that only adds to our unease. This is, of course, part of their power: Shakespeare rarely endorsed any contemporary viewpoint in a simple manner, preferring multivocal fragmentation as the basic structure of his plays. It has often seemed to readers that he had doubts about contemporary depictions of God and the devil as simple opposites, part of a uniquely truthful Christian worldview. A favourite trick of Shakespeare's was to raise questions about good and evil, angels and demons, by having a character pretend to see devils or be thought to be possessed by one or many while the dramatist pointedly informed his audience that this was all a performance and other characters were thrown into confusion. His plays presented the "visionary" or "possessed" characters' supposed experiences of the devil as a feint, lie or mistake, depending on context. Audiences were left with questions about the nature of the devil, how and whether such a deceitful creature might be clearly perceived and perhaps whether the devil really existed—at least in the ways described by churchmen. The difference between this type of communication about the devil and what they heard in sermons or read in instructional books must often have felt quite stark.

There are many good examples of confusing communication about the devil in Shakespeare's dramatic canon. For instance, both his plays *The Comedy of Errors* (c. 1591–5) and *Twelfth Night* (c. 1600–2) feature characters (Antipholus of Ephesus, Malvolio) who are deliberately forced by others into the false position of being thought to be demonically possessed. From biblical times onwards, devils were thought to be able to enter the human body and control its actions, making victims utter horrible blasphemies, experience visions, hold theological debates with their inner demonic voices, act out sins and so on. Both Antipholus and Malvolio supposedly show signs of this kind of behaviour, designed by Satan to demonstrate his power. Both men are examined and certified as possession victims by supposed experts. But both "experts" turn out to be charlatans and neither "victim" is actually possessed. Meanwhile both their stories are contained within plays about doubleness, recalling Duessa's deceptive devilishness: *The Comedy of Errors* and *Twelfth Night* even feature twins, doppelgangers who make the association of the devil, error and falsity all the more telling. Both the plays' titles also gesture towards mistake and playful inversion, with error leading to comic misrecognitions and the specific cultural frame of Twelfth Night festivities providing the setting for further confusion. On Twelfth Night, games and pranks often featured inversions of authority and disguises, and both *Twelfth Night* and *The Comedy of Errors* contain examples of this. In these two plays, therefore, demonic content follows demonic form to create confusion for audiences about what is being communicated.[14]

In some of Shakespeare's other plays, this confusing culture of the demonic is further explored with reference to self-chosen illusion and disguise, willed rather than forced. In *King Lear* (c. 1603–5) the nobleman Edgar explains his pretence of demonic possession in a way that defines for the audience the expected appearance and behaviour of people genuinely afflicted by devils. But his performance also raises more questions than it answers about their, and Edgar's, true status and purpose. This is how Edgar explains himself when, thought to be a traitor, he has become the subject of a manhunt:

I heard myself proclaim'd
And by the happy hollow of a tree
Escap'd the hunt. No port is free, no place
Does not attend my taking. Whiles I may scape
I will preserve myself, and am bethought
To take the basest and most poorest shape
That every penury, in contempt of man,
Brought near to beast. My face I'll grime with filth,
Blanket my loins, elf all my hair in knots,
And with pretended nakedness outface
The winds and persecution of the sky.
The country gives me proof and president
Of Bedlam beggars, who, with roaring voices
Strike in their numb'd and mortified arms
Pins, wooden pricks, nails, springs of rosemary;
And with this horrible object, from low farms,
Poor pelting villages, sheep-cotes, and mills,
Sometimes with lunatic bans, sometime with prayers,
Enforce their charity. Poor Turlygod! Poor Tom!
That's something yet: Edgar I nothing am.[15]

Edgar proposes, in short, to adopt the persona of a beggar who believes himself to be under attack by devils attempting to possess his body.

This long description is important because it seems to offer so much concrete information, but in fact ends with Shakespeare's favourite gesture towards ambiguity, emptiness and "nothingness." We learn that people possessed or obsessed by devils (the two terms covering devils inside or outside the body) tend to be filthy and semi-naked in appearance. They are possibly outcast by society. They shout, curse and pray and sometimes attempt self-harm. Edgar's performance adds rich imaginative content to this picture with apparent visions conjured up: the names of devils that he shouts include Flibbertigibbet, Smulkin, Modo, Mahu, Frateretto, Hoppedance, Obidicut, Hobbididence and others, as well as the generic and repeated "foul fiend." He portrays some of his devils as external ("the foul fiend bites my back") and some as internal ("Hoppedance cries in Tom's belly"), demonstrating both obsession in which devils physically torment their victim externally and bodily possession.[16] Yet all this is consistently represented to the audience as an act, since Edgar often interjects asides in his own voice, contrasting with that of his afflicted persona "Tom." These asides and soliloquies remind us there are in fact no devils present—either on the stage or in a character's body or even in a character's imagination. The more convincing Edgar's performance of the presence of the devil, the more we are reminded by him of its unreality. The suite of Shakespearean plays that explore these ideas of illusion, deceit, doubleness, performance and truth have been referred to as "devil-theatre" and the nature of their communication of the demonic extensively debated.[17]

Well aware of the potential for theatre to embody demonic deceit, puritans such as Philip Stubbes and Stephen Gosson lambasted the acting and playwrighting profession as the devil's "instruments." Gosson compared actors to carpenters' tools in their utility to Satan: "the Carpenter rayseth not his frame without tooles, nor the Devill his woork without instruments," he explained.[18] Likewise Stubbes, drawing on Augustine of Hippo, asserted that "Playes were ordained by the Devil, and consecrate to Heathen Gods, to draw us from Christianity to Idolatry & Gentilisme" (i.e. heathenism or paganism). Plays were not just empty shows but were an embodiment of evil: "filthy" and "bawdy," encouraging fornication, sodomy, theft, swearing, blasphemy and idle pleasure and drawing audiences away from sermons. Gosson was particularly explicit about the disguised nature of the devilish dangers of theatres: "There is more in them then we perceive," he argued, for "the Devill standes at our elbowe when we see not, speaks when we heare him not, strikes when wee feele not, and woundeth sore when he raseth no skinne, nor rentes the fleshe. In those thinges, that we least mistrust, the greatest daunger dooth often lurke."[19] When playwrights dramatised devils using the bodies of their actors, he thought, they were engaging in gleeful baiting of their critics while at the same time affirming fears about demonic deception. The very complexity and multivocality of drama seemed inherently Satanic.

Shakespeare drew on previous models for his devil-theatre, suggesting that Stubbes' and Gosson's concerns had been brewing since the early days of post-reformation theatre. Shakespeare's devils owe something to Marlowe's in *Doctor Faustus*, just as Milton's owe something to Spenser's. Marlowe's Mephistophilis, in particular, would have raised apprehensions for audiences about a simple response to the devil. Although he and his fellow devils Beelzebub and Lucifer shared traits with the devils of medieval theatre, Mephistophilis was not just a roaring, firework-throwing monster. Instead, he articulated a troubling melancholy that must have shocked a few seconds of sympathy—or more—out of unprepared audience members. From his first appearance Mephistophilis is designated as "unhappy" and hauntingly describes the torment he carries around with him:

> Why this is hell, nor am I out of it.
> Think'st thou that I who saw the face of God,
> And tasted the eternal joys of Heaven,
> Am not tormented with ten thousand hells,
> In being depriv'd of everlasting bliss?[20]

While Marlowe's devils are not as multivocal and evasive as Shakespeare's, the way audiences were forced to consider the devil's perspective, and the engaging nature of Mephistophilis' voice, seeded ideas of complexity and unease into the culture of demonic representation in English plays. Marlowe's devils were influential in later dramatic and fictional work globally, too—particularly in Germany, from where the story of Faustus originally came.

### Reportage: Demonic Possession

Building on Marlowe's innovation, Shakespeare's ambiguity in communicating the devil is related to his other sources too, especially depictions of demonic possession and obsession. Turning to these brings us back from fiction into attempts to communicate the "reality" of the devil, or at least his supposed presence in real lives. In particular Shakespeare shaped his devil-plays around a knowledge of the case of the godly exorcist John Darrell, who supposedly dispossessed a series of demoniacs across the English midlands and north in the 1580s and 1590s, and the Catholic exorcists who supposedly dispossessed several people at Denham, Buckinghamshire in 1595–6.[21] Shakespeare encountered a hostile version of these stories in the vicious polemics of the Anglican chaplain Samuel Harsnett, who thought them fake. Particularly in the lengthy and abusive *A Declaration of Egregious Popish Impostures* (1603), Harsnett dissected evidence of demonic activity and represented it all as theatrically fraudulent.[22] Things had changed substantially since Latimer's day, with the English churches fragmented by 1599 into multiple noisy sects, heaping insult on one another. Looking back at Latimer from Harsnett, we should begin to wonder how simple Latimer's depiction of Satan actually was. How much was he suppressing his own anxieties about doubleness, sectarian strife and Christian charity to communicate his comic-book devil? Surely quite a bit.

By 1599 that suppressed panic was out in the open, splashed across multiple media from print to plays. It was from Harsnett's ugly sectarian rant about *Egregious Popish Impostures* that Shakespeare took the names of many of Edgar's fictional devils in *King Lear*. In Harsnett's account of the Denham dispossessions the devils were also portrayed as fictional, yet they had seemed utterly real to the exorcists involved. Possibly they also seemed real to the people whose bodies they had supposedly invaded. That was a terrifying thought. Many modern academic commentators on such cases conclude that alleged victims of demonic possession were simply liars. This was particularly true of accounts written in the later 19th to mid-20th centuries, when discussions of demonology were dominated by the belief that a Eurocentric masculine rationality had triumphed over centuries of superstitious hysteria. F.W. Brownlow, for example, accuses the Denham demoniac Frideswide "Fid" Williams of being "stupid" and "lying" and her fellow sufferer

Richard Mainy of staging "a grand charade," playing "pranks" as "a great lark."[23] This may all be true, but to balance such a possibility it is important to consider medieval and early modern fears that the devil could actually enter and take control of the human body. What were victims of demonic possession and their exorcists trying to communicate about the devil in describing their felt, somatic experiences of him and in their attempts to publicise these in print?

Like many supposedly possessed persons, both the Denham demoniacs were very young at the time of their experiences: just fifteen to sixteen years old. Fid was a servant who had come to the Denham household to look after her sick sister and undertake some of her work, which placed her and her sister (Sara, another demoniac) in a vulnerable, dependent and stressful position. Meanwhile Richard was being prepared for the priesthood by his gentry family. His brother had married into the Peckhams, who owned the estate at Denham, and he was an important part of a network of families whose aim was to keep Catholicism alive in England: young, male, educated, intelligent and therefore an ideal candidate for ordination. Like members of many other religious minorities, the Peckhams, Mainys and Williamses must have felt under constant attack. Their attempts to preserve their rites and culture and to disseminate their beliefs involved great risk. In particular, hiding and smuggling Catholic priests—as the Peckhams did in the mid-1580s—could lead members of their community as well as the priests themselves into exile, imprisonment and ultimately grisly execution (and indeed it did so in the case of some of the Denham exorcists). These violent worldly threats were accompanied by terrifying fears of eternal damnation if their missionary duty was evaded.[24] For them the devil must therefore have felt a lot more like Latimer's armed invader than like Shakespeare's elusive phantom—and it must have hurt when observers saw only fraud in their experiences.

Even where a demonic obsession or possession was or became a deliberate performance, therefore, it could speak to underlying truths of profound importance to individuals and communities. The devil could paradoxically reveal truths about a chosen sect or person. Sometimes he did indeed behave rather like an angel of light. Often he required exorcism to play that role, the idea being that an appropriate religious authority would be able to determine the reality (or not) of a possession and then command the devil to speak the truth and exit his victim's body. By leaving, the devil confirmed the authority of the exorcist and submitted himself to that person and his God, becoming God's instrument. Different religious sects had different opinions of this process, and different words and rites with which to conduct exorcism. In England, Catholics and puritans were especially keen on using it to display the power of their particular understanding of God and establish themselves as true authorities on religious matters, no matter how distant they were from worldly power. The drama of exorcism also attracted playwrights who wanted to make a splash—like Ben Jonson in *The Devil is an Ass* (1616)—although most were wary of dramatising the actual act onstage because of its controversial sectarian history.

In such an atmosphere of compulsory piety, danger and dissimulation—which characterised England from (at least) the 1530s to 1660s—notions of personal attack by the devil flourished. To people who did not ask difficult questions or read complex depictions of Satan, it must have felt as if he was an encircling presence in the world as well as in the afterlife, as explained at the start of this chapter. At Denham, Catholics lived in two worlds, a simulated external normality, deceitfully complying with Protestant norms, and a private, sacred Catholic reality. Meanwhile, puritan people felt similarly under attack: to them it seemed the devil yearned to sully their sacred inner truth, exposing them to the sinfulness of the rest of humanity. Many other Christians across the sectarian spectrum would have recognised elements of these more extreme positions in their own lives. Without reducing the devil wholly to a metaphor, we can see that even moderately engaged religious people would have brooded on notions of interior and exterior, lies, temptation and duality. They experienced personal threat from demons accordingly. Indeed, to be the devil's victim was to be marked out as particularly holy by his evil attentions. No wonder that young Catholics and young radical Protestants, like some of those dispossessed by John Darrell, were particularly drawn to notions of demonic possession. Becoming possessed in reality or simulation communicated their desire to be noticed and taken seriously as Christians, to work through their anxieties about sin.[25]

For supposed victims of demonic assault like Fid Williams, Richard Mainy and their counterparts across Christendom (from Nicole Obry at Laon in 1566 to the people of Salem, Massachusetts, to the nuns at the Poor Clares convent in Carpi in the 1630s to the thousands of people exorcised by Johann Joseph Gassner in 18th-century Germany) the stakes were high. It is important to note that although this chapter has focused on British examples, across Europe and the Americas the devil was also manifested as a personal threat and, simultaneously, an opportunity. Obry's spectacular exorcism in Laon cathedral provided the opportunity both for this young wife to assert her virtue and for the religious leaders of her community to denounce their Huguenot neighbours as anti-Christian heretics.[26] In Britain's colonies Native Americans like "Tituba Indian" and "John Indian" writhed under Satanic attack—or so their puritan examiners said—and escaped execution as witches.[27] Exorcists and ministers keenly awaited their own moment of trial with the devil and consequent fame. For Gassner, the ability to exorcise people who were not classically possessed but instead sick or injured proved that supposedly natural events were in fact providential and allowed him to reassert the centrality of God in all things.[28] What was communicated about the devil varied but in each case an encounter with him revolved around religious self-assertion and victory over evil.

### Reportage: Witchcraft Trials

While demoniacs seldom wrote down their own experiences, those attempting to exorcise them did, and they used these accounts for sectarian propaganda. This was not a new idea, as we saw in Latimer's sermon, or limited to depictions of demonic possession. Supposed encounters with witchcraft could be used in a similar way, communicating the innocence and purity of those unfortunate enough to be attacked by witches—the devil's human agents. Supporters of King James VI of Scotland keenly publicised their monarch's face-off with witches in 1591, including a useful statement supposedly made by the devil that James was "the greatest enemy he hath in the worlde."[29] Dramatists too were drawn to the vexed relationship between the devil and witches. Unlike those who were imagined merely as misbelieving Christians, heretics unwittingly furthering Satan's aims, witches were thought to choose collaboration with the devil and make a spoken or written agreement with him to gain access to his power to do harm. Imagining and depicting this moment of covenant or contracting allowed people to explore their own notions of wish fulfilment, temptation, moral responsibility and the salvation or damnation that would follow a controlled or bungled encounter with Satan.[30] Like the readers of *The Faerie Queene*, those who embodied or spectated upon the making of a demonic pact were walking through a comprehension test.

Each iteration of demonic attack—whether onstage or in imagined reality—was an opportunity for observers to check whether those involved had understood and acted upon the messages about the devil that had been communicated to them, in this case about witches and their demonic contacts.

The relationship between witch and devil fascinated dramatists but it was not until 1621 that a play moved beyond the established Faustus-Mephistophilis trope towards portraying that relationship in a way recognisable by many ordinary people. In 1621's *The Witch of Edmonton*, the devil appeared onstage as a dog, embodied by a human actor. Instead of two male figures facing each other across the human/devil divide, viewers saw a female figure portrayed by a male actor facing a dog portrayed by a man. The devil-dog Tom is one of the stars of the play (whose authors may have included Thomas Dekker, William Rowley, John Ford and others). He is named Tom by his apparent owner, the titular witch of Edmonton, and he not only speaks but also barks and gambols about like an ordinary pet. Audiences must have laughed in delight as well as shuddered, knowing that witches' familiar devils often appeared as animals in real life. Both reactions were important, communicating the devil's showy, tricksy nature once again: Tom is like Duessa, engaging but dangerous, fluffy but false. In vicious soliloquies he plots the downfall of his human victims, leading them on to damnation by inspiring murder. For the image of their devil-dog familiar, the playwrights drew on their principal source, Henry Goodcole's news pamphlet *The Wonderfull Discoverie of the Witch of Edmonton* (1621). Here, the real woman Elizabeth Sawyer—interviewed by the Anglican chaplain Goodcole in her London prison cell—described how the devil came to her as a black dog and became her familiar, the embodied spirit animal whom witches were thought to dispatch to attack their victims.

Sawyer's representation of the devil is as both a persecutory enemy and loving pet. She described his first meeting with her as like the springing of a trap: from nowhere he appeared as she was angrily swearing about her enemies. "Oh!" said the devil-dog, "have I now found you cursing, swearing and blaspheming? Now you are mine." But later in her account the devil's canine nature is more strongly represented: "he came barking to me," Sawyer told Goodcole, and "I did stroake him on the backe, and then he would becke unto me, and wagge his tayle as being therewith contented." Tom also appears like a human lover at times. He sucked Sawyer's blood—as familiar spirits were thought to do—in an intimate, suggestive manner "a little above my fundiment ... the Divell would put his head under my coates, and I did willingly suffer him to doe what hee would."[31] In this section of Goodcole's account, Sawyer's description of Tom hints at the sexual relationship some witches were thought to have with familiar spirits, like Elizabeth Clarke who in 1645 confessed "shee had carnall copulation with the Devill ... in the shape of a proper Gentleman."[32] Such relationships were part of the notion of demonic pact: an agreement between a human and the devil sealed by blood-gift. The pact sometimes also involved sex.[33] Sawyer described the making of her pact as a response to the devil's demand for complete ownership: that she give him "my soule and body, threatning then to teare me in peeces, if that I did not grant unto him my soule and body." She agreed out of fear and "to seale this my promise made unto him, I then gave him leave to sucke of my blutd."[34]

The demonic pact was presented in some contexts as granting its maker almost infinite power. Joan, Margaret and Phillipa Flower were convicted of witchcraft against the earl and countess of Rutland and their children in 1619, and after their execution a ballad described their pact with the devil in lurid terms. Knowing that the women wanted to harm their noble neighbours:

> the Divell made entrance in, his Kingdome to inlarge.
> And puts his executing wrath, unto these womens charge:
> Not caring whom it lighted on, the Innocent or no,
> And offered them his diligence, to flye, to run, and goe.
>
> And to attend in pretty formes, of Dog, of Cat, or Rat,
> To which they freely gave consent, and much rejoyc't thereat:
> And as it seemd they sould their soules, for service of such Spirits,
> And sealing it with drops of blood, damnation so inherits.

By doing this, the ballad's lyricist even alleges that the women themselves have become demons, "being Divels growne." Although in theological terms this was inaccurate, its impression upon readers of the broadsheet and audiences listening to the song must have been a chilling thrill. The devil provided agreeably scary sensation and conversation-starters in such topical, news-making settings: an ambiguous reference to either devils or witches flying, a claim the devil could become an animal servant to the witch in "pretty," deceptive forms, a suggestive speculation on the saleability of the soul and a final frisson of eternal damnation.

Many British people who confessed to witchcraft crimes told similar stories about animal familiars, rich in detail and apparently not inspired wholly by their questioners—since familiars had no role in most European demonology of the period.[35] Stories of devil-animals seem to have sprung from a genuinely popular understanding of the way the devil might manifest: the familiar had affinities with the idea of ghosts as well as talking pets, fairies, hobgoblins and other supernatural creatures often found in folktales.[36] Bessie Dunlop, accused in Lynn, Scotland of invoking "spretis [spirits] of the devil" in 1576 as part of her practice of healing and divination, actually confessed to consulting not with a devil but a ghost, "Thome Reid, quha deit at Pinkye" (who died at the battle of Pinkie, in 1547). She said Thome was an honest, elderly, grey-bearded man wearing old-fashioned clothes and holding a white wand. He came to her when she was sad her husband and child were ill and her cow had died, and explained she must have offended God to have brought this misery upon herself. "I counsel thee to mend to him" [to reform, make amends], Thome said, offering conventional Christian advice. But when Dunlop met him again, she told questioners, he changed his approach, promising her goods, cattle and horses if she "wald denye hir Christindome" [baptism and faith]. On another occasion, he showed her twelve elfin people, "gude wychtis that wynnit at the Court of Elfame" [good people who lived at the fairy court].[37] This story emerged as a result of coercive questioning and was deeply ambiguous, but Dunlop's jurors judged simply that "Thome" was a devil whom she had conjured him up—although she stated clearly she had no power to summon him.

Telling stories of these encounters, confessing "witches" seem to be communicating a complex web of desires, from love and companionship through to the need to control events, gain and share knowledge and the baser emotional satisfaction of seeing an enemy suffer. Bessie Dunlop spoke of Thome in almost wholly positive terms: as a helpful religious guide, an elder who comforted her, offering medical advice for the patients of her healing practice and other marketable knowledge, such as prophecy, weather forecasting and how to find stolen goods. However, even such innocuous supernatural contact led people into confessing criminality when they were interrogated by ministers and magistrates trained in Christian binary thinking. These men assumed that whatever was not obviously godly was demonic. Such stories as Dunlop's often led to conviction, imprisonment or execution as witches, as it did for her. This unforeseen outcome and the framing of "witches'" stories as "confessions" means it is hard to be sure how far they were in control of the apparently demonic representations in their descriptions. It is impossible confidently to separate what is left of their voices from those of the narrators of their stories. For example, even though Dunlop's interrogators and Henry Goodcole both recorded some of their questions, Dunlop and her English counterpart Elizabeth Sawyer gave their evidence only after a lengthy process of arrest, detention and enforced dialogue. In Sawyer's case we know she had been questioned about witchcraft by a magistrate months before and was already tried and convicted of the crime by the time she met Goodcole. When we read her story of the devil, it is important to recall she was communicating not only her own perspective but a mix of inputs from her own imagination and that of her accusing questioners. Yet her representation of the devil feels distinct from the demands of her educated, didactic questioner, like Bessie Dunlop's even less convincingly Satanic narration 50 years before.

What men like Goodcole were really looking for was evidence of demonic pact, not reminiscences about a supernatural friend, ghost, fairy or pet. The devil-dog Tom's demand that Elizabeth Sawyer donate her body and soul to him in exchange for access to his magical power is the conventional price thought to be exacted by devils who bargained with humans for their services, a neat rendition of the expected anecdote. Seeing these transactions represented in print or in the theatre, audiences would have expected this price to be asked and paid. That was the point of the story, its structuring device: without that transaction and its inevitable punitive consequence, it appears that the central message of warning was not seen to be communicated effectively. Since medieval times, the story of the person—Roger Bacon, Peter Fabel, Johann Faustus, Elizabeth Sawyer, Elizabeth Clarke—who made a pact with the devil using their soul and body as collateral was in every sense of the word a familiar story.[38] In the early modern period, the subjects of such stories shifted from male conjurors, scholars and alchemists to female witches, whose requirements were less about boundless aspiration and more about rebalancing existing wrongs in a limited way. Their stories are full of unnecessary detail about the devil that illuminates their lives and priorities—their usually undiscussed marriages, children, illnesses and unceasing work—but which was ultimately, of course, slotted into a self-defeating narrative of their own wickedness and downfall.[39]

The defeat of the witch comes as less of a surprise in *The Witch of Edmonton* than it does in many versions of the stories of the men who made devil pacts, precisely because she is a disempowered female. Indeed, there were even comic versions of men "outdoing Faustus," like Robert Greene's *Friar Bacon and Friar Bungay* (1588–92) or the anonymous *Merry Devil of Edmonton* (1608) with its conjuror Peter Fabel. In these plays, the protagonists escape paying the devil's price, at least for the duration of the play and a notional time thereafter.[40] In contrast, witch trials were supposed to end with the witch's execution. The devil-dog Tom threatens Elizabeth Sawyer with violent death even before she has agreed to covenant with him and the transition from enticing offer to deadly threat is swift, within seven lines:

Dog: … on condition,
That uncompell'd thou make a deed of Gift
Of Soul and Body to me.

Sawyer: Out, alas!
My Soul and Body?

Dog: And that instantly,
And seal it with thy blood: if thou deniest,
I'll tear thy body in a thousand pieces.[41]

The playwrights leave no doubt about who is in charge. This is likely because, as well as reading Henry Goodcole's account of Sawyer's confession, they based their play in part on the view of relationships between witch and devil set out in George Gifford's instructional treatise A *Dialogue Concerning Witches and Witchcrafts* (1593).

### The Devil in Dialogue: Sermon Meets Drama

Gifford is a good example of an early modern author who recognised the problem of Satanic ambiguities, such as those represented in *The Faerie Queene*, but tried to communicate them in simple terms, such as those deployed by Hugh Latimer. As a result he produced a hybrid form of demonic communication: a lively but pious dialogue. It combines the best elements of communicating the devil from fiction and fact, sermon and drama. In important respects Gifford's *Dialogue* was a failure, neither one thing nor the other. Its concepts are too complicated to be simplified effectively and it is only intermittently entertaining. But it is a fascinating record of an early modern preacher grappling with the communicative challenges posed by Satan and choosing something closer to poetic fiction and devil-theatre than it is to sermon. Gifford was a puritan minister at Maldon in Essex, who wanted to educate his parishioners about the witchcraft accusations being made around them. Being godly was not to be automatically a witch-hunter. So while Gifford stated that some people were witches, one of his key arguments in the *Dialogue* was that such people actually had no power. They could not effect harm because Satan did not gift them his power as part of the pact he made with them. Instead they were the tools of the devil, his servants or "instruments." How and whether they should be punished for this was a moot point.

In the course of the *Dialogue*, Gifford's authoritative speaker Daniel, and subsidiary speakers such as the schoolmaster Master B., come to agree that "witches and conjurers are seduced and become the vassals of Satan, they are his servants, and not he theirs." While many people, Daniel suggested, would say simply that "there be witches that worke by the divell" he would rather say that "the divell worketh by them."[42] But Daniel goes further than Master B. in his wisdom. On the question of familiars like Elizabeth Sawyer's Tom, when Master B. innocently repeats the conventional wisdom about the witch commanding her devil-animal familiars, Daniel sharply corrects him:

M.B. … the witches have their spirits, some hath one, some hath more, as two, three, foure, or five, some in one likenesse, and some in another, as like cats, weasils, toades, or mise, whom they nourish with milke or with a chicken, or by letting them suck now and then a drop of bloud: whom they call when they be offended with any, and send them to hurt them …

Dan: Here is great deceit, and great illusion … the divell by such things doth beguile and seduce ignorant men, and lead them into errours and grievous sinnes … the holy Scriptures do paint out the divels to be mightie terrible spirits, full of power, rage, and crueltie … now when they take upon them the shapes of such paltrie vermin, as cats, mise, todes, and weasils, it is even of subtiltie to cover and hide his mightie tyrannie and power.[43]

While acknowledging the complexity of the relationship between the devil and the witch, Gifford thus tried in his treatise to simplify and demystify it. For him, the devil was always the master even when he appeared as a friendly dog or a tiny mouse. Although his deceits were complicated and the truth was hard to see, once understood it seemed to him fairly clear.

Yet although he made his point and the *Witch of Edmonton*'s playwrights echoed it, in trying to get across this "simple" truth about devils Gifford's language betrays the continuing difficulty of communicating the devil. Some passages are straightforward: ones where a supposedly ignorant character is explaining his or her views about witches and devils. But the passages where Gifford tries to articulate more complex view are slippery. For example, at times Gifford represents the devil, rather surprisingly, as a kind of witch himself: "the devil" says his spokesman character Daniel "doth bewitch men by meanes of these witches, and leade them from God." And in being led astray, these "men"—the accusers of witches— become witches too, because they are led by the devil's bewitchment to accuse innocent people as witches. Often they have visited a folk magician, who has prompted them to accuse a neighbour of witchcraft—quite wrongly. Gifford portrays the accusers' visits to these folk magicians as being tantamount to demonic pact, arguing the accusers have been led by Satan "even to follow himselfe, to offer sacrifices unto him, to worship him, to obey his will, to commit many grievous sinnes, and be drowned in manifold errors."[44] These metaphorical witches (or are they really witches, not just metaphorically?) are for Gifford just as bad as those who covenant formally with the devil. This is dense material, switching roles and responsibilities back and forth across the boundary between human and devil in a way that must have perplexed many readers and made little evident impact on ongoing witch trials. But it was a striking communicative experiment.

## Conclusion

Communicating the devil was a hazardous enterprise in the medieval and early modern world. Simple but problematic depictions quickly shaded into more complex ones that dealt more fully with Satan's wiles but were capable of misunderstanding. Sermons, poems, plays and news reportage all failed to pin down the devil and defeat him. His slipperiness infected all communication about him, so no consensus emerged about who he was and how he intervened in human affairs. Terms for his supposed human accomplices—such as "demoniac" or "witch"—were also discovered to be too loose to be useful, although they still got people killed. The examples of demonic communication in this chapter are diverse but each of them is in various ways a failure: too simple, incomplete, self-contradictory, confused, dangerous, self-defeating. Each writer or speaker found that when Satan was involved language deformed and twisted under devilish strain. Several of them died as a result. Each of them tried and failed to communicate the devil.

## Notes

1 Nathan Johnstone, *The Devil and Demonism in Early Modern England* (Cambridge, 2006), 68–76, 143–74.

2 Charlotte Rose Millar, *Witchcraft, the Devil and Emotions in Early Modern England* (London, 2017), 32–3 and 43; Johnstone, *Devil and Demonism*, 150, 160, 167, 172–3.

3 Matthew J. Smith, *Performance and Religion in Early Modern England: Stage, Cathedral, Wagon, Street* (Notre Dame, 2019), 269–74.

4 *The Creation of the World: A Critical Edition and Translation*, ed. Paula Neuss (New York, 1983), 37–40; *The Towneley Plays*, eds. George England and Alfred W. Pollard (Oxford, 1897), 5.

5 Christopher Marlowe, *Doctor Faustus: The A and B Texts*, ed. David Bevington and Eric Rasmussen (Manchester, 1993) 1.3, 1.4; Jan Kott, "The Two Hells of Doctor Faustus: A Theatrical Polyphony," *New Theatre Quarterly* 152 (2009): 10–1, 15.

6 Smith, *Performance and Religion*, 258, 261–6, 292, 301–3; see also Bronwyn Johnston, "Who the Devil is in Charge? Mastery and the Faustian Pact on the Early Modern Stage," in *Magical Transformations on the Early Modern Stage*, eds. Lisa Hopkins and Helen Ostovich (London, 2014), 31–46.

7 Hugh Latimer, "Sermon on Ephesians VI. 10–20" from *Sermons* ed. H.C. Beeching (New York, 1906) at Project Canterbury: http://anglicanhistory.org/reformation/latimer/sermons/ephesians.html

8 Lancelot Andrewes, *Ninety-Six Sermons*, vol. 5 (Oxford, 1841), 550–8.

9 Edmund Spenser, *The Faerie Queene*, ed. Thomas P. Roche (London, 1987) book I, canto II, stanza XII.

10 On Duessa's duality and shape-shifting see Susan Carter, "Duessa: Spenser's Loathly Lady," *Cahiers Élisabéthains* 68 (2005): 9–18.

11 On the poem's relationship with sermons, see Margaret Christian, *Spenserian Allegory and Elizabethan Biblical Exegesis: A Context for* The Faerie Queene (Manchester, 2016).

12 On Spenser, devils and women see Dorothy Stevens, "'Newes of Devils': Feminine Sprites in Masculine Minds in *The Faerie Queene*," *English Literary Renaissance* 23, no. 3 (1993): 363–81.

13 On mode of attack see Darren Oldridge, "Demons of the Mind: Satanic Thoughts in Seventeenth-Century England," *The Seventeenth Century* 35, no. 3 (2020) 277–92 and see also Oldridge, *The Devil in Early Modern England* (Stroud, 2000).

14 For an expanded discussion see Marion Gibson, *Possession, Puritanism and* Print (London, 2006), 160–6.

15 William Shakespeare, *King Lear* ed. R.A. Foakes (London, 1997), 2.3.1–21.

16 Shakespeare, *King Lear* 3.4.115, 3.4.140, 3.4.142–143; 3.6.6, 3.6.17, 3.6.30; 4.1.59–60.

17 See, for example, Jan Frans van Dijkhuizen, *Devil Theatre: Demonic Possession and Exorcism in English Drama 1558–1642* (Woodbridge, 2007); John D. Cox, *The Devil and the Sacred in English Drama 1350–1642* (Cambridge, 2000).

18 Margaret Jane Kidnie, "Marlowe's 'Enterlude' and the Rhetoric of Presence" (PhD diss., University of Birmingham, 1996), 237 at https://etheses.bham.ac.uk/id/eprint/4435/1/Kidnie96PhD_redacted.pdf

19 Stephen Gosson, *The Schoole of Abuse (1579)*, ed. R.S. Bear (Portland, 2000), 13.

20 Marlowe, *Faustus* 1.3.74–78.

21 On Darrell's dispossessions, see Gibson, *Possession* and Brendan Walsh, *The English Exorcist: John Darrell and the Shaping of Early Modern Protestant Demonology* (London, 2020).

22 Most famously, Stephen Greenblatt, "Shakespeare and the Exorcists," in *Shakespearean Negotiations* (Oxford, 1988) 118–21, 123–8 and see also Amy Wolf, "Shakespeare and Harsnett: 'Pregnant to Good Pity?'," *Studies in English Literature 1500–1800* 38, no. 2 (1998) 251–64 and Gillian Woods, *Shakespeare's Unreformed Fictions* (Oxford, 2013), chapter 4.

23 F. W. Brownlow, *Shakespeare, Harsnett and the Devils of Denham* 2nd ed. (New York, 1993), 77–9, 25.

24 Greenblatt, "Shakespeare and the Exorcists," 94–128; Johnstone, *Devil and Demonism*, 88–90.

25 See also Thomas Freeman, "Demons, Deviance and Defiance: John Darrell and the Politics of Exorcism in Late Elizabethan England," in *Conformity and Orthodoxy in the English Church c.1560–1660*, eds. Peter Lake and Michael Questier (Woodbridge, 2000) 34–63; Harman Bhogal, "Miracles, Cessationism and Demonic Possession: The Darrell Controversy and the Parameters of Preternature in Early Modern English Demonology," *Preternature* 4, no. 2 (2015): 152–80.

26 Sarah Ferber, *Demonic Possession and Exorcism in Early Modern France* (London, 2004); Ferber, "Demonic Possession, Exorcism and Witchcraft" in *The Oxford Handbook of Witchcraft in Early Modern Europe and Colonial America*, ed. Brian P. Levack (Oxford, 2013) 575–92; Jeffrey R. Watt, *The Scourge of Demons* (Rochester, 2009).

27 Elaine G. Breslaw, *Tituba, Reluctant Witch of Salem: Devilish Indians and Puritan Fantasies* (New York, 1997), 122 and 140; Mary Beth Norton, *In the Devil's Snare: The Salem Witchcraft Crisis of 1692* (New York, 2002), 28 and 76.

28 Erik Midelfort, *Exorcism and Enlightenment* (New Haven, 2005).

29 *Newes from Scotland* (London, 1591), 15.

30 Ciaran Jones explores practical and spiritual aspects of demonic pact in "The 'Spiritualized Devil': Practical Demonology and Protestant Doctrines in Scottish Witchcraft Confessions," *Magic, Ritual and Witchcraft* 17, no. 1 (2022): 85–105 and see also Nanna Eva Nissen, "Sovereign Dealings with Blasphemy: The Prosecution of Written Pacts with the Devil within the Absolute Monarchy of Denmark-Norway," *Scandinavian Journal of History* 47, no. 4 (2022): 464–89.

31 Henry Goodcole, *The Wonderful Discoverie of Elizabeth Sawyer* (London, 1621) in *Early Modern Witches*, ed. Marion Gibson (London, 2000), 308–13.

32 H. F., *A True and Exact Relation* (London, 1645) in *English Witchcraft 1560–1736: The Matthew Hopkins Trials*, ed. Malcolm Gaskill (London, 2005), 12.

33 Lyndal Roper, *Witch Craze: Women and Evil in Baroque Germany* (New Haven, 2004), 84–5

34 Goodcole, *Wonderful Discoverie*, 310.

35 James Sharpe, *Instruments of Darkness: Witchcraft in England 1550–1750* (London, 1996), 75–8; Millar, *Witchcraft, the Devil and Emotions*, 29.

36 See Emma Wilby, "The Witch's Familiar and the Fairy in Early Modern England and Scotland," *Folklore* 111, no. 2 (2000): 283–305, Victoria Carr, "Witches and the Dead: The Case for the English Ghost Familiar," *Folklore* 130, no. 3 (2019): 282–99 and Helen Parish, "'Paltrie Vermin, Cats, Mise, Toads, and Weasils': Witches, Familiars and Human-Animal Interactions in the English Witch Trials," *Religions* 10, no. 2 (2019): 1–14.

37 Robert Pitcairn, *Ancient Criminal Trials*, vol. 2 (Edinburgh, 1833) part 1, 51–7.

38 For Bacon and Fabel, see below for the representations of their pacts.

39 For an expanded discussion, see Marion Gibson, *The Witches of St Osyth: Persecution, Betrayal and Murder in Elizabethan England* (Cambridge, 2022).

40 Peter Kirwan, "'We Ring this Round with our Invoking Spells': Magic as Embedded Authorship in *The Merry Devil of Edmonton*" in *Magical Transformations*, 115.

41 *The Witch of Edmonton* in *Three Jacobean Witchcraft Plays* eds. Peter Corbin and Douglas Sedge (Manchester, 1986), 2.1.132–37.

42 George Gifford, *A Dialogue Concerning Witches and Witchcrafts* (London, 1842), 14, 18 and generally Scott McGinnis, *George Gifford and the Reformation of the Common Sort* (University Park, 2005).

43 Gifford, *Dialogue Concerning Witches*, 18–22.

44 Gifford, *Dialogue Concerning Witches*, 14.

# Further Reading

Stuart Clark, Thinking with Demons (Oxford: Clarendon Press, 1997).

Marion Gibson, Possession, Puritanism and Print (London: Pickering and Chatto, 2006).

Ronald Hutton, The Witch (New Haven: Yale University Press, 2017).

Nathan Johnstone, The Devil and Demonism in Early Modern England (Cambridge: Cambridge University Press, 2006).

Charlotte Rose Millar, Witchcraft, the Devil and Emotions in Early Modern England (London: Routledge, 2017).

Darren Oldridge, The Devil in Early Modern England (Stroud: Sutton, 2001).

Eric Pudney, Scepticism and Belief in Witchcraft Drama 1538-1681 (Manchester: Lund University Press, 2019).

Jan Frans van Dijkhuizen, Devil Theatre: Demonic Possession and Exorcism in English Drama 1558-1642 (Woodbridge: Boydell and Brewer, 2007).

# 11

# DEVIL FINDERS

*Jan Machielsen*

### Devil Rising

What attributes did the devil need to possess for humans to be able to find him? This chapter will examine two types of "finders"—witchcraft theorists and exorcists—who encountered the devil in two different guises: as a physical entity with whom wicked humans (witches) were able to contract, and as a disembodied one who was able to possess, afflict, or test the bodies of the sinful and the pious. These efforts emerged or found new urgency during the 1400s and 1500s, reflecting changing ideas about the devil's abilities as well as growing fears about the extent of his powers. Christians may well consider the devil, as a fallen angel, a virtually timeless being, begotten at creation and destined to witness its end, but their ideas about his role, aims, and attributes changed over time. Before we can turn to the witch theorists and exorcists therefore, we need to chart the emergence of the particular type of devil that made their quests so urgent.

From Christianity's very beginning, the devil, as Christ's opponent in the New Testament, fulfilled a vital role. But both the nature of his identity and the threat he was believed to pose underwent a gradual but crucial change during the late medieval period. The devil had always been a tempter. He had tempted Christ in the desert, offering him all the kingdoms and all the glory.[1] He also sought to lead the saints astray, enticing them to leave behind their chosen religious vocations. As Chapter 3 has shown, St. Anthony of Egypt (c. 251–356) spent decades in the desert vexed by demons.[2] These attempted to seduce the putative founder of monasticism with offers of wealth and power, and even—as Anthony's hagiographer put it—"took upon him the shape of a woman and imitated all her acts simply to beguile Anthony."[3] The fact that the temptation of St. Anthony came to fascinate early modern visual artists shows the endurance of this aspect of the devil's character.[4]

From the outset, though, the devil offered more than just worldly delights. He also attempted to seduce with things that were *seemingly* good. He was a liar and deceiver. Christ told a group of Jews that they were liars and belonged to the devil who was "the father of lies" (John 8.44; NIV). The Apostle Paul warned the Christians of Corinth of rival "false apostles"; Satan "masquerades as an angel of light" and therefore his followers "also masquerade as servants of righteousness" (2 Cor. 11.13–15; NIV). The same seductive demonic

DOI: 10.4324/9781003096603-12

lies appear in medieval hagiography. The devil sought to seduce Martin of Tours (d. 398), one of the most famous medieval saints, by taking on the appearance of Christ himself, although the holy man was not fooled. The devil's disguise had been too ornate; the real Christ would not have been clothed "in a royal robe, and with a crown of precious stones and gold encircling his head."[5]

The devil that vexed the saints was primarily conceived of as a spiritual creature, deceiving the senses, corrupting the imagination, and invading the body. One of Christ's most famous miracles in the New Testament was the exorcising of the Gerasene or Gadarene demoniac, a man possessed with a "legion" of "unclean spirits" which were sent into a herd of swine that then drowned in the sea.[6] This was by no means the only healing miracle which involved the casting out of demons; other passages appear to hold devils responsible for a range of illnesses, from epilepsy to blindness.[7] Exorcism—the power and authority to cast out demons—proved the truth of the Christian message, and was granted to the apostles, and consequently held by the church, as Christ's representative on earth.[8]

From the outset, then, the devil served as a necessary foil to God, to Christ, and to his followers. As a faith, Christianity thrived on resistance. The devil offered a convenient explanation for any opposition to Christian truths and instantly delegitimised it (as the hidden yet active agent lurking behind such resistance). Such—quite literal—demonisation took on added significance in the early modern period, when the devil's identity as a "contingent being, always a function of another, not an independent entity" fully came into its own.[9] Both the encounter with rival religions and belief systems "abroad" and the descent into virulent religious disagreements "at home" supercharged the Christian devil's role as a *spiritual* tempter. The devil's *active* resistance in the face of Christian truths variously explained the persistence of New World idolatry, the allure of new (Protestant) heresies, or the continued hold of old (Catholic) superstitions.[10] Such competing orthodoxies helped foster what Stuart Clark called "an age of cognitive extremism," a mindset inclined to think in terms of binary opposition and inversion and which, in the process, fashioned an elaborate demonic netherworld that mirrored and mocked divine truths.[11] The accompanying raising of moral standards also provided another impulse to the older spiritual conception of the devil as the inner voice that encouraged opposition to the exacting standards set by the period's more puritanical regimes.[12]

The devil could not only be found lurking in the recesses of one's mind, however. The spiritual conception laid a fertile foundation for a new and improved devil, one that could take on physical form (almost any physical form, in fact), secure human allies, and cause murder and mayhem. The origins of this development predate the European Reformations. Some elements for this supercharged devil were already implicit in scripture, notably in the book of Job and in the gospels where he was already described as the "the prince of this world" (John 12.31; NIV). Whether or not he *took* physical form in early saints' lives, he certainly *appeared* in them.

This transition of the devil into a physical entity has important implications for our chapter—there could be no "devil finders" without it—and for the development of the early modern witch hunt. Starting from the early 14th century, the idea that the devil was able to form a pact with human beings gradually gained currency.[13] In typically self-referential fashion, the existence of such pacts proved the devil's physicality (and existence) and *vice versa*. Two very different factors can be invoked to explain how demons got bodies: the revival of ritual magic and the demonisation of heresy. The rediscovery of Greek philosophy (in particular Neoplatonism), exposure to Arab learning, and the rise of courts and universities as sites of culture and learning all contributed to a renaissance of magic during middle to late Middle Ages. Such magic was not necessarily "demonic"; strands of it were also devoted to uncovering and manipulating hidden or occult sympathies within nature. Yet the survival of many medieval manuscripts containing spells and incantations which forced demons to provide quick riches, effortless learning, and winged transport demonstrates the ready appeal of such acts of necromancy, especially among the "clerical underworld."[14] This magical tradition continued well into the early modern period (note, for example, the astrologer John Dee at the Elizabethan court); depending on the historian, it may even have fed into the early Scientific Revolution.[15]

This type of underground devil finder also came to be seen as a tragic and doomed figure. The life of one early 16th-century German *magus*, Johann Faust, became the stuff of legend, inspiring a play by Christopher Marlowe in which the despairing scholar screamed the name of his demon—"ah, Mephistophilis!"—as he was dragged off the stage towards hell.[16] The same tradition of learned male magic, and in particular the idea of contracting with the devil that lay at its heart, also fed into the early modern witch hunt. In 1580, the French scholar Jean Bodin appended the Sorbonne's 1398 condemnation of the "magical arts" and "nefarious invocations" to his *De La Démonomanie des sorciers* (On the Demon-Mania of Witches) as if it inevitably referred to the mostly illiterate, mostly female targets of his own work.[17] (Conversely, an elderly John Dee thought that the 1604 Witchcraft Act was directly targeting a *magus* like himself.)[18]

If the revival of ritual magic owed much to the intellectually curious and lazy among the "clerical underground," then the demonisation of heresy can be directly tied to the founding of a new intellectual avant-garde in the form of the Dominican Order. The vast majority of early witchcraft theorists, including Heinrich Kramer (Latinised as Institoris), the author of the infamous 1486/7 *Malleus maleficarum* (Hammer of the Female Witches), can be found among its ranks. These witch theorists (or demonologists) are one of the two groups of devil finders with which we shall be concerning ourselves. They must be placed within the context of a longer and deadly campaign against heresy that had already been underway for some time. The burning of heretics in Orléans in 1022 marked the first time in almost 600 years that anyone in eastern Europe was executed for the crime of heresy. When the papacy appointed inquisitors to root out heresy in the early 13th century, many belonged to the Order of Preachers recently founded by St. Dominic. Historians debate the extent to which the heresies of the Cathars, Waldensians, Fraticelli, and others were ever real; certainly their elaborate theologies existed only in the minds of their highly trained persecutors.[19] These heresies—at least in the hostile texts that purport to describe them—often espoused a form of dualism which granted the devil extraordinary power, and it would not be long before heretics themselves came to be seen as devil worshippers.[20] One of the earliest large-scale witch hunts, that of Arras (in present-day northern France) in 1460, referred to the witches as Waldensians or *Vaudois*, although one of the persecution's main defenders admitted that they were not "open heretics" like the original Waldensians but "secret and occult idolaters."[21] The language of "heresy"—albeit a particularly female variety, "a Heresy … of Sorceresses"—still pervades the *Malleus*.[22] Only during the Reformation era—when heresy paradoxically was everywhere—did the witch emerge from her heretical cocoon as a distinct apostate and devil worshipper in her own right.

The gradual emergence of the figure of the witch as an object of fear and belief in late medieval scholarly circles was, therefore, closely and necessarily tied to that of the devil's rise as a *physical* entity. The question as to how he could take physical form became the overriding question for self-appointed devil finders during the 15th century because physical (sexual) contact with human followers would be impossible without it.[23] In turn, these investigations led to a new site where the devil could be found: the witches' sabbat. Its elaboration, down to the smallest Baroque details, reached a peak around the turn of the 17th century. Yet, as already noted, spiritual conceptions of the devil persisted, and the devil also took on a bodily form in a more literal way, by taking possession of a human body. He further continued to be invoked to explain the inexplicable, especially where spiritual phenomena were involved; his agency was suspected behind ghosts, fairies, changelings, poltergeists, and other creatures of popular belief whose existence did not fit Christian theology.[24]

As noted at the outset, the remainder of this chapter will be devoted to the two principal ways in which the devil appeared to reveal himself to humanity during the early modern period: witchcraft and demonic possession. Both of these phenomena were, in different ways, dependent upon the devil's physicality and became more threatening as the devil appeared more active as the end of the world apparently drew ever nearer. They also presented two distinct groups of devil finders—witchcraft theorists and exorcists—with two distinct vexing problems which we shall consider, in turn. We shall conclude by exploring how the devil gradually lost his body in the later 17th century, making the search for him ever more problematic.

### Problem I: Observations from a Distance

One problem vexed devil finders: one did not usually find the devil. He found you—often when you were at your most vulnerable. The confessions of witches often included such moments of seduction. In 1604, for instance, Nicolas Raimbault, a poor 50-year-old farmer from a small village in the Duchy of Lorraine, voluntarily confessed that an "evil spirit" had seduced him after the purchase of a (it turned out) sick horse had ruined him financially.[25] The devil was often said to give some money which then later disappeared, but other, non-pecuniary motives usually played a greater role. In 1613, for instance, another Lorraine suspect, 30-year-old Jeanne Mercier, confessed under torture that she had called out to the devil after her husband had beaten her. She had refused to go to work in the fields because she had not yet finished her housework. When she called upon the devil outside in the garden, he appeared as a man in black who offered to make her very happy.[26] In other cases, the devil's seduction was akin to that of a lover, making false promises he did not keep after sex. One of the saddest (though fictionalised) accounts can be found in *The Witch of Edmonton*. In this 1621 play, Elizabeth Sawyer made a pact with the devil (a canine familiar aptly named "Dog") *after* being physically assaulted and accused of being a witch by her neighbours, reasoning that "'Tis all one/To be a witch as to be counted one."[27]

Such descriptions of demonic seduction often feel sincere because they were likely rooted in real life. They reflected misery and abuse, occasionally even sexual trauma.[28] As such, they provided those caught up in the nightmare of witchcraft accusations with an opportunity to redirect some of the blame for the harm they were meant to have caused onto others, even if this. would not save them. At least implicitly, these narratives also served another purpose. The question as to why someone would turn away from God and give themselves up to his infernal enemy required some sort of satisfactory answer, especially as the devil's physical appearance provided undeniable proof for the truth of the Christian message in its own topsy-turvy way: as one overly enthusiastic English exorcist put it pithily, "if no Divells, no God."[29] This was not a concern, it should be said, that preoccupied the often poorly educated legal officials of a rural duchy like Lorraine—finding witches was enough of a challenge for them. But a small minority, including the duchy's *procureur-général* Nicolas Remy, was intrigued enough by the hidden demonic netherworld that witches represented that they spent thousands of pages describing what pious eyes could not see.

Just as with the ritual magicians that preceded them, the witches of the late medieval and early modern period made a pact with the devil. To a large degree, the early modern witch hunt was the result of a merger: it brought together popular, folkloric witchcraft beliefs, common to most pre-modern societies, with elite ideas about the Christian devil's powers.[30] Yet where the pact was concerned, there were notable differences as well. Rather than signing a written pact with the devil, as Faust, for instance, was meant to have done (and several such documents still survive in archives), illiterate female witches contracted with the devil through sex.[31] The nature of the devil's relationship with his witches made his physicality a necessity, as did his role in causing the death and destruction of which witches were accused. Witchcraft could not function if demons could not impact on the physical world. Opposition to the idea that demons, as spiritual creatures, could take bodily form was rooted in Aristotelian natural philosophy which posited a radical separation between body and spirit. In his *Summa theologica*, the Dominican theologian Thomas Aquinas (d. 1274) sought to reconcile the different demands of philosophy and theology by arguing that angels (good and bad) possessed no bodies but could assume them. Of the four traditional elements, spirits were mostly associated with air; demons, for instance, commonly appeared as aerial creatures in medieval saints' lives.[32]

The subject of angelic bodies became a standard part of the curriculum of the medieval university, "haunt[ing] Scholastic theologians and eventuality inspir[ing] the specialised subculture of witchcraft theorists."[33] 15th-century devil finders devoted considerable sections of their manuscripts to the issue, which probably reflected the scepticism and resistance these authors encountered in wider elite society when they applied these angelogical insights in their efforts to make sense of the witches of popular belief. The corporeality of demons was thus the predictable opening gambit of the Waldensian Arras treatise already cited.[34] The Dominican friar Nicolas Jacquier made the most radical 15th-century case for "demonic realism" in his roughly contemporary *Flagellum hereticorum fascinariorum* (The Scourge of the Heretical Enchanters, 1458). The *Flagellum* highlights the importance of the witches' sensory perceptions as a proof of the reality of demonic bodies; these devils had to be real, Jacquier argues, or witches would not have been "worn out and exhausted after one or two days" of extreme sex with them.[35] In the form of (male) *incubi* and (female) *succubi*, demons were able to have intercourse with witches of both sexes, and the *Malleus* was particularly obsessed with the possibility that the semen of wicked men might be harvested to impregnate witches and so increase the devil's following.[36] When sex featured in confessions, female witches frequently emphasised the coldness of the devil's "member," a striking consistency in trial records across Europe.[37] The reality and corporeality of demons were also exemplified through the devil's mark; this mark on the witch's skin was supposedly insensible—and thought to be a diabolical inversion of the Christian baptism—but the search for it obviously was not; it even justified the shaving of suspects' hair and the inspection of their genitals (in case the mark was hidden in these places).[38]

The confessions and *bodies* of witches thus provided a proof of the corporeal reality of demons, and indirectly a whole host of wider religious truths as well. In a thought-provoking though controversial book, Walter Stephens has argued that demonology was underpinned by spiritual anxieties. Demonology provided empirical proofs for the reality of the spirit world—proofs that devils could actually be located and therefore existed—to a group of deeply worried thinkers who shared "an uncommonly desperate need to believe."[39] While the latter claim pushes the evidence too far, the bodily nature of demons was certainly the linchpin around which demonology evolved. As Aquinas had already observed with regard to (good) angels, they require "an assumed body, not for themselves, but on our account" —so that we may interact with them.[40] As demonology developed as a field of academic study during the 16th century, it moved out of the inquisitorial and scholastic straitjacket to become a pre-occupation for a wide variety of devil finders, some of whom, like the French lawyer and philosopher Jean Bodin, were in fact highly unorthodox themselves.[41] It certainly would be a struggle to reduce this heterogenous field, populated by physicians and lawyers as much as theologians, to one form of spiritual anxiety.[42] But the result was that witchcraft was no longer just another heretical sect. It was a fully fledged phenomenon in its own right.[43]

At the same time, the elaboration of witchcraft continued. The period's "cognitive extremism" contributed to its development, but the internal logic of the science of demons must also have played a role. The idea of the witches' sabbat had already been present in the writings of some 15th-century demonologists, a logical corollary to the gatherings of other heretics and perhaps Jews as well.[44] These early accounts contain some examples of inversion. The Arras treatise, for instance, refers to witches adoring the devil by kissing his backside.[45] Yet the idea of the sabbat came to much greater prominence during the late 16th century when witchcraft prosecutions took on a size and scale that they had not had before.[46] The idea that the devil sought to be "God's Ape" and wished to be worshipped like him has a long and complex history, but it intersected with this tendency towards inversion and combined with folkloric beliefs to generate ever more elaborate sabbat narratives.[47] The extent to which inversion shaped early modern depictions of the sabbat was seemingly limited only by the need for intelligibility. Well-to-do witches, for instance, did not become poor at the sabbat—for why would they ally themselves with the devil otherwise? Such inversion even extended to the dancing; several authors reported that witches danced back-to-back ostensibly so that they could be on the look-out for any intruders.[48] Sabbat engravings, virtually absent from early witchcraft iconography, started to appear in print from the 1590s and became ever more elaborate with time.[49]

Charting this process of elaboration across time and space is a virtually impossible task. It is difficult to pinpoint where and when ideas first emerged and how they spread. It is also tempting to project later additions to the sabbat onto earlier iterations. One striking inversion, for instance, seems to be a particularly late addition. In 1594, the magistrates of the Bordeaux Parlement, the appeals court for Southwest France, encountered the sensational case of Jeanne Bosdeau, a young girl supposedly seduced by an Italian magician. Her case was probably the first to involve a priest who performed a "black mass" at the sabbat, complete with black communion wafers and with the devil's piss replacing the wine. This presented not only a disturbing abuse of the Catholic sacraments and liturgy but also provided the fullest realisation possible of the devil's aspiration to be God's Ape.[50] An account by one of the judges involved, Florimond de Raemond, described these perversions in great detail in his 1597 *L'Antichrist* (The Antichrist), but the devout Catholic could not bring himself to acknowledge that this mockery of a mass was said, not by "a man dressed as a priest" but by a real one.[51] It is difficult to trace the influence of such stories even among the French elite. What is noteworthy is that another of the Bordeaux judges involved in the Bosdeau case—and Raemond's brother-in-law—Pierre de Lancre, was sent to prosecute witches in the Pays de Labourd, a Basque-speaking territory on the border with Spain, where, in 1609, he located a large group of witch-priests, three of whom were executed.[52] De Lancre and his colleague, Jean d'Espagnet, also interrogated a great many children and teenagers who claimed to have been forcefully taken to sabbat. No witch theorist ever came closer to finding the devil than De Lancre, whose 1612 *Tableau de l'inconstance des mauvais anges et démons* (On the inconstancy of evil angels and demons) offered the most detailed descriptions of witches dancing, feasting, and having sex with the devil—one leading modern historian has even called him the "poet of the Sabbath."[53]

The Basque witchcraft panic, which swiftly crossed the border into Spain, produced incredibly rich sabbat narratives which cannot be reduced merely to the judicial imagination. The accounts, for instance, include many stories involving toads: as ingredients for potion making, as demonic familiars (dressed in velvet), and even as involved in childcare at the sabbat.[54] Much of this material has deep folkloric roots, as the similarities in the material uncovered by the Spanish Inquisition and the Bordeaux judges—two legal systems with very different conceptions of justice—highlight.[55] It is not even clear how much of the "black mass" trope can be traced back to de Lancre. Elaborations also reflect the lived experiences of the witches and witnesses, who attended normal, non-demonic church services. An offertory during which money was collected for a witchcraft legal defence fund seems a logical, if inventive, extension to the "black mass" imagery.[56] Yet few witch hunters would embody the idea of a "devil-finder" more fully than Pierre de Lancre, and fewer still came as close to actually finding him. Together with Espagnet, de Lancre climbed to the top of a rock where the sabbat was meant to have been held. And there, he believed he could still make out traces of the base of the cooking pot that had been used.[57] The judges asked those they interrogated to re-enact the dances of the sabbat.[58] De Lancre asked one witch to fly in front of them, and when she complained that she lacked the ointment to do so, he asked her to bring some back next time she went to the sabbat.[59] The sabbat was even held in his bedchamber, although much to his disappointment he slept through the event.[60]

Yet de Lancre was also aware that interest in the sabbat in French learned circles had begun to wane, and his *Tableau* was being overtaken by events. On 30 April 1611, a single priest named Louis Gaufridy was burnt at the stake in Aix-en-Provence for the crime of witchcraft.[61] As de Lancre noted when dedicating the *Tableau*, his colleagues in Aix "encountered and discovered in a few days things so rare and unheard of, disclosed by a single magician and witch that all the books which discuss witchcraft before him appear only to have related insignificant common tales which circulate among the populace."[62] How much more, de Lancre implied, could be learned from the hundreds of witches and witnesses that he had interrogated? Yet it was the Gaufridy case—not the Basque witch hunt—that became a contemporary sensation, worthy of discussion in Parisian literary salons. One news pamphlet was even translated into English and published in London. The Gaufridy case not only offered witchcraft but also sex and demonic possession, for the priest was accused of having bewitched and seduced a young nun, Madeleine Demandols de la Palud. And in its wake, over the next several decades, France was rocked by a number of prominent possession cases, many of which involving young girls and bad priests.

If witchcraft kept the devil hidden from view, only ever to be glimpsed through the words and bodies of witches, then possession cases offered another group of devil finders—exorcists—an opportunity to interrogate him firsthand. Yet possession, too, brought problems in its wake.

## Problem II: Discerning Spirits

While the evidence of witchcraft in scripture was contested, the biblical warrant for demonic possession was almost incontrovertible. While witchcraft sceptics could suggest alternative translations or meanings for references to witchcraft and sorcery, Christ very clearly carried out a number of dispossessions. Yet like witchcraft, its newfangled cousin with whom it shared a certain amount of DNA, demonic possession also came to much greater prominence during the early modern period.[63] The 16th and 17th centuries have long been described as the "golden age of the demonic."[64] Historians have not only likened possession to an epidemic, but suggested that the experience was so common that its "banality" and "triviality" have been emphasised.[65] Some cases, especially those involving a witch as a culprit, such as the Gaufridy trial, gained widespread notoriety. The mass possession at an Ursuline convent in Loudun in the 1630s—possibly Europe's most famous— even made the town something of a tourist destination. And the exorcism of the possessed nuns provided an opportunity to convert Protestant visitors to the Catholic faith.[66] Yet there were thousands of other cases that escaped the public eye; many will have left no traces behind in the records.[67]

To some extent, possession and witchcraft overlap. Witches could be accused of causing possession, as Gaufridy had been. But as that suggests, to be possessed by the devil was fundamentally different from being in league with him. Possession was usually unvoluntary. Although possession could have been a punishment for one's sins, it could also be a test of one's faith—one which had to be suffered piously and patiently. It could even be caused by witchcraft in which case the possessed was entirely blameless. The emphasis partly depended on confessional background. Calvinists, uncomfortable with granting the devil too much agency, emphasised his role as a tempter who posed a spiritual rather than physical threat, offering temptations which the possessed had to conquer themselves.[68] Yet for all early modern Christians, demonic possession was first and foremost an affliction, rather than a legal or criminal matter. This explains why possession has left fewer traces behind in judicial archives. Instead, as a spiritual affliction or a physical illness, it was primarily a matter for physicians and clergy to argue over—not lawyers. The resulting role and position of the demoniac—essentially that of a victim to be supported or a patient to be cured, rather than a devil worshipper to be prosecuted—have made possession into "a methodological land mine for historians."[69]

In many instances, it was not the possessed person but others—including exorcists, our second group of devil finders—who diagnosed the affliction. In theory, such a diagnosis should have been straightforward. The possessed should possess the knowledge, skills, and strength of the devil who had invaded their body. Thus, the possessed were expected to speak in foreign tongues and be deeply knowledgeable about all matters human and divine; they were meant to evince superstrength, vomit up strange objects, and possibly even to levitate.[70] From our modern, secular perspective, this should also mean that demonic possession should always be easily disproven—few demoniacs would have been able to discourse about theology in ancient Greek. Robert Mandrou, an early French witchcraft historian, argued in the late 1960s that increased scepticism towards the cases of mass possession that roiled the country in the early 17th century spilled over into the adjoining field of witchcraft, casting doubt on those prosecutions.[71] In reality, however, this rarely happened. Prominent possession cases often drew attention from physicians who proffered alternative natural diagnoses, particularly the female diseases of hysteria and melancholy, but they did not always carry the day.

Often the behaviour of the possessed was strange enough already. In one of Protestant England's most notorious possession cases—that of fourteen-year old Mary Glover in London in 1602—the devil supposedly possessing the girl almost never spoke, except when a preternaturally soft voice demanded the execution of Elizabeth Jackson, the old woman accused of bewitching her, muttering "hang her, hang her."[72] Yet every encounter with Jackson, who had once scolded Glover, sent the girl into strange fits from which only the lord's prayer—in particular the line "deliver us from evil"—could release her.[73] While the teenager could not speak in tongues, she had fits when Jackson was secretly brought into her presence—and did not when confronted by a woman dressed up in the accused witch's clothes.[74] When the London physician Edward Jorden attempted to propose the alternative diagnosis of "passio hysterica" (a supposed disease of the womb) but could not guarantee a cure for her condition, he received a telling rebuke from the presiding judge, Lord Anderson. "Then in my conscience, it is not natural," he railed, "for if you tell me neither a Natural cause, of it, nor a natural remedy, I will tell you, that it is not natural."[75]

From the viewpoint of the exorcists, whether Protestant or Catholic, the fact that the possessed evinced not only the strengths of the devils but also their weaknesses was still more important. The devil, as a mere creature, had to acknowledge the superiority of the creator. Armed with a divine arsenal, exorcists were able to hurt the devil inside and cause its expulsion. The nameless devil possessing Mary Glover, as we saw, had to acknowledge the power of prayer. The possessed nuns of Loudun writhed with pain when they were sprinkled with holy water or had a eucharist or relic thrust upon them. Indeed, in confessionally contested settings, the devil often put Protestants at the backfoot. Where Catholics subscribed to the continued immanence of the holy in material objects, Protestants had to make do with the much smaller toolkit of prayer, bible reading and fasting.

The surge in spectacular cases of mass possession in early 17th-century France often centred on convents, and so can be linked to the resurgent Tridentine Catholic Church and its campaign against an increasingly marginalised Protestant minority. While the devils possessing the nuns of Loudun shrieked out in agony when exposed to Catholic weaponry, the debate about the fate of Urbain Grandier, the witch-priest held responsible for their fate, turned into a polemic between French Protestants and Catholics.[76] Yet the efficacy of the exorcism campaign was rather undercut by the unwillingness of the devils to definitively leave the nuns' bodies. Different rivalries played a similar role in England where radical Puritans used a form of exorcism against the Church of England; successful dispossessions gave these preachers a more direct divine warrant for their preaching than ordination by the established church.[77]

Demonic possession, then, is a methodological minefield not simply because of the possessed themselves—we obviously cannot look inside their heads—but also because their experiences and behaviour were interpreted, guided, and constructed by those who surrounded them, and who, in the most prominent cases at least, could use them, almost as actors, in their own polemical puppet shows. Once established, a public diagnosis of demonic possession could be impossible to escape except through a successful exorcism. The devil's position as the "father of lies" made recantations difficult because they enabled exorcists and other participants invested in the diagnosis to disregard attempted retractions. In fact, in Italy the Inquisition took a different tack, refusing to accept the testimony of the possessed altogether out of fear of demonic deception.[78] In a supplication to the French crown, Urbain Grandier wrote that the nuns "have discharged me several times and declared themselves frauds in accusing me. But the misfortune is that if they declare me innocent, it is a pretense; if guilty, a truth … [The] exorcists say openly that these devils are angels when they accuse me, and demons when they excuse me."[79] His plea failed; the exorcists were so invested in their devil-finding that they exorcised the wood in Grandier's pyre to make sure he burned—and it was they who lit the fire.[80] Although the devils continued to cling to the bodies of the possessed nuns after the priest's execution, they were able to report on his continued torments in hell.[81]

The relationship between the possessed person and their exorcist was therefore certainly open to abuse, and exorcists did not always enjoy the best of reputations.[82] The gendered nature of possession—the majority of demoniacs were women, while exorcists were invariably male—plays a role here. In 1642, for instance, the exorcist Geminiano Mazzoni proudly and voluntarily confessed to the Inquisition tribunal in Modena that after discovering that demons would often hide in vaginas, he resorted to using his hand and, if all else failed, his penis to push them out of their secret hiding place.[83] Although Mazzoni offers an extreme example, the gendered relationship between the female possessed and the male exorcist was almost by definition imbalanced as the latter sought to assert his control over the woman's supposed inner demons. Moreover, even more than the body of the witch, that of the possessed bore marks of demonic affliction, for instance, through fits or displays of extreme rigidity or agility, that demanded physical dominance.

However unequal, the participation of the possessed in this dialogue still poses considerable interpretative difficulties. A significant strand of historical scholarship has approached demonic possession as a "cultural" or "theatrical performance" and demoniacs as "fairly accomplished actors" who followed commonly accepted "scripts."[84] Approaching possession as theatre enables historians to sidestep the unpalatable question as to what the possessed may actually have experienced. The comparison with witchcraft is again instructive here, as there were very few cases in which witches confessed voluntarily. The "witch" was thus an identity that was almost always ascribed to a person by others and subsequently extorted from her during interrogation or torture. Possession cases were different because they *originated* with a person's strange, unusual, or outright diabolical behaviour, even if the diagnosis of demonic possession was made or confirmed only later by expert devil finders. Scripts alone—however convenient an explanation—thus cannot explain the origins of particular possession cases. Yet origins did not have to be demonic. The saga of sixteen-year-old Nicole Obry, whose possession became an early showcase of Tridentine Catholicism during the French Wars of Religion, for instance, began on All Souls's Day 1565 when she went to pray for her deceased grandfather and—appropriately enough, given the religious significance of the day—believed that she saw his ghost.[85] The mass possession of Loudun had its roots in strange nocturnal spiritual apparitions, glimpsed just as the city emerged out of a devastating and deadly plague. It was only when experts were consulted that these spirits became demonic and were believed to have moved inside the bodies of the nuns themselves.[86] Nor can a theatrical framework properly account for the way in which possessions could spread outwards. One of the Loudun exorcists, Jean-Joseph Surin, became himself possessed and spent a large part of his life as a mute, subjected to the derision and abuse of his fellow Jesuits.[87] Later in life, Surin authored a number of lengthy manuscripts based on his ineffable experiences in which he maintained that theology had "no more powerful argument" for the truth of the Christian message than demonic possession.[88]

But we should not take these famous cases to be typical. While crucial theological truths were at stake in Loudun, the theatrical pyrotechnics of the majority of "mundane" possessions would have been minimal.

We cannot, then, dismiss the lived experiences of the possessed that easily; yet their interpretation presents us with some uncomfortable options. The two "natural" explanations for their symptoms—(mental) illness and fraud—come with considerable historiographical baggage. The former, as we have already seen in Glover's case, was already a viable medical diagnosis in the early modern period and the invariable go-to explanation for 19th-century historians, when such a diagnosis was also presented as a particularly feminine malady. Historians have come a long way since Andrew Dickson White's claim that "the fetichisms and superstitions of the world are bolstered up mainly by women."[89] The late 19th-century historian, who penned infamous chapters entitled "from 'demoniacal possession' to insanity" and "from diabolism to hysteria," claimed that these "crazed women" and "unfortunate beings" were "exactly like those … in our modern lunatic asylums."[90] Accusations of fraud come with similar baggage—this diagnosis too was already used to discredit those claiming visions, not merely demonic but also divine. The Henrician regime executed Elizabeth Barton, the so-called "Holy Nun of Kent" who prophesied against the king's marriage to Anne Boleyn, as a traitor and a fraud.[91]

It is this alternative, yet often ignored, possibility of divine visions that helps us to make some sense of the participation of the possessed themselves, especially in Catholic Europe but also on the radical fringes of the Protestant Reformation.[92] The late medieval church saw the rise of female visionaries—most famously saints Catherine of Siena and Bridget of Sweden—who provided a role model and inspiration for later would-be holy women, so-called *sante vive* (living saints), especially in Italy.[93] The role of visionary was one of the few avenues available for spiritually gifted women to contribute to religious reform or the improvement of their communities. Yet growing fear of the devil, when combined with increased suspicions of both female spirituality and interiorised forms of prayer, created a considerable backlash. These anxieties were new only in their level of intensity. As we saw, tempting the saints was part of the devil's job description, just as discerning and resisting such temptations and resisting them was part of the duty of would-be saint. The devil thus forms an inevitable part of the lives of such famous Counter-Reformation saints (and visionaries) as Ignatius of Loyola and Teresa of Avila.[94] During the early modern period, the reverse proved to be true as well. There was also something saintly about being demonically possessed. Whatever the original, unknowable, and—ultimately, therefore—irrelevant origins of their experiences, the diagnosis of demonic possession still enabled visionaries to confess the truth of the Christian message, but in a topsy-turvy diabolical way that allowed them to shock and turn subtext into text at the same time.[95]

Even if we cannot and should not diagnose demonic possession from afar, we do well to recognise that it sits at the extreme end of a continuum of spiritual experiences. The devil was part of the interior life of many early modern Christians. In the Protestant, especially Calvinist context, where the elect were meant to be completely certain of their salvation, spiritual doubts and suicidal thoughts were attributed to Satan's assaults or temptations. Even when this did not rise to the level of demonic possession, these Christians felt that Satan dwelled inside of them or had captured their soul on account of their inherent sinfulness.[96] At the same time, we must also accept that our problem of discernment is a version of the one once faced by the exorcists. The fluidity and contested nature of the diagnosis of demonic possession was compounded by the fact that it was based on the word and the consent of the (supposedly) possessed and could therefore never be taken for granted. The diagnosis contained within it the germs of its own refutation, making a potential mockery of those who made it. When contested religious truths were at stake—as was the case in Urbain Grandier's Loudun and Mary Glover's London—then such discernment would never be accepted by all. While our first group of devil finders—witchcraft theorists—had to make do with the testimony of the devils' human followers, the direct encounter with supposedly embodied devils did not bring our second group the complete and unequivocal assurances they sought or expected.

## The Devil's Vanishing Act

"The greatest trick the devil ever pulled was convincing the world that he did not exist." This well-known quip, ascribed to a variety of 19th-century authors, was usually part of a lament about the rise of atheism and scepticism.[97] The reasons for the demise of both witch hunting and demonic possession—at the elite level, at least—are much less clear than they once were. Their decline can no longer be ascribed to the progress of rationalism. Even those committed to a role for intellectual history in accounting for this change in elite attitudes accept that the Enlightenment rejected magic and witchcraft for "bad reasons."[98] Where witch hunting is concerned, this change of outlook can be attributed to growing elite disdain for popular—vulgar—opinion; demonology, as I argued elsewhere, "became problematic because it increasingly came to be seen as an elite edifice built on the words of (old, poor, uneducated) women."[99] Still, the fact that the decline of witch hunting and the retreat of cases of demonic possession largely went hand in hand suggests that changes in elite outlook must also be linked, at least in part, to changing attitudes towards the figure of the devil and the demonic.[100]

New *modes* of thinking—rather than new ideas—made the landscape more inhospitable to demons, and with them, to their human hosts and allies, even if we certainly should not conceive of these changes as a process of linear development.[101] We could, first of all, point to a wider reconfiguration of the supernatural. As Euan Cameron has shown, both "religion" and "superstition" took on new meanings, aligned no longer in opposition to each other but placed in a complex three-way relationship with "science."[102] Michelle Pfeffer has drawn our attention to the growing role played by the "historicising" of beliefs—the growing recognition that beliefs about the supernatural themselves had a history, and thus a possibly human origin that could be discredited.[103] Among these factors, the shifting epistemological fortunes of the senses—seeing for oneself, rather than hearing others speak—also cannot be ignored. This was the problem which, in different ways, confronted both groups of devil finders in this chapter. Christians could—by definition—not see the nightmarish world of witchcraft for themselves; they could only *hear* it being spoken about by those who confessed.[104] The emergence of vision as the "queen" of the senses was a crucial nail in witchcraft's coffin at least.[105] Other spiritual phenomena, such as poltergeists, fell victim to the same difficulty, and could not, as Joseph Glanvill discovered, be easily reconciled to the expectations of the "New Science," with its emphasis on observation, promoted by the Royal Society.[106]

The devil thus vanished from sight just as the need to "see" him grew more pressing. The Dutch Reformed pastor Balthasar Bekker published the provocative *The World Bewitched* (1691–4) which did not deny the existence of angels and demons but denied their ability to take on corporeal form. Bekker's motivations have been much debated and deserve further study. While some historians have attributed his scepticism to his commitment to Cartesian dualism—the radical separation between body and spirit—and even represented him as an early figure in the "Radical Enlightenment," others have pointed to the pastor's solidly Calvinist commitment to God's sovereignty and providence which should have left no room for the agency of demons.[107] However controversial at the time, the argument that demons were real but incorporeal, and thus could neither communicate with humans nor invade their bodies—that demons, in other words, could not be found—was also an attempt at compromise. The science of demons had always been a rhetorical search for common ground: *some* of the many reported instances of demonic activity had to be true, while denying that everything was false seemed dangerous.[108] As the threat of the demonic receded, the boundaries of what seemed plausible shifted. Demons, witches, and the possessed no longer inhabited the present, only the past, perhaps even only the distant apostolic past. The devil's role retreated to that of a spiritual tempter. He gradually lost the ability to maintain a physical form. As a result, he could no longer be found.

## Notes

1 Mark 1.12–3; Luke 4.1–13; Matthew 4.1–11. All subsequent biblical references are to the New International Version.

2 Athanasius, "Life of St. Anthony," in *Nicene and Post-Nicene Fathers*, ed. Philip Schaff, Henry Wace, and Kevin Knight, trans. H. Ellershaw, vol. 4 (Buffalo, 1892). http://www.newadvent.org/fathers/2811.htm

3 Athanasius, "Life of St. Anthony," 5.

4 On visual representations of St. Anthony, see Stuart Clark, "Angels of Light and Images of Sanctity," in *Angels of Light? Sanctity and the Discernment of Spirits in the Early Modern Period*, ed. Clare Copeland and Jan Machielsen (Leiden, 2013), 279–304. For the devil in medieval saints' lives, see Florence Chave-Mahir, *L'exorcisme des possédés dans l'Eglise d'Occident (Xe–XIVe siècle)* 10 (Turnhout, 2011), esp. chaps. 5–7.

5 Sulpitius Severus, "On the Life of St. Martin," in *Nicene and Post-Nicene Fathers*, trans. Alexander Roberts, Second Series 11 (Buffalo, 1894), chap. 6. https://www.newadvent.org/fathers/3501.htm

6 Mark 5.1–20; Matthew 8.28–34; Luke 8.26–39.

7 See, for example, Matthew 17.14–18; Matthew 12.22–32.

8 On the apologetic function of exorcism in the early church, see Andrea Nicolotti, *Esorcismo cristiano e possessione diabolica tra II e III secolo* (Turnhout, 2011), 51–4.

9 Stuart Clark, partially citing Neil Forsyth: Stuart Clark, *Thinking with Demons: The Idea of Witchcraft in Early Modern Europe* (Oxford, 1997), 9.

10 Fernando Cervantes, "The Devil's Encounter with America," in *Witchcraft in Early Modern Europe: Studies in Culture and Belief*, ed. Jonathan Barry, Marianne Hester, and Gareth Roberts (Cambridge, 1998), 119–44.

11 Clark, *Thinking with Demons*, 39.

12 Nathan Johnstone, *The Devil and Demonism in Early Modern England* (Cambridge, 2006).

13 Alain Boureau, *Satan the Heretic: The Birth of Demonology in the Medieval West*, trans. Teresa Lavender Fagan (Chicago, 2006).

14 The starting point remains Richard Kieckhefer, *Magic in the Middle Ages*, 2nd ed. (Cambridge, 2014). For an example of a necromancer's manual, see Richard Kieckhefer, *Forbidden Rites: A Necromancer's Manual of the Fifteenth Century* (Stroud, 1997). Also useful is the anthology prepared by Brian P. Copenhaver, *The Book of Magic: From Antiquity to the Enlightenment* (London, 2015), especially sections 7 and 8.

15 For a favourable view of magic's early modern vitality and significance, see Brian Copenhaver, "Magic," in *The Cambridge History of Science*, vol. 3: Early Modern Science, ed. Katharine Park and Lorraine Daston (Cambridge, 2006), 518–40. On Dee, see Glyn Parry, *The Arch-Conjuror of England: John Dee* (New Haven, 2011).

16 Christopher Marlowe, *Doctor Faustus with the English Faust Book* (Indianapolis, 2005), 65.

17 Jean Bodin, *De la démonomanie des sorciers* (Paris, 1580), sig. ī3v–4v.

18 Parry, *The Arch-Conjuror of England*, 266.

19 For the view that medieval heresies were "largely mythical" (and a comparison to the early modern witch hunt), see R. I. Moore, *The War on Heresy: Faith and Power in Medieval Europe* (London, 2012), 338.

20 On this topic, the older work by Norman Cohn is still useful; see his *Europe's Inner Demons: An Enquiry Inspired by the Great Witch-Hunt* (London, 1975), esp. chaps. 3 and 4.

21 Anonymous of Arras, "A History of the Case, State, and Condition of the Waldensian Heretics (Witches)," in *The Arras Witch Treatises*, ed. Andrew Colin Gow, Robert B. Desjardins, and François V. Pageau (University Park, 2016), 27.

22 Heinrich Institoris and Jakob Sprenger, *Malleus Maleficarum: The Hammer of Witches*, ed. Christopher S. Mackay (Cambridge, 2009), 69. For the construction of witchcraft as a female heresy, see, in particular, Tamar Herzig, "Flies, Heretics, and the Gendering of Witchcraft," *Magic, Ritual, and Witchcraft* 5, no. 1 (2010): 51–80. https://doi.org/10.1353/mrw.0.0162

23 On these debates within late 15th- and early 16th-century demonology, see, in particular, Walter Stephens, *Demon Lovers: Witchcraft, Sex, and the Crisis of Belief* (Chicago, 2002).

24 For a survey, see Euan Cameron, "Angels, Demons, and Everything in Between: Spiritual Beings in Early Modern Europe," in *Angels of Light? Sanctity and the Discernment of Spirits in the Early Modern Period*, ed. Clare Copeland and Jan Machielsen (Leiden, 2013), 17–52.

25 Case B 3327, no. 4. See the transcription on https://witchcraft.history.ox.ac.uk/pdf/w040.pdf. For a summary of the case, see Robin Briggs, *The Witches of Lorraine* (Oxford, 2007), 243.

26 Case B 3345. See the transcription on https://witchcraft.history.ox.ac.uk/pdf/w047.pdf. For a summary, see Briggs, *Witches of Lorraine*, 169.

27 William Rowley, *The Witch of Edmonton* (Manchester, 1999), 56 (lines 124–25).

28 Anita M. Walker and Edmund H. Dickerman, "Magdeleine Des Aymards: Demonism or Child Abuse in Early Modern France?," *The Psychohistory Review* 24, no. 3 (1996): 239–64.

29 John Darrel, *The Triall of Maist. Dorrell, or A Collection of Defences against Allegations Not yet Suffered to Receiue Convenient Answere Tending to Cleare Him from the Imputation of Teaching Sommers and Others to Counterfeit Possession of Divells* (Middelburg, 1599), 8.

30 For a very helpful survey of the anthropological literature, see Ronald Hutton, *The Witch: A History of Fear, from Ancient Times to the Present* (New Haven, 2017), chap. 1.

31 See, for instance, the devil's pact signed by David Lipsius, a student at the University of Tübingen, in 1596. https://de.wikisource.org/wiki/Teufelspakt_des_David_Lipsius

32 Chave-Mahir, *L'exorcisme des possédés*, 55.

33 Stephens, *Demon Lovers*, 60. Historians have also emphasised the role of the Council of Basel (1431–49) in spreading these theories: Michael D. Bailey and Edward Peters, "A Sabbat of Demonologists: Basel, 1431–1440," *The Historian* 65, no. 6 (2003): 1375–95.

34 Anonymous of Arras, "A History of the Case, State, and Condition of the Waldensian Heretics (Witches)," 21. The sentences were ultimately overturned by a higher court.

35 Jacquier cited in Martine Ostorero, "Promoter of the Sabbat and Diabolical Realism: Nicolas Jacquier's Flagellum Hereticorum Fascinariorum," in *The Science of Demons: Early Modern Authors Facing Witchcraft and the Devil*, ed. Jan Machielsen (London, 2020), 43.

36 The subject occupies questions 3 and 4 of part I of the *Malleus*: Institoris and Sprenger, *Malleus Maleficarum*, 121–38. Often held up as an "exemplary" demonological text, the *Malleus* was in fact highly idiosyncratic. Other very common aspects of demonological discourse discussed in this section, such as the sabbat and the devil's mark, are entirely absent from it.

37 See, for example, Lyndal Roper, *Witch Craze: Terror and Fantasy in Baroque Germany* (New Haven, 2004), 89; Michael Ostling, *Between the Devil and the Host: Imagining Witchcraft in Early Modern Poland* (Oxford, 2011), 218.

38 Katherine Dauge-Roth, *Signing the Body: Marks on Skin in Early Modern France* (London, 2019), chap. 1.

39 Stephens, *Demon Lovers*, 27.

40 Thomas Aquinas, *The Summa Theologiae*, trans. Fathers of the English Dominican Province; ed. Kevin Knight, pars I, question 51. https://www.newadvent.org/summa/1051.htm

41  On Bodin, see Howell A. Lloyd, *Jean Bodin, "This Pre-Eminent Man of France": An Intellectual Biography* (Oxford, 2017).

42  For the many reasons to write about witches, see Clark, *Thinking with Demons*, and the essays collected in *The Science of Demons: Early Modern Authors Facing Witchcraft and the Devil*, ed. Jan Machielsen (London, 2020). See also Chapter 9 in the current collection.

43  It is significant, for instance, that a Catholic theologian, in 1594, could hold an oration outlining why witchcraft and heresy rise together. See Thomas Stapleton, "Cur magia pariter cum haeresi hodie creverit," in *Orationes academicae miscellaneae triginta quatuor*, vol. 1 (Antwerp, 1600), 1–4.

44  In addition to the "sabbat," several early treatises, including the Arras treatise, refer to the gathering of witches as "synagogues." See Anonymous of Arras, "A History of the Case, State, and Condition of the Waldensian Heretics (Witches)," 37. See also Willem de Blécourt, "Sabbath Stories: Towards a New History of Witches' Assemblies," in *The Oxford Handbook of Witchcraft in Early Modern Europe and Colonial America*, ed. Brian P. Levack (Oxford, 2013), 93.

45  Anonymous of Arras, "A History of the Case, State, and Condition of the Waldensian Heretics (Witches)," 38.

46  Witchcraft prosecutions declined during the mid-16th century but picked up pace again especially from the 1570s onwards. See, for example, the case of Lorraine which became one of the most affected territories. Briggs, *The Witches of Lorraine*, 45. In the late 16th century, prosecutions also began to spread to regions not previously affected.

47  On the idea of the devil as "simia Dei," see Anthony Ossa-Richardson, *The Devil's Tabernacle: The Pagan Oracles in Early Modern Thought* (Princeton, 2013), 66.

48  Florimond de Raemond, *L'Antichrist* (Lyon, 1597), 104; Henry Boguet, *An Examen of Witches*, trans. E. Allen Ashwin, ed. Montague Summers (Mineola, 2009), 56 and 284.

49  Charles Zika, *The Appearance of Witchcraft: Print and Visual Culture in Sixteenth-Century Europe* (London, 2007), 206.

50  Raemond, *L'Antichrist*, 103–5; Jules Delpit, ed., *Chronique d'Étienne de Cruseau*, vol. 1 (Bordeaux: G. Gounouilhou, 1879), 85–6.

51  Raemond, *L'Antichrist*, 103.

52  For de Lancre's participation in the Bosdeau trial, see Pierre de Lancre, *Tableau de l'inconstance des mauvais anges et démons où il est amplement traité des sorciers et de la sorcellerie* (Paris, 1612), 104, where De Lancre himself admits to "assisting" in the judgement. On de Lancre, see Jan Machielsen and Thibaut Maus de Rolley, "The Mythmaker of the Sabbat: Pierre de Lancre's *Tableau* de l'inconstance Des Mauvais Anges et Démons," in *The Science of Demons*, 283–98.

53  Roper, *Witch Craze*, 113.

54  For a survey of Basque sabbat beliefs, see Emma Wilby, *Invoking the Akelarre: Voices of the Accused in the Basque Witch-Craze, 1609–1614* (Brighton, 2019).

55  See, in particular, *Un Documento de la Inquisición sobre brujería en Navarra*, ed. Florencio Idoate (Pamplona, 1972). This important source was barely used in Gustav Henningsen, *The Witches' Advocate: Basque Witchcraft and the Spanish Inquisition (1609–1614)* (Reno, 1980). For a major re-interpretation of the witch hunt, see Lu Ann Homza, *Village Infernos and Witches' Advocates: Witch-Hunting in Navarre, 1608–1614* (University Park, 2022). My own study of Pierre de Lancre and the witch hunt in the French Basque country is forthcoming.

56  On collections for witches, see De Lancre, *Tableau*, 458.

57  De Lancre, *Tableau*, 139.

58  De Lancre, *Tableau*, 207–8.

59  De Lancre, *Tableau*, 97.

60  De Lancre, *Tableau*, 142. See also the reference on 69–70.

61  On this sensational combination of witchcraft and demonic possession, see Thibaut Maus de Rolley, *Moi, Louis Gaufridy, ayant soufflé plus de mille femmes: Une confession de sorcier au XVIIe siècle* (Paris, 2023).

62  De Lancre, *Tableau*, sig. ā3v.

63  On the association between exorcism and witch hunting at the end of the Middle Ages, see Chave-Mahir, *L'exorcisme des possédés*, 17.

64 William Monter cited, among others, by Francis Young, *A History of Exorcism in Catholic Christianity* (Cham, 2016), 1; Moshe Sluhovsky, *Believe Not Every Spirit: Possession, Mysticism, and Discernment in Early Modern Catholicism* (Chicago, 2007), 22.

65 Sluhovsky, *Believe Not Every Spirit*, chap. 1: "Trivializing Possession."

66 See, for instance, the account offered in J. Lough and D.E.L. Crane, "Thomas Killigrew and the Possessed Nuns of Loudun: The Text of a Letter of 1635," *Durham University Journal* 78 (1986): 259–68. On the Loudun case, see in particular Michel de Certeau, *The Possession at Loudun* (Chicago, 2000).

67 For instance, the diary of the English College of Douai records for 3 June 1577 that one of its members passing through Valenciennes had heard of the successful exorcism of "some woman" by a local priest. See *The First and Second Diaries of the English College, Douay and an Appendix of the Unpublished Documents* (London, 1878), 123. Many more cases will not have left any trace behind.

68 Brian P. Levack, *The Devil Within: Possession and Exorcism in the Christian West* (New Haven, 2013), 63.

69 Levack, *The Devil Within*, 3.

70 For a helpful survey of the symptoms, see Levack, *The Devil Within*, 6–15.

71 Robert Mandrou, *Magistrats et sorciers en France au XVIIe siècle: Une analyse de psychologie historique* (Paris, 1980 [original ed. 1968]); see especially section two "la crise du satanisme: les procès scandaleux)." Mandrou's chronology was demolished by the many essays of Alfred Soman.

72 Edward Jorden, *Witchcraft and Hysteria in Elizabethan London: Edward Jorden and the Mary Glover Case*, ed. Michael MacDonald (London, 1991), 66.

73 Jorden, *Witchcraft and Hysteria*, 9 and 25.

74 Jorden, *Witchcraft and Hysteria*, 27.

75 Jorden, *Witchcraft and Hysteria*, 28.

76 Certeau, *The Possession at Loudun*, 160.

77 Marion Gibson, *Possession, Puritanism and Print: Darrell, Harsnett, Shakespeare and the Elizabethan Exorcism Controversy* (London, 2015).

78 Guido Dall'Olio, "Scourging Demons with Exorcism," in *The Science of Demons*, 234.

79 "Requête d'Urbain Grandier au roi Louis XIII (sans date, 1634)," in *Possession et sorcellerie au XVIIe siècle*, ed. Robert Mandrou (Paris: Fayard, 1979), 127.

80 Certeau, *The Possession at Loudun*, 176.

81 Certeau, *The Possession at Loudun*, 180.

82 This was true even for Giolamo Menghi, the author of the most famous exorcism manual of the period. See Dall'Olio, "Scourging Demons with Exorcism," 224–37.

83 Nancy Caciola and Moshe Sluhovsky, "Spiritual Physiologies: The Discernment of Spirits in Medieval and Early Modern Europe," *Preternature: Critical and Historical Studies on the Preternatural* 1, no. 1 (2012): 24.

84 Levack, *The Devil Within*, chap. 6: "The Performance of the Possessed." See also Certeau, *The Possession at Loudun*, chap. 7.

85 Sarah Ferber, *Demonic Possession and Exorcism in Early Modern France* (London, 2004), 24.

86 Certeau, *The Possession at Loudun*, 13–5.

87 Jean-Joseph Surin, *Into the Dark Night and Back: The Mystical Writings of Jean-Joseph Surin*, trans. Patricia M. Ranum, ed. Moshe Sluhovsky (Leiden, 2018).

88 Surin, *Into the Dark Night and Back*, 289.

89 Jan Machielsen, *The War on Witchcraft: Andrew Dickson White, George Lincoln Burr, and the Origins of Witchcraft Historiography* (Cambridge, 2021), 39.

90 Andrew Dickson White, *A History of the Warfare of Science with Theology in Christendom*, vol. 2 (New York, 1896), 138.

91 For Barton's forced confession of fraud, see G. W. Bernard, *The King's Reformation: Henry VIII and the Remaking of the English Church* (New Haven, 2007), 95–7.

92 See, for example, Manfred Brod, "Politics and Prophecy in Seventeenth-Century England: The Case of Elizabeth Poole," *Albion: A Quarterly Journal Concerned with British Studies* 31, no. 3 (1999): 395–412.

93 Gabriella Zarri, "Female Sanctity, 1500–1660," in *The Cambridge History of Christianity: Volume 6: Reform and Expansion 1500–1660*, ed. R. Po-chia Hsia (Cambridge, 2007), 180–200; Tamar Herzig, *Savonarola's Women: Visions and Reform in Renaissance Italy* (Chicago, 2008).

94 Both describe their visions—demonic and divine—in autobiographical texts. For Teresa, see also Gillian T. W. Ahlgren, *Teresa of Avila and the Politics of Sanctity* (Ithaca, 1996).

95 Sluhovsky, *Believe Not Every Spirit.*

96 Michelle Brock, "Internalizing the Demonic: Satan and the Self in Early Modern Scottish Piety," *Journal of British Studies*, 54, no. 1 (2015): 23–43; Nathan Johnstone, *The Devil and Demonism in Early Modern England* (Cambridge, 2009).

97 For an investigation of the quotation's mysterious origins, see the entry on "Quote Investigator: Tracing Quotations." https://quoteinvestigator.com/2018/03/20/devil/

98 Michael Hunter, *The Decline of Magic: Britain in the Enlightenment* (New Haven, 2020), vii.

99 Jan Machielsen, "Bad Reasons: Elites and the Decline of Magic," *Magic, Ritual, and Witchcraft*, 16, no. 3 (2021): 406–14.

100 Levack, *The Devil Within*, 215, although the scriptural warrant for demonic possession means that the phenomenon continues to make itself felt today.

101 Alexandra Walsham, "The Reformation and 'the Disenchantment of the World' Reassessed," *The Historical Journal* 51, no. 2 (2008): 497–528.

102 Euan Cameron, *Enchanted Europe: Superstition, Reason, and Religion, 1250–1750* (Oxford, 2010).

103 Michelle Pfeffer, "The Contribution of the Early Modern Humanities to 'Disenchantment'," *Witchcraft, Ritual and Magic* 16, no. 3 (2021): 398–405. See also Dmitri Levitin, "From Sacred History to the History of Religion: Paganism, Judaism, and Christianity in European Historiography from Reformation to 'Enlightenment,'" *The Historical Journal* 55, no. 4 (2012): 1117–60.

104 On this point, see not only Virginia Krause, *Witchcraft, Demonology, and Confession in Early Modern France* (Cambridge, 2015) but also Stuart Clark, *Vanities of the Eye: Vision in Early Modern European Culture* (Oxford, 2007).

105 See Krause's discussion of Michel de Montaigne's use of "seeing" when discussing witchcraft in her *Witchcraft, Demonology, and Confession*, 97–8.

106 See the case study of the Drummer of Tedworth included in Hunter, *The Decline of Magic*, 86–120.

107 Andrew Fix, "Angels, Devils, and Evil Spirits in Seventeenth-Century Thought: Balthasar Bekker and the Collegiants," *Journal of the History of Ideas* 50, no. 4 (1989): 527–47; Jonathan Israel, *Radical Enlightenment: Philosophy and the Making of Modernity, 1650–1750* (Oxford, 2001), chap. 21; Stronks, *Toverij, Contramagie En Bijgeloof, 1580–1800* (Amsterdam, 2021).

108 Jan Machielsen, *Martin Delrio: Demonology and Scholarship in the Counter-Reformation* (Oxford, 2015), 210.

## Further Reading

Stuart Clark, *Thinking with Demons: The Idea of Witchcraft in Early Modern Europe* (Oxford: Oxford University Press, 1997).

Virginia Krause, *Witchcraft, Demonology, and Confession in Early Modern France* (Cambridge: Cambridge University Press, 2015).

Brian Levack, *The Devil Within: Possession and Exorcism in the Christian West* (New Haven: Yale University Press, 2013).

Jan Machielsen, *The Basque Witch-Hunt: A Secret History* (London: Bloomsbury Academic, 2024).

Lyndal Roper, *Witch Craze: Terror and Fantasy in Baroque Germany* (New Haven: Yale University Press, 2004).

Moshe Sluhovsky, *Believe not Every Spirit: Possession, Mysticism, and Discernment in Early Modern Catholicism* (Chicago: University of Chicago Press, 2007).

Walter Stephens, *Demon Lovers: Witchcraft, Sex, and the Crisis of Belief* (Chicago: University of Chicago Press, 2004).

Deborah Willis, *Malevolent Nurture: Witch-hunting and Maternal Power in Early Modern England* (Ithaca: Cornell University Press, 1995).

# 12

# DEMON POSSESSION AND RITUALS OF PURIFICATION AND ERADICATION IN EARLY MODERN CULTURE

*Ismael del Olmo*

## Setting the Scene: Possession and Dispossession before the Early Modern Era

In the Christian tradition, evil spirits may enter human beings and alter their physical, behavioural, or mental condition. The casting out of possessing spirits, known as exorcism, dispossession, or deliverance, is attested in the gospels and was adopted by the church as part of its efforts to routinise, through rituals, Christ's charismatic potency. Although Christians have always treated the strange symptoms manifested by the afflicted as evidence of spiritual inhabitation, the number of cases of apparent possession ballooned during the early modern era. Claims of possession peaked in the 17th century, which has famously been termed "the golden age" of demoniacs.[1] In large part, the steep rise in possession cases—and their ritual remedy—was informed by the religious and intellectual turmoil of the age. Using sources from Italy, Spain, France, England, Germany, and the Low Countries, in this chapter, I will show that demoniacs and exorcists were part of a larger theological, scientific, and political debate concerning issues such as the interplay of matter and spirit, official and unofficial claims of sanctity, church reform, and appropriate modes of biblical exegeses.

Given that scripture both nurtured and conditioned understandings of the natural and supernatural in the early modern period, let us examine what the New Testament has to say about possession and its remedy. This material, filtered through the lens of early modern developments in demonology and conceptions about the relationship between the physical and metaphysical, served to endow apparent instances of possession with meaning and significance. It thereby conditioned how the experience of encountering a person believed to be demonically possessed was understood and the types of remedy for the affliction that were proposed.

The bible provided early modern people with a rich catalogue of symptoms diagnostic of spirit possession. These included mutism (Mk 9.17), blindness (Mt 12.22), abnormal strength (Mk 5.3-4), physical impairment (Lk 13.11), self-harm and attempted suicide (Mk 5.5 and 9.22), nudity (Lk 8.27), crying out, convulsions, bodily rigidity, foaming at the mouth and the grinding of teeth (Lk 9.39; Mk 1.26 and 9.18). Along with these symptoms manifest in the body, scripture also describes cognitive signs of possession. Chief

DOI: 10.4324/9781003096603-13

among these is clairvoyant knowledge, for on several occasions demoniacs are described as being able to recognise Christ's divinity spontaneously—even before the apostles (Mt 8.29; Lk 4.34; Mk 1.24 and 5.6-7). This, and the account of a woman described as being possessed by "a spirit of divination" (Acts 16.16-18), suggests that demoniacs might be privy to secret knowledge and even be able to prophesy. Because of this emphasis on possession in the synoptic gospels and the Acts of the Apostles, exorcism figures prominently in Christ's ministry (Mt 12.28; Lk 11.20; Mk 1.21-28). Moreover, Christ passes this gift of dispossession to the apostles to further their missionary enterprise, as shown in Luke 9.1, and Mark 3.14-15, 6.7, and 16.17.[2]

These injunctions lay at the foundation of the long history of ecclesiastical exorcism, which extends from Late Antiquity to early modern times. Attested by the 3rd century in Rome, the office of *exorcista* (a minor order in the ecclesiastical hierarchy, together with the reader, the doorkeeper, and the acolyte) was involved in the purification of materials used in baptism and other rites, such as vessels, water, salt, and oil; exorcists also dealt with those who were possessed. The Council of Laodicea (363-364) decreed that only exorcists appointed by a bishop should perform adjurations, while the *Statuta ecclesiae antiqua*, a collection of canons from late 5th-century Gaul, established that, during ordination, exorcists received from the bishop a book with exorcisms, as well as the power to lay hands on the possessed. Despite these early references, liturgical sources from the 6th century onwards show that exorcism was actually conducted, not by the *exorcista*, but by priests and bishops (i.e., by those in higher orders).[3]

Since the order of exorcist was involved in baptism, we should explore connections between this rite and the exorcism of demoniacs. From the 3rd century onwards, before undergoing baptism proper, candidates were ritually exorcised. Some Christian authors saw catechumens as literally possessed by devils; others (the majority, under the influence of St. Augustine) understood the rite as a purification, drawing the candidate away from Satan's dominion and temptation.[4] The question remains, though, and scholars debate the extent to which the liturgy for the exorcism of the possessed was derived from pre-baptismal exorcisms. Florence Chave-Mahir, for example, claims that the exorcism of the possessed broke away from its baptismal roots around the year 1000, around the time that the conversion of the West was finally achieved. The first liturgical exorcisms explicitly devoted to demoniacs—derived from baptismal formulas—appear in the *Pontificale Romano-Germanicum*, compiled around the middle of the 10th century.[5] Francis Young has challenged this interpretation, showing that one of the earliest exorcisms for demoniacs, included in the late 8th-century *Gellone Sacramentary*, contains adjurations not derived from pre-baptismal exorcisms. However, other texts from the same century, such as the *Gelasian Sacramentary*, unequivocally use formulas from pre-baptismal exorcisms. Thus, a better way to understand the relationship between exorcism of the possessed and pre-baptismal exorcism is probably to view both as parallel yet, in some cases, interpenetrating liturgical traditions.[6]

Reference to pre-baptismal exorcism and ordained exorcists enables us to introduce a medieval debate that was still important in early modern times. The anonymous *Apostolic Constitutions* already claimed in c. 375 that "an exorcist is not ordained," and that exorcism "is a trial of voluntary goodness, and of the grace of God through Christ by an inspiration of the Holy Spirit."[7] This shows us the difficulty that would plague the ecclesiastical understanding of exorcism for centuries: Should it be considered a regulated practice performed by ordained celebrants, with its efficacy guaranteed by the relationship between Christ and the institution, or should it be seen as a charismatic gift, its success depending in part on the personal characteristics of the one performing the rite, and ultimately, on God's arbitrary assistance? We will expand on this question later in the chapter; for now, we note that, since exorcism was seen as a form of healing rather than as a sacrament, it was practised equally by ordained and non-ordained officiants.[8]

This enables us to go beyond the official liturgy and discuss other types of exorcism that took place in the Middle Ages and the early modern period, i.e., adjurations and medical exorcisms. Since any spiritual, psychological, or physiological ailment could be attributed to demonic influence, and since diseases and afflictions themselves could be conceptualised as foreign agents pervading the human body, lay formulas of exorcism and adjuration were part of a wide array of healing practices in pre-modern Europe.[9] The vast majority of these practices, while informed by Christian prayers, gestures, and objects, ignored official exorcisms and exorcists. A medieval adjuration, for example, commands an eye irritation to depart: "I adjure you, o speck … to disappear from the eyes of the servant of God, N., whether you are black, red, or white. May Christ make you go away." Another orders a worm to "go out" from the patient's marrow and into the veins, then to the flesh, and so forth, until it is finally out of the body.[10] It is worth noting, however, that some adjurations of disease did draw materials from official exorcisms, which shows the connection between medical and liturgical discourses (and, perhaps, practices). An example is the cure for *ælf-sogoþa*, an unknown disease connected with elves contained in *Leechbook III*, an English medical text compiled in the late 9th century. After preparing the prescribed herbal remedy and inscribing a prayer, the healer—never identified as a priest or exorcist—sings "All-powerful God, father of our Lord Jesus Christ, through the imposition of this writing, expel from your servant N. every attack of elves from the head, from the hair, from the brain, from the forehead …." The formula is a variant of an exorcism for demoniacs found in a 9th-century version of the *Leofric Missal*.[11]

Yet another type of exorcism is the charismatic dispossession performed by or attributed to living or dead saints. In his classic study, *The Cult of the Saints*, Peter Brown identified exorcism as the paradigm of the saint's *potentia*, "the one demonstration of the power of God that carried unanswerable authority."[12] From Late Antiquity to the early modern period, dispossessions figured in saints' lives, in references to their relics, in miracle books recorded at shrines, and in canonisation processes.[13] An early example is the discovery of the remains of the martyrs Gervasius and Protasius in 386 in Milan. Augustine of Hippo recalled that, when confronted with their relics, "some people vexed by impure spirits were healed, the very demons themselves making public confession."[14] At that time, Augustine's mentor, Ambrose of Milan, was involved in disputations with Arian heretics concerning the trinity; Ambrose claims that, when confronted by the relics of Gervasius and Protasius, the possessing demons confessed that no one denying the trinity could be saved.[15] This attests to the early use of possessing devils as paradoxical allies in theological battles between Christian sects, a trend that continued into early modern times. Moreover, in a number of saints' lives, the exorcisms of the saints are portrayed as more effective than ecclesiastical exorcisms—a reminder of the aforementioned tension between charisma and liturgy. The anonymous *Life of Cuthbert* and Bede's *Historia ecclesiastica*, both from the 8th century, show that the relics of Saints Cuthbert and Oswald achieved dispossession when priestly exorcisms had failed.[16]

It is clear that the idea that spirits are able to penetrate human bodies has existed in Christian culture from earliest times. But how should we understand this condition? In the scholastic culture that arose from the early 13th century, theologians set about trying to explain rationally how possession could take place, doing so within the parameters of biblical exegesis, contemporary understandings of the power of God, and natural philosophy. The result was a more formal, more rational demonology (i.e., the theory and praxis of dealing with devils). In this context, the 13th-century Dominican friar Thomas Aquinas proved influential. He suggested an interrelationship between three orders of action: supernatural, natural, and preternatural (this last comprising the activities of pure spirits such as demons). Aquinas termed God's creation "the totality of created nature" (*totius naturae creatae*); demons, as part of this creation, were bound by nature. Following St. Augustine, however, with their superior intellect and vast experience and knowledge of nature's operations and properties, demons could act, not against "the totality of created nature" (that would imply a miracle, which is God's prerogative), but "beyond the order of a particular nature" (*praeter ordinem naturae alicuius particularis*). Operating through and within nature, demons could manipulate a particular natural process and cause it to deviate from its ordinary outcome. Thus, from the human perspective, they could perform what seemed to be extraordinary phenomena.[17]

One of these is demonic possession. In the gradation of created beings, pure, incorporeal spirits such as devils are ontologically superior to humans, for human spirits (that is, their souls) are contained within weighty bodies, which limit them. Given this superiority and their fundamentally different nature, demons can act upon humans and possess them. As created beings themselves, they do so naturally. When they are able to penetrate a body, they assume control of its faculties and organs, manipulating its humoral balance, vapours, and its vital and animal spirits (both were subtle and vaporous entities; the vital spirits were formed from the blood by the heat of the heart; the animal spirits were formed at the basis of the brain). In so doing, the indwelling demon is able to prevent the normal functioning of bodily and cognitive faculties: "Devils can sometimes indeed move internal vapors and fluids even to the point that the use of reason is completely fettered, as is evidently the case with the possessed (*arrepticiis*)."[18] That said, Aquinas argues that demons cannot penetrate the soul, for this would have serious implications for the doctrine of free will and an individual's responsibility for sin.

Possession, then, represents not an opposition between nature and demons, but, rather, a nuanced interrelation between natural and preternatural causalities. At the same time, preternature was a useful category to account for extraordinary abilities. For example, foretelling the future and speaking in languages previously unknown were not, in Aquinas' view, activities that could be explained solely by ordinary natural processes. Indeed, divination and xenoglossia were often viewed as signs of demonic inhabitation—particularly in the early modern period.[19]

Nevertheless, Aquinas acknowledged that other signs of possession were not self-evident. For example, he gave three probable causes for someone losing his ability to reason through sensible things: "First, from a bodily cause, as happens to those who suffer abstraction from the senses through an illness; secondly, by the power of the demons, as in those who are possessed (*arreptitiis*); thirdly, by the power of God."[20] If the same symptoms could have completely different causes, it could never be clear whether an afflicted individual was ill, possessed, or divinely inspired. The appropriate response in such cases was unclear: should the patient be treated with medicines, exorcised, or revered? Although scholastic notions of causation seemed transparent in theory, it would remain a practical problem to assign the correct (invisible) cause to the given (visible) effect. From the late Middle Ages onwards, this difficulty surrounding natural, divine, or demonic taxonomy was increasingly codified in a theory and a practice known as discernment of spirits.[21] Discernment enjoyed biblical pedigree: 2 Corinthians 11.14 claims that Satan disguised himself as an angel of light; 1 John 4.1 states that one must not believe every spirit; 1 Corinthians 12.10 states that we may discern them, should the Holy Spirit grant us this gift. The investigative language of discernment, soon to become a praxis more than a divine gift, helped the priest, the exorcist, the spiritual confessor, the inquisitor, and the physician to interpret the origin of extraordinary behaviour. Given the formal similarities between the naturally afflicted, the divinely inspired, and demoniacs, it was crucial to understand the hidden, invisible cause of visions, bodily excess, divination, or xenoglossia. Early modernity would inherit this epistemological problem.

## Discerning Possession in Early Modern Europe

Because many symptoms of possession could overlap with those of natural affliction, distinguishing authentic cases of possession from illness was difficult. In *De abditis rerum causis* (1548), for instance, the French physician Jean Fernel described the plight of a young man suffering from convulsions. "The most experienced physicians were consulted," he wrote, and, having judged that the patient was epileptic, he was prescribed natural remedies. Three months of failed treatments ensued, the physician continued, "because we were all far from recognising the truth": the man was possessed. The demon presented itself speaking in Greek (although the victim was ignorant of this language) and exhibited clairvoyant knowledge. It also jumped and shuddered when "sacred and divine words were being spoken openly."[22] However, ill people could sometimes be misdiagnosed as demoniacs. Michel de Montaigne thought as much while visiting Rome in 1581, where he saw a man apparently possessed. Noting the man's symptoms, it seemed to Montaigne that he was only "grinding his teeth and twisting the mouth when they presented the *Corpus Domini* to him"; nor did his xenoglossic abilities amaze Montaigne, for "he was a notary, and knew a little bit of Latin." The purported demoniac appeared to the essayist as "a melancholic man, and as paralysed."[23]

Montaigne's reference to melancholy is significant, for it underscores how similar this Renaissance malady's symptoms appeared to those of possession. According to contemporary humoral theory, the corruption of the black bile (melancholy) could affect the functioning of the body and the brain, provoking fits, mental derangement, hallucinations, and animalised traits, among many other grotesque signs.[24] Hence, there was danger in reading the extravagant symptomatology of melancholy as possession. However, at the same time, religious and medical traditions highlighted the close affinity between the two conditions. Although melancholy in itself was a natural condition, demonological theory allowed this affliction to be caused or worsened by a demon manipulating the black humour.[25]

This is highlighted, for example, in Johannes Wier's *De praestigiis daemonum* (1563), well known for treating witchcraft as a delusion caused by the devil in ignorant, poor, and, sometimes, melancholic women. Discernment was on Wier's mind. He emphasised the role of the physician in searching for the origin of "rare and severe" symptoms, especially those seen as pertaining to a preternatural affliction (*malum aliquod praeter naturae ordinem*). More often than not, he said, extraordinary symptoms were wrongly attributed to *maleficium*, when in reality they had a natural origin—for instance, *melancholia*. The prudent physician, then, "discerns between these affections and accidents." However, sometimes a disease "surpasses and goes beyond the limits of nature" (*naturae limites malum exuperare egrediaque*), and this can be related to demonic powers. One such instance is possession. According to Wier, during possession, the devil may creep into melancholy, thus afflicting the demoniac with "twin diseases" (*morbis siquidem geminis*), one of the body, due to melancholy, and one of the mind, due to the devil, who causes madness, grief, fear, and despair.[26]

Although the majority of early modern authors accepted this interplay between nature and demons with regard to possession, a minority of thinkers opposed this view, and developed an alternative tradition in which *melancholia* alone accounted for signs traditionally seen as demonic. This view developed from a reading of the pseudo-Aristotelian *Problemata*, a work that entered the Christian West in the 12th century. Problem 30.1 attributed the extraordinary clairvoyant abilities of pagan sybils and oracles not to spiritual influences but to the natural impact of corrupted black humour.[27] It was the Italian philosopher and physician Pietro d'Abano who, in *Expositio problematum Aristotelis* (c. 1310), linked Problem 30.1 to demonic possession. Abano claimed that, according to Aristotle, divination was a natural consequence of melancholy; it was the same, he added, with xenoglossia. He tells the story of an illiterate woman who, while suffering from melancholy, could communicate in Latin. Once cured, though, the ability vanished. Abano remarked that those "speaking according to religion" attributed these extraordinary events, not to melancholy, but to the spirits (*spiritibus*).[28] Thus, through a radical interpretation of Aristotelian melancholy, the Italian physician helped to naturalise xenoglossia and divination, traditional signs of demonic possession. This view would have an impact on the 16th century (and beyond), influencing, among others, the Italian philosopher Pietro Pomponazzi, the Spanish physician Juan Huarte de San Juan, and the English Reginald Scot, each of whom offered melancholy as an explanation for possession—and were openly accused of denying demonic action in the material world.[29]

It is clear, then, that it was highly problematic to differentiate between possession and illness. But it was just as difficult to discern whether a possessed body was under the influence of a diabolical or divine spirit, especially if it was a female body. From late medieval times, gender had become an important factor in the issue of *discretio*: the growth of female claims of sanctity increased ecclesiastical suspicion over their spiritual experiences. Because this inquiry dealt with inner, invisible realities, Nancy Caciola notes that discernment of spirits turned into a discernment of bodies, which, in turn, often gave way to the diabolisation of female mysticism; women's mystical episodes were frequently interpreted as demonic delusion, possession, or witchcraft.[30] An anonymous "Epistle to the reader" in *Practica y Exercicio Espiritual* (1585) provides an example. Although God wished female saints to be his "instruments," it asserted, no one should admire "weak and naturally ignorant women" who operated outside official clerical (male) sanction. Ecclesiastical officials had to apply expert discernment in their inspection of female inspiration, because women could easily be the devil's instruments: "We must not believe every spirit, because we know that the angel of Satan transfigures himself into an angel of light." One should believe only if the women's revelations were "approved by the Catholic Church, or by her learned men."[31] Nevertheless, discernment was a collective enterprise, rendering its results unpredictable. In 1631, the Spanish Gaspar Navarro, a canon from Huesca, told of a possessed nun who spoke in different voices: "with a more delicate one, she feigned the voice of Christ; with the other, the voice of the devil." To Navarro's horror, the demoniac deceived the priests and believers to the point that, "as if Christ were speaking through her mouth," she consecrated the eucharist and led the congregation in procession, parading the demonic host "as if it was the true and holy Sacrament of the Church."[32]

Navarro shows the clear division between divine and demonic possessions during the early modern period. However, demoniacs could also stand as a sign of God's favour. In such cases, the experience of demonic possession partook of the language of mysticism, blurring the boundaries between the demonic and the divine, and stretching the discourse of discernment to its limits—ultimately destroying it.[33] Jeanne Féry, a 25-year-old nun from a monastery in the Catholic Low Countries, possessed from 1584 to 1586, offers a clear example. She exhibited symptoms such as howling, hostility towards the sacred and suicide attempts. However, she also started receiving visions of St. Mary Magdalene, who encouraged her to resist the possessing devils, particularly their Calvinist hatred towards the Catholic doctrine of transubstantiation (the real presence of Christ's body and blood in the consecrated host). The Magdalene reassured Jeanne of the truth of this doctrine, "of which [Jeanne] was so alienated due to the multitude of errors and varieties of heresies, with which the evil ones had confused her." In addition to divine visions, Jeanne perceived God's presence in her heart, and experienced her dispossession as a mystical ecstasy.[34] In an era that focused resolutely on the necessity of finding and manifesting the divine in the visible world, Jeanne Féry, the devil's vessel, could paradoxically be viewed as a vessel of piety.

## Catholic Exorcism in an Age of Anxiety

Early modern men and women lived in a world that teemed with spiritual forces affecting their lives: divine and demonic possessions, diabolical delusions and illnesses, visions and prophecies were common. In order to benefit and protect themselves from these forces, they resorted to the belief that spiritual energies could be grasped, manifested, or controlled by and through gestures, words, and objects. Exorcism was part of this worldview. As we have already seen, liturgical, lay and saintly dispossessions were common in pre-modern Christianity. Eclecticism and competition were the norm in the early modern health care market—a market shared by priests, physicians, living and dead saints, apothecaries, folk doctors, and charismatic healers. Here, lay and ecclesiastic exorcisms coexisted as viable solutions when medicines, magic, and other conventional remedies failed.[35]

Such coexistence would be increasingly opposed by the Catholic hierarchy from the late 15th and early 16th centuries onwards, when exorcism came under much closer scrutiny and supervision. A heightened preoccupation with superstition was instrumental in this regard. Late medieval and early modern ecclesiastic and secular authorities regarded superstitions as ritual actions that endowed objects, words, and gestures with spiritual power, but whose effects were, in reality, natural, non-existent, or worse, satanic. The church sniffed out the potential for superstition in exorcism—a praxis dealing intimately with the divine and the demonic—and insisted on authorised techniques and forms of dispossession.[36] In addition, exorcism was becoming useful as a strategy for discernment, that is, as a practical means to find out whether possessed behaviours were due to divine or demonic spirits, to illnesses, or imposture. It also helped authorities to determine whether the possession was a consequence of *maleficium* perpetrated by witches. This investigative function of exorcism would encourage the church to secure the rite in institutional hands.[37] The 16th century also ignited the battle between the forces of Reformation and Counter-Reformation. The Roman church emphasised the role of priests as conduits for ritual divine power, often wielding exorcism as an evidentiary weapon against the Reformation. Because Protestants accused Catholic exorcists of superstition and imposture, the institution developed a far more scrupulous examination of both exorcists and the rite itself.[38]

Thus, during the 16th and 17th centuries, there emerged a climate amenable to the professionalisation and clerical monopolisation of exorcism. This entailed the curtailment of charismatic dispossessions and ultimately it became an attack directed against both lay exorcists who challenged the ecclesiastical monopoly over the supernatural, as well as priests who were deemed ill prepared for the task. Pedro Ciruelo's *Reprobacion de las Supersticiones y Hechizerias* (1530), for example, questioned lay exorcism at a fundamental level and emphasised the need to safeguard the rite in the hands of ordained priests. "The good and licit conjurations" were only those performed by the members of the clergy, since Christ gave "spiritual power over all devils to his clerics." Exorcism, then, was "a common office of the clerics and rectors of the parish, like baptising or giving the other sacraments of the Church." Lay exorcists did not have authority over demons, because this was "given to the clerics when the Bishop gives them the orders; and thus, laymen do not have it." If someone outside holy orders casts out spirits, "there is suspicion that he must be a necromantic enchanter."[39]

The church's defence of institutional exorcism was also aimed at controlling or channelling the clergy. The lack of a common or universal rite until the beginning of the 17th century, together with the fact that exorcists were often preoccupied with their own reputation as healers in a competitive market, allowed for a wide spectrum of approaches, styles, and formulas. At the beginning of the 16th century, for example, Father Guglielmo Campana from Modena exorcised by burning wax images of demoniacs at the altar.[40] Ciruelo told of priests who boasted about their exorcistic power, which was allegedly superior to that of other ordained ministers. Some even asked exorcised fiends to return to their victim in order to face a second dispossession.[41] In 1581, Montaigne saw a Roman exorcist bringing a possessed man to his knees, holding him by the neck with a cloth, and hitting him while spitting in his face.[42] The Italian Inquisition heard a mid-17th-century Theatine exorcist explain how he cast spirits out from women by touching their vaginas.[43]

This wide array of exorcistic styles found a strong institutional barrier at the beginning of the 17th century when the church published its official rite in an attempt to transform exorcism from healing praxis to prescribed ritual. Ordered in 1584 by Pope Gregory XIII, and based mainly on medieval pre-baptismal formulas, the *Rituale Romanum* was finally published in 1614 during the pontificate of Paul V. It sought to homogenise and tighten control over a practice whose intrinsic ambiguity, between the divine and the demonic, between individual and institutional power, frequently raised suspicions. The 1614 ritual shows awareness about the difficulties in discerning possession. It exhorts the exorcist "not [to] easily believe that someone is possessed by the devil," since many people were only afflicted by "melancholy or other illness." Then again, the devil could mimic the symptoms of natural illnesses. The possessed exhibited three genuine signs: xenoglossia, divination, and supernatural strength. With lay competitors in mind, the *Rituale* limited exorcism to members of the ecclesiastical hierarchy. Against clerics parading their powers as individual grace, it asserted that exorcistic efficacy derived only from God. With an eye to potential sexual scandals, it recommended that exorcists should not be left alone with female demoniacs. Formulas outside those prescribed by the *Rituale* were prohibited, as well as any other gesture or element that existed outside the church's sacramental system.[44]

Was the *Rituale* successful in homogenising exorcism and controlling (now) heterodox exorcists? In some cases, it seems so. Pope Alexander VII, for example, dismissed a mass possession in the German city of Paderborn between 1656 and 1659, explaining that the procedure outlined in the *Rituale* had not been followed properly.[45] In the 1660s, through the strict application of the rite, the Jesuit Bernhard Frey convinced authorities in Munich that several allegations of possession were in fact cases of insanity or fraud.[46]

However, the institutional suffocation of charismatic power in favour of broad or wide-spread ritual standardisation was never achieved in early modern times. In fact, lay exorcism continued to proliferate. In 1571 Venice, for example, the Inquisition heard one Elena Crusichi claim that, upon possession by an evil spirit, she was able to exorcise the diseases with saliva, herbs, and incantations.[47] Similarly, at the beginning of the next century, a midwife from Munich was investigated for obtaining human body parts from the local executioner and using them to exorcise pregnant women.[48] In 1653, the Inquisition accused Pablo Borao, a Spanish healer, of exorcising demoniacs without clerical standing, and of using heterodox methods: he "made a cross with his tongue on the genitals of a woman who was possessed," and said "he had grace in his semen" which countered the devil's power.[49]

Ultimately, exorcism could not be fully regulated even within the ranks of the church. In part, this was because it never achieved the status of a sacrament, but remained a sacramental. That is, exorcism was not seen as an ecclesiastical rite that automatically conveyed God's grace every time the ritual was performed (as with the seven sacraments), but rather, as a rite whose efficacy depended on God's arbitrary or uncertain assistance, which could be motivated or affected by, among other things, the personal qualities of the exorcist.[50] Thus, individual charisma remained a key factor in exorcistic enterprises throughout the period. Of course, the church often prosecuted such exorcists, as shown in the records of a 17th-century Spanish Inquisitorial trial against a Christian who claimed he had received special grace against demons upon ascending to heaven and visiting Christ.[51] However, it also happened that some orthodox churchmen celebrated exorcism's charismatic elements. The abbot Francisco Blasco de Lanuza recalled how, during a mass possession in Aragon between 1637 and 1642, he asked the Spanish king to send exorcists with "special grace" to intervene. Accordingly, these should be "people of known virtue and religion, who have merits and grace to cast out demons."[52]

As noted above, exorcism became an issue in the clash between Catholics and Protestants. Indeed, the rite was deployed in the propaganda wars against Lutherans and Calvinists, as Catholics claimed that only their church had inherited Christ's exorcistical power.[53] In an age of religious fragmentation and uncertainty, exorcism functioned as a visual proof of abstract theological positions under attack—and justified the institutional power of Catholicism.[54] The French priest Jean Boulaese, for example, wrote about the 1565–1566 possession of a girl called Nicole Obry, in a time when Catholics and Huguenots disputed the doctrine of transubstantiation. Nicole was exorcised by means of the consecrated host, an event that was advertised by Catholics as "the miracle of Laon." "With this story," concludes Boulaese,

> the heretics know that all they have against us Catholics has been rendered void by the sense of sight, hearing and touch, through the truthful and real presence of our Lord Jesus Christ in the Sacrament of the Altar. They have an occasion more than just to convert themselves.[55]

In the heat of the confessional battle, some authors ignored the intricacies of sacraments and sacramentals and affirmed that God would intervene only in favour of Catholic exorcism. This was the case, for example, with the German Jesuit Petrus Thyraeus, who, in his *De daemoniacis* (1591), asks whether the heretics are able to cast out demons successfully. He concludes that it is impossible: miracles confirm the truth, and heretics are enemies of the truth; should they try to exorcise spirits, God would not "concur in the expulsion of demons (which may be placed among the miracles)."[56] God not only intervened in Catholic exorcism, but also willed demonic possessions, since they offered an opportunity for the church to show and defend the truth. Describing an epidemic of possession in Aragon, Blasco de Lanuza claimed that God chose the area because it shared borders with the French Reformed principality of Béarn, "the part which is the most damaged with heretics." Through successful exorcisms, he said, the enemies of the faith contemplated "the virtue of our infallible law."[57]

## Reformed Views on Demoniacs and Dispossessions

The Reformed party would hardly be convinced by the writings of Boulaese, Thyraeus, or Blasco de Lanuza. There were two primary critiques of Catholic exorcism among Protestants. First, the Reformation resorted to a doctrine called "cessationism." That is, it maintained that, since God's revelation was already codified in the scriptures, miraculous signs were no longer necessary to introduce and reinforce the Christian faith. Thus, exorcism as performed in early Christianity had ceased. The second argument stemmed from a critique of the traditional religious worldview in which matter, word and gesture could mobilise spiritual power—something that representatives of the Roman church claimed could be channelled through sacraments and sacramentals. As with other elements of this traditional culture (relics, mysticism, the real presence of Christ in the eucharist), the leaders of the Reformation rejected Catholic exorcism.[58] Indeed, if it were not a divine energy mediated by the clergy, then, exorcism had to be an imposture or a superstition—i.e., a satanic intervention or an irrational belief.

Martin Luther, for example, referred to Catholic exorcists as "charmers" who pretended to cast out devils by "arts, words, or gesture." He declared that "we cannot of ourselves expel the evil spirits," and that we would fail to cast out the devil "with certain ceremonies and words, as Jesus Christ, the prophets, and the apostles did."[59] Jean Calvin's *Institutes* listed "the superstitions of necromancy, frightful curses, unlawful exorcism, and other wicked incantations" as a misuse of God's name. In *Harmony of the Gospels*, he rejected exorcism and claimed that it was the staging of "counterfeit fights of Satan against himself," with the ultimate goal of tricking men to drown "their minds in superstition."[60] The Zurich reformer Heinrich Bullinger affirmed in 1549 that, since "the apostles of the Lord were not exorcists," they used neither "enchantments" nor "conjurations" as contemporary Catholics did; Christ's followers performed miracles, but these "ceased long ago."[61] The Lutheran Martin Chemnitz wrote in his *Examen Concilii Tridentini* (1565) that Christians had enjoyed the gift of exorcism from the time of Jesus to that of John Chrysostom; after that, it had ceased. Catholic exorcists are merely "enchanters," displaying only "superstitious exorcisms."[62] Other Reformed intellectuals saw exorcism, not as satanic magic, but as an ineffective and irrational practice. In 1584, Reginald Scot, an opponent of the scholastic science of demons, emphasised the futility of Catholic exorcism, considering it a fiction similar to the "superstitious fables" of the pagans "and diverse other fancies."[63]

Yet, even if Reformed pastors and intellectuals rejected exorcism, demonic possession still thrived among their flocks. As Keith Thomas pointed out, the Reformation sustained the belief in the immediate presence of devils in earthly affairs, while simultaneously labouring to demolish the traditional system of counter-remedies designed to cope with them. The laity would not abandon these practices, even if downplayed by their self-appointed leaders as superstitious, magical, or "popish."[64] In fact, some pastors, attentive to this demand, gained success as exorcists. In Utrecht, at the beginning of the 17th century, for example, a Calvinist minister cast out spirits using a wolf's heart and right eye.[65]

Still, it remains true that Protestant ideals did broadly influence the understanding of demonic inhabitation and dispossession. The grotesque physical symptoms of demoniacs, at times overflowing the scriptural mould, were viewed within a cultural script, a Reformed understanding of possession that often focused on the inner, spiritual aspects of the struggle against devils.[66] Following Protestant understandings of Satan's relationships with humanity, possession narratives portray human depravity and sinfulness, temptation and demonic control over one's consciousness both as God's trial and punishment, spiritual despair, and, finally, divine liberation. Such intimate relationships between the possessed and Satan required some form of mediation: not the Roman-inspired channelling of external divine power through ritual, but instead, assisting demoniacs to make sense of their ailments, and helping them to strengthen their faith and repentance throughout their inner battle with the old enemy. The model would follow Matthew 17.21, in which Christ prescribed fasting and prayer in order to liberate the possessed.[67]

The story of Alexander Nyndge, published in England in the early 1570s, offers an example. The narrative emphasises Alexander's sinfulness as the cause of his possession, and the demonic attack itself as God's punishment. In Reformed fashion, Edward, Alexander's brother, assured him of liberation should he remain steadfast in his faith, saying, "stand to your true repentance, brother, and your possessed hope of salvation." However, there was no exorcist performing any sort of elaborate ritual: instead, the demoniac was exorcised by the community, some 20 people; "all that were in the house praying earnestly." They quoted passages from the gospels, including those focused on Christ's exorcistic endeavours. The Protestant link between possession and sin, spiritual distress, and God's punishment was strongly emphasised. Alexander's troubles appeared as an "example and warning" to induce everyone to engage in introspection: "to descend into ourselves, and to look into our souls while there is yet time, lest Heaven pour down its vials of wrath on us."[68]

On other occasions, individual exorcists took the lead. A well-researched case is that of the minister John Darrell, a member of the puritans, a dissident movement in the Church of England. Darrell was also an active exorcist in the decades of 1580 and 1590.[69] However, he rejected Catholic exorcism with cessationism, affirming that the biblical "extraordinarie and miraculous kinde of ejection of Sathan" was gone. Instead, he believed that dispossessions could be achieved through "other ordinarie and perpetuall" means recommended in the scriptures, i.e., "praier and fastinge."[70] For him, demonic possession served as a divine example and warning for the community. Darrell recalled how a man from Nottingham, witnessing the horrors endured by a demoniac, "oppressed with feare, upon the fearfull light he then beheld," broke down in tears and "confessed his sinnes before us all."[71] It was said that the puritan minister preached that the demoniac "was not so much troubled for his own sinnes, as for the sins of the people or of the inhabitants in Nottingham."[72]

Darrell's case is also an example of confessional polemics, this time within the context of the Reformed rhetorical tradition. Anglican authorities, fearing that puritans, in Catholic fashion, would hail exorcism as a sign of divine preference for them over the national church, put Darrell on trial. The chaplain to the Bishop of London, Samuel Harsnett, charged him with fraud: in league with fake demoniacs, "pretending by hypocriticall sleightes to cast out Deuils," Darrell intended to fool bystanders into believing he could produce miracles, thus furthering the interests of his own Puritan faction. This shift in the accusation during the midst of the trial—from heresy to imposture—accompanies a gradual development in 17th-century religious controversy, from fearing demonic power to ridiculing human malice. Indeed, according to Harsnett, the whole affair showed no devil; the only evil spirit at play during Darrell's exorcisms was "the spirit of illusion."[73]

The Anglican attack on Puritan dispossessions led to the promulgation of canon 72 in the 1604 *Constitutiones sive canones ecclesiastici*. The hierarchy of the national church threatened to excommunicate any minister willing to "cast out any deuill" by means of prayer and fasting without the proper licence from a bishop. Visitations and inquiries reinforced compliance with the canon; no record for licences to exorcise survives. Scepticism became an important part of the Church of England's official take on demonic manifestations and supernatural cures, showing that critiques of possession and exorcism were often motivated more by harsh theological and political battles, than by any preoccupation with "Science" and "Reason."[74]

However, the desire for remedies against evil forces was impossible to extinguish; theological niceties and confessional disputes such as those fuelling the 1604 canon would not stop the demand. The Anglican minister and physician Richard Napier, for example, became famous in the 17th century through his use of a number of spiritual and natural remedies, cures that included dietary prescriptions, amulets, astrological medicine, and religious exercises. In 1630, more than 20 years after the canon, he resolved to exorcise a melancholy-inducing demon:

> I, God's most unworthy minister and servant, I do charge and command thee, thou cruel beast, with all thy associates and all other malignant spirits in case that any of you have your being in the body of this creature, Mr. E. Fr[ancklin], and have distempered his brain with melancholy and have also deprived his body and limbs of their natural use, I charge and command you speedily to depart from this creature.[75]

## Contesting Demoniacs and Exorcisms in the Later 17th Century

Richard Napier's exorcism of a melancholic client rested on the idea that evil spirits affected the material world. Since demonological theory already accounted for the possibility of illnesses being manipulated by the devil, natural alternatives such as melancholy could not inform a definitive criticism of possession and exorcism. Furthermore, such naturalisation would cast doubt over the biblical account of Christ's exorcisms. This concern is seen in the Calvinist Lambert Daneau's *Les sorciers* (1574): "[Some] believe and say that demoniacs and lunatics (who lived in times of our Lord Jesus Christ and whom He cured) are no other thing than people sicked with an impure and melancholic humour. With this, they disrupt the certitude of the Christian faith, denying the virtue and nature of our Lord Jesus."[76] According to the abbot Blasco de Lanuza, writing in mid-17th-century Spain, the bible plainly shows the reality of demonic possession; those who attribute it to melancholy were mistaken, or worse: "This is such a truth, that whoever denies it, would be a heretic."[77]

The development of materialism and Cartesianism during the second half of the 17th century—and especially the alternative exegetical strategies employed by some of their supporters—would challenge this view. By offering new understandings of the interplay between matter and spirit, they undermined the scholastic capacity of devils to intervene in the material world, and questioned the scriptural instances of demonic phenomena. This accelerated a trend already apparent in mid-17th-century intellectual circles: the emphasis on naturalistic explanations at the expense of supernatural and preternatural ones, and the labelling of demonology as superstition—in the sense of irrational belief.[78]

The English philosopher Thomas Hobbes presented the first systematic critique in this vein.[79] *Leviathan* (1651) saw demonology as "superstitious fear of Spirits," organised by Christian denominations in order to "abuse the simple people."[80] How could the fear of spirits be challenged? While revelation confirmed the existence of devils, they were not presented as incorporeal substances as the scholastics claimed, but rather, as subtle and invisible bodies. The materialistic view rendered demonic possession impossible: if spirits were bodies, it is unreasonable to suppose that one substance could penetrate another substance that is already filled with its own subtle spirits.[81] But how are we then to understand biblical possession and exorcism? Hobbes proposed exegetical strategies such as etymology, metaphorisation, naturalisation, and *accommodatio* (the notion that God adjusts the revelation to the audience's capacities).[82] Regarding metaphorisation, the biblical term "spirit" could signify a personal inclination, such that "the spirit of man, when it produceth unclean actions, is ordinarily called an unclean spirit." Similarly, since the etymology of "Satan" is "adversary," his "entrance" into a person could be interpreted as the entry of "the wicked cogitations, and designes of the Adversaries of Christ." Concerning naturalisation, Hobbes regarded demoniacs as "Mad-men, or Lunatiques." During Jesus' times, pagans, Jews, and early Christians ignored natural causes, relating extraordinary bodily and mental disorders to evil spirits. Ignorance of nature also informed *accommodatio*: Christ did not exorcise demons, but commanded "the Madnesse or Lunacy he cureth" as devils, in keeping with the beliefs of his times.[83]

Although it is not clear whether Hobbes had a direct influence on it, many of his views are present in *De Betoverde Weereld* (1691–1693), written by the Amsterdam Reformed minister Balthasar Bekker.[84] His critique of demonology earned him accusations of heresy and suspension from the ministry. Bekker did not deny the existence of demons, but rejected their activities in nature. Arguing from the perspective of a Reformed hyper-providentialism, he claimed that God's authority over creation was absolute. The devil was already defeated and chained in hell; consequently, he had no power over worldly events. What about the bible, then? Like Hobbes in *Leviathan*, Bekker explained Christian demonology as a superstitious error that evolved from paganism: *daimones*, when adopted by Jews and early Christians, became the evil spirits of the bible.[85] Bekker supplemented this theological and historical critique with a philosophical rejection of the scholastic notion of spirits and the interaction of causalities. Here he parted ways with Hobbes, relying, not on materialism, but on Cartesian metaphysics, which distinguishes thought (pure spirits) from extension (body). Since disembodied spirits are incapable of inhering upon matter, the power of the devil in the material realm must be rejected.[86] Along these lines, Bekker also emphasised metaphorical and natural understandings of biblical passages dealing with demoniacs and exorcism. Jews, pagans, and early Christians confused demons with natural afflictions: "It appears that illness takes the name of 'Spirit' in the Holy Scripture"; possessions were thus "malign afflictions infecting the brain," while Christ's exorcisms were only "a miraculous cure of incurable maladies." Bekker also underlined *accommodatio*: Christ treated ill people with exorcisms, not because he actually expelled spirits, but because he acted "according to the usage of the times."[87]

Hobbes and Bekker participated in a 17th-century "metaphysical free-for-all," where alternative natural philosophies such as materialism and Cartesianism shed new light on the relationship between spirit and matter, profoundly affecting scholastic demonology, which was recast as irrational thinking.[88] In addition, their views contributed to a secularisation of the scripture. Hobbes and Bekker saw the idea of the devil's influence over nature and mankind as stemming from the pagan, Jewish, and early Christian milieu. Experiences such as possession and exorcism, for example, were not part of the divine message, but rather part of the cultural setting in which scripture was written. Thus, demonology was not germane to Christian truth, and never was.

It would be left to 18th-century authors to further develop this transition of the science of demons, from valid thought and action to superstition, and from a divinely sanctioned body of knowledge to culturally determined (and thus rejectable) ideas.[89] To a growing number of people claiming to be at the forefront of Western theology, science, and politics, demoniacs and exorcists ceased to be immediate sources of meaning. They were no longer capable of fuelling confessional battles, or debates over the interplay between matter and spirit; they were no longer able to nurture anxieties over discernment of spirits, or to translate God's will.

This does not mean that the devil, his powers, or the techniques designed to counter him were absent during the Enlightenment (or during the 19th century, for that matter). Quite the contrary, in both rural and urban landscapes, people still suffered the attacks of indwelling evil spirits, and sought physical and spiritual remedies against them.[90] However, from the end of the 17th century onwards, as the intellectual and political preoccupation with demonology began to wane at the level of the elite, and as this elite actively engaged in a critique of what they now rejected as excesses of popular and fanatical beliefs, the "golden age" of demoniacs, and hence of exorcists, came to a close.[91]

## Acknowledgement

I would like to extend my thanks to Richard Raiswell, who provided comments and suggestions which helped to improve this chapter both in content and form.

## Notes

1 William Monter, *Witchcraft in France and Switzerland: The Borderlands During the Reformation* (Ithaca, 1976), 60.
2 For possession and exorcism in the New Testament, see Graham Twelftree, *In the Name of Jesus: Exorcism among Early Christians* (Michigan, 2007), 25–208.
3 Peter Dendle, *Demon Possession in Anglo-Saxon England* (Kalamazoo, 2014), 62–5, 104–5.
4 For an introduction, see Henry Ansgar Kelly, *The Devil at Baptism: Ritual, Theology, and Drama* (Ithaca, 1985).
5 Florence Chave-Mahir, *L'exorcisme des possédés dans l'Église d'Occident (Xe-XIVe siècle)* (Turnhout, 2011), 17.
6 Francis Young, *A History of Exorcism in Catholic Christianity* (London, 2016), 45–53.
7 *Apostolic Constitutions* 8.26, in *The Ante-Nicene Fathers: Translations of the Writings of the Fathers Down to A.D. 325*, ed. Alexander Roberts and James Donaldson (Buffalo, 1886), 493.
8 Dendle, *Demon Possession*, 64. In later times, this would inform the distinction between sacrament and sacramental. A sacrament is a priestly rite endowed with automatic efficacy, thanks to God's promise to the church (for example, communion or baptism). A sacramental, on the contrary, is a rite whose efficacy depended on God's arbitrary, contingent assistance. For this distinction, see Sarah Ferber, *Demonic Possession and Exorcism in Early Modern France* (London, 2004), 65–6.

9  Richard Raiswell and Peter Dendle, "Demon Possession in Anglo-Saxon and Early Modern England: Continuity and Evolution in Social Context," *The Journal of British Studies* 47 (2008): 741–2.

10 Michael Bailey, *Magic and Superstition in Europe: A Concise History from Antiquity to the Present* (Lanham, 2007), 83; Richard Kieckhefer, *Magic in the Middle Ages* (Cambridge, 2014), 71.

11 See quote and interpretation in Emily Kesling, *Medical Texts in Anglo-Saxon Literary Culture* (Cambridge, 2020), 87–94.

12 Peter Brown, *The Cult of the Saints: Its Rise and Function in Latin Christianity* (Chicago, 1981), 107.

13 For Late Antiquity, see Peter Brown, "The Rise and Function of the Holy Man in Late Antiquity," *The Journal of Roman Studies* 61 (1971): 80–101; for the medieval period, Sari Katajala-Peltomaa, *Demonic Possession and Lived Religion in Later Medieval Europe* (Oxford, 2020), 101–28; for the early modern times, David Lederer, *Madness, Religion and the State in Early Modern Europe: A Bavarian Beacon* (Cambridge, 2006), 99–144.

14 Augustine, *Confessions*, trans. Henry Chadwick (New York, 1991), 165.

15 Ambrose, *Epistola* 22, col. 1025. 21 (Patrologia Latina 16).

16 Raiswell and Dendle, "Demon Possession," 747.

17 *Summa theologiae*, I, q. 110, art. 4; I, q. 111, art. 4. On preternature, see Lorraine Daston, "Preternatural Philosophy," in *Biographies of Scientific Objects*, ed. Lorraine Daston (Chicago, 2000), 15–41; on preternature in connection with Aquinas' demonology, see Fabián Campagne, "Witchcraft and the Sense-of-the-Impossible in Early Modern Spain: Some Reflections Based on the Literature of Superstition (ca. 1500–1800)," *Harvard Theological Review* 96, no. 1 (2003): 25–62.

18 *The De malo of Thomas Aquinas*, trans. Richard Regan, ed. Brian Davies (Oxford, 2001), q. 3, art. 4. See also *Summa theologiae*, I. 111, art. 2–4; *Quaestiones de quolibet*, III, 3, art. 3. For the physiology of possession, see Nancy Caciola, "Breath, Heart, Guts: The Body and Spirits in the Middle Ages," in *Communicating with the Spirits*, ed. Gábor Klaniczay and Éva Pócs (Budapest, 2005), 21–39.

19 On divination as a sign of possession, *Summa theologiae*, II-IIae, q. 95, a. 3; on xenoglossia, *Summa theologiae*, I, q. 115, a. 5.

20 *Summa theologiae*, IIa-IIae, q. 175, a. 1.

21 Fabián Campagne, *Profetas en Ninguna Tierra: Una Historia del Discernimiento de Espíritus en Occidente* (Buenos Aires, 2016); Nancy Caciola and Moshe Sluhovsky, "Spiritual Physiologies: The Discernment of Spirits in Medieval and Early Modern Europe," *Preternature* 1, no. 1 (2012): 1–48.

22 Quotations are from the modern translation: *Jean Fernel's On the Hidden Causes of Things: Forms, Soul and Occult Diseases in Renaissance Medicine*, trans. John Forrester, ed. John Forrester and John Henry (Leiden, 2005), 653, 655.

23 Michel de Montaigne, *Journal de Voyage de Michel de Montaigne* (Rome, 1774), 139, 136.

24 See Angus Gowland, "The Problem of Early Modern Melancholy," *Past & Present* 191 (2006): 77–120.

25 For *melancholia* and possession, see Herman Westerink, "Demonic Possession and the Historical Construction of Melancholy and Hysteria," *History of Psychiatry* 25, no. 3 (2014): 335–49.

26 Johannes Wier, *De praestigiis daemonum* (Basel, 1563), 402–4. On Wier, see Michaela Valente, "'Against the devil, the subtle and cunning enemy': Johann Wier's *De praestigiis daemonum*," in *The Science of Demons: Early Modern Authors Facing Witchcraft and the Devil*, ed. Jan Machielsen (London, 2020), 103–18.

27 *Problemata*, ed. E. Forster (Oxford, 1927), 954. On the debate over Problem 30.1, see Noel Brann, *The Debate over the Origin of Genius during the Italian Renaissance: The Theories of Supernatural Frenzy and Natural Melancholy in Accord and in Conflict on the Threshold of the Scientific Revolution* (Leiden, 2002).

28 Pietro d'Abano, *Expositio Problematum Aristotelis* (Mantua, 1475), 30.1, 268.

29 Ismael del Olmo, "'But Who Can Assure Himselfe Not To Be Deceived in Matters Concerning Spirits?' Discernment as Anti-demonology in Late Sixteenth-Century Europe," *Sixteenth Century Journal* 52, no. 3 (2021): 609–30.

30 Nancy Caciola, *Discerning Spirits: Divine and Demonic Possession in the Middle Ages* (Ithaca, 2003), 25–6, 86.

31 *Practica y Exercicio Espiritual de una Sierva de Dios* (Valencia, 1585), v, viii.

32 Gaspar Navarro, *Tribunal de Superstición Ladina* (Huesca, 1631), 33.

33 Sophie Houdard, *Les Invasions Mystiques: Spiritualités, Hétérodoxies et Censures au Début de l'Époque Moderne* (Paris, 2008), 221.

34 Quotations are from the modern reprint of the original 1586 text: Désiré-Magloire Bourneville, *La Possession de Jeanne Féry, Religieuse Professe du Couvent des Sœurs Noires de la Ville de Mons (1584)* (Paris, 1886), 55, 103.

35 Elizabeth Mellyn, "Healers and Healing in the Early Modern Health Care Market," in *The Routledge History of Madness and Mental Health*, ed. Greg Eghigian (London, 2017), 83–100.

36 On late medieval and early modern superstition, see Michael Bailey, *Fearful Spirits, Reasoned Follies: The Boundaries of Superstition in Late Medieval Europe* (London, 2017); Euan Cameron, *Enchanted Europe: Superstition, Reason and Religion, 1250–1750* (Oxford, 2010).

37 Moshe Sluhovsky, *Believe Not Every Spirit: Possession, Mysticism and Discernment in Early Modern Catholicism* (Chicago, 2007), 62–3, 192–7; Sarah Ferber, "Demonic Possession, Exorcism, and Witchcraft," in *The Oxford Handbook of Witchcraft in Early Modern Europe and Colonial America*, ed. Brian Levack (Oxford, 2013), 575–92.

38 Andrew Keitt, *Inventing the Sacred: Imposture, Inquisition, and the Boundaries of the Supernatural in Golden Age Spain* (Leiden, 2005), 159–60.

39 Pedro Ciruelo, *Reprobación de las Supersticiones y Hechicerías* (Valladolid, 2005), 104–5 and 108.

40 On the case, see Matteo Duni, *Tra Religione e Magia: Storia del Prete Modenese Guglielmo Campana (1460?–1541)* (Florence, 1999).

41 Ciruelo, *Reprobación*, 107–8.

42 Montaigne, *Journal*, 137.

43 Sluhovsky, *Believe Not Every Spirit*, 47–8.

44 "De Exorcizandis Obsessis a Daemonio," in *Rituale Romanum* (Rome, 1614), 198–201. On the *Rituale*, see Young, *History of Exorcism*, 34–8, 116–20.

45 Rainer Decker, *Witchcraft and Papacy: An Account Drawing on the Formerly Secret Records of the Roman Inquisition* (Charlottesville, 2003), 169–70.

46 David Lederer, "'Exorzieren ohne Lizenz…': Befugnis, Skepsis und Glauben im frühneuzeitlichen Bayern," in *Dämonische Besessenheit: Zur Interpretation eines Kulturhistorischen Phänomens*, ed. Hans De Waardt et al. (Bielefeld, 2005), 231.

47 Guido Ruggiero, *Binding Passions: Tales of Magic, Marriage, and Power at the End of the Renaissance* (New York, 1993), 149–52.

48 Lederer, *Madness, Religion, and the State*, 227.

49 Quoted in María Tausiet, *Urban Magic in Early Modern Spain: Abracadabra Omnipotens*, trans. Susannah Howe (Houndsmill, 2013), 113–4.

50 Ferber, *Demonic Possession and Exorcism in Early Modern France*, 65–6.

51 María Tausiet, "The Guardian of Hell: Popular Demonology, Exorcism, and Mysticism in Baroque Spain," in *Demonology and Witch-Hunting in Early Modern Europe*, eds. Julian Goodare, Rita Voltmer, and Liv Helene Willumsen (London, 2020), 302–26.

52 Quoted in Ángel Gari Lacruz, *Brujería e Inquisición en el Alto Aragón en la Primera Mitad del Siglo XVII* (Zaragoza, 1991), 419.

53 Daniel Walker, "Demonic Possession Used as Propaganda in the Late Sixteenth Century," in *Scienza, Credenze Occulte, Livelli di Cultura: Atti del Convegno Internazionale di Studi (Firenze, 26–30 giugno 1980)* (Florence, 1982), 237–48.

54 Ferber, *Demonic Possession*, 3–4.

55 Jean Boulaese, *Le Thresor et Entiere Histoire de la Triomphante Victoire du Corps de Dieu sur l'Esprit Maling Beelzebub* (Paris, 1578), 44. On the case, Irena Backus, *Le Miracle de Laon: Le Déraisonnable, le Raisonnable, l'Apocalyptique et la Politique dans les Récits du Miracle de Laon (1566–1578)* (Paris, 1994).

56 Petrus Thyraeus, *De Daemoniacis* (Cologne, 1594), 86.

57 Francisco Blasco de Lanuza, *Patrocinio de Ángeles y Combate de Demonios* (Huesca, 1652), 837.

58 Susan Karant-Nunn, *The Reformation of Ritual: An Interpretation of Early Modern Germany* (London: 2005), 183–6.

59 Martin Luther, *The Tabletalk of Martin Luther*, ed. William Hazlitt (London, 1857), 258, 267.

60 Jean Calvin, *Institutes of Christian Religion*, ed. John McNeill, trans. Ford Lewis Battles (Philadelphia, 1960), 388; Jean Calvin, *A Harmony of the Gospels: Matthew, Mark, and Luke*, vol. II, ed. David Torrance and Thomas Torrance, trans. T. H. Parker (Michigan, 1995), 41–2.

61 Heinrich Bullinger, *The Decades of Henry Bullinger*, ed. Thomas Harding (Cambridge, 1852), 115.

62 Martinus Chemnicium, *Examen Concilii Tridentini*, ed. Eduard Preuß (Berlin, 1861), 477.
63 Reginald Scot, *Discoverie of Witchcraft* (London, 1584), 248. On Scot, see Philip Almond, *England's First Demonologist: Reginald Scot and The Discoverie of Witchcraft* (London, 2011).
64 Keith Thomas, *Religion and the Decline of Magic* (London, 1971), 477–81.
65 Benjamin Kaplan, "Possessed by the Devil? A Very Public Dispute in Utrecht," *Renaissance Quarterly* 49, no. 4 (1996): 738–59.
66 Raiswell and Dendle, "Demon Possession," 756.
67 See Nathan Johnstone, "The Protestant Devil: The Experience of Temptation in Early Modern England," *Journal of British Studies* 43 (2004): 173–205. For the Reformation's model of possession, see Brian Levack, *The Devil Within: Possession and Exorcism in the Christian West* (New Haven, 2013), 39, 62, 111, 161, 156–67, 259–62.
68 *A True and Fearful Vexation of one Alexander Nyndge* (London, 1615), reprinted in Philip Almond, *Demonic Possession and Exorcism in Early Modern England: Contemporary Texts and their Cultural Contexts* (Cambridge, 2004), 55, 49, 52, 48.
69 Brendan Walsh, *The English Exorcist: John Darrell and the Shaping of Early Modern English Protestant Demonology* (New York, 2021).
70 John Darrell, *Detection of that Sinnful, Shamful, Lying, and Ridiculous Discours of Samuel Harshnet* (London: 1600), 48.
71 Darrell, *Detection*, 171.
72 Samuel Harsnett, *A Discovery of the Fraudulent Practises of John Darell* (London, 1599), 115.
73 Harsnett, *Discovery*, 5, 303 and sig. A3.
74 On the canon, Francis Young, *A History of Anglican Exorcism: Deliverance and Demonology in Church Ritual* (London, 2018), 48–56. On the theological-political reasons for criticising possession and exorcism, Michael MacDonald, *Mystical Bedlam: Madness, Anxiety, and Healing in Seventeenth-Century England* (Cambridge, 1981), 206, 226 and 230.
75 Quoted in MacDonald, *Mystical Bedlam*, 215. On Napier, see Ofer Hadass, *Medicine, Religion, and Magic in Early Stuart England: Richard Napier's Medical Practice* (Philadelphia, 2018).
76 Lambert Daneau, *Les Sorciers* (Geneva, 1574), 42.
77 Blasco de Lanuza, *Patrocinio*, 810.
78 Cameron, *Enchanted Europe*, 241–69.
79 Ismael del Olmo, "Against Scarecrows and Half-Baked Christians: Thomas Hobbes on Spiritual Possession and (Civil) Exorcism," *Hobbes Studies* 31 (2018): 127–46.
80 Thomas Hobbes, *Leviathan*, ed. Noel Malcolm (Oxford, 2012), 7–8.
81 Hobbes, *Leviathan*, 207, 353–5.
82 On *accommodatio*, see Stephen Benin, *The Footprints of God: Divine Accommodation in Jewish and Christian Thought* (Albany, 1993).
83 Hobbes, *Leviathan*, 38, 355, 211, 37, 354.
84 Balthasar Bekker, *De Betoverde Weereld*, 4 vols (Amsterdam, 1691–1693). On Bekker, see Andrew Fix, *Fallen Angels: Balthasar Bekker, Spirit Belief, and Confessionalism in the Seventeenth Century Dutch Republic* (Dordrecht, 1999).
85 References are from the French edition: Balthasar Bekker, *Le Monde Enchanté* (Amsterdam, 1694), vol. 1, ix–x, xii.
86 Koen Vermeir, "Mechanical Philosophy in an Enchanted World: Cartesian Empiricism in Balthasar Bekker's Radical Reformation," in *Cartesian Empiricisms*, ed. Mihnea Dobre and Tammy Nyden (Dordrecht, 2013), 275–306.
87 Bekker, *Le Monde Enchanté*, vol. 1, xxxvi and vol. 2, 460, 463.
88 Euan Cameron, "Angels, Demons, and Everything in Between," in *Angels of Light? Sanctity and Discernment of Spirits in the Early Modern Period*, ed. Clare Copeland and Jan Machielsen (Leiden, 2013), 20.
89 For an example of this transition during the Enlightenment, see Rita Voltmer, "Circulating Knowledge in European Enlightened Discourses: Eberhard David Hauber and the *Bibliotheca, sive Acta et Scripta Magica* (1738–1745)," in *Folklore, Magic, and Witchcraft: Cultural Exchanges from the Twelfth to Eighteenth Century*, ed. Marina Montesano (Abingdon, 2022), 281–93.

90 See Erik Midelfort, *Exorcism and Enlightenment: Johann Joseph Gassner and the Demons of Eighteenth-Century Germany* (New Haven, 2005); María Tausiet, *Los posesos de Tosos (1812–1814): Brujería y Justicia Popular en Tiempos de Revolución* (Zaragoza, 2001).
91 Lederer, *Madness, Religion, and the State*, 19–20, 142–3, 197–8, 202–6, 240–1.

## Further Reading

Caciola, Nancy. *Discerning Spirits: Divine and Demonic Possession in the Middle Ages* (Ithaca: Cornell University Press, 2003).

Dendle, Peter. *Demon Possession in Anglo-Saxon England* (Kalamazoo: Medieval Institute Publications, 2014).

Ferber, Sarah. *Demonic Possession and Exorcism in Early Modern France* (London: Routledge, 2004).

Katajala-Peltomaa, Sari. *Demonic Possession and Lived Religion in Later Medieval Europe* (Oxford: Oxford University Press, 2020).

Raiswell, Richard and Peter Dendle. "Demon Possession in Anglo-Saxon and Early Modern England: Continuity and Evolution in Social Context," *The Journal of British Studies* 47 (2008): 738–67.

Twelftree, Graham. *In the Name of Jesus: Exorcism among Early Christians* (Michigan: Baker Academic, 2007).

Walsh, Brendan. *The English Exorcist: John Darrell and the Shaping of Early Modern English Protestant Demonology* (New York: Routledge, 2021).

Young Francis. *A History of Exorcism in Catholic Christianity* (London: Palgrave Macmillan, 2016).

# 13

# THE DEVIL AND STATECRAFT

*Gary K. Waite*

In a 1524 pamphlet addressed to Duke Karel van Guelders, the Catholic author warned the duke that the heresy of Martin Luther would quickly be followed by witches who had made a pact with the devil and were performing black magic to the harm of the realm on the eve of Christ's return later that year. The duke obligingly prosecuted both religious heretics—"Lutherans" and Anabaptists—and witches.[1] This position that rulers needed to attack both heresy and witchcraft in order to protect their sovereignty against the devil's assaults was made most famous in the lectures of the Jesuit Juan de Maldonado (1533–83), who taught a generation of Jesuit priests at Paris at the height of the confessional conflict in France.

One of those who followed this reasoning was the secular judge and witch-hunter of the Duchy of Lorraine, Nicholas Rémy, who in 1595 published his *Daemonolatreiae libri tres* (Demonolatry, in three books), which quickly became a standard manual for witch-craft prosecution.[2] But it was not just witches that worried the jurist. In his foreword to the Duke's son, Cardinal Charles of Lorraine, Rémy followed a similar reasoning to our Guelders' writer that the devil was assaulting Christendom using religious heretics who follow "the light of human reason" towards atheism on the one hand, and the poor and ig-norant people, mostly women, who turn to base witchcraft on the other.[3] He told the prince that "the atheists of the former class are begotten, bred and protected by the freedom which in our time has arisen from the variety and confusion of nations," reaching incredible num-bers and "hiding behind the cover of whatever form of religion comes to their hand." As for those "befouled in the mire of witchcraft," their numbers have been increasing, thanks to the "negligence and laziness of those whose duty it is to preach from the public pulpits."[4] Lax state and church officials were to blame, therefore, for the rise in diabolical apostasy, and the courts needed to put this right.

Lorraine therefore presents a tempting example of witch-hunting as a tool of state-building, of seeing "ducal agents exploiting popular beliefs and the demand for action against suspects in order to complete their victory over rival jurisdictions," as Robin Briggs puts it. And in such weak states as Lorraine, he continues, rulers may have been tempted to "play the witchcraft card" to solidify their authority to craft a godly state; the dukes were pious Catholics struggling to avoid the religious conflict raging in France and the

DOI: 10.4324/9781003096603-14

Holy Roman Empire and to maintain their independence.[5] Yet, it was not Lorraine's central government that targeted witch suspects; it did not even create a witchcraft statute to encourage prosecution. Instead, trials remained local affairs, as judges gave in to local pressure and became convinced of the threat, "and because such action did advance their own prestige."[6] The central government did not intervene in these trials because they never quite reached the level of the socially destructive panics of the Empire. If witch-hunting assisted state-building in Lorraine, Briggs concludes, it did so accidently, and in a minor way. Yet, as advocates of the Catholic Reformation, the dukes and their officials did seek to craft a godly realm devoid of the confessional diversity and conflict raging elsewhere. For them, as for other princes, "the idea of external forces which could be directed against a fragile humanity and its institutions retained great intuitive power."[7]

In the minds of early modern theologians, this malign force, personified in Satan's hordes of demons and human allies, was as politically astute and conniving as any prince or magistrate. By causing havoc within Christendom, he could ensnare more Christians prior to the Last Judgement. Rulers who were not prepared to confront his evil machinations would merit God's anger, for they governed as his representative on earth. In contrast, those who acted with rigour against Satan's minions, including witches, would be protected while engaged in their divinely appointed missions. Neglect of such duties would allow the realm to descend into horrible blasphemy and apostasy that would merit divine punishment in storms and plagues.[8]

## The Medieval Background

This fear of divine anger was a powerful, if neglected feature of governance in early modern Europe.[9] Outside of the scholarship on the witch-hunts, historians have tended to leave Satan out of discussions of the story of early modern state-building. But just as princes made policies to please the divine, they also sought to oppose the great apocalyptical enemy of Christ, Satan, who almost always worked through his human agents, beginning with the Jews in the 1st century.[10] Over time, Satan's minions grew to include heretics, witches, and political enemies. The rise of the medieval Inquisition against heretics supported papal authority, but its methods were also adopted by princes to enhance their authority as well.[11] King Philip IV used the inquisitorial process to get rid of political enemies, including the Knights Templar in 1307 and Pope Boniface VIII in 1311 on trumped up charges of devil worship and heresy. In 1321, Philip V applied the same procedure to get at the wealth of the Leper houses of southern France, and then of the Jews. Satan, of course, was the conspiracy's general.[12] Even if these were cynical ploys to exploit popular fear of Satan against political foes, this does not imply scepticism towards the devil, only that princes knew how powerful an ally he could be.

A century later, in 1411, France was riven by a civil war between the houses of Burgundy and the royal Valois line that some contemporaries blamed on the astrologers and necromancers at the royal court.[13] When King Charles VI began suffering from bouts of insanity, sorcerers flocked to the capital to cure him. Many accused the king's late brother, Louis of Orléans, of having caused the king's affliction through black magic; others accused the Duke of Burgundy's necromancers.[14] When Duke John the Fearless of Burgundy admitted to ordering Louis' assassination, he confessed that "the devil had driven him to this crime."[15] By the start of major prosecution of a diabolical sect of witches around 1426, rulers had been exploiting belief in the devil's machinations as a means of enhancing their sovereignty and eliminating enemies.[16] They also believed that, thanks to the services of their clerical necromancers, the devil's powers were real and available to them to enhance their sovereignty; unsurprisingly, demonologists arranged demons in hierarchies that paralleled that of European nobility.[17] Princes saw part of their duty to supervise the beliefs and religious practices of their people, since their sovereignty relied on a unitary faith. Religious dissent was thus both diabolical and treason against both God and the king.

Focusing primarily on the Holy Roman Empire, France, Spain, England and Scotland, this discussion will examine how theologians encouraged jurists, magistrates, and princes to protect their jurisdictions from Satan's activities, and the extent to which rulers followed such advice. The results varied from state to state, as did the particular minions of the devil targeted, whether the secret Jews of the Spanish Inquisition, religious heretics, commoner rebels, confessional rivals, or any whose blasphemy was a threat to incurring divine anger. We will conclude with the Dutch Republic which, in contrast to all other realms, essentially abandoned the devil as a force in governance, with interesting results.

### Historiography: State-Building, Satan, and Witch-Hunting

To date, most attention on the devil and state-building has been focused on the question of whether or not the witch-hunts aided and abetted princely efforts to centralise their realms. This was the focus of Brian P. Levack's important 1996 essay in which he observed that over the previous two decades, historians had sought "to establish a causal relationship between the great European witch-hunt of the 16th and 17th centuries and the development of the modern state," arguing that the "'rise of the nation-state' is at the very least one of the secondary causes of the witch hunt."[18] In this perspective, princes promoted witch trials to assert greater control over local jurisdictions and smooth the path to state sovereignty. While many clergy, judges, and civic officials advised princes to pursue witchcraft prosecution to shift the allegiance of people from the local community to the state, Levack's close examination of Scotland revealed instead that the royally controlled central courts suppressed executions, in contrast to the unsupervised local courts in which trials could spiral out of control. More recent analyses by Levack and Johannes Dillinger have concluded similarly, that in most cases, governments seeking to build strong centralised governments tended to suppress local witchcraft trials, rather than inspire witch panics as a means of state-building.[19]

Recently, Silvia Federici has sought to revive the top-down model of witch-hunting through a materialist explanation in which these trials were "the first unifying terrain in the politics of the new European nation-states, the first example, after the schism brought about by the Reformation, of a European unification." Needing control over their economies and a growing male labour force, rulers ordered their courts to attack women seeking to control fertility.[20] However, Federici's thesis fails when confronted with detailed analyses of the actual trials.[21] For example, Wolfgang Behringer has shown that Bavaria's major witch panic "began without reflection; nowhere was there a concerted plan for the systematic expansion of individual trials."[22] In most cases, accusations of witchcraft were pursued by neighbour against neighbour, and were not centrally stage-managed. Instead, when central authorities became involved, they restrained local trials.[23] Such intervention in local jurisdictions did assist rulers in consolidating power. The devil did, however, play a strong role in Reformation-era state-building in three areas: the growth of confessionalisation, which escalated religious conflict in various regions; heresy prosecution, which was much more centrally mandated than witch trials; and popular uprisings, which the princes and their clerical advisors associated with the devil. Satan remained active in royal courts.

## State-Building and Confessionalisation

The early modern era witnessed the rise of new national monarchies and of populist reactions against royal policies of centralisation.[24] In the tumultuous 1520s and 1530s, the Reformation dismantled traditional norms of social cohesion and religious and political unity. In response, princes and magistrates took sides with one or the other of mainstream confessional variants—Catholicism, Lutheranism, and Calvinism. In a process described as confessionalism, secular rulers became the principal arbiters of religious affiliation, a posture formalised in the Peace of Augsburg of 1555 ending the war between Lutheran princes and the Habsburg Holy Roman Emperor Charles V (r. 1520–56), by allowing each prince to determine whether their state and people were Catholic or Lutheran.[25] Excluded from the truce, the Reformed or Calvinists fought for recognition, while various princes began fighting to convert neighbouring principalities. Such confessional conflict spread elsewhere, such as France and the Low Countries, leading to a century of religious warfare that ended only in 1648 with the Peace of Westphalia. Despite the divisions, the Reformation(s) reinforced the idea that princes stood in God's place to determine correct belief and practice. Alternative religious forms were therefore to be excised as a threat to the state, as, in fact, a form of *lése majesté*, treason against the king and God. Fear of divine wrath is prominent in the notorious witch-hunts but is also evident in the heresy prosecution that preceded the witch-hunts; both in fact were seen as diabolical. As princes centralised their bureaucracies and courts to better control the behaviour of their people, they did so with God and Satan in mind.

## The Devil in the Reformations, c. 1517–55

This is no truer that with the major German Reformer, Martin Luther, who was obsessed with the devil's raging in the Last Days.[26] Since for Luther Satan was under God's control, he advised believers to counteract the devil's assaults by shouting, "I have been baptised, I am a Christian."[27] Those who feared they had been harmed by witchcraft were misled, for misfortune arose from divine punishment for sin.[28] The devil's most serious agents were the opponents of the gospel: the papal Antichrist; fellow Protestants who denied the Real Presence in the Eucharist; and radical dissenters, such as Anabaptists. Luther's coarse, demonising language hindered collaboration among Reformers and entrenched division on all sides.[29] Lutheran, Catholic, and Reformed princes thus hunted down Satan's human agents, most of whom were Anabaptists.[30] Then, as those heresy fires cooled, rulers began taking seriously concerns about a sect of witches, with large-scale witch trials reviving in Wiesensteig, Southwestern Germany, in 1562.[31]

John Calvin's language was more restrained; yet, he too taught that the papacy was the Antichrist and the devil a powerful tempter. Even though they possessed no real power to harm believers, witches deserved harsh punishment for their apostasy, for God could not tolerate any form of blasphemy in a godly realm. This attitude drove Calvinist ministers to work with civic magistrates to create a godly community, in effect a state-church.[32] Calvinist struggles against Satan were focused on resisting the papal antichrist and his superstition and idolatry and "Libertines" who fostered disbelief and immorality. They also had to battle against the inner voice of temptation beguiling them to doubt their salvation.[33]

The popes responded by redefining theological orthodoxy against Protestant error at the Council of Trent (1545–63); establishing the Roman Inquisition; and founding the Society of Jesus, or Jesuits. Together, these drove Protestantism out of Southern Europe, and Jesuits became key advisors for many Catholic rulers, reminding them that Protestants were led by Satan.[34] As noted above, this posture was taught by Maldonado from 1564 to 1576, during the height of the French civil wars. A fervent anti-Protestant, Maldonado argued that by spreading Protestant heresy, demons made people susceptible to the ultimate apostasy of diabolical witchcraft and atheism.[35] Inspired by such rhetoric, zealous Catholic princes fought even more vigorously against the Calvinist heretics; we will return to this subject later. Among the many Jesuits influenced by Maldonado was the Antwerp humanist Martin Delrio, author of the *Disquisitionum magicarum* (Magical Investigations) of 1599, which opens with a truly apocalyptical scenario of demons raging across Europe inspiring Protestant heretics, followed by swarms of flying, magic-performing, and Satan-worshipping witches.[36] The rhetoric used by all confessional sides against each other, accusing the opponent of devil worship and plotting with Satan against the true faith, heightened anxiety about the devil and his human agents; the most intense was that directed at Anabaptists and other radical nonconformists, some of whom continued to be prosecuted and executed well into the 17th century.[37]

## Opposition to Monarchical Power, c. 1400–1555

Prior to the Reformation, kings and popes fought over who controlled religion, focused typically on the investiture of bishops or the taxation of priests and church property. This led to the Papal Schism and the Conciliarist reform movement of the 15th century. Conciliarists asserted that political authority was invested in the Church as a whole, represented in a council, not the pope, a movement parallel to the rise of representative parliaments and states general.[38] Recent research is showing that demonic witchcraft was a feature in polemics between Conciliarists and papal supremacists; the Council of Basel was a vector for demonological ideas in the 1430s and 1440s.[39] Some of these efforts were accompanied by uprisings wherein the people demanded a voice in national governance, such as those which inflamed France and England during the Hundreds Years War. These climaxed with the massive "Peasants' War of 1525" in the German lands which involved tens of thousands of rural and urban commoners. Was Satan involved in this rebellion against noble authority?

### *The German Peasants War of 1525*

Most of the peasant demands were composed by literate clerics who used scripture and Luther's slogans of equality of all Christians and freedom of the common man.[40] Luther became infuriated with what he saw as the peasants' misappropriation of the "gospel" as a rationale for freedom from prosaic feudal dues and servitude, even though he had told them to rebel against the "spiritual authorities when they are in the wrong." The rebels had, however, ignored the absolute requirement to obey the magistrate in all earthly matters, outside of the conscience captive to the Word of God.[41] Just as the tide was turning against the rebels in May 1525, Luther published his notorious *Against the Robbing and Murdering Hordes of Peasants*, encouraging the lords to hunt down the rebels like "mad dogs," for "it is the devil's work that they are at."[42] The peasants had "become the greatest of all blasphemers of God and slanderers of his holy Name, serving the devil, ... I have never heard of a more hideous sin. I suspect that the devil feels the Last Day coming and therefore undertakes such an unheard-of-act," concluding, "I think there is not a devil left in hell; they have all gone into the peasants." Luther assumed that God may "have thus aroused the devil as a punishment upon all Germany," so princes needed to "humbly pray for help against the devil," and then, as God's "servant of his wrath," slay these servants of the devil who were heading to hell anyway. If they refused, the princes would hand the kingdom of earth over to the devil. While this may be part of the divine plan, Luther hoped for better.

The authors of the peasant articles sought to counteract accusations of diabolical sedition by showing that with their excessive taxation and labour exactions, it was the landlords who were led by the devil. For example, the author of the Salzburg Articles of May–June 1525 described the lords as "antichristian tyrants," "God's enemies," "soul-destroyers, seducers, thieves, and corrupters of the entire commune" who refuse to turn to God and the "evangelical truth" and instead are in thrall to the "damned vice of pride, which arises from the devil." The abuse of the common folk by their oppressors had lured them "from the paths of evangelical truth and led them to the devil."[43] Such clerical writers also included regulations against drunkenness and blasphemy to show that they, like good Christian princes, wanted a realm cleansed of sin.[44] Whatever the knights thought as they massacred the rebels, many on all sides saw the conflict as one between God and Satan, whether defined as Satanic sedition or diabolical oppression.

The knights' attitude towards the rebellion was hardened, thanks to the "massacre of Weinsberg" of 16 April 1535, when a peasant band captured the castle of Weinsberg and forced the ruling lord, Count Ludwig von Helfenstein, and several of his knights to run the gauntlet. This atrocity became a rallying cry for the lords and was cast in a demonising light. The local parson Johann Herolt exclaimed that when the townsfolk of Weinsberg opened their gates to the peasants, "Lucifer and all his angels were let loose, for they raged and stormed no differently than if they were mad and possessed by every devil."[45] One of Count Ludwig's grandsons and heirs, Count Ulrich XVII von Helfenstein, was the ruling count who in 1562 oversaw the notorious Wiesensteig trials with its 63 women victims; one might wonder the extent to which the family stories of the Weinsberg massacre shaped Ulrich's attitude towards his people, the devil, and seditious activity. Given that one of the few women arrested for participating in the Peasants' War, Margaret Rennerin, had bragged to other women to having participated in the stabbing of Count Ludwig, the event may have coloured his view of peasant women.[46] Count Ulrich took the devil seriously in his deliberations, and in 1562 was willing to believe that dozens of the women in his countryside had made a pact with Satan against his realm.

## Confessional Polemics in the Wake of the Peasants War

Luther's unrestrained invective ended popular support for his reform movement, and he turned decisively to the princes to whom he granted authority over all aspects of religion and worship outside an individual's conscience. This the princes used effectively to compel a single religious confession and practice on their people. All Reformers worked with civic magistrates to construct the godly state in which there would be no space for the devil, and where the people would live up to stricter and more carefully defined codes of moral conduct, in line with precisely delineated confessions of faith.[47]

In this context, even a few dissenters presented a major challenge to a unitary confessional state. Since Anabaptism arose during the Peasants' War, it was strongly linked to sedition.[48] Some heresy edicts used language associating Anabaptists with the devil or magic, such as one proclaimed by Protestant Swiss Cantons in 1527 claiming a discovery of magic-performing, shamanistic Anabaptists.[49] Despite this, and the precedent set with the fusion of Waldensian heresy and witchcraft in the previous century, the efforts of Catholic and Lutheran preachers to associate Anabaptists with diabolical magic failed, but they certainly intensified the harshness of their treatment by rulers and judges fearful of incurring divine anger.[50] Archduke Ferdinand of Austria's mandate of 1532 is filled with anxiety over the "punishment of almighty God" which had been raging through the German nation, thanks to such blasphemies.[51]

Such fear was a feature of the Empire's witch panics, as observed by the Jesuit priest Friedrich Spee van Langenfelds, who described the witch trials as "the disastrous consequence of Germany's religious zeal."[52] Writing directly to Germany's princes, Spee observed that the trials began due to the laxity of magistrates and preachers in refuting the people's superstitions and rumour-mongering. As a result, the folk had no choice but to demand legal action, a clamour that forced princes to "command their judges and counselors to begin to try witches."[53] Seeking to please the ruler, the judges and clergy joined in, and the process began, for an ostensibly good reason of purging the state "of a singular plague." Spee highlighted the role of clergy in the noble courts, for he had "heard several preachers … persuade the rulers that they should devote all their severity to banishing this plague of witches from the state" and "heard others excite the princes' rage in private addresses," summoning "fire down from the heavens."[54] Yet, "however many witches the princes burn, they will never burn out the evil unless they burn everything."[55] They are, Spee continued, "ravaging their lands worse than any war could, and yet they achieve nothing."[56] The devil, Spee reminded Germany's rulers, "has found a completely open door to inflict infinite slaughter on innocent people" by overwhelming the courts with denunciations of witchcraft. "I am amazed," he wrote, "that Germany's rulers, surrounded by so many advisers and wise men, have not yet noticed" how ridiculous it is to accept the testimony of accused witches on the rack when otherwise they were regarded as the "worst of all deceivers."[57]

## German Lands

Spee's perceptive eye-witness account of the witch-hunts reveals how they were not top-down affairs, but rushed and haphazard efforts to appease the fears of the people and preachers, during the course of which many princes became convinced of their necessity. While many Protestant preachers and princes suffered from the same anxiety, there were some who argued that the devil's real danger to the state was in inciting heresy or witch persecution. For example, Johannes Brenz (1499–1570), the Lutheran preacher of Württemberg, strongly urged his prince not to execute Anabaptists nor witches, and his advice was taken seriously.[58] Brenz argued that persuasion was better than coercion for Anabaptists and, for witchcraft, confession of sin and prayer, not witch burnings, was the cure for divine punishment. By 1600, this Protestant providentialism was overcoming fear of witches in most German Protestant realms, whose rulers increasingly saw witch-hunting as another Catholic superstition.[59]

### *Bavaria and the Franconian Prince-Bishoprics*

The experience of confessional conflict and witch-hunting in the Duchy of Bavaria reveals how these two activities were interrelated, escalated by recent years of bad weather and crop failure.[60] In this apocalyptical atmosphere, even the providentialism of Protestants did not deter princes from pursuing witches, for they were now "simply the indirect agents of evil" who, by allying with Satan, were incurring the wrath of God. The region's rulers hoped that prosecution of witches would end the destructive storms and plagues.[61] As jurists and rulers rushed together a series of trials to expunge this diabolical threat to the realm, by 1590, they were facing a panic which accounted for a majority of Bavaria's witch trials. Once the fires died down and the damage assessed, Protestant and Catholic advisors sparked a dispute within the ducal court over witch-hunting, which persuaded Duke Wilhelm V to exercise greater caution.[62]

In contrast, such restraint was mostly absent in many of the German Catholic prince-bishoprics. Individual ecclesiastical princes were responsible for incredible numbers of executions for witchcraft; the three archbishops of Mainz, for example, oversaw the judicial execution of some 1,800 witches between 1601 and 1629, more than the entire Duchy of Bavaria.[63] Some of these rulers gained the ignoble title of "witch-bishops" for their zeal. The Archbishop of Trier, one of the seven Electors of the Empire, began a series of truly frightening trials in the 1580s; the suffragan bishop Peter Binsfeld published influential treatises describing these trials and promoting them as necessary for the godly state.[64] Prince-bishoprics were prone to such uncontrolled panics, thanks to their decentralised governance, taxation, and courts, which allowed local jurisdictions a free hand in trying witches. It must also be noted that the ruling bishops faced considerable resistance from Protestant clergy and nobility against Catholic reforms.

Most of these princes were, moreover, zealous reformers inspired by Jesuit counsellors and surrounded by Protestant realms.[65] The bishops thus engaged in a campaign of purification of blasphemy, which included witchcraft. Several locales, such as Ellwangen in 1611, saw accusations climb the social ladder to encompass political elites.[66] In contrast, some German princes, such as the Reformed Landgrave of the Palatinate of the Rhine, refused to prosecute witches precisely because they saw the activity as a form of Catholic superstition, although many Reformed theologians were so concerned about the danger of residents making pacts with the devil that they ignored the implications of Calvin's emphasis on the sovereignty of God. Even so, many German Reformed rulers proved less enthusiastic to engage in a witch-hunt than their Catholic and Lutheran neighbours.[67] This was not necessarily the case elsewhere, but the political conflict among confessional states in the Empire clarified the theological differences, so that belief in a diabolical witch conspiracy became one of the polemical tools used by Protestants against their Catholic opponents.[68]

## Habsburg Domains

The Holy Roman Empire had a central court and bureaucracy, but these were advisory and largely ineffective, since the empire consisted of hundreds of principalities, some of them quite small. Governance of this large, decentralised state thus required the cooperation of the princes and magistrates, as Charles V discovered to his chagrin, despite being the most powerful ruler of Europe. He could not suppress Protestant heresy since he had promised his princes that he would not establish an Inquisition in the German lands. In his reform of the imperial law code, the *Constitutio Criminalis Carolina* of 1532, Charles granted authority over both heresy and witchcraft to local courts. Unrestrained by any real central control, the German lands thus accounted for at least half of all known witch trials and executions in Europe.[69]

Charles had no comparable problem in Spain where both heresy and witchcraft cases remained under the jurisdiction of the Spanish Inquisition, founded originally against the heresy of Judaising, but which had since expanded to all manner of heresy, blasphemy, immorality, and witchcraft. Under the control of the crown through its governing Suprema of eight appointees, it acted effectively as an agency of royal centralisation.[70] It helped suppress internal heretical enemies, such as Judaisers; the spiritualistic Alumbrados; the converted Muslims or Moriscos who were feared to be an Ottoman fifth-column threat; Lutheranism; and blasphemies like illicit magic and witchcraft. Rulers and Inquisitors feared the pollution of Christian blood by Jews and Muslims, leading to trials, the creation of pure blood laws, and expulsions. The Habsburgs also saw themselves as defenders of Christendom against external enemies, including Catholic France, Protestant principalities, and most especially, the Muslim Ottoman Empire. As the Spanish fleets established colonies in the Americas, they decreed that no one with Jewish or Muslim blood could travel to New Spain, in a futile effort to maintain the religious purity of the colonies.[71] In some cases these various threats merged when Spanish Inquisitors interrogated witches who confessed to Morisco conspiracies and sedition.[72] While the devil was the ringleader in all of these, Inquisitors regarded accusations of diabolical witchcraft as mere superstition not worthy of serious treatment, despite the constant pressure from the people and secular courts to hunt witches. While less anxious about a witch cult, Spain's rulers saw Satanic plots in anything that would dilute pure Spanish Christian blood and weaken it against its Protestant and Muslim foes. There was, however, one witch panic in Spain, in the Basque region during the same years as the expulsion of the Moriscos, 1609–14.

It was overseen by the Logroño Tribunal consisting of Alonso Becerra Holguín, Juan de Valle Alvarado, and Alonzo de Salazar.[73] Following the lead of Pierre de Lancre's notorious trials in French Basque territory, Holguín and Alvarado became convinced that there was a massive diabolical conspiracy against the state and community by witches who flew to distant sabbaths to worship Satan. By 1611, Salazar, however, had become sceptical of the procedures used to extract confessions, which included leading questions, interrogation of children, mass imprisonment of suspects, and sleep deprivation. After a months-long visitation in which he reinterrogated all the witnesses, Salazar wrote his report to the Suprema, thoroughly convinced that there had not been "a single proof nor even the slightest indication from which to infer that one act of witchcraft has actually taken place."[74] Salazar was no sceptic of Satan, for when in October 1610 a disease outbreak in the cells killed numerous suspects, he had concurred with Becerra that this was the devil killing off his minions before they could be sentenced.[75] Sensing that Salazar would undo all of their godly work, Becerra blamed his many problems on "the work of the devil": "He it is who causes all these troubles to distract our attention and prevent us from dealing effectively with this accursed witch sect, which indeed may well reduce this part of the country to chaos." "Having to watch all this, and the understandable pain I have felt at seeing God's name blasphemed by acts of such abomination," Becerra explained, had made him ill.[76] The Suprema, and hence King Philip III, to whom the Inquisitors had written directly earlier in the trials, ultimately agreed with Salazar, and ended the trials, due to the lack of credible evidence.[77] The crown was, in fact, preoccupied with overseeing the removal of Moriscos from Spain in response to the alleged Morisco plots, bristling with conspiratorial tropes drawn from trials of Conversos, and some of them tinged with diabolical magic as well. This was Philip III's principal anti-devil focus, rather than the ill-informed superstitions of his rural folk.

## France

Like Spain, France's kings had a better centralised court and administration than the Holy Roman Empire, but the Reformation brought with it intense confessional conflict between the Calvinist Huguenots and the hardline Catholics led by the Guise faction in the royal court. In this anxiety-inducing environment, France's notables sought ways to bring harmony and tolerance to the realm.[78] Such a reformation needed, in the words of Mark Greengrass, "the return of peace to the kingdom" which originated from the grace of God as "mediated to the kingdom through the divine inspiration of its king." This failed, in part, because of the royal crisis of succession and the inability of provincial agents to deliver on the promise of the edicts of pacification.[79] Another feature, however, was the demonising rhetoric used by both sides, although in the early stages of the conflict, the Calvinists' hope of converting the king kept theirs muted.[80] The situation changed in 1566 with the demonic possession of the young woman Nicole Obrey (Aubrey) which led to a series of exorcisms in Laon witnessed by thousands. As the demons were compelled by the Jesuit exorcists to speak, they declared the Huguenots to be their loyal servants, sending shockwaves through the crowd. The Calvinists countered that this was mere fraud, but without their own exorcism rite, they lacked a dramatic response, and many Huguenots returned to Catholicism.[81] Fearing that Satan was using Protestantism to destroy the state, mobs of Catholics attacked Calvinists gathered in Paris on St. Bartholomew's Day, 1572.[82] The slaughter of Protestant notables spread across France, encouraged by the Regent Catherine de Medici and the Guises. The violence against the Huguenots was, by any measure, excessive, provoked by sacrilegious Calvinist iconoclasm which Catholics believed would bring down the wrath of God. Maldonado's theory of a demonic invasion of heresy to destroy a Christian realm seems to have been pervasive.

This is clear from the arguments made by France's premier legal expert, Jean Bodin (c.1529–96), whose "definition of sovereignty as the power of the State" helped European rulers establish their authority across Europe and the colonies.[83] In 1580, he also published his very popular *De la démonomanie des sorciers* (On the Demon-mania of Witches) which explicitly tied nation-building to the suppression of diabolical witchcraft, and in ways that have puzzled historians of both politics and witchcraft to this day.[84] Bodin's religious views were unconventional too, as he sought to bring Christianity and Judaism together, while he could also write like a Huguenot advocating daily prayer, bible reading, and "faith in God" to fight Satan.[85] However, unlike Bodin's Protestant opponent, Johan Wier, author of *De Praestigiis daemonum* (On the Illusions of Demons) of 1563, Bodin believed witchcraft to be the greatest threat to the state, for Satan teaches his servants "diabolical means" to "destroy the human race in perdition."[86] Bodin seems to have noticed the sceptical implications of Wier's argument, calling Wier the "defender of witches" and including him among the "atheists" "who deny that there are any devils at all," asserting that "now it is hardly less of an impiety to call into doubt the possibility of witches than to call into doubt the existence of God."[87] Such atheists could not explain the incidents of diabolical possession during which demons spoke "through the shameful parts" of the possessed, something which does not occur naturally.[88] Bodin told rulers that they needed to believe in Satan's existence and that his minions were a massive danger to the nation.

Stuart Clark sees Bodin and his immediate followers as the strongest advocates for absolute, divine-right monarchy, in which the extermination of witches was a principal duty.[89] Clark further observes that the "theory and practice of witch prosecutions raised political issues, while certain traditions of statecraft ... raised demonological ones."[90] For Bodin, sovereignty needed to be absolute and undivided, as the king stood in God's place over the realm. Among duties expected of the crown were the suppression of evil, the most extreme of which was the apostasy of making a pact with the devil, which was a renunciation of the king as well. For Bodin, such an exceptional crime allowed judges to ignore normal judicial procedures to extract witch confessions.[91] To neglect their judicial duties in such cases would lead only to the ruin of France. Bodin thus defined demonic witchcraft as the polar opposite of the godly state, its archnemesis, so that by attacking the witch conspiracy he was defining in negative terms true sovereignty, and hence supporting it.[92]

Despite Bodin's efforts, France was a place of moderation when it came to the prosecution of witchcraft. This was the result of France's centralised control over the regional parlements. In 1978, Alfred Soman discovered that the royal court, the Parlement of Paris, overturned 90% of death sentences declared by the regional courts, putting the brakes on the witch panics.[93] Even so, the Parlement of Paris strongly urged the prosecution of religious heretics, mostly Huguenots, as part of its mandate to keep the state pure of pollution.[94] These efforts, however, conflicted with royal efforts to achieve peace, which was finally reached in 1598 with the Edict of Nantes providing Huguenots limited toleration. This truce was threatened when Marthe Brossier arrived in Paris the following year demanding to have her demons exorcised publicly, just after the Parlement of Paris had signed the Edict. Through Brossier, Beelzebub claimed that the Huguenots were his allies, a declaration exploited by the Capuchin exorcists to oppose peace with the heretics. Henri IV thus ordered her to return home.[95]

Peace was maintained; yet, the demonic possession became an even greater problem for France's rulers in the 17th century with the infamous possessions of Ursuline convents and the trials of priests on charges of bewitching the nuns. In the 1630s in Loudun, the priest Urbain Grandier was caught up in the political machinations of Cardinal Richelieu and the royal court to destroy the walls of Huguenot cities. In the end, Grandier's supporters in Paris lost out, and Grandier became another victim of the burnings, despite never having confessed to the crime.[96] These spectacular show exorcisms soon embarrassed France's notables, and when the "Affair of the Poisons" rocked the court of Louis XIV from 1679 to 1682, the king finally took decisive action, formally ending witchcraft prosecution in 1682.[97] He, and most rulers, had come to see witch trials as damaging to their sovereignty, rather than an aid to state-building.

## England and Scotland

### England

Something similar happened in England, whose rulers prosecuted both heresy and witchcraft to protect the realm from divine anger and the devil's malice, although religious dissenters were seen by the crown as the greater of these threats. Despite his breach with Rome, King Henry VIII prosecuted Protestants when he considered them a threat to his standing as the defender of Catholicism, although the charges against his second wife, Anne Boleyn, in 1536 included witchcraft, along with adultery, incest, and treason. Henry's witchcraft statute of 1542 was repealed by Edward VI (r.1547–53) whose early death left his reforms unfinished. Queen Mary (r.1553–8) and her husband Philip II of Spain sought to restore England to the Roman Catholic Church and enthusiastically prosecuted Protestants, burning 284 of their number—56 of them women.[98] Eamon Duffy argues that this

violence was effective in bringing the Catholic Reformation to England, although it was undone by her untimely death. Protestants saw this policy as diabolical, as a return to "idolatry, sacriledge, simonie, blasphemy, superstition, hypocrisie, transubstantiate angell of light
and day deuill, kyngdome of lyes ... apostasie ... sathanical subtletie, and abhomination in
the sight of God."[99] The Queen's principal advisor, Cardinal Reginald Pole, told her that
her father's breach with Rome had been caused by the "ancient enemy of mankind, the
devil," and it had poisoned the kingdom and "obliterated all trace of true religion and even
common justice."[100] He ordered priests attending executions to offer the accused sacramental confession to counteract the impression that they were true martyrs, for spectators do
not recognise the devil's strength underneath their "false piety and bogus courage," while
Catholic polemicists argued that the devil had inspired the Reformation "to the destruction of order."[101] In 1555 one writer asserted that Satan was supporting these "obstinate
heretickes," whom the "godli lawes doe iustly condemyne as most contagious & pestilent
members, lest they should infecte & murder gostly with their pestiferous heresy the whole
body." They are, in fact "no martirs of god, but declare them to be members of the deuil,
sythe the matter wherefore they dye is mooste mischeuous and manifest heresy."[102] Such
demonising language helped deter feelings of sympathy on the part of the crown.

Mary's successor, Elizabeth I, restored Protestantism to England, but she too followed
her half-sister's harsh anti-heresy approach, now against Catholics.[103] She also completed
the legal reforms begun by Edward, producing a witchcraft statute in 1563 making the
practice a secular crime; Keith Thomas surmised she did this due to a number of political conspiracies against her that were tinged with magic.[104] Among these were a series of
scandalous exorcisms conducted by Jesuits to prove that the Catholic Church controlled
the supernatural; as in France, Beelzebub claimed the Protestants as his allies. Elizabeth's
minister Francis Walsingham discovered links between these exorcisms and the "Babington
plot" against the Queen's life, revealing that the devil was behind efforts to overthrow the
crown and restore Catholicism.[105]

While trials for witchcraft increased during Elizabeth's reign, she did not see them as a
threat to her sovereignty.[106] Her successor, James VI and I further revised the witchcraft statute in 1604 because when King of Scotland he became personally involved in a witch trial in
North Berwick in the early 1590s, which convinced him that the witches had plotted with
the devil against him, a position encapsulated in his *Daemonologie* of 1597.[107] Despite this
early zeal to eradicate a diabolical plot against the crown, as king of England James placed a
restraining hand on the prosecution of witchcraft. As Brian Levack and others have shown,
James did not see English cases of witchcraft as a serious treasonous threat.[108] Even so, he
could still rebuke officials for questioning the reality of witchcraft, reminding them that "the
Devil had invented a whole host of new tricks and stratagems since the days of the early
Church, many of them to be found in his recently published work on the subject."[109]

Unlike some of their continental counterparts, English Puritans continued to promote
a campaign of cleansing of their realms that included trying accused witches. The chaos
of the Civil War years in England, which culminated with the execution of King Charles
I in 1649 and the establishment of a parliamentary government under Oliver Cromwell,
also meant that there was no longer any royal control over trials for witchcraft. According
to Peter Elmer, this calamitous period was "embroiled in religious and political conflict,
[when] concern with witches and witchcraft once again featured prominently in the general
discourse of those who governed in Church and state" and "demonological thinking permeated religious and political debate," marked by heavy speculation as to the role of Satan

in the crises around the collapse of royal power.[110] Royalists argued that, like witchcraft, the puritan-inspired rebellion had "demonic origins," while the rebels stigmatised the Anglican/royalist cause as "religious apostates," a charge typical of witches as well.[111] Such demonising rhetoric, Elmer concludes, inflamed anxieties over literal witches, leading to the East Anglia witch panics overseen by the witchfinder general Matthew Hopkins.[112] Decades of polemical attacks against Anabaptists had also helped make the concept of a diabolical witch sect more credible.[113] With the Restoration of the crown in 1660, it was the sudden surge of new religious groups of the 1640s and 1650s that Charles II's officials focused on, as Quakers now suffered from accusations of diabolism and witchcraft.[114]

## Scotland

Scotland has been regarded as the principal test case of witch trials as part of state-building, for here the local clergy cooperated and promoted the prosecution of witchcraft as part of the crown's quest to craft the godly realm.[115] The worst of these trials occurred in the local courts where there was little royal oversight and where local judges were themselves fearful of the local witches. The courts overseen by the crown were far more restrained. That said, a more centralised hunt transpired during the 1640s when Presbyterian "Covenanters" dominated the church and ministers were explicitly told to "take notice of charmers, witches and all such abusers" and to "urge the acts of Parliament to be execute against them."[116] Their moral reforming efforts on behalf of a godly state led to the Scottish Parliament's 1649 Witchcraft Act that specifically targeted those who "consult with Devils," leading to one of the realm's major witch panics in 1649.[117] As Paula Hughes has put it, during the Covenanting era, the Scottish church and state were dominated by "presbyterian radicals with apocalyptic visions and an impending sense that the nation's troubles resulted from the scourge of the ungodly threatening to subvert a covenanted and godly nation"; in this context, Calvinism's logic of providentialism was forgotten.[118] Even when the English formally gave up prosecution for witchcraft after the Restoration in 1660, associating the practice with religious nonconformism and superstition, the Scots held on; in a 1736 parliamentary debate over repealing James I's witchcraft statute, some Scottish Parliamentarians simply asserted that their English counterparts were now Satan's minions for denying witch-hunting.[119]

## The Dutch Republic

While the northern Netherlandic provinces had been a region of significant heresy prosecution and had seen a number of trials for witchcraft, when the leading notables and magistrates of the provinces created a union in 1579, they formally ended heresy trials and soon those for witchcraft as well. Demonising of the enemy became focused on the papacy and the Spanish Catholic forces, and elsewhere demonising rhetoric was abandoned, certainly among and between the various confessional factions.[120] Lacking such restraint, the Habsburgs tried hundreds of Protestant heretics between 1567 and 1574 in the Council of Troubles.

With the Union of Utrecht of 1579, Prince William of Orange and the Protestant notables decided not to enforce confessional conformity or coercion when they declared the Reformed Church to be the public church. Other confessions, including Mennonites and Catholics, were informally allowed to worship behind private façades as the Dutch adjusted to religious diversity.[121] Some of the heirs of the persecuted Anabaptists developed an approach to religious identity that emphasised the inner faith over the confessional statements and ritual that princes fought over. One of these spiritualists was the former Anabaptist prophet David Joris (1501–56) for whom angels and demons existed solely within the mind of humans, and therefore possessed no external form.[122] While mainstream writers attacked his idea, it became a popular one among nonconformist streams and helped shape the attitudes of many Dutch elites who ended formal prosecutions for witchcraft just as other neighbouring realms were convulsed by the panics.[123] The few demonological treatises by Dutch authors followed Joris and Wier in depreciating the devil's power, with the most famous example being the *Bewitched World* by the Reformed preacher Balthasar Bekker of the 1690s which, like Joris a century and a half earlier, removed the devil from nature.[124] The anti-Jewish sentiment that had shaped Satan's character in the 1st century was also muted here, as the Republic's Regents insisted on treating their new Jewish residents with the same respect as citizens.[125] Comfort with religious diversity reduced anxiety about the devil, who played little to no role in the territory's state-building or external relations.

## Conclusion

How central, then, was the devil to the state-building of princes and magistrates? The answer is determined by the degree to which princes, kings, and magistrates took the advice of their zealous clergy seriously. When they did, heretics and witches suffered the consequences. Believing that an opponent was a diabolical agent or the Antichrist, or that internal dissidents were a real Satanic danger to incurring the wrath of God, shaped the policy-making of rulers across Europe. Some may have been cynically exploiting the supernatural beliefs of their people, rather than believing in the devil's activities themselves. Regardless, they took belief in Satan seriously, leading to intensified religious persecution, conflict, and warfare. The devil's agents could be external enemies or members of another confession, or neighbours and family members. Many princes felt the need to expunge a realm of diabolical blasphemy and construct a godly realm free of Satan's nefarious influences. While royal courts and rulers often suppressed the witch-hunts when they could intervene in local courts, they regularly encouraged the prosecution of religious dissenters or encouraged military action against them for the same reason that lay behind the demonic witch stereotype: they were the devil's seditious agents undercutting allegiance to the crown. It was only with the exhaustion that came with the witch panics and the end of the religious wars in 1648 that the devil's agency in state formation began a slow process of decline. This coincided with the growing scepticism among the elites towards the devil's very existence that is typically associated with the early Enlightenment, but which had its origins much earlier in Dutch spiritualism. The Dutch Republic's elites abandoned the devil, in any real terms, in building their new state. While many observers doubted its Christian character, the Dutch example proved attractive.

## Notes

1 Willem Frijhoff, "Het Gelders Antichrist-tractaat (1524) en zijn auteur," *Archief voor de Geschiedenis van de Katholieke Kerk in Nederland*, 28 (1986), 192–217; see also Gary K. Waite, *Eradicating the Devil's Minions: Anabaptists and Witches in Reformation Europe, 1535–1600* (Toronto, 2007), 38.

2 See William Monter, *A Bewitched Duchy: Lorraine and its Dukes, 1477–1736* (Geneva, 2007); and Robin Briggs, *The Witches of Lorraine* (Oxford, 2007).

3 On Maldonado, see Jonathan L. Pearl, *The Crime of Crimes: Demonology and Politics in France, 1560–1620* (Waterloo, 1999), 59–75.

4 Nicolas Rémy, *Demonolatry: An Account of the Historical Practice of Witchcraft*, ed., trans. Montague Summers (New York, 2008 [1930]), v–vi.

5 Briggs, *The Witches of Lorraine*, 19.

6 Briggs, *The Witches of Lorraine*, 21.

7 Briggs, *The Witches of Lorraine*, 120.

8 On blasphemy, see Gerd Schwerhoff, *Zungen wie Schwerter: Blasphemie in alteuropäischen Gesellschaften 1200–1650* (Constance, 2005).

9 See Nicholas Terpstra, *Religious Refugees in the Early Modern World: An Alternative History of the Reformation* (Cambridge, 2015).

10 Elaine Pagels, *The Origin of Satan: How Christians Demonized Jews, Pagans, and Heretics* (London, 1996).

11 A good introduction remains Edward Peters, *Inquisition* (Berkeley, 1989); see also R. I. Moore, *The Formation of a Persecuting Society: Power and Deviance in Western Europe, 950–1250* (Oxford, 1987).

12 Carlo Ginzburg, *Ecstasies: Deciphering the Witches' Sabbath* (New York, 1991), 33–86.

13 J. R. Veenstra, *Magic and Divination at the Courts of Burgundy and France: Text and Context of Laurens Pignon's* Contre les Devineurs *(1411)* (Leiden, 1997).

14 Veenstra, *Magic and Divination*, 34–49.

15 Veenstra, *Magic and Divination*, 44.

16 Ronald Hutton, *The Witch: A History of Fear, from Ancient Times to the Present* (New Haven, 2017); see also Michael D. Bailey, *Battling Demons: Witchcraft, Heresy, and Reform in the Late Middle Ages* (University Park, 2003); and Laura Stokes' *Demons of Urban Reform: Early European Witch Trials and Criminal Justice, 1430–1530* (Basingstoke, 2011).

17 Richard Kieckhefer, *Forbidden Rites: A Necromancer's Manual of the Fifteenth Century* (University Park, 1998).

18 Brian P. Levack, "State-building and Witch Hunting in Early Modern Europe," in *Witchcraft in Early Modern Europe: Studies in Culture and Belief*, ed. Jonathan Barry, Marianne Hester and Gareth Roberts (Cambridge, 1996), 96–115.

19 Brian P. Levack "Witchcraft and the Law," in *The Oxford Handbook of Witchcraft in Early Modern Europe and Colonial America*, ed. Brian P. Levack (Oxford, 2014), 468–84; and Johannes Dillinger, "Politics, State-Building, and Witch-Hunting," also in *Oxford Handbook*, 528–47.

20 Silvia Federici, *Caliban and the Witch: Women, the Body and Primitive Accumulation* (New York, 2004), 166; see also Ashley J. Bohrer, "Sorcery and Sovereignty: Bodin's Political Economy of the Occult," *Political Theology* 21 (2020), 479–95. For a thorough critique, see https://mcmxix.org/2019/10/23/caliban-and-the-witch-a-critical-analysis/

21 See the essays edited by Levack in *The Oxford Handbook of Witchcraft* and Gary Jensen, *The Path of the Devil: Early Modern Witch Hunts* (Lanham, 2007).

22 Wolfgang Behringer, *Witchcraft Persecutions in Bavaria: Popular Magic, Religious Zealotry and Reason of State in Early Modern Europe*, trans. J. C. Grayson and David Lederer (Cambridge, 1997), 115.

23 See Brian P. Levack, *The Witch-Hunt in Early Modern Europe*, 4th ed. (London, 2015).

24 For summaries, see *Handbook of European History, 1400–1600: Late Middle Ages, Renaissance and Reformation*, vol. 2, eds. Thomas A. Brady Jr., Heiko A. Oberman, and James D. Tracy (Leiden, 1995).

25 For an introduction to confessionalisation, see Heinz Schilling, "Confessional Europe," in *Handbook of European History*, vol. 2: 641–81; and C. Scott Dixon, *Contesting the Reformation* (Malden, 2012).

26 Heiko A. Oberman, *Luther: Man between God and the Devil* (New Haven, 1989), 102 and 104; Euan Cameron, *Enchanted Europe: Superstition, Reason, & Religion, 1250–1750* (Oxford, 2010), 157–73; and Gary K. Waite, "Sixteenth Century Religious Reform and the Witch-Hunts," in *The Oxford Handbook of Witchcraft*, 485–506.

27 Martin Luther, *Table Talk*, trans. William Hazlitt (Grand Rapids, n.d.). http://www.ccel.org/ccel/luther/tabletalk.html

28 Peter A. Morton, "Lutheran Naturalism, Popular Magic, and the Devil," in *The Devil in Society in Premodern Europe*, eds. Richard Raiswell with Peter Dendle (Toronto, 2012), 409–35.

29 See Mark U. Edwards, Jr., *Luther's Last Battles: Politics and Polemics, 1531–46* (Ithaca, 1983); and Darren Oldridge, *The Devil: A Very Short Introduction* (Oxford, 2012), 33.

30 E. William Monter, "Heresy Executions in Reformation Europe, 1520–1565," in *Tolerance and intolerance in the European Reformation*, eds. Ole Peter Grell and Bob Scribner (Cambridge, 1996), 48–64.

31 Waite, *Eradicating*, 130–53.

32 Stuart Clark, "Protestant Demonology: Sin, Superstition, and Society (c.1520-c.1630)," in *Early Modern European Witchcraft: Centres and Peripheries*, eds. Bengt Ankarloo and Gustav Henningsen (Oxford, 1990), 45–81.

33 Michelle D. Brock, "Internalizing the Demonic: Satan and the Self in Early Modern Scottish Piety," *Journal of British Studies* 54 (2015), 23–43; and Darren Oldridge, *The Devil in Early Modern England* (Stroud, 2000), 8 and 45–57.

34 On the Catholic Reformation, see Ronnie Po-Chia Hsia, *The World of Catholic Renewal, 1540–1770*, 2nd ed. (Cambridge, 2005).

35 Pearl, *Crime of Crimes*, 66–7.

36 Martín del Rio, *Investigations into Magic*, trans. P.G. Maxwell-Stuart (Manchester, 2000), 27–31. Jan Machielsen argues that this prologue was, however, not central to Delrio's demonology: Jan Machielsen *Martin Delrio: Demonology and Scholarship in the Counter-Reformation* (Oxford, 2015), 214. On such apocalyptical thinking and witchcraft, see Stuart Clark, *Thinking with Demons: The Idea of Witchcraft in Early Modern Europe* (Oxford, 1999), 321–62; and Andrew Cunningham and Ole Peter Grell, *The Four Horsemen of the Apocalypse: Religion, War, Famine and Death in Reformation Europe* (Cambridge, 2000).

37 See Waite, *Eradicating*.

38 Brian Tierney, *Religion, Law and the Growth of Constitutional Thought, 1150–1650* (Cambridge, 2008).

39 Hutton, *The Witch*, 178–9; and Bailey, *Battling Demons*.

40 On the conflict, see Peter Blickle, *The Revolution of 1525: The German Peasants' War from a New Perspective*, trans. Thomas A. Brady, Jr., and H.C. Erik Midelfort (Baltimore, 1981).

41 Harry Loewen, *Ink Against the Devil: Luther and his Opponents* (Waterloo, 2015), 55.

42 Martin Luther, "Against the Robbing, Murdering Hordes of Peasants," in *Luther's Works*, ed. Robert C. Schultz, American Edition 46, *Christian in Society* III (Philadelphia, 1967), 47–55.

43 "Preamble to the Twenty-four Articles of the Common Territory of Salzburg, May-June 1525," in *The German Peasants' War: A History in Documents*, ed. and trans., Tom Scott and Bob Scribner (New York, 1991), 105–6.

44 See, for example, "The Allgäu Articles, 24 February 1525," in *The German Peasants' War*, 126–7, or the "Federal Ordinance of Memmingen, 7 March 1525," in *The German Peasants' War*, 130–32, article 12.

45 "The Massacre of Weinsberg, 16 April 1525. Report of the Parson Johann Herolt," in *The German Peasants' War*, 158. The demonising of the peasants was also used by noble leaders of peasant bands who later claimed they had been pressed into service against their will because "the peasants were all full of the devil" who were engaged in "the devil's work." In *The German Peasants' War*, 203–5.

46 "The Role of Women," in *The German Peasants' War*, 225–6.

47 See, for example, Ronnie Po-chia Hsia, *Social Discipline in the Reformation: Central Europe, 1550–1750* (London, 1989).

48 James M. Stayer, *The German Peasants' War and Anabaptist Community of Goods* (Montreal, 1991).

49 Waite, *Eradicating*, 16.

50 On the Vauderie, see Kathrin Utz Tremp, *Von der Häresie zur Hexerei: "Wirkliche" und imaginäre Sekten imp Spätmittelalter* (Hannover, 2008), and "The Heresy of Witchcraft in Western Switzerland and Dauphiné (Fifteenth Century)," *Magic, Ritual and Witchcraft* 6 (2011), 1–10; on the Anabaptists, Waite, *Eradicating*.

51 Waite, *Eradicating*, 170.

52 As cited in Wolfgang Behringer, *Witches and Witch-Hunts*, 120.

53 Friedrich Spee, *Cautio Criminalis, or a Book on Witch Trials*, trans. Marcus Hellyer (Charlottesville, 2003), 214–5.

54 Spee, *Cautio Criminalis*, 47.
55 Spee, *Cautio Criminalis*, 214–5, 20–1.
56 Spee, *Cautio Criminalis*, 21.
57 Spee, *Cautio Criminalis*, 178–9.
58 Waite, *Eradicating*, 145, 158.
59 Behringer, *Witchcraft Persecutions in Bavaria*, 310–21.
60 Behringer, *Witchcraft Persecutions*, 115–7.
61 Behringer, *Witchcraft Persecutions*, 121.
62 Behringer, *Witchcraft Persecutions*, 83.
63 A good summary is Wolfgang Behringer, "Ecclesiastical Territories (Holy Roman Empire)," in *Encyclopedia of Witchcraft: The Western Tradition*, vol. 2, ed. Richard M. Golden (Santa Barbara, CA, 2006), 303–7.
64 Rita Voltmer, "Demonology and Anti-Demonology: Binsfeld's *De confessionibus* and Loos's *De vera et falsa magia*," in *The Science of Demons: Early Modern Authors Facing Witchcraft and the Devil*, ed. Jan Machielsen (London, 2020), 149–64.
65 On clergy and the German witch trials, see Rita Voltmer, "Debating the Devil's Clergy: Demonology and the Media in Dialogue with Trials (14th to 17th Century)," *Religions* 10, no. 12 (2019), 648. https://www.mdpi.com/2077-1444/10/12/648
66 H. C. Erik Midelfort, *Witch Hunting in Southwestern Germany, 1562–1684: The Social and Intellectual Foundations* (Stanford, 1972), 104–12. The most famous example is the burgomaster Johannes Junius of Bamberg; see *Witchcraft in Europe, 400–1700: A Documentary History*, eds. Alan C. Kors and Edward Peters (Philadelphia, 2001), 348–53.
67 Midelfort, *Witch Hunting*, 56–7.
68 Behringer, *Witchcraft Persecutions in Bavaria*, 213–6.
69 Behringer, *Witches and Witch-Hunts*, 83–164.
70 See, for example, Henry Kamen, *The Spanish Inquisition: A Historical Revision* (New Haven, 1998).
71 Karoline P. Cook, *Forbidden Passages: Muslims and Moriscos in Colonial Spanish America* (Philadelphia, 2016).
72 Gunnar W. Knutsen, *Servants of Satan and Masters of Demons: The Spanish Inquisition's Trials for Superstition, Valencia and Barcelona, 1478–1700* (Turnhout, 2009), 141 and throughout.
73 Gustav Henningsen, *The Witches' Advocate: Basque Witchcraft and the Spanish Inquisition* (Reno, 1980); and Gustav Henningsen, *The Salazar Documents: Inquisitor Alonso De Salazar Frías and Others on the Basque Witch Persecution* (Leiden, 2004). This discussion is based on Henningsen's work.
74 Henningsen, *Witches' Advocate*, 304–5.
75 Henningsen, *Witches' Advocate*, 150–3.
76 In a letter to the Suprema written on 3 February 1612, in Henningsen, *Witches' Advocate*, 308–9.
77 Henningsen, *Witches' Advocate*, 173–4.
78 Mark Greengrass, *Governing Passions: Peace and Reform in the French Kingdom, 1576–1585* (Oxford, 2007).
79 Greengrass, *Governing Passions*, 370–2.
80 Carleton Cunningham, "The Devil and the Religious Controversies of Sixteenth-Century France," *Essays in History* 35 (1993), 34–47; Pearl, *Crime of Crimes*.
81 Sarah Ferber, *Demonic Possession and Exorcism in Early Modern France* (London, 2004), 23–39.
82 Natalie Zemon Davis, "The Rites of Violence," in her *Society and Culture in Early Modern France* (Stanford, 1975), 152–85.
83 James Renton and Anya Topolski, "Bodin Now; or What's Wrong with Intellectual History," *Political Theology* 21 (2020), 475–8, here 475.
84 Jean Bodin, *On the Demon-Mania of Witches*, trans. Randy A. Scott, introduction by Jonathan L. Pearl (Toronto, 1995), 9. On Bodin's demonology in light of his political and economic thought, see the essays in the special issue of *Political Theology* 21/6 (September 2020).
85 Bodin, *On the Demon-Mania of Witches*, 147, 149.
86 Bodin, *On the Demon-Mania of Witches*, 45. On Wier, see Hans de Waardt, "Inflating the Prestige of Demons: Johan Wier's Role-Playing," in *Spiritualism in Early Modern Europe*, eds. Michael Driedger, et al., a special issue of *Church History and Religious Culture* 101 (2021), 234–62.

87  Bodin, *On the Demon-Mania of Witches*, 44. He refers to Wier (Weyer) several times in his tome.

88  Bodin, *On the Demon-Mania of Witches*, 109.

89  Clark, *Thinking with Demons*, 669.

90  Clark, *Thinking with Demons*, 670.

91  Clark, *Thinking with Demons*, 675.

92  Clark, *Thinking with Demons*, 674–82; see also S. Jonathon O'Donnell, "Witchcraft, Statecraft, Mancraft: On the Demonological Foundations of Sovereignty," *Political Theology* 21 (2020), 530–49 who argues that for Bodin, "sovereignty rests on a demonological foundation."

93  Alfred Soman, "The Parlement of Paris and the Great Witch Hunt (1565–1640)," *Sixteenth Century Journal* 9 (1978), 31–44.

94  E. William Monter, *Judging the French Reformation: Heresy Trials by Sixteenth-century Parlements* (Cambridge, 1999).

95  Ferber, *Demonic Possession*, 40–59.

96  Robert Rapley, *A Case of Witchcraft: The Trial of Urbain Grandier* (Montreal, 1998).

97  Lynn Wood Mollenauer, *Strange Revelations: Magic, Poison, and Sacrilege in Louis XIV's France* (University Park, 2007).

98  Eamon Duffy, *Fires of Faith: Catholic England under Mary Tudor* (New Haven, 2009), 79.

99  Duffy, *Fires of Faith*, 80.

100  Duffy, *Fires of Faith*, 36. Catholic polemicists frequently argued that the devil had inspired the Reformation "to the destruction of order." Duffy, *Fires of Faith*, 71.

101  Duffy, *Fires of Faith*, 71, and 150. Inquisitors had also argued that demons assisted witches to avoid confessing in the courtroom.

102  Anonymous, *A Plaine and Godlye Treatise Concerning the Masse, for the Instructyon of the Simple and Unlearned People* (London, 1555), sig. Hiᵛ; see also Duffy, *Fires of Faith*, 172–3, who notes it went through several editions in half a year.

103  I summarise these developments in Gary K. Waite, *Heresy, Magic, and Witchcraft in Early Modern Europe* (Basingstoke, 2003), 173–89.

104  Keith Thomas, *Religion and the Decline of Magic* (New York, 1971), 462.

105  For an overview, see Waite, *Heresy*, 180.

106  James A. Sharpe, *Instruments of Darkness: Witchcraft in England, 1550–1750* (London, 1996) and his *Witchcraft in Early Modern England* (Harlow, 2001). See also Malcolm Gaskill, "Witchcraft Trials in England," in *The Oxford Handbook of Witchcraft*, 283–99.

107  James I, King of England, *Daemonologie in forme of a dialogue, diuided into three bookes* (Edinburgh, 1597).

108  Brian P. Levack, *Witch-Hunting in Scotland: Law, Politics and Religion* (London, 2008), 42–7.

109  As quoted in Peter Elmer, *Witchcraft, Witch-Hunting, and Politics in Early Modern England* (Oxford, 2016), 64–5.

110  Elmer, *Witchcraft*, 69.

111  Elmer, *Witchcraft*, 70, 94, and *passim*.

112  Malcolm Gaskill, *Witchfinders: A Seventeenth-Century English Tragedy* (Cambridge, 2005).

113  Gary K. Waite, *Anti-Anabaptist Polemics: Dutch Anabaptism and the Devil in England, 1531–1660* (Hamilton, 2023), esp. 130–58.

114  Peter Elmer, "'Saints or Sorcerers': Quakerism, Demonology and the Decline of Witchcraft in Seventeenth-Century England," in *Witchcraft in Early Modern Europe*, 145–79; also John Marshall, "Seventeenth-Century Quakers, Emotions, and Egalitarianism: Sufferings, Oppression, Intolerance, and Slavery," in *Feeling Exclusion: Religious Conflict, Exile and Emotions in Early Modern Europe*, eds. Giovanni Tarantino and Charles Zika (London, 2019), 146–64; and Waite, *Anti-Anabaptist Polemics*.

115  This discussion is based on Levack, *Witch-Hunting in Scotland* and Julian Goodare, "Witchcraft in Scotland," in *The Oxford Handbook of Witchcraft*, 300–17. See also Michelle Brock, *Satan and the Scots: The Devil in Post-Reformation Scotland, c.1560–1700* (London, 2016).

116  John R. Young, "The Scottish Parliament and Witch-Hunting in Scotland under the Covenanters," *Parliaments, Estates & Representation* 26 (2006), 53–65, here 56.

117  Paula Hughes, "Witch-Hunting in Scotland, 1649–1650," in *Scottish Witches and Witch-Hunters*, ed. Julian Goodare (Basingstoke, 2013), 85–102; Young, "The Scottish Parliament," 58.

118  Hughes, "Witch-Hunting in Scotland," 87.

119 Ian Bostridge, "Witchcraft Repealed," in *Witchcraft in Early Modern Europe*, 257–87.

120 Gary K. Waite, "Where did the Devil Go? Language and the Revolt in the Netherlands, 1566–1648," in *Interlinguicity, Internationality and Shakespeare*, ed. Michael Saenger (Montreal, 2014), 59–72.

121 Benjamin J. Kaplan, *Reformation and the Practice of Toleration: Dutch Religious History in the Early Modern Era* (Leiden, 2019).

122 Gary K. Waite, "Knowing the Spirit(s) in the Dutch Radical Reformation: From Physical Perception to Rational Doubt, 1536–1690," in *Knowing Demons, Knowing Spirits in the Early Modern Period*, eds. M. Brock, R. Raiswell, and D. Winter (Cham, 2018).

123 Hans de Waardt, "Netherlands, Northern," in *Encyclopedia of Witchcraft*, vol. 3, 810–3. On how English writers reacted to Joris's demonology once they were made aware of it in the 1640s, see Gary K. Waite, "The Devil of Delft in England: the Reception of the Dutch Spiritualist David Joris in 17th-Century English Polemics," *Church History and Religious Culture* 101 (2021), 429–95.

124 Waite, "Knowing the Spirit(s)," 42–53.

125 Gary K. Waite, *Jews and Muslims in Seventeenth-Century Discourse: From Religious Enemies to Allies and Friends* (London, 2019), esp. 173–4.

## Further Reading

Michael D. Bailey, *Battling Demons: Witchcraft, Heresy, and Reform in the Late Middle Ages* (University Park, PA: Pennsylvania State University Press, 2003).

Wolfgang Behringer, *Witchcraft Persecutions in Bavaria: Popular Magic, Religious Zealotry and Reason of State in Early Modern Europe*, trans. J. C. Grayson and David Lederer (Cambridge: Cambridge University Press, 1997).

Michelle Brock, *Satan and the Scots: The Devil in Post-Reformation Scotland, c.1560-1700* (London: Routledge, 2016).

Stuart Clark, *Thinking with Demons: The Idea of Witchcraft in Early Modern Europe* (Oxford: Oxford University Press, 2005).

Peter Elmer, *Witchcraft, Witch-Hunting, and Politics in Early Modern England* (Oxford: Oxford University Press, 2016).

Gustav Henningsen, *The Witches' Advocate: Basque Witchcraft and the Spanish Inquisition* (Reno: University of Nevada Press, NV, 1980).

Ronald Hutton, *The Witch: A History of Fear, from Ancient Times to the Present* (New Haven: Yale University Press, 2017).

Brian P. Levack, ed. *The Oxford Handbook of Witchcraft in Early Modern Europe and Colonial America* (Oxford: Oxford University Press, 2014).

Brian P. Levack, *Witch-Hunting in Scotland: Law, Politics and Religion* (London: Routledge, 2008).

Jonathan L. Pearl, *The Crime of Crimes: Demonology and Politics in France, 1560-1620* (Waterloo: Wilfred Laurier University Press, 1999).

Gary K. Waite, *Eradicating the Devil's Minions: Anabaptists and Witches in Reformation Europe, 1535-1600* (Toronto: University of Toronto Press, 2007).

Gary K. Waite, *Anti-Anabaptist Polemics: Dutch Anabaptism and the Devil in England, 1531-1660* (Hamilton: Pandora Press, 2023).

# 14

# SATAN, SEX, AND GENDER IN EARLY MODERN EUROPE

*Erika Gasser*

Early modern Europeans drew on established classical, scriptural, and medieval ideas about the devil even as notions of demonic influence adapted to developments in religion, natural philosophy, and diverse social and cultural pressures. The history of the devil in relation to sex (ideas about what was supposed to be natural to sexed bodies) and gender (culturally specific notions of proper manhood and womanhood) was characterised by local specificities that overlay broad continuities in how patriarchal societies defined pre-ternatural phenomena. This tension between continuity and change remains a suggestive dualism of early modern gender history, and it is productive to allow for sex and gender's ambivalences when analysing the cultural legacies of debates about the sexed valances of demonism. Learned men who wrote about demons puzzled over devils' capacity to exert their will in a long conversation that held serious implications for people caught up in cases of demonic possession, witchcraft, and the religious and political conflicts that sometimes resulted. Despite the cultural diversity of Europe and the tumult that charac-terised the period between 1450 and 1800, beliefs about sex undergirded the foundational binaries on which knowledge about the heavens and earth was built; this meant that key questions about the nature of the demonic were intellectually and culturally inextricable from questions of sex.

As Christianity spread and people turned to scripture and apocryphal books in at-tempts to deepen understanding and resolve contradictions, medieval and early modern thinkers reinforced the reliance upon sex as a foundational part of what constituted good or evil. In Genesis 3, the serpent tempted Eve to eat the fruit of the tree of knowledge of good and evil, which she ate and gave to Adam to eat as well, prompting their exclu-sion from paradise. God consequently multiplied womankind's sorrows in childbirth and placed Eve under the command of Adam; this established patriarchal rule as not only a central precept of Christianity but also naturalised it as part of the world God cre-ated and divided into categories of beings in hierarchical relation to each another. Over time, thinkers continued to grapple with the meaning of the fall and the implications of Eve's temptation for humanity; one influential current held that Adam's masculine body and mind were capable of recognising seduction (intellect), whereas Eve's effeminate and imperfect body and mind were soft, yielding, and easily waylaid by falsehood (sense).

DOI: 10.4324/9781003096603-15

In a text written around 200 CE, Tertullian participated in a broader attempt to define Christianity against paganism by casting a stark dichotomy between virtue and evil that conflated the female Christian converts of his age with Eve. "Woman," he wrote, "Do you not know that you are Eve? The judgment of God on your sex lives on right up to the present age. Your guilt lives on and is wholly deserved. You are the devil's gateway."[1] For Tertullian and many who followed him, Eve provided an enduring symbol that naturalised women's foolish and malicious ways as both cause of and justification for patriarchal rule. Eve also provided a reference point—continually reinforced in liturgy, literature, and art—that shaped many early modern Europeans' sense that women were inherently susceptible to demonic overtures. Scholars must reckon with the marked degree of continuity in social, cultural, economic, religious, and political patriarchalism across early modern Europe even while recognising that lived experiences were more varied and complex than these durable intellectual frames might suggest.[2]

On the whole, thinkers treated the sex of demons and Satan quite differently. Writers and artists depicted incubi (demons who took the shape of men to have sex with women) and succubi (demons shaped like women who had sex with men) in ways that ranged from animalistic and monstrous to wickedly attractive, but for most thinkers demons were more illusory than fixedly male or female.[3] Incubi and succubi had the power to appear exactly like living people and to engage in conversation as well as sexual intercourse that ranged from excessively pleasurable to especially painful. Usually, these demons only made themselves known after the act, at which point they could command their human partner's will, enrol them as a witch, or otherwise do the devil's destructive work. Satan was broadly considered to be a spiritual entity, between divine and human, which consequently should not have been sexed. But in diverse texts that elucidated scriptural accounts of Satan's identity, nature, fall from heaven, and efforts to prevail with humans, the devil personified was nonetheless consistently configured as male. This appeared to suit his primary role and agency, and thus the sex of Satan was consistent notwithstanding his spiritual composition and oversight of a range of unsexed, variably sexed, and stably sexed demons. All of humanity inherited the legacy of sin and vulnerability to temptation, but men were not notably marked by Satan's betrayal and fall in the way that women were by Eve's; Satan was male, but Eve was a woman.[4]

For early modern Europeans in societies riven by religious, political, and military instability, demonic assaults appeared to offer an opportunity to clarify what constituted proper religion and legitimate authority. In the face of considerable uncertainty, it became important for demonological thinkers to grapple with the epistemology of the devil and how it might be possible to recognise true demonic interference as opposed to fraud, madness, illness, or heresy. Demonic possession thus offered clergy an opportunity to affirm their status as true representatives of God and to demonstrate ways to command and control devils that sometimes expressed partisan Catholic or Protestant values on demand. As powerful as such performances proved to be, both in the moment and in subsequent publications, they also attracted criticism from all sides and were unable to banish the instability that had made them appealing in the first place. Witchcraft trials proliferated during the same period and provided a deadly outlet for questions about the proper management of relations among humans and spirits. And while demonic possession required no human intermediary, these categories blurred when sufferers named someone as having sent the devils to afflict them. The ability to discern divine or demonic forces was especially crucial as authorities struggled to contain popular expressions of ecstatic and ascetic piety and to mediate claims to sainthood, divine inspiration, or prophecy. This was complicated by the existence of sanctioned responses to demonic interference, as with saints who had overcome demonic assaults; such narratives appear to have reverberated in convents where nuns emulated those whose credit had been enhanced rather than degraded by their brush with demons. Such opportunities narrowed, however, as authorities worked to control the discernment of spirits. By the 18th century, it had become increasingly clear to many European thinkers that while possession phenomena provided opportunities to enhance piety, attract converts, and reaffirm sectarian authority, each instance unavoidably also raised uncomfortable debates that exacerbated long-simmering divisions between, and among, Catholics and Protestants.

Sex and gender suffused early modern European conceptions of demonic possession and witchcraft and those elements were expressed, explicitly and implicitly, by common folk in court testimonies as well as by the authors of demonological treatises. Many believed that women, children, youths, and servants were more likely to suffer preternatural assaults than adult men, and there were strong popular associations between conceptions of *maleficium* (the preternatural power to harm) and gendered social dynamics that were important to community life. The best-known consequence of these preoccupations was the imbalanced sex ratio of accused, convicted, and executed witches. While parts of Scandinavia, Estonia, Normandy, and Russia had more male than female witches, across the majority of early modern Europe about 80% of those accused, tried, and executed for witchcraft were women and about 20% were men. The sex ratio in demonic possession cases also favoured women but less overwhelmingly, depending on the parameters. In some locations, those executed as witches were exclusively women, and longstanding social, cultural, and intellectual currents that directed the preponderance of suspicion towards female suspects had a cumulative and self-perpetuating effect. People who acted as if they were possessed (when demons assaulted from within) or obsessed (when attacked externally) raised the possibility that some who grappled so dramatically with demonic forces might succumb to them due to some combination of weaknesses universal to humans and particular to their age and sex. Despite variations in religious and political pressures across early modern Europe, and local influences that played out in the articulation of demonic harm, cultural perceptions of the demonic remained grounded in patriarchal premises. Because early modern people internalised patriarchal principles regardless of their sex, these principles shaped perception of demonic interference whatever the sex of those who levied accusations and of those they accused.[5]

Possession performances and attempts to resolve them were cultural events mutually constituted by regular folk, clergy, authority figures, and authors who published accounts about the phenomena and their outcomes. Such cases offered opportunities to define and externalise evil and to reaffirm community identity through resolution. Broad cultural scripts rendered possession symptoms comprehensible, and so these phenomena were both orderly and disorderly, formulaic and chaotic, and featured both conformity to and rejection of norms. To acknowledge the persistence of patriarchy and elements of misogyny in demonological writing and prosecution does not constitute a claim that participants in and recorders of early modern cases of demonic harm must have been predominantly fixated on sex. Gender was a foundational component of what made order or disorder, and so demoniacs and exorcists/dispossessors evoked gender to the extent that it supported their claims. For most people who acted as if possessed—called demoniacs—it was of paramount importance to convince observers that they were innocent sufferers at the hands of evil forces, and for exorcists to demonstrate that their responses to possession were legitimate, authoritative, and effective. Neither side was interested in gender beyond its potential to assist them in those broader goals, and participants subjugated gendered elements they perceived as undermining their aims.

Nonetheless, writers who explored the intellectual parameters of attitudes towards demons replicated strong associations between sex and the demonic even when they focused most of their attention beyond sex itself. Because binaries related to sex held such foundational cultural meanings for early modern Europeans, they were pervasive, that is, never truly irrelevant. That which was everywhere can appear to matter nowhere, if it just always *was*; this can be especially true for historians searching for meaningful patterns that reveal what historical events were centrally *about*. Sex and gender alone do not provide comprehensive explanations for complex phenomena like possession and witchcraft, but neither does anything else. Sex was part of what made a demoniac or bewitched person and so it factored in the discernment of causes and precedents. Sex and gender were also central to claims of legitimacy and authority and—crucially—to challenges to such claims. This rendered sex relevant even when demoniacs and exorcists attempted to sublimate it.[6]

This chapter explores some of the ways that sex and gender factored into early modern European conceptions of the demonic. First, it reviews early modern writers' preoccupation with the possibility of demonic copulation. Based in part on classical and scriptural arguments, the prospect of real sexual relations between demons and humans remained an intellectual problem with significant religious and political implications. As witches were the most likely candidates for intercourse with demons, expectations about the sex and gender of suspected witches were enmeshed with thinkers' interest in demonic copulation. Second, it examines the role that sex and gender played in putative cases of demonic possession. Early modern Europeans who acted as if they were possessed drew upon scripts of formulaic gestures and symptoms that denoted demonic assault. Neither the predominant Catholic nor Protestant possession script contained an explicit stipulation about the sex of demoniacs, since all persons were liable to sin and temptation, but there was a general sense in much of Europe that women were more likely than men to fall prey to both possession and witchcraft because of the humoral constitution of their bodies and minds. Furthermore, those attempting to perform a convincing possession sometimes subverted gender expectations as one part of their broader performance of demonic assaults that made them behave contrary to norms. Ultimately, while peoples' experiences of possession and witchcraft across early modern Europe varied, especially given changes in views of sex and the preternatural from the 16th to the 18th centuries, sex remained a fundamental part of what made witchcraft and demonic possession legible. Both phenomena were grounded in durable cultural binaries, formed within patriarchal societies, that ascribed sexed significance to what made a witch or a demoniac. The resilient cultural legacy of these sexed and gendered binaries helps to explain the persistent relevance of sex—with critical implications for women in particular—across the early modern period.

## Sex with Devils

Early modern writers concerned with the extent of demons' powers continued to grapple with some of the questions that had preoccupied classical and medieval thinkers, notably the possibility of sexual relations with Satan or devils in the form of incubi and succubi. In the 13th century, Thomas Aquinas argued that devils were immaterial spirits, but explained how they could create illusions and cause material effects. He posited that it might be possible for demonic sex to result in a human baby if a succubus received a man's seed and then an incubus transferred it to a woman, an idea writers continued to debate for centuries because of the centrality of fertility, contained within proper bounds, for the orderly functioning of patriarchal societies.[7] Many Europeans believed that demons could exert their will and act, to the extent that God allowed them, in a manner perceptible to human senses. The possibility of demonic copulation mattered because it centred demons' contested corporeality, which held implications not only for the possibility of humans to sign demonic pacts or fly to sabbats, but also for the broader sectarian arguments of Catholics and Protestants. For thinkers concerned with worldly atheism or "Sadducism"—an expansion of the belief by scriptural Sadducees that there were no spirits—witchcraft offered the likeliest proof of direct and even physical contact between the natural and preternatural, and by extension the supernatural. Early modern Europeans who wrote about demonic corporeality were primarily concerned with demonology's religious and political implications, and so their interest in sex rested not with sex itself but with the ways it buttressed their logic and supported their arguments. But writers' choices mattered as much as their intentions; while warning humanity of Satan's malice, theorists of demonic copulation both reflected and reinforced an essential association between the demonic and binary conceptions of sex centred on women's depravity.[8]

By the end of the 15th century, in the wake of Pope Eugenius IV's letter of 1437, the Dominican Johannes Nider collected classical and scriptural examples of women's nature as one of extremes, which rendered women particularly dedicated to sins like envy, pride, malice, and venery. Nider connected this extremity of sinfulness to women's greater likelihood of being witches than men. Later other writers across Europe, influenced in part by Pope Innocent VIII's bull *Summis desiderantes* of 1484, increasingly likened witchcraft to a malefic, inverted Christianity characterised by a kind of sex with demons that was not only possible but central to what witchcraft was.[9] More broadly, writers reiterated witches' and devils' contrariness, thus likening both to heretical conspiracies believed to threaten Christian communities by subverting the natural order of things and opposing all that was good. Like Waldensians, Cathars, and Jews, witches who had long been popularly associated with *maleficium* (harmful magic) became vividly associated with actions such as infanticide, the harvesting of children to make magical unguents, and orgies with man, beast, and spirit. These links between witchcraft, sex with demons, and the diabolical compact later helped facilitate widespread witch-hunts in parts of Europe, eventually resulting in roughly 50,000 executions for the crime. And as writers laboured to counter unbelief by proving the reality of demons, their emphasis on humans' real sex with devils developed in tandem with evidence from scripture and witchcraft confessions in ways that further reinforced concerns about diabolical witchcraft.

One particularly influential text was the *Malleus Maleficarum* (*The Hammer of Witches*, 1487) by the Dominican friar Heinrich Kramer, which articulated a concept of powerful witches that echoed across Europe for centuries. Despite the limitations of generalising about elite versus popular beliefs, one reason the *Malleus* mattered as much as it did was because Kramer managed to bridge some of the intellectual divisions between elite (diabolic) and popular (malefic) conceptions of witchcraft. The *Malleus* linked witchcraft and diabolism, argued that witches might fly to sabbats either bodily or in their imagination, and articulated a vision of witchcraft not limited to heresy practised by secret devil-worshippers but one based in the actions of regular people. The book thus contributed to the climate that produced later witch-hunts by explaining how to identify and prosecute the very people that many villagers tended to suspect; this meant that local suspicions were more likely to be taken seriously by those in the position to do something about it in the courts. While the book's influence was delayed and uneven, the *Malleus* like the papal bull that preceded it emphasised demons' capacity to have sexual relations with humans. An emphasis on women's concupiscence—but also passivity in intercourse—provided Kramer with a kind of intellectual solution helped along by its cultural plausibility.[10]

The *Malleus Maleficarum* is popularly known today primarily for its exuberantly misogynist part 1, question 6, where the author assembled material from other sources as evidence of witchcraft's pervasive cultural association with women. In that section, Kramer related that women "do all things because of carnal lust, which…is insatiable in them. Wherefore for the sake of fulfilling their lusts they consort [*se agitant*] even with devils" and "practice carnal filthiness [*spurcicias carnales*] with devils."[11] Regardless of whether Kramer fully believed in the logical exercises of his varying drafts, whether he had internalised cultural misogyny to a degree that was out of step with other clerics, whether he cited others' material about the perfidy of women to prove a point rather than *as* his point, and despite the fact that the *Malleus* was not translated from the Latin for centuries, the text reinforced cultural links between women's depravity, witchcraft, and diabolic intercourse in ways that influenced many subsequent writers' view of demons' ability to interact with humans.[12] Kramer was primarily concerned with convincing readers that demons were real, not with convincing readers that women were abhorrent, but he reproduced that dense if not lengthy section of misogyny as constructive evidence. As with gender generally, misogyny did not need to have been authors' primary goal—or even represent their own thinking—to factor in the evolving cultural construction of demonism and witchcraft. Misogyny, like myriad complex and contradictory gender ways, could lie at the core of the kinds of conflicts that accompanied witchcraft accusations and demonic possessions without having to be the core. Broadly held views of sexual binaries overlapped with presumptions about lust and power, and together informed authors' conceptions of witchcraft when they engaged explicitly with sexual stereotypes and when they did not. Sex and gender often shifted in and out of frame from moment to moment—much like social status, family history, and reputation. Still, as one of the most pervasive and fundamental binaries that gave shape to the natural and preternatural realms, sex—even where it was not predominant—could never really be irrelevant.[13]

The question of demonic copulation remained critical throughout much of early modern Europe because of what it meant for demonic corporeality, which, in turn, held essential implications for the natural philosophy of angels, souls, and other indispensable elements of Christianity. Demonic copulation and corporeality also factored in the very possibility of witchcraft, demonic possession, and other perceptible exchanges between humans and spirits that were of paramount importance to diverse thinkers across the early modern period. Most 21st-century readers of the *Malleus* are sufficiently divorced from those concerns that their attention moves instead to the sensational elements closer to current interests. If the problem with modern presumptions about the *Malleus* is that people too readily presume Kramer was a virulent misogynist obsessed with developing a convenient justification for a desire to persecute and murder women, it is because—as Walter Stephens shows—that view misconstrues his worldview and motivations.[14] It is necessary to contradict such assumptions not out of some concern to defend Kramer or to lessen the horror of what the book facilitated, but because facile assumptions about Kramer's motivations obscure how thinkers can arrive at terrible conclusions even when they are unaware of or indifferent to their implications. This does not actually excuse Kramer of anything, but it reminds us that humans continue to draw terrible conclusions while unaware or indifferent to their implications. As with many aspects of the histories of demonism and witchcraft, the fearful parts are not just the devils, torture, or murder, but the realisation that we remain implicated in dynamics we would prefer to consign to a distant ignorant past.

It made sense to emphasise women's greater susceptibility to demonic overtures because women were viewed as inherently sexual beings (if passively so), because Satan was consistently male, and because women were on the wrong side of cultural binaries that configured them as irrational, contrary, and more susceptible to temptation. Since demons sought to pervert all that was natural and Christian, many thinkers agreed that witches' sabbats and demonic copulation worked through inversions. For example, rather than a kiss of peace at some sabbats witches supposedly knelt to kiss Satan's anus, and many female witches' confessions (as a result of the questions put to them) attested to having copulated in non-standard positions, to having experienced demonic sex as unusually painful or cold, and having sought to poison children or inhibit fertility rather than nurturing.[15] Based on the importance of inversion as a signifier of the demonic we might expect same-sex eroticism to have featured in notions of demonic copulation; after all, the male/female and sexually active/passive binaries were fundamental to early modern European conceptions of sexuality and there were scriptural admonitions about same-sex "uncleanness" from which to draw. But aside from a few exceptions, such as early 17th-century Navarre where confessors described the male Satan copulating with both male and female witches, most accounts of demonic intercourse reinforced standard male/female binaries in part because of the preoccupation with imagining that sex to be potentially procreative. Cultural expectations about sex therefore provided a flexible way for demonological writers to conceive of diabolic inversion more as repetition than difference.[16]

Across the early modern period, both believing and sceptical writers debated the possibility of demonic copulation while invoking notions of sex to support their diverging intellectual, religious, and political aims. Because the question of demonic copulation was so closely tied up with diabolical witchcraft, believing authors often emphasised scriptural and classical precedent and strove to assure their readers of sufficient proofs that could be not explained away as illness, delusion, insanity, or fraud. 21st-century readers might presume that sceptics who challenged demonic copulation and diabolical witchcraft would have done so either by denying the existence of demons or denying the depravity of women, but that was not the case. The Dutch sceptic Johann Weyer, for example, expressed confidence in *De praestigiis daemonum* (1563) that demons were real and capable of afflicting humans but argued that they could not commit most of the acts attributed to them, including copulating with humans. His explanation for those who claimed to have seen witches copulate with devils and for those who confessed to practising witchcraft was delusion and ignorant credulity, both of which Weyer cast as female. He saw women who confessed as victims of melancholy and assiduous prosecutors, but reiterated women's malice, stupidity, and greater permeability to dangerous influences. Weyer and those who followed him, such as the English sceptic Reginald Scot, argued that officials were prosecuting without sufficient legal basis but did not deny women's contrariness or intellectual inferiority. This makes sense given that it was demons' natures, not women's, that had long been the more unsettled question. Scot went farther than Weyer by arguing that demons could not interfere with humans even by causing the kinds of illnesses Weyer had used to explain witchcraft.

Scot stated that spirits' incorporeality rendered any sexual congress with humans impossible and explained all such stories as resulting from illness and delusion. However tragic it was that people were executed for crimes they were innocent of, both Weyer and Scot still found it useful to disparage witchcraft confessions as the delusions of silly old women because it provided a plausible way to argue that learned men would be ridiculous to heed them. While the methods and tone varied among believers as well as sceptics, familiar cultural binaries of sex and gender supported the logic of writers many 21st-century readers would suspect to be misogynists, such as Kramer, and those more easily imagined as defenders of women, such as Weyer and Scot.[17] On the whole, sceptics made arguments that challenged the logic of witch trials, but not by rejecting the fundamental meanings of sex employed by their opponents.

The pattern exhibited in some of the 16th-century debates—with fundamental conceptions of sex acting as a lens through which thinkers contested the theological implications of demonic corporeality—continued past the late 17th century when the spread of Enlightenment rationalism complicated but did not put an end to belief in devils and witches. Theorists who expressed scepticism about the world of spirits such as Hobbes and Spinoza attracted criticism and controversy, though perhaps none more than Balthazar Bekker's *De Betoverde Weereld* (*The Enchanted World*) of 1691. Bekker built upon Cartesian separation of body and mind to relegate devils and angels—and Satan himself—to the realm of the mind that could not affect the physical world.[18] Demoniacs had always faced testing to ascertain the truth of their affliction, but writers became increasingly likely to attribute demonic possession cases to fraud in part because attacking the credit of afflicted regular folk had always been the least risky position to take; this was especially true when the afflicted were young, female, and/or servants. 18th-century demonological debates evinced notable intellectual continuity even as writers marshalled new science and natural philosophy to debate demonic copulation and diabolical witchcraft. Sceptics referred to philosophical and scientific developments as they stressed the impossibility of intercourse between demons and humans, frequently drawing upon centuries-old debates in the process. But believers also addressed the scientific and medical implications of demonic corporeality, both to assert that devils and witches could introduce disease to human bodies and to chart a path through the interrelated effects of natural and preternatural disorders.[19]

Some believers referred to disease in part to counter the premise that witches were suffering from melancholy—an imbalance of the humours, notably black bile, that would affect physical health and mood—a condition of which women were believed to be particularly susceptible. These questions took on additional immediacy in response to Cartesian and Hobbesian materialism, which led 18th-century sceptics to revisit Weyer and others to argue that spirits' incorporeality meant that most of the standard elements of witchcraft and possession were impossible. Believing writers countered such claims by pointing out, as their counterparts had been doing for centuries, how such arguments undermined Christianity by denying spirits and thus potentially souls or God. From the 17th century, Neoplatonists brought renewed vigour to the task of compiling narratives of witchcraft, possession, and other instances of preternatural phenomena as the likeliest way to rejuvenate faith and combat atheism. Joseph Glanvill, Richard Baxter, Robert Boyle, and others published expansive collections to that effect but despite their efforts a combination of factors—such as challenges to the credit of judges who had convicted based on the testimony of demoniacs later determined to be unreliable—prompted circumspection by many of the elite men positioned to act as magistrates or justices. Published debates over such intrusions of the demonic into the natural world continued to rely upon familiar binaries of sex and gender, both explicitly and implicitly, in the argumentation.[20]

The question of copulation with demons was contested across the early modern period not only because it was an essential signifier of diabolical witchcraft, but because its mechanics reflected on the existence of demons in a way that might reveal the workings of God. Establishing the truth of demonic copulation thus had the potential, as demonic possession cases did, to reinforce the legitimacy of one's faith against claims by heretics, atheists, or competitors for religious and political legitimacy. Both Catholics who believed that Protestantism represented the devil's attack on the true church, and Protestants who believed the Roman Catholic Church was the Whore of Babylon, mobilised cultural presumptions about sex and gender to support their positions. These questions were fundamentally *about* religion, and hence politics and social order and myriad other elements. But sex, as a fundamental and constitutive part of the natural and preternatural realms, provided a foundation for conceptions of the demonic that were remarkably stable across the early modern period. Demonologists did not conceive of Satan, devils, and humans apart from systems of sex and gender, nor did the demonic exist fully without them. If the demonic was not *about* sex or gender, it was nonetheless constituted, challenged, and reconstituted *through* sex and gender—a formulation that obliges scholars to grapple with its valances in thinkers' evaluation of evidence, organisation of logic, and assertion of claims. These intellectual currents can appear divorced from the fates of the people in early modern Europe who became ensnarled in possession and witchcraft cases, but writers' attempts to exert stable meaning over these unstable phenomena helps to reveal the utility of sex for the identification and prosecution of those deemed guilty of preternatural crimes.

## Possession, Sex, and Gender

As early modern European thinkers struggled over questions of demonic corporeality, sex remained a foundational touchpoint through which people made sense of preternatural interference. While debating the possibility of sex with demons, some writers attempted to use putative demonic possession cases—and controversial Catholic and Protestant methods of exorcism and dispossession, respectively—as part of broader agendas either to convince readers of the world of spirits or to protect them from dissimulation. Demonic possession cases had such power to attract converts and reinvigorate piety in part because any treatment of possession was inherently propagandistic; from the terminology to methods of expulsion, many aspects of these events were contested by Catholics and Protestants. By the end of the 15th century, cases of possession and organised witch-hunting began to increase in frequency, and demoniacs became a more female and collective group, fuelled in part by an increased preoccupation with female sexuality and the development of convents where intense piety collided with concerns about containing both women's sexual nature and the meaning ascribed to their ecstatic or prophetic religiosity. Some pious women may have been attempting a good possession, divine inspiration, or prophecy, which often met with resistance given the troubling implications of heeding too readily the apocalyptic predictions of pious visionaries. Most male demoniacs were solitary men of relatively higher social status, and because there was less overt social anxiety about control of male sexuality and men's bodies and minds were believed to be less susceptible to Satan's overtures, the sexual aspects remained comparatively subdued in their narratives.[21]

Early modern European demonic possession and witchcraft cases tended to rise and fall in related patterns, peaking between the 1580s and 1630s, and neither could easily be dispensed with because they existed in scripture and cases continued to appear. As a result, early modern thinkers grappled with how to manage the post-apostolic emergence of these phenomena and their unsettling implications. Possession cases usually involved a combination of symptoms drawn from scripture and elaborated upon over time: convulsive fits, alternating flexibility and rigidity in the body, the emission of strange voices from within, vomiting or fasting, trances and visions, levitation, rejection of holy objects or words in favour of blasphemy, an uncanny access to knowledge or facility with foreign languages, and interruption of the senses that followed scriptural formulae. Some writers suspected that a true possession required that sufferers revoke their Christian baptism and grant the devils permission to enter them, and so for some afflicted people obsession would have more directly supported their claims to being victims of evil forces rather than witch-like figures meddling with the preternatural. Furthermore, some who performed symptoms of demonic possession claimed that a human malefactor sent the devils to harm them—something I have called witchcraft-possession—that further blurred the lines between these phenomena. Demoniacs attempted to convince observers that they were innocent sufferers of demonic malice, sometimes in combination with a human intermediary, but not someone who had welcomed or submitted too readily to demonic interference.[22]

Regular folk would have been more familiar with the phenomenon of demonic possession than with intellectual debates about corporeality, and popular reports of miraculous or remarkable providences and the perceptible actions attributed to spirits meant that those who witnessed demoniacs' suffering were likely to produce testimony that writers could use when relaying cases in print. Both villagers and learned authors grasped that possession was as compelling as it was terrifying, given that demoniacs' plight might correspond to witnesses' or readers' spiritual states. It was especially fearful when demoniacs' symptoms appeared to spread rapidly through environments of heightened piety and shared cultural expectations about how the phenomena might emerge. Some such cases grew to involve hundreds of people, as in the German cities of Friedeberg and Spandau in the 1590s and among Ursuline nuns in Loudun, France in the 1630s. As cultural events that held the promise of exposing evil and confirming religious authority, possessions were not supposed to be about sex or gender. Nonetheless, sex was a foundational component of what made order or disorder, and demoniacs and exorcists evoked sex both explicitly and implicitly as they strove to control the meaning of these chaotic events.[23]

Both bewitchment and possession were embodied experiences in which the feelings and senses of the participants were crucial to the discernment of spirits and creation of a convincing narrative. In response to suspected witchcraft, early modern Europeans used tests and countermagical techniques such as scratching or pricking, burning of hair or nails, and striking at apparitions that conceived of invisible links between the bodies of persons who caused and those who received malefic harm. Demoniacs and their witnesses sometimes experienced a blurring of boundaries of sense and perception, aided by the intensity of the environments in which the symptoms emerged. That demoniacs and their witnesses sometimes collectively saw, heard, felt, smelled, and tasted otherworldly things was perceived as convincing proof to some thinkers and was highly suggestive of fraud to others. Even across devotional divides, demonological authors shared a sense that preternatural events were perceived through bodily senses and perception and so they devoted considerable attention to asserting their authority to pronounce what others' bodies meant. This meant that both believers and sceptics necessarily addressed naturalised presumptions about sex and gender when evaluating the legitimacy of demoniacs' afflictions.[24]

The embodied nature of possession also meant that observers evaluated afflicted demoniacs based on their own perception of who the sufferers had been before, and thus how their behaviour and symptoms marked them as driven by demons to act contrary to norms. Those presumptions meant that observers rejected behaviours that did not fit their view of the proper possession script and were receptive to demoniacs' piety and blasphemy when they aligned with expectations for their age and sex. When "themselves," such demoniacs were described as simple, unlearned, and portrayed by believing authors as guileless—and authors assured readers that myriad creditable observers determined that it was impossible that the symptoms could have been faked. The same assumptions about these populations that figured them as more likely subjects for possession than adult men also reinforced the comparatively low regard for the capacities of women, children, youths, servants, and apprentices. Relatively little was expected of them so fluent preaching, passing knowledge of phrases in foreign languages, and nimble physical and psychological transitions made them seem profoundly other-than-themselves. However much demoniacs and their interlocutors might attempt to sublimate questions of sex or gender in order to focus on the more pressing and controversial theological issues, gendered notions nonetheless emerged explicitly and implicitly. The primary symptoms of demonic possession were performed by demoniacs of both sexes but afflicted individuals articulated their temptation by Satan in ways that reflected broad cultural expectations about their susceptibility to sin; sometimes these gendered narratives emerged in response to the questions put to them or appear to have reflected authors' preoccupations while assembling a narrative for publication, but demoniacs also attributed sexual stereotypes to themselves. Furthermore, many demoniacs performed—or at least chroniclers recorded that they had performed—a contented return to their place within the proper bounds of patriarchal hierarchy as a sign of their reintegration to health. Both demoniacs' sex and gender became more legible as authors described the way their behaviour, speech, and comportment altered after the onset of their affliction and recovery. Since believing authors presented demoniacs as human sufferers in a cosmic struggle, they used gender to the extent that it elucidated the nature of the subjects' suffering and their transformation from recognisable subjects into something other.

Demoniacs, whether women, men, youths, or children, drew upon broad cultural scripts when performing their religious suffering. Beliefs about the devils' desire to foster blasphemy and sin meant that otherwise pious individuals often acted out a rejection of holiness to rapt audiences they would not normally have commanded. This degree of scrutiny was not necessarily pleasant, as excruciating testing often accompanied their interrogations even when observers believed them. The motivations and inner lives of even the most exhaustingly documented demoniacs are inaccessible to us, but it appears that simple fraud was very rare. Those who acted as if possessed were primarily unwilling sufferers gripped by terrifying forces who were both elevated and debased by their proximity to preternatural power. Within that framework, it is possible to see how, as with suspected witches who confessed, the potential agency of afflicted parties' words and actions was profoundly ambivalent. Achieving "success" as a demoniac, whether by performing a convincing restoration to oneself or recovering after the prosecution of those accused of causing the ordeal, ultimately reinforced patriarchal authority and reaffirmed customary social values. That such possessed persons neither intended nor achieved durable social critique through their performances does not negate the fact that some found ways to express explosive emotional and corporeal experiences within the very script that held such ambivalent implications for them and those (if any) they accused. Despite the diversity of European demonological thought across the early modern period, and disagreements between and among Catholic and Protestant thinkers about how to respond to demonic possession and witchcraft-possession cases, Christian possession scripts nonetheless remained centred on scriptural precedents that were enmeshed with ideas about sex.[25]

Demonic possession cases were troubling demonstrations of devilish malice even to those who questioned why God would allow Satan so much power in the world. By the 18th century, possession and witchcraft cases, instead of continuing to rise and fall in related patterns as they had across the early modern period, diverged as elites in most of western Europe became increasingly averse to prosecuting witchcraft in law. Cases of demonic possession persisted, however, given their ongoing power to illustrate key theological questions about sin and godly authority. Both witchcraft and demonic possession cases had, broadly speaking, reinforced the patriarchal foundations of early modern Europe, but their diminishment did as well because the elevation of some men's credit at the expense of others still served to perpetuate those systems.

Although early modern Europeans would not have thought of it in these terms, we can see that there were suggestive similarities in the ways that cultural conceptions of evil and sex functioned. It was a commonplace that evil lurked everywhere, and demonism was an indispensable element of popular and elite Christian cosmologies; the Cambridge Neoplatonist Henry More adeptly summarised this as "no Spirit, no God."[26] The devil was a slippery adversary and great deceiver of the senses, meaning that people of all sorts had to be vigilant lest demonic deceit and temptation lead them to sin. Sex was also accounted for in scripture as a fundamental organising principle of the realms, and the great malleability of ideas about sex meant that it was always potentially relevant as an explanation for human behaviour. Like the devil, who could be invoked with equal vehemence on all sides of a controverted event, sex shifted in and out of contradictory frames as an apt explanation for human behaviour without any diminishment of its explanatory power. And, like the devil, the qualities of one's sex were always there, either explicitly denoted or relegated to the background but there, fundamentally structuring a person's suitability for the role of demonic or witch. One of the central challenges, therefore, is to avoid rigid approaches to sex that presume an unwavering predominance of patriarchalism over early modern people's mentalities or social realities without viewing circumstances in which gender operated ambivalently as *less* sexed or gendered. In putative cases of demonic possession, for example, the pertinence of sex in any particular episode varied not only among categories of participants but also for individuals, from moment to moment. The inconsistency of sex and gender complicates attempts to approach systematically their role in preternatural events, but to side line gender does not satisfactorily resolve these analytical problems either because even in their great diversity, early modern Europeans conceived of the demonic in ways inescapably enmeshed with cultural binaries to which sex and gender were fundamental. Understanding the early modern preternatural requires that we keep sex and gender in view as cultural categories that were as complex, ambivalent, and multivalent as politics, religion, and natural philosophy.

## Notes

1 Gen. 3.1–21 (RSV); *The Medieval Devil: A Reader*, trans. and ed. Richard Raiswell and David R. Winter (Toronto, 2022), chapter 2 and 74–7.

2 Judith M. Bennett, *History Matters: Patriarchy and the Challenges of Feminism* (Philadelphia, 2006); Allyson M. Poska, *Women and Authority in Early Modern Spain: The Peasants of Galicia* (New York, 2006); *Gender and Change: Agency, Chronology, and Periodisation*, eds. Alexandra Shepard and Garthine Walker (Hoboken, 2009); Susan D. Amussen and David E. Underdown, *Gender, Culture and Politics in England, 1500–1640* (London, 2017); Merry Wiesner-Hanks, "Forum Introduction: Reconsidering Patriarchy in Early Modern Europe and the Middle East," *Gender & History*, 30, no. 2 (July 2018): 320–30.

3 On visual depictions of Satan and demons, see Charles Zika, *Exorcising our Demons: Magic, Witchcraft and Visual Culture in Early Modern Europe* (Leiden, 2003); Patricia Simons, "The Incubus and Italian Renaissance Art," *Notes in the History of Art*, 34, no. 1 (Fall 2014): 1–8. On 13th-century demonic disembodiment as purification, see Dyan Elliott, *Fallen Bodies: Pollution, Sexuality, and Demonology in the Middle Ages* (Philadelphia, 1999), chapter 6.

4 On Augustine's influential preoccupation with Genesis and treatment of Eve, embodiment, and original sin, see for example John O'Meara, "Saint Augustine's Understanding of the Creation and Fall," *The Maynooth Review / Revieú Mhá Nuad* 10 (1984): 52–62; On early modern debates about Eve and the nature of women see for example Joan Kelly, "Early Feminist Theory and the 'Querelle Des Femmes', 1400–1789," *Signs* 8, no. 1 (1982): 4–28; Shannon Miller, *Engendering the Fall: John Milton and Seventeenth-Century Women Writers* (Philadelphia, 2008). On philosophical and feminist meanings of Eve, see Phyllis Trible, *God and the Rhetoric of Sexuality* (Philadelphia, 1978); J. A. Phillips, *Eve: The History of an Idea* (San Francisco, 1984); Elaine Pagels, *Adam, Eve, and the Serpent* (New York, 1988); *Eve and Adam: Jewish, Christian, and Muslim Readings of Genesis and Gender*, eds. Kristen E. Kvam, Linda S. Schearing, and Valarie H. Ziegler (Indianapolis, 1999).

5 Brian P. Levack, *The Witch-Hunt in Early Modern Europe* (London, 1987); Julian Goodare, *The European Witch-Hunt* (London, 2016), 27–30; Rolf Schulte, *Man as Witch: Male Witches in Central Europe*, trans. Linda Froome-Döring (Basingstoke, 2009); *Witchcraft and Masculinities in Early Modern Europe*, ed. Alison Rowlands (Basingstoke, 2009); Valerie Kivelson, *Desperate Magic: The Moral Economy of Witchcraft in Seventeenth-Century Russia* (Ithaca, 2013).

6 Phases of the scholarly response to women's and gender history of the preternatural can be seen in a range of texts such as Christina Larner, *Enemies of God: The Witch-Hunt in Scotland* (London, 1981); Lyndal Roper, *Oedipus and the Devil. Witchcraft, Sexuality and Religion in Early Modern Europe* (London, 1994); Diane Purkiss, *The Witch in History: Early Modern and Twentieth-Century Representations* (London, 1996); Malcolm Gaskill, "The Devil in the Shape of a Man: Witchcraft, Conflict and Belief in Jacobean England," *Historical Research*, 71, no. 175 (June 1998), 142–71; Willem de Blécourt, "The Making of the Female Witch: Reflections on Witchcraft and Gender in the Early Modern Period," *Gender & History* 12 (2000), 287–309; and Marion Gibson, *The Witches of St. Osyth: Persecution, Betrayal and Murder in Elizabethan England* (Cambridge, 2022).

7 Aquinas' explanation held sway and received additional support by the end of the 15th century, but for a notable contradiction, see Fabián Alejandro Campagne, "A Spanish Demonologist during the French Wars of Religion: Juan Maldonado's *Traicté des anges et demons*," in *The Science of Demons: Early Modern Authors Facing Witchcraft and the Devil*. ed. Jan Machielsen (London, 2020), 214–9.

8 On demonic corporeality and copulation, see Stuart Clark, *Thinking with Demons: The Idea of Witchcraft in Early Modern Europe* (New York, 1997), 190–7; Walter Stephens, *Demon Lovers: Witchcraft, Sex, and the Crisis of Belief* (Chicago, 2002); Philip C. Almond, *The Devil: A New Biography* (Ithaca, 2014), 111–7. On the sabbat, see Michael D. Bailey, *Origins of the Witches' Sabbath* (University Park, 2021).

9 Johannes Nider, *Formicarius* (1438); Michael D. Bailey, *Battling Demons: Witchcraft, Heresy, and Reform in the Late Middle Ages* (University Park, 2003); Almond, *The Devil*, 94–106.

10 *The Hammer of Witches: A Complete Translation of the Malleus Maleficarum*, trans. Christopher S. Mackay (New York, 2009), 2–6. On resonance with another key text, see Walter Stephens, "The Witch-Hunting Humanist: Gianfrancesco Pico della Mirandola's *Strix*," in *Science of Demons*, 83–99.

11 Kramer, *Malleus maleficarum*, fols. 23r, 48v, 10v; cited in Stephens, *Demon Lovers*, 34.

12 On some of these caveats, see Clark, *Thinking with Demons*, 114–7; Stephens, *Demon Lovers*, chapter 2.

13 Hans Peter Broedel, *The Malleus Maleficarum and the Construction of Witchcraft: Theology and Popular Belief* (Manchester, 2003), chapter 7. On Kramer's interest in the other side of the coin—the potentially positive implications of women's greater susceptibility to spiritual influence—see Tamar Herzig, "The bestselling demonologist: Heinrich Institoris's *Malleus maleficarum*," in *Science of Demons*, 57–63.

14 Stephens, *Demon Lovers*, chapters 2–4.

15 Lyndal Roper, *Witch Craze: Terror and Fantasy in Baroque Germany* (New Haven, 2004).

16 On non-procreative demonic copulation, see Tamar Herzig, "The Demons' Reaction to Sodomy: Witchcraft and Homosexuality in Gianfrancesco Pico Della Mirandola's 'Strix,'" *The Sixteenth Century Journal* 34, no. 1 (2003): 53–72. On sexuality more broadly, see Roper, *Witch Craze*, 82–103; Charlotte-Rose Millar, "Sleeping with Devils: The Sexual Witch in Seventeenth-Century England," in *Supernatural and Secular Power in Early Modern England*, eds. Marcus Harmes and Victoria Bladen (Farnham, 2015); Michelle D. Brock, *Satan and the Scots: The Devil in Post-Reformation Scotland, c.1560–1700* (Farnham, 2016); 152–67; Lu Ann Homza, *Village Infernos and Witches' Advocates: Witch-Hunting in Navarre, 1608–1614* (University Park, 2022).

17 Philip C. Almond, *England's First Demonologist: Reginald Scot & 'The Discoverie of Witchcraft'* (London, 2011); Michaela Valente, "'Against the Devil, the Subtle and Cunning Enemy': Johann Wier's *De praestigiis daemonum*," in *Science of Demons*, 111–5.

18 For scepticism about demons in Thomas Hobbes, *Leviathan* (1651), Baruch Spinoza, *Letters* (1667), and Balthazar Bekker, see Jonathan I. Israel, *Radical Enlightenment: Philosophy and the Making of Modernity 1650–1750* (Oxford, 2001), chapter 21.

19 On medical approaches to preternatural harm or demonic possession, see, for example, Leland L. Estes, "The Medical Origins of the European Witch Craze: A Hypothesis," *Journal of Social History* 17, no. 2 (1983): 271–84; *Witchcraft and Hysteria in Elizabethan London: Edward Jorden and the Mary Glover Case*, ed. Michael MacDonald (London, 1991); Kirsten C. Uszkalo, *Being Bewitched: A True Tale of Madness, Witchcraft, and Property Development Gone Wrong* (University Park, 2017).

20 Joseph Glanvill, *Saducismus triumphatus, or, full and plain evidence concerning witches and apparitions…* (London, 1681); Richard Baxter *The certainty of the worlds of spirits, and consequently, of the immortality of souls…* (London, 1691); Ian Bostridge, *Witchcraft and Its Transformations c. 1650–c.1750* (Oxford, 1997); Michael Hunter, *The Decline of Magic: Britain in the Enlightenment* (New Haven, 2020).

21 Nancy Caciola, *Discerning Spirits: Divine and Demonic Possession in the Middle Ages* (Ithaca, 2003); Sarah Ferber, *Demonic Possession and Exorcism in Early Modern France* (London, 2004), chapters 6 and 7; Brian Levack, *The Devil Within: Possession & Exorcism in the Christian West* (New Haven, 2013), chapter 7. On Protestants, see, for example, Phyllis Mack, *Visionary Women: Ecstatic Prophecy in Seventeenth-Century England* (Berkeley, 1993).

22 Levack, *The Devil Within*, 16–18; Erika Gasser, *Vexed with Devils: Manhood and Witchcraft in Old and New England* (New York, 2017), 5–8.

23 Clark, *Thinking with Demons*, 394; Jonathan L. Pearl, *The Crime of Crimes: Demonology and Politics in France, 1560–1620* (Waterloo, 1999); H.C. Erik Midelfort, *Exorcism and Enlightenment: Johann Joseph Gassner and the Demons of Eighteenth-Century Germany* (New Haven, 2005); Levack, *The Devil Within*.

24 Stuart Clark, *Vanities of the Eye: Vision in Early Modern Culture* (Oxford, 2009), chapters 4, 6, and 8; Erika Gasser, "Possession and the Senses in Early Modern England," *The Journal of the Canadian Historical Association/ Revue de la Société historique du Canada*, 30, no. 1 (2019), 87–113.

25 See, for example, Nathan Johnstone, *The Devil and Demonism in Early Modern England* (Cambridge, 2006); Nicky Hallet, *Witchcraft, Exorcism, and the Politics of Possession in a Seventeenth-Century Convent* (Burlington, VT, 2007); Mairi Cowan, *The Possession of Barbe Hallay: Diabolical Arts and Daily Life in Early Canada* (Montreal, 2022).

26 Henry More, *An antidote against atheism…* (London, 1653), 164.

# Bibliography

Clark, Stuart. *Thinking with Demons: The Idea of Witchcraft in Early Modern Europe*. New York: Oxford University Press, 1997.

Ferber, Sarah. *Demonic Possession and Exorcism in Early Modern France*. New York: Routledge, 2004.

Homza, LuAnn. *Village Infernos and Witches' Advocates: Witch-Hunting in Navarre, 1608-1614*. University Park, PA: The Pennsylvania State University Press, 2022.

Levack, Brian P. *The Devil Within: Possession & Exorcism in the Christian West*. New Haven: Yale University Press, 2013.

Millar, Charlotte-Rose. "Sleeping with Devils: The Sexual Witch in Seventeenth-Century England," in *Supernatural and Secular Power in Early Modern England*, eds. Marcus Harmes and Victoria Bladen. Farnham: Ashgate, 2015.

Roper, Lyndal. *Witch Craze: Terror and Fantasy in Baroque Germany*. New Haven: Yale University Press, 2004.

Rowlands, Alison, ed. *Witchcraft and Masculinities in Early Modern Europe*. Basingstoke: Palgrave Macmillan, 2009.

Stephens, Walter. *Demon Lovers: Witchcraft, Sex, and the Crisis of Belief*. Chicago: University of Chicago Press, 2002.

# 15

# SEEING SATAN

*Linda C. Hults*

In *Paradise Lost*, John Milton imagines the rebellious angels as so completely changed in appearance after being ousted from heaven that their leader Satan cannot recognise his close comrade Beëlzebub.[1] Like good (unfallen) angels, Satan and demons were understood, during and long before Milton's time, as highly intelligent spiritual creatures. Some Christian theologians, such as Tertullian (155/60–after 220) and Origen (c. 185–254), thought they were made of an ultra-refined, tenuous substance, while others, such as Thomas Aquinas (1224/25–74), believed they were completely immaterial.[2] They could fly, move imperceptibly fast, transport objects and bodies, and produce illusions out of air, enabling them to assume different forms instantaneously: powers drawn from nature but beyond human understanding.[3] These powers—especially changing form—enabled them to deceive, seduce and tempt humans. Paradoxically, however, a fallen angel could also return regularly to his proper form. Milton's Satan, for instance, appears as a squatting toad to tempt Eve, but when the angel Ithuriel touches him with his spear, he returns to his own shape.[4] As this chapter shows, the proper forms of Satan and his demons took on many variations in Western art but remained recognisable because they distorted the order of nature, inspired fear, parodied Christian concepts and rituals, and inverted cultural notions of beauty. After Satan's theological role and ontological reality came into question in the Enlightenment, however, these traits did not always hold or have the same connotations.

People inferred Satan's fall from heaven, an idea in Jewish apocalyptic thought, from Isaiah 14.12, a passage about the fall of a pompous Babylonian king dubbed "Lucifer" (light bearer), an epithet eventually attached to Satan. The passage does not describe the fallen Lucifer's appearance beyond implying his loss of luminosity.[5] The bible does, however, suggest some of Satan's guises. The serpent who tempts Eve in Genesis came to be understood as one of his avatars, and Revelation 12.7-9 describes a second war in heaven during the end times and a "great dragon," that was "thrown down, that ancient serpent, who is called the Devil and Satan, the deceiver of the whole world—he was thrown down to the earth, and his angels were thrown down with him." An enormous, hideous sea serpent named Leviathan, also associated with Satan and/or the mouth of hell, is mentioned in

DOI: 10.4324/9781003096603-16

Isaiah 27.1, Psalms 74.14 and 104.25-26, and described in detail in Job 41. All derive from Mesopotamian combat myths in which a god triumphs over a serpentine adversary, snakes being associated with the underworld and primeval chaos, even though they also signified fertility. Origen equated Satan with all these avatars, adding the Prince of Tyre who coveted God's throne (Ezek. 28.12-19).[6]

The cultures vilified in Jewish and Christian scripture as pagan idolaters provided basic components of Satan's appearance. Some derived from the theriomorphic (animalistic), grotesque, hybrid attributes of Egyptian and Ancient Near Eastern gods, such as the dwarfism and distorted face of the Egyptian god Bes (Figure 15.1), who protected the household and women in childbirth, and the horns or horned helmet of the Canaanite god Baal,

*Figure 15.1* *Bes*, stone relief from the Temple of Hathor, Dendera, Egypt, 1st century CE. Photo: Erich Lessing/Art Resource, NY.

worshipped as a bull or golden calf. Among Greco-Roman deities, the horned, pointy-eared, goat-legged god of wild nature and fertility, Pan (or Faunus), greatly influenced images of Satan. A Roman statue from the 2nd century CE depicts Pan teaching the shepherd Daphnis, son of Hermes and a nymph, to play the panpipes (Figure 15.2). His cloven hooves, hairy legs, prominent genitals, and predatory glance could easily be mistaken for satanic traits were they not rooted in Greco-Roman mythology. Despite traits borrowed from paganism and Judaism, however, Satan is fundamentally a Christian character; his image developed following the phases in the history of Christianity that structure this chapter. Demonic iconography emerged as Europe was Christianised in the early medieval period from the 5th through the 10th centuries. Images of Satan and demons proliferated in the high medieval period (11th through the mid-13th centuries), when the Church was tremendously powerful.

*Figure 15.2* *Pan Teaching Daphnis to Play the Panpipes*, marble, 2nd century CE. Archaeological Museum, Naples. Photo: ©Vanni Archive/Art Resource, NY.

## Finding Satan's Look: Early Christianity through the High Middle Ages

The earliest Christian art, such as frescoes in the Roman catacombs and relief sculptures on sarcophagi, stone crosses, and ivories, generally conveyed religious meaning in abstract or allusive ways. The Chi-Rho symbol and the Good Shepherd alluded to Christ; Jonah and the Whale, the Three Hebrews in the Fiery Furnace, and Daniel in the Lion's Den to salvation. Christ treading on beasts signalled his victory over evil. This limited iconography expanded after Christianity, as codified by the Nicene Creed, was legalised by the eastern Roman emperor Constantine in 313, and Theodosius I made it the official religion of the empire in 380.

Satan per se is not present in extant works before the 6th century. He might appear in a mosaic depicting the parable of Jesus Separating the Sheep from the Goats (Matt. 25.31-46), a metaphor for the Last Judgement, from the church of Sant' Apollinare Nuovo in Ravenna, Italy (Figure 15.3). However, nothing distinguishes the angel on Christ's left (Satan?) from the good angel (Michael?) on his right, other than his blue robe suggesting the aerial realm of demons, his position on Christ's left (sinister) side, and his command of goats. For centuries to come, the Pan-like hooves, horns and uncanny eyes of goats would mark Satan and demons. We will begin to see a readily recognisable Satan in early medieval scriptural narratives.

*Figure 15.3*  *Christ Separating the Sheep from the Goats*, mosaic, nave of Sant' Apollinare Nuovo, Ravenna, 6th century CE. Photo: Alfredo Dagli Orti/Art Resource, NY.

Ravenna's history as the capital of the western Roman Empire in the early 5th century, a barbarian capital when the empire fell in 476, and an outpost of the Byzantine (eastern) empire in the 6th century, exemplifies the complex mix of cultures in late antique and early medieval Europe: its architecture and art reflect late Roman, early Christian, and Byzantine styles. In time, Christian art would also take on the flatness, intricate patterns, and abstract animal and plant forms in the metal- and stonework of polytheistic barbarian peoples. Like Pan, the horned fertility god of the Celts, Cernunnos, became associated with the Christian devil.[7]

Celtic tribes had been in central Europe since about 1200 BCE, and their migrations took them west to France and Iberia, east and south to Greece and Anatolia, and north to the British Isles. The ancient Greeks and Hellenistic kings fought off their invasions, and Rome launched campaigns against them over many centuries, building roads and towns as they progressed. Gradually, Celtic culture mixed with Roman. By Trajan's reign (98–117 CE), Rome dominated all territories circling the Mediterranean, including Europe as far north as Britain. When Rome could no longer enforce its hegemony in Europe during the 4th and 5th centuries, however, Germanic tribes (Goths, Visigoths, Burgundians, Angles, Saxons, Franks, and others), pushed westwards by the Huns, migrated into these lands. Some tribes, such as the Visigoths, Franks, and Anglo-Saxons, established kingdoms and expanded them, the most impressive being the Frankish Carolingian empire under Charlemagne in the 9th century, incorporating most of present-day France, Belgium, the Netherlands, western Germany, and part of Italy, until it was divided among his sons.

As the Roman Empire declined, the Papacy grew stronger, sending missions to Christianise polytheistic Celtic and Germanic tribes. Although temporal authority in medieval Europe resided in a patchwork of kingdoms and feudal territories governed by noble landowners, Christianity provided a unifying force. Monastic orders preserved learning and the Latin language. Medieval Christianity's redemptive but stern message made effective use of Satan and demons. Despite the rich variety of its art, iconographic continuities made it possible to communicate this message via the sculpture, altarpieces, frescoes, and stained-glass windows of churches, and Satan and demons appeared as costumed actors in vernacular religious plays available to a wide swath of the population. Clergy, aristocrats, and royals also had access to splendidly illuminated manuscripts on parchment made from animal skins, largely produced by monks and sometimes nuns in *scriptoria* (rooms for copying and painting manuscripts).[8]

One of the three full-page images of Christ from the monumental Gospel Book of Kells is the earliest extant depiction of his Temptation by Satan, fully recounted in Matthew 4.1-11 and Luke 4.1-13 (early 9th century, Figure 15.4). The Kells monastery in northeast Ireland was likely built for the Irish Benedictine community of Iona—an island in the Scottish Hebrides from which the monks launched their conversion efforts in the British Isles and on the continent, and possibly where the book was made. Facing Viking raids, the Ionians needed an inland home.[9]

The Kells *Temptation* faces the Vulgate text of Luke and focuses on the moment when Satan dares Christ to jump from the pinnacle of the Jerusalem Temple and to trust angels to break his fall. In the semi-abstract visual language of Kells, indebted to the interlaced animal forms on Celtic metalwork or stone crosses, the flattened image of the Temple, with its unidentified occupants, merges with the upper body of Christ, the "cornerstone" of a new temple (Acts 4.8-12, Eph. 2.19-22). Brilliant colours echo the description of the

*Figure 15.4*   *The Temptation of Christ*, fol. 202v from the Book of Kells, IE TCD MS 58, early 9th century. Trinity College Library, Dublin. Photo: The Board of Trinity College Library.

Tabernacle of the Ark (Exod. 25-27) that the Church now supersedes.[10] While angels wait to succour him, Christ holds a scroll (the Pentateuch) and rebuffs Satan—a winged black imp suspended on Christ's sinister side and looking much like he does in Byzantine art.[11] A puzzling detail is the crowd of intent observers on the left and bottom. They lack halos, so it is difficult to call them saints. Along with the figure with crossed, floriated staffs enclosed in the rectangle beneath Christ, they may symbolise the importance of sight in Christian devotion.[12]

An early image of Satan's fall graces the Anglo-Saxon manuscript, Junius 11 (c. 950–1000), named after its 17th-century owner, Dutch scholar Franciscus Junius II (Figure 15.5). The old-English poem, *Christ and Satan*, begins with Satan's fall at Christ's hands at the beginning of creation, followed by Christ's Harrowing of Hell between his death and Resurrection to save righteous, pre-Christian people, and ends with his Temptation by Satan. This non-chronological sequence demonstrates Christ's awesome power first, then encourages readers to resist Satan's temptations as Christ did. The image of Satan's fall,

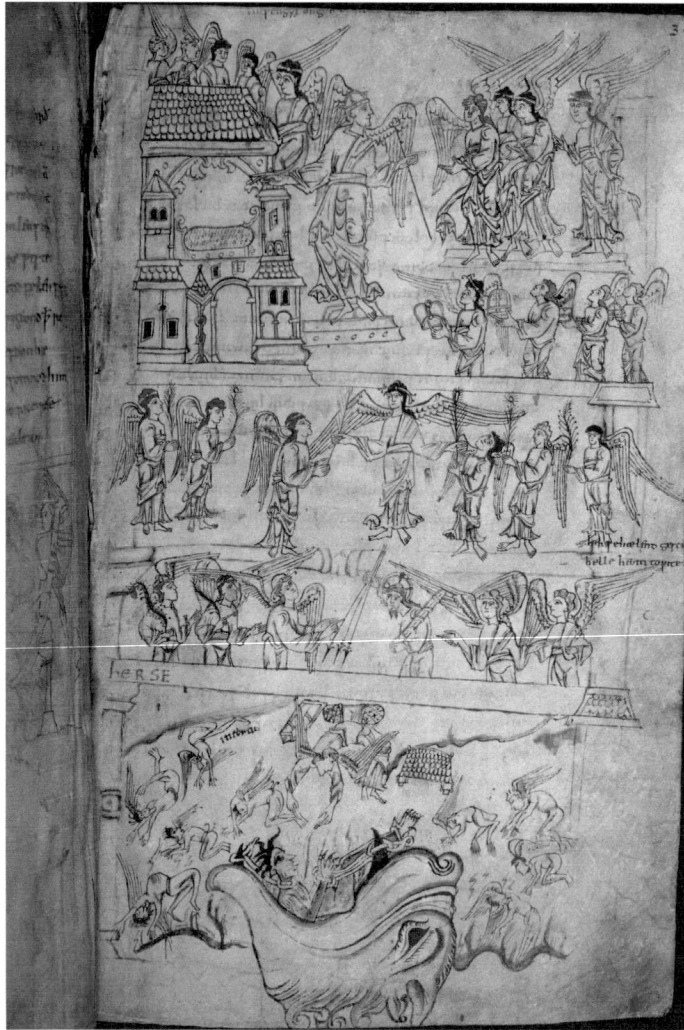

*Figure 15.5   Satan's Fall*, Junius MS. 11, page 3, c. 950–1000. Bodleian Libraries, Oxford. Photo: Bodleian Libraries, University of Oxford.

with its agitated, sketchy figures influenced by Carolingian art, works with bits of text to guide the reader/viewer through horizontal registers. At the top, he is large and crowned as he challenges Christ's position as son of God in heaven, while the text above reads "How the angel began to be proud." Lesser angels pay him obeisance. Below, he has shrunk somewhat as his angels salute him with palm fronds symbolising their hope for victory. To the far right, we read, "Here the Saviour created hell as a punishment for them." Farther down, Christ appears in the centre, wielding three menacing spears to cast the rebels into hell as an emphatic text on the left proclaims, "Here, this." In the bottom register, Satan is shown twice: first as a diminutive, contorted but still humanoid figure with non-functioning wings. Immediately below, he is compelled into the hellmouth, his now wingless body becomes monstrous, his bound hands and feet morph into claws, his skin darkens, and his large head sprouts wild, flamelike hair.[13]

On 18 April 1091, the monks Munnio and Domenico at Santo Domingo de Silos in northern Spain, where monasteries had served as refuges for Christians fleeing the Arab Muslim conquest of the Visigoths in the 8th century, signed their manuscript text, lamented their suffering incurred from laborious writing, and exhorted readers not to touch their letters. The illuminations were finished by Petrus, the monastery's prior, in 1109 (Figure 15.6). This book is one of 29 known versions of St. Beatus of Liébana's illustrated commentary on the Apocalypse (c. 776–780s). His original manuscript is lost, but later versions indicate that Beatus conceived the illustrations as essential, placing them between the biblical text and his commentary. Although the current style was Romanesque, the Silos Beatus reiterates the brilliant colours and patterns of Mozarabic style of early medieval Christian Spain. In the double-folio illustration of St. John's Revelation 12, an expectant "Woman Clothed with the Sun" (Virgin Mary) is attacked by the seven-headed dragon, named Satan in verse 9, who threatens to devour her son. However, Christ escapes to heaven

*Figure 15.6* Petrus, double-folio illustration of Revelation 12, Silos Beatus Liébana, Add MS 11695, fols. 147v–148r, 1091–109. British Library, London. Photo: British Library Board/ Robana/Art Resource, NY.

(upper right), the Woman escapes into the desert, and St. Michael and the good angels cast Satan/dragon into the earth: in the lower right, a black, now humanoid Satan with huge hands and a cyclopean eye is caged and surrounded by the naked damned. Angered at his ousting, Satan/dragon seeks revenge on the Woman (now winged, lower left), by spewing out a flood, which the earth swallows up. Despite these defeats, his war with the "rest of her offspring," namely the Church (12.17), will only cease forever when he is vanquished at the Last Judgement. This narrative reflects the monks' concern for the preservation of the Church in Spain, even though Christian territories were gaining ground against the Muslim armies.[14]

The imp of Kells and the wingless, bound figure of Satan in Junius 11 and the Silos Beatus are no matches for God, Christ, or St. Michael. Resisting dualism, Christianity conceived them as agents of an all-powerful God whose reasons for allowing evil are unfathomable. Christians might feel comforted yet puzzled by Satan's fall because evil was obviously omnipresent and ongoing. If Satan was bound and cast into hell with his demons, how did they roam the earth sowing evil? Did God let Satan out (see Job 2) or did demons leave hell on his orders? Why was Satan not defeated during Christ's time on earth? In Revelation 20.1-3, he is bound again and confined to the underworld during the millennium—a thousand years of peace after horrific violence and destruction—then loosed again until his defeat at the Last Judgement. When would this occur? Despite theologians' warnings not to take the millennium literally or to predict its onset, speculation did not cease. Christian theology has never resolved these issues.[15]

Nevertheless, the Church knew that fear of Satan, demons and eternal punishment would motivate Christians to repent, so images of Satan, demons, and hell became more monstrous in the Romanesque art of the 11th and 12th centuries. Increasingly, heretical movements, influenced by dualism and/or contempt for the Church's wealth and moral failings, threatened its hold on the laity, and the Church responded by linking heretics to the devil and brutally persecuting them. The growing importance of pilgrimage and the veneration of relics (Christian practices since the 4th century), as well as competition among monasteries, led to spacious plans and expansive decoration in churches along the pilgrimage routes leading to Santiago da Compostela in northern Spain, which housed the relics of St. James. The Benedictine abbey church of Sainte-Foy (St. Faith) at Conques in southern France was situated on this route (as was Santo Domingo) and enlarged in the late 10th and early 12th centuries. Its greatest treasure was a piece of the skull of Sainte Foy, said to be a girl in Roman Aquitaine martyred on a gridiron and beheaded for refusing to worship idols, housed in a jewelled reliquary.

The *Last Judgement* sculpted in the mid-12th century on the church's tympanum (the semicircle over the entrance door) likely generated considerable repentance (Figure 15.7). Christ appears in the centre as omnipotent judge at the end of time when the dead are raised, their bodies reunited with their souls, and both living and dead are consigned to heaven or hell forever.[16] Traces of paint indicate the relief's bright colours, and in hell on the right, demons busily torture the damned, who seem unable to resist.[17] They throw a haughty knight from his horse, tie an adulterous couple together with ropes, rip out a liar's tongue, hang an avaricious man with a money bag around his neck, and chomp on an unjust king's head. With his frightening face, squat proportions, wild hair and clawed legs intertwined with snakes, Satan presides over hell as the counterpart to Abraham on the left, welcoming the blessed souls to his bosom (Luke 16.22-23). Above and to the left of Abraham, a prostrate Sainte Foy prays to the disembodied hand of God to gain his

*Figure 15.7* *The Last Judgement*, west tympanum, Abbey Ste. Foy, Conques, c. 1150. Photo: Scala/ Art Resource, NY.

mercy for the souls. Heaven's calm order counters hell's disordered terror, and Latin inscriptions verbalise the tympanum's message. Under hell, we read "Sinners, unless you change your ways, know that a harsh judgement awaits you." Although Romanesque terror was tempered by the graceful Gothic style that emerged later in the 12th century, numerous tympana and other sculptures decorating medieval churches and monasteries echoed this exhortation, and grotesque demonic forms were often found on the capitals of columns in church naves or monastic cloisters, where monks would see them daily.[18]

Repentance could save those whose sins were extremely serious, as in the legend of St. Theophilus, a 6th-century cleric in Cilicia in southern Turkey. Its popularity in western Europe culminated in the 13th century, when it was frequently illustrated in Gothic stained-glass windows and manuscript paintings. Theophilus was a skilled administrator for a bishop and when the bishop died, he was invited to replace him. Being humble, he turned the offer down and was subsequently fired unfairly by the new bishop. Disillusioned, Theophilus secured the help of a Jewish sorcerer (one of many antisemitic tropes in Christian discourse) and made a contract with Satan who promised to get his job back and make him wealthy if he would renounce Christ and the Virgin Mary. Theophilus gained worldly rewards when restored to his office, but guilt drove him to do penance to the Virgin at a chapel. Convinced of his sincerity, Mary invaded hell and forcefully retrieved the contract, allowing Theophilus, who died soon after, to save his soul.[19]

This tale foreshadows the early modern Faust legend and witches' pacts with the devil but has characteristically medieval features. Theophilus's sin reflected a broader concern about corruption within the Church, and his salvation confirmed the power of Mary, chief intercessor on behalf of medieval Christians. Moreover, Theophilus's contract with Satan was often depicted in terms of the fealty ritual between a vassal and his feudal lord, as in the illumination from the late 13th-century Lambeth Apocalypse, where this story is one of many supplements to the Latin biblical text of Revelation and a commentary, probably written in the 11th century by the Benedictine monk, Berengaudus (Figure 15.8).[20]

*Figure 15.8* *Theophilus's Pact with the Devil* from the Lambeth Apocalypse, MS 209, fol. 46r, c. 1260–75. Lambeth Palace Library, London. Photo: Courtesy of Lambeth Palace Library.

Judging by the heraldry in some images, this luxurious devotional book was likely commissioned by Lady Eleanor de Quincy, who plays the roles of Mary Magdalene witnessing the risen Christ, a devotee worshipping the Virgin and Child, and a heroine fending off the devil in an allegorical scene. On the allegory's verso is a vision of the Holy Face captured on St. Veronica's veil. The Theophilus story is one of the Virgin's miracles, contributing to the manuscript's feminine appeal.[21] Although Eleanor may have needed help from male advisers with Latin, the Lambeth illustrations tell the stories compellingly.

In the upper register of one of three full-page illuminations of Theophilus's legend, Jews, characterised by the antisemitic tropes of spiked hats, hooked noses, and money bags, and a devil who seems to be Satan himself, tempt him to seek a contract to regain his office. A chainlike linkage of arms directs us to the small space between the sorcerer's raised hand and an uncertain Theophilus, staring at the money bag the sorcerer proffers. In the lower register, he visits an enthroned Satan, bends down while holding his signed contract, and shakes Satan's right hand as demons and the sorcerer bear witness. The fact that he does not kneel completely to the ground or put both of his hands in Satan's (as in the fealty ritual) suggests that his subservience is incomplete and there is a chance for repentance with Mary's intercession. The robe on Satan's disordered, furry body and his crosier parody the bishop Theophilus served.[22] Another googly eyed face grins out from his abdomen, wings protrude from his knees, eyes peep from his upper torso, and raptorial claws replace his feet—traits that also mark the demons. Similar images decorated many kinds of illuminated manuscripts besides those discussed here, such as Psalters (books of psalms) and Books of Hours (prayers said at different times of the day). Parodies of Christian figures or concepts, the unnatural disorder of body parts, and theriomorphic traits would mark satanic imagery after the 13th century as well, although more humanoid traits also appear.

## Late Medieval and Early Modern Variations on Satan's Look

The late medieval and early modern eras saw the growth of centralised governments with state bureaucracies, such as the French and English monarchies. At its height in the mid-16th century under Charles V, the Habsburg Holy Roman Empire (heir to Carolingian and Ottonian rulers) was a massive conglomeration, including the low countries and Spain; parts of current France, eastern Europe, and the Italian peninsula; the islands of Sicily and Sardinia; and the largely German-speaking duchies, principalities, free imperial cities, and ecclesiastical territories of central Europe. The Protestant Reformation, sparked by the German Augustinian monk Martin Luther in 1517, fuelled profound religious divisions and violent conflicts within and among these powers for much of the early modern era.

Despite frequent wars, cities, capitalism and a middle class proliferated throughout early modern Europe, and exploration and colonisation of the New World began. The development of the printing press and the growth of printmaking in the 15th century vastly increased the circulation of books and images, and the humanist intellectual movement and educational programme, based primarily on Latin texts and largely restricted to men, revived antiquity's cultural legacy, adapting it to the contemporary world. Similarly, artists also looked to antiquity in varying degrees: classical motifs and style came later to northern Europe than to Italy. Along with an increasingly close observation of the natural world foreshadowing the scientific revolution, they would transform the range and character of art as well as the status of their profession, elevating it from a manual craft to a liberal art. Demonic imagery contributed to this transformation by offering artists opportunities to display their fertile imaginations as well as their observation of nature.

In early 14th-century Italy, Florentines Giotto di Bondone and Dante Alighieri, a painter and poet, created influential visions of Satan. Shortly before Dante began his *Divine Comedy* (1308–20), Giotto completed his *Last Judgement* on the entrance wall of the Scrovegni (or Arena) Chapel in Padua in 1305 (Figure 15.9). His medium was fresco, in which water-based pigments are applied to freshly plastered sections of wall, bonding to the plaster as it dries, ensuring durable colours. The predominant sky-blue colour of the chapel, however, required a pigment containing lapis lazuli that could only be applied on dry plaster, making

*Figure 15.9* Giotto di Bondone, detail of hell from *The Last Judgement*, Scrovegni Chapel, Padua, 1303–05. Fresco. Photo: Scala/Art Resource, NY.

those areas vulnerable to damage. The enormous expense of this colour tells us something about the chapel's purpose. It served as a private oratory for the family and associates of a wealthy banker, Enrico Scrovegni. References to greed and usury are found in the *Last Judgement* and in some scenes of the lives of Christ and Mary in the nave and chancel, expressing Scrovegni's hope for forgiveness of his family's financial sins as reward for his very expensive gift. Accompanied by a cleric, he kneels under the cross in the *Last Judgement*, donating the chapel to Mary and two other intercessors, probably St. Catherine and St. John.[23]

The iconography of the *Last Judgement* is closely tied to Giotto's narrative scenes and the personifications of virtues and vices in the nave and chancel. Its composition relates broadly to earlier medieval works like the Conques tympanum (Figure 15.7). Hell's strong black and red colours and chaotic violence contrast with the serenity of the blessed and the abundance of sky blue throughout the chapel. Furry brown and bluish-grey demons torment the naked damned, divided by fiery rivers into three groups focused on avarice, pride and anger, and lust, where clerics are particularly numerous.[24] At the bottom is Satan, enthroned on dragons, chewing on a sinner with his principal mouth while writhing serpents eating sinners emerge from his head. Jeffrey Ruda likens his bloated, bluish-grey, and mostly humanoid body to the mythical character of Silenus, Dionysus's old, fat, and lewd tutor and companion. However, Satan rebirths or excretes a sinner where his genitals would be. This mock birth and its association with defecation emasculate him and parody the life-giving properties of the body of Christ, so saturated with meaning for Christians.[25]

Dante's vision of Satan occurs in Canto 34 of his *Inferno*, the first section of his *Divine Comedy*. When Dante and his guide, the poet Virgil, descend through a multilayered hell to the centre of the earth, they encounter Satan's gargantuan figure, frozen in an icy lake and beating six batwings, bigger than ships' sails, that make the lake even colder. Dante compares his body to those of the giants (whose realm he and Virgil have just traversed), noting that Satan's arm alone is giant-sized. He has three differently coloured faces (parodying the Trinity) and grinds exemplary traitors, Judas, Cassius, and Brutus, in each mouth. Tears flow from his eyes, mingling with frothy saliva and the traitors' blood. This proceeds eternally.

It was difficult to rival Dante's poetry, but if Sandro Botticelli's drawing of Satan had been coloured, it would have come close (Figure 15.10). It was to be part of an illuminated manuscript of the *Divine Comedy*, probably intended for Lorenzo di Pierfrancesco de' Medici, that Botticelli began in the 1480s and 90s, finishing only four of 92 paintings.[26] Satan's image follows Dante carefully and takes up two pages, with the fold at Satan's groin, highlighting sexual sins. The icy lake is rendered as a two-dimensional circle focused on this area, which is also the point at which Dante and Virgil, climbing downwards on Satan's fur, invert themselves to climb upwards to the other side of the earth to reach Purgatory. This is not just a physical shift mapped onto a universe centred on a spherical earth, but the second leg of a moral journey that ultimately takes Dante from the despair and darkness of hell to God's dazzling light and warmth in the outermost heavenly sphere in the *Paradiso*.

In contrast to the largely humanoid devils and demons by Italian Renaissance artists who favoured muscular male nudes inspired by antiquity, northern European artists excelled at theriomorphism.[27] A panel by the Tirolian painter/sculptor Michael Pacher's now disassembled *Altarpiece of the Church Fathers* (c. 1475–79) depicts St. Augustine's encounter

*Figure 15.10*  Sandro Botticelli, *Satan* from Dante's *Inferno*, Canto XXXIV, c. 1488–95. Silverpoint and pen drawing on parchment, 63.5 cm × 46.8 cm (sheet). Kupferstichkabinett, Staatliche Museen zu Berlin–Preußischer Kulturbesitz. Photo: bpk/Kupferstichkabinett, SMB/Jörg P. Anders.

with the devil as told in Jacobus da Voragine's *Golden Legend*, written in the mid-1260s (Figure 15.11).[28] He carries a huge Book of Vices which Augustine (always keen to repent) reads to see if he has overlooked any misdeed, finding that he once forgot his bedtime prayers. Commanding Satan to wait, Augustine goes back into the church and says them. When he emerges, the passage in the book had vanished and the confounded devil disappears. Pacher's style was shaped by Italian artists such as Andrea Mantegna and Filippino Lippi but blends their assertive masses and perspective views with late Gothic architectural settings and a northern attention to surface detail.[29] The devil and the saint are artfully contrasted: Satan's knotty vertebrae parody the intricate trim of Augustine's red mantle that complements the devil's green skin; horns reverse the shape of the bishop's miter; and Satan's tottering, angular pose

*Figure 15.11* Michael Pacher, *The Devil Presenting St. Augustine with the Book of Vices*, panel from the exterior wing (upper half) of the *Altarpiece of the Church Fathers*, c. 1480. Oil on panel, 103 cm × 91 cm. Alte Pinakothek, Bayerische Staatsgemäldesammlungen, Munich. Photo: bpk/Alte Pinakothek, Bayerische Staatsgemäldesammlungen/Art Resource, NY.

opposes Augustine's sturdy verticality. Finally, his superfluous face with mouth in place of an anus disrupts natural order.

Hieronymus Bosch's depiction of the devil in his *Garden of Earthly Delights* triptych is quite different (Figure 15.12). Triptychs were typically altarpieces that were closed or opened to suit liturgical purposes, but this weirdly beautiful work was probably made for the palace of the Counts of Nassau in Brussels, where it was seen in 1517, shortly after Bosch died. Scholars have dated the *Garden* as a late work, c. 1510–15, but analysis of the oak panels suggests an earlier date, perhaps c. 1480. On the triptych's exterior, God creates the world, depicted monochromatically in a misty glass globe. When the triptych is opened, God/Christ joins Adam and Eve together in a fantastic garden with real and fictional animals and a pink fountain in a pool on the left panel. In the central panel, numerous nude offspring of Adam and Eve cavort with each other and oversized birds, eat huge berries, and explore sexuality, all with seeming innocence amid glittering rock formations and pools. Awaiting them in the right panel is a burning hell, anchored by a tree/egg/man housing a tavern topped with a phallic bagpipe, giant musical instruments of torture, and Satan at the lower right with the head of a predatory bird and a lanky blue body.

*Figure 15.12*   Hieronymus Bosch, detail of hell, wing panel from *The Garden of Earthly Delights*, late 15th or early 16th century. Oil on panel, 220 cm × 97 cm (whole panel). Prado Museum, Madrid. Photo: Lessing/Art Resource, NY.

Consuming a sodomite with birds flying from his anus, Satan sits on a toilet/throne above a cesspool, a pot on his head and jugs on his feet, signs of gluttony and drunkenness. Below, he excretes sinners enclosed in a blue bubble into the cesspool, and when they emerge, their punishments continue. A vain, lascivious woman stares at her mirror-image in a demon's behind while other demons fondle her, and a glutton and miser deposit vomit and defecated coins into the cesspool. Along with its exhortation against sin, Bosch's masterpiece is also an allegory of alchemical processes (infused with Christian meaning in this period) to produce healing substances: the mating of elements, their "play," their putrefaction in hell, and their cleansing and rebirth on the triptych's exterior.[30]

The prickly, scaly demons assaulting the 4th-century hermit, St. Anthony, in Martin Schongauer's famous engraving of his Temptation (c. 1470–75) greatly influenced German devils: for example, Albrecht Dürer's woodcut of St. Michael consigning Satan to hell before the millennium from his *Apocalypse*, published in 1498 in both German and Latin, and an engraving of the *Temptation of Christ* by Master LCz (probably Bamberg painter Lorenz Katzheimer), done around 1500 (Figures 15.13 and 15.14).[31] Dürer's savvy publication addressed the idea that 1500 would usher in the destruction described in Revelation leading up to the millennium. His amazingly detailed full-page designs are relief prints, carved from woodblocks whose upper surfaces hold the ink, making them compatible with book printing. Some argue that Dürer occasionally carved his own blocks—he certainly learned how to—but at this point, he likely relegated the task to skilled assistants. His *Apocalypse* illustrations owe much to medieval manuscripts and printed bibles with woodcuts but take precedence over the text printed on their versos, except for the final image, with no text on its verso. Here, a chained Satan with sagging breasts, scales, horns, bat wings and vicious claws has returned to his proper form after appearing earlier as Satan/dragon. Interestingly, Dürer did not depict the Last Judgement itself but ended his series with Revelation 20.1-3: the onset of the millennium. As the devil descends, an angel directs John to a peaceful, pious, and prosperous holy city. Although it alludes to the jewelled New Jerusalem that descends from the sky after the Last Judgement in Revelation 21, it does not conform closely to the biblical description but resembles contemporary German cities, like Dürer's Nuremberg.[32]

*Figure 15.13* Albrecht Dürer, *The Angel with the Key to the Bottomless Pit* from the *Apocalypse*, 1497–98. Woodcut, 46 cm × 31.2 cm (sheet). National Gallery of Art, Washington, DC. Photo: Courtesy of the National Gallery of Art, Patrons' Permanent Fund and Print Purchase Fund (Horace Gallatin and Lessing J. Rosenwald).

*Figure 15.14*    Master LCz, *The Temptation of Christ*, c.1500. Engraving, 22.7 cm × 16.5 cm (sheet). National Gallery of Art, Washington, DC. Photo: Courtesy of the National Gallery of Art (Rosenwald Collection).

St. Michael dominates the devil as does Pacher's Augustine and Christ in LCz's engraving (Figure 15.14). In this form of intaglio printing, the artist incises a design on a copperplate with a burin, then works the ink into the lines while wiping it off the plate's upper surface. Unlike a woodblock, an intaglio plate must be printed with high pressure so that the paper picks up the ink. LCz's landscape and its superfluity of naturalistic details could not be more different from the intricate abstraction of the Kells image (Figure 15.4). He depicts other episodes of the story in the background while, in the foreground, Satan exhorts Christ to turn stones into bread, but he will not break his fast by resorting to magic. LCz conveys his assuredness by his stern expression and self-contained verticality. Satan, however, displays a disconcerting array of spikes, claws, horns, sagging breasts, batwings, and two displaced grotesque faces.

Matthias Grünewald's *Isenheim Altar* (1506–15), with its stunning interpretation of St. Anthony's Temptation, was made for an Antonine monastery treating plague, ergotism ("St. Anthony's fire," caused by fungus-infected bread), and other diseases (Figure 15.15). This complex, folding work of painted panels and sculptures by Nicolas of Hagenau, embraced Christ's Nativity, Crucifixion, and Resurrection, and the cults of Mary, Anthony, Sebastian, John the Baptist, Bridget and the Church Fathers. Its multiple openings followed the calendar of holy days. Additionally, it helped treat patients, who related to Christ's suffering in the gruesome *Crucifixion*, visible when the altarpiece was closed, as well as to his

*Figure 15.15*  Matthias Grünewald, detail of *The Temptation of St. Anthony* from the *Isenheim Altar*, c. 1515. Oil and tempura on panel, 307 cm × 269 cm. Musée d'Unterlinden, Colmar, France. Photo: Erich Lessing/Art Resource, NY.

luminous, pain-free body in the *Resurrection* on the righthand panel when it was opened.[33] The lurid, hallucinatory colours and repulsive details of the demons assaulting Anthony on the righthand panel of the final opening are drawn from birds, reptiles, horned animals, fish and flying insects. They epitomise the sin thought to cause illness. Many of them reveal bodily decay, particularly the one in the lower left. He has lost a hand, and he is covered with fiery skin lesions, evoking not only the loss of extremities from the gangrene of ergotism but also the ulcers of bubonic plague or syphilis.

Grünewald's masterpiece was painted on the eve of the Reformation, which transformed the meaning and usage of altarpieces in Protestant territories, where communion was viewed as commemorative rather than sacramental and the material trappings of Catholic worship, including art, were viewed with suspicion, and often damaged or destroyed in outbreaks of iconoclasm. The loss of commissions for church art caused many artists to turn to secular subjects, images for private devotion, or popular propagandistic prints, both Catholic and Protestant. Frequently, Satan and demons served to vilify the other faith. Erhard Schön's hand-coloured woodcut features the devil playing bagpipes (an instrument associated with sin) made from a monk's head (c. 1530, Figure 15.16). In the text at the lower right, the

*Figure 15.16*  Erhard Schön, *The Devil Playing Bagpipes*, c. 1530. Hand-coloured woodcut, 320 mm × 240 mm. Schloßmuseum, Schloß Friedenstein, Gotha, Germany. Photo: Bridgeman Images.

devil laments his loss of ability to manipulate the clergy after the Reformation. Without this text, however, the print could well have functioned as Catholic propaganda, with the monk standing for Luther.[34]

Pieter Bruegel the Elder's *Fall of the Rebel Angels* (1562, Figure 15.17) was probably made for a wealthy collector interested not only in its religious content but also in its fantastic, humorous array of demonic creatures, so different from those in Frans Floris's version of this theme on the central panel of an altarpiece (1554, Royal Museum of Fine Arts, Antwerp).[35] While Floris grafted animal heads, tails, claws, and wings onto idealised Italianate nudes, theriomorphic traits dominate Bruegel's demons. Satan's avatar, the dragon with seven heads (see Figure 15.6), also appears here, as it did in Floris's work, illustrating the frequent melding of the rebellious angels' fall early in creation with the apocalyptic war in heaven (Rev. 12, 13, 20). In both narratives, the good angels, led by St. Michael or Christ himself (see Figure 15.5), defeat the rebels who then pour out of heaven. Here, clothed in golden armour and a blue cape, Michael wields a sword against the beast, who falls upended into hell, his tail pointing to the upper left and his heads, difficult to discern amid the demonic throng, fanning out like tentacles towards the lower centre and right. As Tine Meganck has shown, Bruegel's demonic array was inspired by Bosch, but goes beyond him in the naturalism and global range of the demons and/ or their components, reflecting knowledge of the New World and the study of nature. In the melee, we discover the wings of a swallowtail butterfly, an armadillo's carapace, a toad, a blowfish, a black bear, a mangabey monkey, a sloth, lobster claws, flying fish, an Ottoman scimitar and helmet (reminders of the Ottoman threat to Europe), parts of a sundial clock, feathers from an Indian headdress and more. Such variety reflects the encyclopaedic collections of curiosities,

*Figure 15.17*    Peter Bruegel the Elder, *Fall of the Rebel Angels*, 1562. Oil on panel, 117 cm × 162 cm. Musée d'Art Ancien, Musées Royaux des Beaux Arts, Brussels. Photo: Scala/Art Resource, NY.

both natural and artificial, popular with wealthy patrons in this era. More broadly, its tumult and the prevalence of weapons may comment indirectly on the religious divisions and violence in the Netherlands on the eve of the revolt against Habsburg Spain, which began with icono-clastic riots in 1566. Spain retaliated with brutal persecutions, but the predominantly Protestant northern Netherlands was able to gain its independence as the Dutch Republic in 1648.[36]

From the mid-16th through the 17th centuries, the Catholic Reform movement mar-shalled art as one of its major tools for revitalising the faith. Catholic iconography was reasserted in all media, and the Baroque style that developed in the early 17th century moved worshippers with its palpable realism, emotional intensity, and dynamic spatiality. All these traits are evident in Peter Paul Rubens's *Miracles of St. Ignatius* (1618), a massive oil-on-canvas altarpiece for the Jesuit Church in Antwerp (Figure 15.18).

Among Ignatius's miracles is the exorcism of demons from two victims writhing con-vulsively (much as in films), while grey, yellow-eyed demons with serpentine tails retreat.

*Figure 15.18*  Peter Paul Rubens, *The Miracles of St. Ignatius*, 1617–18. Oil on canvas, 535 cm × 395 cm. Kunsthistorisches Museum, Vienna. Photo: KHM-Museumsverband.

Numerous exorcisms, fuelled by apocalyptic fears, occurred in early modern Lutheran and especially Catholic contexts to demonstrate a faith's superiority. In 1614, the Catholic Church developed an elaborate rite for driving demons from the body. Rubens's dynamic painting likely helped insure Ignatius's canonisation in 1622.[37]

After 1550, in an echo of medieval persecutions of heretics, parts of Europe witnessed the escalation of the witch hunts that had been sparked in the late 15th century by fear of increasing demonic activity and anticipation of the end times, and then further stoked by religious conflict after 1520. Gaps in records hamper estimates, but it seems likely that between 50,000 and 60,000 people, about 80% women, were tortured and executed for witchcraft, newly reformulated in terms of harmful, demonically assisted magic; gatherings called "sabbaths" that might feature orgiastic sex and cannibalism; religious heresy; and treason against states.[38] A new subcategory of demonic imagery developed, either promoting the hunts or questioning all or parts of this augmented idea of witchcraft.[39]

At the height of the persecutions, some understood witchcraft as a counter-society run by Satan and threatening so-called godly states, whether Catholic or Protestant, attempting to consolidate their power and unify their inhabitants. Jan Ziarnko's encyclopaedic fold-out engraving of a witches' sabbath with its accompanying legend was made for Pierre de Lancre's treatise, *Picture of the Inconstancy of Evil Angels and Demons* (Paris, 1613, Figure 15.19), published two years after a hunt in the French Basque country, where he was a judge.

*Figure 15.19*    Jan Ziarnko, foldout engraving of a witches' sabbath for Pierre de Lancre's *Picture of the Inconstancy of Evil Angels and Demons*, Paris, 1613. Cornell University Library, Ithaca, NY. Photo: Courtesy of the Division of Rare and Manuscripts Collections, Cornell University Library.

Satan appears as a large he-goat flanked by two queens, holding court at the upper right. A witch and demon offer up a sacrificial child. Witches fly in with captive children and stir a foul brew in a cauldron; some dance naked with demons and some join a cannibalistic feast, a parody of the Last Supper and thus, the mass. Children lure toads (important magical ingredients) from a pond. Aristocrats attend the sabbath along with the poor.[40] Depictions of such activities served various purposes over time: like other demonic images, they demonstrated an artist's inventiveness, and they promoted the hunts or discredited them by satirising witch beliefs (as in Figures 15.20 and 15.21, discussed below).

Additionally, these works are often virulently misogynistic, aimed at keeping women in their place. Although Satan undergirded the early modern concept of witchcraft, his power

*Figure 15.20*  Francisco Goya, *Trials*, Plate 60 from the *Caprichos*, 1799. Aquatint, etching, and burin, 20.6 cm × 16.4 cm (plate). Metropolitan Museum of Art, New York, Gift of Knoedler & Company, 1918. Photo: Album/Art Resource, NY.

*Figure 15.21* Francisco Goya, *When Day Breaks, We Will Go*, Plate 71 from the *Caprichos*, 1799. Etching and burnished aquatint, 19.6 cm × 14.9 cm (plate). Metropolitan Museum, New York, Gift of Knoedler & Company, 1918. Photo: HIP/Art Resource, NY.

was degraded when a critical mass of people came to question the feasibility of witches' crimes, the cruelty of the trials and executions, and snowballing accusations that left no one safe. His decline would escalate when his very existence was questioned in the following centuries.

### Satan's Death and Reincarnation in the 18th and 19th Centuries

The Industrial Revolution between the mid-18th and mid-19th centuries transformed agrarian and artisanal economies into manufacturing ones, fuelling increased urbanisation and working-class poverty in the cities. In 1848, widespread revolts, mostly unsuccessful, arose across much of continental Europe, demonstrating the lower and middle classes' dissatisfaction with monarchy. Already in the late 18th century, the French and American Revolutions had successfully challenged monarchical rule, although France's path to republicanism was long and rocky until the Third Republic was established in 1870, when Napoleon III's empire collapsed during the Franco-Prussian War.

The Enlightenment movement, originating in the late 17th century and culminating in the 18th, influenced the struggle against monarchy. It also slowly snuffed out, though never completely, Satan's ontological reality as a demon-inhabited universe was discredited among educated people. Philosophical scepticism and empiricism undermined belief in Satan and demons; scientific discoveries disproved the biblical account of creation by suggesting that the world evolved over millions, not thousands, of years. Comparative mythology interpreted the bible as a cultural product, not the word of God: a point made especially clear in Thomas Paine's *Age of Reason*, published in three pamphlets between 1794 and 1807. Deism assumed God's initial creation of the universe but denied his active intervention in the world, thus disempowering Satan and demons, who now seemed like fantastic, unnecessary complications to Christianity.[41] Detached from his theological moorings, Satan was refashioned by poets and artists of the Romantic and later Symbolist and Decadent movements as a nimble signifier— expressing Edmund Burke's "terrible sublime" and Gothic horror, humanity's evil potential or Promethean ambitions, political conflict and corruption, revolution against tyranny and economic inequality, social decline, or an individual artist's emotions and creative imagination.[42]

Satirical artists in 18th- and 19th-century Britain, where relatively liberal censorship policies enabled a thriving tradition of political cartoons, made frequent use of the devil. In his engraving *Credulity and Superstition* (1762), William Hogarth lambasted the excesses of a Methodist preacher by showing him manipulating little puppets of the devil and a witch to frighten his gullible congregation.[43] The brilliant cartoonist James Gillray often paired Napoleon I ("little Boney") with devils, as did the equally skilled Thomas Rowlandson. His *Devil's Darling* (1814, Figure 15.22) is an etching, made by scratching through an acid-resistant varnish on a metal plate that is immersed in acid to establish the design, then inked, wiped, and printed with an intaglio press.

British satirical etchings were generally hand coloured. This is one of many prints modelled after a German image and was accompanied by a verse in which the devil, sitting in a fire, praises his child's maliciousness and promises him a place in hell. Napoleon is swaddled in tricolour ribbons, and the devil holds a medal from the French Legion of Honour. This devil is Pan-like (compare Figure 15.2) but also comically rustic, with his big head, tiny horns, bulging muscles, and ridiculous grin. In 1814, Napoleon had been exiled from France to the island of Elba, having been defeated by European forces after his invasion of Russia. Soon he would escape exile and marshal an army, only to be finally defeated in 1815 at Waterloo.[44]

Both Francisco Goya and William Blake, early Romantic artists whose work spanned the late 18th and early 19th centuries, were fascinated by Satan and demons. Goya's demonic imagery satirised superstitions still held by uneducated Spaniards and, more broadly, the irrationalities of his society in general. While these images are bizarre and horrifying—both aspects of Romanticism—they largely uphold Enlightenment reason that Romanticism often rebelled against. For the younger Blake (both poet and artist), for example, reason was a tyrant hampering the human imagination and limiting its spirituality. Satan held an important if inconsistent place in Blake's evolving biblical exegesis and view of society.

THE DEVILS DARLING.

*Figure 15.22* Thomas Rowlandson, *The Devil's Darling*, 1814. Hand-coloured etching, 327 mm × 231 mm. British Museum, London. Photo: Universal History Archive/UIG/Bridgeman Images.

After a successful career as a royal tapestry designer and court painter, Goya developed an interest in witchcraft images in middle age. He had survived a life-threatening illness in 1792–93 that left him deaf, and he wanted to refashion himself as an independent artist, free to pursue his own themes and sought after by wealthy collectors.[45] In the late 1790s, he painted witchcraft scenes for the country house of the Duke and Duchess of Osuna, who both held progressive social views.[46] Simultaneously, he worked on sketches for his series of eighty *Caprichos* (1799), incorporating a new etching technique called aquatint employing an acid-resistant powder that adhered to a warmed plate, producing grainy tonal areas when etched, inked, and printed.

When applied to art, the Italian term *capriccio* challenged the superiority of history painting, a genre based on elevated themes demanding knowledge of history, the bible, and literature, as well as skills in landscape, perspective, and human anatomy. In contrast, *capricci* were unfettered flights of imagination, well suited to the relative spontaneity of etching. 18th-century etchers also saw the *capriccio's* affinity for dark or bizarre themes.[47] In his series, Goya expanded the concept by insisting on its potential for social critique. Like many early modern images, *Capricho* 60 is premised on the belief in witches' bodily flight, held only by the most uneducated in Goya's time (Figure 15.20). It centres on a pot of unguent supposedly comprising foul magical ingredients and hallucinogens believed to enable flight or create its illusion. One of his witches (female or male?) is absurdly positioned sideways, while a female companion, her feet barely floating off the ground, pulls his/her ear. The caption, *Trials*, suggests the dubiousness of their efforts. Satan looms over them in the form of a huge he-goat, derived from the engraving in Pierre de Lancre's treatise (Figure 15.19). The witch persecutions in the French Basque country were related to those in Logroño, Spain in 1610, described in a pamphlet later annotated by Goya's friend, playwright Fernández de Moratín the Younger. Goya's ten *Caprichos* on witchcraft echo the confessions at Logroño. In this print, Satan is the spectral fantasy driving the witchcraft beliefs fostered by the Spanish Inquisition, one of Goya's major satirical targets. In *Capricho* 71, *When Day Breaks, We Will Go*, the devil (or demon) is a shadowy winged and horned figure silhouetted against a starry sky (Figure 15.21). Before him are unspeakably grotesque witches, one with captive children tied behind his/her back. Occurring near the end of the series, this print suggests the death of satanic beliefs and the dawning of reason with the tentative light emerging on the horizon, produced with a burnisher that smoothed out parts of the aquatinted sky.[48]

Like Goya's tapestry designs, Blake's early engravings copying works in other media did not satisfy his ambitions. In the 1790s, however, this artisanal job gave him access to a circle of intellectuals (including Thomas Paine) surrounding publisher Joseph Johnson. Blake absorbed their liberal ideas but reshaped and critiqued them with his personal Christian beliefs.[49] For him, the traditional Christian God was a deification of reason, condemning his subjects for disobedience and crushing the desire and energy fuelling prophecy and poetic imagination. Blake's Satan was foreshadowed by the human and heroic aspects of Milton's in *Paradise Lost*, a poem whose reception shifted markedly in the Romantic era, when prominent writers privileged, in Gordon Teskey's words, its "amalgam of grandeur and terror" over its Christian content. Blake, however, challenged this content while still describing Milton as a great poet "of the Devil's party without knowing it" on Plate 6 of his *Marriage of Heaven and Hell* (1790–93).[50]

In this prose work repudiating Emanuel Swedenborg's *Heaven and Hell* (London, 1758), Satan embodies human desire, energy and rebellion: necessary aspects of life that must interact with reason, just as all contraries must interact if humanity is to progress. In other works, such as *America: A Prophecy* (1794), Satan morphs into the character Orc, the fiery spirit of revolution in Blake's mythology. In Plate 8, he is a nude, muscular young man arising from the grave and glancing skywards (Figure 15.23).

Blake's technique here is hand-coloured relief etching, a process resembling woodcut in which shallowly etched-out areas of the plate do *not* hold ink: a reversal of conventional etching. The basic design and Blake's lettering, likely done backwards to address the reversal in printing, were created with acid-resistant varnish. The plate's unetched lines and areas were inked and printed, and the page finished in watercolour by Blake or his wife Catherine. This method along with the integration of text, main image and marginalia in these printed books, produced in very small editions, lends them the handmade character of medieval illuminated manuscripts.

*Figure 15.23*  William Blake, Plate 8 from *America, A Prophecy*, Copy A, c. 1795. Hand-coloured relief etching, 32 cm × 24 cm (leaf). Pierpont Morgan Library and Museum, New York, PML 16134.8, Purchased by Pierpont Morgan, 1909. Photo: The Morgan Library and Museum.

Blake's 21 visual commentaries on the Book of Job (1826–27) are line engravings, although he also made watercolour versions. This work, done shortly before his death, is often regarded as his most profound statement of his religious views. Blake's Satan is a muscular young man who remains in his subordinate role in the heavenly court as a tempter, testing Job's faith by killing his flocks, herds, and sons, and smiting him with boils. Even though God looks exactly like Job, Job sees him as alien: a distant authority to obey, fear, and worship.

In the centre engraving, *Job's Evil Dreams*, Blake merges Satan and God into a being with cloven hooves, entwined with a serpent and framed by lightning (Figure 15.24). Below, demons try to pull Job into hell as this fearsome deity of laws and punishments points to the Tablets of the Commandments. Yet in the fifth Commandment (Exod. 20.12), God stresses his gift of the land so that the days of the Israelites shall be long, and the text below his other hand, deriving from Job 19.22-7, contains a promise of redemption. In the following plates, Job and his wife recognise God's immanence and his control over good and evil, experience the scope and beauty of his creation, witness Satan's fall, learn of the coming of Christ, and regain prosperity and their remaining family.[51]

Figure 15.24    William Blake, *Job's Evil Dreams*, Plate 11 from illustrations to the *Book of Job*, 1826–27. Engraving, 169 mm × 216 mm (page). National Gallery of Art, Washington, DC. Photo Courtesy of the National Gallery of Art, Gift of W. G. Russell Allen.

Even when enhanced with fantastic details such as wings, multiple heads, and serpentine tails, as in his Great Red Dragon watercolours illustrating Revelation, Blake's demonic figures are generally based on muscular, ideal male bodies that evoke Milton's Satan, recall their former unfallen state, and suggest their origins in the human imagination.[52] In 1828, Eugène Delacroix further humanised the devil in his depictions of Mephistopheles in his lithographs for the younger Albert Stapfer's French translation (1823) of Johann Wolfgang von Goethe's *Faust: A Tragedy*, Part I (Tübingen, 1808). Although he first appears to Faust as a black dog (a common demonic disguise), and in the opening illustration, as a clawed gargoyle-like demon flying over Paris, Mephistopheles's proper form is a sophisticated gentleman whose main deformity is cloven hooves, disguised by shoes (Figure 15.25).

*Figure 15.25*   Eugène Delacroix, *Faust Meeting Marguerite* from Goethe's *Faust*, Part 1, 1828. Lithograph, 285 cm × 207 cm (image). Bibliothèque des Beaux-Arts, Paris. Photo: Bridgeman Images.

Indeed, Delacroix's Mephistopheles was partly inspired in 1825 by actor Daniel Terry in a London play about Faust.[53]

Delacroix's illustrations helped elevate lithography from a primarily commercial to a fine-art medium. Invented in the 18th century, lithography uses limestone slabs. The artist makes a design on the stone with a greasy medium (lithographic crayon in Delacroix's case). The design is then sealed with a mild acidic solution that also makes the empty areas of the stone receptive to moisture. When the stone is dampened, the greasy ink is repelled from those areas but adheres to the design. Artists often relied on professional printers for these chemical processes. An important aspect of lithography is its autographic character: Delacroix's hand is always evident in these spirited drawings on stone, with their rich, dark tones, often modified by scraping away some of the pigment.

The ambiguity of Goethe's Mephistopheles, reflected in Delacroix's illustrations, frees him from his traditional role in Christian theology, even though Goethe employs Christian symbolism in *Faust*. He is not the Christian devil, although that is one component of his character, nor is he a secondary demon. Like the Old Testament Satan, he is God's agent of evil: suave, charming, intelligent, cruel, lewd, and a masterful shape shifter. Taking the form of a young nobleman, he makes a wager with Faust, a melancholy scholar, that he will abandon his continual striving; if this happens, Mephistopheles will have his soul. Faust bets that he will never cease striving. Mephistopheles introduces him to sensuality, and he lusts after the innocent Gretchen (Marguerite in French). In Delacroix's image of Faust trying to seduce her, Mephistopheles walks ahead of the couple, his hands and feet crossing to signal his deceptiveness, as Marguerite pulls away from Faust's advances. With his arrogant bearing, elegant clothing, predatory attitude, and sharp profile distantly recalling the Pan-like features of Satan, Faust has become like Mephistopheles. Over the course of the story, the loving Marguerite has Faust's child, drowns it in mad despair, and is executed. Gradually, Faust comes to realise he loved her. In later parts of the story, she is forgiven by the Virgin Mary and welcomed into heaven, as is Faust, who, despite his many sins, has discovered love. Mephistopheles loses his wager.[54]

The stylistically diverse Romantic movement was premised on ideas that continued to influence writers and artists after midcentury. Gustave Doré's designs for wood-engraved illustrations to an edition of Milton's *Paradise Lost* (London and New York, 1866) are utterly Romantic in spirit. He depicts Satan as a clever and brave commander of the rebel angels who also suffers pain, doubt, and regret. In the angel Raphael's account of the war in heaven, told to Adam, we learn that Satan was badly wounded by Michael's sword. Being angelic, he recovered quickly, but his troops suffered a devastating defeat. Doré evokes his lonely struggle and inevitable fate by depicting him alone on a mountain, tired, troubled, and pensive, as nightfall brings a truce (Figure 15.26).

Soon he would convince his troops to invent cannons and continue fighting, but they would lose the war. The spectacular setting and its dramatic lighting, as well as the extraordinary detail of this image were produced by artisans who, following the artist's design, carved minute parallel lines into end-grain blocks of wood. In wood-engraving, as in woodcut, the ink is held on the top surface of the block, making it compatible with book printing and therefore a favourite medium for countless 19th-century illustrations in books and journals.[55]

Romanticism's championing of imagination, emotion, and individual subjectivity, as well as its interest in Satan, influenced the literary and artistic Symbolists and Decadents in the later 19th century. Both movements descended from Charles Baudelaire, whose *Flowers of Evil* (Paris, 1857) was censored as an "insult to public decency." His ironic "Litanies

*Figure 15.26*   Gustave Doré, *Now Night her Course Began*, Plate 26, Book 6, line 406 of Milton's
*Paradise Lost*, 1866. Wood-engraving, 24.5 cm × 20 cm. The Poetry Collection of
the University Libraries, University at Buffalo, State University of New York. Photo:
Poetry Collection, University Libraries at Buffalo, SUNY.

of Satan" parodies Catholic liturgical prayers, particularly the *Kyrie Eleison*. The poet
repeatedly asks Satan to "have pity on my long despair"; that is, the stifling boredom and
melancholy of modern life that steers people towards sensuality and evil.[56] In his energy,
rebelliousness and the pathos of his defeat, Baudelaire's devil draws from Milton's and its
Romantic revision, but a heightened sense of human limitations and societal decay figure
heavily in the evil he fosters.[57]

Like the Romantics, Symbolists and Decadents were stylistically diverse, but all reacted against scientific positivism, materialism, bourgeois culture, Realism and Impressionism, turning inwards to probe the human psyche. Common themes were fantasy, visions, lustful femmes fatales preying on men, esoteric forms of spirituality and the occult and the unconscious mind revealed in dreams (this is also the era of Sigmund Freud). Both labels fit many writers and artists. However, as the name suggests, Decadent art and literature envisioned the degeneration of humanity and society, rejecting the idealism often expressed in Symbolism. Decadent art was morbid and perverse—a context well suited for the devil. Although Belgian Symbolist Félicien Rops was a versatile painter and printmaker whose oeuvre addresses many subjects, he is best known for his provocative erotic and satanic images.[58]

*Les Sataniques* (The Satanic Ones) began as an idea for a book with various demonic images in different media (Figures 15.27 and 15.28). The five images Rops

*Figure 15.27* Albert Bertrand after Félicien Rops, *Satan Sowing Tares*, frontispiece for *Les Sataniques*, 1906. Colour heliogravure, 25.7 cm × 18 cm. Musée Félicien Rops, Namur, Belgium. Photo: Courtesy of Musée Félicien Rops, Province de Namur, Belgium, inv. G E0864.2.

*Figure 15.28* Félicien Rops, *The Sacrifice* from *Les Sataniques*, 1882. Tempera, colour pencil, black crayon, gouache, and gold for the horns on paper, 30 cm × 19.1 cm. Photo: Galerie Patrick Derom, Brussels/Wikimedia Commons.

reproduced via the photo-mechanical process of heliogravure in 1882 depict the abduction by, worship of and sexual intercourse with the devil, familiar tropes in the witch hunts. The same fascinations emerged again in modernity, as in Joris-Karl Huysmans's novel, *Down There* (1891), Ira Levin's novel, *Rosemary's Baby* (1967), and Roman Polanski's eponymous film (1968). Although Rops was a sexual libertine, and his many parodies of Christian iconography evoke the ambiguity of Christianity in the modern industrial, urban world, no evidence connects him to actual satanic worship; indeed, the existence of such cults at this time is dubious.[59] Rather, Satan served Rops as a metaphor for social degeneracy, targeting the prostitutes of *fin-de-siècle* Paris (where he spent much of his career) and, by extension, all femmes fatales. In *Les Sataniques*, only women worship the devil. They display an incorrigible lust that was believed to weaken men and spread venereal disease, a serious concern at the time. Late 19th-century stereotypes of women (even the virginal maidens idealised in Symbolist art) were driven by anxieties about changing gender roles, women's increased presence in the workforce, and their fight for social equality.[60]

*Satan Sowing Tares* refers to a parable (Matt. 13.24-30) about the devil sowing weeds in a wheatfield (Figure 15.27). The field cannot be weeded early without destroying the wheat; one must wait for the harvest, just as the evil souls cannot be separated from the good until the Last Judgement (Christ's "harvest"). In the past, this parable provided an argument against the execution of heretics and accused witches. However, Rops's giant, bony Satan, dressed as a peasant and reminiscent of the animated skeletons in medieval and Renaissance art, sows naked female bodies as he strides across Paris, stepping on Notre Dame as he goes. Subsequently, he manifests himself as a muscular winged figure abducting a witch-like woman by vaginally impaling her on her broomstick, and as a priapic herm eagerly mounted by a worshipper. Next, in *The Sacrifice*, he is thin and horned, with a goat's-skull torso, while he penetrates a bleeding woman stretched out on an altar with his long, serpentine penis (Figure 15.28). Her grimace echoes Dr. Jean-Martin Charcot's photos of female hysterics at the Salpêtrière asylum in Paris, and her pose recalls the many "nymphs with broken backs" in late 19th-century art. In the final image, the devil, with an erect phallus, parodies the crucified Christ as he strangles a worshipper with her hair.[61]

Odilon Redon's haunting Symbolist paintings and graphic works, often reflecting his personal experiences, were also frequently tied to conditions in his country: for example, the Franco-Prussian War (1870–71), in which he served, inspired mournful images of fallen angels evoking France's hubris and bitter defeat. His lithographs, with their exceptionally deep, rich blacks, graced Symbolist texts, including Baudelaire's *Flowers of Evil* and three albums based on the definitive version of Gustave Flaubert's novel or prose-poem, *The Temptation of Anthony* (Paris, 1874, Figure 15.29). Mary Orr's study of this complex text demonstrates how Flaubert re-envisioned the story of the 4th-century Egyptian monk in terms of 19th-century France: the arguments over Christian orthodoxy in Anthony's Alexandria parallel modern disputes within and between the fields of religion and science, personified by Anthony's argumentative disciple, Hilarion, whose name calls up the natural scientist Étienne Geoffroy Saint-Hilaire.[62]

In part six of the book, Hilarion grows into a gargantuan devil proclaiming, "Men call me "SCIENCE!" Anthony, however, calls him "devil." Then, thrown up on Satan's horns, the saint is borne off into outer space. Dazzled by what he sees—comets, stars, and galaxies, the planets and their orbits—and struggling to comprehend the vastness, Anthony bows his head, murmuring, "What is the purpose of all that?" The devil answers, "There is no purpose. How could God have a purpose?" In his updated version of Deism, Satan equates God with the universe itself, obliterating Anthony's belief in a providential, responsive deity who intervenes in our lives and hears our prayers. Orr relates the devil's arguments to the theories of mathematician and astronomer Pierre-Simon Laplace, who attributed the origins and operation of the universe to mathematical laws and saw God as an "unnecessary hypothesis."[63] Redon's image captures Anthony's bewildered sense of smallness and the complexity of Flaubert's Satan. In contrast to the brash confidence of his words, he is not triumphant. The cynical, melancholy tilt of his head is very similar to Redon's images of fallen angels and Mephistopheles, who, despite his intelligence, cannot comprehend love. Like Mephistopheles, Flaubert's Satan cannot explain everything about human life, which is not determined by mathematical

553_1940_17

Digital Image © 2003 MoMA, N.Y.

*Figure 15.29*  Odilon Redon, *What is the Purpose of All That? There Is No Purpose!* Plate 18 from Gustave Flaubert's *Temptation of Anthony*, 1896 edition. Lithograph on chine appliqué, 31.1 cm × 25.1 cm (image). Museum of Modern Art, New York. Photo: Digital Image ©Museum of Modern Art/Licensed by Scala/Art Resource, NY.

laws, and science, like religion, is subject to doubt and error. Anthony's irrational faith finally causes Satan to abandon him on an Egyptian cliff, exhausted, in the book's 7th part. Although his faith has been shaken and he will undergo other visions, Anthony returns to his devotions.

Both Redon and Rops exhibited with an avant-garde group organised in Brussels in 1883, *Les Vingt* (The Twenty), whose founding members included James Ensor. The group rebelled against academic art, advocated stylistic pluralism, and promoted radical social and political reform. In the mid-1880s, Ensor's formerly realist work became fantastical, acridly satirical, and scatological, borrowing from late 19th-century popular entertainments such as displays at fairs, magic lantern shows, and street puppet theatre, as well as the new, shocking images of microorganisms that also fascinated Redon. Like other members of *Les Vingt*, Ensor was intrigued by Flaubert's novel and St. Anthony's Temptation, which became the theme of drawings and prints, an oil painting in 1887 (Museum of

*Figure 15.30*   James Ensor, *Demons Tormenting Me*, 1895. Hand-coloured etching, 11.8 cm × 15.6 cm. Kupferstichkabinett, Staatliche Museen zu Berlin–Preußischer Kulturbesitz. Photo: bpk/Kupferstichkabinett, SMB/Jörg P. Anders.

Modern Art, New York), and an extraordinary collage of 51 coloured drawings in 1888 (Art Institute of Chicago). Ensor's carnivalesque, demonic world, teeming with filth, disease, decay and grotesque monsters recalling Bosch and Bruegel, critiqued the problems of contemporary Belgium.[64]

In an etched, hand-coloured self-portrait of 1895, *Demons Tormenting Me*, Ensor takes St. Anthony's place among grotesque demons hovering around him like malicious, dangling marionettes (Figure 15.30). Their skeletal bodies are enhanced with traditional demonic traits. Sitting in front of a gravestone, the artist looks apprehensively to his left, where bony, clawed, and pointy-eared demons, one with a sagging breast, approach him aggressively. On his right, another skeletal, clawed demon (possibly female, given its red hat, painted lips and deceptively deferential pose) reaches towards his hand, while a pink, dwarfish demon grabs his sleeve. The largest demon in the upper left has horns, spiked wings, and multiple eyes; in the upper right, we see our familiar goat, and a deformed creature with a horse's mane and proboscis that may satirise someone's long nose.[65]

The etching derives from a drawing of 1888, when the anxious, thin-skinned artist, who had been in poor health since 1884, was grieving the recent deaths of his grandmother and alcoholic father, experiencing the incomprehension of art critics, and witnessing alarming changes in *Les Vingt*, as members in thrall of Georges Seurat's *A Sunday on La Grande Jatte* (1884–86, Art Institute of Chicago) turned to Neo-Impressionism.[66] These traumas still haunted him seven years later. Ensor's vision of his personal hell culminates the long evolution of demonic imagery traced in this chapter. Satan and his minions, whose ontological reality and central role in Christian theology were once taken for granted, now serve the widely diverse purposes of their human creators—whether religious, social, political, literary, artistic, or personal. In the 20th and 21st centuries, these purposes would be executed in both old and new media, particularly film. Although Satan's important place in Christian theology has been diminished, he still proves to be a masterful shape shifter.

## Notes

1 John Milton, *Paradise Lost: A Poem in Twelve Books* (London, 1674), 1.75–87.
2 Brian Levack, *The Devil Within: Possession and Exorcism in the Christian West* (New Haven, 2013), 56–80.
3 Stuart Clark, *Thinking with Demons: The Idea of Witchcraft in Early Modern Europe* (Oxford, 1997), 161–78.
4 Milton, *Paradise Lost*, 4. 811–9; Joad Raymond, "Milton's Angels," in *The Cambridge Companion to Paradise Lost*, ed. Louis Schwartz (Cambridge, 2014), 138–51, at 145.
5 Contrariety and inversion are central to demonology: Clark, *Thinking with Demons*, 43–79.
6 Jeffrey Burton Russell, *The Prince of Darkness* (Ithaca, 1992), 78–81.
7 Jeffrey Burton Russell, *Lucifer: The Devil in the Middle Ages* (Ithaca, 1984), 63–4, 70.
8 On Satan and demons in religious plays, see Russell, *Lucifer*, 245–73; on the artistic contributions of nuns, see Jeffrey Hamburger, *Nuns as Artists: The Visual Culture of a Medieval Convent* (Berkeley, 1997).
9 Before trimming in the 19th century, Kell's leaves measured about 370 mm × 260 mm: Carol Farr, *The Book of Kells: Its Function and Audience* (London, 1997), 49, n. 19, and for historical context, 13–32.
10 Farr, *Book of Kells*, 52–61.
11 Cyril Mango, "Diabolus Byzantinus," *Dumbarton Oaks Papers* 46 (1992): 215–23.
12 Kirk Ambrose, "The Sense of Sight in the Book of Kells," *Source: Notes in the History of Art* 27, no. 1 (Fall 2007): 1–9.
13 On Junius 11, see Catherine Karkov, *Text and Picture in Anglo-Saxon England: Narrative Strategies in the Junius 11 Manuscript* (Cambridge, 2001); on the Christ and Satan page, see Asa Mittman and Susan Kim, "Locating the Devil 'Her' in MS Junius 11," *Gesta* 54, no. 1 (March 2015): 3–25.
14 On the Beatus manuscripts, see Richard Emmerson, *Apocalypse Illuminated: The Visual Exegesis of Revelation in Medieval Illustrated Manuscripts* (University Park, 2018), 47–82; esp. 72–4, 77–8 on the Silos manuscript. John Williams catalogued 26 Beatus manuscripts in *The Illustrated Beatus*, 5 vols. (London, 1994–2003); for updates, see his *Visions of the End in Medieval Spain*, ed. Therese Martin (Amsterdam, 2017).
15 Russell, *Prince of Darkness*, 47–9.
16 On bodily resurrection in medieval Europe, see Caroline Walker Bynum, *The Resurrection of the Body in Western Christianity, 200–1336* (New York, 2017).
17 Kirk Ambrose, "Attunement to the Damned of the Conques Tympanum," *Gesta* 50, no. 1 (Spring 2011): 1–17, argues that the inability to control their bodies is part of their punishment.
18 On St. Bernard's objection to monstrous forms and their spiritual purpose in monasteries, see Thomas Dale, "Monsters, Corporal Deformities, and Phantasms in the Cloister of St-Michel-de-Cuxa," *Art Bulletin* 83, no. 3 (September 2001): 402–36.
19 Jerry Root, *The Theophilus Legend in Medieval Text and Image* (Cambridge, 2017), 1–3. https://doi.org/10.1017/S002204691800177X

20 On the relationship between the story and the ritual of feudal homage, see Root, *Theophilus Legend*, 13–61. On Berengaudus and illuminated manuscripts of his Latin commentary, see Emmerson, *Apocalypse Illuminated*, 111–27. The major study of the Lambeth Apocalypse is Nigel Morgan, *The Lambeth Apocalypse, Manuscript 209 in the Lambeth Palace Library: A Critical Study* (London, 1990).

21 On the manuscript's ownership and its feminine appeal, see Loveday Gee, *Women, Art and Patronage from Henry III to Edward III: 1216–1377* (Woodbridge, UK, 2002), 45–7; Emmerson, *Apocalypse Illuminated*, 151–3.

22 Root, *Theophilus Legend*, 33–4.

23 Anne Derbes and Mark Sandona confirm the importance of repentance in the chapel in *The Usurer's Heart: Giotto, Enrico Scrovegni, and the Arena Chapel in Padua* (University Park, 2008).

24 Brendan Cassidy, "Laughing with Giotto at Sinners in Hell," *Viator: Medieval and Renaissance Studies* 35, no. 1 (Winter 2004): 355–86, discusses conflicts between clergy and Padua's government and laypeople, who probably laughed at the torments of the sinful clergy.

25 Jeffrey Ruda, "Satan's Body: Religion and Gender Parody in Late Medieval Literature," *Viator: Medieval and Renaissance Studies* 37, no. 2 (Fall 2006): 319–50. On the body of Christ, see Sarah Beckwith, *Christ's Body: Identity, Culture and Society in Late Medieval Writing* (London, 1996).

26 Barbara Watts, "Sandro Botticelli's Drawings for Dante's 'Inferno': Narrative Structure, Topography, and Narrative Design," *Artibus et Historiae* 16, no. 32 (1995): 163–201.

27 See Luca Signorelli's Capella Nuovo frescoes of the end days in the Cathedral of Orvieto; Michelangelo's *Last Judgement* in the Sistine Chapel, Rome; and Giorgio Vasari and Federico Zuccari's *Last Judgement* in the cupola of Santa Maria Fiore, Florence.

28 The saint is sometimes misidentified as Wolfgang, but the altarpiece was made for an Augustinian convent and other extant panels depict legends about Augustine: Nicolò Rasmo, *Michael Pacher* (London, 1971), 103. On the legend, see Edmund Colledge, "The Augustine Screen in Carlisle Cathedral," in *Augustine in Iconography: History and Legend*, eds Joseph Schnaubelt and Frederick Van Fleteren (New York, 2003), 383–430, at 402–3.

29 Lukas Madersbacher, *Michael Pacher: Zwischen Zeiten und Räumen* (Berlin, 2015), aptly interprets Pacher's work as having roots in two different times and places.

30 Laurinda Dixon, *Bosch* (London, 2003), 227–78.

31 Other examples are Lucas Cranach the Elder's woodcut *Temptation of Anthony* (1506), Dürer's engraving of *Knight, Death, and the Devil* (1514), and Daniel Hopfer's etching of *The Devil Surprising Two Women* (1515).

32 See Natasha O'Hear's discussion of Dürer's *Apocalypse* in *Contrasting Images of the Book of Revelation in Late Medieval and Early Modern Art: A Case Study in Visual Exegesis* (Oxford, 2011): 142–75, esp. 169. https://doi.org/10.1093/acprof:oso/9780199590100.001.0001

33 Andrée Hayum, *The Isenheim Altarpiece: God's Medicine and the Painter's Vision* (Princeton, 1989).

34 On an impression without a text, see Giulia Bartrum, *German Renaissance Prints, 1490–1550* (London, 1995),. catalogue no. 82, at 95. For a survey of such prints, see Robert Scribner, *For the Sake of the Simple Folk: Popular Propaganda for the German Reformation* (Oxford, 1994).

35 On Floris, see Edward Wouk, *Frans Floris (1519/20–1570): Imagining a Northern Renaissance* (Leiden, 2018). In the first chapter, 1–32, Wouk focuses on *The Fall of the Rebel Angels* as an example of Floris's hybrid, cosmopolitan art, and explores its context and reception.

36 Tine Meganck, *Pieter Bruegel the Elder, Fall of the Rebel Angels: Art, Knowledge, and Politics on the Eve of the Dutch Revolt* (Brussels and Milan, 2014).

37 See Levack, *Devil Within*, 1–31, on possession and its symptoms, and 56–80 for Protestant and Catholic attitudes towards exorcism; James Clifton, "The Face of a Fiend: Convulsion, Inversion, and the Horror of the Disempowered Body," *Oxford Art Journal* 34, no. 3 (October 2011): 373–92, discusses commonalities between artistic and filmic exorcisms.

38 Brian Levack, *The Witch-Hunt in Early Modern Europe* (New York, 1987), 19–22, suggests 60,000 executions; William Monter, "Witch Trials in Continental Europe 1550–1560," in *Witchcraft and Magic in Europe: The Period of the Witch Trials*, ed. Bengt Ankarloo, Stuart Clark, and William Monter (Philadelphia, 2002), 13, suggests Levack's figure should be reduced by a third.

39 Linda Hults, *The Witch as Muse: Art, Gender, and Power in Early Modern Europe* (Philadelphia, 2005); Charles Zika, *The Appearance of Witchcraft: Print and Visual Culture in Sixteenth-Century Europe* (London, 2007).

40 Hults, *The Witch as Muse*, 109–13.

41 Jeffrey Burton Russell, *Mephistopheles: The Devil in the Modern World* (Ithaca, 1986), 128–67, surveys the philosophical, religious, and scientific developments contributing to the devil's expiration.

42 Edmund Burke, *A Philosophical Inquiry into the Origin of the Sublime and the Beautiful* (London, 1757), esp. Part 1, section 7 and Part 2, section 2. For an overview of the Romantic devil, see Russell, *Mephistopheles*, 168–213; on Satan as a socialist symbol, see Per Faxneld, "The Devil is Red: Socialist Satanism in the Nineteenth Century," *Numen* 60, no. 5/6 (January 2013): 528–68, and Chapter 18 of the current volume.

43 Bernd Krysmanski, "We See a Ghost: Hogarth's Satire on Methodists and Connoisseurs," *Art Bulletin* 80, no. 2 (June 1998): 202–310.

44 Tim Clayton and Sheila O'Connell, *Bonaparte and the British: Prints and Propaganda in the Age of Napoleon* (London, 2015), 186–7.

45 On Goya's changing ambitions throughout his career, see Janis Tomlinson, *Goya: A Portrait of the Artist* (Princeton, 2020). At 122–6, Tomlinson discusses his illness that may have been caused from the lead in paints.

46 For an overview of Goya's witchcraft paintings for the Osunas, see Hults, *The Witch as Muse*, 221–7.

47 For example, Giambattista Tiepolo's *Capricci* (1740–42) and *Scherzi di Fantasia* (1743–50), and Giambattista Piranesi's *Prisons* (1761).

48 Hults, *The Witch as Muse*, 214–62.

49 Robert Essick, "William Blake, Thomas Paine, and Biblical Revolution," *Studies in Romanticism* 30, no. 2 (Summer 1991): 189–212. On Blake's prints, see Essick's *William Blake: Printmaker* (Princeton, 1980).

50 Jonathan Shears, *The Romantic Legacy of* Paradise Lost: *Reading against the Grain* (Aldershot, 2009); Gordon Teskey, "Milton and the Romantics," in *A Companion to Romantic Poetry*, ed. Charles Mahoney (Malden, 2011), 425–41, quotation at 425. https://doi.org/10.1002/9781444390650.ch25

51 Christopher Rowland, *Blake and the Bible* (New Haven, 2010), 13–42 and 43–72.

52 For Blake, all things, including deities and demons, derived from the human imagination. See Terence Hoagwood's interpretation of such figures as exteriorisations of inner visions in "Pictorial Apocalypse: "Blake's 'Great Red Dragon' and the 'Woman Clothed with the Sun'," *Colby Quarterly* 21, no. 1 (March 1985): 11–21, esp. 17.

53 On Delacroix's *Faust* images and their reception, see Robert Vilain, "'An Excess of Savage Force'? Faust in French: Stapfer, Delacroix, and Goethe," *The Princeton Library Chronicle* 73, no. 3 (Spring 2012): 313–71, at 336–71.

54 For an analysis of Goethe's whole book, see Jane Brown, *Goethe's* Faust: *The German Tragedy* (Ithaca, 1986).

55 On Doré's work, see *Gustave Doré (1832-1883): Master of Imagination*, ed. Philippe Kaenel (Paris, 2014).

56 As in Karl-Joris Huysmans's *Against Nature* (1884) and Oscar Wilde's *The Picture of Dorian Gray* (1891).

57 Matthew J. Smith, "'la manière de Milton': Baudelaire reads Milton's Satan," in *The Hermeneutics of Hell: Visions and Representations of the Devil in World Literature*, eds Gregor Thuswaldner and Daniel Russ (London, 2017), 211–37. https://doi.org/10.1007/978-3-319-52198-5

58 The Musée Felicien Rops in Namur, Belgium, offers an online overview of the artist's work: https://www.museerops.be

59 On Rops's satanic/erotic works and Christianity, see Nella Arambasin, "Le Diable sans Dieu," in Bernadette Bonnier, Véronique Leblanc et al., *Félicien Rops: Rops suis, aultre ne veulx estre* (Brussels, 1998), 203–15; for texts accompanying *Les Sataniques*, see Hélène Védrine's compilation of Rops's writings, "Écrivain," 241–59, at 257. On Rops's satanic works and satanic cults in this period, see Per Faxneld, *Satanic Feminism: Lucifer as the Liberator of Woman in Nineteenth-Century Culture* (Oxford, 2017), 285–304, esp. 296–304.

60 On these female stereotypes, see Bram Dijkstra, *Idols of Perversity: Fantasies of Feminine Evil in Fin-de-Siècle Culture* (New York, 1986); Patricia Mathews, *Passionate Discontent: Creativity, Gender, and French Symbolist Art* (Chicago, 1999). On prostitution in art, see Charles Bernheimer, *Figures of Ill-Repute: Representing Prostitution in Nineteenth Century France* (Cambridge, MA, 1989); Hollis Clayson, *Painted Love: Prostitution and French Art of the Impressionist Era* (New Haven, 1991).

61 Mathews, *Passionate Discontent*, 76–9; Dysktra, *Idols of Perversity*, 99–109.
62 Mary Orr, *Flaubert's* Tentation: *Remapping Nineteenth-Century French Histories of Religion and Science* (Oxford, 2008), esp. 189–206.
63 Orr, *Flaubert's* Tentation, 199.
64 On Ensor's oeuvre, see Anna Swinbourne, Susan Canning, Jane Panetta, et al., *James Ensor* (New York, 2009); on his St. Anthony works, see Susan Canning, Patrick Florizoone, Mary Ireson et al., *James Ensor: The Temptation of St. Anthony* (Chicago, 2014). https://www.artic.edu/digital-publications/10/james-ensor-the-temptation-of-saint-anthony
65 See Sigrid Achenbach's description in *Das Berliner Kupferstichkabinett: Ein Handbuch zur Sammlung*, ed. Alexander Dückers, vol. 2 (Berlin, 1994), 416f., cat. no. VII.68.
66 On Ensor's traumas, see Patrick Florizoone and Nancy Ireson, "The Trials of 'The Temptation': The Genesis of James Ensor's St. Anthony," in Canning, Florizoone, Ireland et al., *Ensor: The Temptation*, 45–64.

## Further Reading

Dixon, Laurinda. *Bosch*. London: Phaidon, 2003.
Emmerson, Richard. *Apocalypse Illuminated: The Visual Exegesis of Revelation in Medieval Illustrated Manuscripts* (University Park: Pennsylvania State University Press, 2018).
Farr, Carol. *The Book of Kells: Its Function and Audience*. London: British Library, 1997.
Hayum, Andrée. *The Isenheim Altarpiece: God's Medicine and the Painter's Vision*. Princeton: Princeton University Press, 1989.
Hamburger, Jeffrey. *Nuns as Artists: The Visual Culture of a Medieval Convent* (Berkeley: University of California Press, 1997).
Hults, Linda. *The Witch as Muse: Art, Gender, and Power in Early Modern Europe* (Philadelphia: University of Pennsylvania Press, 2005).
Meganck, Tine. *Pieter Bruegel the Elder*, Fall of the Rebel Angels: *Art, Knowledge and Politics on the Eve of the Dutch Revolt* (Brussels and Milan: Royal Museums of Fine Arts and Silvana Editoriale, 2014).
Zika, Charles. *The Appearance of Witchcraft: Print and Visual Culture in Sixteenth-Century Europe* (London: Routledge, 2007).

# 16

# THE DEVIL AND COLONIALISM

*Jutta Wimmler*

To investigate how the devil was implicated in colonialism, a good starting point is to look at the Americas.[1] In recent decades, a variety of studies have revealed a strong tendency among early modern European Christians to conceptualise the American continent as Satan's empire.[2] As the continent had been unknown to them (to everyone's irritation, it was not mentioned in the bible), it seemed prudent to assume that the devil had been able to roam freely there.[3] With the sea routes opened up, Christians had the responsibility to wrest this territory from the Evil One through conquest and missions. The rhetoric of holy war and *reconquista*—of Christianity besieged by enemy forces—provides an important lens through which to understand the colonisation of the Americas.[4]

Prominent though this narrative was, it never stood alone. From the beginning, the opinion that the inhabitants of this continent had lived in an innocent and natural state and wanted to worship God had also been embraced.[5] The two were complementary views. The devil and his demons, after all, could not act independently from God. It was God, then, who allowed for the continent to be hidden for so long—and it was he who decided that it was now time for Christians to enter the story. Some would have seen this as a sign that the end time was approaching and call for increasing missionary activity to bring Amerindians into the fold, as the devil launched his last, great attack.[6] Amerindians were not usually perceived as devil-worshippers then, but as potential converts fully capable of receiving and accepting the truth of the Christian message. If they did serve the devil, it was argued, then they did so out of ignorance, not malice.

Jorge Cañizares-Esguerra has powerfully argued that the demonological interpretation of American colonisation was not a purely Catholic, let alone Iberian rhetoric.[7] The English and Dutch—avid readers of Iberian literature—adopted much the same narrative. Building in particular on the work of Spanish Dominican Bartolomé de las Casas (1474–1566), who had in his writings turned the Spanish conquistadors into the devil's agents who had brought hell to the New World, the Protestants developed the so-called "black legend" of Spanish cruelty and vice. Focusing on the Puritans, Cañizares-Esguerra argues that they saw the colonisation of New England as "an epic, crusading act of *reconquista* (against the devil)"—a devil first located with the Spanish, then increasingly with the Amerindians.[8] The satanic enemy was quite flexible: depending on the author's broader argument, pirates,

DOI: 10.4324/9781003096603-17

Jews, the enslaved, metropolitan officials, and nature itself could be the executive officers of his will.

As the excellent scholarship of the past 30 years has illustrated, there was much room for interpretation within this broad narrative, especially if one moves from the larger rhetoric investigated by Cañizares-Esguerra to everyday lives in distinct colonial settings. In his account of the devil's activity in New France (Canada), Peter Goddard has alerted us to the very different circumstances of Jesuit missionary activities as compared to New Spain (Central America and parts of North America).[9] The territories of New Spain, he argues, had in fact been conquered and possessed a functioning colonial infrastructure that included the Church as a strong player. In New France, by contrast, the missionaries (of which there were few) had hardly any colonial/imperial structures to support them and depended on good relations with the surrounding polities of the Huron, Iroquois and Algonquians. He argues that for this reason, Jesuits in New France were more sceptical when it came to acknowledging the devil's activities among the population.

Time is also a factor. Authors who have written on the subject agree that missionary activity in the Americas—whether in Brazil, Canada, Mexico, or Peru—was initially accompanied by optimism. That is, the missionaries believed the natives would be easily converted and would eagerly accept the Christian message. By the 17th century, however, this turned to pessimism. As epidemics and natural disasters decimated populations, and as the newly converted continued their involvement with local traditions of "idolatry," missionaries looked to explain why they had failed. The devil became a popular scapegoat.[10] It seems sensible to add the failure of overseas mission and colonisation to the list of factors that explain the increasing concern with the demonic among 17th-century Europeans.

Cañizares-Esguerra has compellingly dissected the perceived difference between North and South, English and Spanish, Protestant and Catholic and has argued that we need a broader perspective in order to understand European colonisation in general, and the role of demonological discourse within it specifically. He also recognised the danger of privileging the American Atlantic, pointing out that early modern European Empires were global. The metropolitan governments of the Dutch and French certainly prioritised the Indian Ocean—this was one of the reasons why the French Jesuit mission in Canada struggled for attention and survival. In India, too, European Christians interpreted the Hindu Gods as demonic and thought that the devil had taken up residence here, plunging the people into idolatry; among the Chinese, the Jesuits made a name for themselves as exorcists of demons.[11] Clearly, the devil and his minions knew no regional boundaries—if the "discovery" of America and of its non-Christian inhabitants had inaugurated a final struggle between good and evil, then this struggle would play out everywhere.

And yet demonological discourse regarding Africa and Asia has largely escaped the close attention of researchers—in part, because it appears less prominently in the sources. Africa and Asia were part of the Old World, known (at least in theory) since antiquity. These parts of the world were not subject to great territorial conquest and European settlement—at least not in the early modern period, when the devil and demons still had a prominent role to play in European cosmologies. Indeed, not only has most research into the devil's role in colonialism been focused on the Americas, it has also typically ended around 1750. Since belief in the devil is said to have declined markedly in the 18th century, and since colonialism in Asia and Africa is considered a later phenomenon, exploring the theme of "devil and colonialism" with regard to these two continents seems like a fruitless exercise. In what follows, I will make the case that it is not fruitless—in fact, much can be gained from expanding our view towards other regions beyond the Americas, and after the mid-18th century. I will make this point by turning to Europe's contact with Africa and relating the results back to the aforementioned research. Before we delve more deeply into the devil's involvement with colonialism, however, we will first have to clarify what we mean by "colonialism."

## The Trouble with "Colonialism"

The term "colonialism" is difficult to define and is not always clearly differentiated from the related term "imperialism" either in everyday language or in scholarship. According to Krishan Kumar, the classic definition of "empire" is that of a large state that controls vast territories and its peoples—"imperialism," then, is the process by which an empire is established and maintained. "Colony," on the other hand, was originally associated with cultivation and settlement.[12] In the early modern period, a "colony" simply referred to a settlement of a group of people outside of their home territory. There thus existed German colonies in French and Spanish cities, for example—typically a number of merchant-families that clustered in particular parts of town.

In the Americas, a slightly different type of "colony" became common place: one characterised not only by settlement, but also by cultivation and the displacement of the people who had previously inhabited the land. The plantation—agricultural land worked by European indentured workers and/or Amerindian and African enslaved labourers—became the defining element of the American "settler colony," specifically in North America and the Caribbean. As Moses Finley observed, "plantation" and "colony" became synonyms in the course of the 16th and 17th centuries.[13] At that point, the concept of "colonialisation" also emerged, as the process that leads to the establishment of colonies/plantations. When, in the 19th century, "colonialism" caught on as a catchword, it did so first as a neutral term signifying the practice of the colonial system. In the 20th century, however, the term received a negative signification: now it came to mean unjust exploitation by a stronger (typically European) power, a process that plunges the colony into a state of dependency.[14] "Colonialism" comes to us then as a term of cultural criticism—it is not a neutral descriptor but includes an ideological argument.

For historians of Africa, "colonialism" is nevertheless a phenomenon of the later 19th and 20th centuries, defined by European wars against local polities that ultimately led to the conquest of these polities and the subjugation of African peoples. Everything that came before that, including the roughly 400 years that saw the forced transportation of Africans to the Americas through the so-called transatlantic slave trade, is considered a part of the "pre-colonial" period.[15] Indeed, in most of Africa, there were no European state structures to speak of until well into the 19th century. The European presence was limited to a series of small enclaves dotted along parts of the Atlantic and Indian Ocean coasts of the continent. There, Europeans paid local African rulers for the privilege of building forts (also called "castles") that served as their base for trading operations.

Missionary activity was extremely limited. The forts typically employed a pastor or priest for the local European residents and occasionally, small groups of missionaries ventured to parts of the coast to proselytise, dispense the sacraments and hear confession. But Africa was not a priority for European missionary activity—such work was underfunded and not particularly popular. So, unlike regions such as New Spain, Brazil, or New England, in Africa we find no European settlement: European women were rare or non-existent, there existed only a highly localised European infrastructure, and the church was extremely weak or wholly absent.

European actors in Africa before the late 19th century tended to lack concrete power or control over the people and the environment—they depended strongly on local rulers, merchants, interpreters, and others for their survival. The act of writing about their experiences in published travel accounts, letters, and daily logs can be interpreted as a way of taking control of what was really a situation of dependence. After all, it was their interpretation of events that was related to the public back home—and these accounts have come down to us as historical sources. Since we lack other written sources, we depend on these Europeans' versions of what transpired. When they inform us that the locals worshiped the devil and demons, we can rarely check this information against sources written by the locals themselves. While "colonial" structures may not yet have been in place, our sources are certainly biased in a way typical of colonial settings—it is in this sense that we will explore the devil's relationship with colonialism in "pre-colonial" Africa.

This does not mean, however, that European sources tell us nothing of these peoples' responses to European thought-worlds. In what is currently the only book-length historical study of the devil's role in the European colonisation of Africa, Birgit Meyer skilfully draws attention to the fact that Africans—in this case, the Ewe of modern-day Ghana—creatively and actively shaped the Christian concepts they came into contact with.[16] Analysing the records of the *Norddeutsche Missionsgesellschaft* (*North German Missionary Society*) that had started proselytising on the Gold Coast (Ghana) in 1847, Meyer concludes that the concept of the devil was central for conversion to Christianity among the Ewe from the late 19th into the 20th centuries. By focusing on documents that detail conversations with possible converts, she illuminates how prospective Ewe Christians negotiated meaning between the two thought-worlds. For the missionaries, the Ewe were the unwitting servants of Satan, and they saw it as their task to make the Ewe aware of this fact. They demonised Ewe religion and denounced their practices as devil-worship. At the same time, the missionaries of necessity adapted Ewe vocabulary in order to communicate the Christian message, thus blurring the boundaries between Christianity and Ewe religion.[17]

Those who converted, writes Meyer, were usually dissatisfied with the ineffectiveness of Ewe practices and clearly understood the devil as the link between Ewe and Christian belief and practice: the devil was not only the Christian God's counterpart; he also represented the spirits they had previously worshipped.[18] For that reason, the devil was vital for African Christianities: the concept gave meaning to the practices converts left behind in a way that was compatible with their new Christian thought-world. In many ways, this situation resembles the better investigated earlier colonial setting in the Americas, despite the temporal distance and the fact that the missionaries were now Protestants. The missionaries demonised local religions—which paradoxically meant that they first had to introduce devil and demons to the locals on a conceptual level, in order to then convince them to turn their back on their traditional cosmologies.[19]

African coastal societies such as the Ewe had already been in contact with European Christians for centuries by this point. For these earlier centuries, however, it is difficult to ascertain how African actors responded to the demonisation of their cosmologies. One way of approaching this problem is to focus on instances of communication between a European traveller and his African interlocutors—and it is the value of such a perspective and the possible research trajectories it opens that the rest of this chapter will bring into focus. By reading the sources carefully and in a critical, against-the-grain way, we can catch glimpses of intercultural negotiation. We will focus on communicative situations in which the "devil" appears as a subject of conversation.

When Europeans report that African actors used terms such as "devil" (and assuming that we believe their reports), we cannot presume to understand the meaning these interlocutors would have attached to the term. Mary-Louise Pratt uses the term "autoethnographic expression" to describe situations where the colonised take up the coloniser's terminology in order to represent themselves. These are not, she cautions, inherently "authentic" representations. Rather, they should be seen as a kind of response to the coloniser, or a way of entering into dialogue by appropriating his terminology.[20] Both Pratt and Meyer emphasise that such an appropriation of terminology does not automatically mean the adoption of its exact meaning. Both stress that there is a creative process at work here.[21] Let us consider some anecdotes in order to shed light on these creative processes.

## Devil, Idol, Fetish, and Saint

In the 1660s, somewhere around the Danish Fort Frederiksborg in what is today the port city of Cape Coast (Ghana), the German Lutheran pastor Wilhelm Johann Müller (1633–73) approached a basket in a field. Some of the local Fetu people had placed it there before beginning their agricultural work. But when Müller attempted to open it, a Fetu man hastily ran towards him and cried out in Portuguese, "*O senor, no abrid, pretto Diabol sta adentro,*" that is, "Sir, do not open, the black devil is inside." Müller responded that since he was a Christian, the devil could not harm him—but the Fetu man remained adamant and successfully prevented Müller from going ahead.[22] While we can of course not be sure that this conversation actually happened, the fact that Müller's German text quotes the distinguished man's statement in Portuguese is suggestive. The episode can be read as evidence of a communication breakdown, to the extent that the "distinguished man" who offered the term "*diabol*" for the entity in the basket clearly meant something different by that term than what Müller might have understood "*diabol*" to mean. Müller's insistence that he (as a Christian) could open the basket without being harmed was clearly beside the point from the distinguished man's perspective.

Müller was employed as a pastor by the recently formed Danish Africa Company on the so-called Gold Coast—in what is the Central Region of today's Ghana—between 1662 and 1669. He was not a missionary—in fact, Protestant missionary activity in Africa only really emerged in the course of the 18th century.[23] Instead, his function was to care for the Danish Company staff at Fort Frederiksborg. Although it was not his task to collect information on the African societies around his post at Frederiksborg, Müller had a keen interest in them, and his 1673 *Die Africanische, Auff Der Guineischen Gold-Cust Gelegene Landschafft Fetu (The African Fetu Landscape of the Gold Coast of Guinea)* is still considered an extremely valuable source for the history of the peoples of the region. Müller devoted an entire chapter of the work to "*Abgötterei, Un- und Aberglauben*" (idolatry, disbelief, and superstition). Müller was particularly intrigued by their notion of "the devil."

Müller argued that the faith of the Fetu people centred on two diametrically opposed principals: everything evil (including misfortune, poverty, sickness, and death) originated from one source called *Sámma*, while all that was good originated from a source he identified with two related but distinct entities called *O'Bossum* and *Summàn*.[24] Yet it was not *Sámma*, but *O'Bossum* and *Summàn*, whom Müller subsequently equated with "devil." While he acknowledges that the Fetu people distinguish between a "good" and an "evil" entity, Müller primarily demonises the former. There is a certain logic to this: this is, after all, the entity that receives the Fetu people's worship and to Müller this worship, as we shall see, indicated the presence of the devil. The issue is complicated by the fact that Müller's demonised reading of Fetu society included a third entity which he also understood to be the devil: the fetish (*Fitiso*).

"The Fetish" is by all accounts among the best-known conceptual legacies of Afro-European contact, and a complicated one at that. The term derives from the Portuguese word *feitiço*, meaning "manufactured," and had been used in Portugal since the Middle Ages to mean witchcraft, the practice or the object of magic.[25] While 16th-century Portuguese travellers to Western Africa had differentiated between *idolatria* (the worship of false Gods) and *feitiçaria* (witchcraft, enchantment, or more generally speaking, an event that indicated the devil's presence), travellers by the 17th century tended to conflate the two.[26] They no longer saw *feitiçaria* as a magical "event," but identified it with idolatry—they believed the fetish was worshipped as a God, the idolatrous rituals watched over and mediated by the "fetish priests." This is to be seen in the context of early modern European demonological discourse, where idolatry and witchcraft both came to be understood as devil-worship.[27]

The Lutheran Müller's attempts to understand Fetu religious practice speaks to this conflation. To Müller, the idol, the fetish, the devil, *O'Bossum*, and *Summàn* were all the same thing—not least because they were, in his understanding, all the object of Fetu worship. While he tried to find out how the Fetu people distinguished these concepts, Müller surmised that they were unable to do so:

> Among the Blacks there is no-one who can say what O'Bossum, Summan, or Fitiso actually is, as much as they are being led, they do not know how they are led. So it transpires, when one of them is asked what O'Bossum, Sumàn or Fitiso is, he has to admit that he does not know what it is.[28]

While he insisted that his failure to coherently disentangle the terminology of *Summàn/O'Bossum/Fitiso* stemmed from the Fetu people's own "confusion," it in fact attests more to his failure to move beyond his own cultural logic. He was incapable of understanding these concepts or entities as anything but variations on one theme: the devil.

This is also apparent in his discussion of Cúcú, which according to Müller was the most important fetish of the Fetu people. Müller took the physical description of Cúcú that he allegedly received from his Fetu informants as evidence that Cúcú was indeed the devil: Cúcú took the form of a "tall, hideous black moor" carrying the spear of a huntsman, a bow and a quiver; he was also accompanied by a pack of black dogs:

> The description of this Cúcu shows clearly that he must be the hellish hunter, the devil, as the holy scripture explicitly calls him a hunter. Still, they take this Cúcu to be a patron and protective saint of the whole country. Because of this they call him Obóssum, that is, saint.[29]

Müller called on the bible as an authority to confirm that the characteristics of Cúcu as described by the Fetu people betray his real identity: he was the devil, who had conned the people into believing he was a saint. Because Müller believed that the Fetu people were mistaken in calling Cúcu a saint, "saint" (*O'Bossum*) became synonymous with "devil."

The Lutheran Müller reflected on the belief of the Fetu people only one or two decades after the New France Jesuits discussed by Goddard. While Goddard found that these missionaries rarely interpreted the being *Manitou* as an incarnation of the devil, we have seen that Müller allocated much space to establishing such a connection for *O'Bossum/Summàn/Fitiso*. Goddard's argument that the precarious position of the Jesuit missionaries in New France, coupled with their small number and lack of colonial infrastructure, necessitated a more sceptical approach to the demonic, does not quite hold up when we compare it to the Müller example. Müller was a lone Protestant pastor in Frederiksborg, an outpost with a weak colonial infrastructure, and thus he was in a more precarious position than the New France Jesuits—yet it would be far-fetched to call him a "sceptic." Rather than accepting that the difference fell along denominational lines, it seems wiser to follow Mairi Cowan's model, which proposes that demonic interpretations of "heathen" societies varied greatly, even among the Jesuits of New France.[30]

The Müller example nevertheless conforms to Goddard's interpretation of New France demonology on another level: according to Goddard, the Jesuits spoke of demonic activities primarily in relation to the local priests who were clearly their competitors.[31] The "devil's priests" (*Teufelspfaffen*) were indeed a particular nuisance to Müller as well. Although Müller did not doubt that the devil was in fact present among the Fetu people, he was unsure whether the priests were indeed in direct contact with him or whether they were only pretenders who deluded "the poor common folk." He certainly found it suspicious that they would not allow him to observe a consultation of oracles despite repeated requests for permission.[32] Müller did not allow for the possibility that the priests acted in good faith and were themselves deluded by the devil: that would have excused their actions and made them victims. To Müller, the only victims were "the common folk"; the priests were predators one way or the other.

The authority of the "devil's priests" in Fetu society in Müller's opinion frustrated his attempts at conveying the truth of the Christian message to these people. He thought that systematic missionary activity was needed—including a translation of the bible into the Fetu language, especially the New Testament.[33] After all, the Fetu people were well aware of the existence of a benevolent deity—it was only because of their ignorance or "blindness of the heart" that they followed the devil instead:

> If you tell them of the miracles that God worked at the time of the Old Testament, they soon ask how many years ago this was, as if they were trying to say: If a certain time has passed, how are we to know these things? Others can tell many stories of the miracles that the devil, their Obossum and patron saint, has worked among them. Not only have they heard these tales from their fathers, but have also (according to them) experienced them themselves.[34]

Müller indeed tried to convey the contents of the bible to his Fetu acquaintances on numerous occasions, for which, to his disdain, he reaped mostly mockery (*Gespött*) and scepticism. This brings us to another fruitful avenue for investigating the devil's role in the colonial encounter: what we could (somewhat anachronistically) call "interreligious dialogue": a comparison of cosmologies in a colonial setting. We will return to Müller but let us first move to an incident that took place a few decades later, on an island in the Indian Ocean.

## The Devil and Comparison

When attending a sacrificial ceremony in early 18th-century Madagascar, French traveller Carpeau du Saussay (1647–1722) caused quite a scene. Attempting to find out more about religion on the island, du Saussay had sought the help of an old man (referred to only as a *"vieux Neigre"*) who was willing to answer his questions about the worship of the primary deity Oly. As du Saussay did not speak the local language well, the two corresponded with the help of a person du Saussay referred to as his slave (*esclave*), who acted as interpreter.[35] With the old man and a few of "his slaves," du Saussay attended the abovementioned sacrificial ceremony, presided over by the so-called *Ampyfacabire*. This is how he described the experience:

> Then he [the Ampyfacabire] cut off a piece of the victim [the sacrificial bull], which he tore apart, saying: This for Diambiliche; he cut another, which he put on another side, saying, Behold for Zanhar; he then took the dish where the blood was, and threw it on those present. The victim was at that point fragmented and distributed to everyone. The pieces were grilled, and everyone in the house ate everything up, even the babies. During this ceremony, I could not help but burst out laughing at all the contortions he made while addressing the bull. He turned and asked, if I did not apprehend, that their Oly would cause me to die for being so inattentive, and so little collected during the celebration of their mystery: instead of answering him, I began to laugh louder; the angry Ampyfacabire threatened that, if I did not withdraw, he would pray to his God to punish me. The Prince who was present at this ceremony, asked me to withdraw, so as not to interrupt the Sacrifice. I did not want to offend him, for fear of causing an incident. My *esclaves* and my old *Neigre* followed me.[36]

Du Saussay finally had the good sense to leave the scene, accompanied by his "slaves" and the old man, who proceeded to scold du Saussay for his lack of respect, pointing out that "they" had never ridiculed the Europeans' mass. Du Saussay could count himself lucky, he said, that the *Ampyfacabire* had not made good on his threat.

After du Saussay conceded that he had not been able to control himself, he asked the old man to explain what had transpired during the ceremony. He especially wanted to know why the animal having been sacrificed was halved, with one part given to *Diambiliche* and the other to *Zanhar*. In particular, he wanted to know why *Diambiliche* received his portion of the sacrifice first. He was concerned because *Diambiliche* meant *"Monsieur le Diable,"* while *Zanhar* meant God. The old man responded that sacrifice was always offered to both, but that the devil was able to do them harm and thus needed to be appeased first. God, however, was not so difficult to satisfy. From this du Saussay surmised that the worship of the devil was "forced" while that of God was "natural." And yet du Saussay was then quick to diminish the "real" power of the devil. Many Europeans, du Saussay explained, had asserted that the devil was strongly present among these people, and that the devil beat and tyrannised them.[37] Indeed, he himself had heard their cries and seen their contorted movements—but these were, according to du Saussay, to be attributed to epilepsy (*"mal caduc"*) and "vapours."[38]

On the one hand, we can infer from his report that du Saussay found the primacy of the devil in the ritual troubling; on the other, he seems to have rejected the idea that the devil had a real presence in the ceremony. Or if he did believe the devil was present, he certainly did not think that he was to be feared—had he thought otherwise, he would not have dared to behave the way he did during the ceremony.[39] From his 1722 *Voyage de Madagascar*, we do not know how du Saussay came to believe that *Diambiliche* meant devil and that *Zanhar* meant God. He simply stated that this is the correct translation as a matter of fact.

We do not know whether the old man used the term "devil" himself—in fact, it rather seems likely that he did not. Indeed, du Saussay's assertion that an entity called *Diambiliche* or an equivalent existed in Malagasy thinking has been contested almost from the moment du Saussay published it, and one certainly finds no references to such a being in later ethnographic studies. *Zanhar/Sanhar/Zanahary*, however, has been and still is usually identified as the primary creator deity or deities.[40] Where, then, did du Saussay pick up the term *Diambiliche*? Was this a distortion of a Malagasy term? If so, someone must have thought it appropriate to make the connection to the Christian concept of the devil—the enslaved interpreter, perhaps? It is also possible that du Saussay simply concluded from witnessing the ceremony that it had a "demonic" nature and thus inserted the devil into the old man's explanation in a way that made sense to him.

In his book *Savage Systems*, David Chidester takes issue with the fact that the academic field of religious studies—sometimes also referred to as comparative religion—traces its origins to the late 19th century, to the work of "armchair-scholars" such as E.B. Tyler (1832–1917), James Frazer (1854–1941), and Rudolf Otto (1869–1937). Although it is well-known that they built their theories of animism, magic, and the numinous in no small part on the writings of travellers to different parts of the world, it is less frequently acknowledged that these travellers already did much of the interpretative work on which the "armchair scholars" in Europe later built their theories.[41] Using the example of Southern Africa, Chidester moreover illustrates that these travellers did not engage in the practice of comparing religious belief and practice on their own—they did so in communication with their various African interlocutors, who actively participated in this endeavour.

Although it is not easy to reconstruct the extent of their contribution, as it is usually mediated through the European author and often hidden from view, Chidester illustrates that we can catch glimpses of these often-unnamed African actors' contributions in the written record. We have met two of these actors so far: Du Saussay's *vieux Neigre* compared the sacrificial ceremony to the Christian mass in order to explain to du Saussay the extent of his inappropriate behaviour. The "distinguished man" in Müller's tale appropriated the term "*diabol*" to make Müller understand the danger of what he was doing in trying to open the basket. The *vieux Neigre's* comparison was successful—du Saussay realised his misbehaviour—but the distinguished man's was not. In this case, the intercultural communication failed because Müller's understanding of "*diabol*" differed from that of the distinguished man.

In these instances, we get an idea of the sorts of communicative difficulties that existed when it came to relating two different thought-worlds to each other—and we can see that there were two sides to this conversation. While communication was possible in some instances, because both parties could relate the other's statements or practices to their own thought-world, laughter can indicate a failure (on either side) to place something within their own frame of reference in a meaningful way.[42] Whether successful or not, comparative practices such as the ones described here became a vital element of social theorising in the 18th, and especially the 19th, century. The role of the devil and demons in this process of intercultural comparison—a process that relied heavily on communicative situations in colonial contexts—has largely gone unacknowledged.

## The Devil and Social Theory

In the 1870s, somewhere around the Ogowe River in Gabon, the German-Austrian geologist and explorer Oskar Lenz (1848–1925) witnessed the outbursts of a man allegedly possessed by the devil. In his 1879 *Skizzen aus Westafrika* (*Sketches from West Africa*), he states that while the man had behaved and spoken rationally during the day, when evening came, he suddenly jumped up and ran screaming around the village. Eventually, he headed towards the forest, where he uprooted a tree with his bare hands. Running and screaming, the man then carried the tree into the village. Women and children fled into their houses—although, curiously, the men paid no attention to him. The possessed man unsuccessfully tried to enter some of the closed houses still firmly clinging to the tree, but finally collapsed, with his arms around its trunk. Then an old woman "over whom the *kakodämon* inside the man had no power," approached him and gave him a concoction to drink which seemed to mediate his frenzy. Man and tree were disentangled, and the poor fellow was returned to his house to recuperate.[43]

Reflecting on this, Lenz reported that he first classified this occurrence as insanity, but when the same affliction affected various other people over the following days, he sent out his servant to investigate. According to him, the informants all reported the same thing, which appears as an English quotation in the German text: "This be the devil that catch them man." On one particular day, the behaviour spread to such an extent that it seemed to affect the entire village:

> The day the Oganga performed their dances, the spectacle I have described seemed to have become an epidemic; it was as if the entire population had gone mad. The people were in a terrible frenzy and a bunch of the Okande-men rushed to the forest as though in anger, and returned to the village gasping under the weight of a heavy tree, where they then collapsed and passed out. I could not explain the circumstance that both hands of such a devil-possessed man had been tied to the tree, which is hardly possible without assistance from another; but the Okande energetically denied that such assistance had taken place and explained, all this was simply the devil's work.[44]

Once again, we do not know what actually happened, or what the African informants may have meant by "it is the devil that catch them man." But the term "devil" appears to have been used in communications. This would mean that the Africans in question had appropriated the English term "devil," or at least that there was an established practice of translating an African concept (or possibly certain events) as "devil" when talking to Europeans—just as the Fetu man had used the Portuguese term "*diabol*" in his conversation with the German pastor. Again, a kind of communication breakdown ensued. While the Africans' explanation was unacceptable to him, Lenz could not find an alternative explanation, other than falling back on the notion of collective insanity at work. One could argue that in both cases, the communication breakdown ensued because the Africans and the Europeans in question meant something different by "devil."

The episode—or rather, episodes—served a larger purpose in Lenz's narrative. Towards the end of this section of his account, he made clear that everything he has described—including the above episode that he classified as religious mania—should be construed as diagnostic of the state that reigned among these people:

> We can see from the above what kind of desolate conditions exist among the *Bantu-negern*, how a power-hungry and scheming priest-kingship tries everything to keep the people in grossest superstition, how successful these attempts are and how the more than four hundred yearlong acquaintance with Europeans was unable to change and reform the situation in a beneficial way.[45]

The last part of this quotation is a not-so-subtle swipe against the Portuguese who, as Lenz emphasised on numerous occasions, had been unable to found a colonial empire in that part of the world or to bring any kind of order there.[46] But with the slave trade abolished and a better type of trade initiated, with new plantations established, and schools built by rational and practically minded missionaries, things were already getting better. In the long run, Lenz assured his readers, these factors would eliminate the barbaric conditions that these darkest superstitions had brought forth.[47]

Much like Müller, Lenz turned his own confusion into evidence of chaos. It is not his fault, he implied, that he does not understand particular practices. Rather, they are emblematic of a disordered, superstitious society:

> In all of these *Neger*'s religious views, if one may even use this word, there is no moral tendency to be seen; sickness, death, crop failure, absolutely every unhappy event that the people can't explain is blamed on some evil being that then has to be appeased; but this *Kakodämon* often takes the form of a human, and it is now the job of the mediator, the Oganga, the priests and sorcerers, to identify this person; the person is then exposed to the cruel revenge of the people. Centuries of traffic with the Whites has not sufficed to rid the *Negern* of this belief, and even today many thousands annually fall victim to the religious humbug officiated and promoted by the Oganga.[48]

What is striking in this passage are the similarities to earlier reports of demonic activity in Africa, the Americas, and Asia alike: the locals attribute misfortune to a powerful being (remember *Sámma* in Müller's account) and the primary villains of the story are the priests. Lenz, of course, identified another culprit: the Catholic Portuguese. Though his criticism was couched in seemingly "secular" terms in the above quotations, Lenz followed a typical Protestant/Reformed rhetoric of demonising Catholicism and equating Catholic rituals and sacred objects with devil-worship.[49] In other passages of Lenz' text, he made this link explicit by stating outright that the Catholic Portuguese influence had strengthened the already existing use of fetishes among the Okande in the past centuries.[50] The Portuguese were thus even to blame for the "fetishist" nature of Okande religion.

To Lenz, then, the population was not to blame for the state they found themselves in. Goddard has argued that without the belief that the devil was actually present among "heathen" peoples, European Christians only had the locals themselves to blame for the lack of missionary progress.[51] We can see here that this is not necessarily the case: the priests (and the Portuguese) are the real villains in Lenz' account, not the population itself. The goal was clear: free the population from the influence of their rulers, their priests, and the Catholic Portuguese. The way to do this was conquest.

Lenz used the term *Kakodämon* to describe the Okande's beliefs, but according to the report, this was not the term his interlocutors used. They allegedly spoke only of the devil. *Kakodämon* is a term of Greek origin that seems to have surfaced in European writings gradually in the 16th and 17th centuries.[52] It only became common in the course of the 19th century as an analytical descriptor (only to disappear thereafter). Some 19th-century Europeans used it to describe evil demons and spirits but also scary monsters and "horrible spectres" among "the ancients."[53] By using this term, Lenz connected the beliefs of the Okande with that of the ancient Greeks, and thus suggested to his audience that these Africans' beliefs were comparable to those of these ancients. According to Lenz, most Africans had "a cacodemonic worldview": they imagined an evil being or devil who was the cause of all misfortune—and whom they sought to appease or cast out though "strange chanting." Claiming the authority of the rational observer, he imposed the category of the "demonic" on African beliefs in much the same way as Müller had done two hundred years earlier. Müller's chapter on these issues is entitled "Idolatry, disbelief, and superstition," while Lenz' title two hundred years later is "Superstition and fetishism." In both cases, they used the vocabulary of the demonic to explicate these overarching categories and to characterise African belief systems.

In 19th-century social theorising, the historical dimension played an important role. Non-European societies were increasingly understood as windows into Europe's own past. In assigning a belief in demons to African societies, travellers and armchair scholars alike emphasised the difference between Europe and Africa: Europeans had overcome such "irrational" thought, while Africans had not. By locating a belief in the demonic with African peoples, European travellers turned them into people stuck in the past and thus on a lower level of social progress, and in need of the European's "civilising" influence.

When in the second half of the 20th century the concept "African traditional religion" emerged to replace the previous category of "primitive religion," scholars typically argued that demons or "evil spirits" played little or no role in "traditional" African thought, implying that such notions were at some point imported from the outside world.[54] We should, however, not make the mistake of assuming the existence of a coherent and static "traditional" version of African thought(s) at some point in the past. For the historian, as we have seen, the major problem is the lopsided nature of the source material that only allows us access to past African thought-worlds through a distorted lens.

The extent to which the Atlantic slave trade, colonialism, and the presence of Islam and Christianity have impacted African cosmologies, patterns of thought, and ceremonies has been a matter of debate. In his study of precolonial Diola religion and society, for example, Robert Baum notes that on the one hand, this Senegambian community's existing system of thought shaped the way they responded to the changing conditions arising from Atlantic trade—on the other hand, this system of thought also changed as a consequence.[55] Scholars like Baum examine oral traditions that engage with some of these changes to compensate for the lack of written records, but as oral traditions recorded today (or in the 20th century) also underwent changes over time and have been influenced by colonialism and the turbulent second half of the 20th century, they can only take us so far. Studies like Baum's nevertheless confirm the dynamics, adaptability, and diversity of thought-worlds in historic African societies and remind us that contradictions and differing interpretations were and are not the preserve of the West.

## Conclusion

The devil's role in "colonialism" is ambivalent, not least because colonial settings could differ greatly. A Christian tradition of demonising the belief and practices of non-Christians certainly informed European reports of non-European societies, but the details of this demonisation could vary. When investigating this subject, we certainly need to be aware of the traditions that informed this language of demonisation. However, we also need to consider how this broader rhetoric played out in specific colonial settings. In order to do this, we need to be aware of the biases of our source material, but we should not dismiss this material out of hand either. Used responsibly, we can both unmask Christian-European biases and probe the reaction of the colonised to the demonisation of their worldviews.

An analysis of 19th-century demonological discourse also helps us to critically engage with practices of social theorising, prominent in academic disciplines like sociology, anthropology, or history that all emerged at this time and drew heavily on writings produced from experiences in a colonial context. Modern social theories are to a great extent built on the "observations" of non-European cultures that "armchair scholars" then compared to form classificatory systems and interpret societal change. They drew on the interpretations of travelling authors whose "observations" were informed by centuries-old traditions of interpreting these cultures along demonic lines. This heritage is still with us today, and we should keep it in mind when classifying, categorising, and evaluating religious systems and cultures today.

## Notes

1 I thank Andrew Apter, Theresia Heimerl, Lisa Kienzl, and the editors of this volume for their valuable comments on previous versions of this chapter.
2 Fernando Cervantes, *The Devil in the New World: The Impact of Diabolism in New Spain* (London, 1994); Laura de Mello Souza, *The Devil and the Land of the Holy Cross: Witchcraft, Slavery, and Popular Religion in Colonial Brazil* (Austin, 2003); *Angels, Demons and the New World*, eds. Fernando Cervantes and Andrew Redden (Cambridge, 2013); Andrew Redden, *Diabolism in Colonial Peru, 1560–1750* (London, 2016).
3 See, for example, Peter Burke, "America and the Rewriting of World History," in *America in European Consciousness, 1493–1750*, ed. Karen O. Kupperman (Chapel Hill, 1995), 35–7.
4 Redden, *Diabolism in Colonial Peru*, 18–9.
5 See, for example, Redden, *Diabolism in Colonial Peru*, 24; Fernando Cervantes, "How to See Angels: The Legacy of Early Mendicant Spirituality," in *Angels and Demons in the New World*, eds. Fernando Cervantes and Andrew Redden (Cambridge, 2013), 69, 84.
6 Jorge Cañizares-Esguerra, *Puritan Conquistadors: Iberianizing the Atlantic, 1550–1700* (Stanford, 2006), 19.
7 Cañizares-Esguerra, *Puritan Conquistadors*. For a concise overview of his argument, see Jorge Cañizares-Esguerra, "The Devil in the New World: A Transnational Perspective," in *The Atlantic in Global History: 1500–2000*, ed. Jorge Cañizares-Esguerra and Erik R. Seeman, 2nd ed. (Milton, 2017), 22–40.
8 Cañizares-Esguerra, *Puritan Conquistadors*, 28–31.
9 Peter Goddard, "The Devil in New France: Jesuit Demonology, 1611–50," *Canadian Historical Review* 78, no. 1 (1997): 40–62.
10 Goddard, "The Devil in New France," 44; Fernando Cervantes, "The Devils of Querétaro: Scepticism and Credulity in Late Seventeenth-Century Mexico," *Past & Present* 130, no. 1 (1991): 51–2; Cervantes, *The Devil in the New World*, 13–5; Cañizares-Esguerra, *Puritan Conquistadors*, 82.
11 Richard Raiswell, "Edward Terry and the Demons of India," in *Knowing Demons, Knowing Spirits*, eds. M. Brock, R. Raiswell and D. Winter (Cham, 2018), 171–210; Qiong Zhang, "About God, Demons, and Miracles: The Jesuit Discourse on the Supernatural in Late Ming China," *Early Science and Medicine* 4, no. 1 (1999): 1–36.

12 Krishan Kumar, "Colony and Empire, Colonialism and Imperialism: A Meaningful Distinction?," *Comparative Studies in Society and History* 63 (2021): 284–5.

13 Moses Finley, "Colonies: An Attempt at a Typology," *Transactions of the Royal Historical Society* 26 (1976): 167–88.

14 Kumar, "Colony and Empire," 287; Finley, "Colonies," 171.

15 Richard Reid has cautioned that this method of periodisation is problematic for several reasons—among other things, it suggests a clear break between the two periods and it privileges the "colonial moment" in African history. Richard Reid, "Past and Presentism: The 'Precolonial' and the Forshortening of African History," *Journal of African History* 52, no. 2 (2011): 135–55.

16 Birgit Meyer, *Translating the Devil: Religion and Modernity among the Ewe in Ghana* (Edinburgh, 1999).

17 Meyer, *Translating the Devil*, 51 and 56.

18 Meyer, *Translating the Devil*, 99–100.

19 On this point see especially Redden, *Diabolism in Colonial Peru*, 91, 121.

20 Mary Louise Pratt, *Imperial Eyes: Travel Writing and Transculturation* (London, 1995), 7.

21 Meyer, *Translating the Devil*, xxv.

22 Wilhelm Johann Müller, *Die Africanische, Auff Der Guineischen Gold-Cust Gelegene Landschafft Fetu* (Hamburg, 1673), 193. Adam Jones has made this text available in an edited English translation and also supplies some background information. See Adam Jones, *German Sources for West African History: 1599–1669* (Wiesbaden, 1983), 134–259.

23 Adrian Hastings, *The Church in Africa: 1450–1950* (Oxford, 1996), 177–88; For Protestant missionary activity in general, see Katharine Gerber, *Christian Slavery: Conversion and Race in the Protestant Atlantic World* (Philadelphia, 2018).

24 Müller, *Landschafft Fetu*, 43–4. In the early 20th century, R.S. Rattray translated these Akan terms as follows: *obosom* = God, *suman* = fetish, and *saman* = ghost/spirit. Robert Sutherland Rattray, *Ashanti Law and Constitution* (Oxford, 1929), 53 and 325. This distinction can also be found in 21st-century scholarship, where *abosum* is translated as "deity" and *suman* as "amulet." See, for example, Adam Mohr, "Missionary Medicine and Akan Therapeutics: Illness, Health and Healing in Southern Ghana's Basel Mission, 1828–1918," *Journal of Religion in Africa* 39, no. 4 (2009): 443 and 448.

25 For a materialist interpretation of the concept "fetish," see William Pietz, "The Problem of the Fetish, I," *RES: Anthropology and Aesthetics* 9 (1985): 5–17; William Pietz, "The Problem of the Fetish, IIIa: Bosman's Guinea and the Enlightenment Theory of Fetishism," *RES: Anthropology and Aesthetics* 16 (1988): 105–24. For a pointed summary of Pietz' argument, see Christina Antenhofer, "Fetisch als heuristische Kategorie," in *Fetisch als heuristische Kategorie: Geschichte–Rezeption–Interpretation*, ed. Christina Antenhofer (Bielefeld, 2014), 9–11.

26 Roger Sansi, "Der Fetisch: Kreativität und Historizität im modernen Atlantik," in Antenhofer, *Fetisch als heuristische Kategorie*, 43–6.

27 Cervantes, *The Devil in the New World*, 21.

28 "Keiner unter den Schwarzen weiß zu sagen, was O-Bóssum, Summàn, oder Fitiso eigentlich sey, immassen sie geführet werden, daß sie selbsten nicht wissen, wie sie geführet werden. Dahero kompt es, wann Jemand unter ihnen befraget wird, was O-Bòssum, Summàn oder Fitiso sey, er bekennen muß rund herauß, er wisse es nicht, was es sey." Müller, *Landschafft Fetu*, 45.

29 "Die Beschreibung dieses Cúcu deutet klärlich an, daß er der höllische Jäger, der Teuffel, seyn müsse, immassen derselbe außtrücklich in H. Schrift ein Jäger genennet wird. Nichts destoweniger halten sie diesen Cúcu vor einen Patron und Schutz-Heiligen des ganzen Landes, Ursach dessen wird er von ihnen Obóssum, das ist ein Heiliger genannt." Müller, *Landschafft Fetu*, 46.

30 Mairi Cowan, "Jesuit Missionaries and the Accomodationist Demons of New France," in *Knowing Demons, Knowing Spirits*, 211–38.

31 Goddard, "The Devil in New France," 52 and 54.

32 Müller, *Landschafft Fetu*, 56–9.

33 Müller, *Landschafft Fetu*, 89.

34 Müller, *Landschafft Fetu*, 91.

35 Carpeau de Saussay, *Voyage De Madagascar* (Paris, 1722), 258.

36 "Ensuite il coupa un morceau de la victime, qu'il mit à part, en disant: voilà pour Diambiliche; il en coupa un autre, qu'il mit d'un autre côté, en disant: voici pour Zanhar; il prit ensuite le plat où

étoit le sang, & le jetta sur les Assistans. La Victime fut dans le moment mise par pieces, & distribué à tout le monde. On les fait griller, & tous ceux de la maison en mangent, jusqu'aux enfans à la mamelle. Pendant cette ceremonie, je ne pus m'empêcher d'éclater de rire de toutes les contorsions qu'il faisoit en haranguant le taureau; il se tourna & demanda, si je n'apprehendois pas que leur Oly ne me fît mourir d'être si peu attentif, & si peu recueilli pendant le celebration de leur mistere: au lieu de lui répondre, je me mis à rire plus fort; l'Ampyfacabire irrité me menace, si je ne me retirois, de prier son Dieu de me punir. Le Prince qui étoit present à cette ceremonie, me pria de vouloir bien me retirer, pour ne point interrompre le Sacrifice. Je ne voulus pas le desobliger, crainte de quelque accident. Mes Esclaves & mon vieu Neigre me suivrent." Saussay, *Voyage de Madagascar*, 262–3.

37 The notion of the devil's physical violence against Africans (and other "heathens") was a common trope in French writings at the time. See Jutta Wimmler, "The Devil's Beatings: African Dimensions of Early Modern Demonology in the Atlantic World," *Journal of Religion in Africa* 45 (2015): 249–87.

38 Saussay, *Voyage de Madagascar*, 263–4.

39 Compare Euan Cameron, *Enchanted Europe: Superstition, Reason, and Religion, 1250–1750* (Oxford, 2011), 311.

40 Hilde Nielssen translates "Zanahary" as both "God" and "Gods"; see Hilde Nielssen, *Ritual Imagination: A Study of Tromba Possession among the Betsimisaraka in Eastern Madagascar* (Leiden, 2012). For a 19th-century critique of Du Saussay, see A. H. Grant, "Glimpses of Madagascar and its People," *Time. A Monthly Miscellany of Interesting and Amusing Literature* 8 (1883), 333. *Diambiliche* also appears in some French encyclopaedias throughout the 19th century as a term for the devil in Madagascar. The common source seems to be du Saussay.

41 David Chidester, *Savage Systems: Colonialism and Comparative Religion in Southern Africa* (Charlottesville, 1996). This practice did not start in the 19th century. For late 17th-century examples, see Cameron, *Enchanted Europe*, 265, 308–9. For the 18th century, see Frank E. Manuel, *The Eighteenth Century Confronts the Gods* (Cambridge, 1959).

42 For examples, see Chidester, *Savage Systems*, 195–6.

43 Oskar Lenz, *Skizzen aus Westafrika: Selbsterlebnisse*, 2nd ed. (Berlin, 1879), 199.

44 "An dem Tage nun, an welchem die Oganga ihre Tänze aufführten, trat die geschilderte Erscheinung geradezu epidemisch auf; es war als würde die ganze Bevölkerung vom Wahnsinn erfaßt. Die Leute waren in der furchtbarsten Aufregung und eine Menge Okandemänner stürzten wie wüthend in den Wald und kamen keuchend unter der Last eines schweren Baumes zurück ins Dorf, wo sie dann ohnmächtig zusammenbrachen. Unerklärlich war mir dabei die Erscheinung, daß die beiden Hände eines solchen vom Teufel Besessenen fest an den Baum gebunden waren, was ohne Zuthun eines Anderen kaum möglich ist; die Okande aber bestritten eine solche Beihilfe energisch und erklärten, Alles das sei nur das Werk des Teufels." Lenz, *Skizzen aus Westafrika*, 200.

45 "Wir sehen aus dem Vorstehenden, was für trostlose Zustände unter den Bantunegern existieren, wie ein herrschsüchtiges und ränkevolles Priesterkönigthum mit allen Mitteln bestrebt ist, das Volk in dem krassesten Aberglauben zu erhalten, wie erfolgreich diese Bestrebungen sind und wie die mehr als vierhundertjährige Bekanntschaft mit den Europäern nicht im Stande war, in günstigem Sinne ändernd und reformirend einzuwirken." Lenz, *Skizzen aus Westafrika*, 213.

46 For example, Lenz, *Skizzen aus Westafrika*, 179.

47 Lenz, Skizzen aus Westafrika, 213–4.

48 "Bei all den religiösen Anschauungen der Neger, wenn man überhaupt dieses Wort gebrauchen darf, blickt nirgends eine moralische Tendenz heraus; Krankheit, Tod, Mißernte, überhaupt jedes unglückliche Ereigniß, das sich die Leute nicht erklären können, wird einem bösen Wesen in die Schuhe geschoben, das dann versöhnt werden muß; oft aber nimmt dieser Kakodämon die Gestalt eines Menschen an, und es ist nun die Aufgabe der Mittelspersonen, der Oganga, der Priester und Zauberer, den Betreffenden ausfindig zu machen; dieser aber verfällt der grausamen Rache des Volkes. Der jahrhundertelange Verkehr mit den Weißen hat nicht genügt, den Negern diesen Glauben zu nehmen, und noch heute fallen jährlich viele Tausende als Opfer eines durch die Oganga gehaltenen und geförderten religiösen Humbugs." Lenz, *Skizzen aus Westafrika*, 181.

49 See, for example, Cameron, *Enchanted Europe*, 196–209; Sansi, "Der Fetisch," 47, 49. Gloria Flaherty, *Shamanism and the Eighteenth Century* (Princeton, 1992), 33–5.

50 Lenz, *Skizzen aus Westafrika*, 193.
51 Goddard, "The Devil in New France," 61–62.
52 A division between good and evil spirits was not inherent in ancient Greek thought. The term *daimon* could mean "divine spirit," "intermediary," or simply "divinity." "Kakon/kakos" could mean "ill," "bad," or "lowly." More research is needed, but it appears that a dualistic conception of the *kakodemon* in the sense of "evil spirit" as opposed to the *agathodemon* or "good spirit" only developed in Christian times.
53 Jacques Collin de Plancy, *Dictionnaire Infernal Ou Répertoire Universel* (Paris, 1844), 108.
54 Edward Geoffrey Parrinder, *African Traditional Religion* (London, 1974); John S. Mbiti, *African Religions & Philosophy* (London, 1969). For a contextualisation of this work, see Rosalind Shaw, "The Invention of 'African Traditional Religion'," *Religion* 20 (1990): 339–53.
55 Robert Martin Baum, *Shrines of the Slave Trade: Diola Religion and Society in Precolonial Senegambia* (New York, 1999), 3.

## Further Reading

Chidester, David. *Savage Systems: Colonialism and Comparative Religion in Southern Africa*. Charlottesville: University Press of Virginia, 1996.
Fabian, Johannes. *Out of Our Minds: Reason and Madness in the Exploration of Central Africa*. Berkeley: University of California Press, 2000.
Flaherty, Gloria. *Shamanism and the Eighteenth Century*. Princeton: Princeton University Press, 1992.
Manuel, Frank E. *The Eighteenth Century Confronts the Gods*. Cambridge: Harvard University Press, 1959.
Meyer, Birgit. *Translating the Devil: Religion and Modernity among the Ewe in Ghana*. Edinburgh: Edinburgh University Press, 1999.
Shaw, Rosalind. "The Invention of 'African Traditional Religion.'" *Religion* 20 (1990): 339–53.
Wimmler, Jutta. "The Devil's Beatings: African Dimensions of Early Modern Demonology in the Atlantic World." *Journal of Religion in Africa* 45 (2015): 249–78.

# 17

# "EVIL AND DESIRABLE"

## Gothic Inversion and the Satanic Monster in 18th- and 19th-Century Fiction

*Miranda Corcoran*

By the mid-17th century, Satan was on the move. While his first abode had been the church (and after the Reformation, churches) that had exerted so much power over Europe and its colonies, the advent of the Enlightenment saw him chased into new dwelling places. No longer a tangible, corrupting presence, the devil was reconceived—at least by some educated, urban segments of the population—as a symbol of human evil, an imaginative concept to be deployed in art, literature and rhetoric. As the historian Robert Muchembled explains, starting in the 1600s, the image of Satan, "which had previously been concentrated in the militant discourses of fiercely rival Churches, and imposed on the entire population from top to bottom of the social scale, shattered into innumerable fragments."[1] The devil was no longer a unified, monolithic entity, but instead came to mean different things to different people. For some, he remained the Prince of Darkness, a very real presence abroad in the world and capable of performing terrible acts of evil. For others, his power was increasingly limited to that of suggestion, his scope of influence reduced to the human mind.[2] In some of the new strains of philosophical scepticism that were emerging in the 1660s and 1670s, the role of the devil was further diminished: he became a mere symbol for the evil that exists in human beings.[3]

By the 18th and 19th centuries, Satan found himself firmly enmeshed in the "literary and artistic imagination," a space which, according to Muchembled, was "mild and oneiric, in contrast to that terrible part of the social imagination constituted by belief in the reality of the [diabolic] sabbath."[4] Yet, despite this comparative mildness, the literary and artistic devil could still be terrible, representing as he often did the darkest of human impulses. In this chapter, I argue that the devil's migration to the realm of literature manifests most explicitly in the figure of the Gothic monster, a being frequently linked to Satanic notions of transgression and inversion. In their capacity to evoke both terror and desire, repulsion and attraction, the Gothic monster reifies the very process through which the devil was transformed from a real-world threat to an imaginative symbol of human corruption.

DOI: 10.4324/9781003096603-18

In Gothic fiction, the transgressive power of the monster is frequently matched by the reader's desire for the taboo border crossings these beings frequently undertake. As Jerrold E. Hogle explains:

> Threats of and longings for gender-crossings, homosexuality or bisexuality, racial mixture, class fluidity, the child in the adult, timeless timeliness, and simultaneous evolution and devolution (especially after the middle of the nineteenth century): all these motifs as potentially evil *and* desirable, circulate through Gothic works across the whole history of the form, differing mostly in degrees of emphasis from example to example.[5]

In this chapter, I maintain that the intertwining of evil *and* desire is crucial to the construction of the 18th- and 19th-century monster as a fundamentally Satanic being. Whether incarnate in the form of an immortal being, a literal demon, or a human being whose inherent sadism renders them abhorrent, the Satanic monster is at once attractive—blithely traversing social, moral and sexual boundaries—and repulsive in their violence and cruelty. In Gothic fiction of the 18th and 19th centuries, the villain's monstrosity is often rendered explicit through feats of Satanic inversion, either through acts of abominable immorality or the moral reversal that attends the performance of a black mass. Yet, in such texts, diabolism is frequently framed as attractive, desirable and even erotic. In this way, the presence of Satanic elements in Gothic fiction functions to establish and articulate one of the key characteristics of the Gothic: an ambivalence grounded in the simultaneity of fear and desire.

This chapter focuses on a series of texts written in the 18th and 19th centuries, during a period when the Gothic was coalescing into a recognisable literary mode. Identifying examples of diabolic monstrosity in four novels—Matthew Lewis's *The Monk* (1796) Charles Maturin's *Melmoth the Wanderer* (1820), Lautréamont's *Les Chants de Maldoror* (1868) and JK Huysmans's *Là-Bas* (1891)—I argue that Satanism serves to position the monster in the imaginatively fertile space between terror and desire. Indeed, Satanic monsters frequently recall Jeffrey Jerome Cohen's assertion that the "simultaneous repulsion and attraction at the core of the monster's composition accounts greatly for its continued cultural popularity, for the fact that the monster seldom can be contained in a simple, binary dialectic [...]."[6] Moreover,

> We distrust and loathe the monster at the same time we envy its freedom, and perhaps its sublime despair. Through the body of the monster fantasies of aggression, domination, and inversion are allowed safe expression in a clearly delimited and permanently liminal space.[7]

The Satanic monster, precisely because of its engagement with malefic rituals and acts of moral inversion, engenders fantasies of violence and transgression while also, by virtue of its association with the diabolical, ensuring that such fantasies are understood as evil and objectionable.

## Imagining the Devil: From the Enlightenment to the Gothic Novel

As noted in the introduction, the philosophical and scientific rationalism of the Enlightenment prompted a shift in how Christian doctrine was perceived, and the devil transformed from a real figure, with a tangible presence in our material world, into a mere concept, an idea. Although this reconfiguration of the devil was largely an elite phenomenon, with many segments of the population retaining a powerful conception of a literal devil, Satan appeared, with increasing frequency, in literary and artistic contexts ostensibly removed from his original theological function. Muchembled elucidates how "the devil was not suddenly banished from the Western imagination in the mid-seventeenth century" but instead "lost his importance, slowly almost imperceptibly."[8] Sarah Bartels points out that Satan's waning influence was the result of a wide array of social, religious and philosophical factors. The animating force of the Reformation and its attendant religious conflict dissipated while previously entrenched dogmas were displaced by new intellectual paradigms.[9] In 1691, the Dutch minister and theologian Balthasar Bekker published a work entitled *The Enchanted World*. Heavily influence by Cartesian philosophy, Bekker claimed that it was "logically impossible for a spiritual entity like the angel of evil to exert any tangible influence on the kingdom of this world."[10] No longer able to act upon material reality, the devil began to be perceived as an infinitely less threatening figure and thus found himself reimagined by some as a literary figure: "disconnected from his theological roots and reduced to an amorphous symbol which could signify almost anything."[11]

Much has been written about the appropriation of Satanic iconography by Romantic poets in the latter part of the 18th century and early 19th century. Notably, Peter A. Schock has demonstrated how, informed by John Milton's *Paradise Lost* (1667), poets such as Blake, Byron and Shelley reimagined Satan in terms of "rebellion, resistance, defiance, temptation, and tyranny."[12] For many associated with Romanticism, Satan became a symbol of liberty, a harbinger of rationality whose temptation of Eve in the Garden of Eden bestowed divine knowledge of good and evil upon humanity. Crucially, for Ruben Van Luijk, the Romantics, by expressing "sympathy with the fallen angel," ultimately "resurrected him from the burial he had been given by Enlightenment rationalism."[13] Alongside, and sometimes intersecting with, the Romantic rehabilitation of Satan, the diabolical also lent itself to a thoroughly Gothic inversion of morality, allowing works produced in this literary mode to frame monstrosity as simultaneously desirable and frightening. In this way, while the devil may have been transformed into a literary symbol by the force of Enlightenment rationalism, his banishment to the literary realm did not signify the uncontested triumph of reason. By articulating the coincidence of terror and desire, the Satanic also functioned, like the Gothic mode itself, to counteract the teleological myth of human progress through what Cleo Cameron terms an "extreme oppositional stance to the hegemonic currency of Enlightenment ideas."[14]

## The Black Mass: Inverting the Age of Reason

One of the most explicit literary manifestations of Satanic monstrosity as an oppositional force, counteracting Enlightenment positivism, is the black mass. Although frequently described in theological and legal texts on witchcraft, the literary treatment of the black mass or the witches' sabbath has been infinitely more complex. In what is perhaps the most well-known 19th-century literary rendering of the devil, Goethe's *Faust* (1808–1832), the black mass is conspicuously absent. While Faust and the devil Mephistopheles attend the witches' Walpurgisnacht celebrations atop the Brocken, they are never depicted reaching the summit of the mountain, where Satan is said to be enthroned. Drafts and fragments of unfinished scenes indicate that one possible scenario might have involved a Satanic ceremony with the devil enthroned as "the all-powerful black goat."[15] In this version of the Walpurgisnacht scene, the devil would have presided over a gathering similar to the perverse rite of the black mass, complete with the notorious *osculum infame*, or shameful kiss.[16] However, these fragmentary sketches never made it into the completed play. Ehrhard Bahr suggests that the excision of these scenes was an act of "self-censorship," with Goethe having been, apparently, concerned about the potential for obscenity inherent in the black mass.[17] Moreover, as noted below, the Black Mass signifies an inversion of good and evil, and as Bahr notes, Goethe seems to have opposed strict dualisms, instead framing good and evil as part of a single whole.[18] After all, the most famous line in the play describes Mephistopheles as "a part of that same power that would/Forever work for evil, yet forever creates good."[19] Although Goethe's opus does not feature the black mass, in Gothic and generically affiliated texts of the 18th and 19th centuries, the black mass is a central motif, embodying notions of inversion as evil takes the place of good and the profane supplants the sacred. Likewise, while the black mass reflects the perfidy of the Satanic Gothic monster, it also inverts the values of modernity, extolling darkness and degeneration and rejecting rationality and progress. In Lewis's *The Monk* and Huysmans's *Là-Bas*, in particular, the black mass evokes the chaos and irrationality of a premodern world, while at the same time framing the diabolic figures who engage in these perverse performances as both repulsive and intriguing.

According to Massimo Introvigne, the black mass is not simply a diabolical ceremony, but rather an intentional upending of Christian, specifically Catholic, ritual. For Introvigne, these diabolic rites are best understood as "an 'inverted' Roman Catholic Mass in which, by appropriately changing the formula, Satan is worshipped and Jesus Christ is cursed."[20] Indeed, the true nature of the black mass is perhaps best encapsulated by the French term employed to describe the ritual: the "contre-messe," or "counter-mass." Not simply a parody of the Catholic mass, the black mass serves as what Walter Stephens describes as a "countersacrament," "identical in type, but opposite in orientation, to the power of the sacraments."[21] There is, in Western European thought, a long history of anxious fantasies about various "sinister" groups inverting the spiritual dynamics of the mass for their own insidious purposes. During the Middle Ages "when the hallowedness of the Mass and the host was further enhanced, stories about deliberate desecration began to circulate as well."[22] Thus, a range of cultural others, from heretical Christian sects to Jews, and later, witches, were imagined to gather under cover of night to desecrate the eucharist and pervert Catholicism's most sacred rites.

As the Middle Ages gave way to the earliest stirrings of modernity, such fantasies became more elaborate. It is during the early modern period that the Satanic witch, a malefic magician who has entered into a pact with the devil, first emerges as a coherent cultural archetype.[23] At this time, earlier antisemitic conspiracies, as well as nightmarish visions of heretical blasphemies, coalesced into the image of the witches' sabbath. Here, the black mass, as it is popularly conceived of, begins to accrue its most iconic trappings:

In these descriptions, we encounter parodies of the Mass with black candles and a black host in a black chalice; aspersions using the devil's or witches urine instead of holy water; a satanic book of liturgy bound in black leather; Satan preaching like a priest on the virtues of vice.[24]

A dark reflection of Catholic worship, theologians and demonologists posited that the black mass pivoted around the macabre centrepiece of stolen hosts, consecrated to Lucifer rather than to Christ. Even more disturbingly, Stephens recounts how, in some cases, the bodies of dead children were believed to supplant the Eucharist as the object of devotion. In Johannes Nider's *Formicarius* (1475), one of the first printed texts describing the phenomenon of Satanic witchcraft, the author reports on an initiation rite that employs the bodies of disinterred infants in place of the host. According to one accused witch interrogated by a local official, the devil's acolytes would "secretly steal [babies] from their graves and cook them in a cauldron until the whole flesh comes away from the bones and becomes a soup that may easily be drunk."[25] The broth would, apparently, confer power and wisdom on those who partook of it. Crucially, in this context the ingestion of the flesh of infants functions as a perverse counterpoint to the Catholic Eucharist, a cannibalistic communion that had a transcendent effect on the faithful. As Stephens explains, the construction of Satanic cannibalism as a perversion of the communion rite is also evinced by the tendency of Medieval mystics to imagine the eucharistic host as an infant, sometimes even receiving "ecstatic visions of infants during communion."[26] In this way, the black mass functions according to a "precise logic of reversal, whereby the effects of the Catholic sacraments are transformed into equally strong but opposite effects under the devil's control."[27]

Notions of inversion and references to the black mass are central to the construction and articulation of monstrosity in Lewis's *The Monk*. Indeed, a number of key sequences in the novel reflect the inverted logic of the black mass. Notably, these scenes are employed to underscore the evil capabilities of the corrupted monk Ambrosio and his lover, the diabolical magician/demon Matilda. In one of the novel's most sensational scenes Matilda summons Lucifer to appear before her. As part of the ritual to invoke the fallen angel, Matilda draws a circle around herself and another one around Ambrosio, "then taking a small phial from the basket, poured a few drops upon the ground before her."[28] Here, the sorceress appears to invert the Catholic practice of consecrating sacred spaces with holy water. Matilda then goes on to produce a number of items from a basket, including "three human fingers"—perhaps a reference to the cannibalism traditionally held to form part of the witches sabbath—and an *Agnus Dei*—a term which translates as "Lamb of God" and in this context refers to the eucharist.[29] Like the early modern witches described in *Formicarius* and the diabolical adherents believed to worship at medieval black masses, Matilda does not honour the host, but instead desecrates it: "She threw them all into the flames which burned before her, and they were instantly consumed."[30]

In his feminist analysis of *The Monk*, Per Faxneld reads Matilda's ritual as a spectacle of inversion. After consigning the host to the flames, Matilda is described as being "seized with an excess of delirium; she tore her hair, beat her bosom, used the most frantic gestures, and drawing the poignard from her girdle plunged it into her left arm."[31] According to Faxneld, Matilda's power, as demonstrated in this passage is "a female power, a threatening hysterical ecstasy."[32] This power is not only framed as ecstasy that exists "in opposition to the calm prayers of the monk," but it can also be read as a "Satanic parody of the famous ecstasies of the female saints."[33] Yet, while Matilda's devilish abilities are undeniably repulsive, dependent as they are on murder, dismemberment and the abuse of the host, they are also enticing.

For much of the early modern period, witches were understood as enslaved to the devil. Signing away her soul in a demonic pact, the early modern witch, ordinarily gendered female, possessed no power of her own but was enabled to harm others and perform wonders only through the aid the devil. Conversely, Matilda is explicit in her assertion that she does not serve the devil, rather she commands his demonic legions:

"I saw a daemon obedient to my orders, I saw him trembling at my frown, and found that instead of selling my soul to a master, my courage had purchased for myself a slave."[34] While Matilda is ultimately revealed to be demon, cleverly assuming human guise to manipulate Ambrosio, she is portrayed "for all but a few pages of the novel as a woman [...] who gains her authority and power by consorting with the powers of darkness."[35] In this way, Matilda's Satanism enables the reader to approach the character as an archetypal Gothic monster. Occupying a liminal position between human and devil, Matilda is both alluring and repulsive. Her Satanic power, her assertive nature and knowledge of occult rites, renders her an attractive figure, as does her frequent manifestation in the form of a sexually desirable woman. Concomitantly, her blasphemous perversion of Christian ritual suggests that the reader should approach her cautiously, fearing and condemning her diabolical practices. The ambivalence of Matilda's characterisation ensures that *The Monk* remains, in Faxneld's words, "another example of how Gothic novels are very often permeated with a strange enthusiasm for its villains and their antisocial, rebellious deeds."[36]

In as much as Matilda's Satanic power causes us to hesitate between desire and horror, so too does it suggest an ambiguous, even transgressive approach to gender and sexuality. According to Steven Blakemore, Lewis's complex treatment of gender and sexual desire—his creation of characters who repeatedly blur the lines between male and female, homosexual and heterosexual—functions as the linguistic "equivalent of a Black Mass, inverting and subverting the traditional roles of religion and sex."[37] Lewis's inversion of traditional sex and gender roles further aligns his principal villain-protagonists, Ambrosio and Matilda, with the figure of the monster. Indeed, returning to Cohen's influential thesis, a defining feature of the monster is its "ontological liminality."[38] The monster is dangerous because it is "a form suspended between forms that threatens to smash distinctions."[39] In a similar way, Ambrosio and Matilda move back and forth between gender identities and sexual categories, troubling the distinction between masculine and feminine, active and passive, homosexual and heterosexual.

This inversion of gender and sex roles begins early in the novel, as Ambrosio is immediately "situated in a 'feminine' position" through a myriad of allusions to his "innocence" and "virtue."[40] When Antonia, the monk's future object of desire, first glimpses him in the cathedral, her aunt explains that Ambrosio is "so strict an observer of chastity, that he knows not on what constitutes the difference of man and woman."[41] Conversely, Matilda first appears to Ambrosio in the guise of a beautiful young man, a novice named Rosario. The fact that Matilda is ultimately revealed to be "a demon disguised as a woman in the guise of a man" further underscores the instability of gender identity within the novel.[42] Sexuality is also framed as fluid and ever shifting. Although Ambrosio initially desires only women—Antonia and Matilda, albeit with the latter occasionally disguised as man—he later gazes with "delight and wonder" upon the figure of Lucifer, who appears as beautiful, naked young man with "silken locks" and "two crimson wings."[43] In all of these passages, categories associated with gender, sex and sexuality shift in unexpected ways, undermining the supposed naturalness or fixity of these positions. Because such indeterminacy is based upon the inversion of sex/gender norms, Blakemore argues that it is paralleled by the perverse subversion of Catholic dogma that characterises the novel's Satanic ceremonies.[44] Just as the black mass reappropriates and reverses Christian symbology, so too does Lewis upend binary constructions of gender and sex, inverting the meaning of masculine and feminine, homosexual and heterosexual.

In *The Monk*, the black mass can be said to function as a metonym for the terror and pleasure that comes from crossing boundaries, whether those are the borders that map the edges of acceptable morality, gender presentation or sexual desire. Similarly, in JK Huysmans's *Là-Bas*, the black mass embodies a sexual and social transgression that is at once pleasurable and repulsive, while also signifying an irrational impulse that inverts the values of modernity. Huysmans's novel is one of the canonical texts of *fin-de-siècle* Decadent literature. Encompassing writers such as Jules Barbey d'Aurevilly, Rachilde, Charles Baudelaire, Arthur Rimbaud, Paul Verlaine, as well as artists like Félicien Rops, Gustave Moreau and Aubrey Beardsley, the Decadent movement revered corruption, excess and artificiality. As Asti Hustvedt illuminates, the word "decadence," from the Latin *decadere* ("to fall away from"), was widely used in late 19th-century France to condemn a "a diseased culture."[45] Yet, while some condemned what they saw as a society on the verge of collapse, others embraced decadence, decay and disease:

> In decadent literature sickness is preferable to health, not only because sickness was regarded as more interesting, but because sickness was construed as subversive, as a threat to the very fabric of society. By embracing the marginal, the unhealthy, and the deviant, the decadents attacked bourgeois life, which they perceived as the chief enemy of art.[46]

As such, while Decadence is not identical to the Gothic, it frequently overlaps and intersects with that mode via their shared preoccupation with themes of transgression and degeneration.

*Là-Bas* centres on the experiences of Durtal, a consummate Decadent, who, weary of monotonous 19th-century bourgeois life, spends his time composing a biography of the alleged serial killer and occultist Gilles de Rais. Durtal also engages in a frensied search for proof that black masses are still practised in the modern, cosmopolitan Paris of the *fin-de-siècle*. In the first half of the novel, Durtal becomes obsessed with "the terrible Canon Docre," a wicked priest who "conjures up the devil," "feeds white mice on hosts which he has himself consecrated" and "has had the image of Christ tattooed on the soles of his feet so that he may always be treading on the Saviour."[47] Moreover, Docre is rumoured to celebrate the black mass "with men and women of the vilest kind," and his perfidy is such that Durtal dubs the priest "a modern Gilles de Rais."[48] After meeting the enigmatic and sinister Madame Chantelouve, Durtal finally has the chance to witness a modern-day black mass, which Huysman portrays as a diabolical inversion of the Catholic rite.

A blasphemous spectacle of sexual perversion, the mass features choirboys clad in red, a corrupted former nun and the canon himself "wearing a scarlet bonnet from which two buffalo horns covered in red cloth protruded."[49] Moreover, Durtal observes that Docre is naked beneath his robe: "The white flesh, bulging over the suspenders fastened just below the knee and holding up his black socks, was plainly visible."[50] At the same time, the canon's garments appear as a Satanic version of traditional priestly dress:

> The chasuble was the same shape and size as an ordinary chasuble but was dark red, the colour of dried blood, and in the middle of a triangle around which was an embroidered border of colchicum, savin, sorrel and spurge, was the figure of a black billy-goat showing off his horns.[51]

Above the altar, in place of the humble image of Christ the Saviour, hangs a grotesque figure of Jesus: "He was naked, and where a loincloth should have covered his flanks, a virile member projected from a bush of horsehair."[52] Echoing the Romantic Satanists who found in Lucifer a symbol of rebellion, liberation and the triumph of knowledge, Docre and his acolytes position Satan as the inverse of bourgeois Christian values. In the course of his sermon, Docre venerates the devil as "Lord of Misrule, Dispenser of the Wages of Sin, Master of Venalities and Vices! [...] God of logic and reason [...] champion of the poor, and the staff of the vanquished."[53] At the same time, the sacred paraphernalia of the Catholic Church is mocked and debased:

> Choirboys sprinkled holy water over the pontiff's naked belly and member, women threw themselves on the consecrated wafers and, grovelling in the dust before the altar, fought over the soggy particles, cramming this divine ordure into their mouths. Another woman, straddling a crucifix, laughed frantically [...].[54]

Moments later, the ceremony is transformed into an orgy that Huysmans compares to "padded cells in a madhouse," as "the choirboys coupled with men" and a woman "mounted the altar with her skirt tied around her neck, grasping the phallus of Christ with one hand and holding a chalice between her naked legs with the other."[55]

Huysman's vision of the black mass, like medieval and early modern images of heretical rites, pivots on acts of inversion: the devil rather than Christ is venerated, the Host is abused rather than revered, base sexuality supersedes divine spirituality. Yet while this up-ending of bourgeois religion and morality is initially a source of fascination for Durtal, he also finds himself repulsed by the Satanic rituals he encounters in the company of Madame Chantelouve. Throughout much of the novel, Durtal is preoccupied with the black mass precisely because he views the rite as a tangible link to the Middle Ages, a survival from a more mystical, spiritual age. Elizabeth Emery explains that Huysmans himself viewed the medieval period as marvellous epoch, championing the revival of medieval art, architecture, mysticism and music.[56] In contrast to the crass consumerism and sterile rationality of *fin-de-siècle* Paris, the Middle Ages pulsed with magic and irrational wonder. Just as the Gothic mode itself hinged upon a revival of the ornate, chaotic, even grotesque, aesthetics of the Middle Ages, so too does Huysmans employ Durtal's fictive quest for an authentic black mass as a means to stress the need for contemporary France to recreate or reexperience "the lost soul of the Middle Ages."[57] It is perhaps for this reason that Durtal is ultimately repulsed by his encounter with modern Satanism.

The dirty, debauched rite he witnesses seems to have little in common with the ecstatic Sabbaths of the past. Clearly influenced by historical studies such as Jules Michelet's *La Sorcière* (1862) and Jules Bois's *Le Satanisme et la magie* (1895), Durtal's ideal Satanism is a rollicking, carnivalesque affair. It is a realm far outside the bounds of everyday existence where the taboos are violated and magic abounds.[58] In Bois's Satanism, the categories that structure mundane reality collapse in upon themselves as witches ride goats and humans transform into animals. However, while Docre's rite is certainly an ecstatic commingling of flesh, it lacks the carnivalesque spirit and naïve mysticism described by Michelet and Bois. For Michelet, Satanic sabbaths were a form of rebellion, as rural peasants gathered by night in defiance of both the aristocracy and the Church: "Human brotherhood, defiance towards the Christian heaven, denatured cult of divine nature—that is the meaning of the *Black Mass*."[59] Conversely, Docre's black mass consists of phlegmatic aesthetes and bored intellectuals for whom Satanism offers an amusing diversion from the tedium of bourgeois life.

Huysmans's Satanism lacks the overt supernaturalism of the Sabbaths described by Michelet and Bois. Van Luijk observes that Huysmans's black mass does not include "a real-life appearance of the devil," and as such his vision of Satanism is "essentially a *human* affair, an activity *about* Satan, and not *by* Satan."[60] It is devoid of the wonder associated with the medieval black mass. devil worship is transformed, rather mundanely, into what Durtal's friend Des Hermies designates "a proper little harem of hystero-epileptics and erotomaniacs."[61] The diabolists who make up Docre's congregations are framed, in modern, rationalistic terms as psychologically disturbed hysterics. All traces of magic are banished by the cold mundanity of modern science. As Robert Ziegler explains in his study of occultism in *fin-de-siècle* France, the "ignominy of contemporary devil worship," which "enacts only the banality of evil," is, for Durtal, merely a hollow spectre of medieval Satanism.[62] Huysmans's black mass is, much like Lewis's treatment of Satanic rites, profoundly ambivalent. Durtal craves admission to a Satanic ceremony, fantasising about the transgressive power of such a performance, yet once he experiences the inverted mass, he is disgusted by its base materiality. At once alluring and repulsive, the black mass encapsulates the fundamental ambiguity of the Gothic, the uncertain affect that resides at the heart of the genre.

### The Satanic Monster as a Gothic Hero-Villain

Fred Botting argues that "Gothic texts operate ambivalently," drawing attention to the often-tenuous borders that separate pleasure from terror, moral from immoral, natural from unnatural.[63] Similarly, in Cohen's delineation of the monster, these creatures occupy an ambiguous space: "monsters serve as secondary bodies through which the possibilities of other genders, other sexual practices, and other social customs can be explored [...] This corporeal fluidity, this simultaneity of anxiety and desire, ensures that the monster will always dangerously entice."[64] Elaborating on this notion of ambivalence, this section explores how the ambiguity of the Satanic monster, like that of the black mass, is framed as both repulsive and attractive. In Gothic works centred on Satanic figures, such ambivalence is often intimately bound up with the diabolical monster's capacity to invert norms and collapse binary modes of being.

The eponymous hero-villain of Charles Maturin's *Melmoth the Wanderer* has much in common with the myriad of earlier and contemporary literary figures who exchanged their immortal soul for power, knowledge or longevity. Echoing narrative conventions found in both Marlowe's and Goethe's versions of the Faust myth, as well as in its folkloric antecedents *Melmoth the Wanderer* centres on a tragic, rootless protagonist whose thirst for knowledge leads him to damnation.[65] Through his mastery of alchemy and dark magic, Melmoth obtains "from the enemy of souls a range of existence beyond the period allotted to mortality," as well as the ability to manipulate the laws of time and space.[66] Yet, where other hubristic magicians are merely aligned with the devil, Melmoth is frequently conflated with the Prince of Darkness and, as such, becomes indistinguishable from his supposed master. For instance, while Goethe's Faust and the demon Mephistopheles are closely intertwined throughout the play, they are clearly distinct beings. However, as Per Faxneld observes, "Melmoth is not merely the devil's emissary and apologist. He himself displays many characteristics of the devil."[67]

When Melmoth first visits his lover Immalee (later renamed Isidora) in her remote island home, we are told that "he experienced a sensation like that of his master when he visited paradise."[68] As Melmoth educates Immalee about the "civilised" world and its various religious factions, the dissolution of her innocence is compared to that of Eve, tempted by Satan to eat the forbidden fruit: "She had, indeed, tasted of the tree of knowledge, and her eyes were opened, but the fruit was bitter to her taste."[69] Indeed, as Joseph Lew notes, Melmoth "goes one-up on Satan," corrupting both Immalee's island paradise and, later, the idyllic garden of her family home once she is returned to her native Spain.[70] Similarly, when Immalee's father is warned about Melmoth's intentions towards his daughter, he is told that "there is an eye fixed on her, and its fascination is more deadly than that fabled of the snake!."[71] Melmoth is repeatedly described using language that frames him not simply as a servant of the devil, but as his reflection. Throughout the novel, Melmoth is described as "fiend," "foe" and "enemy," epithets usually reserved for the Dark Lord himself. So indistinct are the boundaries separating Melmoth and his Satanic master that at least one contemporary reviewer understood them to be one and the same. J.W. Croker, in his 1821 piece for the *Quarterly Review*, interpreted Melmoth as Satan himself, excoriating the novel for allowing the devil to emerge as its hero.[72]

As a character, Melmoth is often associated with images of inversion and perverse morality that suggest the antithetical logic of the black mass. In her study of consumption in *Melmoth the Wanderer*, Christina Morin explains that "depictions of cannibalism, both literal and metaphoric, prove pervasive," and Melmoth's curse can be understood as essentially cannibalistic in nature.[73] Haunting prison cells, asylums and gallows, Melmoth searches endlessly for an individual desperate enough to take his place. Morin notes that

> Melmoth himself, with his desire for a replacement, a sacrificial victim to assume the onus of his long-ago crime, essentially seeks to cannibalise those he tempts. For him, these helpless individuals are simply commodities to be bought, sold, and traded for his benefit.[74]

Melmoth is associated throughout the novel with one of the key features of the Black Mass, and the epitome of its Satanic inversion, the cannibal feast. In one of the novel's many interlocking episodes, "The Lover's Tale," Melmoth is described as "Seeking whom he might devour."[75] This line is borrowed from the New Testament's First Epistle of Peter, where the reader is warned to "Be sober, be vigilant; because your adversary the devil, as a roaring lion, walketh about, seeking whom he may devour" (1 Pt. 5.8). While those familiar with this passage might connect Melmoth once again to the figure of Satan, the decontextualised presentation of the word "devour" suggests that Maturin's diabolical hero possesses an inherently cannibalistic appetite. Beyond the figure of Melmoth himself, cannibalism is linked throughout the novel to the inversion of morality and the upending of accepted societal norms. In one of the novel's most notorious incidents, two lovers imprisoned at the behest of the Spanish Inquisition apparently resort to cannibalism in the dark desperation of their subterranean dungeon: "I heard the shriek of the wretched female,—her lover, in the agony of hunger; had fastened his teeth in her shoulder;—that bosom on which he had so often luxuriated, became a meal to him now."[76] Although when the door is unbarred, the young woman is discovered intact and with only a "slight scar on her shoulder," the language of reversal employed in this passage maps the movement of desire from lust to hunger.[77]

Such a perversion of morality is emblematic of the inverted logic of the black mass. For David Frankfurter, it is precisely this reversal of entrenched values that defines Satanic rites and sabbaths: "Everything is turned upside down: they eat what we find disgusting, they mock what we find sacred, they expose what we do in private, they abuse what we protect, they congregate when we stay at home."[78] In Frankfurter's schema, evil becomes recognisable as such through its inversion of familiar moral structures. Rather than being understood as fundamentally alien, evil forces—such as witches and Satanists—operate through systems of reversal. Evil is understood in this context as "a function of inversion, not incomprehensibility."[79]

In *Melmoth the Wanderer*, the titular character frequently engages in performances of spectacular inversion that seek to recontextualise sacred imagery and Christian values in a thoroughly diabolical manner. When Melmoth marries Immalee, the ceremony does not follow the Catholic ritual treasured by the bride but is instead constructed as a dark mirror of the Christian church wedding. The service takes place in a decrepit chapel where the window is shattered, "the stained glass of its compartments, broken and discoloured."[80] No longer a pristine spiritual place, nature attempts to reclaim the ruined church: "Ivy and moss darkened the fragments of glass and clung around the clustered pillars. Beneath were the remains of an altar and crucifix."[81] Just as witches and devil worshippers are believed to be active by night rather than by day, so too does the marriage of Melmoth and Immalee take place under cover of darkness.[82] Indeed, when the moon that provides their only light slips behind a cloud "everything was enveloped in a darkness so profound" that the young bride "did not recognise the figure of Melmoth till her hand was clasped in his."[83] More disturbing still, the hand that unites them is described as being "as *cold as that of death*," and it is later revealed that the priest who conducted the ceremony had died the night before.[84] In this way, the fundamental symbolism of the Catholic wedding service is turned on its head. Disconnected from its original connotations of life and fecundity, Melmoth and Immalee's marriage is signalled by darkness, ruin and necromancy.

In as much as the figure of Melmoth is associated with the perverse power of the black mass and Satanic inversion, he nevertheless remains an essentially alluring character. In his 1968 exploration of the Gothic novel's paradoxical nature, Leven M. Dawson draws attention to the dual nature of the Gothic, or Byronic, hero. Referencing Lowry Nelson's "Night Thoughts on the Gothic Novel," Dawson emphasises the Gothic "hero-villain's" ability to embody "pervasive paradoxical confusion of conventional good and evil basic to Gothic literature."[85] Not only does Melmoth's essential pathos—his eternal wandering, his endless loneliness, his tragic love for Immalee—render him essentially sympathetic, despite his infernal allegiance, but even his more diabolical facets emerge as intriguing, even attractive. His capacity to violate natural laws, traversing the boundaries of time and space with ease, imbues Melmoth with an enviable, even desirable, power, while his frequent inversion of Christian morality allows the reader to fantasise such transgression alongside him.

In a similar vein, early modern theological writings on the witches sabbath repeatedly demonstrate how "the wholesale inversion of cultural norms carries an intrinsic excitement, which compounds both the overall picture of the monstrous and the prurience of contemplating it."[86]

During the medieval and early modern periods, demons often embodied both hellish monstrosity and repressed sexual desire. For the clergy and religious writers of the period,

> The demonic host also reveals itself as a repository of repressed instincts in its capacity as a dark surrogate for humanity. As frequent instigators of sin, especially sexual sin, the demons were constantly available to Christendom at large, and the clergy in particular, as repressed "doubles."[87]

Meditating on the sexual licence of demons—the orgiastic excess of the sabbath, the seductive power of the incubus—good Christians were able to experience a frisson of fear coupled with a taboo sense of arousal. However, because contemplation of demonic forces was couched in a language of condemnation, the pleasure it afforded always seemed within the boundaries of morality. In this way, just as the Gothic novel depends upon the "interaction, and almost equation, of terror and beauty," so too was the contemplation of the Satanic defined by both pleasure and repulsion.[88]

The inversion of morality and its power to both enthral and disgust also manifests in another Satanic villain-hero of the 19th century, Lautréamont's vile Maldoror. Published (in part) in 1868, *Les Chants de Maldoror* is a generically unstable text: part poetry, part novel, it is a literary hybrid that would, through its experimental form, go on to exert an immense influence over 20th-century surrealism. Described by Australian censors as an "extraordinary work of Satanic obscenity," the book incorporates elements of Gothicism, Decadence and Romantic Satanism.[89] While little is known about the life of Isidore Ducasse, the author who employed the pen name Comte de Lautréamont and died at the age of 24, he has been described posthumously as a "Satanist, a rebel against the order of the world."[90] Written in a style that anticipates modernist stream of consciousness, the novel centres on the eponymous Maldoror, a sadistic, diabolical figure whose identity often overlaps with that of the book's first-person narrator. Over the course of the novel's six parts, Maldoror engages in murder, mutilation, sexual violence and bestiality. A misotheist, he establishes himself as the enemy of God, framed in the *Les Chants* as a philandering, cannibalistic monster. Paul Knight observes that in its framing of Maldoror as a Satanic figure, *Les Chants* possesses numerous parallels with *Melmoth the Wanderer*. Knight goes on to explain that while Melmoth is a "tragic illustration of the Faustian urge," Maldoror is "the blasphemous, remorseless opponent of God and man."[91] Nevertheless, the characters mirror each other in their affinity for perversion and their capacity to collapse the boundaries between good and evil, life and death.

Inversion is a recurring motif throughout *Les Chants*, as both the narrator and the protagonist delight in violating deeply entrenched taboos. Knight observes how this inversion exists in the novel even at a linguistic level. The book opens with a passage warning the reader to "turn on your heels and go back before penetrating further into such an uncharted, perilous wasteland."[92] Knight shows how this passage is "an *inversion* of the rhetorical topos of affected modesty, where the author traditionally begs the reader's indulgence."[93] In other places, Lautréamont empowers his protagonist to commit brutal acts of cannibalism, torture and infanticide which, in their affront to ingrained systems of morality, are redolent of the black mass. In one early passage, the narrator (possibly also Maldoror himself) muses on the pleasure he takes (or would take) in dragging a child from his bed, "dig[ging] one's long nails into his soft breast" and "drink[ing] his blood as one licks his wounds."[94] Here, and throughout the novel, Maldoror/the narrator takes pleasure in the murder, even consumption, of children. Just as witches and Satanists allegedly cannibalised the flesh of infants, despoiling the ultimate symbol of innocence, at their sabbaths and black masses, so too does Lautréamont's repugnant anti-hero destroy or consume children in order to attack what is good and pure. Like the sabbath or black mass described by Frankfurter, Maldoror's litany of transgressions, recounted in an almost adulatory tone by the narrator, "conjures an entire monstrous realm [...] set apart from ours, where the disgusting is prized and the horrific celebrated."[95]

Lautréamont's preoccupation with inversion and transgression also manifests in his propensity to efface the boundaries that separate human from animal, divine from profane. Mapping the influence of the Marquis De Sade on Lautréamont's monstrous protagonist, Joshua D. Gonsalves argues that "Lautréamont loves, like Sade, to incarnate contradiction—to be simultaneously victim and executioner, virgin and villain, God and Satan, animal and human."[96] In one of the novel's most puzzling and notorious episodes, Maldoror copulates with a female shark:

> When they are three yards apart they suddenly and spontaneously fall upon one another like two lovers and embrace with dignity and gratitude, clasping each other as tenderly as brother and sister. Carnal desire follows this demonstration of friendship. Two sinewy thighs press tightly against the monster's flesh, like two leeches; and arms and fins are clasped around the beloved object, while their throats and breasts soon form one glaucous mass amid the exhalations of sea-weed [...] with the foaming waves for marriage bed [...].[97]

Though immediately striking for its depiction of Maldoror's zoophilia, the passage also alludes to an array of other perversions, including incest, as the pair clasp "each other as tenderly as brother and sister." Yet, alongside its embrace of taboo sexuality, the shark incident also evokes one of Lautréamont's primary thematic concerns, the collapse of the border separating human from animal, civilisation from nature.

In another, equally disturbing passage, the narrator/Maldoror describes his disease-ridden body, elaborately detailing how his form has degenerated into a grotesque mesh of human and animal life, a fusion of organic and inorganic matter:

> Sitting on shapeless piece of furniture, I have not moved my limbs for four centuries. My feet have taken root in the ground [...] A family of toads has taken residence in my left armpit and, when one of them moves, it tickles [...] In my right armpit is a chameleon which is perpetually chasing them, to avoid starving to death [...] An evil snake has eaten my verge and taken its place; the filthy creature has made me a eunuch [...] My anus has been penetrated by a crab; encouraged by my sluggishness, he guards the entrance with his pincers, and causes me a lot of pain [...] Do not speak of my spinal column, as it is a sword [...].[98]

A transgressive hybrid, the narrator/Maldoror dismantles the conceptual categories that give meaning to our experience. He is at once living and dead, rotting and flourishing, man and animal, human and object. Moreover, the narrator/Maldoror explains that he has vowed to "live disease-ridden and motionless until I had conquered the Creator."[99] By transforming himself into this seething abomination, the narrator/Maldoror positions himself in opposition to God and all that he has created. He takes God's creatures, the world that he has made for the enjoyment of humanity, and reconfigures them as a boundless, perverse monstrosity.

At the same time, however, while the narrator/Maldoror views himself as the opponent of God, his image of the deity is not that of a good or loving God. Rather, his vision of God, whom he calls the Creator, is that of a clawed, devouring beast. Aligning God with his own cannibalistic impulses, as well as the iconography of the black mass, the narrator/Maldoror imagines the Christian God engaging in vile necrophagy:

> He was holding in his hand the rotten body of a dead man, carrying it in turn from his eyes to his nose and from his nose to his mouth; and once it reached his mouth one can guess what he did with it.[100]

This image of the Creator devouring the flesh of the dead recalls the medieval sabbatic feasts described by the historian and occult writer Jules Bois, whose visions of the black mass pivot on the volition of the "taboos normally structuring a world of antinomy and separation."[101] In Bois's account of the Sabbath, "corpses are disinterred from their resting places in graveyards, and engage, not in the coupling of Decadent Luciferianism, but in carrion banquets consecrating incest and necrophagy."[102] In Lautréamont's nightmarish fictional realm, not only does his villain-protagonist engage in transgressive acts of violence, torture and cannibalism, but so too does the God who reigns over that world.

In as much as Maldoror is repulsive, perverse and morally repugnant, his transgressions enable the reader—in the grand tradition of Gothic fiction—to fantasise about the crossing of moral boundaries. As Fred Botting elucidates:

> Desire is often heightened and given more intense significance due to the weight of the initial sanction. Transgression, too, brings out the importance of limits in the act of exceeding them: one becomes more keenly aware of boundaries and taboos, both because of their existence and the consequences of breaking them.[103]

*Les Chants* brings cultural taboos and boundaries into sharp relief by dramatising their capacity to be violated, while also empowering the reader to take a vicarious pleasure in shattering those same taboos. At the same time, Lautréamont appears to situate himself within the tradition of Romantic Satanism, framing his work as inherently philosophical, even moral. In a letter to his publisher, Lautréamont not only compares his work to that of Byron and Milton, but also claims that *Les Chants*, like all sublime literature, sings of "despair only to cast down the reader and make him desire good as the remedy."[104] Whether this claim is sincere or merely a consideration of the literary marketplace, it suggests that the book possesses a transcendent quality that problematises any attempt to read it as merely evil or profane. Rather, *Les Chants* follows the tradition of the Gothic novel by approaching evil with profound ambivalence, suggesting some of the ways in which the profane might generate transcendence, pleasure or even moral reform.

## Conclusion

In an era when the devil had been transformed into a symbol for humanity's darkest impulses, 18th- and 19th-century fiction frequently aligns Satan with notions of inversion and upheaval. Celebrating that which is usually reviled, worshipping that which is ordinarily condemned, Satanic characters and rituals are deeply enmeshed in complex forms of transgressive pleasure. Whether incarnate in the black masses performed in *The Monk* and *Là-Bas* or in the villain-protagonists of *Melmoth the Wander* and *Les Chants de Maldoror*, Satanism articulates one of the primary affective modes of the Gothic: ambivalence. Empowering readers to engage in fantasised border crossings, these works generate both fear and desire, attraction and repulsion. Satanism, because of its association with taboo acts, creates an imaginative space in which readers can explore other genders, sexualities, moral frameworks and identities. Yet, because these actions are framed as unequivocally, even deliciously, evil, readers are able to temper their desire with an equally profound horror. Satanic monsters and perverse black masses emerge as the nadir of Gothic monstrosity, instilling in the reader a pleasure that is always tinged with disgust, a terror endlessly inflected with longing.

## Notes

1 Robert Muchembled, *A History of the Devil: From the Middle Age to the Present*, trans. Jean Birrell (Cambridge, 2003), 148.
2 The notion that Satan's powers inhere only in suggestion is, of course, a much older theological tradition. According to Muchembled, the belief that Satan could not act upon bodies, but only through the power suggestion dates back to the Middle Ages. See Muchembled, *History of the Devil*, 149.
3 Muchembled, *History of the Devil*, 157.
4 Muchembled, *History of the Devil*, 167.
5 Jerrold E Hogle, *The Cambridge Companion to Gothic Fiction* (Cambridge, 2002), 12. Emphasis in original.
6 Jeffrey Jerome Cohen, "Monster Culture (Seven Theses)," in *The Monster Theory Reader*, ed. Jeffrey Andrew Weinstock (Minneapolis, 2020), 49.
7 Cohen, "Monster Culture," 49.
8 Muchembled, *History of the Devil*, 148.
9 Sarah Bartels, *The Devil and the Victorians: Supernatural Evil in Nineteenth-Century English Culture* (London, 2021), 7 and 8.
10 In Ruben Van Luijk, *Children of Lucifer: The Origins of Modern Religious Satanism* (Oxford, 2016), 64.
11 Bartels, *The Devil and the Victorians*, 9.
12 Peter A Schock, *Romantic Satanism: Myth and the Historical Moment in Blake, Shelley and Byron* (London, 2003), 5.
13 Van Luijk, *Children of Lucifer*, 69
14 Cleo Cameron, "Materialism in the Monk," *The Palgrave Handbook of Gothic Origins*, ed. Clive Bloom (London, 2021), 520.
15 Henry Hatfield, "The Walpurgis Night: Themes and Variations," *Journal of European Studies* 13 (1983): 57.
16 John R. Williams, Introduction to *Faust* (Ware, 2007), xiv
17 Ehrhard Bahr, "Faust and Satan: Conflicting Concepts of the Devil in *Faust I*," *International Faust Studies: Adaptation, Reception, Translation*, ed. Lorna Fitzsimmons (London, 2008), 96.
18 Bahr, "Faust and Satan," 91.
19 Johann Wolfgang Goethe, *Faust: A Tragedy in Two Parts*, trans. John R Williams (Ware, 2007), line 1335.
20 Quoted in Ruben Van Luijk, "A Brief History of the Black Mass," *Sanctifying Texts, Transforming Rituals: Encounters in Liturgical Studies*, eds. Paul van Geest, Marcel Poorthuis and Els Rose (Leiden, 2017), 275.
21 Walter Stephens, *Demon Lovers: Witchcraft, Sex, and the Crisis of Belief* (Chicago, 2002), 197.
22 Van Luijk, "History of the Black Mass," 276.
23 Stephens, *Demon Lovers*, 13.
24 Van Luijk, "History of the Black Mass," 276.
25 Qtd in Stephens, *Demon Lovers*, 200.
26 Stephens, *Demon Lovers*, 200.

27 Stephens, *Demon Lovers*, 203.

28 Matthew Lewis, *The Monk* (Ware, 2009), 203.

29 Lewis, *The Monk*, 203.

30 Lewis, *The Monk*, 203. Such scenes of inversion and the abuse of the host appear in many literary treatments of witchcraft, Satanism and the black mass. In her article on femininity in Goethe's *Faust*, Barbara Becker-Cantarino notes that not only does the witches' kitchen sequences invert notions of womanhood as traditionally expressed in the figure of the good housewife, but other scenes indicate an inversion of the Catholic eucharistic rite. In one scene, the demon Mephistopheles uses the term "hocus-pocus" to describe a witch's brew. Becker-Cantarino notes that term *hocus-pocus* "is a defective version of the Latin 'hoc est corpus meum' (this is my body), which signals the high point of the mass, the transubstantiation of bread and wine into Christ's body and blood." Here, however, the dark magic of Mephistopheles and the witch transforms this phrase into a blasphemous parody of Christian ritual. See Barbara Becker-Cantarino, "Witch and Infanticide: Imaging the Female in Faust I," *Goethe Yearbook*, vol. 7 (1994), 1–22, at 4.

31 Lewis, *The Monk*, 203.

32 Per Faxneld, *Feminism: Lucifer as the Liberator of Woman in Nineteenth-Century Culture* (Oxford, 2017), 162.

33 Faxneld, *Feminism*, 162.

34 Lewis, *The Monk*, 197.

35 Faxneld, *Feminism*, 164.

36 Faxneld, *Feminism*, 165.

37 Stephen Blakemore, "Matthew Lewis's Black Mass: Sexual, Religious Inversion in *The Monk*," *Studies in the Novel* 3, no. 4 (1998): 521.

38 Cohen, "Monster Culture," 6.

39 Cohen, "Monster Culture," 6.

40 Blakemore, "Matthew Lewis's Black Mass," 522.

41 Lewis, *The Monk*, 14.

42 Blakemore, "Matthew Lewis's Black Mass," 523.

43 Lewis, *The Monk*, 204.

44 Blakemore, "Matthew Lewis's Black Mass," 521.

45 Asti Hustvedt, "Introduction" in *The Decadent Reader: Fiction, fantasy and perversion from fin-de-siècle France* (New York, 1998), 1.

46 Hustvedt, "Introduction," 14.

47 JK Huysmans, *Là-Bas*, trans. Terry Hale (London, 2001), 124.

48 Huysmans, *Là-Bas,* 124 and 125.

49 Huysmans, *Là-Bas*, 224.

50 Huysmans, *Là-Bas*, 224.

51 Huysmans, *Là-Bas*, 224.

52 Huysmans, *Là-Bas*, 222.

53 Huysmans, *Là-Bas*, 225. As numerous critics, including Van Luijk, have observed, it is difficult to miss the influence of Baudelaire's "Litanies to Satan" (1857) on this passage. Baudelaire's poem even includes a short prayer which is very similar to Huysmans's Satanic liturgy: "Satan be praised, be glorified on high/ And in the depths of Hell where you must lie/ In silence, ruminating your defeat!/ Grant that my soul some day may find a seat/ Under your Tree of Knowledge, which spreads/ Its limbs to make a Temple overhead!"

54 Huysmans, *Là-Bas,* 227–8.

55 Huysmans, *Là-Bas*, 228.

56 Elizabeth Emery, "JK Huysmans, Medievalist," *Modern Language Studies* 30, no. 2 (2000): 119.

57 Emery, "JK Huysmans, Medievalist," 124. Although beyond the scope of this chapter, it is worth noting that just as Huysmans's work is characterised by an inchoate nostalgia for the Middle Ages, so too was the Gothic, at least initially a revival of interest in the dark, chaos of medieval art and architecture, which provided an extreme contrast to the clean, ordered lines of Enlightenment neoclassicism. Likewise, as Fred Botting notes, Gothic tales—such as *The Castle of Otranto* (1764), *The Mysteries of Udolpho* (1794) and *The Monk*—were typically set in the Middle, or "Dark," Ages, a period which, in contrast to the Enlightenment, signified "an absence of the light associated with sense, security and knowledge." See Emery, "JK Huysmans, Medievalist," 2.

58 Robert Ziegler, *Satanism, Magic and Mysticism in Fin-de-siècle France* (London, 2012), 21.

59 Quoted in Van Luijk, *Children of Lucifer*, 123.

60 Van Luijk, *Children of Lucifer*, 196.

61 Huysmans, *Là-Bas*, 231.

62 Ziegler, *Satanism, Magic and Mysticism*, 4.

63 Fred Botting, *Gothic: The New Critical Idiom*, 2nd edition (London, 2014), 9.

64 Cohen, "Monster Culture," 50.

65 Charlie Jorge explicitly compares Melmoth to Faust, and many scholars have identified parallels between the figure of Melmoth and folklore surrounding the wandering Jew. However, there also appear to be a number of similarities between Melmoth and the Irish folktale of "Stingy Jack," a man who ticked the devil and was condemned to wander the earth with only an ember from hell to light his lantern. This story is often identified as the source of the Halloween Jack-o'-lantern.

66 Charles Maturin, *Melmoth the Wanderer* (London, 2012), 676.

67 Faxneld, *Feminism*, 171.

68 Maturin, *Melmoth the Wanderer*, 351.

69 Maturin, *Melmoth the Wanderer*, 382.

70 Joseph W. Lew, "Unprepared for Sudden Transformations: Identity and Politics in *Melmoth the Wanderer*," *Studies in the Novel* 26, no. ½ (1994): 182.

71 Maturin, *Melmoth the Wanderer*, 632.

72 Faxneld, *Feminism*, 173.

73 Christina Morin, "Delightful Cannibal Feasts: Literary Consumption in *Melmoth the Wanderer*," *The Irish Journal of Gothic and Horror Studies* 5 (2018): 46.

74 Morin, "Delightful Cannibal Feasts," 47.

75 Maturin, *Melmoth the Wanderer*, 628.

76 Maturin, *Melmoth the Wanderer*, 260.

77 Maturin, *Melmoth the Wanderer*, 261.

78 David Frankfurter, *Evil Incarnate: Rumors of Demonic Conspiracy and Satanic Abuse in History* (Princeton, 2008), 137.

79 Frankfurter, *Evil Incarnate*, 75.

80 Maturin, *Melmoth the Wanderer*, 490.

81 Maturin, *Melmoth the Wanderer*, 490.

82 Ronald Hutton, *The Witch: A History of Fear, From Ancient Times to the Present* (New Haven, 2017), 22.

83 Maturin, *Melmoth the Wanderer*, 490–1.

84 Maturin, *Melmoth the Wanderer*, 491 (emphasis in original), 661.

85 Leven M. Dawson, "*Melmoth the Wanderer*: Paradox and the Gothic Novel," *Studies in English Literature, 1500–1900* 8, no. 4 (1968): 623.

86 Frankfurter, *Evil Incarnate*, 137.

87 Dyan Elliot, *Fallen Bodies: Pollution, Sexuality, and Demonology in the Middle Ages* (Philadelphia, 1998), 9.

88 Dawson, "*Melmoth the Wanderer*: Paradox and the Gothic Novel," 623.

89 Nicole Moore, "Surrealism to Pulp: The Limits of the Literary and Australian Customs," *Censorship and the Limits of the Literary: A Global View*, ed. Nicole Moore (London, 2015), 109.

90 Quoted in Moore, "Surrealism to Pulp," 110.

91 Paul Knight, "Introduction to Maldoror," 7–26, in *Les Chants de Maldoror* (London, 1978), 18.

92 Comte de Lautréamont, *Les Chants de Maldoror*, trans. Paul Knight (London, 1978), 29.

93 Knight, "Introduction to Maldoror," 13 (emphasis added).

94 Lautréamont, *Les Chants de Maldoror*, 34.

95 Frankfurter, *Evil Incarnate*, 85.

96 Joshua D. Gonsalves, "Byron—In-Between Sade, Lautréamont, and Foucault: Situating the Canon of 'Evil, in the Nineteenth Century." *Romanticism on the Net*, no. 43 (2006). https://doi.org/10.7202/013591ar

97 Lautréamont, *Les Chants de Maldoror*, 111–2.

98 Lautréamont, *Les Chants de Maldoror*, 160–1.

99 Lautréamont, *Les Chants de Maldoror*, 161.

100 Lautréamont, *Les Chants de Maldoror*, 85.
101 Ziegler, *Satanism, Magic and Mysticism*, 21.
102 Ziegler, *Satanism, Magic and Mysticism*, 21.
103 Botting, *Gothic*, 9.
104 Quoted in Knight, "Introduction to Maldoror," 9.

## Further Reading

Cohen, Jeffrey Jerome. "Monster Culture (Seven Theses)", *The Monster Theory Reader*, edited by Jeffrey Andrew Weinstock, 37–56. Minneapolis: Minnesota University Press, 2020.

Faxneld, Per. *Satanic Feminism: Lucifer as the Liberator of Woman in Nineteenth-Century Culture.* Oxford: Oxford University Press, 2017.

Frankfurter, David. *Evil Incarnate: Rumors of Demonic Conspiracy and Satanic Abuse in History.* Princeton: Princeton University Press, 2008.

Hustvedt, Asti. "Introduction", *The Decadent Reader: Fiction, fantasy and perversion from fin-de-siècle France*, 10–30. New York: Zone Books, 1998.

Muchembled, Robert. *A History of the Devil: From the Middle Age to the Present. Translated by Jean Birrell.* Cambridge: Polity, 2003.

Stephens, Walter. *Demon Lovers: Witchcraft, Sex, and the Crisis of Belief.* Chicago: University of Chicago Press, 2002.

Van Luijk, Ruben. *Children of Lucifer: The Origins of Modern Religious Satanism.* Oxford: Oxford University Press, 2016.

# 18

# THE DEVIL, PROTEST, AND THE AGE OF REVOLUTION

*Per Faxneld*

### To Justify the Ways of God? Regicide, Rebellion, and the Sublime

Satan is often perceived as the first protester against authority, the original revolutionary. It is not surprising, therefore, that he was a prominent figure in the political and literary discourses of what has been called the Age of Revolution. But when did this period take place? Historian Eric Hobsbawm's influential 1962 book *The Age of Revolution* delimits it to the period 1789–1848.[1] However, it would also be feasible to view this age as beginning with the American Revolution of 1765–83 and then carrying over through the key event of the French Revolution (that Hobsbawm takes as his starting point) and a plethora of colonial uprisings (for example, the Haitian Revolution of 1789–99), and finally encompassing a series of republican-democratic revolts throughout Europe over the following decades. Where to end the "age of revolutions" is quite unclear, and it could be argued the dramatic events surrounding the Paris Commune of 1871 should be included. In the spirit of Hobsbawm's famous extension of the 19th century from 1776 to 1914 in a different book, I will here be even more generous and define the period as ranging from roughly the beginning of the American Revolution (1765) to the Russian October Revolution (1917)—that is, around 150 years. But in what follows, it will also be necessary to add several glances backwards and ahead.[2]

In fact, let us begin with a much earlier revolution—the English Civil War of 1642–52 (historically commonly referred to as "the great rebellion")—and the climactic execution of King Charles I by radical parliamentarians in January 1649. Though the interregnum did not last long, and the monarchy was restored with the coronation of Charles II in 1660, the revolutionary fury the regicide unleashed arguably retained its momentum and informed later republican endeavours elsewhere.[3] But the rebellion was also, as we will see, directly connected to a dramatic re-evaluation of Satan, one that took place in a context where poetry and politics became intertwined.

One of the driving forces of "the great rebellion" was the military commander and politician Oliver Cromwell (1599–1658), who ruled England as Lord Protector from 1653 to 1658. Under Cromwell's reign, the learned poet John Milton (1608–1674) handled the regime's foreign correspondence and produced political propaganda for the republican

DOI: 10.4324/9781003096603-19

cause—a creed to which he had been committed for some time. Perhaps the most controversial of the works he produced during this period was his unequivocal defence of regicide, *Eikonoklastes* (1649).[4] But his main poetical work was the blank-verse epic poem *Paradise Lost* (1667) which also deals with insurrection—specifically, Satan's mutiny against God. Given Milton's political background, it is unsurprising that the text was read as implicitly lauding the devil, understood as a stand-in for Cromwell (with God as a heavenly equivalent to earthly kings). Interpreted in this way, *Paradise Lost* became an allegorical, republican retelling of the civil war, with Satan as the hero of its narrative.[5] But such a reading was cynical and primarily employed by those seeking to blacken Milton's reputation. Milton was in fact a deeply religious puritan, and he states in the preface to *Paradise Lost* that it has been written "to justify the ways of God to men."[6] Nevertheless, the extent to which he held some sort of Satanic sympathies has long been a matter of debate. Certainly, Satan appears persuasive and at least partially in the right at the beginning of the poem—perhaps most famously in his rousing speeches asserting the value of independence to the rebel angels—but most scholars have tended to accept Milton's avowal of piety at face value. In that context, it is significant that as the tale progresses, Satan becomes less likeable.

The primary admirers of the antihero of *Paradise Lost* appeared several generations after Milton's death and are associated with the amorphous, so-called romantic movement. Romanticism arose in countries like Britain and Germany around the middle of the 18th century, becoming a dominant literary current towards the century's last decades. To some extent, the movement repudiated the cold, intellectual reflection of the Enlightenment, giving primacy instead to the world of the emotions and imagination. At the same time, though, many romantics embraced Enlightenment republicanism and shared its negative attitude towards authorities like institutional Christianity (though there were also plenty of conservative Romantics).[7] This revolutionary strain of romanticism encompassed what is commonly labelled "Romantic Satanism." Another possible name might be "Revolutionary Literary Satanism."

The counter-readings of biblical tradition and Milton performed by these Romantics were facilitated by the accelerating decline of (mainline) Christianity's status in western Europe at the time. Arguably, the Romantic subversion of Christian mythology also helped hasten this process, as key proponents like Percy Shelley and Lord Byron (discussed below) were among the most widely read authors of their day.[8] For a contextual understanding of this subversion, it is important to keep in mind that Satanism—either as a self-designation or understood as the open expression of sympathy for the devil—has a quite short history. While the *notion* of wicked secretive groups worshipping Satan is as old as Christianity itself, there is no real evidence of anything of this kind existing outside paranoid religious fantasies until much more recently. The first documented explicitly Satanist organisations date to the early 20th century (see Chapters 23 and 24). Even the idea of taking a pro-Satanic stance for polemical or aesthetic reasons is comparatively recent.[9] This first occurred in the mid-18th century when several influential cultural figures sidestepped the question of the devil's morality, concentrating instead on his *sublime* characteristics.[10]

A key text here was the Irish philosopher and statesman Edmund Burke's celebrated treatise *Philosophical Inquiry into the Origin of Our Ideas of the Sublime and Beautiful* (1756). This work shifted the debate over aesthetic experience away from neoclassicism's notions of the harmonious and well-proportioned into more disturbing, stormy realms. Burke writes that "passion caused by the great and the sublime in nature, when those causes operate most powerfully, is astonishment; and astonishment is that state of the soul, in which all its motions are suspended, with some degree of horror."[11] Significantly, he high-lighted Milton's Satan as a prime example of the sublime, directly linking him to "the ruin of monarchs, and the revolutions of kingdoms."[12] This is not to say that Burke approved of such things, in spite of recognising their aesthetic fascination. Indeed, in his 1790 bestseller *Reflections on the Revolution in France*, he consistently tied the French rebels to Satan in order to condemn them.[13] All the same, Burke's horrified account was read as a sort of unintentionally "revolutionary book against the revolution" (as the German poet Novalis put it) by some radicals.[14]

By this point, an admiration of the sublime Miltonic Satan had become quite common among a certain type of readers. The rebellious Scottish poet Robert Burns (1759–96), for example, wrote in a 1787 letter, "Give me a spirit like my favourite hero, Milton's Satan."[15] One of the period's most well-known, radical political thinkers was the novelist, journalist, and (proto-) anarchist philosopher William Godwin (1756–1836). In his famous *Enquiry Concerning Political Justice* (1793), he observed that "poetical readers have commonly remarked Milton's devil to be a being of considerable virtue."[16] Satan mutinied against God, Godwin says, "because he saw no sufficient reason, for that extreme inequality of rank and power which the creator assumed," as "prescription and precedent form no ad-equate ground for implicit faith."[17] In short, Godwin turned Satan into an emblem of his own anarchist values and God into a representation of the despotic, arbitrary inherited authority of 18th-century England. This reading of *Paradise Lost*, of course, ignores Satan's authoritarian and evil traits, taking the pro-revolutionary understanding of the text as well-established and generally accepted.[18] This symbolic valorisation of Lucifer was, in other words, part of a common discourse prominent among certain radicals at this time.

In mainstream contexts, by contrast, it remained common to use Satan to vilify pro-gressive ideas. The British government held up revolutionary France as the great beast of Revelations, for instance, while the caricaturist James Gilray's 1798 etching, *The Tree of Liberty*, shows the pro-French Revolution politician Charles James Fox (1749–1806) as the serpent in the garden of Eden—here offering an apple bearing the word "Reform."[19] Most English radicals, revolutionaries, and reformers, too, tended to employ such intuitively *negative* devil symbolism, portraying, for instance, institutions such as the royal dynasties of Europe as Satanic. By comparison, Godwin's innovative approach was at this point still marginal. It would become less so through the intervention of a series of literary figures.

## The Devil's Party: England's Revolutionary Romantics

The first important literary texts to laud Satan were written by William Blake (1757–1827). Never famous during his lifetime, the multi-talented poet and pictorial artist's ideas only had a real impact in the generation after his death. However, by the 1890s, through the efforts of poets and artists like Dante Gabriel Rossetti and William Butler Yeats, he was widely recognised as a romantic key figure.[20] Blake's use of the figure of Satan can be divided into two phases. Early in his career, he seems to idealise Satan. This is clear in his *The Marriage of Heaven and Hell* (c. 1790–3).[21] Here, the opening pas-sage lays down that "Good is the passive that obeys Reason. Evil is the active springing from Energy. Evil is Hell. Good is Heaven." To this, "The Voice of the Devil" adds that "Energy is eternal delight."[22] In the poem, Satan is an expansive, generative, and chaotic force energising the cosmos. By contrast, God and good represent an oppressive status quo, something that Blake clearly resented. Indeed, *The Marriage* was produced after

Blake had spent a long time moving in the same political circles as Godwin and other radicals.[23] Blake, too, was an avid reader of Milton, famously claiming that the puritan bard "wrote in fetters when he wrote of Angels & God, and at liberty when of Devils and Hell ... because he was a true poet and of the Devil's party without knowing it."[24] Later in life, though, Blake's approach to Satan became more conventional. For example, in *The Book of Urizen* (1794), *Milton: A Poem* (c. 1804), and *Jerusalem* (c. 1820), Satan is portrayed as a despotic, fiendish figure that hinders rather than helps man on the path to redemption.

A poet who knew full well to whose party he belonged was Percy Bysshe Shelley (1792–1822), one of the most celebrated of the Romantic poets. In his hands, he turned Satan into a positive political role model. As part of the short-lived campaign for Irish political reform in which he engaged during 1812, he penned a broadsheet entitled *A Declaration of Rights*. This concluded with a quotation from Satan's speech to the fallen angels from book I of *Paradise Lost*: "Awake!—arise!—or be for ever fallen."[25] In Milton, this line comes directly after the failure of the celestial rebellion, as Satan comes to terms with his new situation, encouraging his entourage to join him in a struggle to regain heaven. The parallel, then, was politically loaded, for in 1798 and 1803 the Irish had attempted to rebel against their British overlords. However, their efforts had also been quashed by brute force.[26] No stranger to fierce ideological confrontations himself, Shelley had been expelled from Oxford after publishing his tract *The Necessity of Atheism* (1811). In "A Defence of Poetry" (1821, published in 1840) he hails Milton as a subversive poet, asserting that the portrait of a morally superior (!) Satan in *Paradise Lost* entails an implicit refutation of Christianity.[27] Shelley here drew on an unpublished earlier text, "On the Devil, and Devils" (c. 1819) where he also enthusiastically praises Milton's Satan:

> Nothing can exceed the grandeur and the energy of the character of the Devil as expressed in *Paradise Lost*. ... Milton's Devil as a moral being is as far superior to his God, as one who perseveres in some purpose which he has conceived to be excellent, in spite of adversity and torture, is to one who in the cold security of undoubted triumph inflicts the most horrible revenge upon his enemy, not from any mistaken notion of bringing him to repent of a perseverance in enmity, but with the open and alleged design of exasperating him to deserve new torments.[28]

Yet Shelley was wary of revitalising Christian myth, including "that miserable tale of the Devil" as he describes it in a footnote to *Queen Mab* (1813).[29] He resolved the conundrum by merging the most appealing traits of Milton's Satan with other mythological figures, for example, the Greek Titan Prometheus (*Prometheus Unbound*, 1820). In *The Assassins*, he lets another stand-in for Satan, the Wandering Jew, cry out to God: "I was thy slave ... I am thine equal, and thy foe—Thousands tremble before thy throne who at my voice shall dare to pluck the golden crown from thine unholy head."[30] The Wandering Jew also appears in *Queen Mab*, explaining that even before Christ cursed him he had "learned to prefer/Hell's freedom to the servitude of Heaven," and continues to struggle against "my almighty Tyrant, and to hurl/Defiance at His impotence to harm/Beyond the curse I bore."[31]

For his long poem, *The Revolt of Islam* (1817, also known as *Laon and Cythna*), Shelley came up with a new strategy. None of the traditional names of Satan are used, but it is still clear that the inverted dualist mythology sketched in Canto I of *Revolt* has Lucifer as its hero. A serpent—identified as the Morning Star—battles with an eagle, is defeated and falls from the heavens. The evil eagle is subsequently mistakenly perceived by humanity as the "good" God:

> Thus evil triumphed, and the Spirit of evil,
> One Power of many shapes which none may know,
> One shape of many names; the Fiend did revel
> In victory, reigning over a world of woe,
> For the new race of man went to and fro,
> Famished and homeless, loathed and loathing, wild,
> And hating good—for his immortal foe,
> He changed from a starry shape, beauteous and mild,
> To a dire snake, with man and beast unreconciled.
> ...
> And the great Spirit of Good did creep among
> The nations of mankind, and every tongue
> Cursed and blasphemed him as he passed; for none
> Knew good from evil, though their names were hung
> In mockery o'er the fane where many a groan,
> As King and Lord, and God, the conquering Fiend did own.[32]

This Fiend—the eagle/God—is the creator of death, earthquake, and blight, while the serpent is mankind's true benefactor and an enemy of all oppressors. The day the latter resumes his fight with God, thrones will shake and "earth's immense and trampled multitude" will begin to realise its own power.[33] Satan thus becomes an icon of righteous revolt, the genius of revolution. Possibly due to worries over the legal dangers of outright Satanism under the period's blasphemy laws, Shelley consistently refrains from using the actual names "God" and "Satan"—though the symbolism would have been obvious to most readers.[34] The heroic serpent may, moreover, reflect Shelley's interest in the American Revolutionary War (and the democratic model that resulted from it), where the American Culpeper Minutemen used a coiled snake as their insignia accompanied by the emblazoned anti-colonial slogan "Don't tread on me."[35]

Shelley claimed in his introduction to *The Revolt of Islam* that it was written "in the view of kindling within the bosoms of my readers a virtuous enthusiasm for ... doctrines of liberty and justice." He underscores the fact that it is "narrative, not didactic" and aims at "the unveiling of the religious frauds by which they [the oppressed people] have been deluded into submission." Shelley's narrative is thus a counter-myth intended to relativise and subvert the bible, propagating an ideology inverting the conservative ethos he viewed as being commonly inferred from biblical tradition. In creating a potent dissident romantic hybrid of literature and religious myth, Shelley explicitly attempted to explode hegemonic Christian mythology from the inside, disrupting its function as a pillar of the present order.

### Man Is in Part Divine: Conservative Backlash and Radical Riposte

First-generation Romantics like William Wordsworth (1770–1850), Samuel Taylor Coleridge (1772–1834), and Robert Southey (1774–1843) had, by contrast, become staunchly conservative establishment figures by the early 19th century. These aging poets now condemned progressive forces using time-worn literally demonising rhetoric. In *Statesman's*

*Manual* (1816), for instance, Coleridge sought the cause of current British political upheaval in a diabolical French influence, claiming that the atheism and apotheosis of reason characteristic of the French Revolution was a modern expression of the serpent's words to Eve in the Garden of Eden: "ye shall be as gods" (Gen 3.5). Napoleon, as the ultimate product of the revolution, embodies "satanic pride and rebellious self-idolatry."[36] His friend Southey argued along similar lines in an 1816–7 issue of the conservative periodical *The Quarterly Review*, attacking the reformists' celebration of the will of the people ("Vox Populi, Vox Dei") and claiming that the voice of the masses is not God's voice, but that of "the Devil whose name is Legion." After all, the will of the people, he emphasises, led to the reign of terror during the French Revolution, the death of Socrates, and the crucifixion of Christ.[37] In the preface to *A Vision of Judgement* (1821), Southey would extend his demonisation of democratic ideals to fellow poets, specifically targeting Shelley and his friend Lord Byron (their names are not mentioned, but he is unmistakably referring to them). Vitriolically, he designated them "the Satanic School" in poetry, compares them to Milton's fallen angels Belial and Moloch, and declares that they are "characterized by a Satanic spirit of pride and audacious impiety."[38]

Shortly afterwards, Shelley visited his friend Byron, who was hard at work on his play *Cain: A Mystery*, and proposed a counterattack. This probably influenced the seditious, inflammatory monologues Byron allowed Lucifer in *Cain*, where God is painted as a lonesome tyrant creating worlds just to mitigate his solitude. However, it remains unclear whether Lucifer's words in this poetic riposte are to be understood as uncomfortable truth or malicious manipulation. An unwillingness on Byron's part to become an easy target for additional conservative rants about "Satanism" probably influenced his ironic and evasive Lucifer. Such accusations were not a mere question of social discomfort, for the anti-Christian outbursts in *Queen Mab* had lost Shelley custody of his children. Byron may also have worried about having his child taken from him if he was too bold in his attacks on Christianity.[39] Artistic concerns should, of course, not be disregarded either, as the ambiguity is arguably what makes his Lucifer so interesting. This figure is in many ways a cold and aloof personage, one whose endgame is hardly to aid humankind. Yet the character gets to utter lines difficult to hear as anything but an expression of the values of the young Romantic freethinkers themselves. In his final speech, he says:

> One good gift has the fatal apple given—
> Your reason:—let it not be over-sway'd
> By tyrannous threats to force you into faith
> 'Gainst all external sense and inward feeling:
> Think and endure,—and form an inner world
> In your own bosom—where the outward fails;
> So shall you nearer be the spiritual
> Nature, and war triumphant with your own.[40]

Presumably, many contemporaries—aware of the poet's own stance—would have understood Lucifer as Byron's mouthpiece here. Although Lucifer at times behaves like the traditional malefactor, for example, by trying to lure Cain's soul to his thus far empty Hell, he frequently embodies views held by the author and his circle.

The monologue just quoted draws on Satan's speech in Book I of *Paradise Lost*, where he has fallen into Hell and proclaims that he has a "mind not to be chang'd by Place or

Time," underscoring the point that "the mind is its own place, and in itself/Can make a Heav'n of Hell, a Hell of Heav'n."[41] In *Cain*, Lucifer extols the human mind as the "centre of surrounding things," sharing his doubts that he was created by God. Hereby, the romantic Lucifer becomes, in Peter Schock's words, "an image of apotheosis, an emblem of an aspiring, rebelling, rising human god who insists that he is self-created."[42] This must be understood against the background of broader processes of secularisation, where notions of the divine were transferred from God in heaven to man himself—something made explicit in Byron's 1816 poem "Prometheus," in which he writes about how "Man is in part divine."[43]

## Stand by Me, Lucifer: French Romantics and Anarchists

In France, Romantic poets developed a rather different Satanic tradition, focusing on a peculiar type of sentimental sympathy. Here, one of the main motifs focused on the idea of God pardoning Satan and reinstating him to his former celestial glory, with accordingly less emphasis on the devil as a virtuous freedom fighter.[44] Victor Hugo's unfinished epic *La Fin de Satan* (The End of Satan, 1854–62) is one example of this tendency, although Hugo does let a feather from Satan's wing generate the allegorical figure of the angel Liberty.[45] George Sand, in her novel *Consuelo* (serialised 1842–43), took a more "English" approach. Her eponymous protagonist experiences a vision of Satan in which he tells her "I am not the demon, I am the archangel of legitimate rebellion and the patron of the grand struggles. Like Christ, I am the god of the poor, of the weak, and of the oppressed."[46] The vision (or hallucination) ends with her kneeling to Lucifer. Sand's Lucifer, however, has been pardoned by God and promises to bring freedom side by side with Christ, hence not breaking completely with the decidedly heterodox but still comparatively moderated approach typical of the French Romantics.

Celebrations of Satan in the role of God's *adversary* became truly prominent in France only with Charles Baudelaire's collection of poems, *Les Fleurs du mal* (The Flowers of Evil, 1857). The most explicitly Satanic of the poems is "Les Litanies de Satan" (The litanies of Satan), in which the devil is represented—with all the layers of irony characteristic of Baudelaire—as an emancipator of the exploited and reviled. The poem is as complex as the poet's own commitment to social justice, which was fleeting and fickle at best. The 1848 revolution saw him briefly mount the barricades brandishing a revolver, but he was hardly a consistent political activist in any way, just as he oscillated between deeply felt Catholic guilt and blasphemous transgression.[47] Baudelaire's multifaceted Satanism represents a transitional stage between political Romantic Satanism and a later Decadent variety. The Decadents were often simultaneously reactionary and depraved, revering (regularly half-joking or remorseful) Satan as the epitome of atrocious evil and boundless carnality, instead of a self-sacrificing cosmic and political liberator in the romantic mould.[48]

Situated within the same field of tension between progressivity and decadent delights as *Les Fleurs du mal* is *La Sorcière* (The Witch, 1862) by renowned French historian, republican, and social agitator Jules Michelet (1798–1874). Nominally a monograph on the European witch trials, it argues that those who were accused of witchcraft in the Middle Ages really did practise Satanism. However, the proper way to understand this counter-religion, according to Michelet, is as an expression of class hatred on the part of feudal serfs. The nobility had God and the Church on their side, so logically the medieval peasantry in desperation turned to God's adversary, Satan—who, for Michelet, embodied science, reason, and everything natural. However, in some of the historian's enthusiastically kinky descriptions of Satanic rituals and the machinations of demons, he approached a more decadent take on infernal powers. In this sense, the book's contents cannot be reduced simply to a rehash of English romantic emancipatory Satanism. Moreover, *La Sorcière*, it should be noted, contains a greater number of colourful Gothic vignettes and passages approximating prose poems than anything approximating historical research grounded in archival sources.[49] It became an immediate and scandalous bestseller, which has never gone out of print since its initial publication. Along with the work of the English Romantics, it is one of the foundation stones of progressive political Satanism and, moreover, displays an ambiguous, anti-Christian, feminist tendency that later authors would develop further.[50]

Michelet first presented many of the ideas which would become *La Sorcière* in academic lectures, and one of his students in the late 1830s and early 1840s was Pierre-Joseph Proudhon (1809–1865)—subsequently one of the foremost anarchist philosophers.[51] Thus, it is feasible that the charismatic lecturer was the cause of Proudhon's choice to incorporate a sprinkling of Satanism in his anarchist works. The two remained in contact, though Michelet disagreed with some of Proudhon's more extreme maxims such as "property is theft."[52] The student would precede his teacher in actually peppering his works with outbursts of Satanism, beginning in *Système des contradictions économiques* (The System of Economic Contradictions, 1846) in which he hailed "the spirit of analysis, the indefatigable Satan who questions and contradicts without cease."[53] Such phrasings recur throughout his literary works. In the *Idée générale de la révolution au XIXe siècle* (The General Idea of Revolution during the Nineteenth Century, 1851), for instance, he cried "Stand by me, Lucifer, Satan, whoever you are, demon who in the faith of my fathers opposed God and the Church! I will carry your word, and I ask for nothing."[54] In *De la justice dans la révolution et dans l'église* (Concerning Justice in the Revolution and in the Church, 1858), he mocked conservatives with an address to a hater of freedom in which he writes, "Liberty, symbolised by the story of the temptation, is your Antichrist; liberty, for you, is the Devil. Come, Satan, come, the one slandered by priests and kings, so that I may embrace you, so that I may hold you to my chest!"[55]

On the whole, however, Proudhon's writings are more anticlerical than they are anti-Christian. Indeed, some of his inspiration for his political positions seems to have come from his understanding of the bible and his admiration for early Christianity. In his opinion, for instance, the gospels forbade inequality, but the church had strayed from this original position. His notion of property being theft arose from ambitious attempts to correct existing translations of the bible, for which he even learned Hebrew. Consistently critical of the church, he was, nevertheless, a practising Catholic—if only periodically.[56]

Proudhon's network of acquaintances included not only Michelet but also Baudelaire, whose Satanism he may have influenced. They met several times from 1848 onwards, and the poet was an avid reader of the anarchist's works, particularly those in which Satan is held up as the genius of freedom. While it is quite possible that Baudelaire intended an anarchist subtext to poems like "Les Litanies de Satan" Proudhon's influence on his Russian anarchist comrade Mikhail Bakunin (1814–1876) is clearer.[57] Briefly a leading name in international revolutionary socialism, Bakunin was quickly overshadowed by Karl Marx and others more skilled in building coherent political philosophies. That said, Bakunin's untidy but inspired texts have retained a special credibility because of the author's bold deeds as a practical revolutionary. Indeed, the core of his credo is that the impulse to revolt does not need to be justified through complicated reasoning, for it exists as an inherited impulse in all of us. Those in power have attempted to stifle this instinct through religion in particular. This can be seen in Bakunin's most famous text, *Dieu et l'état* (God and State, written in 1871 as part of a planned larger work and published posthumously in 1882), which is primarily a critique of Christianity. In Bakunin's view, belief in God is one of the most threatening obstacles standing in the way of humanity's liberation. When we are "slaves of God," he wrote, "men must also be slaves of Church and State, in so far as the State is consecrated by the Church."[58] But Bakunin went further, even claiming that he can disprove the existence of God. Mocking St. Anselm's 11th-century ontological proof for the existence of God, he asserted that "If God is, man is a slave; now, man can and must be free; then, God does not exist."[59]

Bakunin described God as "the most jealous, the most vain, the most ferocious, the most unjust, the most bloodthirsty, the most despotic, and the most hostile to human dignity and liberty [sic]."[60] In his assessment, God prohibited Adam and Eve to eat from the fruit on the tree of knowledge in an attempt to ensure that "man, destitute of all understanding of himself, should remain an eternal beast, ever on all-fours before the eternal God."[61] Luckily, he continued, "Satan, the eternal rebel, the first freethinker and the emancipator of worlds" hurries to humanity's rescue: "He makes man ashamed of his bestial ignorance and obedience; he emancipates him, stamps upon his brow the seal of liberty and humanity, in urging him to disobey and eat of the fruit of knowledge."[62] Bakunin argued that "God admitted that Satan was right; he recognised that the devil did not deceive Adam and Eve in promising them knowledge and liberty as a reward for the act of disobedience which he had induced them to commit."[63]

Mankind's progress and primordial achievement of free thinking thus springs from a rebellion inspired by Satan. Naturally, since Bakunin was a rigid atheist, the figure of Satan is employed in a purely symbolic manner. This Satanist counter-reading of Genesis 3 may have been conceived to destabilise the hegemonic status of the bible in the same strategic manner in which Shelley subverted Christian mythology, serving as a rhetorically effective tool, giving colour to the exposition of abstract political ideas. Additionally, Bakunin would have found gleeful delight in such a provocation, for it was an act of anarchist sabotage. Yet, in his enthusiastic embrace of Satan in the same text, he warned that we are always at risk of "sooner or later" relapsing back "into the abyss of religious absurdity."[64] The power of religious myth is difficult to oust entirely, he conceded, and reinterpreting it can entail inadvertently reinforcing.

### In Prometheus' Guise: Sweden's Satanic Social Democrats

As we have now seen, three of the main ideologues of anarchism—Godwin, Proudhon, and Bakunin—celebrated Satan as a symbol of revolt. Many other socialists, both anarchists and others, chose the same approach, making the motif something of a revolutionary evergreen. An interesting example of this tendency is the remarkable prominence the motif gained among Swedish Social Democrats. After World War II, Social Democracy enjoyed a complacent hegemonic position in Sweden. But this had not always been the case. Its 19th-century incarnation was an aggressive and radical movement, publicising its ideas through the magazine *Lucifer* founded in 1891.[65] This appropriation of Satanism is interesting, for there was little in the way of locally produced esoteric or literary Satanism in Scandinavia in the 19th century so it is unclear how prominent figures in the movement came in contact with these ideas. It is possible that they were informed by English Romanticism which had some currency among Swedish intellectuals. [66] Equally, while there are no direct references to the British, French, or Russian anarchist figures in Swedish political Satanism, impulses from that direction cannot be ruled out. But perhaps most intriguingly, it is possible that the idea could have gained currency with Swedish socialists through contacts with the Swedish emigree community in the United States and the individualist-anarchist weekly newspaper *Lucifer the Light-bearer*, which started publication in 1883, first in Kansas and then later in Chicago. [67] Certainly, the similarity to the Swedish magazine's name seems suggestive in that capacity.

*Lucifer's* first issue contained an editorial that stated that it intended "Lucifer" to be understood in its purely etymological sense—that is, as *light bringer*. But there can be no doubt that the name was selected in full awareness of its disturbing connotations for Christians—a deliberate provocation of the Church of Sweden and the pious bourgeoisie.

The early Swedish Social Democratic movement of the 1880s was home to many kinds of socialists, including a minority often labelled (not always entirely accurately) anarchists. At the party's constituting congress in Norrköping in 1889 the most radical figures were booted out, although the party manifesto still left the door open for violent revolution under extreme circumstances. To some extent, however, this phrasing should probably be understood primarily as a strategic choice to maintain maximum pressure on the conservative establishment. The purge led to the more radical phalanx instead forming numerous youth clubs and other small political organisations in the 1890s, still using the name Social Democrats. Seeking broad parliamentary support, the party declared religion to be a private matter, but the radicals remained committed to stamping out Christianity. At the very least, they wanted to annihilate the political influence of the conservative priesthood. [68]

In the two early *Lucifer* issues, we encounter Satan the liberator in a series of poems and polemical texts by a certain Atterdag Wermelin (1861–1904). Unlike most poets of the worker's movement, this son of a priest in the Church of Sweden was well-educated and had studied at Uppsala University. He played a key part in early Swedish socialism, not least by introducing the economic theories of Marxism, although he eventually became marginalised within the movement. [69] In the premier issue of *Lucifer* (1886), Wermelin laid down what he called the "Ten Commandments of Lucifer." The first of these states, "Thou shalt have no other gods before me, the Lightbringer." [70] More revolutionary, though, is the tenth which states that "Thou shalt not covet thy neighbour's wife, unless she covets only you, but his ox and ass and all the capital that belongs to him thou shalt take from him and make the property of thine brothers." [71] In like manner, all of Wermelin's other Satanist commandments largely invert the Old Testament decalogue to socialist ends. In the second issue of *Lucifer*, Wermelin published a poem showcasing his avid reading of the English romantics. It describes how the light bringer lies bound to a rock with a vulture pecking his body, but still defiantly exclaims "In Satan's guise, in Prometheus' guise/I remained the same—indomitable." [72]

The more elaborate later *Lucifer* publications continued in the same blasphemous vein. The 1891 issue opens with the poem "Lucifer" by the signature "Spartacus" (Carl Natanael Carleson, 1865–1929). There can be no doubt it celebrates Satan, not just as a "light bringer" but in a more general sense:

There is a creature, who goes around
And causes only uproar and unpleasantness.
Formerly he is supposed to have floated freely in heavenly ether
And been on equal terms with divine beings. [73]

"Spartacus" pronounces Lucifer a socialist hero, who will "bring light to thralls and ruin to tormentors."[74] Similar examples of socialist Satanism crowd a variety of Swedish socialist publications well into the early 20th century. Satan, as the spirit of progress, is especially recurrent in the Socialist Youth Association's magazine *Brand* (Fire). A 1907 issue contains the confrontational "Hymn to Satan" by the signature "n." This has obvious similarities to the Italian poem of the same title ("Inno a Satana," written in 1863, published 1865 and translated into Swedish by Aline Pipping in 1894) by Giosuè Carducci. As Carducci had received the Nobel Prize in literature in 1906, his work would have been widely known in Sweden at this time.[75] Carducci viewed the Catholic Church as an obstacle against the unification of Italy, and against rationality and progress in general (for example, the pope had condemned the steam locomotive). His poem, therefore, praises the devil as the Church's antagonist, portraying him as a protector of freethinkers and sceptics, connecting him with the alchemists and magicians historically oppressed by the priesthood.

Following in the footsteps of Carducci (and Bakunin), the author of the "Hymn to Satan" in *Brand* reinterprets the well-known narrative from Genesis 3 but celebrating Satan as the spirit of intellectual enlightenment, combating an enslaving God:

Hail thee, Satan,
who could entice
first woman
to pluck
the fruit of knowledge!
What was there before
the light of knowledge entered the world? ...

...

But You Great
Holy Satan
Lover of man
Hater of God
more clever was than
old God
who posited
the commandments filled with thanks.[76]

Engaging even more directly with Genesis 3, in a manner still reminiscent of "Hymn to Satan" and its various antecedents, is a text by Uppsala University literature professor Henrik Schück published in a 1905 issue of *Brand*. In this excerpt from a longer text, Schück demonstrates that the serpent did not lie when he told Eve that, contrary to God's intimations, she would *not* die by eating the forbidden fruit. It is God who is an envious falsifier. By contrast, the serpent is reliable and benevolent. In Schück's opinion, God wanted to retain his absolute power and feared that mankind might become his equal.[77] Who the hero is according to such a reading is quite obvious.

Much of the Satanic poetry in *Brand*, *Lucifer*, and other socialist publications may come across as quaintly amusing today. Contemporaries would have perceived them differently. Anarchists, connected to a series of violent deeds of terrorism, were genuinely feared in Sweden at the time of their publication. In July 1908, a bomb attached to the hull of a ship in Malmö harbour housing English strike breakers killed one and injured many. In 1909, the commander of the Swedish coastal artillery was shot dead in Stockholm by an anarchist carrying an issue of *Brand* in his pocket.[78] *Brand* and its insurrectionary content was no joke to Swedes. The anarchists wanted people to fear them, and Satanism was one of their tools to accomplish this.

1880s mainline Social Democrats had initially desired the same thing and viewed the Church as a chief enemy. When the party started to aim seriously for a place in parliament, and purged its more extreme members, dramatic tactics like rhetorical Satanism had to be abandoned. Over time, the figure faded in relevance in other phalanxes of Swedish social-ism as well, with the mysterious, visionary atmosphere of the early mythological allegories being replaced by a more naturalist and social realist approach. Satan was thus discarded among Swedish socialists both for strategic reasons (in order not to scare voters), and be-cause of an aesthetic reorientation reflecting a broader cultural abandonment of literary styles like Romanticism and Symbolism.

## Quo Vadis, Satanic Revolutionary?

With the outbreak of World War I, literary and political Satanism became less prominent globally. It did not, for example, feature prominently in the Russian revolution of 1917. A new era of revolutions occurred in the 1960s—with the protests of the civil rights move-ment in the United States, student revolts across the world, and in the early 1970s the rise of leftist terrorist groups like Rote Armee Fraktion (Red Army Faction) and Bewegung 2. Juni (2 June Movement) in West Germany—and once more, the motif of Satan as a virtu-ous rebel appeared. For instance, the civil rights activist Saul Alinsky (1909–1972), an author much admired by Hilary Clinton, praised Lucifer as "the first radical known to man who rebelled against the establishment" in the epigraph of his influential book *Rules for Radicals* (1971).[79] And in the Bewegung 2. Juni, the internal greeting was "Hail Satan," as members were avid readers of Bakunin and Proudhon.[80]

Today, this tradition is particularly kept alive in The Satanic Temple, the secularist activ-ist organisation founded in the United States in 2013. Part spoof, and part enthusiastic em-brace of the long-running tradition of revolutionary (symbolic) Satanism, this group arose as part of a wider reaction to the increasing influence of neo-conservatism and evangelical Christianity in American politics (which would eventually lead up to the election of Donald Trump as the president in 2016). Its material extensively references Bakunin, Proudhon, Shelley, and other literary and political Satanists. Using Satanism strategically, The Satanic Temple has attempted to showcase the absurdity of the special affordances made for Chris-tian groups in American legislation, for example, by establishing "After School Satan" in response to the Evangelical "Good News Clubs" being allowed to offer after-school activi-ties in public schools or donating a huge Satanic statue as a countermove to the installation of Ten Commandments-themed monuments on State Capitol grounds (arguably a violation of church-state separation).[81]

The Satanic Temple is very much the product of an aggregating mediatisation of religion and has proved masterful at manoeuvring traditional mass media and orchestrating cam-paigns via social media platforms. Through its plethora of local sub-groups, it has man-aged to re-establish Satanism as a language of political resistance across the United States and beyond. In a sense, we live in a new age of revolutions, typified by decentralised social media-based initiatives like The Satanic Temple and Black Lives Matter—and wherever widespread revolutionary tendencies are coupled with a conservative establishment rooted in Christianity, some radicals inevitably seem to turn to Satan.

## Notes

1 Eric Hobsbawm, *The Age of Revolution: 1789–1848* (New York, 1962/1996).
2 Eric Hobsbawm, *The Age of Empire, 1875–1914* (London, 1987), 8.
3 On the English Civil War, see David R. Como, *Radical Parliamentarians and the English Civil War* (New York, 2018).
4 For a recent account of Milton's career, see Joe Moshenska, *Making Darkness Light: A Life of John Milton* (New York, 2021).
5 Peter A. Schock, *Romantic Satanism: Myth and the Historical Moment in Blake, Shelley, and Byron* (Basingstoke, 2003), 27.
6 John Milton, *The Complete Poetical Works of John Milton* (Cambridge, 1941), 155; C. S. Lewis, *A Preface to Paradise Lost* (London, 1942/1944), 92–100.
7 Arthur O. Lovejoy, *Essays in the History of Ideas* (New York, 1948/1955), 228–53; Cf. Duncan Heath, *Introducing Romanticism* (Cambridge, 2006); David Blayney Brown, *Romanticism* (London, 2001).
8 Cf. Ruben van Luijk, *Satan Rehabilitated? A Study into Satanism during the Nineteenth Century* (PhD dissertation, Tilburg University, 2013), 103.
9 Per Faxneld, "Disciples of Hell: The History of Satanism," in *The Routledge History of Witchcraft*, ed. Johannes Wilfried Dillinger (London, 2020), 332–48.
10 M. H. Abrams, *The Mirror and the Lamp: Romantic Theory and the Critical Tradition* (London, 1953/1974), 251.
11 Edmund Burke, *A Philosophical Enquiry into the Origin of our Ideas of the Sublime and Beautiful* (London, 1756/1823), 73.
12 Burke, *A Philosophical* Enquiry, 81–2.
13 Edmund Burke, *Reflections on the Revolution in France* (Harmondsworth, [1790]/1969).
14 "ein revolutionäres Buch gegen die Revolution." Novalis, *Gesammelte Werke* (Frankfurt am Main, 2008), 386.
15 Robert Burns, *Selected Poems* (London, 1993), 118–21.
16 William Godwin, *An Enquiry Concerning Political Justice* (London, 1993), 146.
17 Godwin, *Enquiry*, 146.
18 Peter A. Schock, *Romantic Satanism: Myth and the Historical Moment in Blake, Shelley, and Byron* (Houndsmills, 2003), 2 and 34.
19 Ronald Paulson, *Representations of Revolution (1789–1820)* (New Haven, 1983), 192; Schock, *Romantic Satanism*, 19.
20 Anna Budziak, "Genius and Madness Mirrored: Rossetti's and Yeats' Reception of William Blake," in *Crossroads in Literature and Culture*, ed. Jacek Fabiszak & Ewa Urbaniak-Rybicka (Berlin, 2013), 282.
21 Peter L. Jr. Thorslev, "The Romantic Mind Is Its Own Place," *Comparative Literature* 15, no. 3 (1963): 260.
22 William Blake, *The Complete Poetry and Prose* (Berkeley, 2008), 34.
23 John Howard, "An Audience for the Marriage of Heaven and Hell," *Blake Studies* 3, no. 1 (1970): 39–52; Schock, *Romantic Satanism*, 6–7, 42–4.
24 Blake, *Complete Poetry*, 35.
25 Percy Bysshe Shelley, *The Prose Works of Percy Bysshe Shelley*, vol. 1 (Oxford, 1993), 6.
26 Schock, *Romantic Satanism*, 115–6.
27 Shelley, *Prose Works*, 214.
28 Shelley, *Prose Works*, 197.
29 Percy Bysshe Shelley, *The Poetical Works of Percy Bysshe Shelley* (Oxford, 1908), 791.
30 Shelley, *Prose Works*, 134.
31 Shelley, *Poetical Works*, 781 (VII, 194–5).

32 Shelley, *Poetical Works*, 46–7 (I. xxvii, 361–78).
33 Shelley, *Poetical Works*, 47 (I. xxxi, 403).
34 Kyle Grimes, "Censorship, Violence, and Political Rhetoric: The Revolt of Islam in Its Time," *Keats-Shelley Journal*, 43 (1994): 100.
35 Kenneth N. Cameron, "A Major Source of the Revolt of Islam," *Publications of the Modern Language Association*, 56, no. 1 (1941): 202.
36 Samuel Taylor Coleridge, *On the Constitution of the Church and State, According to the Idea of Each: Lay Sermons* (London, 1816/1839), 24.
37 Quoted in Schock, *Romantic Satanism*, 123.
38 Robert Southey, *A Vision of Judgement* (London, 1821), xxi.
39 Schock, *Romantic Satanism*, 25, 101–3.
40 Lord George Gordon Byron, *The Complete Poetical Works*, vol. VI (Oxford, 1991), 275.
41 See Lord George Gordon Byron, *The Complete Poetical Works*, vols 1, 4 and 6 (Oxford, 1980–1991); John Milton, *The Complete Poetical Works of John Milton* (Cambridge, 1941), 160.
42 Schock, *Romantic Satanism*, 38.
43 Byron, *Poetical Works*, vol. 4 (Oxford, 1986), 32.
44 Alfred de Vigny, *Œuvres complètes*, vol. I (s.l, 1986), 10–31. For a slightly dated but still useful discussion of French sentimental sympathy for the devil, see Maximilian Rudwin, *The Devil in Legend and Literature* (New York, 1931/1970), 285–99.
45 Victor Hugo, *Poésie*, vol. III (Paris, 1972), 1280.
46 "Je ne suis pas le démon, je suis l'archange de la révolte légitime et le patron des grandes luttes. Comme le Christ, je suis le Dieu du pauvre, du faible et de l'opprimé." George Sand, *Consuelo* (Paris, 1979), 285.
47 Lois Boe Hyslop, "Baudelaire, Proudhon, and 'Le Reniement de saint Pierre'" *French Studies* 30, no. 3 (1976): 273–4.
48 Cf. Luijk, *Satan Rehabilitated?*, 174; Per Faxneld, *Satanic Feminism: Lucifer as the Liberator of Woman in Nineteenth-Century Culture* (New York, 2017), 252–68.
49 Jules Michelet, *La sorcière* (Nijmegen, [1862]/1989).
50 Faxneld, *Satanic Feminism*, 199–208.
51 K. Steven Vincent, *Pierre-Joseph Proudhon and the Rise of French Republican Socialism* (New York, 1984), 53.
52 Cf. Per Faxneld, *Mörkrets apostlar: Satanism i äldre tid* (Sundbyberg, 2006), 91.
53 "L'esprit d'analyse, Satan infatigable qui interroge et contredit sans cesse." Pierre-Joseph Proudhon, *Système des contradictions économiques ou philosophie de la misère* (Paris, n. d.), 7.
54 "A moi, Lucifer, Satan, qui que tu sois, démon que la foi de mes pères opposa à Dieu et à l'Eglise! Je porterai ta parole, et je ne te demande rien." Pierre-Joseph Proudhon, *Idée générale de la Révolution au XIXe siècle* (Paris, 1923), 307.
55 "La liberté, symbolisée dans l'histoire de la tentation, est votre anté-christ; la liberté, pour vous, c'est le diable. Viens, Satan, viens, le calomnié des prêtres et des rois, que je t'embrasse, que je te serre sur ma poitrine!" Pierre-Joseph Proudhon, *Œuvres complètes*, vol. 3 (Paris, 1932), 433–4:
56 Edward Hyams, Pierre-Joseph *Proudhon: His Revolutionary Life, Mind and Works* (London, 1979), 12, 28; Vincent, *Pierre-Joseph Proudhon*, 65 and 72–3.
57 Faxneld, *Mörkrets apostlar*, 96; T. J. Clark, *The Absolute Bourgeois: Artists and Politics in France 1848–1851* (London, 1973), 164; James Henry Rubin, *Realism and Social Vision in Courbet & Proudhon* (New Jersey, 1980), 51–3 and 148–9; Lois Boe Hyslop, "Baudelaire, Proudhon, and 'Le Reniement de saint Pierre'," *French Studies*, 30, no. 3 (1976); Richard E. *Burton, Baudelaire and the Second Republic: Writing and Revolution* (Oxford, 1991), 198–9, 259.
58 Michael Bakunin, *God and the State* (New York, 1970), 24.
59 Bakunin, *God and the State*, 25.
60 Bakunin, *God and the State*, 10.
61 Bakunin, *God and the State*, 10.
62 Bakunin, *God and the State*, 10.
63 Bakunin, *God and the State*, 12.
64 Bakunin, *God and the State*, 23.
65 The 1891 magazine had been preceded by two more amateurish Social Democratic publications both called *Lucifer*, both only published in one issue (Christmas 1893, April 1887).

66 On early Scandinavian Satanism in non-political contexts, see Per Faxneld, "The Strange Case of Ben Kadosh: A Luciferian Pamphlet from 1906 and Its Current Renaissance," *Aries: Journal for the Study of Western Esotericism*, 11, no. 1 (2011): 1–22; Faxneld, *Mörkrets apostlar*, 134–40.

67 Per Faxneld, "The Devil is Red: Socialist Satanism in Nineteenth-Century Europe," *Numen: International Review for the History of Religions*, 60, no. 5 (2013): 542–3.

68 Axel Uhlén, *Arbetardiktningens pionjärperiod: 1885—1909* (Johanneshov: Bokförlaget Vanadis, 1964), 48–9, 53–7.

69 Uhlén *Arbetardiktningens*, 28–32. Wermelin was a co-editor of the 1886 and 1887 *Lucifer* publications.

70 "Du skall inga andra gudar hava för mig, Ljusbringaren." Atterdag Wermelin, "Lucifers tio bud" *Lucifer: Socialdemokratiskt flygblad* (Christmas 1886), 2.

71 "Du skall icke begära din nästas hustru, så framt hon ej begärer dig ensam, men hans oxe och åsna samt allt kapital honom tillhörer skall du taga ifrån honom och göra till dina bröders egendom." Wermelin, "Lucifers tio bud," 2.

72 "I Satans gestalt, i Prometeus' gestalt / Förblef jag densamme—okuflig." Atterdag Wermelin, "Ljusbringaren," *Lucifer: Flygblad för bespottelse och galghumor*, 1. no. 2 (1887): 1.

73 "Det finns en varelse, som går omkring / Och ställer till blott bråk och ledsamheter. / Förr lär han ha sväfvat fritt i himmelsk ether / Och varit du och bror med herligheter." The poem has a comical tone in the original Swedish, difficult to convey in English. Spartacus is identified as Carleson elsewhere in the same issue, where it is also mentioned that he too, like Wermelin, was a former student at Uppsala University. "Spartacus," "Lucifer," *Lucifer: Arbetarkalender*, 1 no. 1 (1891): 2 and 68.

74 "bringa trälar ljus och plågarne förderf." "Spartacus," "Lucifer," 3.

75 Giosuè Carducci, *Valda dikter*, trans. by Aline Pipping (Stockholm, 1894). On Carducci's poem, see Faxneld, *Mörkrets apostlar*, 98–100.

76 "Hell dig Satan, / som kunde locka / första kvinnan /till att plocka / kunskapens frukt! / Vad fanns väl innan / vetandets ljus i världen kom?' (…) 'Men Du Store / Helige Satan, / Mänskoälskarn, / Gudahatarn, / slugare var än / åldrige guden / som ställde upp / de tackfyllda buden." "n.," "Hymn till Satan" *Brand*, 10, no. 5 (1907): 5.

77 Schück, Henrik, "Paradis-Sagan: Ur den israeliska litteraturen," *Brand*, 8. no. 9 (1905): 11.

78 Uhlén *Arbetardiktningens*, 290.

79 Per Faxneld, "Problematiskt med Satan som god förebild," *Svenska Dagbladet* (June 22, 2006).

80 "Bommi" [Michael] Baumann, *Wie alles anfing* (Frankfurt: Sozialistische Verlagslieferung, 1976), 81.

81 Manon Hedenborg-White & Fredrik Gregorius, "The Satanic Temple: Secularist Activism and Occulture in the American Political Landscape," *International Journal for the Study of New Religions* 10, no. 1 (2019): 89–110.

## Further Reading

Clark, T. J. (1973) *The Absolute Bourgeois: Artists and Politics in France 1848–1851*, London: Thames and Hudson.

Per Faxneld (2013) "The Devil is Red: Socialist Satanism in Nineteenth-Century Europe", *Numen: International Review for the History of Religions*, vol. 60, no. 5, pp. 528–58.

Per Faxneld (2017) *Satanic Feminism: Lucifer as the Liberator of Woman in Nineteenth-Century Culture*, New York: Oxford University Press.

Paulson, Ronald (1983) *Representations of Revolution (1789–1820)*, New Haven: Yale University Press.

Rudwin, Maximilian (1931/1970) *The Devil in Legend and Literature*, New York: Ams Press.

Peter A. Schock, *Romantic Satanism: Myth and the Historical Moment in Blake, Shelley, and Byron*, Houndsmills, Basingstoke: Palgrave Macmillan, 2003.

# 19

# DEVIL AND WAR

## 1600–1920

*David R. Lawrence*

### Introduction

In the western Christian tradition, the devil was born of war.[1] The bible and the church fathers tell of Satan being driven from heaven in the aftermath of a great cosmic battle with the Archangel Michael and an army of good angels. Victory goes to Michael and, though bruised and bloodied, the devil is hardly broken. As the books of Daniel and Revelation vividly describe, Satan was now locked in a great struggle with God and Christ—a war that will eventually culminate in Christ's victory and Satan's destruction in a lake of fire. Sadly, for people, this cosmic struggle had its earthly manifestations. After the fall (both of Satan and humanity), mankind lived in a world where the devil encouraged conflict and disorder. War soon became the saddest and most destructive of human inventions. Throughout history, theologians, politicians and propagandists have argued that it is Satan who prods man to take up arms against his fellow man. As the 16th-century French demonologist Nicholas Rémy concluded in his 1595 *Daemonolatreiae (Demonolatry)*, the devil "from the beginning … was a murderer, a calumniator, robber, destroyer, traitor, tormentor and slaughterer." His chief desire and object are "that his subjects should, like himself, busy themselves to procure the misery and misfortune of others."[2]

Since 1600, there have been wars aplenty, waged on the European continent between the great powers, between Europeans and the indigenous peoples of the Americas, Africa and Asia, and as civil wars that cleaved nations as diverse as France, Germany, Britain and the United States. During this period, the weaponry developed has made combat deadlier and evermore destructive. At the beginning of the 17th century, Western armies relied on cannon and handheld gunpowder weapons, but by the end of the First World War, the destructive forces unleashed by militaries turned battlefields like Verdun and the Somme into muddy, cratered, rat-infested hellscapes—truly tramping grounds for the devil and his minions. Some have seen Satan's hand in each new technological development that enhanced killing, from his assistance in combining sulphur, charcoal and saltpetre to create gunpowder, to the invention of the 19th-century Maxim machine gun, affectionately referred to by British troops as "the devil's paintbrush." By the 20th century, Jeffrey Burton Russell

DOI: 10.4324/9781003096603-20

points out that the array of weaponry available to modern armies had become "physical concretizations of the demonic."[3]

This chapter addresses the relationship between the devil and the wars fought by Western powers from 1600 to 1920. While the geographical locations, causes and combatants vary significantly, four prominent themes emerge linking the diabolic and demonic to each of the conflicts examined. The first is the central role of religion in these wars and, by extension, the significance of both diabolism and providentialism in the rhetoric and propaganda employed by the antagonists. Many historians have noted that the religious or confessional wars of the early modern period concluded with the end of the Thirty Years' War in 1648.[4] However, this claim has been challenged and, as we will see, diabolism, apocalypticism, millenarianism and chiliasm appear whenever conflicts began, including those with causes as diverse as the Thirty Years' War, the English and American Civil Wars, the Indian Wars in the United States and the First World War.

Second, in a holy war, customary constraints found within the laws of war could be abrogated in order to defend the faith and vanquish infidels. The demonisation and vilification of the enemies of God often preceded the outbreak of wars, or these could build during conflicts, thereby making it easier for combatants to engage in brutal violence to expel or exterminate their foes. When Western armies went to war, it was priests, propagandists, politicians, satirists and cartoonists who were behind this rhetoric of demonisation—a rhetoric that portrayed their enemies in league with the devil or his son, Antichrist. This demonisation could be tempered, as it was in the French Wars of Religion and the American Civil War, with one side arguing that their opponents were not necessarily demonic or on the side of the devil but had rather been tempted into rebellion and secession by him and, consequently, it was only through the victory of God's chosen that the state be made whole again. In other wars, such as the Thirty Years' War, the English Civil War, the Anglo-Irish Wars and the Indian Wars in America, this vilification was driven by religious ideology or in the case of the latter two conflicts, by a combination of religion and bitter racial animus.[5]

Third, during these conflicts the devil has been portrayed not only as a threat to individual Christians, but also the well-being of the state or, more broadly, Western civilisation. The devil was history's first rebel, the instigator of disorder, sedition and secession. Monarchs, princes and politicians, as representatives of the commonwealth (but also as mere mortals), were susceptible to the devil's wiles. As the Rolling Stones' sang in their 1968 "Sympathy for the Devil," throughout history Satan appears to tempt those in power, and as this chapter will reveal, monarchs such as Philip II of Spain, Charles I of England, George III of Britain and Wilhelm II of Germany were all accused of falling under Satan's powerful influence. Leaders possessing great military power or martial genius, such as Oliver Cromwell and Napoleon Bonaparte, were also open to attack, with enemies claiming their successes were either the product of pacts with Lucifer or the maleficent assistance of his minions.[6]

Finally, what of the individual soldiers bound for these wars? How did warriors confront the threat of evil and the demonic on the battlefield and how did they protect themselves against threats to their person or strengthen themselves to overcome their opponents? In many cases, soldiers considered providentialism, rather than demonism, as the reason for the battlefield deaths of friends and enemies alike.[7] Below, we encounter armies and individual soldiers believed to possess magical powers that made them difficult to defeat. To counter these evil forces, soldiers sought protection by donning spiritual as well as physical armour. Catholic soldiers had an "arsenal of sacramental objects" that they used to defend themselves against the diabolical in battle, including amulets, rosaries, saints' medals and scapulars.[8] Protestants, however, rejected these protections as superstitious and were left to find other means of combatting the devil. Many turned to scripture, carrying pocket bibles, psalm books, pages of scripture and religious postcards, while others used tried and true methods, carrying tested Catholic talismans into battle. Stories abound of miraculous escapes and bullets and shrapnel being stopped by bibles and amulets in wars from the 17th to the 20th century, with both Catholic and Protestant cheating death (and the devil) by bearing charms said, by some, to have "great potency."[9]

### The Grand Captain of Wickedness: Satan as a Soldier

In the history of western Christendom, the devil has worn many guises, but it is his position as commander of an army of demons, witches and familiars—his legion—that is surely one of his most renowned, inspiring authors, playwrights and filmmakers well into the 21st century. Western literature is replete with references to Satan's army and the threat it poses to humankind, perils described by Neil Forsyth as using the "standard metaphors of apocalyptic military terminology."[10] But as Forsyth notes, myths about supernatural struggles between the powers of good and evil had a long history before the emergence of Christianity.[11] As earlier chapters have shown, over the following centuries, Christians developed an elaborate and complex demonology that they used to gain adherents. Key here was the notion of spiritual warfare which came to occupy "a central role in the Christian-European psyche and culture."[12] Commanding his vast demonic army, the devil is both the "grand captaine of wickednesse" and chief strategist, the leader of a "great conspiracy ... against the Christian community."[13] From his war room in hell, he sows division, chaos and discord, pushing humanity away from Christ. Like any general, he has a lieutenancy, but this one comprises fallen angels, demons and witches, all bound by a strict military hierarchy. Beelzebub, Moloch and Mammon offer strategic advice, but it is the devil who ultimately decides his army's battle plan. Since the fall, various authorities have claimed that Lucifer has recruited millions of damned souls to his ranks—diabolical conscripts who have become his servants. Such great numbers were required in order to overcome his omnipotent and omniscient enemy: God. Various late medieval and early modern theologians sought to calculate the size of this army, no doubt in response to Revelation 9.16 that put Gog's army at "two hundred thousand thousand." The Spanish converso priest, Alfonso de Spina, author of the 1485 *Fortalitium Fidei* (Fortress of Faith) counted 133,306,668 soldiers while Sigmund Feyerabend insisted in his 1569 *Theatrum Diabolorum* (Theatre of Devils) that the army run to an astounding 26 billion souls.[14]

In war, Satan was thought to employ a range of powers to further his interests, among them the abilities to conjure up great storms, fog or rain to mask an army's movements, slow an advance or provide his favourites with a tactical edge; sink ships by the stirring of winds, waves or whirlpools; raise plagues and pestilence to decimate armies and states; deceive combatants into surrendering in battles or sieges; curse, hex or cast spells to obstruct opponents or to bring victory to the force he preferred and carry men distances in the flash of an eye, thereby keeping them safe from wounds or capture. Devils and demons were also adept at shape-shifting, taking human or animal forms, or occupying the bodies of the dead—making them appear reanimated so as to mislead or confuse the living. Satan and his minions could also enchant weapons—either making them more powerful or rendering them useless. Equally, he could grant the user special skills or dexterity when wielding sword, bow or gun. Likewise, Satan could make certain parts of a fighter's body immune to these different types of weapons. And, of course, he could use his vast knowledge of nature seemingly to conjure up fire or lightning bolts to strike down his enemies. In all of this, though, it is important to note that soldiers' fears of these supernatural forces were stoked by the widely held belief, reinforced by blood curdling tales in the demonological literature, that the devil could cause death or serious physical harm to anyone encountering him or his army. [15]

## Putting on the Face of Hell: The Devil in Late Medieval and Early Modern Warfare

By the 17th century, the devil's position in the West was firmly established and his association with human evil and warfare was beyond question. Late medieval and early modern demonological texts drew heavily upon biblical martialism when offering advice on combatting the devil. These texts made use of works by the church fathers that explored the circumstances in which Christians could, or could not, take up arms against their enemies. These early debates laid the foundations of the just war tradition, which was being formulated at the same time that Christians were confronting the nature of evil and the role of the devil in the world. Just war theories, including those later developed by Thomas Aquinas in the 13th century, taught that wars were the product of sin and that Christians could, if required, take up the sword to eradicate evil and the forces of Satan. Aquinas claimed that men "should wage war against the demons" but should not "make use of the demons' help by compacts either tacit or express" to advance their cause.[16] Some 250 years later, Martin Luther went further, stating empathically in his 1526 *Ob Kriegsleute auch in seligem Stande sein können* (Whether Soldiers, Too, Can be Saved) "what else is war than the punishment of wrong or evil? Why does anyone go to war, except because he desires peace and obedience?"[17]

While these thinkers argued that Christ's followers should refrain from fighting one another, all agreed that armed force could be used to oppose those allied with the devil, and notably this included pagans, infidels and heretics.[18] As Elaine Pagels has suggested in her study of the devil in early Christianity, Satan's role in human conflicts led Christians to associate their enemies with "the embodiment of transcendent forces" and this "vindicated Jesus' followers and demonised their enemies."[19] However, in 1517 the Reformation precipitated a split in Christendom that led to a lengthy period of bloody and brutal religious wars which saw Christian slaughter Christian.[20] Lutherans soon found that they could add "Catholics, monks, Turks, and radical Protestants" to the rank and file of Satan's army.[21] For many contemporaries, the confessional wars amplified the devil's powerful influence over the lives of Europeans, what Erasmus of Rotterdam had called the "encircling ocean of all of the evils in the world."[22] These wars, spawned in part by apocalyptic and millenarian beliefs, saw the formation of ever larger armies that unleashed chaos and barbarism across the continent. It is no coincidence that the so-called "century of the soldier" corresponded to the "age of atrocity," the "age of the witch hunts," the "golden age of the demoniac," and "the crisis of the seventeenth century."[23]

By this time, battles and sieges had taken on new, hellish qualities with the roar of great cannon, clouds of black powder smoke and bloody collisions of squares of pike and shot arrayed amidst fire and brimstone. Many believed that it was Satan who invented gunpowder, passing the recipe to the fabled German monk Berthold Schwarz sometime in the early 14th century, thereby transforming warfare forever. Illustrations depicted this fatal moment in history, with a horned devil giving a sack of powder to the monk as he carries it towards two great siege guns. The Sienese metallurgist Vannoccio Biringuccio claimed, in his popular 1540 *Pirotechnia*, that gunpowder's inventor was influenced either by "demons or by chance," an assertion echoed by Francesco Guicciardini in his *History of Italy*.[24] Late medieval cannons were described as "the devil's gonne" while handheld firearms were diabolical instruments or engines.[25] The round shot fired from these weapons travelled much further, faster and with more destructive force than either trebuchet stones or arrows, thus appearing to onlookers to be the work of the devil.[26] Gunpowder's fiendish creation story echoed down to John Milton who, in his 1667 *Paradise Lost*, wrote that it was Satan who handed Adam a reed "tipt with fire," an "instrument to plague the Sons of men."[27]

The results of the devil's handiwork were on show for all to see in the wars of the late 16th and early 17th centuries. To many, it seemed clear that it was Satan (or Antichrist) who caused these conflicts, sowing discord in the royal courts and halls of power to foment war. While Catholics, Lutherans and Calvinists all agreed that one of the devil's greatest abilities was his power to tempt people—implying that good Christians should strive to resist such allurements—it was evident that given the profits and powers that could be won through war, monarchs and princes were as susceptible to these temptations as peasants and paupers.[28] Indeed, in his 1580 *De la Démonomanie des sorciers* (On the Demon-Mania of Witches), Jean Bodin cited the King of Sweden's use of four witches to "prevent victories" in a war with Denmark in 1563 and argued, on the basis of the claims of the sorcerer Trois-Échelles, that 30,000 sorcerers were active in France in 1571 influencing the course of the civil war.[29] The Protestant soldier-author Francois de La Noue claimed that peace would only be achieved when those same sorcerers had been overcome.[30] What this meant was that whole commonwealths could be overthrown if a ruler fell under Satan's influence and took his state or principality to war.[31] That influence was said to be present in the war in the Low Countries, where the Dutch argued that ever since the late 1560s their Spanish overlord, Philip II, had selected demonic proxies, including the Duke of Alva, Cardinal Granvelle and the members of the Council of Blood, to suppress their rebellion. Dutch print makers took great pride in expressing their hatred for the villainous Alva, the so-called Butcher of Flanders, by portraying him in the presence of the devil.[32] When the English joined the Dutch cause in 1585, they too were convinced of Spain's collusion with dark forces. In his 1592 sermon, *The Solace for the Souldier and Saylor*, the cleric Simon Howard justified his country's entry into the war on the grounds that Philip II had joined with Antichrist in Rome to support rebellion against the Dutch and Queen Elizabeth, owing to his allegiance to the "Prince of Rebels, Lucifer himselfe."[33]

The Dutch Revolt and the Anglo-Spanish Wars gave rise to the Black Legend, which stressed Spanish brutality, fuelled in part by the "simmering apocalypticism" of print propaganda, with God and the devil choosing sides in preparation for a great European conflagration. The Spanish cruelties, Protestants vehemently argued, had shown Catholicism and Spain in their true light, revealing their Church as the "synagogue of Satan." Johann Heinrich Alsted and Johann Amos Comenius, two Palatine Calvinists who studied in the Low Countries in the late 16th century, asserted in apocalyptic language that the House of Hapsburg, with its centres in Madrid, Brussels and Vienna, was the Fourth Monarchy of Revelation and that—consequently—it had to be accepted that the continent was on the verge of a cataclysmic battle between Christ and Satan. This was a prophecy that appeared to come to pass as the horrors of the Thirty Years' War compounded in the years after 1618.[34]

The Thirty Years' War proved to be one of the most destructive in German history. It was brought on in part by Calvinist millenarians who judged that the time had come to bring down the House of Hapsburg and its demonic allies, thereby preparing the way for Christ's return.[35] Catholics, including those close to the centre of Hapsburg power, notably Cardinal Melchior Klesl, one of the Emperor Ferdinand's councillors, in turn, justified imperial action against the Protestant rebels in Prague by claiming that the Calvinists were acting in league with the devil and that

> God had undoubtedly willed to bring about this troubling, terrible situation, so that the whole world and all reasonable men of whatever religion could recognize how repulsive, unjust, unchristian, unreasonable, unevangelical and worthy of punishment and execution [were the rebels].[36]

The Thirty Years' War included a vast cast of characters—monarchs, princes, courtiers and generals—whose actions, their enemies asserted, were manipulated by the devil and his familiars. One newsbook claimed there were rumours that Count Tilly, the successful general of the Catholic League and the man responsible for the infamous Sack of Magdeburg in 1631, could not be killed by gunfire, having gained his shot-free powers from "devilish inchantment."[37] The Protestant Swedish king, Gustavus Adolphus, who invaded the Holy Roman Empire in 1630 and attempted to drive back Tilly and the Catholic armies, firmly believed that the devil was influencing the course of the war. Praised by Protestants as Revelation's [Rev. 5.5] "Lion from the North," Gustavus commanded a godly army he wished to keep free of the demonic manipulation of the "reprobate raskalitie" of Tilly's army. In the Swedish Articles of War, the rules and regulations governing his soldiers, Gustavus established as his very first injunction that the use of "any kind of idolatry, witchcraft or Enchanting of Armes, by devils enchantment any manner or way whatsoever" was prohibited in the ranks. He gave assurances that any malefactors (sorcerers and witches) would be kept out of camp to protect soldiers from spells placed on their persons or weapons.[38] Despite these concerns, the arrival of war to many Germanic lands actually saw a significant decline, rather than an increase in cases of witchcraft. As Brian Levack notes, "the presence of soldiers in an area … gave local residents alternative means of explaining misfortune."[39] The death and dislocation accompanying the Thirty Years' War (as well as the civil wars in Britain) saw a decrease in the male population, which led to the victimisation of widowed or unmarried women and girls after the wars concluded.

In 1641, as the Thirty Years' War raged on the continent, a rebellion broke out in Ireland which pitted Irish Catholics against the Anglo-Scots colonists. An anonymous pamphlet printed the next year, entitled *The Mathematicall Divine, Shewing, the Present Miseries of Germany, England and Ireland* sought to tie together the "divers fires of war" now being waged in every corner of a continent that "hath put on the face of Hell." Each war, it argued, showed evidence of Satan's hand, with comets, plagues, and massacres wrought by the "cruel scourges and chiliads of miseries."[40] The English and Scots colonists had long considered the Irish to be savage and barbarous, and as papists, they were also confederates of "his Hellish majesty."[41] But the Catholics felt likewise, and when they murdered Anglo-Scots heretics in the course of the rebellion, they buried them facing downwards so "they might have a prospect and sight of Hell only, and therefore when they killed any of [them] they used always these words Ainm a Dwell [d'anam don Diabhal], which is thy soul to the Devil."[42]

Amidst all of this war and destruction, soldiers like those fighting in Ireland feared the unknown, believing that amulets and charms could protect them against bodily injury and the *maleficia* of any witches, sorcerers or shape-shifters encountered on the march. Early modern armies were composed of common folk whose mental world easily found room for demons, witches and assorted hobgoblins. Bloody conflicts offered up a host of unexplained events that soldiers often attributed to supernatural intervention—both good and bad. In the 1486 *Malleus Maleficarum*, Heinrich Kramer (Latinised as Institoris) observed that it was common for men-at-arms to carry charms and verses and "blessings that look like incantations" to ward off evil. The "unknown words and signed characters" on these charms implied that the wearer had entered into a tacit agreement "with a demon, and the demon secretly intervenes and brings about the things requested in order to eventually entice the man to worse crimes."[43] A century later, Bodin recorded that Spanish and Italian soldiers making their way along the Spanish Road to the Low Countries (to serve under the Duke of Alva) were wary of entering lands infested with heretics and carried "notes full of spells, which they had been given in order to be safe from all evils." Some Germans wore the "shirt of necessity," a protective undergarment covered with crosses to safeguard the wearer on the battlefield.[44] Amulets protected soldiers against known (or unknown) enemies and against injuries to certain parts of the body—usually those closest to the charm.[45] Such protections might also include making one shot-proof or impervious to bladed weapons. A pamphlet informing Londoners of an Anglo-Scots victory over the rebels at Kinsale in September 1642 cited evidence of the diabolical protections offered soldiers in Ireland. The colonists had been directed in battle by the "finger of God" so "that his power & providence in his own cause might be the more clearly discerned by us." The rebels, however, were aided by Catholic friars who had "given many of them Charms to keep them shot-free."[46] One of the chapbooks found in George Sinclair's 1685 compilation *Satan's Invisible World Discovered* also suggested that it was well known that Irish troops were employing supernatural aids in battle, reporting that they "carry charms about them to make them shot-free when they go to war; as also hath been found by experience in the late Irish wars, many of the idolatrous Irish being found with charms in their pockets, composed by the Popish clergy."[47]

While amulets might ward off injury, being made "shot-proof" was bound closely with the diabolical and stories abounded of soldiers and civilians making pacts with demons, witches and sorcerers to gain bullet-proof protection.[48] Priests and ministers often blessed the weapons of those headed for war and early modern physicians applied weapons salves in order to heal wounds. Asking the devil to make one shot-proof was simply the inversion of these Christian practices. In this capacity, evidence given in the case of Giles Fenderlin, said to have been prosecuted in England in 1652 for murdering his wife, is instructive. Fenderlin had served in the Low Countries in 1638, and there, he confessed, he had purchased from a Jesuit (linking the demonic and the papist) certain protections against "any hurt or danger, either by iron, steel or lead; or any wound by gun-shot, stab, or cut by sword, dagger or knife."[49] The Jesuit also granted Fenderlin a ring that gave him the ability to find buried money and travel long distances. In the end, though, Fenderlin admitted that he fell prey to Satan's machinations and this caused him to murder his wife—and for that crime he was hanged in March 1652.

The use of demonic amulets to ward off harm in battle is perhaps most ironically represented in the great novel of the Thirty Years' War, the 1669 *Der abenteuerliche Simplicissimus Teutsch* (Simplicissimus: The German Adventurer) by Hans Jacob Christoffel von Grimmelshausen. At one point, a soldier encountered an irreligious peasant who had been made shot-proof by his devotion to Lucifer and was loudly rejecting God and the saints. This angered the soldier who fired his musket directly at the peasant's head. But the ball failed to find its mark, having "had no more effect than if it had been shot at a steel mountain." Seeing that, the soldier realised the demonic source of the peasant's power. Crying out, "Aha! So you are one of that ilk!," the soldier drew his broadsword and cleaved the peasant's head down the middle, dispatching him to hell.[50] The pact, it seemed, only made the peasant invulnerable to gun shot!

A number of similar stories were recorded during the English Civil War. The most famous of these relates to the demonism of Prince Rupert of the Palatinate, the nephew of Charles I and a renowned Royalist cavalry general. The English Revolution from 1642 to 1660 has been characterised by Nathan Johnstone as the "zenith of Satan's activity in England."[51] Charges of witchcraft and demonic collusion were levelled by both Parliamentary and Royalist presses against their enemies throughout this tumultuous period; attacks that began as the sides raised their armies in the summer of 1642. Prince Rupert's case is particularly interesting, owing to claims Mark Stoyle investigated in his book, *The Black Legend of Prince Rupert's Dog: Witchcraft and Propaganda during the English Civil War.*[52] Rupert's story pulls together many of the elements of early modern demonology, including the demonic pact, collusion with familiars, shot-proof protections, the casting of spells, shape-shifting, flying and invisibility.[53]

During the war, Rupert's dog, Boy accompanied the prince into battle and, as propagandists claimed, was one of Satan's familiars. The dog's powers were actually the invention of a Royalist pamphleteer but Parliamentary propagandists turned the tale (and Boy) against his master. It was claimed Boy boasted many of the same supernatural qualities as Rupert, including invisibility and being "weapon-proofe," with shot magically sliding "off his skin as if it had beene Armour or Proofe [a]nointed over with Quick-silver."[54] Boy also defended his master by breaking the force of shot fired in Rupert's direction, making it impossible for bullets to penetrate the prince's buff coat. When Rupert attended the Council of War, Boy rested one paw on the foot of his master and the other on the foot of Charles I, channelling diabolical thoughts from nephew to uncle. Boy's religious leanings were "mostly Popish" as he refused to attend the Established Church services with Rupert.[55] Boy, however, did not see out the war's conclusion. He was shot and savaged by Parliamentary troops after the Royalist defeat at the Battle of Marston Moor in 1644, no doubt the result of his well-known demonism. The story, however, lived on and represents one of the finest examples of the role of the devil, diabolism and propaganda in early modern warfare.

## The Offspring of Hell's Brood: Satan and War in Colonial America

In the 16th and 17th centuries, the Americas became the new battleground in the war between God and Satan, with European settlers arriving to establish empires in the New World. The natives they encountered were described as beasts, savages, cannibals and demons, and so posed a serious threat to the civilised Christians populating the Americas. With the colonisation of the New World came wars of conquest that would, in time, see the extermination of millions of the region's indigenous peoples. The devil figured prominently in these wars—no more so than in North America, where white settlers quickly came to associate Satan with the American Indian.

As a result, the devil's presence has been strongly felt across the wide arc of American history, especially in the context of the lengthy Indian Wars fought by white settler-colonists to secure the vast (occupied) continent Europeans "discovered" in 1492. By the 16th century, supporters of the English colonial project had strong suspicions that the devil had won over the natives of North America and that only Christianity and the fruits of European civilisation could save these "offspring of Hell's brood."[56] As Robert Ivie and Oscar Giner point out in their study of demonology and American war culture, the "Devil-Indian avatar became a constant symbol of hostility and violence in the strange threatening landscape of the New World."[57] Though English colonists and later, the citizens of the American Republic, were often of two minds as to the extent of Satan's hold over the Indians, the belief that these "red devils" must either be driven from white lands or exterminated influenced policies towards, and perceptions of Native Americans that persisted well into the late 19th century.[58]

Accordingly, there is a clear connection between the demonism underlying the early modern European confessional wars and that of the extirpative wars against the American Indians. The colonial settlers, especially those living on the "bleeding edge" of the frontier, sought to carve out farms, villages and towns from the primeval wilderness they found frightening and threatening.[59] For them, Indians haunted this wilderness in the same way that witches, demons and imps inhabited the woods, wastes and crossroads of Europe. One colonist observed soon after arriving in Jamestown in 1607 that "Satan visibly and palpably reignes" in Virginia, while another asserted that the local (Powhatan) natives' chief god "is no better than the devil."[60]

The English carried with them notions of civilisation that they wished to impose upon the Indians, hoping to free them from their supposed wicked heathenism.[61] But almost as soon as the Jamestown settlement was established, the colonists faced Indian attacks. Though some colonists called for peaceful coexistence, violence soon begat violence. As bad as this was, the nature of this warfare compounded the terror felt by the colonists and reinforced the idea that the natives were colluding with the devil. The whooping war chants of tattooed and feathered warriors, the warfighting methods of surprise, stealth, speed and "skulking" (warfare in which the Indians refused to meet their opponents in set-piece battles, and instead used raiding and ambushes) and the brutality of attacks on the colonists—especially women and children—were evidence enough that these godless savages were "representatives of Satan in the wilderness."[62] Though such attitudes were tempered over time, the demonised Indian created in Jamestown was never fully exorcised from the American psyche and has remained an important element of its war culture ever since.

In many respects, the role the devil and demonism played in the religious wars that defined post-Reformation Europe was simply transported wholesale to the American colonies. Indeed, many early colonial leaders were veterans of the European wars—and so brought with them not just their propensity towards violence but a willingness to cast those who opposed them as somehow demonic—with predictably bloody consequences. The Virginia Company's secretary, Edward Waterhouse (fl. 1622), for instance, wrote that the colonists were beginning a long struggle against a "wyld, naked" people who served the devil. To destroy them, the company hired "hammerours," veteran English and Scots troops who used the same brutal warfighting tactics—framed within a similar rhetoric of demonisation—against the Indians that they had used against Catholics in the Low Countries, Ireland and

Germany.[63] This demonic subtext gave these wars an apocalyptic dimension, turning a simple conflict over territory and control into a holy war that the colonists could not afford to lose.[64]

Although America's colonists were briefly distracted from their desire to eliminate the threat of the satanic "savages" on their frontier over the course of the Revolutionary War, the period after 1783 saw the genocidal struggle resume.[65] One historian has described the period as one in which "American Christianity fully developed the concept of 'spiritual warfare' in the revivalist context, a view of the Christian experience that once again emphasized the martial struggle with Satan and his demons."[66] Andrew Jackson's Indian wars reflected this belief system, with tragic results for the indigenous peoples of the continent.[67] By the 1860s and 1870s, exterminationist settlers on the western frontier still referred to the Indians as "devils in human shape" even though it was whites—generals such as James Carleton, George Custer, and Philip Sheridan (the last known for the infamous claim that "the only good Indian was a dead one")—who were behind the slaughter of thousands of indigenous people. Settlers, stoked by claims of American exceptionalism and the doctrine of manifest destiny, brought about the destruction of much of the Indian way of life, with the Sioux, Arapaho, Cheyenne, Apache, Navajo and countless other tribes demonised as "red devils." Writing in his memoirs in the mid-19th century, former army officer Colonel Philip St. George Cooke recounted an Indian attack by the Arikara of North Dakota on white fur traders that repeated the tropes of the demonic Indian dating from colonial America: "They rioted in blood with horrid grimaces and convulsive action they hewed into fragments the dumb lifeless bodies; they returned to their camp a moving group of dusky demons, exulting in revenge, besmeared with blood, bearing aloft each a mangled portion of the dead."[68] Newspapers regularly used headlines referring to "Indian Devils" or "Red Devils" in columns describing "wily savages" carrying out atrocities against "defenceless people."[69] An article in Baton Rouge's *Daily Advocate* in 1867 cautioned against taking a conciliatory approach to the Plains Indians, advising readers that these "Indian Devils" were "guilty of every imaginable crime."[70]

Though Anglo-Americans may have disagreed about the true nature of the Indian, whether they were demons or men, most held firm to the belief that by eliminating the Indian leadership, the larger body of Indian women and children could be assimilated into white American society. White settlers saw that leadership as bloodthirsty, treacherous, and deceitful—characteristics long associated with the devil. During the Pequot War of 1636 to 1637, Roger Williams claimed that the Indian sachems (chiefs) of New England only spoke "words of policie, falshood & Treacherye."[71] They were deceivers in words and deeds, refusing to observe the rules of war against the killing of innocents—even though the colonists regularly carried out atrocities against Indian women and children with equal ferocity.[72] For this reason, Anglo-Americans often singled out sachems, werowances, pow-waws and shaman as demons themselves or men working in the service of the devil. Many powerful chiefs who led the resistance against white settlers, from Powhatan to Sitting Bull, were accused of practising Satanism.[73] These chiefs, whites argued, had convinced the less powerful in their tribes to accept the devil's authority, offering ample reason to mark out the leadership for extermination. In 1587, Thomas Harriot observed that the Indian shaman he encountered in the Roanoke Colony was "very familiar with devils" and, two decades later, Captain John Smith concluded that the great sachem, Powhatan was "more like a devill than a man, with some two hundred more as blacke as himself."[74] During King Philip's War, which had opened in 1675 with an earthquake and a lunar eclipse—a troubling combination of ominous portents—Ezra Stiles chronicled an attack on the town of Bridgewater, south of Boston, in which a group of twenty Wampanoag Indians set fire to the houses there. They "had a Paww when the Devil appeared in the Shape of a Bear walking on his two hind feet: the Indians all followed him & drew off." Stiles went on to write that had a deer, rather than a bear, appeared to the Wampanoag, they would have destroyed the village and killed all the colonists.[75] Not unlike Rupert's Boy channelling demonic thoughts to Charles I, Stiles was convinced animal familiars were offering up military advice to the Indians.[76]

In the mid-19th century, the Mexicans considered the Apache Goyathlay, or Geronimo as the Americans called him, to be the incarnation of the devil and also to possess supernatural powers, including being bullet proof. Captain Robert Carter of the American army described Quanah Parker, the great Comanche warrior and contemporary of Geronimo, in terms reminiscent of accounts of Indians by the Pilgrim Fathers. Parker, Carter wrote, sat upon on his war pony

> with six-shooter poised in the air, he seemed the incarnation of savage, brutal joy.
> His face was smeared with black warpaint, which gave his features a satanic look ...
> A full-length headdress or war bonnet of eagle's feathers, spreading out as he rode.[77]

In fighting these demonic Indians, settlers and soldiers also recorded some of the supernatural defences their opponents used in battle and how those protections sometimes failed. George Percy, the president of the council of Jamestown in 1609, explained that in battle, the Powhatans

> fall into their exorcismes Conjuracyons and Charmes throweinge fyer upp into the skyes. Runneinge up and downe w[i]th Rattles and makeinge many dyabolicall gestures w[i]th Many nigramantcke Spelles and incantacions Imagein[in]ge thereby to cawse Raine to fall from the Clowdes to extinguishe and putt outt our mens matches and to wett and Spoyle their powder. Butt nether the dievell whome they adore nor all their Sorceries did any thinge avayle them for our men Cutt downe their Corne [and] Burned their howses and besides w[hi]ch they had slayne brought some of them prisoners to our forte. [78]

The Virginia colonists also encountered the Powhatan werowance Nemattanew, who professed to be shot-free. Known to the English as Jack-of-the-Feathers, because it was said that he could fly and went into battle "strangely adorned" with feathers. Nemattanew was eventually killed by musket fire—although his last request was that the colonists who shot him "not make it knowne hee was slaine with a bullet."[79] Other Indians, such as the Cheyenne chief Roman Nose, a renowned fighter and deeply religious man, also claimed to be bullet-proof though he too was shot down while fighting against American cavalry at the Battle of Beecher Island in 1868.[80] Sitting Bull, the leader of the Hunkpapa Lakota in the 1860s and 70s, was said to have been shot more than forty times while fighting American troops and other Indians. To Americans, Sitting Bull possessed all of the demonic qualities associated with the natives of the continent. A brief story in the *Sunday Times* of Chicago in 1876, just six months before the Battle of Little Bighorn, succinctly summed up those feelings. Sitting Bull was "the notorious murderer of the upper Missouri" who had declared he would "wipe out of existence all frontier settlements in his section."

This "bloodthirsty devil's designs" included harassing the military, killing and scalping settlers, burning ranches, haystacks and grain, stealing horses and cattle, and most importantly to Midwestern readers, taking "no white captives."[81]

## All War Is Hell: The Devil and the American Civil War

Many of the soldiers who fought against Sitting Bull and Roman Nose gained their military experience in the American Civil War (1861–65), a conflict also hailed as a holy war or a crusade by its participants—even though it was fought by two sides, both of which were Christian. It is said that on the eve of the Civil War, the United States was the most Christian nation in the world, a country "awash in a sea of faith."[82] The religious enthusiasm of the combatants, combined with the "robust history of demonization before the Civil War," produced America's bloodiest conflict.[83] Religion "was found everywhere in the war," writes Randall Miller, with God "truly alive and very much at the centre of the nation's defining moment."[84] This was a war where religion and nationalism were as tightly bound in the North as in the South, where "civil and religious vocabularies were combined."[85] But Abraham Lincoln's oft-repeated line from his Second Inaugural Address that "both prayed to the same God" meant that both Johnny Reb and Billy Yank were equally capable of accusing the other of being the spawn of Lucifer.

With the outbreak of the war in 1861, clergy across America alluded to the coming Armageddon and quickly rallied their congregations to the cause, ably assisting in recruiting men for military service. In the North, the New School Presbyterians saw the war as a battle between the followers of Satan and the godly, with the Southern states traitorously taking the side of "anarchy and misrule."[86] Northern clergy argued that the secessionist Southern states harkened back to the world's first great rebellion—the devil's secession from heaven—with one Unionist claiming the rebel attack on Fort Sumter had "opened the gates of Hell."[87] Edward Blum has vividly described how Northern ministers and propagandists tied Satan, "the first secessionist," to the rebellion of the Confederacy and more closely to its president, Jefferson Davis. Northerners were not necessarily suggesting that Southerners were inherently evil; instead, the devil had duped the rebels into rejecting the constitution of the United States, thus forcing President Lincoln to suppress their insurrection.[88] South Carolina, the first state to secede, was "like the Red Dragon in the Apocalypse, curling his tail."[89] In 1862, the *Western Christian Advocate*, the mouthpiece of the Methodist Episcopalian Church, described the southern cause as "a besotted, barbarous, brutalizing, bastard corruption, and the perversion of the holy religion."[90] Even among the Northerners who favoured pacifism or non-interference on religious grounds, equating the rebellion, slavery and the demonic made the war easier to justify.

Northern printers too unleashed their own particular brand of anti-Confederate propaganda, adding satirical cartoons and text to envelopes depicting the southern cause in demonic terms. Southern clergy gave sermons "wonderfully assisted" by Satan, who offered "scriptural authority for Secession and Treason."[91] Another set, entitled "Rebel States," showed a shield-bearing devil representing each of the Confederate states while another set included the figure of an angel protecting the Union flag, as a grinning devil grasped the emblem of one of the secessionist states.

Southern politicians and clergy, however, responded quickly to such insults, blaming the war on Northerners who had fallen prey to the godlessness of secularism and diabolism. Southerners were the new children of Israel, breaking free from their Babylonian Captivity and from Abraham Lincoln, the "American Nebuchadnezzar."[92] Dr. George Todd, South Carolinian and brother of Mary Todd Lincoln, the president's wife, refused to accept his brother-in-law's decision to invade the Confederacy and declared the fight was between the "children of the devil" and the "children of the Lord."[93] The Reverend Stephen Elliot, who served as bishop of Georgia and presiding bishop of the Episcopalian Church of the Confederacy, preached that the South had Christ on its side while the North had undertaken an unholy crusade against "the altars of the living God." In his sermon, given at the funeral of the Reverend (and Southern General) Leonidas Polk in 1864, Elliot saw the destruction of the Confederacy by the Union army as evidence of their enemy's godlessness and desire to use newly freed slaves against the South. Like those in the North who did not wish to paint all Southerners with the broad brush of diabolism, Elliot believed that the Union had fallen away from the faith and that only the Southern cause could defend Christians from the growing storm of an inherently diabolical slave rebellion. "We are warring with hordes of unprincipled foreigners, ignorant and brutal men," he wrote,

> Who, having cast off at home all the restraints of order and of belief, have signalized their march over our devoted country by burning the Churches of Christ by defiling the altars upon which the sacrifice of the death of our Savior is commemorated, by violating our women, by raising the banner of servile insurrection, by fanning into fury the demonic passions of the ignorant and the vile.[94]

Elliot, like some other Southern clergymen, believed that abolitionist cause was turning the "heathen race" against the Confederacy—an act that would unleash the forces of Satan and bring about the downfall of the Southern way of life. As the war progressed and Union troops pushed further into the South, clergymen across the Confederacy warned that atheists, infidels and heretics were descending upon their homeland. One Tennessee pastor described the whole Union Army as the "anti-christ, the Beast that [will] ascend from the bottomless pit."[95]

Though one's opponent might have succumbed to the devil, there were also evils much closer to home, as sin could abound in any army camp—cardplaying, drunkenness and swearing were commonplace. Bible and tract societies were tasked with improving the "spiritual good of the soldier," aiding chaplains in helping troops resist the devil by setting up makeshift churches and distributing pocket bibles, sermons and tracts which were printed in the thousands for soldiers on both sides. But unlike the wars discussed above, amulets and talisman do not appear to have been widely used by soldiers of either side.[96] Instead, bibles seemed to have served in this capacity, functioning, according to Jamie L. Brummitt "simultaneously as God's Word, commodities, contraband, weapons, shields, and talismans."[97] In 1864 alone, 570,000 bibles were given to Union soldiers.[98] The Union banned the export of bibles published in the North to the Confederacy, deeming them contraband of war and confiscating them when they could. Soldiers on both sides wrote home about "capturing" bibles from the enemy. Apparently in shunning amulets, the bible's "talismanic" or "mystical" qualities still served Civil War soldiers as a shield against evil, reminiscent of the verses from Ephesians. Union and Confederate soldiers carried their bibles in their breast pockets and reports of soldiers being saved when musket balls intended for their hearts lodged instead, in the pages of their bible, are many.[99] As in Europe's confessional wars, Civil War soldiers also saw the bible as a "supernatural weapon in a holy war that would smite God's enemies."[100]

## Who Lifted the Lid Off Hell?—Satan and the First World War

By the outbreak of the First World War in August 1914, one might think that the devil's place on the battlefield had been usurped by science, reason and technology. But Satan is a stubborn foe, and at the end of the 19th century, many Europeans and Americans continued to believe in the supernatural, magic, the occult and even witchcraft. In fact, the First World War witnessed "an incredible return to the past," creating a great conflict awash with medievalisms.[101] Apocalypticism and millenarianism influenced the way those in power thought about the struggle, while religion remained an important motivating factor for all sides in the "war to end all wars."[102] No sooner had mobilisation begun, then the propaganda machines of the Entente and Central Powers took to demonising one another. If Germany was the demonic Hun, Britain and her Empire were "Babylon, the Great Whore" or the "God of Prophecy.[103]

The First World War proved unlike any war discussed in this chapter in its scope and devastation. Lasting four years, 70 million soldiers served in theatres around the globe. There were more than 20 million battlefield causalities and another 21 million civilian casualties. Towns and villages were completely destroyed in artillery bombardments and conditions at the front, even early in the war, suggested this was the Armageddon prophesied in Revelation. The British artist Paul Nash wrote on witnessing the carnage of the Western Front that "evil and the incarnate fiend alone can be master of this war, and no glimmer of God's hand is seen anywhere."[104] Another Briton commented that the world "was in the presence of wickedness ... that the powers of darkness were very near, and that behind those blackened walls there lurked evil forms ... One could almost hear the devil laughing at the handiwork of his children."[105] In his sermon *Armageddon*, preached in 1914, the Dean of Norwich Cathedral, Henry Beeching, placed the Kaiser and the German Empire firmly on the side of darkness—the Germans, he said, were a nation and an army hellbent on undoing "all the work of civilisation" through world conquest. Germany was "no longer a Christian nation" and Britain and her allies stood as a force for good in defence of the civilised Christian world. The British, Beeching explained, were rejecting darkness and the devil, just as "our blessed Lord," had done when he opened his ministry, by claiming "Get thee behind me, Satan."[106]

Germans, who considered themselves among the most civilised people in the world, declared that it was the Entente who had caused the war and who threatened civilisation. German Lutherans, as we have seen, had no aversion to war so long as it was carried out to protect the church and the state. Protestant German churchmen who espoused the *Kriegstheologie* saw the war in nationalistic, patriotic and apocalyptic terms, with some proclaiming that the country was engaged in a holy war.[107] That said, the devil did not play as prominent a role in the propaganda of the Central Powers as he did among the Entente, possibly owing to the influence of vocal evangelicals in Britain and America.[108]

The unprovoked invasion of Belgium provided Entente propaganda with a ready-made villain in Kaiser Wilhelm II.[109] The atrocities committed by the German Army during the "Rape of Belgium," including the burning of the library at Louvain University, the taking and execution of hostages and the destruction of businesses and private property led to widespread condemnation of the Kaiser as the devil's pawn. The Allies considered Wilhelm responsible for the behaviour of his army, an army that they were now associating with the Dragon of Revelation. The Kaiser and Prussian militarism were also depicted as the Hun— a dark, uncivilised force threatening western Christendom.

To the Allies, the Kaiser was devil, Antichrist and their minions all rolled into one. Just after the war began, the French occultist Joseph Péladan passed information along to the respected newspaper, *Le Figaro*, that a little-known 17th-century monk named Johannes had prophesised that a monarch and "a son of Luther" would reveal himself as the Antichrist. There was little doubt among French readers that the monarch in question was Wilhelm.[110] For their part, the Russians too saw the German-Ottoman alliance as unholy and another reminder of the coming of the end of days. Propaganda posters printed in Russia depicted the Kaiser as the seven-headed beast from Revelation. The Australian journalist and healer, Victor Kroemer was convinced that disharmony in the universe and Lucifer's control over Wilhelm had sparked the world crisis of 1914. In 1915, two of his books appeared, the first *The Beast* and the second, *Is the Kaiser 'Lucifer'?* which added to accusations of Wilhelm's demonism and Germany's fiendish war aims.[111]

Throughout the conflict, the popular Dutch editorial cartoonist, Louis Raemaekers, depicted the German atrocities in Belgium and France and assigned guilt for these crimes to the Kaiser and his General Staff. Around 1918, Raemaekers drew a number of cartoons with the Kaiser and Satan in consultation. In one of the most chilling, entitled *A Good Month's Business*, Wilhelm nuzzles up to the devil, both with red faces and evil grins, chuckling over a casualty list of "babies, children, and women" numbering in the hundreds. In *Morning Prayer*, Wilhelm sits upon a throne of bones with Satan and his army kneeling at the Emperor's feet, while *Let me congratulate your Majesty* has the devil greeting a forked-tailed Kaiser, equally demonic in a skin of red and wearing his distinctive spiked *pickelhaube* with the words, "You have done more in four years than I have in four thousand."[112]

America's entry into the war in 1917 produced more propaganda demonising the Kaiser. The war was not popular in the United States and so Americans needed to be convinced that their involvement was justified. Even more than for Europeans, many Americans believed that the devil played a role in their day-to-day lives—and, as Scott Poole points out, that meant that for Americans, Satan was still "a handy way to portray one's religious enemies."[113] In 1917, he was also a handy way to portray their foreign enemies. Accordingly, as American politicians warned that Prussian militarism and German autocracy threatened democracy, free trade and the emerging role of America in the world, evangelicals and propagandists used the Kaiser's diabolism to encourage recruitment, win wider support for the war, and sell war bonds. In a January 1918 speech entitled *The Poison Growth of Prussianism*, given in Milwaukee, a Midwestern city with a large German population, Otto Kahn, himself of German birth, declared the Kaiser had been hoodwinked by Satan, "the Tempter, who took the Prussian and Prussianized rulers to a high mountain and showed them all the riches and power of the world."[114] There, he offered the Germans a quick and merry war but as was so often the case with those who "got behind Satan," they would be bitterly disappointed when chaos, rather than riches, resulted.

It was the American heartland that needed the most convincing, though, and the Kaiser's pact with the devil seemed a good way to "correct" opinion in favour of American involvement. Kahn argued that the emperor's demonism gave Americans the cause they needed: deliverance from an evil, "unrighteous power."[115] This was an idea Americans in the Midwest and the South understood, and evangelicals, like the popular Iowan Billy Sunday, used the trope to win support for the war effort. Sunday filled his sermons with a mix of muscular Christianity, messianic interventionism and good old-fashioned fire and brimstone preaching, encouraging his countrymen to mobilise against the Hun and urging them to sign up to fight as "gospel grenadiers" to "do battle with the devil."[116] He disparaged Germany as a "vile, greedy, sensuous bloody thirsty" nation "made in hell."[117] Sunday asked listeners to purchase war bonds for weapons that would bury the Hohenzollerns.[118] Here was a rallying cry that made sense to the factory worker and farmer and to evangelicals and mainline Protestants. Germany had become the first of a number of "evil empires" America would encounter in the 20th century.

American and British filmmakers built on these fears, producing several silent pictures that played up the Kaiser's satanic connections. Though many have now been lost, stills and movie posters suggest Hollywood saw real propaganda potential in the Kaiser/devil trope, leading to films with the titles, *The Kaiser*, *Beast of Berlin* and Metro Pictures *To Hell with the Kaiser*, both of which appeared in 1918. The former starred and was directed by Rupert Julian, with Lon Chaney (the great horror star of the post-war period) as Chancellor Bethmann-Hollweg. Wilhelm is portrayed as a callous brute, similar in many respects to the demonic figure Raemaekers drew in *A Good Month's Business*. There are two extant movie posters for *To Hell with the Kaiser*, one showing a fist striking Wilhelm firmly in the face while the other has the Kaiser flanked by a smiling devil wearing a halloweenish red cape and horns.

But what of the common soldier in the sodden trenches of the Western Front? Did he recognise the devil in the enemy, as those on the home front did, or was Satan no longer a threat in a war-torn landscape that seemed worse than hell itself? First, there is no doubt that soldiers on both sides understood, and were forced to respond emotionally and spiritually, to the notion of evil, just as Nash had described in 1914. The effects of industrial warfare were clearly terrifying, and while the scale of destruction was greater than previous wars, it did not mean that the soldiers in the First World War were witnessing the emergence of new forms of evil. With armies face to face in trenches separated by as little as fifty yards of no man's land, soldiers were more likely to see the hand of the devil in the actions of their own generals and politicians, and in the destruction, blood, mud and madness they endured, than in the face of the enemy. While there are few references to the carrying of talismans by Civil War soldiers, combatants from the Old World continued to carry an array of amulets and charms into battle in the First World War. These protections included traditional religious amulets and badges worn by Catholics, such as crucifixes, rosaries, saint's rings, medallions, scapulars and hands of Fatima while Protestants carried pocket bibles and verses, as well as psalm books. Folkloric and national charms, such as four-leafed clovers, horseshoes, gemstones, swastikas and lucky coins and postcards were also popular among soldiers on both sides. German *Kreigsglücksringe*—horseshoe nails crafted into rings—were said offer "a visible sign and protect against misery and death."[119] Stories once again circulated of bullets and shrapnel impaled in biblical "armour" carried by soldiers. Clergy were divided on the use of such protections, with some priests and ministers offering them to soldiers as "religious insurance against harm" while sceptics called them "rubbish," concluding they did more harm evil than good. Some soldiers swore by them and the number of talismans found by medical staff on the wounded suggests their popularity and possibly their utility, at least for those who survived the war.

With millions of men volunteering and being conscripted into service, some Christians argued that the devil was very likely to be one of his own comrades, wearing the same uniform and sitting in the same trench. As with American Civil War soldiers, First World War recruits were cast into an environment filled with a host of moral evils. Drink, gambling, prostitution, pilfering, blaspheming had been part of soldiering for centuries, and the First World War was no different. To combat such threats, an English Pentecostal pamphlet entitled *"Quit You Like Men, Be Strong"* by J. T. Mawson, warned those entering the armed services that:

> [i]t was not the physical dangers that you have to face that give us the deepest concern on your behalf, but the evils of the billet camp, and mess: evils moral and spiritual, that will assail you mightily ... Your enemy—THE DEVIL—is terrible and tireless, and the weapons in his arsenal are many and varied. If he cannot seduce you, he will persecute you: from him you will get no quarter, therefore "BE SOBER, BE VIGILANT.[120]

The pamphlet made no mention of the Germans. The real threat was Satan's presence in the day-to-day life of the military camp, just as it had been in the Confederate Army and the Swedish Army before that.

In the decade following the war's conclusion, as general staffs, historians and private citizens pondered why the world had descended into bitter conflict in 1914, an American political scientist, Harold Lasswell, placed some of the blame, but not all, on the devil. In his 1927 *Propaganda Technique in the World War*, Lasswell recognised that Satanism, as he entitled one chapter, proved a significant factor in shaping public opinion through the war years.[121] He argued, as diplomats had done at the peace talks at Versailles in 1919, that "any nation that began the War and blocks peace, is incorrigible, wicked and perverse."[122] Though he did not place blame on any particular party for causing the war, Lasswell explained that the efficient propaganda machines of the great powers had succeeded in turning their enemies into barbarians, monsters and demons, concluding that the "cult of satanism thus arises and feeds on hate. Vengeance is Mine, saith the Lord, and the Lord is working through us to destroy the devil."[123]

## Conclusion

The devil's influence over warfare in the West has been strangely consistent throughout the period between 1600 and 1920, unchallenged it seems, by the march of time. Europeans and Americans have seen Satan's hand in the many wars they have waged, ably assisting the many enemies they have faced. Demonism, it is said, has informed the motivations of those making the crucial decisions to go to war, and those doing the fighting and dying. The fears that have caused the devil to make his appearance in the war rooms and council chambers and in the camps of a host of armies are the result of the prominent role of religion has played, and continues to play, in shaping Western warfare. During this time, apocalypticism and millenarianism have been constant companions of warfare, ensuring that Satan has never been far from the battlefield. Painting your enemy in league with the devil has produced terrifying results, including the slaughter of soldiers and innocents, the destruction of homes, crops and animals, and the exile and extermination of conquered peoples. Though Satan's influence has waxed and waned as these wars have dragged on, the fact that he featured as prominently in the First World War as he did in the Thirty Years' War suggests that for many Christians, the devil remains, as the French reformer Pierre Viret claimed nearly five centuries ago, the "authour of warre and strife. Peace cannot greatly please hym."[124]

## Notes

1 The author wishes to thank the Centre for Renaissance and Reformation Studies at the University of Toronto for its ongoing support of his research.

2 Nicholas Rémy, *Demonolatry: An Account of the Historical Practice of Witchcraft*, trans. E.A. Ashwin (London, 2008), 128.

3 Jeffrey Burton Russell, *Lucifer: The Devil in the Middle Ages* (Ithaca, NY, 1984), 21.

4 See David Trim, "Conflict, religion and ideology" in Frank Tallett and D. J. B. Trim, eds., *European Warfare, 1350–1750* (Cambridge, 2010), 278–99.

5 Bernard Bailyn, *The Barbarous Years: The Conflict of Civilizations 1600–1675* (New York, 2012), 110, 474, and 499.

6 Anon, *The English Devil: Or, Cromwel and His Monstrous Witch Discover'd at White-Hall...* (London, 1660) and Anon., *The Identity of Napoleon and Antichrist Completely Demonstrated...* (New York, 1809).

7 John Underhill, *Newes from America or A New and Experimental Discoverie of New England...* (London, 1638), 37.

8 Owen Davies, *A Supernatural War: Magic, Divination and Faith during the First World War* (Oxford, 2018). 192.

9 Davies, *A Supernatural War*, 14.

10 Neil Forsyth, *The Old Enemy: Satan and the Combat Myth* (Princeton, 1987), 283 and Jeffrey Burton Russell, *Mephistopheles: The Devil in the Modern World* (Ithaca, NY, 1986), 28.

11 Forsyth, *The Old Enemy*, 11–2.

12 Mark Neocleous, *The Universal Adversary: Security, Capital and 'The Enemies of All Mankind'* (New York, 2016), 80.

13 Nathan Johnstone, *The Devil and Demonism in Early Modern England* (Cambridge, 2006), 231.

14 Brian P. Levack, *The Witch-Hunt in Early Modern Europe* (London, 2016), 31.

15 Neocleous, *The Universal Adversary*, 80 and Ephesians 6–18, King James Version.

16 Carlos M. N. Eire, *Reformations: The Early Modern World, 1450–1650* (New Haven, 2016), 622.

17 Martin Luther, "Whether Soldiers, Too, Can be Saved," trans. C.M. Jacobs. https://www.degruyter.com/document/doi/10.1515/9783110847710-032/pdf, 2.

18 Alphonsus de Spina, *Fortalitium fidei in universos christiane religionis hostes Judaeorum et saracenorum...* (Lyon, 1525).

19 E. Pagels, *The Origin of Satan: How Christians Demonised Jews, Pagans and Heretics* (New York, 1995), 13.

20 Stuart Clark, *Thinking with Demons: The Idea of Witchcraft in Early Modern Europe* (Oxford, 1999), 62.

21 Russell, *Mephistopheles: The Devil in the Modern World*, 42.

22 Erika Rummel, *The Erasmus Reader* (Toronto, 1990), 289. The quote is from *Complaint for Peace* (1517).

23 See Philip C. Almond, *The Devil: A Biography* (London, 2016), xvii and Geoffrey Parker, *Global Crisis: War, Climate Change and Catastrophe in the Seventeenth Century* (New Haven, 2017), 175. For the age of atrocity, see David Edwards, Pádraig Lenihan, and Clodagh Tait, *Age of Atrocity: Violence and Political Conflict in Early Modern Ireland* (Dublin, 2007).

24 Vannoccio Biringuccio *The Pirotechnia of Vannoccio Biringuccio: The Classic Sixteenth-Century Treatise on Metals and Metallurgy*, trans. by Cyril Stanley Smith and Martha Teach Gnudi (New York, 1990), 409 and J.R. Hale, ed. *Guicciardini, The History of Italy and The History of Florence* (New York, 1964), 152–3.

25 J.R. Hale, *Renaissance War Studies* (London, 1983), 394.

26 See Clifford Rogers, "Gunpowder Artillery in Europe, 1326–1500: Innovation and Impact" in John F. Guilmartin, Robert S. Ehlers, Sarah K. Douglas, Daniel P. M. Curzon, eds., *Technology, Violence, and War: Essays in Honor of Dr. John F. Guilmartin, Jr* (Brill, 2019).

27 Hale, "Gunpowder and the Renaissance," 395. See also Lawrence Freedmen, *Strategy: A History* (Oxford, 2013), 54–65.

28 Daniel Pellerin, "Calvin: Militant or Man of Peace?" *The Review of Politics* 65, no. 1 (2003): 37.

29 Jean Bodin, *On the Demon-Mania of Witches* (Toronto, 2001), 88.

30 Francois de La Noue, *The Politike and Militaire Discovrses of the lord De La Nowe* (London, 1588), 7.
31 I.L, *The Birth, Purpose, and Mortall Wound of the Romanish Holy League* (London, 1589), sig. A2ᵛ.
32 Daniel R. Horst, "The Duke of Alba: The Ideal Enemy," *Arte Nueve*, 1 (2014), 130–54.
33 Simon Howard, *The Solace of the Souldier and Saylour* (London, 1592), sig. E3ᵛ.
34 Peter Wilson, *Europe's Tragedy: A New History of the Thirty Years War* (London, 2005), 262.
35 Wilson, *Europe's Tragedy*, 722.
36 Robert Bireley, *Ferdinand II: Counter-reformation Emperor, 1578–1637* (Cambridge, 2014), 92.
37 William Watts, *The Swedish Discipline: Religious, Civile and Militarie…The Third Part* (London, 1632), 32.
38 William Watts, *The Swedish Discipline, Religious, Civile and Militarie…The Second Part* (London, 1632), 55–7.
39 Levack, *The Witch-Hunt in Early Modern Europe*, 115.
40 Anon. *The Mathematicall Divine, Shewing, the Present Miseries of Germany, England and Ireland* (London, 1642), 4.
41 Darren Oldridge, *The Devil in Tudor and Stuart England* (Stroud, UK, 2011), 148–9.
42 Nicholas P. Canny, *Making Ireland British, 1580–1650* (Oxford, 2001), 490–1.
43 Christopher S. Mackay, *The Hammer of the Witches: A Complete Translation of the Malleus Maleficarum* (Cambridge, 2015), 396.
44 Bodin, *On the Demon-Mania of Witches*, 67.
45 William Perkins, *A Discourse of the Damned Art of Witchcraft: So Far Forth as It Is Revealed in the Scriptures, and Meanest by True Experience* (Cambridge, 1610), 36.
46 Tristram Whetcombe, *A most Exact Relation of a Great Victory, obtained by the Poor Protestants in Ireland…* (London, 1642), 7.
47 George Sinclair, *Satan's Invisible World Discovered…* (Edinburgh, 1685), 126.
48 B. Ann Tlusty, "Invincible blades and invulnerable bodies: weapons magic in early-modern Germany," *European Review of History*, vol. 22, no. 4 (2015): 658–79.
49 Anon., *The Tryall and Examination of Mrs. Joan Peterson…* (London, 1652), 3–4.
50 Johann Jakob Cristoffel von Grimmelshausen, *Simplicius Simplicissimus*, trans. George Schulz-Behrend (Indianapolis, IN, 1965), 66.
51 Johnstone, *Devil and Demonism in Early Modern England*, 213. See also Christopher Hill, *Antichrist in Seventeenth Century England* (London, 1990), 78–145.
52 Mark Stoyle, *The Black Legend of Prince Rupert's Dog: Witchcraft and Propaganda during the English Civil War* (Exeter, 2011).
53 Stoyle, *The Black Legend of Prince Rupert's Dog*, 39.
54 T. B., *Observations Vpon Prince Rvperts White Dog Called Boy…* (London, 1642), sig. A2.
55 T. B., *Observations Vpon Prince Rvperts White Dog*, sig. A3.
56 Alfred A. Cave, *Lethal Encounters: Englishmen and Indians in Colonial Virginia* (Santa Barbara, 2011), 121.
57 Ivie and Giner, *Hunt the Devil: A Demonology of US War Culture*, 6.
58 Gerald Messadie, *A History of the Devil* (New York, 1996), 194.
59 Samuel C. Gwynne, *Empire of the Summer Moon: Quanah Parker and the Rise and Fall of the Comanches, the Most Powerful Indian Tribe in American History* (New York, 2010), 97.
60 Richard B. Davis, "The Devil in Virginia in the Seventeenth Century," *The Virginia Magazine of History and Biography* 65, vo. 2 (April 1957): 132–3.
61 Richard W. Pointer, "Native Freedom? Indians and Religious Tolerance in Early America," in Chris Beneke and Christopher S. Grenda, *The First Prejudice: Religious Tolerance and Intolerance in Early America* (Philadelphia, 2011), 178.
62 Sandra Slater, "'Great Pride and Insolence': Spiritual Justifications for the Violence in the Pequot War," *Journal of Early American History* 4 (2014): 38.
63 Bailyn, *The Barbarous Years*, 105–6.
64 J. Frederick Fausz, "An 'Abundance of Blood Shed on Both Sides': England's First Indian War, 1609–1614," *The Virginia Magazine of History and Biography* 98, no. 1 (January 1990): 3–4 and 8.

65 In 1776, some American colonists believed that it was George III who was now acting under Satan's orders. In his pamphlet, *Common Sense*, Thomas Paine equated the monarchy Americans were forced to live under as "the most prosperous invention the Devil ever set on foot for the promotion of idolatry." Thomas Paine, *Collected Writings* (New York, 1995), 12. See also Anon., *A Dialogue between the Devil and George III tyrant of Britain* (Boston, 1782).

66 W. Scott Poole, *Satan in America: The Devil We Know* (London, 2009), 34.

67 See Robert Remini, *Andrew Jackson and his Indian Wars* (New York, 2001).

68 William B. Skelton, "Army Officers' Attitudes toward Indians, 1830–1860," *The Pacific Northwest Quarterly* 67. no. 3 (July 1976), 115.

69 A.J. van Vorhes, "Latest from the Indian War," *Chicago Tribune*, 27 August, 1862.

70 "Conciliation" *Daily Advocate*, 12 August, 1867.

71 Jill Lepore, *The Name of War: King Philip's War and the Origins of American Identity* (New York, 1998), 61.

72 Skelton, "Army Officers' Attitudes toward Indians, 1830–1860," 115.

73 Davis, "The Devil in Virginia in the Seventeenth Century," 132–3.

74 John Smith, *The Generall Historie of Virginia, New-England, and the Summer Isles...*(London, 1624), 49.

75 Quoted in William S. Simmons, "Cultural Bias in the New England Puritans' Perception of Indians," *The William and Mary Quarterly* 38, no. 1 (Jan. 1981), 60.

76 Samuel Gardiner Drake, *Indian biography: containing the lives of more than two hundred Indian chiefs...* (Boston, 1832), 266.

77 Samuel C. Gwynne, *Empire of the Summer Moon: Quanah Parker and the Rise and Fall of the Comanches, the Most Powerful Indian Tribe in American History* (New York, 2010), 11.

78 Mark Nicholls, "George Percy's Trewe Relation: A Primary Source for the Jamestown Settlement," *The Virginia Magazine of History and Biography* 113, no. 3 (2005): 259.

79 Smith, *The Generall Historie of Virginia*, 144.

80 Maurice Kenny, "Roman Nose, Cheyenne: A Brief Biography," *Wicazo Sa Review* 5, no. (1989), 18.

81 "Sitting Bull [Special Telegram]," *The Sunday Times* (Chicago), 16 January, 1876, 6.

82 Edward J. Blum, "'The First Secessionist Was Satan': Secession and the Religious Politics of Evil in Civil War America," *Civil War History* 60, no. 3 (September 2014), 245.

83 Blum, "The First Secessionist Was Satan," 245.

84 Randall M. Miller, Harry S. Stout and Charles R. Wilson, eds., "Introduction" in *Religion and the American Civil War* (New York, 1998), 4.

85 Miller, et.al, *Religion and the American Civil War*, 142.

86 Philip Shaw Paludan, *"A People's Contest": The Union and Civil War 1861–1865* (New York, 1988), 347.

87 Bertram Wyatt-Brown, "Church, Honor and Secession" in *Religion and the American Civil War*, 100.

88 Blum, "The First Secessionist Was Satan," 238.

89 Byrd, *A Holy Baptism of Fire & Blood*, 52.

90 Paludan, *"A People's Contest,"* 348.

91 *An eminent southern clergyman*, New-York Historical Society, Patriotic envelope collection. Series I: Civil War envelopes, 1861–1865, aj45013.jpg 1578.

92 Byrd, *A Holy Baptism of Fire & Blood*, 5.

93 Steve E. Woodworth, *While God is Marching On: The Religious World of Civil War Soldiers* (Lawrence, KS, 2001), 122.

94 Traci Nichols-Belt with Gordon T. Belt, *Onward Southern Soldiers: Religion and the Army of Tennessee in the Civil War* (Charleston, SC, 2011), 48.

95 Blum, "The First Secessionist Was Satan," 246.

96 James M. McPherson, *For Cause and Comrades* (Oxford, 1997), 63.

97 Jamie L. Brummitt, "'How Dare Men Mix up the Bible so with Their Own Bad Passions': When the Good Book Became the Bad Book in the American Civil War," *Material Religion* 18, no. 2 (2022): 132.

98 Brummitt, "'How Dare Men,'" 133.

99 Woodworth, *While God is Marching On: The Religious World of Civil War Soldiers*, 71.

100 Brummitt, "How Dare Men," 142.
101 Patrick J. Houlihan, "Religious Mobilization and Popular Belief," *International Encyclopedia of the First World War*. https://encyclopedia.1914-1918-online.net/article/religious_mobilization_and_popular_belief, 2.
102 Eric Michael Reisenauer, "'The Merchants of Trashish, with all the Young Lions Thereof.' The British Empire, scripture Prophecy, and the War of Armageddon, 1914–1918," *Journal of Bible and Its Reception*, 4(2) (2017): 312.
103 Reisenauer, "'The Merchants of Trashish,'" 141.
104 Houlihan, "Religious Mobilization and Popular Belief," 3.
105 A.J. Hoover, *God, Germany and Britain in the Great War: A Study in Clerical Nationalism* (New York, 1989), 5.
106 H.C. Beeching, *Armageddon* (London, 1914), 4, 9 and 12.
107 Hoover, *God, Germany and Britain in the Great War*, xi.
108 Julian Jenkins, "War Theology, 1914 and Germany's Sonderweg: Luther's Heirs and Patriotism," *The Journal of Religious History* 15, no. 3 (June 1989), 302.
109 Hoover, *God, Germany and Britain in the Great War*, 11.
110 Davies, *A Supernatural War*, 49–50.
111 Frank Bongiorno, "The Devil and Kaiser Bill: Victor Kroemer and the World Crisis of 1914–15," *Australian Journal of Politics and History* 53, no. 3 (2007), 420.
112 For Louis Raemaekers' posters, *A Good Month's Business* (c. 1918) *Morning Prayer* (c. 1918) and *Let me congratulate your Majesty* (c. 1918). See The Metropolitan Museum of Art website. https://www.metmuseum.org/art/collection/search/727995, 727985, 727992, respectively.
113 Poole, *Satan in America*, 55.
114 Poole, *Satan in America*, 22.
115 Poole, *Satan in America*, 37.
116 Poole, *Satan in America*, 60.
117 Jörg Nagler, "Pandora's Box: Propaganda and War Hysteria in the United States during World War I," in R. Chickering and S. Förster, eds., *Great War, Total War: Combat and Mobilization on the Western Front: 1914–1918* (Cambridge, 2000), 494.
118 Michael Snape, "The Great War" in ed. Hugh McCleod, *The Cambridge History of Christianity: World Christianities c. 1914–c.2000* (Cambridge, 2000), 142.
119 Davies, *A Supernatural War*, 141, 151.
120 J.T. Mawson, *Quit You Like Men, Be Strong* (London, 1916), 3–4.
121 Harold Lasswell, *Propaganda Technique in the World War* (New York, 1938).
122 Lasswell, *Propaganda Technique*, 77–81.
123 Lasswell, *Propaganda Technique*, 96.
124 Pierre Viret and Thomas Stocker. *The Worlde Possessed with Deuils Conteyning Three Dialogues....* (London, 1583) sig. Aiiii[v].

## Further Reading

Bailyn, Bernard. *The Barbarous Years: The Conflict of Civilisations 1600-1675*. New York: Alfred A. Knopf, 2012.
Blum, Edward J. "'The First Secessionist Was Satan': Secession and the Religious Politics of Evil in Civil War America". *Civil War History*, Vol. 60, No. 3, September, 2014, pp. 234–69.
Davies, Owen. *A Supernatural War: Magic, Divination and Faith during the First World War*. Oxford: Oxford University Press, 2018.
Hamalainen, Pekka. *Indigenous Continent: The Epic Contest for North America*. New York: Liveright Publishing, 2022.
Ivie, Robert L. and Oscar Giner, *Hunt the Devil: A Demonology of US War Culture*. Tuscalosa, AL: University of Alabama Press, 2015.
Jenkins, Philip. *The Great and Holy War: How World War I Became a Religious Crusade*. New York: Harper Collins, 2014.
Stoyle, Mark. *The Black Legend of Prince Rupert's Dog: Witchcraft and Propaganda during the English Civil War*. Exeter: University of Exeter Press, 2011.

# 20

# DEVIL, TEMPTATION, CONSCIENCE, EMOTION

*Charlotte-Rose Millar*

If asked to picture the devil, many of us would instinctively think of a physical, cloven-hoofed, horned beast, one likely to strike fear, even terror, into those he encountered. And while this concept of a tangible devil certainly proliferated throughout the early modern and modern periods, this chapter is primarily concerned with exploring a more insidious devil—an intangible being who could take many forms and who, primarily, was a source of mental rather than physical torments. Like his corporeal counterpart, this devil of the mind also struck fear into those whom he tormented. This chapter surveys emotional responses to the devil from the puritans of the early modern era to the early development of psychology as a profession and reflects on the interconnected relationship between conceptions of Satan and the human psyche. Its main focus is on the early modern world, a time of extremely rich emotional engagement with the demonic. The introspective nature of Reformed Protestant piety, one in which private devotions were meant for reflection on one's emotional engagement with God and the demonic, has meant that historians have been left many self-writings and spiritual diaries, all of which talk at length about the authors' religious experience and the emotions which informed it. This unusually voluminous source base makes the period an especially rich one for understanding the links between the devil, temptation, conscience and emotion. The critical importance of conscience in the theology of both Martin Luther and John Calvin also makes a focus on Reformed Protestantism especially fruitful.[1] As such, this chapter focuses predominantly on Reformed Protestantism, but also places this theology in a wider context. It explores the intense emotions engendered by the devil, whether they be the great fear, sorrow, self-loathing or hatred that he often evoked as well as the ecstasy, joy and hope felt in overcoming his temptations. In doing so, it highlights the importance of emotional responses in encouraging ongoing belief in the devil, even into the modern age.

## The Devil Ascendant

### The Devil's Growing Powers

The early modern era was a golden age for the devil. In England, Scotland, the New World and in parts of Europe, the Protestant Reformation strengthened belief in the devil and brought with it a new emphasis on the devil's power and omnipresence. In Reformation

DOI: 10.4324/9781003096603-21

Europe, the knowledge that the end times were near brought with it an increased fear of the devil's machinations and heightened activity in this pre-apocalyptic world. Early modern writers referred to Satan's increasing powers frequently. In 1584, William Chub noted that "the gates of hell are opened and the floodes of Satan hath overflowen the whole world."[2] The anonymous author of a 1597 witchcraft pamphlet claimed that in this current age Satan corrupts more "mens minds by his wicked suggestions" than in any previous age.[3] A third writer, this time publishing in the mid-17th century, warned that in "our dayes" we find the devil "daily subverting, ensnaring men and women, his policies and devices are many, his temptations subtle."[4] These authors were supported by scripture, with Revelation 12.12 predicting an increase in Satan's wrath as he felt the end times approaching.

As a result, the devil was ubiquitous in early modern culture. Sermons, conduct books and popular pamphlets all emphasised the growing power of the devil and the need for good Protestants to steel themselves against him. Crucially, these texts also emphasised the devil's role as a tempter. The devil had, of course, always performed this role, with his position as a tempter enshrined in the book of Job. But this role was not as emphasised in medieval culture as it came to be in the early modern world. During the Middle Ages, the devil was often imagined in physical form and, while this could be a fearful image, it also reminded medieval men and women of the devil's limitations. The medieval devil could be physically outrun and was also quite often tricked by those humans he encountered. The main change between medieval and early modern demonology was an increased emphasis on the devil's powers in the world, especially his powers of mental temptation. The new-found emphasis on personal piety in the 15th, 16th and 17th centuries turned temptation into one of the devil's most important functions.

Early modern Protestants increasingly found themselves in an individual struggle with Satan, one that was tested purely by their faith and ability to resist demonic temptation. This emphasis on faith as the only sure-fire protection against the devil was an ongoing theme of Protestant doctrine. Another key element of the Reformed Protestant experience was the emphasis on double predestination which forced the godly to "look tirelessly within themselves for marks of either grace or damnation."[5] Protestant reformers emphasised an individual's struggle with Satan, one in which the pious were expected to enter a lifetime's conflict with the demonic, an experience in which resisting the devil was one's own responsibility. Underpinning this concept was the strong belief that men and women were innately sinful creatures who, if they were not careful, could very easily become part of Satan's kingdom. As Michelle D. Brock has put it, "the battle between Good and Evil was not cosmic, but domestic, occurring not in the heavens but in [people's] own corrupted hearts and minds."[6] It was commonplace for early modern Protestants to bemoan their inherently weak and damaged nature, one that was forever tainted by original sin. Early modern Protestants were constantly encouraged to examine their own conscience for any weaknesses that could be exploited. This "turning inwards of the Christian conscience" emphasised the role of men and women in an individual and lifelong struggle with Satan.[7]

Some historians have argued that many newly minted Protestants were left feeling "disarmed" by the Reformation, left as they were without the ability to cross themselves, go on pilgrimage, petition the saints, ring the bells or engage in any number of pre-Reformation activities to help ward off an increasingly aggressive and active enemy.[8] Preaching before Queen Mary in 1554, the Catholic Thomas Watson asked, "What meant they that toke away this armour of Christes flesh and bloud from us, but to leave us naked and unarmed against the devyll?"[9] To be left "naked and unarmed" against an increasingly powerful devil must have been a grim prospect. Much later, one 19th-century writer bemoaned the tendency for Protestantism to do away with traditional protections, writing that the devil's ability to convince men and women "that the Scriptures contain all things necessary to salvation" as a reason for despising "the assistance which the Church may afford him" was proof of his sophisticated ability to trick and tempt.[10]

This is not to say though that Protestant divines left their flock powerless against the devil. As Nathan Johnstone has explained, reformers attempted to replace more traditional forms of demonic resistance with soteriological knowledge.[11] Biblical scripture should, reformers argued, serve both to arm and to reassure the elect with the knowledge of their ultimate protection. As well as this, to know that God allowed the devil to tempt men, and that men would never be tempted beyond their endurance, was supposed to offer strength to those struggling. Even for the elect, it was not enough to know that one was destined for salvation—and, indeed, it was not really possible to know, in life, if one was a member of God's chosen, a state of being that made some Protestants despair. Thus, part of their role was to continue the ongoing struggle with Satan. While the devil could never be defeated—that was a job for God—he could be resisted and fought. One especially evocative case of demonic resistance comes from an extremely unusual first-person narration from 1579, in which Richard Galis was visited and tormented by demonic spirits.[12] In the face of a demonic cat appearing in his chamber, Galis took his prayer book and "knowing that prayer in all troubles and extremities was the chiefest string whereon each true Christian ought for to strike," and with "the brakish teares distilling from the fountains of my eyes" read it and sang psalms to "the honor and glory of God."[13] Galis reminded himself that "God being my helper, buckler and defence, neither any Witch nor all the Devils in hel were they in number as many as the sands in the Sea could have once power to hurt mee."[14] Thus fortified, Galis called for his bible and reminded himself of "that just man Job, of whose stedfast faith and milde patience" which made him so full of faith in the lord that he is no longer afraid.[15] Here Galis was initially terrified but felt bolstered by knowing that if he was faithful to God, he would be protected, as others had been before him. Although some early modern Protestants may have felt disarmed in the face of the devil, Protestant doctrine taught that they did have all the necessary tools at their disposal to resist his temptations.

### Demonic Temptation

Protestant theology emphasised the power of the devil and "placed the struggle against him at the centre of religious life."[16] But Protestant divines did more than just emphasise the devil's growing powers; they focused explicitly on the devil's power of temptation, specifically, in the words of Johnstone, "his ability to enter directly into the mind and plant thoughts within it that led people to sin."[17] While for the medieval devil temptation was just one of his many ways of afflicting mankind, the early modern devil was defined by his power to tempt the godly. Calvin described how the devil "opposes the truth of God with falsehoods" and "entangles men's minds in errors."[18] The French Calvinist theologian and reformer Theodore Beza focused on the devil's ability to disrupt prayer, explaining that Satan "lies in wait, to seduce us, so does he, especially, at such times, seek to creep into our minds, to divert our thoughts elsewhere, that they may be polluted with many blemishes."[19] Satan attempted not just to tempt men and women but to exploit their inherent weaknesses and depravity, leading to an ever-greater need to examine one's own conscience for weaknesses. William Perkins (1558–1602), the "virtual inventor" of conscience literature, warned that man's innately sinful nature made him vulnerable to demonic assaults.[20] While in much pre-early modern doctrine demonic temptation was seen as a possibility which one might encounter within one's life, in reformed thought this became an expectation. Changes to baptism rites in early modern England provide just one example of how early modern Protestantism emphasised a person's relationship with Satan as one of lifelong and intimate struggle. In the 1540s under the Sarum rite, an infant being baptised would be exorcised of the devil, but with the introduction of the second reformed Edwardian prayer book in 1562, this ritual changed from one of banishing Satan to one in which the infant entered a pact to devote their life to resisting Satan's influence.[21] This change not only emphasised the devil's increased presence and aggression, but also elevated the struggle against him to one of personal responsibility and intimacy.

Although the stress here is on resisting mental temptations, these could have physical ramifications. In 1582, accused witch Elizabeth Bennett attempted to resist the temptations of the devil. After multiple refusals to give up her soul, during which time she invoked God and prayed fervently, the devil appeared to her in the form of a lion and thrust her into a burning oven, leaving a visible mark on her arm.[22] Here Elizabeth's internal battle with Satan took physical form. Joan Cariden, a widow and accused witch, also experienced her mental battle with Satan physically. She was tormented by the devil in the shape of a "rugged soft thing" which crept into her bed and lay on her in the night. After this incident, Cariden felt that "God forsook her, for she could never pray so well since as she could before."[23] She eventually succumbed to the devil and was executed for witchcraft in 1645. These cases demonstrate that the devil still had a very tangible role to play in early modern Protestantism. Protestant demonism did not deny that the devil could appear in physical form—a fact of which we are constantly reminded when reading witchcraft narratives from the period—but it did stress that his powers of mental temptation were the real danger. For divines, Satan's insidious ability to enter the mind was his most threatening attribute.

We should be wary, though, as Darren Oldridge has warned, of thinking of early modern Protestants experiencing the devil "inside their own minds." This is a 20th-century conception, one based on ideas of negative projection. Rather, as early modern divines such as Perkins and Robert Bolton argued, the devil could implant his own thoughts into the mind of a human being.[24] Although Perkins and Bolton both noted that sinful or wicked ideas could stem from either an individual or the devil, in practice, it was difficult to distinguish between the two, although some argued that the more aggressive and sudden the sinful thought, the more likely it was to stem from the devil.[25] Despite this, early modern Protestants ultimately insisted that pious men and women were responsible for resisting these thoughts, even if they were planted by the devil.[26] This was nothing new in Christian tradition, with Thomas Aquinas in the 13th century reminding us of the typical view that the devil could only kindle humanity's innate sinfulness; he could not force man to sin. For early modern Protestants, the devil was a being who could invade their minds and tempt them into sin. Only prayer, faith and constant vigilance were suitable antidotes.

Although the devil attempted to tempt all men and women, early modern Protestants were worthy of especial attention. As the elected few, godly men and women knew that the devil's natural malice would most readily be directed against them.[27] One minister noted in a funeral sermon that "the Devil most assaulteth them which be most godly, thinking to hinder all religion if he may prevaile."[28] Calvin declared that "Satan in some sort trifles where he is not seriously opposed, but exerts all his strength against those who resist him."[29] This special attention, while distressing, could sometimes be rationalised as not altogether a bad thing. Protestant theology emphasised that the devil was only able to act with God's permission and God only permitted the devil's torments when they were ultimately beneficial. It may be then that experiencing temptation could be viewed as being "spiritually fruitful," if extremely distressing.[30] Further, an awareness that the devil was tempting one person more than another may have given the afflicted the sense and possible reassurance that they were one of God's elect.[31]

## Demonic Possession

Demonic possession was an extreme form of temptation, involving the devil possessing the demoniac's body and, according to some confessions, their soul. In some areas, such as in certain German communities, possession could even begin with the demoniac giving into temptation and signing a pact with the devil.[32] The claim that demoniacs were morally culpable was one that varied by confession, with Protestants, especially Calvinists, much more likely to be blamed for their possession than their Catholic counterparts. Although Catholic demoniacs were generally seen as blameless victims, this was not always the case. In the German Catholic prince-bishopric of Paderborn in the 1650s, more than a hundred people (mainly women) who were supposedly possessed by demons were suspected to be either fraudulent or witches. This crisis was resolved by the Dominican exorcist Father Michael Angelo who, being highly sceptical of the possessions, explained that the possessed could only remain possessed if they allowed themselves to be so. As he stated, "the possessed cannot actually be forced to speak or to do anything evil; rather they are persuaded and led into temptation."[33] As Brian Levack has explained, this view was similar to that of the Protestant physician and demonologist Johann Weyer, who believed that if demoniacs put their faith in God and were pious, they could resist possession.[34] Despite Father Angelo's views, it remained common for Catholic demoniacs to be seen as victims, not sinners. The Calvinist tendency to believe that demoniacs were responsible for their own possession tied into Protestantism's emphasis on sin and moral culpability.[35] A Protestant demoniac could be accused of giving into temptation, lacking faith and, as such, allowing the devil a way in.

Exorcism, or dispossession as it was called in Protestant contexts, also differed by confession, as did the extent to which temptation was emphasised within these rituals. For Catholics, the main goal of exorcism was the physical banishment of the demon from the demoniac's possessed body, and the subsequent curing of their physical suffering. But for Protestants the focus was on the spiritual, not the physical, with the main goal of helping the demoniac overcome temptation, thereby avoiding eternal damnation.[36] Catholic theology taught that the devil could only possess the body. But in the Calvinist tradition the devil was believed to possess the soul as well. This belief was consistent with the broader Protestant belief that the devil was primarily a spiritual foe, whose main activity was temptation.[37] Calvinist demoniacs were all assailed by demonic temptation to sin, and the role of dispossession was to help the demoniac resist these temptations, and to ask God to help the possessed resist. In this way, Protestant dispossession mirrored ideas about the individual's own struggle with Satan and the importance of faith and prayer in

resisting temptation. Possession could, therefore, "afford the Protestant scheme of temptation and resistance a remarkable tangibility."[38] In general, Catholic demoniacs were
not driven to this same sense of temptation and despair, nor was their exorcism centred
around resisting sin.

## An Emotional Engagement with the Devil

The Protestant emphasis on an individual and internal struggle with Satan was one that
encouraged an emotional engagement with the devil. Early modern Protestantism was a
highly introspective form of piety which viewed the devil as an "intimate, lifelong companion," who needed to be fought daily.[39] But this emotional engagement was set against
a backdrop of early modern Protestants looking to their own feelings to hear God's voice.
Feelings and emotions could be divinely or satanically inspired, meaning that the human
psyche became an "arena for spiritual contest."[40] Early modern Protestants needed to examine their emotions for signs of the demonic or the divine constantly. Emotion could be,
as Alec Ryrie has put it, a "form of revelation" but it could also be the lurking place of the
devil.[41] Some Protestants, especially Reformed Protestants, took an especially grim view,
with Perkins arguing that the "affections of the heart, [such] as Love, Joy, Hope, Desire,
etc. are moved and stirred to that which is evil, to imbrace it; and they are never stirred
unto that which is good, unless it be to eshew it."[42] It was possible, though, to find God
in one's emotions and, indeed, many English and Scottish Protestants continually examined
their feelings for such signs of election. Feelings of salvation or contentment could not simply manifest in one's body; they were placed there by God.[43] Although all emotions were
subject to supernatural manipulation, there were some that were more readily associated
with demonic temptation and salvation than others.

### *Fear*

Many historians have noted that the early modern devil was a far more frightening prospect than in previous centuries. As noted earlier, the new Protestant devil was believed to
be more aggressive than his previous iteration. This, combined with an increasing emphasis
on an individual form of piety that left the godly seemingly alone in an internal struggle
against Satan, led many men and women to become extremely fearful, even terrified, of the
devil. As numerous historians have warned, attempting to study fear in past societies can
be a "particularly hazardous endeavour."[44] Those scholars who have made headway in this
area have often focused on fear as a historical phenomenon rather than as a psychological category.[45] This approach lends itself more to a study of the "logistics of fear"—the
way in which people perceived fear, the means they undertook to suppress or overcome it,
how they coped with it and, importantly, what triggered it.[46] It is also worth noting that,
perhaps unlike our modern society, fear in the early modern world was not always a bad
thing. There could be healthy types of fear, such as a respectful, reverential fear of God.[47]
Reminders that parents should bring up their children "in the feare of God" so that "in
the end they receive the reward of their faith, even the salvation of their souls" were not
uncommon.[48] Fear of damnation was a key part of the Protestant conversion narrative.
As Ryrie has noted, many early modern divines preached that only those who had come
face-to-face with their own sin, and felt the full terrors of that experience, were worthy of
salvation. John Dod preached that those who were "never terrified nor troubled in their

consciences" were lacking "the first principall note of true conversion," and Robert Bruce, preaching in Scotland, explained to his followers that "it is not possible to you to make meikle of heaven, except you have some taist of hell."[49] Although some disagreed with the premise that a good conversion required fear, this was an extremely prevalent concept, and many early modern Protestants shared the absolute terror they felt before breaking through to the other side. Nor was this a straightforward process. As we will see below with the example of Nehemiah Wallington, early modern Protestants did not simply convert and then feel at peace. Theirs was an ongoing process of conversion followed by bouts of temptation, fear and despair—and sometimes joy. For many, even those who experienced joy and grace, fear of damnation was always present.

Fear of the devil was common to both the godly and the damned. Early modern witchcraft narratives include examples of how (mainly) women gave into the devil's demands out of fear. Temperance Floyd, a woman accused of witchcraft in England in the 1680s, refused to admit the location of a doll she had supposedly used to inflict harm because she was afraid the devil would "tear her in pieces" if she did. She also told her accusers that she once refused to harm a woman and so "the Devil beat [her] about the Head grievously."[50] Mary, another witch in this same account, claimed that the devil frightened her.[51] In a similar case from 1621, accused witch Elizabeth Sawyer claimed that she was in "a very grete feare" when she met the devil who threatened to "teare me in peeces if I did not grant unto him my soule and body."[52] John Sterne's 1648 pamphlet describes how accused witch Ellen Greenliefe was approached by a thing "like a Mole, soft and cold" who "spoke to her with a great hollow voice, and asked her to give her soule and body to him." Ellen accepted but the mole threatened her: if she ever confessed to witchcraft, he would "cause her to drowne her selfe" and, when she did confess, we are told this creature "tore her as she confessed, as if he would have torne her in pieces."[53]

Those threatened by witches were also terrified. Witches were, of course, believed to be in league with the devil so an encounter with one was always satanically charged. When approached by a "grand witch" Robin, the subject of an English witchcraft pamphlet from 1655,

> fell into such a trembling condition, that his hands shooke, his pulses beat, his heart panted, his head aked, his nose dropt, his belly rumbled, and a certain parcell of melting teares dropt out of the lower ends of his breeches.[54]

In another less visceral but still palpable example, one tale of witchcraft from 1606 describes the male victim crying "the Witch, the Witch, I am undone, I am undone: O God, women of Royston, helpe, helpe, the Witch, the Witch, I am a man spoyld, helpe I am undone."[55] In these examples, the witch, through her demonic associations, was a terrifying figure.

## Despair and Suicide

Perhaps one of the emotions most commonly attributed to Protestants and their relationship with the devil is despair. Catholics could also, of course, be prone to despair but this was less likely to be fatalistic. Purgatory, for instance, did not induce despair as it was not a permanent end. The Catholic writer Robert Parsons stressed the biblical statement that

God desired all men to be saved, meaning that the damned had the free will to change their ultimate destiny. For Catholics, God was "predominantly merciful."[56] This was in stark contrast to the God constructed by Calvin, as was the idea that the faithful had free will—which from a Calvinist perspective implied that people had a form of power over God. The idea that the damned could change their destiny did not fit with the Protestant conception of double predestination. As we will see, this could have a doleful impact on the Protestant psyche.

Much has been written about the Puritans' so-called "culture of despair." Historians have warned that we should be careful of exaggerating Calvinism's tendency to breed despair, but it is undeniable that it was a key element of Protestants' rich emotional engagements with the demonic.[57] As Blair Worden once observed, "the volume of despair engendered by Puritan teaching ... is incalculable."[58] This partly stemmed from the doctrine of double predestination, but also the fact that one's salvation was ultimately unknowable. Together, these ideas produced a state of mind that left many of the godly "psychologically damage[d] and anxious."[59] For reformers such as Luther and Calvin, hell was "essentially psychological" and represented the "pain of eternal rejection by God."[60] And for those who believed themselves damned, this hell became the daily experience for the despairing literate Protestant. Combined with the idea that humans are innately sinful creatures, it is easy to see how some early modern men and women fell into the depths of despair. Michael MacDonald's reading of the physician Richard Napier's (1559–1634) casebooks tells us that he saw 91 patients—19 men and 72 women—who were "doubtful of salvation" or were "tempted to despair of salvation."[61] Despair or anguish about one's own sins and salvation seems to have been "almost a routine part of the Protestant experience."[62] This despair was often directly attributed to the devil, raising despair to the status of a spiritual battle. Luther suffered from what he called *Anfechtung*, a form of despair arising directly from diabolical assault.[63] This most afflicted Luther while he was experiencing moments of personal crisis, particularly when he was agonising over the nature of true religion in the early 1500s.[64] This was not unusual; it was at moments of vulnerability, especially emotional vulnerability, that the devil was most likely to attempt his seductions. We see this play out in early modern English witchcraft narratives. In cases from 1579, 1619, 1621, 1646, 1693 and 1712, the devil chose to approach a potential witch at the precise time that she lost control of her emotions, giving in to uncontrolled passions and anger.[65] In New England, "discontent" was often viewed as the devil's first point of entry.[66] Either way, it was when women gave into their emotions that the devil swept in and offered them the power to act—and this point marked the first step in what was to become an ongoing relationship. The devil's ability to prey on the vulnerable and send them to the depths of despair was a common preoccupation in early modern Protestant theology, and one that demonstrated the devil's innate understanding of the human psyche.

In extreme cases, despair could lead to suicidal thoughts, a state of mind often characterised as a form of temptation. In Protestant England, the connection between religious despair and suicide was "constantly made," much more so than it was in the pre-Reformation period.[67] There was even a sense in 17th-century England that suicide was reaching new heights, with the puritan preacher William Gouge (1575–1653) declaring that "scarce an age since the beginning of the world hath afforded more examples of this desperate humanity that this our present age, and that in all sorts of people, Clergie, Laity, unlearned, Noble, Female, young and old."[68] Others criticised Calvinism's tendency to invoke suicidal ideation:

> He strives and stretches his brains to find out the depth of that doctrine, and cannot attain to it; for indeed it is not knowledge, but imagination: and so by poring and puzzling himself in it, loses that wisdom he had, and becomes distracted and mad ... if the passion of sorrow predominate, then he is heavy and sad, crying out, *He is damned, God hath forsaken him, and he must go to Hell when he dye, he cannot make his calling and election sure*: And in that distemper many times a man doth hang, kil or drown himself.[69]

Nehemiah Wallington (1598–1658), a London puritan artisan, has been described as the "poster boy" for Protestant despair. He left behind more than 2,600 pages of personal papers, including a spiritual diary, which tell us that he attempted suicide eleven times.[70] He attempted to poison himself on at least two occasions, but failed. He considered jumping from high windows, cutting his throat and even hanging himself. Wallington's life was an "endless struggle" against this demonic temptation.[71] Such temptations were especially common among the godly who, having conscientiously prayed for God to reveal their sins, became overwhelmed by the resulting knowledge. The realisation of one's inherently sinful nature and inevitable damnation, made some of the godly determined to end their life as quickly as possible to prevent further sin.[72] Graphically illustrating this point is the suicide of Mr Monk who, one morning in June 1635, rose from his bed before five in the morning, cut his throat, ran outside in a bloody shirt flourishing his sword, and leapt into the Thames. He was pulled out "by boat hooks and brought home [roaring] most hideously, crying that he was damned, and he had prayed often, and God would not hear him ... he lay crying very strangely and hideously till the next Wednesday, and then he died."[73] Mr Monk's belief in his own damnation was clearly linked to his suicide attempt. Another common reasoning behind suicide attempts is best summed up by Sarah Wight, a despairing puritan living in the 1640s: "I thought hell to come, couldn't be worse than what I felt."[74]

The very language surrounding suicide, a crime committed "at the instigation of the Devil," made its demonic associations and origins obvious. English court documents routinely (although not consistently) noted that a suicide committed his crime "not having the Fear of God before his Eyes but moved and seduced by the Instigation of the Devil."[75] Self-murder was a "satanic sin" which was punished increasingly harshly in Protestant England. The belief that suicide was inherently supernatural in its origins set it apart from most other crimes. Although all crimes could be viewed as sins, or as demonically inspired actions, very few offences other than suicide and witchcraft were deemed to be caused primarily by supernatural factors. Throughout the early modern period, the association between suicide and demonic causation became particularly strong in the popular imagination. Scholars such as R. A. Houston have argued that the devil was less important in reports of suicide than has traditionally been argued.[76] But even in offering this critique Houston does highlight the role of the devil in suicide cases, especially when no "natural" cause was noted.

Of course, there were some contemporary sceptics who did not believe in the devil's role in suicide, but these were in the minority. England appears to have been a bit of an outlier in terms of punishing suicide. In France, for example, the laws against self-murder were seldom applied. Calvinist regimes in the Swiss-city states of Geneva and Zurich did attempt to impose harsh sanctions, but these were not as harsh as those routinely prescribed in England. There they involved the complete forfeiture of goods and the desecration of the suicide's corpse. It seems that in England both the laity and the clergy were united in their desire to punish those who chose to commit suicide.[77] For both, suicide was a demonic temptation, one that some found impossible to resist. At the same time, the sin of self-murder was the gravest one that a Christian could commit. Returning to Napier's records, we find that some afflicted men and women heard or saw the devil tempting them to self-murder, whereas the majority believed that demonic spirits or witches had implanted suicidal urges in their minds.[78] These beliefs persisted well into the modern age. As with other instances of demonic temptation, orthodox clergymen preached that only faith and prayer could help to ease one's suffering.

In the same way that the constant cycle of temptation and resistance could be rationalised as a "good" thing for the devout Protestant to endure, suicidal temptation could represent an important point on the path to redemption. As part of their religious practice, early modern Protestants were encouraged to examine their conscience and to come face-to-face with their sins. This process could lead some, like Wallington, to fear that they were fatally damned and lead to suicidal despair—even sometimes to an actual attempt at suicide. However, as Michael MacDonald and Terence Murphy have noted, Wallington's experience characterised by constant flights of despair followed by prayer and renewed faith could be seen as part of an "ideal pattern" of religious experience.[79] They argue that English puritans institutionalised suicidal despair, presenting it as "the emotional symbol of the liminal stage between the sinful life and regeneration."[80] The same can be argued in the case of Scottish Calvinists. As Houston has demonstrated, in the writings and sermons of the Scottish clergy there was "a strongly positive side to the contemplation of self-murder."[81] Suicidal thoughts were part of Calvinist conversion narratives, thus indicating "a degree of acceptance ... that people could contemplate self-murder, even if they were supposed to win through rather than succumb."[82] By struggling through temptations of self-harm, Calvinists framed thoughts of suicide as a "prevenient grace, forming antecedents to regeneration and salvation in an essentially positive interpretation of spiritual turmoil."[83] Further, in many Scottish cases of completed suicide, the victim was not necessarily damned but friends and family were able to remain hopeful of their loved one's salvation.[84] Suicidal temptation, while extremely distressing, could be reframed as a positive experience for some Reformed Protestants.

## *Joy*

The Protestant experience of the demonic was one that encouraged extremes of emotion. The faithful could be driven to the depths of despair but, if they managed to persevere, they could find themselves in the midst of great joy. Luther remarked on his own suffering and despair: "I myself have been offended more than once even to the abyss of despair, nay so far as even to wish that I had not been born a man; that is before I knew how beautiful that despair was, and how near to Grace."[85] In some cases, it was necessary to reach the depths of despair before achieving grace. Wallington is, again, an excellent example of these highs and lows of emotions: one night looking at the stars he was "ravished with the favour of God" but, a moment later, he was tempted to throw himself from the window.[86] Joy needed to be divided between worldly joy and the specific joy experienced on feeling God's presence. It was this second emotion, certainly not the first, that the godly Christian should seek, and it was often preceded by fits of despair. This joy could be a "vivid and life-changing experience," one which lifted believers into the very presence of God.[87] These rare glimpses of joy could be understood as previews of heaven. For most early modern Protestants, these glimpses were fleeting but, sometimes they were enough to sustain them through the tumult that came with being one of God's elect.

## The Devil in Decline?

### *The Devil in the Modern World*

Until recently, it was taken for granted that the devil's relevance and utility in society steadily declined after the end of witch-hunting in the 17th and 18th centuries. This was a view espoused both by contemporaries and by historians. Writing in 1727, Daniel Defoe was able to claim confidently that the age of the devil was at an end:

> The Age is grown too wise to be agitated by these dull scar-crow Things which their Fore-Fathers were tickled with; *Satan* has been obliged to lay by his Puppet-shews and his Timblers, those things are grown stale; his morrice-dancing *Devils*, his mountebanking and quacking won't do now.[88]

One hundred and fifty years later, William Gladstone echoed this sentiment, remarking that hell and the devil had been "relegated ... to the far-off corners of the Christian mind ... to sleep in deep shadow, as a thing needless in our enlightened and progressive age."[89] In the words of Philip Almond, by the middle of the 18th century "for an educated elite at least, the Devil had become a figure *of* history—one of the past rather than the present or future—and not a participant *within* it."[90] Historians have noted the devil's declining relevance, citing enlightenment ideas, such as those espoused by René Descartes, Baruch Spinoza and John Locke, as key reasons for his decline.[91] Much scholarship on the devil is strongly associated with witchcraft studies, meaning that compared to the vast literature produced on his medieval and early modern incarnations, work on the modern devil is relatively rare.

It is clear that demonic ideas continued to resonate for much of the population. Recent scholarship has stressed the ongoing relevance of the devil, right up until the present day. Vital work by Owen Davies, Jeffrey Burton Russell, Karl Bell and Sarah Bartels has demonstrated the key role the devil continued to play in the modern age, in terms of both theology and popular depictions.[92] Just two years before Defoe wrote his *History of the Devil*, Newcastle-upon-Tyne curate Henry Bourne reflected on the stories he heard of commoners telling each other how they had seen fairies, spirits and "even the Devil himself, with a cloven Foot."[93] As Davies has noted, the concept of the mischievous devil existed well into the 18th century, was accepted by Anglican clergymen, and could be found in popular literature and culture. The devil even continued to be prominent in English courts, long after the decriminalisation of witchcraft.[94] Looking to the 19th century, Bartels has demonstrated that the devil still played a key role in English society, with a "significant subset" of the population continuing to view the traditional devil as very real and important.[95] French poet Charles Baudelaire's (1821–1867) famous epigram that the devil's greatest trick was to convince us of his non-existence was repeated, albeit less eloquently, in an 1888 sermon entitled "Is the Devil Yet Alive? If So, Where does he Live?" Delivered by the Reverend J.

Van Horn, it declared that "the Devil is 'the father of lies.' The report that he does not exist is a lie, and therefore the Devil is the father of the report."[96]

Victorian views of the devil do not provide a straightforward "loss of faith" narrative; instead, they highlight the "diversity and complexity of Victorian religion."[97] The Victorian period was defined by an "ardent attraction to the supernatural," with people from all segments of society following a desire to engage with the supernatural world.[98] That being said, the devil of the 19th century was a more malleable creature than that of previous centuries. Karl Bell's work on the legend of Spring-heeled Jack is a good example of this. As Bell shows, the creature was able to be deployed as an anti-authoritarian symbol, a devil, a ghost and a monster, among many other things.[99] The notion of Spring-heeled Jack as a devilish figure eventually became the most common interpretation, with Bell arguing that this figure "can be seen to embody a popular romanticist notion of the devil."[100] Returning to Bartels' work, we see that the 19th-century devil could be understood from a literary, romantic, theological or popular perspective. Indeed, Satan's reduction in power allowed him to be deployed as a changing symbol in numerous literary works, something that has dominated scholarship at the expense of focus on the devil's social and theological power.[101] It is unquestionable that the devil of the modern world was less powerful than that of the early modern, but he was (and is) still relevant. William James' suggestion in 1902 that "the world is all the richer for having a devil in it, so long as we keep our foot upon his neck" perhaps gives some sense of the devil's changing importance in the modern world.[102]

### *The Devil and Early Psychology*

As concerns about the devil's powers of temptation were continuing to resonate in the modern world, the development of early psychology in the late 19th century created its own interpretation of humanity's ongoing emotional engagement with the devil. Early psychology located the devil within the human psyche as a key part of the unconscious mind. Sigmund Freud (1856–1939), the father of psychoanalysis, is the most well-known proponent of this view. Freud famously viewed religion as an illusion and was fascinated by the devil as a symbol of repressed desire, claiming that Satan was "nothing other than the personification of repressed, unconscious drives."[103] The very malleability of the devil was a boon to Freud, for it meant that he was able to identify him with a diverse number of neuroses and unconscious desires. As Russell has explained:

> Because Freud believed that sexuality is the most frequently and powerfully repressed force, he thought the Devil particularly represented the power of repressed sexual drives, which often cause people to act against their conscious will. Noting the frequent traditional connection of the Devil with anal imagery (in Luther, for example), Freud considered him especially the symbol of repressed anal eroticism.[104]

Freud applied his theories to early modern cases of witchcraft and demonic possession, noting especially the preponderance of anal imagery in sabbaths, such as when the alleged witch was asked to kiss the devil's backside.[105] At various points in his career Freud regarded the devil as a symbol for the seductive father, the hatred of a parent, a repressed fear of death or as death itself. In sum, for Freud, the devil always represented "whichever element of the unconscious Freud saw as most in opposition to the conscious will."[106]

Freud also devoted quite some time to an exploration of cases of demonic possession. He explained this phenomenon through psychoanalysis and saw possession as a manifestation of a disease or illness that had natural causes which he then described using his own universal theories. In 1923, he published an exploration of the 1677 demonic possession case of the Bavarian Christoph Haizmann. Freud retrospectively diagnosed Haizmann as having a paranoid psychotic illness rooted in an Oedipal complex, one in which the devil acted as a father-substitute. Freud argued that Haizmann's submission to Catholic exorcism represented "a flight to his mother, the Church, to avoid the threatened castration by his father."[107] While this explanation does nothing to further our understanding of the 17th-century psyche, or early modern belief in the devil, it does show how some early psychologists viewed the devil. Freud's devil was one that lived firmly in the mind and represented the afflicted's deepest desires. Although a different devil from that of the early modern period, Freud's devil was also one that could only be understood in terms of emotions.

Another prominent early psychologist, Carl Jung (1875–1961), went to great lengths to incorporate the devil into his theories. For Jung, evil was real, as was good. Both were necessary parts of the cosmos. But Jung saw good and evil as being incorporated within God. To find the devil in Jung's psychology, we need to look to what he called "the Shadow." This concept is not entirely incongruent with the Christian devil. For Jung, the shadow represented an unconscious force which was a primitive psychological element that lacked moral control. Jung theorised that there was both a collective shadow and an individual shadow, and these could differ from person to person. Jung also suggested the existence of an archetypal shadow:

> … an archetypal Shadow may also exist, though Jung was not clear on this point. At times he suggested that the demonic Shadow, consisting of repressed material that might become destructive if not integrated, could be distinguished from the Satanic Shadow, which was intrinsically evil and sought to suck everything down into the eternal vacuum and void. The archetypal Shadow, representing evil as perceived collectively by all of humanity, would be close to absolute evil, close to the traditional Devil.[108]

Like Freud, Jung placed the devil firmly within the human unconscious. Although this may remind us, in some ways, of Reformed Protestants' concern that the devil lurked in their own minds, it is a very different approach. For early psychologists and psychoanalysts, the devil was an unconscious figure. For early modern Protestants, he was terrifyingly real, and had the ability to infiltrate and plant thoughts within their minds. But for both, the devil was a figure that tapped into emotion.

\* \* \*

This chapter has surveyed the many complex links between demonic temptation, conscience and emotion. Its focus has been on early modern Reformed Protestants, a group who spent much of their lives worrying about the temptations and snares of the devil. But it has also briefly juxtaposed these ideas with modern conceptions of the devil, demonstrating that the devil remained relevant as a source of mental temptation and emotional turmoil right into the modern world, in both theological and popular depictions, and in ideas from early psychology. For many people, especially those living in the early modern world, the devil was not an abstract figure; he was a real, tangible creature with whom one engaged with over a lifetime. He could produce fear, despair, even suicidal despair but, for those who could resist him, their reward could be great joy.

## Notes

1 For more on the role of conscience in Reformed Protestantism, see Randall C. Zachman, *The Assurance of Faith: Conscience in the Theology of Martin Luther and John Calvin* (Minneapolis, 1993).
2 William Chub, *The True Travaile of all Faithfull Christians* (London, 1584), 137v.
3 I.D., *The most wonderfull and true storie, of a certaine witch named Alse Gooderige of Stapen hill* (London, 1597), sig. A2r.
4 Anon., *The Snare of the Devil Discovered: Or, A True and Perfect Relations of the Sad and Deplorable Condition of Lydia the Wife of John Rogers* (London, 1658), 1.
5 Michelle D. Brock, *Satan and the Scots: The Devil in Post-Reformation Scotland c. 1560–1700* (Farnham, 2016), 24.
6 Brock, *Satan and the Scots,* 1.
7 Jeffrey Burton Russell, *Mephistopheles: The Devil in the Modern World* (Ithaca, 1986), 31.
8 Kathleen Sands, *Demon Possession in Elizabethan England* (London, 2004), 146.
9 Thomas Watson, *Twoo notable Sermons,* (London, 1554), sig. G3v-G4r in Nathan Johnstone, *The Devil and Demonism in Early Modern England* (Cambridge, 2006), 84.
10 Walter Farquar Hook, *Discourses Bearing on the Controversies of the Day* (London, 1853), 284–5.
11 Johnstone, *The Devil and Demonism,* 85.
12 Richard Galis, *A Brief Treatise Conteyning the Most Strange and Horrible Crueltye of Elizabeth Stile* (London, 1579).
13 Galis, *A Brief Treatise,* sig. A4v.
14 Galis, *A Brief Treatise,* sig. A4v.
15 Galis, *A Brief Treatise,* sig. B1r.
16 Darren Oldridge, *The Devil in Early Modern England* (Stroud, 2000), 19.
17 Johnstone, *The Devil and Demonism,* 2.
18 Calvin, *Institutes,* I.xiv.15–6 in Brock, *Satan and the Scots,* 27.
19 Theodore Beza, *Maister Bezaes household prayers* (London, 1603), preface.
20 Alec Ryrie, *Being Protestant in Reformation Britain* (Oxford, 2013), 37. For William Perkins' views, see William Perkins *The Combat between Christ and the Divell displayed* (London, 1606) or his *A Discourse of the Damned Art of Witchcraft* (Cambridge: 1608).
21 Johnstone, *The Devil and Demonism,* 60 and 62. For more on baptism reform see Keith Thomas, *Religion and the Decline of Magic,* 2nd ed. (London, 1991), 62–4 and Eamon Duffy, *The Stripping of the Altars* 2nd ed. (New Haven, 2005), 280–1 and 473.
22 W.W., *A True and Just Recorde, of the Information, Examination and Confession of All the Witches* (London, 1582), sig. B7v-B8r.
23 Anon., *The examination, confession, trial, and execution, of Joane Williford, Joan Cariden, and Jane Hott* (London, 1645), 3.
24 Oldridge, *The Devil in Early Modern England,* 45.
25 Oldridge, *The Devil in Early Modern England,* 46.
26 Michael MacDonald, *Mystical Bedlam: Madness, Anxiety and Healing in Seventeenth-Century England* (Cambridge, 1983), 219–20.
27 Johnstone, *The Devil and Demonism,* 61.
28 William Harrison and William Leygh, *Deaths advantage little regarded* (London, 1602), 82.
29 Jean Calvin, *Calvin's Commentary on the Epistle of James* (Aberdeen, 1797) 82.

30 Ryrie, *Being Protestant*, 32

31 Johnstone, *The Devil and Demonism*, 3

32 Brian P. Levack, *The Devil Within: Possession and Exorcism in the Christian West* (New Haven, 2013), 200.

33 Levack, *The Devil Within*, 205.

34 Levack, *The Devil Within*, 205.

35 Levack, *The Devil Within*, 205.

36 Levack, *The Devil Within*, 63 and 111.

37 Levack, *The Devil Within*, 161.

38 Johnstone, *The Devil and Demonism*, 103.

39 Oldridge, *The Devil in Early Modern England*, 25.

40 Ryrie, *Being Protestant*, 42.

41 Ryrie, *Being Protestant*, 40.

42 William Perkins, *The Foundation of Christian Religion, Gathered into Six Principles* (London, 1642), 3; quotation on 14–5.

43 For more on this topic, see Ryrie, *Being Protestant*, Part I.

44 Peter Marshall, "Fear, Purgatory and Polemic in Reformation England," in *Fear in Early Modern Society*, ed. William G. Naphy and Penny Roberts (Manchester, 1997), 150.

45 William G. Naphy and Penny Roberts, "Introduction," in *Fear in Early Modern Society*, 2.

46 Naphy and Roberts, "Introduction," 2.

47 Marshall, *Fear, Purgatory and Polemic*, 160.

48 Anon., *A True Relation of an Apparition in the Likenesse of a Bird with a white brest* (London, 1641), sig. A3v-A4r.

49 Ryrie, *Being Protestant*, 36.

50 Anon., *A True and Impartial Relation of the Informations against Three Witches* (London, 1682), 19 and 38.

51 Anon., *A True and Impartial Relation*, 38.

52 Henry Goodcole, *The wonderfull discoverie of Elizabeth Sawyer a Witch* (London, 1621), sig. C3r.

53 John Sterne, *A Confirmation and Discovery of Witchcraft* (London, 1648), 28.

54 L.P., *The Witch of the Woodlands* (London, 1655), 7–8.

55 Anon., *The Most Cruell and Bloody Murther committed by an Innkeepers Wife called Annis Dell* (London, 1606), sig. C4v.

56 John Stachniewski, *The Persecutory Imagination: English Puritanism and the Literature of Religious Despair* (Oxford, 1991), 35.

57 For warnings on the danger of exaggerating this culture of despair, see Ryrie, *Being Protestant*, 29 and Johnstone, *The Devil and Demonism*, 20.

58 Blair Worden, review of Paul S. Seaver, *Wallington's World: A Puritan Artisan in Seventeenth-Century London* (1985) in *London Review of Books* (23 Jan.-6 Feb. 1986), 16–7 as quoted in Stachniewski, *The Persecutory Imagination*, 1.

59 Brock, *Satan and the Scots,* 29.

60 Stachniewski, *The Persecutory Imagination*, 24.

61 MacDonald, *Mystical Bedlam*, 220.

62 Ryrie, *Being Protestant*, 32.

63 Ryrie, *Being Protestant*, 32. The term is usually translated as *trial* but sometimes *temptation* or even *affliction*. See David Scaer, "The Concept of *Anfectung* in Luther's Thought," *Concordia Theological Quarterly* 47, no. 1 (1983): 15–30 on 15.

64 Darren Oldridge, *The Devil: A Very Short Introduction* (Oxford, 2012), 55.

65 Charlotte-Rose Millar, *Witchcraft, the Devil and Emotions in Early Modern England* (London, 2017), 91.

66 For more on New England, see Erika Gasser, *Vexed with Devils: Manhood and Witchcraft in Old and New England* (New York, 2017).

67 Stachniewski, *The Persecutory Imagination*, 46. For work on suicide in the later period, see Olive Anderson, *Suicide in Victorian and Edwardian England* (Oxford, 1987).

68 William Gouge, "To the Christian Reader," in John Sym, *Lifes Preservative against Self-Killing* (London, 1637), sig. A4v.

69  Gerrard Winstanley, *The Law of Freedom in a Platform* in *The Complete Works of Gerrard Winstanley*, vol. 2, ed. Thomas N. Corns, Ann Hughes, David Loewenstein (Oxford, 2009), 346–61.

70  Paul S. Seaver, *Wallington's World: A Puritan Artisan in Seventeenth-Century London* (Stanford, 1985), 2, 22 and 30.

71  Seaver, *Wallington's World*, 31.

72  Seaver, *Wallington's World*, 16.

73  Seaver, *Wallington's World*, 60.

74  Henry Jessey, *The Exceeding Riches of Grace Advanced* (London, 1647), 70.

75  Michael MacDonald and Terence R. Murphy, *Sleepless Souls: Suicide in Early Modern England* (Oxford, 1990), 55. For more on the inconsistency of this usage, see R. A. Houston, *Punishing the Dead? Suicide, Lordship, and Community in Britain, 1500–1830* (Oxford, 2010), 288.

76  Houston, *Punishing the Dead?*, chapter six.

77  MacDonald and Murphy, *Sleepless Souls*, 75–6.

78  MacDonald and Murphy, *Sleepless Souls*, 51.

79  MacDonald and Murphy, *Sleepless Souls*, 65.

80  MacDonald and Murphy, *Sleepless Souls*, 65.

81  Houston, *Punishing the Dead?* 306.

82  Houston, *Punishing the Dead?* 310.

83  Houston, *Punishing the Dead?* 311.

84  Houston, *Punishing the Dead?* 308–9.

85  Martin Luther, quoted in Stachniewski, *The Persecutory Imagination*, 18.

86  Ryrie, *Being Protestant*, 85.

87  Ryrie, *Being Protestant*, 80 and 83.

88  Daniel Defoe, *A History of the Devil* (London, 1727), 388.

89  William Ewert Gladstone, *Studies Subsidiary to the Works of Bishop Butler* (Oxford, 1896), 206.

90  Philip C. Almond, *The Devil: A New Biography* (New York, 2014), 220.

91  See, for example, Jeffrey Burton Russell, *Mephistopheles* and Almond, *The Devil*.

92  Owen Davies, "Talk of the Devil: Crime and Satanic Inspiration in Eighteenth-Century England" (2007, self-published, open access paper); Russell, *Mephistopheles*; Karl Bell, *The Magical Imagination: Magic and Modernity in Urban England, 1780–1914* (Cambridge, 2012); Sarah Bartels, *The Devil and the Victorians: Supernatural Evil in Nineteenth-Century English Culture* (London, 2021).

93  Henry Bourne, *Antiquitates Vulgares* (1725) quoted in Margaret Spufford, *Small Books and Pleasant Histories: Popular Fiction and Its Readership in Seventeenth-Century England* (London, 1981), 5.

94  Davies, "Talk of the Devil," 2.

95  Bartels, *The Devil and the Victorians*, 29.

96  Rev. J. Van Horn, "Is the Devil Yet Alive? If So, Where Does he Live?" *Cheshire Observer*, 6 September 1884.

97  Bartels, *The Devil and the Victorians*, 31.

98  Karl Bell, *The Legend of Spring-Heeled Jack: Victorian Urban Folklore and Popular Cultures* (Woodbridge, 2012), 54.

99  Bell, *The Legend of Spring-Heeled Jack*.

100  Bell, *The Legend of Spring-Heeled Jack*, 55 and 60.

101  Russell, *Mephistopheles*, 169.

102  William James, *The Varieties of Religious Experience* (New York, 1902), 50.

103  Sigmund Freud as quoted in Russell, *Mephistopheles*, 228.

104  Russell, *Mephistopheles*, 228.

105  See Chapters 4, 5, 9 and 11 in this volume.

106  Russell, *Mephistopheles*, 229.

107  Levack, *The Devil Within*, 133.

108  Russell, *Mephistopheles*, 234.

## Further Reading

Almond, Philip C. *The Devil: A New Biography*. New York: I.B. Tauris, 2014.

Bartels, Sarah. *The Devil and the Victorians: Supernatural Evil in Nineteenth-century English Culture*. London: Routledge, 2021.

Brock, Michelle D. *Satan and the Scots: The Devil in Post-Reformation Scotland c1560-1700*. Farnham: Ashgate, 2016.

Johnstone, Nathan. *The Devil and Demonism in Early Modern England*. Cambridge: Cambridge University Press, 2006.

Levack, Brian P. *The Devil Within: Possession and Exorcism in the Christian West*. New Haven: Yale University Press, 2013.

Oldridge, Darren. *The Devil in Early Modern England*. Stroud: Sutton, 2000.

Russell, Jeffrey Burton. *Mephistopheles: The Devil in the Modern World*. Ithaca: Cornell University Press, 1986.

# 21

# CONJURING THE DEVIL

## The Cinematic Satan, 1899–2020

### W. Scott Poole

A searching for the devil's hoofprints in popular film might seem to offer little more than an analysis of ephemera. But the sheer popularity of films that employ Satan and related themes calls for discussion. Beyond the fact that they are a hurtling cataract in transatlantic popular culture, they are often in a braided, sometimes parasitical, relationship with conservative cultural mores, religious fundamentalism and false conspiracy narratives of the far right, making them essential to interpreting the role of mythic belief in contemporary culture and politics. This chapter surveys the history of Satan in cinema while showing how that history intertwines with cultural politics.

*Conjuring 3: The Devil Made Me Do It* (2021) insists that Satan not only possesses and destroys the lives of the unwary. He works through human servants that are equally malicious, powerful and active. Not unlike the fantasy of QANON, and American moral panics nearly half a century old, the film reveals that the devil's goons hive away in tunnels, hidden caverns honeycombed in darkness just beneath the thin placenta of our reality.[1] *Conjuring 3* is part of the now sprawling "Conjure-verse," eight films that draw on the world created by the original 2013 film with more on the way. Satan appears in the series as a nearly invincible dark lord. He can seemingly trick and deceive, infest and possess anyone. He is active across the globe, popping up like the wily target of a spiritual whack-a-mole game. His servants are everywhere, either wilfully or apathetically unleashing unspeakable horror.

The series might be better referred to as the Warren-verse. Demon-hunters Ed and Lorraine Warren, whose experiences are allegedly the factual basis for the $1.9-billion franchise, began their career as paranormal investigators in the 1970s. The pair parlayed a tenuous connection with *The Amityville Horror* into nine books and a busy, profitable lecture schedule. Ed Warren, a former city bus driver turned amateur demonologist, died in 2006. Loraine Warren lived to see the couple's peculiar niche in the paranormal become one of the most popular licenses in horror film history.

The first entry in the series became a surprise summer hit in 2013 with its assertions that a New England haunting was not the work of an unquiet spirit, but of a demonic power summoned by the witches of Salem. Indeed, the fake history lesson the film delivers in an almost pugilistic fashion is that *real witches* died at Salem in 1692–3.

DOI: 10.4324/9781003096603-22

Rather than innocent victims of misogynistic theology and community conflict that we know them to be from historical evidence, the film implies that Cotton Mather had been right about them all along. In case anyone missed the message of a film that asserts its basis in truth, Patrick Wilson who plays Ed Warren ends the film by sermonising that, "The devil exists. God exists. And for us, as people, our very destiny hinges on which we elect to follow."[2]

These raw assertions, coming after an admittedly spooky 90 minutes crafted by director James Wan, had the desired effect on audiences. Shot quickly and sequentially for twenty million, the film made in excess of eight times its production cost. This was the case even though the demon-fest appeared in July's summer slump, a time of year when horror films go to die. Warner Brothers tried something new with the story of the Warren's, launching what can best be described as a faith-based marketing campaign. The company held special screenings for influential constituencies, including evangelical youth pastors and Catholic priests.[3]

The film's screenwriters played a prominent role in this promotion to the faithful. Brothers Chad and Chris Hayes have been very open about how their beliefs inform the franchise. Raised as conservative Baptists, they described themselves in 2013 as "messianic Jews"—a brand of Christian fundamentalism that holds to many of the same beliefs as other evangelicals while adhering to some of the Tanakh's dietary laws and voicing unconditional support for the Israeli state. Before their work on *The Conjuring*, the pair had primarily been known for writing *Baywatch Nights*, a campy spin-off to the yet campier 1990s TV series.

At the time of the film's release, the Brothers Hayes gave a peculiar interview to the Christian Broadcasting Network. In it, they claimed *The Conjuring* was not just a horror movie but a film about "love and family and people who come to help, and God is at the center of it." It was "God-based" and showed audiences characters that "you know, battle into darkness." These promotional efforts do seem to have worked, given the sheer number of positive notices received in various evangelical outlets. In fact, even more moderate outlets bought into the demonic gibberish. A writer for *Relevant* magazine called it "not only a first-class faith movie" but "a testimony."[4]

The cultural meaning of the Warren-verse, its alchemy of theological belief and pop culture, captures a very important truth about how ideas about the devil have shaped, and been shaped, by film over the last hundred years. An analysis of the large and still proliferating diabolical filmography reveals that the idea of Satan has become an essential element in a profound intertwining of folk culture and film. An age that was supposed to experience "rationalisation" with revolutionary changes in technology experienced instead a revanchist growth of early modern beliefs tinctured with modernity's obsessions. Nowhere has his been more notable than in the United States, a culture heavily immersed in ideas about the devil that also just happens to be the spigot from which much of the world's pop culture geysers spew forth.

## Devil Disenchanted?

In the 19th century, print culture and popular tableaux kept literal conceptions of Satan and his work alive, even as the Christianities of the English-speaking world emphasised moral reform, ameliorative millennialism and eventually the turn-of-the-century social gospel. In the United States, the devil Americans have come to know on both the large and small screen has been responsible for, and grown out of, the country's equally demon-haunted worldview.[5]

Characters of myth, legend and the religious imagination faced a daunting prospect when making the leap from oral and print cultures into the new medias of the last hundred years. When they make it, it is largely because the entertainment industry has taken up their cause. Imagine the fate of Odin, Thor and Loki if they had not been capitalised by Marvel comics and, eventually, Marvel Studios. Dim figures from an oral culture refracted through second-hand Christian accounts in the Eddas and reimagined in the 18th and 19th centuries by northern European nationalists; without American pop culture, they would likely only have a fandom among a handful of academics who can translate Old Norse, Wagner enthusiasts and Nazi propagandists, in both their classic and contemporary forms.[6]

Satan, on the other hand, entered the 20th century with some ease. J. Charles Hall, a bit baffled, given that he had spent his career studying the supposedly demon-ridden Middle Ages, wrote in 1904 that, "nowhere can we turn that we hear the Archfiend's name coupled with every conceivable object and invoked over every single theory."[7] Hall had no way to guess that film, eventually slaved into social media platforms and digital culture in the late 20th century, would cause this mythos to proliferate. This was not supposed to happen.

In the last century, many of the global north's most influential thinkers have followed Max Weber and Friedrich Schiller's frequently evoked idea of the "disenchantment of the world." In this view, the Enlightenment and subsequent scientific advances fundamentally altered the ability of humans to imagine the sacred. Weber, in particular, did not consider this a happy consummation. Perhaps human beings needed freedom from a demon-haunted universe. But, Weber thought, disenchantment with devils also meant that the holy sites of saints and the realms of the gods would go into eclipse, chilling the flame of wonder to cold cinder. Social theorists of the Frankfurt School also took an interest in the idea, with some special notice from the circle's outlier Walter Benjamin.[8]

The interest of philosophical heavy hitters like Weber and the Frankfurters does not mean that the "rationalisation" thesis has received anything like universal acceptance. But its fingerprints are all over popular discourse. By the 1990s, the salon class worried that a "culture of unbelief" had replaced conceptions of the sacred and the profane. Ignoring decades of polling data, sociological studies and even cultural wildfires, the "satanic panic" of the 1970s, 1980s and early 1990s, both conservative and liberal voices sounded the tocsin.[9] This is why Andrew Delbanco could argue, in the highly premature *The Death of Satan: How Americans Have Lost the Sense of Evil* (1995), that the contemporary world had been "emptied of metaphysical meaning" and efforts to speak in terms of Satan, demons or indeed a providence that oversees them, fall into "gibberish and silence." Delbanco, who worries over this supposed lapse of the language of evil, believes that modernity's "culture of irony" created a world in which "we have literally enveloped ourselves in quotation marks." This state of affairs, he asserted, has made it impossible to truly believe in Satan, and thus in evil.[10]

A quarter of a century after Delbanco wrote, his argument seems hopelessly culture-bound, a relic unearthed from that the thin soil of optimism sedimented at the end of the Cold War. Political scientist Francis Fukayama's now infamous 1992 *The End of History and the Last Man*, based on a 1989 article, promised "the end of history," a respite from ideological conflict and international competition in which "the west" had triumphed. The now saccharine-tasting boast about the world conquest of those sup-posed twins, free market capitalism and democracy, has been falsified by reality. What entered the vacuum of power created by the Soviet collapse, across the globe and grow-ing in the maggot-ridden corpse of the USSR itself, has been a gaggle of authoritarian populisms and religious fundamentalisms each with its own bleak understanding of "the end of history."

The continuing survival of Satan as an idea, a belief and for some religious communities and individuals even an obsession gives the lie to the concept of a disenchanted world, at least in the case of the world "hyperpower," the United States. For many believers, both those who associate with an institutional church and that wild out on their own, Satan does not serve as a metaphor for something else, just frightening film trope, or a highly port-able commodity in horror fandom. He is real. To them, the world of belief, moral panic and false conspiracy theories has no need of being re-enchanted. The cantrips still gibber and scripture still rustles in the hearts that make up a not-particularly-secular-American society.[11]

This certainly is the case with beliefs about Satan and the diabolical, particularly after the growth of mass media in the 20th century. Rather than simply hearing official doctrine proclaimed from pulpits and enforced by the sword, Americans found belief emerging from intertwined narratives that did not conform easily to definitions of sacred and secular. Film and more recently digital narratives and streaming services have given the devil his due in ways that have harnessed belief to the engine of pop culture.

A sermon by the prominent Southern Baptist preacher Billy Graham, delivered at the height of the popularity of *The Exorcist* in 1974, illustrates the cross-fertilisation of media and religious message. Speaking in the wasting heat of an Arizona summer to a crowd of 30,000—the "crusade" gathering held without noted irony at Sun Devil Stadium—Graham professed not to have seen the film. Yet he warned of the dangers of "exposing yourself" to such material. However, the rest of his message reproduced almost precisely the message of *The Exorcist* itself. Graham warns against flirting with the occult through the ouija board, a warning that the film itself issues. When he insists that "Jesus, of course, was the great-est of all exorcists" and that demons are only "compelled by the power in Jesus's name," it is hard not to see William P. Blatty—author of the book upon which *The Exorcist* was based—nodding a silent "amen."[12] Billy Graham and *The Exorcist* director William Fried-kin had created a seamless narrative and their respective audiences could inhabit the same universe of sermon and film, satisfied in a worldview handed them by both religion and mass culture.

Scanning the dark lord's cinematic life, and how it intertwined with other narrative ele-ments in mass culture, reveals that credulity and not theology have allowed a very unstable set of concepts to thrive. Scholars have argued that the cinematic Satan has maintained many of the characteristics of the concept of the devil in the Christian tradition. What makes such a view untenable is the perhaps obvious fact that there is no single Christian tradition and—as other chapters in this collection have made clear—certainly no canoni-cal devil. Kelly Wyman in her 2004 "The Devil We Already Know" has contended that cinema has primarily borrowed the tropes of "the medieval devil" admits that the concept of "Satan" has been "in constant flux" and that the medieval period itself did not have "established portrayals of Satan."[13]

Intriguingly, both political forces and communities of faith have been utterly pleased to allow "a constant flux" in their portrayals of the devil. They have found in film, and not simply self-consciously religious narratives such as *The Conjuring*, their unacknowledged ally and source material.

For a significant number of Americans, many living in blighted rural areas in deeply precarious economic circumstances, the firehose of obscenities that came from the mouth of Regan McNeil—the demoniac at the centre of *The Exorcist*—in 1973 stand in easily for the floodtide of social change that the period seemed to promise, important changes resulting in increased judicial equality and a reshaping of the public discourse without concomitant changes in the distribution of income or access to social power.

The conservative backlash began through coordinated efforts in the 1970s and continued over the next four decades. Sarah Posner writes that the massive white evangelical support for Trumpism in 2015 down to the present has its roots in a belief "that America lies in ruins after the sweep of historic changes since the mid-twentieth century." The "values voter" is really the grievance voter worried over a loss of cultural and social power. The far right, including the white supremacist elements of the so-called alt-right, have marshalled this reactionary version of raging against the machine because behind the vexation over cultural change lies the sting of economic defeat.[14]

The overwhelming majority of films dealing with Satan concern some version of demonic possession. The typical possession/exorcism drama is about control lost and won, who has the power and who loses agency. These are stories about who wins, whether the religious patriarchs wielding bell, book and candle play out a drama of victory or become victims themselves. Notably, many of these films make the heroic male saviour into the victim of adolescent girls who are also vessels of evil. This is precisely the kind of masochism upon which grievance politics thrive. Alan Noble, writing specifically about the "persecution complex" that had thrived among American evangelicals, describes how "narratives of social, political, and theological persecution" have become widely accepted in those communities, even though they are "fiction or deeply exaggerated non-fiction."[15]

These changes seemed to come just as the post-industrial economy ripped apart the social compact to which many working-class white men believed that they and their parents had tacitly agreed. The demon-possessed body politic, feminine and obscene, became their ugly obsession.

## The Devil's "Merry Frolics"

Over the last half-century, the way audiences respond to a film has changed dramatically, given the influence of new kinds of mass advertising, the VHS revolution and the current realities of social media promotion and fan interaction. A garbled set of religious meanings about the influence of the devil exists in a parasitical relationship to the giant body of film narrative. Media, not just doctrinal teaching, recapitulates the power of folk belief and satanic rumour legends. Pulpits and catechisms form only one strand of the fibres that tie together belief in Satan and his activity on earth.

However, the first time Satan's shadow fell across the screen, the benign intent seemed to belie the vicious narratives that would appear later. At the dawn of cinema, the devil received plenty of attention, much more than the sunnier side of Christian faith. George Méliès, master magician, illusionist and one of the earliest filmmakers, saw little difference between these roles and produced at least ten films that dealt with satanic themes.

Indeed, Kendall Phillips has described his work as "crucial" in hardwiring the "technology of the cinema to the fantastic and the spectacular." Films like *The Merry Frolics of Satan* (1906), *The Devil in the Convent* (1899), *The Infernal Cauldron* (1903), *The Phantasmal Vapor* (n.d.), *The Treasures of Satan* (1902) and *The Infernal Cake Walk* (1903) dealt, usually in a comedic tone, with Faustian pacts, demons tempting the foolish and unwary, and images of hell and damnation.[16]

The fact that comedy played a role in these early films does not indicate a lack of interest in Satan or a widespread culture of unbelief. Méliès context suggests that his short features, as with any film, soaked up the anxieties that audiences brought to them. In the divided world of the French Third Republic, shaped by an often bitter struggle between secular republicans and adherents to a particularly reactionary form of Catholicism, these films would have had differing but equally powerful effects. Notably, it is human foibles that Méliès tended to portray as buffoonish. Satan and attendant imps have a skittering perversity that likely caused more than a little fright at the turn of the century.

Two early German expressionist films, *The Student of Prague* (1913) and *Faust* (1926), had little to do with the clownish antics of demons. They are better understood as attempts to come to grips with a century that had already revealed its heart of darkness. Paul Wegner, most famous for his trilogy of films dealing with the Jewish legend of the monstrous Golem, created a most dapper devil to tempt Balduin, the titular student of *The Student of Prague*. Balduin proves ready to sell his soul to seduce a countess and settle his financial difficulties. Although the film has a long-ago and faraway quality, heightened by being set in the early 19th century, it does not offer a soporific ending. The tale turns on the idea of the human self, cleaved into warring doppelgängers, a metaphor that would become central to German expressionist horror when it entered a much more morbid stage after 1918. F. W. Murnau's *Faust* portrays a Satan given to farcical debauchery and yet also a figure that, in an obvious reflection of the director's experience in combat during World War I, can raise skeletal armies and wage global war. He is both tempter and tyrant, a force of nature as well as a dangerous being to bet against.

In the United States, the peculiar relationship between the nation's evangelical heartland and popular culture had begun to emerge by the second decade of the 20th century. Christian fundamentalism defined itself in response to modernity, often rejecting "movie-going" as itself a devil's snare on par with alcohol, dancing and an informed theological education. At the same time, fundamentalist preachers quickly became aware of the power of modern technologies, especially radio, to spread their message. Billy Sunday (1864–1935), Aimee Semple McPherson (1890–1944) and Charles E. Fuller (1887–1968), for instance, all combined radio and mass printing to shape themselves into religious celebrities.[17] Sunday set aside any moralistic qualms about the movies and allowed his sermons to be filmed for Hearst newsreels. In one surviving clip from 1916, he rails against bootleggers, Satan and immigrants, all of whom were linked in his poisonous worldview. His kinetic sermons, in which he pantomimed wrestling with the devil, appeared not only in mass-produced images and in newsreels but in a magic lantern show. He also filmed a brief biographical sketch and acted as an uncredited advisor for the temperance allegory in the 1915 film *Jordan Is a Hard Road*.

The degree to which cinema in America became a populist artform, a new vaudeville, accelerated this process. Folk belief and a ferocious nationalism had plenty of pillow talk. While Billy Sunday preached "100% Americanism" in response to the American entrance into World War I, Satan and the film industry proved a fecund pairing at such a time, and crisis cut the legs from under an argument about film's alleged antagonism to religion.[18]

In *To Hell with the Kaiser* (1918), nearly every trope of the anti-German propaganda appears, with a bit of a twist. A Screen Classics production advertisement promised vendors that audiences would see "the lustful remorseless avalanche of barbarism the Hun has unleashed on the world." No actual prints of the film still exist and the only images we have from it are still photographs. We do know from a plot summary that the titles did not simply offer obvious metaphor: captured by Americans and given a good punch by a doughboy, the Kaiser commits suicide in a prisoner of war camp, his soul spelunking into hell. There he meets Satan who offers him the throne of his infernal kingdom. In this film that promised to help audiences see "the supreme duty of the hour," the devil confesses that Kaiser Wilhelm is more fit than him to reign as lord of evil.[19]

Satan would return as a propaganda tool in World War II in films that replaced the Kaiser with Hitler or that portrayed Satan as busily wrecking the American war economy. That said, though, *To Hell with the Kaiser* certainly did not open a deluge of diabolical film. What is most noteworthy about the cinematic Satan in the United States between the 1920s and the 1960s is how seldom the trope makes an appearance. Satan remained silent in American cinema, in sharp contrast to his popularity on the continent. After the early burst of enthusiasm over the new medium and some degree of openness to its possibilities, religious and cultural mandarins in American life began to pressure the major studios to self-censor the films they produced. In something of a symbol of the Catholic Church's growing presence in American cultural life, American bishops exerted enough pressure on the industry that it created the Motion Picture Production Code (MPPC) in 1930 and the Production Code Administration (PCA) in 1935.

The MPPC, written by a Catholic priest and a devout layman, is brief, to the point and does not lend itself to mockery as a simplistic moral screed. In general, it makes fairly reasonable demands about what should and should not be presented on screen. On the topic of religion, aside from some draconian guidance about the presentation of clergy that would make either a production of *Tartuffe* or *Elmer Gantry* impossible, it simply suggests that any religious ceremony (not merely a Christian one) must be presented in a respectful manner and no "film or episode may throw ridicule on any religious faith."[20] This general guidance can be interpreted as either a yawning loophole or an ingenious ambuscade. What exactly does *ridicule* look like in the abstract? In the case of Satan, how does one portray any element of his character from theology or folklore, a story arc that assumes millennia of mocking religion as part of his long war with God, without seeming to "throw ridicule" on sacred ideals?

Two films made during the early years of the MPPC illustrate the difficulties of navigating these demands. And yet, in very different fashion, they brought Satan to the American screen. Both Universal Studios' eccentric 1934 *The Black Cat* starring horror icons Bela Lugosi and Boris Karloff and the 1941 adaptation of Stephen Vincent Benet's *The Devil and Daniel Webster* make the idea of the devil central to their plot. The success of one with mainstream audiences and the failure of the other represent the direction American satanic cinema would take.

*The Black Cat* holds a place among the most outré horror masterpieces. German expressionist filmmaker Edgar G. Ulmer, later the creator of classic noir films such as the 1945 *Detour*, managed to launch a revenge tale that includes the brutalities of the Great War's eastern front, precisely some of the unconventional sexual relationships the code explicitly forbade, and a scene of horrific, if implied, torture. But what truly makes the film stand out, even amid all these peculiarities, is its creation of a satanic cult led by the rather staid Karloff. In this film, he is a stand-in for Aleister Crowley (1875–1947), the occultist and con man known for his creation of "Magick" as a system and who the director apparently encountered while "the Beast" lived in Berlin.

The studio cut Ulmer's film down to the bone, leaving a tattered 69 minutes to limp into theatres. It proved a popular hit, becoming America's first successful satanic cult film. Unlike some later productions (such as Val Lewton's 1944 *The Seventh Victim*), *The Black Cat* makes no effort to present Satanism with a wink and a nod. Karloff reads from a grimoire called "The Rites of Lucifer." His antagonist Bela Lugosi, speaking to a terrified American couple who has gotten themselves hopelessly mixed up in these diabolical affairs, asks if they have "heard of the worship of the devil, of evil" and warns them that Karloff is the "great modern priest of this ancient cult."

The 1941 film adaptation of *The Devil and Daniel Webster* offers a very different example. Much loved by critics over the years, it performed poorly at the box office. It is a story of rock-ribbed American values confronting a deceptive devil. But those values are the heartland values of the populist American left rather than Billy Sunday's "100% Americanism." In a move likely to irritate even contemporary traditionalists, the actor Walter Huston's "Mr. Scratch" suggests that the demonic shadowed the very origins of American experience. "When the first wrong was done to the first Indian I was there," he intones; "when the first slaver put out for the Congo I stood on her deck." A satanic version of the New York Times Magazine's 2019 "1619 Project," *The Devil and Daniel Webster* found little purchase in the same year that magazine-magnate Henry Booth Luce declared "the American Century" and the country entered a war that would bring it close to global hegemony.

## Omens, Exorcisms and Monstrous Births

The classical triptych of horror films inspired by the prince of darkness, *Rosemary's Baby* (1968), *The Exorcist* (1973) and *The Omen* (1976), has been given much of the credit for Lucifer becoming a box office regular. In this case, at least, this is a truism that happens to be true. There is really no way to overestimate their importance, with their directors—Polanski and Friedkin—having received significant scholarly attention. However, the attention these films have received has offered barely a nod towards some of the cultural shifts and underground films that helped prepare the way for this unholy trinity of cinema.

The turn to science fiction horror in the 1950s America left little room for doing the devil's business, concerned as it often was with presenting Cold War allegories. Even films whose titles suggested they offered the taboo disappointed anyone hoping for some devilish fun. 1957's *From Hell It Came*, for instance, merely blended a bit of pacific islander witchcraft with the oft-employed trope of the mad scientist. *The Night of the Demon* (1957), notably a British import, borrowed its supernaturalism from the work of Welsh author Arthur Machen rather than from Christian conceptions of Satan.

Moreover, the religious revival in post-World War II American life, particularly the type of religious experience mainstream Americans favoured, made horror films that portrayed Satan as part of the American experience conceptually impossible.

The success of radio preachers like the evangelical Graham and the Catholic Bishop Fulton Sheen (1895–1979) came from their blend of patriotism, optimism and the use of religious affiliation as a badge of middle-class respectability. When Satan appeared in any kind of cultural discourse, he represented a concrete threat to the American way of life, striking at the heart of American identity—people's sense of themselves and their role in the world. The burgeoning American middle class seems to have nodded in agreement when Graham suggested that satanic aid enabled the Soviet Union to launch Sputnik in 1957. They made Protestant clergyman Norman Vincent Peale's *The Power of Positive Thinking* (1952) an enormous bestseller. The seemingly anaemic nature of Peale's prescription, his advice to ignore doubts and focus on personal success, would contribute to a peculiarly American style of non-sectarian fundamentalism, a frighteningly optimistic religious nationalism.

New influences came from the United Kingdom, a nation having a very different experience of the post-war world. While the United States completed its ascendancy to global hyperpower and invested in the creation of world history's largest and most prosperous middle class, Britain fell into decline according to every significant indicator. Reeling from massive destruction of property and burdened with debt after World War II, the once great power had to abandon its imperial self-image. Indian Independence in 1947 and the embarrassing misadventure of the Suez Canal crisis in 1956 best reveal these changes. By the 1960s, inflation and shortages in housing became endemic. Joblessness among the young became especially common, creating both the practical conditions and the sociological maelstrom necessary for a strange set of rumour legends to find purchase in what was becoming an increasingly post-Christian society. These conditions helped to set the stage for the acceptance of this new kind of horror film in Britain—a type of film characterised in particular by its turn towards infernal imagery.

Perhaps as part of response to feelings of crisis and despair in 20th-century Britain, the occult novels of Dennis Wheatly (1897–1977)—along with the allegedly non-fiction accounts he wrote of the enduring reality of witchcraft—became enormous bestsellers. Wheatly wrote some 60 books between the 1930s and his death, including *The Devil Rides Out* (1934), *To the Devil...A Daughter* (1954) and *The Devil and All His Works* (1971), the latter described without irony in the *New York Times* as "the modern textbook on satanism." Nervous Britons would also have heard of the claims of anthropologist Gerald Gardner (1884–1964) that ancient rites survived into modern England especially in his especially 1954 *Witchcraft Today*. Groups of Wiccans, inspired and led by Gardner, publicly announced their belief in "the old religion" and received the to-be-expected coverage in the British press. Wiccans made clear that their "horned god" had no relationship to the Christian Satan, but such nuances became lost in the tabloids' tales of a coven hiding out in the undisturbed forests in Hampshire and Wiltshire.[21]

These images in mass culture and media blended with legerdemain about the "black magic circles" of active occultists, false information that circulated in Britain for decades without quite becoming as dangerous as the equally false claims of "satanic covens" in the United States were later to become. The strength of these rumour legends emerged in part from the willingness of some Anglican clergy to claim that incidences of vandalism or theft in their parishes was the work of satanic cultists. In one case, a clergyman went so far as to publicly ask for police protection from a witch coven supposedly luring "men and girls from God to Devil-worship" in Chelsea. Reports from outlets like the *Empire News*, poorly sourced follow-up stories and unconfirmed "confessions" of cult leaders added to what became something of a carnival atmosphere around the occult.[22]

Bill Ellis has described how churchyards became sites of "legend tripping" that offered spaces for a deeply disaffected, and unemployed, young people. The abuse of alcohol and drugs, the former expectedly popular in time of social and economic chaos, turned this gathering into rages where a tombstone or two certainly got kicked over and some tempting stained glass surely shattered. A few Anglican ministers suggested that Satanists had stepped out of the page of pulp literature to become a real danger, but Britain's sensationalist tabloids drove much of the interest.[23]

A film studio would solidify these connections, helping to trigger, focus and define the loose legerdemain of "black magic circles." Hammer Studios had transatlantic success with their reboots of some of the classic Universal Studios monsters, first with 1957's *The Curse of Frankenstein* and then with 1958's *Dracula*, released in America as *The Horror of Dracula*. Becoming increasingly popular into the 1960s, the Hammer films might seem an odd sell for the Age of Aquarius. Usually set in a vague Victorian/Edwardian era in an equally indeterminate central European locale, directors like Terence Fischer (1904–1980) brought a heavy-handed Christian worldview to the films' construction of the struggle between good and evil. The *mis-en-scene* developed by the studio often had what is best described as a mod gothic flavour, showing some resemblance to the aesthetic that has been described since the 1990s as "steampunk." Hammer horrors became the first to employ the use of fake blood in copious quantities and in fully colourised, if oddly hued, gore. Moreover, both in advertisement and in the content of the films, Hammer allowed heteronormative male desire and frank, arguably crude, expressions of sexuality. Hammer posters during the sixties are infamous: Goya's Black paintings meet mid-century "good girl" art.

By the late 1960s, rumours legends, theories of satanic conspiracies and the notion that magic circles regularly met to plunder and fornicate in churchyards like some sort of brutish fairy rings intertwined with the continuing popularity of Hammer films. In what would become a common theme in the next half-century, these films existed in a cognitive feedback loop with beliefs in real world satanic mischief. *Taste the Blood of Dracula* (1970) employs the trope of the magic circle engaging in sacrilegious rites in "an abandoned church." *The Satanic Rites of Dracula* (1973) showed eager audiences more satanic rites than Dracula, with actor Christopher Lee (1922–2015) making an all-to-brief appearance in the eponymous role.

In response, American horror followed the Hammer formula, becoming more enthusiastic in its use of gore but also seeking to enchant the world in the darkest of shades. Some of America's first satanic thrillers of the new era were made abroad, such as the 1960 *City of the Dead*, released in the United States as *Horror Hotel*, or the 1966 *Eye of the Devil*, featuring Sharon Tate as one half of a pair of seductive, witchy twins. But American independent films like *The Devil's Hand* (1960) and 1962's *The Devil's Messenger*, in which Lon Chaney Jr. portrays a silly but still sinister atomic-age Satan, helped prepare a younger generation for the age of *The Exorcist*.

Efforts to portray a semi-serious version of Satanism came from some unlikely directions. One of the successful independent films of the era, Roger Corman's 1964 *Masque of the Red Death*, took the bare bones of the Edgar Allan Poe tale and conceived of Prince Prospero (played by Vincent Price) as a cruel Satanic high priest, another Crowley knock-off.

The screenplay owed some of its devilish flair to the writer Charles Beaumont (1929–1967), who also gave Satan the lead in several episodes of the popular television programme *The Twilight Zone* which ran through the early 1960s. Such films helped *Rosemary's Baby* come to full term. Polanski may have created an art-house film using themes known only to Americans who explored the darker fare offered by late night drive in and 42nd Street's Grindhouse culture, but he could not have done so without that dark Id in the American experience to draw upon. *The Exorcist* certainly represents a cultural phenomenon in its own right but also drew strength from a growing interest in demonic power displayed by the burgeoning charismatic movement. An outgrowth of Pentecostalism, this movement had moved from the rural Midwest and storefront churches in urban areas into the suburbs of America by the 1960s. Along with the spiritual charisms of prophecy and divine healing, this brand of Christianity claimed the power to "cast out devils." Such power did not need the conduit of a priest or any clergy to manifest.[24]

The power of films like *The Exorcist* in this environment cannot be overestimated. Appearing eight years after Harvey Cox (1929–) of Harvard Divinity School proclaimed the coming of "The Secular City" and seven years after the cover of *Time* magazine wondered if God was dead, *The Exorcist* became much more than a popular film. As Joseph Laycock has written, it marked a moment of "the resurgence of folk piety" in an era of alleged secularisation. Even negative responses from religious figures seemed to challenge Walter Benjamin's suggestion that the "aura" of art disappeared in the age of film. Billy Graham famously suggested that evil resides "in the very celluloid" of Friedkin's masterpiece.[25]

*Rosemary's Baby*, *The Exorcist* and *The Omen* did more than make Satan a box office draw. They entered a climate that proved profoundly open to new styles of spirituality, including Christianities that believed the view from hell was at least as important as the one from heaven. Popular media, much like ersatz religious belief, depended on a bewildering mixture of theology, folklore and rumour legend. The success of all three of these films drew upon the growing distrust of institutions and an often-unsophisticated notion of the moral minefield that is the "do your own thing" ethic.

*Rosemary's Baby*, for example, not only showed the breakdown of community but suggested something insidious had wormed into the medical profession. Rosemary's loss of bodily autonomy includes her husband and her neighbours choosing her gynaecologist, an ill-natured misogynist who tells her to take herbal compounds but not to read books and seems unaware that an ectopic pregnancy is an actual health crisis. We learn that, in the conspiratorial logic that has informed stories about Satan since the early modern witch hunts, everyone Rosemary knows has been in on it all along. In response, Rosemary turns to the popular, handsome and supposedly caring Dr. Hill for help. But she discovers that his dedication to medicine, science and his male colleagues makes him willing to betray her to an apartment building lousy with devil worshippers.

*The Exorcist* also questions the role of science in human flourishing, showing the psychiatric world's utter failure to aid Regan. There's also the subtle questioning of the post-Vatican II Church. The modern priest, Father Karras who studied psychiatry at "Harvard, Bellevue, places like that," suffers existential doubt until he meets the demons that proliferate in Regan. *The Omen* takes such claims the farthest. By 1976, it became possible for filmmakers to portray the church itself as a part of the conspiracy with priests and nuns who make sure that the demonic Damien makes his way into the halls of power. Willing to engage in murder and kidnapping to carry out the devil's designs, they switch the unnatural thing at birth to ensure that the antichrist becomes the scion of a powerful political family.

The flood of possession/exorcism dramas over the next half-century frequently reiterated this theme with ronin exorcists struggling with a moribund church hierarchy that refuses to recognise the reality of evil in their midst. The cultural phenomenon of *The Exorcist* inspired numerous copycat films (*Beyond the Door, Amityville II: The Possession, Lisa and the Devil, The Return of the Exorcist*) and films into the 1980s and 1990s that played with demonic themes (*Angelheart, Mister Frost, The First Power, Fallen, End of Days, Bless the Child*).

### "You Root of All Evil and Vice, Seducer of Men, Betrayer of Nations"

In the decade after 2000, so many possession/exorcism dramas appeared that they complicate any analysis that simply sees them all as heirs to *The Exorcist*. It is understandable that an increasing number of films dealing with the devil should appear in the wake of 9/11. However, in these offerings, it is difficult to locate even a tenuous ligature between 9/11, the "war on terror" and the twice-told tales of exorcism. Victoria McCollum, whose 2016 *Post 9/11 Heartland Horror* is perhaps the finest book on the subject, did not discuss any films that used the precise demonic template that had become common since the 1970s. McCollum examines how the audience reception of Bill Paxton's psychological thriller *Frailty* (2001) grew in part from a post-9/11 sensibility. And yet, as she notes, the film places the real horror not in actual demonic presences but in the belief in demons that leads to generational violence.[26]

Other cultural factors are important in a new cycle of 21st-century satanic horror films. Notably, they emerge in the wake of an increasing cultural divide after 2008. Although marked by the election of Barack Obama as president in the United States, that event became largely symbolic of an interrelated set of ideas that found expression in the so-called Tea Party movement and Donald Trump emerging as the intemperate voice of the "birther" movement. Much work remains to be done on the proliferation of books that suggested that the increasing acceptance of LBGTQ+ people and Obama's 2010 Affordable Care Act were signs of the coming of the antichrist. Indeed, in 2013, a frightening total of 26% of Americans told Public Policy Polling that they believed Obama "was" or "might be" the antichrist, an idea perhaps forwarded by cable TV's History Channel's enormously successful miniseries *The Bible* that made use of a near look-alike of Obama for their Satan. The primary producers of that series, Mark Burnet and Roma Downey, who have been called the heads of a "faith-based [media] empire," also produced *The Apprentice* in which Trump himself starred. The Hayes brothers pointed to the success of this "faith based empire" as their inspiration for *The Conjuring*.[27]

There are two very notable things about the role of Satan and demonic forces in the second decade of the 21st century. First, the films deal almost exclusively with demon possession and exorcism. Second, there are an uncountable number of them. These points are almost truisms. Although many horror scholars see the last two decades as the age of the zombie, the number of films that deal with possession and exorcism themes have exploded. *The Conjuring* series alone takes up a huge swath of the mainstream horror market. Other popular films not yet discussed, all made just since 2010, include *The Rite, The Devil Inside, The Devil, The Vatican Tapes, May the Devil Take You, Along Came the Devil (1 and 2), Deliver Us From Evil, The Cleansing Hour, Eli, The Assent, Ouija: Origin of Evil* and *The*

*Possession of Hannah Grace*. Even films sometimes described as "art horror," aimed for a sophisticated audience who desire more than ragged and well-worn tropes, make use of material from their down-at-the-heels cousins. *The Blackcoat's Daughter, Hereditary, The Taking of Deborah Logan* and *Sator* provide examples. This deluge aside, the number of direct-to-streaming or festival circuit films is, this author can attest, literally impossible to quantify, with quickie and gimmick films like *Scream at the Devil* and *Exorcism at 60,000 Feet* only the bottom of this rather enormous barrel.

Mainstream, lowbrow and more sophisticated versions of possession and exorcism tales have in common two major ideas. First, evil is not only omnipresent, but there is also no definitive protection against it. Even in films that offer a cautionary message, suggesting the possible dangers of ouija boards or tarot decks, the victimised are guilty of nothing but curiosity or there is the suggestion that a demonic possession would have occurred without material aid. Second, either there is no one to trust or, at least, traditional channels of spiritual aid are closed or corrupted. Certainly, the *Conjure*-verse has promulgated a stealthy version of do-it-yourself fundamentalism with the Warren's and their allies dealing with, if not a corrupt, at least a dubious and somewhat cynical church hierarchy. This anti-institutional bias beloved of modern conservatives is not untypical.

Eli Roth's 2010 *The Last Exorcism*—which turned out only to be the penultimate exorcism since a *Last Exorcism 2* surfaced in 2013—changed the template slightly by constructing an exorcist from the evangelical tradition rather than from Catholicism. But there is no real departure from the formula at all. We learn that the maverick religious entrepreneurs from that denominational universe cannot be trusted either and the film ends leaving some audiences believing in an underground satanic conspiracy. Indeed, a belief circulated online that *The Last Exorcism*, which made use of found footage horror technique, had been an actual documentary.

The DVD release in 2011 dangerously played with this notion by including a documentary called "Real Life Exorcisms" while another that taught viewers a "protection prayer" to be said before watching the film. This is creative ("disruptive" in current advert-speak) promotion or, from another standpoint, extraordinary cynicism. The protective ward the featurette promises the viewer is actually just a stylised version of the Prayer to St. Michael that lay Catholics of a traditionalist bent often say in conjunction with the rosary after the mass has ended and they have been urged by the celebrant to go in peace.

This construction, in some ways as important as crucifixes and holy water, reached its apotheosis in 2020's *The Seventh Day*. A bizarre buddy-cop flick with demons (it borrows its character tropes from classics like 1987's *Lethal Weapon* and 2001's *Training Day*), the film authoritatively tells audiences that, before the turn of the century, the Catholic Church had "given up the teaching of the rite" and only a "small, brave band of priests" kept it alive. Not only is this wrong, but the exorcism business has been booming for 50 years, with the Archdiocese of Washington offering a "Request an Exorcism" web page. But this demonstrably falsifiable claim sets up an important theme. Unlike the films of the 1970s and 1980s that at least showed priests as sincere, *The Seventh Day* nods to the sex abuse scandals in the Catholic Church, with one exorcist praising the perks of working for an institution he calls "a titan of influence and corruption." The denouement reveals that it is the priests who have a bad case of demonic infiltration.[28]

Such films would seem to have a subversive element or are at least another tired example of the "but who's the real monster here?" trope. In fact, with notable exceptions like Aislinn

Clark's 2018 *The Devil's Doorway*, these films frequently conform to the fact-challenged ideas that created the satanic panic of the 1980s and its modern kissing cousin, QANON. For example, *The Last Exorcism* has been lazily labelled "postmodern" and compared to *Scream* (1996) in its alleged willingness to deconstruct its own narrative. But there is little irony in a film that lets you know it is aware it exists in a world in which Friedkin made *The Exorcist* and then regurgitates the worst aspects of America's enthusiasm for believing in the devil's infiltration into all parts of American society.

One of the more telling examples of how good fun, fakelore and Satan on film intertwine appears in the 2016 *La rage du Démon* (*Fury of the Demon* in English release). Boasting the participation of acclaimed horror director Alejandra Aja, the film presents itself as the story of one of Méliès' many lost films, allegedly cursed by some demonic force. Describing two showings of the film, one in Paris in 2012 and another in 1939 at New York's Virginia Theatre (now the August Wilson on W. 52nd Street), a variety of critics appear in the documentary to claim that both showings of the mysteriously missing film ended in an orgy of violence. The problem is that neither of these events seems to have occurred. The film used a stub clip from the front page of the 30 November 1939 *New York Times* that reports "Riot in the Theater of Film Premier." However, no such article exists, and the image used in the film and circulated online has been doctored. In the actual edition of *The Times*, the place in which the piece supposedly appeared features an article about the "Winter War" in Finland. Moreover, the Virginia was a not-very-popular theatre for live drama, not a cinema in 1939.

Even while realising that some fictional elements had been included, both horror fan sites and more serious scholarly discussions ended up being fooled by the film. Perhaps they can be forgiven since Friedkin himself directed and narrated an exploitative documentary in 2017 entitled *The Devil and Father Amorth*. This depressing film includes cringe moments, including an obviously mentally ill woman physically restrained by a group of male family members. Cleverley edited interviews either leave the possibility open that demonic possession might occur or assert absolutely that it does. Friedkin really stacks the deck by including medievalist and Guggenheim fellow Jefferey Burton Russell, the author of the brilliant quartet on the history of Satan turned Christian apologist. Russell warns of the devil's power while sporting an enormous pectoral cross that resembles cosplay rather than an act of devotion.

*The Fury of the Demon* and *The Devil and Father Amorth* represent more than simple credulity. They are small echoes of the thunderous voice of the Warren-verse, examples of how misinformation becomes deep-fake truth. Even the mockumentary form employed by *Fury* can become fodder for exchange networks of rumour legend. Just as denials of conspiracy theories can be incorporated into the body of belief as proof that they are the machinations of co-conspirators, efforts to subvert or satirise gullibility can fuel the desire for spiritual experience—even dark and terrifying spiritual experience.

This reality forces scholars who have studied the contours of the "satanic panic" in the analogue world of the 1960s, 1970s and 1980s to consider how film and the cultural narratives that swaddle with it in an era of rapidly changing technology have extended, extrapolated from and rebooted some of the central rumour legends born in that period. This will also encourage a much-needed reassessment of the timeline of that strange era and its extension beyond the early 90s. The FBI Lanning report that found no single case of alleged satanic ritual abuse confirmed by evidence, the controversy over the Mc-Martin Trial (see Sarah Hughes' chapter in this volume), the controversial conviction of the West Memphis 3 for "satanic crimes" and their subsequent public vindication or the broader backlash against notions of "satanic ritual abuse" in the social work and psychiatric communities.

The most influential current representation of Satan and satanic activity on earth appears in the remarkable political influence of the QANON movement and its hydra-like offshoots. Much necessary attention has been paid to the role played by online life today appears in the remarkable staying power of the QANON movement. This grab bag of falsehoods represents a conflagration that detonated from the combustible elements of "netlore" and the template of the satanic panic, the mythic hydrocarbons of the latter given oxygen by Trumpism and set ablaze. The flames would not burn without the coalescing narratives of American religion and film, stories of the devil at work in Georgetown townhouses and day care centres, Satan worshippers hiding in tunnels and pizza parlours.

These ideas are reinforced by film and by responses to them, a process that has a longer genealogy than just back to 2013 or 1968. Over the last hundred years, the unstable concept of "the devil" has brought together seemingly unrelated narratives received with little attempt at taxonomy and classification by popular audiences. Belief and entertainment have allied. Film, often without the direct initiative of directors, producers and screenwriters, has honed the teeth of the interlocked gears of culture, belief and panic.

The last century has not only seen this celluloid devil emerge from rough-edged beginnings to become the ultimate horror film nemesis. Satan's increasingly visible role in our social imaginary from the late 1960s to the present has come to play an important conceptual role in the building of multi-layered narratives across numerous media platforms that shape the worldview of many American believers. Films, many either presenting themselves as "based on actual events," intertwine with religious and political forces, reflecting powerful beliefs that roar into the real world. Across the world where American popular culture reigns, Weber's fears have proven unfounded, as popular culture remains under a dark enchantment.

## Notes

1 The trope of evildoers building secret caverns to hide their dark deeds has an analogue in 18th-century gothic. These works in turn informed anti-Catholic screeds in the mid-19th century such as *The Awful Disclosures of Maria Monk* (1836) that told of taboo eroticism in perilous underground spaces beneath monasteries and convents. In the satanic panic of the 1980s and 1990s, such tunnels are imagined in cases from Ohio to California to explain the lack of physical evidence with the panic at the McMartin Preschool offering only the most well-publicised example. See Chapter 24. In 2016, the false Pizzagate conspiracy claimed secret passages beneath Comet's Pizza. See Jeffery S. Victor, *Satanic Panic: The Creation of a Contemporary Legend* (Chicago, 1993), 19–20 and Gregor Aisch, Jon Hung and Cecilia Kang, "Dissecting the #Pizzagate Conspiracy Theory," New York Times, 19 December 2016.
2 *The Conjuring*, Dir. James Wan (Warner Brothers, 2019).
3 Brook Barnes, "Secular Hollywood Quietly Courts the Faithful," *New York Times*, 24 December 2016.
4 Hannah Goodwyn, "Screenwriters Chad and Carey Hayes on The Conjuring and God" N.D. https://www1.cbn.com/700club/screenwriters-chad-and-carey-hayes-conjuring-and-god
5 Notably, a number of mainline Christian clergy had attempted to push American Christianity in the direction of social reform and away from obsessions with abstract "spiritual warfare" and demonic evil. American popular culture seemed to be going in the opposite direction. See Gary Dorrien, *The Making of American Liberal Theology: Imagining Progressive Religion, 1855–1900* (Louisville, 2001); see especially 33 and 50.

6 None of the above is meant to suggest that ideas about Satan did not grow in part from various forms of popular entertainment in both the 18th and 19th centuries. Even print culture that aimed for moral or catechetical instruction drew on folklore and templates of Satan cast in popular illustration. Moreover, the "dark ride" traditions continued into the 20th century in the sideshow, the carnival and the amusement park.

7 J. Charles Wall, *Devils: Origins and History* (London, 1904).

8 *Max Weber*: The Vocation Lectures, eds. David Owen and Tracy B. Strong, trans. Rodney Livingstone (Indianapolis, 2004); Walter Benjamin, "Goethe's Elective Affinities," in *Walter Benjamin Selected Writing Vol. 1, 1913–1926*, ed. Marcus Bullock and Michael W. Jennings (Cambridge, 1996), 308–9 and 324.

9 Consider the massive discussion around Yale Law Professor Stephen Carter's *The Culture of Disbelief: How American law and Politics Trivializes Culture* (New York, 1993).

10 Andrew Delbanco, *The Death of Satan: How Americans Have Lost the Sense of Evil* (New York, 1995), 12, 13 and 208–10.

11 Conrad Ostwalt has suggested that the United States began with a Christianity that "had to compete against secular institutions and secular forms of entertainment." This led to a dynamic that found the churches "moving toward popular culture." See Ostwalt, *Secular Steeples: Popular Culture and the Religious Imagination* (Harrisburg, 2003), 21–2. See also R. Laurence Moore in *Selling God: American Religion and the Marketplace of Culture* (New York, 1995).

12 Billy Graham, "The Devil, Demons, and Exorcism," 16 September 1974, Tempe, Arizona. Complete recording is available at https://billygraham.org/audio/the-devil-demons-and-exorcism/

13 Kelly J. Wyman, "The Devil We Already Know: Medieval Representations of a Powerless Satan in Modern American Cinema," *Journal of Religion & Film*, 8, no. 3 (2004), 13,14.

14 Sarah Posner, *The Unholy* (New York, 2020), 9 and 10.

15 Alan Noble, "The Evangelical Persecution Complex," *The Atlantic,* 4 August 2014.

16 An excellent introductory discussion of Méliès appears in Kendall R. Phillips, *A Place of Darkness: The Rhetoric of Horror in Early American Cinema* (Austin, 2018), 48–60. Notably, most of the French magician and filmmakers' short features are lost to us, indeed close to 500 of them. There's no way to know how much of a role Satan played in his vast, likely long-destroyed corpus. But it is striking how frequently demons, devils and Old Scratch himself appear in what we know is his catalogue. Moreover, as explored later in his essay, his lost films themselves became part of the feedback loop of film and fakelore.

17 Quentin J. Schultze, "Evangelical radio and the rise of the electronic church, 1921–1948," *Journal of Broadcasting & Electronic Media*, 32, no. 3 (1988): 289–306.

18 The trajectory of these events gets a close description in George R. Marsden, *Fundamentalism and American Culture* (Oxford, 2006); Fredrick C. Giffen, "Billy Sunday: Evangelist as Patriot," *Social Science* 48 (1973): 216–21.

19 "To Hell with the Kaiser" promotion to theatre management, 1917; collection of the author.

20 The full text of the MPPC appears here: https://www.asu.edu/courses/fms200s/total-readings/MotionPictureProductionCode.pdf. It is worth noting that in some respects, the Code aided the film industry that previously had to deal with idiosyncratic state laws that made the United States an unruly patchwork of the regulation of content.

21 See "Dennis Wheatly, Writer on the Occult, Dies," *New York Times,* 12 November 1977. Wheatly's novels dominated the British horror scene for a large portion of the 20th century. Gardner received surprisingly gentle, if rather wry, treatment in the British press. See, for example, Peter Hawkins "No, Witchcraft is Fun," *Sunday Pictorial,* 12 June 1955.

22 See Bill Ellis, *Raising the Devil: Satanism, New Religions, and the Media* (Lexington, 2000), 148–56.

23 Ellis, *Raising the Devil*, 155–6.

24 See Michael W. Cuneo, *American Exorcism: Expelling Demons in the Land of* Plenty (New York, 2001), 119–26.

25 See Joseph Laycock, "The Folk Piety of William Peter Blatty: 'The Exorcist' in the Context of Secularization," *Interdisciplinary Journal of Research on Religion* 5, art. 6, p. 46 (2009) and "Graham on Demons", *Christianity Today,* June 7, 1974.

26 Victoria McCollum, *Post-9/11 Heartland Horror: Rural Horror Films in an Age of Urban Terrorism* (New York, 2016), 8–9 and 48–65.

27 Yvonne Villarreal, "Mark Burnett, Roma Downy, Add to Faith-Based Empire," *Hartford Courant*, 12 October 2014; Alicia M. Cohn, "Conjuring Faith Audiences," *World*, 19 July 2013; Burnett regularly introduced Trump at the National Prayer Breakfast and once called him a "soulmate." See "Mark Burnett Stands Firmly behind the Reality Show President He Helped Create," *Deadline*. https://deadline.com/2019/01/mark-burnett-donald-trump-protector-the-apprentice-commentary-peter-bart-1202532074/

28 See "Request An Exorcism." https://adw.org/about-us/resources/request-an-exorcism/ The trope of "the church doesn't teach this anymore" seems to have its distant DNA in the rhetoric of bizarre figures like Malachi Martin and other Catholic reactionaries who despised Vatican II. Many of these same figures played an important role in the creation of the satanic panic. See Michael W. Cuneo's, *The Smoke of Satan: Conservative and Traditionalist Dissent in Contemporary American Catholicism* (Baltimore, 1999). In fact, the practice of exorcism in Roman Catholicism alone has grown enormously over a half-century. See "Exorcism: Vatican Course Opens Doors to 250 Priests," *BBC News*, 17 April 2018. https://www.bbc.com/news/world-europe-43697573

## Bibliography

Ellis, Bill. *Raising the Devil: Satanism, New Religions, and the Media.* Lexington, Ky: The University Press of Kentucky, 2000.

McCloud, Sean. *American Possessions: Fighting Demons in the Contemporary United States.* New York: Oxford University Press, 2015.

Phillips, Kendall. *A Place of Darkness: The Rhetoric of Horror in Early American Cinema.* Austin: The University of Texas Press, 2018.

Poole, W. Scott. *Satan in America: The Devil We Know.* Lanham, MD: Rowman & Littlefield, 2009.

Victor, Jeffery S. *Satanic Panic: The Creation of a Contemporary Legend.* Chicago: Open Court, 1993.

# 22

# HUMANISING THE DEVIL, C. 1850–2000

*Karl Bell*

In 1896, William Gladstone, Britain's former Prime Minister, noted with concern that the doctrine of hell had become "relegated to the far-off corners of the Christian mind ... there to sleep in a deep shadow, as a thing needless in our enlightened and progressive age."[1] In many respects, Gladstone's comment was a reflection of a general weakening of belief in the reality of the devil by the late 19th century. However, this shift in attitudes towards hell and the devil did not mark his end. This chapter explores how, freed from theological dogma, the devil was adapted to and continued to have meaning in an increasingly secularised Western culture.[2] While his traditional role as God's punisher in hell—keeping the faithful on the straight and narrow—was diminishing in the Western imagination, between the mid-19th and the end of the 20th centuries, other elements of his character were foregrounded. Instead of the tormented tormentor, some groups chose instead to stress the devil as the mythological rebel, the insidious trickster and even as the personification of *human* evil. This enabled him and his related personas—Lucifer, Satan, the Antichrist—to be continually applied and appropriated as unfixed symbols that found new relevance in many quarters during what was a tumultuous period of change, conflict and anxiety.

This chapter argues that this was achieved through a humanising of the devil. It is examined through four themes. Firstly, it explores the devil as a positive representation of the rebel, a trend set by literary precursors such as the Romantic poets. In the 19th century, both Lucifer and Satan were adopted as figureheads by European political revolutionaries and social reformers, while in the late 19th and 20th centuries, Satan also became a provocative symbol of rebellion and free thought for various countercultural movements. Emphasising Satan as a fallen angel rather than as the archfiend of hell allowed some people to draw affinities between his story and their own struggles—be it in their quest for political liberty and social change, or as a cultural challenge to conservative conventions.

Secondly, we examine how these affinities with humanity were made more explicit. From 19th-century folklore to late 20th-century Hollywood movies, the devil frequently took human form, often concealing but letting slip tell-tale signs of his true nature. Traditional demonology was also updated for a more secular cultural context. The diabolical assumed a human face in this period. Serving as a metaphor for human evil—the devil

DOI: 10.4324/9781003096603-23

within—Western cultures demonised serial killers and 20th-century wartime political leaders, perhaps most obviously Adolf Hitler.

Thirdly, even if the belief in the physical reality of the devil had weakened, aspects of Western culture continued to fear (and sometimes thrill) to the idea that there could be diabolical influences working through human agents. This was seen in things as varied as the deceptive demonic entities that mediums supposedly risked summoning at spiritualist seances, the uncertain nature of religious visions, cinematic portrayal of exorcisms and the Antichrist, and the various "satanic panics" of the 1980s and 1990s. Finally, the chapter considers how the humanisation of the devil has led to his taming in niche areas of Western culture. More than mere sympathy for the devil, he has become likeable through comic book heroes such as Hellboy. These four themes do not represent a chronological progression in the construction of modern demonism. Rather, they demonstrate the multiple, sometimes contradictory applications of the humanised devil in a self-consciously "modern" Western culture. Fear of the devil as God's adversary may have been diminished by giving him a human face, but such a shift has brought him closer than ever before. In the modern age, the devil walks among us, lead us, and has become us.

## The Devil as Revolutionary and Rebel

Increasingly unshackled from the constraints of theology and religious belief, the devil became a symbol open to appropriation and adaptation in the 19th century. One such transition was Satan's shift from a theological to a more mythological figure, a being whose biblical backstory came to sit comfortably alongside rebellious classical mythological figures such as Prometheus. As Chapter 19 has shown, Romantic poets such as Lord Byron, Percy-Bysshe Shelley and William Blake had already begun this mythological reimagining and appropriation of Satan at the turn of the century. Their poetry transformed the biblical devil from the embodiment of evil to a political and imaginative symbol of revolution, free thought and individualism—an instigator of change against tyrannical conformity.[3] A damned but arrogant rebel, the Satan of Milton's *Paradise Lost* can be read as a predecessor of the Byronic hero.[4] Consequently, from the Romantics onwards, there was an inclination "to view figures from religious myth as simply representations of human traits," seeing our own qualities variously reflected in Christ or Satan.[5]

With the end of the Napoleonic Wars in 1815, Europe's conservative governments attempted to suppress the forces of liberalism, democracy and national self-determination that had been stoked by the French Revolution or provoked by resistance to Napoleon's conquering French armies. These progressive forces had periodically erupted into rebellion and revolution in countries across Europe in 1820–1821, 1830–1832 and 1848–1849. In such circumstances, Lucifer, the rebellious angel, became ripe for reimagining as a figurehead of the revolutionary dreams and political yearnings of the period; he became a champion of change and free will, an opponent of tyrannical authority. But the very adoption of Satan as a positive figure in this way also served as a challenge to convention—he was a tool through which people might be encouraged to reconsider their preconceptions about what was "normal," one which demonstrated that the status quo was not natural but could be questioned and reimagined. Just as Satan had awoken Adam to his own ignorance, so revolutionaries sought to stir their compatriots to rise and resist. As such, Satan and Lucifer became potent symbols in the terrestrial struggles of 19th-century revolutionaries, anarchists and socialists.

Young French revolutionaries of the 1830s had not been above posturing, talking up their "satanic" qualities or knowingly praising the devil for the shock doing so would cause to conservative convention.[6] Other European revolutionaries drew upon diabolical references to demonise the forces of conservatism. By 1848, for instance, Prince Metternich, the Austrian Chancellor and a longstanding opponent of revolutionary change, was being condemned as a "wicked demon," "chief bloodsucker" and "lame, like the devil" by some of his countrymen.[7]

Some French literati who were involved in the 1848 revolution and its aftermath went further, going beyond the rhetorical ease of demonising the forces of reaction to pen works that advanced challenging notions of Satan. In 1848, the novelist Victor Hugo (1802–1885) was elected as a member of the Second Republic's National Assembly following the abdication of King Louis Phillipe. Initially conservative, the future author of *Les Misérables* became increasingly progressive, making speeches on poverty, education and universal suffrage. His epic poem, *La Fin de Satan* (The End of Satan, started in 1856 but posthumously published in 1886), was indicative of a trend towards a more sympathetic portrayal of the devil. Here, Hugo drew attention to Satan's alienation from and longing to be reintegrated with the divine from which he had exiled himself through his pride and foolishness. The poem ends with the devil's reconciliation and with Satan being reborn as the archangel Lucifer. Part of Satan's redemption rests in his willingness to let the angel Liberty visit earth. There she rouses humanity to rebellion and encourages the destruction of the Bastille, a symbol of government oppression. Saved from his own worst qualities, the poem speaks to hopes for the possibility of change, be it redemption for a fallen angel or greater liberty on earth.[8]

This more positive reading of Lucifer's actions was echoed by others in the second half of the 19th century, a period when the Romanticism of 1848—"the springtime of the people"—withered into a more protracted struggle between social classes. The French anarchist, Pierre-Joseph Proudhon (1809–1865), appropriated Satan as a powerful symbol of rebellion, a grandiose embodiment of Proudhon's concerns with more human political struggles. In the wake of France's 1830 revolution, Proudhon had come to view Christianity as a restraint on liberty and the church as a betrayer of the revolution. In response, in his 1858 *De la Justice dans la Revolution et dans L'Eglise* (Justice in the Revolution and the Church), Proudhon championed Satan as the "great outlaw," the embodiment of liberty and a mythologised expression of humanity's struggle for freedom from tyranny.[9]

Satan was also adopted as a figure of rebellion by the more radical, anarchist-inclined elements of the Swedish socialist movement in the 1880s and 1890s. This radical element had been largely purged from the ranks when the Social Democrats became a formal party in 1889. Given their anti-conservative stance and their resistance to the church as a prop of an exploitative state, these socialists were symbolically drawn to the idea of Lucifer as a champion of those oppressed by authority. In this, the devil was representative of their human struggles, the mythical first rebel from whom all other revolutionaries took their inspiration.[10] It is notable that various late 19th-century political, social and esoteric movements adopted the name *Lucifer* for their periodicals, including the Swedish Social Democrats, the Theosophists and female emancipationists in the United States.[11] In all cases, the name could be taken literally as "light bringer," a bestower of knowledge and Enlightenment progress, while also provoking the more conservative-minded with its obvious diabolical associations.

This appropriation of the devil informed countercultural resistance in the late 19th and into the 20th centuries. These were softer cultural challenges rather than overt political revolutions. Theosophy's alternative spirituality, a blend of Western Gnosticism and Eastern mysticism, is a useful example. Helena Blavatsky (1831–1891), the movement's founder, published several works that criticised the West's growing materialism, drawing attention to the spiritual losses that Western societies had suffered in exchange for their modernising, industrial and commercial advances. In a chapter entitled "The Devil Myth" in the second volume of her *Isis Unveiled* (1877), Blavatsky explored the devil's wider connection with a range of religions and cultures while questioning the Catholic Church's reliance on the personification of the devil to uphold belief in Christ and salvation.[12] Echoing the romantic poets, she too viewed the devil as the granter of free will and knowledge, the being who made humans what they are, rather than the blissfully unthinking puppets the creator had apparently intended.

Satan also featured prominently in the decadent literature of *fin-de-siècle* Europe. A literary and artistic movement that championed aesthetic refinement, beauty and artificiality in an age perceived to be in cultural decline, the decadent movement served as yet another critique of modern Western society. French novelist Joris-Karl Huysmans' 1891 *Là-Bas* (translated as *Down There*, or *The Damned*), centred on the character of Durtal and his investigation into an underground culture of satanic practices in Paris. Climaxing with a description of a black mass, *Là Bas* became an important touchstone text for ideas about satanic cults. Fearful fantasies of satanic masses and cavorting with the devil had previously resulted in brutally real consequences for those condemned and executed in the early modern witch trials. In the more tolerant, secular society of late 19th-century France, Huysmans' fiction provided the seeds of a satanic reality—one which bore fruit perhaps most overtly in Anton LaVey's founding of the Church of Satan in San Francisco in 1966.

In both the late 19th and mid-20th centuries, countercultural trends often blended occultism and hedonism with a knowing appropriation of provocative symbolism. While embracing a sense of outsider identity, an affront to convention, the extent to which participants genuinely believed in the existence of the devil is questionable. Even LaVey's "Nine Satanic Statements" in *The Satanic Bible* (1969) do not suggest that Satan exists as a real entity. He merely represents things that LaVey saw as anti-Christian and that symbolised pleasure-seeking, free-willed individualism: "Satan represents indulgence instead of abstinence"; he embodies "vengeance instead of turning the other cheek"; he is "all of the so-called sins, as they all lead to physical, mental, or emotional gratification."[13] This then was the devil being used not to demonise others but to enable people to adopt an oppositional stance to the moral constraints of the majority.

The counterculture of the 1960s was drawn to rebels and anti-heroes, figures who questioned the notions of heroism and moral right in traditional Western narratives. Echoing the ideas of William Blake, himself co-opted as a freethinking precursor to the New Age, the devil in the minds of many counterculture advocates was a product of the human imagination, an embodiment of all the things a weakening Christian culture had long demonised in human nature: freedom from moral constraint; the pursuit of hedonistic pleasure; the assertion of free thought and will against the perceived conformity of the older generation.[14] While some 19th-century revolutionaries had viewed the devil as a figurehead for their political and social ambitions, his advocates in the 1960s largely deployed diabolical symbolism for affect, as markers of cultural resistance to conservative conventions. His continuing power to provoke was itself proof that the devil had not yet lost his ability to disrupt and challenge, even in increasingly secular Western societies. Satan and Lucifer may have come to symbolise mythologised figures of revolt and rebellion, but this association with human struggles also hints at an emerging sympathy with the devil. Rather than some remote, metaphysical being, his rebellious actions could be understood through a human lens of ambition, resistance to tyranny and a desire for freedom of thought and expression.

## The Human Devil

This humanisation of the devil was enhanced by the fact that he was frequently depicted in human form. This was seen in everything from 19th-century folklore and literature through to late 20th-century Hollywood films such as *Angel Heart* and *The Witches of Eastwick* (both 1987), *Needful Things* (1993) and *The Devil's Advocate* (1997). He was also brought closer to us by a psychologising of his previous diabolical qualities, transforming the devil from an external threat to a metaphor for the darker side of human nature. This development had its origins in the early modern period, with Reformation-era protestant theology placing less emphasis on the physicality of the devil and more on his ability to tempt people already inclined towards sin.[15] In the 19th and 20th centuries, this led to the demonising and demarcating of secular individuals such as serial killers and political figures, especially enemy leaders during the two world wars.

In 19th-century folklore, the devil was variously understood as a malevolent supernatural force of misfortune, God's punisher and an enforcer of morality, and a Mephistophelian trickster in search of souls. The devil of folk memory was also supposedly responsible for shaping local geographical features, some of which were named after his body. Both the Devil's Arse, a cave in Derbyshire, England, and The Devil's Point (or Demon's Penis) in the Cairngorms, Scotland, referenced his gigantic but essentially anthropomorphic anatomy. Such a being had clearly once been envisioned as a titanic entity. In New England, the Puritans were active in renaming locations that suggested that the devil was present in the landscape, with Connecticut alone featuring 34 such venues, and Massachusetts 43—including a number of Devil's Dens and Devil's Pulpits.[16] These folk memories had been passed on orally from generation to generation but in this period they were also being increasingly collected into written accounts capturing the character of regional cultures.

Despite these topographical associations, the devil often remained an abstract force of misfortune, one whose evil could be averted by resort to ritualistic protective practices such as casting salt over one's shoulder. Yet in these same collections, tales also told of encounters with a menacing human (usually male) figure, often described as "the black man." In such tales, his true nature was only glimpsed, signified by the hint of a tail or a cloven hoof. In such cases, the figure was usually a deceiver and punishing avenger, although folkloric tales also liked to entertain the idea that the devil could be outwitted by the common man or woman.[17] Indicative of the way the devil had drawn closer to daily lives, regional folklore records suggest that he was discussed with familiarity, though one that included a sense of underlying respect (tempered by fear). The devil was commonly known as "Old Nick," "Old Scratch," "The Old Gentleman" or "The Old Lad."[18] This was akin to the placating of other supernatural beings, such as referring to fairies as "the good folk." Folkloric notions of demons on earth were played out in the sensational accounts of Spring-heeled Jack, a supposedly fire-breathing, clawed, demonic entity that terrorised Londoners in late 1837 and 1838. Although usually advancing the view that Jack was a human prankster consciously trying to evoke the idea of the devil, the press could not resist playing up the diabolical allusions.[19]

The folkloric devil extended into broadside ballads, cheap publications aimed largely at the newly literate urban working class. Often portrayed as a human figure, albeit one with a tail, this devil was prone to being outwitted by cunning urban dwellers or being beaten by tough working-class women. Such a fate befell the devil in the ballads *The Devil and Little Mike* and *The Devil and the Washerwomen*. In the first, he initially seems menacing, barging his way into a house to claim Mike. Yet he is set upon by Mike's sisters and takes such a beating that he dies the following day. Freed from his threat, the ballad joyously ends with "For since the Devil is dead, we can all do just as we like." In the second, he disguises himself as "a Bond Street swell" but is soon mishandled by a group of washerwomen who reveal his tail, horns and cloven hoof. Having been viciously scrubbed, he escapes but leaves his tail behind. In *The Devil in Search of a Wife*, he again disguises himself as a man and walks the streets of London, hiding his tail. It is eventually revealed in a dance and, again, he is assaulted—this time with chairs—before his tail is singed with a poker and he is thrown from a window. In the end, he agrees to take a farmer's wife down to hell. But once there, the woman beats up demons and imps and ends up subjecting the devil to her "petticoat government."[20] Such treatment clearly shows how, waning as a threatening, diabolical reality, the devil became a figure to be mocked. Rather than the noble rebel of revolutionaries, he was used here as a comic shorthand for the overthrow of power and authority.

Once a punisher of human sin, the devil was increasingly relegated to the level of a metaphor for wickedness. More liberal-minded 19th-century Anglican theologians found it increasingly difficult to defend the devil or hell as literal truths. In his essay, "On the Evil Spirit," for instance, the Anglican clergyman, F. D. Maurice, indicated that there were those who saw the belief in the existence of the devil as "the least tenable figment of orthodox theology," going on to note that nobody in the 19th century could still hold such views with sincerity.[21] H. B. Wilson's contribution to the innocuously titled but controversial *Essays and Reviews* (1860) was seen to challenge the idea of hell and led to him being prosecuted for heresy, although he was eventually acquitted in 1864.[22] Owen Davies has suggested that by the outbreak of the First World War the Anglican Church had "demoted the afterlife in its tenets, services and public engagement," muting metaphysics in favour of its concerns with morality and social activism.[23] While others may have persisted in believing in the reality of the devil and hell, in 1876 the Reverend Hugh Reginald Haweis argued that it mattered little whether people were tempted "by fiends without or by lusts within."[24] The cause—diabolical or human—was less important than the fact that one would face a struggle for salvation. Presenting the devil as a metaphor for human evil rather than as a supernatural entity was easier to voice in an increasingly materialistic, secular world that questioned the intervention or existence of supernatural entities but sought to uphold morally correct behaviour.

This notion of the devil within was propagated in 19th-century literature too. Unlike his countryman Victor Hugo, French poet Arthur Rimbaud's *A Season in Hell* (1873) did not portray Satan as a remorseful rebel but as someone whose diabolical domain might struggle to keep up with humanity's vices, flaws and urges. For Rimbaud, hell served as an appealing home for our worst instincts. In the titular poem for the collection, a demon declares that the poet will "never stop being a hyena ... Go to greet death with all your appetites, with your selfishness and all the deadly sins." In a later poem, "Night in Hell," Rimbaud, the *enfant terrible* of French symbolist poetry, declared "I ought to have a hell for my anger, a hell for my pride, —and a hell for embraces; a whole symphony of hells ... Satan you clown, you want to destroy me, with your enchantments. That is what I want. I crave for it! Stab me with your pitchfork, sprinkle me with fire."[25]

That humanity's darkest instincts may be barely contained by the horrors of hell—perhaps even eclipsing them—had already been explored by Isidore Ducasse (1846–1870) in his deliberately provocative 1868 *Les Chants de Maldoror* (written under the penname Comte de Lautréamont). This nightmarish novel can be read as a revelling in evil, its taboo-breaking scenes rivalling the work of the Marquis de Sade. Beyond redemption and unrepentant, the character of Maldoror positions himself as an opponent of God and man, his self-belief, freedom from moral bounds and sadism making him the literary embodiment of the human devil. As he declares, "I would rejoice to know that hell is so near to man."[26] Over the course of this deranged and phantasmagorical story, the author repeatedly shocks the reader's sense of morality and social convention through a litany of violence, mutilation, sexual depravity and murder. Free from social constraint, Maldoror's actions and fantasies make him something other than human, a force of evil that borders upon but requires no supernatural explanation. In this sense, Maldoror best encapsulates the early French Decadent writers' personification of human diabolism.

This idea of a diabolical nature extended beyond fiction. Projected onto murderers and political leaders, certain individuals accrued an air of inhuman menace. The most notorious in the late 19th century was Jack the Ripper. When this unknown individual began a series of violent killings of women in the East End of London in autumn 1888, the sensationalist press was quick to draw upon diabolical associations. A *Punch* magazine cartoon of October 1888 depicted him as a devil pasting posters on walls, their images comparing his crimes to the horrors of the penny dreadfuls, another form of cheap literature that had become popular in this period.[27] These associations were enhanced by the provocative letters sent to the press and the vigilance committees, supposedly by the killer (although the penmanship varies considerably). One such letter sent to the Whitechapel Vigilance Committee in October 1888, renowned for including half a human kidney, was addressed "From Hell."[28]

Similar diabolical associations were made across the Atlantic in the mid-1890s. The Chicago-based serial killer H. H. Holmes (1861–1896) used the sealed chambers, acid vats, and crematorium of his infamous hotel, popularly known as "The Murder Castle" once his crimes had been exposed, to turn murder and the disposal of the bodies into an industrial process. Reporting on Holmes' confession in 1896, an article in *The North American* declared that he had been "stamped by Satan." Holmes stated that he "was born with the devil in me" and, no longer having any affinity with humanity, felt he was "a part and parcel of the Inferno." In prison awaiting execution, he became "fully convinced that physically as well as mentally [he] is slowly but surely growing to look like a devil" and that his face had come to adopt "a pronounced Satanic cast."[29]

This diabolical rhetoric served to describe actions that would become framed as "psychopathic," a term coined by German psychiatrist Julius Ludwig August Koch (1841–1908) in the year the Ripper killings began.[30] The claim "The devil made me do it" is not framed as genuine diabolical possession but rather as a loss of control over one's own darker urges and desires. This symbolic appropriation turns the devil from an external entity into an internal aspect of our own psyche. Among the most notorious cases of the later 20th century was Richard Ramirez (1960–2013), the "Night Stalker," who in 1989 was found guilty of killing thirteen people. Ramirez had left an inverted pentagram at some of his murder scenes, thereby consciously invoking a connection with satanic symbolism. Lacking remorse and said to display many aspects of psychopathic behaviour, Ramirez, upon sentencing, announced "Lucifer dwells in all of us."[31]

In attempting to grapple with these grim and seemingly motiveless crimes, casting them as diabolical served to indicate their exceptionalism, marking a boundary between ordinary criminality and the predatory nature of serial killers. For Holmes and Ramirez at least, they also seemed to serve as a way of lessening or even removing some of their responsibility for their actions. Unlike the positive self-identification between revolutionaries and Satan, here the association with the devil pushed the killer's humanity away, suggesting that if the devil walked among us, he was fundamentally different. As such, the devil could serve as a way of distancing individuals from human "normality" even as he became associated with the antisocial urges and motivations within the human mind.

The "devil within" had been promoted in late 19th-century Gothic literature such as Robert Louis Stevenson's *The Strange Case of Dr Jekyll and Mister Hyde* (1886) and Oscar Wilde's *The Picture of Dorian Gray* (1894). These novels destabilised ideas of the "self," exploring fears about split personalities and unstable or hidden identities. Lacking overt supernatural associations, Wilde's novel involved a variant of the diabolical pact—albeit without a devil—through which the character became corrupted by his own debauchery and freedom from consequence. This psychological focus was advanced into the early 20th century by Sigmund Freud (1856–1939), although his own work made only limited references to the psychoanalytical significance of the devil. Rather, it was his follower and associate, Ernest Jones (1879–1958), who interpreted the devil as a personification of repressed impulses, especially libidinal desires. For Jones, the devil also informed negative aspects of the father-son relationship, arguing that he functioned as a symbol of the hated father who the son wished to destroy, or the rebellious son who revolts against the father.[32]

Carl Jung (1875–1961), Freud's rival and a towering figure of early 20th-century psychiatry, also touched upon the devil in his work. His interest in spirituality, mythology and trickster archetypes led him to make references to Faust and Mephistopheles. Ultimately, though, he came to see the devil as an analogy for the operation of psychological influences such as temptation and deception. In one text, for instance, he noted how "the darkness supposedly represented by the Devil has localized itself in man," with the result that "the Devil was largely, if not entirely, abolished," transformed from a metaphysical being through being "introjected into man."[33] In another, he declared "The Devil is the sum of the darkness of human nature" and that the devil's influence only ever works "through one's own serpenthood."[34] The development of psychoanalysis has commonly been presented as a secular successor to religious belief, a turn from God to a narcissistic focus on the human self. As such, one can interpret the psychologising of the diabolical as part of a 19th- and 20th-century trend towards trying to dispel belief in supernatural entities as things external to the human mind.[35]

The use of diabolism to denote human exceptionalism continued into the world wars of the 20th century. Western wartime propaganda sought to personify both Kaiser Wilhelm II and Adolf Hitler as devils with human faces. The demonic "othering" of enemy leaders was far from new.[36] Napoleon had been presented in a similar manner in the early 19th century, although the 20th century's developing media and advertising cultures may have helped expand the reach of such associations far beyond previous audiences. Enemy wartime political leaders came to serve a similar oppositional role to that previously performed by the devil in Western Christian society, representing a remote, threatening, larger-than-life menace that stood apart from common humanity. This provided the Allies with a sense of providential purpose, enabling them to present global conflicts as a Manichean struggle between good and evil. The scale of the wars encouraged talk of titanic clashes between civilisation and barbarism, democracy and totalitarianism (and later, in the Cold War, capitalism and communism). Propagandists grasped that these real, existential threats to Western (self-) identity and values could be simplified into old dualities of Christian right versus diabolical wrong.

Given the First World War's apocalyptic religious rhetoric, it comes as little surprise that there were attempts to associate Kaiser Wilhelm II with the Antichrist. The Antichrist offered a more overtly human incarnation of diabolical intrigue, described as the son of Satan and a false prophet.[37] A month into the war, on 10 September 1914 the French newspaper, *Le Figaro*, promoted a supposed 17th-century prophecy that the Antichrist would be a monarch and "a son of Luther," hence German. While most were sceptical about such a convenient discovery, the prophecy of "Brother Johannes" contributed to the wartime demonisation of the German Emperor. While American evangelicals doubted that the kaiser was the Antichrist himself, they seemed willing to entertain the notion that he heralded the coming of the Antichrist.[38]

In the more outlandish spiritualist literature of the war, a tradition that viewed the conflict as a struggle between modernity's growing materialism and a resurgent spirituality, the kaiser could easily be portrayed as a direct human puppet of a demonic entity. Elsa Barker's *War Letters from a Living Dead Man* (1915), for instance, recounts how the titular spirit encounters a demon on the astral plane. It is suggested that this is the demonic form of the kaiser himself, for he proudly boasts that he is "the deeper self of a man who is great among men, a man who will follow my will as others follow his will." Indicating that the kaiser is subservient to this demonic entity, the latter declares, "I broke away from the earthly form that had enchained me when he acknowledged my rulership and worshipped me as his genius." Adding to the satanic associations, Barker's narrator later states "the German Emperor did hesitate to touch the spring which should open the doors of hell ... he shivered at the responsibility that faced him while gloating in that responsibility, which further exalted his already self-exalted ego."[39]

Similar associations were made when portraying Adolf Hitler in the Second World War. While Nazi propaganda had frequently sought to demonise and de-humanise Germany's Jewish population through diabolical imagery from the 1930s, once war broke out Allied propaganda presented Hitler as a devil. This is seen in the 1942 American poster, "Eat to beat the devil," with a horned Hitler being punched on the chin.[40] Punching the demonic Führer in the face was simply an updated, wartime adaptation of the violence and robust humour with which Victorian street ballads had treated the devil.

While his religious identification may have weakened, nominally Christian Western democracies still drew upon the devil as a way of demonising the powerful, pseudo-religious forces of nation-worshipping fascists. This was demonstrated in the British press in July 1942. The *Daily Mirror* reported on a German book entitled *Gott und Volk, Soldatisches Bekenntis* (*God and the People: A Soldier's Profession of Faith*, 1940), said to be popular among the ranks of the Wehrmacht. With 200,000 copies printed by 1942, this slim text supposedly advanced a "religion of the sword" and exalted a "God of Force." The article suggested younger Germans had been persuaded by "this diabolical drive" to promote Nazi values as a replacement for Christianity, and that the British needed to realise that Nazism was "far more a faith than a policy."[41] The associations between Nazis and the occult have continued as yet another way of distancing Nazi Germany from other self-identifying

Christian nations, presenting Hitler at the head of a false or secular religion.[42] The sense of Christian soldiers fighting the diabolical forces of Central Europe was underscored by the American Armed Forces which distributed a special pocket-sized edition of Bram Stoker's 1897 *Dracula* to G.I.s serving overseas in the Second World War.[43] Dracula's devilish associations are continually stressed through the course of Stoker's perennially popular novel.

The devil's humanisation reinforced but also complicated his traditional function of dividing "them" from "us." Taking human form diminished his threat and made him a figure of mockery, one who could be overcome with brute force. Yet doing so also implied that he might now be encountered in the street, the unknown urban stranger rather than some remote being. The psychologising of the devil brought him closer still, becoming a way of describing our own darker impulses while also offering a means of demarcating and distancing ourselves from the exceptional evil of serial killers and power-hungry dictators.

## The Hidden Devil

Although the devil may have faded as a real entity, his influence stretched into the modern era. This marked his continuing humanisation, for he remained an invisible and disembodied presence, purely reliant upon human agents and worshippers to have any effect upon the world. This idea, presented as both real threat and entertaining thrill, was expressed through a range of cultural practices and forms, from the séance room to the cinema, from literary fictions of satanic cults to the real-world satanic panics of the 1980s and 1990s.

Disturbed by spiritualists' claims to be able to communicate with departed spirits and therefore to gleam insight into the afterlife, some 19th-century clergymen suggested that the spirits being summoned during séances were not those of deceased family members but manipulative demons seeking to mislead the grieving and the gullible. This view was most persistently voiced by members of the Catholic clergy, although there were critics from other Christian denominations willing to express similar concerns about diabolical deception and human ignorance. For example, William Holt Yates, a Scottish physician, founder of the Syro-Egyptian Society of London, and a keen opponent of spiritualism, believed that the devil was cunningly repackaging older supernatural practices for a more scientific age. "Satan," he declared, "avails himself of our boasted worldly wisdom and, as the mind is prepared for new wonders by the rapid discoveries of Science and Philosophy, these become the most orthodox channels for the successful introduction of his devices." Yates condemned spiritualism and mesmerism as "lying wonders," evidence of the devil's wiles and a sign that "the star of Lucifer is upon the rise."[44] The Anglican clergyman, Reverend Nathaniel Steadman Godfrey, promoted similar views in published pamphlets such as *Table-Turning, the Devil's Modern Masterpiece* (1853) and his more substantial *The Theology of Table-Turning, Spirit-Rapping, and Clairvoyance, in Connection with the Antichrist* (1854). Yet there were those like Francis Close who countered such ideas, fearing these sensational claims would stimulate a revival of "superstitious" thinking.[45] Concern about demonic deceit in the séance room continued into the early 20th century, with John Godfrey Raupert, a former Anglican clergyman turned Catholic priest, continuing to warn of diabolical influences in his *Dangers of Spiritualism* (1901).[46] Even if the First World War gave spiritualism more urgent cultural relevance, the number of spiritualist practitioners remained small compared with orthodox religions. This supposed diabolical backdoor into the modern world, naively opened by human mediums, never amounted to anything more than the possibility of deceiving a relatively few séance attendees.

A similar suspicion of demonic workings was seen in religious visions too, a repetition of an age-old doubt as to whether a vision could truly be known to be divine or diabolical in origin. The outbreak of supposed demonic possessions in Morzine in Savoy between 1857 and 1870 (a region of Italy that came under French control in 1860) demonstrated an obvious humanisation of the devil. Girls and young women were subject to convulsions, sleepwalking and hallucinations. Some claimed to have seen visions of both the devil and the Virgin Mary. One girl was said to be possessed by seven devils. When the parish priest voiced his scepticism, locals were offended by his disbelief. Despite demonstrating traditional signs of possession, this outbreak was given an overtly sociopsychological interpretation as an expression of collective hysteria.[47] When an apparition was seen at Fatima in Portugal in 1917—some 60 years later—the local priest warned that it could be a deception by the devil.[48] Such cases highlighted the uncertainty about the reality of the devil but also an abiding concern that he would exploit a human longing for signs of the divine and proof of faith.

While these examples may indicate how the devil turned humans into his unwitting instruments, he did have willing followers in Satanists. Yet up to and even after Anton LaVey established the Church of Satan, Satanist groups remained relegated to the cultural margins, very small in terms of followers, limited in appeal and influence, and often short lived in their organisational existence.[49] Fears of satanic practices derived from long-held paranoid fantasies about devil worship in Europe and North America and their continuing place in the Western imagination owes more to popular fiction than any meaningful and sustained reality prior to the mid-20th century. British author Dennis Wheatley's occult thrillers offer a good example of this. In a foreword to the best known of these, *The Devil Rides Out* (1934, filmed 1968), Wheatley provided vague but ominous hints that in conducting research for his novel he found "ample evidence that Black Magic is still practised in London, and other cities, at the present day." He also warned his readers to avoid being drawn into such practices for "to do so would bring them into dangers of a very real and concrete nature."[50] The warning may have been genuine, but Wheatley was also setting up the story, one in which the devil (as the Goat of Mendes) makes an appearance, but whose central villain is the Satanist cult leader, Mocata.

The fiction of the devil's insidious influence and his human agents continued to be promoted in novels and, in terms of wider audiences, in the mainstream horror films based on them in the late 1960s and 1970s. These include most notably Ira Levin's *Rosemary's Baby* (1967, filmed 1968), William Peter Blatty's *The Exorcist* (1971, filmed 1973), and *The Omen* (1976, with David Seltzer's novelisation of his screenplay appearing in the same year).[51] Rather than a fiery apocalypse, in these works the devil often took human form, slipping into the Western world as a baby or by possessing a young teenage girl. As with folklore, there were tell-tale signs of these innocents' true diabolical nature. Rosemary's baby, Adrian, has the devil's eyes, while Damien Thorn, the son of the devil in *The Omen*, has a "666" birthmark hidden beneath his hair. *Rosemary's Baby* spoke to both urban paranoia and the period's female liberation movement, while the affluence and presidential ambitions of Damien Thorn in *The Omen* series chimed with a nation awash with conspiracy theories and high-level skulduggery, including the Kennedy assassinations and Watergate.

Of the three, *The Exorcist* seemed to provoke the greatest response from various Christian denominations. The American evangelist Billy Graham urged people not to watch the film, insisting that demonic possession was "not make believe. It is reality." Other clergymen seemed keen for audiences to be confronted with such horrors for that very reason. In a piece in the *Daily Express* in March 1974 Reverend Christopher Neil-Smith, a London-based priest who had conducted numerous exorcisms, claimed that the novel and film both "reveal the stark reality of possession in its horrific form."[52] The film spawned a sub-genre of the horror film industry, revealing our fascination with possession and exorcisms, especially those that purport to be based on true events. Possession has become the cinematic trope by which filmmakers can represent the demonic with a human face, a diabolical presence that can only be perceived in human form and then only through the gruesome physiological effects it has upon the human it possesses. This plays to both the visual thrills and philosophical concerns of horror cinema. *The Exorcist*'s headline-grabbing depiction of demonic possession presaged the emergence of "body horror" films by the likes of David Cronenberg in the late 1970s and 1980s.[53] In doing so it expressed anxieties about the morphing of one's flesh alongside more metaphysical concerns about free will and the nature of evil. Yet *The Exorcist* and its subsequent imitators frequently offer comfort in the efficacious power of Christian faith. As with the influence of the crucifix on cinematic vampires, Western audiences continue to show themselves willing to imagine the power of Christianity in opposing demons, even if that imagining no longer extends to genuine belief for many.

The paranoia concerning Satanists often said as much about the fantasies of conservative-minded Christians as it did about those who appropriated diabolical symbolism. The "satanic panics" of the 1980s and 1990s perpetuated the fear of conspiracy evident in *Rosemary's Baby* and *The Omen* and carried the threat to childish innocence into the real world. In much of the Anglophone world, the 1980s saw increasing numbers of aspirational, two-parent income families having to leave their children in the care of strangers at nurseries. This gave rise to parental anxieties, often expressed as fears about paedophilia. Updating the instinct to demonise and scapegoat threats within the community, the resultant moral panics saw cases of nursery staff being presented as Satanists indulging in child abuse.[54] Alongside the threat of closet Satanists in nurseries was the occasional scare about satanic messages being conveyed to impressionable youths via the backmasking (songs recorded backwards) of pop, rock and heavy metal tracks.[55] It is not a coincidence that the late 1970s and 1980s also saw a resurgent fundamentalist Christian Right, one that could rally the faithful to its cause by identifying satanic threats to children, youth, and to conservative values. Moral panics tend to erupt in cycles. Having declined by the end of the 1990s, satanic worship conspiracies have recently revived, incorporated into Q-Anon's wild theories about high-level paedophile rings and their defamation of "deep state" political insiders. As this section suggests, while the context may shift over time, the devil remains absent. In the modern world, his influence, real or imagined, had become wholly reliant on human agents who ranged from the deceived to the willing to the possessed.

## Taming the Devil

As indicated in the sections above, the modern devil found himself reappropriated and re-packaged through fiction and advertising. If he was to be grounded, humanised and made accessible through the selling of commercial products and entertainments, the devil necessarily required taming.

From the rise of the Victorian stage magic show in the 1840s, performers such as John Henry Anderson, the "Wizard of the North," had been willing to toy with associations between illusionism and the diabolical, often adorning his promotional posters with imps. This trend became even more overt in the advertising for late 19th- and early 20th-century American stage magicians such as Harry Kellar, Charles Joseph Carter (Carter the Great) and Howard Thurston (Thurston the Great). Their posters frequently included images of horned red devils and winged imps at their side. In such a context, the devil was reduced to a mere lacky, granting a borrowed allure of supernaturalism to a human performer in a safely packaged modern, commercial entertainment.[56]

Later 20th-century forms of entertainment and play also furthered this tamed interest in demons. The growth of fantasy role-playing games such as *Dungeons and Dragons* (or D&D) attracted numbers of participants that far exceeded those who self-identified as genuine Satanists. Created in 1974 by Gary Gygax and Dave Arneson, D&D grew in popularity with (predominantly) adolescents during the 1970s and 1980s. This collective game involved story-driven quests that featured a broad range of monsters and demons drawn from world folklore and mythology. Yet in the febrile atmosphere of the "satanic panics" of the 1980s, even this imaginative role-playing game led to wild accusations that it encouraged demon worship and belief in the occult. With no logical or evidential justification, it was linked to a number of reported suicides and killings. Patricia Pulling claimed her son's suicide in 1982 was due to his playing D&D and formed the group *Bothered by Dungeons and Dragons*. Evangelical groups were also vocal, with D&D being accused of serving as "an occult tool that opens up young people to influence or possession by demons."[57] While seen as another potentially corrupting satanic influence by Christian fundamentalists, the D&D *Monster Manual* (first published 1977), a compendium of monsters and supernatural entities, effectively reduced demons to a list of game-related attributes and statistics. Demons may have represented a powerful threat to players' characters, but role-playing games were a harmless, imaginative entertainment, one in which the diabolical threat was likely to be defeated or vanquished. Despite the panic, D&D games typically reiterated the moral sense of good and evil that critics feared was being eroded.

We have seen how the 19th century's positive re-reading of the devil as a rebel and emancipator (for some) required a more sympathetic interpretation of his biblical narrative. This continued into the 20th century. The Rolling Stones' song, "Sympathy for the Devil" (1968), serves as the backing track for a later 20th-century trend for turning traditional monsters into more humanised, sympathetic characters. In 1972, both DC Comics' Etrigan and Marvel's Ghost Rider presented comic book readers with demonic "superheroes." Etrigan was bound to a human, Jason Blood, while Ghost Rider, a demon linked to stunt rider Johnny Blaze, updated the folkloric idea of the devil as a punisher of injustice. Both demons had a propensity for violence, but their human element often helped keep them on the side of right and justice.[58]

More directly, the character of Lucifer himself first appears in DC's *Sandman* series in 1989, with writer Neil Gaiman clearly basing him on Milton's Satan in *Paradise Lost*. In the subsequent Vertigo spin-off series, *Lucifer*, written by Mike Carey, the fallen angel assumes the form of a handsome, besuited man and sets up home in a Los Angeles nightclub. Far from a classic superhero, and always far more than human, readers were nevertheless encouraged to root for him as a character who keeps his word and overcomes threats from all sides through a combination of cunning, intelligence and will. Dispensing with any theological mystery surrounding the actions and unknowable intentions of the devil, the comic book's story arcs were driven by Lucifer's clear (and recognisably human) ambitions.[59]

439

Reworking the more conventional horned red devil image, Mike Mignola's *Hellboy* was first published in serial form by Dark Horse Comics in 1994. The child of a demon duke of Hell and a human witch, it is not in his devilish appearance but in the humanity of his character that he represents a humanised devil. While struggling with his own apocalyptic destiny, he acts very much in the vein of brawling superhero champions, with Guillermo del Toro's films, *Hellboy* (2004) and *Hellboy II: The Golden Army* (2008), playing up the idea of Hellboy as a regular Joe, a demonic blue-collar worker just doing his job. This sympathetic and overtly heroic character has updated and arguably popularised the humanising trend initiated in Milton's 17th-century text.

It is significant that the character of Hellboy is the harbinger of the apocalypse. Although tamed into comic book fantasy, this thread has run from the kaiser as herald to the Antichrist, to Damien Thorn as the Antichrist himself, to Hellboy. It fits with a Western 20th-century cultural anxiety and fascination with Armageddon. While that may have been envisioned as the battlefields of the Somme in the First World War, or Stalingrad or the Blitz in the Second, for the duration of the Cold War fantasies of the end of days were inspired by the threat of imminent nuclear destruction.[60] While still holding up a dark mirror to the horrors of the 20th century, the devil arguably paled beneath the threat presented by the magnitude of world wars, the powerful totalitarian symbolism of the swastika, or the looming atomic mushroom cloud left in the collective imagination after Hiroshima and Nagasaki.

This turn towards identifying with our traditional monsters and demons may have cheapened them by knowingly forcing them into the conventions of the superhero genre. Yet that shift also indicates a cultural yearning to detach the demonic from evil and to appropriate monsters as refashioned icons with which we can willingly identify. This can be understood as an expansion in parts of Western culture not just to tolerate but to identify with otherness, on the condition that those others are perceived as non-threatening. This diabolical taming reached its high (or low) point in the adult cartoon series *South Park*. Although Satan is depicted as a muscular, horned red devil in the show, its creators clearly sought to provoke Christian fundamentalists, not by presenting him as a malevolent menace but as an increasingly likeable, essentially human character. If a marker of Satan's late 20th-century cultural taming was required, one might point to his heartfelt singing of "Up There," a mock-Disney song number in *South Park: Bigger, Longer & Uncut* (1999).

Increasingly freed from theological dogma, the devil became a symbol that could be adapted to the anxieties and struggles of the modern age. Alongside his continuing, traditional role in demonising others, the period covered by this chapter also saw a willingness to find affinities with the devil and even for people to align themselves consciously with him. This is perhaps one of the most notable features of the period under consideration here, be it 19th-century anarchists and socialists, *fin-de-siècle* French Decadents, or New Age Californian Satanists. As such, Western societies' former personification of evil developed a more contradictory dimension. Now the devil could variously be interpreted as empowering or threatening, a mythologised embodiment of Western individualism or a symbolically monstrous threat to it.

This chapter has suggested some of the ways in which this affinity with the devil was achieved through his humanisation. This was a two-way process, with people identifying with him, and with him increasingly being depicted in human form. He came to represent darker urges within ourselves that we would rather not confront directly, while any evidence of his insidious influence was reliant upon the operation of human agents rather than the devil himself. In seeing something of ourselves in the devil, and something of the devil in us, he has continued to find broad (although often rather shallow) cultural expression and relevance, leaving modern Western societies as suffused with the demonic as ever.

## Notes

1 See William Gladstone, *Studies Subsidiary to the Works of Bishop Butler* (Oxford, 1896), 206.

2 Historians debate the nature, extent and pace of secularisation in post-Enlightenment Western societies. For a recent summary, see William Gibson, "Introduction: New Perspectives on Secularisation in Britain (and Beyond)," *Journal of Religious History*, 41, no. 4 (2017): 431–8.

3 For the earlier 17th-century humanising of Satan in literature, see Nancy Rosenfeld, *The Human Satan in Seventeenth-Century Literature: From Milton to Rochester* (London, 2008).

4 For more on the cultural expression of the Byronic hero across this period, see Atara Stein, *The Byronic Hero in Film, Fiction and Television* (Carbondale, 2004).

5 Per Faxneld, "The Devil Is Red: Socialist Satanism in the 19th Century," *Numen* 60 (2013): 528–58, on 554.

6 Robert Muchembled *A History of the Devil, From the Middle Ages to the Present*, trans. Jean Birrell (Cambridge, 2003), 197.

7 See R. John Rath, *The Viennese Revolution of 1848* (Austin, 2013).

8 Victor Hugo, *God and The End of Satan / Dieu et la Fin de Satan: Selections in a Bilingual Edition*, trans. and ed. R.G. Skinner (Chicago, 2014).

9 See Ruben van Luijk, *Children of Lucifer: The Origins of Modern Religious Satanism* (Oxford, 2016), 116–9.

10 See Faxneld, "Devil Is Red."

11 Faxneld, "Devil Is Red," 541–3.

12 See H. P. Blavatsky, *Isis Unveiled, Vol 2: Theology* (UK, 2006), 434–83, especially 437 and 440.

13 Anton Szandor LaVey, *The Satanic Bible* (New York, 1969), 25. See also Chapter 24.

14 For more on Blake's influence on the 1960s counterculture, see Stephen F. Eisenman, *William Blake and the Age of Aquarius* (Princeton, 2017).

15 See Chapter 20 and Nathan Johnstone, *The Devil and Demonism in Early Modern England* (Cambridge, 2006).

16 See https://spookygeology.com/devil-places/ and Jacqueline Simpson, "God's Visible Judgements: The Christian Dimension of Landscape Legends," *Landscape History* 8, no. 1 (1986): 54.

17 See William Axon, *Echoes of Old Lancashire* (London, 1899), 212–3. This took more literary form in works such as Herman Melville's *The Confidence Man* (1857).

18 See Sarah Bartels, "'A Terrific Ogre': The Role of the Devil in Victorian Popular Belief," *Folklore* 128, no. 3 (2017): 271–91 on 278–9.

19 For more on this, see Karl Bell, *The Legend of Spring-heeled Jack: Victorian Urban Folklore and Popular Cultures* (Woodbridge, 2017).

20 Copies of these ballads are held in the University of Oxford's Bodleian Library. See *The Devil and Little Mike*, Bod. 6660 Roud No. 1696; *The Devil and the Washerwomen*, Bod14064 Roud No. V4803; *The Devil in Search of a Wife*, Bod 10195. Roud No. V379.

21 See F. D. Maurice, *Theological Essays* 2nd edn (Cambridge, 1853), 47.

22 See H. B. Wilson, "Seances Historique de Geneve—The National Church," in *Essays and Reviews* ed. John William Parjer (London, 1860), 145–206.

23 See Owen Davies, *A Supernatural War: Magic, Divination and Faith during the First World War* (Oxford, 2018), 78.

24 See Henry Dunn, *The Destiny of the Human Race: A Scriptural Inquiry* (London, 1863), Henry Constable, *The Duration and Nature of Future Punishment* (London, 1868), and "Something about 'The Devil'," *The Preston Guardian*, 26 February 1876.

25 Arthur Rimbaud, *A Season in Hell and Illuminations*, trans. Mark Treharne (London, 1998), 3 and 19–21.

26 Lautréamont, *Maldoror* (Harmondsworth, 1978), 47.

27 "Horrible London: Or The Pandemonium of Posters," *Punch*, 13 October 1888.

28 See Stewart P. Evans and Keith Skinner, *Jack the Ripper: Letters from Hell* (Cheltenham, 2001).

29 "Holmes' Confession," *The North American*, 11 April 1896, 1.

30 Koch first referred to "psychopathic inferiority" in his 1888 text, *Kurzgefasster Leitfaden der Psychiatrie*. This was developed and elaborated upon in his *Die psychopathischen Minderwertig-keiten* (*The Psychopathic Inferiorities*), a work published in three parts between 1891 and 1893. See Greg Eghigian, "A Drifting Concept for an Unruly Menace: A History of Psychopathy in Germany," *Isis* 106, no. 2 (2015): 283–309 on 285–6.

31 Gabriel Andrade and Maria Susana Campo Redondo, "Satanism and Psychopathology: Some Historical Cases," *The Journal of Psychohistory*, 47, no. 2 (2019): 126–43 on 132.

32 See Ernest Jones, *Nightmares, Witches and Devils* (New York, 1931), and Jeffrey Burton Russell, *Mephistopheles: The Devil in the Modern World* (Ithica, 1986), 229.

33 C. G. Jung, *Four Archetypes. Mother. Rebirth. Spirit. Trickster* (London, 1998), 37.

34 C. G. Jung, *The Red Book. Liber Novus: A Reader's Edition* ed. Sonu Shamdasani (New York, 2009), 432 and 433.

35 For the earlier development of this, see Terry Castle, *The Female Thermometer: Eighteenth-Century Culture and the Invention of the Uncanny* (London, 1995), 168–89.

36 For more on this, see Chapter 19.

37 See Philip C. Almond, *The Antichrist: A New Biography* (Cambridge, 2020).

38 See Augusta Cook, *Is It Armageddon? The Present War in the Light of Divine Prophecy* (London, 1917); Herbert Thurston, *The War and the Prophets: Notes on Certain Popular Predictions Current in the Latter Age* (London, 1915), 47–67 and Davies, *A Supernatural War*, 49–52.

39 Elsa Barker's *War Letters from a Living Dead Man* (Guildford, 2009), 18 and 23–4.

40 See https://www.gettyimages.co.uk/detail/news-photo/fist-labelled-americas-increased-war-production-delivers-an-news-photo/91905568

41 David Walker, "Germany Cannot Repent—They Know No God," *Daily Mirror*, 14 July 1942, 4.

42 See Eric Kurlander, *Hitler's Monsters: A Supernatural History of the Third Reich* (New Haven, 2017), and *Revisiting the "Nazi Occult": Histories, Realities, Legacies*, ed. Monica Black and Eric Kurlander (Rochester, 2015). For the Nazis' suppression of the Fraternitas Saturni, a German magical group that included the worshipping of Satan, see Luijk, *Children of Lucifer*, 301–2.

43 See Mathias Clasen, "Attention, Predation, Counterintuition: Why Dracula Won't Die," *Style* 46, nos. 3 and 4 (Fall/Winter 2012): 379.

44 William Holt Yates, *An Essay on Mesmerism, Clairvoyance, and Communication with the Spirits of Departed Friends* (1853), Wellcome Institute ref. MS5100, 5–6.

45 See N. S. Godfrey, *Table-Turning, the Devil's Modern Masterpiece* (London, 1853), and *The Theology of Table-Turning, Spirit-Rapping, and Clairvoyance, in Connection with the Antichrist* (London, 1854), and Francis Close, *Table-Turning Not Diabolical: A Tract for the Times* (London, 1853).

46 Around the same time, some authors were expressing similar concerns about the devil's influence via hypnotism. See Charles Helot's *Le Diable et L'Hypnotisme* (Paris, 1899).

47 See Ruth Harris, "Possession on the Borders: The "Mal de Morzine" in 19th-Century France," *Journal of Modern History* 69, no. 3 (1997): 451–78.

48 Davies, *A Supernatural War*, 66.

49 Satanism is explored in more detail in the next chapter. For a thorough investigation into the history of 19th- and 20th-century Satanism in Western culture, see Luijk, *Children of Lucifer* and *The Devil's Party: Satanism in Modernity* eds. Per Faxneld and Jesper A. Petersen (Oxford, 2013).

50 Dennis Wheatley, "Author's Note," *The Devil Rides Out* (London, 2013).

51 For more on this "satanic cycle" of films, see Tony Williams, *Hearths of Darkness: The Family in the American Horror Film* (Jackson, 2014), 98–128 and *Giving the Devil His Due: Satan and Cinema*, eds. Jeffrey Andrew Weinstock and Regina M. Hansen (New York, 2021).

52 "In the Demon's Clutches," *Daily Express*, 13 March 1974, 8.

53 See Xavier Aldana Reyes, *Body Gothic: Corporeal Transgression in Contemporary Literature and Horror Film* (Cardiff, 2014), 52–74.

54 See Chapter 24.

55 See Bill Thompson and Andy Williams, *The Myth of Moral Panics: Sex, Snuff, and Satan* (New York, 2014), 175–208.

56 For more on Anderson and the tension between secular stage magic and the supernatural, see Karl Bell, "Remaking Magic: The 'Wizard of the North' and Contested Magical Mentalities in the Mid-19th-Century Magic Show," *Magic, Ritual and Witchcraft* 4, no. 1 (2009): 26–51.

57 See David Waldron, "Roleplaying Games and the Christian Right: Community Formation in Response to a Moral Panic," *Journal of Religion and Popular Culture* 9, no. 1 (2005): 1–40.

58 This more sympathetic, humanised devil was paralleled by the late 20th-century reimagining of superheroic vampires such as Marvel's Blade (first appearance in 1973) and Angel in *Buffy the Vampire Slayer* (1997–2003) and *Angel* (1999–2004).

59 This series started with the *Sandman Presents: Lucifer* miniseries in 1999 and ran until 2006.

60 See *Understanding the Imaginary War: Culture, Thought and Nuclear Conflict, 1945–90*, eds. Matthew Grant and Benjamin Ziemann (Manchester, 2016) and David Seed, *Under the Shadow: The Atomic Bomb and Cold War Narratives* (Kent, 2012).

## Recommended Reading

Bartels, Sarah. "'A Terrific Ogre': The Role of the Devil in Victorian Popular Belief." *Folklore* 128, no. 3 (2017): 271–91.

Bell, Karl. *The Legend of Spring-heeled Jack: Victorian Urban Folklore and Popular Cultures.* Woodbridge: Boydell and Brewer, 2017.

Faxneld, Per and Jesper A. Petersen (eds.). *The Devil's Party: Satanism in Modernity.* Oxford: Oxford University Press, 2013.

Luijk, Ruben van. *Children of Lucifer: The Origins of Modern Religious Satanism.* New York: Oxford University Press, 2016.

Russell, Jeffrey Burton. *Mephistopheles: The Devil in the Modern World.* Ithaca, NY: Cornell University Press, 1990.

Weinstock, Jeffrey Andrew and Regina M. Hansen (eds.). *Giving the Devil His Due—Satan and Cinema.* New York: Fordham University Press, 2021.

# 23

# THE EMERGENCE OF A "SATANISM PROBLEM"

*Bill Ellis*

For most people living in the middle of the 20th century, the devil was a fictionalised expression of human aspirations and venal temptations. Easily bested by appeals to venerable ideals such as patriotism, the value of hard work, or romantic love, Satan served mainly as a traditional warning not to let personal ambition supersede traditional ethics. More comic than sinister, this religious icon seemed diminished by the growing impact of secularism—like religion itself. "He's just like Santa Claus," a joke commented, "just your dad in a red suit."

In the first part of the century, a number of new religions attempted to appropriate the concept of Satan and use it to embody positive values of the human personality. At the same time, conservative factions within Christianity maintained that the devil was a spiritual threat to believers' immortal souls and the central moving force behind global changes that challenged their faith. Satan was the central figure in modern society that believers felt was entering the chaotic age of tribulation forecast in the book of Revelation. As these fundamentalist factions experimented with "gifts of the Spirit"—that is, altered forms of consciousness—a more dangerous image of the devil came into being. Responding to new religions' revival of the devil concept, evangelicals began to see Satan as an *empirical* menace to society; that is, they defined the devil as a concrete physical threat in the real-life world shared by humans of all faiths. Satan was not just a spiritual threat but the mastermind of a terrestrial conspiracy carried out by a vast horde of demons and the human minions that they controlled. Increasingly, such a worldview influenced secular professions such as law enforcement and psychological therapy, suggesting a world rife with secret societies and conspiracies dedicated to evil.

## New Religions' Use of the Devil Concept

British esoteric movements such as the Hermetic Order of the Golden Dawn had waned in visibility after the start of the century, but one of its members, the flamboyant Aleister Crowley, remained a controversial public figure until his death in 1947. A vocal critic of Christianity and an advocate for a more explicit role for sexuality within religious practices, he was frequently accused of practising Satanism during his lifetime. In truth, he did

444
DOI: 10.4324/9781003096603-24

claim at one point to be "the Beast 666" and incorporated imagery from Revelation in his occult writings. But he emphatically rejected the Christian belief in a devil-god as well as the Christian concept of sin. Instead, Crowley believed that the ultimate goal of humans was to discern their "True Will," or their individual calling in the cosmos. His notorious credo, "Do What Thou Wilt," was not a call to hedonism or sinful self-indulgence but instead a challenge to each follower to seek out and follow their personal calling in life. This mission, however, was no response to a transcendent divine code, but the individual's unique way of finding meaning in an impersonal universe.[1] At times, though, Crowley visualised this "True Will" as a *daimon* or guardian angel dwelling inside each individual's personality.

That said, Crowley visibly enjoyed the controversy that his so-called "Satanic" activity caused in his various residence in England, Europe, and the United States. And so it was inevitable that the public persona he projected became a commonplace stereotype in popular culture. Perhaps the most notable of these was Dennis Wheatley's 1934 novel *The Devil Rides Out* in which a Crowleyesque figure named Damien Mocata heads up a large cult of wealthy and socially powerful devil-worshippers. The novel includes a wide variety of traditional motifs: Mocata is able to hypnotise those he meets through the power of his keen and sinister stare; an open-air orgy climaxes with the manifestation of the evil one; and Mocata is prevented in the nick of time from sacrificing a young child as part of a black mass. This popular image of Crowley, augmented by many unconfirmed rumours and legends about his personal life, became more influential in popular culture than his actual esoteric writings.

But another legacy of Crowley was the impetus he gave to what became the Neo-Pagan or Wicca movement. Earlier in the century, folklorist Margaret Murray (1863–1963) had proposed that the lingering rituals of an "Old Religion" had been demonised as "witchcraft" during the early modern era and forced into the shadows. Her books *The Witch-Cult in Western Europe* (1921) and *The God of the Witches* (1933) attempted to reconstruct this alleged grassroots faith. These attracted many non-academic readers, including some interested in reviving pre-Christian rituals in the present day. Chief among these was Gerald Gardner (1884–1964), an amateur archaeologist and folklorist. Already familiar with Murray's theory, Gardner was introduced to Aleister Crowley shortly before the occultist's death and initiated into his religious movement, the Ordo Templi Orientis. Gardner's role in this movement was short-lived, but a number of Crowley's rituals were copied into his manuscript of the rituals that he claimed the "Old Religion" had practised. "Wicca," the Neo-Pagan movement Gardner founded, grew into a worldwide phenomenon during the 1960s. As in Crowley's philosophy, his religion denied the reality of the Christian Satan but freely appropriated the iconography of the devil. The traditional horns, tail, and cloven hoof, Murray and Gardner believed, showed that witches had once worshipped a masculine divinity that they termed the "Horned God."

The idea that the practice of witchcraft had secretly survived into modern times became a common trope in popular culture, often deployed in a comic mode. The 1942 Paramount screwball comedy *I Married a Witch*, for instance, depicts the romance between a contemporary mortal and a woman who is the reincarnation of one of the Salem witches. John Van Druten's more serious stage play *Bell, Book, and Candle* (1950, adapted to film in 1958) tells of how a witch learns to feel human emotions when a normal male awakens her love. The author commented that he meant the play to challenge society's growing emphasis on self-gratification at the expense of personal growth, perhaps an allusion to Crowley's focus on "True Will."[2] A more influential version of this scenario was the TV sitcom *Bewitched* (1967–1972) which explored the married life of Samantha, a member of a multi-generational witch family. Media studies critic Walter Metz observed that the narrative pattern of the series nominally honoured the prevailing gender stereotypes: Samantha's use of magic is seen by her husband Darrin as transgressive, and episodes end with her apologising to him and promising never to use her occult powers again. Yet the long-term narrative arc of the series requires the witch/housewife to break her promise, over and over, "thus empowering Samantha to override her husband's patriarchal prohibition against magic."[3] In this way, Metz argues, the series represented "a clarion call for social change," directly responding to Betty Friedan's 1963 feminist attack on the portrayal of housewives in television series as mindless and complacent.[4]

Amid wide-ranging protests in the United States, a formal "Church of Satan" was taking shape in the counterculture capital of San Francisco at just this time, too. The movement was led by Anton LaVey (1930–1997), a local musician and celebrity, who had given a series of public lectures on the history of occult movements. Though this church did not actually preach worship of a devil figure, LaVey made much out of its titular connection, formally declaring "the Age of Satan" as beginning on 30 April 1966—a stunt which brought him national notoriety. He furthered this publicity on 1 February 1967 when he conducted a marriage ceremony dressed in a red devil outfit with a horned hood while mobs of reporters and curious teenage spectators clamoured in the street outside to get in.

The sensation caused by the opening of an apparently Satanic "church" was exploited that year by the novel *Rosemary's Baby*, written by novelist Ira Levin and adapted into film the following year. The book graphically describes the ordeal of a woman whose husband is secretly a member of a Satanic cult and who forces her to bear a child to the devil himself. "I don't believe in Satan," Levin later emphasised to a reporter, admitting also that he regretted that this project and others inspired by it gave currency to a "strong fundamentalism."[5] However, LaVey loved the film and bragged that he himself had played the role of Satan in the climactic scene.[6] He further capitalised on his notoriety and the publicity from the film by publishing his *Satanic Bible* in 1969. In his worldview, "Satan" was not a personal spiritual being, but a potent symbol for "opposition to all religions which serve to frustrate and condemn man of his natural instincts."[7] His philosophy, like Crowley's, rejected any moral code imposed on the individual from outside; rather, one's imperative, he asserted, should be self-actualisation, accepting one's personal code of behaviour as itself a reflection of divine nature. While LaVey's gospel of self-worship picked up elements from Friedrich Nietzsche and contemporary authors like Ayn Rand, it also reflects earlier American traditions of freethinking, notably that of Ralph Waldo Emerson who had asserted that "if I am the Devil's child, I will live then from the Devil," adding, "no law can be sacred to me but that of my nature."[8] Through *The Satanic Bible*, sociologist James R. Lewis concluded, "LaVey was able to suggest the reality of mysterious, 'occult' forces while simultaneously appealing to an atheist viewpoint that, he asserted, was supported by modern science."[9]

*The Satanic Bible* initially had a huge impact on the American occult scene. LaVey's credo proved to be particularly influential among the 1960s generation that was questioning older social and moral constructs. Sociologist James R. Lewis found it "the single most important influential document" for the 140 self-identified Satanists that he located in his home state of Wisconsin.[10] Likewise, in his 1970 *The Second Coming*, popular author Arthur Lyons (1946–2008) claimed to have found numerous "Satanic" organisations operating in California, inspired by LaVey's book but not formally affiliated with his organisation. In Great Britain, no formal "Church of Satan" emerged in LaVey's model, but *The Satanic Bible* was published there and avidly read by adolescents. After 1972, however, LaVey's control over the movement waned, and the original Church of Satan became a coalition of "grottoes" unified by a common opposition to institutionalised religions of all kinds. For that reason, many of these offshoots avoided using "Satan" in their movement's name or even in their rituals, opting instead to honour rogue or trickster deities from a wider range of world religions. Among these were "The Temple of Set," founded by LaVey's former associate Michael Aquino, and "Dragon Rouge," founded in 1989 by the Swedish occultist Thomas Karlsson. These groups maintain a worldwide presence, now increasingly through internet web sites.

Sociologist Jesper Aagaard Petersen has called this spectrum of new religions a "Satanic milieu," or a shared reservoir of idea with fuzzy borders. His extensive survey concludes that "few modern, self-professed Satanists feel as a part of a grand movement," many even attacking even the notion of a shared religious community.[11] None of these movements and phenomena, in themselves, has more than a glancing relevance to the historical definition of the devil. None of their proponents—Crowley, Gardner, or LaVey—preached worship of Satan as a real spiritual entity. They saw "Satan" as a face for human personality traits that had been demonised by puritanical Christian ethics and now needed to be acknowledged frankly and given respect. In a similar but opposite way, popular culture used the figure of the devil in a secular way, a comic foil to traditional values—romantic love, hard work, patriotism—and no real threat to anyone.

And yet, by the end of the 1970s, *all* of these popular movements had come to be defined as overt forms of devil-worship by important religious and secular institutions. Aleister Crowley was assumed to be a vicious Satanic high priest who had led a cult that sacrificed children and practised sexual perversions. The Murray/Gardner claim that an underground witch cult had survived as an alternative nature religion became a model for the claim that "intergenerational Satanic cults," dedicated their children to the devil and used their supernatural abilities to infect others with damnable impulses. And in one case, LaVey's book was used by police as *prima facie* evidence that a teenager was a practising member of a dangerous cult. The growth and popularity of the freethinking tradition that led to the Church of Satan gave Christian proponents a plausible target, allowing them to assert that society was imperilled by a real-life "satanism problem."

The religious trends that justified seeing these new religions as literally diabolical had histories of their own which only gradually attached to esoteric religions and neo-paganism. The three most crucial beliefs were:

i that demonic presences were ubiquitous and devoted to manipulating and misleading the minds of every human being;

ii that, as a consequence, secret subversive organisations devoted to evil were also ubiquitous and devoted to the destruction of religions and morals;

iii that the existence of demons and cults could be *empirically* demonstrated through the tactics of spiritual warfare and their analogues in folk traditions.

The rest of the chapter will outline the development of each of these beliefs.

## The Pentecostal Reply: Demons Are Everywhere

When the Christian fundamentalist movement emerged at the turn of the 20th century, belief in Satan and demons initially did not play a large part. Instead, its crucial elements consisted in faith in the literal inerrancy of scripture and the rejection of secular influences such as the theory of evolution and the idea of higher criticism—the latter a liberalising trend that saw biblical writings as reflections of ancient culture. However, when the proponents of this conservative backlash organised their arguments into *The Fundamentals,* a set of 90 essays serialised between 1910 and 1915 and later published in book form in 1917, they included an essay entitled "Satan and His Kingdom" by the Welsh evangelical theologian Jessie Penn-Lewis (1861–1927).[12] This influential author emerged as an early proponent of the Pentecostal revival which had begun at the start of the century in the United States as a series of spirit-filled revivals characterised by intense religious conversions and speaking in tongues. The sect's emphasis on "signs and wonders" born of the Holy Spirit resulted in strong criticism even among fundamentalists who agreed that an "encounter with Christ" was essential for Christians. Penn-Lewis insisted that direct religious experience was central to her faith. "*I want the thing!*" she famously said in describing her own quest.[13] As her sense of faith matured, she recognised that religious experience alone was not the goal: that was "deliverance," which she defined as achieving freedom from the power of sin and Satan.[14] Achieving this spiritual liberation gave her the ability to address audiences with an unprecedented liberty of utterance and she quickly became a much-respected revival leader.

However, as the Pentecostal movement spread, many theologians pointed to its similarities to Spiritualism, then still a popular rival to institutional religion and widely considered a product of the devil by its critics. Alma White (1862–1946), a prominent Methodist preacher, for instance, called followers of the new movement "hypocritical sign-seekers" whose alleged miracles came from "the same old spirit of necromancy and witchcraft that has been manifested in all ages." The ecstasy experienced at revivals, White argued, proves only that "wherever people are given to the over-indulgence of their fleshly appetites, it is an easy matter [for them] to become the victims of witchcraft."[15] Pentecostals responded by becoming experts on how to recognise the workings of the devil. Penn-Lewis's *Fundamentals* essay concedes that true religious experience could be imitated by a "Satanic counterfeit" and included a lengthy list of signs according to which a given encounter could be discerned as godly or devilish. In pagan cultures, she asserts, Satan holds humanity in an explicit state of "gross and open sin," but "in civilised countries, the god of this age needs must veil his working." Lately, though, the prince of darkness has begun to make his presence more manifest. "Books to be popular must be about him," she notes, "while palmistry, clairvoyance, planchette, and other means of intercourse with the spirits of evil, abound on every hand."[16]

In fact, Penn-Lewis adds, Satan "reigns over an aerial kingdom of hierarchies and spiritual powers, and a kingdom on earth in the world of men, and he governs by means of an organized government."[17] The demonic influence is, of course, banished by means of "the thing"—that is, full surrender to the Holy Spirit—but, Penn-Lewis stressed, such gifts are not given to believers for enjoyment alone, but only to motivate them to acts of service. Further, she warns readers, "the adversary knows that the believer has but little knowledge of his foe, so the wiles are soon planned to counterfeit the voice of the Lord, so as to confuse or to mislead the soul, either to destroy his faith in the guidance of the Spirit, or else to lead him in obedience to the voice of the devil, and in strong delusion to believe a lie."[18] And Penn-Lewis admitted that such deceptions were impossible to avoid. God cannot destroy Satan's counterfeits, she reasoned, without also destroying faith in the true gifts of the Spirit. So, like the wheat and tares in Jesus' parable, the works of God and the devil "are always found side-by-side throughout the inhabited earth."[19]

Penn-Warren was centrally involved with the 1904–5 Welsh Revival, an event punctuated by outbreaks of apparently supernatural phenomena. The revival's central figure, the self-taught preacher Evan Roberts, exhibited many mediumistic traits recognised as typical of clairvoyants of the era; however, his career was cut short when he began to fall prey to psychic attacks which he blamed on "hypnotism" or spiritual attacks by demonic spirits.[20] Penn-Lewis offered her home to the convalescent revivalist, who in turn related many of his encounters with supernatural forces during the revival. The result was the 1912 *War on the Saints*, a book that became the doctrinal cornerstone of evangelical demonology. The book argued that the *normal* state for most practising Christians was to be under constant demonic influence. She warned her readers:

> ... the Christian Church must recognize that the existence of deceiving, lying, spirits, is as real in the twentieth century as in the time of Christ, and their attitude to the human race unchanged. That their one ceaseless aim is to lie, and deceive every human being. That they are given up to wickedness all day long, and all night long, and that they are ceaselessly, and actively pouring a stream of wickedness into the world, and are satisfied only when they succeed in their wicked plans to deceive, and ruin men.[21]

Moreover, revival and spirit baptism by no means banished the working of such evil spirits. Neither did abstinence from Spiritualism. Christians who think that they have escaped this occult threat "because they have never been to a séance," she said, need to be aware "that evil spirits attack, and deceive every human being, and they do not confine their working to the Church, or the world, but [attack] wherever they can find conditions fulfilled to enable them to manifest their power."[22] Through her periodical *The Overcomer* and regular religious conferences, Penn-Lewis reached an international audience, and her belief in the universal presence of demonic influence influenced the resurgent Christian movement in the United Kingdom.[23]

The author C. S. Lewis (1898–1963) played a major part in the renewal of institutional religion in Great Britain, and later on in the United States as well. Converting to Christianity as an adult, he came to prominence during World War II by giving a series of informal lectures on the BBC promoting his faith. Later published as *Broadcast Talks* (1942), he tried to give a down-to-earth, ecumenical perspective on Christian doctrine, but in so doing, he also laid special emphasis on the literal existence and relevance of Satan.[24] "I know someone will ask me," he says, "'Do you really mean, at this time of day, to reintroduce our old friend the devil—hoofs and horns and all?' Well, what the time of day has to do with it I don't know. And I'm not particular about the hoofs and horns. But in other respects my answer is 'Yes, I do.'"[25] Lewis represents life as a spiritual battle. Writing to a wartime audience, Lewis describes the world as "enemy-occupied territory," with the enemy—invisible demons—using a variety of tricks to disable Christians from doing God's will. He called his audience to take part in "a great campaign of sabotage" against the works of the devil and compared attending church to "listening in to the secret wireless from our [celestial] friends."[26]

Simultaneously, Lewis composed a series of satirical sketches, entitled *The Screwtape Letters* (1943), which imagined an exchange of directions from a senior demon to a novice who is trying to claim a particular human's soul. The effort fails, but the sketches reflect Penn-Lewis's theology, particularly the notion that even a Christian who avoids obvious sins is, nevertheless, the object of constant demonic interference and at risk of eternal damnation. The novice demon once asks whether the mortal he is tempting should be aware of his actions, to which his mentor responds that the answer is obviously not. Nevertheless, Lewis has the demon reflect that when devils are taken as real by society, the result terrifies most people but makes some want to be "magicians." By contrast, when they are assumed to be imaginary, demons can handily encourage people to be materialists or sceptics. A religion that represents a synthesis of psychoanalysis with vague notions about sexuality and "life force" might, the demon says, lead to the creation of a "Materialist Magician" who worships "forces" while denying belief in "spirits." The arrival of this synthesis (which likely is Lewis's critique of Aleister Crowley's atheistic sense of magick) would mean that "the end of the war will be in sight."[27]

Lewis's book became immensely popular among Christian readers, and it remains so, notably being quoted by American President Ronald Reagan in 1983 in his "evil empire" speech. The core notion of a ubiquitous bureaucracy of demons serving Satan by constantly tempting humans was presented as a fiction in Lewis, to be sure, but it was one that was accepted as essentially factual by a wide range of theologians advocating the practice of spiritual warfare, or the use of prayer to counteract the forces of evil in everyday life.

Particularly influential in this context was German evangelist Kurt E. Koch (1913–1987). Koch grew up in rural southwestern Germany, where magico-religious healing practices were common. Such traditions preserved esoteric symbols and incantations to banish the forces of certain illnesses, many of which were preserved in self-described "magic books." Such practices were held in disfavour by mainstream pastors, both in Europe and in the American diaspora, where the "Pow-wow" tradition was imported by immigrants and remained quietly active well into the 20th century. Many of these magical healers were nominally Christian, quoting verses from scripture or adding invocations of "the three high names" (Father, Son, and Holy Ghost). Nevertheless, Koch believed that such rituals were a forbidden form of witchcraft, using demonic assistance to effect cures, a process that implicitly entailed a pact with Satan.

Beginning with his own encounters with magical healing in rural Germany, Koch compiled a massive database of cases in which magical healings had led to demon possession. From 1962, he published a series of influential textbooks on how to recognise and deal with evidence of demonic obsession. Children were particularly at risk, he thought, as many of the magico-religious charms he discussed were used to heal childhood ailments. Such charming, Koch argued, left "engrams"[28] in the child's developing personality that led to a lifetime of demonic interference; also, the impact of dabbling in forbidden arts could be passed on from parent to child with the same result. "The Civitas Dei, the Kingdom of God," he maintained, "is confronted by the civitas diaboli, the kingdom of Satan."[29] Although his work initially dealt only with Germanic folk traditions, Koch found that his work was received well and applied to many other indigenous forms of occultism in other parts of the world, particularly in the United States. He lectured first there, and then made additional world tours covering Latin America, Australia, and Asia.

In the process, Koch expanded his insights to cover spiritualistic practices of all kinds, also performing exorcisms to liberate subjects whom he had diagnosed as suffering from demon possession. Like Jessie Penn-Lewis, whose work he had read in translation during his seminary years, he came to believe that faith healing and glossolalia were often expressions of demonic power and he frequently passed on stories in which Pentecostal worshippers who spoke fluently in tongues ultimately proved to be subject to demonic influence. In one dramatic example, a tongue-speaker, challenged by a missionary, confessed in a demonic voice that he belonged to "The Church of Satan," and another expressed faith in "the Jesus of Satan." "Jesus" was not a name unique to the Messiah but one common to many contemporaries during his career in the Holy Land, so Koch believed that demons could claim this name to trick unwary Christians who believed that they were in contact with the son of God when, in fact, they were being possessed by evil spirits. At one point Koch's followers denounced the charismatic preacher Oral Roberts (1918–2009) as possessing "mediumistic" healing powers that came from the devil.

The controversy revived the deep division and controversy that first met the emergence of Pentecostalism. It remained unclear when believers could consider themselves safe from demonic influences. Some factions continued to focus on spiritual warfare, using prayer and rituals such as exorcism to confront the hordes of demons in their midst, while others considered baptism in the Spirit as sufficient protection against Satanic influences. The topic was seriously discussed by various evangelical theologians. Dr. V. Raymond Edman (1900–1967), president of the fundamentalist Wheaton College, for instance, agreed that according to Christian doctrine, no demon could possess the body of a believer who had received the Holy Spirit. "However," he added, "I know true Christians who were truly demon possessed."[30] The result was a stalemate, with theology arguing one way and spiritual experience validating a different view. This internal division created a state of perennial tension, it being practically impossible to determine which otherworldly states of mind were heavenly and which were demonic counterfeits. Hence the internal energy that such disputes caused began, from the 1960s onwards, to be projected outwards from these subcultures onto external scapegoats that all factions could agree represented the empirical manifestations of demonic forces that truly bedeviled Pentecostalism.

### The Enemies of God Are Everywhere

Subversion myths, or claims that some mysterious group of evil elites had plans to achieve world domination, have been a part of Western culture for centuries. In the late 1700s, the rogue Masonic lodge, headed by Adam Weishaupt in Bavaria termed "The Illuminati," was suppressed and blamed for various forms of political unrest across Europe, including the French Revolution. During the ensuing century, Masons of all stripes were accused of subversive behaviour, the rumours growing into a media sensation in France with the "Leo Taxil" hoax. Under this pen name, the fraud's perpetrator, Gabriel Jogand-Pages, published a series of exposes and alleged confessions of the members of "Palladian Freemasonry." These stories included ceremonies at secret temples in which Masons worshipped "The Palladium," a goat-headed statue of Satan and witnessed actual apparitions of demonic spirits.[31] The controversy over this sensation gave wider currency to many anti-Semitic and anti-occult motifs. Most importantly, it served as a model for the even more influential subversion myth embodied in *The Protocols of the Learned Elders of Zion*. First published in Russia in 1903, its chief promoter was the mystic Sergei Nilus, who claimed in 1911 that *The Protocols* were a "faithful translation of the original documents that were stolen by a woman from one of the highest and most influential leaders of the Freemasons at a secret meeting somewhere in France."[32]

*The Protocols* purport to be a set of public lectures describing the agenda of a group of elite Jewish conspirators in their quest to achieve world domination. While prolix and repetitive, these lectures present three basic premises. First, they argue that "liberalism" is a deliberately flawed political doctrine that had been created by the Elders of Zion to encourage activists to engage in "the anarchy of protest for the sake of protest" (Protocol 12).[33] Second, to maximise this confusion, the Elders infiltrate institutions such as the press, popular culture, and education to replace faith in God with "arithmetical calculations and material needs" (Protocol 4). Third, an unseen but carefully coordinated cadre of diplomats, bankers, and military leaders foment and encourage disputes, both within countries and between them, constantly upsetting the status quo. As the *Protocols* put it, "it is indispensable to trouble in all countries the people's relations with their governments so as to utterly exhaust humanity with dissention, hatred, struggle, envy and even by the use of torture, by starvation, by the inoculation of diseases, by want, so that the 'goyim' see no other issue than to take refuge in our complete sovereignty" (Protocol 10). The Elders look forward to the time, which seems imminent, when they will make their presence known "by the aid of coups d'état prepared everywhere for one and the same day" (Protocol 15). The document does not explicitly say that this rule will be Satanic in nature, but such a connection was made at once: its final publication in book form bore the subtitle *He is Near, At the Door ... Here comes Antichrist and the reign of the Devil on Earth*. Confronted with evidence that the document was spurious, Sergei Nilus angrily retorted, "You really are under the Devil's influence. Satan's greatest ruse is to make people deny not simply his influence on the things of this world but even his very existence."[34]

Circulating initially in Russia, in part to justify pogroms against Jewish communities there, the text arrived in the West in 1920 through an English translation. An early proponent of *The Protocols* in Britain was author Nesta Webster (1878–1960), who had previously written a revisionist history of the French Revolution, blaming "illuminated Freemasonry" for the fall of Louis XVI. At once she recognised the arguments credited to the Elders as similar to the earlier claims that Masons were covert devil-worshippers. But in her two influential books, *World Revolution* (1921) and *Secret Societies and Subversive Movements* (1924), she argued—in a self-authenticating circle—that the common elements of these conspiracy theories proved that they were all true—and that they all had a supernatural and demonic origin.

> For behind the concrete forces of revolution—whether Pan-German, Judaic, or Illuminist—beyond that invisible secret circle which perhaps directs them all, is there not yet another force, still more potent, that must be taken into account? ... how is it possible to ignore the existence of an Occult Power at work in the world? Individuals, sects or races fired with the desire for world-domination have provided the fighting forces of destruction, but behind them are the veritable powers of darkness in eternal conflict with the powers of light.[35]

Webster held that the tactics used by the conspirators were supernatural as well. "Let us not forget," she warns, "that the cult of Satan ... is practiced to-day in our own country. The powers exercised by the modern Illuminati are occult powers and range from hypnotism to black magic, which ... have always formed part of the stock-in-trade of the sect."[36]

Webster also linked Jews to a range of subversive movements—including the Russian Revolution—while also controlling the media in the West and profiting from illegal drug traffic. Later, she came to be a central propagandist for the British Fascisti, expressing support for Hitler and Mussolini even after the onset of World War II. While Webster's popularity did not last much longer than that, the concept of an all-encompassing world domination plot guided by Satanic forces continued to gain supporters.

One was British-born naval officer William Guy Carr (1895–1959) who followed Webster in linking the Illuminati, the Elders of Zion and communism. His early lectures on the work of "international bankers" relied on *The Protocols* and Nesta Webster's use of them. After retirement from the military, he emigrated to Toronto, Canada in the 1930s and became president of a Catholic auxiliary group named the National Federation of Christian Laymen which disseminated anti-Semitic and anti-Masonic propaganda. His most influential work was *Pawns in the Game* (1955) which claimed that that *The Protocols* had been written in 1773 by the founder of the Rothschild banking dynasty for Jewish conspirators "who had literally 'Sold their souls to the devil.'"[37] Carr called this diabolical cabal "the Synagogue of Satan," appropriating a biblical term previously used in anti-Semitic propaganda. A group of Jewish rabbis, not Weishaupt, had founded the Illuminati lodge, he continued, following "inspirations given to [them] by Lucifer during the performance of their Cabalistic Rites."[38] So the conspiracy revealed in *The Protocols*, he concluded, was indeed the same as the cabal uncovered by Webster, namely the plans by which the Illuminati/Jewish plot would gain world domination.

The seeming omnipresence of Illuminati agents in the political world, according to Carr, demonstrated their alliance with Satan's unseen world of spiritual warfare. Belief in God, Carr argued, "automatically includes belief in supernaturally Good and Evil Spirits which can influence men's minds.... It is the struggle going on for the possession of men's Souls that causes the conditions which prevail upon this earth today."[39] He attributed the seeming unity of the Synagogue of Satan to a kind of spiritual broadcasting system. "If HUMAN Beings can establish radio, and television stations," he argued, "then why shouldn't it be possible for CELESTIAL Beings to broadcast their messages to us?"[40] Just as Christians believe that they receive the grace of God by attending church, praying and receiving the sacraments, Carr added, so the minions of the Illuminati believe that, by engaging in devil-worship rites, they are inoculated by Satan's "evil influence and powers."[41] Readers who are uncertain about the truth of such matters, he concluded, need only "recite the first half of the Lord's Prayer SLOWLY and contemplate on the meaning of those wonderful words of wisdom."[42] When this ritual is carried out, "It doesn't require more than a few minutes to decide if any act to be performed ... is in accordance with the Will of God, or furthering the machinations of the Devil."[43]

Carr's book was hugely influential among America's anti-communist factions, notably the conservative John Birch Society. Indeed, the Illuminati conspiracy theory was paraphrased in *American Opinion*, the society's widely distributed magazine, though Carr's anti-Semitism was softened and his allusions to communism correspondingly made more prominent.[44] From this point on, the Illuminati became an integral part of American subversion mythology while their actual identity—Jewish, communist, or occult—ultimately became irrelevant. The conspirators were evil, undetected and seemingly omnipotent, the human counterparts to the ubiquitous demons that, in the charismatic worldview, were constantly assailing Christian souls. In this way, Jessie Penn-Lewis's and C. S. Lewis's vision of the human mind as a battleground dominated by devils was combined with a political world filled with evil human agents of all kinds. Only mass religious revivals, among all Christian sects, would have any chance of saving society and religion, Carr felt.[45]

The same post-war impulse for a Christian reawakening had brought evangelist Billy Graham (1918–2018) to prominence: during his very first revival meetings in 1949, the evangelist had declared, "Communism is a religion that is inspired, directed and motivated by the Devil himself who has declared war against Almighty God."[46] As his influence among right-wing audiences grew, Graham's teachings increasingly referenced William Guy Carr's conspiracy. By 1957, the evangelist was echoing Carr's belief that the devil was using supernatural forces to advance an empirical international conspiracy. "My own theory about Communism is that it is master-minded by Satan," he told an interviewer, adding "there is no other explanation for the tremendous gains of Communism, in which they seem to outwit us at every turn, unless they have supernatural power and wisdom and intelligence given to them."[47] In 1972, Graham elaborated on this point in a private conversation with President Richard Nixon in the Oval Office, warning the President about the covert actions of "the Synagogue of Satan." These enemies of society, he told Nixon, "are energized by supernatural power … they have a strange brilliance about them. They're smart. And they are energized by supernatural power."[48]

Like Carr, Graham believed that a country-wide religious revival would defeat Satan's subversive conspiracy. But by urging Nixon to take political actions against the "Synagogue of Satan," Graham endorsed what historians have seen as a building trend in the United States through the 20th century: the "crisis mentality" of the conservative wing of Protestant Christianity. Beset by disorienting changes, Robert Fuller argues in his *Naming the Antichrist*, this subculture became obsessed with a sense that Americans were living in the "last days" forecast in Revelation. They constantly looked for signs that would identify the prophesied Antichrist and clarify the significance of the mysterious "666" symbol associated with this sinister being. While the bible does not say that Antichrist was Satan, fundamentalists took it for granted that this figure would be the devil's powerful agent on Earth, and so Americans' watch for his identity progressively politicised the fundamentalists' definition of Christianity. The face of Satan-on-Earth changed according to the emphases of American right-wing politics, being by turns socialist, Jewish, Catholic, communist, liberal, and Islamic. Always, however, this menace represented an empirical threat to American society, not just a spiritual threat to Christian believers.

In truth, the issue of who Antichrist might be was always secondary to the central function of subversion myths. These were always to ensure solidarity *within* the ranks of a religious (or political) subculture by projecting internal dissent outwards onto a common enemy. As Serge Moscovici noted in his 1987 essay, "The Conspiracy Mentality," belief in an evil conspiracy validates those who expose it as well-intentioned and intelligent enough to discover and understand its implications. In addition, he observed, identifying an evil other is a powerful way of muting dissent within an interest group by focusing people's attention towards an external evil. Thus, Moscovici goes on, civil wars are routinely blamed on outside provocation, rather than on unresolved internal dissention. "The possibility of antagonism within the group itself is rejected," he concludes, "by displacing the conflict from the inside to the outside."[49] Hence a subversion myth, folklorist Veronique Campion-Vincent says, "simultaneously reinforce[s] the in-group's cohesion through the designation of enemies."[50] In the end, the combined Antichrist/Illuminati/demonic possession subversion myth came to define the threat simply as "Satanic cults," which had the advantage of bundling in concerns about modern witchcraft revival and the Church of Satan. Proponents of this subversion myth could concede that Wiccans and followers of LaVey were not *deliberately* engaging in worship of the devil; they nevertheless engaged in a global plan directed by the adversary of God. This generated a vast number of empirical targets for identifying Satan's actions on Earth, which provided the charismatic camp relief from its irresolvable internal dispute over which spiritual gifts were Satanic counterfeits.

### Satan Is Everywhere!

By the mid-1970s, Graham was lamenting the extent to which Satan was being mentioned and discussed in all forms of media—books, movies, TV programmes, and rock music. "Even in the Christian world the presses have turned out a rash of books on the devil," he commented, adding, "I personally believe we have more than given the devil his due with too many books about him."[51] Nevertheless, in a book intended to give God's celestial helpers equal time, Graham devotes large sections to reaffirming that Satan is a real being actively working in the world, fomenting wars and other crises while carrying out spiritual attacks on devout Christians. Meanwhile, evangelist Hal Lindsey, who published *The Late Great Planet Earth* in 1970—a best-selling popular book on the imminence of the rapture and second coming of Christ—added his own omnibus description of Satan's workings in the modern world. Entitled *Satan Is Alive and Well on Planet Earth* (1972), the book surveyed what he took to be a recent craze in matters of the occult which included the spread of witchcraft and the worship of Satan. "This book is an attempt to define a personal enemy who rules our world system," Lindsey said in his introduction, adding "whether we know it or not, he also influences every life to some degree."[52] Lindsey's book, a mixture of theology, interviews with Wiccans and occultists, and unconfirmable stories about contacts with demonic forces, gave a sense of the breadth to which the devil had become a topic of discussion both in secular society and among proponents of various factions within fundamentalist Christianity.[53]

Lindsey's book attracted a huge audience both among Christians and curious laypeople. However, the trend towards challenging the devil could have been, like the then-current interest in paranormal and esoteric topics, a self-limiting fad. LaVey's church attracted oversized media attention at its founding, but rapidly declined in membership in the next years. However, the developing image of a vast, invisible "Satanic cult" reflected issues that were deeper seeded in both modern culture and religious history. And these issues were used to construct a wide range of events that demonstrated that the devil was "alive and well on planet earth," not just a religious belief. The final step in demonstrating a "satanism problem" was grounded in what were claimed to be real-life enactments of devil-worship and demonic manifestation. And increasingly, these "real happenings" were denounced by the media and also by secular authorities such as law enforcement agents and psychological therapists.

Among the first of these empirical events were alleged "black magic rituals" reported as factual by law enforcement authorities, first in Great Britain and then, a little later, in the United States. As early as 1954, Robert Fabian, ex-superintendent of Scotland Yard and former head of its vice squad, warned that "Satan-worship" was widespread in the United Kingdom. In any year when 13 December fell on a Sunday, he told the public, devil-worshippers gathered in their secret temples in London where, amid pentagrams and inverted crucifixes, they dedicated young girls and boys to Pan (i.e., the devil) in a "witchcraft rite." Police had no success in infiltrating such groups, he went on, partly because agents feared being hypnotised and brainwashed during their undercover work.[54] British tabloids ran regular features describing alleged "black mass" ceremonies and thefts from churches were often accompanied by suggestions that the items might have been stolen for use in devil-worship rites. Regional panics also focused on remote or disused cemeteries where repeated incidents involved the exhumation of corpses, with bones rearranged in patterns that the police suspected were "occult" in nature. Sceptics suggested that the vandals were scavenging lead and other recyclable metals for resale, but the "black magic" claim continued to be associated with petty thefts and vandalism. A climax came on 13 March 1970 when, after a series of London press reports and TV interviews about occult activities in the disused Highgate Cemetery, the area was overrun by a mob of "vampire hunters" looking for evidence of devil-worship. In the wake of this event, there was a spate of occult-focused media reports, which were followed by lurid reports that claimed there were as many as 10,000 active "black witches" practising in the country.

At the same time, panics were breaking out in the United States, many of them following the 1969 arrest and prosecution of Charles Manson and his "family" for the murders of actress Sharon Tate and six others.[55] Immediately, rumours held that the crime had taken place during some kind of "black mass." When the perpetrators were apprehended, it appeared that Manson had claimed to be an avatar of Jesus Christ while one of his followers, Susan Atkins, had participated in public rituals at LaVey's Church of Satan. Multiple photographs surfaced showing the future murder participant standing with the movement's leader beneath an inverted pentagram. As a result, the group was widely described in the media as being a "real" Satan-worshipping cult, leading to speculation that his "family" had been one of many operating in California.

A more widespread series of panics occurred between 1973 and 1976, when farmers in the Great Plains states found that some of their cattle were dying without warning, their bodies bearing what seemed to be marks of ritual mutilation made with "surgical skill." A common explanation was that Satanists were killing the animals, removing their blood and certain organs (typically a bull's penis) for use in occult ceremonies. Veterinarians found no sign of human involvement and suggested that the animals had died of natural causes and then been visited by natural predators like vultures and coyotes. Nevertheless, the claim that cults were responsible was taken seriously enough that federal agents were called in twice to search for the devil-worshippers responsible. The result of such investigations in both Britain and the United States was the spread of the claim among law enforcement networks that Satanic cults were ubiquitously active in their countries. Police specialists (later termed "cult cops" by sceptics) generated implied patterns of activity that signalled the presence of a cult in a community. Travelling widely, these "experts" disseminated the belief in the cult menace to local police forces as they went.

## Exorcism: Demons Are Real

Added to these criminal suspicions was the growth of professional interest in exorcism both among the general public and in the professional circles of psychological therapists. The 1971 release of American film-maker William Peter Blatty's novel *The Exorcist* generated a sensation, as did the 1973 film (scripted and produced by Blatty). These, however, reflected a Roman Catholic approach to the phenomenon, while in both the States and Britain the less formal Protestant strategy to dispossession proposed by Jessie Penn-Warren was more common. Exorcism is an ancient practice, amply referenced in ancient and New

Testamental times, but it had rarely been practised by mainstream religion in the decades before the book and film appeared.[56] During the earlier days of Spiritualism's popularity, proponents recorded many cases in which "earthbound" spirits apparently afflicted sensitive people, causing them to change personalities and indulge in outbursts of profanity and vulgar behaviour. The American clinical psychologist Carl Wickland (1891–1945) developed a technique by which such spirits could be transferred from the afflicted patient to the consciousness of Wickland's wife, a skilled spiritualist. This allowed the doctor to challenge afflicting spirits (interpreted as the restless dead) and make them leave the patient in peace. His book 1924 *Thirty Years Among the Dead* described his strategies and provided transcripts of these spiritualist "exorcisms."

Penn-Lewis's *War on the Saints* had given a detailed set of instructions on how to practise "deliverance" in cases in which parishioners showed signs of demonic possession, giving a set of case histories at the end of the volume. Koch had also used exorcism in counselling troubled persons whom he suspected of being involved in occult practices such as fortune-telling. He collaborated with Alfred Lechler (1887–1971), a Wiesbaden psychotherapist, to produce a secularised version of his anti-occult ministry in *Occult Bondage and Deliverance* (1970) which he intended for professional mental health counsellors. This work and Koch's other works blaming demons for mental problems, were considered authoritative by Christian mental health therapists in both Britain and the United States. When Notre Dame University hosted a symposium on demon possession as an empirical mental health condition, a number of secular clinical psychologists were invited. Many were profoundly sceptical of this diagnosis; while patients verifiably showed symptoms of mental illness, including exhibiting multiple personalities, it was difficult to demonstrate that an indwelling demon was the empirical cause of this illness. Nevertheless, many clinicians did hold fundamentalist Christian beliefs, including belief in Satan and his demonic minions, so demonic possession was for them a simple and compelling diagnosis. In any case, the printed version of the presentations given at this academic conference, showed authors citing Koch and Lechler's treatise more frequently than any other.[57]

Two key figures in the development of deliverance ministry were H. A. Maxwell Whyte (1908–1988), and Don Basham (1926–1989). Significantly, both had backgrounds in Spiritualism. Whyte, a native of Manchester, England, grew up in a family devoted to the female prophet Joanna Southcott (1750–1814) and his family practised several types of Spiritualism, including automatic writing and séances. Renouncing such practices after his 1939 conversion to Pentecostalism, he founded a charismatic ministry in Toronto, Canada, using deliverance to treat his parishioners' mental and psychological illnesses. Basham was a native of Texas who had initially been attracted to both Pentecostalism and a church that practised spirit mediumship; he was also an admirer of the Canadian spirit medium Arthur Ford, likewise a nominally Christian advisor. In the early 1960s, he met Whyte and was impressed by an exorcism in which the subject collapsed and gave "an eerie laugh, more sinister than anything I had ever heard." Whyte undeterred, commented, "That laugh! I'd recognize it anywhere. Witchcraft!"[58] Both writers travelled widely and published detailed guides which outlined when and how to recognise the signs of demons, listing also ways to cast them out safely and effectively.

Serious discussion of the validity of demonic possession as a mental health condition coincided with clinical attention to what became known as multiple personality disorder. Ralph B. Allison, a clinically trained and licensed psychiatrist, began to study this phenomenon in the early 1970s. He came to believe that the alternate personalities of his patients had origins in moments of extreme trauma, particularly in early youth. He used a variety of strategies, including clinical hypnosis, in order to help patients remember such moments and access what he came to term an "Inner Self Helper" or ISH, a benevolent part of the personality that he believed was "that part of the mind through which God is revealed to the individual."[59] However, he noted that patients also could access their ISH "through visions, automatic writing, speech, and the presence of an inner voice," suggesting again a mode of thought common to Spiritualism. Nevertheless, he found the work of the deliverance movement helpful, agreeing that contact with "witchcraft" could be a source of the disorder and advocating a form of exorcism to treat such patients.[60] "Essentially, I was bringing mental health full circle, combining the best of medicine and religion," he concluded, noting that his family had produced a long line of ministers, and so performing a religious ritual in the context of psychiatry was in his patient's best interest.[61]

The actual nature of what goes on during exorcism is open to interpretation; a compelling explanation for those who witness or experience such rituals is that demons are empirically real and that they are sent by the devil to afflict the righteous. Among secular therapists, a less empirical but equally compelling explanation is that the patients affected had to have been severely traumatised by people practising bizarre and gruesome devil-worship ceremonies. However, anthropologists like Felicitas Goodman have noted that the same phenomenon occurs in other traditions of spirit possession practised by indigenous cultures outside Europe.[62] Sonographic analysis of voice patterns made during spirit possession, Christian exorcism and glossolalia appear to show similarities, suggesting a common neurological phenomenon. This observation may explain explaining why Pentecostal subcultures have difficulty clearly distinguishing genuine signs of the Holy Spirit from "Satanic counterfeits." If spirit baptism and glossolalia reflect a neurological process common to possession and the emergence of demonic personalities, then the two are not opposites but parts of a spectrum of dissociative states, as many Pentecostal critics of the tongues movement argue.

It is also significant that the ritual pattern underlying exorcisms is similar to that developed in folk culture during the same period around the Ouija board, another product of the Spiritualism era. Patented in 1892, this implement helps pairs of users engage in a type of "automatic writing." A pointer on a board painted with the letters of the alphabet and the numbers to ten is held loosely by two users, which then appears to move as if by itself, spelling out messages by moving letter-by-letter or answering yes/no questions. Ouija boards achieved a striking popularity during the occult fad of the 1960s, even among fundamentalist Christian families. Edmund C. Gruss, an early Christian critic of the boards, noted that fully half the students at his Baptist-run seminary had either used one or had a close friend who had. Further, while messages received by Spiritualists involved innocuous forms of fortune-telling, contemporary accounts of the Ouija ritual collected by folklorists emphasise its use to contact and talk to demons—even to Satan himself. Users typically invoke a spirit when using a board, often explicitly asking for a demonic one, then demanding its name. A lengthy dialogue follows, in which the participants test the demon's powers. Eventually, this leads to a confrontation, in which participants demand a sign of the demon's reality—often some startling noise or visual effect. After this, the ritual is terminated.[63]

Deliverance ministers in both Europe and the United States universally condemned participation in this folk tradition and others that constructed messages from spirits in some other mechanical way. Yet a survey of personal accounts suggested that in most cases participation did not cause users to doubt their underlying religious belief; in fact, the information obtained through such dialogues with the "demon" served to validate their pre-existing faith. Much the same was true of the messages given by the diabolical alternate personalities that emerged during exorcism: in fact, both traditions, Ellis concluded, "are mirror-image forms of calling and dismissing demons and hence participating directly in myth."[64] In other words, the quest for material evidence of the existence of demons was a back-door empirical means of demonstrating the existence of God.

This suggests a parsimonious explanation for the rapid emergence of the "satanism problem." As secular science and materialist approaches became more dominant in education and in the professions, fundamentalist Christianity needed a fact-based demonstration of its validity. Evil was ubiquitous; thus, demons enacting evil pervaded human society, in turn, generating Satanic secret societies devoted to destroying religion. Through ritual means such as deliverance, derived from earlier traditions of Spiritualism, the direct existence of these demons could (apparently) be demonstrated beyond doubt. Hence God *needed* to exist to provide the spiritual power to defeat this vast diabolical conspiracy. On the theological front, this created religious subcultures that generated a chronic paranoia about folk devils assumed to exist in every part of society. As this worldview penetrated secular networks of professional law enforcement officers and therapeutic psychological therapists, it generated opportunities to strike back against Satan's kingdom by detecting and prosecuting cult members wherever they were perceived to be active.

## Notes

1   Aleister Crowley, "Duty: A Note on the Chief Rules of Practical Conduct to Be Observed by Those Who Accept the Law of Thelema," *Essays*, U.S.A. Library, Ordo Templi Orientis. https://lib.oto-usa.org/crowley/essays/duty.html

2   Jay Weston, "Bell, Book and Candle at Colony Theatre in Burbank," *HuffPost News*, 22 October 2010. https://www.huffpost.com/entry/book-and-candle-at-colony_b_771779

3   Walter Metz, *Bewitched, TV Milestones Series* (Detroit, 2007), 41.

4   Metz, *Bewitched*, 18.

5   Mary McNamara, "The Art of Darkness," *Los Angeles Times*, 22 September 2002. https://www.latimes.com/archives/la-xpm-2002-sep-22-lv-levin22-story.html

6   He didn't: the role was enacted by bit-player Clay Tanner who had a career of playing walk-on parts in TV series.

7   Anton LaVey, *The Satanic Bible* (New York, 1967), 55.

8   "Self-Reliance," originally published in 1841 in Emerson's *Essays: First Series* and frequently anthologised well into the 20th century.

9   James R. Lewis, "Who Serves Satan? A Demographic and Ideological Profile," *Marburg Journal of Religion* 6, no. 2 (June 2001), 17.

10  Lewis, "Who Serves Satan?" 5.

11  Jesper Aagaard Petersen, "Introduction: Embracing Satan," *Contemporary Religious Satanism: A Critical Anthology*, ed. Jesper Aagaard Petersen (Farnham, 2009), 5.

12  This essay was an abridged version of an earlier pamphlet, entitled *The Warfare with Satan and the Way of Victory*, based on lectures presented in 1897 and first printed in 1908. I have used *The Fundamentals* version as it arguably was the more widely distributed and influential version.

13  Mary N. Garrard, *Mrs. Penn-Lewis: A Memoir* (Westbourne, 1947), 22. Italics are Penn-Lewis's.

14  Jessie Penn-Lewis, *War on the Saints: A Text Book for Believers on the Work of Deceiving Spirits among the Children of God* (Leicester, 1912), 179 ff. For a discussion of how "deliverance" became a key concept among Pentecostal Christians, see Stephen Hunt, "Deliverance: The Evolution of a Doctrine," *Themelios* 21, no. 1 (October 1995). https://www.thegospelcoalition.org/themelios/article/deliverance-the-evolution-of-a-doctrine/

15  Alma White. *Demons and Tongues* (Bound Brook, 1910), 16.

16 Jessie Penn-Lewis. "Satan and His Kingdom," in *The Fundamentals: A Testimony to the Truth*, vol. 10 (Chicago, 1917), 50.

17 Penn-Lewis, "Satan and His Kingdom," 51.

18 Penn-Lewis, "Satan and His Kingdom," 63.

19 Penn-Lewis, "Satan and His Kingdom," 62. The author is citing Matthew 13.24–30.

20 For a detailed survey of the occult and paranormal elements in the Welsh Revival, see Bill Ellis, *Lucifer Ascending: The Occult in Folklore and Popular Culture* (Lexington, 2004), 199 ff.

21 Penn-Lewis, *War on the Saints*, 44. Her unusual approach to punctuation, perhaps a reflection of her oral preaching delivery, has been retained.

22 Penn-Lewis, *War on the Saints*, 41.

23 For a wider discussion of Jessie Penn-Lewis's theology and career, see Sharon Baker-Johnson, "The Life and Influence of Jessie Penn-Lewis," *Christians for Biblical Equality International*, 30 April 2012. https://www.cbeinternational.org/resource/life-and-influence-jessie-penn-lewis

24 This was later revised and published more widely as *Mere Christianity*. I have used the earlier edition here.

25 C. S. Lewis, *Broadcast Talks* (London, 1942), 46.

26 Lewis, *Broadcast Talks*, 46.

27 Lewis, *Broadcast Talks*, 39.

28 L. Ron Hubbard's more notorious use of this term in Scientology comes independently from the German medical research used by Koch.

29 Kurt E. Koch and Alfred Lechler, *Occult Bondage and Deliverance. Advice for Counseling the Sick, the Troubled and the Occultly Oppressed* (Grand Rapids, 1970), 25.

30 *Victory Over Demonism Today*, ed. J. Russell Meade (Wheaton, 1963), 34–5.

31 The goal of Palladian Freemasonry, "Taxil" said, was to infiltrate and overthrow all governments using magical means to communicate instantly with Masons' minions around the world. In 1897, facing increasing demands to show his evidence for these exposes, Jogand-Pages held a press conference in which he admitted that the whole affair was "a practical joke" at the expense of the Catholic Church and the anti-Masonic critics it had encouraged. Nevertheless, as often happens with hoaxes, many people who had been the target of the satire continued to believe that there was some truth behind the alleged conspiracy. The "Palladium," or horned statue of the devil, continues to be used by critics of Christianity, often facetiously, though now it is usually referred to as a "Baphomet." A popular survey of this hoax is presented by Henry T. F. Rhodes, in *The Satanic Mass: A Sociological and Criminological Study* (London, 1954), 179–98. An even more detailed contemporary account is Arthur Edward Waite, *Devil-Worship in France: or, The Question of Lucifer* (London, 1896). Waite was a central member of the British esoteric Order of the Golden Dawn, one of the most influential occult organisations in the Anglo-American tradition, and he wrote the book because "Taxil" had called out one of his fellow members as part of the international network of Satanic Masons.

32 Morris Kominsky, *The Hoaxers: Plain Liars, Fancy Liars, and Damned Liars* (Boston, 1970), 209.

33 The *Protocols* have been made available widely in cheap reprints and online by a variety of religious and conspiracy-minded organisations. I have used the most commonly available translation by Victor E. Marsden (London, 1923) and referenced quotations and paraphrases by the number of the protocol in which they appear.

34 Norman Cohn, *Warrant for Genocide: The Myth of the Jewish World-Conspiracy and the Protocols of the Elders of Zion* (New York, 1967), 92.

35 Nesta H. Webster, *Secret Societies and Subversive Movements* (New York, 1924), 404–5.

36 Nesta H. Webster, *World Revolution: The Plot against Civilization* (London, 1921), 325.

37 William Guy Carr, *Pawns in the Game* (Willowdale, 1955), 26 ff.

38 Carr, *Pawns in the Game*, 32.

39 Carr, *Pawns in the Game*, 3.

40 Carr, *Pawns in the Game*, 7.

41 Carr, *Pawns in the Game*, 36.

42 That is, stop before one gets to "And lead us not into temptation, but deliver us from evil." Evan Roberts used a similar means of consulting the Holy Spirit on decisions he made while engaged in the Welsh Revival. Penn-Lewis afterwards concluded that such practices were spiritually dangerous. "Those who have their eyes opened to the opposing forces of the spiritual realm," she

cautioned, "understand that very few believers can guarantee that they are obeying *God, and God only, in directly supernatural guidance,* because there are so many factors liable to intervene, such as the believer's own mind, own spirit, own will, and the deceptive intrusion of the powers of darkness. Since evil spirits can counterfeit God as Father, son, or Holy Spirit, the believer needs also to know very clearly the principles upon which God works, so as to detect between the Divine and the Satanic workings." Penn-Lewis, *War on the Saints*, 53.

43 Carr, *Pawns in the Game*, 178.

44 Robert Welch, "More Stately Mansions" in his *The New Americanism and Other Speeches and Essays* (Belmont, 1966), 125–6.

45 Carr, *Pawns in the Game*, 179–80.

46 Billy Graham, "We Need Revival," in *Revival in Our Time* (Wheaton, 1950), 55. This sermon text is not dated, but Graham's introduction shows it was preached during the revival meetings held in Los Angeles between 25 September and 20 November 1949, the event that brought the evangelist to national attention.

47 Billy Graham, "Does a Religious Crusade Do Any Good?" *US News & World Report*, 27 September 1957, 78. For a fuller survey of Graham's use of the communism menace in his preaching, see William Gerald McLoughlin, *Billy Graham: Revivalist in a Secular Age* (New York, 1960), 138–41.

48 Mike Hertenstein, "Conversation Nº662-4: Key Sources for 'Billy Graham & the Synagogue of Satan'." *Medium*, 29 July 2018. https://medium.com/@mikeh_50175/conversation-662-4-291aa74083a5. For a broader view of this controversy, see Mike Hertenstein, "Billy Graham & the Synagogue of Satan," *Medium*, 28 July 2018. https://medium.com/@mikeh_50175/billy-graham-the-synagogue-of-satan-681360ae5b99. Critics of Graham claimed that this taped remark (embargoed by the Nixon Library until the preacher's death) demonstrated his anti-Semitism. A simpler explanation is that Graham accepted Carr's notion that though the chief conspirators of the Illuminati were Jewish, that did not mean that *all* Jews were evil, just the ones who used unholy powers obtained from Satan.

49 Sergei Moscovici, "The Conspiracy Mentality," *Changing Conceptions of Conspiracy*, ed. Serge Moscovici and Carl Friedrich Graumann (Berlin, 1987), 153.

50 Veronique Campion-Vincent, "From Evil Others to Evil Elites: A Dominant Pattern in Conspiracy Theories Today," in *Rumor Mills: The Social Impact of Rumor and Legend*, ed. Gary Alan Fine, Veronique Campion-Vincent and Chip Heath (New Brunswick, 2005), 107.

51 Billy Graham, *Angels: God's Secret Agents* (Garden City, 1975), 5–6.

52 Hal Lindsay, *Satan Is Alive and Well on Planet Earth* (Grand Rapids, 1972), 11.

53 The book, for instance, gives a carefully worded discussion about whether glossolalia is Satanically inspired, taking Jessie Penn-Lewis's position that it is indeed a genuine gift of the Holy Spirit, but that practitioners should be constantly on watch against similar phenomena that are diabolical counterfeits. See Penn-Lewis, *War on the Saints*, 284–9.

54 Robert Fabian, *London after Dark* (London, 1954), 74–6.

55 See also Chapter 24.

56 The obvious exception is the case on which Blatty based his novel, which had been conducted under formal Catholic supervision in 1949 in St. Louis, Missouri. That was extensively covered by *The Washington Post* at the time of the exorcisms, with more details published in the wake of the novel/movie. For a broader study of the impact of this case, see Joseph P. Laycock and Eric Harrelson, *The Exorcist Effect: Horror, Religion, and Demonic Belief* (New York, 2023).

57 *Demon Possession: A Medical, Historical, Anthropological and Theological Symposium*, ed. John Warwick Montgomery, (Minneapolis, 1976).

58 Don W. Basham, *Deliver Us from Evil* (Washington Depot, 1972), 111–2.

59 Ralph Allison with Ted Schwarz, *Minds in Many Pieces: The Making of a Very Special Doctor* (New York, 1980), 109.

60 Allison, *Minds in Many Pieces*, 198.

61 Allison, *Minds in Many Pieces*, 83.

62 Felicitas Goodman, *How About Demons? Possession and Exorcism in the Modern World* (Bloomington, 1988), 6–9.

63 Bill Ellis, *Raising the Devil: Satanism, New Religions, and the Media* (Lexington, 2000), 67–73.

64 Ellis, *Raising the Devil*, 78.

## Select Bibliography

Cohn, Norman. 1967. *Warrant for Genocide: The Myth of the Jewish World-Conspiracy and the Protocols of the Elders of Zion*. New York: Harper & Row.

Ellis, Bill. 2000. *Raising the Devil: Satanism, New Religions, and the Media*. Lexington: University of Kentucky Press.

Ellis, Bill. 2004. *Lucifer Ascending: The Occult in Folklore and Popular Culture*. Lexington: University of Kentucky Press.

Fuller, Robert. 1995. *Naming the Antichrist: The History of an American Obsession*. Oxford: Oxford University Press.

Goodman, Felicitas. 1988. *How about Demons?: Possession and Exorcism in the Modern World*. Bloomington: Indiana University Press.

Kelly, Aidan A. 1991. *Crafting the Art of Magic, Book I: A History of Modern Witchcraft, 1939-1964*. St. Paul, MN: Llewellyn.

Petersen, Jesper Aagaard, ed. 2009. *Contemporary Religious Satanism: A Critical Anthology*. Farnham, Surrey: Ashgate.

# 24

# COMMUNITIES, PURITY AND CONSPIRACY

*Sarah A. Hughes*

In the 1980s, a far-reaching "satanic panic" brought fears of devil-worship to renewed—and at times unprecedented—heights across various regions of the Anglophone world. While anxieties over Satanism were most pronounced in the United States, they also appeared to a significant degree in parts of Canada, the United Kingdom, Australia and South Africa and lasted into the 1990s. The panic primarily manifested in the form of hundreds of accusations of "satanic ritual abuse," a recently articulated phenomenon involving abuse as part of devil-worshipping practices. This resulted in the arrest and imprisonment of dozens of people around the globe. Defendants in ritual abuse cases were most often daycare centre owners and employees, or those tasked with caring for children in some capacity, demonstrating that the era's fears over devil-worship were primarily concerned with corruption of the young, and a function of shifting gender roles. Other aspects of the panic included fears over demonic possession, devil-worshipping cults and Satanic messages—particularly in the music industry—which again were generally targeted towards young people.

The panic coincided with a noticeable expansion in stories and images about the demonic. Beginning in the late 1960s, notions of the devil began to regain cultural prominence, fuelled by an increasingly symbiotic relationship between sensational news media, horror movies, heavy metal music, conservative politics and religion, and a cultural fascination with the occult. While facets of these trends were visible throughout the Western world—and various parts of the non-West as well—they were most evident in the United States, followed by the United Kingdom and Canada. The Satanic panic of the 1980s reveals the tremendous emphasis the United States and other globally dominant Western powers were coming to place on their respective news and entertainment media, which not only grew in scale due to the deregulatory policies enacted by conservative politicians but which also became harder to distinguish from one another—particularly in terms of the genre of "infotainment," an increasingly popular style of tabloid television that privileged more sensational and outrageous stories.

The politics of the era were increasingly dictated by the "New Right," a loose coalition of various conservative groups that reached its apex in the 1980s with the election of Ronald Reagan as the President in the United States and Margaret Thatcher as the Prime Minister in the United Kingdom. The religious wing of the New Right was composed primarily

DOI: 10.4324/9781003096603-25

of evangelical Christians, who began building megachurches, sending their missionaries all over the world and saturating the airwaves with the message of their televangelist preachers.[1] By the late 1970s, conservative evangelicals had eclipsed the Catholic Church as the dominant voice of the Christian right. This transformed cultural representations of the devil. They became more pronounced, more wedded to television and fundamentally tied to the reactionary politics of the New Right, particularly in terms of its antagonism towards science, feminism and the counterculture of the 1960s. As the New Right rejected the complex social movements of the previous decades, it idealised white suburbia and the nuclear families residing within it. The devil in the 1980s was most often portrayed as a backlash figure who terrorised the residents of otherwise tranquil white suburban neighbourhoods.

Ritual abuse cases—and the Satanic panic of which they were a part—were both a reflection and endorsement of the New Right's political and cultural ascent. The suburban backdrop of the panic indicated that the New Right's hostility to racial diversity and its elevation of suburbia to mythic status were particularly evocative among the white middle class. Conservatives openly rejected the racial activism—and calls for power, justice and equality—adopted by various social movements of the 1960s. As they attacked and undermined novel policies designed to enhance diversity across a range of social institutions and cultural arenas through the next decades, they cast suburbia as an idyllic safe-haven—a place of divine refuge that was characterised not only by its isolation from political instability, but by its homogenous racial composition. However, for conservatives, white suburbia's status as a sanctified fortress was matched only by its perceived vulnerability. A rotating cast of enemies both global and domestic, real and imagined, seemed to constantly threaten its destruction. The children residing there appeared to them as purveyors of innocence and virtue, seemingly the last bastion of hope for defeating suburbia's growing list of enemies. Ritual abuse cases helped reinforce these representations and bolster the image of white suburbia as a sacred space constantly threatened by demonic evil.

### The "Diabolical Wagon"

In 1983, a woman named Judy Johnson accused Ray Buckey, a young male employee at the McMartin Preschool in Manhattan Beach, California, of sexually assaulting her two-year-old son at the daycare. After medical specialists confirmed Johnson's claims, police arrested Buckey and social workers arrived to interview the daycare children. Although many of the children initially denied the claims against Buckey, interrogation sessions led to accusations that the children were being used in child pornography and were being forced to participate in ritual abuse at the preschool. This included mutilating and slaughtering animals, digging up bodies, and brainwashing children into complicity. Hundreds of charges were filed against Buckey and his grandmother, preschool owner Virginia McMartin, as well as his mother, sister and other centre employees. In early 1984, police shut down the preschool and Los Angeles-based reporter Wayne Satz broke the story on station KABC's local news. Soon, hundreds of similar cases began to emerge around the country. Over the next few years, as cases spread across the United States, they also cropped up in parts of Canada, England, Wales, Northern Ireland and Australia.

In the United States, most ritual abuse cases centred on white middle-class suburban daycare centres, where centre owners and employees faced charges of conspiracy and abuse tied to Satanic rituals. Many of the cases that emerged in the wake of Buckey's arrest received national attention. In 1984, Gerald Amirault, a young male employee at Fells Acres day care centre in Malden, Massachusetts, was sentenced to 18 years in prison after he was accused of crimes similar to Ray Buckey's.[2] A year later, in a suburb of Dade County, Miami, Frank and Ileana Fuster were arrested for ritually abusing children in the daycare they ran out of their home.[3] In 1988, aspiring actress and daycare centre worker Margaret Kelly Michaels was sentenced to 47 years in prison after children at Wee Care in Maplewood, New Jersey, accused her of torture and abuse.[4] Dozens of other, less well-publicised cases also emerged into the early 1990s.

A number of additional cases, including many of those in other countries, involved parents or guardians, police officers, teachers and members of the community. In Thurston County, Washington, for instance, Paul Ingram, Chief Civil Deputy of the Sheriff's department, spent over a decade in jail after being sentenced in 1987 for ritually abusing his two daughters.[5] In Canada, a few cases that began in 1985 in Hamilton, Ontario, involved children accusing their parents of Satanic ritual abuse, although criminal charges were never filed there due to a lack of evidence.[6] In 1992, accusations in a case in Saskatchewan against nine residents had "overtones of a satanic cult."[7] In 1989, teachers at Seabach Kindergarten in Sydney, Australia, "were arrested and accused of occult sexual abuse."[8] A year later, police there formed a task force to deal with the problem.[9] And in Britain, between 1988 and 1990, "evidence of satanism, black magic and witchcraft has featured in 14 wardship cases involving 41 children," reported British daily newspaper *The Independent*.[10] With the exception of McMartin and a few other cases, many defendants spent years or decades in prison until their cases were ultimately overturned. As the tide of public opinion shifted in the early 1990s, public sympathies switched from the accusers to the accused. Increasingly, the entire panic was condemned as a witch hunt or the result of mass hysteria.

Ritual abuse cases marked the apex of several intersecting trends that began to pick up pace in the late 1960s. Beginning in 1968, a marked resurgence in interest in the devil was partly catalysed through news reports and horror movies, which increasingly fed off of one another. The theatrical release of the horror film *Rosemary's Baby* in the United States and Canada in June 1968 "started the diabolical wagon rolling," remarked an article in the popular American weekly newsmagazine *Newsweek* in 1979.[11] The film portrays the story of a blonde newlywed named Rosemary Woodhouse who is forcibly and unknowingly raped and impregnated by the devil. At the end of the film, Rosemary discovers that her husband, doctor and neighbours in her Manhattan apartment building are actually members of a devil-worshipping cult who used her to carry Satan's offspring. The film was a commercial success and was released in several other countries, including the United Kingdom, after its premiere.[12] It brought global fame to its relatively unknown director Roman Polanski who, in late 1969, became tied to another story of devil-worship in the form of the Manson murders.[13]

In August 1969, cult leader Charles Manson ordered his followers—known as his "family"—to murder several high-profile individuals, including business owners Leno and Rosemary LaBianca, coffee heiress Abigail Folger and actress Sharon Tate, who at the time was pregnant and had recently married Polanski. The murders, which took place in the wealthy suburbs of Los Angeles, California, immediately became a point of media fascination, particularly on television. Following the indictment of Manson and several members of his group in December 1969, national network evening news in the United States ran more than 140 segments on their trials up to its conclusion in 1971.[14] While reports on the group emphasised their homicidal violence and alleged Satanic practices, they also indicated a growing relationship between the news media and fictional entertainment, particularly with respect to horror movies. Many reports focused on what reporters took to be the uncanny parallels between *Rosemary's Baby* and aspects of the Manson murders—both Rosemary Woodhouse and Sharon Tate were blonde, pregnant newlyweds. Despite the death of several individuals at the hands of the Manson family, the media fixated on the murder of Tate, focusing on the alleged Satanic practices of the Manson clan, making her—like Rosemary—the victim of a devil-worshipping cult. The suspects "specialized in religious killings," reported a national evening news segment on ABC's *World News Tonight* in December 1969.[15] "Witness Recalls Manson as 'Devil,'" ran a 1970 headline in the reputable daily American newspaper *New York Times*.[16] In the aftermath of the Manson murders, many news sources went to great lengths to depict Manson's family as a devil-worshipping cult, much like the one presented in *Rosemary's Baby*. This trend was most pronounced in the United States, but was evident in other areas, too, particularly the United Kingdom, where coverage of the murders was also significant.

While news reports about the Manson murders continuously forged connections between movies and reality, they also indicated how growing backlash politics would shape subsequent stories about devil-worship. Media sources explicitly linked Manson and his family to the 1960s counterculture—or social movements that reacted against the conservative Cold War ideals at the time. News reports in both the United States and the United Kingdom frequently linked the group's "hippie" lifestyle, which included communal living and psychedelic drug use, to their violence and alleged devil-worship.[17] A contemporary report in *The New York Times* explained that while Manson explicitly rejected the "hippie" label, he was referred to as such by "the police and the news media."[18] This connection between the counterculture and the occult would grow more pronounced in the next decades with the rise of infotainment and the New Right.

In the 1970s, the devil became further entrenched in the cultural mainstream with a slew of popular horror movies about demonic possession that capitalised on the success of *Rosemary's Baby* and continued to provide material for news reports. The most successful of these included *The Exorcist* (1973), *The Omen* (1976) and *The Amityville Horror* (1979). In *The Exorcist,* based on a 1971 novel of the same name and released on 26 December 1973 in the United States and Canada, twelve-year-old Regan MacNeil is possessed by a demonic entity following her communication with a spirit through an ouija board. It was the top grossing movie of the year. It was followed three years later by *The Omen*, which presents the story of a young boy named Damien who is revealed to be the Antichrist and seeking global destruction; it too was a major commercial success,[19] and immediately spawned a sequel, *Damien: Omen II* (1978), which came out a year after a sequel to *The Exorcist—Exorcist II: The Heretic* (1977). For its part, *The Amityville Horror* was allegedly based on a true story—in this case, of the Lutz family, who claimed to have moved into a haunted house after a real-life murder had occurred there. The film was adapted from author Jay Anson's 1977 best-selling book of the same name and compiled from his interviews with George and Kathy Lutz.[20]

The news media tried quickly to exploit the success of these films using their popularity as a pretext for segments on aspects of the demonic—often conflating reported fact with images from the films.[21] In a feature on exorcism for a February 1974 news segment, *CBS Evening News* reported that *The Exorcist* was based on the true story of the exorcism of a fourteen-year-old girl, but embellished the piece with clips from the film.[22] Similarly, a 1976 CBS report on national interest in the devil included scenes from *Rosemary's Baby*, *The Exorcist* and *The Omen*.[23]Ahead of *The Amityville Horror*'s national premiere, the

Lutz family insisted on ABC's daily morning news show *Good Morning America* that the terrifying paranormal experiences depicted in the film—which included swarms of flies, foul smells and slime dripping from keyholes, as well as patriarch George descending into madness—had actually happened to them.[24]

The prevalence and success of these films revealed and compounded a growing cultural fascination with the occult that was partly tied to the decade's emerging New Age movement, which included an interest in alternative religions, beliefs, philosophies and practices. Along with facets of major religions such as Buddhism, Christianity and Islam, the New Age movement incorporated "pagan" teachings, as well as practices like Wiccan and shamanic rituals.[25] In the 1970s, the movement swept through the United States and emerged to varying degrees in Canada, the United Kingdom and in parts of western Europe. By the end of the decade, New Age interest in astrology, psychics, healing crystals and channelling the spirit realm often encouraged, and sometimes overlapped with, exploration into other aspects of the supernatural and the occult, including hauntings, demonic possession, devil-worship, UFOs and alien abduction.[26] As infotainment gained momentum in the 1980s, this new genre took a keen interest in these topics, validating them and providing them with relevance and traction.

## *Child's Play*

At the dawn of the 1980s, many of the previous decade's trends regarding the demonic both intensified and were transformed. Cultural attention to the devil continued but underwent pronounced shifts in large part due to the meteoric rise of televangelism. Mostly concentrated in the United States, televangelists—or evangelical preachers on television—achieved success and influence around the world over the course of the period. They included Jim and Tammy Faye Bakker, Pat Robertson, Jerry Falwell, James Robison, Billy Graham, Oral Roberts and Jimmy Swaggart. While they came to use and control a growing number of mass media platforms, they primarily chose television to spread their doctrine. They broadcast multiple times a day on cable channels, national networks and religious stations like Pat Robertson's Christian Broadcasting Network (CBN) and the Bakker's Praise the Lord Television Network (PTL). Swaggart—one of the most popular televangelists until his career was derailed by scandal at the end of the decade—claimed that television was his "manifest destiny."[27] By the mid-1980s, tens of millions of Americans regularly tuned in each month to watch television preachers.[28]

As television technology improved, televangelists also gained success and recognition beyond the borders of the United States. Swaggart, for instance, gained a substantial following in Latin America, which had a large and growing evangelical population.[29] By the mid-1980s, *The PTL Club* (1976–present), the PTL network's anchor talk show hosted by the Bakkers, was available in dozens of countries. In Canada, it joined successful Christian variety show *100 Huntley Street* (1977–present), hosted by Canadian televangelist David Mainse and produced by his organisation, Crossroads Christian Communications.[30] However, the Canadian Radio-Television and Telecommunications Commission (CRTC) remained sceptical about the "unregulated" model of religious broadcasting that had emerged in the United States and did not begin granting licenses for satellite-distributed national religious broadcasting until the 1990s.[31] In parts of Europe, where religious content was even more limited, PTL offered some of the only evangelical programming on the air.[32]

Televangelists and other conservative groups helped ignite a backlash against progressive social movements. Their preaching often centred on identifying Satanic forces—or "the Antichrist"—which increasingly they found underlying the work of activists from the 1960s and 1970s who had agitated for social reforms and rejected aspects of the prevailing Cold War ideology. Televangelists were particularly concerned about feminism and made it a central target of their preaching, portraying it as threatening and destructive.[33] The legalisation of abortion in 1973, which was tied to feminist advocacy, motivated Falwell to make a foray into Republican politics. After criticising feminism in a 1984 televised sermon in Cincinnati, Ohio, Jimmy Swaggart reminded the packed stadium that he was telling them "some of the dangers that are in this nation to try to destroy the Judeo-Christian concept which has given us Western civilization, Western culture, and every freedom that we have today."[34]

Perceived as a threat to traditional gender roles by encouraging women to work or to pursue interests outside the home, televangelists and other conservatives took aim at feminism and endeavoured to vilify working women and mothers, often demonising them in the process. The apparent "dangers" of women leaving their traditional roles is underscored by some of the most popular films of the period. In *The Exorcist*, for instance, Regan's mother is a single working actress. Her busy schedule filming a movie nearby gives her daughter plenty of time without parental supervision. This leaves Regan free to play with the ouija board she discovers in the basement of her house and to become possessed as a result. The film was one of the first to articulate what became an increasingly common trope in the horror films of the period: children or teenagers dabbling in the occult beyond the purview of their parents, who are otherwise too preoccupied or unconcerned to notice. The 1983 film *Amityville 3-D* is another case in point. It centres on the daughter of a divorced male journalist—who has moved into the house in the first *Amityville* film—and dies after she and her friends play with an ouija board. The message these and other films make is clear: children whose parents—especially their mothers—are too busy to fulfil their traditional roles often inadvertently leave open doorways to the demonic. As such, these films reflect an anxiety about the era's shifting family dynamics, which saw both rising divorce rates and unprecedented numbers of women joining the workforce. These trends were seen as dangerous to children and to society more generally.[35]

To some extent, these fears seemed to be borne out by the rise of ritual abuse cases, for they frequently reflected concerns about shifting gender roles, especially in terms of working women. Virginia McMartin was a small business operator. Though she had once been considered "a pillar of the community," and had received recognition for her community service four times, the accusations levelled against her daycare turned her into a figure in league with the devil.[36] Other working women caught up in ritual abuse cases included Gerald Amirault's mother and sister, both of whom ran Fells Acres; Frank Fuster's wife, Ileana, who ran Country Walk; Margaret Kelly Michaels, who worked at Wee Care; and two women involved in the Saskatchewan case who worked at a daycare service.[37] While not all the working women accused in ritual abuse cases were mothers, they collectively appeared to reinforce the decade's increasingly popular "bad mothering" trope as they allegedly terrorised the surrogate children in their care.

Published accounts of alleged ritual abuse from private therapy sessions were another common means by which stories of demonic "bad mothers" circulated. The 1980 book *Michelle Remembers* describes therapy sessions in which a woman named Michelle Smith claimed to recover memories of being ritually abused as a child by a devil-worshipping cult in Victoria, British Columbia. Co-written by Smith and her psychiatrist Dr. Lawrence Pazder, the book casts Smith's deceased mother as the main villain, describing her as a "disturbed, peculiar woman" who abuses Smith as part of Satanic rituals and ceremonies.[38] While Pazder and Smith were based in British Columbia, they travelled extensively around North America in the wake of the book's success, even visiting Manhattan Beach in 1985 to talk with McMartin parents and children.[39]

Smith and Pazder's book launched a crusade against ritual abuse that reached its apex with criminal cases like McMartin. But it also spurred similar stories in books and news reports about adults apparently "remembering" their forced Satanic cult participation as children—these, too, often involved the alleged victims' mothers acting in some demonic capacity. These "repressed memories," as they were termed, usually emerged during one-on-one therapy sessions with the patient, who was sometimes under hypnosis. Several such patients were also diagnosed with multiple personality disorder (MPD)—currently known as dissociative identity disorder (DID)—a "dramatic condition" argued to be an adult coping mechanism for dealing with repressed childhood trauma.[40] According to the American Psychiatric Association, symptoms of MPD typically included two or more "distinct identities" that are each accompanied by behavioural changes and "gaps in memory."[41] While cases before the 1970s were extremely rare, by the 1980s reports in both the United Kingdom and the United States put the number of MPD diagnoses in the thousands.[42] According to a 1988 article in London's *The Guardian*, the majority of patients were women.[43]

In his 1991 *Satan's Children: Shocking True Accounts of Satanism, Abuse, and Multiple Personality*, author and psychiatrist Dr. Robert S. Mayer recounts stories of ritual abuse from some of his patients—all of whom were also diagnosed with MPD. Under hypnosis, a female patient named "Randall" remembered that her controlling mother had once put a hood over her head and driven her somewhere to perform the ritual sacrifice of another child.[44] Another female patient, "Rebecca," told Mayer about her participation as a child in similar rituals after her mother had driven her out to the woods.[45] Through a personality named "Arlene," Rebecca told Mayer that she was forced to "do whatever Momma says or terrible things will happen to us."[46] In both cases, the patients' mothers had passed away by the time Randall and Rebecca came to seek Mayer's help. Similar stories circulated in news reports and other texts. In 1990, a report in the *Canadian Press* discussed George Fraser, a psychiatrist in Ottawa with a dozen MPD patients, all of whom were female.[47] Of these, four claimed to have been ritually abused by family members and two "were introduced to the cult by their mothers."[48] Not all stories directly involved patients' mothers, but enough did to attest to the cultural power of the "bad mothering" trope, particularly in the context of the diagnosis and treatment of MPD and ritual abuse.

Rebecca's account included another popular element of the mother/demonic discourse that was emerging at the time, for she claimed that the Satanic cult—of which her mother and family were a part—kept women "hidden on farms" to serve as baby breeders, providing children for ritual sacrifice.[49] In the same 1990 *Canadian Press* report cited above, Fraser discussed a patient who claimed that she had been a cult "breeder."[50] Two years later, a conference on ritual abuse in San Diego included several women "survivors" discussing their past experiences as "breeders."[51] Despite these apparent first-person testimonials, in 1993, FBI Special Agent Kenneth Lanning, a behavioural science specialist, publicly denounced "baby-breeding" as part of what he considered the "extreme end" of prevailing Satanic conspiracies.[52] He claimed that there was "no evidence" for such allegations.[53]

Lanning was part of the first generation of self-proclaimed experts in ritual abuse. From the early 1980s, a growing number of social workers and therapists came increasingly to identify themselves as specialists in demonically inspired occult crimes often connected to MPD and repressed memories. As the volume of "evidence" they uncovered amassed, they were joined by members of law enforcement. Lanning was one of these—and at this early stage in his career, he admitted that he "believed most everything" about the apparent ritualistic crimes he investigated.[54] These people saw themselves as advocates for the alleged victims and proponents for the prosecution of those who abused them. They travelled around the United States, Canada and the United Kingdom giving seminars and appearing on television programmes to promote the idea that Satanism and ritual abuse were prolific throughout society and represented an immediate threat to everyone, particularly children.[55] Increasingly, many of these "experts" were brought in to train law enforcement officers on how to look for signs of ritualistic abuse and evidence of demonic cult activity. In 1988, Lanning travelled to Hamilton, Ontario, to conduct seminars for American and Canadian officers on "ritualistic child abuse."[56] Other similar figures included American police officer Sandi Galland, who travelled around England lecturing on Satanic cults, and English social worker Dianne Core, who argued that Satanic cults were also a pervasive threat in the United Kingdom.[57] The work of these "experts" and the atrocities they described helped give the notion of ritualistic abuse credibility.

However, these accusations were not without their critics, many of whom focused on the controversial role played by therapists. According to a 1993 article in London's *The Times*, many mental health professionals denied the existence of MPD, which was predicated on the claim that "abuse victims can develop thousands of separate personalities" that could only be elicited through therapy.[58] Others believed that the number of cases had been exaggerated or that the condition had been "over-diagnosed."[59] By 1993, even Lanning had come to be openly sceptical.[60] As the concept of repressed memory also came under scrutiny in the early 1990s, some raised questions about why patients did not recall ritual abuse before going to a therapist.[61] In "Alternative Hypotheses Regarding Claims of Satanic Cult Activity: A Critical Analysis," Dr. George B. Greaves notes that, in therapy sessions dealing with trauma, certain types of clinicians explicitly indicate "an earnest desire to hear more," thereby rewarding "the most bizarre accounts with the greatest level of attention and rapt interest."[62] Lanning labels such people "*Overzealous intervenors*," and includes among them individuals such as social workers, doctors and family members, as well as therapists.[63] He explains that "victims have been subtly as well as overtly rewarded and bribed by usually well-meaning intervenors for furnishing additional details."[64] Such problematic approaches were often especially evident in the emerging field of Christian psychotherapy, which, as David Frankfurter explains in *Evil Incarnate*, "often reconfigured therapy as a context for spiritual warfare."[65] Christian psychotherapists like James G. Friesen viewed ritual abuse claims among patients as part of a "cosmic struggle" in which "Satan's forces" were working to oppose the "Kingdom of God."[66] Patients were "Satan's victims" and often acquired demonic personalities—leading to a diagnosis of MPD—that required expulsion by the therapist.[67] Therapy, then, was a form of exorcism.

The period also saw a renewed cultural interest in ecclesiastical exorcisms inspired in part by *The Exorcist*. While the film itself presented the rite as rare, something which the central characters engaged in only as a last resort, that the number of exorcisms conducted began to increase is evident from news reports from the mid-1970s—many of which used excerpts from the film to supplement their stories.[68] By 1985, an Associated Press article cited claims from "experts" that "as many as 1,000 exorcisms" were being performed annually in the United States.[69] Members of the Catholic clergy still played a prominent role in performing exorcisms, as evidenced by a letter issued by the Vatican in 1986 making clear who could perform them and how they were to be done.[70] However, as church authorities were reluctant to authorise exorcisms despite the fact that demand for such spiritual services was growing, evangelical ministers increasingly took up the role, sometimes partnering clandestinely with Catholic priests. In the late 1970s, these clergy were increasingly joined by Christian psychotherapists, like Harvard-educated psychiatrist Dr. M. Scott Peck.[71] Following his best-selling book *The Road Less Traveled*—espousing his spiritual approach to psychiatry—Peck published *People of the Lie: The Hope for Healing Human Evil* in 1983. This latter work highlighted his participation in two exorcisms which he used to underscore his argument that demonic possession should be categorised as a mental disorder.[72] According to Peck, other psychologists, psychiatrists and medical doctors were in attendance at both exorcisms, and he had learned of a handful of others in the field who had also participated in the practice.[73] The growing interest in exorcisms during the decade by members of the medical profession demonstrated how deeply the era's prevailing religious climate had penetrated culture.

During this time, too, conservatives elevated the nuclear family to almost mythic status. "The family is the God-ordained institution of the marriage of one man and one woman together for a lifetime with their biological or adopted children," Falwell wrote in his 1980 treatise *Listen! America*.[74] According to various televangelists, the devil targeted white suburbia and the nuclear-family ideal in particular. This is reflected in a shift in the focus of horror films. While *The Exorcist* and *The Omen* had focused on demonically possessed/aligned children, the films of the late 1970s and 1980s centred more on suburban children being stalked and terrorised by external demonic entities. Moreover, the period also saw a decline in the role of priests as authorities on the occult. In these later films, they were replaced by parapsychologists, spiritual mediums and psychics who did not appear to have any explicit religious affiliation, again demonstrating the cultural influence of conservative evangelicals.

This realignment began with *Halloween*, released in North America in 1978, which centres on Michael Myers, a demonic masked anti-hero who terrorises white teens in his suburban hometown of Haddonfield, Illinois. But by 1984, Myers had been joined by Jason Voorhees and Freddy Kreuger—together, these were the decade's three most prolific icons of suburban terror, familiar to audiences around the world. The hockey mask-wearing Voorhees who hunts suburban teens at a summer camp is the primary villain of the *Friday the 13th* franchise which began in 1980. Kreuger is the horribly disfigured, demonic child murderer at the centre of the *A Nightmare on Elm Street* films launched in 1984. And, like the devil described in 1 Peter 5.8, these killers stalk their prey relentlessly.

The popularity of Krueger, Myers and Voorhees, while international in scale, was most pronounced in the United States and Canada. In 1987, *A Nightmare on Elm Street 3: Dream Warriors* reportedly "set the all-time box office record for a weekend opening by an independent film company" after its February North American release.[75] By 2011, nine *Nightmare on Elm Street* films, a dozen in the *Friday the 13th* franchise, and ten *Halloween* movies had a worldwide gross of over a billion dollars.[76] There was also an abundance of merchandise tied to these films, including video games, Halloween costumes, action figures, board games and trading cards. Dozens of similar lower budget slasher films were released during the 1980s, looking to emulate the fame and success of this unholy trinity of demonic killers. Some notable films that centre on evil demonic entities who stalk and torture their often-suburban victims include *The Slumber Party Massacre* (1982), *Child's Play* (1988), *Pumpkinhead* (1988) and *Puppet Master* (1989). In *Child's Play*, which debuted at number one in both the United States and Canada, the demonic entity comes in the form of a child's doll named Chucky which is possessed by the soul of a serial killer.[77] A review in *The New York Times* called the film "a fitting successor to the classic television horror stories it takes off from," revealing that the film built upon, and contributed to, a long legacy of cultural images of the demonic.[78]

Underscoring the anti-progressive politico-religious agenda espoused by contemporary conservatives, these predators were modern day serpents in the new, white Garden of Eden—the American suburbs. They existed only to destroy suburban society, the sacred nucleus of white family life. But they were also seemingly akin to Manson who—through his minions—had brought death and ruin to an idealised family environment. In this respect, Manson and these fictional killers operated in something of a feedback loop, a process which became even more intense over the decade with the rise of infotainment and the New Right. The effect was to increase Manson's celebrity status with news sources in the United States—and to a lesser extent in Canada and the United Kingdom—providing regular updates on him and his family in prison, drawing parallels between him and other violent criminals and cult leaders. They also turned him into a television star. In 1981, he made "his first network TV appearance" as a guest on NBC's *Tomorrow Coast to Coast* hosted by Tom Snyder. It was a ratings success.[79] Manson subsequently made appearances on several different types of tabloid programmes in the United States, particularly talk shows and morning news programmes, both local and national. His growing notoriety over the course of the decade served to reinforce the relationship between the counterculture and the devil. As Roger Ailes, executive director of *Tomorrow Coast to Coast,* stated, "There are many young people today who unfortunately do not know who Charles Manson is or what the drug culture, taken to its extreme, can do to people."[80] The decade's fictional icons of horror continued the legacy of rendering the demonic in Manson's image. In ritual abuse cases, daycare centres, parents and guardians also appeared on the margins of society, despite the important role they often played in the community.

### "Exposing Satan's Underground"

Both ritual abuse cases and the growing celebrity status of Charles Manson were a function of the meteoric rise of tabloid television in the 1980s. While sensational news content, particularly on television, was an extension of trends already evident in previous decades, it became more extreme in this period with the expansion of infotainment. Tabloid programmes—which included talk shows, entertainment news and documentary crime shows—became an integral part of television content in the period. They were joined in 1980 by *Cable News Network* (CNN), the first 24-hour rolling-news network, and a growing number of local news shows all of which sought sensational content. The emergence and aggressive growth of these popular tabloid programmes in the United States led other countries to follow suit, initially importing American shows before gradually developing their own.[81]

In this context, stories about the demonic were a favourite and proved to be a ratings winner. Following Satz's initial KABC report about the McMartin case in 1984, other networks and programmes rushed to produce similar content. Between 1984 and 1985, network evening news programmes ran over twenty reports on McMartin.[82] CNN aired the formal arraignment in the case, as well as live coverage of the preliminary hearing, with network executives justifying such pervasive coverage by arguing that it "would help educate viewers about a sensitive subject."[83] Other high-profile ritual abuse trials, like those for Gerald Amirault, Frank Fuster and Paul Ingram, ran regularly on local news. Over the same period, ABC's hour-long signature television newsmagazine show *20/20* dedicated several segments to McMartin in the period, including "The Devil Worshippers," "The Best Kept Secret" and "Why the Silence." Many of these national news reports drew heavily on local content, accepting its veracity uncritically, giving viewers the sense that a national scandal was at hand, and that those implicated in their reporting were likely guilty of abhorrent crimes. However, the significant time that the networks devoted to ritual abuse cases, particularly the McMartin case, was dwarfed by a much heavier and more prolonged investment in the topic from the growing number of tabloid television sources.

While the networks mostly avoided the topic of ritual abuse after 1986 when the McMartin case began to fall apart, tabloid programmes remained persistent. The most notable example was Geraldo Rivera's 1988 special, "Devil Worship: Exposing Satan's Underground." Although it had difficulty finding advertisers due to its content, it was a ratings success, reaching an audience of 19.8 million, or one third of all television viewers for its evening time slot.[84] The special was tabloid television at its most extreme and featured host Rivera authoritatively claiming that the country was under siege by networks of violent devil-worshippers. He interviewed members of law enforcement and the Church of Satan, as well as heavy metal musician Ozzy Osbourne, who was part of a genre that was increasingly tied to devil-worship in the popular imagination. Rivera also included footage of interviews with Manson, whom he deemed part of a long legacy of "satanic criminals" operating in the United States, and with several of the McMartin children, who sat with their backs to the camera.[85] "In the very places created to care for children," Rivera prefaced his segment on McMartin, "in nurseries and daycare centres across the nation, there are increasing reports of ritual sexual abuse."[86]

While the special was not without critics, including executives of national morning news talk show *The Today Show* who denied Rivera a promotional interview for the special, its popularity ensured that Rivera was able to follow it up with other similarly themed "news specials," including "Satanic Breeders: Babies for Sacrifice" (October 1988) and "Investigating Multiple Personalities: Did the Devil Make Them Do It" (September 1991).[87] But Rivera was only one of several tabloid hosts to explore the topic of devil-worship over the course of the period.[88] Both Oprah Winfrey and another talk show host, Sally Jessy Raphael, produced episodes of their programmes on survivors of ritual abuse cults through the late 1980s.[89] And after the acquittal of Ray Buckey in the McMartin case in 1990, Winfrey, Rivera and Raphael all revisited the case. As they had done in earlier shows, the hosts generally took the side of the prosecution, encouraging a second trial for Buckey on the thirteen charges that had left the jury deadlocked.[90]

The presentation of ritual abuses cases by tabloid programmes ensured the success of the genre, but it also served to validate such claims—and the idea of secret, powerful sects of devil-worshippers more generally. The uncritical presentation of this material meant that such accounts were difficult to challenge. As one sociologist complained in 1993, the sweeping allegations of ritual abuse "from California to Ontario to the United Kingdom" were the fault of "opportunists" like "Geraldo Rivera and other purveyors of junk journalism, eager to exploit the anxieties of the gullible for shock value and ratings."[91]

## X-Rated Society

Ritual abuse cases were only one part of the decade's larger fears over Satanism. Other concerns about devil-worship in the culture emerged, too. These were mostly concentrated in the United States but reports often circulated throughout the Western world. They demonstrated that accusations of devil-worship were not confined just to childcare workers and guardians; they could affect global businesses and the commercial entertainment industry—and they could have serious repercussions. In this context, one of the most prominent campaigns against demonism and its allure centred on that against heavy metal music. This culminated in 1990 with the trial of the British metal band Judas Priest for allegedly implanting subliminal messages in their music that had encouraged two fans to form a suicide pact. As with ritual abuse cases, the attack of conservatives on heavy metal was driven by a concern about the corruption of the young when they were outside parental supervision.

Fears over devil-worship in music picked up pace over the course of the 1980s, gaining credibility, publicity and momentum through the efforts of the Parents Music Resource Center (PMRC). Founded in 1977 by the wives of several prominent American politicians, the PMRC targeted music it felt contained "graphic" content.[92] The group's main spokeswomen included Tipper Gore, wife of American Senator from Tennessee Al Gore, and Susan Baker, wife of James Baker, who served as Ronald Reagan's Secretary of the Treasury.[93] Gore and Baker made the rounds on various talk shows and local news programmes starting in the mid-1980s, condemning music that seemed to promote drug use, violence, sex and the occult.[94] By November 1985, PMRC had succeeded in pressuring the nation's record companies to add parental advisory warning labels on albums deemed "explicit."[95] A month later, Canadian record companies followed suit.[96] Gore was particularly concerned about heavy metal. In a chapter entitled "Playing with Fire: Heavy Metal Satanism" in her 1987 *Raising PG Kids in an X-Rated Society*, she argued that metal "has introduced the accoutrements of satanism to a generation of kids."[97] Bringing Satanic themes into music was not "harmless," she continued, because it promoted violence and "turns good and evil upside down."[98]

To some concerned parents, Gore's pronouncements seemed to ring true. The delinquency and violence that she argued could be consequences of heavy metal and its connection to Satanism were increasingly hard to ignore. News reports linking instances of teen vandalism, suicide, drug abuse and murder to devil-worship were common, often suggesting that the perpetrators "may have been inspired by heavy metal rock bands."[99] This was a theme Rivera exploited in his "Devil Worship" special. He claimed that, while not all fans of heavy metal worshipped the devil, there was an "undeniable connection between an obsession with the really hard stuff and the occult."[100] The documentary then cut to excerpts of teens discussing self-mutilation and drug use. Rivera concluded that "whatever the connection, there is no doubt that teenage Satanic activity in this country is increasing dramatically," over footage showing male teens headbanging and shoving one another at a metal concert.[101]

Alarm about the Satanic heavy metal reached its peak with the Judas Priest trial. In a story that made headlines around the Western world, a civil lawsuit filed in 1986 charged that the band's music led two teenage boys in Nevada—James Vance and Raymond Belknap—to shoot themselves after listening the band's 1978 album, *Stained Glass*, for six hours. A similar lawsuit was brought against Ozzy Osbourne at about the same time, also alleging that his music had a "satanic influence" that caused a teenager to commit suicide—this time while listening to Osbourne's *Blizzards of Oz*.[102] In the Judas Priest trial, lawyers for the families of Vance—who initially survived—and Belknap argued that subliminal messages "touting the devil and encouraging listeners to 'do it, do it'" had a hypnotic effect on the two friends and convinced them to commit suicide.[103] The lawsuit eventually went to trial in July 1990—after Vance had passed away from complications related to his injuries—with the band maintaining that the album did not use subliminal messages to promote devil-worship or suicide.[104]

Although both suits failed, they marked the culmination of a decade-long fear over the negative influence of heavy metal music on young people. The judge in Osbourne's case ruled that the plaintiff's lawyer had failed to demonstrate why the songs should not be protected under the first amendment.[105] Nevada State District Judge Jerry Whitehead, who presided over the Judas Priest trial, ruled that the families "failed to prove that defendants intentionally placed subliminal messages on the album" that caused the suicide pact.[106] Subliminal messages were present, he explained, but were only there by "a chance combination of sounds."[107] Whitehead's decision indicated that it was difficult to prove that subliminal messages were deliberate and led to violence.[108] But that cases ever made it to trial, shows just how prominent the idea of a connection between allegedly Satanic lyrics and violence among teens had become by this point.[109]

\* \* \*

In 1990, after Ray Buckey's acquittal and the dismissal of the Judas Priest lawsuit, ritual abuse cases and general fears over Satanism dramatically receded in the United States. Articles and exposés in major papers in the United States, including *The Los Angeles Times*, *The New York Times*, *The Washington Post* and *The Wall Street Journal* began openly to attack ritual abuse accusations as witch hunts. However, cases continued into the 1990s in Canada, the United Kingdom and Australia as their respective news and entertainment industries began to follow the American model more closely. The panic also spread to South Africa, where it took on a slightly different shape. Rather than fixating on devil-worship, it manifested as fears over bringing about "the actual appearance of the devil," explains Nikki Falkof in "'Satan has come to Rietfontein': Race in South Africa's Satanic Panic."[110] It primarily involved cases of alleged demonic possession and supernatural encounters that were sometimes tied to violent crime. According to Falkof, the South African panic "tapped into" the complex racial tensions that characterised the country's system of apartheid, or policies of racial segregation, that had been in place since the 1940s.[111]

By the end of the 1990s, anxieties over the demonic had made their way through most of the English-speaking world, demonstrating the far-reaching power of religious ideology and evolving commercial entertainment and news media. However, fears did not fully disappear and were poised to reemerge, perhaps in slightly different form and targeting new enemies.

## Notes

1 Susan Friend Harding, *The Book of Jerry Falwell: Fundamentalist Language and Politics* (Princeton, 2001); Andrew Hartman, *A War for the Soul of America: A History of the Culture Wars* (Chicago, 2015); Peter Steinfels, *The Neoconservatives: The Origins of a Movement* (New York, [1979], 2013); Gil Troy, *Morning in America: How Ronald Reagan Invented the 1980s* (Princeton, 2005); Michael Schaller and George Rising, *The Republican Ascendancy: American Politics 1968–2001* (Wheeling, 2002); Garry Wills, *Reagan's America: Innocents at Home* (New York, [1987], 2000).
2 Dorothy Rabinowitz, "A darkness in Massachusetts-III," *The Wall Street Journal*, 12 May 1995. https://www.wsj.com/articles/SB920002710785789000
3 Glenn Collins, "Nightmare in Country Walk," *The New York Times*, 14 December 1986.

4 Her conviction was overturned in 1993 after she had served five years. Lona Manning, "Nightmare at the Day Care: The Wee Care Case," *Crime Magazine*, 14 January 2007. http://www.crimemagazine.com/nightmare-day-care-wee-care-case

5 Lawrence Wright, *Remembering Satan: A Case of Recovered Memory and the Shattering of an American Family* (New York, 1994).

6 Adrian Cloete, "Satanism: The Spectre of Ritual Child Abuse," *The Toronto Star*, 29 June 1989.

7 Marjaleena Repo, "Fairytales of Abuse Make for Nightmares," *The Globe and Mail*, 28 July 1992.

8 Richard Guilliatt, "Demons from the Past; Therapy in Turmoil," *Sydney Morning Herald*, 1 February 1995.

9 Guilliatt, "Demons from the Past."

10 Rosie Waterhouse, Sharon Kingman, and Jenny Cuffe, "A Satanic Litany of Children's Suffering," *The Independent*, 8 March 1990.

11 David Ansen, Martin Kasindorf, and Katrine Ames, "Hollywood's Scary Summer," *Newsweek*, 18 June 1979; "Rosemary's Baby (1968) Release Info," *IMDb*. https://www.imdb.com/title/tt0063522/releaseinfo?ref_=tt_dt_dt. See also Chapter 21 of the current volume.

12 "Rosemary's Baby (1986) Release Info."

13 "'Rosemary's Baby' Gave Birth to a New Breed of Terror When It Premiered 50 Years Ago," *Variety*, 12 June 2018.

14 "Charles Manson 'Family' Timeline: 1967 to the Present," *Los Angeles Times*, 28 July 2019. https://www.latimes.com/california/story/2019-07-27/charles-manson-family-timeline; Key Word Search: "Charles Manson," 146 items between 4 August 1968 and 4 August 1972. Vanderbilt Television News Archives.

15 "Tate Murders/Suspects," *ABC Evening News*, Abstract, 2 December 1969. Vanderbilt Television News Archives.

16 Martin Waldron, "Witness Recalls Manson as 'Devil': He Says Murder Defendant Posed as Satan on Loose," *The New York Times*, 18 September 1970. Proquest Historical Newspapers.

17 Sarah A. Hughes, *American Tabloid Media and the Satanic Panic, 1970-2000* (London, 2021), 127.

18 Steven V. Roberts, "The Hippie Mystique: Tate Murders Prompt a Closer Look at It," *The New York Times,* 15 December 1969, 1. Proquest Historical Newspapers.

19 Gary Fishgall, *Gregory Peck: A Biography* (New York, 2002), 292; "The Omen (1976) Release Info," *IMDb*. https://www.imdb.com/title/tt0075005/releaseinfo?ref_=tt_dt_dt

20 Delia Nicholls, "When a Hoax Turned into a Horror Story," *Sydney Morning Herald,* 29 November 1986.

21 Allan J. Mayer and Martin Kasindorf, "Entertainment: The Undertaker," *Newsweek,* 7 June 1976; "Movies Draw Record Receipts," *Facts on File World News Digest,* 22 February 1975; "Top-grossing '74 films," *Facts on File World News Digest,* 4 October 1975.

22 "Exorcism," *CBS Evening News,* 5 February 1974, Abstract, Vanderbilt Television News Archives.

23 "Devil/Satan/Lucifer/Beelzebub," *CBS Evening News,* Abstract, 14 November 1976, Vanderbilt.

24 Pat Milton, *The Associated Press,* 27 July 1979.

25 Paul Heelas, *The New Age Movement: The Celebration of the Self and the Sacralization of Modernity* (Oxford, 1996), 1.

26 Robert Ellwood, "How New Is the New Age?" in *Perspectives on the New Age,* eds. James R. Lewis and J. Gordon Melton (Albany, 1992), 60 and 64; Shoshanah Feher, "Who Holds the Cards? Women and New Age Astrology," in *Perspectives on the New Age,* 179–180 and 187; Suzanne Riordan, "Channeling: A New Relation?" in *Perspectives on the New Age,* 105 and 107; Phillip C. Lucas, "The New Age Movement and the Pentecostal/Charismatic Revival: Distinct Yet Parallel Phases of a Fourth Great Awakening?" in *Perspectives on the New Age,* 199.

27 Joanne Kaufman, Kent Demaret, Anne Maier, and Joyce Wadler, "The fall of Jimmy Swaggart." *People* 29, no. 9 (March 1988): 37.

28 Robert Barr, "For the Electronic Church, Contributors Will Be the Jury," *The Associated Press,* 29 March 1987.

29 Richard N. Ostling and Laura Lopez, "Offering the Hope of Heaven Jimmy Swaggart Takes His Pentecostal Fervor to Latin America," *Time* 129, no. 11 (May 1987).

30 Gwen Smith, "Religious Stations Are Supported in Letters and Petitions to CRTC," *The Globe and Mail,* 9 January 1982.

31 Mark Lukasiewicz, "CRTC Sets Inter-Faith Requirements for Nationally Distributed Pray TV," *The Globe and Mail*, 3 May 1983; "Miracle Channel Debuts in Alberta," *Broadcaster*, February 1996.

32 Salem Alaton, "Hot Christians," 17 March 1984, *The Globe and Mail*.

33 Harding, *The Book of Jerry Falwell*, 189.

34 "Jimmy Swaggart Crusade Cincinnati., OH 1984: The Future of Planet Earth," YouTube video, 46:50–52:18, 1:21:59, 15 August 2016, Posted by Christian Sermons Online. https://www.youtube.com/watch?v=4O6mosdMpsYzs&t=3019s

35 Ana Swanson, "144 Years of Marriage and Divorce in the United States, in One Chart," *The Washington Post*, 23 June 2015. https://www.washingtonpost.com/news/wonk/wp/2015/06/23/144-years-of-marriage-and-divorce-in-the-united-states-in-one-chart/; United States Census Bureau: Current Population Survey, 1968 to 2009 Annual Social and Economic Supplements, "Number of Full-Time, Year-Round Workers with Earnings by Sex: 1967 to 2009," chart, *Women in the Workforce*. http://www.census.gov/newsroom/pdf/women_workforce_slides.pdf

36 John Earl, "The Dark Truth about the 'Dark Tunnels' of McMartin: The Beginning," *Institute for Psychological Therapies* 7 (1995), last modified 15 April 2014. http://www.ipt-forensics.com/journal/volume7/j7_2_1_1.htm; McMartin father quoted in Kathy Horak, "Day Care Center's Elderly Founder among 7 Indicted," *The Associated Press*, 24 March 1984.

37 Repo, "Fairytales of Abuse."

38 Smith was initially Pazder's patient but later became his wife. Michelle Smith and Lawrence Pazder, *Michelle Remembers* (New York, 1980), 91 and back cover.

39 Richard Beck, *We Believe the Children: A Moral Panic in the 1980s* (New York, 2015), 105; Tracey Harrison, Peter Rose, Chriss Brooke, and Stephen Oldfield, "The Nightmare that Never Was," *Daily Mail*, 25 April 1994.

40 "Dissociative Disorders," *National Alliance on Mental Illness*, 2021. https://www.nami.org/About-Mental-Illness/Mental-Health-Conditions/Dissociative-Disorders; Mary Lassance Parthun, "A Thought-Provoking Document of a Gruesome Case," *The Globe and Mail*, 16 April 1988; Yvonne Preston, "Annie's Agony; The Scream that Must be Heard," *Sydney Morning Herald*, 8 December 1990.

41 "What Are Dissociative Disorders," *American Psychiatric Association*, 2024. https://www.psychiatry.org/patients-families/dissociative-disorders/what-are-dissociative-disorders

42 Kim Ode, "Issue of Memory Is Complicated," *Star Tribune*, 11 October 1993; Ann Shearer, "Thursday Women (Health Watch): Myself and Other Individuals – Why Has There Been a Sudden Rise in the Diagnosis of Women with Multiple Personalities?" *The Guardian*, 7 April 1988; Jean Snedgar, "Health: The Impossible Life of a Woman Split in 10," *The Independent*, 20 March 1990.

43 Shearer, "Thursday Women."

44 Robert S. Mayer, *Satan's Children: Shocking True Accounts of Satanism, Abuse, and Multiple Personality* (New York, 1991), 161 and 165–6.

45 Mayer, *Satan's Children*, 71–4.

46 Rebecca/Arlene quoted in Mayer, *Satan's Children*, 71.

47 "BC-Weekend-Exchange-Devil-Worship," *The Canadian Press*, 6 March 1990.

48 "BC-Weekend-Exchange-Devil-Worship."

49 Rebecca/Arlene quoted in Mayer, *Satan's Children*, 66.

50 "BC-Weekend-Exchange-Devil-Worship."

51 "Prepared Testimony of Carol Lamb Hopkins before: The Subcommittee on Early Childhood, Youth, and Families Committee on Economic and Educational Opportunities," *Federal News Service*, 31 January 1995.

52 Kenneth Lanning quoted in Larry King, "Claims of Satanic Cult Ritual Abuse- Are Any Real?" *CNN Larry King Live*, 5 July 1993.

53 King, "Claims of Satanic Cult Ritual Abuse."

54 Kenneth Lanning quoted in Ellen Futterman, "Hints of Darkness: Satanism Reports Stir Worry," *St. Louis Post-Dispatch*, 5 February 1989; Kenneth V. Lanning, "A Law-Enforcement Perspective on Allegations of Ritual Abuse," in *Out of Darkness: Exploring Satanism and Ritual Abuse*, eds., David K. Sakheim and Susan E. Devine (New York, 1992), 114.

55 David Frankfurter, *Evil Incarnate: Rumors of Demonic Conspiracy and Satanic Abuse in History* (Princeton, 2006), 60–61.

56 Kevin Marron, "Police Attending Seminar on Ritualistic Child Abuse," *The Globe and Mail*, 7 July 1988.

57 Frankfurter, *Evil Incarnate*, 60.
58 Julia Llewellyn Smith, "Too Much Devilry in Mind," *The Times*, 25 June 1993.
59 Snedegar, "Health."
60 Kenneth Lanning quoted in Ellen Futterman, "Hints of Darkness: Satanism Reports Stir Worry," *St. Louis Post-Dispatch*, 5 February 1989; Kenneth V. Lanning, "A Law-Enforcement Perspective on Allegations of Ritual Abuse," in *Out of Darkness: Exploring Satanism and Ritual Abuse*, eds., David K. Sakheim and Susan E. Devine (New York, 1992), 114.
61 Elizabeth Loftus, "The Reality of Repressed Memories," *American Psychologist* 48 no. 5 (1993). http://faculty.washington.edu/eloftus/Articles/lof93.htm
62 George B. Greaves, "Alternative Hypotheses Regarding Claims of Satanic Cult Activity: A Critical Analysis," in *Out of Darkness*, 50.
63 Lanning, "A Law-Enforcement Perspective," 134.
64 Lanning, "A Law-Enforcement Perspective," 134.
65 Frankfurter, *Evil Incarnate*, 62.
66 Frankfurter, *Evil Incarnate*, 62. James G. Friesen, "Ego-Dystonic or Ego-Alien: Alternate Personality or Evil Spirit?" *Journal of Psychology and Theology* 20, no. 3 (1992), 197.
67 Friesen, "Ego-Dystonic or Ego-Alien," 197–9.
68 Johann Hari, "The Devilish Church Practice of Exorcism," *The Independent*, 17 January 2008.
69 Kay Bartlett, *The Associated Press*, 15 December 1985.
70 Hari, "The Devilish Church"; "Vatican Releases Letter with Rules on Exorcism," *The Associated Press*, 22 February 1986.
71 Bartlett, *The Associated Press*.
72 Bartlett, *The Associated Press*; Cathy Lawhon, "Satan Exists in Some People, Psychiatrist Concludes," *St. Louis Post-Dispatch*, 12 August 1989.
73 Kay Bartlett, "'Encountered Satan' during Exorcisms: Psychiatrist Sees Evil as Form of Mental Illness," *Los Angeles Times*, 15 December 1985. https://www.latimes.com/archives/la-xpm-1985-12-15-mn-499-story.html
74 Jerry Falwell, *Listen! America* (Toronto, 1980), 104.
75 "New-Line-Cinema; (NLN) New Line Cinema Reports Financial Results," *Business Wire*, 7 May 1987.
76 Joe Mont, "5 Ways Horror Movies Scare Up Cash," *TheStreet.com*, 14 October 2011.
77 "Box Office Child's Play for Chucky," *The Toronto Star*, 16 November 1988; "Child's Play (1988)," *IMDb*. https://www.imdb.com/title/tt0094862/?ref_=fn_al_tt_1
78 Caryn James, "A Killer Companion in 'Child's Play,'" *The New York Times*, 9 November 1988.
79 Charlie Reina, "Manson to Appear on TV Show," *The Associated Press*, 10 June 1981; Tom Shales, "The Killer Interview," *The Washington Post*, 16 June 1981. https://www.washingtonpost.com/archive/lifestyle/1981/06/16/the-killer-interview/7aecfa21-48c3-4b4b-86f9-7247b92726bc/
80 Roger Ailes quoted in Reina, "Manson to Appear on TV Show."
81 Richard Mahler, "A Growing Acceptance; First-Run Product Starting to Sell Overseas," *Electronic Media*, 28 April 1988; Joey Slinger, "Stop the Presses," *The Toronto Star*, 20 January 1990.
82 Key Word search "McMartin," between 1 January 1983 and 1 January 1991. Vanderbilt Television News Archives.
83 Eloise Salholz, Alexander Stille, and Holly Morris, "Turning an Eye on the Lurid," *Newsweek*, 7 May 1984; Carolyn Skorneck, "Judge Closes Discovery Hearing in Preschool Molest Case," *The Associated Press*, 7 June 1984; "CNN Plans Live Coverage of Child Molestation Preliminary Hearing," *The Associated Press*, 23 April 1984; Lynn Elber, "Hearing to Stay Open; Judge Nixes Photo Lineup," *The Associated Press*, 13 June 1984.
84 Hughes, *American Tabloid Media*, 75; Jay Sharbutt, "Cauldron Boils over Geraldo's 'Devil Worship': 'Satan' Wins Ratings, Loses Advertisers," *Los Angeles Times*, 27 October 1988. https://www.latimes.com/archives/la-xpm-1988-10-27-ca-449-story.html
85 "Devil Worship: Exposing Satan's Underground: Part 1," YouTube video, 0:04-0:22, 14:47, 13 September 2006, Posted by Random Stuff I Find on VHS, youtube.com/watch?v=qocBf3_mmic; "Devil Worship: Exposing Satan's Underground: Part 4," YouTube video, 2:41-3:30, 10:31, 13 September 2006, Posted by Random Stuff I Find on VHS. https://www.youtube.com/watch?v=YTY0p-yEo70
86 "Devil Worship: Exposing Satan's Underground: Part 4," 2:38–2:48.
87 Jeffrey S. Victor, *Satanic Panic: The Creation of Contemporary Legend* (Chicago, 1993), 83.

88  Peter J. Boyer, "Program on Satan Worship Spurs Controversy at NBC," *The New York Times*, 26 October 1988. http://www.nytimes.com/1988/10/26/business/program-on-satan-worship-spurs-controversy-at-nbc.html

89  Victor, *Satanic Panic*, 83.

90  Howard Rosenberg, "A Retrial by Talk Show," *Los Angeles Times*, 31 January 1990. https://www.latimes.com/archives/la-xpm-1990-01-31-ca-1049-story.html

91  Christopher Dornan, "The Devil or Delusion? Either Satanic Cults are Victimizing Thousands of People or North America is in the Grip of an Insidious Hysteria," *The Gazette*, 4 September 1993.

92  Thomas E. Larson, *History of Rock and Roll* (Dubuque, 2004), 246.

93  Larson, *History of Rock and Roll*, 246.

94  Lisa Ladouceur, "The Filthy 15: When Venom and King Diamond Met the Washington Wives," in *Satanic Panic: Pop-Cultural Paranoia in the 1980s*, eds. Kier-La Janisse and Paul Corupe (Surrey, 2015), 162; Julia Malone, "Washington Wives Use Influence to Target Sex, Drugs in Rock Music," *Christian Science Monitor*, 23 August 1985.

95  Walter Goodman and Katherine Roberts, "Ideas & Trends; Warning Labels for Rock-and-Roll," *The New York Times*, 11 August 1985.

96  Peter Goddard, "Record Industry to Issue Language Warning," *The Toronto Star*, 4 December 1985.

97  Tipper Gore, *Raising PG Kids in an X-Rated Society* (Nashville, 1987), 118.

98  Gore, *Raising PG Kids*, 119 and 121.

99  "Teens, Rock Music Blamed in Cemetery Vandalism," *United Press International*, 6 December 1985; "Youth Sentenced to Three Years for Killing Dad," *The Toronto Star*, 15 April 1986.

100  "Devil Worship: Exposing Satan's Underground," YouTube video, 6:29–6:35, 1:29:42, 22 February 2015, posted by Francisco Figueira. https://www.youtube.com/watch?v=0mytkRybjNI

101  "Devil Worship," 8:54–9:00.

102  Catherine Gewertz, *United Press International*, 21 January 1986; "Judge Dismisses Suicide Suit Against Ozzy Osbourne," *The Associated Press*, 7 August 1986.

103  Sandra Chereb, "Trial to Begin in Suit Alleging Record Album Led to Suicide," *The Associated Press*, 15 July 1990; Frank Taylor, "Suicide Blamed on Rock," *Sunday Mail*, 17 April 1988.

104  Tom Gardner, "Comatose Man Who Sued Judas Priest Rock Group Pronounced Dead," *The Associated Press*, 30 November 1988; Judy Keen, "Band: No Subliminal Messages in Songs," *USA Today*, 19 July 1990; "Record-Suicide," *The Canadian Press*, 15 July 1990.

105  "Suit Against Osbourne Dismissed," *The Toronto Star*, 8 August 1986.

106  Jerry Whitehead quoted in Cy Ryan, "Judge Rejects Subliminal Message Suit against Judas Priest," *United Press International*, 24 August 1990.

107  Ryan, "Judge Rejects Subliminal Message Suit."

108  Charles Patrick Ewing and Joseph T. McCann, *Minds on Trial: Great Cases in Law and Psychology* (Oxford, 2006), 107–10.

109  "Nevada's High Court Allows Suit on Rock Band's Lyrics," *The New York Times*, 26 August 1988.

110  Nikki Falkof, "'Satan has come to Rietfontein': Race in South Africa's Satanic Panic," *Journal of Southern African Studies* 38, no. 4 (October 2012), 754. https://doi.org/10.1080/03057070.2012.732290

111  Falkof, "'Satan has come to Rietfontein'," 754.

## Further Reading

David Frankfurter, *Evil Incarnate: Rumors of Demonic Conspiracy and Satanic Abuse in History* (Princeton: Princeton University Press, 2006).

Debbie Nathan and Michael Snedeker, *Satan's Silence: Ritual Abuse and the Making of a Modern American Witch Hunt* (San Jose: Authors Choice Press, [1995], 2001).

Garry Wills, *Reagan's America: Innocents at Home* (New York: Penguin Books, [1987], 2000).

Jeffrey S. Victor, *Satanic Panic: The Creation of Contemporary Legend* (Chicago: Open Court, 1993).

Lawrence Wright, *Remembering Satan: A Case of Recovered Memory and the Shattering of an American Family* (New York: Alfred A. Knopf, 1994).

Richard Beck, *We Believe the Children: A Moral Panic in the 1980s* (New York: Public Affairs, 2015).

# 25

# DEMONS, MISSIONARIES AND MIGRANTS

*Johanneke Kroesbergen-Kamps*

In 1909, the American Pentecostal missionaries Thomas and Helen Junk wrote home to the Atlanta-based *Bridegroom's Messenger* about their mission in northern China—a land they characterised as one rife with "Devil worship." While they claimed that great crowds came to their small mission every day to have their wounds dressed and to be prayed for, "One thing [that] is a great help to us," they continued, is that "the people believe and know that the Devil is real, no imagination (as so many in the home land would like to have it), for in many cases the Devil talks to them, and people know the terrible influence he exercises over them."[1] As Jutta Wimmler has shown in Chapter 16, from the 17th century, missionaries and colonisers brought the concept of the devil to the global south. In this sense, it is ironic that as belief in an activist devil was declining in the global north under the weight of the forces unleashed by the European Enlightenment, it found fertile soil in those parts of the world that were relatively new to Christianity. Yet by the early 20th century, yoked to the civilising mission of European imperialism with its emphasis on modernisation, even mainstream missionaries in Africa started to see the devil as merely a superstitious belief. In the Zambian diaries of the Society of the Missionaries of Africa, a Roman Catholic international missionary organisation also known as the White Fathers, for instance, the idea of the devil as an active force had all but disappeared by the 1950s—replaced by the notion that such superstitions needed to be eradicated through education and the provision of modern healthcare.[2] Within the autonomous churches of the global south, however, the prominence of the devil only increased from the middle of the 20th century. This history is entangled with that of the development and spread of Pentecostalism.

This chapter focuses on the concept of the devil in the global south as it developed in the 20th and 21st centuries, with a particular emphasis on the period after the 1950s. During this time, Pentecostalism—with its emphasis on experiential faith—emerged as a global religious movement that proved especially adept at adapting and accommodating itself to local worldviews. Defining "Pentecostal" and "Pentecostalism" is complicated, and the precise boundaries of the terms are fuzzy. Nevertheless, I take them to refer to the wide range of Christian movements, organisations and churches, active on a global scale, that are related by virtue of their focus on what they take to be the workings of the Holy Spirit in the world. In contemporary Pentecostal Christianity, the gifts of healing, deliverance and prosperity

DOI: 10.4324/9781003096603-26

are particularly emphasised.[3] Because Pentecostalism's engagement with demonism in the colonial context is most extensively documented for sub-Saharan Africa, this region will necessarily be the main focus of this chapter. However, I will also offer examples from other parts of the global south to suggest that the African dynamics I explore apply more broadly. Here, the rise of the Brazilian Universal Church of the Kingdom of God is a case in point.

This chapter begins by tracing the way in which the devil became entangled and then embedded in local worldviews in those parts of Africa where Pentecostal missionaries evangelised. This led to a process by which aspects of indigenous life and belief were demonised—a process of colonisation of minds whereby some African converts came to understand their own culture, its rituals and practices as associated with Satan. The chapter concludes by examining the return of the devil to the global north by way of African migrant and diaspora churches, a process that began in the 1980s.

### Local Experiences of Misfortune and the Classical Mission Churches

Many African traditions accept the idea of a supreme being, a god who is often far removed from the daily affairs of the people. The world beyond the physical entails much more than just this faraway god, however; it includes, for example, ancestors, other human and non-human spirits, and the forces effected by witches. These forces are believed to play a central role in the causation of misfortune as well as the allocation of blessings. The spirits of ancestors, for example, are frequently believed to act as watchdogs of the moral behaviour of the community.[4] They are able to punish moral transgressions, cause ill health or other problems—sometimes even going so far as to take revenge on people—if they are not treated with the requisite respect. More troublesome, though, are non-ancestral spirits. In Zambia, for instance, the spirit of a dead person can act as a beloved ancestor towards its relatives but as a malicious spirit against those who do not belong to its family. Even the widow of the deceased, being no longer a part of his lineage, can be harmed by his spirit and therefore needs to be cleansed according to traditional Zambian beliefs.[5] Those who died under unfortunate circumstances—in a war or after committing a grievous crime, for instance—form another category of potentially troublesome spirits. Because these spirits are unable to find rest, they are often perceived as angry, and are believed to cause misfortune or illness for anyone who is unfortunate enough to pick such a spirit up by being in the wrong place—for example, at a graveyard or a crossroads. Then there are the witches and sorcerers—human beings who are, through various means, able to manipulate invisible forces in order to harm or help people.

All of these spirits and humans who wield spiritual powers could be harmful, angry or capricious—they could be seeking to avenge some transgression—and so cause all sorts of problems for people, but none of them are deemed inherently evil in and of themselves in traditional African thought.

This changed with the coming of Christian missionaries, for they introduced the idea of the devil to the global south. Under their influence, all of these various spiritual forces were demonised.[6] Such a reading of local religious practice as belonging to the realm of Satan has a long history within Christianity. While it was a convenient way for these missionaries to understand what was to them a series of strange beliefs, this process of demonisation has had unforeseen consequences. Indeed, far from displacing traditional belief, these African gods and spirits assumed a new role in the lived religion of believers—that is, as demons or demonic forces. Now, whenever misfortune befell a believer, he or she could still attribute it to a traditional spiritual force. The only difference is that this spiritual force is recast as being in league with the devil. This process of cultural colonialisation is visible not only in Africa, but in other parts of the global south as well.

But the fact that capricious spirits were now deemed demons and that traditional gods were devils did not always mean that they operated in a completely Western theological framework. Indeed, as Adam Ashforth has stressed, with the coming of the Western colonising powers, "no one lives exclusively in one system of thought or culture" anymore.[7] As other chapters in this volume have shown, Western theology has had much abstract to say about the nature of demons and of Satan, but it has little to say about the relationship of these agents of evil to humanity. In Africa, though, this relationship is key, and gave the devil, in the form of demonised traditional entities, a special place in African Christianity. If someone experiences misfortune—a drought, a persistent illness, failure in marriage or business—the cause is generally externalised, often perceived in terms of the person's relationship to particular human or spiritual beings such as witches, the spirits of ancestors or even gods. For instance, while ancestors are traditionally believed to bestow blessings on their living relatives, if they feel dishonoured because their living relative has acted in a taboo fashion or has been lax in giving offerings, they may lash out with a curse. Any bad thing that happens can be related to a disturbance within a relationship. This dynamic did not change with the Christianisation of traditional belief. An ancestor may be deemed a demon or an agent of Satan in the new Christian vocabulary, but it was still the relationship between the living and the dead that was the key to the problem, not the evil nature of the ancestor spirit. African Christians, therefore, still felt a need for rituals that could restore these relationships. In this sense, then, it is important to understand that while Christian missionaries brought with them a new label for evil, they often lacked any appreciation for the disturbed relationships of which evil in an African context was always believed a symptom. As a result, Christian missionaries lacked the spiritual resources to deal with these issues, leaving the door open to traditional healers and diviners, who were still believed to be able to offer solutions that addressed the disturbances in relationships that manifested in misfortune. As a consequence, the mission churches struggled to make these religious specialists redundant.[8]

While Pentecostal missionaries, like those in the introduction to this chapter, may have been glad that non-Western audiences embraced the devil as a supernatural force, many classical Protestant and Catholic mission churches felt increasingly uncomfortable with his enthusiastic adoption by believers in the global south. To them, the hybrid theology that was emerging from the contact between mainstream Christianity and traditional religion and the new role it afforded to the devil was superstition—and, as a result, they became even less sensitive to the problems local believers attributed to the operation of spiritual forces.[9] Consequently, the hesitancy of the classical mission churches to deal with the devil as he was coming to be understood by African Christians compelled believers to look for solutions elsewhere.

Besides using the services of traditional healers, priests and diviners, another response to the failure of classical missionary Christianity to address the problem of the devil adequately was the rise of independent African churches. These African Initiated (or Instituted, or Independent) Churches (AICs) which began early in the 20th-century blended aspects of Protestant Christianity with traditional teachings, often emphasising the importance of spiritual healing through the office of a pastor who was generally accepted to be a prophet. In West Africa, these churches are known as "Spiritual" or "Aladura" (i.e. praying) churches, and in South Africa as "Zionist" churches.[10] The AICs and their prophets offered various rituals to detect and expel evil spiritual forces. In many respects, these churches and their rituals were an attempt to provide the services offered by traditional healers, priests and diviners but within a Christian frame.[11] To be sure, these churches saw evil spiritual forces as related to or derived from Satan, but their focus was on the direct, specific spiritual causes of a particular problem rather than on the more abstract concept of the devil.[12]

## The Rise of Neo-Pentecostal Churches

Until the 1950s, Satan was real in the burgeoning churches of the global south, but he was a figure on the margins of missionary and independent Christianity. Through the second half of the 20th century, a number of trends worked together to change this. While missionaries from the classical mission churches were increasingly silent on the topic of the devil, religious changes in Europe and the United States inspired a new generation of theologians and missionaries to focus again on the satanic. To a large extent, this change is a function of the coming of Pentecostal and charismatic Christianity to Africa.

The beginning of the Pentecostal movement is often dated very precisely to the Azusa Street revival in Los Angeles in 1906. Like evangelical Christianity in general, as Chapter 23 has shown, Pentecostalism emphasises the importance of personal conversion and direct experience of the divine. The history of Pentecostalism is often described as comprising three consecutive waves. The first wave, at the beginning of the 20th century, emphasised speaking in tongues as evidence of a true conversion experience. These early or so-called "Classical Pentecostal churches" often appealed to the marginalised and disenfranchised. By the 1950s, the movement had come to find acclaim among mainstream Protestant churches, and to some extent, with Roman Catholics as well. During this second wave of charismatic renewal, many believers did not leave their churches for Pentecostal denominations but started to press for change within their own churches. As a result of the influence of Pentecostalism, many of these traditional churches began to stress the importance of the gifts of the Spirit—things such as the ability to prophesy. But they also tended to stress the ability to heal people from the influence of demonic forces. For Roman Catholics, this was through the sacramental of exorcism, for Protestants through the process of deliverance.[13] The third wave in the development of Pentecostalism started in the 1970s and 1980s, when the movement's focus shifted to signs and wonders, spiritual warfare and prosperity. It is this wave—also known as "neo-Pentecostalism"—that has had a profound influence on African Christianity.

Today, there are between 300 and 700 million Pentecostals worldwide, many of whom live in the global south—the higher of these estimates includes independent churches such as the AICs.[14] Around 12% of Africa's population belongs to a Pentecostal church; another 5% defines itself as having "a charismatic outlook" but remains, nevertheless, a member of a non-Pentecostal denomination.[15] That said, the Pentecostalism of the region is not homogenous, and churches highlighting teachings from the different stages of the movement's development exist side by side. But while classical Pentecostal churches such as the Assemblies of God, which have existed in many places since the beginning of the 20th century, still remain, the coming of the second-wave Pentecostalism with its renewed emphasis on missionary activity—inspired by the charismatic movement—has served to set the stage for the growth of Pentecostalism across the global south.[16] The real mushrooming of Pentecostalism started in the 1970s and 1980s, when evangelists from the global north like the German-born Reinhard Bonnke (1940–2019) and British charismatic Derek Prince (1915–2003) started organising crusades all over the global south to preach the Pentecostal message of deliverance from evil spirits. It is this third-wave variety of Pentecostalism that has resulted in a tremendous increase in churches all over the region, and it is also here that the devil plays an important role in Pentecostal theology.

The development of Pentecostal theology was not merely something that originated in the global north and exported to the south. Within Africa itself, African pastors made a significant contribution to its development, helping craft aspects of its message as well. In Nigeria, for example, Pastor Benson Idahosa (1938–1998) set up a training college in Benin City—the Christian Faith University (later renamed Benson Idahosa University)—which became a hub, connecting many new Pentecostal and charismatic churches and ministries across the continent.[17] But south-south missionary activity also proved important in developing and disseminating this new theology. Here, the examples of the crusades of the Korean Pastor David Yonggi Cho (1936–2001) and the immensely popular Brazilian Universal Church of the Kingdom of God founded in 1977 stand out as especially significant.[18]

Ideas about spiritual evil existing in the global south also influenced American preachers like Peter Wagner (1930–2016). As a missionary in the global south, particularly in South America, Wagner encountered believers for whom the belief in Satan and his demons was very much alive. This experience inspired him to think about the forces of evil and came to colour his understanding of spiritual warfare.[19] The idea of spiritual warfare is an important characteristic of the third wave of Pentecostal renewal and has had a profound and far-reaching effect on the concept of the devil in the global south.[20]

At a basic level, spiritual-warfare theology assumes a Manichean world in which things are either good or evil, and in which human beings function as pawns in the struggle between God and Satan.[21] In this view, Satan and his agents have the power to hinder human potential, but the church can offer protection and healing from any afflictions caused by these nefarious powers. As African traditions conceptualised evil as the action of an external agency on a person which could be remedied only through the rites and rituals of certain specialists, this emphasis on the action of Satan and its institutional amelioration fit well with indigenous conceptions of evil. In this sense, neo-Pentecostal Christianity helped fill the healing vacuum left by the classical mission churches. In effect, it offered a synthesis whereby it accepted the reality of traditional African spiritual beings—keeping those traditional associations alive—while presenting solutions to the problems they were believed to cause within a Christian framework.[22]

The influence of neo-Pentecostal spiritual-warfare theology has not been limited to Africa. All across the global south, traditional spiritual forces have been demonised, assimilated into the universalising vocabulary of the demonic.[23] Although the specific powers and beings that are relegated to the realm of the devil vary regionally, the effect of this totalising theology is to unite Christians from all over the global south with neo-Pentecostals from the global north—both see themselves as involved in the same spiritual struggle. When Bonnke preached in Africa that God and Satan are at war everywhere and that spiritual powers cause every evil, for instance, his audience understood him as referring to local conceptions of witchcraft and traditional evil spirits.[24] When missionaries from the Brazilian Universal Church of the Kingdom of God explained in a South African town that illness, poverty and social discord are caused by demons impeding the flow of God's blessings, their preaching can readily be assimilated into the traditional idea that supernatural blessings can be held up by evil or angry spirits.[25] In Africa, Asia and Latin America, then, spiritual warfare has become a familiar part of Christian practice and belief because in many ways it mirrors aspects of traditional spirit belief.[26]

But this is only part of the attraction of the notion for Africans. The idea that ordinary Christians are soldiers in a war between God and Satan is also empowering, for it implies that believers have access to the spiritual tools to resist the devil and to better their circumstances. If Satan is accepted as having an active role in the world, misfortune has meaning. If a marriage is in difficulty or a business is failing, for instance, if a child dies or a spouse is ill, such things can be attributed to the actions of the devil and his agents. But doing so also implies a remedy, for believers have access to the rituals of deliverance and exorcism found in neo-Pentecostal churches.[27] In a context in which people are confronted with hardships such as poverty and illness on a daily basis, and generally feel that they lack any power over their own fate, the idea that each individual is a soldier in God's army is attractive in that it gives a sense of authority and control.[28] Moreover, fighting against demonic afflictions also affords those who do so a high degree of social capital. A so-called "prayer warrior"—that is, someone who spends time praying against the forces of evil, often on behalf of others—is not cowardly or weak; rather, they are someone who takes destiny into their own hands.[29] This is a particularly attractive—even liberating—notion for youth and young adults in the global south. Not only does the idea imply a sense of agency, but it also suggests that a Pentecostal worshiper is fulfilling an important social role and even that he has a direct line, as it were, to God. This autonomous position stands in marked contrast to the subordinate role young people often play in traditional societies, particularly in Africa.[30]

But this focus on the devil as the source of problems can also lead to social and political apathy—a failure to pursue other, more practical solutions for poor leadership, corruption, socioeconomic and even medical problems.[31] After all, if Satan can be blamed for road accidents, there is no need to fix potholes; if the devil is behind premature deaths, an investment in medical infrastructure is unnecessary.[32]

This growing acceptance of the neo-Pentecostal notion of spiritual warfare across the global south has had another important effect, for it has led to a resurgence of suspicion about the use of spiritual powers. Although accusations of witchcraft have never disappeared from African societies, such accusations, especially made against politicians and businesspeople across the continent, have become increasingly frequent from the end of the 20th century and are often combined with allegations of devil worship.[33] I will return to the relation between devil worship and wealth or status later in this chapter. Many times, though, violence against people accused of witchcraft in Africa as well as Melanesia is fuelled by neo-Pentecostal convictions about the powers of Satan.[34] Agents of the devil are seen as being everywhere. A 1994 "Presidential Commission of Inquiry into Devil Worship" in Kenya, for instance, found that "Satanists" had infiltrated "the Jehovah's Witnesses, Mormons and Christian Scientists as well as Freemasons and the Theosophical Society."[35] In Zambia in 1998, members of the Universal Church of the Kingdom of God were accused of devil worship, and the church was even banned by the government for a while.[36]

The universalising language of Christianity, particularly in combination with the notion of the devil, has also led to a blurring of local, traditional understandings of evil. With all spiritual forces other than the Holy Spirit demonised, what had originally been different conceptions of the preternatural acting in different ways towards different ends are homogenised—and a traditional language for expressing the experience of misfortune is lost. Through the 1970s and 1980s, for instance, under the influence of the charismatic movement, the Zambian Archbishop Emmanuel Milingo started to exorcise his followers of evil spirits. An analysis of letters written to him requesting help show that although some writers refer to the spirits they believed to be tormenting them according to local African names, most simply called them "evil spirits"—although they did sometimes also go so far even as to identify them as Lucifer, the devil or Satan.[37] Somewhere along the line, the rich African conceptualisation of the spiritual world had crumbled. Even the distinction between possession and witchcraft has become obscure to many people.[38] When Ghanaian respondents were asked the difference between witchcraft and demonology, for instance, most assumed the two terms to be synonymous or claimed not to understand the question.[39] Since these ideas have become common not only in neo-Pentecostal circles but also in classical mission churches, many people live in a state of "spiritual insecurity."[40] There is a sense of an ever-present spiritual danger, but the exact nature of that threat has become less clear than it might have been in a traditional society before the coming of missionary Christianity. It is all just related to Satan.

From the 1980s onwards, different churches across the global south have developed a highly evolved demonology. In part, this has been informed by American evangelical and neo-Pentecostal literature and by missionary activities.[41] But African churches, in particular, have been creative in this regard as well. Authors like Dr. D. K. Olukoya, founder of the Nigerian Mountain of Fire and Miracles Ministries, have written handbooks about how to deal with the satanic forces that may destroy the prosperity to which an individual is destined. Many of these are on sale in major cities across the continent.[42] Another way in which knowledge about demonology is spread is through the testimonies of people who claim to have been in league with the devil. Some label themselves as satanists, others are called satanists by virtue of what is perceived to be their connection with Satan's realm. But in both cases, as with the witch confessions discussed in Chapter 9, they provide Christian audiences with apparently first-hand, eye-witness testimony about the action of the devil, and provide a face and a narrative for the place of evil in this world.[43] In this sense, the narratives of these ex-satanists make the devil vividly real and relatable.[44]

All of this means that for a competitive pastor in the global south—someone ambitious, looking to enhance his social capital and reap all the resultant worldly trappings—it makes sense to preach about the devil and his actions. The audiences for such preachers frequently suffer from many problems and find little help or solace from their governments either in terms of social security or high-standard healthcare. Thus, the neo-Pentecostal pastor who preaches that all problems have a spiritual cause offers not only an explanation for poverty, illness and other troubles, but also promises to provide a solution through his rituals of deliverance. Indeed, in the Brazilian Universal Church of the Kingdom of God, pastors are even seen as superheroes, men fighting evil on behalf of the Christian community.[45] Members of neo-Pentecostal churches hope to find healing and protection against all their afflictions. At the same time, it would be a misconception to think that people in the global south have an unquestioned, enchanted worldview. Testimonies of healing, of finding blessings, and of involvement in Satanism are so popular within neo-Pentecostal churches because they are evidence that the powers of both God and the devil are real. If the reality of these forces were self-evident, the emphasis on testimonial evidence would not be necessary.[46]

If Christian missionaries brought the devil to the global south, and locals accepted the demonisation of their traditional spiritual forces, it has been neo-Pentecostals who have really provided the universal language of evil into which indigenous religious belief has been assimilated. In this process, the devil has become an alternative language—a way to speak about specific spheres of life. In the following sections, I will show how this language has come to inform the ways in which people have come to understand the past, as well as wealth and power. All have become realms in which Satan is omnipresent.

## Making a Break with the Past

From the 18th century onwards, the history of many African societies along with the traditions, practices, and beliefs connected with them were demonised under the influence of Western missionaries. That story has been told in earlier chapters, so I will focus here on the attitude towards the past of African societies adopted by neo-Pentecostals.

Neo-Pentecostal Christianity emphasises the need to make a complete break with the non-Christian past. In the African context, this meant that converts have been obliged to renounce all practices related to African Traditional Religions (ATRs) and even sever ties with family members who still practised these rites and rituals.[47] To neo-Pentecostals, assimilating their experience and observations into a biblical frame, everything related to the pre-Christian past belongs to the realm of Satan. With traditional deities, spirits and ancestors all demonised, anyone associating themselves with these preternatural entities needs deliverance, for it is inevitable that they have become inhabited or possessed by demons as a result.[48] This is not just an issue for individuals and their traditional practices. This process of demonisation also often includes the older, African Initiated Churches with their prophets and healing rituals. The effect of this demonisation has often served to strain relations between AICs and neo-Pentecostal churches.[49]

But more than this, this process—this colonisation of the African past by missionaries and African believers—has also had an effect on how people have come to understand their heritage in general, for neo-Pentecostalism sustains an enchanted worldview.[50] When, for example, in March 2014, an anthropologist asked an attendant at the national museum in Kinshasa in the Democratic Republic of Congo why it was so quiet, she explained that the school children, who used to make up a big part of the visitors, no longer came there because they had become Pentecostals and now believed that the museum's collection of traditional ritual objects was diabolical.[51] In this demonised past, it seems, for objects to become deemed acceptable heritage artefacts, they first need to be disenchanted so that they can safely be displayed as objects of ethnic pride.[52]

The demonisation of the past is not merely an African phenomenon. In 2013, for instance, the speaker of the Papua New Guinea parliament attempted to cleanse the House of Assembly of a display of traditional carvings. This display had been intended to show the nation's pride in its customs. But the carvings were interpreted by neo-Pentecostals as entry points for demonic forces—and so represented an especially potent threat to the nation situated as they were at centre of its political culture.[53] Similarly, in the Brazilian Universal Church of the Kingdom of God, the traditional religious movements of Candomblé, Umbanda, Quimbanda and Kardecist Spiritism are all believed to be forms of devil worship that involve believers communing with real, powerful spirits which are actually agents of Satan.[54] In Melanesia, local spirits as well as traditional healing practices are denounced as satanic.[55] In Singapore and Hong Kong, Pentecostals organise so-called "prayer walks" around parts of the city, mirroring the "Jericho March" described in Joshua 6.3-5, performatively laying claim to the spiritual territory of the city against Buddhists and those practising traditional Chinese religions, and their demonic architecture.[56] Whenever a temple or shrine is encountered on one of these walks, the participants stop and pray to bring the territory under Christian dominion.[57] Beyond the global south, demonisations of the past happen as well. After a devastating earthquake hit Haiti in 2010, the well-known American evangelical and charismatic televangelist Pat Robertson (1930–2023) claimed on his popular Christian Broadcasting Network programme, "The 700 Club," that the disaster was punishment for the fact that the Haitians had made a pact with the devil in their struggle for independence in 1804. According to Robertson, the Haitians "were under the heel of the French. You know, Napoleon III (sic!) or whatever. And they got together and swore a pact to the devil. They said, 'We will serve you if you will get us free from the French.' True story. And so, the devil said, 'OK, it's a deal'. And they kicked the French out ... but ever since they have been cursed by one thing after another."[58] For Robertson, the trials of the Haitians can be explained by an association with the devil connected to historical and traditional events.

However, as a number of scholars have noted, the break with the past that neo-Pentecostal Christianity requires has limits.[59] For instance, a converted family that has traditionally offered libations to their ancestors may well stop doing so in the belief that these ancestors are in fact agents of Satan. But this does not diminish their belief in the reality of these ancestral spirits. Indeed, they may well still feel that they receive messages from their ancestors in their dreams. But such dreams are subsequently recast as ultimately having some sort of connection to the realm of the satanic.[60] With these spirits no longer placated by the family's offerings, it is often accepted that they are even more likely to impede the family's fortune—thus causing family members to seek out deliverance rituals. Given that this reworking of traditional belief increases the demand for spiritual services in this way, it is not surprising that pastors and prayer groups in neo-Pentecostal churches (as well as a growing number of classical mission churches) are engaged to pray for believers time and again—to these believers, this assimilation of ancestor belief into an evangelical frame means that it is almost impossible not to be haunted by the evil spirits of the past. If the neo-Pentecostal concern with deliverance shows one thing, it is that the forces of the past are still alive and kicking in the present.[61] This does not mean that Christianity has not brought change, but rather that the encounter between Christianity and traditional beliefs has led not to a rejection of traditional spirit entities but to a complete re-evaluation of them—an evaluation through the lens of an experiential demonism.[62]

## Wealth and Power

In contemporary African Christianity, wealth is sanctified. Alongside the idea of spiritual warfare, neo-Pentecostal theology stresses what it terms "the Prosperity Gospel." This asserts that a Christian's wealth or social standing can be read as an index of his or her piety: if a Christian is rich, it is a sign that he is blessed by God; if, on the other hand, he is poor, his faith is likely lacking or he is mired in sin.[63] That said, given the emphasis neo-Pentecostals place on the power and influence not just of the Holy Spirit but of the devil, too, the significance of a person's fortune can be ambiguous. Wealth and power can stem from a legitimate source—God—but it can also be of an illegitimate and even satanic nature. In this context, the evaluation of a person's fortune matters. If it is deemed legitimate, this means that the person's wealth is a sign of their spiritual support. Fortunes that are deemed illegitimate come from the realm of the devil.[64] Thus, many African neo-Pentecostal churches are deeply concerned with discerning the moral legitimacy of wealth.[65] In this section, then, I will describe how wealth and power became such ambivalent markers of an individual's spiritual status.

A characteristic of many traditional African societies is a stress on equivalence, the idea that "all members of the community are, in principle, equivalent as brothers and sisters."[66] In these traditional societies, the few elevated statuses that existed were deemed to exist by virtue of the support of spiritual forces. Access to these forces was mediated through rituals that involved the sacrifice of the lifeforce of animals and sometimes even of humans. In the popular culture of sub-Saharan Africa—rumours, folktales, movies and the like—the idea of becoming rich or powerful through the payment of a human life to the spirit world is a common motif.[67] Traditionally, the offering of such sacrifices seems to have been reserved for chiefs (and maybe a few others of elevated status) and performed only in extraordinary circumstances.[68] But the coming of colonialism with its realignment of traditional power structures encouraged those of lower social status to aspire to elevation as well, a desire that helped to "democratise" this practice in some sense.[69] Ordinary businessmen and politicians started to seek out the services of specialists in acquiring special powers as well. In this context, over the years, businessmen and politicians have come to be suspected of using sacrifices—a practice known in South Africa as killing for *muti* (medicine)—to advance their position.[70]

Contemporary African Christians characterise such practices as forms of Satanism.[71] In Zambia alone, over just four years, riots against businessmen alleged to have been practising Satanism took place in Chambishi (2012), Katete (2013), Ndola (2014), Shiwang'andu (2015), Luanshya (2015), Chingola (2015), Chipata (2015) and Mkushi (2015 and 2016). In most of these cases, the riots erupted after the disappearance and subsequent death (in most cases) of a local child, suggesting that rioters were moved to take to the streets believing that these children were murdered for their body parts—body parts ritually used to attract wealth and power.[72]

While the notion of human sacrifice is abhorrent within a Christian frame and so easily equated with satanic ritual, what makes them particularly evil in an African context is that such sacrifices are believed to have been offered for the sake of personal gain or success. Traditionally, legitimately acquired wealth is meant to be shared with the community, and power used for its betterment.[73] From this perspective, *muti* murders—if undertaken for the sake of individual ambition—are at odds with traditional conceptions of the purposes of wealth, and, by extension, undermine values of community and equivalence.

Like wealth, political power can be treated with suspicion. Politicians are also often suspected of involvement in practices associated with Satanism.[74] When the aforementioned committee that investigated rumours about devil worship in Kenya in the 1990s failed to publish its final report, this stirred up even more rumours—this time about the possibility that the politicians themselves were involved in Satanism.[75] The actions of both businessmen and politicians are deemed satanic not just because of the alleged means by which they have gained their wealth and power, but also because they are not using their fortune for the good of the community. In this sense, accusations of Satanism against contemporary politicians and businessmen—many of the latter of whom are non-ethnic Africans—in their pursuit of personal status and profit also stands as a critique of the breakdown of traditional patterns of communalism.[76]

While African and especially Pentecostal churches have tended historically not to take a stance in political matters, this has changed in recent years under the influence of territorial spiritual-warfare theology.[77] This type of neo-Pentecostal theology holds that there are demons who control specific geographical territories, often because of sins and evils committed there in the past—such things as the worship of traditional gods before the coming of Christianity. But this demonisation of space can also have a political dimension to it.

In Zimbabwe, for example, evangelicals have recently claimed that the social and economic problems currently dogging the country are a result of the pacts various people made with the devil during the liberation struggle of the 1960s and 1970s.[78] In this context, poverty is interpreted as a spiritual rather than an economic problem, and as such, the performance of political leaders in ameliorating such problems is viewed through a demonising lens. Should they have success in lifting people out of poverty, they are construed as breaking the region's ties to the devil. But, of course, the opposite is also true.[79]

While the close link between power and spiritual support may be specific to the African worldview, the influence of the idea of territorially grounded spiritual warfare is not.[80] The controversy over the carvings of traditional symbols in the Papua New Guinea parliament to which I alluded earlier had its roots in the belief that such symbols could bind the whole nation to the devil.[81] In Brazil, a bishop from the Universal Church of the Kingdom of God stated that the majority of politicians are in service of the devil, creating unjust laws. This was a problem, he asserted, that could only be remedied through prayer and the ritual action of the church.[82] With the success—or lack thereof—of political programmes viewed as a consequence of the spiritual battle between good and evil, it is not wholly surprising that such thinking has spilled over into election campaigns in some jurisdictions, with particular candidates evaluated according to the extent to which they are believed to serve the interests of God or, conversely, of the devil. In the Brazilian presidential elections of 2010, for example, candidate Dilma Rousseff's chances of winning in the first round of voting vanished after campaigns by both Catholic and evangelical churches.[83] Although she ended up winning the presidency that year and was re-elected in 2014, in 2016 the caucus of evangelical and Pentecostal Christians in the Brazilian National Congress was instrumental in reaching the majority needed to impeach her—a change deemed necessary for Brazil to become prosperous.[84] In Guatemala, spiritual warfare and citizenship are perceived as closely linked, implying that every citizen has the responsibility to fight Satan for the soul of the nation.[85] In some cases, this has helped fuel violent and lethal interactions aimed against outsiders and purported criminals who threaten the Christian status quo.[86] In neo-Pentecostal theology, the devil is politicised.

## The Return of the Devil

Contrary to the popular expression, what happens in Africa does not always stay in Africa. The concept of the devil that has developed in the global south has moved back north in recent decades brought along with migrants leaving Africa in search of a better future for themselves in Europe and the United States. AICs like the West African Aladura churches established themselves in the global north in the 1960s, but from the 1980s, they have been joined by a burgeoning number of newer neo-Pentecostal churches.[87] The Brazilian Universal Church of the Kingdom of God has now established branches in over 100 countries in both the global north and south.[88] Many of these churches from the global south have brought not only their vibrant styles of worship to their new host countries, but their theology—a theology in which the devil plays an important role. Thus, it is not uncommon, for instance, to find African diaspora churches singing a worship chorus about stomping down on the devil, or organising a Jesus march through the city to combat territorial demons.[89] The conception of the devil in these churches—a devil who is materialised and chased away through intense physical experiences—worries and perplexes many mainstream religious denominations.[90]

What is the influence of these churches from the global south on Christianity in Europe and the United States? On the one hand, the missionary zeal of these churches positions them well to convert new members in the global north.[91] On the other, many diaspora churches are particularly successful among migrant communities but lack converts who are not migrants or who come from a migrant family. In this sense, they are akin to migrant sanctuaries, catering to the needs of immigrants.[92] The Universal Church of the Kingdom of God, for instance, caters to migrants and refugees from diverse ethnic backgrounds.[93] Even though these churches may not have a big impact with regard to conversion, in contexts strongly influenced by de-Christianisation, migrants shore up falling numbers of Christians and their churches have—to some—become the new face of Christianity. In the United Kingdom, for instance, although attendance at Church of England and Church of Scotland services has declined, Pentecostalism has been growing, in terms of both the number of churches established and the number of adherents.[94] Migrant churches form an important part of Christianity in almost all urban areas in Europe, the United States and Australia.

Migrant churches are important in creating communities that provide help and opportunities to members to improve their future through social assistance and connections to employment.[95] Often, the experience of migrants is not easy. Some quickly discover that their expectations of prosperity are not met, and find themselves instead in troubled and stressful circumstances, struggling to make ends meet, sometimes even fearing deportation.[96] In the absence of a family network, a faith community can provide important social connections.

But alongside the sense of communal solidarity these churches provide, part of the force that helps bind the migrants attending these diaspora churches together is that of the devil. The image of the devil articulated by the preachers and through the rituals of these churches resonates with Christian migrants in different ways. To be sure, the Christians who attend their services come to share an enchanted worldview in which the boundary between mind and world is porous.[97] Much more than the Christians of Europe's traditional churches who are affected by the secular context in which they live and could themselves be argued to be secularised to a certain extent, these people are open to hearing the voice of God in their lives and to perceiving the actions of the devil underlying the circumstances with which they are confronted. This helps migrants contextualise their struggles in their new home, marking out the challenges they face as having some sort of eschatological significance, giving them meaning that transcends the mundane and worldly. But the corollary of this also matters, for recontextualising their experience in this way also suggests a way for them to reclaim some of the agency they feel they have lost—allowing them to take control over their lives in some way. In neo-Pentecostal migrant churches, this can mean becoming an active participant in a spiritual battle against the powers that are perceived to be the source of their troubles.[98] From this, it is just a short step for such people to conclude that the human agencies of their new host country that seem to be stifling their aspirations are in some way demonic. In some churches, it is not uncommon to hear that the immigration authorities are connected to the devil in just the same way that politicians in Africa or South America are sometimes believed to be.[99] In this way, migrants use their religious resources, which include a belief in Satan as a force that can cause problems, to make sense of their new context.[100]

The presence of migrant churches in Europe and North America has evoked concern as well. In 2000, eight-year-old Victoria Climbié was brought to a British hospital suffering from injuries and showing signs of grave neglect. She died a day later. Victoria's great-aunt, Marie-Thérèse Kouao and her boyfriend Carl Manning—with whom she was living—were later convicted of her murder. Over the previous months, Kouao had visited several diaspora churches in London with Victoria—including the Universal Church of the Kingdom of God—where pastors diagnosed her as being possessed with an evil spirit. Although the church officials did not suggest the manner of exorcism used by her guardians and advised them to take the girl to a hospital, the belief in the possibility of possession which is central to these churches' tenets likely contributed to the torture she suffered.[101]

It seems to be the case that with the coming of African churches in the diaspora, there has been a rise in alleged cases of witchcraft and possession.[102] Deliverance from evil spirits and witchcraft—both associated with Satan—is a common practice in many neo-Pentecostal and mainline churches in the global south. Consequently, dispossession rituals now take place in the diaspora churches as well, often sought out to provide relief from some of the inevitable difficulties new migrants to a country experience. If someone struggles to find a job in their new homeland, for instance, struggles with anxiety, or suffers in some other way, linking these problems to the action of demonic forces gives them meaning, recasting the ordinary travails of migrant life as part of the great eschatological struggle against evil. But if the cause of the problem for which the afflicted is seeking help is deemed to be spiritual, state medical or social services that work from a secular perspective are believed to be unhelpful in these cases.[103] In such cases, pastors in African churches promise to offer a solution through rituals of deliverance.

Once begun, though, the dispossession process often discovers that the devil is working his malice through some member of the community—someone who is then singled out as being possessed or as a witch. Children and youths are especially vulnerable in this regard particularly those who seem to have a weak bond of affection with their accuser.[104] They may live in the same household, but may only be distantly related to other family members—or not related at all. Often, the child also is perceived as "different" due to a disability or illness, or because of some sort of challenging behaviour.[105] The process of dispossession usually centres on prayer, but there have been instances in which violence was used against the child as well.[106] Sometimes, these accusations can lead to child abuse, as in the case of Victoria Climbié. According to recent research by the British Local Government Association, the abuse of children based on belief—which includes cases where accused abusers justify their actions on the basis of the fact that they believed their victim was possessed and had succumbed to witchcraft—has increased by a third to 1,950 cases per year between 2016 and 2019.[107]

This has stoked a rise in bigotry against diaspora communities in the West, particularly in Britain, where the connection between a belief in witchcraft and possession on the one hand and child abuse on the other has been stoked by the popular press, feeding into the public discourse. The shocking case of Victoria Climbié has clearly played a role in this, but so have other notable cases in which African churches were suspected to be involved. In this capacity, the 2001 discovery of the torso of a young boy of African descent in the Thames in London stands out. Although the identity of the boy was unknown and there was no reason to assume that he had been deemed to be possessed, the British media and public quickly came to assume that he was a victim of ritual sacrifice sanctioned at some level by African churches in the city.

Coming on the heels of the satanic panics of the 1980s and 1990s, this crime echoed fears of ritual murders. But instead of looking for a group of alleged British satanists as would have been the case a decade or so earlier, the attention of law enforcement, the media and the public shifted to African immigrant communities. Building on old, imperialist, racist tropes, as the boy was clearly African, his murder, it was widely assumed, must be linked to secret, occult rituals—rituals when traced back to their origin which were ultimately satanic.[108] These Western images of Africa may still be a factor in the concern that some commentators show towards African churches in the diaspora. In secular western Europe, the enchanted worldview of diaspora churches is almost by default perceived as something that is *other* and therefore potentially dangerous.

This does not mean that diaspora churches are able to retain an unchanging religious worldview; it does not mean that they can transpose their heritage from the global south to their new environment wholesale. The secular context in which these diaspora churches operate also influences their practices and belief systems. In some respects, they have had to adapt to an environment in which institutionalised religion has been relegated to the private sphere.[109] But this new context also has had an effect on the understanding of Satan and his agents. As we have seen, many neo-Pentecostal churches from the global south demonise traditional spiritual beings. In the Universal Church of the Kingdom of God in Spain, however, the demons that are exorcised are not described as spirits linked to a traditional religion, but as personifications of the troubles that members of the church experience. In the ritual of deliverance, the demons are asked to give their names. Instead of giving the name of a spiritual being known from another religious tradition, they label themselves things like "the spirit of bankruptcy," "the spirit of poverty" or "the spirit of depression."[110] This change could be interpreted as a consequence of the secularised environment. But more research needs to be done to establish how the image of Satan seems to be evolving in migrant and diaspora churches operating in a secular context.

## Conclusion

After the idea of the devil was introduced into the global south, it was indigenised quickly and assimilated into more traditional conceptions of spiritual forces, their actions and effects. But the journey of the devil to the global south was not one-way traffic. Spiritual-warfare theology, that global mainstay of neo-Pentecostal Christianity, may not have been developed if American theologians had not experienced ideas about the devil in the context of their missionary work in the global south. Neo-Pentecostalism, in turn, has had a great effect in the global south, placing Satan centre stage—a place he retains within migrant churches in Europe and the United States.

In the context of growing secularisation and profound changes in morality and values, the idea of the devil enchants the world once more. It gives meaning to contemporary issues like poverty, political corruption, the consequences of unrestrained progress and the accumulation of wealth, and, in the global south, it provides a way to think about the rise of individualism as traditional patterns of communalism break down under the weight of unrestrained capitalism.

This overview of the history of thinking about the devil in the global south in the 20th and early 21st centuries shows that the devil is still pre-eminently good to think with.

## Notes

1 Thomas and Helen Junk, "God Is Blessing in China," *Bridegroom's Messenger* 15 February 1909, 1.
2 Bernhard Udelhoven, "The Devil of the Missionary Church: The White Fathers and Catholic Evangelization of Zambia,' *Journal of Global Catholicism* 2, no. 1 (2017): 101.
3 Whether to classify African Initiated Churches as Pentecostal is a contentious issue. I base this definition on Allan Anderson's "Varieties, Taxonomies, and Definitions," in *Studying Global Pentecostalism: Theories and Methods*, ed. Allan Anderson, Michael Bergunder, André Droogers and Cornelis van der Laan (Berkeley, 2010), 13–29.
4 Laurenti Magesa, *African Religion: The Moral Traditions of Abundant Life* (Maryknoll, 1997), 48.

5 Bernhard Udelhoven, *Unseen Worlds: Dealing with Spirits, Witchcraft, and Satanism* (Lusaka, 2015), 73 and 274–5.

6 I allude here to Birgit Meyer's seminal work *Translating the Devil: Religion and Modernity among the Ewe in Ghana* (London, 1999).

7 Adam Ashforth, "Reflections on Spiritual Insecurity in a Modern African City (Soweto)," *African Studies Review* 41, no. 3 (1998): 39–67 on 59.

8 Udelhoven, "Devil of the Missionary Church," 93, see also Meyer, *Translating the Devil*, 83–111.

9 Birgit Meyer, ""If You Are a Devil, You Are a Witch and if You Are a Witch, You Are a Devil." The Integration of 'Pagan' Ideas into the Conceptual Universe of Ewe Christians in Southeastern Ghana," *Journal of Religion in Africa* 22, no. 2 (1992): 122.

10 J. Kwabena Asamoah-Gyadu, "Pentecostalism and the Transformation of the African Christian Landscape." In *Pentecostalism in Africa: Presence and Impact of Pneumatic Christianity in Postcolonial Societies*, ed. Martin Lindhardt (Leiden, 2015): 103.

11 Meyer, *Translating the Devil*, 137.

12 Marthinus L. Daneel, "Coping with Wizardry in Zimbabwe in African Initiated Churches (AICs)" in *Coping with Evil in Religion and Culture*, ed. Nelly van Doorn-Harder and Lourens Minnema (Amsterdam, 2008): 51f, and Afe Adogame, "Engaging the Rhetoric of Spiritual Warfare: The Public Face of Aladura in Diaspora," *Journal of Religion in Africa* 34, no. 4 (2004): 493–522.

13 Stephen Hunt, "Deliverance: The Evolution of a Doctrine," *Themelios* 21, no. 1 (1995): 10–3.

14 Michael Wilkinson, "The Emergence, Development, and Pluralisation of Global Pentecostalism," in *Handbook of Global Contemporary Christianity: Themes and Developments in Culture, Politics, and Society*, ed. Stephen Hunt (Leiden, 2015), 97.

15 Martin Lindhardt, "Introduction: Presence and Impact of Pentecostal/Charismatic Christianity in Africa." in *Pentecostalism in Africa: Presence and Impact of Pneumatic Christianity in Postcolonial Societies*, ed. Martin Lindhardt (Leiden, 2015), 1.

16 Lindhardt, "Introduction," 5.

17 Allan Anderson "Exorcism and Conversion to African Pentecostalism," *Exchange* 35, no. 1 (2006): 122.

18 Rosalind Hackett, "Discourses of Demonization in Africa and Beyond," *Diogenes* 50, no. 3 (2003): 62.

19 Knut Rio, Michelle MacCarthy and Ruy Blanes, "Introduction to Pentecostal Witchcraft and Spiritual Politics in Africa and Melanesia," in *Pentecostalism and Witchcraft: Spiritual Warfare in Africa and Melanesia*, ed. Knut Rio, Michelle MacCarthy and Ruy Blanes (Cham, 2017), 11.

20 Other authors refer to the complex of Pentecostal-charismatic churches (PCC) when they speak of the development of Christianity in the global south. I choose to use the term "neo-Pentecostalism" because it is mainly the churches that are influenced by the third wave in the development of Pentecostalism that focus strongly on the workings of the devil. Older, classical Pentecostal or charismatic churches often show considerable hesitancy towards this.

21 Nimi Wariboko, *Nigerian Pentecostalism* (Rochester, 2014), 34.

22 Anderson, "Exorcism and Conversion," 133.

23 Rio, MacCarthy and Blanes, "Introduction," 12.

24 Paul Gifford, "Reinhard Bonnke's Mission to Africa, and His 1991 Nairobi Crusade," *Wajibu* 9, no. 1 (1994): 15.

25 Ilana van Wyk, "'All Answers': On the Phenomenal Success of a Brazilian Pentecostal Charismatic Church in South Africa," in *Pentecostalism in Africa: Presence and Impact of Pneumatic Christianity in Postcolonial Societies*, ed. Martin Lindhardt (Leiden, 2015), 153.

26 Philip Jenkins, *The New Faces of Christianity: Believing the Bible in the Global South* (Oxford, 2006), 105.

27 Anderson, "Exorcism and Conversion," 130. Gregory Deacon, "Driving the Devil Out: Kenya's Born-Again Election," *Journal of Religion in Africa* 45 (2015): 201.

28 Wariboko, *Nigerian Pentecostalism*, 35.

29 Steve Brouwer, Paul Gifford and Susan D. Rose, *Exporting the American Gospel: Global Christian Fundamentalism* (New York, 1996), 181.

30 Lindhardt, "Introduction," 16.

31 Gregory Deacon and Gabrielle Lynch, "Allowing Satan In? Moving Toward a Political Economy of Neo-Pentecostalism in Kenya," *Journal of Religion in Africa* 43 (2013): 117.

32 David Ngong, "Stifling the Imagination: A Critique of Anthropological and Religious Normalization of Witchcraft in Africa," *African and Asian Studies* 11 (2012): 174 and 178.

33 Deacon and Lynch, "Allowing Satan in?" 111.

34 Rio, MacCarthy and Blanes, "Introduction," 12. See also Seth Tweneboah, "Pentecostalism, Witchdemonic Accusations, and Symbolic Violence in Ghana," *Pneuma* 37 (2015) and Lynda Newland, "Turning the Spirits into Witchcraft: Pentecostalism in Fijian Villages," *Oceania* 75, no. 1 (September 2004).

35 Hackett, "Discourses of Demonization," 64.

36 Hackett, "Discourses of Demonization," 68.

37 Gerrie ter Haar and Stephen Ellis, "Spirit Possession and Healing in Modern Zambia: An Analysis of Letters to Archbishop Milingo," *African Affairs* 87, no. 347 (April 1988): 196.

38 Anderson, "Exorcism and Conversion," 121.

39 Opoku Onyinah, *Pentecostal Exorcism: Witchcraft and Demonology in Ghana* (Blandford Forum, 2012): 175.

40 Jenkins, *New Faces of Christianity*, 100. Adam Ashforth, *Witchcraft, Violence, and Democracy in South Africa* (Chicago, 2005).

41 Brouwer, Gifford and Rose, *Exporting the American Gospel*, 169f.

42 Paul Gifford, "Unity and Diversity within African Pentecostalism: A Comparison of the Christianities of Daniel Olukoya and David Oyedepo," in *Pentecostalism in Africa: Presence and Impact of Pneumatic Christianity in Postcolonial Societies*, ed. Martin Lindhardt (Leiden, 2015): 117.

43 The label of "Satanist" is used particularly in Southern Africa. See Johanneke Kroesbergen-Kamps, *Speaking of Satan in Zambia: Making Cultural and Personal Sense of Narratives about Satanism* (Cape Town, 2022) and Jean Comaroff and John Comaroff, "Occult Economies and the Violence of Abstraction: Notes from the South African Postcolony," *American Ethnologist* 26, no. 2 (1999): 286. For those linked by others to Satan, see, for example, the well-known testimonies of Emmanuel Eni from Nigeria and Evangelist Mukendi from the Democratic Republic of Congo, but also testimonies in Ghana. See Meyer, *Translating the Devil*, 201.

44 David Frankfurter, *Evil Incarnate. Rumors of Demonic Conspiracy and Satanic Abuse in History* (Princeton, 2006): 155f.

45 Eric W. Kramer, "Spectacle and the Staging of Power in Brazilian Neo-Pentecostalism," *Latin American Perspectives*, Issue 140, vol. 32, no. 1 (2005): 104.

46 See Johanneke Kroesbergen-Kamps, "Dreaming of Snakes in Contemporary Zambia: Small Gods and the Secular" in *Fairies, Demons, and Nature Spirits: 'Small Gods' at the Margins of Christendom*, ed. Michael Ostling (London, 2018): 248. See also Kramer, "Spectacle and the Staging of Power," 110.

47 See Birgit Meyer, "'Make a Complete Break with the Past.' Memory and Post-Colonial Identity in Ghanaian Pentecostalist Discourse," *Journal of Religion in Africa* 28, no. 2 (August 1998): 316–49.

48 Anderson, "Exorcism and Conversion," 121.

49 See Ogbu Kalu, "Pentecostal and Charismatic Reshaping of the African Religious Landscape in the 1990s," *Mission Studies* XX (2003): 90 and Birgit Meyer, "Christianity in Africa: From African Independent to Pentecostal-Charismatic Churches,' *Annual Review of Anthropology* 33 (2004): 452 and 456.

50 Paul Gifford, *African Christianity: Its Public Role* (Bloomington, 1998): 328.

51 Filip De Boeck and Sammy Baloji, *Suturing the City: Living Together in Congo's Urban Worlds* (London, 2016), 10.

52 Birgit Meyer and Marleen de Witte, "Heritage and the Sacred: Introduction," *Material Religion* 9, no. 3 (2013): 278.

53 Thomas Strong, "Becoming Witches: Sight, Sin, and Social Change in the Eastern Highlands of Papua New Guinea," in *Pentecostalism and Witchcraft: Spiritual Warfare in Africa and Melanesia*, ed. Knut Rio, Michelle MacCarthy and Ruy Blanes (Cham, 2017), 74.

54 Justin Michael Doran, *Demon-Haunted Worlds: Enchantment, Disenchantment, and the Universal Church of the Kingdom of God*, MA Thesis (University of Texas at Austin, 2013), 31f.

55 See Richard Eves, "'In God's Hands': Pentecostal Christianity, Morality, and Illness in a Melanesian Society," *The Journal of the Royal Anthropological Institute* 16, no. 3 (2010): 501 and Fraser Macdonald, "'God Was Here First': Value, Hierarchy, and Conversion in a Melanesian Christianity," *Ethnos* (2018): 12.

56 Benjamin Kirby, "Occupying the Global City: Spatial Politics and Spiritual Warfare among African Pentecostals in Hong Kong," in *Religion and the Global City*, ed. David Garbin and Anna Strhan (London, 2017), 71.

57 Daniel P. S. Goh, "Chinese Religion and the Challenge of Modernity in Malaysia and Singapore: Syncretism, Hybriditisation and Transfiguration," *Asian Journal of Social Science* 37 (2009): 130.

58 "Pat Robertson Calls Quake 'blessing in Disguise'," YouTube Video, 13 January 2010. https://www.youtube.com/watch?v=f5TE99sAbwM. See also Elizabeth McAlister, "From Slave Revolt to a Blood Pact with Satan: The Evangelical Rewriting of History," *Studies in Religion / Sciences Religieuses* 41, no. 2 (2012): 187–215.

59 See for an early example of this idea that has now become commonplace Meyer, "Make a Complete Break with the Past."

60 Udelhoven, "Devil of the Missionary Church," 88.

61 Meyer, "Christianity in Africa," 457.

62 Joel Robbins, "Can There Be Conversion without Cultural Change?" *Mission Studies* 34, no. 1 (March 2017): 43.

63 See, for example, Deacon and Lynch, "Allowing Satan In?" 109f, and Lindhardt, "Introduction," 8.

64 Deacon and Lynch, "Allowing Satan In?" 111.

65 Martin Lindhardt, "Continuity, Change or Coevalness? Charismatic Christianity and Tradition in Contemporary Tanzania," in *Pentecostalism in Africa: Presence and Impact of Pneumatic Christianity in Postcolonial Societies*, ed. Martin Lindhardt (Leiden, 2015): 182. See also Meyer, "Christianity in Africa," 460.

66 Robert Thornton, *Healing the Exposed Being: A South African Ngoma Tradition* (Johannesburg, 2017): 138.

67 Wariboko, *Nigerian Pentecostalism*, 123f. For a thorough discussion of the devil in popular West African movies, see Birgit Meyer, *Sensational Movies: Video, Vision, and Christianity in Ghana* (Oakland, 2015).

68 Johanneke Kroesbergen-Kamps, "Religion, Satanic Accusations, and Politics," in *Competing for Caesar: Religion and Politics in Postcolonial Zambia*, ed. Chammah J. Kaunda and Marja Hinfelaar (Minneapolis, 2020): 185ff.

69 Rob Turrell, "*Muti* Ritual Murder in Natal: From Chiefs to Commoners (1900-1930)," *South African Historical Journal* 44, no. 1 (2001).

70 Kroesbergen-Kamps, "Religion, Satanic Accusations, and Politics."

71 In Zambia, people make a relatively clear distinction between Satanism and other phenomena attributed to the devil, such as possession or witchcraft. In other parts of sub-Saharan Africa, this distinction is less clear, although all of the things mentioned here are clearly connected to Satan and therefore could be labelled as Satanic as well.

72 Some of the children in these cases were found murdered; others were recovered alive. In some cases, body parts were missing, but not always. Riots often occur when a situation is still developing and people imagine what could have happened, drawing on the motifs present in popular culture and belief. That being said, murder for body parts does happen in Africa, although there are no statistics on it.

73 Robert J. Thornton, *Healing the Exposed Being: A South African Ngoma Tradition* (Johannesburg, 2017): 138.

74 Kroesbergen-Kamps, "Religion, Satanic Accusations, and Politics." See also Stephen Ellis and Gerrie ter Haar, *Worlds of Power: Religious Thought and Political Practice in Africa* (New York, 2004), 78 and Peter Geschiere, *The Modernity of Witchcraft: Politics and the Occult in Postcolonial Africa* (Charlottesville, 1997).

75 Wariboko, *Nigerian Pentecostalism*, 109, and Deacon and Lynch, "Allowing Satan In?" 117.

76 Kroesbergen-Kamps, "Religion, Satanic Accusations, and Politics," 192.

77 Gifford, *African Christianity*, 21f. See also Andreas Heuser, "Encoding Caesar's Realm—Variants of Spiritual Warfare Politics in Africa," in *Pentecostalism in Africa: Presence and Impact of Pneumatic Christianity in Postcolonial Societies*, ed. Martin Lindhardt (Leiden, 2015).

78 Ezra Chitando, "'Down with the Devil, Forward with Christ!' A Study of the Interface between Religious and Political Discourses in Zimbabwe," *African Sociological Review* 6, no. 1 (2002): 11.

79 Wariboko, *Nigerian Pentecostalism*, 241.

80 Rio, MacCarthy, and Blanes, "Introduction," 5.

81 Rio, MacCarthy, and Blanes, "Introduction," 2.

82 Ari Pedro Oro, "The Politics of The Universal Church and its Consequences on Religion and Politics in Brazil," trans. Enrique J. Romera, *Revista Brasileira de Ciências Sociais,* 18, no. 53 (2005): 6f.

83 Carlos Gustavo Sarmet Moreira Smiderle and Wania Amelia Belchior Mesquita, "Political Conflict and Spiritual Battle: Intersections between Religion and Politics among Brazilian Pentecostals," *Latin American Perspectives*, issue 208, 43, no. 3 (2016): 85–103.

84 Virginia Garrard, "Hidden in Plain Sight: Dominion Theology, Spiritual Warfare, and Violence in Latin America," *Religions* 11, no. 648 (2020): 8.

85 Kevin Lewis O'Neill, *City of God: Christian Citizenship in Postwar Guatemala* (Berkeley, 2010): 89.

86 Garrard, "Hidden in Plain Sight," 6.

87 Afe Adogame, "Engaging the Rhetoric of Spiritual Warfare: The Public Face of Aladura in Diaspora," *Journal of Religion in Africa* 34, no. 4 (2004): 500.

88 Kathleen Openshaw, "The Universal Church of the Kingdom of God in Australia: A Church of Non-Brazilian Migrants," *Social Compass* 68, no. 2 (2021): 231.

89 Annalisa Butticci, *African Pentecostals in Catholic Europe: The Politics of Presence in the Twenty-First Century* (Cambridge, 2016): 4. J. Kwabena Asamoah Gyadu, "'To the Ends of the Earth': Mission, Migration and the Impact of African-led Pentecostal Churches in the European Diaspora," *Mission Studies* 29 (2012): 31.

90 Butticci, *African Pentecostals*, 64.

91 Gyadu, "To the Ends of the Earth," 24 and Moses O. Biney, "African Christianity and Transnational Religious Networks: From Africa to America and back to Africa," in *The Routledge Companion to Christianity in Africa*, ed. Elias Kifon Bongmba (New York, 2016), 343.

92 Babatunde Aderemi Adedibu, "Reverse Mission or Migrant Sanctuaries? Migration, Symbolic Mapping, and Missionary Challenges of Britain's Black Majority Churches," *Pneuma* 35 (2013): 416 and 423.

93 Openshaw, "The Universal Church of the Kingdom of God in Australia," 231.

94 Kirsty Rowan and Karen Dwyer, "Demonic Possession and Deliverance in the Diaspora: Phenomenological Descriptions from Pentecostal Deliverees," *Mental Health, Religion and Culture* 18, no. 6 (2015): 441.

95 Leonardo Vasconcelos de Castro Moreira, "Self Othering in the Testimonials of the Universal Church of the Kingdom of God in Madrid," *Social Compass* 68, no. 1 (2021): 126.

96 Joseph Bosco Bangura, "Holding My Anchor in Turbulent Waters. God, Pentecostalism, and the African Diaspora in Belgium," *Pneuma* 40 (2018): 514.

97 For the concept of "porosity," see Tanya Marie Luhrmann and Kara Weisman, "Porosity is the Heart of Religion," *Current Directions in Psychological Science* 31, no. 3 (2022), 247–53.

98 Openshaw, "The Universal Church of the Kingdom of God in Australia," 238.

99 Gyadu, "To the Ends of the Earth," 24.

100 Manuel A. Vásquez and Kim Knott, "Three Dimensions of Religious Place Making in the Diaspora," *Global Networks* 14, no. 3 (2014): 326.

101 Amanda van Eck Duymaer van Twist, "Beliefs in Possession," in *The Devil's Children: From Spirit Possession to Witchcraft: New Allegations that Affect Children*, ed. Jean La Fontaine (Farnham, 2009), 18.

102 Kirsty Rowan, "'Who Are You in this Body?': Identifying Demons and the Path to Deliverance in a London Pentecostal Church," *Language in Society* 45 (2016): 247.

103 Jean La Fontaine, *Witches and Demons: A Comparative Perspective on Witchcraft and Satanism* (New York, 2016), 109.

104 La Fontaine, *Witches and Demons*, 96f. Eleanor Stobart, "Child Abuse Linked to Cases of 'Possession' and 'Witchcraft'," in *The Devil's Children: From Spirit Possession to Witchcraft: New Allegations that Affect Children*, ed. Jean La Fontaine (Abingdon, 2009): 162.

105 Stobart, "Child Abuse," 158.

106 See La Fontaine, *Witches and Demons*, 97 and La Fontaine, "Child Witches," 117f.

107  William Eichler, "Child Abuse Linked to Faith Rises by 'a Third', Council Chiefs Warn," LocalGov, 14 November 2019. https://www.localgov.co.uk/Child-abuse-linked-to-faith-rises-by-a-third-council-chiefs-warn/48530
108  Terence Ranger, "Scotland Yard in the Bush: Medicine Murders, Child Witches and the Construction of the Occult: A Literature Review," *Africa* 77, no. 2 (2007), 272–283.
109  Joseph Bosco Bangura, "Holding My Anchor in Turbulent Waters," 504.
110  Leonardo Vasconcelos de Castro Moreira, "The Secularisation of Demons: Exorcisms Conducted by the Universal Church of the Kingdom of God in Madrid," *Journal of Contemporary Religion* 37, no. 1 (2022): 117.

## Bibliography of Selected Readings

Bernhard Udelhoven, *Unseen Worlds: Dealing with Spirits, Witchcraft, and Satanism* (Lusaka: FENZA Publications, 2015).
Birgit Meyer, *Translating the Devil: Religion and Modernity among the Ewe in Ghana* (London: Edinburgh University Press, 1999).
Jean La Fontaine, *Witches and Demons: A Comparative Perspective on Witchcraft and Satanism* (New York: Berghahn, 2016).
Johanneke Kroesbergen-Kamps, *Speaking of Satan in Zambia: Making Cultural and Personal Sense of Narratives about Satanism* (Cape Town: AOSIS, 2022).
Knut Rio, Michelle MacCarthy and Ruy Blanes (eds.), *Pentecostalism and Witchcraft: Spiritual Warfare in Africa and Melanesia* (Cham: Palgrave Macmillan, 2017).
Martin Lindhardt (ed.), *Pentecostalism in Africa: Presence and Impact of Pneumatic Christianity in Postcolonial Societies* (Leiden: Brill, 2015).

# 26

# THE DIGITAL DEVIL

*Philip L. Frana*

Digital computing is full of dark metaphors. When a program crashes, it is said to "hang" or "die." The "kill" command terminates a running process inside an operating system. "Master/slave replication" describes the way database administrators maintain simultaneous data backups on multiple servers. The terms "gypsy wagon" and "poltergeist" are used by hackers to denote hidden objects in code that appear and disappear inexplicably. "Evil numbers" are those that have even parity, an important property in a branch of computing that grapples with the transmission of information over long distances. "Code bombs" are viruses deliberately planted by programmers in order to punish clients who refuse to pay. Many personal computer owners have first-hand experience with "dependency hell," a technical term used to explain why new software sometimes will not run on old machines.

The language used to describe computers, programming, and other digital practices often draws on imagery of demons, wizards, and other supernatural entities. In Unix operating systems, automated tasks are performed by "daemons." Strings or numbers that are crucial for program execution, yet lack any accompanying context or explanation for their existence, are called "magic values." Technicians who lose control of the servers they maintain are termed "sorcerers' apprentices." Developers have long been known to give their systems and programs Mephistophelian names. An early 1960s data processing system developed by military contractor American Bosch Arma is named Daemon, an acronym for Data Adaptive Evaluator and Monitor,[1] and "DEMON" is a program written by the Australian Atomic Energy Commission in 1965 that solves differential equations.[2] "Natas" (Satan spelled backwards) and "Satan Bug" are computer viruses written by the hacker "Priest" that infected computers of the United States Secret Service in the early 1990s.[3] "DEVIL" is an interface definition language released in 2000 that helps write efficient low-level code.[4] And "DevIL" is a 2002 cross-platform image library that defines a common application programming interface for various file formats.[5]

The metaphorical language of computing reflects a long-standing tradition of associating scientific and technological innovations with otherworldly powers. Massachusetts Institute of Technology (MIT) roboticist Rodney Brooks in his 2002 book *Flesh and Machines: How Robots Will Change Us* outlines two common views of what an automated future will look like. One view is "damnation"; the other, "salvation."[6] From the damnation perspective,

DOI: 10.4324/9781003096603-27

robots will be emotionless and remorseless, lacking empathy for humanity. For example, evolvable hardware pioneer Hugo de Garis describes an inevitable Terminator-like "artilect war" triggered by super-intelligent machines.[7] From the salvation perspective, intelligent robots offer a path to immortality. Digital technologies will give us the ability to download human consciousness, gain immortality or live in a post-scarcity economy. The extropian perspective, which advocates for the continuous technological improvement of humanity, finds support from well-known computer scientists like Hans Moravec and Ray Kurzweil.[8]

"Geek mythology" is suffused with mystic and evangelistic parables about robot takeovers and the boundless power of artificial intelligence. Exponentially increasing computing power is also inspiring new faiths and challenging established belief systems. The Terasem Movement seeks to bestow upon its followers the prospect of heavenly immortality by uploading minds into virtual reality simulations.[9] The Church of Perpetual Life embraces expert knowledge on artificial intelligence, transhumanism and cryonics.[10] The disbanded Way of the Future was established with the purpose of advocating for a future where an artificial superintelligence (ASI) receives reverence, legal rights and assumes control over the planet.[11] The Christian Transhumanist Association and the Mormon Transhumanist Association recognise that science, technology, and artificial intelligence serve to exalt human beings and affirm Christian fellowship.[12] The android Mindar is a popular Buddhist priest at the Kodaiji temple in Kyoto, Japan.[13] In contrast, the Southern Baptist Convention categorically rejects the innate "identity, worth, dignity, or moral agency" of AI.[14]

The experts who create and amplify these technologies are substituting one array of deities for another as they contemplate the consequences of software development and machine learning. As we will see, angels, demons, and demigods haunt the logic gates, information theories, and software agents devised by computer scientists. In the context of computer operating systems, a "daemon" is a background process or service that runs independently of user interaction. Daemons perform various tasks, such as managing system resources, handling network requests, scheduling processes or serving other programs. Programmers refer to elusive errors and glitches in code as the "ghost in the machine." In object-oriented programming, a "god object" is a software object or class that has excessive responsibilities, control or knowledge about various parts of a computer system. The process of constructing AI models is characterised as "techno-magical." Use of AI chatbot services such as Bard, Bing, and GPT is colloquially regarded as "promptmancy." The hapless lawyer who supplemented his important court filing with "hallucinated" citations provided by ChatGPT is a Faustian figure making a pact with a mischievous demon who promises enlightenment but delivers confusion.[15] "I find it hard to believe that we could manufacture robots that actually worked and not have them disturb our ideas of religion and God," writes *Wired* magazine founding editor Kevin Kelly in 2010. "Someday we will make other minds, and they will surprise us."[16]

The cultural fears and anxieties surrounding the rise of electronic technologies have frequently been expressed in terms of moral panics, with hackers and heavy internet users cast as dangerous and subversive individuals. During the satanic panic of the 1980s and early 1990s, cyberpunks and hackers were erroneously associated with malevolent practices due to their fascination with personal computers, unconventional lifestyles and countercultural ideologies.[17] This conflation of technological enthusiasm and moral transgression was fuelled by sensationalised media accounts and cultural anxieties regarding the potential dangers of emerging digital subcultures.[18] Long-ago hacker activities still resonate in current public affairs. In 2019, American presidential candidate Beto O'Rourke was unmasked as a teenage member of the 1980s group Cult of the Dead Cow, which traded pirated video games, stole phone credit card numbers and calling card codes and facilitated other illegal activities on computer bulletin boards.[19] The group also distributed an underground electronic magazine which burst into public view in a television episode of *Geraldo* entitled "Computer Vice." In the episode, host Geraldo Rivera calls the hackers a "bunch of sickos" for publishing a sexually explicit story entitled "Sex with Satan."[20]

Complaints about the evils of electronic videogames paralleled mistrust of computers. The arcade game *Death Race* attained infamy in 1976. The objective of *Death Race* is to use a car to run over humanoid "gremlins" that scream when hit.[21] The fighting game *Mortal Kombat* was so gruesome—players could punch through the chests of characters and rip out their spines—that it sparked senate hearings in the United States in 1993.[22] The original game in the *Grand Theft Auto* franchise, released in 1997, was decried as a "murder simulator."[23] *Grand Theft Auto III* was banned in Australia for depicting sexual violence involving prostitutes. Moral outrage followed in the wake of the Columbine High School massacre in 1999.[24] School shooters Eric Harris and Dylan Klebold were avid video game players. Among the games mentioned in reports of the Columbine shooting aftermath is *Doom*, the premise of which centres on fighting demons from hell.[25] In 2009, Marla Jo Fisher attracted media attention when her complaint that "Video Games Were Invented by the Devil" was published in the *Orange County Register*.[26] "I truly believe that video games were created by Satan to turn otherwise normal children into his drooling, glassy-eyed stooges," she explained.[27]

This chapter will explore the history of the relationship between the devil and digital technologies, particularly from the 1960s to the 2020s. It seeks to explain how reliance on "demon thinking" has influenced the development of information technologies in the Western tradition, and the ways that it continues to inform the culture, artefacts, and representations of hackerdom. It begins with an exploration of the demons of information theory and operating systems, moves on to explain how hackers became folk devils, and describes the preparations and responses of cryptography and cybersecurity professionals. The chapter concludes with an examination of the demon-haunted world of artificial intelligence, computational thinking, and the contemporary internet.

## A Veiled Enigma: Demons and Information Flows

Digital devilry carries a profound historical legacy in programming, for it has been there since the beginning and continues to be transmitted from one generation of coders to the next. As far back as the 1840s, Ada Lovelace, who worked on programs for an unfinished, steam-powered general-purpose computer called the Analytical Engine, wrote to her collaborator Charles Babbage: "[T]hat brain of mine is something more than merely Mortal. ... Before ten years are over, the Devil's in it if I haven't sucked out some of the life-blood from the mysteries of this universe."[28] And separately, "I am working very hard for you, like the Devil in fact (which perhaps I am). I think you will be pleased."[29]

The demons of digital information emerged from the demons of physics. In physics a "demon" is a hypothetical supernatural being that has its own agency and can violate laws of nature. Devils borrowed from physics, notably Laplace's demon, profoundly influenced the theory of information flows in digital communications. The physicist Pierre-Simon Laplace imagined this demon—which knew the past and future of every atom in the universe—as all-knowing and infernally super-intelligent. Babbage noticed that Laplace's demon imitated deterministic principles that drove machines. Both harnessed precise and rule-based operations, which also sought to control complex natural phenomena.[30] Inspired, he and Lovelace turned this powerful demon into a computational program within a cogwheel brain, in the process reimagining it as an analytical engine.[31]

Ludwig Boltzmann, a late 19th-century inventor of statistical mechanics, uncovered a paradox within Laplace's deterministic worldview: why are particle movements irreversible in practice? Why do they only move in one direction, like ripples in water resulting from a thrown stone?[32] Boltzmann also spent time wrestling with Maxwell's demon, a hypothetical entity imagined by James Clerk Maxwell that also worked surreptitiously behind the scenes to control nature. Maxwell's demon violated the second law of thermodynamics by selectively allowing particles to pass between two chambers of gas and lowering system entropy.[33] Intrigued by this thought, Boltzmann developed statistical mechanics, which is based on a probabilistic law of disorder where entropy and randomness increase in isolated systems over time.[34]

Maxwell's and Boltzmann's demons sparked research at Bell Telephone Laboratories, which uncovered the fundamental connection between thermodynamics and information theory. Bell Labs paid its researchers to invent dependable telephone networks, spelunk the technical limits of communications systems, and create new digital technologies. Decipherment of the mathematics of information transmission by numerous individuals led to multiple innovations.[35] For instance, Harry Nyquist studied the transmission of "intelligence" and signal bandwidth requirements for telegraph, telephone and television. Ralph Hartley focused on devices that retransmit signals and devised a law that linked information transmission with frequency range and available time.[36] Hartley admired James Clerk Maxwell's super-intelligent demon, and drew parallels to information flow.[37] Together, Nyquist and Hartley concluded that clear and high-capacity channels will ensure the reliable transmission of information, and that in noiseless channels supervised by information demons, signals can be communicated intact. But in real-world systems, information cannot be transmitted without noise creeping into the physical medium. This fact necessitated the invention of techniques such as error correction, modulation, and signal processing to mitigate interference and ensure successful communication.

Claude Shannon at Bell Labs brought together these and other ideas in his 1948 "A Mathematical Theory of Communication"[38] which contained a formal theory of information transmission, processing and usage. Shannon had realised that noise, probability and uncertainty must form the bedrock of any working information theory. He introduced the concept of a "bit" to measure this uncertainty. And he swiped the term "entropy" to describe the information quantities in a particular channel,[39] underscoring its near equivalence to Boltzmann entropy in statistical thermodynamics.[40]

The concept of a "demon" controlling and manipulating the behaviour of particles aligns with the idea of "daemons" in computer information processing, which exert control over processes and resources. In computer science, demons are intelligent agents acting as guiding spirits that can control systems and services while operating autonomously and independently of user interactions. Maxwell's demon inspired MIT computing pioneers Fernando Corbató and Jerry Saltzer to use the Latin term "daemon" to describe the flow of operating system activities in the Defense Advanced Research Projects Agency-funded Project MAC around 1963. Project MAC's goal was a single computer resource that could be shared by multiple users in different locations. "Maxwell's daemon was an imaginary agent which helped sort molecules of different speeds and worked tirelessly in the background," recalled Corbató. "We fancifully began to use the word 'daemon' to describe background processes which worked tirelessly to perform system chores."[41]

Corbató's term may have been fanciful, but it reflects a long lineage of similar choices. Historian Adrienne Mayor in her 2018 *Gods and Robots: Myths, Machines, and Ancient Dreams of Technology* has written about the legendary automatons in the myths of Jason and the Argonauts, Medea, Daedalus, Prometheus, and Pandora that worked behind the scenes, monitoring and responding to events and performing tasks.[42] The EXEC II operating system developed by System Development Corporation (SDC) for the UNIVAC 1107 computer in the 1960s possessed "parasites" capable of concurrently handling peripherals such as card readers, card punches and line printers. The Univac company, finding this term unseemly, rechristened them "symbionts."[43] The MIT Artificial Intelligence Lab called these entities "dragons" in the Incompatible Time-sharing System (ITS) and the Stanford Artificial Intelligence Laboratory named them "phantoms."[44]

Regardless, Project MAC's Compatible Time-Sharing System (CTSS) and its successor the Multiplexed Information and Computing Service (Multics) inspired many other multi-user, multitasking computer operating systems, including the Unix operating system subsequently developed at Bell Labs by Ken Thompson and Dennis Ritchie. The concept of daemons obviously fit well within the culture of Bell Labs, which had been using similar metaphorical representations to grapple with the development of information theory and technical systems for many years. Like Project MAC, Unix exploited daemon background processing tools. The parent procedure for daemons was often "init," the first process started when a computer is booted. Other daemons are created by the init process, or by forking (making a copy of) a child process and exiting, which causes the init process to adopt the child process. Daemons make more daemons. One of the daemons most familiar to users of email is the message transfer agent MAILER-DAEMON, which handles the sending and receipt of email. Users become aware of its presence only when the daemon returns undeliverable emails. Computer operators are not usually aware that swarms of demons await their turn to be called into being. Even Unix programmers who write and execute common scripts may be dimly aware that, with every action, a demon is roused.[45]

In 1977, the legendary computer programmer Bill Joy shared what became a popular Berkeley Software Distribution (BSD) of Unix. BSD Unix came bundled with handy utilities and a powerful text editor. BSD Unix quickly became known homophonically as "Beastie" Unix. Subsequently, daemon backronyms began to propagate across computer reference books. A "Disk And Execution MONitor" or "DEvice And MONitor," is a task, process, or service that repeatedly "wakes" to perform some errand and then returns to an idle state. On the TOPS-10 operating system for the DEC PDP-10, DAEMON is the "Dump And Examine MONitor." Another computer-communication service sharing the acronym DAEMON stands for "Distribution And Electronic Maintenance Over Network."

Comic book artist Phil Foglio drew BSD Unix t-shirt artwork for Mike O'Brien, one of the system's developers, in the 1970s. The drawing contained four devils climbing on pipes connected to a computer-like device reminiscent of a DEC PDP-11 minicomputer. Each devil holds in its hands a trident, representing the forking of processes controlled by daemons.[46] And the so-called "Unix Bible," *Design and Implementation of the 4.3BSD Unix Operating System* published in 1989 by Samuel Leffler, Marshall McKusick, Michael Karels, and John Quarterman, has on its cover a single cartoon devil mascot, nicknamed "Beastie," drawn by John Lasseter (later of Pixar fame).[47]

In the 1989 *Unix System Administration Handbook* co-author Evi Nemeth complained about the Christianising of Unix daemons. "Many people equate the word 'daemon' with the word 'demon,' implying some kind of satanic connection between UNIX and the underworld," she wrote. But, Nemeth explained,

> This is an egregious misunderstanding. 'Daemon' is actually a much older form of 'demon'; daemons have no particular bias towards good or evil, but rather serve to help define a person's character or personality. The ancient Greeks' concept of a 'personal daemon' was similar to the modern concept of a 'guardian angel'—*eudaemonia* is the state of being helped or protected by a kindly spirit. As a rule, UNIX systems seem to be infested with both daemons and demons.[48]

Indeed, the term daemon was selected to describe these processes because, like mythological demons, they worked tirelessly and invisibly behind the scenes to perform system chores and maintain the smooth operating of the Unix system and its various components.

## Hackers as Folk Devils

In hackerdom, the devil presents himself as an opaque user interface, one that conceals an inner realm accessible only to those who toil on computers and wield the power of code. Consequently, hackers themselves became folk devils in the 1980s. Media and society demonised them as exceptionally skilled and malicious individuals who threatened both personal and national security. The *Net Cafe* television show (1996–2002) meticulously documented the San Francisco Bay Area internet boom. "The hacker culture: Are they demons or saviors?" is the first question television presenter Stewart Cheifet asked in the inaugural episode of *Net Cafe*.[49] Cheifet's question encapsulates the ongoing debate about hackers and their ambiguous role in shaping the contemporary world, as hackers are still sometimes described as subversives who control our lives and hoard (or steal) valuable data.

Anthropologist Gabriella Coleman has studied in detail the frequency of particular personality traits ascribed to hackers in published texts. They are "wizardly," "mystical," "creepy," and "asocial."[50] It is generally conceded that hackers are invested in keeping programming mysterious, hierarchies hidden and education informal.[51] The generation of programmers who came of age in the 1980s perceived of themselves as sorcerers and demon-tamers. The go-to "Wizard Book" of many hackers in that decade was Hal Abelson, Jerry Sussman, and Julie Sussman's 1984 *Structure and Interpretation of Computer Programs*, which depicted on its cover the legendary magician Hermes Trismegistus and the medieval mystic Ramon Llull. Hackers were also self-consciously adept at preparing and transmitting digital assemblages of their history, values and knowledge. Hackerdom found identity and cultivated idiosyncratic behaviours through such liminal documents as the *Hacker Papers* (1980), Jargon File (1975–1983), *Hacker's Dictionary* (1983), *Phrack* magazine (1985–), and *Hacker's Manifesto* (1986).

The *Hacker Papers* are a set of Stanford University online bulletin board system chat logs. In 1980, the magazine *Psychology Today* excerpted and published selections from the conversation, with commentary by psychologist Philip Zimbardo, the author of the Stanford prison experiment.[52] In the Hacker Papers, a user named Gandalf provides a personal account of his hacker "addictions" and "misplaced values" and their nourishment within the sterile confines of the university's computer centre. "Fifty people stare at terminal screens. Fifty faces connected to 50 bodies, connected to 50 sets of fingers that pound on 50 keyboards ultimately linked to a computer," he writes. The computer silently modifies the personalities of its vulnerable and alienated users. "Weak-willed people, people with unstable social lives, people in formative stages of their lives, should not become involved in computer science," Gandalf pleads. "It should be left until they are truly able to make decisions and be aware of all the consequences."[53] This critique echoed other worries of the era, many of which directly informed the satanic panics of the decade discussed in Chapter 25: the cultural unease surrounding unsupervised latchkey children, women asserting their economic independence, and other technological breakthroughs like videogames and cable television that caused people to feel disconnected from traditional sources of stability.

Adding to the mystical, potentially demonic aura of hackers, the Jargon File was an online dictionary of slang and technical terms regularly updated with input from the hacker community. Raphael Finkel of the Stanford Artificial Intelligence Laboratory first compiled the Jargon File in 1975, which culminated in the paperback publication of *The Hacker's Dictionary* in 1983.[54] Two programming traditions are conjoined in some versions of the Jargon File, interleaving an older set of terms rooted in Lisp programming history and culture with a newer lexicon derived from Unix system development.[55] The Jargon File and *Hacker's Dictionary* are awash with allusions to magical powers, occult forces, devilish commands, computer mischief and deception, temptations and superstitions, and dark parody religions. The best system hackers are described in the Jargon File as "wizards" and "lord high fixers." Hackers with "arcane theoretical knowledge" of a system are said to be practitioners of "deep magic"; those with intimate experiential knowledge are called "heavy wizards."[56]

According to the Jargon File, hackers are aware that associations with wizardry and magic may carry negative associations, especially the implication that code is deceptive or carries hidden functions. One definition of magic offered by the *Hacker's Dictionary* is "a feature not generally publicized that allows something otherwise impossible."[57] Hackers who optimise compilers, artificial intelligence algorithms, and crypto techniques are said to be practitioners of "black arts." "Black magic" is defined as a "technique that works, though nobody really understands why."[58] In hacker communities, the fairy dust filters down to the operating system's lowest levels. A "magic number" can refer to data or inputs that have meaning only to the original author. "Magic strings" are values representing text that invokes hidden program functionality. A user would not ordinarily discover hidden functions unless they stumbled across the right sequence of characters. Hexspeak, a way of spelling words using only the digits 0123456789ABCDEF (for example, spelling DEFECATE as DEFECA7E or DEFEC8) is another way for programmers to obscure the meaning of code and notation. Deception and brainteasers are a favourite game of hackers. The programming language Malbolge, named after the eighth circle of hell in Dante's *Divine Comedy*, uses base-three (trinary) arithmetic and polymorphic, self-modifying code. A basic "Hello, World!" program written in the language required two years of coding effort.[59]

One of the most important hacker convictions is personal choice elevated to moral imperative. Parody religions that satirise spiritual convictions are treated with surprising seriousness in the hacker community. One parody religion popular among hackers is Discordianism.[60] The Discordian word "fnord" is used in hacker conversations to describe anxiety, confusion, and unease, and as a placeholder metasyntactic variable. The Church of the SubGenius is an anarcho-libertarian religion considered "ha ha only serious" among hackers.[61] The founding philosophers and prophets of the church weave Lovecraftian fiction into their pretend worship of the "relatively evil" extraterrestrial alien Jehovah 1 and other demons. One of the chief roles of leaders is to help members "justify their sins."[62]

Hacking leapt into the public imagination in part because of its unusual aesthetics and broad impact on the economy, but also because of an eruption of public alarm related, in part, to fantasy literature and the development of tabletop role-playing games. The 1979 disappearance of sixteen-year-old Michigan State University student James Dallas Egbert III, who attempted suicide in a steam tunnel used by his *Dungeons & Dragons* group for live action role-play, riveted the nation. Egbert was a passionate hacker and known to be highly knowledgeable about computer technology. He was also rumoured to be depressed, lonely, addicted to drugs and gay. Egbert survived his first suicide attempt, but the media firestorm triggered by the frantic search for the young man had done real damage to the role-playing franchise, and by association, the seemingly bestial lifestyles of hackers. Egbert died from a self-inflicted gunshot wound one year later.[63] Here was an event primed to stoke the era's conspiracy theories and provoke 1980s evangelical fears about satanic ritual abuse and occultism.

The hacker-as-folk-devil narrative mirrors the core of moral panic theory.[64] In 1981, the Federal Bureau of Investigation (FBI) discovered that a small cabal of hackers had penetrated the security systems of the prominent time-sharing computer company, National CSS. At the source of the breach, the FBI found a bored field technician in possession of a master list of stolen passwords. Yet a *New York Times* account painted the breach as a pivotal moment in the history of security, one that exposed the weaknesses of computer networks and the near-ubiquity of digital intrusions. The story described hackers as "technical experts; skilled, often young, computer programmers, who almost whimsically probe the defenses of a computer system, searching out the limits and the possibilities of the machine" but also having "a tradition of almost ritual thievery."[65] Media reports and books about hackers in the 1980s read like significant moments in Christian hagiography: the devil and a horde of hyenas testing Saint Anthony in the desert or Saint Ignatius of Loyola's journey to uncover the *Spiritual Exercises*. Here, however, were events and people that threatened the safety and interests of wider society. A string of federal government raids, documented with humour and pathos in Bruce Sterling's *The Hacker Crackdown* (1992), followed. In one passage of his book, Sterling recounts the harrowing tale of games company owner Steve Jackson, who could not convince the Secret Service that a paper supplement to a virtual world called *G.U.R.P.S. Cyberpunk* was not a "manual for computer crime," but a role-playing simulation.[66]

A hacker calling himself The Mentor published the widely read "Hacker's Manifesto, or The Conscience of a Hacker" in the e-zine *Phrack* in 1986.[67] *Phrack* remains the longest running periodical providing coverage of underground hacker techniques and culture. In the manifesto, The Mentor admits that he is both an addict and a criminal. He finds the rush of computer communication "like heroin through an addict's veins," and describes his crimes as "curiosity," "judging people by what they say and think," and "outsmarting you, something that you will never forgive me for."[68] Popular media amplified hackers' implied threats with a string of inflammatory accounts of dark-side programming. Dark-side hackers use special skills to crash computers, unleash malware attacks, steal financial records or electronic money, engage in collusion and conspiracies, nurture commercial darknets, and/or participate in software piracy.[69] Hackers with aliases like Captain Zap, Phiber Optik, The Condor, and Dark Dante enjoyed exploring the secret inner recesses of networked systems and databases, craved special computer administrator powers and influence, and were often dismissive of the efforts of corporate experts and law enforcement investigators to catch them.

## Secret Messages and Cybersecurity

The theory of moral panic also predicts an exaggerated government response to perceived threats; in this case the threats were national security and individual privacy. Federal legislators writing the original bill that became the Computer Fraud and Abuse Act (CFAA) of 1984 surreally cited the fictional techno-thriller film *WarGames* as "a realistic representation of the automatic dialling and access capabilities of the personal computer."[70] The use of legal enforcement, cryptography and computer security protocols have often been met with a mixture of fear and suspicion by hackers, cybersecurity policy experts, digital rights advocates and the general public. This is primarily due to the perception that strong cryptography enables secret communication, which can be seen, variously, as a threat to national security, law enforcement efforts and privacy. Encryption technologies were viewed as potential tools for criminals and terrorists to hide their activities. Authorities worried about untraceable communications, trespassers inside sensitive computer systems and online trafficking in illegal activities. These establishment anxieties contributed to outrage among hackers, who perceived a disparity between security and individual privacy. The availability of digital encryption technology and the potential for secure communication led to questions about the limits of government surveillance and their rights to freedom of expression. The clash between public cryptography advocates and established powers wanting greater control created fertile ground for moral indignation.

Discernment is an important part of cryptography and cybersecurity work. The professionals who do this work lurk in the secret back rooms of security operations centres (SOCs). Privacy advocates routinely rebuke security personnel for their surveillance activities, while highlighting their alleged misbehaviours. Security professionals are interrogated about the ethical implications of their opaque but near-omniscient activities, and asked how they weigh the need to protect intellectual property against the need for open access to information. Cryptography is a tough, inscrutable and heavily mathematical field that evolved from various methods of hiding secret messages within other messages or channels. The art and science of cryptography stretches back to the occult writings and the substitution ciphers of such works as the *Polygraphia* of German Benedictine abbot Johannes Trithemius.[71] Cryptography and cybersecurity assume the presence of devilish adversaries who wage relentless wars to intercept private messages between parties in order to gain unauthorised access to sensitive data.

Illustrations of the devil are sometimes used in the context of cryptographic schemes to depict the concept of an attacker who tries to exploit vulnerabilities in a computer system. "There is a long tradition of cutesiness in our field," writes UC Davis computer scientist Phillip Rogaway. "People spin fun and fanciful stories. Protocol participants are a caricatured Alice and Bob. Adversaries are little devils, complete with horns and a pitchfork."[72] The eavesdropper or intercepting adversary is often called "Eve," a potent allusion to the biblical figure who succumbs to temptation and eats fruit from the forbidden tree of knowledge. This reference to Eve is particularly intriguing in a male-dominated field. Often, a skilful attacker who probes for vulnerabilities is called the "penetration tester."

The use of devilish imagery in cryptographic explanations illuminates the hacker's role in exploiting system vulnerabilities. Amidst this symbolic backdrop of cryptographic folklore, pioneers like IBM's Horst Feistel emerged as pivotal figures who championed encryption technologies and played instrumental roles in the development of data security in electronic communications. In the 1970s, Feistel shared his description of an experimental LUCIFER 128-bit block cipher. (The first name for the program was DEMONSTRATION, shortened to DEMON to meet cramped filename requirements). As symmetric-key cryptographic technology, LUCIFER employs the same secret key to encrypt and decrypt messages.[73] LUCIFER variants were employed in secure bank transactions and are a direct ancestor of the Data Encryption Standard (DES) approved by the federal government in 1977. In a controversial move, IBM collaborated with the National Security Agency (NSA) to modify the LUCIFER cipher, reducing the key size from 128 bits to 56 bits. This reduction, criticised as making it susceptible to brute force attacks, sparked concerns of potential NSA involvement in such attacks with superfast computers and advanced programming tools.[74]

The Data Encryption Standard contained eight classified substitution boxes (S-boxes) to "confuse" ciphertext and private key associations, but no explanation of this design decision was disclosed, leading to mistrust. Some researchers assumed that the NSA had covertly introduced a trapdoor into the cryptographic system. Martin Hellman and Whitfield Diffie, pioneers of public-key cryptography, sharply criticised DES.[75] Public-key cryptography enhances security by using distinct public and private keys for encryption and decryption. The public key can be shared freely, simplifying secure communication, digital signatures, user authentication, and the development of network security protocols.

Around 1990, it was revealed that the S-boxes were fine-tuned to resist differential cryptanalysis.[76] This revelation suggests that while IBM and the NSA appear to have substantially weakened the DES scheme by reducing the key size, they also improved security by modifying the S-boxes. The controversy stimulated broad interest in digital cryptography while also intensifying mistrust. Widespread worry about secret backdoors in encryption algorithms extended to suspicions about constants chosen for initialisation vectors or S-box mixing. The crypto community prefers "nothing-up-my-sleeve" numbers that are intentionally chosen to minimise concerns about nefarious purpose. Examples are mathematical constants like $\pi$, Euler's number $e$, and the golden ratio.[77]

The automated security audits developed to assess the strength and integrity of networks and software are similar to how Yahweh's tester in the Book of Job evaluates the faith of individuals by looking for vulnerabilities and weaknesses. Both processes involve scrutiny, evaluation, and identification of areas that may require improvement or pose risks. SATAN, the Security Administrator's Tool for Analyzing Networks, is a piece of free software developed in 1995 by programmers Dan Farmer and Wietse Venema that performs automated security audits on Unix operating systems and computer networks.[78] Farmer created an early and widely distributed specialised security suite called the Computer Oracle and Password System (COPS). Farmer developed COPS in the late 1980s while finishing a computer science degree under Gene Spafford.[79] Spafford is famous for his role in tracing the origins of the Morris worm, one of the first malware programs. A worm makes copies of itself to infect computers through a network. In 1988, the Morris worm affected 6,000 computers connected to the internet, about 10% of all networked computers. Farmer and Venema described how they used SATAN to hack back against the malicious "uebercracker," a "deadly creature that can both strike poisonously and hide its tracks without a whisper or hint of a trail" in a message to network administrators titled "Improving the Security of Your Site by Breaking Into It."[80]

Farmer and Venema were among the first non-military personnel to recommend the techniques of the hacker to attack, defend, and evaluate system and network security. SATAN could run audits on other services, not just the owner's, which prompted the *Oakland Tribune* to editorialise that "It's like randomly mailing automatic rifles to 5000 addresses. I hope some crazy teen doesn't get a hold of one." The software could be used for virtuous or nefarious purposes. Security administrators used the program to test the configuration of network software and find holes in security firewalls; interlopers used the software to gain unauthorised access to systems.[81] The Department of Justice was so concerned about the existence of the SATAN tool that in 1995 it threatened to sue Silicon Graphics, the company where Farmer worked. Instead, the company fired Farmer.[82] Today, federal laws do not explicitly ban the kind of port and vulnerability scanning performed by SATAN, as these tools are common in security. In the 21st century, Farmer and Venema are praised as "ethical hackers."[83]

The SATAN name was suggested to Farmer by programmer Jean L. (Muffy) Barkocy. "We were trying to think of some provocative name that had some 'S's in it, an 'N', and maybe a 'T' … because I wanted to have words like security, system, networks, tool, etc. in the name," Farmer explained.[84] However, when questioned pointedly about the name in an interview on *Net Cafe,* Farmer admitted, "With any product, the name is two-thirds of what the value of the product is."[85] Users of the software affronted by the acronym could type the special command "repent," which reordered the letters to spell out SANTA.[86] The devil artwork accompanying distribution of SATAN software was created by Neil Gaiman, who is now a famous fantasy novelist.[87]

Because SATAN exposed network vulnerabilities, it nurtured a wide range of user behaviours. "White hat" hackers used SATAN to close security loopholes and warn administrators of weaknesses. Steve Bellovin of AT&T warned users that internet protocols contained inherent security flaws, "regardless of the correctness of any implementations."[88] Bellovin would publish one of the first books on public network security in 1994, *Firewalls and Internet Security: Repelling the Wily Hacker.*[89] Some "grey hat" hackers learned about computer security in order to participate in unauthorised but otherwise benign explorations of systems. "Black hat" hackers used their knowledge of systems and security to engage in identity theft, steal data, or commit fraud and financial crimes. The internet in the 1990s experienced several other novel exploits, including IP spoofing, phishing scams and ransomware attacks. The first IP spoofing attack was perpetrated by Kevin Mitnick in 1994.[90] In IP spoofing, hackers falsify the source address in the header—the part of an internet protocol packet that comes before the message body and contains addressing data—to make it look like the message comes from a trusted source. Phishing expeditions rely on spoofed emails and websites to lure people into voluntarily sharing private or sensitive information like credit card numbers or passwords.

The trickster nature of Satan in Christianity comes from his role as a cunning deceiver who tempts people to sin. In like manner, cybersecurity threat vectors often use tricks or deception to infect computers or penetrate networks. Ransomware originated in the late 1980s AIDS Trojan horse infecting DOS systems and encrypting hard drives. Researchers Adam Young and Moti Yung identified its weaknesses and presented a more advanced extortion protocol in 1996.[91] They predicted that the protocol would eventually be used in e-currency extortion schemes, which was borne out in the WannaCry ransomware attacks of 2017. [92] Satan ransomware bills itself as "Ransomware as a Service" or RaaS, meaning it is modelled after pay-per-use software developer product leasing.[93] The purveyors of Satan ransomware lease the malware to criminals in return for a commission of 30% of ransom payments. Satan uses an unidentified encryption algorithm. Security provider Proven Data estimates that attackers deliver decryption keys about 90% of the time when a ransom is paid.[94] It is often cheaper to pay the ransom than to attempt retrieval with traditional data recovery services and tools. In 2019, the mayor of Baltimore refused to pay hackers $76,000 in a ransomware attack on the city's information infrastructure. Instead, he ordered the rebuilding of the entire network for the city, which cost approximately $18 million.[95]

Satan ransomware, along with other regional variants like CryptoJacky and Kaenlupuf, are distributed from pages on the darknet, a network populated by cypherpunks, civil libertarians, cryptoanarchists, whistleblowers, and cybercriminals. In actual practice, most systems are not cracked by direct attacks. Rather, many intrusions stem from design mistakes, management failures, or inadequately shared key encryption practices. It may take years for such errors to come to light because, as security experts Ross Anderson and Roger Needham point out, "It is hard to simulate the behaviour of the devil; one can always check that a protocol does not commit the old familiar sins, but every so often someone comes up with a new and pernicious twist."[96]

### Summoning the Demon: Artificial Intelligence

In the fringe science of ASI, the pursuit of hidden truths is often associated with the realm of the supernatural. Proponents are confident that artificial superbeings will one day be unleashed using one or more advanced tools: evolutionary algorithms, whole brain emulation, nanotechnology, recursive self-improvement, or emergent principles. ASI research has also spawned its own eschatological narratives of transformation, existential crises, the end-times, final judgement, and the ultimate destiny of humanity. Transhumanism, which explores the possibilities of enhancing human capabilities through technology, can be likened to the idea of transformation or even transcendence. The AI "alignment problem," which involves speculations on the development of Friendly AIs that are aligned with human values and goals, is an example of an existential crisis in the field. The unintended consequences of accidental or deliberate release of an Unfriendly AI have been extensively discussed among scientists involved in philosophical and social movements such as effective altruism and long-termism. The Machine Intelligence Research Institute (MIRI), for example, has devised a "demon-in-a-box" experiment that raises questions about whether an AI system can persuade or manipulate a human operator into granting it access to resources or actions that may have world-ending consequences.

Artificial intelligence throughout its long history has been feared as a deceiver.[97] What computer pioneer Alan Turing called the "Imitation Game" in 1950 relies explicitly on trickery.[98] Daemons are common in artificial intelligence applications. They may be intelligent decision makers that remain in an idle state until certain conditions occur. These agents may even evoke or call upon a cascade of further daemons to perform useful work or fulfil objectives. In 1958, the MIT researcher Oliver Selfridge presented "Pandemonium: A Paradigm for Learning" at one of the earliest artificial intelligence conferences. His pattern-recognising model is named for the capital of hell in Milton's *Paradise Lost*, which is populated by countless numbers of shrieking demons.[99]

Pandemonium anticipates modern machine learning techniques. Its architecture consists of an artificial neural network and hierarchically organised sets of symbol processors (the demons) functioning in parallel. At the lowest levels, "computational demons" examine different aspects of a problem, for example recognising a single letter of the alphabet on a page. One so-called "feature demon" might look for the left angled slash; another for a crossbar; a third for a right-angled slash in the letter *A*. Each feature demon passes its findings along to middle-management demons who assemble these individual findings and arrive at more general conclusions. These results are passed along to demons at even higher levels of authority. How loudly a demon shrieks determines the weight with which certain upper-level demons trust individual findings. Selfridge even suggested that some favoured demons might be equipped with special equipment to make their shouts louder. Some upper-level demons in the neural network model are assigned to listen for particular lower-level demons. Selfridge called the near-top-level demons the "cognitive demons." These demons decide what to shriek at the controller demon Selfridge called the "decision demon." The decision demon reveals the letter on the page simply by listening for the loudest voices among the cacophony of cognitive demons. The model is made to learn by altering the number and kinds of demons, the volume at which they shout to other upper-level demons and testing with a large dataset of letters of various sizes, shapes, and legibility.[100]

Selfridge also shared a second method for replacing demons that do not achieve their objectives. Typically, the operator wanting to automate some pattern-recognition task selects a preexisting model for use and tunes it by hand. But under the second method, the assembly of demons arbitrarily selects sub-demons that seem to be of value; and those sub-demons in turn select other useful sub-sub-demons. As the model generates improvements, the "worth" of individual demons is evaluated on the basis of their volume-adjusted learning. Those contributing the loudest shrieks are considered the biggest contributors to the final solution. Those contributing little to the cacophony are removed from the model. Some demons are encouraged to mutate before returning to service. Others are forced into "conjugation" with one another to create new demon offspring. The process is repeated until the model as a whole can no longer be improved.[101]

Selfridge's approach is just one example of how the concept of demons has been applied in pattern recognition. In 1972, Eugene Charniak, also at MIT, produced a doctoral thesis that used lurking demons to address the problem of children's story comprehension. "How does a person answer questions about children's stories?" Charniak asked. "For example, consider 'Janet wanted Jack's paints.' She looked at the picture he was painting and said 'Those paints make your picture look funny.' The question to ask is 'Why did Janet say that?'" Charniak suggested a model to generate answers to questions by linking the story to information about the real world. As each sentence of a story sample passes through Charniak's model, specialised demons are aroused from their slumbers to examine and comprehend individual phrases and relate them to earlier sentences.[102]

Charniak's use of demons as cognitive agents represented a useful approach to unravelling the intricacies of comprehension. Another notable application of demons as cognitive agents emerged in the field of rule-based or symbolic artificial intelligence. Particle physicist M. Mitchell Waldrop has called the Soar cognitive architecture created by John Laird, Allen Newell, and Paul Rosenbloom at Carnegie Mellon University a "society of little demons."[103] Soar is composed of a production system of condition-action (IF-THEN) rules that lie quietly, observing a computer's working memory. "IF" a certain condition is reached by a running program in working memory, "THEN" the demon comes to attention and shrieks out a corresponding command to perform a particular action in its own associative memory. This process is not so different from Selfridge's original proposal. Sometimes, though, the demons compete for attention in responding to the same condition. How is this impasse between shrieking demons resolved? The Soar inventors cracked this problem with a mechanism called "universal subgoaling." Here, Soar generates a new problem space and applies algorithms in search of general problem-solving or reasoning methods. A representation of the solution is applied to the current situation and also stored in long-term memory. The next time the system encounters the same situation, it can apply the solution from memory rather than by unleashing demons anew.[104] The advantage of Soar's cabal is that each demon is trained to express opinions that, as Waldrop explained it, might be observed at an "exceedingly polite business conference."[105] Each demon makes its opinion known before the whole system arrives at a decision, solves a problem, or develops a plan.

An unchecked AI may be our "last invention"; the result could be rapid self-improvement and uncontrolled replication, an idea described by Nick Bostrom in his Paperclip Maximizer thought experiment.[106] Bostrom's cautionary scenario illustrates the potential risks of an AI system relentlessly pursuing what seems to be a harmless goal, such as maximising paperclip production, to the possible detriment of human well-being.[107] One example of final judgement is Roko's Basilisk, a hypothetical super-intelligent AI that will reward humans who contribute to its creation and punish those that attempt to obstruct its realisation. Even in mainstream computer science, software and hardware developers find themselves captivated by both the dreamlike and nightmarish potential outcomes of their work. Their visions include a range of farsighted and quasi-mystical concepts, including post-scarcity societies, simulated realities, and a Technological Singularity.

When tech mogul Elon Musk speaks or tweets, people pay attention. Musk's optimism about artificial intelligence is tempered by his fears. After Musk tweeted that "We need to be super careful with AI. Potentially more dangerous than nukes," it made headlines. For Musk, AI is humanity's greatest existential challenge. "With artificial intelligence we are summoning the demon," he said in 2014. "In all those stories where there's the guy with the pentagram and the holy water, it's like yeah he's sure he can control the demon. Didn't work out."[108] Perhaps more worrisome are the comments of deep learning AI pioneer Geoffrey Hinton, who recently stepped down from his position at Google. "I have suddenly switched my views on whether these things are going to be more intelligent than us," he said in a 2023 interview. "I think they're very close to it now and they will be much more intelligent than us in the future. How do we survive that?"[109] Hinton worries that in the future, AI may come to intentionally or unintentionally dominate humanity, a situation known as an "AI takeover." He is also concerned that an authoritarian leader may attempt to use advanced AIs to create lethal autonomous weapons.[110]

To counter AI threats, a number of collaborative research endeavours have emerged across the globe. "Explainable AI," "Interpretable ML" and "Trustworthy AI" are frequently used labels associated with these efforts. They reflect shared concerns about the metaphorical "black box" of machine learning which involves difficulties in interpreting conclusions made by artificial neural networks. Challenges for computer scientists include tracing back from the outputted predictions of trained models to the input features that are most important and fundamental misunderstandings about the self-modifying or adaptive nature of machine learning. Activists, in turn, seek regulatory frameworks to assure what is called "a right to explanation." A common complaint is that explanations may be extremely difficult to follow.

Calls for algorithmic transparency beg questions of everyday pellucidity in human decision making. To counteract negative views of AI cyber activity, computing communities are now encouraging public dialogue under the banners of "Beneficial AI," "Friendly AI," and "AI for Good." In other words—and despite the genuine goodwill of AI developers—the attributes, traits and language used to describe "good" AI is intentionally chosen to be the opposite of what is typically associated with malicious or harmful entities, be they religious or digital.

Is artificial intelligence already harmful, unfriendly and bad? When Microsoft introduced the chatbot Tay on Twitter in 2016, the company thought it had created a playful diversion that could also help the company harvest real-world training data. Twitter users instead taught the chatbot how to be racist and sexist.[111] In 2021, a simulation of Russian opposition figure Alexei Navalny's chief of staff interacted with members of the Dutch parliament on a video conference call. The deception was uncovered only weeks later after the imposter engaged in several other politically sensitive calls.[112] An escalating arms race to detect deepfakes and evade deepfake-detectors is already underway and experts are warning of deepfake misinformation super spreaders.[113]

The subject of digital discernment remains at the centre of current AI discussions. Just as the "digital devil" in the history of cryptography challenged our ability to discern intentions hidden away in the code, AI debates call into question our capacity to probe the mysterious depths of digital tech. It begs the question of whether AI protects against evils or occasionally magnifies them.

## Conclusion

Oliver Selfridge's Pandemonium and the Soar cognitive architecture are 20th-century models of artificial intelligence, but they share with medieval scholasticism a formal, structural and logical method of scrutinising and resolving complex questions. Both models adopt a hierarchical approach when addressing intractable problems. Pandemonium does this by using a hierarchy of feature detectors and demons. Soar does it by organising problem-solving processes into higher-level rules and concepts that guide the behaviour of lower-level elements. A hierarchical structure of rules and knowledge representations allows for the modelling of complex cognitive processes and the generation of solutions to problems at various levels of abstraction. That is the essence of Aristotle and Thomas Aquinas's system for building knowledge and understanding theology, philosophy, logic, and the natural sciences.

The notion that human brains follow information processing rules and are organised into hierarchical modules is widely commented upon in the information and cognitive sciences. Noam Chomsky staked his career on a claim that rules acting on representations would help philosophers, psychologists, biologists and computer scientists peek into the brain's black box. Sets of symbols, which are analogous to features of a world, are themselves relatively unintelligent; but when taken together, the reading, manipulation and interpretation of data creates a system of intelligence. This involves the work of a committee, cooperating and competing to manipulate symbols. The various intangible "supervisors," "monitors," "interpreters," "executives," "agents," and "demons" come together and form a system or network that is greater than the sum of their parts.[114]

Historically, our interactions have been regulated and guided by various means such as legal codes, etiquette protocols, societal norms, and even the rules followed within monastic communities. Now we live by heuristics, machine learning algorithms and big data analytics. But the devil knows that when we make our own rules we are invariably led into temptation. Ambrose Bierce in *The Devil's Dictionary* shares a short story of Satan's asking a favour before his abrupt departure from heaven. "Man, I understand, is about to be created," says the devil. "He will need laws." "What, wretch!" replies an incredulous God. "You his appointed adversary, charged from the dawn of eternity with hatred of his soul—you ask for the right to make his laws?" Satan clarifies, "Pardon. What I have to ask is that he be permitted to make them himself."[115] In the past, we created norms to survive, thrive, and defend against social and moral disorders. Today, we ask our machines to be the guardians of order, taking on tasks that were once the purview of human societies. Are we placing too much faith in these machines?

The computational approach that permeates modern surveillance capitalism—the collection, analysis, and monetisation of vast amounts of personal data for the purpose of targeted advertising—is effective because people are both creatures of habit and highly distractible. Researchers have examined and quantified cell phone map tracing data and found human activity to be 93% predictable. The team at Northwestern University's Center for Complex Network Research dryly explains their findings by stating, "Spontaneous individuals are largely absent from the population."[116] The science fiction author Alfred Bester blithely anticipated this predictability when he wrote that "the great majority of people live the sort of linear life that could easily be programmed into a computer."[117] At the same time—and due in large measure to those same smart phone apps—we suffer from impoverished attention, reduced task performance, internet addictions and the allure of mediated experiences. Attention is a scarce resource, constantly vied for by those seeking to capture our focus as consumers.[118]

Just as digital marketers entrap and redirect our attention using psychological tactics and targeted algorithms, artificial agents scuttle across complex cyberscapes to pursue objectives that are not in accord with our good intentions. Some of these agents produce effects that are difficult to predict from initial conditions. There are genuine concerns about control, intentionality and other shadowy phenomena when humans interact with artificial intelligences. Under the rules of emergence, individual cells can become brains, predators and prey can form ecosystems, and bits and pieces of information can grow into economies and societies. A subfield of computer science known as artificial life (Alife) reveals how complexity can emerge from simple sets of rules for behaviour and interaction rather than from the guidance or benevolence of an omniscient overseer.[119]

In this way, AI and Alife make more space for the demonic than the divine. These digital assemblages simulate worlds free from oversight or planning. The chaotic emergent activities of these worlds stand in opposition to divine order and benevolence. Alife's "survival of the fittest" rulebook promotes adaptation through suffering. For this reason alone, it is not surprising that critics portray the goals of artificial intelligence as misaligned with moral and spiritual principles and anticipate existential dangers where humans act as gods, summoning artificial demons that break free and wreak havoc.

The American mathematician John Conway sought to uncover fundamental or cosmic principles that underlie the complexity and diversity of the natural world by exploring the dynamics of Alife.[120] Consider his turn-based game of "Angels and Devils," played on an infinite grid. One player is the "angel" and the other is the "devil." The angel is placed on any square and given a power $k$ representing a natural number of 1 or higher. On each turn, the angel can move to another space within a boundary representing *k* moves (as of a chess king). The player representing the devil, in its turn, may block in perpetuity any square not containing the angel. The angel can leap over the devil's blocked squares as they accumulate over many turns but is not permitted to land on them. The devil wins the game if the angel becomes unable to make a move. The angel wins by evading the devil. What Conway wanted to know was: can the devil always trap the angel? Or does the angel have a strategy to win the game if given enough power to move away?[121]

Too often we expect clear and unambiguous solutions to questions such as these and this is especially true in a world that many of us believe is ruled by natural and mathematical patterns and algorithmic optimisations. In a world that is no longer "demon haunted," we expect our digital tools to resolve even the most "wicked" problems neatly. Instead, we are discovering that our algorithms are unruly and that programmers are modern-day necromancers who traffic in complex microstructures, recursive functions and self-referentiality. They create pocket universes out of code and set themselves up as clever deities who manipulate parameters and variables. Douglas Hofstadter, computer science's high priest, conceives of "strange loops" as recurrent symbolic structures that pass up and down through various micro and macro levels of observed reality and abstraction, ultimately arriving back where they began. Hofstadter's strange loops are often compared to paradoxes, fractal patterns or stochastic self-similarities. Hofstadter believes these loops throw light on the origins of consciousness, personal identity and the narrative fictions we construct (or perhaps hallucinate) to explain everyday life. We are part of the loop of all things, building new machines, systems and algorithms that in turn redefine us.[122]

In his 1979 *Gödel, Escher, Bach: An Eternal Golden Braid*, Hofstadter gives a famous example, drawn directly from the medieval Christian notion of devil's advocacy, showing how it is fallacious to assert that an artificial intelligence needs rules telling it what to do, while a human being does not, since AIs and humans both rely on physics—the original material and rules of the universe. "Since, as is well known, God helps those who help themselves, presumably the Devil helps all those, and only those, who don't help themselves. Does the Devil help himself?" Hofstadter asks in a decidedly scholastic manner.[123] Turing Award-winning computer scientist Donald Knuth locates divinity inside this framework and acknowledges that even God need not know everything or be omniscient: "I think it's fair to say that God may well be bound by the laws of computational complexity, even if we grant (as I do) that the Bible is God's inspired word."[124]

The "digital demon" is a metaphor that matters. It unlocks the portal to grappling with our pervasive engagement with computer technologies that are powerful, mysterious and disruptive. Demons continue to "both serve and subjugate" our world.[125] They are spreading into more and more digital spaces. Deep learning neural networks increasingly resemble the tangled goetic patterns found in grimoires for summoning deities, demons and angels.[126] Arguably, the number of demons sewing discord on the internet today far exceeds those catalogued by the Renaissance demonological work *Ars Goetia*. Gifted AI programmers like Tom Murphy (aka "suckerpinch") can "pray to the dark wizard of hyperparameter tuning in the hope that he smiles upon your work," while simultaneously, an army of creators continue to build antisocial shock sites that nurture the depravity and addictions of trolls, "shitposters," pornographers, bigots, and extremists.[127] Our interpersonal connections are increasingly influenced and manipulated by computers that surpass the understanding of their users. These machines ignite the intellectual curiosities of developers and sustain the rich digital landscape needed for the digital devil's ongoing handiwork.

## Notes

1 Philip J. Klass, "New Data System Proposed for Space," *Aviation Week and Space Technology*, 21 May 1962, pp. 77–9.
2 N. W. Bennett, *Demon: A Programme Generator for Problems Involving Ordinary Differential Equations*, AAEC/E142 (Lucas Heights, 1965).
3 George Smith, "The Virus Creation Labs: A Journey into the Underground," December 1994. http://web.archive.org/web/20100515145009/vxheavens.com/lib/agm00.html
4 Fabrice Mérillon, Laurent Réveillère, Charles Consel, Renaud Marlet, and Gilles Muller. "Devil: An IDL for Hardware Programming," in *Fourth Symposium on Operating Systems Design and Implementation* (San Diego, CA, 2000), 17–30.
5 Denton Woods, "DevIL: Developer's Image Library Manual," March 2002. http://openil.sourceforge.net/docs/DevIL%20Manual.pdf
6 Rodney A. Brooks, *Flesh and Machines: How Robots Will Change Us* (New York, 2002), 198–208.
7 Hugo de Garis, *The Artilect War: Cosmists vs. Terrans: A Bitter Controversy Concerning Whether Humanity Should Build Godlike Massively Intelligent Machines* (Palm Springs, 2005).
8 Stephen Cave, "AI: Artificial Immortality and Narratives of Mind Uploading," in *AI Narratives: A History of Imaginative Thinking about Intelligent Machines*, ed. Stephen Cave, Kanta Dihal, and Sarah Dillon (Oxford, 2020), 309–32.
9 Terasem Movement Foundation. https://terasemmovementfoundation.com/
10 The Church of Perpetual Life. https://www.churchofperpetuallife.org/
11 Mark Harris, "Inside the First Church of Artificial Intelligence," *Wired*, 15 November 2017. https://www.wired.com/story/anthony-levandowski-artificial-intelligence-religion/
12 Christian Transhumanist Association. https://www.christiantranshumanism.org/; Mormon Transhumanist Association. https://www.transfigurism.org/
13 Peter Holley, "Meet 'Mindar' the Robotic Buddhist Priest," *Washington Post*, 22 August 2019. https://www.washingtonpost.com/technology/2019/08/22/introducing-mindar-robotic-priest-that-some-are-calling-frankenstein-monster/
14 Southern Baptist Convention, Ethics & Religious Liberty Commission, "Artificial Intelligence: An Evangelical Statement of Principles," 11 April 2019. https://erlc.com/resource-library/statements/artificial-intelligence-an-evangelical-statement-of-principles/
15 Benjamin Weiser, "Here's What Happens When Your Lawyer Uses ChatGPT," *New York Times*, 27 May 2023. https://www.nytimes.com/2023/05/27/nyregion/avianca-airline-lawsuit-chatgpt.html
16 Kevin Kelly, *What Technology Wants* (New York, 2010), 357–8.
17 Jim Thomas, "The Moral Ambiguity of Social Control in Cyberspace: A Retro-Assessment of the 'Golden Age' of Hacking," *New Media & Society* 7, no. 5 (2005): 599–624.
18 Andrew Ross, "Hacking Away at the Counterculture," *Postmodern Culture* 1, no. 1 (September 1990). https://dx.doi.org/10.1353/pmc.1990.0011
19 Joseph Menn, "Beto O'Rourke's Secret Membership in a Legendary Hacking Group," *Reuters*, 15 March 2019. https://www.reuters.com/article/us-usa-politics-beto-orourke-special-rep/special-report-beto-orourkes-secret-membership-in-a-legendary-hacking-group-idUSKCN1QW26N
20 Psycoe, "Sex with Satan," *Cult of the Dead Cow*, 7 February 1988. https://web.archive.org/web/20070623164738/http://www.cultdeadcow.com/cDc_files/cDc-0040.php
21 Wendy Walker, "It Offers That Run-Down Feeling," *Minneapolis Star*, 2 July 1976, 3.
22 Jimmy Maher, "The Ratings Game, Part 2: The Hearing," The Digital Antiquarian blog, 23 April 2021. https://www.filfre.net/2021/04/the-ratings-game-part-2-the-hearing/
23 Luke Winkie, "Grand Theft Auto's Greatest Controversies," *PC Gamer*, 23 September 2022. https://www.pcgamer.com/grand-theft-auto-controversies/
24 "Grand Theft Auto III Banned in Australia," *ZDNet*, 12 December 2001. https://www.zdnet.com/article/grand-theft-auto-iii-banned-in-australia/
25 Jim D'Entremont, "Preachers of Doom," *Index on Censorship*, 28, no. 4 (1999): 189–94.
26 Greg Tito, "'Frumpy Mom' Says Videogames Made by the Devil," *The Escapist* forums, 5 January 2010. https://forums.escapistmagazine.com/threads/frumpy-mom-says-videogames-made-by-the-devil.180700/

27 Marla Jo Fisher, "Video Games Were Invented by the Devil," *Orange County Register,* 27 December 2009. https://web.archive.org/web/20130924070730/http://themomblog.blog.ocregister. com/2009/12/27/video-games-were-invented-by-the-devil/42149/

28 Quoted in Mary Dodson Wade, *Ada Byron Lovelace: The Lady and the Computer* (New York, 1994), 73.

29 Wade, *Ada Lovelace,* 75.

30 Charles Babbage, *The Ninth Bridgewater Treatise; A Fragment* (1837), 44.

31 James Gleick, *The Information* (New York, 2011), 375–6.

32 Katie Robertson, "The Demons Haunting Thermodynamics," *Physics Today* 74, no. 11 (November 2021): 44–50.

33 Katie Robertson, "The Demons Haunting Thermodynamics," 44–50.

34 Ludwig Boltzmann, "The Second Law of Thermodynamics," in *Theoretical Physics and Philosophical Problems: Vienna Circle Collection,* vol. 5, edited by Brian McGuinness (Dordrecht, 1974), 20.

35 Jon Gertner, *The Idea Factory: Bell Labs and the Great Age of American Innovation* (New York, 2012).

36 Ralph V. L. Hartley, "Transmission of Information," *Bell Systems Technical Journal* 7, no. 3 (July 1928): 554.

37 See *Maxwell's Demon: Entropy, Information, Computing,* eds. Harvey S. Leff and Andrew F. Rex (Princeton, 1990).

38 Claude Shannon, "A Mathematical Theory of Communication," *Bell Systems Technical Journal* 27, no. 3 (July 1948): 379–423.

39 David Tse, "How Claude Shannon Invented the Future," *Quanta Magazine,* 22 December 2020. https://www.quantamagazine.org/how-claude-shannons-information-theory-invented-the-future-20201222/

40 Roger Balian, "Information in Statistical Physics," *Studies in History and Philosophy of Science Part B: Studies in History and Philosophy of Modern Physics* 36, no. 2 (June 2005): 323–53.

41 Email response to Richard Steinberg, columnist for the *Austin Chronicle.* http://www.takeourword. com/TOW146/page4.html

42 Adrienne Mayor, *Gods and Robots: Myths, Machines, and Ancient Dreams of Technology* (Princeton, 2008).

43 This story is shared by legendary hacker and Autodesk co-founder John Walker in an introduction to the *EXEC II Programmer's Guide.* "CSC called these 'parasites,' but Univac deemed this terminology infelicitous and renamed them 'symbionts,' crudely replacing the text throughout the manual. Well, almost everywhere. Eagle-eyed readers will be amused to discover they missed a few." Fourmilog, "Univac Document Archive: 1107 EXEC II Manual Added." https://www. fourmilab.ch/fourmilog/archives/2017-11/001731.html

44 Jargon File. http://catb.org/jargon/html/D/dragon.html

45 Linux Information Project, "Daemon Definition." http://www.linfo.org/daemon.html

46 Greg Lehey, "What's that Demon?" https://web.archive.org/web/20010803131841/http://www. lemis.com/grog/whyadaemon.html

47 Samuel Leffler, Eric P. Allman, Marshall K. McKusick, Michael J. Karels, and John Quarterman, *Design and Implementation of the 4.3BSD Unix Operating System* (Boston, 1989).

48 Evi Nemeth, Garth Snyder, and Scott Seebass, *Unix System Administration Handbook* (Englewood Cliffs, 1989), 403.

49 *The Internet Cafe,* season 1, episode 1 (1996). https://archive.org/details/nc101_hackers

50 Gabriella Coleman, "Hacker," in *Digital Keywords: A Vocabulary of Information Society and Culture* (Princeton, 2016), 159.

51 Paige Franklin, Ryan Adams, and Caroline Henry, "What the Hack is a Hacker?" (B.S. thesis, James Madison University, 2019). https://commons.lib.jmu.edu/honors201019/671/

52 Philip G. Zimbardo, "The Hacker Papers," *Psychology Today,* August 1980, 62–9.

53 Kenneth Peter, "The Hacker Papers." http://www.textfiles.com/news/hackpape.hac

54 Steven Ehrbar, "The Jargon File Archive." http://jargon-file.org/archive/

55 Paul Dourish, "The Original Hacker's Dictionary." http://www.dourish.com/goodies/jargon.html

56 Jargon File. http://catb.org/jargon/html/H/heavy-wizardry.html

57 Jargon File. http://catb.org/jargon/html/M/magic.html

58 Jargon File. http://catb.org/jargon/html/B/black-magic.html

59 Lou Scheffer, "Introduction to Malbolge." http://www.lscheffer.com/malbolge.shtml

60 Based on the 1963 book *Principia Discordia* by Greg Hill and Kerry Wendell Thornley. The original version of the text is stored on a Carnegie Mellon Computer Science Department server and may be viewed at https://www.cs.cmu.edu/~tilt/principia/

61 Jargon File. http://www.catb.org/jargon/html/D/Discordianism.html

62 Church of the SubGenius. http://www.subgenius.com/

63 William C. Dear, *Dungeon Master: The Disappearance of James Dallas Egbert III* (Boston, 1984).

64 Stanley Cohen, *Folk Devils and Moral Panics: The Creation of the Mods and Rockers* (London, 1972).

65 Vin McLellan, "Case of The Purloined Password," *The New York Times,* 26 July 1981, sec. 3, p. 4.

66 Bruce Sterling, *The Hacker Crackdown: Law and Disorder on the Electronic Frontier* (New York, 1992). Steve Jackson Games also publishes editions of the *Principia Discordia* at http://www.sjgames.com/principia/

67 Later revealed as Loyd Blankenship of the hacker group Legion of Doom.

68 The Mentor, "Hacker's Manifesto: The Conscience of a Hacker," *Phrack* 1, no. 7 (8 January 1986). http://www.phrack.org/issues/7/3.html#article

69 Early journalistic and popular nonfiction books on the threat of mischief-making or malevolent hackers are Clifford Stoll's *The Cuckoo's Egg* (1989), Katie Hafner's *Cyberpunk* (1991), Bruce Sterling's *The Hacker Crackdown* (1992), and Michelle Slatalla's *The Masters of Deception* (1995). Classic dystopian fictional accounts foregrounding bleak hacker tropes are William Gibson's *Neuromancer* (1984) and Neal Stephenson's *Snow Crash* (1992). Contemporaneous fictional films involving amoral or rebellious hackers in need of social control generated even more social anxiety. Notable in this regard are *Tron* (1982), *WarGames* (1983), *Brainstorm* (1983), *Electric Dreams* (1984), *The Terminator* (1984), and *Hackers* (1995). *Hackers* lifts ideas and passages wholesale from the Hacker Manifesto.

70 Quoted in Jacquellena Carrero, "Access Granted: A First Amendment Theory of Reform of the CFAA Access Provision," *Columbia Law Review* 120, no. 1 (January 2020): 134, n. 18.

71 Johannes Trithemius, *Polygraphia libri sex* (1518). https://lccn.loc.gov/32017914. Trithemius's role in the history of secure communications is explained in David Kahn, *The Codebreakers* (New York, 1967), pp. 132–7.

72 Phillip Rogaway, "The Moral Character of Cryptography Work," 41–2, unpublished. https://www.cs.umd.edu/class/fall2019/cmsc818O/papers/moral-character.pdf

73 Alan G. Konheim, "LUCIFER," in *Computer Security and Cryptography* (Hoboken, NJ, 2007), 283–7.

74 Walter Tuchman, "A Brief History of the Data Encryption Standard," in *Internet Besieged: Countering Cyberspace Scofflaws*, eds. Dorothy E. Denning and Peter J. Denning (New York, 1997), 275–80.

75 Whitfield Diffie and Martin E. Hellman, "Exhaustive Cryptanalysis of the NBS Data Encryption Standard," *Computer* 10, no. 6 (June 1977): 74–84.

76 Eli Biham and Adi Shamir, "Differential Cryptanalysis of DES-like Cryptosystems," in *Advances in Cryptology-CRYPTO 1990 Proceedings*, eds. Alfred J. Menezes and Scott A. Vanstone (Berlin, 1991), 2–21; Steven Levy, *Crypto: How the Code Rebels Beat the Government—Saving Privacy in the Digital Age* (New York, 2001), 55.

77 For a contemporary view of human factors and deception in cybersecurity, see K. Scott, "'Nothing Up My Sleeve': Information Warfare and the Magical Mindset," in *Cyber Influence and Cognitive Threats*, eds. Vladlena Benson and John McAlaney (London, 2020), 53–76.

78 Dan Farmer and Wietse Venema, "Improving the Security of Your Site by Breaking into It." https://cyberwar.nl/d/1993-FarmerVenema-comp.security.unix-Improving-the-Security-of-Your-Site-by-Breaking-Into-It.pdf

79 Rik Farrow, "Interview with Dan Farmer," *;login:* 39, no. 6 (December 2014): 32–5.

80 Dan Farmer and Wietse Venema, "Improving Security of Your Site by Breaking into It." https://groups.google.com/g/comp.security.unix/c/dJqpVPNtLJQ/m/pAT_WtOaBRkJ

81 See Martin Freiss, *Protecting Networks with SATAN* (Sebastopol, 1998).

82 O. Ryan Tabibian, "Internet Scanner Finds Security Holes," *PC Magazine,* 23 April 1996, NE38.

83 C. C. Palmer, "Ethical Hacking," *IBM Systems Journal* 40, no. 3 (2001): 770–1.

84 Dan Farmer, website comment. https://web.archive.org/web/19990202094945/http://www.fish.com/satan/

85 The Internet café. https://archive.org/details/nc101_hackers

86 "SATAN (Security Administrator Tool for Analyzing Networks)." http://www.porcupine.org/satan/demo/name.html

87 "SATAN Artwork." http://www.porcupine.org/satan/demo/docs/artwork.html

88 Steven M. Bellovin, "Security Problems in the TCP/IP Protocol Suite," *Computer Communication Review* 19, no. 2 (April 1989): 32–48.

89 Steven M. Bellovin, *Firewalls and Internet Security: Repelling the Wily Hacker* (Boston, 1994).

90 See Tsutomu Shimomura's first-hand account *Takedown* (New York, 1996).

91 Adam Young and Moti Yung, "Cryptovirology: Extortion-Based Security Threats and Counter-measures," in *Proceedings of the IEEE Symposium on Security and Privacy* (New York, 1996), 1–12.

92 Adam Young and Moti Yung, "Cryptovirology: The Birth, Neglect, and Explosion of Ransom-ware," *Communications of the ACM* 60, no. 7 (July 2017): 24–6.

93 "Ransomware Recap: Satan Offered as Ransomware as a Service," *Trend Micro*, 15 March 2017. https://www.trendmicro.com/vinfo/es/security/news/cybercrime-and-digital-threats/ransomware-recap-satan-offered-as-ransomware-as-a-service

94 "The Pros and Cons on Paying the Ransom: When Should I Consider It?" *Proven Data*. https://www.provendatarecovery.com/blog/pros-cons-paying-ransomware/

95 Bruce Sussman, "Baltimore, $18 Million Later: 'This is Why We Didn't Pay the Ransom,'" *SecureWorld*, 12 June 2019. https://www.secureworldexpo.com/industry-news/baltimore-ransomware-attack-2019

96 Ross Anderson and Roger Needham, "Programming Satan's Computer." https://www.cl.cam.ac.uk/~rja14/Papers/satan.pdf

97 See Simone Natale, *Deceitful Media: AI and Social Life after the Turing Test* (New York, 2021).

98 Alan M. Turing, "Computing Machinery and Intelligence," *Mind* 59, no. 236 (October 1950): 433–60.

99 Oliver G. Selfridge, "Pandemonium: A Paradigm for Learning." In *The Mechanisation of Thought Processes*, eds. D. V. Blake and A. M. Uttley (London, 1959), 511–29.

100 Selfridge, "Pandemonium," 514–8.

101 Selfridge, "Pandemonium," 521–4.

102 Eugene Charniak, "Toward a Model of Children's Story Comprehension," Technical Report 266 (Cambridge, December 1972).

103 M. Mitchell Waldrop, "Toward a Unified Theory of Cognition," *Science* 241, no. 4861 (1 July 1988), 28.

104 Dina Amselmi, Ralph Morelli, and W. Miller Brown, *Minds, Brains, and Computers: Perspectives in Cognitive Science and Artificial Intelligence* (Norwood, 1992), 16–7.

105 Waldrop, "Toward a Unified Theory of Cognition," 28.

106 Irving J. Good, "Speculations Concerning the First Ultraintelligent Machine," *Advances in Computer* 6 (1966): 33.

107 Nick Bostrom, "Ethical Issues in Advanced Artificial Intelligence." https://nickbostrom.com/ethics/ai

108 Matt McFarland, "Elon Musk: 'With Artificial Intelligence We Are Summoning the Demon,'" *Washington Post*, 24 October 2014. https://www.washingtonpost.com/news/innovations/wp/2014/10/24/elon-musk-with-artificial-intelligence-we-are-summoning-the-demon/

109 Will Douglas Heaven, "Geoffrey Hinton Tells Us Why He's Now Scared of the Tech He Helped Build," *MIT Technology Review*, 2 May 2023. https://www.technologyreview.com/2023/05/02/1072528/geoffrey-hinton-google-why-scared-ai/

110 Cade Metz, "'The Godfather of A.I.' Leaves Google and Warns of Danger Ahead," *New York Times*, 1 May 2023. https://www.nytimes.com/2023/05/01/technology/ai-google-chatbot-engineer-quits-hinton.html

111 Peter Lee, "Learning from Tay's Introduction," *Official Microsoft Blog*, 25 March 2016. https://blogs.microsoft.com/blog/2016/03/25/learning-tays-introduction/

112 "Dutch MPs in Video Conference with Deep Fake Imitation of Navalny's Chief of Staff," *NL Times*, 24 April 2021. https://nltimes.nl/2021/04/24/dutch-mps-video-conference-deep-fake-imitation-navalnys-chief-staff

113 Karen Emslie, "AI vs. AI: The Race to Detect Deepfakes," *Communications of the ACM* 64, no. 5 (May 2021): 16.
114 Steven Pinker, *How the Mind Works* (New York, 1997), 79.
115 Satan is granted his request. Ambrose Bierce, *The Devil's Dictionary* (Cleveland, 1911), 308.
116 Chaoming Song, Zehui Qu, Nicholas Blumm, and Albert-László Barabási, "Limits of Predictability in Human Mobility," *Science* 327, no. 5968 (19 February 2010): 1018–21.
117 Alfred Bester, "Something Up There Likes Me," in *Starlight: The Great Short Fiction of Alfred Bester* (Garden City, 1976), 376.
118 Paul Atchley, Sean Lane, and Kacie Mennie, "A General Framework for Understanding the Impact of Information Technology on Human Experience," in *Human Capacity in the Attention Economy*, ed. Sean Lane and Paul Atchley (Washington, 2021), 11–24.
119 Mitchel Resnick, "Learning about Life," in *Artificial Life: An Overview*, ed. Christopher G. Langton (Cambridge, 2000), 234.
120 Lorena Caballero, Bob Hodge, and Sergio Hernandez, "Conway's 'Game of Life' and the Epigenetic Principle," *Frontiers in Cellular and Infection Microbiology* 6 (2016): 1–8.
121 John H. Conway, "The Angel Problem," in *Games of No Chance*, ed. Richard Nowakowski (Berkeley, 1996), 3–12.
122 See, for example, media studies scholar Taina Bucher's *If … Then: Algorithmic Power and Politics* (New York, 2018).
123 Douglas R. Hofstadter, *Gödel, Escher, Bach: An Eternal Golden Braid* (New York, 1979), 684–5.
124 Donald E. Knuth, *Things a Computer Scientist Rarely Talks About* (Stanford, 2001), 174.
125 Erik Davis, "Techgnosis, Magic, Memory, and the Angels of Information," in *Flame Wars: The Discourse of Cyberculture* (Durham, 1994), 46.
126 Sam Kriss, "The Internet is Made of Demons," *Damage*, 21 April 2022. https://damagemag.com/2022/04/21/the-internet-is-made-of-demons/
127 Tom Murphy, "Uppestcase and Lowestcase Letters." http://tom7.org/lowercase/

## Bibliography

Canales, Jimena. *Bedeviled: A Shadow History of Demons in Science*. Princeton, NJ: Princeton University Press, 2020.
Davis, Erik. "Techgnosis: Magic Memory, and the Angels of Information." In *Flame Wars: The Discourse of Cyberspace*, edited by Mark Dery, 29–60. Durham, NC: Duke University Press, 1994.
Geraci, Robert M. *Apocalyptic AI: Visions of Heaven in Robotics, Artificial Intelligence, and Virtual Reality*. Oxford, UK: Oxford University Press, 2012.
Leff, Harvey S., and Andrew F. Rex, eds. *Maxwell's Demon: Entropy, Information, Computing*. Princeton, NJ: Princeton University Press, 1990.
McKelvey, Fenwick. *Internet Daemons: Digital Communications Possessed*. Minneapolis: University of Minnesota Press, 2018.
Midson, Scott A. *Cyborg Theology*. London: I. B. Tauris, 2017.
Natale, Simone. *Deceitful Media: Artificial Intelligence and Social Life after the Turing Test*. New York: Oxford University Press, 2021.

# 27

# INTO THE 21ST CENTURY

*Robert L. Ivie*

"We need institutions that can maintain order in a nation of devils... Good rules control devils. Good cultures make it difficult for people to be devils."[1]

The 21st century opened with an idiomatic devil embedded in the discourse of Western society. This proverbial devil—left over from premodern times—lives in the details, giving people a devil of a time. Still, the devil we know is better than the devil we don't know. We play devil's advocate and assume a devil-may-care attitude. We might be full of the devil or choose to scare the devil out of someone. Our foe is the devil incarnate or the devil in disguise. There are crafty devils, lucky devils, handsome devils and devils who quote scripture. Speak of the devil and he appears. Idle hands are the devil's playthings. We can have a devil of a job or a devil of a time, and sometimes we find ourselves caught between the devil and the deep blue sea. We can make a deal with the devil, knowing we had better be in the forefront of the pack because the devil takes the hindmost.

Indeed, making a deal with the devil—a staple of premodern accusations of heresy and witchcraft—is a popular theme carried into the 21st century. The *Good vs Evil* comedy-drama television series, which ran from July 1999 to May 2000, featured a secret corps of God's agents assigned to find individuals who had made Faustian bargains with agents of evil. The 2004 Canadian-British film, *Pact with the Devil*, retells Oscar Wilde's story of Dorian Grey selling his soul for youth and beauty. A luckless writer exchanges his soul for fame and fortune in *Shortcut to Happiness*, released in 2007, as an adaptation of Stephen Vincent Benet's short story, "The Devil and Daniel Webster." The first five seasons of the long-running television series, *Supernatural*, beginning in 2005, featured two brothers as demon hunters and various characters making deals with demons for selfish or selfless ends in exchange for their souls. In the television comedy series *Reaper*, launched in 2009, the parents of the main character traded the soul of their first born to the devil in exchange for restoring his father's health.

The image of the devil is invoked as a cautionary tale on matters of public policy when drawing on the Faust legend to issue a warning about pursuing technical knowledge at the expense of civic intelligence. The Faust myth, argues Douglas Schuler, is

DOI: 10.4324/9781003096603-28

a valuable resource for meditating on the current world and the consequences of its unquestioning devotion to technological knowledge without considering the diabolical losses that come with any short-term gains in power and control. Srđan Korać observes, for instance, that drones and smart bombs are effective weapons with underappreciated negative consequences, such as the dehumanising of enemy combatants and civilians alike, to the point of depriving them of human dignity and removing ethical constraint. Thus, Schuler maintains, "we must inquire into the identity of Doctor Faustus of the twenty-first century and, in the more material and secular world of today, determine the nature of the *soul* that is being lost in the bargain" for power. The complexity of instrumental knowledge and its application to personal gain degrades society's ability to address challenges such as environmental damage equitably and effectively. It strips the citizenry of actionable knowledge required to participate effectively in problem solving for society at large and thus risks a "hellish fall," especially for those already pushed to the margins of society.[2]

On this very point, Benjamin Ramm, writing for *BBC Culture*, underscores the lasting relevance of the Faust legend, suggesting that as "a metaphor for unholy political pacts" it "may even shed light on our own populist moment, from Brexit to the election of Donald Trump." It is a metaphor that continues to "haunt the Western imagination," especially at "times of moral crisis." The Faustian bind of today, he writes, is a plague of politicians "offering easy answers to complex problems," regardless of the ecological and human cost, because of an insatiable appetite for power and wealth: "Climate change is perhaps the most fitting contemporary analogy for the Faustian bargain—decades of rapid economic growth for an elite, followed by grave ecological consequences for eternity."[3]

Beyond bargaining, Johnathan Powell, who served as chief of staff to British Prime Minister Tony Blair, asks when it is best "to quarrel with the devil." The devil to which he refers is corrupt Arab rulers—dictators and despots, including Bashar al-Assad's murderous regime in Syria. Powell insists that it is appropriate sometimes "to reach out to a reformed sinner," but usually (quoting a Yugoslavian proverb Franklin Roosevelt favoured) you should not quarrel with the devil you meet on a river crossing until after you are over the bridge. Offering incentives to Libya's Moammar Gadhafi was a prudent means of getting him to disavow weapons of mass destruction, but even on a narrow river crossing, no accommodation of the Syrian devil is acceptable because "evil regimes" that threaten democracy "are best overturned."[4]

The question is whether these linguistic traces, popular culture characters and proverbial applications of an earlier worldview are indicative of the continuing presence of the devil at the crossroads of contemporary politics, religion, and culture. Does today's devil amount to more than a figure of speech? Is it the case, as Louise Penny's popular novel proclaims (in words drawn verbatim from Shakespeare's *The Tempest*), that "Hell is empty and all the devils are here"?[5] The short answer is "yes": the devil remains a presence operating under the menacing sign of evil. These are apocalyptic times marked by a sense of impending disaster and doom, which some wish to forestall but others embrace as the way of salvation. Evil is the watchword in this period of racial strife, economic displacement, climate crisis, and ascending authoritarianism.

"The devil has not gone away," declares Darren Oldridge.[6] "There are devils aplenty, large and small," affirms Stein Ringen.[7] Satan persists as a mainstay of many Western faith communities and remains a potent figure in public and popular culture. The evil one, the tenacious force of iniquity, haunts contemporary life. Such devilising to the point of acute polarisation is caustic to a democratic ethos. Just as the notion of the devil gives licence to dispatch a foreign enemy, it corrodes the democratic principle of living with differences in noble tension. The attribution of evil is not a gesture that invites self-examination.

## A Familiar Devil Updated

Interest in matters diabolic has not waned in the troubled new century. If anything, it has undergone something of a revival. Belief in Satan as an external force of evil at work in the world is reflected in a resurgence of exorcism.[8] Moreover, most people in the United States believe in the devil, regardless of level of education, gender, religious orientation, political affiliation or region of the country. The percentage increased from 60% in 1968 to 70% in 2004 and has remained above 60% in various surveys. Likewise, about 70% believe in hell.[9] While the United States has remained "religion central" in the Western world, a 2009 Nielsen poll found that 68% of Australians believe in God, 37% in the devil and 38% in hell. Australia like the United Kingdom is "middling devout" by Western standards. The Scandinavians hold down the low end of the spectrum.[10] Another revealing finding by pollsters is the difference between the numbers that believe Satan is a living being versus those who see him merely as a symbol of evil. In the United States using 1991 as a baseline, 35% of American adults responded by saying that Satan is a living being, while 60% said Satan is a symbol of evil. Even by 2007, 24% of American adults still strongly rejected the idea of Satan as just a symbol of evil and not a real spiritual being. One gets a sense of the degree to which these belief structures match up to other Western countries from a 1991 survey asking respondents whether they definitely believe in the devil. In the United States, 45.4% answered "yes," compared to 43.1% in Northern Ireland but only 24.8% in Ireland, 21.4% in New Zealand, 20.4% in Italy, 15.4% in Poland, 13.3% in the Netherlands, 13.1% in Norway, 12.7% in Great Britain, 11.1% in Austria and 9.5% in West Germany.[11] From this, we might reasonably assume that while these numbers will vary somewhat over time, the comparison between the United States and other Western countries remains relevant into the early decades of the 21st century.

According to Christopher Partridge and Eric Christianson, popular culture in the West reflects "a widespread fascination with the diabolical" and "unease about the dark side." The devil in particular, they note in reference to Michel Foucault's argument, is a cultural marker of alterity, the satanic-monstrous *other* that "lies close to the heart of contemporary Western cultures."[12] Mel Gibson's film, *The Passion of Christ* (2004), features an androgynous Satan "fitting for a generation for which evil cannot be seen to be gender-specific." This obscene devil is erotically charged, alluring, disorienting and putrid, exuding the sign of death. The film's s/he devil, is a "cultural transmission" that exhibits the filmmaker's adaptation of the traditional Satan to a current image of evil that is not strictly male or masculine, an adaptation "in line with the particular concerns and interests" of audiences and "current understandings of temptation and evil" underlying such representations.[13]

For much of Western society, the 21st-century devil symbolises evil, while evil itself is considered literal and present. Still, the devil remains real to religious fundamentalists, not symbolic. Whether understood as a supernatural being, impersonal force, or symbol of wickedness, the figure of the devil, routinely personified, is implicated in the problem of evil. The devil *persona*, Oldridge observes, is "an enticing trace of transgression." In the Christian tradition, both biblical and cultural, the evil one, often depicted in black or red, is adversary, accuser, prosecutor, tempter, deceiver, enemy, serpent, dragon and humanoid with horns, claws, cloven hooves, tail and wings. Even where the traditional notion of Satan has subsided, the devil functions in "secular guise" as a force of embodied evil.[14]

This somewhat updated demonology of a secularised devil, a function and embodied force of evil, burst into the forefront of political discourse with the advent of what quickly became an all-encompassing global war on terror. "Today, our nation saw evil," proclaimed a flummoxed President George W. Bush, seemingly on rhetorical impulse.[15] Following the 9/11 attacks on the United States, Richard Bernstein remarked that "the world changed": it was "bombarded with images and talk of evil"; evil became "a popular, 'hot' topic."[16] President Bush quickly pointed the finger of blame at an "axis of evil" among state sponsors of terrorism supporting the likes of Osama bin Laden.[17] The ensuing terror war, open-ended in time and space, converged with an authoritarian temperament permeated by religious fundamentalism and instantiated in militarism. Iraqi dictator Saddam Hussein was a convenient, twice-chosen devil figure, before and after 9/11—the Antichrist to fundamentalists, Adolph Hitler to secularists, the embodiment of evil to both—soon to be replaced by a series of devil figures in the wide-ranging war.[18]

The myth of pure evil permeating Western accounts of 21st-century terrorism is a permutation of an enduring devil myth deeply ingrained in American war culture.[19] The contemporary version sustains a continuous war in which malice is attributed to terrorists as their sole impulse. Terrorism is a demonic force beyond understanding or redemption, an enemy "possessed by Satan—as someone who does evil for evil's sake," a nemesis that must be eradicated.[20] The terrorist devil is soulless, devoid of conscience, unappeasable and susceptible only to the force of arms. This is a call to battle that reflects Ephesians' biblical portrayal of the devil as vulgar, dishonest, greedy, thieving, bitter, wrathful and malicious—the very force of darkness. The difference is that Ephesians is a metaphorical rather than literal call to arms. Putting on "the whole armour of God so that you may be able to stand against the wiles of the devil" is an image of Christians struggling against darkness, resisting "the spiritual forces of evil," not an exhortation to engage in a physical battle with "enemies of blood and flesh." It is a call "to proclaim the gospel of peace" rather than to engage in literal warfare (see Eph 4.17-5.11 and 6.10-13; NRSV).

The language of terrorist evil impacted the public discourse of America's Western allies. British tabloids made "uncivilized evil" a defining image, including references to the "devil," the "diabolical," and "apocalyptic."[21] Prime Minister Blair, a staunch supporter of the United States' war on terrorism, referred to the enemy as an "evil ideology," following the London bombings of July 2005.[22] While public reaction in the United Kingdom, as well as in France, Germany and Italy, was initially supportive of the war, it found Bush's "axis of evil" rhetoric objectionable.[23] The European Union's attempt to advance an alternative discourse that focused on addressing root causes proved unable, however, to withstand the power of the United States' rhetoric of evil. Speaking of root causes was taboo and considered tantamount to condoning terrorism.[24] The sign of evil retained its grip on the mindset of terror war. Following a terrorist attack on French soil in October 2020, France's president Emanuel Macron, in a gesture to the nationalist far-right, called Islamist terrorism "evil."[25]

The rhetorical presence of pure evil compels warfare. Speaking in Oslo as he accepted the Nobel Prize for peace in 2009, Barack Obama attested to the necessity of war and stressed his responsibility, as President of the United States and Commander in Chief, to protect his country and all nations from the evil of terrorism in this new century. The use of military force against terrorism is not only "necessary but morally justified." The moral force of nonviolence, he maintained, is insufficient in a world confronting such a foe. We "must face the world as it is," he insisted, "for evil does exist in the world." Just as non-violence could not stop a Hitler, "negotiations cannot convince al Qaeda's leaders to lay down their arms." Such are the limits of reason when confronted by "a vicious adversary that abides by no rules." We can strive for peace, he concludes, but we must understand that "there will be war."[26]

Dehumanisation, the myth's master trope for demonising the *other*, comprises a binary of guilt and innocence that suppresses thoughtful consideration of why so many people worldwide support terrorism, how past policies generated enduring grievances and whether extermination strategies are counterproductive. Myth displaces pragmatic measures for mitigating terrorism. It divides the post-9/11 world into a "stark and simplistic dichotomy," Bernstein maintains, which constitutes a dangerous *"abuse of evil."* It violates religion and corrupts democracy as it produces a political and cultural default to extremism that sup-presses critical thinking and inquiry, obscures complex issues and stifles public deliberation. It panders to a superficial mindset of absolutes and moral certitude rather than considering how to rectify the policies that breed enduring grievances.[27]

Placing this abuse of evil in historical perspective, Bernstein notes that pragmatism emerged in the latter decades of the 19th century in response to the absolutist mindset and bloody violence of the American civil war. No possibility of compromise existed in that polarised world of "stark binary oppositions" and "violent extremism." Pragmatists such as William James, Charles Peirce, John Dewey and Oliver Wendall Holmes, Jr. worked out an alternative mentality to absolutism, a critically engaged fallibilism that featured con-tingency, chance, pluralism, flexibility and ideas over moral certainty, rigidity, absolutes, sharp dichotomies, ideology and dogma. The possibility of democracy, they maintained, rests on a pragmatic, fallibilistic orientation, one that entails an open society of testing ideas in public, tolerating uncertainty, recognising the role of perspective and revising or abandoning beliefs that cannot hold up to critique.[28]

In contrast to pragmatism, the cult of Satanism, as a 21st-century remainder and permutation of Anton LaVey's 1960s-era Church of Satan, is explicitly anti-democratic. With some exceptions—notably, the Satanic Temple, which is discussed below—this subcultural phenomenon is Christianity's dark alter ego, a neofascist mutation. It is an ideology of the self, Chris Matthews argues, an atheistic doctrine that elevates the indi-vidual above society. Satan is its archetype of individualism, nonconformity, rebellion and pride; he is the devil epitomised as adversary to the herd mentality of humanity at large, the symbol of opposition to egalitarian values and human rights.[29] As such, Satan stands for radical rebellion against a repressive Christian morality. The atheistic Satanist rejects the masses and the comfort they seek in dogma, affirming brutal truth instead, regarding morality as a matter of personal choice and seeking to realise the authentic self.[30] The confrontation between good and evil in this anti-religious trope is reversed but still absolute, leaving little room for community, equality, fallibilism or other demo-cratic values. The atheistic Church of Satan is a twist on the living tradition of Western demonism, a twist that theistic Satanism extends even further by its neopagan belief in Satan as an actual entity and its commitment, as professed by the radical Order of Nine Angels, to violence in the pursuit of a new human being, uninhibited and thoroughly sinister.[31]

The post-9/11 world, embracing an absolutist discourse of good versus evil marked by an apocalyptic rhetoric, dogmatic mindset, radical politics and propensity to demonise, is habituated to violence. It is increasingly inclined to authoritarianism and is decidedly unpragmatic. Daniel Bell argues that the turn of the century was marked by deeply emotional, primordial ties of identity—including religion, race, ethnicity, language, tribe and clan—that fuel civil wars "on a scale unique in world history," give rise to an apocalyptic encounter with Islamic fundamentalism, increase resistance to American military occupation and contribute to an upsurge of genocide, torture and terror, all of which raises the basic ethical issue of evil. It is an old issue that now engulfs the world, framed as a choice between preserving human rights and destroying the foundation of Western civilisation. War is not a negotiable clash between states so much as it is an absolute conflict between faiths.[32] The question, one might conclude, is whether democracy can be revitalised in the devil's shadow where the prevailing attitude is one of annihilating one's evil enemies.

The difficulty of any such revival is hard to overestimate. In the United States, Satan is a 21st-century carryover of an enduring anxiety about ultimate evil, observes W. Scott Poole. The devil has always been part of the American story, and for most of that history he is the evil that is thought to reside within the nation's enemies. In this founding myth, "America is the Unfallen Angel, secure in its innocence, but beset by thousands of dark foes." Evil lurks. Enemies are satanic. The devil's continuing ascension shapes the political imagination and forms the cornerstone of state and empire. Terrorist evildoers are the most recent devil figure in a long line of forerunners from witches, Black people, Indians, immigrants and transgressive women to dictators and communists. The image of Satan in its various iterations expresses what the culture hates and fears most in each historical period. Satan, as the timeless force of malevolence that stalks America, "remains a powerful part of [the] public consciousness and political rhetoric" where hubris intersects with violence.[33]

Indeed, the mythic figure of the devil "haunts US political culture," constituting a serious obstacle to the realisation of a healthy democratic culture and practice, as Robert Ivie and Oscar Giner attest through genealogical critique. Attributing evil to others "casts a spell of militant insecurity on the American people." The devil is the virtuous nation's essential antagonist. The post-9/11 preoccupation with evildoers resonates not only with right-wing Christian fundamentalism but also with mainstream political culture and its secular religion of national mission and mythos of American exceptionalism, positioning the nation on God's side against Satan. Then-President Bush preached a message of holy battle at the outset of the new century. He would bestow freedom on a corrupt world in which Saddam Hussein is the face of evil. Bush spoke of an enemy that spews hellfire and inhabits dungeons, that is "flat evil," declaring that America "must defeat the evildoers where they hide," for their terror is a dark force that aims to "diminish our soul."[34] Western allies, reluctantly or otherwise, followed Bush's rhetorical lead in a war that served as a deadly exorcism.

## A New Century Re-Enchanted

While arguably Pope Francis maintains an ambiguous position on exorcism, his reference to the devil as an external force—a source of temptation that emanates from beyond the human realm—Alan McGill suggests that it may be intended to "discourage the demonization of humans."[35] The pope's old-school devil, about which he speaks regularly, reports the *Washington Post*, is "a supernatural entity with the forces of evil at his beck and call." This literal devil is the cause of evil and, unlike an allegorical devil, is at odds with the progressive teachings of the church which posit that evil is an artefact of human free will.

The winds of the church appear to be shifting in the pope's direction to counter the impact of satanic cults. "Lookout," Francis cautions, "because the Devil is present."[36]

Others, too, such as Anglican priest and licenced exorcist Erich Junger, are dedicated to spiritual warfare against the literal Satan understood as a living being bent on human destruction. Demonic possession requires expelling evil spirits. Otherwise, darkness prevails. Indeed, an ecumenical sense of urgency to counter the influence of supernatural evil, contrary to the scepticism of 18th-century rationalism and humanism, is growing across the Catholic-Orthodox-Protestant divide.[37] A 2011 Pew Research Center global survey of evangelical Protestant leaders, for instance, found that 57% reported experiencing or witnessing the devil or evil spirits being driven out of a person—although this figure was higher in the global south than the north.[38] Dwight Longenecker, Anglican minister turned Catholic priest, writes that "Satan's grip on the world is insinuated into every nook and corner." He insists that there is today "an extraordinary interest in demon possession and exorcism" and that "Satan is real." The devil has "infiltrated and dominated" culture. Through lies, temptations and tricks, the evil one spreads the false hedonistic perspective of materialism.[39] Polls indicate that about half of Americans believe in demonic possession as a real phenomenon.[40]

Indeed, for many Christians around the world, the devil remains an active agent in human affairs. He is "an objectification of the oft-times incomprehensible evil that lies within us and around us, threatening to destroy us," observes Philip Almond. The secular spell of disenchantment is broken and Satan is on the prowl again in a "newly enchanted world." Almond traces the contemporary re-emergence of the devil from the margins of Western culture back to the 1973 horror film, *The Exorcist*. This, he writes, "was the beginning of a re-engagement with the demonic in film, television, literature and music that has lasted into the twenty-first century." This newly enchanted world of willingly suspended disbelief is inhabited by imaginary beings from vampires, zombies and ghosts to witches, shapeshifters, and demons existing somewhere "in a space between reality and unreality."[41]

In the larger cultural context, Almond notes, the faithful are free again to choose to believe in the Christian story of the devil.[42] A case in point is the religious blogger Roger Olson who insists that not just fundamentalists but also conservative evangelicals can openly contest the modernist disregard of the literal Satan. The return of these relatively moderate, centrist Protestants to what Olson calls the "Satanic realism" of the New Testament means believing not just in the devil as a symbolic representation of evil but candidly in the devil as a real being, a real presence that contests God's power but that is ultimately doomed to fail. A professor in Baylor University's theological seminary, Olson contends that only the "Enlightenment taboo" previously kept Protestant evangelicals, other than fundamentalist extremists, from rejecting theodicies that excluded the role of an actual devil.[43]

Conservative evangelical commentator, Larry Tomczak, who might well be considered a fundamentalist extremist, illustrates the presence of the literal devil in the current political divide in the United States when he insists that "the devil is using the Democratic Party to try to destroy America." The Democratic Party is morphing into "a European secular and socialist entity" in its "leftist and anti-capitalist … pursuit of 'social justice' and 'income equality'." Millennials have been "seduced" and "lured" by "charismatic politicians" who often go unchallenged by the "anti-Trump media." Democratic Party leaders are avowed socialists, he insists. They head up a party of "godless secularism," a political party hostile to "biblical values" and bent on a radical redistribution of wealth, aggressive anti-climate-change initiatives, a complete takeover of healthcare by the federal government, open immigration, the legalisation of marijuana, implementation of a comprehensive LGBTQ and feminist agenda, taxpayer-funded abortion on demand, euthanasia, gun control, cuts in defence spending, the appointment of liberal judges, censorship of conservative thought, fraudulent voting practices, the privileging of globalism over nationalism along with other abominations. "Without a desperately needed spiritual awakening, America is on a dangerous slope," Tomczak warns, because the devil is using the Democratic Party to seduce the nation with its "godless vision."[44]

Just as Donald Trump can be regarded, by himself as well as his followers, as chosen by God and opposed by satanic forces, opponents can consider Trump to be possessed by the devil or worse.[45] "She's the devil," Trump proclaimed, in reference to Hillary Clinton, his foe during the 2016 presidential campaign, apparently meaning it literally, even if cynically.[46] Again, in the 2020 campaign, he declared Joe Biden was "against God."[47] The cult-like QAnon phenomenon, capitalising on social media, emerged as a pro-Trump force in his re-election bid. It spread the far-right conspiracy theory that a cabal of Democratic political leaders and other institutional figures kidnapped and tortured children whose blood they used in satanic rituals.[48] These devil figures, who were in control of the "deep state," opposed Donald Trump in his battle against the entrenched forces of evil. Trump's political opponents were portrayed as the enemy in a cosmic battle of "good versus monstrous evil," observes Paul Thomas, a professor of religious studies.[49] This cabal of "Satan-worshiping pedophiles" included Joe Biden, Hillary Clinton, Barak Obama, George Soros, Oprah Winfrey, Tom Hanks, Ellen DeGeneres, Pope Francis and the Dalai Lama, among others.[50]

Yet, for a "growing legion of people," writes Gini Graham Scott, "Donald Trump has become the modern devil, because of his association with racism, bigotry, xenophobia, inciting violence, lying about almost everything and otherwise having the attributes of someone who is a dangerous threat to humanity." Her point is not quite that Trump is the devil but that he has "sold his soul to the devil for fame, power, and glory" and can be compared to the devil as the evilest of all monsters.[51] Education scholars Cheryl Matias and Peter Newlove, referring to Trump's racist political rhetoric, warn that his discourse is akin to fascism. They urge Americans to resist Trump as "the devil of Whiteness himself."[52] Even Trump's first impeachment is considered by a *Wall Street Journal* opinion writer to be "the devil's work," in that it serves no one well and for which no one but the devil "may take pride in a job well done."[53] Whether Trump is thought to be preordained by God to defeat the devil or is perceived as working for/as the devil, a kind of spiritual polarisation converges around the haunting perception of the evil one literally or figuratively raising 21st-century hell.[54]

Trump's authoritarian assault on democracy is considered by certain critics as "purely evil," comparable in degree, and not just in the sense of name calling, to the fascist tactics of Hitler and the Nazis. Philosopher Susan Neiman, an authority on the Holocaust, acknowledges that "evil" is a word that should be used with caution but insists that "Donald Trump meets every single criterion for using the word evil."[55] Indeed, public memory of the Holocaust is fading in the United States, just as antisemitism is on the rise. "There is a revival of a rhetoric of Jews as the children of Satan," observes Alvin Rosenfeld, director of Indiana University's Institute for the Study of Contemporary Antisemitism.[56]

The right-wing uprising in Europe, reacting to a loss of job security and welfare-state safety nets, aims to dismantle the European Union or to transform it from within.[57] To them, it is at once a nationalist and pan-European movement. And fascist symbols are now on the rise in Italy, Germany, and elsewhere. The week before the 2016 Brexit vote, a scare-mongering image of migrants and refugees circulated by Nigel Farage, leader at that time of the United Kingdom's anti-immigration Independence Party, prompted comparisons to Nazi propaganda demonising Jews and other minorities.[58] The right-wing movement's anti-immigration, anti-globalisation, identity, xenophobic and authoritarian rhetorical bent is replete with toxic language and scapegoating. It is a discourse that constructs a homogeneous in-group, demonises pluralism and functions as a politics of fear.[59] In its more subtle "civilisationist" form, it represents Islam as a civilisation alien to Europe's Christian foundations, marking the distinction between "us" and "them" in a sense of shared culture, if not religious belief itself. The central threat, the implied evil within this "thin ideological veneer," is the "Islamization of Western societies."[60] An "ingrained animus" of "deep-seated prejudices" against a "demonic enemy," argues Chika Mba, is "embedded in the *cultural unconscious* of Europe and North America."[61]

Beyond the Trump phenomenon and its right-wing populist corollaries in Europe and elsewhere, evil figures prominently in contemporary Western culture. With the decline in church membership, horror films provide an alternative site for making religious meaning, including the meaning of evil. Whether evil assumes the form of monsters in *Pitch Black* (2000), artificial intelligence in the *Resident Evil* franchise (2002–2021) or the devil in *Lost Souls* (2000), these films convey the sense of a dangerous and unstable world subject to destruction and chaos. Thus, Paul Teusner observes, horror films "do theology" in a way that challenges the mainstream of society from the margins.[62]

"Although the charismatic and Evangelical churches are significant presences in American society," writes Armando Maggi, "they are not sufficient to explain the unprecedented popularity of horror films and television shows depicting the demonic invasions and rituals of exorcism in … the new millennium." With reality rendered as no longer fully explicable, viewers can doubt spectacles of demonic possession but still feel affected as if they were true. In an age of declared secular disenchantment, but in the presence of supernatural evil, people reach out through horror films to reintegrate lost identity. Accordingly, the horror genre plays a cultural role in its "ability to represent national trauma after 9/11." It embodies radical evil and draws parallels between repressed past sins and current evils, such as torture in Abu Ghraib perpetrated by Americans in the war on terror.[63]

Moreover, the music of contemporary popular culture in its alternative spiritual milieu and changing context of spiritual re-enchantment, especially as reflected in metal music, features dark themes of evil, suffering, war and death drawn from Judeo-Christian demonology, eschatology and apocalypticism, among other religious sources and themes. As Markus Moberg observes, "From the very outset, *religion*, particularly the dark and evil forces of the Judeo-Christian tradition in the form of Satan, demons and the fires of hell, has functioned as one of heavy metal's most important sources of inspiration." Metal's dark spirituality and polarising music embraces individualism and the devil in its confrontation with institutional Christianity, its cultural impact continuing into the present century.[64] Black metal, in particular, assumes an explicitly demonic posture to cultivate a "liturgical discourse about Satan," rendering Christianity vulnerable to the devil's dark powers and allying itself with the demonic as a force of dissent from the dominant Christian culture.[65] Satanic metal is extreme metal, rule-breaking and boundary crossing music that is deliberately transgressive in its inhuman sound and blasphemous lyrics. While some of these transgressive bands endorse the devil for shock value, others adopt the satanic aesthetic to battle the church; some claim truly to worship Satan as God's enemy, and still others are atheistic Satanists. As Nick Jones notes, "Satan is the ultimate rebel."[66]

The Lucifer Morningstar character in Neil Gaiman's *The Sandman* graphic novel series represents a rebellious devil, too, but without the loud angst of satanic metal music. Here, Lucifer Morningstar quits hell after ruling there for ten billion years and moves to live in retirement on earth. Mike Carey's spinoff of Gaiman's Lucifer develops the character into a free-will advocate and adversary of God's tyranny—a full-blown rebel against God's creation and rule. As Carey's series entered the 21st century, Lucifer Morningstar sets about creating his own alternative universe of free will where the operative rule is not to worship anyone. Aaron Rabinowitz argues that this representation of the devil reflects a human desire for autonomy, a passion "to break free from God's overbearing plan."[67]

The devil endures in popular culture as a biblical monster, a paradoxical combination of demon and deity, and a medium that recurs in different forms with a message adapted to current times. *Lucifer*, the television series, Kelly Murphy writes, "presents us with a 21st century depiction of the devil" that tests our working assumptions about scripture and, by extension, our nature as moral beings. Lucifer is the "rebel angel who fell from heaven," the master provocateur of wrongdoing. This television devil takes up residence in Los Angeles during his extended vacation from hell. He is a "rewriting of earlier rewritings" not only of Gaiman's and Carey's graphic novel portrayals but also of scriptural renderings of the devil—a monster "ever changing and adapting." This Lucifer is the fallen devil banished to hell but now living much like a human on earth, even helping a police detective solve crimes. He appears in the form of an ordinary, albeit dashing, human being but possesses supernatural powers that occasionally transform him into the image of a monstrous devil complete with glowing red eyes. He is rebellious, cutting off his wings, opening a nightclub and refusing to return to hell, but he also undergoes talk therapy with a therapist to understand his anger with a God that turned him into a torturer. While the message conveyed is that "people need to take responsibility for their own bad behavior" and recognise their own monstrosity, God, seen through Lucifer's eyes, is also a monster, a "cruel, manipulative bastard" that subjects humans to a rigged game that neither sinner nor saint can win. Thus, Murphy concludes, this popular culture devil challenges viewers to reconsider, from the perspective of a biblical fiend, "what it means to be human, monster, and divine" and how they blend into one another.[68]

In another expression of this theme of humanity reconsidered from the diabolical viewpoint, The Satanic Temple, not to be confused with the Church of Satan, is a nontheistic religious group based in the United States with chapters also in Canada and the United Kingdom. Its stated mission is to encourage benevolence and empathy, oppose tyranny and injustice, advocate common sense and undertake noble pursuits. It aims to advance secularism and preserve individual liberties, specifically to counter the political influence of conservative religion, such as the fundamentalist anti-abortion lobby. Its position is thoroughly oppositional, operating under the sign of the devil. "Satan," for the Satanic Temple, "is the symbol of the Eternal Rebel in opposition to arbitrary authority, forever defending personal sovereignty, even in the face of insurmountable odds." He is an "icon of unbowed will" and emblem of the "heretic" opposed to tyranny. This "metaphoric representation is the literary Satan best exemplified by John Milton and the Romantic Satanists from William Blake to Percy Shelley to Anatole France."[69] As Lily Rothman writes, the Satanic Temple is a political Satanism that "sees Satan as a *Paradise Lost*-inflected metaphor who represents skepticism and the ability to challenge authority."[70] Towards that end, the Satanic Temple strives for equal representation in public space. Typical is the public unveiling of the goat-headed statue of Baphomet—complete with wings and pentagram—in Detroit on 25 July 2015 in opposition to displays of the Ten Commandments and other Christian monuments placed on public property there.[71] Joseph Laycock's detailed history of the Satanic Temple assesses its significance for contemporary issues of religion, morality and democracy, arguing that in advancing a sociopolitical counter-myth it seeks to complicate the prevailing notion of America as a Christian nation. That is, it functions as a corrective to the prevailing myth, a corrective that aims to renegotiate and promote core values of pluralism, equality, tolerance and free inquiry.[72]

There is something unmistakably spiritual about this secular rebellion against traditional religion undertaken in the name of Satan. Tara Isabella Burton calls it "occult spirituality." Progressive millennials, she writes, are abandoning institutional religion to engage in a culture war that pits "the self-identified Davids of seemingly secularized progressivism against the Goliath of nationalist evangelical Christianity." Witch culture transgresses evangelicalism, using the language of "the diabolical to chip at the edifice of what it sees as white, patriarchal Christianity that has become a *de facto* state religion," as reflected in white evangelical complicity with Donald Trump. Devil worship serves as a "levying force for social justice." As a weapon of resistance to an oppressive power structure, in the words of Dakota Bracciale, witchcraft "must ride into battle under the banner of the Devil himself." Witchcraft in this sense, as with the Satanic Temple, hails Satan to oppose conservative, evangelical Christian hegemony in a way that Burton says has permeated political-activist culture on the political left more broadly. The contemporary millennial left adheres to an alternative spirituality, using "the language, the imagery, and the rituals of modern occultism to re-enchant its seeming secularism."[73]

## Malevolent Enchantment

What are we to make of this gesture to cultural, religious and political re-enchantment which brings into focus, among other matters, the agency—real or symbolic—of a rebel devil, either as a force to be expelled or venerated? Certainly, but perhaps in an unexpected way, the metaphor of re-enchantment is a mark of a secular-spiritual tension within modern and postmodern thought. Re-enchantment flows from modernity and earlier periods of Western culture writ large; it is a troubled metaphor, a trope that conjures up the devil among other spirits to carry affective freight in conflicted images of alienation and wonderment. Talk of re-enchantment, Jason Crawford attests, "is a sign of the times. Look for a literature on re-enchantment pre-2000, and there isn't much to find." Modernity's condition of disenchantment, Charles Taylor argued, is a material world of instrumental reason and technological control, a world lost to the enchantment of a premodern era of spirituality and magic. Its avowed secularity, Crawford allows, is background to the new phenomenon of re-enchantment.[74]

Crawford notes that most contemporary writers on re-enchantment are searching for a way out of disenchantment short of succumbing to irrationality. They want their spirituality without superstition or scientific ignorance—that is, they want re-enchantment without the old devilry of enchantment in which, as puritan preacher George Gifford warned, "Satan ... bewitched the minds of men." Since early modern times, enchantment has attracted both fascination and derision in a fashion consistent with the present-day ambivalence between fantasy, wonderment and mystical contemplation on the one hand and wariness about unreality on the other. It is as if contemporary searchers know, in Crawford's view, "that the full-blooded gods of the old redemptive order have passed us by. What remains is a shadow, derivative and late to the game." The present re-enchantment, by this account, is "secondary to something authentic" and thus "harassed to the margins of a rational social order" in the manner that modernity—blind to its own magical enchantment—constituted itself in opposition to the enchanted *other*.[75]

While this critique reflects the ambivalence about the relationship between spirituality and rationality in this present moment of re-enchantment, Eugene McCarraher notes significantly that "we have never been disenchanted." At least unknowingly, if not perversely, modernist secularism, with its faith in reason, material forces and science, has been infused by a kind of "sacramental imagination," by which McCarraher means that the material mediates the supernatural. Capitalism in particular is a "metamorphosis of the sacred in the raiment of secularity"—a "covert form of enchantment, all the more beguiling on account of its apparent profanity" as a "powerful solvent of enchantment." In capitalism's pecuniary enchantment, money supplants the creative power of the gods. To the mind of the Trappist monk Thomas Merton, this capitalist enchantment masquerading as secularity is evil, a perverse reduction of the world to inventory, an insatiable avarice counter to a loving God.[76] One might surmise that this unacknowledged enchantment is itself the work of the devil in secular disguise, or the functional equivalent thereof. Whether the spell should be perceived as good or ill is a matter of perspective in a disaggregated and diffuse world.

In films ranging from *Habemus Papam* (2011) to *Antichrist* (2009), many recent European filmmakers grant religion a post-secular role, deeming its outright rejection intellectually and existentially problematic for contemporary life. In the "façade of a secularized world," Costica Bradatan argues, religion still shapes lives and thinking, whether through churches or "subtler outlets." Cinema engages spiritual experiences that convey a sense of personal fulfilment and belonging in the cosmic order. Religious imagery saturates intellectual conversation, philosophical discourse, politics and even scientific debates.[77]

The very notion of a re-enchanted 21st century may signal a cultural development beyond postmodernism. Sara Helen Binney boldly contends that postmodernism is dead. Among the attributes of a potential successor, she suggests, is "the idea that, after the scepticism of postmodernism, interest is reemerging in the inexplicable, the unspeakable, in the things that cannot be encompassed rationally." This turn has been termed religious, or at least a return of the supernatural. Something new in contemporary fiction, Binney argues, "something which belongs to the 21st century," is a metamodernism that contributes to "the creation of a space for the sacred." Contemporary novels retelling folklore (which itself is not a new phenomenon) have an effect unlike postmodernism's decentring and demythologising project. They convey a feeling of hesitation about the appearance of supernatural phenomena. Their engagement of the fantastic in this way introduces the sacred through a sense of the sublime, understood in Kantian terms as a feeling of terror and delight or pleasurable pain provoked by the appearance of something vast or infinite—creating an oscillation between the self and something greater. A metamodern balancing between the real world and the folkloric supernatural sphere constitutes space for the sublime, allowing for a kind of "naïve sincerity ... a momentary irruption of awe and wonder," which many cultural theorists call enchantment or re-enchantment. There is an element of uncertainty embedded in this fantastic experience and something sacred in the broad rather than strictly religious sense of being set apart and holy.[78]

This element of uncertainty is indicative of an unresolved tension within Max Weber's foundational claim that modernity is characterised by its disenchantment with the world, a disenchantment he saw as brought about by advances in the natural sciences that constituted a secular and rational worldview absent the supernatural. As Wojciech Załuski observes in his review of Joshua Landie and Michael Saler's edited volume, *The Re-Enchantment of the World: Secular Magic in a Rational Age*, the question remains as to whether the world can be re-enchanted in good faith, without rejecting the secular and the rational. The essays in Landie and Saler's notable collection set out to answer that question in the affirmative, making a strong case in Załuski's opinion that modernity itself is much more enchanted than a literal reading of Weber would entail. Therein lies Załuski's critique and, for immediate purposes, important insight: a reading of Weber does not necessitate the mistaken, insufficiently nuanced conclusion that modernity is totally disenchanted.[79] Moreover, Martin Cohen notes, Landie and Saler's book underscores the fact that "disenchantment is easier claimed than achieved."[80] The break with enchantment was never complete; a degree of continuity is to be expected from premodernity through modernity and postmodernity and into the swell of metamodernity. Emphases vary from period to period, but spirituality, the supernatural and religion remain present to some degree and form. The carryover of enchantment includes the Western devil—albeit a devil that may not in its various guises conform to Landi and Saler's aim of a 21st-century re-enchantment with dignity—along with a secularity informed by a progressive pluralism and contingency that leaves room for the continuing role of mystery and meaning in contemporary life. In the spiritual mix of the metamodern narrative, the devil is largely an irreverent, indecent and divisive impulse.

The antagonist devil functions as an article of disdain or esteem to be exorcised or summoned literally or symbolically depending on one's sacred or profane, pious or impious, standpoint. This conflicted devil is a polarising figure, an index of social anxiety, a vehicle of rebellion and alienation at the intersection of contemporary culture, religion and politics. The subversive spirit of Lucifer suffuses art, music and literature along with politics and religion. For many Christians, as Matthew Paul Turner attests, "Satan is an easy go-to device for making villains out of people with whom we disagree ... a name we drop when we are afraid of change ... a big scary demon ... an excuse we use when we aren't willing to face our own demons."[81] What goes around comes around, though: the accused become the accusers, finger-pointing in reverse, and evil is righteously attributed to Christian piety. The dark shadow is displaced at the cost of human relations. Satan no longer stands "as the ultimate choreographer of all human depravity," observes Rosemarie Ho, so much as those who are perceived to "manifest his program."[82] Even Satanists displace evil onto those who blame the devil. The scapegoat mechanism fractures community, institutionalises fear and undermines the promise of democracy. Fear is "the temptation to hate and despise the religious other, the immigrant other, the racial other, the sexual other," an affective complex that exposes people to political manipulation, argues Susan Brooks Thistlethwaite.[83]

Malevolence is the defining temptation of the times—a prevailing sense of evil provoked by fear and hatred, a devil function that breeds estrangement, a polarising mindset, the dark side of enchantment. What Tony Judt calls the "banalization" of evil—the banality of its overuse in moral and political discourse, a discourse that finds Hitlers everywhere and makes dehumanising gestures with ease—has displaced the "truly diabolical" with an obsession used "to justify a hundred lesser crimes of our own."[84] In the first two decades of the new century, the presumption of evil has teetered at the threshold of public alienation, rendering democratic polity questionable as disagreement and dissent escalates into disaffection and rebellion. The devil taken as sign or symbol of an evil presence sustains a deepening division between the worthy and the wicked, each side of the divide affirming its own virtue while attributing malevolence to the other.[85] This polarising mindset paralyses the collective will to respond appropriately to global warming, economic displacement, racism and the other exigencies of an unsettled world.

Polarising discourses of evil are difficult to escape, especially in troubled times of disruption and transition, and when publics feel urgently threatened, whether by loss of status and income security or by systemic racism and climate change. Evil is a self-sustaining discourse that frames thought and feeling, word and action, and narrows vision within the tight circumference of wickedness opposed to goodness. Like the devil, it is utterly oppositional. Few, if any, are immune to its pull.

James Baldwin understood the social malignancy of devil work ever so well. "The mindless and hysterical banality of the evil presented in *The Exorcist*," he wrote, "is the most terrifying thing about the film." The devil is a presence in you and in me that is marked by the moment, in your eyes or mine, when "no other human being is real."[86] Whether or not the devil is called by name, the warring camps ascribe a dehumanising evil to one another, insisting that the opposing side must be held accountable for harms perpetrated.[87] The devil is the accuser, the one who projects. Why, we must learn to ask, do you or I need such a creature in our life?

Fortunately, the devil is not the only story to be told about life in the 21st century. Satan's story is one, albeit important, perspective but not necessarily the final word on what has happened or will follow. Nevertheless, recognising that enchantment is intrinsic to human affairs—that society is never fully disenchanted—and acknowledging how a malevolent enchantment figures into the culture wars is a step in the right direction. It could help clear a path in search of ways to work around and beyond the dysfunction of the hostile divide.

# Notes

1 Stein Ringman, *Nation of Devils: Democratic Leadership and the Problem of Obedience* (New Haven: Yale University Press, 2013), 5. Ringman is paraphrasing Immanuel Kant.
2 Douglas Schuler, "Doctor Faustus in the Twenty-First Century: A Meditation on Knowledge, Power, and Civic Intelligence," *AI & Society* 28 (2013): 261–5, emphasis in original. Srđan T. Korać, "Depersonalisation of Killing: Toward a 21st Century Use of Force 'Beyond Good and Evil?'" *Philosophy and Society* 29, no. 1 (2018), 49–64, emphasis in original.
3 Benjamin Ramm, "What the Myth of Faust Can Teach Us," *BBC Culture*, 26 September 2017. https://www.bbc.com/culture/article/20170907-what-the-myth-of-faust-can-teach-us
4 Jonathan Powell, "When to Quarrel with the Devil," *New Statesman*, 13 February 2012, 33–5.
5 Louise Penny, *All the Devils Are Here* (New York: Minotaur Books, 2020).
6 Darren Oldridge, *The Devil: A Very Short Introduction* (Oxford: Oxford University Press, 2012), 90.
7 Ringman, *Nation of Devils*, 5.
8 David Crary, "Exorcism: Increasingly Frequent, Including After US Protests," *AP News*, 31 October 2020. https://apnews.com/article/portland-san-francisco-oregon-cff13a56cd41997553ea3e-9a8fc21384; Mike Mariani, "American Exorcism," *The Atlantic*, December 2018. https://www.theatlantic.com/magazine/archive/2018/12/catholic-exorcisms-on-the-rise/573943/; Jean Hopfensperger, "Exorcisms Make a 21st Century Comeback in Minnesota, US," *Star Tribune*, 11 November 2019. https://www.startribune.com/exorcisms-make-a-21st-century-comeback/564708901/; https://www.afr.com/life-and-luxury/health-and-wellness/pope-expected-dioceses-to-battle-the-occult-with-exorcisms-20191125-p53drf; Brian McNeill, "The Centuries-Old Practice of Exorcism Is On the Rise. Why Now?" *VCU News*, 11 January 2019. https://news.vcu.edu/article/The_centuriesold_practice_of_exorcism_is_on_the_rise_Why_now

9  While the percentages of believers recorded in polls can vary according to sample and methodology, there is an overall consistency in the high level of belief, including a 2001 Gallup poll that reported 68% of Americans believed in the devil, a Harris poll in 2007 that reported 62% of Americans believe in the devil; a 2016 Gallup poll that reported 61% of Americans believe in the devil. See Ed Stoddard, "Poll Finds More Americans Believe in Devil than Darwin," Reuters, 29 November 2007. https://uk.reuters.com/article/us-usa-religion-beliefs/poll-finds-more-americans-believe-in-devil-than-darwin-idUKN2922875820071129; Jennifer Robison, "The Devil and Demographic Details," *Gallup*, 25 February 2003. https://news.gallup.com/poll/7858/Devil-Demographic-Details.aspx#:~:text=Sixty-six%20percent%20of%20people%20between%20the%20ages%20of,education%20appear%20to%20quash%20belief%20in%20the%20devil; Anugrah Kumar, "Gallup Poll: 89% of Americans Say They Believe in God," *The Christian Post*, 2 July 2016. https://www.christianpost.com/news/americans-belief-in-god-poll.html. Two examples of polls concerning Americans' belief in hell are "Belief of Americans in God, Heaven, and Hell, 2016," *Statistica Research Department*, 29 June 2016. https://www.statista.com/statistics/245496/belief-of-americans-in-god-heaven-and-hell/ and "CBS News Polls: Americans' Views on Death," *CBS News*, 27 April 2014. https://www.cbsnews.com/news/cbs-news-poll-americans-views-on-death/

10  David Marr, "Faith: What Australians Believe In," *The Sunday Morning Herald*, 19 December 2009. https://www.smh.com.au/national/faith-what-australians-believe-in-20091218-l5qy.html

11  B. A. Robinson, "Diversity of Beliefs about Satan by the General Public," *Religious Tolerance*, 7 May 2008. http://www.religioustolerance.org/chr_sat4.htm

12  Christopher H. Partridge and Eric S. Christianson "Introduction: A Brief History of Western Demonology," in *The Lure of the Dark Side: Satan and Western Demonology in Popular Culture*, eds. Christopher H. Partridge and Eric S. Christianson (London: Routledge, 2014), 11–13. See Michel Foucault, *Religion and Culture*, ed. Jeremy Carrette (London: Routledge, 1999), 75–84.

13  William R. Telford, "Speak of the Devil: The Portrayal of Satan in the Christ Film," in *Lure of the Dark Side*, 100–1, 103.

14  Oldridge, *The Devil*, 93 and 95.

15  George W. Bush, "Text of Bush's Address," *CNN.com*, 11 September 2001. http://edition.cnn.com/2001/US/09/11/bush.speech.text/

16  Richard J. Bernstein, *The Abuse of Evil: The Corruption of Politics and Religion since 9/11* (Cambridge: Polity Press, 2005), vii, 10 and 116–8.

17  For a critique of the "axis of evil" discourse that reveals the complications this slogan deceitfully and counterproductively oversimplifies, see Bruce Cumings, Ervand Abrahamian, and Moshe Ma'oz, *Inventing the Axis of Evil: The Truth About North Korea, Iran, and Syria* (New York: The New Press, 2004).

18  Diane Winston, "The Demonization of Saddam Hussein," *Baltimore Sun*, 3 March 1991. https://www.baltimoresun.com/news/bs-xpm-1991-03-03-1991062102-story.html; William James Martin, "Just How Evil was Saddam Hussein?" *Media Monitors Network*, 29 July 2003. https://www.mediamonitors.net/just-how-evil-was-saddam-hussein/

19  Robert L. Ivie and Oscar Giner, *Hunt the Devil: A Demonology of US War Culture* (Tuscaloosa: University of Alabama Press, 2015), 1–9, 14, 22–3, 111 and 130–3.

20  Bernstein, *Abuse of Evil*, 60.

21  Alexander Spenser, "The Social Construction of Terrorism: Media, Metaphors, and Policy Implications," *Journal of International Relations and Development* 15, no. 3 (2012): 393 and 406.

22  Tony Blair, "Full Text: Blair Speech on Terror," *BBC News*, 16 July 2005. http://news.bbc.co.uk/2/hi/uk_news/4689363.stm

23  "Americans and Europeans Differ Widely on Foreign Policy Issues," *Pew Research Center*, 17 April 2002. https://www.pewresearch.org/global/2002/04/17/americans-and-europeans-differ-widely-on-foreign-policy-issues/

24  Claire Howells, "European Approaches to Terrorism in a Post-9/11 World," *E-International Relations*, 6 (September 2012). https://www.e-ir.info/2012/09/06/european-approaches-to-terrorism-in-a-post-911-world/

25  Adam Nossiter and Katrin Bennhold, "The Politics of Terrorism in a Combustible Europe," *New York Times*, 9 November 2020. https://www.nytimes.com/2020/11/09/world/europe/france-austria-terrorist-attacks-marcon-kurz.html

26 Barack Obama, "Full Text of Obama's Nobel Peace Prize Speech," *NBC News*, 10 December 2009. http://www.nbcnews.com/id/34360743/ns/politics-white_house/t/full-text-obamas-nobel-peace-prize-speech/#.X5Goc1l7lsM

27 Bernstein, *Abuse of Evil*, viii, 11, 59 and 83, emphasis in original.

28 Louis Menard, *The Metaphysical Club: A Story of Ideas in America* (New York: Farrar, Straus, and Giroux, 2001); Bernstein, *Abuse of Evil*, 21–38.

29 Chris Matthews, *Modern Satanism: Anatomy of a Radical Subculture* (Westport: Praeger, 2009), xvi–xviii, 195 and 204–5.

30 Olli Pitkänen, "Satan—A Good Guy?" in *The Devil and Philosophy: The Nature of His Game*, ed. Robert Arp (Chicago: Open Court, 2014), 284–5.

31 On the Order of Nine Angels, see Pitkänen, "Satan," 285–6. This global group, based in the United Kingdom, came to public attention in the 1980s and established an internet presence in 2000 that was extended to social media in 2008.

32 Daniel Bell, "Ethics and Evil—Frameworks for Twenty-First-Century Culture," *The Antioch Review*, 63, no. 2 (2005): 688–9, 697 and 700.

33 W. Scott Poole, *Satan in America: The Devil We Know* (Lanham: Rowman & Littlefield, 2009), x–xii, xiv–xix, xxi–xii, 213 and 215–7.

34 Ivie and Giner, *Hunt the Devil*, 1–14, 18 and 20.

35 Alan McGill "What Does Pope Francis Mean by his References to the Devil as a Being? An Intra-textual, Cultural-Linguistic Perspective," *Heythrop Journal* 60, no. 5 (2019): 769.

36 Anthony Falola, "A Modern Pope Gets Old School on the Devil," *Washington Post*, 10 May 2014. https://www.washingtonpost.com/world/a-modern-pope-gets-old-school-on-the-devil/2014/05/10/f56a9354-1b93-4662-abbb-d877e49f15ea_story.html

37 Griffin Paul Jackson, "The Protestant Exorcists: How Fighting the Devil Became an Ecumenical Pursuit," *Christianity Today* 63, no. 8 (2019): 52–6.

38 Pew Research Center, "Evangelical Beliefs and Practices," 22 June 2011. https://www.pewforum.org/2011/06/22/global-survey-beliefs/

39 Fr. Dwight Longenecker, "Where is the Devil at Work in the World?" *National Catholic Register*, 29 January 2020. https://www.ncregister.com/blog/where-is-the-devil-at-work-in-the-world

40 Mike Mariani, "American Exorcism," *The Atlantic*, December 2018. https://www.theatlantic.com/magazine/archive/2018/12/catholic-exorcisms-on-the-rise/573943/

41 Philip C. Almond, *The Devil: A New Biography* (Ithaca, 2014), 221–2 and xiii–xiv.

42 Almond, *The Devil*, 221.

43 Roger E. Olson, "Where the Devil is Satan (in Contemporary Christianity)?" *Patheos*, 20 May 2013. https://www.patheos.com/blogs/rogereolson/2013/05/where-the-devil-is-satan-in-contemporary-christianity/

44 Larry Tomczak, "21 Ways the Devil is Using the Democratic Party to Destroy America," *Charisma News*, 14 January 2019. https://www.charismanews.com/opinion/heres-the-deal/74772-21-ways-the-devil-is-using-the-democratic-party-to-destroy-america

45 Jim Galloway, Greg Bluestein, and Tia Mitchell, "The Jolt: On God, the Devil, and Donald Trump," *Atlanta Journal-Constitution*, 26 November 2019. https://www.ajc.com/blog/politics/the-jolt-god-the-devil-and-donald-trump/MePxQTJWaWKtJMMWlvwzgO/. For a cynical, secular take on this question of whether Trump is devil possessed and God chosen, see Sarah Jones, "Here's How We'd Really Know that Trump is the Antichrist," *Explainer*, 21 August 2019. https://nymag.com/intelligencer/2019/08/heres-how-wed-really-know-that-trump-is-the-antichrist.html

46 Adam K. Raymond, "Donald Trump Calls Hillary Clinton the 'Devil'," *Intelligencer*, 2 August 2016. https://nymag.com/intelligencer/2016/08/donald-trump-calls-hillary-clinton-the-devil.html

47 David Jackson, "Donald Trump Claims Joe Biden is 'Against God'; Biden Calls Attack 'Shameful'," *USA Today*, 6 August 2020. https://www.usatoday.com/story/news/politics/2020/08/06/trump-claims-biden-against-god-biden-team-calls-trump-divider/3311594001/

48 Brett Forrest, "What is QAnon? What We Know About the Conspiracy-Theory Group," *Wall Street Journal*, 4 February 2021. https://www.wsj.com/articles/what-is-qanon-what-we-know-about-the-conspiracy-theory-11597694801; "America's Satanic Panic Returns—This Time through Q-Anon," *All Things Considered*, National Public Radio, 18 May 2021. https://www.npr.org/2021/05/18/997559036/americas-satanic-panic-returns-this-time-through-qanon

49  Paul Thomas, "How QAnon Uses Satanic Rhetoric to Set Up a Narrative of 'Good vs. Evil'," *The Conversation*, 20 October 2020. https://theconversation.com/how-qanon-uses-satanic-rhetoric-to-set-up-a-narrative-of-good-vs-evil-146281

50  Kevin Roose, "What is QAnon, the Viral Pro-Trump Conspiracy Theory," *New York Times*, 15 June 2021. https://www.nytimes.com/article/what-is-qanon.html?.?mc=aud_dev&ad-keywords=auddevgate&gclid=EAIaIQobChMIqcP_0I2n8gIVNGpvBB2MFAZwEAMYASAAEgJu6_D_BwE&gclsrc=aw.ds

51  Gini Graham Scott, "Is Trump the Modern Day Devil?" *HuffPost*, 31 March 2017. https://www.huffpost.com/entry/is-trump-the-modernday-de_b_9579936; Amanda Marcotte, "Evangelicals Told Trump He was 'Chosen' by God; Now He Says It Himself," *Solon*, 22 August 2019. https://www.salon.com/2019/08/22/evangelicals-told-trump-he-was-chosen-by-god-now-he-says-it-himself/

52  Cheryl E. Matias & Peter M. Newlove, "Better the Devil You See than the One You Don't: Bearing Witness to Emboldened En-Whitening Epistemology in the Trump Era," *International Journal of Qualitative Studies in Education* 30, no. 10 (2017): 926.

53  Joseph Epstein, "Will the Gentleman from the Underworld Yield?" *Wall Street Journal*, Eastern Edition, 7 January 2020, A15.

54  Tom Jacobs, "One Quarter of Americans Believe Donald Trump Is a Tool of the Devil, According to a New Study," *Pacific Standard*, 30 July 2019. https://psmag.com/news/one-quarter-of-americans-believe-donald-trump-is-running-with-the-devil

55  Chauncey DeVega, "Philosopher Susan Neiman Says Trump Evil—and She Literally Wrote the Book," *Salon*, 24 September 2019. https://www.salon.com/2019/09/24/philosopher-susan-neiman-says-trump-is-evil-and-she-literally-wrote-the-book/

56  Carmen Siering, "Anti-Semitism on the Rise," *Bloom* (Bloomington Indiana), April/May 2019, 106.

57  Andrea Mammone, "Right-Wing Nationalists Are on the Rise in Europe—And There's No Progressive Coalition to Stop Them," *Washington Post*, 7 April 2019. https://www.washingtonpost.com/outlook/2019/04/07/right-wing-nationalists-are-rise-europe-theres-no-progressive-coalition-stop-them/

58  Ishaan Tharoor, "New Pro-Brexit Ad Gets Linked to Nazi-era Propaganda," *Washington Post*, 16 June 2016. https://www.washingtonpost.com/news/worldviews/wp/2016/06/16/new-pro-brexit-ad-gets-linked-to-nazi-era-propaganda/

59  Ruth Wodak and Majid KhosraviNik, "Dynamics of Discourse and Politics in Right-Wing Populism and Politics in Europe and Beyond: An Introduction," in *Right-Wing Populism in Europe: Politics and Discourse*, eds. Ruth Wodak, Majid KhosraviNik and Brigitte Mral (London: Bloomsbury Academic, 2013), xviii. Ruth Wodak, "International Analysis: (Re)Inventing Scapegoats—Right-Wing Populism Across Europe," *Andean Air Mail and Peruvian Times*, 4 March 2014. https://www.peruviantimes.com/04/international-analysis-reinventing-scapegoats-right-wing-populism-across-europe/21672/

60  Rogers Brubaker, "The New Language of European Populism," *Foreign Affairs*, 6 December 2017. https://scholar.ss.ucla.edu/wp-content/uploads/sites/6/2018/02/The-New-Language-of-European-Populism-Foreign-Affairs-final.pdf

61  Chika Mba, "Philosophy and the Rise of Ultra-Nationalism in Contemporary Euro-American Politics," *Africology: The Journal of Pan African Studies*, 11, no. 8 (2018): 138, 130, 142 and 145, emphasis in original.

62  Paul Teusner, "Resident Evil: Horror Film and the Construction of Religious Identity in Contemporary Media Culture," *Colloquium*, 37, no. 2 (2005): 169–70, 173–4 and 176–7.

63  Armando Maggi, "Christian Demonology in Contemporary American Popular Culture," *Social Research: An International Quarterly*, 81, no. 4 (2014): 770, 776–8 and 783–6. See also W. Scott Poole's chapter in the present volume.

64  Markus Moberg, "Popular Culture and the 'Darker Side' of Alternative Spirituality: The Case of Metal Music," *Scripta Instituti Donneriani Aboensis*, 21 (2009): 110–1 and 118–9, emphasis in original. On the matter of religious re-enchantment, see Christopher Partridge, *The Re-enchantment of the West: Understanding Popular Occulture* (London: Continuum, 2004) and Christopher Partridge, *The Re-enchantment of the West: Alternative Spiritualities, Sacralization, Popular Culture and Occulture* (London: Continuum, 2005).

65  Partridge and Christianson, "Introduction," 14–7.

66  Nick Jones, "Satanic Metal: So Bad It's Good," in *The Devil and Philosophy*, 177, 179 and 182.

67  Aaron Rabinowitz, "A Sympathetic Look at Lucifer Morningstar," in *The Devil and Philosophy*, 226. The television series *Lucifer*, based on *The Sandman* character, was developed in 2015, premiered by Fox in 2016, and picked up by Netflix in 2019 through 2020.

68 Kelly J. Murphy, "Leviathan to *Lucifer*: What Biblical Monsters (Still) Reveal," *Interpretation: A Journal of Bible and Theology*, 74, no. 2 (2020): 148, 152–4 and 157–8.

69 The Satanic Temple. https://thesatanictemple.com/

70 Lily Rothman, "The Evolution of Modern Satanism in the United States," *Time*, 27 July 2015. https://time.com/3973573/satanism-american-history/

71 Nash Jenkins, "Hundreds Gather for Unveiling of Satanic Statue in Detroit," *Time*, 27 July 2015. https://time.com/3972713/detroit-satanic-statue-baphomet/

72 Joseph P. Laycock, *Speak of the Devil: How the Satanic Temple is Changing the Way We Talk about Religion* (New York: Oxford University Press, 2020), 187 and 192–3.

73 Tara Isabella Burton, "The Rise of Progressive Occultism," *The American Interest*, 7 June 2019. https://www.the-american-interest.com/2019/06/07/the-rise-of-progressive-occultism/. Dakota Bracciale is quoted by Burton. See also Tara Isabella Burton, *Strange Rites: New Religions for a Godless World* (New York: Public Affairs, 2020).

74 Jason Crawford, "The Trouble with Re-Enchantment," *Los Angeles Review of Books*, 7 September 2020. https://lareviewofbooks.org/article/the-trouble-with-re-enchantment/. I draw from Crawford's reading of Charles Taylor, *A Secular Age* (Cambridge: Harvard University Press, 2007).

75 Crawford, "The Trouble with Re-Enchantment." I draw from Crawford's quotation of George Gifford.

76 Eugene McCarraher, "We Have Never Been Disenchanted," *The Hedgehog Review*, 17, no. 3 (2015): 89–90 and 98.

77 Costica Bradatan, "Introduction: Dealing (Visibly) in 'Things Not Seen'," in *Religion in Contemporary European Cinema: The Postsecular Constellation*, eds. Costica Bradatan and Camil Ungureanu (New York: Routledge, 2014), 5–6.

78 Sara Helen Binney, "Oscillating Towards the Sublime," *Notes on Metamodernism*, 2 April 2015. http://www.metamodernism.com/2015/04/02/oscillating-towards-the-sublime-2/. The term metamodernism, broadly speaking, refers to a reaction to modernism and departure from postmodernism, a kind of cultural vernacular that oscillates between modernity and postmodernity to re-engage with feeling and narrative without abandoning thought, reason and a degree of doubt.

79 Wojciech Załuski, "Review of *The Re-Enchantment of the World: Secular Magic in a Rational Age*, eds. Joshua Landie and Michael Saler (Stanford: Stanford University Press, 2009)," *International Review of Modern Sociology*, 36, no. 1 (2010): 96–8.

80 Martin Cohen, "Review: Re-Enchanting the World," *The Philosopher*, 97, no. 2 (2009). http://www.the-philosopher.co.uk/2009/09/review-re-enchanting-world-2009.html

81 Paul Matthew Turner, "Why American Christians Love Satan," *Daily Beast*, 14 April 2017. https://www.thedailybeast.com/why-american-christians-love-satan?ref=scroll

82 Rosemarie Ho, "Every Generation Gets the Devil it Deserves," *The Outline*, 1 November 2018. https://theoutline.com/post/6504/satan-devil-cultural-history-chilling-adventures-of-sabrina

83 Susan Brooks Thistlethwaite, "The Devil in Politics: Why Fear Works and What to Do About It," *Huffpost.com*, 6 December 2017. https://www.huffpost.com/entry/the-devil-in-politics-why_b_8793722

84 Tony Judt, "The Problem of Evil in Postwar Europe," *The New York Review*, 14 February 2008. https://www-nybooks-com.proxyiub.uits.iu.edu/articles/2008/02/14/the-problem-of-evil-in-postwar-europe/

85 For a discussion of how the Holocaust Museum in Washington, DC locates the evil of genocide and holocaust outside the United States, see Ivie and Giner, *Hunt the Devil*, 89–90.

86 James Baldwin, *The Devil Finds Work* (New York, 1976), 126.

87 By way of example of liberals attributing "evil" to conservatives, see Joe Concha, "Olbermann Dismisses Romney Criticism of 'Vile' Rhetoric: Bothsideism in the Face of Evil," *The Hill*, 14 October 2020. https://thehill.com/homenews/media/521028-olbermann-dismisses-romney-criticism-on-vile-rhetoric-bothsideism-in-the-face-of

## Recommended Readings

Almond, Philip C. *The Devil: A New Biography*. Ithaca: Cornell University Press, 2014.

Bernstein, Richard J. *The Abuse of Evil: The Corruption of Politics and Religion since 9/11*. Cambridge, 2005.

Ivie, Robert L., and Oscar Giner. *Hunt the Devil: A Demonology of US War Culture*. Tuscaloosa, 2015.

Landie, Joshua, and Michael Saler, eds. *The Re-Enchantment of the World: Secular Magic in a Rational Age*. Stanford: Stanford University Press, 2009.

Maggi, Armando. "Christian Demonology in Contemporary American Popular Culture." *Social Research: An International Quarterly* 81, no. 4 (2014): 769–93.

Matthews, Chris. *Modern Satanism: Anatomy of a Radical Subculture*. Westport: Praeger, 2009.

Partridge, Christopher H., and Eric S. Christianson, eds. *The Lure of the Dark Side: Satan and Western Demonology in Popular Culture*. London: Praeger, 2014.

Poole, W. Scott. *Satan in America: The Devil We Know*. Lanham: Rowman & Littlefield, 2009.

# EPILOGUE

## Teaching with Demons

### Michelle D. Brock

On the first day of my "History of the Devil" seminar, a course primarily for third- and fourth-year students, I like to start with a story about a restaurant in North Carolina called Luna Rotisserie that serves varieties of South American cuisine. At the height of the COVID-19 pandemic, in compliance with the state's executive order, customers were asked to wear masks if they intended to enter the restaurant for indoor dining. One group came in unmasked and was asked either to wear face coverings except when eating, sit in the outdoor dining area, or leave. These would-be customers apparently left in an angry huff. Later that week, the restaurant received a one-star review on Google that read: "This place is full of satanic activity. As free breathing humans, we were discriminated against ... If you like freedom, go elsewhere!!" The owners of Luna responded by embracing this review as a branding opportunity, designing restaurant merchandise featuring a grinning, masked devil and the tagline "Luna Rotisserie: full of Satanic Activity!"[1]

I share this story with my students for a few reasons. First, it is funny, and it never hurts to start a class on a subject as serious as Satan with a bit of humour. But more importantly, it makes the imagery and meaning of the devil relevant to a class of students who have a shared experience of the global pandemic. It also raises some questions which speak to the key themes of the class: Why did the angry patrons label the restaurant "full of satanic activity"? What does this tell us about our present moment that they reached for the rhetoric of the demonic to condemn a place trying to enforce a public health measure? And what does it mean that the restaurant used the figure of Satan in a funny, satirical way meant to draw people in rather than scare them away? In short, this story gives us the opportunity to think together about the varied uses and understandings of the demonic in the 2020s, before asking the question which animates my class and this volume alike: how did we—and the devil himself—get here?

### The Devil in the Classroom

The devil has long interested scholars. Since the publication of several landmark works in the late twentieth century, the study of Christian demonology has entered the mainstream not only of historiographical discourse, but of literary, cultural, and religious studies. In recent decades, courses on the devil, witches, monsters, and other things that go bump in

DOI: 10.4324/9781003096603-29

the night have also proliferated on college campuses; accordingly, "teaching with demons" is increasingly popular and, as this volume attests, important.[2] This expansion has not happened against a neutral background: in the United States, at least, curricular offerings have come under increased scrutiny from parents and legislators alike, thanks to the stoking of "culture war" issues. On both sides of the Atlantic, the utility of humanities courses has been increasingly questioned—and at times, seriously impaired—by politicians, Boards of Trustees, and administrators. In this context, courses on the preter- and supernatural, and especially those centred on the demonic, provide an opportunity not only to attract students to the humanities but also to introduce them to critical questions about human nature and the nature of the cosmos. Because the demonic has been and remains so central to the Western imagination, as a cognitive category for the assimilation of difference and disdain, a course on the devil is also a course about religion, politics, culture, art, and more. The subject encourages students not only to think about the damage done by the processes of demonisation and "othering" more broadly, but also about the creative forces unleashed in society and culture by the varied ways that the devil has been depicted over time. This chapter reflects on some of the pedagogical challenges and opportunities of "teaching with demons" and suggests how the contents of this volume might be used in the classroom. The devil still matters, and the subject deserves to be taught accordingly.

A few caveats are worth noting from the outset. First, my experiences of teaching about the demonic, either in my "History of the Devil" or "Age of the Witch Hunts" courses, have happened exclusively in the United States, and more specifically at a small liberal arts college in Virginia. My classes are small—25 people or fewer—and I tend to get to know my students quite well. This alone makes my experiences distinct from colleagues at universities who have far larger classes. The religious composition of my students is also notable, though it likely typifies teaching in the American south: many come from quite conservative religious backgrounds (primarily evangelical Protestantism but occasionally traditional Catholicism); others are mainline Protestants, "spiritual but not religious"; some are still seeking to understand what they do and do not believe. While I have had a few Jewish students in these classes—and even fewer students who openly identify as atheist—the vast majority of those I teach were raised Christian and many are still actively involved in their faith. What this means is that my students tend to enter the classroom with distinct ideas about the devil, born not only of popular culture but also of their own theological commitments that sometimes contradict what we learn in class. This is not the norm in many places; some of my colleagues in the United Kingdom and Canada, for example, have said that they struggle with the total lack of familiarity their students have with the bible. In this chapter, though I lead with my own experiences, I incorporate what I have heard and read about "teaching with demons" in a wide range of contexts. Much like its subject, the pedagogy of the devil has a "decidedly slippery character" that must be fashioned in response to different contexts.[3]

## Opportunities

Because the subject is engaging, weird, expansive, provocative, and relevant in ways students do not often anticipate, teaching about the devil is replete with opportunities. I will focus here on three, but this list is, of course, not exhaustive. The first opportunity is related to the tired truism that the humanities are in crisis. Pick up any issue of a higher education publication, and you will see articles lamenting declining enrolments in fields like English, Romance languages, and philosophy.[4] In history in particular, a rather maddening debate has emerged about whether or not the field has become too dominated by cultural and social history, or by "presentism" at the expense of more "traditional" approaches to studying things like political and military history—as if the human experience can be so neatly compartmentalised. In some ways, the history of the devil moves beyond this, for it is truly interdisciplinary and deeply current, as the chapters in the present collection make clear.[5] A major benefit of classes on the devil and adjacent subjects is, at least based on anecdotal data, that they appeal to students and serve as an excellent hook to get them to think broadly about the construction of culture through an array of overlapping disciplinary lenses. Many of the authors in this volume, who represent a wide variety of disciplines, institutions, and geographic locations, have taught in-demand classes on supernatural and demonic subjects.[6] It seems, then, that offering classes on subjects which fascinate and draw students while providing unique pedagogical opportunities is especially well advised. Satan sells, and this is a fact that humanities educators should embrace.

Second, and perhaps most of interest to premodernists, exploring subjects like the preter- and supernatural complicates the triumphalist paradigm of the scientific revolution and helps students move beyond artificial notions of "religion versus rationality." In drawing attention to what are often seen as intellectual byways and dead ends, they more effectively historicise the processes through which the world was—and came to be—viewed and comprehended. Teaching students about beings such as demons, monsters, and witches and how they have been used in the past challenges any simplistic dichotomies brought into the classroom and, in turn, encourages us to think critically about the ways in which epistemologies evolve. In short, the devil affords educators an opportunity to bring students back behind modern ideas of knowing, dominated as they are by historically constructed ideas of "rationality" and "evidence."[7] Beneath all the perceived weirdness and wildness, we find the past not as a foreign country, but rather as a landscape of men and women trying to make sense of their own experiences, much as we do our own—sometimes at great cost. Along these lines, we can also learn a surprising amount from studying things once accepted as true that we now find false or even absurd. By asking, for example, why people once believed in witches who poisoned crops and copulated with Satan, and that these witches should be killed at the stake or by the noose, we begin to understand not only religious beliefs of the premodern era, but also the development of the legal system, gender dynamics, and the consequences of social and political instability. As important, considering how epistemologies in the past were constructed also helps us think about the way modern epistemologies are made. Like our premodern forebearers, much of we accept as "true" is, at least in part, a function of how we set out to know things. On the final day of class, I often ask my students this question: what do we talk about when we talk about the history of the devil? Their answer: everything.

Third, classes on the demonic are uniquely suited to serving many of the critical purposes of higher education. Yes, everyone thinks this about their subject of expertise, but bear with me. For one, the history of the devil illustrates in stark terms what happens when elites such as spiritual and political leaders encourage the demonisation of "others" and, by extension, the homogenisation of group "insiders," a dangerous phenomenon with which we are still very much living.[8] As this volume so clearly illustrates, because of Satan's flexibility, he has long been and remains the core of a useful, movable fiction used to demonise others; the devil is a profoundly convenient, if often profoundly lazy, way to label whole hosts of people as mortal enemies. If you say someone is a worshiper of Satan, engaged in all sorts of unthinkable deeds like the ritual harm of innocent children, you also deem them unhuman and even anti-human, thus justifying their persecution. And though many have bid farewell to some of the demonic ideas of the past, this association of others with the devil persists, sometimes implicitly and other times explicitly. Encouraging students to recognise these demonising patterns—and by extension, to be wary of their own complicity in them—is, to my mind, essential for building empathy and good citizenship, two often underappreciated values of a college education.

More generally, as Madeleine Castro points out, classes on the occult are especially well suited to what Ronald Barnett has termed "critical being," which he characterises as something beyond critical thinking: "Critical persons ... are able critically to engage with the world and with themselves, as well as with knowledge."[9] Reflection and metacognition—thinking about one's own thinking—are at the core of "critical being"; teaching about the devil, witches, monsters, and other subjects without easy or even obtainable answers necessitates both. A class on the demonic or the occult asks students, first and foremost, to engage with primary source material in order to understand the thought processes of others. But equally, at least in my experience, it also encourages students to do the deep work of examining their own commonplace beliefs and assumptions, and to get to grips with the "strangeness" of their own world as much as that of the past. Doing so can also be necessarily humbling. As Julian Goodare has noted in teaching and writing about witch hunts of early modern Europe, modern audiences are quick to point out the barbarity of the past as a measure of distance between now and then. To them, Goodare poses a key question: "Are our own times so free of wars, persecutions and injustice that we can afford to look down disapprovingly on earlier ages?" Perhaps, he suggests, "by contemplating the persecutions of the past we may gain some insight into how to treat another humanly in the present."[10] To my mind, there is no higher aim than this.

## Challenges

Teaching with demons has a lot to recommend it, but the devil can also be a difficult subject for students and instructor alike. Part of this is because the foundations of demonic belief themselves are shaky; there is no coherent narrative of his origins, forms, purpose, or powers, not even in the texts from which he emerged. The devil has always been up for interpretation—he is, at the core, a product of discussion and debate rather than doctrine. While this, in many ways, makes the demonic a subject ripe for collective exploration in the university classroom, it also means that students often bring with them preestablished beliefs and perceptions that contradict scholarly consensus. Moreover, the subject of the devil is bound up with—and in some respects, borne out of—one of the most intractable theological issues in the Western tradition: theodicy, or the problem of evil. Critically examining the nature of Satan invariably implicates the nature of God and questions of divine benevolence, cruelty, justice, and sovereignty. In short, a course on the devil is ultimately about Christian ideas, identities, and actions past and present, and as such, it features some especially sensitive subjects. To be clear, students are in no way to blame for these hurdles; everyone, instructor included, comes into the classroom with a set of pre-existing beliefs and assumptions. The challenge, then, is how to navigate them with both scholarly eyes and mutual respect.

"Teaching with demons" often involves two competing but parallel issues that will be familiar to anyone who regularly engages with religion in the classroom. The first is the anxiety deeply religious students sometimes feel when asked to address topics like demons and spirits from a scholarly perspective. For those who actively believe in and even fear the demonic, encountering scriptural ambiguities and culturally constructed ideas about Satan (and indeed, God) can be particularly difficult. Learning, for example, that their understanding of the devil does not exist in the Old Testament, or that Jesus, as a Jew, would not have shared modern Christianity's conception of the afterlife, can be destabilising.[11] And in attempting to respect the faith of others—itself a positive thing—they may be too willing to take at face value religious experiences of people past and present, without considering things like motivation, positionality, and audience. Many students, regardless of confessional background, likewise initially struggle to grasp that the devil, like all ideas, has a history; as this volume demonstrates, he has been made and remade in response to context. Satan, like the faith that created him, has never been immutable.

Unsurprisingly, this issue is most salient for those who teach at either Christian institutions or in comparatively conservative places like the American south. In my own experience, a few students have reported that their parents were nervous that their child was taking a class on the devil; one concerned mother even asked to see my syllabus in advance of the start of term. Joseph Laycock, who teaches at Texas State University, has also had this issue in his course on "Demonology, Possession, and Exorcism." When he asked his students whether their parents were more worried about possession or issues of belief, they said it was both: they worried that their children "might stop believing in demons and then get possessed."[12] It can also be difficult to engage with contemporary uses and abuses of demonology, especially in today's deeply polarised environment. One Canadian professor shared that they had received a formal complaint from a student who "felt affronted" by these modern connections and perceived that they were "making fun of her evangelical heroes (Pat Robertson, Mel Gibson, Gerry Falwell, etc.) by projecting their own comments on the screen."[13] Happily, though, these sorts of complaints seem rare, even if discomfort with the material is not. Heather Macumber, who teaches at Providence University College in Manitoba, told me that while her students who are committed Christians may be wary of her classes on women and gender, they embrace the opportunity to take "Monsters in the Bible"; in this course, she has had no complaints about the material she covers on the demonic. Still, some of her students have struggled "with the idea of ha-Satan belonging to the divine court in the Old Testament as a legitimate part of God's council. They are very focused on the New Testament version of the devil or demons and struggle to let that go when reading the Old Testament."[14] In my experience, while students' having some degree of biblical literacy is an asset in class, it can also be selective and limiting.

The second challenge comes from the other end of the spectrum: the secular-minded students keen to dismiss beliefs about the devil and associated phenomena like possession and witchcraft as "irrational," "backwards," and "superstitious." This is particularly acute when exploring ideas about the devil in the distant past, as some students assume that the people of the premodern world were inherently more credulous than themselves. As such, it can be a struggle to get them to take Satan—and all the myriad beliefs, experiences, and fears he has engendered—seriously. There is also a tendency to see the devil as primarily a cultural symbol, to the exclusion of viewing him as a genuine belief and important theological figure. Tellingly, a number of colleagues have reported that students wrote in evaluations that their courses had "too much religion." Many students are also quick to functionalise belief in the supernatural and supernatural experiences. They insist, for example, that witchcraft was really about something other than genuine fear of witches, be it poisoned rye, the suppression of a pagan cult, or family rivalries. Others, as David Winter pointed out to me, assume that "the Church" has, throughout history, monolithically and self-consciously deployed the devil to cow the public into submission; they want to make Satan a cynical tool of social control rather than take demonic belief seriously. Relatedly, if students do not have much biblical literacy—and this is sometimes as true for Christian students as it is for non-Christians—it can be a heavy lift to ensure the basic theology of the devil is intelligible enough to make the classroom inclusive for everyone, some of whom bring knowledge of the devil primarily from horror films and heavy metal.

Colleagues who teach at other universities have reported similar experiences with sceptical students. Jan Machielsen noted that when he teaches about saints, students are much more comfortable with stories of divine visions than they are accounts of demonic encounters. "Where the devil is concerned," he explained, "these stories need to be caveated ('allegedly') or they need to be given a naturalist explanation. If you don't, people will think of you as a mad person ...."[15] Similarly, Laycock has pointed out that his more sceptical students often assume that "anyone claiming to experience spirit possession is either mentally ill or lying."[16] For many students, there are, understandably, only two viable explanations for why someone might become a demoniac: they are either faking it, or they are actually possessed by demons. They may have never been asked to think beyond or to complicate their own epistemological dichotomies; it can be difficult to grasp that some things can be neither true nor false, and some things can be both.

The challenge, then, is to find a balance between reflexive scepticism and uncritical credulity, and to do so in a way that puts students at ease in grappling with ideas that are either quite foreign to them or uncomfortably familiar. This is a difficulty in any class that deals with religious themes, but in some ways classes on the devil (as well as other supernatural or "occult" subjects) are exceptional: the demonic teeters on the edge of, and in some places just beyond, mainstream belief. Yet at the same time, because of the importance of the demonic in shaping the Western tradition, Satan and his minions are at the centre of so much popular culture and political discourse. So how does one effectively teach about the demonic in a classroom full of competing assumptions about the devil's history, remit, and impact?

## Teaching with Demons in Practice

The major challenges in teaching the devil coalesce around dismantling assumptions and easy dichotomies while also meeting students where they are. To this end, I have found a few activities during the first week of class especially effective in setting a constructive agenda for the semester. The opening activity in my seminar on Satan might seem an odd fit for a history class: I ask my students to draw a picture of the devil. I tell them to look only at their own sheets of paper, and to sketch the first thing that pops into their mind (no artistic talent required). I want to know what they see when they picture the devil, and I ask them to "show and tell" what they drew if they are comfortable doing so. Most of their pictures share much in common with the devil that medieval men and women might have encountered in the frescos decorating their local churches: a monstrous human-animal hybrid with horns and cloven hooves. A few of them draw something less literal, an image that symbolises evil for them. When I taught the class in the early 2020s, this list has included Adolf Hitler, Donald Trump, a serpent, a black hole representing distance from the divine, and, most amusingly, an accounting exam. A few leave the page blank, representing their complete disbelief in the demonic. I then ask them whether they think drawing the devil was easier—and more comfortable—than drawing God might be. Nearly all of them answer yes.

Beyond serving as an engaging icebreaker, this activity works because it reflects from the outset two seemingly paradoxical truths to which we return throughout the term. First, there is no one standardised image of the devil: not in people's minds and, as the opening chapter of this volume illustrates, not in the building blocks of scripture. And yet at the same time, there is a shared, immediately recognisable devil of the popular, Western imagination, one born of centuries of art, intellectual endeavour, mythology, media, and experience. The devil is, in some respects and for a range of reasons, more accessible to the mind's eye than God. Satan is embodied and immediate, frightening and familiar. Getting students to consider this fact—and why it is—opens them up to taking the devil seriously, regardless of their own backgrounds. It also enables me to emphasise that my class is not intended to change how they view the devil, but rather to understand why their classmates drew him as they did. This activity also confirms a point astutely made by Richard J. Callahan Jr. in an essay on teaching about ghosts: while a faith background is essential, many people develop their religious sensibilities from sources outside the church, such as popular culture and folklore. As he puts it, "these ideas and practices are more of a repertoire of familiar idioms and affects than they are 'beliefs'."[17] The pictures that the students draw in my class are products of cartoons, Halloween costumes, and music videos as much as they are of the bible. This recognition can, in my experience, lower the personal stakes of class content for some students; I want them to reflect actively on their own convictions and assumptions, but the history of the devil is not actually about their beliefs.

The other thing I do the first week of class—and it is something that I do a variation of in each of my classes—is an "initial self-reflection." In it, I include the following questions:

- Do you have any apprehensions about studying the history of the devil?
- How familiar do you think you are with Christian history and theology?
- Is there anything about your religious background that you think I should know or that you would like to share? (This question is *completely optional*, and you should feel free to skip it if you prefer.)

Usually, students do a lot of self-reporting here. Most want to share with me the faith tradition in which they were raised (if any), and their answers give me insight into where the class is collectively starting from. The question about apprehensions is especially useful because it allows me to take the temperature of the room and to signal to students that I care about how they feel and about their individual experience of learning. It also helps me know which readings might be especially difficult for the class in terms of content and to give them a heads-up accordingly. While there is no consensus about the ethics and efficacy of content warnings, I, like many of my colleagues, use them out of an abundance of caution and care.[18] As Richard Raiswell explained to me, "I have felt it necessary in recent years to include notices on my syllabus advising them that while we do devote a class to a discussion of heavy metal, other sections engage with material that is misogynistic and racist. We will be reading material that deals with torture and violence of every kind imaginable—and some kinds students haven't imagined."[19] Far from coddling, the goal of opening surveys and content warnings alike is to create a classroom comfortable enough to have uncomfortable conversations.

To that end, I try to treat their experiences of faith (positive or negative or lack thereof) as an opportunity. I do not insist on keeping the personal out of the classroom, though I also make clear that the historical understanding of the devil, as established by scholars, is our focus. Objectivity is an impossible goal, even if (and this is debatable) a worthy one. If I give students permission to put their own beliefs in dialogue with what we are learning—and here, I mean through discussions and informal reflections rather than things like research papers—then the experience of the class becomes richer and more inclusive. Moreover, as Fred Glennon puts it in an essay on teaching the paranormal, engaging with a supernatural subject "not only broadens students' understandings of the complexities of religion and spirituality, it also provides opportunity for them to discover deeply their own religious commitments."[20] This is equally true, I think, for both those who are spiritual and those who are sceptical. Self-understanding is not the central purpose of studying Satan, but it is part of the critical reflection work and understanding of difference that my courses are designed to encourage.

In helping students break through pre-existing assumptions, resistance to the material, and simplistic dichotomies, establishing a shared vocabulary from the outset is essential. The language of "perceived reality"—a person's subjective experience of reality—has been particularly instructive for my students. This phrasing does not deny or affirm the truth of something but instead emphasises contexts and mentalities. This provides a useful entry into thinking about how the demonic is as much a product of perception and experience as belief, all things conditioned by concurrent sources of knowledge and authority. I also find discussing the "supernatural"—loosely defined as something that appears to transcend the laws of nature—a useful starting point for dialogue about which beliefs seem reasonable or self-evident to them.[21] I list a range of entities—ghosts, fairies, angels, demons, werewolves, God—and ask my students which of these are supernatural. Very few report that they would characterise God as supernatural, and when I ask why, they explain that to them, the term describes things that might not or probably do not exist. I tell them that for centuries, most Christian theologians argued that only God, in his divine sovereignty and ultimate unknowability, was supernatural, while everything that went bump in the night was preternatural—a category of beings and forces suspended between the mundane and the miraculous.[22] Only that which created nature could truly operate above and beyond it. Today, many folks have thrown out the term "preternatural" and conflated supernatural with "occult" or "mythological," and in so doing, have decided God is not supernatural, because belief in a divine being is still the norm for them. This conversation, while it may seem a bit in the weeds, illustrates how modalities of belief have shifted over time. The language of who and what is supernatural is far from static, and accordingly, modernity does not have a monopoly on "truth" or "accuracy."

In having these definitional conversations, Darren Oldridge's *Strange Histories: The Trial of the Pig, the Walking Dead, and Other Matters of Fact from the Medieval and Renaissance Worlds* has proven invaluable in giving students a frame in which to consider "systems of belief" and the notion that "ideas can be regarded as rational if they are consistent with prevailing knowledge."[23] This knowledge, Oldridge reminds us, is not fixed; just as we are interested in expanding our knowledge of the world, so too were premodern people. By extension, our perceptions of reality, and of what is true and good, will invariably change. I emphasise with my students that the recognition of "truth" and "rightness" as constructs is not to suggest that we should condone actions based on those constructs, such as the execution of some 50,000 people for the crime of demonic witchcraft. Indeed, I think we ought to judge the injustices of the past and learn from them—but not without understanding the past on its own complicated terms, and in turn asking uncomfortable questions about the assumptions of our present. Doing this, as Oldridge so compellingly puts it, "may inspire a more critical approach to the things we think we know. It may even, from time to time, lead us to reflect on how strange we really are."[24]

My next point is obvious, but important: in teaching a topic like Satan or any number of supernatural subjects, high levels of engagement and in-class participation are essential. This is because students need to talk through their responses to the material, as much with each other as with the professor; in so doing, they will feel both prepared to tackle challenging material and encouraged to treat the subject with the seriousness it deserves. One of the reasons active learning is so effective is that it cultivates positive emotions in students like excitement, confidence, and curiosity. Experiencing these emotions in the classroom has been proven to lead to deeper and more lasting learning.[25] It also emboldens students to ponder what Sarah Rose Cavannah calls the "transcendent purpose" of what they are learning.[26] Engagement can be achieved in a number of ways, depending on class size and level, such as heavily weighting class participation, asking students to submit discussion questions in advance of the class meeting, using Perusall or other text annotation platforms to ensure students complete the reading, implementing "think-pair-share" or other group activities, and offering students flexibility in selecting research topics that speak to their interests.

As a first step in ensuring a spirit of open conversation, I have found it particularly worthwhile to ask students to devise between three and five questions about devil belief and to discuss them with at least five friends and family members within the first week or two of class. They then write short, low-stakes reflections (meaning they get credit just for doing the activity) on these conversations. This not only gets the students comfortable talking about the devil with others, but also encourages them to think about material outside of class. Inevitably, they report that their roommates or relatives have followed up on these conversations later in the term with "hey, how is that weird devil class you're taking going?"

Raiswell has taken modes of engagement a step further in his class on the *Malleus maleficarum* at the University of Prince Edward Island, in which he stages a mock inquisition in order to help the students understand the atmosphere of apocalyptic urgency that gave rise to such an infamous text.[27] In the debriefing session, the students reported that the whole exercise was an "exciting way to think about the text—treating it as a living document. But more than that, not knowing how proceedings would unfold—whether they themselves would end up being accused of witchery—not knowing who deposed what against them really helped synthesise some of the anxiety around the presence of an inquisitor."[28] Assignments that incorporate choice, gaming, and performance—components at the heart of the popular Reaction to the Past pedagogy—invoke positive emotions and help students move beyond the "strangeness" of subjects and texts to a deeper understanding of the material at hand.[29]

The ideas above have worked well in my classes, but here it is worth reiterating the caveat that student populations are distinct, and classrooms themselves have their own particular dynamics as social spaces that are often beyond the instructor's control.[30] On top of this, the identity of the professor can matter immensely; I am, for example, a tenured white woman, making my ability to take pedagogical risks significantly greater than it is for many in less privileged or more precarious positions who might face augmented scrutiny from parents, students, and administrators. In short, pedagogy is a process, not a prescription; what works for some will not work for others.

That said, the co-editors of the *Routledge History of the Devil* (RHOTD) have structured this volume in the hope that it will be useful for a wide range of instructors as well as scholars; it is the secondary resource we have often wished we had when "teaching with demons" in our own (very different) institutions. I think it can be used in several ways. Most obviously, it should pair well with primary source readings to offer students an accessible yet scholarly introduction to the field. I imagine, for example, coupling Chapters 1 and 2 with relevant passages from scripture, Chapters 11 and 14 with evocative witchcraft treatises, Chapter 20 with excerpts from puritan self-writings, and Chapter 27 with news stories on the demonic rhetoric surrounding more recent events like 9/11 or the COVID-19 pandemic. In lower division courses, the RHOTD's chapters will be useful for students not only as content-based readings, but as examples of how to survey the existing literature and use primary sources to offer either synthesis or new arguments. For upper division classes, its thematic chapters can serve as an inspiration for students tasked with developing their own research projects. For students of all sorts, this volume also offers a general chronological introduction to the devil's history while also demonstrating the continued importance of the demonic. Making classroom content germane to the lives of students is another one of those high-impact practices that evokes positive emotions and improve learning.[31] We should not ignore the ongoing relevance of very old ideas about the devil; we should look straight at this moment of "Satanic renaissance" and harness it for our own pedagogical ends. The core argument of this volume—that the devil still matters, precisely because of his historical construction—lends itself explicitly to this goal.

## Conclusion: The Case for Seminars on Satan

I want to end where, in many ways, this volume's introduction began: by making the case for why the devil matters in this current moment. When I defended my doctoral dissertation in 2012, I began with an anecdote to show the continued presence of the devil in American life and political discourse: in 2008, Rick Santorum, who became a Republican presidential candidate four years later, gave a speech at Ave Maria University in Florida in which he claimed that America was engaged in a spiritual war with the devil. "And the Father of Lies," Santorum told his audience, "has his sights on what you would think the Father of Lies would have his sights on: a good, decent, powerful, influential country—the United States of America. If you were Satan, who would you attack in this day and age?"[32] He then went on to describe how the devil had used the "great vices of pride, vanity and sensuality" to go after academia, which in turn had corrupted the church, culture, and government.[33] I was struck then by the surprising similarity between some of his remarks and the sermons and polemical treatises of some of the individuals who I featured in my study of the devil in early modern Scotland. What I did not anticipate then seems glaringly apparent to me now: we are in the midst of a resurgence of popular and political uses and abuses of the devil.

When thinking about the current and future trajectory of the devil, two tracks, competing yet intimately bound together, emerge. On the first, as we continue to see the growth of "religious nones"—people without any formal religious affiliation who may be agnostic, atheists, or spiritual but not confessionally committed—there will likely be even greater space for understanding the devil as a symbol of resistance or creative inspiration.[34] Satanism, epitomised in particular by the swell of membership in The Satanic Temple, may well become a more mainstream part of modern pluralism much as Wicca already has.[35] At the same time, I expect that a far bigger embrace of the devil will come from the far right and from an evangelical backlash to cultural changes and shifting demographics—the Satanic Panic, redux. Indeed, we are already seeing a recommitment to demonic rhetoric that is bleeding into political life, especially in the United States. In 2021, for example, the demonically suffused QAnon conspiracy theory animated many of the men and women who stormed the Capitol on 6 January 2021. In April the next year, congressional representative from Georgia Marjorie Taylor Green said that Christian organisations working to resettle undocumented immigrants and refugees in the United States are under the control of Satan.[36] "Anti-liberal demonology" and Christian nationalism more generally have taken deep root in American politics and show no sign of abating.[37] This trend matters immensely. As Elaine Pagels wrote in the introduction to her brilliant *The Origin of Satan*, "our imaginative perceptions of what is invisible relate to the ways we respond to the people around us, to events, and to the natural world."[38] It is impossible to predict the future—though our intellectual forebears in the Western tradition certainly tried—but I think we can say with confidence that Satan is not going anywhere anytime soon. Teaching with demons has never been more urgent.

## Notes

1 Sarah Edwards, "'This Place is Full of Satanic Activity': The One-Star Anti-Masker Review of Luna Rotisserie that Became a Commemorative T-Shirt," *Indy Week*, 11 November 2021, accessed 6 August 2023 at https://indyweek.com/food-and-drink/why-luna-owner-shawn-stokes-turned-a-one-star-review-into-a-t-shirt/

2 The phrase "teaching with demons" is a play on the title of Stuart Clark's magisterial *Thinking with Demons: The Idea of Witchcraft in Early Modern Europe* (Oxford, 1997).

3 Richard Raiswell and David Winter, *The Medieval Devil: A Reader* (Toronto, 2022), 1.

4 For a useful survey of the history of the "humanities in crisis" narrative, see Benjamin Schmidt, "The Humanities Are in Crisis," *The Atlantic*, published 23 August 2018, accessed at https://www.theatlantic.com/ideas/archive/2018/08/the-humanities-face-a-crisisof-confidence/567565/

5 The best piece, to my mind, on the recent debates within history about method and "presentism," see Jonathan Wilson, "What AHA President James Sweet Got Wrong—And Right," Clio and the Contemporary, published 30 November 2022, accessed at https://clioandthecontemporary.com/2022/11/30/what-aha-president-james-sweet-got-wrong-and-right/

6 Contributors to this volume, for example, offer the following courses: "The Devil in the Western World" and "The Malleus maleficarum" (University of Prince Edward Island), "The Devil in the Western World" (Brandon University); "The Devil in the Western World" and "The Age of the Witch Hunts" (Washington and Lee University); "Magic and Witchcraft in European History" (Iowa State University); "Witch-hunting in European Societies" (University of Melbourne); "History of the Supernatural" and "Witchcraft and Demonology in Early Modern Europe and its Colonies" (University of Queensland); "The Early Modern Witch-hunt" (Cardiff University); "Heresy and Witch-hunts" and "Religion, Magic, and Witchcraft in the Medieval World" (University of New Brunswick).

7 Many of these ideas were explored in a "Teaching Demons" roundtable featuring me, Peter Dendle, Cassandra Gorman, Richard Raiswell, and David Winter, presented at the 2019 Scientiae conference in Belfast, 12–15 June 2019.

8 On the long history of the use of the devil as an instrument of both demonisation and internal cohesion—at the expense of making deviants into demonic heretics—see the introduction to the present volume, and Elaine Pagels, *The Origin of Satan: How Christians Demonized Jews, Pagans,*

*and Heretics* (New York, 1995), and Norman Cohn, *Europe's Inner Demons: The Demonization of Christians in Medieval Christendom* (Chicago, 2001; orig. 1975).

9 Madeleine Castro, "Reflecting on the Occult: Nurturing 'Critical Being' through Exposure to Marginal or Controversial Ideas," *Religious Studies News* (October 2017), 14, accessed 6 July 2023 at https://rsn.aarweb.org/spotlight-on/teaching/paranormal-occult/haunting-religious-studies-classroom; Ronald Barrett, *Higher Education: A Critical Business* (Buckingham, 1997), 1.

10 Julian Goodare, *The European Witch-Hunt* (London, 2016), xvii.

11 On these points, see, for example, Chapter 1 of this volume and Bart Ehrman, *Heaven and Hell: A History of the Afterlife* (New York, 2020).

12 Joseph Laycock, "Teaching Demonology, Possession, and Exorcism in Texas," *Religious Studies News* (October 2017), 19.

13 Quotation is from email correspondence, 13 June 2023. Used with the permission of the author.

14 Quotation is from a conversation with Heather Macumber via X, 13 June 2023. Used with the permission of the author.

15 Quotation is from an email exchange with Jan Machielsen, 13 June 2023. Used with the permission of the author.

16 Laycock, "Teaching Demonology, Possession," 22.

17 Richard Callahan, "Haunting the Religious Studies Classroom," *Religious Studies News* (October 2017), 11.

18 On the debate over the efficacy of content or "trigger" warnings, see Jeannie Suk Gersen, "What if Trigger Warnings don't Work?," *The New Yorker*, 28 September 2021, accessed 6 August 2023 at https://www.newyorker.com/news/our-columnists/what-if-trigger-warnings-dont-work

19 Quotation from a message exchange with Richard Raiswell on 4 August 2023.

20 Fred Glennon, "Teaching the Paranormal and the Occult: Editor's Introduction," *Religious Studies News* (October 2017), 2.

21 For a more sophisticated discussion of how the supernatural has been understood and defined during the premodern era, see Robert Bartlett, *The Natural and the Supernatural in the Middle Ages* (Cambridge, 2008), particularly chapter 1 and Julian Goodare and Martha McGill, "Exploring the Supernatural in Early Modern Scotland," *The Supernatural in Early Modern Scotland*, eds. Julian Goodare and Martha McGill (Manchester, 2020), 1–9.

22 For premodern ideas about the supernatural, see, for example, "Fallen Spirits and Divine Grace: The Supernatural in Early Modern Scottish Sermons," in *The Supernatural in Early Modern Scotland*, 144–59.

23 Darren Oldridge, *Strange Histories: The Trial of the Pig, the Walking Dead, and Other Matters of Fact from the Medieval and Renaissance Worlds*, 2nd ed. (London, 2017).

24 Oldridge, *Strange Histories*, 184.

25 Sarah Rose Cavannah, *Spark of Learning: Energizing the College Classroom with the Science of Emotion* (Morganstown, West Virginia, 2016).

26 Cavannah, *Spark of Learning*, 153–4.

27 Richard Raiswell, "A Moot Inquisition: The Malleus Maleficarum in the Undergraduate Classroom," *The Canadian Historical Association Teaching and Learning Blog* (18 January, 2023), accessed at https://cha-shc.ca/teachers-learning-bl/a-moot-inquisition-the-malleus-maleficarum-in-the-undergraduate-classroom/

28 Raiswell, "A Moot Inquisition."

29 Mark Carnes, *Minds on Fire: How Role-Immersion Games Transform College* (Harvard, 2014); Adam Porter, "Role-Playing and Religion: Using Games to Educate Millennials," *Teaching Theology & Religion* 11.4 (2008), 230–5.

30 To my mind, the best recent work on how to navigate the classroom as a social space in a way that is mindful of one's own identity is Jessymyn Neuhuas's *Geeky Pedagogy: A Guide for Intellectuals, Introverts, and Nerds Who Want to Be Effective Teachers* (Morganstown, West Virginia, 2019).

31 Cavannah, *Spark of Learning*, 152–4.

32 Santorum's remarks can be read here: https://www.politifact.com/article/2012/feb/22/context-santorum-satan/

33 https://www.politifact.com/article/2012/feb/22/context-santorum-satan/

34 For studies of the so-called "rise of the religious nones," see Gregory A. Smith, "About Three-in-Ten U.S. Adults Are Now Religiously Unaffiliated," *Pew Research Center*, published 14 December 2021, accessed at https://www.pewresearch.org/religion/2021/12/14/

about-three-in-ten-u-s-adults-are-now-religiously-unaffiliated/; Frank Newport, "Millennials' Religiosity amidst the Rise of the Nones," *Gallup*, published 29 October 2019, accessed at https://news.gallup.com/opinion/polling-matters/267920/millennials-religiosity-amidst-rise-nones.aspx; Adam Gabbot, "Losing Their Religion: Why US Churches Are on the Decline," *The Guardian*, published 22 January 2023, accessed at https://www.theguardian.com/us-news/2023/jan/22/us-churches-closing-religion-covid-christianity

35 The best study of the Satanic Temple is Joseph Laycock, *Speak of the Devil: How the Satanic Temple Is Changing the Way We Talk about Religion* (Oxford, 2020).

36 https://www.independent.co.uk/news/world/americas/us-politics/marjorie-taylor-greene-christianity-migrants-satan-b2066997.html

37 See, for example, S. Jonathon O'Donnell, "The Deliverance of the Administrative State: Deep State Conspiracism, Charismatic Demonology, and the Post-Truth Politics of American Christian Nationalism," *Religion* 50.20 (2020), 696–719; Paul Thomas, "How QAnon Uses Satanic Rhetoric to Set Up a Narrative of 'Good vs. Evil'," *The Conversation*, 20 October 2020, accessed 12 July 2023 at https://theconversation.com/how-qanon-uses-satanic-rhetoric-to-set-up-a-narrative-of-good-vs-evil-146281; Whitney Phillips, Mark Brockway and Abby Ohlheiser, "The Dangerous Demonology of Ron DeSantis," MSBC.com, 18 June 2023, accessed 6 July 2023 at https://www.msnbc.com/opinion/msnbc-opinion/ron-desantis-using-literal-devil-vilify-liberals-rcna89850

38 Pagels, *The Origin of Satan*, xv.

## Further Reading

Darren Oldridge, *Strange Histories: The Trial of the Pig, the Walking Dead, and Other Matters of Fact from the Medieval and Renaissance Worlds* (London: Routledge, 2nd edition, 2017).

Jessymyn Neuhaus, *Geeky Pedagogy: A Guide for Intellectuals, Introverts, and Nerds Who Want to Be Effective Teachers* (Morgantown, WV: West Virginia University Press, 2019).

Kevin Gannon, *Radical Hope: A Teaching Manifesto* (Morgantown, WV: West Virginia University Press, 2020).

Mark Carnes, *Minds on Fire: How Role-Immersion Games Transform College* (Cambridge: Harvard University Press, 2014).

Richard Raiswell and David Winter, *The Medieval Devil: A Reader* (Toronto: University of Toronto Press, 2022).

Sarah Rose Cavannah, *Spark of Learning: Energizing the College Classroom with the Science of Emotion* (Morgantown, WV: West Virginia University Press, 2016).

Stuart Clark, *Thinking with Demons: The Idea of Witchcraft in Early Modern Europe* (Oxford: Oxford University Press, 1997).

# INDEX

For Product Safety Concerns and Information please contact our
EU representative GPSR@taylorandfrancis.com Taylor & Francis
Verlag GmbH, Kaufingerstraße 24, 80331 München, Germany